D1431702

The Culture and Commerce of Texts

The Culture
and Commerce of Texts

*Scribal Publication
in Seventeenth-Century England*

Harold Love

Foreword by David D. Hall

University of Massachusetts Press
Amherst

Originally published in 1993 by the Clarendon Press of Oxford University Press as *Scribal Publication in Seventeenth-Century England.* This edition is reprinted by arrangement with Oxford University Press and Harold Love.

Library of Congress Cataloging-in-Publication Data

Love, Harold, 1937–
    [Scribal publication in seventeenth-century England]
    The culture and commerce of texts : scribal publication in seventeenth-century England / Harold Love ; foreword by David D. Hall.
        p. cm.
    Originally published: Scribal publication in seventeenth-century England. Oxford : Clarendon Press, 1993.
    Includes bibliographical references and index.
    ISBN 1-55849-134-1 (pbk. : alk. paper)
    1. English literature—Early modern, 1500–1700—Criticism, Textual.
2. Literature publishing—England—History—17th century.
3. Authors and readers—England—History—17th century. 4. Music—Publishing—England—History—17th century. 5. Manuscripts, English—History—17th century. 6. Scriptoria—England—17th century. 7. Manuscripts, English—Editing. 8. Transmission of texts. 9. Scribes—England. I. Title.
PR438.T42L68 1998
820.9'004—dc21   97-40966
                                                                                      CIP

British Library Cataloguing in Publication data are available.
This book is published with the support and cooperation of the University of Massachusetts, Boston.

FOREWORD

"The great grey goose of bibliography has laid a golden egg." So I declared some years ago in reviewing Harold Love's *Scribal Publication in Seventeenth-Century England* (as the cloth edition of the book was titled) for the newsletter of the American Antiquarian Society's Program in the History of the Book in American Culture. Reading it for the second time, I turn its pages with an even greater sense of admiration for what Love has accomplished. His is a model account of how the materiality of the text impinges on and intersects with the practices of authorship, reading, censorship, and the publication and distribution of books, printed or handwritten. The significance of this book lies as well in how its author is persistently historical in his understanding of terms and categories that can slide off into generalities or abstractions.

Consider the deceptively simple word *publication.* A central argument of this book is that the circulation of handwritten texts in seventeenth-century England can properly be understood as a system of publication—that is, of making public and distributing texts that otherwise seem private, hidden, or divorced from the book trades. Within this system Love differentiates several modalities of publication. The materiality of the scribal text—the qualities of paper, ink, and handwriting, as in the choice of "hands"—figures in this analysis, as does the wider politics of publication in a situation where some writers shrank from exposing themselves to the "stigma of print" and many others ran the risk of offending the government by publishing outside the normal frameworks of licensing and censorship. When Love turns to the practice of reading and introduces the concept of "scribal communities," his analysis achieves the same richness as we follow him in learning how texts were shared and reproduced within different milieus. That the workings of the economy, the courts, and the government depended on handwritten forms and other scribally produced texts is a point Love makes almost in passing, although its implications for the history of the book, and for any argument about the significance of the technology of printing, are many.

We do not have to guess at these implications, for Love pursues them himself in challenging the adequacy of concepts like the "logic of print," the power of writing, and the "presence" of orality. His critique reminds us that the history of the book is an unstable coalition of subjects, methods, and framing questions, leavened with large assertions about change over time within Western culture. For Love, the framing question arises out of the intersection of literary history and bibliography—How were literary texts transmitted and published?—a question he has answered by broadening our understanding of publication, by demonstrating the intertextuality of poems that circulated in manuscript "miscellanies," and by enabling us to recognize the participation of "scribal communities" in the making of texts. His greater achievement is to manifest the enduring usefulness of a bibliographically informed literary history as a means of joining together the materiality of texts with the politics and economics of writing and reading. That so many aspects of book history achieve coherence in this work is a tribute both to the remarkable skills of Harold Love and to the discipline he represents.

David D. Hall

PREFACE

THE realization that this book needed to be written emerged from an interest in the editorial problems posed by the writings of Rochester and other Restoration authors of libertine and state verse. The period since 1960 has seen a remarkable growth in our understanding of the importance of manuscript copies to the circulation of these writings, and the first serious attempts by editors to reconstruct lost authorial texts from the highly variant copies. However, most of these attempts limited their concern to the individual poems, excluding any but the most perfunctory investigations of the larger manuscript anthologies in which most of them were to be found. This was understandable in that traditional approaches to recensional editing offer no satisfactory methodology for determining the relationships of such complex and heterogeneous wholes; but it also meant that the editorial enterprise was considering only one part of the available evidence.

It seemed obvious that if answers to this problem were to be found it could not be through any narrow technical analysis of variant readings, but had to embrace an understanding of the culture of transmission within which the proliferation of copies took place. It was equally clear that this culture was a very sophisticated one with links back to the period before the invention of printing when all texts were circulated in handwritten copies. From this realization that a wider context had to be found for a textual problem came the awareness that the context was a topic of even greater interest than the problem.

This account of the origins of my interest in the subject will explain the way in which it has been approached. Where the book draws on my own research into manuscripts and their transmission, this is mostly from the field just indicated; otherwise, in considering the periods and areas of the vast, multiform enterprise that I call by the name of scribal publication, my contribution has largely been one of collecting and interpreting the work of other scholars. The appreciation that such a book was necessary might just as easily have come to a worker in a very different speciality— say parliamentary compilations, cathedral music or scribally transmitted prophecies—and the resultant perception of the nature of scribal publication would necessarily have been a different one, not simply because of differences in the expert knowledge brought to bear, but because the very subject has no objective status independent of the point of view from which it is constructed. What is presented is to be seen as a model to aid in seeking solutions for practical problems but one that will itself continually require modification in the light of the solutions arrived at.

The decision to restrict this study to seventeenth-century examples followed from my initial concern with the generation of Rochester: to look any further into the past would make it difficult to assume continuity of practices. Obviously, much of what is said would also hold true of the generation of Sidney and Spenser, and examples have occasionally been borrowed from the 1590s. Yet it will be evident from what follows that the accession of James I precipitated a situation in which, for a variety of reasons, texts of great political and intellectual importance were deliberately reserved for the scribal medium. At the other end of our time scale, the accession of Anne provided a natural terminus, not because texts ceased to be circulated in manuscript, but because such texts (with the possible exception of John Dyer's newsletters) had lost the centrality to ideological debate which can still be claimed for them in the 1690s.

The chance to lay a foundation of research for this book was offered under ideal circumstances by the Cambridge University Library through the award of the Munby Fellowship in Bibliography for 1986–7. Among the many individuals who contributed guidance and suggestions during that year I owe a particular debt to David McKitterick, who encouraged the publication of an early summary of my findings in the *Transactions of the Cambridge Bibliographical Society*, and Sheila Lambert, who guided my first attempts to acquire an understanding of the scribal publication of parliamentary documents, as well as passing on invaluable references to her own and others' writings. Beyond that, Anne Barton, Howard Erskine-Hill, Paul Hartle, Mary

Hobbs, Robert D. Hume, Ian Jack, Peter Jones, Elizabeth Leedham-Green, Richard Luckett, Jeremy Maule, Don McKenzie and Arthur Sherbo all contributed helpful advice or useful leads for which I am grateful. At a later stage, following a break to complete a book on a nineteenth-century topic, I was able to draw on the vast expertise of Peter Beal and Hilton Kelliher. But my greatest debt is undoubtedly to Keith Walker, who heroically read the entire typescript, besides being a continual source of wit, wisdom, hospitality and obscure journal articles which would otherwise have escaped my notice.

It was my great fortune during the period of writing to have the services of two enthusiastic and highly skilled research assistants, Meredith Sherlock and Dianne Heriot. Their contribution both to this book and to the edition of Rochester in which I hope to apply its discoveries has been very considerable. I am also much in debt to my colleagues in the Monash University English Department, Philip Ayres, Geoff Hiller, Clive Probyn and Chris Worth, all of whom made valuable comments on draft chapters, and Denise Cuthbert and Mark Allinson for many useful leads regarding Marvell and Donne respectively. Wallace Kirsop and Brian McMullin of the Monash Centre for Bibliographical and Textual Studies and Richard Overell, Monash's Rare Books Librarian were generous, as always, in answering bibliographical and booktrade enquiries.

This book draws widely on my 'Scribal publication in seventeenth-century England', *Transactions of the Cambridge Bibliographical Society* 9 (1987), 130–54. An early version of Chapter 7 appeared as 'The editing of Restoration scriptorial satire' in *Editing in Australia*, ed. Paul Eggert, Canberra, 1990, pp. 65-84, while the opening section of Chapter 4 draws on my 'Manuscript versus print in the transmission of English literature, 1600–1700', *Bibliographical Society of Australia and New Zealand Bulletin* 9 (1985), 95–107.

References cited at any stage by short-title are included in the bibliography; others should be sought through the index.

Clayton, Victoria   H.L.

Author's Note to the Paperback Edition

Since this book was first published, two particularly valuable studies have extended our understanding of its topic. These are Arthur F. Marotti, *Manuscript, Print, and the English Renaissance Lyric* (Ithaca, N.Y., 1995) and H. R. Woudhuysen, *Sir Philip Sidney and the Circulation of Manuscripts, 1558–1640* (Oxford, 1996). Peter Beal's important Lyell Lectures are to appear as *In Praise of Scribes: Manuscripts and Their Makers in Seventeenth-Century England.*

H.L.
July 1997

CONTENTS

ILLUSTRATIONS

ABBREVIATIONS

BIHR	*Bulletin of the Institute of Historical Research*
BL	British Library
BNYPL	*Bulletin of the New York Public Library*
BSANZ Bulletin	*Bulletin of the Bibliographical Society of Australia and New Zealand*
CSP(Dom)	*Calendars of state papers: domestic series*
CTB	*Calendars of treasury books*
ELN	*English language notes*
EMS	*English manuscript studies*
HMC	*Historical Manuscripts Commission*
IELM	Beal, Peter, comp. *Index of English literary manuscripts. Volume 1 1450–1625* and *Volume 2 1625–1700* (London, 1980–92)
M&L	*Music and letters*
MLR	*Modern languages review*
N&Q	*Notes and queries*
PBA	*Proceedings of the British Academy*
POAS (Yale)	*Poems on affairs of state. Augustan satirical verse, 1660–1714*, gen. ed. George deF. Lord 7 vols. New Haven, 1963–75.
P&P	*Past and present*
PRO	Public Record Office
RES	*Review of English studies*
SB	*Studies in bibliography*
SEL	*Studies in English literature*
SP	*Studies in philology*
STC	*A short-title catalogue of books printed in England, Scotland and Ireland and of English books printed abroad 1475-1640*, first comp. by A. W. Pollard and G. R. Redgrave; 2nd edn, rev. and enlarged by W. A Jackson, F. S. Ferguson and Katharine F. Pantzer (London, 1976–86)

The Culture and Commerce of Texts

PART I

SCRIBAL PUBLICATION

I

THE PHENOMENON

In publishing this Essay of my Poeme, there is this great
disadvantage against me; that it commeth out at this time,
when Verses are wholly deduc't to Chambers, and nothing
esteem'd in this lunatique Age, but what is kept in Cabinets,
and must only passe by Transcription . . .

Michael Drayton (1612)[1]

I might have had one Word here by Way of Reflection upon
the happy Times we are just now coming to; Times I
remember very well to have seen before, when Printing
being not in use, I mean as to News-Papers, State-Tracts,
Politicks, &c., Written Scandal shall revive, and the Nation
shall swarm with Lampoon, Pasquinade, written Reflec-
tions, Characters, Satyrs, and an inconceivable Flood of
written News-Letters.

Daniel Defoe (1712)[2]

THAT many of the texts known to an educated English reader of
the seventeenth century would have been encountered in
manuscript rather than in print is hardly news: the collections of
major British and United States libraries contain many thousands
of testimonies to this fact. That some of this material was the
creation of professional scribes, whose work was distributed
through organized markets, while less widely known, is also a
matter of record—the advent of the press did not extinguish older

---

[1] 'To the generall reader', *Poly-olbion*, in *The works of Michael Drayton*, ed. J. William
Hebel (Oxford, 1961), iv, p. v. The idea is repeated in his 'To . . . Henery Reynolds
Esquire', ll. 187–95 (ibid., iii. 231).
[2] *A review of the state of the British nation*, viii. 708 (facsim. ed. A. W. Secord (New York,
1938), book 21).

methods of publication through manuscript. That certain seven-teenth-century poets, among them Donne, Corbett, Strode, King, Carew, Pestell, Marvell, Cotton, Katherine Philips, Traherne, Rochester and Dorset, wrote primarily for scribal transmission is amply acknowledged by their editors and confirmed by the formidable list of sources for the best-known of these given in Peter Beal's volumes of the *Index of English literary manuscripts*.[3] What is lacking to date has been an awareness that each of these things is a part of a larger phenomenon—scribal publication—which had a role in the culture and commerce of texts just as assured as that of print publication. The aim of this book is to explore the nature of this phenomenon and to propose terms for its further investigation.[4]

In doing so it will be necessary to draw connections between fields of enquiry which, for reasons that invite consideration, have not been seen as related. Between 1952 and 1978 the Clarendon Press published the distinguished Gardner and Milgate editions of Donne's poetry.[5] The main textual sources for these were manuscript collections circulated during Donne's lifetime, others written after his death, and a first printed collection which was itself reliant on scribally published exemplars.[6] Over much the same period David M. Vieth was working on his path-breaking study of the scribal transmission of Rochester's verse, *Attribution in Restoration poetry*, and the edition which drew on its findings.[7] The earlier volumes of the Donne edition were available to Vieth, and

[3] Peter Beal, *Index of English literary manuscripts. Volume 1 1450–1625. Volume 2 1625–1700* (London, 1980–).

[4] These matters were originally raised in my 'Scribal publication in seventeenth-century England', *Transactions of the Cambridge Bibliographical Society* 9, no. 2 (1987), 130–54. There is a also a lucid statement of the issues in Hilton Kelliher's review of Beal, *IELM*, i/1 and 2 in *Library*, 6:4 (1982), 435–40.

[5] John Donne, *The divine poems*, ed. Helen Gardner (1952), *The elegies and the songs and sonnets*, ed. Helen Gardner (1965), *The satires, epigrams and verse letters*, ed. Wesley Milgate (1967) and *The epithalamions, anniversaries and epicedes*, ed. Wesley Milgate (1978). The poems are currently being re-edited for the Variorum Donne to be published by the University of Missouri Press.

[6] Discussed in Alan MacColl, 'The circulation of Donne's poems in manuscript' in A. J. Smith, ed., *John Donne: essays in celebration* (London, 1972), pp. 28–46; *The first and second Dalhousie manuscripts: poems and prose by John Donne and others, a facsimile edition*, ed. Ernest W. Sullivan II (Columbia, Mo., 1988), pp. 201–8 and Beal, *IELM*, i/1, 243–568.

[7] David M. Vieth, *Attribution in Restoration poetry: a study of Rochester's 'Poems' of 1680* (New Haven, Conn., 1963); *The complete poems of John Wilmot, Earl of Rochester*, ed. David M. Vieth (New Haven, Conn., 1968).

his own work to the Donne editors for all but their first volume. The two projects were concerned with very similar traditions of copying and distribution and faced identical problems in endeavouring to construct texts from a multiplicity of witnesses. Yet neither cites the findings or textual arguments of the other or shows any sign of having drawn on them. The example is far from unique: editors of seventeenth-century poetry have generally shown a quite staggering lack of interest in authorial traditions other than the one in which they were directly engaged.

This is hard to understand when, as is so often the case, the most characteristic mode through which verse was circulated to its readers was the miscellany containing work by a number of writers, rather than the manuscript devoted to the work of a single poet. Miscellanies have usually been treated simply as quarries for texts of individual writers and as providers of dating evidence. Rare is the editor who, like Vieth in his study of the major Rochester source Yale MS Osborn b 105, pauses to consider how the larger context provided by the miscellanies may have influenced the writing or reading of the individual poem.[8] From the earlier Stuart period, only Mary Hobbs's study of miscellanies circulated by Henry King and Arthur F. Marotti's of the social context of Donne's poetry can be said seriously—and successfully—to have confronted such questions.[9] To Hobbs the miscellany is a communal as well as an individual construct, to be read for what it shows us about the communities in which it was created and revised. The interest of the case is heightened by the fact that King was himself a scribal publisher of miscellanies, presenting his own poems intermixed with those of friends. Marotti emphasizes that miscellanies (whether manuscript or printed) 'often give the impression that they retain a sense of the social environment of the verse they collect' in presenting 'courtly or satellite-courtly poems written on particular (if conventionalized) social occasions'. Removed from this setting the poems

---

[8] See Vieth, *Attribution*, pp. 56–100 and *passim*.

[9] Mary Hobbs, 'An edition of the Stoughton manuscript (an early seventeenth-century poetry collection in private hands, connected with Henry King and Oxford) seen in relation to other contemporary poetry and song collections', London University Ph.D. thesis, 1973 and 'Early seventeenth-century verse miscellanies and their value for textual editors', *English manuscript studies 1100–1700* 1 (1989), 182–210; Arthur F. Marotti, *John Donne, coterie poet* (Madison, Wis., 1986), pp. 5–13.

suffer a decontextualization which it is one of the tasks of the historicist critic to reverse.[10] The possibilities of interpretation open to an early reader would always have been governed by the wider context provided by the miscellanies, and the fact that particular poems would tend to cluster with others from the same circles. Any attempt to enter that first reading experience must always take account of the company poems were accustomed to keep.

It must also be stressed—genealogical analysis of variants hardly being an exact science—that the transmissional history of the poem can often be understood only through that of the miscellanies in which it is encountered. It is certainly the case that the ability to derive a whole family of miscellanies from a particular scriptorial archive vastly simplifies the task of creating stemmas for their individual items. For the Restoration period, Vieth's pioneering work on the scribal publication of verse in the 1670s and 1680s is valuably supplemented by W. J. Cameron's detailed analysis of the surviving output of a scriptorium of the 1690s specializing in verse miscellanies.[11] If Cameron's findings are correct, which I believe to be the case, the texts of Restoration state and libertine verse contained in a substantial body of manuscripts can be assumed, in the absence of countervailing evidence in the variants themselves, to derive from single archetypes. Unfortunately, scholarly information about these matters is not abundant, and when it does exist is too often ignored. Cameron's hypothesis has drawn no follow-up work prior to the present study. Even Hobbs's important findings languished for many years in an unpublished Ph.D. thesis. The problem is not simply one of editors and critics being too absorbed in particular authors, works or manuscripts to reach out to the wider culture of transmission, but of a blindness to the nature and persistence of this culture.

This observation is not intended to denigrate editors. Editing is hard enough work as it is without adding new methodological requirements. There are also many practical difficulties affecting research. The manuscript heritage is now widely dispersed over

[10] Marotti, pp. 12, 11.

[11] W. J. Cameron, 'A late seventeenth-century scriptorium', *Renaissance and modern studies* 7 (1963), 25–52 and 'Transmission of the texts' in *Poems on affairs of state. Augustan satirical verse, 1660–1714*, gen. ed. George deF. Lord (New Haven, Conn., 1963–75), v. 528–38. Collations by the present author of texts from the manuscripts concerned have always supported Cameron's results.

Britain, North America, Europe and even Japan. Microfilms (necessarily regarded by many libraries as a means of fund-raising) and travel are both expensive. While most libraries with large manuscript collections give strong support to the work of scholars, others, through tradition or penury, insist on restrictive rules for the use of their materials. Frequently funds for an expensive acquisition may only be available if first publication is reserved for the purchasing institution, which will not necessarily possess the scholar best fitted for the job. Above all, awareness of the existence of problems is something which is itself dependent on the progress of scholarship. It was not until such editions as the Oxford Donne and Suckling, Vieth's and Keith Walker's editions of Rochester, the monumental Yale *Poems on affairs of state* series and Ernest W. Sullivan's edition of the Dalhousie miscellanies were in existence that the transmissional challenges posed by scribal publication fully revealed themselves to literary scholars.[12] As late as 1955 it was still possible for an Oxford edition to dismiss the manuscript tradition of a scribally published poet with the remark: 'most of the manuscripts containing poems written by or attributed to Corbett are commonplace books of little authority, and sometimes compiled, in part at least, from printed sources', and to refer the reader to 'the printed catalogues of the great libraries' for further information.[13] Finally, it should be remembered that literary editors normally work to provide the kinds of texts required by critics. An author-centred critical ideology will assign less importance to the wider structures that connect sources than one which is concerned with the intertextual workings of language, or which, in foregrounding the role of the reader, requires that more information be given about the historical circumstances of reading.[14]

It will also be evident that the making of historical connections is

[12] *The works of Sir John Suckling*, ed. Thomas Clayton and L. A. Beaurline (Oxford, 1971); *POAS (Yale)*; Vieth, *Complete poems*; *The poems of John Wilmot, Earl of Rochester*, ed. Keith Walker (Oxford, 1984); Sullivan, *Dalhousie manuscripts*. For the other editions mentioned see nn. 5 and 6 above.

[13] *The poems of Richard Corbett*, ed. J. A. W. Bennett and H. R. Trevor-Roper (Oxford, 1955), p. lvii. For a refutation of these assumptions, see Hobbs, 'Early seventeenth-century verse miscellanies', pp. 183–4.

[14] These relationships are further explored in D. C. Greetham, 'Textual and literary theory: redrawing the matrix', *SB* 42 (1989), 1–24 and '[Textual] criticism and deconstruction', *SB* 44 (1991), 1–30.

7

hindered by the existence of scholarly lines of demarcation, of which the most glaring is the year 1660. Vieth, as well as neglecting the example of Donne, makes no reference to Carew, who performed a literary role in the court of Charles I which was a direct model for that which Rochester was to adopt at the court of Charles II, and whose work was distributed through similar modes of scribal publication.[15] The reason for this is not hard to seek. Literary scholars working on the earlier Stuart period define themselves as Renaissance specialists, inhabiting a different conceptual as well as historical world from those working on the later Stuart period who define themselves as Augustan specialists. Those Renaissance specialists who concern themselves with Caroline authors further define themselves as studying the end of a process of development which reached its highest point with Shakespeare, while Restoration scholars see themselves as occupied with the beginning of a process which is to reach fruition in Pope and the eighteenth-century novelists. Despite the existence of the *Oxford book of seventeenth-century verse* there is no such subject as seventeenth-century literature in our academies. Historians acknowledge the same divide. W. K. Jordan, writing in 1960, could think 'of no scholar who has done really significant work on both sides of the watershed, who has moved easily and freely in both historical environments'.[16] It is not hard today to think of exceptions to this generalization, especially in the fields of economic, ecclesiastical and legal history, but it still has force. Differences in interest and professional approach become hypostatized into a belief that there was a sharp and decisive break in the development of English culture in 1660—a year which, in actuality, saw a massive attempt to obliterate all political change that had taken place since 1641. But, if chronological and ideological divisions within one discipline are enough to blind literary scholars and some historians to continuities in scribal practice, how much more serious are those that separate them from scholars in other disciplines—from musicologists, historical socio-

---

[15] The similarity extends to the first printed edition of each writer's verse having been an unauthorized collection of mixed authorship hastily set from a scribally published miscellany immediately following his death.

[16] *The restoration of the Stuarts, blessing or disaster? A report of a Folger Library conference held on March 12 and 13, 1960* (Washington, DC, 1960), pp. 47–8.

logists, historians of science and medicine, legal scholars and codicologists, and these from each other? For the scribal transmission of verse is something that can be treated only when we have a sense of the very much wider enterprise of which it was only one part. The same agencies, both private and professional, which created the verse miscellanies were employed in a large variety of other fields, all of which throw light on each other, but few of which have been studied comparatively.

Scribal publication, then, is a perfect example of what Don R. Swanson has called 'undiscovered public knowledge'. By this he means knowledge that exists 'like scattered pieces of a puzzle' in scholarly books and articles, but remains unknown because its 'logically related parts . . . have never all become known to any one person'.[17] In the remainder of this chapter, I will demonstrate this principle, and the method to be followed in the rest of the book, by bringing together scattered pieces of work on two fields which to date have only been studied as isolated phenomena—the scribal publication of parliamentary proceedings and the provision of manuscript copies of viol consort music—and then by pointing to some ways in which these illuminate both each other and the larger phenomenon. This will also be an opportunity to consider what use is to be made of such knowledge once assembled.

NEWSLETTERS, SEPARATES AND PARLIAMENTARY COMPILATIONS

Political documents—state papers, short polemical tracts, and reports of parliamentary proceedings—were copied in larger quantities than any other kind of scribally published text and, for that reason, reveal more about the production of copies in general. But before we consider the case of the proceedings, it will be necessary to review the history of two contributory sub-types of the scribally published text, the manuscript newsletter and the 'separate'.

At the beginning of the seventeenth century the practice was

---

[17] Don R. Swanson, 'Undiscovered public knowledge', *Library quarterly* 56 (1986), 116. See also Roy Davies's review of this and other papers by Swanson in 'The creation of new knowledge by information retrieval and classification', *Journal of documentation* 45 (1989), 273–301.

already established of country gentlemen receiving news and political information on a regular basis from a town informant. Lawrence Stone notes that 'by the 1590s Peter Proby was writing regularly to the Earls of Shrewsbury, Derby, Pembroke, and Hertford, and many others of the nobility during their absences from Court'.[18] The extensive correspondence between John Chamberlain and a circle of friends headed by Dudley Carleton, Ralph Winwood and Lancelot Andrewes represents a stage before this custom had become professionalized. Chamberlain, an enquiring Londoner, traded information largely acquired in Paul's Walk for friendship, influence and more information, and not for money; yet he was operating in a mode which was already being pursued as a means of livelihood.[19] The advent and growing influence later in the century of the printed coranto and newspaper did not initially affect the newsletter trade, as much more could always be said in a letter than could be uttered in print. The very secretiveness of the operation cast a gloss over what might otherwise have been regarded as rather ordinary news. A 'Factor of newes for all the Shieres of *England*' in Jonson's *Newes from the new world discover'd in the moone* (1620) acknowledges this when he complains: 'I would have no newes printed; for when they are printed they leave to bee newes; while they are written, though they be false, they remaine newes still.'[20] A well-organized newsletter writer, with good sources of information, would soon build up a network of customers, who would pay a subscription to receive the letters. John Pory received a remarkable £20 a year from Lord Scudamore for his weekly letters in 1631–2, and Edward Rossingham was rumoured in 1640 to be charging 'not under' the same sum.[21] (Another source estimated Rossingham's income at £500 a year, suggesting a clientele of about the maximum size that could be written to on a weekly basis by a

[18] *The crisis of the aristocracy 1558–1641* (Oxford, 1965), p. 388.

[19] For Chamberlain, see *The letters of John Chamberlain*, ed. N. E. McClure, 2 vols (Philadelphia, 1939) and Wallace Notestein, *Four worthies* (New Haven, Conn., 1957), pp. 29–119. His 'knot of friends', a small 'scribal community' of the kind that will be discussed in Ch. 6, is treated in Notestein, pp. 37–8.

[20] *Ben Jonson*, ed. C. H. Herford and Percy and Evelyn Simpson (Oxford, 1925–52), vii. 514–15. The idea is repeated in *The staple of newes*, I. v. 46–50 (ibid., vi. 295).

[21] William S. Powell, *John Pory 1572–1636. The life and letters of a man of many parts* (Chapel Hill, NC, 1977), p. 55; *Proceedings of the short parliament of 1640*, ed. Esther S. Cope in collaboration with Willson H. Coates, Camden Society, 4:19 (London, 1977), p. 35.

single writer who also had to devote time to information gathering.[22]) After the Restoration Henry Muddiman charged £5 a year for a weekly letter, Giles Hancock between £4 and £6, and Will Urwin a reputed £10, while the average price for written news in 1709 was '£3 or £4 *per annum*'.[23] If demand for services should outstrip the power of the writer's own pen, clerks would be employed to duplicate a standardized form of the letter. However, the fiction was usually maintained that the letter was a personal communication between gentlemen, and in two surviving files of Rossingham's letters duplicated passages are supplemented by other material apparently unique to the recipient.[24] When in 1696 Ichabod Dawks's newsletter reached a circulation that made the transition to print unavoidable, he tried to retain something of the old exclusiveness by having a special script typeface cast.[25]

Despite this air of confidentiality, the circulations of some newsletters may have risen to several hundred copies. Jonson's fictional factor writes his 'thousand Letters a weeke ordinary, sometim⟨e⟩ twelve hundred', supplying his customers, to order, with Puritan, Protestant or 'Pontificiall' [i.e. Catholic] news.[26] This is no more to be taken literally than the outrageous claims of the other news-gatherers in this and *The staple of newes*; but the real-life model for the satirical portrait was genuine enough: a body of scribal journalists engaged in a profitable trade, some of whom will have specialized in personalized service to a small group of clients (and charged accordingly) and others in the distribution of a cheaper, standardized product to as many as practicable. In 1688 Sir Roger L'Estrange noted on an inflamma-

[22] Stone, p. 389. The claim was made by William Cavendish, Duke of Newcastle, in a memorandum to Charles II written shortly before the Restoration.

[23] Peter Fraser, *The intelligence of the secretaries of state and their monopoly of licensed news 1660–1688* (Cambridge, 1956), pp. 40, 128; HMC, 11th rep., app., vii. 20; Henry L. Snyder, 'Newsletters in England, 1689–1715, with special reference to John Dyer—a byway in the history of England' in Donovan H. Bond and W. Reynolds McLeod, eds, *Newsletters and newspapers: eighteenth-century journalism* (Morgantown, 1977), p. 8.

[24] Cope, p. 36. Of course, it is possible that what appears to be unique in the files, those to Lords Scudamore and Conway, was differentially recycled in other letters of the same week.

[25] Described in Stanley Morison, *Ichabod Dawks and his 'News-Letter'; with an account of the Dawks family of booksellers and scriveners, 1635–1731* (Cambridge, 1931), pp. 18–32.

[26] *Ben Jonson*, vii. 514. Cf. *The staple of newes*, I. v. 13–17 (ibid., vi. 294). The rivalry between newsletter and newspaper suppliers may be overstated. John Pory, a leading newsletter writer, maintained a close relationship with Nathaniel Butter, the pioneer coranto publisher.

tory newsletter: 'The Paper Enclosed is an Original of One Dyer, a Coffee-man in White-Fryers. There cannot upon a Fair Computation be so Few as Five Hundred Copies of it Spread over y^c Kingdom.'[27] In this case what we have is not satirical exaggeration, but an educated guess by a well-informed official. In the case of the official newsletters issued during the reign of Charles II as a domestic counterpart to the printed *London gazette*, circulations of well over a hundred are recorded. During the late 1660s, Joseph Williamson, under-secretary to secretary-of-state Arlington, sent letters to 122 correspondents within Britain and fifty-four overseas (though not to all of these simultaneously).[28] A staff of five clerks was required to maintain this output. Henry Muddiman's letter had a circulation of around 140 at the close of 1665 when it was still issued from Arlington's office, but undoubtedly increased this after February 1666 when it came under the patronage of the other Secretary.[29] Giles Hancock, the leading Whig newsletter writer of the 1680s, often brought 'above thirty letters to the post', a figure which to Fraser suggests a total of 'well over a hundred correspondents'—there being by this time three posts a week out of London as well as an efficient daily delivery system within the metropolis and surrounding boroughs.[30] From the 1650s there was a brisk demand from coffee houses, which were in effect also reading rooms. In 1683 Nathaniel Thompson recorded that the (mostly Whig) newsletter writers had 'foisted their Shams . . . at the constant Pension of 4, or 5s. a week from each Coffee-house'.[31]

The newsletter, then, was a stable and successful genre of scribal publication and one that maintained a function for some decades after the advent of the printed newspaper. However, it was not the

---

[27] BL MS Add. 41805, f. 93. This appears to be the earliest reference to Dyer's famous letter. For its later history, see Snyder, 'Newsletters'.

[28] For their names and addresses, see Fraser, pp. 140–4, 153–5.

[29] J. G. Muddiman, *The king's journalist 1659–1689: studies in the reign of Charles II* (London, 1923), pp. 258–64. Muddiman had originally produced his letter for Williamson, but changed masters after a dispute over the mixed public and entrepreneurial nature of his operation (Fraser, pp. 30, 34, 49). Williamson's ideal was one of a confidential exchange of information with the recipients of his letters.

[30] Fraser, p. 128, citing William Cotton's memorandum, *CSP (Dom.) 1683–4*, pp. 53–4.

[31] *Loyal Protestant and true domestic intelligence*, no. 239, 1 March 1682/3, p. 2. See also Fraser, pp. 114–21 and Muddiman, p. 219. Fearing competition from Thompson's printed newspaper, the newsletter writers arranged for a 'scandalous Villain' to harrass his hawkers and customers.

only scribal source of information on current happenings. Individuals who subscribed to newsletters were also likely to have large collections of the documents that historians call 'separates' and that were sometimes referred to in their own time as 'pocket manuscripts'.[32] Bibliographically the separate is an individually circulated short manuscript which was written as a unit, and not assembled from elements copied at varying times and places (which would be an 'aggregation'[33]). In the usage of historians it refers exclusively to texts of a political or ideological nature, but there is no reason why it should be restricted to this sense and it is convenient to be able to speak of poetical or theological separates. The most common format was the same as that favoured for the newsletter—a whole or half-sheet bifolium with the first three pages written on and the last left blank for addressing—but texts written over two or three sheets and quired or stab-sewn may also be so described. (Anything beyond this would comprise a manuscript book.) A separate usually contains a single text such as a speech or short treatise, but will sometimes present a 'linked group' of closely related items—for example epigrams on the same subject. Any more heterogeneous assemblage of texts becomes a 'compilation'.[34] In practice any text initially published as a separate, and that had a reasonably wide circulation, is likely to be known today both from true separates, as just defined, and from later copyings into compilations, commonplace books or volumes of 'collections'.

That political separates were produced in enormous numbers is made clear by the quantity that survive today: some can still be found in fifty or more contemporary copies. (Several tracts by a single author, Sir Robert Cotton, survive in such numbers.) While we can only speculate about the number that were once in circulation, the evidence of newsletters, whose surviving copies can be measured against an estimate of total circulation, would suggest that the loss rate has been considerable. Conservatively assuming a circulation of 200 a week for Dyer's letter, the 300 copies located by Snyder (pp. 8–9) for 1709–10 would represent

---

[32] e. g. on the title-page of Burleigh's *Certain precepts* (London, 1617).

[33] For this term, see Cameron, 'Scriptorium', p. 27.

[34] A compilation, as a single manuscript with heterogeneous contents, is distinct from an aggregation, which is joined together from a variety of pre-existing manuscripts.

only 1.5 per cent of those produced. For earlier separates the additional hazards of the Civil War and the great fire would have to be allowed for, as well as the fact that 'loose papers' were in constant demand for a variety of domestic uses. (An important Mary, Countess of Pembroke autograph was acquired 'among other broken books to putt up Coffee pouder'.[35]) These copies circulated by a variety of means. Chain copying by private individuals was probably the most important, but there is also evidence for commercial production by law scriveners and by booksellers, particularly those in the vicinity of the Inns of Court who dealt in legal manuscripts as well as printed books. The separate might also circulate as an adjunct to the newsletter, as is noted by Powell in his study of John Pory:

> In addition to payment for his regular newsletters, Pory also sold his patrons copies of 'excellent discourses' which he copied from various sources available to him in London. The speech of Sir Benjamin Rudyerd, 28 April 1628, may have been such an item. On 22 September 1631, in a postscript to a regular letter to Sir Thomas Puckering (which was also shared with Sir Thomas Lucy), he offered for ten shillings each an assortment of 'discourses' by Mons. de Rohan, a 'character' of Cardinal Richelieu, an 'apology' of the cardinal, and 'a pathetical Remonstrance' of the princes assembled before the Holy Roman Emperor in Leipzig. Lucy agreed to share the cost of these with Puckering. Several pieces which must have been prepared in this category are included among Pory's letters: the Rudyerd speech of 28 April 1628; Dr Mainwaring's submission, 21 June 1628; the king's speech to both houses, 26 June 1628; 'Certain speeches whereof one Mr Melvin a Scottishman is accused', 26 June 1628; and 'A true recital of what hath passed', 30 October 1630.[36]

The pieces named include four parliamentary reports of a kind which received very wide circulation in manuscript and which survives today both as actual separates and as transcripts entered from separates into albums and compilations.[37]

[35] Samuel Woodford's note, cited in *The triumph of death and other unpublished and uncollected poems by Mary Sidney, Countess of Pembroke (1561–1621)*, ed. G. F. Waller (Salzburg, 1977), p. 24. Jayne Ringrose records how Richard Rawlinson rescued several important collections of papers which had been sold to be used as waste. (' "I collect and I preserve": Richard Rawlinson 1690–1755 and eighteenth-century book collecting', *Book collector* 39 (1990), 36.)

[36] Powell, *John Pory*, p. 56.

[37] See, for example, the list of manuscript sources for speeches given in *Proceedings of the short parliament*, pp. 292–318.

The most extensive study to date of the political separate and newsletter in their relationship to larger unities was published in 1921 by Wallace Notestein and Frances Relf in the introduction to their edition of the commons debates of the 1629 parliament.[38] Once again, their discussion concentrates on one particular mode and occasion of scribal publication, only intermittently raising its gaze to the wider picture, but the material is of such richness that a great deal is suggested about that picture. More importantly, the hypotheses advanced by Notestein and Relf and the discussions of their findings by other historians permit us to consider how far practices observed in a particular field of scribal publication can be assumed to apply in other fields where evidence for them may not be so strong. The question is a vital one in that it is only if a positive answer is given, and the conditions defined under which such an answer would be valid, that we can hope to use a generalized model of the procedures of scribal publication in the search for historical explanations.

Prior to 1921 the proceedings of the parliament had been known from the scribally published *A true relation of every day's proceedings in parliament since the beginning thereof being the 20th of January 1628* [i.e. 1628/9]. This is available in print in editions of 1641, 1654 and 1707 and the 1751 *Parliamentary history*, as well as having been reproduced in part by Rushworth in the second volume of the *Collections*.[39] But the texts of the three editions differ from each other in a great many details, and also from the text in the *Parliamentary history* which appears to have been conflated from 1707 and two manuscript sources. The editors discovered that none of the printed editions possessed authority, but that they were simply taken from whatever manuscript happened to be available to the printer. Their own edition drew on forty-eight contemporary manuscripts of the *True relation*, the survivors of what must have been a much larger body once in circulation. A new census would undoubtedly uncover additional sources.[40]

Circulation on this scale of a scribally published text is not in

---

[38] *Commons debates for 1629* (Minneapolis, 1921), pp. xi–lxv.

[39] *CD 1629*, p. xv.

[40] One such, purchased from a law bookseller in the year of the parliament, is described in Edward Hughes, 'A Durham manuscript of the *Commons debates* of 1629', *English historical review* 74 (1959), 672–9.

itself unusual, but the nature of its contents makes the *True relation* a valuable witness to the processes of its creation, production and distribution. For a start it should be noted that it is neither a newsletter nor a separate but a compilation formed out of independently circulating separates of parliamentary speeches, messages and declarations, together with linking passages of a diary-like nature.[41] The 1921 edition lists fifty-eight copies then known of seventeen elements found in the compilation, which survive independently of it as separates or miscellany transcripts *from* separates. While a few may have been copied from the *True relation* itself, there can be no doubt that most of this transmission was distinct from and, in its origins, prior to that of the compiled text. Notestein and Relf differed from most editors of historical documents in possessing practical skills in the genealogical analysis of textual variation. This allowed them to dispose very quickly of an earlier hypothesis that the manuscripts were descended from a single archetype which could be reconstructed by applying the method of Lachmann. Instead they diagnosed a situation similar to that to which some contemporary Chaucer scholars attribute variations in the order of the *Canterbury tales*: namely that several compilers created differing versions of the larger text (four in the case of the *True relation*) by making their own selection and ordering of the currently available materials.[42] According to this view, the differences arose from variations between the summaries (of which for one period two were available) and differences in the choice and placing of separates.

As regards the general availability by 1629 of separates of parliamentary speeches and declarations, there was no shortage of evidence. Despite regularly renewed attempts to enforce the ancient principle of secrecy, such materials had been freely circulating since the time of Elizabeth. For the reigns of James I and Charles I they survive in 'untold numbers'.[43] Moreover, these are generally of quite a different cast from the brief versions of the same materials found in the 'newsletter' sections of the *True relation*

---

[41] *CD 1629*, pp. 271–2.

[42] For the possible Chaucerian parallel, see Ralph Hanna III, 'The Hengwrt manuscript and the canon of *The Canterbury tales*', *English manuscript studies 1100–1700* 1 (1989), 64–84.

[43] *CD 1629*, p. xxii.

or the hurriedly scribbled accounts sometimes found in members' personal diaries. Notestein and Relf observe:

The separates are obviously the product of leisure. They have, most of them, full, rounded sentences, they are not at all conversational in style, but rather oratorical and flowing. They are full of delightful allusions to scripture and to the classic writers. They reveal in every way the fact that they have been 'written up'. They give the names of the speakers in full and present the speeches in a formal, full-dress pattern. They are finished productions intended for a wide circulation.[44]

Among a wealth of attendant evidence gathered from the period 1610–42 were cases where members circulated their speeches in a different form from that in which they had been delivered, or even speeches which had never been delivered at all. At other times, speeches were deliberately misattributed under illustrious names or compiled on the basis of second-hand reports.[45] It is clear that there were many active note-takers in parliament who could probably have passed on a fair report of a speech; but it is equally clear that the circulation of speeches by the author was an important form of political activism. The editors cite comments by Simonds D'Ewes, Peter Heylyn, Bulstrode Whitelock and John Nalson relating to this practice, as well as the following from the preface to Thomas Fuller's *Ephemeris parliamentaria*:

Some *Gentlemen, Speakers* in this *Parliament*, imparted their *Speeches* to their *intimate Friends*; the transcripts whereof were multiplied amongst others (the penne being very procreative of issue in this nature:) and since it hath happened that the *Gentlemens Originalls* have in these *troublesome* times miscarried, yet so that the *fountain* (as I may say) being dried up, hath fetch't this water from the *channell*, & they have again supplied their losses from those to whom they civilly communicated a *copy* of their paines.[46]

Some parliamentary documents, including legal arguments, were available to members from the Clerk's book and could be copied at their request in the Clerk's scriptorium. This material was of

[44] *CD 1629*, pp. xx–xxi.
[45] *CD 1629*, pp. xxii–xli.
[46] Thomas Fuller, *Ephemeris parliamentaria* (London, 1654), ¶¶1ᵛ; cited *CD 1629*, pp. xxviii–xxix. Lord Digby's speech on Strafford's attainder was given by him 'to John Moore a com[m]on writer to write 20 copies' (ibid., p. xl; BL MS Harl. 163, f. 396ᵛ).

particular interest to the legal profession, and there is every reason to suppose that copies were sought by legal stationers for further duplication. Separates of actual speeches would appeal to a much wider public, embracing leading county families (many separates show marks of mailing), foreign diplomats, politically involved clergymen, and members of both houses, some of whom possessed large collections of separates.[47]

Some separates of speeches show signs of being compiled by outsiders with an imperfect grasp of parliamentary procedure. This, together with the very wide circulation achieved by the standard separates and the apparent rapidity with which they became available, led Notestein and Relf to hypothesize that professional 'venters of manuscripts' played a significant role in their multiplication.[48] This was certainly so by the early 1640s when Samuel Pecke, a scrivener, actually had a stall in Westminster Hall for the sale of parliamentary speeches and proceedings, though one would be surprised if this was a location of long standing.[49] Stationers or newsletter writers might acquire a copy directly from the author (in which case, as with Sir John Eliot's speeches, the resulting text would be a good one), might draw on notes taken from a member, or might cobble up a version of their own from verbal reports. A Commons resolution of 25 January 1641 drew a lively picture of 'loose beggerly schollers who did in Alehowses invent speeches of and make speeches of members in the Howse' which were then sold to stationers.[50] None the less, the *CD 1629* editors' claim that separates were 'parliamentary speeches, etc., gathered by ignorant, careless and often unscrupulous scriveners in roundabout ways and hastily put together for immediate circulation' (p. xli) probably underestimates the amount of what will subsequently be called 'author' and 'user' publication involved. More caution should also have been extended with regard to the time range of the evidence cited (much of which is from the early 1640s) and of the manuscripts

---

[47] *CD 1629*, pp. xxxi–xxxiv.
[48] p. xxxiv. Evidence is presented from the D'Ewes diaries and the Borlase 'newsletters' suggesting that separates were normally received 'about a week after the delivery of the speech' (p. xxxiii).
[49] Muddiman, p. 10.
[50] BL MS Harl. 162, f. 351ᵛ; *CD 1629*, p. xxxv.

themselves—bearing in mind that material relating to the parliaments of Charles I continued to be copied for several decades.[51] As regards the dating of sources, it makes sense to assume that a separate that survives as a separate is probably fairly close to the event: the average life expectancy of unbound separates before and during the Civil War years is unlikely to have been high.[52] It was separates aggregated into bound volumes or texts recopied into compilations or personal miscellanies which were more likely to be preserved to the present day. The 1629 *True relation* is itself one of these larger compilations and in some sources has become incorporated into others of still wider scope. However, the dates of surviving sources are of little significance when a later copy simply replaced an earlier one. The real problem to be resolved is whether the overall population of copies shrank from a large base, grew from a small one, or maintained a roughly stable profile over the crucial decades. At present there is no way of choosing between the three models. Genealogical analysis can demonstrate the existence of lost intermediaries but has no method for estimating the number of texts intervening between a surviving document and the nearest common ancestor. In the end we must rely on a broader assessment of the vitality of the trade in separates and compilations at the time of the parliament, a matter in which evidence from fields of scribal publication other than the political has to be considered.

As well as investigating the circulation of separates, Notestein and Relf also had to explain the diary-like accounts of proceedings in which the separates are embedded, and for which they use the term 'newsletters'. This reflects their belief that these were compiled outside the House by newsgathering professionals drawing on information from members. There are examples of parliamentary newsletters in an account by Pory of a day in the

[51] However, the copy cited in Hughes, 'A Durham manuscript' was certainly written in the year of the parliament, being inscribed 'August the 10th, 1629, John Heath empt Londino a W. Walbanck'. The parties to this transaction seem to have been John Heath of Durham who entered Gray's Inn on 8 August 1620 and Matthew Walbanck, bookseller at Gray's Inn Gate, or a member of his family.

[52] Some reasons for this have already been suggested. More generally P. J. Croft observes that '"Loose papers"—i.e. manuscripts written on unbound sheets—are the most intrinsically vulnerable of all types of record, and survive only when they become incorporated with other papers at an early date' (*Autograph poetry in the English language* (London, 1973), i, p. xv). Parliamentary separates would have suffered further as documents which some would regard as risky to keep.

1610 parliament (of which he was himself a member) and material forwarded in 1640 by Rossingham.[53] Newsletter-like accounts also survive for the 1628 parliament (BL MS Stowe 366, 367) and for the Short and Long Parliaments, but none external to the *True relation* for 1629.[54] This is not an overwhelming objection to the newsletter hypothesis, since such material would be expected to have a low survival rate, especially once it was also available in larger retrospective compilations. Moreover, it is possible that newsletter accounts (which were technically in contempt of parliament) would have been burnt after reading—a practice enjoined on his customers by Pory.[55] On the other hand, a circulation on the scale envisaged by Notestein and Relf would surely have left some trace of itself in the form of a particular letter or two bearing an address. In the absence of this, the strongest evidence for the newsletter hypothesis remains the one that first suggested it—namely the presence of the diary-like material in each of the four recensions of the *True relation*, with the implication that four separate compilers (whether stationers, newsletter writers or private individuals) were independently in possession of copies. However, Notestein and Relf fail to consider, and by this failure do not exclude, the possibility that the summary of proceedings may only have become available after the end of the session. Neither do they consider whether the four recensions may have arisen within a single scriptorium.

Validation (though not proof) for the last possibility is provided by an account of two scriptoria of the 1670s run by the Whig booksellers Thomas Collins and John Starkey which specialized in the provision of exactly this kind of material:

There are two booksellers shops (viz. John Sterkey's and Thomas Collen's, living neer Temple Bar) that poyson both City and country with false newes.

To these shops are sent every afternoon

1. All novells and accurents so penned as to make for the disadvantage of the King and his affairs.

---

[53] Powell, pp. 65–9; Cope, pp. 36–7.

[54] *CD 1629*, pp. xlii–xlv. For the Stowe MSS, see *Commons debates 1628*, ed. Robert C. Johnson, Mary Frear Keeler, Maija Jansson Cole and William B. Bidwell (New Haven, Conn., 1977–8), i. 20–3 and below.

[55] Powell, p. 54.

II. All resolutions of Parliament that are either voted or a preparing for vote in either House, perfect true, or artificially corrupted, or penned by halves on purpose as may make most for the Faction.

III. All speeches of the most eminent members of each House that way affected, upon every business, are also sent them.

IV. Addresses also intended and at any time preparing by either House are here to be had in copies.

All these are thus disposed as followeth.

To these shops, for those things, every afternoon do repair severall sorts of people.

1. Young lawyers of both the Temples and the other Inns of Court, who here generally receive their tincture and corruption.

2. Ill-affected citizens of all sorts.

3. Ill-affected gentry.

4. The emissaries and agents of the severall parties and factions about town.

Against the time of their coming the Masters of those Shops have a grand book or books, wherein are registred ready for them, all or most of the forenamed particulars; which they dayly produce to those sorts of people to be read, and then, if they please, they either carry away copies, or bespeak them against another day.

These take care to communicate them by Letter all over the kingdome, and by conversation throughout the City and suburbs.

The like industry is used by the masters of those shops, who together with their servants are every afternoon and night busied in transcribing copies, with which they drive a trade all over the kingdome.

You may at present there have a copy of the intended address to his Majesty which the Houses have not yet agreed to.[56]

What is described here is exactly the kind of organization which

[56] BL MS Egerton 3329, fol. 57; Andrew Browning, *Thomas Osborne, Earl of Danby and Duke of Leeds 1632–1712* (Glasgow, 1944–51), iii. 2–3. A file of Collins's newsletters for 1688 is preserved in BL Add. MS 34487. For the scribal publication of parliamentary votes and proceedings after 1660 see Fraser, pp. 124–6. The 'Preface to the reader' of *A coppy of the journal-book of the House of Commons for the sessions of parliament begun at Westminster the 21. day of October, 1678. and continued until the 30. day of December next following* (London, 1680) justifies the printing of proceedings from the currency of inaccurate manuscript copies: '*Besides which there are many other most remarkable passages worthy our curiosity and knowledge, and very instructive both as to what has past, and towards what is to come; none of which should have been thus exposed (though this juncture of time gives so great a liberty to the Press) had not this very thing been handed about in Manuscripts to the great charge, as well as the great abuse of inquisitive Gentlemen, by imperfect Coppies; for what that Honorable House thinks fit to be lock'd up in their Archives, ought not to be exposed without their leave; but when any such secrets; are stolen abroad, it can be thought no ways unbecoming to make them speak the truth, and correct the mistakes that are incident to a hasty pen; so that here you shall find onely such Lapses as are inseperable to the Press*'

21

might have given rise to all stages of the creation of the *True relation* and perhaps even its division into four separate recensions. This division could have happened as the result of copying by several scribes simultaneously from an exemplum in the form of loose sheets, or from copying over a longer time span from an exemplum whose constituent elements were not stable (what will later be described as a 'rolling' as opposed to a 'static' archetype), or, designedly, as the result of preparing recensions to suit the knowledge and interests of particular customers.[57] It is true that the date of the document is 1675 not 1629 but the claim is not made here that the existence of the Starkey and Collins operations at a later period implies that of a predecessor using the same techniques—simply that, now the new model is admitted, the existing textual evidence requires to be reassessed and new evidence sought that would permit us to test the possibility. This cannot be performed from the *CD 1629* record of variations which, as a matter of policy, omits all readings 'whose only service would be to show the worth of particular manuscripts' (p. 3). Moreover, not all sources were collated in their entirety (p. 276). None the less, it remains possible that the advanced techniques of genealogical analysis which are described in Chapter 8, if applied to a fresh collation, could permit a preference to be established for one model over the other.

To say this is to assert that the *True relation* still remains a document in need of explanation, and that this explanation can only be provided when we possess a much fuller understanding not only of its own textual history but of the regularities (such as they may have been) of scribal publication over a much broader prospect.

($A2^r$–2^v). A Commons debate of 29 October 1678, cited by Fraser (p. 124), mentions a Mr Cole (perhaps Elisha Cole the author and writing master) as a supplier of parliamentary separates and that they were available 'sometimes for 6*d.* sometimes for 12*d* according as they were considerable'. The theme is renewed in the preface to *A true copy of the journal-book of the last parliament* (London, 1680), $A3^r$: '*The purchace of so many written Coppies as have been dispers'd at so great rates (notwithstanding the many imperfections they are fraught withal) demonstrates sufficiently, the vallue curious people sets upon them; how much more acceptable therefore must they needs be when purged from their Errors, and brought down to such a reasonable price, as to afford Gentlemen the benefit of them in their Libraries, without any great Tax upon their Purses'*.

[57] Cope, pp. 35–7, regards this last possibility as the most likely cause of the variations among texts of the diurnal of the 1640 parliament.

THE SCRIBAL PUBLICATION OF CONSORT MUSIC FOR
VIOLS

My other example of a specialized study of scribal publication is the admirable *Thematic index of music for viols* published by the Viola da gamba Society of Great Britain.[58] Although the index includes printed as well as manuscript sources, its interest for us lies in its being an exhaustive inventory of surviving examples of a particular class of seventeenth-century, scribally circulated text. Within this class, our concern will be with the sources of consort music written for three to six viols.

The consort of viols was introduced into England by Italian court musicians during the reign of Henry VIII. During the later years of Elizabeth it became a favourite with amateurs, with the result that the reigns of James I and Charles I saw an outpouring of fantasias for the combination by Alfonso Ferrabosco II, Orlando Gibbons, John Coprario, John Ward, Richard Deering, William Lawes, John Jenkins and a number of lesser lights. The viol fantasia with its 'perpetuall grave course of fugue' maintained its popularity through the Commonwealth, when, as Roger North put it, 'many chose rather to fidle at home, than to goe out, and be knockt on the head abroad'.[59] However, after the Restoration, a shift of taste towards a lighter, more homophonic idiom based first on French and later on Italian models led to the neglect both of the instrument (in favour of the violin family) and the fantasia style. Purcell's fantasias, written in the early 1680s, are the last significant contribution to viol consort literature.

Consort music was and remains primarily players' music, giving each performer both an individually rewarding voice in the ensemble and a unique spatial perception of the interrelationship of the musical lines. It is most satisfactorily performed with the players in a ring facing inwards towards each other, the role of the listener, if any, being that of an eavesdropper. Roger North found an ideological value in this '*respublica* among the consortiers', contrasting it with the 'unsociable and malcreate behaviour' of 'some violin spark, that thinks himself above all the rest, and above

---

[58] Comp. Gordon Dodd, first instalment (London, 1980), with further instalments 1982, 1984 and 1987.

[59] *Roger North on music*, ed. John Wilson (London, 1959), pp. 25, 294.

23

the musick itself also, if it be not screwed up to the top of his capability'.[60] Such music encoded an idealized image of the gentry as a community of equals while, at the same time, providing release from the tensions of hierarchy in the state and in the family. In refusing a dominant role to any single part it was also asserting— even when played by musicians who were political royalists—a consensual conception of the ideal state.[61] The culturally and ideologically competing ideal of a dominant, ornate melody line supported by a subservient chordal continuo was frowned on by admirers of the viol, though most of their favourite composers eventually adjusted to it.[62] It also altered the social relationships of playing, making the accompanists subordinate to the soloist and the soloist in turn subordinate to the listener.

The kind of circle in which the consort style was cultivated is indicated by the learned nature of its counterpoint and the fondness of composers from Lawes onward for striking dissonances and bold modulations. It is not surprising to find either that Oxford maintained a strong tradition of consort playing or that several composers for the medium held appointments in the private music of James I and Charles I.[63] This was music for educated, often intellectual, music lovers who would themselves in most cases have been players. Seeing that to play the five and six part fantasias, which were the crown of the repertoire, required the continued presence of a group of competent performers in one place, there was a strong tendency for consort music to be associated with music-loving gentry families such as the L'Estranges, Norths,

[60] North, *Roger North*, p. 222. His words acquire interesting resonances from Patrick Collinson's use of the term 'republic' in *De republica Anglorum, or history with the politics put back* (Cambridge, 1990), pp. 18–35.

[61] This was not lost on left-wing musicologists of the 1930s and 1940s. See in particular Ernst Meyer's pioneering studies of the consort repertoire, *Die mehrstimmige Spielmusik des 17. Jahrhunderts in Nord- und Mitteleuropa* (Kassel, 1934) and *English chamber music* (London, 1946; rev. edn as *Early English chamber music* (London, 1982)), and John Manifold, *The amorous flute* (London, 1948), p. 14.

[62] For opinions to this effect see North, *Roger North*, p. 222 and Thomas Mace, *Musick's monument* (London, 1676), pp. 233–4.

[63] For music at Oxford, see Bruce Bellingham, 'The musical circle of Anthony Wood in Oxford during the Commonwealth and Restoration', *Journal of the Viola da gamba Society of America* 19 (1982), 6–70. Court appointments of the principal viol composers are detailed in *Records of English court music*, ed. Andrew Ashbee (Snodland, 1986–), greatly extending the work of H. C. de Lafontaine, *The king's musick* (London, 1909). The 'private music' was the inner circle of court musicians who played in the sovereign's own apartments.

Brownes, Packers, Bolles's, Cliffords, Hattons, Fanshawes, Hamonds, Maules and Pastons.[64] Children would be instructed and consorts directed (from the organ) by visiting music masters who in many cases were also composers for the medium.

The Viola da gamba Society's index demonstrates how profoundly reliant the players of viol consort music were on manuscript transmission. Of hundreds of surviving fantasias for the instruments written between 1600 and 1680, only a few in three parts by Gibbons, Lupo, Coprario, Young and Locke and some lightweight four and five part pieces by Michael East ever appeared in print.[65] The rest were published scribally by their

[64] The L'Estranges are discussed in Pamela Willetts, 'Sir Nicholas Le Strange and John Jenkins', *Music and letters* 42 (1961), 30–43 and 'Sir Nicholas Le Strange's collection of masque music', *British Museum quarterly*, 29 (1965), 79–81, and Andrew Ashbee, 'A further look at some of the Le Strange manuscripts', *Chelys* 5 (1973–4), 24–41; the Norths in North, *Roger North*, Pamela J. Willetts, 'John Lilly, musician and music copyist', *Bodleian Library record* 7 (1962–7), 307–11 and Margaret Crum, 'The consort music from Kirtling, bought for the Oxford Music School from Anthony Wood, 1667', *Chelys* 4 (1972), 3–10; the Brownes and Packers in Andrew Ashbee, 'Instrumental music from the library of John Browne (1608–1691), clerk of the Parliaments', *Music and letters* 58 (1977) 43–59, Nigel Fortune (with Iain Fenlon), 'Music manuscripts of John Browne (1608–91) and from Stanford Hall, Leicestershire' in *Source materials and the interpretation of music: a memorial volume to Thurston Dart*, ed. Ian Bent (London, 1981), pp. 155–68, and David Pinto, 'William Lawes' music for viol consort', *Early music* 6 (1978), 12–24. Information on other families will be found in Margaret Urquhart, 'Sir Robert Bolles Bt. of Scampton', *Chelys* 16 (1987), 16–29 and *Sir John St Barbe Bt. of Broadlands* (Southampton, 1983); Lynn Hulse, 'John Hingeston', *Chelys* 12 (1983), 23–42 (the Cliffords of Skipton Castle); David Pinto, 'The music of the Hattons', *RMA Research chronicle* 23 (1990), 79–108 (the Hattons and Fanshawes); Margaret Crum, 'A seventeenth-century collection of music belonging to Thomas Hamond, a Suffolk landowner', *Bodleian Library record* 6 (1957–61), 373–86; Calum McCart, 'The Panmure manuscripts: a new look at an old source of Christopher Simpson's consort music', *Chelys* 18 (1989), 18–29 (the Maules); Pamela Willetts, 'Musical connections of Thomas Myriell', *Music and letters* 49 (1968), 36–42 and 'The identity of Thomas Myriell', *Music and letters* 53 (1972), 431–3; Philip Brett, 'Edward Paston (1550–1630): a Norfolk gentleman and his musical collection', *Transactions of the Cambridge Bibliographical Society* 4 (1964), 51–69; and Andrew Ashbee, 'A not unapt scholar: Bulstrode Whitelocke (1605–1675)', *Chelys* 11 (1982), 24–31. John Harper, 'The distribution of the consort music of Orlando Gibbons in seventeenth-century sources', *Chelys* 12 (1983), 3–18 discusses the collections of Thomas Myriell, John Merro, John Browne and Narcissus Marsh (with bibliography). Craig Monson's valuable *Voices and viols in England, 1600–1650: the sources and the music* (Ann Arbor, Mich., 1982) discusses a wide range of surviving sets of manuscripts including those of Myriell, Hamond and Merro. Sets of unknown provenance are closely analysed for clues as to their geographical and institutional origins.

[65] Collections of dances, masque tunes and pieces arranged for broken consort did appear in print and may have been used by viol ensembles (as were madrigals) but were not primarily meant for them. The small corpus of printed ensemble music for lyra viol represents a separate tradition of the instrument.

composers for direct sale to players (some of whom will have been their pupils) or as part of their work for their patrons. Collections of fantasias consolidated into part books were also available, with some pieces evidently composed as sets for this purpose.[66] Once available in this form, new compositions moved quickly through the network of music-loving families, either by private copying or by purchase.

An insight into the quantity of material in circulation may be gained from the most popular of the composers, John Jenkins, whose entries in the *Thematic index* occupy seventy-six pages. The manner in which Jenkins operated as a publisher of his own music is illustrated by Roger North (born in 1651) who as a young man was closely associated with the by then elderly composer. North's account is of special interest because Jenkins's methods of reaching his public need not have been very different from those of a poet, a scholar or a writer of political tracts. By this stage of his life, Jenkins had long been a pensionary of a succession of music-loving, royalist households who welcomed his visits and would often have a room permanently reserved for his use. During his stays Jenkins would instruct the children of the house, supervise consort playing, copy and compose. North speaks of 'horsloads' of his works being 'dispersed about' and states that 'the private musick in England was in great measure supplyed by him'.[67] North himself occasionally acted as Jenkins's distributor by delivering copies of new compositions to the viol virtuoso, Dietrich Steffkins.[68] Transmission was not restricted to England. On one occasion

A Spanish Don sent over to the late S'P. Lely, the leaves of one part of a 3 part consort of his, with a desire to procure the rest, *costa che costa*; for his musick had got abroad and was more esteemed there than at home. I shewed him the papers, but he could tell nothing of them, when or where they were made, or might be found, onely he knew they were his owne.[69]

---

[66] Examples are the sets of six six-part fantasias by Orlando Gibbons and William White. The production and sale of partbooks of vocal music by a well-organized scriptorium of the late sixteenth century is discussed in Philip Brett, 'Edward Paston'; however, that all the manuscripts discussed were written for Paston is to be doubted. As with the verse and political miscellanies, there was considerable overlap between the different collections offered for sale, forcing assiduous collectors of new material into purchasing items they already had.

[67] North, *Roger North*, p. 345.

[68] Ibid. 21, 298, 347.

[69] Ibid. 296.

The channel of communication in this case is likely to have been Henry Butler, an English viol player at the Spanish court whose pupils included Philip IV and his son Don Juan.[70] Apart from some pieces said to have been contributed to Christopher Simpson's *The division viol* in 1659, there is no evidence that Jenkins sought print publication for any significant body of his music.[71] He was content with scribal publication and lived in comfort on the proceeds from it. It was Nicola Matteis, according to North, who made the discovery that higher returns could be made from printing music than from selling it in manuscript.[72]

What the case of Jenkins demonstrates is exactly what we would expect from the rich scribal heritage revealed by the *Thematic index*. Viol consort music, along with the related lyra-viol repertoire and fantasia suites and airs for violin, bass viol and organ, circulated through an extensive and well-organized network of copyists to a scattered but enthusiastic amateur clientele to whom it offered both an aesthetic and, as suggested earlier, an ideological satisfaction. But this circulation represented only one aspect of a much wider participation by the families concerned in the culture of scribal publication. That this was the case is evident at every turn; but for the moment a few instances must suffice. The first of these is the career of Roger North as writer for the scribal medium. North, besides his activity as a player and copyist of music, was a voluminous author of tracts, treatises and essays most of which remained unprinted during his lifetime. As a lawyer he belonged to a profession still predominantly dependent on the handwritten word; but in the long years of his retirement his conception of himself was clearly as an essayist, philosopher and family historian. He was also an inveterate reviser and reworker of material, deriving later treatises out of the materials of earlier ones.[73] Franciscus Korsten advances the opinion that North was his own

[70] Ian Woodfield, 'The first Earl of Sandwich, a performance of William Lawes in Spain and the origins of the pardessus de viole', *Chelys* 14 (1985), 40–2; Elizabeth V. Phillips, 'Henry Butler and the early viol sonata', *Journal of the Viola da gamba Society of America* 21 (1984), 45–52. Butler was active at the Spanish court between 1623 and 1652. Charles I of England was also a competent viol player.

[71] North, *Roger North*, p. 347.

[72] Ibid. 356. See also pp. 64–5 below.

[73] See Wilson on this point in *Roger North*, p. vii, and Mary Chan, 'Roger North's *Life* of Francis North', *RES* NS 42 (1991), 191–211.

sole intended reader; but this seems to be contradicted both by the public nature of the forms he chose for his writing and their frequently pedagogical tone.[74] While it is possible that he wrote with the expectation of posthumous print publication, it is more natural to see him as an heir to the tradition, which will be discussed in subsequent chapters, of the scribally published treatise, bearing in mind that such texts were frequently restricted by design to a single copy.[75] If Korsten is right, it may only be because North was a scribal author who had outlived his natural readership. For his deep identification with the culture of the inscribed word, the fifty-six volumes of his manuscripts in the British Library are sufficient evidence.[76]

A wider involvement in scribal publication was also displayed by another of Jenkins's patrons, Sir Henry North, baronet of Laxfield, Suffolk.[77] The evidence for this lies in the personal miscellany of John Watson, a fellow of Queens' College, Cambridge who in 1661 became vicar of Mildenhall in the same county.[78] Watson's manuscript, which will be discussed in more detail later, is of special value because it records the donors of separates that were copied into it, together with the date of copying. Among the contributors of texts was Jenkins himself, bringing poems by Sir Henry and his chaplain Clement Paman, as well as two poems of his own, one being an elegy on Lord Digby North.[79] However, Sir Henry and his wife Sara are also present in the volume as writers or transmitters of poems and inscriptions. Among these is 'Tush, look for no ease from Hippocrates', marked 'A Song in Sr H. North's Eroclea. transcribd

---

[74] F. J. M. Korsten, *Roger North (1651–1734): virtuoso and essayist* (Amsterdam, 1981), p. 23.

[75] See below, pp. 70–2.

[76] BL Add. MSS 32,500–32,551. For descriptions of these, see Mary Chan and Jamie C. Kassler, *Roger North. Materials for a chronology of his writings. Checklist no. 1* (Kensington, NSW, 1989), pp. 65–91. The whereabouts of other Roger North manuscripts are given in ibid. 50 and P. T. Millard, 'The chronology of Roger North's main works', *RES* NS 24 (1973), 283–94. North's (anonymous) print publications are described in Korsten, pp. 24–5.

[77] The Norths of Laxfield and Mildenhall were descended from Henry, second son of Roger, second Baron North (1531–1600). The Norths of Kirtling (Roger's branch) derive from John, the eldest son. There is an account of the family in Dale B. J. Randall, *Gentle flame: the life and verse of Dudley, fourth Lord North (1602–1677)* (Durham, NC, 1983).

[78] J. and J. A. Venn, *Alumni Cantabrigienses. Part I. From the earliest times to 1751* (Cambridge, 1924–7), iv. 349.

[79] BL MS Add. 18220, ff. 11^r–13^r, 37^r–37^v.

Nov: 26 1668' and 'Sr H. North Baronet Auto^r 1659'.[80] Since no printed work of this title survives, it must be assumed that *Eroclea* was a scribally circulated text—either a collection of poems along the lines of Lovelace's *Lucasta* or a play. Watson seems to have served as a conduit of literary separates in and out of Suffolk, receiving material from his brother Thomas in London and friends at Cambridge, and returning satires, neo-Latin verse and funerary inscriptions by Suffolk and Norfolk writers. The inclusion of the words of anthems and songs, along with the presence of Jenkins as a donor, suggests that the transmission of musical manuscripts may have gone hand in hand with that of literary texts.[81]

Two other viol-playing families have a quite explicit link with the scribal communication of non-musical texts. John Browne as Clerk of Parliaments from 1638 to 1649 and again from 1660 was, during sessions, at the head of the most important scriptorium in England, while Sir Roger L'Estrange served as press-licenser and propagandist for Charles II. Although the story of L'Estrange involuntarily playing in a viol consort before Cromwell is well-known, it is not generally realized that he was also a composer for the instrument.[82] His professional concern was with printed books and pamphlets, yet he thoroughly understood the political influence of scribally circulated texts and twice memorialized Charles II on the need to control them. On the second of these occasions he noted tellingly that 'not one of forty [libels] ever comes to the Presse, and yet by the helpe of Transcripts, they are well nigh as Publique'.[83]

Another kind of link between musical and nonmusical kinds of scribal transmission is suggested by the activities of Sir Nicholas Le Strange (Roger's brother). This enthusiastic viol-player brought to his music-making the skills and enthusiasm of an experienced

---

[80] Ibid., ff. 25^v–26^v.

[81] Composers besides Jenkins mentioned as having set texts in the volume are Benjamin Rogers, Sylvanus Taylour and Thomas Bradbury.

[82] For the compositions, see *Thematic index*. The allegation that he had played for Cromwell led to him being nicknamed 'Noll's fiddler'. His own account of the event is given in his *Truth and loyalty vindicated* (London, 1662), p. 50. Walking in St James's Park, he heard music from John Hingeston's room at Whitehall. Entering, he found some viol players who asked him to join them. While they played, Cromwell entered, listened for a while, and left.

[83] 'Mr L'Estraings Proposition concerning Libells, &c.', 11 Nov. 1675, reproduced in Ch. 2.

textual critic. In the years following his marriage in 1630 he assembled a large body of viol consort music in part books.[84] These were written by four copyists, including Sir Nicholas himself and John Jenkins. (Pamela Willetts has proposed that one of the remaining hands is that of the composer Thomas Brewer who was retained as a house musician.[85]) The filling of the books was itself a labour of many years, but what is equally remarkable is that Le Strange regularly acquired books from other players and, with the help of his amanuenses, carefully collated their versions with his own. A record was made of all differences, including obvious errors, and such details as the order of items in the borrowed volumes. The two largest Le Strange collections, now BL Add. MSS 39550–4 and Royal College of Music MS 1145, contain between them records of twenty-one collated sources identified as Couzens, Sheppy, Pettus, Drury, Dunn, Donne 2^d, Holland, Harman, Couzens Score: B:, Pettus: 2d: coppy, Gibbs, Francklin, Staresmore, Fowler, Ives, Rampley, Barnard score: B:, Mr Fanshaw Score: b:, Bromall, Mr Collins, and Mr Coleman.[86]

The most noteworthy thing about this procedure is that it was possible for Sir Nicholas and his amanuenses to have access to such a large number of manuscripts. If, as Andrew Ashbee suggests, they were borrowed for use at Hunstanton, and this reflected a wider code of trust and generosity among possessors of manuscripts, it could well be that the use made of the single manuscript copy (whether in this or other fields) was far wider than we would expect.[87] But the more significant point is that this vast exercise (reminiscent of the work of editors of parliamentary compilations) was not even necessary. By scoring problematical passages from his partbooks and consulting with his resident professionals, Sir Nicholas would have had little difficulty in finding an acceptable solution for any progression that displeased his ear. The mammoth labour of comparison springs from what is not a musician's but a

---

[84] Listed in the *Thematic index* under 'The Le Strange manuscripts'.

[85] Willetts, 'Sir Nicholas Le Strange and John Jenkins', p. 40.

[86] Ashbee, 'A further look', p. 28. Willetts, 'Sir Nicholas Le Strange and John Jenkins', pp. 39–40 suggests some identifications. Sir Nicholas also obtained manuscripts from Jenkins's early patrons the Dereham family, from Coprario's friend Richard Ligon, and from the Jacobs family.

[87] Ashbee, 'A further look', p. 28. Sir Robert Cotton's free and easy way with both his own and other people's manuscripts suggests the same.

bibliophile's or philologist's fascination with the vagaries of signification arising from scribal transmission: it reflects a love of the medium quite as much as a love for music.[88] This wider concern with the medium is also evident in his 'Merry passages and jeasts', the manuscript collection of jokes and anecdotes for which he is principally remembered.[89] A further question that arises is to what extent his tastes in music were an outgrowth of the scribal culture to which he belonged rather than representing an autonomous aesthetic preference. (This problem arises again in the relationship between the spread of 'country' political views in the early decades of the century and the tendency of political separates to be concerned with court scandal and imagined conspiracies. Which was giving rise to which?)

Yet another kind of interpenetration of music and scholarship is found in the career of the first Baron Hatton of Kirby, born in 1605. David Pinto has established that the Hatton musical manuscripts formed a substantial part of the collection left to Christ Church, Oxford in 1710 by Dean Aldrich, making them one of the most important family collections of the century. But Hatton was also 'a generall sercher of all antiquityes concerning the whole kingdome, but cheifelye Northamptonshire his own country'. His collection included 'almost a hundred bookes of his owne abstracting, of very choyce antiquityes' in addition to those prepared for him by assistants.[90] In his case major achievements in the collection and transcription of historical records went hand in hand with a concern to secure and copy music. The fate that sent his historical manuscripts to Bodley and the British Library and the musical manuscripts to Christ Church fractured what at Kirby Hall had existed as a unified expression of a preoccupation with the scribally transmitted text.

[88] A striking analogy between the activities of the editor and the musician is drawn by Fuller, *Ephemeris parliamentaria*, loc. cit.: 'And may the *Reader* be pleased to take notice that this *Book* is no *Monochord*, or *Instrument* of a *single string*, no nor is it a *single Instrument*; but the exact result of many collections. We have compared *varias lectiones*, or rather *varias auditiones*, the copies as they have been taken by severall *Auditours*.'

[89] BL MS Harl. 6395. Edited as '*Merry passages and jeasts': a manuscript jestbook of Sir Nicholas Le Strange (1603–1655)*, ed. H. F. Lippincott (Salzburg, 1974). One use for these anecdotes would have been during the prolonged periods of tuning customary among viol players.

[90] Pinto, 'The music of the Hattons', p. 87; draft letter from Sir Symon Archer to Thomas Habington, 27 December 1637 in *The life, diary, and correspondence of Sir William Dugdale*, ed. William Hamper (London, 1827), p. 171 n.

CONCLUSION

In this chapter we have looked at three different products of scribal publication—verse miscellanies, parliamentary compilations and consort music for viols. It is not entirely true that the existing scholarship is narrowly restricted to one or the other field (musicologists and literary scholars have some areas of contact), but it is valid to claim that they have never been acknowledged as separate aspects of a common phenomenon—the publication of texts in handwritten copies within a culture which had developed sophisticated means of generating and transmitting such copies. Not all consumers of scribally published texts will have had verse miscellanies on their bookshelves, parliamentary compilations discretely locked in their cabinets and part books of viol music in their music chests, but some will certainly have done so, and, in any case, these are but three of a multitude of genres of the scribally published sign. It would be a mistake to assume too great a degree of regularity and too high a degree of organization in the procedure by which scribal texts were written, copied and communicated; but that there were such regularities and such organization will already be evident, and it will be one task of this book to explore them. Since the bibliographical aids necessary for a comprehensive survey of primary sources are still largely lacking, the majority of my material will be drawn from already available scholarship but with new research offered where this is necessary and appropriate.

As part of this process, we need first of all to acquire an empirical understanding of the phenomena. Information about scribal practice across the sequence authorship, production and distribution needs to be collected and classified, and new information sought about matters that reveal themselves as significant. Patterns in this information must be recognized and a variety of models considered for the working of each stage of the process of publication. Certainly we will need to look more closely at how far it is valid to extrapolate from one field or genre to another. Is the enormous success of John Jenkins as a scribal author-publisher typical or atypical? How far were his methods similar to or different from those of poets like Donne and King, thinkers like Filmer and Sir Thomas Browne, or historians like Camden and

32

Cotton? Do Roger North's thousands of pages of manuscript discourses devoted to a wide range of learned enquiries have anything to tell us about the intended social function of the even larger and no less varied body of discourses inscribed by Isaac Newton? But another, no less important kind of understanding will need to be theoretical and interpretative, embracing a broader consideration of the functioning of the scribal medium within seventeenth-century society. We must seek through a process of recontextualization to understand the ways in which scribal publication served to define communities of the like-minded. We must also consider what the scribally published text has to tell us about how information of all kinds was constituted, encountered and encoded by seventeenth-century readers. Beyond these lie other questions (considered in Chapter 4) concerning the ways in which scribal and print media project their respective metaphors of the nature of knowledge, how the reader and the writer are constructed by the scribal text, and how the 'presence' of the writer is projected through the two media. All these things will have a bearing not simply on how we interpret what we find but on what kinds of information it is necessary to look for.

While new research will be required to pursue some of these topics, it must be stressed again how much information about scribal publication is already available under Swanson's category of 'undiscovered public knowledge'. Swanson presents three models for this. The first is the case where evidence that would refute or require the modification of a conjecture has been assembled in ignorance of the original conjecture. The second is where the conclusions '*a* proves *b*' and '*b* proves *c*' have been reached without the bibliographical connections being made that would permit the further hypothesis '*a* proves *c*'. The third is where 'many individually weak tests of a theory can be combined into the equivalent of a much stronger test'.[91] It is this third category, illustrated by Swanson from the early history of investigation into the link between smoking and lung cancer and by Roy Davies from the emergence of Chaos theory in mathematics, which has the most direct relevance to the present

---

[91] Swanson, pp. 108–13; see also Davies 277–87. Historians will recognize Swanson's third category as the means used to secure the conviction of Strafford in 1641.

enquiry. A passage cited by Davies from James Gleick's *Chaos* could hardly be more pertinent to the problem in hand:

A mathematical discovery was understood by mathematicians, a physics discovery by physicists, a meteorological discovery by no one. The way ideas spread became as important as the way they originated. Each scientist had a private constellation of intellectual parents. Each had his own picture of the landscape of ideas, and each picture was limited in its own way. Knowledge was imperfect. Scientists were biased by the customs of their disciplines or by the accidental paths of their own educations.[92]

In our case what remains 'undiscovered' is a whole dimension of seventeenth-century culture, one which has been the subject of endless minutely detailed research, and which is everywhere apparent, and yet one which has never been addressed as an entity in its own right.

[92] Davies, p. 283, Gleick, *Chaos: making a new science* (London, 1988), pp. 181–2.

2

'PUBLICATION' IN THE SCRIBAL MEDIUM

CHAPTER 1 introduced some sub-traditions of scribal publication, but postponed the question of how we are to define the term. This will require some finesse. When we speak today of an unpublished manuscript we mean an unprinted manuscript, but we now need to consider how handwritten texts are to be classed as published or unpublished within a culture in which scribal transmission might be chosen without any sense of its being inferior or incomplete.

Although our modern usage of 'publish' excludes the notion of *scribal publication, there is no problem about recovering it. There* is already a tendency to speak of a sound recording, a video, or computer software as having been published. We do not regard a new poem read during a radio broadcast as having been published on that occasion, but it would not be a contradiction of our other usages if we were to do so. The ancient world accepted the idea of publication by declamation, with a new epic or history being read aloud to an audience prior to its distribution in written form. E. A. J. Honigmann has argued that for Shakespeare 'the theatre gave the primary form of publication'.[1] A corollary of this wider conception was that it became possible for the same text to be published in more than one medium. Francis Beaumont in his commendatory poem printed with the first quarto of Fletcher's *The faithful shepherdess* speaks of the printing of the play as 'This second publication'—performance being the first.[2] A present-day

---

[1] *The stability of Shakespeare's text* (London, 1965), p. 191.
[2] 'To my friend Maister *John Fletcher* upon his Faithfull Shepheardesse', l. 40, in *The dramatic works in the Beaumont and Fletcher canon*, gen. ed. Fredson Bowers (Cambridge, 1966–), iii. 491; cited Honigmann, loc. cit.

parallel is the notion of a 'pre-publication' text of a scientific paper—in effect one awaiting print publication but freely available in electronic form. No-one would deny that these papers are already published: it is simply that they still await a redundant further publication in a more privileged medium, by which time (such is the pace of science) they may possess only archival interest. Margaret Anne Doody, writing of her novel, *The alchemists*, expresses a literary author's sense of the phenomenon of double publication. Although the book, written between 1965 and 1968, had not been print-published at the time, 'it had been published in an older sense (as it had been read in manuscript by a group of readers)'. Revising it for the press in 1980 she 'felt as if it had been completed, and that in some peculiar sense it was a trespass to return to work begun nearly fifteen years ago'.[3]

The root sense underlying all these usages is of publication as a movement from a private realm of creativity to a public realm of consumption. The problem is to determine whether any given text—in our case a text transmitted through handwritten copies— has made this transition. We will need to recognize both a 'strong' sense in which the text must be shown to have become publicly available and a more inclusive 'weak' sense in which it is enough to show that the text has ceased to be a private possession. A further condition is that scribal publication should be something more than the chrysalis stage of an intended print publication. This would exclude manuscripts circulated for comment and correction prior to printing or in order to attract a sheaf of commendatory verses.[4] However, Pope's circulation among his friends of the *Pastorals* might well be included since the manuscript, like that of its successor, *Windsor forest*, was obviously meant to be enjoyed in its own right as an example of skilled calligraphy.[5]

[3] 'Taking it up again', *London review of books*, 21 March 1991, p. 17.

[4] For the first of these practices we might instance Dryden's circulation of drafts of sections of his translation of the *Aeneid* (*The works of John Dryden*, gen. eds H. T. Swedenberg, jun. and Alan Roper (Los Angeles, 1956–), vi. 868). The second is discussed in Franklin B. Williams, jun., 'Commendatory verses: the rise of the art of puffing', *SB* 19 (1966), 8–9. *Annalia Dvbrensia* (London, 1636; ed. Christopher Whitfield (London, 1962)) employed the same technique to assemble a volume of celebratory poems on Robert Dover's '*Olimpick Games vpon Cotswold-Hills*'.

[5] See *Pastoral poetry and An essay on criticism*, ed. E. Audra and Aubrey Williams (London, 1961), pp. 38–40 and the facsimile edition in Maynard Mack, 'Pope's pastorals', *Scriblerian* 12 (1980), 85–161. Pope has noted the names of the twelve readers of the manuscript. The

Publication in our strong sense is usually equated with the provision of large numbers of copies, and some kinds of scribal publication do fulfil this criterion. Prior to the invention of print there had been entrepreneurial stationers who functioned in a way similar to modern print publishers—obtaining texts, arranging for them to be copied in whatever numbers were needed, and supplying them to public bookshops. In the great cities of the ancient world, *bibliopolae* duplicated texts in scriptoria where slaves copied simultaneously from dictation. In the late middle ages scriptoria producing prayer books, bibles and books of hours developed elaborate routines through which sections of a book could be worked on successively by scribes, artists and illuminators. Medieval universities supported the development of an educational book trade and established collections of manuscripts from which students could make their own copies. Eventually secular stationers emerged who specialized in vernacular manuscripts, an early English example being Lydgate's publisher, John Shirley.[6] 'Scribal editions' of the fifteenth century were sometimes comparable in size with those of the early printers. Marcel Thomas cites an order to a fifteenth-century Flemish scriptorium for 400 copies of a university text, with which we can compare the 250 to 500 copies John Feather estimates as the norm for early printed editions.[7] Texts so issued must be regarded under any criteria as published.

In other cases, the scribally circulated text would have had a much more restricted availability than the average printed text. But is this difference to be regarded as one of kind or merely of

Windsor forest manuscript is praised by Audra and Williams as 'an example of Pope's superb craftsmanship in lettering' (p. 129), while Robert M. Schmitz, *Pope's Windsor forest 1712. A study of the Washington University holograph* (St Louis, Miss., 1952), p. 7, considered that Pope 'had penned the *Pastorals* manuscript as if he had learned the art of lettering in the best scriptorium'. This suggests that Pope saw scribal transmission as having its own integrity, independently of print-publishing; and yet the objection could be made that his calligraphy was directed towards recreating the effect of a *printed* page. In fact he had taught himself his script by imitating typography.

[6] See Cheryl Greenberg, 'John Shirley and the English book trade', *Library*, 6:4 (1982), 369–80. Further information is available in H. S. Bennett, 'The production and dissemination of vernacular manuscripts in the fifteenth century', *Library*, 5:1 (1946–7), 167–78, and the papers gathered in Jeremy Griffiths and Derek Pearsall, eds, *Book production and publishing in Britain 1375–1475* (Cambridge, 1989).

[7] Introduction to Lucien Febvre and Henri-Jean Martin, *L'apparition du livre*, 2nd edn (Paris, 1971), pp. 35–6; Feather, *A history of British publishing* (London, 1988), p. 8.

degree? A book printed in an edition of 500 copies is only available to a maximum of 500 purchasers; moreover, the only potential readers who would be able to take advantage of that availability would be those who had learned of the publication's existence, knew where copies were to be obtained and were interested (and affluent) enough to take advantage of this information between its appearance on the shelves and the return of any unsold copies for pulping. We might assume that a copy of a print-published work would subsequently be obtainable from a library or through the second-hand book trade, but even this is not always the case: a large body of material classified as ephemera or as disposable is not preserved by anyone. Scribal publication, operating at relatively lower volumes and under more restrictive conditions of availability than print publication, was still able to sustain the currency of popular texts for very long periods and bring them to the attention of considerable bodies of readers. The material difference is that it did this through small increments rather than through one explosive provision of copies. Whereas the printed book for which there was no immediate requirement would be ready in a warehouse, new copies of the scribal text only came into existence in response to the desire of prospective readers. So while the survival of a text in a large number of manuscript copies is certainly evidence for its having been published, the fact that it only survives in two or three does not mean that it had not made the crucial transition from private status which would allow us to include it, under our weak sense, in the same category.

This weak sense, in rejecting availability as the primary criterion of published status, invokes an alternative criterion of publication as an activity carried out by a special kind of person called a publisher. In present-day print publication this activity embraces the procurement or commissioning of the book from an author, the editing of the text into a form suitable for production, the contracting out of the printing and binding, the promotion and advertising of the book, the maintaining of stocks of the edition, and its distribution on mutually agreed terms of sale to retailers. The publisher is also required to provide capital for the production stage of the venture and to assume certain responsibilities under the laws relating to copyright, libel and deposit. Even a simple act of desk-top publication, in which the various parties of these transactions may be united in a single individual, will still involve most of the stages described. This definition has the advantage that the 'privately printed' or 'not published' book can be admitted to the category of publications, for there can be no doubt that the defining activities of the publisher have been performed, the only difference being in the method used to secure distribution. Its limitation is that the activities of the modern print-publisher are not a very satisfactory model for those of the seventeenth-century scribal publisher. They also diverge in a number of ways from the activities of the seventeenth-century print-publisher, for whom publishing was still a subsidiary operation to bookselling, printing or binding.

None the less, this freer conception of publication as a social activity is a useful one for our present enquiry. It has always been present in the legal sense of the word as it applies in libel and treason cases. In the case of Oscar Wilde, the publication of a libel was constituted by the act of leaving a card addressed to Wilde at his club.[8] By this ritualized transfer the text of the message was agreed to have moved from the private to the public realm and Wilde was permitted to sue the Marquess of Queensberry. In a wider context, this moment at which a text passes from one to the other domain may be defined as being that at which the initiating agent (who will not necessarily be the author or even acting with the approval of the author) knowingly relinquishes control over the future social use of that text. Once this has happened, the text must be regarded as possessing a potential for wider availability, this potential being realized or not realized according to the subsequent decisions of those to whom power over the text has been transferred. The transmissional history of Donne's *Biathanatos* will help to illustrate this.

Donne wrote his treatise in 1607–8 with no apparent thought of publication through the press. Its argument—that suicide was not in all circumstances to be condemned—made him cautious about who was allowed to see it. In a letter of 1619 to Sir Robert Ker he tells us 'no hand hath passed upon it to copy it, nor many eyes to

---

[8] Richard Ellmann, *Oscar Wilde* (New York, 1988), p. 438. A relevant treason case is that of Edmund Peacham in 1615 where one of the legal issues considered was whether statements made in notes for an undelivered sermon could be regarded as constituting treason.

read it: onely to some particular friends in both Universities, then when I writ it, I did communicate it'.[9] So, if we are to say that it was published at the time of writing, it was published, like Doody's *The alchemists* or Pope's *Pastorals*, by allowing a series of readers to see a single manuscript. The crucial issue is whether this is to be seen as a private or as a public transaction. Donne's view of the case is clarified by another statement in the same letter when he tells Ker that he is at liberty to show it to 'any that your discretion admits to the sight of it' but that he must observe the condition of warning them that it is a book 'written by *Jack Donne*, and not by *D. Donne*' (p. 22). This constitutes a partial surrender of control over the social use of the text to Ker; however, Donne conditionally envisages a more complete one, saying 'Reserve it for me, if I live, and if I die, I only forbid it the Presse, and the Fire'—in other words, in the event of his death, the text should be treated as published, but only through the scribal medium. In this instance Donne did retrieve the copy, and it was only some years later at the request of the future Lord Herbert of Cherbury that he is known to have allowed another to be made. The process described shows control over the social use of the text being relinquished through a series of separate declarations. The initial circulation among university friends might still, perhaps, be classified as private; however, the letter to Ker involves both an actual and a provisional waiving of control. The later supplying of a copy to Herbert was an outright relinquishing, since Donne had no way of preventing Herbert (or any other person who acquired a copy) from making it available for further copying. While debate is still possible over the precise point at which we should locate the transition from the private to the public realm, the stages by which such a transition could take place are clearly illustrated. This sense of publishing as a surrender of control over the future use of the manuscript constitutes our 'weak' definition, the only additional condition being that the surrender should take place in a context where there was some practical likelihood of the text entering public channels of communication. In a century where the practice

---

[9] *Letters to severall persons of honour* (London, 1651), p. 21. See also *Biathanatos*, ed. Ernest W. Sullivan II (Newark, NJ, 1984), pp. xli, xlvi–xlvii. Sullivan is too hasty in assuming that the copy circulated by Donne was a holograph: it could have been a scribal copy made under Donne's direction.

of copying was almost universal among the educated this is not a
difficult condition to satisfy.

Jonson's 'An epigram to my muse, the Lady Digby, on her
husband, Sir Kenelme Digby' illustrates a related process by which
a patron or friend might be entrusted with a copy on the explicit
understanding that he or she would bring it to wider attention.

> O! what a fame 't will be?
>> What reputation to my lines, and me,
> When hee shall read them at the Treasurers bord,
>> The knowing *Weston*, and that learned Lord
> Allowes them? Then, what copies shall be had,
>> What transcripts begg'd? how cry'd up, and how glad,
> Wilt thou be, *Muse*, when this shall them befall?
>> Being sent to one, they will be read of all.[10]

In this case the author is the publisher in the weak sense in
surrendering control over the poems to his friend Digby, who
becomes the publisher in the strong sense by reading them to a
circle of connoisseurs whose approval will create a demand for
transcripts.

The desire to make a piece of writing public, or to keep it
private, may also be evident from its own nature. Sir Thomas
Browne wrote of the unauthorized 1642 printing of *Religio medici*:
'He that shall peruse that worke, and shall take notice of sundry
particularities and personall expressions therein, will easily discerne
the intention was not publik: and being a private exercise directed
to my selfe, what is delivered therein was rather a memoriall unto
me then an example or rule unto any other.'[11] Dudley, Lord North
hardly had need to explain that his poems 'were designed, as they
tell you, to a domestique confinement, impatient of public view':
the only reason that could have led him to print them (albeit in a
'private Edition') was that in the disturbed circumstances of the
Civil War they were 'obnoxious to a sodain destruction'.[12] More
generally, much as a gentleman or lady was not in a fit state to

---

[10] *Ben Jonson*, viii. 263.
[11] *Religio medici and other works*, ed. L. C. Martin (Oxford, 1964), p. 1. The work was one
which 'being communicated unto one, . . . became common unto many, and was by
transcription successively corrupted untill it arrived in a most depraved copy at the presse'
(loc. cit.).
[12] *A forest promiscous of several seasons productions* (London, 1659), pp. A2ᵛ, 172.

appear out of doors until he or she had been elaborately clothed, so a piece of writing was not ready to appear before readers until it had reached a required state of finish. In private letters, wrote Sprat in 1668, 'the Souls of Men should appear undress'd: And in that negligent habit they may be fit to be seen by one or two in a Chamber, but not to go abroad into the Streets'.[13] Anything lacking the required finish remained a piece of private writing improperly exposed to public view—the argument of Wycherley's poem 'To Sir George Etheridge, on his shewing his verses imperfect':

> Be wise, and ne'er to publick View produce
> Thy undrest Mistress, or unfinisht Muse;
> Since either, by that *Dishabilé*, seem
> To hurt their Beauties in our good Esteem:
> And easier far we kind Impressions make,
> Than we can rooted Prejudices shake.
> From Nature learn, which *Embrio*'s does conceal,
> Thine, till they're perfect, never to reveal.[14]

What is objected to here is not simply the showing round of inferior work but a sense that the rules governing the constitution of a public realm are being violated by an interposing of materials from the private realm (where a sweet disorder in the dress might be attractive rather than otherwise).

This suggests that the dress of texts, in the sense of appearance as well as style, might offer grounds for positing a published status. A finely written manuscript in a large format using good paper invites and may be said to expect readers just as the semi-legible private scrawl (writing in dishabille) indicates an indifference to them. An intention (if no more) to publish might also be suspected when the text in question has adopted a polished public style or employs a recognizably public form of discourse, such as the political satire, the pedagogical treatise or the formal epistle. Criteria such as these can be used to supplement designations based on the proven fact of public accessibility or knowledge, such as that

[13] Preface to his edition of Cowley's *Works*, in *Critical essays of the seventeenth century*, ed. J. E. Spingarn (Oxford, 1957), ii. 137.

[14] *The posthumous works of William Wycherley, Esq.* (London, 1728), p. 182; also in my *Restoration verse* (Harmondsworth, 1968), p. 301. Geoffrey Hiller has drawn my attention to the frequency with which dedications by Elizabethan and Jacobean writers refer to their work being dressed in the livery of the noble dedicatee.

revealed by the history of *Biathanatos*, of the author's transactions with readers. Of course a work intended, like *Religio medici*, for strictly private use might become a public possession against its author's wishes. The same applies to personal letters, generally regarded as unsuitable for print publication, but which were frequently made available for recopying. Sprat, in acting as Cowley's literary executor, would not permit the printing of private correspondence.[15] On the other hand, Hearne's journals show him, in the early decades of the eighteenth century, regularly transcribing letters which had been lent by colleagues and expecting that his own letters would be read and valued by future scholars. Attitudes had undoubtedly changed during the intervening years, but the difference of medium may well have been the crucial one. Even Sprat does not assume that private correspondence was meant solely for the recipient. In any case, once a private letter had begun to be freely copied it became a published text irrespective of the wishes of the recipient, and might even be included in specialized anthologies such as Folger MS V a 321.[16] Such cases reflect the ease with which a text could be introduced to a public, duplication requiring nothing more than a pen and a willingness to use it.

Such a framing of the field of scribal publication still excludes the case of a text communicated within a closed circle of readers on the understanding it is not to be allowed to go beyond the circle. Examples would be documents circulated within a family, like the copies of Dudley North's poems written out by his widow for each of her children, or among tightly knit groups of officials, county neighbours or courtiers.[17] Lawrence Squibb's *A book of all the several officers of the Court of Exchequer*, written in 1642 as a guide to the practice of the court, was recopied many times (sixteen manuscripts are known) and revised on at least two occasions but appears to have circulated only within a small circle of Exchequer officials and politicians with whom they had dealings.[18] Here

[15] Spingarn, ii. 137.

[16] Reproduced in facsimile with facing transcriptions in *A seventeenth-century letter-book*, ed. A. R. Braunmuller (Newark, Del., 1983). The volume is a mixture of formal and personal letters with a few non-epistolary texts.

[17] For the North example, see Randall, *Gentle flame*, pp. 100–2. Cases falling under the other categories are discussed in Ch. 5.

[18] J. D. Alsop, 'A 1721 version of Squibb's 1642 treatise on the Exchequer', *Library*, 6:6

individual control over the social use of the text has been replaced by the control of a community, creating a status delicately balanced between the public and the private. In such cases, and assuming there was no broader transmission of the text concerned, it should be the nature of the community that determined the issue. If it was genuinely closed, and the text could only achieve wider circulation through a violation of trust, private status may be allowed. (An example here would be Marvell's letters to the Corporation of Hull, which contain frequent warnings that they should not be allowed to come to other eyes. An occasion when Marvell felt confidentiality had been breached drew a swift reprimand.[19]) But many communities within which manuscripts circulated were not of this kind: their membership was relatively fluid and a reader sympathetic enough to the aims of a group to be interested in the texts that were circulating within it would probably not find it difficult to be accepted into the network. The analogy in modern print publishing would be that of a learned society or book club whose publications were only available to members but which placed no barriers against gaining membership.

A further difference between scribal and print publication is that, while a printed text is published in a large number of copies on a single occasion, the manuscript text must usually be regarded as republished as often as it is copied. There is an exception to this in the 'scribal editions' of multiple copies of a given exemplar which were sometimes commissioned by commercial dealers; but the mass of surviving manuscripts are the outcome of a discontinuous series of acts of publication in editions of one. In order to mediate between this aspect of scribal publication and the print model, it will be helpful to distinguish between an initiatory and a replicatory act. The first is what happens when a private possessor of a text (who, as mentioned earlier will not necessarily be the author or even acting in accordance with the author's wishes) facilitates its first going forth into the world, while the second is

---

(1984), 366–9; *A book of all the several officers of the Court of Exchequer*, ed. W. H. Bryson, in *Camden miscellany* 26 (London 1975), pp. 77–136. For the manuscripts and their relationship see Bryson, pp. 80–95.

[19] *The poems and letters of Andrew Marvell*, ed. H. M. Margoliouth, 3rd edn, rev. Pierre Legouis with the collaboration of E. E. Duncan-Jones (Oxford, 1971), ii. 166.

what happens when some individual owner of a subsequent copy permits that copy to be available for recopying. The distinction can be demonstrated through the example of John Hollond's 'The navy ript and ransacked', a treatise of 1660 on the way contractors and shipyard-owners were cheating the crown.[20] Hollond published the work by presenting a single copy to James, Duke of York, in his capacity as Lord Admiral. (This was the initiatory act and deprived the author of control over the future social use of the text.) The Duke passed on the copy to Sir William Coventry who showed it to Pepys. Pepys took a copy for himself and Coventry kept the Duke's copy. However, the three seem to have agreed that it was much too hot to go any further and after only one replicatory act its transmission was brought to an end. It could of course be argued that Hollond's treatise was in the nature of a confidential report—in which case no further circulation might have been envisaged or desired—but neither the text, the writing nor the snappy title suggest this; moreover, Hollond's earlier 'A discourse of the navy' had enjoyed wide circulation in manuscript.[21] The importance of this replicatory power is that it provides us with a scribal counterpart to the notion of 'going out of print'. A text will continue to multiply until interest in it fails and no further replications take place. But this process will be distributed, not centralized, with each copying demanding a separate act of will to continue the life of the text. As we have just seen, the power could also be used in a negative sense to suppress a text by withholding it from any potential future copyists. English law of the time took cognizance of this negative aspect of the replicatory power by insisting that anyone encountering a libel had an obligation to destroy it.[22]

The criteria proposed will have shown how the term 'scribal publication' is to be used in this book and what kinds of manuscripts are covered by it. Naturally, other ways of making

---

[20] John Hollond, *Two discourses on the navy*, ed. J. R. Tanner (London, 1896), pp. lxix–lxx.

[21] Ibid., pp. lxviii–lxix.

[22] Lord Chief Justice Richardson, in a judgement of June 1632, ruled that 'if it concern a publique person the libell must be shewed to the Kings Councell or some competent judge, but if it concerne anie private person he that findeth it must burne it'. *Reports of cases in the courts of Star Chamber and High Commission*, ed. S. R. Gardiner, Camden Society, NS 39 (London, 1886), p. 152.

the distinction are possible and would lead to a different assignment of published or unpublished status: my aim here has been simply to provide discriminations which would be useful to the task in hand and not in flagrant disregard of our present-day notions of publication. If a greater stress has been laid on the text's potential for wider replication than on its practical availability, this is because that potential was far more easily realized by an intending reader in the manuscript than in the print medium. A text that was of pressing interest, and whose existence had become known through word of mouth, would never lack copyists. It is true that a certain critical population of copies had to be achieved before exemplars would be readily available, much as a certain level is necessary to ensure the survival of a living species. But, once that was done, the process of multiplication would be driven by cultural energies quite as powerful as those which sustained the printed text.

MODES OF PUBLICATION

Having looked at means of distinguishing published from unpublished texts, our next task will be to decide how various kinds of scribal publication are to be distinguished from each other. Here it will be helpful to begin with three predominant categories of manuscript (omitting mixed examples): the authorial holograph, the copy made by a specialist scribe, and the copy made by an individual who wished to possess the text. It is often possible to assign a manuscript to one of these categories on appearance alone. The authorial copy may contain interlinear revisions of a kind which no scribe could have devised. The scribal copy is usually written in a clear, regularly formed hand with consistent page numbering and catchwords on every page. Virtuosic displays of penmanship may also be evident. A copy written in a rapid, untidy hand is probably personal, though not all personal copies are so written, and some private transcribers matched the professionals for the care and beauty of their script. Of course, these distinctions—when they can be made—will not always reveal the mode of publication employed, since, if the scribe was a professional, he or she may still have been working under the author's direction or for someone who wished to possess a copy.

46

But the classification does suggest the three agents most likely to have performed acts of publication: the author, the stationer or scrivener for whom manuscripts were articles of commerce, and the intending reader.

On this basis I would like to propose that there are three main modes of scribal publication which I will call author publication, entrepreneurial publication and user publication. The first of these is self-explanatory; the second embraces all copying of manuscripts for sale by agents other than the author; the third covers the vast field of non-commercial replication whose most durable outcome was the personal miscellany or volume of 'collections'. The textual tradition of any given work will probably include more than one of these modes. Thus, a seventeenth-century text put into circulation in copies prepared by its author might subsequently be copied for sale or for personal use. Copyists, too, may have found themselves acting in more than one role, as in the case of the privately employed scribe who took a secret extra copy for subsequent sale. But, if we are prepared to ignore some marginal imprecisions, this tripartite distinction will be found to be of service in relating particular instances of scribal publication to the general definitions that were proposed at the beginning of this chapter.

Author publication occurs when the production and distribution of copies takes place under the author's personal direction. Writers from the gentry and aristocracy were particularly likely to publish in this way owing to what J. W. Saunders has called the 'stigma of print' but it must also be regarded as the common way of securing readers for works of which only a small number of copies was required or when a subsequent process of user publication was assumed and perhaps courted.[23] An important criterion for identifying author publication is the presence of signed dedications or epistles to particular persons. Two manuscripts of Sir John Davies's *Nosce teipsum* (first circulated in the early 1590s) contain dedicatory verses to Henry Percy, ninth Earl

---

[23] J. W. Saunders, 'The stigma of print: a note on the social bases of Tudor poetry', *Essays in criticism* 1 (1951), 139–64. Complementing the 'stigma' was a sense of the higher prestige of the handwritten text. Humfrey Wanley, in describing a book of engravings prepared for Louis XIV, notes 'This Painter ha's gotten the Prints purposely wrought-off for him, without the Words, which are added, for Magnificence-sake, by a fine Pen' (*The diary of Humfrey Wanley 1715–1726*, ed. C. E. Wright and Ruth C. Wright (London, 1966), i. 89.)

of Northumberland, and a not-yet-knighted Edward Coke respectively. All four manuscripts of the complete text contain a verse address to Queen Elizabeth, who must also therefore have received a copy.[24] A second criterion is the presence of passages or corrections in the author's own hand, or those of known amanuenses—the clue that allowed Crum and Hobbs to identify a number of manuscripts as issued under the supervision of Henry King.[25] A third is that the text is correct and accurate, though this is more useful in the negative sense that a text containing frequent obvious errors, or evidence of sophistication, is unlikely to have emanated from the author.[26] Many author-publishers wrote their own copies; but another common method was to have them prepared by an experienced scribe, as when Milton made use of Henry Lawes for the scribal publication of *Comus* following its successful performance in September 1634. Lawes's preface to the 1637 printed text explains that 'Although not openly acknow-ledg'd by the Author, yet it is a legitimate off-spring, so lovely, and so much desired, that the often copying of it hath tir'd my pen to give my severall friends satisfaction, and brought me to a necessitie of producing it to the publick view'.[27] Lawes here represents the pre-print circulation as a gentlemanly labour on behalf of friends; but hard-working musicians could rarely afford such luxuries and he probably expected a return of gifts from his presentations. An example of an authorially supervised master copy is the manuscript of Sir Arthur Gorges' 'The Olympian Catastrophe' (Huntington

[24] *The poems of Sir John Davies*, ed. Robert Krueger (Oxford, 1975), pp. 3–5; Beal, *IELM*, i/1, 215–16. Author publication is assumed only for the dedication copies, not for subsequent copies that might include the dedications.

[25] Manuscripts produced by scribes working under King's direction are described in *The poems of Henry King*, ed. Margaret Crum (Oxford, 1965), pp. 48–9 and Mary Hobbs, 'The poems of Henry King: another authoritative manuscript', *Library*, 5:31 (1976), 127–35 and 'The Stoughton manuscript', *passim*. Manuscripts of work by other poets in a scribal hand but with authorial revisions are cited in Croft, *Autograph poetry*, i, p. xv.

[26] In cases where authors acted as scribes as well as publishers, they were as likely to make mistakes in transcribing as anyone else: the difference is that they were much more likely to recognize and correct them. For an example of a holograph text containing a large number or corrected transcriptional errors, see Anthony S. G. Edwards, 'The author as scribe: Cavendish's *Metrical visions* and MS Egerton 2402', *Library*, 5:29 (1974), 446–9.

[27] John Milton, *A masque. The earlier versions*, ed. S. E. Sprott (Toronto, 1973), p. 39. Robert K. Root, 'Publication before printing', *PMLA* 28 (1913), 417–31, draws on letters of Petrarch and Boccaccio to illustrate a late-medieval practice in which the work was directed to a patron or dedicatee under the assumption that it would be first revised and then put into circulation by him.

Library MS Ellesmere 1130). Here the scribe, who had originally done his best to produce a clean copy, was required by the author to make 'hundreds of alterations' in the form of superscriptions and paste-ons.[28] The only conceivable use for such a manuscript would be as an exemplar for others.[29]

Some cases of author publication have already been mentioned in Chapter 1, including those of John Jenkins as a composer-publisher and the members of the Caroline parliaments who distributed separates of their speeches. The production of newsletters should also be seen as a specialized form of author publication. Otherwise it is to be found across the entire range of seventeenth-century writing. Important prose texts such as Sir Robert Cotton's *A short view of the long life and reign of Henry the third*; Sir John Davies's *Whether the king of England by his prerogative may set impositions, loans or privy seals without assent of parliament*; Sir Robert Filmer's *Patriarcha*; Halifax's *The character of a trimmer*; Sir John Harington's *A supplie or addicion to the catalogue of bishops*; Sir Thomas Herbert's *Memoirs of the two last years of the reign of King Charles I*; Sir Roger Owen's *Of the antiquity, ampleness, and excellency of the common laws of England*; Raleigh's *A dialogue between a counsellor of state and a justice of the peace*; John Selden's *Table talk* (the 'author' in this case being Richard Milward); Henry Stubbe's *Account of the rise and progress of Mahometanism* and Sir Roger Twysden's *Certain considerations upon the government of England* all appear to have been given to their first readers through author-controlled duplication.[30]

[28] *The poems of Sir Arthur Gorges*, ed. Helen Estabrook Sandison (Oxford, 1953), p. lvii. The alterations are categorized on pp. xlix–lii.

[29] A set of three master-copies from the late-17th-cent. scriptorium studied by W. J. Cameron (Folger MS M. b. 12) also survives in a form heavily reconstructed by excisions and paste-ons. See Cameron 'Scriptorium', *passim*.

[30] For information on the transmissional histories of these texts (the titles of which are often variable), see William A. Jackson, 'Sir Robert Bruce Cotton's *A short view of the long life and raigne of Henry the third*', *Harvard Library bulletin* 4 (1950), 28–37; Beal, *IELM*, i/1, 231–2 (Davies); Peter Laslett, 'Sir Robert Filmer: the man versus the Whig myth', *William and Mary quarterly*, 3:5 (1948), 523–46 and Gordon J. Schochet, 'Sir Robert Filmer: some new bibliographical discoveries', *Library*, 5:26 (1971), 135–60; *The works of George Savile Marquis of Halifax*, ed. Mark N. Brown (Oxford, 1989), i. 343–54 and Beal, *IELM*, ii/1, 507–15 (Halifax); R. H. Miller, 'Sir John Harington's *A supplie or addicion to the catalogue of bishops, to the yeare 1608: composition and text*', *SB* 30 (1977), 145–61; Beal, *IELM*, i/2, 424–7 (Raleigh); Ernest A. Strathmann, 'Ralegh's *Discourse of tenures* and Sir Roger Owen', *HLQ* 20 (1956–7), 219–32; *Table talk of John Selden*, ed. Sir Frederick Pollock (London, 1927), pp. xi–xxiv; James R. Jacob, *Henry Stubbe, radical Protestantism and the early Enlightenment*

Part I

Reflecting on the huge body of amateur verse written during the early years of the century, Dennis Kay has written

Any educated person in the sixty years leading up to the English Civil War is liable to have written verses of some kind. The practice was recommended by educational theorists—some children's verses have survived—and many individuals continued to write, as the occasion struck them, into later life. The survival rate of such exclusively amateur pieces is, inevitably, not high, especially in cases where an author's subsequent career or status required a display of *gravitas* with which a reputation as a poet might appear inconsistent. Even a poet as renowned and as reputedly influential as Sir Edward Dyer is known today only through fragments. Yet new discoveries are constantly made, sometimes of substantial bodies of notable work—Sir Robert Sidney is the most striking recent instance—but more usually of individual pieces.[31]

Dyer was one of the casualties of scribal publication: Robert Sidney a lucky survivor. The great bulk of this verse was distributed by its authors. Among the better-known poets, Alexander Brome, Sir John Davies, Donne, Harington, the two Herberts, King, Marvell and Katherine Philips all seem to have taken a supervisory role in the production and circulation of copies of their works, contrasting in this with Strode, Corbett. Carew, Cotton, Rochester and Dorset, who were more inclined to let circulation take its course.[32] Both groups were sustaining a preference carried over from the reign of Elizabeth when, as Saunders has shown, there was a sharp distinction between the courtier or gentleman poet for whom print publication would have been a social disgrace, and more humbly born aspirants for patronage who turned to the press as a means of self-advertisement.[33] Insofar as this position changed in the early years of the seventeenth century, it was in that the communication of manuscripts became so widespread a practice that the search for

(Cambridge, 1983), pp. 64–5, 76–7, 99, 126, 138, 140–3, 159–62; Frank W. Jessup, *Sir Roger Twysden* (London, 1965), p. 189. Many other widely read texts could be cited.

[31] Dennis Kay, 'Poems by Sir Walter Aston, and a date for the Donne/Goodyer verse epistle "alternis vicibus"', *RES* ns 37 (1986), 198.

[32] Beal's introductions in *IELM*, i and ii indicate when a significant number of surviving manuscripts come from the authors or their amanuenses and contain well-informed judgements about the circumstances of early copying. Otherwise the reader is referred to the standard scholarly editions of these writers.

[33] Saunders, pp. 150–9.

preferment could be pursued through that medium alone. (Massinger, Drayton and Abraham Holland comment abrasively on this phenomenon from the point of view of print-publishing poets.[34])

The most studied case of author-published poetry is that of Donne, who printed very little verse in his lifetime, and always with misgivings. Instead, the poems obtained wide circulation then and for some years after his death in manuscript volumes of which MacColl knew of 'some forty collections of varying size, and over a hundred miscellanies'—a figure since enlarged.[35] These first appeared among a circle of friends and patrons from whom they percolated to a wider readership. The emphasis on large collections is important, as Donne followed the practice of the classical poets in structuring his output into groups determined by genre. MacColl's contention that 'with the exception of verse letters and occasional pieces he rarely gave out copies of single poems' has been disputed by Marotti and Sullivan; but there can be little doubt that, even if not personally responsible, he lent his assistance to the assemblage of the larger, composite groups of satires, elegies, verse letters and ultimately 'works'.[36] It is clear from the history of *Biathanatos*, already considered, and from a letter requesting Sir Henry Goodyer to return a volume of poems, that some of this circulation was regarded by Donne as remaining in the private sphere.[37] But this was partly a reaction of his later life when the poems of his youth were an increasing embarrassment. The extreme rarity of autographs of the poems suggests that he used scribes to produce copies. While there is no evidence that he accepted payment for manuscripts of his verse, there would have been gifts from patrons. Otherwise the circulation of poems

[34] For Massinger, see Peter Beal, 'Massinger at bay: unpublished verses in a war of the theatres', *YES* 10 (1980), 190–203; for Drayton p. 3 above; and for Holland, p. 217 below.

[35] MacColl, p. 29. A new census of sources will be appearing with the Variorum Donne.

[36] MacColl, p. 41; Marotti, p. 15. Helen Gardner's belief that at least one of these collections originated from Donne himself has been questioned by Sullivan who insists that 'no evidence exists that Donne ever successfully collected his poems' (*Dalhousie manuscripts*, p. 10). Ted-Larry Pebworth, 'John Donne, coterie poetry, and the text as performance', *SEL* 29 (1989), 61-75, goes further in presenting a Donne for whom 'once the poetic gesture [had] been made and received' the poem became expendable and might not even be preserved (p. 65). According to this view, the collections are the creation of the coterie, not the author.

[37] *Letters*, p. 197; MacColl, p. 35.

helped to confirm friendships with like-minded contemporaries (several of whom were themselves poets) and to advertise Donne's suitability for advancement in state and church.

Similar methods were also employed by Henry King who used Oxford scribes, including Thomas Manne, the chaplain of his college, Christ Church, to circulate a regularly updated miscellany of poems by himself and friends. At Cambridge during the 1630s, Crashaw also made use of scribes to put his poems into circulation.[38] John Watson's commonplace book, drawing on largely Cambridge material from between the 1640s and the late 1670s, besides confirming that the scribal circulation of verse was still in a flourishing condition, identifies a number of pieces as having been received directly from their authors, those named being Joseph Arrowsmith, Robert Gaton, John Jenkins, Sir Henry North, Matthew Pool, Thomas Townes and Roger Wolverton. Arrowsmith, a fellow of Trinity, had a comedy, *The reformation*, performed by the Duke's Company in 1673. Gaton, Pool and Townes were dons; North, Watson's patron in the country; Jenkins, at that stage, a member of North's household; and Wolverton a physician.

A further issue to be noted under the topic of author publication is its effect on conceptions of the activity of composition. Even among print-publishing writers, then and now, it is not hard to find examples of texts which remain obstinately in process, being revised or updated at each new edition through the writer's lifetime, and after it too as editors wrestle with the multitude of authorial possibilities.[39] While we should be wary of assuming that this is the natural condition of *all* writing (a proportion of authors have always refused to alter any feature of a work once written), it is one that was actively encouraged by the scribal medium, where changes could be made from copy to copy rather than from edition to edition. Sometimes these revisions would be recorded as corrections to a master-manuscript like that of Gorges' *The Olympian catastrophe*. In that case no derived copies survive; but

[38] For King, see n. 25 above. Crashaw's use of scribes is discussed in *The poems English Latin and Greek of Richard Crashaw*, ed. L. C. Martin (Oxford, 1957), pp. xlvi, lv–lvii, lxi–lxii, lxiv and xciii.

[39] The cases of Auden, Graves, Hardy, James, Whitman, Wordsworth and Yeats immediately suggest themselves.

with the Lauderdale translation of the *Aeneid* we possess not only a palimpsestic master copy of book four (Royal Irish Academy MS 12 B2 25) but the author's own notes identifying three scribes by name and the numbers of revised readings introduced at certain transcriptions.[40] The Sidneian psalms, to be considered in the following section, are another case of a text subject to incessant revision, although in this case neither of the two putative master copies survives. The term serial composition is proposed for this phenomenon.

The ideal of creativity revealed in such cases is a gradualistic one. Freed from the print-publishing author's obligation to produce a finalized text suitable for large-scale replication, the scribal author-publisher is able both to polish texts indefinitely and to personalize them to suit the tastes of particular recipients. This practice denies the sharp distinctions which can be drawn for print-published texts between drafts, the 'authorized' first-edition text, and revisions which are fully reflected on and well spaced in time. It also militates against our identifying any particular text as the embodiment of a 'final intention', for while the process of revision may in some instances be one of honing and perfecting, it may equally be one of change for change's sake or of an ongoing adaptation to the expectations of readers. Versions produced in this way do not so much replace as augment each other. In some instances they seem to grow from a lifestyle in which the activity of altering a text was more important than its outcome. Lauderdale's revisions to his *Aeneid*, made during his exile with James II at Saint-Germain, would be hard in many cases to describe as improvements, but seem rather to betray a mind in search of occupation. Roger North's perpetual recasting of the material of his treatises suggests a similar preference not to finalize. Had he been writing for the press, publication would have directed him to new projects and relieved him of the burden of the old; but it would also have deprived him of an activity, which was obviously greatly to his taste, of sitting down with his loved papers and engaging in largely superfluous acts of redrafting. Mary Countess of Pembroke's lifetime of work on the translation of the psalms begun by her

[40] Analysed in Margaret Boddy, 'The manuscripts and printed editions of the translation of Virgil made by Richard Maitland, fourth Earl of Lauderdale, and the connexion with Dryden', *N&Q* 210 (1965), 144–50. The printed editions were posthumous.

brother, Sir Philip Sidney, while stimulated by a sense of family and religious duty, was also the result of an unwillingness to bring an absorbing activity to too precipitate an end. While the later versions are certainly tauter and more polished than the earlier ones, much variation is of the gratuitous kind that could just as well be unmade or further varied. It is a mistake in such cases to assume that revision is the consequence of a Platonic impulse towards the perfected, unalterable text. No doubt in some cases it was, but one should never overlook Ong's insight that this ideal is itself a function of print culture.[41] The model for such revision may well be closer to that of a musican playing variations on a favourite theme.

For the print-published author who wished to employ a scribe-like flexibility, there was the recourse of marking up copies of an edition with handwritten alterations. Two copies of Sir William Killigrew's *Five new plays* (1666) exist in this form, while there are manuscript corrections, believed to be by the author, in almost every copy of the 1651 quarto of D'Avenant's *Gondibert*.[42] A striking example from after our period is the 1739 Dublin *Verses on the death of Dr Swift* in which spaces were left in the notes to be filled in by hand prior to sale, but no surviving copy contains the suppressed text in full.[43]

WOMEN WRITERS AND THE SCRIBAL MEDIUM

The stigma of print bore particularly hard on women writers, as they themselves pointed out. Anne Finch, Countess of Winchilsea, praised Lady Pakington, the reputed author of *The whole duty of man*, as having combined the 'Skill to write' with the 'Modesty to hide'.[44] The alternative to 'hiding' one's work would often be to

[41] Walter J. Ong, *Orality and literacy: the technologizing of the word* (London, 1982), pp. 121–3.

[42] Joseph S. Johnston, jun., 'Sir William Killigrew's revised copy of his *Four new plays*: confirmation of his claim to *The imperial tragedy*', MP 74 (1976), 72–4; John Horden, 'Sir William Killigrew's *Four new plays* (1666) with his *Imperial tragedy* (1669): a second annotated copy', *Library*, 6:6 (1984), 271–5; Beal, *IELM*, ii/1, 310–11.

[43] See Clive Probyn, 'Swift's *Verses on the death of Dr. Swift*: the notes', SB 39 (1986), 47–61.

[44] 'On the death of the honourable Mr. James Thynne', l. 41 in *The poems of Anne, Countess of Winchilsea*, ed. Myra Reynolds (Chicago, 1903), pp. 56–9.

find a metaphorical equation drawn between an eagerness to appear in print and sexual immorality, as in Lovelace's lines

> Now as her self a Poem she doth dresse,
> And curls a Line as she would do a tresse;
> Powders a Sonnet as she does her hair,
> Then prostitutes them both to publick Aire.[45]

Lady Mary Wroth, after having run into trouble over the print publication in 1621 of her *roman à clef*, *The Countesse of Montgomery's Urania*, kept the second part and a play derived from it in manuscript.[46] Even so pious an undertaking as the Sidneian psalms was never printed.[47] This was not for want of merit: the work was highly admired in its time and sixteen manuscripts survive as a testimony to its wide distribution. Sir John Harington, in an aside in his *Treatise on play*, which itself remained confined to the scribal medium, thought the Countess of Pembroke was being too restrictive:

seing it is allredy prophecied those precious leaues (those hims that she doth consecrate to Heauen) shall owtlast Wilton walls, meethinke it is pitty they are unpublyshed, but lye still inclosed within those walls lyke prisoners, though many haue made great suyt for theyr liberty.[48]

Whether print publication was what Harington had in mind, or simply a fuller release of the sequence in manuscript is not made clear. (He had sent three of the poems to Lucy Countess of Bedford and left eight among his own papers but may have lacked a

---

[45] *The poems of Richard Lovelace*, ed. C. H. Wilkinson, corr. repr. (Oxford, 1953), p. 200. Wycherley's lines on Aphra Behn, 'To the Sappho *of the Age, suppos'd to Ly-In of a* Love-Distemper, *or a* Play', are an even more blatant version (*The complete works of William Wycherley*, ed. Montague Summers (London, 1924), iii. 155–6). For further instances of the accusation, see Jacqueline Pearson, *The prostituted muse: images of women and women dramatists 1642–1737* (Hemel Hempstead, 1988), pp. 6–14.

[46] *The poems of Lady Mary Wroth*, ed. Josephine A. Roberts (Baton Rouge, La., 1983), pp. 28–38.

[47] For the textual history of this work see Mary Sidney, *Triumph of death*, pp. 18–36; *The psalms of Sir Philip Sidney and the Countess of Pembroke*, ed. J. C. A. Rathmell (New York, 1963), pp. xxvii–xxix; and Noel Kinnamon, 'The Sidney psalms: the Penshurst and Tixall manuscripts', *English manuscript studies 1100–1700* 2 (1990), 139–61. Sir Philip's share of the cycle is included in *The poems of Sir Philip Sidney*, ed. William A. Ringler, jun. (Oxford, 1962), pp. 265–337. An OET edition is being prepared by Margaret P. Hannay and Kinnamon.

[48] *Nugae antiquae: being a miscellaneous collection of original papers* (London, 1769–75), ii. 6.

complete set.[49]) The work of Noel Kinnamon and the editors of the Sidneian psalms has given us a fairly full picture of the Countess's activity as a writer for and publisher in the scribal medium. At the time of Sir Philip's death in 1586 only forty-three of the 150 psalms had been translated. The Countess proved an inveterate improver both of her brother's work and of her own as it proceeded, the changes showing up as variants between successive manuscripts. Master copies were kept in London as well as at Wilton, with changes made to one not necessarily being transported to the other. The conjectural ancestor X which gave rise to ten of the surviving sources is assumed to have been the London master on the grounds that it was there the Countess would have received most requests for copies. The considerable extent to which sources are found to preserve unique authorial readings indicates that the process of publication remained firmly under the writer's control.

Katherine Philips ('Orinda'), the most admired woman poet of the century, built her reputation largely through manuscript transmission, initially within a circle of intimates in Ireland and later on a wider scale. Elaine Hobby lays stress on her status as a published author through the scribal medium:

In part, the image of Orinda that has come down to us is dependent on the belief that her writing was really a secret and private affair, her poems passed around only in manuscript form to a few trusted friends. This is an anachronistic distortion of the method of 'publication' that she used: circulation of manuscripts was the normal way to make writing public before the widespread use of printed books, and was a method that continued to be popular in court circles throughout the reign of Charles II, at least. Such a description also fails to consider the fact that, as a royalist poet married to a leading parliamentarian, she had positive reasons for avoiding too much public attention during the 1650s, which was when she did most of her writing. Bearing these factors in mind, we find that the evidence suggests that she was actually a well-known writer. . . . The 'public' she was interested in reaching was the coterie of court and leading poets, not the wider world.[50]

[49] See Rathmell, pp. xxvii, xxix. John Davies of Hereford praises the Countess's reticence, along with that of her fellow writers Lucy Countess of Bedford and Elizabeth Lady Cary, commending them in that 'you presse the *Presse* with little you haue made' (*The muse's sacrifice*, in *The complete works of John Davies of Hereford*, ed. Alexander B. Grosart (repr. New York, 1967), ii. 5).

[50] Elaine Hobby, *Virtue of necessity: English women's writing 1649–1688* (London, 1988), p. 129.

Towards the end of Orinda's life collections of her verse were circulating in manuscript, one of these forming the basis of an unauthorized printed edition in 1664 which so greatly distressed her that she tried to have it suppressed. One surviving collection was prepared by a professional scribe after Orinda's death as a gift to her friend Lady Montague (the Mary Aubrey and 'Rosania' of her poems).[51]

The poems themselves yield numerous clues about Orinda's methods as author-publisher. A large group among them is addressed to various members of a circle of English admirers of the French *précieuse* spirit who were known to each other by pastoral names and cultivated 'platonic' friendships. New poems can be assumed to have travelled rapidly through this circle, and some of its members would have built up personal collections of the verse. A second group of poems, printed at the head of the posthumous 1667 edition, is addressed to members of the royal family. The link between the two groups was Sir Charles Cotterell, Master of Ceremonies at the court of Charles II, and, as 'Poliarchus', a leading spirit of the *précieuse* circle. Through Cotterell's advocacy the poems became well known at Whitehall. Roger Boyle, Earl of Orrery, in a verse epistle written during Orinda's lifetime alludes to 'the praises of th'admiring Court' and displays a personal acquaintance with a wide range of her work.[52] A verse address by Orinda to Anne, Duchess of York is evidently meant as the dedicatory poem to a lost manuscript collection of the poems. Through such means Orinda was able to establish herself as a known and noted writer with only one, involuntary appearance in print.

[51] National Library of Wales, Aberystwyth, MS 776–B. Claudia A. Limbert, 'Katherine Philips: another step-father and another sibling, "Mⁿ C: P.", and "Polex:"', *Restoration* 13 (1989), 2–6, has suggested that Sir William Temple (and not Sir Charles Cotterell, as earlier believed) was the compiler of this collection. For a census of the surviving manuscripts, see *The collected works of Katherine Philips*, ed. Patrick Thomas (Stump Cross, 1990–), i. 41–50. The availability of Philips's work in manuscript raises doubts about Allan Pritchard's use of parallels between poems in her 1667 collection and Marvell's 'The garden' to argue for a date of composition in the late 1660s for 'The garden'. It is also possible that Philips had seen 'The garden' in manuscript, reversing the assumed direction of influence. ('Marvell's 'The garden': A Restoration poem?', *SEL* 23 (1983), 371–88.) However, Pritchard's wider plea for scepticism towards the traditional Marvell datings is fully justified.

[52] *Poems by the most deservedly admired Mⁿ Katherine Philips, the matchless Orinda* (London, 1678), b1ʳ–1ᵛ. The two had met in Dublin in 1662.

Scribal publication, then, provided an avenue for those women poets who either through preference or lack of access eschewed the press. However, literary writings circulated in this way were quantitatively of minor significance besides the texts by women writers dealing with the practical conduct of the household, the preparation of food and clothing and the treatment of illness. Personal collections on these subjects were regarded with great pride by their compilers. The will of Dame Johanna St. John, signed on 7 March 1704, carefully instructs that her 'great Receit Book' was to go to her eldest daughter Anne Cholmondeley, and her 'Book of receits of cookery and Preserves' to her granddaughter, Johanna Soame. But for her other manuscripts she showed no such concern: in leaving her private cabinet to another granddaughter, she specified that she 'would have the papers therein burned first'.[53]

PROFESSIONAL AUTHORSHIP AND THE SCRIBAL MEDIUM

While much of the transmission so far described was of a social or peer-group-bonding nature (a matter to be discussed in Chapter 5), there is evidence that scribal publication, when undertaken in a sufficiently hard-headed spirit, could be more profitable than publication through the press. Print publication offered the writer two chances of income—a payment from the bookseller, and the gift that was expected to follow a dedication; however, booksellers would often jib at any payment at all. The point of view of one representative of the trade, writing in 1624, was that any self-respecting author would not expect it:

And most of the best Authors are not soe penurious that they looke soe much to theire gaine, as to the good they intend Religion or State. They are too Mercenary that write bookes for Money, and theire couetuousnes makes theire labours fruitles, and disesteemed.[54]

The £5 offered to Milton for the first printing of *Paradise lost* was by the standard of its time a generous payment: it was only the steep rise in the value of literary property which took place from the 1690s that made it seem exploitative. The response of authors

---

[53] Frank T. Smallwood, 'The will of Dame Johanna St. John', *N&Q* 214 (1969), 346.
[54] BL MS Add. 18648, f. 18ʳ; cited in Allan Pritchard, 'George Wither's quarrel with the stationers: an anonymous reply to *The schollers purgatory*', *SB* 16 (1963), 37.

to such attitudes was naturally a hostile one. George Wither's *The schollers purgatory* (1624) vigorously presents the case of the aspiring professional. That of the part-time author is hinted at in a *bon mot* recorded by Sir Nicholas Le Strange: 'A Gentleman usd to say of Booke-Sellers, that they were like lice, bredd of the sweat of a Mans Braine, and upon that they live.'[55] Under some agreements the author would not be paid in cash but copies of the book which then had to be turned into money by whatever means presented themselves.[56] Scribal publication offered the resourceful author the chance of higher rewards. Once the charges of copying and paper had been met, the presentation of a work in manuscript to a well-disposed patron could be expected to bring in a sum commensurate with that from the dedicating of a printed book. The presentation could then be repeated to other patrons, as Cosmo Manuche did when he prepared separate dedication copies of *The banished shepherdess* for the Queen Dowager Henrietta Maria and James, third Earl of Northampton, or Daniel when he reassigned his 'Epistle to the Lady Margaret, Countess of Cumberland' to Elizabeth, Lady Hatton.[57] Moreover, once the scribe had been paid, the author was the direct recipient of all benefits, having to surrender nothing to a middleman.

Much author publication was really a form of begging. Giacomo Castelvetro's dedication of his manuscript treatise, *Brieve racconto di tutte le radici, di tutte l'erbe et di tutti i frutti, che crudi o cotti in Italia si mangiano* (1614), to Lucy Countess of Bedford is accompanied by a plea that she should continue the pension he had received from her brother.[58] On 23 November 1660, while searching the room of an impoverished scholar named Robert Gaton who had committed suicide, John Watson discovered the

[55] *Merry passages and jeasts*, p. 141.

[56] One well-documented case of this practice is discussed in my 'Preacher and publisher: Oliver Heywood and Thomas Parkhurst', *SB* 31 (1978), 227–35. Heywood, a victim of the 1662 ejectment of Nonconformists from their livings, obtained a substantial part of editions of his books either as part of his contract or by purchase at a discount. These were distributed to his co-religionists (lists of whose names have been preserved) with 'guilded' copies sometimes provided for influential patrons. While it appears that at least some of these books were distributed gratis by Heywood, it can be assumed that their cost to him was eventually covered by contributions from his 'hearers'.

[57] Williams, 'Castle Ashby manuscripts', pp. 395–8; Arthur Freeman, 'An epistle for two', *Library*, 5:25 (1970), 226–36.

[58] *The fruit, herbs and vegetables of Italy*, trans. Gillian Riley (Harmondsworth, 1989), p. 47.

manuscript of a short poem 'May't please! here is a wearied Bee from hive' which he judged to have been prepared '*pro formâ mendicandi*'.[59] Others were more persistent, or perhaps successful, and the miscellanies of seventeenth-century verse contain many thinly disguised appeals for favour or subvention. The plea did not have to be direct: verse in praise of a patron's house, person or family, a funeral elegy for a relative, or a piece which simply agreed with views the patron was known to hold would produce the same effect, and, when presented in a reasonably dignified way, was an accepted part of the vocation of letters. Neither did the response have to be in cash: houseroom, wine, clothing or assistance in some suit for preferment would be just as welcome.

> Commend this Olio of this Lord, 'tis fit,
> Nay ten to one but you have part of it;
> There is that justice left, since you maintain
> His table, he should counter-feed your brain.
> Then write how well he in his Sack hath droll'd,
> Straight there's a Bottle to your chamber roll'd.
> Or with embroidered words praise his *French* Suit,
> Month hence 'tis yours, with his Mans curse to boot . . .
> Or spin an Elegie on his false hair,
> 'Tis well he cries, but living hair is dear;
> Yet say that out of order ther's one curl,
> And all the hopes of your reward you furl.[60]

Such addresses were part of the machinery of the patron-client relationship—expressions of allegiance to a social superior who in turn was expected to advance the fortunes of the petitioner. None the less, properly handled, and directed to a variety of patrons, they could offer a resourceful writer better returns in money or kind than the sale of the same texts to a print publisher.

One writer, Richard Flecknoe, daringly transposed this practice into print. His numerous books of epigrams (almost an annual event at one stage of his life) are rich in thinly disguised begging poems, many addressed to members of the Cavendish family.[61] The books themselves, of which fourteen out of thirty-two were published 'For the author' and only ten bear the imprint of a

---

[59] BL MS 18220, f. 4.
[60] Lovelace, 'On *Sanazar's* being honoured', *Poems*, p. 194.
[61] See my 'Richard Flecknoe as author-publisher', *BSANZ bulletin* 14 (1990), 41–50.

bookseller, were themselves distributed as a form of begging. In one epigram, he frankly confesses that

> To you, from whom I can't so much as look
> For charges of the *binding* of my *Book*;
> Much less the *Printing*, why should I present
> It now? but only out of Compliment?
> And I don't like such Compliments as those,
> When one gets nothing, and is sure to lose.[62]

Flecknoe is a useful because unusually blatant witness to a practice that was already well established in manuscript. But print had the drawback that these machinations were on public display, a matter that must have contributed to the contempt in which Flecknoe was held by Dryden.[63] Flecknoe's readers can hardly have failed to notice that, on the death of patrons, poems written in their honour were sometimes transferred to other recipients—a practice much less risky in manuscript.[64]

The exclusivity of the scribal medium made it ideally suited to another form of the client–patron relationship in which the writer produced numerous pieces specifically tailored to the taste of the patron and his friends. Nashe's claim of 1592—'I haue written in all sorts of humors priuately, I am perswaded, more than any yoong man of my age in England'—appears to refer to light-hearted pieces, now mostly lost, written for the circle of Lord Strange in the early 1590s.[65] The same kind of dependence can be seen in the long series of papers on administrative questions prepared by Sir Robert Cotton for Henry Howard, Earl of Northampton.[66] Shakespeare's sonnets are another outcome of a sustained client–

[62] *Epigrams of all sorts* (London, 1671), p. A4ʳ. See also Anton Lohr, *Richard Flecknoe. Eine literarische Untersuchung* Leipzig, 1905), p. 104.

[63] Discussed in my 'Shadwell, Flecknoe and the Duke of Newcastle: an impetus for *Mac Flecknoe*', *Papers on language and literature* 21 (1985), 19-27.

[64] For examples see Love, 'Richard Flecknoe', p. 44. Kay, 'Poems by Sir Walter Aston', pp. 206–7 and n. 37 cites parallel cases from manuscript elegies on Prince Henry.

[65] *The works of Thomas Nashe*, ed. R. B. McKerrow, rev. F. P. Wilson (Oxford, 1958), i. 320. For Nashe and Strange see Charles Nicholl, *A cup of news: the life of Thomas Nashe* (London, 1984), pp. 87–98. Nicholl's identification of Strange as the dedicatee of 'The choice of valentines' is confirmed by Folger MS V. a. 399, ff. 53ᵛ–7ʳ. For the circulation of writings by Nashe in manuscript, see *Works*, v. 136.

[66] Cotton's work for Northampton is described in Kevin Sharpe, *Sir Robert Cotton 1586–1631: history and politics in early modern England* (Oxford, 1979), pp. 114–28 and Linda Levy Peck, *Northampton: patronage and policy at the court of James I* (London, 1982), pp. 103–17. See also below, pp. 83–9.

patron relationship, the earlier decades having an unmistakable status as gifts presented singly or in small groups during the client's regular visits to wait upon the patron.[67] (The opening scene of *Timon of Athens* shows an Athenian version of such a visit.) This would still hold even if the 'story' of the sonnets was a fiction, since it would be a fiction styled around the known conditions of the client's service and the patron's acceptance; moreover, the poems could still have performed the function of a client's gift to a patron who was not the young man presented in them. Moving from the known to the unknown, and from the opening years of the century to the 1670s, it is tempting to see Traherne's industry as a composer of prose meditations (while obviously congenial) as tailored to the tastes of his patron and employer, the elderly Sir Orlando Bridgeman.[68] Not all these cases qualify as examples of scribal publication but they illustrate how an author working in the scribal medium could be just as professional in outlook as his print-orientated counterpart.

Consideration of the links between author publication and the search for patronage leads irresistibly to Andrew Marvell, who made his way during the 1650s to a position which Hilton Kelliher has accurately described as that of Cromwell's own laureate and the 'official verse-propagandist of the new state'.[69] This was done with very little exposure by name in print, though a few texts appeared anonymously. Instead his preference was always to direct poems along precisely calculated paths within networks of patronage. His Latin verse address to Nathaniel Ingelo was composed in order that it should be seen (as it was) by 'the learned Queen Christina, whom it flatters at length', while the 'Horatian ode', although not directly addressed to Cromwell, was very probably meant to reach his hands.[70] Having served these purposes

[67] This is also Arthur F. Marotti's view in 'Shakespeare's sonnets as literary property' in *Soliciting interpretation: literary theory and seventeenth-century English poetry*, ed. Elizabeth Harvey and Katharine Maus (Chicago, 1990), pp. 143–73.

[68] Traherne was chaplain to Bridgeman and his large family. As a famous anecdote concerning Swift records, a chaplain might be required to read meditations aloud to his employer.

[69] *Andrew Marvell poet and politician 1621–78. An exhibition to commemorate the tercentenary of his death* (London, 1978), p. 56.

[70] Kelliher, p. 59. In my reading of the ode, I follow the findings of Denise Cuthbert's meticulous study of the evolution of Marvell's relationship with Cromwell in her Sydney University Ph.D. thesis, 'A re-examination of Andrew Marvell' (1987).

neither poem appears to have circulated further either in print or in manuscript until its appearance in the posthumous *Miscellaneous poems* of 1681, assembled by Mary Palmer. Prior to attaching himself to Cromwell, Marvell had been in the service of another great Puritan leader, Thomas, Lord Fairfax. The hostile references to Cromwell, Fairfax and their cause in the elegy on Lord Francis Villiers (printed anonymously *circa* 1648–9) has led several scholars to reject its somewhat shaky attribution to Marvell; but this is to display a naïve attitude towards the politics of patronage as they affected the scribal medium, especially as Marvell's third major patron was to be Francis Villiers's brother, the second Duke of Buckingham. Over recent decades Marvell scholars have been steadily accumulating evidence for the prior scribal publication of poems from the 1681 collection, but it is only in the case of the post-Restoration satires (mostly excluded from the collection) that this was genuinely extensive.[71] Insofar as a continuing theme can be identified behind Marvell's conduct of his career, it is one of exercising the maximum amount of influence with the minimum amount of visibility. His airy dismissal of Samuel Parker's account of his Cromwellian past was only possible because the 'Horatian ode' and the elegy on the death of Cromwell still remained in manuscript.[72] The second of these seems actually to have been withdrawn at the last moment from the volume of elegies which was to haunt Dryden, Waller and Sprat for the rest of their lives.

Having earlier considered Flecknoe's naturalization into print of the manuscript begging poem, it will be helpful here to consider another area in which print exposed a practice that had previously been earning income for scribal author-publishers. John Jenkins's career as a composer-publisher has already been discussed but not its economic basis. While Jenkins must sometimes have received direct payment or presents in return for manuscripts of his music, Roger North makes clear that his primary support came as a salaried visitor to music-loving houses ('I never heard that he articled with any gentleman where he resided, but accepted what

[71] See Kelliher, *passim*; Pritchard, 'Marvell's "The garden"'; and Margarita Stocker and Timothy Raylor, 'A new Marvell manuscript: Cromwellian patronage and politics', *ELR* 20 (1990), 106–62.

[72] *The rehearsal transpros'd and The rehearsal transpros'd the second part*, ed. D. I. B. Smith (Oxford, 1971), p. 203.

they gave him'), and that such terms were generous enough for Jenkins to be able to leave a number of legacies.[73] This arrangement reflects the conditions of musical life in the country; but in the cities and large towns the professional musician would expect to earn regular income from individual pupils, which would include payment for handwritten tutors and simple 'lessons'.[74] At a later stage the learner would be expected to purchase manuscripts of more advanced compositions, which meant that it was rarely in the composer's interest to publish these in printed form.[75] As late as 1669 it was widely believed that 'no Choice Ayres or Songs are permitted by Authors to come in print'.[76] The price of music so secured was a constant source of complaint. Roger North, for one, had no regrets for an age 'when all passed in MSS, which were not onely hard to get, but often slovenly wrote'.[77]

That having 'lessons' engraved for private sale by the composer could bring even higher returns than the sale of handwritten copies was the discovery of the violin virtuoso Nicola Matteis. North's account of this change is as follows:

> And he found out a way of getting mony which was perfectly new. For seeing his lessons, (which were all *duos*), take with his scollars, and that most gentlemen desired them, he was at some charge to have them graven in copper, and printed in oblong octavos, and this was the beginning of ingraving musick in England. And of these lessons he made books, and presented them, well bound, to most of the lovers, which brought him the 3, 4, and 5 ginnys; and the incouragement was so great, that he made 4 of them.[78]

As in Flecknoe's case, the transition to print illuminates what had previously been buried from sight in manuscript. The musician

---

[73] North, *Roger North*, p. 344.

[74] A practice already established by the late 15th cent. as is shown by Christopher Page, 'The 15th-century lute: new and neglected sources', *Early music* 9 (1981), 11–21. For a 17th-cent. example, carefully fingered for a novice harpsichordist, see John L. Boston, 'Priscilla Bunbury's virginal book', *Music and letters* 36 (1955), 365–73.

[75] Byrd's 'My lady Nevell's book', superbly written for the composer by the Windsor music scribe, John Baldwin, is one famous example.

[76] *The treasury of musick: containing ayres and dialogues* (London, 1669), p. A1'. John Playford's denial of this proposition is, naturally, a self-interested one.

[77] North, *Roger North*, p. 311 and n. 66.

[78] Ibid. 356. For Matteis's place in the history of music engraving in England (which actually dated from 1613), see D. W. Krummel, *English music printing 1553–1700* (London, 1975), pp. 152–9.

selling individual engraved lessons directly to his pupils or presenting 'books' of these to patrons in return for a 'present' of three, four or five guineas a time would have earned far more than by a sale of his copy to a regular print-publisher supplemented by a single dedication. Moreover, by paying for and retaining the plates he could produce repeated small editions to suit requirements. The good fortune of Matteis lay in his having enough pupils and patrons to be his own print publisher, having graduated to this from scribal publication. It is likely that other manuscripts arising from the teacher–pupil relationship, such as writing-copy-books, dance manuals, devotional works and materials for the study of foreign languages, were sold or 'presented' in the same way, and at the same high prices.

THE AUTHOR PUBLICATION OF PLAY TEXTS

The pre-1641 theatres, always cautious about print publication, tolerated the scribal publication of play-texts, at least from the early 1620s and probably earlier.[79] Humphrey Moseley in his introduction to the 1647 Beaumont and Fletcher folio mentions copies having been made available by actors to their 'private friends', the manuscript of Fletcher's *Bonduca* (BL Add. MS 36758) being one such presentation copy, in the hand of Edward Knight, the King's Men's prompter.[80] A second scribe was responsible for a manuscript of *Beggars' bush* and a royal presentation copy of Suckling's *Aglaura*.[81] The King's Men also made regular use of Ralph Crane's services in order to produce play-manuscripts whose purpose was, in M. A. Buettner's words, 'either to present

[79] W. W. Greg in the *The editorial problem in Shakespeare*, 3rd edn (Oxford, 1954) expressed his position in the following words: 'I am not aware that any private transcript can be dated before 1624, when the scandal over *A Game at Chess* created a sudden demand, but it is quite possible that isolated copies may have been produced earlier' (p. 45). This is a fair assessment of the position as regards surviving manuscripts but has to be questioned on the basis of those lost ones which served as the basis of unauthorized printed editions. John Jowett, 'Jonson's authorization of type in *Sejanus* and other early quartos', *SB* 44 (1991), supports Greg's position on the equally contestable grounds that 'the drama simply did not belong to an élite culture in the sense that metaphysical poetry did' (p. 255).

[80] *Comedies and tragedies written by Francis Beaumont and John Fletcher gentlemen* (London 1647), p. A4ʳ; W. W. Greg, 'Prompt copies, private transcripts, and the "playhouse scrivener"', *Library*, 4:6 (1926), 148–56; *The dramatic works in the Beaumont and Fletcher canon*, iv. 151.

[81] *Dramatic works*, iii. 227.

to aristocratic patrons or to sell in the marketplace'.[82] Only a handful of Crane's manuscripts survive—the existence of others being inferred from the study of printed texts for which they are believed to have served as copy—but none of these is a working playhouse manuscript; nor would the expensive services of a skilled scribe be wasted on such utilitarian documents as prompt-books, plots and actors' sides.[83] In August 1624 Crane was called on to assist with the scribal publication of Middleton's banned *A game at chess*. Three of the six surviving manuscripts are in his hand, two others being wholly or partly in that of the dramatist. The question whether Crane's copies are to be regarded as examples of author or of entrepreneurial publication is answered by the fact that one of them contains a dedication signed by Middleton to 'the Worthlie-Accomplish'd, Mr: William Hammond'

> This, which nor Stage nor Stationers Stall can Showe,
> (The Common Eye maye wish for, but ne're knowe)
> Comes in it's best Loue, wth the New-yeare forth,
> As a fit Present to the Hand of Worth.[84]

Middleton then was the director of the enterprise: moreover, while undoubtedly expecting a return for his own and Crane's labours, he was keen to preserve the gentlemanly fiction of an exchange of gifts. The practice of presenting plays as new-year-gifts to a patron is also alluded to in Heywood's dedication of the 1633 printed text of *The Jew of Malta* to Thomas Hammon of Gray's Inn, this time with an apology that the donor had no better gift to offer.[85]

---

[82] '*A game of chess*' *by Thomas Middleton: a textual edition based on the manuscripts written by Ralph Crane*, ed. Milton Arthur Buettner (Salzburg, 1980), p. 1.

[83] A partial exception is Crane's transcript of *Sir John van Olden Barnavelt*, BL MS Add. 18653, which was marked up by a later hand to serve as a prompt-book. F. P. Wilson, 'Ralph Crane, scrivener to the King's Players', *Library*, 4:7 (1926), points out that the hand of this manuscript is 'less calligraphic' than his other copies and that it is a folio, whereas the private transcripts are quartos (pp. 202–3). For a consideration of the evidence for lost manuscripts, see T. H. Howard-Hill, *Ralph Crane and some Shakespeare first folio comedies* (Charlottesville, Va., 1972).

[84] '*A game of chess*', p. 44. Crane's transcript of Middleton's *The witch* (Bodleian MS Malone 12) contains a similar dedicatory epistle from the author to Thomas Holmes. However, that of Fletcher's *The humorous lieutenant* as *Demetrius and Enanthe* (Harlech collection) is by Crane himself, indicating entrepreneurial publication.

[85] 'I had no better a New-yeares gift to present you with; receive it therefore as a continuance of that inviolable obliegement, by which, he rests still ingaged; who as he ever hath, shall always remaine, *Tuissimus*' (*The complete works of Christopher Marlowe*, ed.

The 1650s found a large body of play manuscripts in circulation, some of these, no doubt, being survivors from the theatres' own collections but others emanating from a tradition of author publication which acquired new life when playwrights were deprived of their regular livelihood by the closing of the playhouses. Sizeable collections of manuscripts of unprinted pre-1642 plays were assembled by the booksellers Francis Kirkman, Richard Marriott and Humphrey Moseley (the third group being the source of the collection diminished by Warburton's cook).[86] The titles contained in these offer a tantalizing view of the wealth of material then available and the seriousness of the subsequent loss, except insofar as some of the plays may survive in Restoration adaptations.[87] In presenting the Beaumont and Fletcher folio of 1647 to the world, Moseley announced with obvious pride that 'Heretofore when Gentlemen desired but a Copy of any of these *Playes*, the meanest piece here (if any may be called Meane where every one is Best) cost them more then foure times the price you pay for the whole *Volume*'.[88] This would seem to indicate the '3 or 4' guineas mentioned by North as customary for a manuscript presented by its author.

Shakespeare may well have put work into circulation through the agency of scribes. As house dramatist for the King's Men, he was unable to print his plays without the approval of his fellow sharers.[89] Bentley judges that he 'did not himself take to the printer any of the plays he wrote for the Lord Chamberlain-King's company'.

Fredson Bowers (Cambridge 1973–), i. 259). For the earlier history of such presentations, see E. H. Miller, 'New year's day gift books in the sixteenth century', *SB* 15 (1962), 233–41. Wilson (p. 200) records that Ralph Crane made an annual gift of a manuscript to John, Earl of Bridgewater.

[86] The contents of these collections are listed on pp. 292–5 of Alfred Harbage, 'Elizabethan–Restoration palimpsest', *MLR* 35 (1940), 287–319 and in his *Annals of English drama 975–1700*, 3rd edn, rev. S. Schoenbaum and Sylvia Stoler Wagenheim (London, 1989), pp. 212–18. 'Hill's list' appears to represent the Kirkman collection. Manuscripts of already printed plays seem to have been of no interest to the collectors.

[87] The argument of 'Elizabethan–Restoration palimpsest'.

[88] *Comedies and tragedies*, p. A4^v. Moseley also complains: 'the *Care & Pains* was wholly mine, which I found to be more then you'l easily imagine, unlesse you knew into how many hands the Originalls were dispersed'. Robert K. Turner discusses the implications of this remark in *Dramatic works*, i. xxx.

[89] See G. E. Bentley, *The profession of dramatist in Shakespeare's time 1590–1642* (Princeton, NJ, 1971), pp. 264–81. The prohibition also applied to his successors Fletcher, Massinger and Brome.

When his plays were published they appeared without any indication of the author's sponsorship—no dedications, no epistles, no addresses to the reader, no commendatory verses from friends, not even a list of characters, and for most of them neither prologue nor epilogue . . . In whatever manner Shakespeare's several plays may have come into the hands of the printers before 1616 (and the possible methods are various) it is reasonably clear that he himself refrained from ushering them into print . . .[90]

The sale or presentation to a wealthy patron of a manuscript of a favourite play would have offered an opportunity for additional income, and is intrinsically no less improbable than other explanations which have been brought forward for the genesis of the manuscripts which served as copy for the better quarto editions. E. A. J. Honigmann singles out *Troilus and Cressida* and the sonnets, both printed by G. Eld in 1609, as possible outcomes of scribal circulation.[91] The play is described as *'neuer stal'd with the Stage, neuer clapper-clawd with the palmes of the vulger'*[92]; moreover, an attempt at print publication in 1602 had proved abortive—suggesting a certain notoriety. Honigmann's proposal that the play would have been read by contemporaries as an allusion to the fall of Essex would link it with other politically suspect material of the kind that, throughout the century, was restricted to manuscript circulation but often eagerly sought in that form.

In the case of the sonnets, we know from Francis Meres's reference in 1598 to their circulation 'among his priuate friends' and the appearance of two poems in *The passionate pilgrim* (1599) that some elements of the cycle were in circulation during the late 1590s. Other sonnets which survive in manuscript sources may also derive from originals of this period.[93] John Kerrigan, while accepting it as an 'inescapable conclusion' that some of the sonnets were 'quietly made public' through manuscript during the reign of Elizabeth, argues that the final form of the cycle, incorporating 'A

---

[90] Ibid. 280. Bentley points to the poor condition of the texts as further evidence against the involvement of a writer who 'did take great pains with his text when he published his poems' (loc. cit.).

[91] 'The date and revision of *Troilus and Cressida*' in *Textual criticism and literary interpretation*, ed. Jerome J. McGann (Chicago, 1985), p. 54.

[92] *The famous historie of Troylus and Cresseid* (London, 1609), ¶2 ʳ.

[93] For the manuscripts of the sonnets, see Beal, *IELM*, i/2, 452–4. Twelve sonnets in all are found in manuscript sources, Sonnet 2 occurring twelve times.

lover's complaint' and the more stylistically complex sonnets, was arrived at between 1603 and its appearance in print in 1609.[94] Despite the stress laid by Katharine Duncan-Jones on the solid professional standing of Thomas Thorpe, the 'adventurer' responsible for the 1609 publication, the absence of an authorial dedication and the riddling quality of Thorpe's salute to Mr. W. H. still leave a distinct odour of the intercepted manuscript—which in this case was of high quality but apparently not a holograph.[95] One possibility to be added to the multitude already canvassed is that Mr W. H. was a scribe charged with the production of copies who had made a surreptitious extra copy for sale to Thorpe. His 'begetting' of the text would consist of his having inscribed it—a common metaphor which will be further discussed in Chapter 4. The question is not without its critical implications, both in small matters (a visualizing reader will wish to know whether the image which should accompany 'That in black ink my love may still shine bright' is one of a printed or handwritten page) and in the broader question of the kind of readership to which Shakespeare was addressing the poems, and whether this varied as the cycle evolved through revision.

The Restoration theatre companies, with their repertoires secured by royal edict, had no reason to oppose the print publication of plays. Scribal publication was now reserved for dramatists who maintained a genteel disdain for the press (like Orinda with *Pompey* and Rochester with *Lucina's rape*) or where performance was prevented, as with Dryden's *The state of innocence*. In his preface to the 1677 quarto, Dryden complained of 'many hundred Copies of it being dispers'd, abroad without my knowledge or consent: so that every one gathering new faults, it became at length a Libel against me'. This is undoubtedly an exaggeration, but since seven manuscripts survive it is not implausible that ten times that number may once have existed.[96]

---

[94] *The sonnets and A lover's complaint* (Harmondsworth, 1986), p. 10. See also pp. 427–33 and the account of the variant texts on pp. 441–54.

[95] Katherine Duncan-Jones, 'Was the 1609 *Shake-speares Sonnets* really unauthorized?', *RES* NS 34 (1983), 151–71. See also Kerrigan, p. 66. The most revealing analysis of the language of the dedication is Donald W. Foster, 'Master W. H., R. I. P.', *PMLA* 102 (1987), 42–54.

[96] *The state of innocence, and fall of man: an opera* (London, 1677), p. b1ʳ. For the manuscripts see Harbage, *Annals*, p. 309. Five of these are discussed in Marion H. Hamilton,

Tellingly, one of these (Harvard MS Thr. 9) contains corrections in Dryden's own hand, suggesting that the tradition may have arisen from author publication. A manuscript of *The Indian emperour* used as a prompt copy for some country-house theatricals has also been traced back to a source close to the dramatist.[97] Among the poems, *Mac Flecknoe* and the collaborative *Essay upon satire* were consciously intended for scribal circulation though the surviving copies all seem to derive from entrepreneurial, not author, publication. Dryden is also said in one contemporary source to have written lampoons.[98]

PUBLICATION THROUGH ONE COPY

A survey of author publication is the most convenient place to address the apparently paradoxical notion of publication through a single copy, lent or rented. (A case of a manuscript being rented is attested to by Simonds D'Ewes.[99]) Circulation of a single copy to a series of readers has already been documented in the case of *Biathanatos* at the beginning of the period and of Pope's *Pastorals* a century later, and may well have been the mode of transmission of some works which were known prior to their first appearance in print but for which there are no surviving manuscripts. Among a number of documented examples is that of Hobbes's *An historical narration concerning heresie and the punishment thereof.* This was

---

'The manuscripts of Dryden's *The state of innocence* and the relation of the Harvard MS to the first quarto', *SB* 6 (1954), 237–46.

[97] See Fredson Bowers, 'The 1665 manuscript of Dryden's *Indian emperour*', *SP* 48 (1951), 738–60. The later 'Douai' manuscript is derived from a printed source (*Works*, ix. 382).

[98] For the manuscripts of *Mac Flecknoe*, see *Works*, i. 428–39; David M. Vieth, 'Dryden's *Mac Flecknoe*: the case against editorial confusion', *HLB* 24 (1976), 204–45; and Beal, *IELM*, ii/1, 407–8. Manuscript sources unknown to Vieth are Leeds University Brotherton MS Lt 54, pp. 1–10 and National Library of Ireland MS 2093, pp. 36–55, making 16 in all. For manuscripts of the *Essay*, written with John Sheffield, Earl of Mulgrave, see Beal, *IELM*, ii/1, 396. The accusation that Dryden wrote lampoons is made in Shadwell's 'Upon a late fall'n poet' ('A sad mischance I sing alas'), Yale MS Osborn b 105, p. 330, with reference to Anne Reeves: 'And thô she had Clapt him o're & o're, / Poxt all Wild:House Spanjards, and Forty more, / Yet he lampoon'd those that call'd her Whore' (ll. 37–9). On 23 February 1699 he sent two lampoon separates to Elizabeth Steward with speculations about their authorship (*The letters of John Dryden*, ed. Charles E. Ward (Durham, NC, 1942), p. 133).

[99] *The autobiography and correspondence of Sir Simonds D'Ewes, Bart., during the reigns of James I and Charles I*, ed. James Orchard Halliwell (London, 1845), ii. 39–40. John Shirley had run a lending service for manuscripts as early as the 15th cent.

written in 1666 to deflect a proposed prosecution of *Leviathan* but never printed during his lifetime. A manuscript was available to Charles Blount in 1678 through Hobbes's bookseller and print publisher, William Crooke.[100] Blount himself circulated a single manuscript copy of *A summary account of the Deists' religion*. Writing in 1686 to Thomas Sydenham, he explained: 'The last time I had the happiness of your Company, it was your Request that I would help you to a sight of the Deists Arguments, which I told you, I had sometimes by me, but then had lent them out, they are now return'd me again, and according to my promise I have herewith sent them to you.'[101] Mary Hobbs cites Aubrey's account of Donne's friend, John Hoskins, whose 'booke of poemes, neatly written by one of his clerkes, bigger then Dr Donne's poemes' disappeared after his son lent it to 'he knowes not who, about 1653'.[102] One of Aubrey's own close friends, the deist James Boevey (1622–95), wrote a kind of personal encyclopedia in thirty-nine volumes covering morality, psychology, economics, politics and the skills of negotiation. Aubrey makes clear that it was composed of actual treatises, not just commonplace books, and that it was 'all in his custodie' but available to his friends.[103] Another revealing case is that of George Hakewill, chaplain to Prince Charles, whose lost tract of 1621 dissuading his master from the proposed Spanish marriage brought about not only his own imprisonment but that of those identified as having read the unique manuscript.[104] Celia Fiennes's narrative of her travels through England survives in a partial holograph and a fair copy in the hand of an amanuensis, it being the latter which was the published text, incorporating a preface and a promise that any

[100] In a letter of 1678 sent to Hobbes through Crooke, Blount writes: 'By your Permission, and Mr. *Crook*'s Favour, I have had the Happiness to peruse your incomparable Treatise of Heresie in Manuscript' (*The oracles of reason* (London, 1693), p. 97). Crooke printed the work after Hobbes's death.

[101] Ibid. 87.

[102] John Aubrey, *'Brief lives', chiefly of contemporaries*, ed. Andrew Clark (Oxford, 1898), i. 418.

[103] Ibid., i. 112–14. For Boevey, see Arthur W. Crawley-Boevey, *The 'perverse widow': being passages from the life of Catharina, wife of William Boevey, Esq.* (London, 1898), pp. 24–38. I have traced manuscripts of treatises by Boevey, but only one (BL Harl. MS 28531) from the list given by Aubrey.

[104] See Arthur Freeman, 'George Hakewill's disgrace and the character of Prince Charles', *N&Q* 215 (1970), 247–9.

errors noted by readers would be corrected in a 'supplement annext to the Book'. The modest statement in the preface that 'it was never designed, soe not likely to fall into the hands of any but my near relations' is called into question by the broadly moralizing tone of what follows; but there is no suggestion that any further copying was envisaged.[105]

Clearly the instances just described inhabit a rather uneasy area between the private and the public. Yet it could be argued that the restriction was not always a chosen one and that some of the authors concerned would have welcomed wider scribal circulation if it were not that they had pressing reasons for confining work to a single copy. The first of these reasons would have been the need to limit knowledge of material that might be judged indecent, heterodox, seditious, or simply too far ahead of its time for a rising statesman, lawyer or cleric. (Borrowers may also have preferred a temporary custody of such perilous writings.) The second reason was the very real danger that a text in uncontrolled circulation would sooner or later be piratically propelled into print. In this connection more credence than is customary should be given to the claims made by authors in the prefaces to printed works that they had been forced to the press by the fear or fact of an unauthorized printing from a corrupt manuscript. Far from being coy attempts to disarm criticism, such pleas identify a real and pressing dilemma for scribally publishing authors. George Wither gave their point of view in 1624 when he complained that if a bookseller 'gett any written Coppy into his powre, likely to be vendible; whether the Author be willing or no, he will publish it; And it shallbe contrived and named alsoe, according to his owne pleasure: which is the reason, so many good Bookes come forth imperfect, and with foolish titles'.[106] Nashe in the 1590s seems to have been acting as an agent for the booksellers Richard Jones and Thomas Newman in obtaining scribally published texts by writers of the Sidney-Pembroke circle for unauthorized print publication.[107]

[105] *The journeys of Celia Fiennes*, ed. Christopher Morris (London, 1947), pp. 1–2.
[106] *The schollers purgatory, discovered in the stationers common-wealth* (London, 1624), p. 121.
[107] Nicholl, pp. 82–5; Christopher R. Wilson, '*Astrophil and Stella*: a tangled editorial web', *Library*, 6:1 (1979), 336–46. Gerald D. Johnson, 'John Busby and the stationers' trade, 1590–1612', *Library*, 6:7 (1985), 1–15, finds a similar pattern in the career of the younger John Busby.

ENTREPRENEURIAL PUBLICATION

Entrepreneurial publication, the second of our three modes, has already been introduced in Chapter 1 through the discussion of professional vendors of parliamentary papers in the reign of Charles I and the operations of the later Starkey and Collins scriptoria in the 1670s. The techniques of production and distribution employed by these agencies are discussed in Chapter 3: our task at the moment is simply to assess the significance of entrepreneurial publication relative to other modes. One important thing to remember is that it was not a new initiative of the seventeenth century but a continuation of established book-trade practice from before the invention of printing. A second is that the skilled manpower required for the scribal publication of separates and manuscript books was amply to hand in the huge number of trained clerks. Throughout the century the work of commerce, the law, the church, the army, the navy and all levels of government was conducted through handwritten documents. Bishops communicated with their parish clergy through written instructions, as did secretaries of state with Lord Lieutenants, Lord Lieutenants with sheriffs, and sheriffs with Justices of the Peace. The business counting house and the attorney's and scrivener's office provided training to young clerks in the skills of the scriptorium which could then be transferred to the book trade. Such training would have covered not simply the production of individual copies but streamlined methods of producing large numbers of copies of a particular text.

Entrepreneurial publication took place when manuscripts were produced and circulated for gain by a scribe or stationer. The term is a little misleading in that not all such copying involved a prior commitment of capital—the cautious trader would produce manuscripts only in response to orders—but it is the best among the available alternatives. ('Commercial publication' would not have distinguished between the activities of authors and those of stationers or entrepreneurial scribes; 'petty commodity publication' while more accurate is too cumbrous.[108]) It was strongly opposed to any notion of authorial control over distribution: such

---

[108] For an application of this Marxist term to printed books, see N. N. Feltes, *Modes of production of Victorian novels* (Chicago, 1986), pp. 3–10.

73

manuscripts would be available to anyone who could pay for them and who was trusted by the vendor. The texts copied would always be ones for which there was a strong public demand and for which no competition was expected from the press. The market produced some publishers, such as Robert Julian, who did not maintain bookshops, but much of the trade remained a sideline of established stationers such as Starkey and Collins already mentioned. An important testimony to this is a document by Sir Roger L'Estrange, presented to the House of Lords in 1675, of which a précis is given in a Historical Manuscript Commission Report, but which is here reproduced in full from the original in the House of Lords Record Office:

> The Question of Libells, extends it selfe (I conceive) to manuscripts, as well as Prints; as beeing the more mischievous of the Two: for they are com[m]only so bitter, and dangerous, that not one of forty of them ever comes to ye Presse, and yet by ye help of Transcripts, they are well nigh as Publique.
>
> For the preventing, and suppressing of Printed Libells, I shall only desire such a generall warrant from his Maty: and Councill, as I have formerly had, to support mee in the Execution of my Duty.
>
> And for Libells in Writing, I do humbly offer this to Consideration. That although Copyes of them may passe indifferently from one to another, by other hands, yet some certain Stationers are supposed to bee ye chiefe, and profest dealers in them, as having some Affinity with their Trade.
>
> And when they come to bee detected, the Com[m]on pretence is, *They were left in my shopp,* or *sent in a Letter, I know not by whom*: which may be true in some cases, though but a shift, for ye greater Part.
>
> In the former case, The stationers may be ordered to call a Hall, and administer an Oath to all their members, neither directly, nor Indirectly, to Countenance, dispense, publish, Print or Cause to bee Printed any such Libells.
>
> And secondly, for a Generall Provision; whoever shall receive, and Conceale any such Libell, without giving notice thereof, to some of his Matyes Justices, within a certain space of time after the receipt of it; let him suffer as an Abettour of it, & if he shall not produce ye person of whom he had it, let him suffer as ye Authour of it.[109]

A feature of this report is that much of its phraseology is taken over

---

[109] 'Mr L'Estraings Proposition concerning Libells, &c.', 11 November 1675, summarized in *HMC, 9th rep., app.*, p. 66b.

from a similar paper of 1662 (PRO SP29/51/10.1), presumably also composed by L'Estrange. This at least confirms that the well-documented popularity of manuscript satires from 1675 onwards was not a novelty, but a continuation of an older practice. A comparable enterprise of the earlier Stuart period would be the production of such a forbidden text as Thomas Scot's *Vox populi*. A spy's report of around 1620 describes a conversation with a scrivener who had received an order from a stationer for twelve copies of the work only to lose it when a rival offered a lower quotation.[110] While each of these examples concerns the sale of forbidden and offensive texts they have implications for the associated trade in less sensational documents. L'Estrange's point about the sale of manuscripts 'having some Affinity' with the stationer's trade would also apply to the copying of perfectly unobjectionable texts which were required in too small numbers to justify printing, or which could be sold more profitably in manuscript than in print.

In other specialist and professional areas we can also assume an involvement by stationers in the entrepreneurial production of manuscripts. Towards the end of the century, the music bookseller John Carr had a 'secretary's office' at his shop at the Middle Temple gate 'for wrighting the theatricall tunes, to accomodate learners and country fidlers'.[111] His better-known contemporary, Henry Playford, regularly included manuscripts in his printed catalogues but may have been only a dealer rather than a scribal publisher.[112] John Bagford sold albums of fragments from medieval manuscripts to a circle of virtuosi who included Pepys, Humfrey Wanley, Hans Sloane and Peter Le Neve.[113] Law booksellers,

---

[110] W. W. Greg, *A companion to Arber* (Oxford, 1967), pp. 176–8. See also pp. 96–7 below.

[111] North, *Roger North*, p. 29 n.

[112] The presence of manuscripts in Henry Playford's sales catalogues is discussed in D. R. Harvey, 'Henry Playford: a bibliographical study', Victoria University of Wellington Ph.D. thesis, 1985, pp. 133–50. See also Lenore F. Coral, 'Music in English auction sales, 1676–1750', University of London Ph.D. thesis, 1974, pp. 74–80. *A curious collection of musick-books, both vocal and instrumental* (London, 1690) has the 'prick'd' music in pride of place at the head of the catalogue. Up-to-date as well as older music was available in manuscript.

[113] See Milton McC. Gatch, 'John Bagford as a collector and disseminator of manuscript fragments', *Library*, 6:7 (1985), 95–114. The practical aim of such collections, whose materials were largely retrieved from old bindings, was to illustrate historically significant hands.

already cited as traders in political separates, also provided treatises and copies of the speeches of eminent judges and counsel. An instance from the beginning of the century illustrates this. Following the union of the crowns of England and Scotland in 1603 there was uncertainty over the rights under the laws of England of Scots born after the union (the *post-nati*). A test case mounted in the Exchequer in 1608 drew on the greatest legal talents of the time, and, although it was known that the material decisions would be printed (the king having issued a patent to that effect to Sir William Woodhouse), reports of speeches by Bacon, Coke, Lord Chancellor Egerton and others were widely circulated as separates and compilations. Egerton complained that 'diuerse vnperfect Reports, and seuerall patches and pieces of my Speech haue bin put in writing, & dispersed into many hands, and some offred to the Presse'. At the request of the king he had to reconstruct his speech from notes and print it together with Coke's detailed report of the judges' arguments, in order 'to preuent the Printing of such mistaken and vnperfect reports of it, as weere already scattered abroad'.[114] The situation described is very similar to that we have already observed in the transmission of parliamentary documents, and, although there is no specific evidence that manuscripts of these actual texts were being commissioned by law stationers in commercial quantities, it perfectly illuminates the circumstances that led to such production. Providers of copies from outside the book trade included industrious secretaries such as Sir Robert Cotton's scribe Flood, who provoked a royal confiscation of the Cottonian library through his trafficking in Sir Robert Dudley's *Propositions delivered to His Majesty*.[115] Likewise, scriveners might market manuscripts on their own account rather than simply copying them for stationers, as Nashe reveals in the preface to *The terrors of the night*:

A long time since hath it laine suppressed by mee; vntill the vrgent importunitie of a kinde frend of mine (to whom I was sundrie waies beholding) wrested a Coppie from me. That Coppie progressed from one scriueners shop to another, & at length grew so common, that it was readie to bee hung out for one of their signes, like a paire of indentures.

---

[114] *The speech of the Lord Chancellor of England, touching the post-nati* (London, 1609), A5^v–A6^r; cited in James G. McManaway, 'Privilege to print', *SB* 16 (1963), 202.

[115] D'Ewes, *Autobiography*, ii. 39–42; Sharpe, *Sir Robert Cotton*, pp. 143–4.

Wherevppon I thought it as good for mee to reape the frute of my owne labours, as to let some vnskilfull pen-man or Nouerint-maker startch his ruffe & new spade his beard with the benefite he made of them.[116]

Entrepreneurial publication is to be suspected whenever a text survives in two or more copies in the same non-authorial hand. In the case of manuscript books, as opposed to unbound separates, one would also need to consider the quality of the script. Such bulky items were produced for a relatively restricted clientele who expected a finished and professional product. The third criterion is textual: a text containing errors and sophistications is unlikely to be an outcome of author publication. An indicative case of an entrepreneurially published book is *The discourse of Mr John Selden Esquire*, better known as *Table talk*. This was a collection of sayings noted down by Selden's secretary, Richard Milward. Its first appearance was through author publication by Milward, who can be assumed to have presented copies at least to the book's four joint-dedicatees, Matthew Hale, Edward Heyward, John Vaughan and Rowland Jewkes. This stage of circulation, which can be dated to 1654–60, appears to be represented now only by the Lincoln's Inn manuscript, which has by far the best text. All but one of the eight other surviving manuscripts appear to be the products of a commercial scriptorium or copies of those products, two being in the same professional hand.[117] The outspoken quality of its political judgements would have debarred the work from print publication just as much under Cromwell as under Charles II and James II, but the revolution of 1688 made it a very timely text indeed, especially to the Whigs, who had probably been its most devout readers in manuscript. The circumstances that led to the 1689 edition are described by Harley in a note on one of his two manuscripts.

This Book was given in 168[incomplete] by Charles Erle of Dorset & Middlesex to a Bookseller in Fleet street in order to have it printed; but the Book seller delaying to have it done Mʳ Tho: Rymer sold a Copy he

---

[116] *Works*, i. 341.

[117] BL Harl. MS 1315, Sloane MS 2513; Bodleian Add. MS A. 201; House of Lords Record Office, Commons MS 10b; National Library of Scotland Adv. MS 23. 6. 13; Yale MS Osborn b. 102; and a manuscript owned by the author (in the same hand as the Edinburgh manuscript). BL Harl. MS 690, was prepared for Edward Stillingfleet, a friend of Hale and Vaughan, by the same amanuensis who transcribed the medieval chronicle with which it is bound.

procurd to Mr Churchill who printed it as it came out in the year 16[incomplete].[118]

This is typical of the way in which scribally transmitted prose treatises finally reached the press, and is further evidence that the better texts of them are still as a rule to be sought among the manuscripts. The involvement of Dorset is particularly interesting as he was also an author of scribally published satires.[119] In several other cases the printing of a bad manuscript led to the subsequent printing of a better one; but this was not to happen with *Table talk*, which continued to be printed in mutilated form until the publication of the Lincoln's Inn manuscript in 1927. A significant point for the present discussion is that both Rymer and Dorset appear to have known where a manuscript was to be purchased.

Commercial involvement must also be suspected in the case of a large body of anti-court treatises and satires that achieved very wide circulation during the reigns of James I and Charles I. As one consults the catalogues incorporating the manuscripts of such seventeenth-century collectors as Stow, Spelman, Cotton, Selden, Dering, D'Ewes, Wood, Pepys, Stillingfleet, Petyt, Strype and Moore, and their eighteenth-century successors Sloane, Harley, Carte and Rawlinson, titles and authors recur over and over again. The best-known of these texts, *Leicester's commonwealth* (attributed to Robert Parsons), *Tom Tell-truth*, *The forerunner of revenge upon the Duke of Buckingham* (attributed to George Eglisham), and *To the Father Rector at Brussels*, also made appearances in print, but always from unauthorized sources. Today they are chiefly known from such printed archives as Rushworth's *Historical collections*, the *Harleian miscellany* and the Somers *Scarce and interesting tracts* and more modern anthologies dependent on these; but it does not take much investigation to discover that the texts of these printed versions are usually both corrupt and heavily sophisticated, and that they were taken from manuscript copies encountered virtually at random. Characteristically such pieces circulated both as separates and in large retrospective collections of political texts, with entrepreneurial involvement likely at both levels. However,

[118] BL MS Harl. 1315, f. 1^v.

[119] See *IELM*, ii/1, 350–81 and *The poems of Charles Sackville, sixth earl of Dorset*, ed. Brice Harris (New York, 1979), drawing on 118 manuscript sources. Harris, p. xxiv, rejects the early printed collections of Dorset's poems as without authority.

we still await detailed study of the transmissional histories of representative texts of this kind and the larger compilations into which they were recopied.

From the same period, it would be strange if there was no entrepreneurial involvement in the circulation of Nashe's pornographic *The choice of valentines* and Heywood's translation of Ovid's *Art of love*—works whose notoriety suggests they were much more widely available than is indicated by the small number of copies that survives.[120] Rosenbach Museum and Library MS 1083/15, whose contents, composed between 1590 and 1630, are correctly described as 'predominantly satiric and occasionally lubricious', is a miscellany of much the same kind as formed the stock in trade of the Restoration scriptoria.[121] Entrepreneurial copying of lampoons during the Restoration period has already been documented and will be discussed in greater detail in Chapter 6. As with so many aspects of scribal publication, information on these matters is often already in existence but quarantined in studies of particular authors, topics or genres.

USER PUBLICATION

User publication covers a vast area of activity in which, as we have seen, it is not always possible to distinguish between the public and the private. Its most characteristic mode was the edition of one, copied by the writer for private use into a personal miscellany or 'commonplace book'; however, this was never an isolated activity since it always involved a transaction between at least two individuals—the copyist and the provider of the exemplar. It is also a mistake to assume that the copy in a personal miscellany marks the terminus of a chain of acts of publication. In practice, individuals who assembled large numbers of scribally published

[120] For *The choice of valentines*, see Nicholl, *A cup of newes*, pp. 90–4 and Beal, *IELM*, i/2, 356. Nicholl (pp. 93–4) connects both it and Marlowe's translation of Ovid's *Amores* with the circle of Lord Strange. For the 'Art of love', see S. Musgrove, 'Some manuscripts of Heywood's *Art of love'*, *Library*, 5:1 (1946–7), 106–12 and Beal, i/2, 220.

[121] See James L. Sanderson, 'An unnoted text of Nashe's "The choise of valentines"', *ELN* 1 (1964), 252–3 and S. A. Tannenbaum, 'Unfamiliar versions of some Elizabethan poems', *PMLA* 45 (1930), 809–21. Marotti, *John Donne*, p. 72 associates the manuscript with the Inns of Court.

documents were also likely to be active transmitters of texts. Where political texts were concerned, the reasons for this will often have been ideological; but it must also have been the case that presenting texts to other collectors, who would reciprocate in kind, was the most efficient way of enlarging a collection. While texts were sometimes copied from book to book, it was more common for them to pass from collector to collector by the medium of separates, which might then be further transmitted in the original or copies. Networks of friends or associates would regularly exchange texts with each other either by a process of chain copying or by a member making copies for the entire group. Individuals might consciously adopt the role of facilitator of the circulation of manuscripts as a means to other kinds of social advantage. The fact that most personal miscellanies rarely record the circumstances of receipt of particular items, and almost never those of further transmission, disguises their dynamic quality as points of transit within networks of copying.

John Watson, as one of those rare collectors who record donors, provides us with an invaluable insight into the sources from which texts arrived first at a Cambridge college and later at a Suffolk parsonage between the 1640s and the 1670s. Having matriculated from Emmanuel College at Easter 1640 he was a fellow of Queens' from 1645 to 1654. In 1661 he became vicar of Mildenhall, holding the post until 1673 which was probably the year of his death. His album, now BL Add. MS 18220, was presented to him in 1667. Its contents are a mixture of new items entered as received and material dating back to the 1640s which was apparently held as separates. He does not indicate when copies of these texts were sent on by himself to other members of his circle of correspondents but there can be little doubt that this happened. In particular, the large number of contributions received from his brother Thomas in London must surely have been matched in kind by texts of Cambridge and Suffolk writers. John Pye, another collector who made notes of receipt and transmission, wrote on one satire 'This was taken vp by one Mr Thwaites man a Gentleman in Leeds Yorks. I had it from Mr Robt Twisse Min^r. of ye new Chappell Tothill streete Westm^r—Wensday. 4th. Decr. 1666'. His transcript of 'Rochester's farewell' bears the inscription: 'from Mr Ellasby of Chiswick 18th. Septb^r 80. Returnd ye originall to him agen 22th

Septb[r] by y[e] boy sealed up'.[122] In positing the post as a means of transporting manuscripts it should be remembered that a regular official service only began in 1635 and that even at the close of the century some mail still had to be entrusted to carriers, waggoners and travellers. However, progress in developing the official service was swift: by 1640 one might 'with safetie and securitie send letters into any part of this Kingdome, and receive an answer within five dayes', while from 1680 London had an efficient 'Penny post' which could return answers within a few hours.[123]

Replicatory user copying of this kind, considered on an individual basis, comprises an act of publication in our weak sense. But viewed as a collective enterprise its significance is far greater than this. The author-publisher who presented a short topical text to a small number of chosen readers would do so in the knowledge that copies would multiply by being transmitted through interlocking networks of friends and neighbours. While Sir Thomas Browne regarded the unauthorized copying of *Religio medici* as an uncalled-for and unanticipated violation of privacy, Rochester must by the close of his career have been fully aware that the placing of a poem into circulation at court would eventually lead to its distribution throughout the entire kingdom. During the reign of the 'Temporary Prince' of the Middle Temple Christmas revels of 1636, his 'Court and retinue' were proclaimed in 'transcripts published from hand to hand' which by 16 January were being copied at Oxford.[124] Where such copying was part of an organized programme of promulgation, associates of the writer would be deputed to multiply texts within their own vicinities or circles of correspondents. Writing to Samuel Hartlib on 13 September 1630, Walter Welles apologized for dilatoriness in circulating transcripts of John Dury's *De theoria pacis*, which he had 'thought to have copied out and sent unto B[ishop] of Armath and others'; however, the exemplar, left with a friend who wished to make a personal copy, had been mislaid following the friend's

---

[122] Yale MS Osborn b 52/1, p. 150; b 52/2 p. 180.

[123] *The humble remonstrance of the grievances of all his Majesties posts of England, together with carriers, waggoners, &c.* (London, n.d. [1642?]), p. 1. Information about postal services in the early 17th cent. can be found in *The inland posts (1392–1672): a calendar of historical documents*, ed. J. W. M. Stone (London, 1987). Letters passing through the official posting system could be opened at will by agents of the secretaries of state.

[124] *The diary of Thomas Crosfield*, ed. Frederick S. Boas (London, 1935), p. 83.

death and only recently retrieved. 'If I had had this last but a fortnight sooner', he continues, 'I had conferred with many friends about it in my late travayles through Northamptonshire and Oxfordshire and Warwickshire and Buck etc. But I undertake it presently to send it to many.'[125]

In some cases user publication might be initiated by some calculated public gesture such as nailing a manuscript to a door, dropping copies of it at court, inscribing it on a wall, tying it to a statue (after the precedent of Pasquino and Marforio in Rome) or leaving it on the table at a tavern or coffee house. A few of hundreds of references that might be cited will illustrate the nature of the practice. On 29 March 1629, following the committal of Sir John Eliot, Selden and five other members of parliament to the tower, the then Bishop Laud noted in his diary that two seditious papers had been found in 'the Dean of Paul's [John Donne] his yard before his house'. A fortnight later a proclamation denouncing the bishops was 'put up upon the Exchange in the day time' and on 17 May two further libels addressed to the king were left at Paul's cross.[126] A later example comes from a letter to Laurence Hyde of 27 October 1676 which mentions a libel against Lord Chancellor Finch as having been fastened to doors at the Rolls and the four Inns of Court.[127] This was in itself an act of publication, but it was also intended to inaugurate a process of user copying. Many satirical epigrams of both the earlier and the later Stuart periods announce themselves as having been given to the world through public posting. Favoured locations were the House of Commons door and those of the king and leading courtiers: others claimed include the 'treason bench' in St James's park and a football found in Spitalfields.[128] It is likely that in many cases the claim was untrue, it being much easier to announce that a satire had been posted in the king's bedchamber than actually to place it

---

[125] Cited from G. H. Turnbull, *Hartlib, Dury and Comenius: gleanings from Hartlib's papers* (Liverpool, 1947), pp. 135–6. The 'many' were to include only 'assured men'.

[126] *The works of the most reverend father in God, William Laud D. D.* (Oxford, 1847–60), iii. 210; *CSP (Dom.)* 1629, pp. 519, 550–1; John Forster, *Sir John Eliot: a biography 1590–1632* (London, 1864), ii. 473.

[127] *The correspondence of Henry Hyde, Earl of Clarendon, and of his brother Laurence Hyde, Earl of Rochester*, ed. Samuel Weller Singer (London, 1828), i. 2.

[128] Nottingham U. L. MS Pw V 46, p. 282 as 'Trees and Bench' (correctly in other sources); *POAS (Yale)*, v. 485–7.

there. But even the invention of such events acknowledges a method by which the readership of a text could be multiplied, first through public display and then through the incentive to subsequent user publication provided by a catchy title.

In any case, the real interest of this mode of transmission lies not so much in how it was done as by whom, because, whatever user publication is, it is not random and unstructured. Instead, since it usually rests on a personal agreement between the donor and the receiver of the text, there is an overwhelming tendency for the networks that have been mentioned to coincide with social groupings of one kind or another—with families, with groups of individuals linked by common beliefs or interests, with institutions such as the court, the diocese or the college, and with geographical entities such as the county. Since an individual could well be a member of a number of these communities, the passage of a text might be a complex and also a very rapid one. Paths of transmission laid down for one kind of document (e.g. parliamentary speeches) were from then on available for the transmission of others (e.g. antiquarian essays, viol music). These facts are mentioned in order to introduce the notion of the 'scribal community' which will be dealt with in more detail in Chapter 5.

SIR ROBERT COTTON AS SCRIBAL PUBLISHER

A name that has already occurred several times in this book is that of Sir Robert Cotton, and in concluding this chapter it will be helpful to consider how our three modes of scribal publication apply to the rich tradition of copying associated with Cotton as an author and with the famous collection of manuscripts which he assembled. Cotton's life and the main stages in the formation of the library have been knowledgeably described by Kevin Sharpe, and what follows will be largely dependent on his findings.[129] However, the perspective of scribal publication is one that shows Cotton and his cultural mission in a subtly different light from that in which Sharpe sees them. The points I wish to emphasize are that the Cottonian library served as a source of new manuscripts as well as a repository for old ones, and that Cotton himself, while no

[129] Sharpe, *Sir Robert Cotton.*

enemy to the press, assumed an equal and in no way diminished role for the handwritten word.

Born in 1571 Cotton belonged to the third generation of English antiquarians, drawing inspiration from the work of Bale, Parker and Leland in the mid-sixteenth century and direct guidance from the generation of his immediate mentor, William Camden. As a teenager in 1586 he was a founder-member of Camden's Society of Antiquaries which, meeting on a regular basis until 1607 and briefly revived in 1614, brought together a fruitful assemblage of historians, legal men, heralds, collectors and administrators.[130] Papers given to the Society circulated quite widely in manuscript but were kept from the press, not appearing together in printed form until Hearne's *A collection of curious discourses* in 1720. (Leland's writings had a similar history.[131]) Its major concern was always with English rather than classical antiquities, although the two merged enticingly in Camden's *Britannia*, first published in 1586 and later greatly revised with Cotton's assistance. In pursuing these and other historical enquiries, Cotton and his friends made long topographical expeditions to study ruins and inscriptions and to collect artifacts and coins; but their main archival project was the preservation of manuscripts, especially the vulnerable survivors of the two great disasters which had overtaken the transmission of historical records in the British isles—the advent of the print-communicated new learning of the Renaissance and the dissolution of the monasteries. The famous library, housed at Cotton's house at Westminister, and now part of the British Library's manuscript collection, was not only the finest private archive of its time but, together with the Tower records, the principal support of research into the history of pre-Reformation England. For government officials the library served in Sharpe's words 'as a state paper office and research institute providing a better service than the unsatisfactory official collections and

---

[130] There is a good, short introduction to the work and personnel of this society in W. R. Gair, 'The politics of scholarship: a dramatic comment on the autocracy of Charles I' in *The Elizabethan theatre III. Papers given at the third international conference on Elizabethan theatre held at the University of Waterloo, Ontario, in July 1970*, ed. David Galloway (Waterloo, Ont., 1973), pp. 100–18. Pauline Croft, 'Annual parliaments and the long parliament', *BIHR* 59 (1986), 155–71, adds the scribally circulated 'Motives to induce an annual parliament' of 1614–21 to the roll of the Society's papers.

[131] See Philip Styles, *Sir Simon Archer 1581–1662* (Oxford, 1946), pp. 5, 25–6.

repositories in the Tower and Exchequer'. Borrowers of Cotton's manuscripts during James's reign comprised 'a *Who's who* of the Jacobean administration'.[132] In this the library differed markedly from the later Harleian collection, whose users, as recorded by Wanley, were primarily committed scholars rather than active statesmen and administrators.[133]

As Sharpe and Gair also show, the antiquarianism of Cotton and his circle was deeply political. Research into the Anglo-Saxon past had originally been inspired by the desire to establish traditions for the English Church which would both prove its original independence of Rome and serve as a defence against Puritan desire for innovation. This project was soon translated to the sphere of national politics with ancient and medieval precedents being sought for the conduct of contemporary affairs. A subject of continuing concern to the Society was the powers and functions of the great officers of the crown, a matter that Cotton himself pursued in papers written for his patron, Henry Howard, Earl of Northampton.[134] This was knowledge with direct bearing on the functioning of government, with Cotton called on more than once to serve as arbiter in demarcation disputes between departments of the administration. In the parliamentary battles of the 1620s antiquarian knowledge had a vital tactical role to play with regard to questions of procedure within the two houses, while also providing precedents to support claims for parliamentary privilege against the exercise of the royal prerogative.[135] During the turbulent 1629 session, Cotton's manuscripts were put to such good use by the opponents of the prerogative that Charles I was driven to a royal confiscation of the library and Cotton himself placed under arrest, an action that reached the stage thinly disguised in Marmion's *The antiquary*.[136] This move was a tacit acknowledgement of the modernity of the king's own ideals of government and the deeply ingrained traditionalism of the 'country' opposition and their common-lawyer allies, albeit their

---

[132] Sharpe, p. 78.
[133] *The diary of Humfrey Wanley, passim.*
[134] A relationship further explored in Peck, *Northampton*, pp. 103–17.
[135] The role of antiquarian scholarship, largely communicated through manuscript, in one such dispute is illustrated in Colin G. C. Tite, *Impeachment and parliamentary judicature in early Stuart England* (London, 1974), pp. 24–53.
[136] Discussed in Gair, 'The politics of scholarship'.

interpretation of the records of the past had been a very partial one. The sense of the political importance of ancient charters, chronicles and parliamentary records was such that both scholars and men of affairs were keen to make personal copies of them, a work that Cotton actively encouraged. Copying was so extensive that when a section of the library was destroyed by fire in 1731 the texts of many of the lost manuscripts had already been preserved through transcription.[137]

This copying of older records was itself a significant part of the scribal culture of the seventeenth century. At a time when libraries were small and restrictive and cataloguing woefully inadequate, the availability of transcripts in private hands was necessary to make historical research possible.[138] Access to a key text such as Robert of Gloucester's chronicle, which did not appear in print until Hearne's edition of 1724, could only be ensured by the possession of a manuscript.[139] The amount of energy that antiquaries of the time were prepared to commit to such copying is astounding. Sir John Birkenhead, a scholar as well as a journalist, who had begun his career as a scribe in Laud's scriptorium at Lambeth, accumulated transcripts of historical records which were reported to have sold after his death for £900.[140] The correspondence of William Dugdale and the various diaries and journals of Simonds D'Ewes record Herculean programmes of transcription by themselves and amanuenses.[141] (D'Ewes was a close friend of Cotton and drew on materials from his collection.) Christopher first Baron Hatton is said to have outlayed 'an hundred poundes

---

[137] Sharpe, p. 83. Hearne noted at the time: 'Many transcripts are dispersed up and down, wch now must be looked upon as very valuable' (*Remarks and collections of Thomas Hearne* (Oxford, 1885–1921), xi. 8).

[138] Andrew G. Watson in his introduction to *The library of Sir Simonds D'Ewes* (London, 1966), pp. 40–5 explains the enormous value of such transcripts to 17th cent. scholars.

[139] See Anne Hudson, 'Robert of Gloucester and the antiquaries, 1550–1800', *N&Q* 214 (1969), 322–33.

[140] Aubrey, *Brief lives*, i. 106.

[141] For D'Ewes see *Autobiography and correspondence*; *The journal of Sir Simonds D'Ewes from the first recess of the long parliament to the withdrawal of King Charles from London* (New Haven, Conn., 1942); and *The diary of Sir Simonds D'Ewes (1622–1624), journal d'un étudiant londonien sous le règne de Jacques 1ᵉʳ*, ed. Elisabeth Bourcier (Paris, 1974). Watson pays tribute to D'Ewes 'incredible industry in transcribing records' while noting that 'this could probably be matched by that of contemporaries' (*The library of Sir Simonds D'Ewes*, p. 7). Dugdale's prodigies of transcription can be sampled in his letter of 16 November 1635 to Sir Simon Archer in *Life*, pp. 151–2.

per ann. in abstracting Records', a figure which, if not exaggerated, could have allowed a handsome stipend to two full-time assistants or a more modest wage to three or four.[142] As with many antiquaries, his primary concern was with the antiquities of his own county, Northamptonshire. There was also some commercial copying: D'Ewes accused Starkey of 'base nundination' in offering transcripts of antiquarian manuscripts for sale; but wasted no time following Starkey's death in October 1628 in purchasing his papers, largely composed of transcripts of Tudor and more recent records.[143]

As well as serving as a centre for the transcription of older texts, the library regularly gave birth to new ones, among which were Sir Robert's own writings issued by him as author publisher. Although he assisted fellow historians in a number of large print-publishing projects, his conception of himself was as an author solely for the scribal medium. Cotton died in 1631. The *STC* shows only three works by him as having appeared in print prior to 1641, and it was not until 1651, with the publication by James Howell of *Cottoni posthuma,* that anything like a comprehensive body of his writings was available in print. But in manuscript Cotton is everywhere. His influential anti-Spanish tract of 1627, *The danger wherein the kingdome now standeth, and the remedie,* survives in fifteen copies in the British Library alone and at least twice that number elsewhere. There were also printed editions—two of 1628 (one set from the other), one in *Cottoni posthuma* and one in Rushworth—but none of these derives from an authoritative manuscript.[144] Cotton's *A short view of the long life and reign of King Henry the third,* written for Prince Henry, and *The manner and means how the kings of England have from time to time supported and repaired their estates,* written for James I, are hardly less common, though this has been obscured by vagaries of attribution and title. Composite editions of his tracts also circulated in manuscript. One such collection, believed to have been destroyed by fire in 1937,

---

[142] Dugdale, *Life,* p. 171 n.

[143] *Autobiography,* i. 294; *The library of Sir Simonds D'Ewes,* pp. 24–6.

[144] The text in *Cottoni posthuma* at least makes sense, though it probably requires emendation in from 20–30 readings. That in Rushworth's *Historical collections* (London, 1659), pp. 471–6 shows signs of heavy editorial reworking. That of the 1628 editions (one of which is the source for the *English experience* reprint) is so corrupt as to be little better than gibberish in places.

consisted of fifteen tracts in chronological order of composition followed by an epicedium.[145] On the other hand the collection in *Cottoni posthuma* does not look particularly authentic. The tracts are not in chronological order, or any kind of order, and four pieces by other authors have crept in.[146] Cotton's most characteristic form of writing was the short essay summarizing the historical precedents relevant to some contemporary administrative question: Sharpe has illuminatingly compared them to the kind of position paper that today might be prepared by a civil servant for a minister. Such pieces, being short, were eminently suited to scribal communication, and also contained the kind of privileged information that would have been carefully guarded from the press. The opportunity to copy Cotton's writings may well have been a bonus to users of the Cottonian library, although it is noteworthy that D'Ewes's greatly-prized copies of three tracts acquired in 1623 are in the hand of Ralph Starkey. These were presumably supplied by Starkey in his capacity as a professional copyist, the price of the three together being thirteen shillings.[147]

One or two glimpses of the day-to-day events of the Cotton household raise the possibility of other kinds of involvement in the transmission of manuscripts. At a dinner attended by Ben Jonson which was later the subject of an official enquiry a manuscript of a poem eulogizing Felton, the assassin of the Duke of Buckingham, was passed round after the meal.[148] The event of 1629 which provided Charles I with his pretext for closing down the library was that a scribe in Cotton's employment was making copies of an outrageously pro-prerogative tract as a means of embarrassing the crown.[149] Incidents such as these, together with Cotton's vigorous

---

[145] *HMC*, 2nd rep., p. 90b; *Guide to the location of collections described in the reports and calendars series 1870–1980* (London, 1982), p. 29.

[146] See Dennis Flynn, 'Three unnoticed companion essays to Donne's "An essay of valour"', *BNYPL* 73 (1969), 424–39. Flynn is too hasty in assuming that Howell's source for the collection was Cotton's own papers.

[147] *The library of Sir Simonds D'Ewes*, pp. 238–9.

[148] Sharpe, p. 212. The poem, beginning 'Enjoy thy bondage, make thy prison know' had a long career in manuscript transmission, still being found in some Restoration state poems collections.

[149] See D'Ewes, *Autobiography*, ii. 39–42. D'Ewes was clearly well informed about the circumstances although his account is designed to place Cotton in the most favourable light and to distance him from the actions of his dependants Flood and Richard James. For further sources for the incident, see Sharpe, pp. 143–4.

scribal publication of his own writings, suggest that the library may well have been as important an agency for the circulation of new manuscript texts as it was for the copying of old ones. Such copying can be viewed both as user publication on the part of the transcribers and as a form of non-commercial entrepreneurial publication on Cotton's. This role, and that of the library in the context of his times, has been well portrayed by Sharpe, but a considerable body of bibliographical evidence still remains unexamined. A full critical edition of Cotton's own writings remains the major desideratum—an enormous task but one that would contribute greatly to our understanding of the production and distribution of scribally published texts. Beyond that we have yet to look throroughly at the substantial body of transcripts of both older and more modern texts which derive from the library and which at present are only identifiable when they belong to collections whose historical link with it is known on external grounds.

3

SCRIBAL PRODUCTION

STUDENTS of seventeenth-century print publication are able to assume certain regularities in the processes of production. The extent of these is disputed, but no one would deny that Joseph Moxon's *Mechanick exercises on the whole art of printing* (1683–4) gives as detailed a description of the skills and technology of typefounding, composition and presswork as we could hope for.[1] Over the few matters where Moxon is silent or ambiguous, printers' manuals from later dates and from other countries are available. In addition, patient, empirical studies of specific editions and printeries have built up an enormous amount of data concerning such matters as compositorial 'fingerprints', the re-use of identifiable printing materials, press correction, cancellation and variations in paper stock. The most famous of these studies, Charlton Hinman's *The printing and proof-reading of the first folio of Shakespeare*, presents us with a production-history of an edition so meticulous that it is hard to imagine what might have been added.[2] The organization of production within the printery is less well documented than the work practices of individual craftsmen, but two monumental studies of the records of particular workplaces—D. F. McKenzie's of the Cambridge University Press over the years 1696–1712 and Keith Maslen and John Lancaster's of the Bowyer printery in the early eighteenth century—shed illumination well beyond the sphere of their immediate concern.[3]

By comparison with this well-mapped terrain, the production

[1] ed. Herbert Davis and Harry Carter, 2nd edn (London, 1962).
[2] 2 vols (Oxford, 1963).
[3] D. F. McKenzie, *The Cambridge University Press 1696–1712: a bibliographical study*, 2 vols (Cambridge, 1966); *The Bowyer ledgers*, ed. K. I. D. Maslen and John Lancaster (London, 1991).

90

practice of scribal publication is largely *terra incognita*. What has been attempted so far in this book is to establish a terminology which can be illustrated from case studies; however, this procedure does not equip us with the means to generalize confidently from the known to the unknown over the wider field of production. The question that now arises is the much more searching one of the representativeness of our existing data, and whether or not it is possible to achieve an assumption of regularities of the kind and to the degree that can be accepted for print publication. In some sections of this chapter the information assembled will inevitably seem slight. This partly reflects limitations of space but also arises from a conviction that areas in which extensive research was not possible within the scope of this project should at least be blocked in, however imperfectly, as an encouragement to those (particularly manuscript librarians and archivists) who are equipped to proceed further. Since our chief concern will be with the work of the paid rather than the amateur scribe, the emphasis will be on entrepreneurial publication and author publication, though some of the findings will also apply to user publication.

In pursuing this aim, knowledge of the conventions of print-production will be vital. The two areas are linked by the fact that their products were designed for a similar, though not identical, social use, and by the involvement in each of booktrade professionals. This does not of itself guarantee that common solutions would have been found to common problems, but does make print practice a fruitful source of hypotheses which can then be tested against the evidence. Besides this, the connection directs our attention to certain methodological problems which have arisen in work on print production, and which would be ignored at our peril.

In the midsummer noon of the McKerrow–Greg–Bowers 'new bibliography', the assumption was too readily made that a printery of the handpress era operated like an efficient modern business overseen by modern managers. Natural human variability and the looser industrial organization of the hand-press era were not allowed for, with the result that the imaginative leap from the data of the page to the activities of the workplace was often made with unjustified confidence. Print bibliographers, and particularly editors, for whom the issue was one of having a basis for textual decision-making, became involved in a process of narrative-building in which the elegance of the narratives was all too often accepted as a badge of their correctness. Or a narrative of some complexity might be constructed which certainly explained the phenomena but was only one of a multitude of ways of doing so. McKenzie's famous 1969 paper, 'Printers of the mind', encouraged a greater realism about the variability of work practices in early printing, but could not wholly prevail against the impulse to assume that physical regularities in the printed book must necessarily correspond to a consistent routine in the process of production.[4] Compositor identification—a much more difficult business than the identification of scribes—remains bedevilled by such assumptions. The lessons which have been learned so painfully by print bibliographers are no less vital for the study of scribal production, in which human variability had even wider scope.

THE RECRUITMENT AND TRAINING OF SCRIBES

Codicologists frequently refer to work as being written in a 'professional' hand. The term does not imply a sharp division into professional and 'amateur' manuscripts, or that the writing of a non-professional would of necessity be less skilled. Some of the most polished and agreeable hands of our period are those of individuals who were not scribes by profession, while paid scribes might write at times in a rapid informal hand. What is implied, rather, is a hand that in its regularity and evenness shows the effects of careful training and long practice, and that remains unvarying over the entire span of the text being copied. It should also be a hand that is well-adapted to the purpose for which the copy was made, which in most cases would mean that it was readily legible. Such a hand might incorporate displays of skill in the use of decorated forms for headings and proper names or in executing intricate flourishes, but it would not project virtuosity as a means of personal expression. Indeed, ideally, it would preserve a certain impersonality, being careful not to intrude on the reader's awareness of the text. In the copying of forbidden texts one will

[4] *SB* 22 (1969), 1–75.

often suspect a deliberate avoidance of idiosyncrasy in order to minimize the danger of identification; in other cases there may be a degree of accommodation to the received style of a particular scriptorium.[5] Such a hand differs as much from that of the cultured gentleman or lady, for whom handwriting, as much as dress or gesture, might be a mode of individuation, as it does from the exhibitionistic displays of another kind of professional, the writing master. The aim then is to enquire what kind of training lay behind the humbler professionalism of the skilled but unvirtuosic craftsman copyist.

Writing as an elementary skill was acquired at home or school, and as a more advanced art might be studied from an engraved copy-book, at a 'writing school' or with a private tutor.[6] The teaching of writing in the 'petty' schools must always have been hindered by the absence of desks. Rosemary O'Day goes as far as to say that it 'was not accepted as one of the skills taught in the elementary school' but this was not true at least of the progressive schoolteachers cited by David Cressy.[7] The 'writing school' taught spelling, arithmetic, the elements of accounting and in some cases shorthand; however, the main emphasis was on training in the customary business hands, and its head was normally an acknowledged writing master.[8] At all levels beyond the elementary, instruction would also cover such matters as the cutting of pens, the mixing of ink, the folding of paper into quires, the ruling of margins, the ensuring of equal lineation, the casting-off of copy,

[5] Such as that of Little Gidding. However, the most striking examples of this second phenomenon are the 'departmental' hands employed in certain areas of the administration and judiciary. L. C. Hector, *The handwriting of English documents*, 2nd edn (London, 1966), pp. 64–8 and 86–97, gives contemporary examples of common-law hand, engrossing hand, Pipe Office hand, Lord Treasurer's Remembrancer's hand, King's Remembrancer's hand and Chancery hand. See also Hilary Jenkinson, *The later court hands in England from the fifteenth to the seventeenth century* (Cambridge, 1927), pp. 68–78.

[6] For further information see Hilary Jenkinson, 'The teaching and practice of handwriting in England', *History* 11 (1926), 130–8, 211–18 and David Cressy, *Literacy and the social order: reading and writing in Tudor and Stuart England* (Cambridge, 1980), pp. 19–41.

[7] *Education and society 1500–1800: the social foundations of education in early modern Britain* (London, 1982), p. 60; Cressy, *Literacy*, pp. 22–7. However, it is significant that most schoolchildren were taught to spell by a vocal method without being allowed to write at the same time (Cressy, pp. 20–1).

[8] A good deal of information about these schools can be gleaned from the biographical section of Ambrose Heal's *The English writing-masters and their copy-books 1570–1800: a biographical dictionary and a biography* (London, 1931).

and the correct placing of catchwords and page numbers. (Page headlines of the kind found in printed books are rare in manuscripts of this period.) An understanding of these matters would be required of anyone seeking employment as a scribe but would not of itself qualify a pupil to perform the work of a clerk or, except under privileged circumstances, that of a secretary—and it is among the ranks of clerks and secretaries that most of our professional copyists are likely to be found. A secretary, as the derivation of the word indicates, was a personal scribe who was privy to his master's secrets. Birth and private recommendation were likely to count as much as skilled penmanship in appointments of this kind, and training would be given directly by the employer. The position of clerk, on the other hand, could not be secured without an initiation into the practices of a particular trade or profession, achieved through a formal apprenticeship or some looser arrangement by which the learner offered unpaid labour in return for instruction.

Evidence has already been presented in this book for the involvement of legal clerks in scribal publication, and it is law writing that best illustrates the nature of scribal training. Edward Chamberlayne suggests that at least a grammar school education was normal for those intending to become 'Clerks to Justices or Lawyers', while fearing that their level of education left them 'longing for Innovations and Changes, and watching for an opportunity to alter the Government both of Church and State'.[9] Legal writing, at whatever level, involved careful drilling in the exact reproduction of standard documents, and some acquaintance with Law French and Latin. In the course of his training, the scribe would be expected to master an engrossing hand as well as a range of hands suitable for correspondence and record keeping, and, since deeds were still frequently written on parchment, he would need to acquire the skills of working with that testing material.

Legal copying not performed by lawyers' clerks was the province of scriveners, whose professional function was one of drawing up contracts, negotiating loans and performing some simpler legal formalities. They also had a statutory responsibility for ensuring the accuracy and authenticity of documents and

---

[9] *The second part of the present state of England*, 12th edn (London, 1684), pp. 334–6.

preventing forgery. Nashe's identification of scriveners as agents of scribal publication makes them of particular interest to this study.[10] The London scriveners, as the Writers of the Court Letter, first appeared as a separate body in 1373 when they broke away from the Writers of the Text Letter who were later to help found the Stationers' Company. In January 1617 the company, by now plagued with members who were not scriveners by profession, was refounded under new letters patent which are reproduced in full in Francis W. Steer's edition of its early documents.[11] These provided for a period of apprenticeship lasting no less than seven years (an eight-year apprenticeship could be secured more cheaply) and for its commencement to be recorded with the company within six months of the sealing of the indentures. On becoming free of the company, the apprentice was entitled to set up in his own right as a scrivener.

Some of the realities of apprenticeships are betrayed in Francis Kirkman's *The unlucky citizen*, in a chapter whose events, insofar as they draw on personal experience, appear to be set around 1650. His hero is bound apprentice to a scrivener who already has two apprentices but apparently no adult clerks. As the youngest apprentice he is expected to perform numerous 'Petty services' besides his writing:

I was to make clean the Shooes, carry out the Ashes and Dust, sweep the Shop, cleanse the Sink (and a long nasty one it was) draw the Beer, at washing times to fetch up Coals, and Kettles; these were the within doors employs, and abroad, I was to go of all errands, and carry all burthens . . . and rather than I should want a Burthen, I was to carry earthen Pots and Pans, and Ox Livers, and Bones for the Dog . . . [12]

In all these matters he was under the direction of the kitchen wench who could at any time order him to leave his writing. Having known this would be his lot, he accepted it without grumbling for three years, but by then, having acquired a good suit and his own watch, he began to resent having to carry burdens. A complaint to his father earned him a beating from his master with a '*lusty Bartoon*

---

[10] See above, pp. 76–7.

[11] *Scriveners' Company common paper 1357–1628 with a continuation to 1678* (London, 1968), pp. 76–113.

[12] Francis Kirkman, *The unlucky citizen: experimentally described in the various misfortunes of an unlucky Londoner* (London, 1673), pp. 35–6.

Cane (the ordinary Weapon with which I was used to be disciplined)' (p. 43). By this time the master's son had become the youngest apprentice, but was naturally free from the menial duties and 'became so insolently proud, as to command me to make clean his Shooes, and do more for him than formerly' (p. 40). The son also took over a clerkship which was the apprentice's main source of fees. In this predicament he undertook the perilous course of covertly undertaking additional legal writing on his own account and hiding it in a trunk.

This part of the citizen's history has introduced us to one potential source of labour for scribal publication, the moonlighting apprentice. The next part leads us to another, the unqualified scrivener. Having absconded from his master, he set up for himself in 'a little *Dog-hole* of a Shop, at the utmost Skirts of *London*' where he wrote letters for sailors' wives and would 'now and then make a Letter of Attorney, or a Deed of Gift . . . or some such Twelve-penny Jobbs' (p. 53). Next, having obtained a release from his former master, he took out indentures with a new one who was a drunkard and needed someone to mind the shop while he spent his days at taverns negotiating loans which were never concluded. With little to do, the apprentice was free to take his first tentative steps in the book trade as translator and print publisher; but he might equally well have been passing his time in copying newsletters or separates.

Kirkman's narrative illustrates some of the circumstances which encouraged young scriveners and their apprentices to undertake copying for the booksellers or for author publishers. A report of 1620 printed in Greg's *A companion to Arber* gives a glimpse of one such transaction:

Althoughe such bookes as vox populi, and other suche as daylie tooe audaciouslie are dispersed, are forbid[d]en and ought by noe good subiect be intertained or openly divulged, yet (as I am lykewayes crediblie given to vnderstand) there bee dyuers stationers soe soone as they heare of anie such bookes, as haue noe publicke authoritie they indevo^r vpon whatsoever condi[ti]on to gett them in theire hands and hopes some younge Fellowes to transcrybe them, & sells them to such Nuefangle persons as will not spare anie charges for acqueiringe such trashe as infatuats the foolishe vulgar wth a misprision of lest-actions, and wth wch they ought not to medle. . . .

To satisfie my selfe more fullie in this particular, I did inquyre of a younge Fellowe a scriviner whoe dwelleth neere to a Stationer who (as I heare) is a man of good meanes whether he had transcrybed anie of the bookes called vox populi to his neighbo[r] the stationer, he did tell mee he had agreed wth him for a dusson, but findinge that he would not wryte them soe cheape as in an other place he could haue them, he had onelie writen one of them, and soe he had taken backe the Copie and putt them out to some other. This stationer as I heare hathe beene before questioned, for ventinge forbiden ware.[13]

Scott's *Vox populi, or news from Spain* was one of the most widely circulated of the anti-Spanish tracts inspired by the proposed match between Prince Charles and the Infanta. Surreptitiously printed copies were available but will have lacked the cachet of the scribally published ones. Having taken his single copy, the scrivener could well have been content to lose the others, as he could now enter production on his own behalf.

The work of the secretary differed considerably from that of the clerk. Where the latter was merely a transcriber, the secretary must be capable, in Angel Day's words, of using 'the *Pen*, the *Wit* and *Inuention* together'.[14] He would need to be within call during most waking hours and might well be, as Donne was with Lord Keeper Egerton and Rowland White with Sir Robert Sidney, on very good personal terms with his employer. Day assures us that 'as hee is in one degree in place of a *servant*, so is he in another degree in place of a *friend*' (p. 106). Polished manners and good connections would be a desideratum. There is a telling picture of the relationship of secretary and employer in III. i of Shirley's *The lady of pleasure* (1635). While the aristocratic master converses wittily with his visitors, the secretary is unobtrusively by his side to take down a letter. Ronald Huebert's modern spelling edition has been cited in order to clarify the stage action:

LORD. [*To Secretary*] Write. 'Madam, where your honour is in danger, my love must not be silent'.
       Enter SENTLOVE *and* [ALEXANDER] KICKSHAW
    Sentlove and Kickshaw!
ALEXANDER. Your lordship's busy.

---

[13] *A companion to Arber* (Oxford, 1967), p. 177.
[14] *The English secretary or methods of writing epistles and letters* (London, 1599); facsim. repr. introd. Robert O. Evans (Gainesville, Fla., 1967), p. 129 (second pagination).

LORD. Writing a letter; nay, it sha' not bar any discourse.

SECRETARY.—'Silent'.

LORD. [*Continues dictation.*] 'Though I be no physician, I may prevent a fever in your blood'. [*To* SENTLOVE *and* ALEXANDER] And where have you spent the morning's conversation?

SENTLOVE. Where you would have given the best Barbary in your stable to have met on honourable terms.

LORD. What new beauty? You acquaint yourselves with none but wonders.

SENTLOVE. 'Tis too low a miracle.

LORD. 'Twill require a strong faith.

SECRETARY.— 'Your blood'.

LORD. [*Dictates.*] 'If you be innocent, preserve your fame lest this Decoy madam betray it to your repentance'. By what name is she known?[15]

Shirley deploys the idea for a further thirty lines during which dramatic use is made of the secretary's vocal catchwords to make a punning comment on the action. The point of the scene is to emphasize the linguistic virtuosity, and through this the high intelligence, of the lord, but the secretary shines with reflected light as the chosen servant of such a paragon. When the lords were less gifted, it became the task of secretaries through their 'sufficiencies' to 'give Lustre unto their Masters glorie'.[16]

A secretary of this kind required social as well as scribal skills. One of his tasks in Shirley's play is to control the admission of callers to the Lord's dressing chamber, confirming Day's prescription that 'His office is likewise to entertaine all maner of suters vnto his Lord' (p. 131). His closeness to the lord made him a person of some power: at the conclusion of Shirley's scene, Sentlove, who fancies himself one of the lord's intimates, expresses chagrin that the appointment of the secretary has been made without his advice.[17]

At this social level, the secretary would probably have university or Inns-of-court training and have entered his service as an avenue to greater preferment. But if his master was a writer or a collector of others' writings he would expect to do regular turns at

---

[15] James Shirley, *The lady of pleasure*, ed. Ronald Huebert (Manchester, 1986), pp. 109–10.

[16] Sir Edward Peyton, 'A discourse of court and courtiers' (1633), BL Harl. MS 364², f. 62ᵛ. The duties of noblemen's secretaries are discussed on ff. 62ᵛ–65ᵛ.

[17] p. 113.

transcription in addition to his other duties, and to serve as a point of relay for documents circulating through author and user publication. Simonds D'Ewes's 'industrious servant' who helped him with his historical research falls into this category as does Lord Herbert of Cherbury's secretary, Rowland Evans, who transcribed his master's *Autobiography*.[18] Another responsibility of a secretary was that he should be able to write a passable imitation of his master's (probably italic) script as well as possessing a well-formed 'secretary' hand.[19] As the century progressed much of the secretary's mystique evaporated—a manual of 1683 translated from Jean Puget de la Serre has the mundane title *The secretary in fashion*—and his ethics declined to the point where he might well become a source by which author-published texts passed into the hands of the entrepreneurs. The same period saw a steady devaluation of his abilities as a penman, for now the aristocracy increasingly wrote their own letters, using a script whose slovenliness proclaimed a modish disdain for the finer arts of the hand.

Women were disqualified from working as scribes both by social custom and by lack of access to education. David Cressy has calculated that only about 10 per cent of seventeenth-century women were literate to the extent of being able to write their names, though the proportion was naturally much higher among the better-off classes and in London.[20] Since it was a fixed article of belief among (male) writing masters that the secretary hand was too difficult for women, they were usually taught only italic. None the less, there is plenty of scattered evidence that as family members they performed the functions of clerks and secretaries. Roger Boyle, first Earl of Orrery is said to have used his daughter Elizabeth as his amanuensis and Edmund Waller his daughter Margaret.[21]

As well as the clerk and the secretary, writing masters are also

---

[18] D'Ewes, *Autobiography*, i. 409–10; N. W. Bawcutt, 'The manuscripts of Lord Herbert of Cherbury's *Autobiography*', *Library*, 6:12 (1990), 133.

[19] These aspects of the secretary's work are discussed and theorized in Jonathan Goldberg, *Writing matter: from the hands of the English Renaissance* (Stanford, Calif., 1990), pp. 266–73.

[20] *Literacy*, pp. 41, 128–9, 144–9.

[21] *The dramatic works of Roger Boyle, Earl of Orrery*, ed. William Clark Smith II (Cambridge, Mass., 1937), ii. 950. The Waller example was contributed by Peter Beal who has encountered many examples in the Waller family papers of what he suspects is her hand.

likely to have undertaken paid copying, especially at the higher-priced end of the market. By this class we are to understand both the directors of writing schools and private tutors who, like the music and dancing master, would normally give lessons by appointment at the homes of their pupils. Today we are most aware of this class through the activities of virtuosi such as Peter Bales, Martin Billingsley and John Davies of Hereford, but these were simply the high-fliers of a profession whose instruction was normally exercised at a more practical level. Heal's *English writing masters* gives us names and varying degrees of biographical information for a considerable number of these; but many others, especially those working out of London, must have escaped his net. Some are no more than names and addresses from Pepys's 'Alphabetical list of the surviving maister-pen-men of England and more particularly in and about the cities of London and Westminster in the year 1699'—a useful guide to future research.[22] Writing masters had a natural and necessary connection with the small circle of booksellers who published engraved copy-books, usually combining this with the sale of maps and prints to wealthy collectors. It would certainly be no surprise if evidence should emerge to link print-sellers such as John Garrett and John Overton with scribal publication.[23] The training of a writing master was normally acquired by study with another writing master. John Ayres, greatly respected by Pepys, began his working life as a footman, was educated at the expense of his employer, and then studied writing with an older virtuoso, Thomas Topham, who was himself a pupil of Richard Gething. Ayres's income at the height of his career was estimated at an impressive £800 a year.[24]

It remains to mention as a possible agent in scribal publication the mysterious 'printer's scribe' whose existence was revealed by James Binns's investigation into the printing of Latin books in England.[25] The scribe's function was one of rewriting difficult

---

[22] Discussed in Heal, pp. xi–xii. Pepys, a keen collector of fine writing, gives a total of 77 names and had secured examples of the script of those he most admired.

[23] For these and their predecessors see Leona Rostenberg, *English publishers in the graphic arts 1599–1700* (New York, 1963).

[24] Heal, pp. 7, 10.

[25] 'STC Latin books: evidence for printing-house practice', *Library*, 5:32 (1977), 5–7. Elkanah Settle blames the errata to his *The conquest of China by the Tartars* (London, 1676) on the transcriber of the press copy.

copy and of making manuscript corrections in printed sheets. While no evidence survives relating to recruitment or training, it is useful to be reminded that printing shops still required the services of a skilled penman. Common-sense would suggest that he was often identical with the proof-reader.

THE PHYSICAL WORK OF THE SCRIBE

As we have just seen, scribes differed from compositors in not being members of a single industry; but all will have had training in certain basic skills of penmanship and in the care and management of the highly refined tools of their vocation. In discussing these tools and the uses to which they were put I draw with gratitude on Michael Finlay's excellent illustrated account in his *Western writing implements in the age of the quill pen* (Wetheral, 1990).

Paper and ink

A consideration of the scribe's equipment should also include the surfaces on which writing was inscribed. 'The Ancients', recalls the English translation of Comenius's *Orbis sensualium pictus*, 'writ in *Tables done over with wax* with a brasan *poitrel*, with the sharp end whereof Letters were engraven, and rubbed out again with the broad end.'[26] The wax-coated table-book was still in use in the seventeenth century, as was that much more durable antique surface, parchment, but the class of writings with which this book is concerned was with negligible exceptions inscribed on paper.

Paper was the product of a technology that was already many centuries old. Its raw material was rags, preferably linen, which for the most part came from discarded clothing: when we turn the pages of an early book, we are actually handling recycled shirts, night attire and underclothes, with perhaps the occasional table cloth. Rags were bought from householders by door-to-door collectors. Delivered to the manufacturer in bales, the cloth was washed, left to rot, sliced and stamped into fragments, and finally reduced to a warmed, aqueous solution of its primary fibres. In this

---

[26] Joannes Amos Comenius, *Orbis sensualium pictus*, facsim. edn introd. James Bowen (Sydney, 1967), p. 186.

form it became the 'stuff' of papermaking. The sheet was made by dipping a hand-held mould into a vat of stuff, the mould consisting of a rectangular arrangement of wires, with sides in the form of a detachable wooden frame. Lifted from the vat, the mould was shaken to help the fibres knit, and the water allowed to drain away through the wires. The sides were then removed and the deposit laid, 'like a thin *pan-cake*', between pieces of felt to await pressing and drying.[27] Consistency within batches depended on the ability of the vatman to judge just how great a quantity to take into the mould. Colour was determined by that of the rags. To make the paper impermeable, it would later be sized by being dipped in gelatine.[28]

The moulds used in seventeenth-century papermaking were of the 'laid' variety with contiguous thin 'wires' running parallel to the longer side and thicker 'chains' placed at intervals parallel to the shorter side. The pattern of the mould will usually be visible when a leaf is held up to the light and is used by descriptive bibliographers to confirm judgements of format. The watermark was a design in wire attached to the upper surface of the mould. Since moulds were used in pairs, any given book is likely to contain two versions of the watermark. The normal position for the mark was in the middle of one half of the sheet, so orientated as to show vertically in a folio leaf. A countermark is often found in the middle of the other half-sheet. While watermarks had originated as manufacturer's symbols, by our period they had largely become indicators of dimensions and grades of paper, with such standard sizes as pot, foolscap and crown actually named from their customary watermarks.[29] Paper of each dimension was carefully identified by makers as being of the printing or writing variety, with the sheet size of the writing version usually smaller than that

[27] The quoted phrase is Evelyn's from his vivid description of paper-making at Byfleet (*The diary of John Evelyn*, ed. E. S. de Beer (Oxford, 1955), iv. 141).

[28] For a concise account of early papermaking, see Philip Gaskell, *A new introduction to bibliography*, rev. impression (Oxford, 1974), pp. 57–60.

[29] The trade names, dimensions and watermarks of the principal sizes are given in Gaskell, pp. 73–5. A contemporary list which also gives prices is reprinted in R. W. Chapman, 'An inventory of paper, 1674', *Library*, 4:7 (1927), 402–8; however, Edward Heawood, 'Papers used in England after 1600. I. The seventeenth century to *c.* 1680', *Library*, 4:11 (1930), 263–99, questions the accuracy of this source suggesting that 'the samples had been disarranged after the list of sorts had been compiled, but before the marks were described' (p. 264).

of the corresponding printing version. Writing paper was also more heavily gelatinized: indeed, much printing paper could not be written on without blurring. Finlay quotes advice from a writer of 1594 that before entering marginalia in a printed book one should first rub the surface with a bag containing resin and sandarach.[30]

Most writing paper used in England during the seventeenth century was imported from France whose makers were favoured by fast-flowing rivers, an abundant supply of linen, and Huguenot business acumen. Duties that for royal ran as high as a pound a ream (500 sheets) were unable to overcome this superiority, and it was only when protected by embargos on French goods during the reigns of William and Anne that English and Dutch makers were prepared to attempt the finer grades required for writing.[31] Thomas Fuller has left a mid-century user's impression of the the various national papers:

Paper participates in some sort of the *Caracters* of the *Countrymen* which make it, the *Venetian* being *neat, subtile* and *courtlike*, the *French, light, slight* and *slender*, the *Dutch thick, corpulent* and *gross*, not to say sometimes also *charta Bibula, sucking up the Ink with the sponginess thereof.*[32]

The careful writer would clearly prefer the French and Italian writing papers to the Dutch. In the earlier part of the century Norman papers, marketed as 'Caen' and 'Morlaix', dominated the market; however, from around 1660 this preference was challenged by mills from the Angoumois whose product, generically described as Rochelle, was also purchased for re-export by Dutch merchants and often bears Arms of Amsterdam or Vryheyt watermarks.[33]

Duties and the labour-intensive method of production meant that paper represented a significant element in any author or

[30] Finlay, p. 33, citing Sir Hugh Platt, *The jewell house of art and nature* (London, 1594), p. 46.

[31] For an account of the difficulties experienced by British paper-makers in resisting French competition, see D. C. Coleman, *The British paper industry 1495–1860. A study in industrial growth* (Oxford, 1958), pp. 3–23 and Marjorie Plant, *The English book trade. An economic history of the making and sale of books*, 3rd edn (London, 1974), pp. 190–205.

[32] *The history of the worthies of England* (London, 1662), p. 144.

[33] A development discussed in Heawood, 'Paper used in England' and R. P. Thompson, 'English music manuscripts and the fine paper trade, 1648–1688', London University Ph.D. thesis, 1988, i. 31–68.

entrepreneurial publisher's investment. The sample prices assembled by J. E. Thorold Rogers from the records of schools and colleges show the price of a quire (24 or 25 sheets) of writing paper at the beginning of the century as 4*d.* or 5*d.* with ruled and 'singing' paper double that price. This probably represents a durable paper suitable for registers and account books, with the regular price per ream (480–500 sheets) of 5*s.* being for a cheaper grade to be used by students or for printing. By the middle of the century the price per quire had risen by about 1*d.* and that of a ream to 7*s.* (still much cheaper on a cost-per-sheet basis); however, there would simultaneously seem to have been a movement to larger sizes at 1*s.* a quire. The very sparse data for the two closing decades of the century suggests a decline in prices during the 1680s followed by a rise to as much as 8*d.* a quire during the French wars which was sustained into the new century.[34] It is likely that the cost of production remained fairly stable, the price increase being the result of continually rising excise and customs charges.

Paper was acquired in sheets, not single leaves, and normally used in the form of a bifolium formed by folding a whole or half sheet. For somewhat longer texts booklets might be compiled by sewing a number of sheets or leaves through stabholes made a little way in from the fold. William P. Williams found several booklets of this kind among the Castle Ashby manuscripts and Pepys must have had something of the same kind in mind when he recorded under 16 April 1666: 'Up, and set my people, Mercer, W Hewers, Tom, and the girl, at work at ruling and stitching my ruled books for the Muster maisters.'[35] The scarcity and expense of the primary medium of writing meant that it was important to extract the maximum amount of use from it. For scribes, as Germaine Warkentin has demonstrated, this must often have been reflected in difficult, much emended authorial exemplars or uncertainties over order in longer texts still in bifoliar form.[36] Apart from the

---

[34] *A history of agriculture and prices in England* (Oxford, 1866–1902), vi. 565–9; vii. 451–3. At 8*d.* a quire, and allowing for the fact that the outer, wrapping sheets might not be usable, the cost of paper for a 200-leaf (400-page) folio book would be around 3*s.* The entering of text in a large hand and the leaving of white space conveyed an unmistakable message of conspicuous consumption.

[35] 'The Castle Ashby manuscripts', pp. 395–6; *The diary of Samuel Pepys*, ed. Robert Latham and William Matthews (London, 1970–83), vii. 100.

[36] 'Sidney's *Certain sonnets*: speculations on the evolution of the text', *Library*, 6:2 (1980), 430–44. Cf. Croft, *Autograph poetry*, i. xv.

work of R. P. Thompson on the heavy, high-quality French papers preferred for music copying, the grades and varieties of seventeenth-century writing paper remain largely unstudied. Papers of the same heavy kind were also used for much scribal bookwork and for some separates, though the latter were usually on flimsier paper suitable for folding and pocketing. An important change noted by Thompson is the introduction during the 1660s of the lighter letter papers known as 'Dutch post' and 'Fine horn' (pp. 64–5); but this is just one episode in a story which at present is understood only in the broadest of outlines.

The ink used in scribal bookwork, being a solution of colouring matter in water, required more careful preparation than the crude, oil-based concoction used in printing. Seventeenth-century writers had a choice between the medieval style of ink coloured with a mixture of vegetable tannins (oak galls) and iron sulphate, and the more ancient kind made by dissolving cakes of lampblack compounded with gum. The first of these had the advantage of reacting chemically with the page. The second produced a deeper black but, because there was no reaction with the writing surface, might eventually peel away from it, and was prone to redissolve if exposed to water.[37] Ferro-tannic ink had no such drawbacks and was generally preferred. Careful writers would manufacture their own ink. Moxon, who was a perfectionist about printer's ink, has left us a recipe for writing ink which is typical of the time:

To a quart of rain-water put 5 ounces of Galls moderately pounded. Stir y^m up every day for 14 dayes together. Then put in 2 Ounce & a half of Copperas [ferrous sulphate] and half an Ounce of gum. Do not put in the gum and Copperas till after ye 14 dayes probatum est A little gum gives it a gloss, & boyling makes thick.[38]

The waiting time could be shortened, with some sacrifice of quality, by leaving the mixture in the sun. For those unwilling to

---

[37] Hector, p. 20; Finlay, p. 26. Recipes by 'E. B.' for both kinds of ink are given in John de Beau Chesne and John Baildon, *A booke containing divers sortes of hands* (London, 1602; facsim. repr. Amsterdam, 1977), p. A2^r. Printing ink also used lampblack as its colouring agent but dissolved it in oil, not water, and underwent chemical change during drying (Gaskell, pp. 125–6).

[38] Moxon, p. 82; from Bodl. MS. Rawl. D 11 20. Cf. Jonson, prologue to *Volpone*: 'All gall, and coppresse, from his inke, he drayneth, / Onely, a little salt remayneth; / Wherewith, he'll rub your cheeks . . . ' (*Ben Jonson*, v. 24).

take such pains ink was also available from stationers and street hawkers. Refinements on the standard recipes were legion, many writing masters having their own secret formulae.

Once used, ink frequently required to be dried. 'We dry a writing', Comenius explains, 'with *Blotting-paper*, or *Calis-sand* out of a Sand-box'.[39] Early blotting paper was simply unsized brown paper and would not have been as effcient as its present-day descendant. The sand-box, also known as the pounce-pot and the sander, did not contain sand but sandarach, a resin imported from Africa. The practice of rubbing paper with a bag containing this substance or sprinkling it from a sand-box, as well as assisting the writing of marginalia in printed books, was also adopted in order to give a sharper outline to writing. One Italian authority, cited by Finlay, recommended finely crushed egg-shells mixed with powdered incense as a substitute.[40] However, others frowned upon the practice because it slowed the speed of writing.

A matter in which the compositor had an undoubted advantage over the scribe was that of correction: once inscribed, the written mark was hard to remove. If there was no alternative, an erasure might be made by scraping, ideally with a long-handled knife with a leaf-shaped blade specially designed for that purpose.[41] This left the paper noticeably thinner and would have required recourse to the sand-box before the erased section could be overwritten: some scribes preferred to conceal it beneath filagree work. But close acquaintanceship with manuscripts will reveal many other devices for coping with misinscription, the simplest of which was to alter the spelling or even the wording of the text. Words struck through or overwritten, words added interlinearly with a caret, and omitted lines written vertically in margins are found even in careful, high-priced scribal bookwork and seem to have been accepted as an unavoidable feature of the medium.

The pen

The near-universal instrument of writing in our period was the incised feather—cheap, wonderfully light in the hand and able

---

[39] Comenius, p. 187.
[40] Finlay, p. 33.
[41] Examples are illustrated in Finlay, colour plate II(i), i and m.

with the aid of a penknife to be cut to whatever width or slant was desired. By cutting the quill to an oblique edge, L. C. Hector explains, 'as long as the pen was held naturally and at a constant angle to the writing-surface the strokes it made were thick or thin according to the angle they made with this edge'. For the round hand that established itself towards the end of the century 'the goose-quill was cut to a symmetrically tapered fine point, which needed frequent 'mending' (that is, recutting) by the writer'.[42] A document in which headings were to be in a larger, thicker and more elaborate style than the body letter, or whose scribe made use of decorative flourishes, small marginalia, or words set off in bold or italic, would require the use of several differently sized and cut quills. The shaping of the nib was quite a tricky operation: a minimum of seven cuts was required, all of which called for a good eye and a firm yet steady hand.[43] For those lacking the skill or the patience to cut and mend their nibs, bundles of quills could be purchased ready cut; however, without recutting, the life of these would be short—perhaps no more than a single day's writing. Prodigies of penmanship by which a long manuscript was written with a single quill could only be achieved through continuous, time-consuming resort to the penknife and perhaps some artificial means of hardening the point. Yet the skill of nib-cutting once acquired permitted the writer to shape a quill exactly to the requirements of the text being inscribed, and to complement the choice of ink and paper.

Music paper, while sometimes printed, was more commonly produced with a specialized pen called a rastrum which could produce up to thirty lines simultaneously, divided into staves. Thompson indicates that this was a skilled craft usually executed for stationers rather than by individual musicians, and that 'the life of a rastrum was not very long'.[44] If it was an assemblage of quills this would certainly have been the case; however, as no example survives, one can at present only speculate about its construction.

The need for any further historical account of the quill and its subsidiary implements, the penknife, the ink-horn and the sand-box, is obviated by the existence of Finlay's thorough study.

---

[42] Hector, p. 19.
[43] Described in Finlay, pp. 10–11 and illustration 29, p. 98.
[44] 'English music manuscripts', p. 82.

Hands

The seventeenth century gave birth to a bewildering variety of hands. There is a widely accepted belief that the overall movement across the period was in this, as in other things (including upper-class dress), one from variety to conformity; but such a view is at best a half-truth. A more accurate model (again as in other things) would be one of of repeated attempts to impose conformity subverted by new assertions of diversity. My view is therefore different from that of L. C. Hector, Anthony G. Petti and Jonathan Goldberg except in recognizing the ultimate triumph of the 'round hand'—but even this was more delayed than is often assumed, and the hand itself less uniform.[45]

In the early years of the century a professional scribe would be expected to write at least two hands, the native secretary and the imported italic. Secretary was a derivative of the fifteenth-century 'gothic' hand of the same name.[46] Those who used it as their regular hand would often use italic for proper names and headings or interpolated passages that required to be distinguished in some way (e.g. letters to be read out in a play). This relationship was rarely if ever reversed: those who wrote italic as their primary hand would simply use another form of italic for such purposes.[47] From its first introduction into England, italic was undoubtedly the hand of greater prestige, being preferred for material to be presented to royal or aristocratic readers; yet the compliment was sometimes a two-edged one. The greater legibility of italic made it suitable for readers whose limited literacy might not have extended to decoding the more complex secretary, which up to the 1620s remained the preferred, everyday hand of the highly educated functionaries who performed the actual work of government. That secretary did not quite so readily yield its

[45] Goldberg, *Writing matter*; Hector, *The handwriting of English documents*; Anthony G. Petti, *English literary hands from Chaucer to Dryden* (London, 1977). Despite my differing on this particular point, I am indebted to all three studies, and make no claim to anything approaching Hector's or Petti's general understanding of the history of written forms, or Goldberg's of the philosophy of inscription. Additional information on hands, along with invaluable specimens and transcripts, will be found in Croft, *Autograph poetry* and W. W. Greg, *English literary autographs, 1550–1650*, 3 vols (London, 1932).

[46] For the origins of the hand, see Petti, pp. 14–20.

[47] Yet it could be argued that the small quotation hand for which Simonds D'Ewes took up his fine-nibbed quill in writing BL Harl. MSS 162–3 has a greater number of secretary features than his larger, much clumsier, text hand.

meaning to a casual glance may have been one of its recommenda-
tions for such users: it could also be written much more rapidly
than italic.[48]

Italic script developed in early fifteenth-century Florence as an
attempt by Humanist scholars to create a hand that would lend
clarity and distinction to manuscripts of classical Latin authors.
Rejecting the late-medieval hands then current, it turned for
inspiration to much earlier models, including ancient inscriptions
(for its capitals) and Carolingian miniscule. Initially restricted to a
small circle of antiquarians, it gained wider currency when it was
taken up by Cosimo de' Medici and then by the Papal chancery,
from which it rapidly spread throughout Europe.[49] As its origins
suggest, and as Goldberg stresses repeatedly, to write in italic called
for a conscious suppression of individuality: the ideal italic was an
impersonal hand, indistinguishable from other well-written
examples of the script. International circulation of the engraved
copy-books of Italian writing masters helped maintain this
uniformity. Secretary, conversely, existed in so many regional and
personal variants within the British Isles as to be rather a broad
family of hands than a single model. Martin Billingsley, betraying
a characteristic writing master's dislike of individuality, wrote in
1618: 'To speake of the kindes of *Secretary*, is (in these dayes) no
easie matter: for some haue deuised many, and those so strange and
disguised; that there is hardly any true straine of a right Secretary in
them.'[50] Indeed, it was both desired and expected that one's
practice in writing secretary should have an individuating
function. When William Bagot in a letter of 1622 to his father
apologized for having shown 'a barren invention' in his use of
secretary hand, this meant, according to Dawson and Kennedy-
Skipton, that his hand 'lacked elegance and individuality'.[51] In fact

---

[48] As a supplement to the examples in Giles E. Dawson and Laetitia Kennedy-Skipton,
Elizabethan handwriting 1500–1650 (London, 1966), a range of bureaucratic secretary from the
early years of the century is conveniently illustrated in Peter Davison, 'King James's Book of
bounty: from manuscript to print', *Library*, 5:28 (1973), 26–53. Example Bg (p. 45) is
especially remarkable.

[49] The origins of italic are discussed in Stanley Morison, *Politics and script*, ed. Nicholas
Barker (Oxford, 1972), pp. 264–78, 290–3 and its later development summarized in Petti,
pp. 18–20.

[50] *The pens excellencie* (London, 1618; facsim. repr. Amsterdam, 1977), p. C3ᵛ.

[51] *Elizabethan handwriting*, pp. 102–3, 9.

the trouble seems to have been that the younger Bagot was incorporating influences from italic, and that his father saw this as a regrettable abnegation of the proper independence of an English gentleman. The cultural implications of this contrast (further explored in Chapter 4) are of obvious importance.

Italic hand on the Renaissance model is still written today by enthusiasts for well-formed script and poses no difficulty for a modern reader. Secretary on the other hand, even when written with care and precision, requires a constant attentiveness which is not simply an effect of the remoteness of its letter-forms from present-day practice, but arises from the greater complexity of these forms—especially the capitals—and the fact that the same scribe may use several versions of a single letter. Some of its more recondite versions have to be learned virtually as separate scripts if they are to be read with fluency. This variety, while it impedes ready legibility, is one of the factors that makes the script so expressive and visually pleasing. Reading it we become acutely aware of the poverty of the typographer's alphabet and those forms of handwriting which have allowed themselves to be dominated by it. As well as this, secretary's strongly cursive nature gave encouragement to all kinds of flourishes and decoration. Both the problems and the advantages are on display in the section of BL Harleian MS 7368 believed to be in the hand of Shakespeare.[52] Petti comments on the use of two or more forms for single letters, drawing particular attention to 'a', 'b', 'g', 'h', 'p', 's' and 't' (p. 87). The impression may have been even stronger if the writer had not been so sparing in his use of capitals. And yet the graphic expressiveness of the hand, whether or not it is Shakespeare's, cannot be denied. Particularly striking is the tension between the compressed profile of those parts of the letters which fall above the base line of the writing and the daring expeditions made below the line in the form of loops, descenders and redundant ascenders. The graphic virtues of italic, while no less real, are of a chaster and less assertive order.

---

[52] Ff. 8–9ᵛ. This is the hand D section of *The booke of Sir Thomas Moore*, part reproduced with discussion in Stanley Wells and Gary Taylor, *William Shakespeare, a textual companion* (Oxford, 1987), pp. 11, 461–7; Croft, i. 23–4; and Petti, pp. 86–7. F. 9ʳ is reproduced in the Library's *English literary manuscripts*, ed. Hilton Kelliher and Sally Brown (London, 1986), p. 23.

It was the typographer's alphabet as much as the influence of italic which was responsible for the demise of secretary. Regular exposure to the printed roman and italic (the former derived from the original humanistic book hand and the latter from its cursive derivative) encouraged a preference for the related inscribed forms. One minority hand, practised, among others, by Esther Inglis, John North and Alexander Pope, was a close simulacrum of printed lettering. Among the last professional copyists of separates to use a personalized, full-blooded secretary was the 'feathery scribe' active from the 1620s to the 1640s whose work is the subject of research in progress by Hilton Kelliher and Peter Beal (see Plate 1). However, the decline of secretary did not bring any diminution of individualism in handwriting, and can even be said to have enhanced it. To supplant secretary, but also the pure italic, came the so-called 'mixed hand' whose origins lie as far back as the reign of Henry VIII and which was to maintain its dominance until late in the century. This hand was, as its name implies, a blending of italic with secretary forms, but the mixture was never a standardized one. Writers could make their own selection from the two traditions, and also had the freedom of alternating forms of the same letter drawn from each (particularly common with capitals). While aspiring to the greater legibility of italic, the mixed hand still offered the scribe a rich field for choice; so, while much of the intricacy and expressive quality of secretary had to be sacrificed, this did not mean that individual hands ceased to be characteristic and distinguishable.

To the elderly Richard Gething, writing in 1645 as a champion of pure italic, the mixed hand was seen, as many present-day writers prefer to see it, as an unskilled italic 'corruptlie taught, especiallie by Mountebancke and circulatorie professors of impossibillities, to the dishonour of our Nation and abuse of learners in generall'.[53] Jenkinson, approaching the topic from another perspective, presents it as a modification of secretary 'written of a size and with an uniform slope taken from the other hand' into which 'all the *Italic* forms gradually penetrated'.[54] Both

---

[53] Facsim. in Joyce Irene Whalley, *The pen's excellencie: a pictorial history of Western calligraphy* (New York, 1980), p. 219, from *Chiro-graphia or a book of copies* (London, 1645).

[54] *Later court hands*, p. 65. An example would be Simonds D'Ewes quotation hand mentioned earlier.

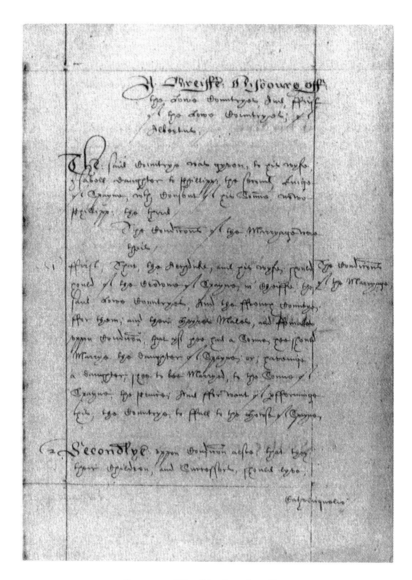

PLATE I. The 'feathery' scribe.

processes were undoubtedly at work; but the time is long overdue for us to forget its supposedly transitional nature and look at it as a hand, or family of hands, in its own right—one that satisfied through the fecundity of its resources. The truth is that pure italic had always been an exotic flower, and it was the greater liberty of the mixed hand that best answered to the eclectic genius of the mid-century. Petti, while noting that the retroflex secretary 'e' survived even in some eighteenth-century hands, implies that the mixed hand was as good as dead by 1680.[55] Yet National Library of Scotland Adv. MS 19. 3. 4, a collection of *very* modish libertine verse copied no earlier than 1688, is in a hand that still shows a strong secretary influence.

None the less, by the end of the century both the mixed hand and pure italic had yielded to the so-called 'round hand'. Palaeographers differ on the criteria used to distinguish this from the less formal versions of italic. Petti helpfully nominates the hands of Marvell and Dryden as early examples, crediting the former with a 'roundness, clarity, smoothness and cursiveness which look forward to the copperplate of the 19th century' and a harmonious balancing of 'long, oval loops above and below the line'; but these features are not so marked in Dryden's script.[56] To Jenkinson, a perfectionist for whom no hand written after 1350 is wholly satisfactory, the round hand is simply a debased italic, written too rapidly 'with a pen wrongly shaped and wrongly held', while Roger North was reminded of pigs' ribs.[57] The round hand satisfied a need for a cursive that could be written at speed while remaining perfectly legible. By comparison the pure italic had been too slow to write, secretary too slow to read and the mixed hand too confusing in its repertoire of letter forms. Round hand spread independently of the writing virtuosi through such down-to-earth publications as *The a la mode secretarie* (1680), *A set of copies of the round hand now in use* (1685), and *A new coppy book of*

---

[55] pp. 20, 132.
[56] Petti, p. 119.
[57] *Later court hands*, p. 10; *The life of the right honourable Francis North, Baron of Guilford* (London, 1742), p. 16. Robert Moore, *Of the first invention of writing. An essay* (London, 1716), uses the term 'Bastard Italian' for the round hand, and attributes its popularization to John Ayres (p. 7). The development coincided with a growing preference for more expanded printing types to which Moxon (pp. 22–3) is a witness.

the round hand, as now practis'd (1702).[58] Stanley Morison designates
it as 'colourless, thoroughly unromantic, and dull . . . a frankly
expeditious script'.[59] Here indeed was a triumph of uniformity,
and yet it was of the nature of the round hand with its simple basic
forms and ease of mastery that it would be written in a great
variety of personal idioms. The division that established itself was
that between a standardized version of the hand suitable for public
documents and fair copies and a 'running hand' with innumerable
variations used for informal correspondence and personal memoranda. Insofar as handwriting sought to emulate the uniformity and
the public status of print it would move more and more in the
direction of copperplate; but even while this happened new
private dialects were establishing themselves.

The professional book hands which are our major concern in
this section range across all the major styles discussed, though
secretary is largely restricted to the first four decades of the
century. Documents written in a self-consciously calligraphic or
elaborately decorated hand are in a minority, and there is a paucity
of manuscripts of the kind quite common in France of a standard
text, such as a prayer book, presented in exquisite calligraphy. A
few manuscripts exist from early in the century using a specialized
form of italic favoured by writing masters, with clubbed ascenders
and descenders. These are likely to be presentation copies for
wealthy patrons. Two handsomely written copies of a condensed
version of Raleigh's *History of the world*, one in a practised italic and
the other in an exceptionally beautiful mixed hand, appear to be
survivors from a larger scribal edition which would have been sold
or presented, but are unrepresentative of a tradition of copying
which aimed above all at the serviceable.[60] Britain certainly had its
skilled writing masters, known today through their copy books,
but these seem generally to have stood aloof from the hurly-burly

[58] Heal, pp. 150, 157, 165.
[59] Heal, p. xxxiii.
[60] University of North Carolina MS CSWR/A96 (signed in five places by Robert
Greville, fourth Lord Brooke) and Emmerson collection, Melbourne (from the library of
the Earls of Bute at Aldenham Abbey). A third manuscript was used by Laurence Echard as
the basis for his *An abridgement of Sir Walter Raleigh's history* (London, 1698). The
Emmerson copy, a small octavo with red-ink margins, containing 402 text leaves plus two
of index, is meticulously keyed to the paragraphs of the original. The small-quarto Chapel
Hill copy is unruled and lacks the keys.

of scribal publication.[61] A masterpiece like the manuscript of the Sidneian psalms written by John Davies of Hereford for Mary Countess of Pembroke was by its very nature a private commission.[62] The identification of scribes is much more difficult when the relatively invariant italic is used, and some pardonable misattributions have resulted from this.

Generally, professional bookwork and the writing of separates encouraged a hand which created no problems of comprehension, which could be sustained evenly through long documents, and which could be written with some speed. Each of these criteria encouraged the use of the mixed or the round hand. In an important series of anthologies written during the 1690s and the early years of the new century which were identified by W. J. Cameron as having been issued by a single entrepreneurial publisher, the work is all in round hand or a mixed hand not far removed from it. In this case it is evident that the entrepreneur had a clear ideal of the kind of hand he preferred and that the scribes did their best to conform to his wishes. In one sequence of three anthologies written by two scribes, now reduced to one volume as Folger MS M b 12, the care and similarity of the two hands and the disciplined method of presenting the texts both suggest a striving for what Cameron characterizes as 'an impersonal, professional norm'.[63] In two other manuscripts commissioned by the same entrepreneur, Bodleian Eng. poet. 18 and Nottingham University Library Pw V 46, one scribe consciously tries to imitate the hand of the other. On some pages the resemblance is so close as to suggest that both are in the same hand, but on others an accumulation of minor differences indicates that this is not the case. Versatility of this kind was a valued skill in the half-world of political and religious intrigue. Goldberg reports a case from 1594 of an imprisoned priest, John Gerard, who, realizing that a document he was about to write might be used to attribute other papers to him, immediately switched to a hand unlike his usual one (not an easy

---

[61] Heal, *English writing-masters* includes both a biographical dictionary of the masters and a bibliography of the copy-books. Examples from several of the books are given in Whalley, pp. 216–37. A recognized master could obtain high prices from connoisseurs for relatively small samples of virtuoso script. There may even have been a resistance to writing longer texts which could have been broken up by others for sale to a number of collectors.

[62] Described in Kinnamon, 'The Sidney psalms'.

[63] 'Scriptorium', p. 31.

thing to do without prior training).[64] A similar versatility was noted in August 1678 when Roger L'Estrange wrote to Secretary Williamson concerning Anne Brewster who had been involved in the surreptitious printing of three Whig pamphlets:

> She is in the House of a person formerly an officer under Cromwell: one that writes three or foure very good Hands, and owns to have been employd in Transcribing things for a Counsellor in the Temple. From which Circumstances one may fayrly presume that all those Delicate Copyes, which Brewster carryed to the Presse, were written by Brewsters Land Lord, and Copyd by him, from the Authour.[65]

Here the concern is with the interface between scribal publication and surreptitious printing, but it would be surprising if the varied hands of Brewster's landlord were not also involved in the production of separates and anthologies, especially as he seems to have done work for Andrew Marvell.

The combination of deliberate disguise, skilled imitation of other hands, and a pride in versatility together with the opportunities offered by the mixed hand for varying letter forms means that there will often be no sure way of determining whether two pieces of work are by the same copyist. Pamela Willetts's study of the music script of Stephen Bing may serve as an example of the difficulties that can arise even when there is fair external evidence for an attribution.[66] It is helpful in such cases if, as well as facsimiles (which are indispensable), a technical description of the alphabets used in each document can be given, allowing the reader to go straight to the crucial forms and words. There is a good model for this in the introduction to the Foakes and Rickert edition of Henslowe's diary.[67]

Writing the manuscript

The work of the scribe would begin with the preparation of ink and paper, which in the second case might involve rubbing or dusting with sandarach. Paper would also need to be folded or cut and folded to form leaves which, later in the century, would often

---

[64] *Writing matter*, pp. 273–4.
[65] PRO SP29/406, f. 49; full document in Kelliher, *Andrew Marvell*, p. 113.
[66] 'Stephen Bing: a forgotten violist', *Chelys* 18 (1989), 3–17.
[67] *Henslowe's diary*, ed. R. A. Foakes and R. T. Rickert (Cambridge, 1961), pp. xliv–l.

be given ruled margins, usually in red. Pepys had paper ruled by 'an old woman in pannier ally'.[68] Sometimes additional folds, rules or lines would be added to guide the writing of columns, or to ensure even lineation. In many manuscripts it is clear that some method, not immediately visible, has been used to direct eye and hand. A technique recommended to children, though perhaps too unsophisticated for adult scribes, was to rule lines lightly with black lead and then rub them out with bread.[69] Otherwise lines could be scratched with a dry point or a temporary impression made with a lute-string.[70] It was possible for the scribe to make use of a ready-bound book, as was done by compilers of private albums and commonplace books; however, it was obviously safer to copy sheet by sheet or quire by quire and bind up afterwards, a practice sometimes betrayed by the presence of an inverted gathering.[71] In any case even new printed books were usually sold unbound at this period. The most common form for the separate was a sheet or half-sheet folded to give two leaves. Three sides were used for text with the fourth left at least half blank to allow for two outer surfaces after further folding, one of which would usually contain the title or an address for delivery. In poetical separates it was usual, and more cost-effective, to fold to a normal folio or quarto gathering for pentameter verse but to a long folio or long quarto for tetrameters.

With ink and paper ready the next concern would be the choice of quill and nib, or of a variety of each. These decisions would be determined by broader considerations regarding design, and would in turn be related to the intended asking price for the product. Moreover, since paper was an even more expensive commodity than it was for printers, careful casting off would be necessary to ensure that a given text was fitted within an agreed number of sheets without any obvious squeezing. Like the compositor, the scribe would choose a standard number of lines

---

[68] *Diary*, vii. 98.

[69] De Beau Chesne, p. A2ᵛ.

[70] For these and other methods of ruling, see Petti, p. 6. The use of a pricking-wheel or pair of dividers to make marks, which then served as a guide for the ruling of lines, was usually restricted to vellum; however, Jayne Ringrose has indicated Cambridge MS Add. 3544 as a paper example.

[71] This should not be confused with the practice of writing in an already bound book from both ends, with the retrograde text upside down.

per page and do his best to maintain a consistent average of words per line. All these matters, corresponding to the printer's choice of measure and fount, would need to be determined before pen was set to paper. The other choice would concern the level of flourish and ornament. Most hands could be written in both plain and decorated versions, the latter, naturally, taking longer to execute and often occupying more space. Here again the choice would be part of an initial decision about the design of the document, which in turn would be a reflection of its purpose and the payment likely to be received for it. Overall the matching of aesthetics to function in a handwritten document was no less deliberate than in a printed one, and usually more so, insofar as here the actual formation of the letters was the responsibility of the workman.

The action of inking the pen is neatly described in 'E. B.'s' line, 'Dip pen, and shake pen, and touch pen for haire'. The 'hair' would be threads from the cloth used to plug the mouth of the inkhorn. Penhold and posture are thus described in the same source:

> Your thombe on your pen as highest bestow,
> The forefinger next, the middle below:
> And holding it thus in most comely wise,
> Your body vpright, stoupe not with your head.
> Your breast from the boord, if that ye be wise,
> Lest that ye take hurt, when ye haue well fed.[72]

The description is supplemented by illustrations of the kind usual in writing manuals of right and wrong versions of the penhold.

The physical needs of the scribe were satisfied by a table and stool, adequate light, a fire in winter, and the modest tools of his trade as they have been described. A chest or cabinet would be desirable for storing paper and written sheets: contemporary illustrations also show papers wedged behind horizontal wooden rails attached to the wall.[73] While most writers' desks appear to be flat, the scholar illustrated in Comenius writes on a small inclined desk resting on a table. Petti regards this as an archaic practice, the new ideal being for the arm to rest directly on the table.[74] Ageing eyes, if unaided by spectacles, might have required the assistance of

---

[72] De Beau Chesne, p. A2^{r-v}.
[73] Cf. Finlay pp. 72, 73, 107, 152.
[74] *Orbis sensualium pictus*, p. 200; Petti, p. 7.

a prism or magnifying glass. Comenius pays particular attention to illumination. In two illustrations the writer's desk faces an open window.[75] The unpleasant smell of tallow candles is mentioned and wax ones recommended. His suggestion that a screen of green glass be placed in front of the candle reminds us that it would have burned less evenly than its present-day counterpart and that the writer would have had to remain very close to it. Finally, being a night-worker, the writer might well have need of a lanthorn which is pictured in a corner of the study. The scribe's cat was a working animal whose task was to protect paper and especially parchment from mice and rats. Most professional writers would have worked from their homes or from the homes of their masters, the business place that was not also a place of residence being rare at this date. Apprentices normally lived in the master's house.

The editorial work of the scribe

Present-day typesetters are not required to question any detail of their copy, this having been prepared for them by another professional, the copy-editor. Their responsibility is to reproduce what is put before them with complete fidelity, leaving any problems to be dealt with by the back-up professional, the proof-reader. Their seventeenth-century predecessor, while maintaining this as an ideal, would have felt obliged to depart from it in practice:

For by the Laws of Printing, *a* Compositer *is strictly to follow his* Copy, *viz.*
to observe and do just so much and no more than his Copy *will bear him out for;*
so that his Copy *is to be his* Rule *and* Authority: *But the carelessness of some good*
Authors, and the ignorance of other Authors, has forc'd Printers *to introduce a*
Custom, which among them is look'd upon as a task and duty incumbent on the
Compositer, *viz. to discern and amend the bad* Spelling *and* Pointing *of his*
Copy, *if it be English* . . .[76]

The compositor, then, had a great deal of latitude in his treatment of the text, including primary responsibility for orthography and punctuation. He was also required to adjust any archaic features to conform to the fashion of the present and to correct obvious errors of sense or grammar. Henry Weber's 1812 edition of Beaumont

[75] pp. 186, 200.
[76] Moxon, p. 192.

and Fletcher records a succession of four well-intentioned miscorrections which took place during resettings of the printed text of *The scornful lady*. The original passage was '*El. Lo.* And say my back was melted when the gods knowes / I keep it at a charge'. Weber's note is:

> It is curious to observe the gradual corruption of this speech. The first quarto reads, 'When the gods knowes.' The second, 'When the God knowes.' The third, 'When God the knowes.' That of 1639, 'When God he knowes.' And the sixth, which is the text-book of the modern editors, 'When Heaven knowes.'[77]

Each of these changes shows a new compositor dutifully trying to make sense out of what appeared to be an error.

Although we have no comparable statement of the responsibilities of the scribe copying a manuscript book or separate, it becomes clear from collating scribally transmitted texts that the same attitude was current. The transcriber no less than the compositor would be expected to impose his own practice with regard to spelling, punctuation and minor points of grammar, to modernize, and to correct solecisms and apparent errors. It was only under exceptional circumstances—most commonly the direct influence of a strong-minded author or patron—that the accidentals of the exemplar would have been regarded as sacrosanct. In addition the scribe would have had to make decisions over the use of the contracted and apocopated forms which were much more widely used than in printing.

Beyond this the scribe must have had a far more acute awareness of the limitations of his exemplar than the compositor. Texts decayed very rapidly in manuscript transmission: by the time Filmer's *Patriarcha* eventually reached the press it was '*so corrupted that it scarce deserved to wear his Name, being not only wretchedly mistranscribed, but strangely mutilated*'.[78] Moreover, there was no public market to which recourse could be had for an ascertained earlier state of the text in question. A professional engagement with the copying of manuscripts cannot but have led to an empirical understanding of the causes of error and the principles of emendation. In cases where the restoration of earlier readings was

---

[77] *The works of Beaumont and Fletcher* (Edinburgh, 1812), ii. 221.
[78] *Patriarcha*, 2nd edn (London, 1685), p. A3'.

impossible, the scribe, as an educated reader with a contemporary's understanding of the matter in hand, would often have felt obliged to provide a plausible substitute. The traces of such interventions are detectable at every stage of editorial work on texts of the period and provide overwhelming evidence that a majority of scribes regarded themselves as having an editorial as well as a transcriptional responsibility. However, we must always be aware that the intention behind such changes was not the scholarly one of recovering original readings so much as the practical one of offering a presentable text, able to perform its perceived social function. The enemy of the modern editor is not blatant nonsense, which must always have been recognizable for what it was, but the pressing urge to produce at least local sense through speculative emendation.

However, some scribes would rather let an error remain, however gross, than perform any act that would compromise the appearance of the written page, while others may well have been over-conditioned by the legal copyist's awareness that even the most trivial error in transcribing a writ, deed or will could have serious consequences. From time to time, especially in the later years of the century, one encounters manuscripts whose tolerance of nonsense is so remarkable that one is forced to hypothesize either a despairing literalism in transcribing a hopelessly corrupt exemplar, or that the scribe had an imperfect command of English. The latter explanation is given plausibility by the steady immigration, especially from the 1680s, of highly educated Huguenots who would have had difficulty in finding regular work as clerks. Two earlier arrivals, Jean de Beau Chesne and Esther Inglis, were distinguished calligraphers.

Where the scribe differed from the compositor was in a generally greater tolerance of variant practices within the same text. Because printers and booksellers, as members of the same industry, were in constant contact with each other and each other's products, they were encouraged to work towards the standardization of spelling, punctuation and usage, a process that by the first decade of the eighteenth century had led to what is recognizably the forerunner of modern practice. Scribal spellings are nearly always more archaic than contemporary printers' spellings and the notion of there being 'right' and 'wrong' alternatives was much slower in gaining force among writers than among printers. The spelling of any given copy was likely to represent the outcome of a tug-of-war between that of the exemplar and the scribe's personal preferences, and considerable changes might occur when a second copy was made by the same scribe from the same exemplar. Or the scribe might have no particular spelling preferences for some (or many) words but rather a range of possibilities to be alternated at whim or in response to the workings of anticipation and perseveration. In some cases variation arises from a sense of being caught between an older system and a more modern one. The use of double letters for long vowels ('shee', 'wee'), double consonants after short vowels, and the '-ie'/'-y' distinction in forms such as 'easie' and 'wyer' is a hangover from a practice widely observed in the earlier years of the century that the printers abandoned in favour of the less phonetic modern forms. Many writers of the mid-century seem to feel that the phonetically accurate form is the proper one but to be unable to prevent the shorter one slipping in from time to time.

The editorial work of the scribe suffered from generally being done on the basis of what had already been read rather than on a knowledge of what was to come. A grammatical incongruity near the beginning of a long sentence might well provoke an emendation when progressing to the end would have shown that it was justified. Writing further would not necessarily lead to recognition of the earlier miscorrection, since the scribe, transcribing phrase by phrase or at most line by line, could not be expected to retain the overall structure of the sentence firmly in memory. Yet editorial thinking could also be surprisingly lateral. The transcriber of 'The visitt', a satire of the late 1670s preserved in Lincolnshire Archives Office MS Anc 15/B/4, was obviously working from a very corrupt, and perhaps only semi-legible exemplar.[79] Yet he was not a negligent workman: marginal additions in a number of texts he copied show that he proof-read his transcriptions and was not ashamed of revealing his omissions. The problems he had with this particular text can be judged by several errors and obscurities he let pass, most notably the mysterious 'matrix Glances' in

---

[79] pp. 20–1. The full text of the satire is given in Ch. 6.

> There was obscene Rotchesters Cheife storys
> Of matrix Glances Dildo and Clittoris

but that there was a mind at work behind the neatly inscribing pen is indicated by the lines

> The Taburn was the next resoult, where I
> Quite weary of there Tipling company
> went home a Cursing of this wretched age
> That Couples each old Lady wth. her Page

In the first line it is obvious from context that the poet wrote 'The tavern was the next resort' but it would appear that what the scribe saw, or thought he saw, in his exemplar was 'The Tyburn was the next result'. What we seem to have is a pair of forms, aberrant in themselves, which have been ingeniously devised to exclude neither possibility, leaving the matter to the judgement of the reader.

Multiplication of copies

Author and entrepreneurial publishers would frequently produce 'scribal editions' of works, especially short separates and newsletters but sometimes quite lengthy volumes. Next to nothing is known about the methods used, but where any degree of haste was involved—which was certainly the case with newsletters—there would have been little point in a number of scribes waiting to have their turn at a single exemplar. Copying from dictation would be one solution to this problem, though one for which we so far lack evidence for our period.

The alternative was to make use of some form of progressive copying. This was a system by which scribes used each other's copied sheets as exemplars, and volumes, or extended separates, might be produced which were an indiscriminate mixture of first, second and perhaps more remote copies. The method was first hypothesized as an explanation of inconsistent agreements found in medieval textual traditions.[80] The simplest form would be for scribe A to pass the first sheet copied to scribe B to use as his exemplar. This would also save B the labour of having to duplicate

---

[80] The medieval form of this practice is analysed in Anne Hudson, 'Middle English' in *Editing medieval texts, English, French, and Latin written in England*, ed. A. G. Rigg (New York, 1977), pp. 45-8.

A's editorial work on the text: he would be able to copy rapidly and mechanically in the knowledge that the version had already been overseen by an experienced professional. If a third scribe was involved in copying, he might well receive sheets from A and B in no particular order representing in one case a first copy and in the other either a first (A's original copy) or a second (B's transcript). The only limiting factor would be that there was a preference for manuscripts to be in the same hand throughout (though there are certainly exceptions to this). Progressive copying should theoretically be detectable by different sections of a given source displaying irreconcilable patterns of agreement, or by one part being rich in unique readings, indicating terminal status, while another lacks such readings, indicating intermediary status. Another conceivable system would see the exemplar divided into separate sections, like medieval *peciae* or cast-off copy in a printing house, which were then passed from scribe to scribe or made the basis of an even more complex form of progressive copying. There is no positive evidence to date that either method was ever actually employed: all that is claimed is that the manufacture of copies would have been a much more prolonged business without it.

The possibility raised in Chapter 1 that the four variant orders of the 1629 *True relation* might have originated within a single agency implies the use of a looser form of shared copying. Here we need to imagine a master text composed of independent units which might have contained alternate versions of some of its elements, or which might have been reconstituted during the course of copying. Once again the claim is not made that this was actually the case, simply that there is nothing implausible in such a proceeding and it should not be overlooked when explanations are sought for the existence of highly variant forms of a composite text.

Scriptoria

Any proven case of progressive copying would indicate that scribes worked in close proximity to each other, if not actually in the same room. There is other evidence that this was often the case. The medieval name for such a room would be a scriptorium, the modern one an office. Defoe, considering in 1712 how he might switch his *Review* from print to scribal production, used neither term but simply spoke of hiring 'some large Hall or Great Room, in the City' and employing 'Thirty or Forty Clarks to write News, Lampoons, Ballads, any Thing in the World besides'.[81] There may be a degree of comic exaggeration in this, and yet in 1683 William Cotton had testified that 'many scores of clerks' were employed by newsletter proprietors, some of whom must have worked in scriptoria similar to those envisaged by Defoe.[82] For our present purposes, 'scriptorium' will be used to designate any communal working space in which the predominant part of the labour performed was that of transcription. In the seventeenth century, when the day-to-day functioning of society was still directed by the handwritten record, government, the law, commerce and the professions all relied on the existence of such working spaces. In many instances scriptoria and their practices stood in an unbroken line of professional descent from medieval forerunners, only the monastic scriptorium having suffered a total extinction of its traditions. The alternative to scriptorial copying was that performed by individuals in their homes or studies. Undoubtedly much production for author and user publication was done in this way, and even entrepreneurial publication may often have involved a farming out of work to individual copyists; but in the writing of newsletters and the large-volume copying of separates there were good reasons why the scriptorial method would be preferred.

Information about the personnel and organization of scriptoria is close to non-existent. The diarist, Thomas Crosfield, records organizing a group of students in Queen's College, Oxford to copy a theological manuscript, but is silent about the actual method employed.[83] The one source which goes into any detail is a report written on 23 October 1674 by Henry Ball on the organization of the scriptorium in the Paper Office at Whitehall in which newsletters were produced for Secretary of State Williamson.[84] In this case (discussed in greater detail in the next

---

[81] *A review*, viii. 708.

[82] *CSP (Dom.)*, *1683–4*, p. 54.

[83] On 21 July 1626 he wrote: 'Mr Provost gave me a moderatours place. imposed a taske upon me to rewrite a MS cuiusdam Sorbonistae adversus potestatem summi pontificis disposui inter pueros'. On 26 July he delivered the manuscript 'à multis peractum' (*Diary*, p. 5).

[84] *Letters addressed from London to Sir Joseph Williamson while plenipotentiary at the Congress of Cologne in the years 1673 and 1674*, ed. W. D. Christie (London, 1874), ii. 159–65.

section) four scribes worked under the close supervision of Ball who himself assisted with copying on post-nights. Williamson's scriptorium supplied letters to over a hundred clients many of whom received more than one letter a week. The rival newsletter, operated by Henry Muddiman under the patronage of the other Secretary's office, had at least as large a clientele and must have organized its copying along similar lines. The difference between the two operations was that Muddiman's, despite its official status, was a money-making operation, while Williamson was prepared to trade free copies of his newsletter for information sent in return.[85] The political newsletter-writers of the period of the Exclusion Bill crisis may well have had larger circulations, and John Dyer's scriptorium, dating from 1688, have been the largest of all. Snyder reports that, in the one case when four copies of Dyer's letter survive for the same day, all are in different hands, and, astoundingly, that 'for 1709 and 1710 for which some 300 copies survive, the hands employed must number fifty or more'.[86] Like all journalists, the newsletter producers worked to strict deadlines. Their clients expected their letters to contain fresh news up to and including the post-day.

THE ECONOMICS OF SCRIBAL PUBLISHING

The fields in which scribal publication held an advantage over print publication were firstly the short text copied in limited numbers for immediate use, and secondly the large, retrospective, regularly updated collection, often of prohibited material, written to order for a wealthy clientele. In the rhythm of production, the first kind of text would predominate during periods of heightened activity, such as law terms and parliamentary sessions, while the second might employ the same scribes in quieter times. When scribal publishers competed at the day-by-day level with the print publisher, their advantage lay in their ability to mobilize manpower very rapidly into the transcription of texts of urgent interest. As far as length was concerned, it was the text occupying a single sheet or less that allowed them superiority over their rivals.

[85] Fraser, *Intelligence*, p. 34.
[86] Snyder, pp. 8–9.

The report on the activities of the Starkey and Collins scriptoria shows how effective the methods of scribal publication were at supplying topical documents to a specialized clientele. While both booksellers were dealing with documents that a printer, more vulnerable to reprisal, might have been reluctant to touch, they were also offering a service that for its flexibility in placing new documents into circulation with the minimum of fuss could not have been duplicated by the rival medium with its cumbrous technology and multiple levels of contract.

The fact that bookselling professionals were involved in both kinds of publication encourages us to hypothesize that methods of costing and remuneration may have been similar. At the very least we would expect there to have been some parity between the earning power of the highly skilled craftspeople active in each field. With the aid of data from the Cambridge University Press, Bowyer and Ackers archives, it is possible to gain a clear notion of printers' costing for the 1690s and early eighteenth century.[87] Most journeymen printers, whether compositors or pressmen, were paid by piecework on a daily contract basis. Compositors were paid at a rate per sheet with higher rates for work likely to cause difficulty. The base rate from which others were calculated was given by Samuel Richardson in 1756 as six shillings a sheet for octavos and duodecimos in English type, but with an acknowledgement that it had earlier been 5s. or 5s. 6d. Two shillings was added for each move down to a smaller typeface on the scale pica, small-pica, long primer and brevier.[88] McKenzie's analysis of the Cambridge accounts reveals a standard rate of 5s. per sheet for quartos in pica and 7s. 6d. per sheet for octavos in pica, the latter figure in close agreement with Richardson's.[89] He also reports enhanced rates for setting in type-sizes larger than English (Richardson only having

---

[87] McKenzie, *Cambridge University Press*; K. I. D. Maslen, 'Masters and men', *Library*, 5:30 (1975), 81–94; D. F. McKenzie and J. C. Ross eds, *A ledger of Charles Ackers: printer of 'The London magazine'* (Oxford, 1968), pp. 12–13; K. I. D. Maslen and John Lancaster, *The Bowyer ledgers*.

[88] Samuel Richardson to William Blackstone, 10 Feb. 1756, in I. G. Philip, *William Blackstone and the reform of the Oxford University Press in the eighteenth century* (Oxford, 1957), pp. 39–42; McKenzie, *Cambridge University Press*, i. 70–80. For the type sizes referred to see Gaskell, pp. 12–16 and Moxon, p. 21.

[89] pp. 78–9. The closest possible approximation to a 'normal standard payment' for composition would be 'almost, but not quite, 4d. for 1000 Pica ens of English text in octavo with or without a scatter of notes' (p. 79).

specified smaller ones). Of course these rates were not just for setting but also covered justification, imposition, the correcting of errors discovered by the proof-reader, and the cleaning and distribution of type after use, besides other small tasks which fell to the lot of the compositor. Any comparison made with the output of a scribe would need to take into account that the word once written was in most instances complete. By any calculation it would be possible to produce several times the written word-length in the time it took to prepare the two imposed formes necessary to print a sheet at the press. Moreover, the printery still needed to add the costs of correction, traditionally one-sixth of the composition charge, presswork and the 'master's third', making the written copy even more competitive.[90] Paper was paid for directly by the bookseller and was not a charge to the printer. While it was in the bookseller's interest to seek the lowest possible quotation from the printer, the prices charged for books of specific kinds and sizes, like those for tradesmen's work, were relatively stable, and there would have been a mutual awareness of the range over which negotiation was possible. Binding was not at this period a concern of the printer, and even the bookshops would usually offer new books for sale in sheets, which customers could then send to their own preferred binder. Short pamphlets were sold stab-sewn with two or three quick stitches. It is probable that much scribal production was also sold unbound. The entering of text in bound volumes of blank leaves was more characteristic of the private keeper of commonplace books than of the commercially produced volume.[91]

In the entrepreneurial production of manuscripts, it is likely that the entrepreneur, for reasons of quality control, would follow the practice of the printing trade in supplying the paper, though we have no evidence on this matter. Whether production was arranged by direct agreement with the scribe or through a middleman such as a scrivener would be immaterial with regard to

---

[90] McKenzie, *Cambridge University Press*, i. 88, shows that both in Cambridge and London presswork was charged around a notional norm of 1s. 2d. per token of 250 copies, with adjustments for ease or difficulty. For overall costs, see McKenzie and Ross, *Ledger*, pp. 12–13.

[91] The presence of blank leaves at the end of a miscellany is not evidence of private origin since it was a regular practice for the scribes of commercial miscellanies to leave space for future additions.

price since the two would be bidding competitively against each other. The cost of the scribe's labour would depend on whether it was charged on a piecework, hourly or salaried basis. In a scrivener's office, apprentices were theoretically unpaid but in practice appear to have been allowed to earn some fees for piecework, while adult clerks would have worked for a combination of fees and salary. Otherwise, copying would be done by individual craftsmen paid by piecework which might be calculated by the page, the sheet or the whole item. As in printing, there must always have been prior agreement as to the number of sheets to be used in the finished copy, with text cast off to allow for this. (A cast-off master copy in the Osborn collection at Yale of a scribally published satire of 1688 is marked 'six sheets' at the beginning and end and divided by ticks into twenty-four sections.[92]) It is possible that for work using an elaborate decorative script, which as well as requiring exceptional skill would be slower to write, payment by the hour may have been considered, by analogy with the practice of engravers.[93] Alternatively, a premium analagous to that given to compositors and pressmen for working with the larger and smaller typefaces might have been allowed. The vital point is that the entrepreneur working in this way would be dealing with a single craftsman able to perform all stages of the production of the written text.

Numerous contemporary records of payment for manuscripts exist but I know of none for copying as such, which is to say for the bare labour of copying positively distinguished from the cost of paper, the commercial value of the content of what was copied and the premium, profit or fee added by the entrepreneur or master. Prices paid for newsletters are of no help at all as they were primarily in return for information, not the written record, which was often destroyed after reading. The prices we need to discover are those paid for the simple copying of workaday texts for which

---

[92] In Yale MS Osborn fb 70, the former Phillipps 8301; see *POAS (Yale)*, iv. 351–2, with illustration following p. 190.

[93] Wenceslaus Hollar charged 1s. an hour, measuring time with an hour glass which could be stopped when he was interrupted (Richard Pennington, *A descriptive catalogue of the etched work of Wenceslaus Hollar, 1607–1677* (Cambridge, 1982), pp. xlviii–xlix.). Hourly rates were also used at times in printing, especially for presswork and correction. A German illustration of a corrector, reproduced in Moxon, p. 407 (fig. 15) shows him, pipe in mouth, with a double hourglass to the left of his desk.

we can supply an approximate word length. Until a range of such evidence is secured, speculation on piecework rates would be fruitless. While analogies with the practices of print publication are suggestive they can never be conclusive. The contrast is between a centralized, highly disciplined trade operating under the supervision of the Stationers' Company, and a tradition of copying that operated on the margins of a variety of trades concerned with the work of the pen but was central to none of them. Insofar as it relied on piecework, our expectation would be of greater variety in its arrangements than is found in the printing trades.

In cases where copying was salaried rather than done on piecework, we are on slightly firmer ground for estimating the cost of the written product. Scribal publication was too small and specialized an industry to have established its own salary structure, but would have been guided by the expectations of scriveners', attorneys' and merchants' clerks, who enjoyed salaries of at least the level enjoyed by other literate skilled tradesmen, which is to say in the range from 10s to £1 per week for a reliable, experienced writer once out of his indentures. In Henry Ball's report of 1674 the wages of the four 'young men' who copied Secretary Williamson's newsletters are given as totalling £120, suggesting an average salary of £30 a year or 11s. 6d. a week, a sum that compares quite well with the average income of a compositor as recorded by McKenzie.[94] This figure, paid for work which was confidential and carried out at unusual hours, would represent the top of the range for relatively junior employees. Their capacities are thus described:

The 4 clerkes that were in the office (besides myselfe) before Mr. Charles, my Lady Portesmouth's gent. came into it, were Mr. Lawson, Mr. Kelly, Mr. Delamain, and Jo. Keeve, amongst which the above-recited letters were most of them divided (according to the fastness of their writing,

---

[94] *Letters to Sir Joseph Williamson*, ii. 165; McKenzie, i. 82. Compositors could greatly increase their incomes by taking on additional work at piecework rates, a few being able to average over £1 a week for considerable periods. Likewise, it was standard practice in many departments of the administration for clerks to supplement their salaries by supplying officially permitted copies of documents. Thus clerks in the customs' house enjoyed the privilege of supplying merchants with copies of the daily bills of entry which showed which goods had been received and by which importers. There was considerable chagrin in 1619 when this right was withdrawn to make way for a printed list (John J. McCusker, 'The business press in England before 1775', *Library*, 6:8 (1986), 210, 213 and n.).

which was equall all but Mr. Lawson, who as yett cannot doe as fast as the other), which being alwayes too much for them by reason of the uncertainty of the posts coming in I alwayes helped them doe a share or as many as I could, and had time to spare from the collecting the coppy and lookeing after the business . . .

The actual production of newsletters was done on Tuesdays, Thursdays and Saturdays; on the three other working days two of the clerks went to the Rolls while the other two made summaries of the information received from Williamson's foreign correspondents. The stints on writing days are thus defined:

The number of the letters that each wrote was, on Tuesday, 16 letters, viz. 4 long letters (which are those that contain the whole week's col(lection?) and 12 short (which is 2 dayes newes only); on Thursday, 13 letters, 3 long and 10 short; and on Satturday 7 long, 4 of 4 dayes newes, and 8 short; but now by Mr. Charles not being able to write above 4 letters a day the business will lye much heavyer upon us all.

Despite working under continuous pressure they have made 'the letters long and farr longer then they were before'.[95] Except in the case of Mr Charles, the appointment forced on them by a royal mistress, the expectation was that the production of fourteen long letters, four containing four days' news, and thirty short letters would occupy three days' work and represent a labour cost of a little under six shillings. The standard format of a newsletter, which would have applied for the longer letters, was a single folded sheet with between three and three-and-a-half pages of fairly densely written text. The four-day and short letters were more likely to occupy three pages of a half-sheet. While any calculation of rates can only be guesswork, we will probably not err too badly if we allow for an output equivalent to around twenty-four full sheets per writer per week, or eight a writing-day, which would give a labour cost of about 3*d*. per sheet. By comparison the lowest rate cited by Thomas Powell in 1623 for copying at the Rolls was 2*d*. a sheet for an additional copy of documents which had previously been engrossed at 4*d*. a sheet in the special hand used for this purpose.[96]

---

[95] *Letters to Sir Joseph Williamson*, pp. 164–5. Evelyn noted in the same year, that Williamson was 'a severe Master to his Servants' (*Diary*, iv. 39).

[96] *The attorney's academy* (London, 1623), pp. 75–7.

The relative cost of scribally and print-published texts

Any notion of a market in manuscripts within which price levels would set themselves as the result of buyer choice and competition between suppliers would be an illusion. As the earlier account of author publication will have demonstrated, many manuscripts were presented in the expectation of a gift or exchange rather than sold for a fixed sum. In the more hard-nosed field of entrepreneurial publication, transactions were of a bespoke nature, with the price a matter of negotiation between the customer and the supplier. None the less there are times when manuscripts appear side by side as items of commerce with printed books and we are able to make direct comparisons between the two kinds of product. Lenore F. Coral cites a catalogue of music issued by Henry Playford in 1698 which contains 'Bassani's Sonata's printed' for 10s. and the same 'fairly Prick'd' for £1. 10s., and Corelli's op. 1–4 for £2 engraved and £6 in manuscript—suggesting that scribally published music was about three times the price of engraved music.[97] This is not much help in establishing a ratio between the handwritten text and the products of letterpress printing but it does establish that 'fairly Prick'd' music was a luxury product for which Playford's customers were prepared to pay high prices, as for practical performance there could have been little advantage over even fair quality engraving.

In other cases it was the forbidden nature of the texts that justified their high price rather than their being in handwritten form. Yet there must also have been cases where the number of copies needed was so low as to make scribal publication more attractive on economic grounds alone. Leaving aside the privileged position of the scribal publisher with regard to texts which could only be printed with danger, and the various non-commercial motives which could lead to the choice of one or the other avenue, there remained an area of low-volume publication in which he was simply able to offer a cheaper service than the printer. It is true that printers did at times produce what appear to us to be abnormally short runs. In the Ackers ledgers, of a later, slightly higher-priced period, we find fifty copies of Elliston's *Devotional offices* (15.25 sheets) at a unit production cost (rounded to the nearest farthing) of

---

[97] 'Music in English Auction Sales', p. 76.

3s 8¾d. per volume; seventy-five three-volume sets of *The journal and proceedings in Georgia* (91.5 sheets octavo) at 14s 7¾d., 100 copies of a sermon of two and a half sheets at 3¼d., and 100 of eight sheets of *The devout communicant's companion* at 11d., prices which even after the bookseller's mark-up would have been strongly competitive with handwritten work.[98] Runs of this length are not uneconomic in any absolute sense: it is simply that over a run of thirty to forty copies the cost of composition was still the predominant element, whereas over one of 5000 this would be negligible. Still, below a certain level, it would have become possible to supply a handwritten copy for less than the cost of a printed one. My own view is that even at twenty copies print was still competitive with manuscript, but that below that we enter an area where the advantage would depend on the capacities of individual craftsmen and the nature of the text. Further interrogation of the figures is ruled out by the difficulty of estimating the cost of presswork over very small runs in which the actual pulling of sheets would be a minor item beside the time spent in make ready; but by any calculation the cost of setting and printing ten copies of a printed sheet can hardly have been less than the cost of a week's labour by a scribe.

None the less, in author or entrepreneurial publication, it was probably only on rare occasions that the question of relative cost was the crucial one in a decision to use one rather than the other medium. For the entrepreneurial publisher, the handwritten text was a specialized product to be sold to the well-off at a handsome premium for its rarity or danger, while for the author-publisher it was simply the accustomed way of addressing a particular kind of readership. In user publication, on the other hand, much copying may well have been undertaken because the employment of the writer's own labour made it a cheaper way of acquiring reading matter than the purchase of printed books. This must particularly have been true of the lesser clergy whose educated tastes were poorly served by stipends which were often well below what could be earned by a clerk or compositor in steady employment. Parson Adams's *Aeschylus* in Fielding's *Joseph Andrews* was not copied out by hand from choice but because he was unable to

---

[98] *Ledger*, pp. 156, 45, 51.

afford a printed edition. Even among the aristocracy, frequently spending well in advance of their receipts, there may well have been a perceived advantage in restricting writings to manuscript.[99]

THE BUILDING OF COMPOSITE COLLECTIONS

The example of the 1629 *Commons debates* enabled us to ask profitable questions about the ways in which larger collections were constructed out of smaller ones. Throughout the century there was an eager demand for collections of related pieces. The bulk of our surviving texts of political material which was originally circulated as separates has come down in this form, and the pattern is repeated in the verse anthologies, the musical part-books, the collections of antiquarian records and other specialized compilations.

Once in circulation, separates of this kind had a strong tendency to cluster. This was because the individual separate usually documented only one part of an ongoing, public process whose records needed to be assembled in much fuller form if they were to be comprehensible. Once related materials had been gathered as bundles of separates, it was often convenient for their owners to copy them into a bound 'paper book', after which the originals might well be abandoned to the kitchen or the privy. The indexed, fair-written volume of satires or political papers, and the set of bound music part-books were in every way easier to use than what they replaced. The entrepreneurial publisher, on the other hand, might well continue to copy from the original bundles, both to economize on labour and so that the resultant collection could be revised and updated at will.

An understanding of the processes by which such collections grew, and varied in growing, is obviously of central importance to any consideration of scribal publication; moreover, it is one that can be obtained to a large extent on the basis of evidence internal to the text. The classic 'rolling archetype' of the scribal publisher is to be considered in a later chapter; but it will be useful here to give examples of the different, because conflationary as well as

---

[99] For the depleted purchasing power of these two classes of reader, see Plant, pp. 42–6. Lawyers, by contrast, were perceived as an exceptionally wealthy group.

appropriative, procedures that gave rise to the parliamentary compilations. Notestein and Relf in their later publication with Hartley Simpson of the 1621 Commons debates present an analysis of a compilation which they call 'the anonymous journal X', which proves to be particularly revealing in this regard. The document was known to them from five principal sources. Of these, MS 1 and MS 2 represent the work in its finished form as 'a day by day narrative in which various accounts, separates, etc., have been put together to make a detailed record of the proceedings of the Commons'.[100] MS 4 and MS 5 contain excerpts from the longer text, with, in the second case, an interpolation from another source. MS 3, on the other hand, is a document of the kind hypothesized as the foundation of the 1629 *True relation*—a connected narrative of the parliament, though in this case not in finished professional form. Instead, it ranges from a fairly detailed and connected record to 'rough jottings which before they grew cold meant something to the original note-taker' (p. 7). Its importance is that it was one of two diary sources used by the compiler of MS 1. The second source does not survive and its contents must be guessed at from those portions of MS 1 which are not derived from MS 3 or other known sources. It would appear that the second source was more comprehensive, but less well written. Comparing the two, the editors state that 'The unknown diary is labored and the work of a persistent person. MS 3 is the work of an intelligent and penetrating mind who is, however, irregular in recording' (p. 10). Our present interest, though, is in the work of the compiler who unified two diary sources and a body of separates into the fuller record represented by MSS 1 and 2. This compiler's work is at times highly skilled and at others rather stupid—perhaps, the editors suggest, because it had been left to an assistant. But overall:

Depending mainly on MS 3 and the unknown source, the compiler has shown skill in weaving his materials together and in reconstructing a narrative from them. If at times he makes errors, he atones for them by an astonishing accuracy at other times. Not only has he shown ability in placing speeches from two or three different records of a day's

---

[100] *Commons debates 1621*, ed. Wallace Notestein, Frances Helen Relf and Hartley Simpson (New Haven, Conn., 1935), i. 6.

proceedings but he has sometimes with ingenuity pieced together from the stray offerings of various accounts a substantially complete version of a single speech. MS 3 will have a speech by Sir T. B. in a few brief sentences. In the compilation those sentences will all appear, each put in its proper place in the whole, a fact which can be readily tested from other diaries. . . . The compiler must have had helpful notes from his unknown source, yet he seems to have realized that the notes in MS 3 were better and to have inserted them whenever he could (p. 8).

Something very similar is described by Fuller as the procedure by which he had constructed the texts of his printed *Ephemeris*:

Sometimes one *copie* charitably relieved another, nor was it long before the defects of the same *copie* were supplied out of that other *transcription*. Thus neither is there being for *Books*, nor *living* for *men* in this world, without being mutually beholding one to another; & he who lends to day, may be glad to borrow to morrow.[101]

and by Simonds D'Ewes in his account of how he compiled a manuscript record of the parliaments of Queen Elizabeth:

I had occasion this instant March to pass over some days in discoursing, journeying and visiting: yet did I spend the greater part of it in transcribing some abstracts of Tower records I had borrowed, and in the beginning of a memorable and great work, which I afterwards finished; which, though it were upon the matter, except some few lines here and there, wholly written by an industrious servant I then kept, who wrote a very good secretary and Roman hand, yet it cost me many months' time to direct, compare, and overview, because it was framed up out of many several manuscript materials, with some little helps gathered out of some printed books. This work contained all the journals both of the Upper House and the House of Commons, of all the Parliaments and Sessions of Parliament during all Queen Elizabeth's reign; gathered out of the original journal-books of both the Houses, which I had the most free use of from Henry Elsing, Esq., clerk of the Upper House, and John Wright, Esq., clerk of the House of Commons. Into which, in the due places, (unless in some few particulars where I was fain to guess,) I inserted many speeches and other passages, which I had in other private journals in MS., and in loose papers. I added also many animadversions and elucidations of mine own where occasion served.[102]

Such intricate mosaic-work, indispensable when the materials at

---

[101] Fuller, *Ephemeris parliamentaria*.
[102] *Autobiography*, i. 409–10.3

hand were independent transcriptions of oral originals, is otherwise encountered only when a scribe or reader had some particular reason to suspect the completeness or accuracy of a scribally transmitted text. But it is valid testimony to a wider practice of agglutinative compilation that characterizes the whole range of scribal publication. At one level, knowledge encountered in fragments, and often further fragmented through the processes of transmission, encouraged a counterpoising activity of reconstitution. At another, new texts of a given kind were added to existing compilations in a process which, once initiated, might well extend to the proportions of a five- or six hundred-page volume. (Examples will be discussed in later chapters.) Whatever else it may be safe to assume about the regularities of scribal publication, there can be no doubt about the strength of this impulse towards the generation of larger and larger forms of the compiled text, a practice that ends only when the upper limit of manageable size is reached, after which, as we will see later, the process becomes one of a simultaneous gaining and shedding of elements. Parliamentary compilations present some of our best, because fullest, evidence of the workings of this process, but will come to be understood, in this as in other respects, only when we are able to study them as part of a much wider practice.

CONCLUSION

Our investigation into the work practices of scribal publishers has revealed a situation not very different after all from that which affects studies of print publication, namely that while the physical work involved in production can be described in some detail, the wider trade context of that work can only be guessed at by inductive reasoning from evidence which is often imperfect and nearly always capable of more than one interpretation. But while a vast and concentrated scholarly enterprise has been directed to assembling the empirical evidence for print publication, that for scribal publication in our period still remains largely unexplored, or, where it has been explored, is dispersed and unintegrated. If the present chapter has not been able to do very much to remedy this situation, it has, I hope, indicated the kinds of evidence we now need to search for and some of the uses to which it might be put.

PART II

SCRIPT AND SOCIETY

4

SOME METAPHORS FOR
READING

THE previous chapters have dealt with the production and transmission of scribally published texts. I would now like to enquire how these were perceived by their original readers to differ from printed and oral texts, a topic that will require a more theoretical orientation than has so far been adopted. We will need for a start to consider, drawing on the insights of Walter J. Ong and Jacques Derrida, how the oral, the chirographical and the printed text each presuppose their own distinct modes of knowing. We will then need to test our theoretically derived predictions against a range of figurative formulations of the acts of reading and inscription actually current during the seventeenth century. Lastly I wish to consider the role played by the handwritten text in the constitution of 'fictions of state'—those figurative constructs that were invoked to legitimize the exercise of political authority.

'PRESENCE' AND THE SCRIBAL TEXT

One of the major debates of contemporary literary theory has centred on whether 'presence' is to be accepted as an inherent constituent of discourse. The concept itself is a complex one, having roots both in the psychology of utterance and in theology (God present in all things as the cause of their being). Ong, drawing on a heady synthesis of Thomistic theology, structuralist anthropology and McLuhanite media analysis, argues that presence is an attribute of the oral which becomes dissipated as words are encoded as writing and print.[1] This position is asserted as part of

[1] See his *The presence of the word* (New Haven, Conn., 1967), *Orality and literacy: the technologizing of the word*, and *Fighting for life: contest, sexuality, and consciousness* (Ithaca, NY,

a broader investigation into the ways in which language and thought are conditioned by the circumstances under which texts are encountered in any given culture—whether orally, chirographically, typographically or electronically. Chirographical transmission represents an intermediate stage between oral and typographical transmission in which the values of orality—and the fact of presence—are still strongly felt. The written word is therefore more likely than the printed word to promote a vocal or sub-vocal experience of the text, and a sense of validation through voice. Because it is easier for an author or, indeed, a reader to intervene in the process of transmission, manuscripts remain 'closer to the give-and-take of oral expression' and their readers 'less closed off from the author, less absent, than are the readers of those writing for print'. A manuscript-based culture preserves 'a feeling for the book as a kind of utterance, an occurrence in the course of conversation, rather than as an object', whereas the printed book is 'less like an utterance, and more like a thing'. Print 'situates words in space more relentlessly than writing ever did', thus giving them the status of objects rather than experiences and separating off the apprehension of meaning from an awareness of presence.[2]

Derrida rejects both this priority assumed for speech and the 'reality' of presence. His first formulation of the deconstructive approach to language was directed against the reliance of Western philosophy on a 'metaphysic of presence' through which speech was credited with a capacity to generate self-validating meaning, while writing, viewed as derivative from speech, was denied this

1981). Ong's work also needs to be placed in the context of a broader body of writing on the ways in which cultures and individuals negotiate their way among oral, chirographic, typographic and electronic modes of communication. Of relevance to the present study are Richard Bauman, *Let your words be few: symbolism of speaking and silence among seventeenth-century Quakers* (Cambridge, 1983); David Cressy, *Literacy and the social order*; Ruth Finnegan, *Literacy and orality: studies in the technology of communication* (Oxford, 1988); Jack Goody, *The interface between the written and the oral* (Cambridge, 1987); Alvin Kernan, *Printing technology, letters and Samuel Johnson* (Princeton, NJ, 1987); D. F. McKenzie, *Bibliography and the sociology of texts* (London, 1986) and 'Speech-manuscript-print' in *New directions in textual studies*, ed. Dave Oliphant and Robin Bradford (Austin, Tex., 1990), pp. 87–109; and Marshall McLuhan, *The Gutenberg galaxy: the making of typographic man* (Toronto, 1962). In opposition to Kernan, Ong and McLuhan, Finnegan doubts the existence of 'a clear-cut and non-problematic association between *literacy* or *orality* on the one hand and specific cognitive processes on the other' (p. 150).

[2] Ong, *Orality*, pp. 132, 125, 131, 121. Cf. Pebworth, 'John Donne, coterie poetry, and the text as performance', pp. 65-6.

capacity. The metaphysic is seen to rest on the two assumptions that there is somehow a point where meaning *begins* and that this is to be identified with the moment at which words find spoken or mental utterance. Deconstruction, as is well known, draws with qualifications on the Saussurean view that, since each signified has to be constituted negatively from other signifieds within language viewed as a system of differences, it can never be self-validating or originary. It is this conception of language as the unfinalizable play of signification which Derrida subsumes under the signifier 'writing' and sets in opposition to the metaphysic of presence. The speaker or subject, who under the metaphysic is the source of validation for meaning, now becomes no more than the 'space' within which the play of signification takes place. However, this view does not negate the traditional 'logocentric' project: Derrida's more radical point is that neither can have meaning apart from the tension of its relationship with the other.[3]

Ong, in criticizing this view, reasserts the metaphysic of presence and with it the proposition that the spoken word is more fully human than the written, but sees the distinction drawn by Derrida as a valid report on the way modes of inscription influence our perception of reality.[4] In his stress on the ability of print to empty words of presence, Ong's perception of its function has a superficial similarity to Derrida's of the more general condition of *écriture*, but, whereas Derrida's 'writing' is premised on a perpetual deferment of closure, Ong sees that print both resists *and* demands closure, the latter because it reduces language to the appearance of an exactly replicable object and because print production is crowded into a single, definitive press run. Moreover, not only does it try to insist that the text presented is final and unalterable

---

[3] The fullest exposition of these views is in Derrida's *Of grammatology*, trans. G. C. Spivak (Baltimore, 1976). There is a lucid summary of his position in Christopher Norris, *Deconstruction: theory and practice* (London, 1982). The papers in which Derrida comes closest to the concerns of the present study are those in which he considers the supposed authenticating power of the written signature as a displaced version of the supposed priority of speech over writing, as in 'Signature, event, context', *Glyph* 1 (1977), 172–97 (also in his *Marges de la philosophie* (Paris, 1972), pp. 365–93). For an acute, deconstructive study of the culture of writing, see Goldberg, *Writing matter*, discussed later in this chapter. Among hostile critiques of deconstruction, particular attention should be given to Anthony Giddens, 'Structuralism, post-structuralism and the production of culture' in *Social theory today*, ed. Anthony Giddens and Jonathan Turner (Cambridge, 1987), pp. 195–223.

[4] Cf. *Orality and literacy*, pp. 101–3.

but it imposes this condition of the text's existence upon its readers as a metaphor of the nature of knowledge, giving rise to what Alvin Kernan describes as 'print's remarkable ability to confer authoritative being and firm truth on its texts'.[5] In this and the other senses discussed, an increase in the perceived objectification of the word through print is to be seen not as a liberation of the possibilities of meaning but as a more rigid form of subjugation. It is the presence-rich chirographic text which becomes the arena of freedom. The freedom offered by typography is narrowly and specifically the freedom *from* presence (Derrida's conception); but it also brings with it a new tyranny arising from the object-like status of the typographic page and the hypostatization of language as possessing a reality independent of specific human acts of utterance and audition.

While the Derridean insight into the constitution of the sign is not an immediate concern of the present discussion, the opposition speech/writing, as formulated by Ong, has obvious bearing on any attempt to theorize the relationship between spoken language and the two kinds of written signifier we are concerned with—the chirographical and the typographical. The notion of 'presence', whether or not regarded as philosophically sustainable, provides us with a method of discriminating between modes of signification as being more or less distanced from a *presumed* source of self-validating meaning. Such a spectrum exists within speech itself to the extent that the capacity of an utterance to invoke the authority of presence is exercised at descending levels of plausibility by the sound of one's own voice, by that of another person addressing one directly, by a voice heard over the telephone, by words heard indistinctly over a public address system in a busy airline terminal, by the raised pitch levels of a diver speaking from within a diving helmet, by the voices of the dead from old recordings, and so on. One might differ over the placing of a particular speech experience on the spectrum but the principle is clear enough. Moreover, there is a point on the spectrum at which certain forms of writing might be regarded as bearing stronger intimations of presence than certain forms of speech. In Chinese tradition such claims are frequently made for calligraphy as against the spoken word, while

[5] *Printing technology*, p. 165.

in the West inscriptions using the writer's blood for ink have always been afforded a highly privileged status, and were generally preferred over vocal attestation in such important matters as pacts with the devil and appointments to the crews of pirate ships. Within the more conventional modes of inscription, a sub-spectrum along the axis chirography–typography–electronography might be formed thus: authorial holograph, scribal transcript, typewritten transcript with manuscript corrections, typewritten transcript without corrections, words printed from copper or steel engraved plates, computer printout, lithographic printing, raised surface printing, baked clay tablets, braille, skywriting with aeroplane, words seen on a TV screen or VDU, neon sign—by each of which the sign is progressively removed from an assumed source of validation in the movement of the author's fingers and relies instead for signifying power on its locus within an autonomous universe of signs.

These concepts need to be applied with some delicacy to writers who persisted in the use of manuscript transmission within a society that was already fully exploiting the possibilities of print; but they also give rise to an expectation that seventeenth-century writers might not only write differently but also adopt different conceptions of the function of writing as they turned from one medium to the other. It is interesting in this respect to note that the major writers of the period tend to display a strong disposition towards one particular medium, and that writers exhibiting these opposed positions often appear chronologically in pairs. Thus, against Spenser as a print-fixated poet, we might set Donne as one committed to manuscript. For Spenser, that *The faerie queene* should be print-published and circulated to as wide a readership as possible was an indispensable premise of its strident nationalism, its Puritan didacticism and its claim to stand as a worthy continuation of the great tradition of European epic.[6] But equally to the point is the look of the poem on the page, its magisterial succession of stanzas, each grounded on the concluding Alexandrine, progressing past with the air of a fleet in full sail—a design that, despite its

---

[6] One could argue, of course, that this is an immense confidence trick on the part of a narrative whose aim is, in Jonathan Goldberg's words, to 'induce frustration [and] . . . deny closure' (*Endlesse worke. Spenser and the structures of discourse* (Baltimore, 1981), p. xii); and one would have to answer that it does this too.

145

Italian and Chaucerian forerunners, seems so perfectly adjusted to the strengths of Renaissance typography. Donne, on the other hand, the leading non-dramatic poet of the next generation, not only rejected print but does not even look particularly distinguished in print. Whereas the typographical designer's art is based on the repetition of standardized visual patterns, whether they be type-pieces, fleurons, or stanzas, within a harmoniously balanced page, Donne's art leads to bizarrely shaped and constantly varied stanzas—even in some cases within the same poem. His stanza pattern for any given poem is determined by the requirements of the thought, without consideration for visual effect, and as the thought is invariably knotty and intricate, so are the stanzas, in a great many instances, straggly and gnarled. In this, in Donne's concentration as a writer on private experience, and in his uncompromising intellectuality, he was consciously opposing the values of the open market and the promiscuously purchasable page created by print.

Shakespeare and Jonson form another such pair, this time contemporaneous. Rejecting Shakespeare's disdain, as a dramatist, for the typographical medium (discussed in Chapter 3), Jonson took extraordinary care over the printing of his plays and in the 1616 folio produced one of the great typographical monuments of his age. In the 1605 quarto of *Sejanus*, as Philip Ayres has pointed out, the very look of the page, with its severe columns of verse flanked by marginal scholia and with the proclamations set in the style of a Roman lapidary inscription with medial stops between each word, was meant as an iconographic expression of its subject.[7] With Dryden and Rochester, to whom we will be returning shortly, the distinction occurs in an exceptionally revealing form. Rochester, the courtier, subscribed to an aesthetic of improvisation in writing as in everything else, being valued as much for his witty conversation as for his verse. He wrote for a small circle of friends, who saw the poems in manuscript, and seems to have had no interest in their future fate. Dryden, 'saturnine' and reserved in

---

[7] 'The iconography of Jonson's *Sejanus*, 1605: copy-text for the Revels edition', in *Editing texts: papers from a conference at the Humanities Research Centre*, ed. J. C. Eade (Canberra, 1985), pp. 47–53. John Jowett, 'Jonson's authorization of type in *Sejanus*', pp. 254–65, argues for the typography of the edition permitting a manuscript-like immediacy of access to the author; however, this was lost in the folio where the play was stripped of its Roman dress to fit the overall design of the volume.

company, found self-expression through the polished period and the balanced couplet, carefully and professionally working up the effects which to Rochester were a matter of spontaneity. His audience was a public not a private one, ranging in size from the 'town' to the nation, and was addressed as a matter of course through print.

Specialists in one medium would sometimes make revealing excursions into the other. Dryden took a holiday from print to write *Mac Flecknoe* which, withheld from the press, circulated alongside Rochester's verse in scribally published miscellanies, and which might well be read as a demonstration to Rochester, who in 'An allusion to Horace' had reproved Dryden for lack of conversational brilliance, of how well a skilled professional could recreate his own manner. *Mac Flecknoe* differs from every other known poem written by Dryden to that date in being vituperative, scatological and riddlingly allusive. But in this Dryden was simply accepting the decorum of the alternative medium with the same skill with which he adapted to any other decorum. By contrast, his other known scribally published work, the collaborative 'Essay on satire', is a polished literary piece which makes no flagrant departure from print decorums. Donne made the transition in the other direction in a small number of highly reluctant appearances in print. These reveal no attempt whatsoever to write down to a wider public. If anything, in the two *Anniversaries*, written in return for the patronage of Sir Robert Drury, and the elegy on the death of Prince Henry, he produced work of exceptional difficulty, even for him. In the opening lines of the elegy he comes close to self-parody in his determination to show that as a scribally publishing poet he was going to make no concessions at all to print.

Too few writers published extensively in both media to permit any more searching analysis of the effects of moving from one to another. If such a study were to be attempted, the best subjects might well be proselytizing writers on social, theological and scientific subjects such as Samuel Hartlib and Henry Oldenburg, who moved freely between the printed pamphlet, the scribal separate and the personal letter as each was found appropriate to the task in hand. Yet, Ong's distinctions would lead us to expect that a preference for the scribal medium would be accompanied by other preferences. Such writing would be more vocal and less visual; it would address a more intimate community of readers with a strong sense of immediacy; it would prefer freer, speech-like rhythms rather than arithmetically regulated metre, and organic notions of form rather than those reliant on a visually inspired symmetry; it would invite the reader to become a writer by annotating, extending or writing an 'answer' to the text presented. The literary comparisons just made suggest that these expectations are often fulfilled, though there are other cases—the pairing of Cowley and Carew would be an example—which appear, at least on first sight, to reverse them.[8] So while the precise working of these predispositions with regard to one and the other medium is something that must be considered on a case-by-case basis, it will do no harm to approach the next stage of our investigation with a sense of certain opposed tendencies in the two media which, while not always followed through, can fairly be regarded as innate. In applying this insight to political thought, our concern will be to demonstrate how attempts to legitimize the exercise of power demand the prior assertion of a point of origin for meaning within one or other of the realms of voice, script and, latterly, print.

METAPHORS OF INSCRIPTION

These general metaphors for the nature of knowledge projected by script and print undoubtedly influenced the attitudes of individual writers and readers towards the two media; but our distinctions need to be refined by reference to the associations between inscription and life actually made by contemporaries. As my point of departure for an examination of these historically contingent associations, it will be convenient to take a series of metaphors for the act of reading which are discussed in the fifth chapter of Ann and John Thompson's *Shakespeare: meaning and metaphor*.[9]

---

[8] Carew, the scribally publishing poet, exhibits a restraint and elegance which is missing from the self-consciously libertarian Cowley with his love of extreme metaphors and cultivation of the unmeasured pindaric form. However, the evidence assembled by Beal (*IELM*, ii/1, 240–1) suggests that Cowley might better be viewed as a scribal author-publisher who suffered from his work being ruthlessly pirated by booksellers. John Kerrigan writes sensitively on Carew's engagement with the scribal medium in his 'Thomas Carew', *PBA* 74 (1988), 311–50.

[9] (Brighton, 1987), pp. 163–206.

Although the Thompsons' concern with this material is cognitive rather than cultural, they cast valuable light on associations which seem to have been habitual to the period and which, by virtue of their presence in writers as influential as Shakespeare and Jonson, were continually being reinforced.

We begin with a very powerful and deep-rooted metaphor which sexualized the material of writing, paper, as female and the acts of reading and writing as displaced versions of sexual domination of the female by the male. The 'procreative' pen has already made its appearance in a quotation from Thomas Fuller.[10] The metaphor of the woman as page finds one of its most familiar expressions in Valentine's 'mad' speech to Angelica in Act IV of Congreve's *Love for love* (1695):

ANGELICA. Do you know me, *Valentine?*
VALENTINE. Oh very well.
ANGELICA. Who am I?
VALENTINE. You're a Woman,—One to whom Heav'n gave Beauty, when it grafted Roses on a Briar. You are the reflection of Heav'n in a Pond, and he that leaps at you is sunk. You are all white, a sheet of lovely spotless Paper, when you first are Born; but you are to be scrawl'd and blotted by every Goose's Quill.[11]

Despite the fashionable Lockean overtones of this passage, the underlying force of the metaphor arises from an equivalence between writing and sex, found very widely in seventeenth-century poetry and drama. Shakespeare's internalization of it is explored by the Thompsons in these terms:

in *Much Ado About Nothing* Leonato misreads Hero's appearance (presumably her blushes) as evidence of her sexual guilt: 'Could she here deny / The story that is printed in her blood?' (4. 1. 121–2). Othello looks for similarly readable signs in Desdemona: 'Was this fair paper, this most goodly book, / Made to write 'whore' upon?' (*Othello*, 4. 2. 71–2). Here the face is not specified and Desdemona as a whole seems to be paper or book. Another instance where the body as a whole is readable occurs in *Measure for Measure* when Claudio acknowledges that Juliet is visibly

---

[10] p. 17.
[11] IV.i. 631–46 in *The complete plays of William Congreve*, ed. Herbert Davis (Chicago, 1967). Another version of the image is found at the close of the act: 'She is harder to be understood than a Piece of Ægyptian Antiquity, or an Irish Manuscript; you may pore till you spoil your Eyes, and not improve your Knowledge' (IV. i. 801–3).

pregnant by remarking, 'The stealth of our most mutual entertainment / With character too gross is writ on Juliet' (1. 2. 154–5). It is striking how regularly when a woman's face or person is in question, it is her sexual guilt or innocence that is to be read from it. The general tendency is for women to be seen as the books or papers which are to be read by men— having been written or printed upon by other men.[12]

The wider currency of images of women as ' "blank pages" waiting to be inscribed by the male pen/penis' (as the Thompsons put it) has been noted by Susan Gubar, for whom 'women have had to experience cultural scripts in their lives by suffering them in their bodies'.[13] A related image is that of the blot as a sign of sexual stigma, as in Fauconbridge's description of himself to his mother as 'The sonne that blotteth you with wedlocks breach' in *The troublesome reign of John, King of England*, Part 1.[14] Drayton's 'The epistle of Rosamond to King Henry the second' offers a concatenation of such imagery:

> This scribbled Paper which I send to thee,
> If noted rightly, doth resemble mee:
> As this pure Ground, whereon these Letters stand,
> So pure was I, ere stayned by thy Hand;
> Ere I was blotted with this foule Offence,
> So cleere and spotlesse was mine Innocence:
> Now, like these Markes which taint this hatefull Scroule,
> Such the blacke sinnes which spot my leprous Soule.[15]

But there is a no less telling absence: the male writer of love poetry may image himself as either the writer or the reader, but will rarely present himself as the surface being inscribed, this being metaphor-

---

[12] Op. cit., p. 177. Further examples from early drama of this analogy are given in Louis Charles Stagg, *The figurative language of the tragedies of Shakespeare's chief 17th-century contemporaries: an index*, 3rd edn (New York, 1982) and *The figurative language of the tragedies of Shakespeare's chief 16th-century contemporaries: an index* (New York, 1984). R. W. van Fossen in his edition of Thomas Heywood's *A woman killed with kindness* (London, 1961) refers to it as a 'favourite idea' of the dramatist (p. 35n.).

[13] Op. cit., p. 177; Susan Gubar, ' "The blank page" and the issues of female creativity', in Elizabeth Abel, ed., *Writing and sexual difference* (Brighton, 1982), p. 81. The Renaissance notion of the body as directly inscribed by metaphorical meanings found wider expression in icon books, allegorical drama, the Quaker practice of public metaphorical acts (discussed in Bauman, *Let your words be few*, pp. 84–94) and the practice of branding felons with a sign indicating their crime (discussed by the Thompsons, p. 109).

[14] *Troublesome reign*, facsim. ed. J. S. Farmer (Edinburgh, 1911), B4'.

[15] *Works*, ii. 133.

ically assigned as the female role.[16] By the same logic, for a woman
to wield the pen is a metaphorical emasculation:

> How would thy masc'line Spirit, Father *Ben*,
> Sweat to behold basely deposed men,
> Justled from the Prerog'tive of their Bed,
> Whilst *wives* are per'wig'd with their *husbands head.*
> Each snatches the male quill from his faint hand
> And must both nobler write and understand,
> He to her fury the soft plume doth bow,
> O Pen, nere truely justly slit till now![17]

Here the metaphor is one of the male being deprived of his penis by
the writing woman, with the last line punning on 'slit' in the sense
of vagina.[18]

Jonathan Goldberg views the sexualization of writing from a
more complex perspective according to which the emphasis in
instruction books on 'the softness and malleability' of the hand that
holds the phallic pen 'suggests feminization even as it founds the
privileged male subject'. As regards women writers, a series of
double entendres in Dekker's *Westward ho!* arising from an attempt
at seduction by a bogus writing master is read by him as an
initiation into 'fornication, fellatio and masturbation'.[19] Gubar's
darker view that women's writing is 'not an ejaculation of pleasure
but a reaction to rending' is closer to the expressed Renaissance
perception (p. 86).

A related topos is what is described by the Thompsons as the
'sex-as-printing' metaphor. One version of this is present in
Fuller's 'Indeed the Press, at first a *Virgin*, then a *chast Wife*, is since
turned *Common*, as to prostitute her self to all Scurrilous
Pamphlets'.[20] However, the aspect of the printing press that most
vividly imposed itself on the Renaissance masculine imagination
was its ability to produce an endless succession of identical copies of

---

[16] An exception needs to be made for the conceit of the image of the beloved being
transferred into the eyes or heart, as in Donne's 'The dampe', l. 4.

[17] 'On *Sanazar's* being honoured', Lovelace, *Poems*, p. 200.

[18] As in the following couplet from a satire on Nell Gwynn ('I sing the story of a
scoundrel lass'): 'To Thee I doe resigne my Youth and Witt / Then dear be kind, and gently
broach my slit' (Ohio State University MS Eng. 15, p. 225).

[19] Goldberg, *Writing matter*, pp. 99–100.

[20] *History of the worthies*, p. 30.

the type-page. In its metaphorical transformation this becomes an image of patriarchally legitimized procreation. The characteristic form of the topos is one which presents the woman as a means whereby a man is able to produce an exact simulacrum of himself ('Your Mother was most true to Wedlock, Prince, / For she did print your Royall Father off, / Conceiuing you'[21]). In the various forms given to this metaphor the woman may be presented as the press, as the sheet of paper 'pressed' by the man, or simply as a text over which the man possesses copyright—but the recurring theme is the precise exactness of the resulting copy. Through this image of a mechanized, unvarying reproduction of a patriarchal exemplum, printing is posited as the agency by which women are reduced to a state of total passivity. This in turn leads us to two other common metaphors, those of the woman as wax which receives an impression from the male ('She caru'd thee for her seale, and ment therby, / Thou shouldst print more, not let that coppy die'[22]) and as the metal which is cast into the form of a medal or coin, these earlier forms of the concept having a typographical analogue in the punchcutter's 'matrix'. Examples of all three metaphors are given by the Thompsons, but a reader familiar with the drama and poetry of the period should have no trouble in recalling further examples.

In yet another transformation, used by Donne in his Latin verses to Richard Andrewes, the press, as woman, shares in the sin of Eve, bringing forth offspring in pain who are destined for death.

> Parturiunt madido quae nixu praela, recepta,
>   Sed quae scripta manu, sunt veneranda magis.
>
> .   .   .   .
>
> Qui liber in pluteos, blattis cinerique relictos,
>   Si modo sit praeli sanguine tinctus, abit;
> Accedat calamo scriptus, reverenter habetur,
>   Involat et veterum scrinia summa Patrum.[23]

---

[21] *The winter's tale*, ll. 2576–9, in *William Shakespeare. The complete works*, ed. Stanley Wells and Gary Taylor (Oxford, 1986), p. 1294; discussed with similar passages in Thompson and Thompson, pp. 177–83.

[22] Sonnet 11, in *Works*, p. 850.

[23] *The poems of John Donne*, ed. H. J. C. Grierson (Oxford, 1912), i. 397, which should, however, be read in the light of H. W. Garrod, 'The Latin poem addressed by Donne to Dr Andrews', *RES* 21 (1945), 38–42. I am in debt to Hilton Kelliher for the identity of the poem's addressee.

These lines are normally quoted in Edmund Blunden's English verse translation which suppresses the metaphors of the original.[24] A more accurate translation would be: 'What presses give birth to with sodden pangs is acceptable, but manuscripts are more venerated. A book dyed with the blood of the press departs to an open shelf where it is exposed to moths and ashes; but one written by the pen is held in reverence and flies to the privileged shelf reserved for the ancient fathers.' Here the surface on which the text was inscribed has ceased to be an element in the metaphor and the contrast is between the patriarchal pen and the press imaged as a woman in perpetual labour.

The figuring of the press in these terms implies a contrasting position for the scribal text—still patriarchal in its mode of inscription, but free from the suggestion of a controlled, iterative procreation of unvarying simulacra. Certainly the handwritten copy could never serve, as the printed one does, as an icon of marital fidelity: the fact that a given copy may contain the inscription of several hands, and might expect to be reinscribed by successive owners, points towards the implications latent in Congreve's scribbled page of a threateningly catholic sexuality. The woman who has allowed herself to be scrawled and blotted by every goose's quill is hardly going to offer any assurance of paternity in her children. (History has provided an appropriate exemplum in the eighteenth-century countess of Oxford whose variously fathered offspring were known as the 'Harleian miscellany'.) In other words, the modes of reproduction characteristic of print and script pointed, at the level of metaphor, towards a socially approved and a socially disapproved mode of procreation. Viewed in this way, script emerges as the seductive, untrustworthy medium whose texts, replicating themselves by suspect means, must always elude possession.

THE VIOLENCE OF THE PEN

However, other metaphorical equivalences are found for both the handwritten and the printed text. John Davies of Hereford in 'The

---

[24] 'Some seventeenth-century Latin poems by English writers', *University of Toronto quarterly* 25 (1955–6), 11.

muse's sacrifice' (1612) puns on pressing as a form of judicial torture.

> But *Poesie* (dismall *Poesie*) thou art
>   most subiect to this sou'raigne *Sottishnesse*;
> So, there's good Cause thou shouldst be out of heart,
>   sith all, almost, now put thee under *Presse*.[25]

Goldberg in *Writing matter* has built a cultural interpretation of considerable scope on the equation which he finds in early writing manuals between inscription and violence. Starting from a metaphorical description of quills as weapons in Vives' Latin dialogue 'Scriptio', he moves on to discuss the prominence given in accounts of the technology of inscription to the penknife, and the way in which the sharpened quill is itself frequently figured as a knife or dagger.[26] A penknife could in fact be an effective weapon—in the last act of *The changeling* De Flores kills himself with one. But the violence Goldberg is concerned with is the institutionalized violence of the Renaissance state, issuing in the form of racism, sexism and colonial exploitation.

Writing is wielded as a weapon through a series of social positions. The knife works: to produce the quill, to produce the writer. The scene of writing, we could assume after Derrida, is always associated with violence; here, with the very materials of his craft, scenes of mutual violence are staged, openings and enclosures that extend and contain the activity of writing. In Vives or Bales, we can see the paths that are taken once the writer has his weapons to hand. But these scenes can be read too on the pages of the writing manuals, in their descriptions of the instruments, in their demarcations of the spheres in which the writer's hand moves.[27]

In introducing Goldberg we have switched from consideration of the relatively simple figurative transformations actually acknowledged by men and women of the time to the imposed constructions of the twentieth-century theorist. The same kind of

---

[25] *Works*, ii, 'The muse's sacrifice', p. 5.

[26] Goldberg, *Writing matter*, pp. 60–107. Goldberg's deconstructionist argument is too complex to be summarized here. I have done no more than to abstract a few themes with direct bearing on my own concerns.

[27] Ibid. 69. A full explication of this passage would need to return to Derrida's critique of Lévi-Strauss in *Of grammatology*, discussed by Goldberg on pp. 16–55.

post hoc structuring lies behind a number of Goldberg's more extravagant conceits, such as the suggestion that writing on vellum with the sharpened pen is a re-enactment of the slaughtering of the animal whose skin provides the surface, or that the image of the pen as plough shows how 'colonial activity extends from the agricultural metaphor that extends from the writing surface'.[28] He also sees a figuration of violence in the dismembered hands that are used to illustrate penholds (synecdoche as the trope of mutilation), and interprets the violence committed by the penknife upon the pen as a metaphorical self-wounding (see his reference p. 99 to the 'castrative economy' of the penhold). None the less, the image his study presents of the 'armed' scribe who wrote with a knife in one hand, for support and erasure, and the pen in the other is an appropriate one for a century which produced Montrose's 'I'll write thy epitaph in blood and wounds', and Marvell's:

> When the sword glitters o'er the judge's head,
> And fear has coward churchmen silenced,
> Then is the poet's time, 'tis then he draws,
> And single fights forsaken virtue's cause.[29]

But otherwise, Goldberg's account of metaphors for writing credits it with a role in instilling submission to established power that conflicts strongly with the view proposed earlier of script as the medium of freedom, intimacy and individuality, and of the scribal text's essential evasiveness and indeterminacy. In fact, both views can claim historical justification. The apparent contradiction arises chiefly from Goldberg's primary concern being with the invariant international hand of the Renaissance, the italic, rather than the bewilderingly diverse local and individual hands. He is also, in a book that misleadingly claims to be a study of handwriting, almost exclusively concerned with engraved and

---

[28] Ibid. 73; see also p. 64. However, something like the first of these metaphors does occur at least once in a seventeenth-century poem, Alexander Radcliffe's 'The swords farewell, upon the approach of a Michaelmas-Term':

> Farewel (dear Sword) thour't prov'd, and laid aside;
> Thy youngest Brother, *Penknife*, must be try'd;
> That thou art best, needs but a thin dispute,
> Thou woundest skin of *Man*, he skin of *Brute*.
> (*The ramble: an anti-heroick poem* (London, 1682), p. 119)

[29] 'Tom May's death', ll. 63–6.

woodcut images of handwriting, i.e. with printed simulacra. In a passage quoted by Goldberg from a letter of Erasmus, Guillaume Budé is reproved for using so individualistic a hand that Erasmus had to transcribe it before he could read it. Goldberg reads this episode as evidence of a 'disciplinary submission' on the part of humanistic pedagogy to power conceived in Foucaultian terms as totalized and superinstitutional.[30] But it is equally a testimony that writing could be a conscious expression of individualism and a rejection of rather than a submission to the values of the unifying nation state or the universal church. This was certainly the view of writers of English secretary hand, for whom, as we saw in Chapter 3, the forming of a writing style was a conscious mode of self-fashioning. The copy book and the standardized hand were objects of admiration only to those who had an untroubled faith in the goodness of popes, princes and courts, or those who found it politic to pretend they did.

The rich variety of actual practice can be seen at a glance by turning from the specimens of copy-book hands in Joyce Whalley's *The pen's excellencie* to actual contemporary manuscripts.[31] To a modern eye even the mixed secretary–italic and the succeeding round hand often show marked variation from individual to individual. Just as striking is the way in which the hand of the same individual can vary, even over short periods of time, suggesting an impatience with the idea of submission to a single unvarying paradigm. The exact replication of the writing master's forms, which Goldberg treats as the norm of pedagogy, would be rejected by the Bagots as sterile; and there must surely have been masters whose aim was to encourage creative invention in the same way as tailors and fencing masters encouraged their pupils to aim at a distinguishing individual excellence. A musical analogy would be the addition of ornaments or divisions to a plain melody, which, again, was meant to be an expression of the performer's individualism and never to be done the same way twice. Guy Miege wrote towards the end of the century:

As to the . . . *Roman, Italian* and *Round Hands*, there are few Men that

---

[30] Goldberg, pp. 114–15.

[31] For representative reproductions of hands of the period, see the collections by Dawson and Kennedy-Skipton, Petti, Croft and Greg cited in Ch. 3.

write them exactly, according to the Models prescribed by Writing Masters. But every one writes as he fancies, and as his Genius leads him. Insomuch that one may truly say, there are as many Hands as there be individual Writers, it being as hard to find an absolute Likeness between two Persons Writings, as it is to find two Faces or two Voices alike. So wisely Nature has provided against the Confusion which must necessarily arise from an universal Likeness.[32]

The uniformizing tendency attributed by Goldberg to writing certainly existed, and finds a representation in metaphor; but, despite the relentless self-advertisement of writing masters, of which his book gives copious documentation, it was strongly opposed in England by the champions of variety. Goldberg takes the writing masters too much at their own valuation when they claim that the whole of humanist culture is grounded in their craft. Similar claims were made by music masters, dancing masters, fencing-masters, cookery instructors (as in *The staple of news*) and self-advertising pedants of all persuasions. When a common hand did in the end establish itself, it was the flexible, utilitarian hand of the business world, not the courtly template of the pedagogues.

SCRIPT AND THE STATE

Apart from its figurative resonances, script had a number of practical functions, *vis à vis* speech and print, as an agent in the exercise of political authority. The New Historicism (of which Goldberg must count as a maverick adherent) has accustomed students of the literature of the period to read texts in the light of a wider social narrative relating to the acquisition of power by the centralizing state at the expense of older, more dispersed forms of authority.[33] This will be one of the issues to be considered later in the present chapter. However, my immediate aim is the more restricted one of taking the system of power as it was then understood and looking at the roles assigned within it to speech, writing and print respectively. Having done this we will be in a better position to consider the more general question of how

[32] *The English grammar*, 2nd edn (London, 1691), p. 119.
[33] Two already classical examples of this kind of analysis will be found in Stephen Greenblatt's essays 'Shakespeare and the exorcists' and 'Martial law in the land of Cockaigne', in his *Shakespearean negotiations* (Oxford, 1988), pp. 94–128, 129–63.

modes of communication contributed to the framing of myths of legitimacy. My concern will be with what speech–act theorists call the 'performative' role of utterance, and with the circumstances under which something analogous to that role can be attributed to script and print.[34] In mixed acts (e.g. a speech read from a written copy), the dominant medium is taken as that in which the authority of the text is seen to be grounded.

During the periods of effective Stuart rule, power was seen as vested in three agencies, the sovereign, the parliament and the courts of law. In the terms of one widely accepted (though not uncontested) myth of legitimation, the authority of the second and third of these was derived from the king but secured by the king's accepting an obligation to maintain the laws of the kingdom. This was a view elastic enough to be acceptable both to James I in his speech to parliament on 21 March 1610 and Pym in pressing for the impeachment of Strafford on 25 November 1640.[35] In each case power could be exercised through utterance, writing or the use of seals, some actions being satisfied by one of these, but others requiring a combination. In the day-to-day exercise of authority, voice remained the dominant medium. On deliberative occasions, the king was counselled through the spoken advice of his ministers and issued his own conclusions vocally to his advisers and parliament, which he would often address in person. When a message was sent to parliament it was usually a spoken message delivered by a royal officer. Otherwise, the king's agreement to policies was to be gained through the spoken persuasion of favourites. In the other main areas of authority, the law and parliament, power was again exercised through utterance. The two houses of parliament enacted their measures through spoken debate and votes. Although each house employed a clerk to record its decisions and communicate its wishes in writing, the director of its proceedings was, appropriately, a 'speaker', though only known by that name in the Commons. The decisions of the law were delivered in a spoken verdict, and the power to influence

[34] As defined in J. L Austin, *How to do things with words*, 2nd edn (Oxford, 1975), a performative utterance is one which accomplishes what it refers to: e.g. 'I sentence you to death'.

[35] See J. P. Kenyon, ed., *The Stuart constitution 1603–1688*, 2nd edn (Cambridge, 1986), pp. 11–13, 191–3.

those decisions was exercised in most instances through the spoken arguments of counsel. (The famous exception to this rule was the court of Star Chamber whose deliberations, though conducted orally, were largely concerned with written presentations.)

In this context of deliberation, writing was secondary to voice in the sense that it rarely possessed a performative function. However, directions for the execution of spoken commands, whether they were those of the king, the courts or the parliament, had always to be in the form of a written instruction. The king's word might be law but his warrant was required before action could be undertaken by his servants. These documents were written not printed, and were validated by signatures and seals. On occasions, one of which is defined by the scrivener in *Richard III*, they needed to be read aloud in order to have legal force. Here the written document possessed a latent authority awaiting release by utterance, rather than one initiated by utterance.

> Here is the indictment of the good Lord Hastings,
> Which in a set hand fairely is engrosst,
> That it may be to day read ouer in Paules:
> And marke how well the sequele hangs together,
> Eleuen houres I haue spent to wryte it ouer . . .
> And yet within these fiue houres Hastings liued,
> Vntaynted, vnexamined, free, at liberty:
> Heeres a good world, the while. (ll. 1977–86)

Writing was also a source of authority where it served as a record of speech uttered on former occasions. Both parliament and the law were deeply reliant on precedents, and a great deal of energy went into unearthing these from old manuscripts. But this knowledge, important as it was, only became actualized as power when it was translated back into voice within the appropriate forum.

Where writing emerged as of at least equal power to speech was through its use for contractual agreements under the law, including transactions relating to the ownership of property. This also applied to contracts between subjects and the crown, whether individual or, in the case of Magna Charta, collective. Agreements between sovereign states were also performed through the signing of written documents. In some of these cases the document can still be regarded as a substitute for an absent voice; but this could not be the case when the signing of a document was, as frequently happened, an application of closure to the rights of voice, or when negotiations were conducted entirely in the written medium. A parliamentary bill still required to be read on three occasions before it could be passed, but a legal writ existed entirely as a written formulation and would never be uttered in words. Indeed it might be composed in Latin or a long-obsolete version of Norman French, this death of speech being the birth of writing in its modern conception as transcending presence. It was the authority attributed to writing as contract that constituted the most effective counter to the exercise of power through voice. Printing, however great its capacity to sway public opinion, was of minimal importance to the institutional exercise of power, even a printed warrant requiring a validating signature or seal.

FICTIONS OF AUTHORITY

At this point in our discussion the discussion of political practice shades over into the discussion of political fictions, particularly those fundamental legitimizing fictions to which any institutional exercise of power must ultimately appeal. Auden's reply to 'the lie of Authority' was to assert 'There is no such thing as the State'.[36] If there is indeed no such thing as the state (which is unquestionably the case), then when we speak of the state we are speaking of a fiction—a construct of the imagination—and if this is so, all other formulations on which the claim to exercise power is based must equally be fictional. This insight is far from being a new one. To Hobbes the state was 'but an Artificiall Man' in whom '*Soveraignty* is an Artificiall *Soul*', the artifice concerned being of the same order as that displayed by 'Engines that move themselves by springs and wheeles as doth a watch'.[37] To Halifax, a political 'Fundamental' was no more than 'a general unintelligible Notion'.

Every Party, when they find a Maxim for their turn, they presently call it

---

[36] W. H. Auden, *Another time* (London, 1940), p. 114.
[37] *Leviathan*, ed. C. B. Macpherson (Harmondsworth, 1968), p. 81. More generally, advocates of social-contract theories of government have never been in a position to demonstrate that the contracts they assumed had ever taken place.

a Fundamental, they think they nail it with a Peg of Iron, whereas in truth they only tie it with a wisp of Straw. . . . Every thing that is created is Mortal, *ergo* all Fundamentals of human Creation will die.[38]

Machiavelli provided a recipe book from which new fictions could be generated.

This nominalist view of power makes it necessary that, if we are to discuss legitimizing codes, we should do so in their nature as fictions, using the tools employed for the analysis of literary fictions, and, in recent years, also for the law as an authored system. For our present purposes these tools can be regarded as narratology and tropology. Fictions of authority are to be understood as topoi or combinations of topoi organized in relationship to themselves and the world by means of figures. 'Figures' here embraces all the verbal devices of classical rhetoric but particularly the master tropes of metaphor, metonymy, synecdoche and irony, both in their local use as devices of style and their extended use as complex tropes and ideological master narratives. Such fictions may be acknowledged as such without losing their societal utility; but their motivating force is usually stronger if they are accepted as possessing a 'real' existence (in the case of abstract nouns) or comprising a true description of events (in the case of originary narratives).

The relative status accorded to voice, script and print within the political structure will be considered first in relationship to the key social fiction that located the origin of all secular power in the king's person.[39] That power might then be actualized either through the royal touch or the royal voice. Touch was exercised directly in the ceremony of ennoblement and indirectly through writing and the use of seals, these representing different degrees of displacement from the validating body. Touch differed from voice in its being part of a chain of legitimation which reached back into the remote past: in the ceremony of coronation, the king was confirmed in his status by the touch of bishops whose own act of

---

[38] *The works of George Savile Marquess of Halifax*, ed. Mark N. Brown (Oxford, 1989), ii. 220.

[39] Rationalizing contemporary versions of this are given by Barclay, Hobbes and Filmer; however, in its purest form, as expounded and accepted by James I, the theory maintained that the king's power devolved immediately from God. The point must be made that, expressed in this form, it was still a relatively recent theory. Both the view that power

ordination linked them directly with the touch of Christ and the apostles. Touch, therefore, was metonymic, extending through contiguity rather than resemblance. Voice, on the other hand, communicable only through the vibrations of air and fading as soon as heard, could claim no such metonymic force and was a purer example of the ability of the royal person to generate new meanings. Here the operative figure is metaphor—each such act being a re-enactment through resemblance of the world-creating logos. In its extreme form, as embraced in practice if not quite in theory by Charles I, the royal utterance was seen as the source not just of self-validating meaning but of all meaning, since that king presumed upon a moral right not simply to temporize but to lie, i.e. to be a legitimizer of contingent as well as originary fictions. Prudently, parliament chose in the end to deprive him of the organs of utterance.

A corollary to what has been said is that any challenge to the accepted hierarchy of modes of communication was also a challenge to the current legitimizing fiction. In the case of Puritan opposition to the crown in the earlier part of the century, this took the initial form of a reorientation of the authority of voice away from the signification-generating monarch to the inspired preacher; yet, the Puritan preacher's inspiration still came from his internalization of the printed Bible; so, despite the great stress laid on vocal attestation, it was the press that provided Puritanism with its locus of validation.[40] Laudian Anglicanism reacted by replacing the pulpit with the altar as the central focus of worship, in effect an attempt to privilege sight over hearing. The other principal challenge was that of the Common Lawyers who appealed from the authority of voice to the authority of script by assembling a vast body of medieval precedents to buttress their case for the political authority of the judiciary and parliament, which for their purposes counted as a court. 'Between 1603 and 1660', David Douglas notes, 'this literature had grown to a vast size, and claims such as those of Edward Coke that the laws of England had remained unchanged through the five successive ages of the

derived from the people and the Cokean view that power was assigned by and under the law were of greater antiquity.

[40] Puritan anxiety over the relative merits of preaching and reading is discussed in McKenzie, 'Speech-manuscript-print', pp. 91, 100–1 and *passim*.

Britons, Romans, Saxons, Danes, and Normans, won a wide acceptance even from well informed men, as did the similar assertions contained in Selden's *History of tithes*.[41] To Coke, like Hooker, there was no 'intelligible sense in which law could be said to be made'.[42] Inherited from remote antiquity, grounded in ancient written records, and incarnate in its various courts with their assigned jurisdictions, the common law of England was the source from which both king and parliament received their powers and to which they must answer when those powers were extended beyond their permitted limits. This represents yet another case of the logocentric search for legitimation through a fiction of origin, and one that, in this case, is still encountered today in the form of the related Blackstonean conception of the common law, though Blackstone's appeal was to the rationality of the law rather than its antiquity.[43] Today that origin is sited within the print and electronic media. In Coke's time it was to be sought principally among written records, but increasingly *through* the medium of printed commentaries and reports (including his own). However, this transporting of legal doctrine and data from script into print was nearly always undertaken with reluctance, partly because it involved a sacrifice of control over power-conferring knowledge and partly because printed law took on a fixed, unnegotiable quality.[44] When the constitutional break with the authority of the crown was made in 1642 it was on the basis foreshadowed by the Common Lawyers rather than the Puritan theocrats.

The rejection of the royal authority by the parliament disposed for the time being of the fiction of a single, signification-conferring voice as the source of political authority, and initially must have seemed to open the way to a babble of mutually competing voices. In this crisis, recourse was had to relegitimation through writing in the form of the personal subscriptions demanded to the Protestation Oath of 1641, the Vow and Covenant of 1643 and the

[41] David Douglas, *English scholars 1660–1730*, 2nd edn (London, 1951), p. 119.
[42] George H. Sabine, *A history of political theory*, 4th edn, rev. T. L. Thorson (Hinsdale, 1973), p. 419.
[43] The collapse of Coke's view and its replacement by Blackstone's is discussed in Robert Willman, 'Blackstone and the 'theoretical perfection' of English law in the reign of Charles II', *Historical journal* 26 (1983), 39–70.
[44] For evidence on this matter see McKenzie, 'Speech-manuscript-print', pp. 97–9.

Solemn League and Covenant of 1644.[45] In testimony to this reinstatement of the authority of writing, the Cromwellian state saw marked advances towards the creation of a civil service of the modern kind in which administrative decisions were based on the study of written reports. The exhaustive private record-keeping of officials of a later date like Pepys, William Petyt and Sir Daniel Fleming was the effect of attitudes imbibed during this period. The legitimizing voice having been at least temporarily silenced, it was important to fill the vacuum with huge bodies of script.

With the coronation of Charles II in 1660 a fiction of authority based on the originary power of the royal utterance was again in place, but it was a fiction that made little attempt to disguise its fictive nature. This was certainly Dryden's view in 'Annus mirabilis'. In recounting a royal visit to the dockyards, he confronts us with a disconcertingly human Charles II:

> Our careful Monarch stands in Person by,
> His new-cast Canons firmness to explore:
> The strength of big-corn'd powder loves to try,
> And Ball and Cartrage sorts for every bore.

Here the royal touch, severed from its sanctifying metonymies, is totally demystified. But elsewhere Dryden's recourse is to a divinizing Mannerist iconography adapted from that applied to Charles I as the royal martyr, and grotesquely inapplicable to his son:

> Mean time he sadly suffers in their grief,
> Out-weeps an Hermite, and out-prays a Saint:
> All the long night he studies their relief,
> How they may be suppli'd, and he may want.[46]

It was not a matter of concern that the two perceptions were irreconcilable. To Dryden at this time the real danger was that fictions that carried too great a charge of conviction could mislead those who relied on them over the real extent of their power. It was enough in this new world if they were expressed with elegance and bravura.

[45] Discussed from the point of view of the history of literacy in Cressy, *Literacy and the social order*, pp. 65–91. Subscription to these by signature or mark was sought, on a parish by parish basis, from all adult males, with those refusing to subscribe being reported to parliament.

[46] *Annus mirabilis: the year of wonders, 1666*, ll. 593–6, 1041–4, in *Works*, i. 82, 98.

THE FRAGILITY OF VOICE

The special value of literary texts to this kind of historical enquiry is that writers, as specialists in the use of figurative language, will often possess a privileged understanding of the figurative nature of belief systems, and be able to engage in a very direct and revealing way with the master narratives of their culture. In the present case, a text of 1595, Shakespeare's *Richard II*, is of great help in understanding the rivalry between the fiction that linked legitimacy with voice and that which sought to found legitimacy in writing.

The opening scenes of the play present us with the workings of a political culture organized round the sovereign authority of the royal utterance. The fact that the power of that utterance is used capriciously in no way detracts from its performative force. The shortening of Bullingbrooke's exile brings the acknowledgement

> How long a time lies in one little word,
> Foure lagging winters and foure wanton springes,
> End in a word, such is the breath of Kinges. (ll. 485–7)

Voice is figured throughout as breath, its validating power here lying not in its metaphorical recapitulation of the *logos* but in its being an emanation of the *pneuma*. Gaunt's attempts to check Richard's irresponsible exercise of the prerogative of voice fail, among other reasons, because he lacks breath (l. 644). The seizure of Gaunt's property is achieved by a single performative utterance:

> Towards our assistance we doe seaze to vs:
> The plate, coine, reuenewes, and moueables
> Whereof our Vnckle Gaunt did stand possest. (ll. 775–7)

Although the decision has to be reiterated for York's benefit, the second version

> Thinke what you wil, we cease into our hands
> His plate, his goods, his money and his landes. (ll. 824–5)

is redundant. The appropriation has already been made by the act of speaking it.

Richard's misfortune lies in being a king who has failed to realize that the logocentric idealization on which his power rests is no more than a fiction: indeed it is not clear that he ever arrives at that realization. This leaves him defenceless against those who are prepared to challenge the fiction of the primacy of voice with an alternative fiction based on the primacy of writing. Gaunt is the first to speak of this power when he laments that England 'leasde out . . . / Like to a tenement or pelting Farme / . . . is now bound in with shame, / With inckie blots, and rotten parchment bonds' (ll. 673–8). Writing as such is not identified specifically with Bullingbrooke, although it is his 'letters pattents' (l. 1194) that provide the justification for his return and other letters and warrants attend his progress; rather it is a force that Richard himself has unwisely tolerated and which, first in the form of the parchment bonds and later in that of the written agreement by the plotters against Bullingbrooke, is to bring about his ruin.

The deposition scene confounds the figurative basis of the authority of voice by showing that Richard's fiction is untenable even in its own terms. The problem is one encountered in even sharper form in a later play, Nathaniel Lee's *The tragedy of Nero*, where the emperor performs an act of autoapotheosis through a performative utterance:

> Great Julius and Augustus you adore;
> And why not me who have their very pow'r?
> To them you daily offer Sacrifice:
> I am a GOD; my self I Canonize.[47]

The problem here is that the authority assumed by the first part of the final line is not conferred until the second. (Descartes' 'cogito ergo sum', which may have helped suggest Lee's line, labours under the same difficulty.) In confuting its originary status even as it claims it, the line reveals what deconstruction would claim as the condition of all utterance, and which is certainly the case of all fictions of authority. Richard's position, however, is the reverse one: trapped within his fiction he must find a way of divesting himself of the authority of voice through the exercise of that authority. The process begins with a dismantling through voice of the subsidiary authority conferred by touch:

> Now, marke me how I will vndoe my selfe.
> I giue this heauie Weight from off my Head,

[47] I. ii. 24–7 in *The works of Nathaniel Lee*, ed. Thomas B. Stroup and Arthur L. Cooke (New Brunswick, NJ, 1954), i. 32.

And this vnwieldie Scepter from my Hand,
The pride of Kingly sway from out my Heart
With mine owne Teares I wash away my Balme,
With mine owne Hands I giue away my Crowne,
With mine owne Tongue denie my Sacred State,
With mine owne Breath release all dutious Oathes;
All Pompe and Maiestie I doe forsweare:
My Manors, Rents, Reuenues, I forgoe;
My Acts, Decrees, and Statutes I denie:
God pardon all Oathes that are broke to mee,
God keepe all Vowes vnbroke are made to thee. . . .

(ll. 2025–37)

Although the words are accompanied by gestures it is the words which give the gestures their performative status. The dismantling of that which cannot be dismantled, because to do so would destroy the power by which the act must be performed, leaves Richard with an identity crisis so severe that he asks for a mirror in order to reassure himself of his own existence—an existence which must now be reconstituted through sight not sound.

Northumberland, as advocate for a competing fiction by which authority is grounded in writing, now demands that Richard read a document specifying

These Accusations, and these grieuous Crymes,
Committed by your Person, and your followers,
Against the State, and Profit of this Land:
That by confessing them, the Soules of men
May deeme, that you are worthily depos'd. (ll. 2045–9)

The purpose of this is not simply to reassure those who are not present to hear Richard's speech-act, but to indicate that the authority of voice is now subservient to the authority of script. However, Richard indignantly refuses to read. Whether or not he can be regarded as having divested himself of the authority of voice, he has said or done nothing that indicates he rejects the primacy of voice over writing. All his abdication has achieved is to create a situation in which the authority predicated under that particular fiction is placed in limbo. Northumberland again presses his paper, arguing that the commons (sharers now in the allocation of power) will not be satisfied unless it is read, but is neatly evaded by Richard:

They shall be satisfy'd: Ile reade enough,
When I doe see the very Booke indeede,
Where all my sinnes are writ, and that's my selfe.
Giue me that Glasse, and therein will I reade. (ll. 2095–8)

Here Richard picks up the metaphor, more usually applied by
Shakespeare to women, of the face as a paper written on by
experience. However, the concession is only a brief one—
moments later the mirror lies shattered, and Richard in effect
rejects any other than a physical submission to Bullingbrooke, a
decision that must now inevitably lead to the stopping of that
breath that can not help but utter power.

The crucial point that emerges as Richard is led away to the
tower is that, while he has been deposed, the fiction that all lawful
authority emanates from the person of the sovereign remains intact
(as it does, in an otiose sense, in Britain today). What has changed
in the play is that it must now be perceived as a fiction rather than
as a truth, a fact that neither Richard nor Bullingbrooke will ever
be able to alter. Bullingbrooke's assumption of kingship as Henry
IV is not accomplished by a performative utterance but by a simple
statement of intention: 'In Gods name Ile ascend the regall throne'
(l. 1936). He will reign as a king whose power has no originary
basis—an *ironic* king whose rule (like that of Claudius in *Hamlet*)
has to be reconstituted at every turn through negotiation. This is
also to define him as a Machiavellian king, one who must
constantly manufacture fictions fitted to compel the obedience of
others without being permitted to have any belief in them himself.
In a tetralogy of plays already written Shakespeare had chronicled
the dire consequences this conception of the rhetoric of statecraft
was to have for Henry's successors. The ideal, clearly, was one of a
more prudent Richard II. His portrait of that king represented a
powerful plea from the stage, an institution whose own rationale
lay in the power to enforce belief in fictions uttered through voice,
for a monarchy that would restore the same authority to the heart
of politics. James I and Charles I were daringly but imperfectly, to
oblige.

In the terms in which it has just been approached, Shakespeare's
play casts a sharp analytic light on the fictions of authority that
were used to confer legitimacy upon Stuart kingship. While it was
Elizabeth who was heard to sigh 'I am Richard II', it was the

personal rule of Charles I which in both its conduct and its conclusion offered the closest parallel to the events of the play. Charles's great innovation in the cultural poetics of kingship was his conferring a primacy on the royal voice over the written record which (despite Shakespeare) probably had no real parallel in previous English history—even the Conqueror had grounded his administration on a book. Charles's seizure in 1629 of the collections of state papers made by Sir Robert Cotton and John Stanesby and in 1635 of Coke's papers may be regarded as a kind of *coup d'état* against the authority of script.[48] Puritanism was as successful and as unsuccessful as Northumberland and Henry in reversing this priority: removing the man, it could never finally extirpate the fiction.

In contrast to Shakespeare's plea for a politics grounded in the authority of voice, Donne asserted the primacy of script. In matters of religion he certainly saw the authority of writing as the higher of the two. Winfried Schleiner sees this as arising from a conviction, shared with Augustine, that sight is 'so much the Noblest of all the senses, as that it is all the senses'.[49] He concludes that 'Although there are some impressive passages stressing the idea of the sacramental power of the word, Donne holds that God's first language addressed itself to the eye'.[50] In the course of a sermon preached in 1623 or 1624 he used an astonishing metaphor in which an originary 'writing' is presented as the master trope of spiritual obligation:

Beloved, the death of Christ is given to us, as a *Hand-writing*; for, when Christ naild that *Chirographum*, that first hand-writing, that had passed between the Devill and us, to his Crosse, he did not leave us out of debt, nor absolutely discharged, but he laid another *Chirographum* upon us, another Obligation arising out of his death. His death is delivered to us, as

---

[48] Stanesby had collected 'sundry manuscripts, journals, and other passages of Parliament, with divers other notes and papers of several natures to the number of about 300 quires of paper, together with some small printed books'. In November 1629 they were seized in his absence by Thomas Meautys one of the clerks of council. On petitioning the council in 1631 he was told 'that he should have none of his papers about the Parliament, as they intended to suppress such kinds of collections' (*HMC, 4th rep.*, p. 54a).

[49] *The sermons of John Donne*, ed. Evelyn M. Simpson and George R. Potter (Los Angeles, 1953–62), viii. 221.

[50] Winfried Schleiner, *The imagery of John Donne's sermons* (Providence, 1970), p. 153. With this should be contrasted the Puritan and anti-Laudian distrust of the visual.

a *writing*, but not a writing onely in the nature of a peece of *Evidence*, to plead our inheritance by, but a writing in the nature of a Copy, to learne by; It is not onely given us to reade, but to write over, and practise; Not onely to tell us *what he* did, but *how we* should do so too.[51]

Here the use of copying from a copy-book as a metaphor for religious duty parallels the ideal documented by Goldberg of the training of the hand as forming an induction into civil obedience. The companion metaphor of the fall and redemption as written contracts or mortgages is a logical extension of Coke's vision of the common law as the most ancient of all systems of power. In a reversal of the Derridean priority, chirocentrism replaces logocentrism, and speech, not writing, becomes the medium of *différance* in politics as well as theology. Remembering Donne's long connection with the law, first as a student at Lincoln's Inn, then as secretary to Lord Keeper Egerton, and latterly as divinity reader at Lincoln's Inn, it is hardly surprising that his God should have become a scrivener. But he is also a scribal publisher! Jeremiah, Donne goes on to tell us, 'when the hand of God had been upon him . . . published Gods hand-writing: not onely to his owne conscience, by acknowledging that all these afflictions were for his sins, but by acknowledging to the world, that God had laid such and such afflictions upon him'.[52] Scribal publication (Donne's own preferred medium for his verse) is here not simply a metaphor for the origin of power, but the model for how its demands are to be both internalized and externalized by the governed.

A different sense of lives lived under the constraint of writing is vividly conveyed by a play from the very end of the century, Congreve's *The way of the world*, whose action involves a complex attempt to contravene the effect of wills, deeds, entails and marriage settlements. Through one of these Lady Wishfort has gained control over part of Millamant's inheritance. Through another, Fainall thinks he has control of his wife's money. Through yet another, Mirabell possesses the whole of Mrs Fainall's estate in trust, thus negating Fainall's document. By Act v there is also a contract 'in Writing' between Mirabell and Millamant. Finally there is the bogus Sir Rowland's 'black box' which Lady

[51] *Sermons*, x. 196. I am grateful to Mark Allinson for drawing my attention to this remarkable passage.
[52] *Sermons*, x. 200.

Wishfort believes gives him the power to reduce Mirabell to poverty. Within the constraints imposed on action by the handwritten word, the rights of voice are fragile. Conversation must always be guarded—the celebrated verbal wit of the play is predominantly a mode of self-disguise.[53] Only in the famous proviso scene, in effect a spoken, extra-judicial addendum to the written marriage contract, is speech allowed to stand as a source of authority in its own right. The shrinking of the role of voice in private life reflects a sense of its wider decline in the nation in the reaction against Stuart logocentrism.

Neither *Richard II* nor *The way of the world* is concerned with the relative status of print and script within this process. For as long as print was seen as institutionally subordinate to both voice and script, its function could be relegated to that of conveying the decisions of authority to the governed. This was certainly the ideal the Stuart monarchs strove to impose through their close supervision of the printing and bookselling trades. But twice in the century the press became an agency of power in its own right. It did this not through acquiring a performative role within the accepted institutionalization of power (though we will see in Chapter 7 that it was in the process of doing this) but through its ability to promulgate new, subversive fictions with an irresistible force and rapidity. The first of these periods was 1641–9 and the second 1677–82, the fiction in each case being a variant on the old theme of anti-Popery.[54]

By the time Dryden came to write *Absalom and Achitophel*, defending Charles II against the second of these crises, he had seen the ingenious inventions of Titus Oates's printed *A true narrative of the horrid plot and conspiracy of the Popish party against the life of His Sacred Majesty* acquire a greater power over the minds of his countrymen than the utterance of a discredited king.[55] Oates's incredibly circumstantial accounts of imaginary papist intrigues bombarded its readers with a whole new construction of reality, richly metonymic and virtually unfalsifiable insofar as anyone

---

[53] The language of the play is considered from this point of view in my *Congreve* (Oxford, 1974), pp. 85–107. For a wider-ranging consideration of the transactional basis of Restoration wit, see D. R. M. Wilkinson, *The comedy of habit* (Leiden, 1964).

[54] Discussed in Peter Lake, 'Anti-popery: the structure of a prejudice' in *Conflict in early Stuart England*, ed. Richard Cust and Anne Hughes (London, 1989), pp. 72–106.

[55] (London, 1679). Dryden's poem appeared in 1682.

challenging the existence of the plot must *ipso facto* be one of the plotters.[56] Indeed, the study of literary realism in English might more profitably commence with the *Narrative* and its imitations than with *Robinson Crusoe*, which surely learned many techniques from it. Oates's fabrications are not in themselves fictions of authority since they do not aspire to a performative force: his title still accepts the sovereign's person as the source of legitimate power. But they do in a number of indirect ways withdraw credibility from voice and script in order to confer it on their own preferred medium of print. The world of Jesuit intrigue as Oates, William Bedloe and the tribe of informers present it is a world of whispers, covert meetings, overheard conversations and secretly transmitted letters and commissions, all directed towards a horrific overthrow of social order. With voice and script branded as the media of concealment and dissimulation, the witnesses can be credited with the heroic, Promethean act of having transferred this concealed information into print where it was available to all and could be properly assessed. This done, the innate power of print-logic could be exploited along the lines suggested by Ong and Kernan. The well-financed managers of their campaign made sure that their various narratives were given to the public in handsome, physically ample folios with engraved portraits and parliamentary imprimaturs. In this way they were able to appeal directly to the power of the printed page to confer objectivity and impersonality upon the texts it presented and to repress any aspiration to dialogue on the part of the reader, releasing language from the grounding in presence which still attended script and voice. The visual suggestiveness of the printed page was able to achieve a tacit displacement of the phonocentric ideal of authority even while the printed text continued to give it lip service.

Dryden in *Absalom and Achitophel* undertook the task of reasserting the validity of the phonocentric ideal under circumstances that were less than ideal. His presentation of Charles as a divine-right monarch at the close of the poem was one way of doing this:

> Thus from his Royal Throne by Heav'n inspir'd,
> The God-like *David* spoke: with awfull fear

---

[56] Cf. *Absalom and Achitophel*, ll. 664–71.

His Train their Maker in their Master hear. (ll. 936–8; *Works*, ii. 33)

Here and in the speech that follows, the grand originary fiction of the royal utterance as an emanation of the logos was being revived with something like its former force for the last time in English history. Metaphor had, for the moment, triumphed over metonymy. But this revival was by now beyond the power of kings to secure for themselves; instead, crucially, it demanded the services of skilled wordsmiths, working in the medium of print. The service that Oates had performed for the Whigs, Dryden now had to perform for the Tories. The responsibility for sustaining fictions of authority had been passed to the professional makers of fictions, a fact that was soon to lead to a vast increase in their remuneration.

What both Shakespeare and Dryden were eventually led to was a view of power very different from Donne's or Foucault's, or that implied by Goldberg's interpretation of the politics of the hand. For them power was neither autonomous nor originary but something immediate and provisional that required to be recreated at every turn through the arts of language. Wise kings—Henry IV, Claudius and Charles II—were always conscious of this fact: foolish ones—Richard II and Charles I—forgot it. Strangely, though, the foolish kings are also the flamboyant performers— royal actors who press the fictive authority of utterance to its extreme, and nowhere more dazzlingly than in the loss of power. But, fatally for themselves, they are actors who have forgotten that legitimacy has no reality beyond their own projection of an originary fiction.

CONCLUSION

What has been said so far in this chapter will have suggested a number of roles for the handwritten text in the exercise of power so defined, and it is now time to summarize the consequence of these for our understanding of scribal publication. The first role was an executive one exercised through warrants, memos and official letters. This was generally little more than a means to allow the prerogative of voice to operate at a distance, and it was, in any case, rare for such documents to enter wider channels of scribal publication. They are to be regarded as bearers of power only by delegation, whether from voice or from other writings.

A second and much more important role was as written contract and legal record—the body of statutes, deeds, charters and written precedents that set the limiting conditions for the actions of both king and parliament. The Stuart monarchs, aided by compliant judges, did their best to push back these limits; but for a sovereign to override, say, the written law of inheritance would be to undermine the very legitimacy of the crown—a Cokean point that Dryden was careful to stress in *Absalom and Achitophel* (ll. 777–80). From the subject's point of view the defence of ancient rights (especially during the 1620s and 1670s) was most effectively pursued by the searching out of ancient documents which purported to guarantee these rights. The circulation of these older records and their supplementation with current ones (e.g. legal judgements and parliamentary proceedings) provided a significant proportion of scribally published texts throughout the century. It is through these that the scribal medium was most valuably a conduit of power.

The role of the scribally published satire or treatise in its relationship to the exercise of power was usually either the illocutionary one of raising issues which would eventually be debated vocally at the heart of the decision-making process or that of reporting back on the functioning of that process. Where this kind of scribally published text comes closest to possessing a perlocutionary function which is not delegated by print or voice is in the essay or poem addressed directly and personally to a powerful individual. Marvell's 'A Horatian ode upon Cromwell's return from Ireland' is interesting here because of the uncanny accuracy with which it foreshadowed policies which for the historical Cromwell still lay some way in the future.[57] A good deal of this writing (in verse as well as prose) filled a function similar to that of a report or position paper circulating in a modern government department—that is as a means of formulating policies for the consideration of the decision-makers. The writers might well themselves be civil servants, either in form, like Sir Robert Cotton, or on a salaried basis, as in the cases of Marvell and

[57] Cuthbert, 'A re-examination of Andrew Marvell', pp. 172–255.

Dryden. In other cases, the perspective is closer to that of the modern journalist advising and criticizing from outside the political system, but often being able to modify and at times to initiate policies. The chief difference between the seventeenth century and ourselves in this respect was that there was nothing corresponding to our sharp professional divide between the executive, the civil service and the press. A wealthy gentleman, like Cotton, attending regularly at court, could be called on for written advice by both the king and leading nobles without ever holding a formal position in the apparatus of state. In the same way a squire who was not a regular attender at court, like Sir Robert Filmer, could circulate political advice in the form of scribally published essays with a fair hope of it reaching the oral decision-makers.

The last and in some ways most fascinating function of the scribal text was that represented by the sceptical philosophizing of Rochester and the pornopolitics of the lampoon. The function of much oppositional satire, both before and after the Civil War, was explicitly that of neutralizing or evacuating the dominant fictions of state without any serious intention of replacing them with new fictions. Rochester's position—worked out in some detail in his adaptation of Fletcher's *Valentinian*—was that while a literal belief in fictions of authority was necessary for the governed it was a severe impediment to governors. Valentinian was hardly to be condemned (by the standards of the 1670s) for his frank summing up of the noble, patriotic Aecius:

> The honesty of this Æcius
> Who is indeed ye Bullworke of my Empire
> Is to bee cherish't for ye good it brings
> Not vallu'd as a merit in the owner
> As Princes are Slaves bound up by Gratitude
> And duty has noe claime beyond acknowledgement
> Which I'le pay Æcius whome I still have found
> Dull, faithfull, humble, Violent, & Brave,
> Talents as I could wish 'em for my Slave

but errs fatally when he treats his own divinity as if it has a factual rather than a fictive basis:

> Did not my Will ye Worlds most sacred Law
> Doome thee to dye

175

And darest thou in Rebellion bee a live
Is death more frightfull grown then disobedience[58]

The presentation of Charles II as a priapic buffoon in Rochester's 'In the isle of Great Britain' and the darker deconstruction of the mysteries of state in the closing stanzas of 'Upon nothing' are variations on the same theme. The important thing, after the disaster of 1649, was that kings and their ministers should never be allowed to place any excessive trust in the power promised by legitimating fictions. The volumes of the lampooners were mirrors in which rulers could read the truth that their authority, however constituted, rested on ingeniously figured lies, and then, if they wished, break the glass.

The other major function of the scribally transmitted text was that of providing physical and ideological definition for class and interest groups within the state. As this requires a different conceptual approach it will be considered a separate chapter.

[58] BL MS Add. 28,692, ff. 14ʳ–ᵛ, 64ʳ. Only the first couplet of the first passage is by Fletcher.

5

THE SOCIAL USES OF THE
SCRIBALLY PUBLISHED TEXT

HAVING investigated the position of the handwritten text within the cultural symbologies of the time, I would now like to transfer attention to its societal functions. At a very simple level it was one of several means of acquiring and transmitting information, to be chosen in preference to other media according to the audience addressed but also because this was usually privileged information, not meant to be available to all enquirers. A second function which was of great importance was that of bonding groups of like-minded individuals into a community, sect or political faction, with the exchange of texts in manuscript serving to nourish a shared set of values and to enrich personal allegiances. (A modern counterpart would be a group of researchers exchanging results and draft papers by electronic mail.) However, the function with which I would like to begin is that of scribal publication as a means by which ideologically charged texts could be distributed through the governing class, or various interest-groups within that class, without their coming to the knowledge of the governed. Clearly this falls far short of accounting for all occasions on which texts were published scribally; but it does provide our best explanation for the vigour of the institution and the care taken to maintain it even when its existence posed a threat to entrenched interests.

The positing of a distinct 'governing class' is something of a simplification, though one that has precedent in the usage of historians. For our present purpose this class is to be seen as constituting the court and its officials, the aristocracy with their families and clients, the gentry, merchants concerned in the financing of state enterprises, and the upper hierarchical levels of the law, medicine, the church, the army and the navy. To these we should add young aspirants to such positions, which would include university and Inns-of-Court students. Apart from peers and, from 1611, baronets, whose status descended by inheritance, membership of the class was still relatively fluid: the acquisition of land would secure admittance, at least to the lower levels, while the loss of it soon led to exclusion.[1] Yet, while there might well be debate over marginal cases, there was a clear sense in the minds of such contemporaries as Gregory King and Edward Chamberlayne that there was such a class and that its members could be numbered.[2] Stuart monarchs, militarily and administratively weaker than their continental counterparts, were forced to rule through a mixture of bluff and negotiation, which meant that their relations with the governing class, or factions within it, were often conducted as a process of dialogue in which the scribally published text played a very significant role.

The internal structure of the governing class was sustained by two forms of exclusion, one operating vertically and the other horizontally. The vertical form was that of social subordination manifest through elaborate codes of deference and the practice of claiming or yielding precedence in a wide range of everyday encounters. Even so simple a matter as walking along a narrow street, taking one's place at a dinner table or going into church would involve continual decisions about whether to domineer or defer. Individuals soon acquired a very sharp sense of their own place and that of others in a hierarchically ordered society, and, while they might compete fiercely for precedence within their own stratum of the hierarchy, would do so out of a belief in the inherent value of precedence as a principle of social organization. The Civil Wars brought only a partial and temporary relaxation of this attitude. The horizontal exclusion was that set up by allegiances claimed and given within specific chains of lordship or patronage which in some cases were still of a recognizably feudal

---

[1] Cf. J. P. Kenyon, *Stuart England*, 2nd edn (Harmondsworth, 1985), pp. 23–7; Peter Laslett, *The world we have lost: further explored* (London, 1983), pp. 238–45.

[2] See Gregory King, *Natural and political observations and conclusions upon the state and condition of England* (London, 1696) and the tabular analysis of his estimates in Laslett, *The world we have lost*, pp. 30–4. Chamberlayne's more particularized account of administrative and social hierarchies can be found in the annual editions of his *Angliae notitiae, or the present state of England* (from 1669).

nature, and which only gradually began to be subsumed under the wider allegiances of party. Such relationships replicated hierarchy within their own vertical structure but distinguished between individuals of similar status by reference to their allegiances upward and downward.

The paths taken by the scribally transmitted text from reader to reader were affected by both kinds of exclusion. In relationships of patronage and dependence, the client would present manuscripts upwards, either as a bid for reward or an expression of gratitude, and would dutifully copy texts transmitted downwards, especially if they were composed or approved of by the patron. The Donne Dalhousie manuscripts illustrate the first of these processes, consisting of texts presented to the Essex family by a variety of writers who sought or enjoyed their patronage; John Watson's transcriptions of writings by Sir Henry North the second process.[3] Exchanges of texts between individuals who belonged to the same stratum of the hierarchy were likely to be an extension of other kinds of mutual sociability. Matthew Locke's widely copied 'Consort of two parts for several friends' exemplifies this relationship among near equals, the title indicating its status as a gift rather than a plea for patronage.[4] However, circulation might follow oblique or erratic paths arising out of shared enthusiasms (antiquarianism, viol-playing, astrology, sedition). An outbreak of oblique transmission might be an indication that long-accepted exclusions were under strain, pointing to stratigraphical stress within the system. Certainly, the impetus to initiate an exchange of texts within a community (or to create a new community out of the exchange of texts) would frequently have a motive that was either reformist or reactionary. A perception of crisis might lead to the near-simultaneous birth of opposed groups, like the Whig and Yorkist circles of scribally publishing poets of the late 1670s.

By its nature scribal publication could hardly proceed at random. Instead, since it usually rested on a personal agreement between the supplier of the text and the copyist, or copyist and recipient, there was a strong tendency for patterns of transmission

---

[3] Sullivan, *Dalhousie manuscripts*, pp. 4–7; BL Add. MS 18220, ff. 9^r, 13^r, 24^r–25^r, 25^v–26^v, 43^r–44^r, 63^v–64^r, 68^r–69^v.

[4] For the sources, and hints at the identities of some of the friends, see Robert Thompson, 'The sources of Locke's consort "For seaverall friends"', *Chelys* 19 (1990), 16–43.

to coincide with pre-existing communities—the court, the diocese, the college, the county, the circle of friends (*vide* John Chamberlain), neighbours or colleagues, the extended family, the sect or faction. For groups such as these, bonded by the exchange of manuscripts, the term 'scribal community' is proposed. The notion of such a community is illustrated by two papers written in the 1940s by Peter Laslett, in which he argues that the gentry of Kent prior to the Civil War constituted an entity of this kind, regularly composing and circulating handwritten treatises on matters of urgent concern to themselves as a group.[5] A circle of the same period, centred in the midlands, which supported the antiquarian research of William Dugdale, is described by David Douglas and Philip Styles.[6] J. S. Morrill characterizes the Cheshire squire, William Davenport, as 'one of a reading circle who received [scribal] pamphlets and then passed them on'.[7] In these cases, and no doubt others, the scribal community coincided with what historians describe as the 'county community', although not all county communities would have been scribal communities in our sense.[8] Craig Monson's *Voices and viols in England, 1600–1650: the sources and the music* adopts a wider geographical perspective, tracing the regional workings of a tradition that was heavily dependent on scribal publication. Other active and substantial communities are described in Kevin Sharpe's account of the circle of political antiquaries centred on the Cottonian library in the reigns of James I and Charles I, and G. H. Turnbull's group biography of the mid-century Hartlib circle.[9] Author and user

[5] Peter Laslett, 'The gentry of Kent in 1640', *Cambridge historical journal* 9 (1947–9), 148–64, and 'Sir Robert Filmer: the man versus the Whig myth', 523–46. In the first of these papers (p. 149) and again in *The world we have lost*, p. 226, he goes as far as to characterize the Kent gentry of the time as a 'dispersed university'.

[6] Douglas, *English scholars*, pp. 31–2; Styles, *Sir Simon Archer*, pp. 27–30.

[7] 'William Davenport and the 'silent majority' of early Stuart England', *Journal of the Chester Archaeological Society* 18 (1975), 121.

[8] For county communities, see in particular Alan Everitt, *The local community and the Great Rebellion* (London, 1969) and *The community of Kent and the Great Rebellion 1640–60* (Leicester, 1966); Clive Holmes, 'The county community in Stuart historiography', *Journal of British studies* 19 (1980), 54–73; and Laslett, *The world we have lost*, pp. 223–8. Historians are divided over how far the example of Kent can be extrapolated to other counties.

[9] Sharpe, *Sir Robert Cotton* (see pp. 83–9 above); Turnbull, *Hartlib, Dury and Comenius*. The Great Tew circle of Lucius Cary, second Viscount Falkland read early work by Hobbes in manuscript and preserved Falkland's own *Discourse on the infallibility of the church*. There is a sympathetic account of the circle and its influence in Hugh Trevor-Roper, *Catholics, Anglicans and Puritans* (London, 1987), p. 174.

publication, in such cases, was often a mode of social bonding whose aim was to nourish and articulate a corporate ideology.

Testimony to this sense of the scribally circulated text as a group possession is given by the changes that will often be made to the contents of collections when they pass through user copying from their original communities into new ones. An exemplary demonstration is given by Mary Hobbs in her study of the anthologies copied by Christ Church scribes for Henry King as author publisher, though also including work by other poets he admired. These were first recopied in other Oxford colleges, representing distinct but closely related scribal communities. They then passed into circulation in London among two very different communities—the Inns of Court and the musicians (who plundered them for song texts). Their passage from community to community was marked by deletions and interpolations to suit the tastes of their new readerships. Thus, the parallel Oxford collections, while repeating most of the Christ Church material, also contain 'turgid elegies on men of other colleges'.[10]

The findings of these scholars point to the advances in our understanding of scribal publication that would accrue from further systematic study of individual communities, such as is currently being undertaken at the University of Sheffield for the Hartlib group. This approach would be particularly illuminating for the four Inns of Court—Gray's Inn, Lincoln's Inn and the Inner and Middle Temple—each of which had its own intellectual traditions, and which, with their unlimited access to legal copyists, were among the most important centres for the circulation of literary and political separates.[11] Laslett's papers, although light on detail, present a plausible picture of the scribal community as a cultural agency, besides explaining why manuscript treatises of a certain kind should have begun to circulate among the gentry of a particular county in the 1620s. Hobbs's and Monson's work complements this by demonstrating how individual collections of texts can be analysed as communal constructs. Sharpe's study of the

[10] Hobbs, 'Stoughton manuscript', p. 155.
[11] A start to this has been made by Marotti, *John Donne* (Lincoln's Inn); Philip J. Finkelpearl, *John Marston of the Middle Temple: an Elizabethan dramatist in his social setting* (Cambridge, Mass., 1969), and Sandra A. Burner, *James Shirley: a study of literary coteries and patronage in seventeenth-century England* (Lanham, 1988), pp. 41–84 (Gray's Inn); however, the concerns of all three remain rather narrowly literary.

Cotton circle shows how a community could coalesce around a single active individual, but one who himself was formed by an earlier community—Camden's society of antiquaries. The instances of Hartlib and later Henry Oldenburg illustrate how a newcomer with no such advantages could become the hub of an active scribal community through diligent performance of a secretarial role in sustaining the circulation of correspondence and manuscript treatises. Oldenburg's function became institutionalized and partially conveyed into the print medium with the foundation in 1662 of the Royal Society, but Hartlib's primary affiliation remained with the scribally orientated world of reserved knowledge. Illuminating with regard to the tendency of scribal reading circles to seek a closer corporate identity is a formal agreement signed in 1642 by John Dury, Comenius, Hartlib and William Hamilton to govern the conduct of their joint research.[12]

Print could also be used to define communities, and we will need to consider how these differed from scribal communities. Lois Potter has shown how Cavalier writers of the interregnum developed a subtle set of interpretative codes which allowed the public text to be read in a factional way, the community as such being defined by its awareness of and willingness to impose those codes.[13] From subsequent decades, we might consider the role the press played for clergy ejected from their livings under the Commonwealth or the 1662 Act of Uniformity or for refusal to take the oaths of allegiance to William and Mary. Denied the pulpit, some turned to the printed tract as a substitute for the spoken sermon, circulating copies gratis to those who could not afford to pay for them, and using the presentation of specially bound copies to wealthy sympathizers as a form of fund raising.[14] For non-jurors the writing and presentation of substantial works of antiquarian scholarship seems to have served a similar function.[15]

---

[12] Turnbull, pp. 459–60.

[13] Lois Potter, *Secret rites and secret writing: royalist literature, 1641–1660* (Cambridge, 1989). For a more theoretical consideration of the stylistics of indirection, see Annabel Patterson, *Censorship and interpretation: the conditions of writing and reading in early modern England* (Madison, Wis., 1984).

[14] This was particularly so of the 1662 ejectees. One well-documented case, that of Oliver Heywood, is discussed in Love, 'Preacher and publisher'.

[15] The careers of George Hickes and Thomas Hearne both suggest this pattern, the difference being that Hickes concentrated on a single large work, his *Linguarum veterum septentrionalium thesaurus* (London, 1703–5), whereas Hearne issued a long succession of

In all these cases we can speak of printed texts as giving rise to 'communities of the book'. The advent of the subscription list late in the century made these communities publicly visible while strengthening the political dimension of book purchase. In an age when the bookseller was also the publisher, the clientele of a particular shop might form a community in its own right, cemented by common tastes and regular meetings at the source of supply. Beyond this, much knowledge about and possession of printed texts would pass by a series of personal transactions among individuals and families: it was only those key texts whose aim was the defence or overthrow of the political *status quo*, and for which every effort was made to ensure indiscriminate circulation, that could be regarded as wholly transcending any particular pre-existing community of sympathizers.

Yet there remain significant differences between the kinds of community formed by the exchange of manuscripts and those formed around identification with the printed text. The most important is that the printed text, being available as an article of commerce, had no easy way of excluding readers. Inherent in the choice of scribal publication—including the more reserved forms of entrepreneurial publication—was the idea that the power to be gained from the text was dependent on possession of it being denied to others. Thus the quadripartite contract of 1642 between Hartlib, Comenius, Dury and Hamilton contained a confidentiality clause concerning the divulging of their productions.[16] The political aspect of this exclusion is laid bare in the introductory epistle to the printed text of *Arcana aulica* (London, 1652), one of a number of English adaptations of Eustace du Refuge's *Traité de la cour*:

It is some years since I first met with it in a Manuscript, and in a Foraign Language . . . I have since that time found it published in *Latine*, but still as nameless as at our first acquaintance. The divulging of it, seriously, I did

editions of medieval chronicles. In each case, the help given to their research by their many supporters (which in Hickes's case included physical concealment) had a strong political colouring.

[16] 'Visum autem est, et datâ fide spondemus, pacta haec foederis nostri . . . non vulgare ad alios, nisi communi consensu: atque id iis solis, quos ejusdem foederis socios fore idoneos confidamus: . . . Nisi forsan et Patronis ac promotoribus, quos suscitabit Deus, eadem haec patere opus videatur, ad intentionis nostrae integritatem demonstrandam' (Turnbull, p. 460).

much lament, and that for a twofold Reason; One was, to see it come abroad so lamely, and so much injured; another was, to finde it divulged at all: For surely, it is a Tract not intended for the unskilful palate of the vulgar. . . . [17]

Du Refuge's exposé of court skulduggery might encourage 'unskilful' readers to imitate what they should abhor; but even abhorring had its dangers when respect for the English court (whether Stuart or Cromwellian) might be threatened. The extreme case of scribally withheld knowledge was the vast individual databases assembled by men such as Simonds D'Ewes, Daniel Fleming, Pepys, Petyt, Newton and Roger North. Print publication implied the opposed view of a community being formed by the public sharing of knowledge. In this sense the printed text was as likely to be directed at the fracturing of existing communities as the formation of new ones. Its function was Promethean: knowledge exposed in print was knowledge which was no longer reserved for the advantage of the few but retailed for the use of the many. Titus Oates in revealing the imaginary secrets communicated in clandestine meetings and covert manuscripts by largely imaginary Jesuits was specifically claiming this heroic status. Print-based communities were characterized by an openness and flexibility that contrasted with the coherence and inward-turned autonomy of the scribal reading circle. However, in rejecting that autonomy, they also sacrificed the ability to distribute kinds of knowledge of which the state did not approve. The printed text was, with a few high-risk exceptions, a censored and controlled text; the scribal text, a free one.

CENSORSHIP AND THE SCRIBAL TEXT

From the notion of scribal publication as a vehicle for ideological debate within the governing class, we would expect to find it at its greatest vigour in the periods preceding the outbreak of national crises rather than during the actual crisis itself. Once the extremity of the situation had become generally acknowledged, the press should logically become the preferred medium for debate as

---

[17] *Arcana aulica: or Walsingham's manual of prudential maxims for the states-man and the courtier* (London, 1652), pp. A5^r–A5^v; discussed in W. Lee Ustick, 'The courtier and the bookseller: some vagaries of seventeenth-century publishing', *RES* 5 (1929), 143–4.

struggling factions looked outside their own class for support and the underclasses took advantage of slackening control. The truth of this hypothesis cannot be tested quantitatively since only the level of print production, and not that of scribal publication, is amenable to accurate measurement; but it is clear enough that the choice of scribal over print publication was often made through a desire to evade censorship, whether it was imposed by the state or was a self-censorship accepted by writers who did not wish to compromise the façade of governing-class solidarity.[18]

It was thus the case that many who would dearly have preferred to have their works appear in print were forced to choose scribal publication by default. Unable to provide a printed text of the Kentish Petition of 1644, George Thomason obtained a separate for his collection, annotating it 'All wch was Receivd wth much thoughtfulness; but m^{r} Rushworth durst not license it to print'. Aware of the dangers of print, governments of all complexions did their best, when it lay within their power, to control it, the goal of this control, as spelled out in a Star Chamber edict of 1637, being that a printed book should contain nothing 'that is contrary to Christian Faith, and the Doctrine and Discipline of the Church of *England*, nor against the State or Gouerment, nor contrary to good life, or good manners, or otherwise, as the nature and subiect of the work shall require'.[19] There was already a natural tendency for scribally published texts to be oppositional, since, where a text supported the position of those who controlled the apparatus of suppression, there would not only be no barrier to its print publication but probably great benefit to be gained from a public declaration of the writer's allegiances. Oppositional texts would find their way to the press in periods when censorship was weak but withhold themselves when it was strong or particularly unsympathetic to the writer's point of view. The history of the print publication of parliamentary proceedings is one example of this: in periods of relative harmony between the crown and parliament both sides were content to accept the traditional

[18] Patterson, *Censorship and interpretation*, p. 7, describes such self-censorship as 'a joint project, a cultural bargain between writers and political leaders'. However, the bargain was one that only applied to print.

[19] *A decree of Starre-chamber, concerning printing, made the eleventh day of July last past* (London, 1637), C1^{r}–C1^{v}.

convention against it; but in times of crisis—notably the 1640s and the early 1680s—parliament waived the rule so its own case could be put to the people. The 1680 vote on this issue was justified publicly as being 'for the benefit of the clerks who supply the whole kingdom with news', confirming the existence of an established system of scribal publication of political information.[20]

One example of a text neatly suspended between the media is Francis Osborne's *Advice to a son*, a deeply disillusioned piece of 'courtesy' literature which could probably only have made its way to the press under the relatively unconstrained circumstances that prevailed towards the end of the interregnum. Its marginal status is confirmed by the fact that, after its first part had appeared in print without hindrance in 1656, the work was twice the subject of attempts at suppression, firstly in 1658 by the Vice Chancellor of Oxford and again in 1676 by the House of Lords. The second section of the *Advice*, 'Love and marriage', which is described as '*a result of more juvenile yeares*' and only included because the author feared '*if let alone, it might hereafter creepe abroad from under a false impression, and one more scandalous to that sexe, than becomes my Complexion or Obligation*', would seem to be a revision of a scribally published forerunner, though I know of no surviving manuscript.[21] There can be no doubt that Osborne's decision to print the book in 1656 was a deliberate one, if possibly opportunistic. But both the genre and the ruthless realism of his paternal advice link it with scribal tradition: it is difficult to think of it as a work conceived from the start for print publication. The *Advice* may be taken as representing a limiting case of what was legally publishable while the press remained controlled, and of preserving, even when circulated in print, much of the character of a subversive kind of wisdom literature which was usually reserved for manuscript. Halifax, Osborne's most distinguished successor in this genre, never intended the *Advice to a daughter* for the press and did his best to prevent the unauthorized edition of 1688.[22]

Censorship was at its most effective during the periods of unchallenged Stuart rule. In the reigns of James I and Charles I, it

---

[20] *HMC, 12th rep., app., vii*, p. 173.

[21] Francis Osborne, *Advice to a son: or directions for your better conduct* (Oxford, 1656), p. 46. For a sympathetic account of the book, see Wilkinson, *The comedy of habit*, pp. 26–43.

[22] *Works of George Savile*, ed. Brown, iii. 355, 357n.

was exercised in the first instance through the Stationers' Company, which had a responsibility under its charter for preventing the publication of offensive writings. In addition, books touching on matters of faith were supposed to be submitted to ecclesiastical licensers.[23] The method of censorship was reviewed in 1643, when parliament replaced the old ecclesiastical licensing arrangement with a new one under which all works intended for the press had to be approved by licensers appointed by itself—the system attacked by Milton in *Areopagitica*. This initiative did not have its intended effect, and soon ceased to be observed with any strictness. Under the Licensing Act of 1662, Charles II provided for a full-time official licenser with powers of investigation and seizure, a post filled with great energy by Roger L'Estrange; however, the act was allowed to lapse from 27 May 1679 to 24 June 1685 and finally dropped for good in 1695.[24] The practical effectiveness of these official attempts at control over the press varied greatly. The Civil War and the Exclusion crisis saw them flouted with impunity by writers of all political persuasions and came closer than any other period to a modern conception of open public debate.

It should be noted that even the existence of Draconian punishments for involvement in the print-publishing of heterodox or treasonable books was not sufficient to prevent the production of dissident texts, either by courageous, ideologically committed printers and booksellers or for under-the-counter sale at a high mark-up by the trade at large. In both cases, the effectiveness of whatever controls were in place at any time depended on the co-operation in enforcing them of the Stationers' Company. This was always a questionable matter since the stationers felt a conflict of interest between the need to appease the government (which protected them from competition and secured the market in copyrights) and the temptation to profit from the strong demand for dissident religious and political texts. During much of the reign of Charles II the printing of banned Nonconformist tracts was organized by a ring of powerful booksellers within the Company

[23] There is a convenient account of the workings of this system in W. W. Greg, *Licensers for the press, &c. to 1640* (Oxford, 1962), pp. 1–4.

[24] For a fuller account of this intricate matter, see F. S. Siebert, *Freedom of the press in England, 1476–1776* (Urbana, Ill., 1965).

whose position protected them from action by their fellows and usually from the exasperated L'Estrange. Licensed printers were blackmailed into working on such texts by the threat of losing their regular work for the booksellers concerned and interlopers shielded from suppression for as long as they co-operated in the plans of the company.[25] Another tactic was for the company to seize sheets printed by unlicensed printers and then assign them to favoured stationers for surreptitious sale.

Once a book had appeared in print, either legally or illegally, powerful means of suppression were available. Punishments of great ferocity were inflicted on authors, printers and booksellers under the laws against treason, libel and *scandalum magnatum* (the libelling of peers), and seizures could be organized in sufficiently disciplined communities. The discovery in 1622 that a standard work of Biblical explication, David Pareus's *In divinam ad Romanos Sancti Pauli epistolam commentarius* (Heidelberg, 1613), gave support to the proposition that 'subordinate magistrates may rise against their Prince if he interfere with religion' led to extraordinary scenes at the universities in which 'every schollar [was] sent for into ye Publick Hall, & ye Keys of theyre studyes demand^d & theyre studyes search't' while they stayd there'.[26] This was followed by epistles from Cambridge declaring 'the books of Dr. Pareus Bucanus condemned to eternal infamy, and forbidden to be read' and from Oxford 'not doubting that all contagion of his doctrine is purged from the University'. All this served as a magnificent advertisement for the book: within days of a solemn burning at Paul's Cross an Oxford student was warning a correspondent: 'Pareus' book must be sent safely wrapped up for fear of discovery.'[27] In another case, discussed by Patterson, the suppression of a printed preface led immediately to its circulation in manuscript.[28]

All this meant that oppositional texts were frequently circulated

[25] The workings of this trade are discussed in John Hetet, 'A literary underground in Restoration England: printers and dissenters in the context of constraints, 1660–1689', Cambridge University Ph.D. thesis, 1987.

[26] *CSP (Dom.) 1619–23*, p. 396; Bodleian MS Wood D 18, 45^v.

[27] *CSP (Dom.) 1619–23*, pp. 426, 421. The particular sensitivity felt about this text arose from the fact that James I was even then engaged in supporting a rising by the Protestants of France against their lawful prince, Louis XIII.

[28] *Censorship and interpretation*, p. 44.

scribally only for lack of opportunity to appear in print. The question here is, once again, whether the manner and content of the work may still have been conditioned by this, albeit involuntary, choice of medium. There are many suggestions that it was. The author torn between the possibilities of script and print publication, but having decided in the end on one medium, would then have to accept the decorum and the genres appropriate to it. The ruling decorum of print was essentially that which governed the public utterances of gentlemen. A certain level of formality was expected; and while opinions could be expressed with brutal vigour they would appear in the dress suitable to the hierarchical status of the author, who would refrain from language that would cause him to lose caste in the eyes of his social inferiors. Scribal publication, since it would not normally come to the eyes of these inferiors and was in most cases anonymous, offered much more latitude. Indeed, the fact that texts so circulated were expected to be oppositional, and that the liberty was available, whether or not accepted, of using language of a frankness and familiarity that would not have been appropriate in print, encouraged the presence of these features even when they were not required. It must have been hard for the writer of a lampoon intended for scribal circulation not to be obscene and not to traduce the great—this was, after all, what readers expected of such texts. A rhetorically aware writer might even feel an aesthetic obligation arising from the doctrine of the three styles to adopt the language of the brothel in such compositions.

One kind of evidence for this is the many cases of scribally circulated texts tidied up and bowdlerized for later appearances in print; a better one might be the conversion downwards for manuscript circulation of a text originally presented in print—though I know of no actual example. However, the shortened text of Marvell's 'To his coy mistress' found in the miscellany of his parliamentary colleague Sir William Haward could conceivably represent a related process by which a poem written for scribal circulation in more refined times was reworked by its author to suit the coarser tastes of the Restoration court.[29] One is also tempted to enlist the malicious scribal circulation in 1603 of a

---

[29] Bodleian MS Don. b 8, pp. 283–4; facsimile in Kelliher, *Andrew Marvell*, p. 53.

speech by an atheist from the printed play, *The first part of the tragicall raigne of Selimus* (London, 1594) under the title 'Certaine hellish verses devysed by that Atheist and traitor Ralegh'.[30] Here the words remained more or less unchanged but the new title and medium gave them a much more subversive significance.

This sense of the scribally published text as intrinsically prone to be oppositional has important implications for any assessment of its role in national politics. While the needs of individual scribal communities would partly have been satisfied from within those communities and by material filtering osmotically from intersecting networks, it is also easy to demonstrate a supplementary process, particularly evident in the cases of parliamentary news and accounts of court scandal, of radial distribution from London. Any consideration of the spread of anti-court attitudes in the decades prior to both the Civil War and the Exclusion crisis must concern itself with the constant stream of political separates dispatched by the newsletter writers of the metropolis to such readers as William Davenport, which then entered local reading networks. While this activity was not an organized one in the sense the term can be used of the trade in printed books, it was still the work of an identifiable group of professionals who, whatever their individual political views or desire to conform to those of their customers, would have understood that court scandal was the hottest and most saleable form of news. But the possibility can not be dismissed that the writers collectively did tend towards an anti-court position. Nathaniel Thompson, writing in 1683, was in no doubt that 'the generality of News-writers about Town are Factious', a judgement endorsed by Peter Fraser.[31] The reason is simple enough: a court sympathizer would not be likely to become involved professionally in the circulation of information which the court desired should remain concealed.

J. S. Morrill, having noted that the material copied out by Davenport between 1613 and 1650 'was (until 1641) consistently anti-government and particularly anti-Court', then wants to

[30] Text in Jean Jacquot, 'Ralegh's 'Hellish verses' and the 'Tragicall raigne of Selimus'', *MLR* 48 (1953), 1–9. For another widely circulated piece of scribally published Raleighana of the same year, see Franklin B. Williams, jun., 'Thomas Rogers on Raleigh's atheism', *N&Q* 213 (1968), 368–70. This was, of course, the year of Raleigh's conviction for treason.

[31] *Loyal protestant and true domestic intelligencer*, no. 239, 1 March 1682/3, p. 2; Fraser, *Intelligence of the secretaries of state*, pp. 127–32.

conclude that 'the selection of these particular types of material rather than others . . . reveals something of his political views'.[32] Yet as far as Davenport's political *actions* were concerned, he seems to have been a man without strong views, inclining if anything to a moderate royalism. One is moved in this case to ask whether there really had been any process of selection at work, or whether Davenport was simply accepting what was brought to him by a medium which was inherently adversarial to authority but which he could not ignore because it was the only source available to him for certain valuable kinds of information. Certainly we can make no judgements concerning the extent of selectivity when we have no information about the range of options from which the selection was made. If we had that information it might well appear that the medium was very much part of the message and that the message of the London scribal journalists and traders in separates was a 'country' one. Moreover, exposure to such material can hardly have failed to have a radicalizing effect when there was no way of testing such confident assertions as Eglisham's that Buckingham had poisoned James I.

While censorship was an important factor in the continuing vitality of scribal publication, it should not be forgotten that, because of the 'stigma of print' or a level of demand that would never have justified printing, many scribally published texts would not have reached the press at any period. Many others—as we have seen—were designed from the start for circulation within a particular circle or coterie within the governing class and drew their political character from this fact. Their power and influence would be in inverse proportion to the extent of their circulation. These factors confirm that a healthy tradition of scribal publication would have existed even had there been no censorship.

SCRIPT AS A MEDIUM OF INFORMATION

So far in this chapter we have looked first at the role of scribal publication in defining communities of the like-minded, and then at the ways in which the choice of medium was influenced by censorship. However, a full understanding of the societal functions of scribal publication can only be achieved through a consideration

---

[32] 'William Davenport', pp. 119, 121.

of how information of all kinds was transmitted within those classes most concerned with the conduct of affairs.[33] This will also be an opportunity to cast some new light on Jürgen Habermas's contention, first advanced in 1962, that late-seventeenth-century England saw the creation of the modern 'public sphere' and to illustrate the contribution made by scribal publication to this development.[34]

A young man of parts and some education wishing to rise in the world during the Stuart period had a choice between two main avenues of advancement. The first of these, already discussed, was the system by which one placed one's talents at the service of a patron (secular or ecclesiastical) who was usually also involved in the search for advancement at a higher level. Most patrons were male, but in the earlier part of the century a number of aristocratic women performed the role with distinction, while after 1660 the leading royal concubines were courted quite as much as leading ministers. The second avenue was commerce, to which the normal point of entry was an apprenticeship to a trade, although a person already possessing some capital might skip this hurdle. Success in both paths depended vitally on the ability to predict the future—to know whose star was rising and whose declining at court and how commodities were likely to perform on the exchange. Moreover, that knowledge had to be possessed if possible before and certainly no later than the rest of one's community.

For an élite to which information was so vital, there were remarkably few printed media through which one could learn of current happenings. Printed corantos made sporadic appearances from the 1620s and flourished for a time during the Civil War and Commonwealth years; but non-official newspapers, especially those dealing with domestic news, were not to enjoy a regular, unthreatened existence until the 1690s.[35] Governments, when they were powerful enough, imposed the severest restrictions on the

[33] A matter more fully considered in F. J. Levy, 'How information spread among the gentry, 1550–1640', *Journal of British studies* 21 (1982), 11–34 and Richard Cust, 'News and politics in early seventeenth-century England', *P&P* 112 (Aug., 1986), 60–90.

[34] *The structural transformation of the public sphere: an inquiry into a category of bourgeois society*, trans. Thomas Burger with the assistance of Frederick Lawrence (Cambridge, Mass., 1989), 57–67.

[35] The official *London gazette* of the post-Restoration years restricted itself to foreign news, while the newspapers of the later years of Charles II were unreliable (see Fraser, *Intelligence of the secretaries of state*, p. 122) and subject to official harrassment.

printing of news, as part of a wider policy of securing a monopoly of information to themselves. Behind this attitude lay not only a conviction that such information should be reserved to those actually concerned in political decision making, but a practical awareness that private information could be traded for new information—a technique brought to its highest point of refinement by Joseph Williamson in the years following the Restoration.

Certainly, for the first few decades of the century, news was still primarily an oral commodity, and its emporium the nave of St Paul's cathedral. Here in the reign of James I, as Francis Osborne recalled,

> It was the fashion of those times, and did so continue 'till these (wherein not only the Mother but her Daughters are ruined) for the principall Gentry, Lords, Courtiers and men of all professions not meerely Mechanick, to meet in *Pauls Church* by eleven, and walk in the middle Ile till twelve, and after dinner from three, to six; during which time some discoursed of Businesse, others of Newes. Now, in regard of the universall commerce, there happened little that did not first or last arrive here: And I being young, and wanting a more advantagious imployment, did, during my aboad in London, which was three fourth parts of the yeare, associate my selfe at those houres with the choycest company I could pick out, amongst such as I found most inquisitive after affaires of State; who being then my selfe in a daily attendance upon a hope (though a rotten one) of a future Preferment, I appeared the more considerable, being as ready to satisfy, according to my weak abilities, their Curiosity, as they were mine:[36]

Another frequenter recorded: 'The Noyse in it, is like that of Bees, a strange hum[m]ing or Buzz; mixt of walking Tonges and feet; it, is a kind of still roare, or Loud whisper.'[37] News of this kind passed with no reliance on writing except insofar as letters may have brought information from the country and other letters returned it again. The nave of the church was no venue for reading.

The decline of 'Paul's walking' has never been properly chronicled. The destruction of the old building by fire in 1666 marked its certain end; but one imagines that it had been in

---

[36] Francis Osborne, *Traditionall memoyres on the raigne of King Iames* (London, 1658), pp. 64–6.
[37] John Earle, *The autograph manuscript of Microcosmographie* (Leeds, 1966), p. 143.

abeyance since the disestablishment of the cathedral under the Commonwealth. Between the Restoration and the fire, Pepys was a frequent visitor to neighbouring bookshops but not it would seem to the old 'walk'. His own oral information-gathering was done at the Royal Exchange and taverns. Into this vacuum, which was eventually to be satisfied by the printed newspaper, came the manuscript newspaper and separate, no longer just a means of retailing news from a predominantly oral culture, but increasingly valuable in their own right as a means by which that information was to be gained and interpreted.

Habermas's notion of the 'public sphere' is specifically associated with the coffee-house culture of the later seventeenth century.[38] Yet it can hardly be denied that, viewed as a medium of oral communication, this culture represented a radical fracturing of the vast information exchange of Paul's into a multitude of separate, more specialized exchanges through which orally transmitted information would have passed more slowly and with less efficiency. (An analogy would be the difference between a series of computer terminals receiving information from and returning it to a large central processor, and a network of PC users who only ever communicated on an informal one-to-one basis.) This new arrangement satisfied one requirement of the new economic order symbolized by the founding in 1694 of the Bank of England by encouraging a more intense communication between those sharing common interests (e.g. insurers at Lloyds) while helping to ensure that certain especially sensitive kinds of information were kept from wider knowledge; but it was still essential for the proper functioning of the system that knowledge of general significance should pass through it rapidly. The fact that this *did* happen was a puzzle even to contemporaries: Mr Spectator could only explain it by positing that the possession of a new piece of news would compel demented individuals to rush from coffee house to coffee house for the prestige of being the first to announce (or whisper) it.[39] But this is purely fanciful. The truth of the matter lies rather in the burlesque diary of no. 154 with its engaging picture of the coffee house as a site of reading in which the customer vainly tries

[38] *Structural transformation*, pp. 32–3, 59.
[39] See the accounts of Peter Hush (no. 457; Addison and Pope) and Thomas Quid-nunc (no. 625; Tickell) in *The spectator*, ed. Donald F. Bond (Oxford, 1965), iv. 111–14, v. 136–7.

to discover whether or not the Grand Vizier has been strangled. That no attempt was made to restore the old grand exchange for oral news, and that it was the new system that sustained the modernizing tendencies in London's intellectual and commercial cultures, would suggest that written and printed information had more than compensated for the loss in efficiency in the circulation of oral news, and was serving, in effect, as the central processor. It is therefore in the sphere of inscription—the printed pamphlet and the scribal separate—rather than that of voice that we should be looking for the architecture of the public sphere.

This new public culture created by writing needs to be further analysed in terms of four phases: production, distribution, consumption and social use. Here production indicates the printing of topical pamphlets (entirely professionalized) and the copying of scribal texts (still largely in the hands of authors and readers). Distribution covers the processes by which short printed texts were made available to buyers (principally through mercury women and hawkers) and scribal texts to their readers (professionally by bespoke sale but otherwise by personal exchange). Consumption embraces the various ways in which a text of either kind could be read (a variety of relationships depending not only on the material form of the text but the physical circumstances under which the reading took place). Finally, social use covers the consequences that followed from the reading (decision on a course of action, oral dissemination of data, debate with other readers, the production of another piece of writing). Since to deal satisfactorily with these matters would require a book rather than a chapter, simplification is essential. In this case it will take the form of describing a number of the subordinate spaces in which the reading of scribal texts took place, and the kinds of production, distribution, consumption and social action that were privileged by those spaces.

SITES FOR READING

On the opening page of *If on a winter's night a traveller*, Italo Calvino presents an inventory of the ways in which reading, as a physical activity, might be undertaken by an Italian of the late 1970s.

Find the most comfortable position: seated, stretched out, curled up, or lying flat. Flat on your back, on your side, on your stomach. In an easy chair, on the sofa, in the rocker, the deck chair, on the hassock. In the hammock, if you have a hammock. On top of your bed, of course, or in the bed. You can even stand on your hands, head down, in the yoga position. With the book upside down, naturally. . . . Stretch your legs, go ahead and put your feet on a cushion, on two cushions, on the arms of the sofa, on the wings of the chair, on the coffee table, on the desk, on the piano, on the globe. Take your shoes off first. If you want to, put your feet up; if not, put them back.[40]

This is reading in the privileged private space of the home; but as the fiction progresses other possibilities are canvassed: listening in a university office to someone's extemporized translation, reading in the context of a seminar, reading from a pile of photocopies in a publisher's office, reading in a café while waiting for someone, reading on a deckchair on the terrace of a chalet, reading on a rocky ledge in the mountains, reading while flying, disembarking and passing through customs, and so on until we finally arrive in a library whose users describe their highly divergent subjective experiences of the text.

There are a number of omissions from this inventory. No one reads in the bath, on the lavatory, in a laundromat, on a bus or train, under the desk during school lessons, or behind a screen of agenda papers at boring meetings. Incomprehensibly to an Australian, no-one lies on the beach reading at intervals between dips in the surf. But on the whole, Calvino offers much valuable data (along with a few postmodern red herrings) to future historians of late-twentieth-century reading. For the seventeenth century we possess no such inventories and must draw on casually encountered information whose representativeness can rarely be ascertained. Some travellers were able to read in a coach, but how easy was it to read in sedan chairs or boats on the river? It was certainly possible to read in the newer churches, since Protestant architects laid great stress on the ability to see in their buildings, but may not have been in medieval survivors. Reading in bed seems to have been regarded as anti-social and a fire-risk. Reading while walking seems to have been common—or is that simply an illusion

[40] *If on a winter's night a traveller*, trans Wiliam Weaver (London, 1982), p. 9.

created by representations of reading in plays?[41] Yet Margaret Clifford, Countess of Cumberland, would walk in the woods with her Bible, depositing it 'in some faire tree' when she wished to meditate on a passage; while the Earl of Essex, confined to his home in 1600, would often walk 'upon his open leades, and in his garden, with his wiffe; now he, now she, reading one to the other'.[42] The practice of browsing in booksellers' shops was well established and would have compensated for the severe lack of public libraries. Did readers read as much as we do, or as quickly? How much more retentive were their highly trained memories than ours? Indeed, how far did the desire to memorize structure the practice of reading? In an age where literacy itself was far less widespread than in the West today, how much reading was communal rather than solitary? Basic questions such as these are often more difficult to answer than that of how seventeenth-century readers used to interpret the texts they read, a matter for which we have no shortage of evidence.[43]

The problem is particularly acute for the reading of the handwritten text. There are many pictorial representations of the act of reading but they rarely allow us to determine whether it is a printed book or a manuscript which is being read. Our evidence, then, must be the messages conveyed by the physical records themselves, drawing in this on the insights of McKenzie and Ong, and our knowledge of the places where reading took place. In the remainder of this chapter I wish to consider four of these sites for reading which were of special importance for the scribally published text—the country house, the coffee house, the court, and the main sites of learned reading, the Inns of Court and universities.

The country house

Outside London and the large towns, the reading of scribally published texts is chiefly associated with the houses of the

---

[41] Cf. Ford, *The broken heart*, I. iii; Shakespeare, *Hamlet*, sc. 7, ll. 1098 ff. and *Richard III*, sc. 15, ll. 2085–8; Webster, *The duchess of Malfi*, v. v.

[42] Aemilia Lanyer, 'The description of Cooke-ham', ll. 83–4 in *Kissing the rod: an anthology of seventeenth-century women's verse*, ed. Germaine Greer *et al.* (London, 1988), p. 48; Rowland White to Sir Robert Sidney, 12 Apr. 1600, cited in Margaret P. Hannay, *Philip's phoenix: Mary Sidney, Countess of Pembroke* (Oxford, 1990), p. 155.

[43] The problem is of course how far methods taught in textbooks of interpretation actually applied in everyday reading. For one point of view on this, see Eugene R. Kintgen, 'Reconstructing Elizabethan reading', *SEL* 30 (1990), 1–18.

aristocracy and the gentry. While some members of these classes could afford to employ secretaries or stewards to do their writing for them, it was common for the lesser landowner to be his own scribe and record keeper. The facility at writing so developed was frequently put to work in user or author publication, and was reflected in a habit of reading that was serious, attentive and solitary.

By the seventeenth century it had become usual for landed families to preserve large bodies of handwritten records. Even the semi-literate and uncultured would still need to retain a considerable amount of documentation relating to the sale and purchase of items relating to the estate. One also encounters an intense concern with family genealogies and the history of land ownership—matters endlessly productive of research. Commenting on one such investigation, Philip Styles notes that 'in that age of transition a certain amount of antiquarian knowledge was necessary to make feudal tenures profitable': in Sir Simon Archer's case one sees 'how easily the lord of the manor merged into the feudal historian'.[44] Where the hereditary landowner was also a justice he might have custody of judicial records of some complexity. If his interests were unintellectual, the collection of manuscripts might stop there; but the squire of the seventeenth century was often far removed from the stereotype of 'a rough unsophisticated countryman who was interested only in the state of his rent-roll and the pleasures of the chase', as J. T. Cliffe puts it. Indeed, in Yorkshire, remote from the traditional centres of education, 247 out of 679 heads of gentry families identifiable in 1642 had spent time at a university, an Inn of Court or a Catholic college, and 93 at both a university and an Inn.[45] Lacking profound learning, the squire might still be a dogged autodidact, like Sir John Newdigate who compiled thematic commonplace books devoted to theology, law, history and husbandry, and aspired to devote between eight and ten hours a day to study.[46] It would also be common for him to have a passionate interest in matters of religion and to be deeply read in

[44] *Sir Simon Archer*, pp. 20, 22. The investigation is described on pp. 15–23.
[45] *The Yorkshire gentry from the Reformation to the Civil War* (London, 1969), pp. 81, 73. See also O'Day, *Education and society*, pp. 88–99.
[46] Vivienne Larminie, *The godly magistrate: the private philosophy and public life of Sir John Newdigate, 1571–1610* (Oxford, 1982), pp. 7–8.

controversial literature. From a man of this type—and they formed at least a significant minority—we would expect not only a keenness to obtain scribally published texts, but a habit of integrating these into a private database, largely written in his own hand.

A description of one such landowner is given in Alan Macfarlane's *The justice and mare's ale*. Sir Daniel Fleming of Rydal Hall, Westmorland, born in 1633, inherited the paternal estate at the age of 19 after brief stays at Oxford and one of the Inns of Court. Of his industriousness as a scribe, Macfarlane gives the following account:

His voluminous personal papers show him to be a truly remarkable man. He combined great intelligence, vast erudition, immense curiosity and great energy, with a love of documents. When his papers were deposited in the Cumbria Record Office in the 1960s they comprised about seventy manilla boxes. There were also roughly 6,000 letters to and from him. There are copies of love letters, books of jokes, series of grocers' bills, payments to harvest workers and many other items. Just the letters concerning the education of his children, when published, filled three bulky volumes. His immense energy and organization is shown in an account book he kept which, if fully published, would run to many volumes. His legal learning is illustrated by his letters and book purchases, but one particularly strong indication is the annotated copy of the *Statutes of the peace* which he kept with him in his judicial business. The first 286 pages are a printed abstract of the legal position in relation to alphabetically arranged subjects such as 'Alehouses', 'Archery', 'Arrests'. These first pages are densely annotated with added topics, modifications, amplifications from all the current legal writers. Not content with this, Fleming then proceeded to fill a further 482 pages in his tiny handwriting with annotations and explanations, with the forms of writs and warrants, with the statutes concerning taxation and the poor, and numerous other topics.[47]

We cannot know to what extent this (to us) prodigious industry at penmanship was typical of Fleming's class at this time; but my own guess would be that it represented a wide social practice, excessive, if at all, only in quantity not kind. Fleming belonged to a

---

[47] Alan Macfarlane in collaboration with Sarah Harrison, *The justice and the mare's ale: law and disorder in seventeenth-century England* (Oxford, 1981), p. 42. For the Fleming MSS, see *HMC, 12th rep., app., pt. vii.*

generation trained by the new bureaucrats of the interregnum in the importance of meticulous documentation, and which also still respected the medieval view of copying as a work of virtue to be instilled in the young to preserve them from debauched courses (an attitude intensified rather than otherwise by Puritanism).

From earlier in the century the autobiographical writings of another learned squire, Simonds D'Ewes, reveal a similar delight in the activities of ordering, filing and transcribing, joined with an often declared conviction of guilt in not keeping up to the targets he set himself. His account of the compilation of his massive scribal edition of the parliamentary papers of Elizabeth's reign has already been quoted in Chapter 3: in this case it was the editorial work that was performed by D'Ewes while the actual copying was done by 'an industrious servant'; however, at the same time D'Ewes himself was also engaged in a transcription of the medieval commentary on the laws of England known as the *Fleta*, switching between editorial work on one project and actual copying in the second. 'The ensuing month of August', runs a typical account from the autobiography, 'was almost wholly spent in transcribing Fleta out of a copy I had of it, and in directing my servant in the penning of the parliamentary journals of Queen Elizabeth's time.'[48] Unlike Fleming, D'Ewes was a professed antiquary, one of a large community of gentleman-scholars; but he shared with the Cumbrian justice an almost fetishistic delight in manuscripts and a passion for transcribing that exceeded any immediate practical need. James Boevey from the age of 14 'had a candle burning by him all night, with pen, inke, and paper, to write downe thoughts as they came into his head; that so he might not loose a thought'.[49]

What is described here is not scribal publication as such but the wider culture of transcription from which it grew. For Fleming, D'Ewes, Boevey and many like them a significant pleasure of reading was that it should be an encounter with their own script— a matter partly narcissistic, partly a reflection of a spirituality turned in upon private experience, and partly a comforting reminder of prodigies of godly labour. But it was also a new and powerful mode of social control, and one which in this case broke with Ong's notion of the residual orality of the chirographic text.

[48] *Autobiography*, i. 409, 435.
[49] Aubrey, *Brief lives*, i. 113.

Ong sees oral culture as 'homeostatic' in its readiness to shed or reconstitute the past whenever the past ceases to serve the needs of the present.[50] In doing so it sacrifices the possibility of controlling the future through the past. These immensely patient labours of transcription, whether it was Fleming's desire to preserve records of his own family and community, Archer's to trace the history of Warwickshire tenures, D'Ewes's to have access to ancient parliamentary and administrative precedents, or Roger North's to preserve his deliberations on an encyclopaediac range of subjects, were a way of capturing the past for future service. D'Ewes put his historical database at the service of parliaments in which he served, while Fleming used his records in pursuing a notorious band of lawbreakers. This pursuit, the subject of Macfarlane's study, was only successful because of Fleming's power to integrate information within his personal archive. But power, once again, resided in the data remaining private—if available in printed form it would have deprived the owner and his allies of a vital advantage. The same clearly applies to the encyclopaedia of 'active philosophy' composed by Boevey after he had 'retired to a countrey life', which handled 'all the Arts and Tricks practised in Negotiation, and how they were to be ballanced by counter-prudentiall rules'.[51] Once again there was knowledge to be shared and knowledge to be reserved.

This kind of country-house reader would have been a writer prior to his being a reader, and with a preference for the products of his own pen. His reading would have been solitary, with a 'closet' away from the bustle of the household set up for writing and where documents could be concealed from prying eyes. (Women readers would have had to be of high social standing before they acquired this privilege, though the example of Dame Sara Cowper (1644–1720) shows that they could be just as industrious as men in assembling large private collections of manuscripts.) The utilitarian nature of much reading, nourished in turn by patient study of the Bible and devotional books, would· have encouraged high levels of concentration. Striking thoughts would be abstracted for preservation in a commonplace book. Among scribally published texts most likely to have passed before

[50] Ong, *Orality*, pp. 46–9.
[51] Aubrey, i. 112.

his eyes would have been newsletters and separates sent from town, and essays and epistles from other educated squires of his district, echoing the practice observed by Laslett in Kent and also evident in the Fleming MSS and the collections of William Davenport.[52] The habits of filing and ordering made necessary by his functions as landlord and justice would also have encouraged the rereading of important manuscripts. A class of writing that would be preserved with especial care was the advices and treatises prepared by parents for the guidance of their children, an important sub-genre that would occasionally break into wider circulation but mostly remained within the extended family.[53] As far as we can judge, the reading of the scribally published text within such a household would be a careful and attentive business, always likely to provoke the complementary activity of writing. What held good for the squire might equally be true of the vicar in his parsonage, whom the squire had frequently appointed.

The cultural ideal of the learned squire is preserved for us in the political genre, common to both the scribal and print media, of the political tract or verse epistle in the form of a 'Letter to a gentleman in the country'. The gentleman in these cases represents a judge to whom the competing innovators of the metropolis submit their causes for censure confident that he will lend his weight to their own side. He is assumed to be deeply versed in history and the constitution (which in a sense he embodies). His political understanding has been nourished by an early study of the classics, and his judgement of human nature by his experience on the bench, but his understanding of the political traditions of the nation is one that has been gained through a first-hand

---

[52] Fleming corresponded frequently on political matters with his neighbours (*HMC, 12th rep., app., vii*, pp. iii–iv), as well as receiving regular newsletters from the Secretary of State's office. For Davenport see Morrill, 'William Davenport', pp. 115–29 and Cust, 'News and politics', pp. 80–3.

[53] Examples already discussed include Osborne's 'Advice to a son' and Halifax's 'Advice to a daughter'. Dame Sara Cowper preserved shorter epistles of this kind to two of her children (Hertfordshire Record Office MS D/Ep F37, pp. 49–55). The well-known letter from Lord Burghley to Robert Cecil, material from which was appropriated by Dame Sara, is available in facsimile in Braunmuller, *A seventeenth-century letter-book*, pp. 276–87. Daniel Fleming's advice to his son, reprinted in Cumberland and Westmorland Antiquarian and Archaeological Society, tract series no. xi (Kendal, 1928), pp. 92–9, is another version of the Burleigh letter, as is the widely circulated 'Admonition of the Earl of Essex to his son'. For the genre at large, see *Advice to a son: precepts of Lord Burghley, Sir Walter Raleigh, and Francis Osborne*, ed. Louis B. Wright (Ithaca, NY, 1962), pp. ix–xxvi.

acquaintance with ancient records. Removed from the factions and hurly burly of the town, he has room in his life for scholarship and reflection. The ideal was realized in men such as D'Ewes, Fleming and Walter Yonge, and for many others it was a construction to be identified with to the limit of their capacities.[54] The reading that informed such a life would be directed towards the past rather than the present, shunning novelty in order to search out time-sanctioned verities. That such a paragon should be addressed in a letter (even if it was a printed one) was a tacit acknowledgement that his concern would be with the products of the pen quite as much as with those of the press. But, as the emergence of this construction was a response to political needs, so was its decline inevitable once the urgency of those needs was no longer felt. Steele's mockery of Sir Roger's devotion to Dyer's letter ('our Authentick Intelligence, our *Aristotle* in Politicks'[55]) was a sign that both the role and the medium were becoming irrelevant.

The coffee house

Habermas's 'public sphere' is most immediately observable in the coffee houses of London. With the decline of Paul's and the Exchange as centralized sources for the dissemination of oral information within the capital, their place was taken by the newcomers, the indiscriminate public space giving way to a variety of more restricted and intimate ones. First known in the early 1650s, coffee houses spread widely in England during the 1660s and 1670s and were the chosen meeting place for men of business as well as men of leisure. From an early period they became highly specialized in terms of clientele, many performing the role of semi-private clubs for patrons of varying trades, faiths or political views. They could also be semi-public places of business, providing an office address for the advertisers of services. At the universities they were seen as disruptive influences. Roger North gives an informed if somewhat jaundiced view of their effect on Cambridge over the decades following the Restoration:

[54] For Yonge, see V. L. and M. L. Pearl, 'Richard Corbett's 'Against the opposing of the Duke in parliament, 1628' and the anonymous rejoinder, 'An answere to the same, lyne for lyne': the earliest dated manuscript copies', *RES* NS 42 (1991), 32 and the sources there cited.

[55] *Spectator*, i. 182–3.

Part II

At that time and long after there was but one, kept by one Kirk. The trade of news also was scarce set up, for they had only the public gazette, till Kirk got a written newsletter circulated by one Muddiman. But now the case is much altered, for it is become a custom after chapel to repair to one or other of the coffee-houses (for there are divers), where hours are spent in talking, and less profitable reading of newspapers, of which swarms are continually supplied from London. And the scholars generally as so entête after news (which is none of their business) that they neglect all for it. And it is become very rare for any of them to go directly to his chamber after prayers without first doing his suit at the coffee-house, which is a vast loss of time grown out of a pure novelty. For who can apply close to a subject with his head full of the din of a coffee-house?[56]

The replacement of the public concourse by the coffee house as the primary venue for the exchange of information had an inevitable effect on the way in which that information was communicated. The confidentiality of coffee-house discussion encouraged a new frankness, much as the brew itself probably encouraged increased mental acuity among drinkers whose nervous systems had not been habituated to caffeine since childhood. Mr Spectator speaks of thrusting his head 'into a Round of Politicians at *Will*'s, and listning with great Attention to the Narratives that are made in those little Circular Audiences'—a description that accords perfectly with Habermas's vision of 'private people come together as a public'.[57] But, as indicated under our earlier informational model, the retreat towards intimacy—and professional specialism—also reduced the quantity and variety of the oral information that entered the place of exchange. For this reason the coffee house had to become a site for reading as well as conversation: early illustrations nearly always show reading matter scattered on the tables. Newspapers, when available, were provided by the proprietor; but newspapers were of dubious value for an understanding of the world—strictly censored during those periods when censorship was possible and unreliable in those periods when it was not. Most vitally, the information they presented was available to hundreds of others

---

[56] Roger North, 'Life of Dr John North', in *General preface and life of Dr John North*, ed. Peter Millard (Toronto, 1984), p. 115. For a very similar attitude towards the impact of the coffee-drinking culture on Oxford, see *The life and times of Anthony Wood*, ed. Andrew Clark (Oxford, 1891–5), ii. 300 and 429.

[57] *Spectator*, i. 3; Habermas, p. 27.

who might be relied upon to be drawing the same conclusions from it.

The role of the coffee houses as centres for the dissemination of newsletters and separates has already been touched upon. They had become dangerous enough by the winter of 1675–6 in their circulation of forbidden documents to provoke an attempt at suppression.[58] Dyer the coffee house man whose inflammatory 1688 newsletter so annoyed L'Estrange was only one of a number of proprietors who were actively engaged in scribal journalism. Will Urwin, of the Will's just mentioned, whose customers included Dryden and the Covent Garden wits, issued a newsletter in 1678 which was delivered by 'a little tapster boy' from his coffee house.[59] Coffee houses were the ideal place to inject new texts into circulation. Being common to both the City and the West End, the coffee-house culture could transfer texts rapidly between milieux which had little other direct contact. A report on radical Nonconformists, apparently dating from the late 1660s, connects them both with coffee houses and the transmission of lampoons:

> The Independents and Anabaptists with some of the fiercer Presbyterians are proud and censorious; Quaker like they will denounce Judgments both upon King & Kingdome upon any pretended Miscariages they doe but heare of.
>
> They are great Frequenters of Coffeehouses and great Improvers of any little matters that is but whispered against the Court or the Government.
>
> These with some hipocriticall Loyalists take paines to divulge any thing that may cast a reproach upon the King, and to disperse any scandalous Verses of which many have been abroad of late.[60]

In an age when many men took delivery of their mail at their coffee house, and where the owner might have his own service for delivering letters, they were an obvious recourse for the aspiring scribal publisher. Within their walls, the newsletter and separate served both as reading matter and as a currency of exchange

[58] Further discussed in Ch. 6, pp. 240–2.

[59] *HMC, 11th rep., app., vii*, p. 20. Further information on the nexus between coffee houses and the writing and circulation of newsletters is given in Bryant Lillywhite, *London coffee houses: a reference book of coffee houses of the seventeenth, eighteenth and nineteenth centuries* (London, 1963), pp. 19–20, under the years 1679, 1683 and 1688, and Fraser, *Intelligence*, pp. 114–21.

[60] 'The state of the non-conformists in England soon after the Restoration. From a MS in the possession of Thomas Astle Esq', BL MS Stowe 185, ff. 175^{r-v}.

between customers. For information, if it was of real value, was always to be traded, not given. Men's clothes had changed by 1660 from the earlier doublet and hose with the cloak for outward protection to the shirt and breeches beneath a knee-length coat with capacious pockets. These pockets were the perfect receptacle for separates. Rochester is known to have carried manuscripts in this way, as does Mr Friendall his daily wad of love letters in Southerne's *The wives' excuse*.[61] In the economy of the coffee house the scribal texts supplied by the proprietor were supplemented by those traded for oral news or other reserved writings by their information-hungry patrons.

In their semi-secretive, semi-public character the newsletters and lampoons exactly mimicked the institutions that played host to them. But our concern now is not with their social function as such but the way in which the nature of the space provided helps identify and define particular kinds of reading. A text might be read aloud by one member of a party to his table-fellows, and perhaps inadvertently to the entire room. In a coffee-house scene in a comedy of 1667 the coffee-master brings a *Gazette* to a table, which, at the suggestion 'Pray let one read for all', is read out while the reader's companions interpolate their questions and comments.[62] Steele, writing in 1711 as 'Abraham Froth', described how it was the custom at Sir Roger de Coverley's in the country 'upon the coming in of the Post to sit about a Pot of Coffee, and hear the old Knight read *Dyer*'s Letter, which he does with his Spectacles upon his Nose, and in an audible Voice, smiling very often at those little strokes of Satyr which are so frequent in the Writings of that Author'.[63] This while not a description of a coffee house may be accepted as a coffee-house custom transposed to the shires. Reading might equally be silent, but it was a silence within the ambience of communion. The solitary kind of reading was necessary to the pursuit of whatever shared goal had brought the patrons of the house together, but what was divined from it still

---

[61] It was from a pocket that Rochester produced the copy of 'In the isle of Great Britain' that he inadvertently gave to Charles II. Cf. also his 'Timon a satyr', ll. 13–16: 'He takes me in his coach and as we go / Pulls out a libel of a sheet or two . . .'. For Mr Friendall see, *The wives' excuse*, v. ii. 52–65 in *The works of Thomas Southerne*, ed. Robert Jordan and Harold Love (Oxford, 1988), i. 330.

[62] Sir Thomas St Serfe, *Tarugo's wiles: or the coffee house* (London, 1667), p. 24.

[63] *Spectator*, ii. 4–5.

needed to be handled with a degree of reserve in that these fellow patrons might also be spies or competitors. The coffee-house reader was both of and not of his particular scene of aspiration, retaining the detachment famously captured in Pope's 'Coffee, (which makes the Politician wise, / And see thro' all things with his half shut Eyes)'.[64] The reading was a necessary preparative to engaging in conversation—the other rationale of the house—but even the conversation, as Alexander Radcliffe noted, was of a different kind from the bonhomie of the tavern.

> A Pox 'o these Fellows contriving,
>   They've spoilt our pleasant design;
> We were once in a way of true living,
>   Improving Discourse by good Wine.
> But now Conversation grows tedeous,
>   O'er Coffee they still confer Notes;
> 'Stead of Authors both learn'd and facetious,
>   They quote onely *Dugdale* and *Oats.*[65]

It is likely enough that the Nonconformists' tendency to 'denounce Judgments' and to be 'great Improvers of any little matters' represents the tone of such conversation quite accurately. It easily slid back into writing in the form of the lampoon or the scribally-circulated essay.

The court

The court as a site of writing has been much studied but is more difficult to focus on as a site of reading. To begin with we need to distinguish the court as the royal household from the court as the centre of the national administration, which was still technically conducted from within the household and to some degree by the same officers. In its first function it was the scene of ceremonies to which any person of suitable social standing could attach themselves under the guise of 'waiting', and which were an excellent opportunity for an exchange of manuscripts. But the

---

[64] iii. 117–18, in *The rape of the lock and other poems,* ed. Geoffrey Tillotson (London, 1962), p. 130. Charles A. Knight writes: 'By serving as the forum where readership moved into conversation, the coffee-house played a role for the periodical essay at least equal to that later played for the novel by the circulating library' ('The literary periodical in the early eighteenth century', *Library,* 6:8 (1986), 242).

[65] 'To the Tune of *Per fas per nefas*', *The ramble,* p. 34.

court was also a community of individuals living in close proximity. At the palace of Whitehall favoured courtiers, concubines, high officers of state and hundreds of servants and officials had apartments or humbler spaces which became their homes, at least for the period when the monarch was in residence. A writer of 1642 has left us a lament for a Whitehall suddenly deserted:

There is no presse at the Wine-Sellor Dores and Windowes, no gaping noise amongst the angry Cookes in the Kitchings, no wayting for the opening of the Posterne-dore to take water at the Stayres, no racket nor balling in the Tenis Court, no throng nor rumbling of Coaches before the Court Gates, but all in a dumbe silence, as the Pallace stood not neere a well peopled City, but as it were the decay'd buildings of ruin'd *Troy*, where scarce a passenger is known to tread once in twenty yeares.[66]

Rochester, writing in the early 1670s, compared life at court to being 'shutt up in a Drumme, you can thinke of nothing but the noise is made about you'.[67] Graham Parry has stressed the self-absorbed quality of the Caroline court in terms that also apply to its Restoration successor, describing it as 'excessively distracted by sophisticated game-playing, insufficiently aware of its dangerous isolation, and indifferent to the growing bitterness in the world outside'.[68]

Within this bustling, self-contained community, it was possible to take meals, to attend plays or worship, to gamble for high stakes at the Groom Porter's, to conduct love affairs, to call on the purveyors of an amazing range of products and services, and to hear and generate gossip. What was difficult to find was any more purposive activity: the 'work' of the courtier was in most cases simply to be physically present in the presence chamber. Sensibly noting that 'men cannot bee allwayes discowrcing, nor women always pricking in clowts', Sir John Harington thought it was 'not amisse to play at some sociable game (at which more than ii may

---

[66] *A deep sigh breath'd through the lodgings at White-hall, deploring the absence of the covrt, and the miseries of the palace* (London, 1642), A3ᵛ.

[67] *The letters of John Wilmot, Earl of Rochester*, ed. Jeremy Treglown (Oxford, 1980), p. 93.

[68] *The seventeenth century. The intellectual and cultural context of English literature, 1603–1700* (Harlow, 1989), p. 35. The court's self-image is elegantly explored in his *The golden age restor'd. The culture of the Stuart court, 1603–42* (Manchester, 1981).

play) wherby the attendawnce may seem the lesse tedious to the players, and the rest that looke on may in a sort intertayn themselvs with the beholding it'.[69] Another way of combating the tedium of such occasions was through the composition and circulation of subversive writings, which must have gained a special piquancy when the victims were also present in the chamber.

The circulation of written texts, then, was part of the everyday current of life in the palace. Most of these were highly topical and quickly rendered out of date by the flow of events. They could also be ruthlessly frank about the real rationale of court life, which was incessant conflict for wealth and influence, with closeness to the sovereign the recognized way of securing this.[70] That most of these texts remained in manuscript was a concession that this rationale should be concealed as far as possible from the governed; however, the existence of networks of scribal publication at the centre of power was a standing invitation to outsiders to seek to obtain manuscripts from these networks and to insert writings into them that promoted their own interests. The rapidity with which material relating to the Somerset scandal (and others) in the reign of James I spread through the kingdom reflects the first of these phenomena, and the penetration achieved by Whig satires of the late 1670s the second. Few of these texts were in any way taxing. 'The court aristocracy of the seventeenth century', Habermas notes, speaking here on a European scale, 'was not really a reading public. To be sure, it kept men of letters as it kept servants, but literary production based on patronage was more a matter of a kind of conspicuous consumption than of serious reading by an interested public.'[71] The scholar courtiers of Elizabeth's reign were supplanted under the Stuarts by men of very different attainments. Attention might still be sought through writing as through dress, sexual attractiveness, polished manners or conversational wit, but not necessarily to more effect.

---

[69] *Nugae antiquae*, ii. 14. He goes on to complain about the hardness of the court chairs and benches.

[70] The rules of this conflict are exposed in Kevin Sharpe's 'Crown, parliament and locality: government and communication in early Stuart England' in his *Politics and ideas in early Stuart England: essays and studies* (London, 1989), pp. 75–100, and in his own and Neil Cuddy's contributions to *The English court from the wars of the roses to the Civil War*, ed. David Starkey (London, 1987), pp. 173–260.

[71] Habermas, p. 38.

The court then was not a place for deep or serious reading. The majority of texts in circulation were short and uncomplicated enough to be produced from pockets in idle intervals of wearisome ceremonies, or as a source of sociable amusement. Pepys, on a hot summer's day in 1666 while on the grass by the canal in St James's Park, found himself 'thinking of a Lampoone which hath run in my head this week, to make upon the late fight at sea and the miscarriages there—but other businesses put it out of my head'.[72] And yet court life did encourage one kind of reading skill, which was that by which texts circulating in the form of separates were interrogated for clues to the current and future configurations of influence. Satire in particular had an important role as a means of undermining the standing of rivals: the malice of court lampooners, whether of Suckling's generation or Rochester's, is rarely if ever gratuitous but needs to be tracked back to the interests of a particular patron or faction. Apart from this, the levity of court reading reflects its function as an escape valve for an institution otherwise characterized by a rigid formality. Where texts of a more seriously informative or monitory kind are encountered which endeavour to address policy issues otherwise than in terms of personalities, it is likely that their intended readership was among the administrators rather then the courtiers (insofar as any sharp division can be made between the two).

Above all, scribally transmitted court writing was an insiders' writing, reflecting the values of an institution that was devoted to the manufacture and maintenance of an image in which it could hardly itself be expected to believe. As such it stands in an antithetical relationship to the idealization of the court in the masques of Jonson, Carew, D'Avenant and Crowne, performed for the benefit of outsiders rather than inmates and subsequently promulgated through the print medium. The frankness, indeed cynicism, of these scribally circulated writings can often be disconcerting when comparison is made with work presented by the same writer in more public forums. Harington's *A supplie or addicion to the catalogue of bishops to the year 1608* is one text whose ambivalences and apparent self-contradictions only make sense when it is firmly seen as the work of one insider writing to another

---

[72] *Diary*, vii. 207.

insider (Prince Henry) about still other insiders (the bishops) whose status as leaders of the church must not be allowed to become confused with their status as fellow-courtiers.[73] What was true of the king's court was equally true of its tributaries. 'Every great courtier', R. Malcolm Smuts points out, 'maintained his own household near Whitehall, each a miniature court in its own right which functioned as the nerve center for its owner's affinity.'[74] In the case of Harington's *Supplie*, it is important to remember that Prince Henry had his own court, distinct from those of his father, mother and siblings, and that this possessed its own political and cultural programme. The levees of great commoners like Somerset and Buckingham were hardly less splendid than those of the king.

The Haward miscellany

One of our best guides to the kinds of texts circulated at the Stuart court is the bulky (721 written pages plus blanks) miscellany assembled between the late 1660s and circa 1682 by Sir William Haward of Tandridge, and now Bodleian MS don. b 8. A note on the manuscript by a later owner, Peter le Neve, identifies Sir William as 'K$^{nt.}$ of the Privy Chamber to King Cha: y^e 1st. Cha: 2^d. and King James the second' and as having enjoyed an apartment in Scotland Yard, the area adjacent to the court, formerly reserved for the use of visiting Scottish monarchs. He was knighted in 1643.[75] His post at court, which he acquired in 1641 and still retained in 1689, was one of forty-eight Gentlemen of the Privy Chamber in Ordinary. Of these Chamberlayne writes:

Their Office is Twelve every Quarter to wait on the Kings Person within doors and without, so long as His Majesty is on foot; and when the King eats in the Privy-Chamber, they wait at the Table, and bring in His Meet. They wait also at the Reception of Ambassadors; and every night two of them lye in the Kings Privy-Chamber.[76]

---

[73] Ed. R. H. Miller (Potomac, 1981). The first printed edition did not appear until 1653. For the manuscripts, see Beal, *IELM*, i/2, pp. 154–5. The importance of appreciating 'the innerness of many of Harington's allusions' is brought out in Patrick Collinson's review, *Library*, 6:4 (1982), 198–200.

[74] *Court culture and the origins of the royalist tradition in early Stuart England* (Philadelphia, 1987), p. 55.

[75] There is a short biographical account of Sir William in W. Paley Baildon, *The Hawardes of Tandridge co. Surrey* (London, 1894), pp. 23–31 which records that he sold his estate at Tandridge in 1681 and that his wife, Martha, died in 1689.

[76] *Angliae notitia: or, the present state of England. The first part*, 10th edn (London, 1677), p.

The privy chamber was intermediate between the presence chamber and the bedchamber, placing its officers closer to the sovereign than the general run of courtiers but not in the inner circle of his intimates. Sir William was also MP for Bletchingley and later Reigate in the pension parliament. A satirical account dated 1670 of the court supporters in that parliament, copied by him into his book, describes him as 'a privy-Chamber-man, & Commission^er for sale of Fee-farme Rents' (p. 256). He was therefore a courtier in the three senses of one who held office within the royal household, of one who supported the crown in parliament, and of one who lived for periods of the year within the royal precinct in Whitehall. (Presumably he would return to his country estate during the summer.) To claim him as a 'typical' courtier would be to go beyond our present knowledge, but the range of interests revealed by his book, covering scandal, politics, poetry, heraldry, constitutional history, law, antiquarianism, geography, but not much religion, is what we would expect of the court of Charles II.[77] His book may therefore be regarded as a kind of net held out to catch whatever scribally published documents came into circulation at Whitehall.

Although the book is composed of transcriptions of material originally encountered as separates, it is not clear how soon after acquisition texts were entered. While the overall tendency of the items is chronological, this could well be the result of one or many *post hoc* reorderings of documents rather than conscientious entering in order of receipt. (Certainly, the position of a text in the volume should only be used with caution in determining its date of composition.[78]) One oddity is that pp. 1–68 were originally left blank and thus contain the last material to be entered, a matter confirmed by handwriting as well as dates. Haward gives no information concerning the subsequent fate of the separates from which he copied, or whether his own book served as an exemplar

159. See also Nicholas Carlisle, *An inquiry into the place and quality of the gentlemen of His Majesty's most honourable privy chamber* (London, 1829).

[77] However, Sir William was at least on good terms with princes of the Church: on 14 Nov. 1685 Evelyn encountered him at dinner with several prelates at Lambeth Palace, noting that 'The Dinner was for cheere extraordinary' (*Diary*, iv. 489).

[78] Paul Hammond, 'The dating of three poems by Rochester from the evidence of Bodleian MS Don. b 8', *Bodleian Library record* 11 (1982–5), 58–9 seems to assume copying in order of receipt; but this can be no more than a hypothesis.

for user publication. Given that separates were a kind of currency around the court and could be used to confirm alliances and attract favour, it is quite likely that the volume was meant as a source book for further transcription as well as a personal record. Nor is there much information about the individuals from whom documents were received. Poems by court authors are often in good texts and correctly ascribed, suggesting they may have been received via author publication; however, Rochester's 'Artemisa to Chloe' bears the uncertain annotation 'This poeme is supposed to bee made by ye Earle of Rochester, or Mr Wolseley' (p. 494). An account of a diplomatic incident involving the British resident at Venice (pp. 60–8) was passed on by John Grenville, Earl of Bath, and a narrative of the naval attack on Bergen by Sir Gilbert Talbot.[79] We must assume that these were connections on which Haward particularly prided himself. On another occasion he may well have seen the original of an epigram placed on the door of the royal bedchamber, since it occurred during his term of waiting and the finder was known to him.[80] But the important point is that, although the names of sources are suppressed, the entire contents of his book had come from donation, exchange or purchase. Behind its carefully inscribed pages lie possibly hundreds of individual transactions.

What prospect of the range of court reading are we given by this volume? To begin with there is a very substantial body of satirical verse, partly written by courtiers about other courtiers, partly drawn from the broader 'state poems' tradition, and partly belonging to an older, more genial tradition of social verse. Overall there are 180 verse items ranging from two-line epigrams to lengthy satires. That there should be a good representation of writing by Rochester (eight items plus some dubia) and the wits of the Buckingham circle is hardly surprising. What is unexpected is the very full coverage of oppositional satire directed at the crown and its policies, especially from what will be described in the next chapter as the 'Marvellian' tradition, centring on the various

---

[79] 'This paper was written by ye Com[m]and of Sr Gilbert Talbott for me, & 'giuen mee by his owne hand on Saturday in ye Euening, being y^e. 21th. of January. 1676/7' (p. 66). A poem by Talbot, 'The Hermite to his Citty Freind' is given on pp. 648–50.

[80] 'About nyne of ye Clocke at night on Friday being y^e. 26th. of November, 1675. This ensueing Distick was found put ouer ye Doore of ye Kings new Bedchamber, & taken downe by Francis Rogers page of ye Bedchamber' (p. 539).

'Advice to a painter poems'. In particular, Haward was diligent in his recording of satires, some of considerable grossness, on the king and members of the royal family.[81] Encountered without knowledge of its provenance one would assume this to be the miscellany of either a Whig sympathiser or an extreme Yorkist rather than a faithful servant of the reigning monarch. Haward sometimes tries to cover himself by using disapproving titles, as with 'An horrid Anagram on the Motto of ye Kings Armes' (p. 539), 'A detestable Libell' (p. 554) and 'A damn'd Ballad of this is the Tyme' (p. 568) as well as a number of items signalled as 'base', but otherwise seems to have been remarkably detached about the undoubtedly treasonable nature of much of his material. (Cognitive dissonance of another kind is suggested when Rochester's(?) pornographic 'Seigneur Dildoe' is followed by 'On the Bible A Pindarique Ode' ('Haile Holy thinge', pp. 478–80) and that in turn by additional stanzas to 'Seigneur Dildoe'.)

As a member of parliament it would be expected that Haward would collect parliamentary separates. These include brief notes on the session commencing 22 November 1669 (pp. 446–7), a committee paper and the famous speech of Lord Lucas against the Subsidy Bill from February 1671 (pp. 198–201, 202–4), an extended parliamentary compilation, of the kind discussed in Chapter 1, for the session commencing 19 February 1673 which saw the passing of the Test Act (pp. 384–409), a journal for the session commencing 20 October 1673 (pp. 467–75), and a scattering of papers, petitions and speeches from other sessions (pp. 156–68, 293–5, 302, 446, 686, 704–6). There are no complete compilations of pre-1660 parliaments, but Haward did transcribe a

---

[81] These include 'To her Matie upon her dancing' ('Reforme, deare Queene, ye errours of your youth'), the two satires on the killing of a beadle by a gang led by the Duke of Monmouth ('Neare Holborne lyes a parke of great renowne', and 'Assist mee, some auspicious Muse, to tell'), several attacks on the Duchesses of Cleveland and Portsmouth, and a gallery of unflattering portraits of the king. Charles, as well as being addressed in several virulent epigrams, is the subject of the longer satires, 'The Chronicle' ('Chast, pious, prudent Charles ye Second'), 'Another base songe' ('I am a senceless thing wth a hye')', 'A base Copy' (Rochester's 'I'th' Isle of great Britaine'), 'The Kings Farewell to Danby' ('Farewell, my deare Danby, my pimpe, & my Cheate'), 'An historicall Poeme' ('Of a tall Stature, & of sable Hue'), 'On Madam Lawson' ('Mee-thinkes I see our Mighty Monarch stand'), besides other pieces attacking his policies rather than his person. Those satires whose first lines have been given will all be found in *POAS (Yale)* i and ii together with page-references to their MS sources; however, the titles and first-lines are as Haward gives them and vary in some instances from those of the Yale editors.

number of parliamentary and administrative separates from the reigns of Elizabeth, James I and Charles I, among them a collection of speeches relating to the Earl of Essex (pp. 75–83), a speech of James I (pp. 169–74), and a list of propositions made by the commons in 1610 concerning the abolition of knights' services (pp. 361–7). Supplementing these are a number of political pieces of an extra-parliamentary kind, including several by or concerned with Shaftesbury at various stages of his career (pp. 370–2, 448–9, 501–2, 523–4, 555–7, 702–3, 713–17). Lauderdale's administration of Scotland is attacked in a discourse dated 1675 on pp. 541–54. Anne, Duchess of York's reasons for embracing the Roman Catholic faith (pp. 562–3) are balanced at pp. 457–63 by her father's letter dissuading her from this course, and at 606–10 by a transcript of a printed narrative of the Pope-burning of 17 November 1679. Pages 661–80 contain two lengthy papers on the king's supposed mariage to Lucy Walters—actually Whig diatribes against the Duke of York. There is also the inevitable linked group of attacks on Buckingham *père* (pp. 108–17).

While not an antiquary in the severe sense of Cotton or D'Ewes, Sir William did have interests in this direction that were strong enough to draw recognition from Evelyn who described him in 1671 as 'a greate pretender to English antiquities &c'.[82] At p. 502 he provides a copy of an inscription found at Beverley minister. The early pages of the volume, which were the last to be written, include exchequer and tower records concerning the office of Constable of the Tower, the patent of creation of Thomas Howard, Earl of Surrey to be Duke of Norfolk in the reign of Henry VIII, an 'An Act concerning ye Title, Name, & Dignity of Earle of Arundell' and an account of the funeral of Richard, Duke of York, the father of Edward IV (pp. 36–42, 49–54). An interest in heraldry reveals itself in pieces on the arms of Gresham (pp. 279–80) and Wriothesley (pp. 420–22) and a report prepared by Haward together with Sir William Dugdale and Walter Chetwind on Wycherley's father Daniel's right to arms (pp. 60–3). 'A Roll of the Peeres of ye Kingdome of Englande' dated 4 February 1673 is given at pp. 373–8 and a transcript of Monck's commission as Captain General of Charles II's armies at pp. 43–9. Diplomatic

---

[82] *Diary*, iii. 598. The Pepysian copy of Robert of Gloucester's chronicle was originally written for Haward.

interests are reflected in some papers from the British ambassador at the Imperial court at Vienna (pp. 33–6) and a narrative by the British resident at Venice of an affront done to him by the Duke of Mantua's gondoliers (pp. 66–8). Haward also transcribed the lengthy charter of the East India Company in the form confirmed by Charles II in 1660 (pp. 310–41) and a treatise by Sir Harry Sheeres on the Mediterranean Sea and the Straits of Gibraltar (pp. 1–22).

Although, as mentioned, there is little evidence in this particular collection of any deep concern with religion, Haward did have a keen interest in prophecies. The prophecy was a genre of scribal publication which knew no boundaries of class or institution and would well for this reason reward specialized study.[83] Texts of this nature in Haward's volume are a versified extract from Nostradamus ('The bloud oth' Just Londons firme doome shall fix', p. 217), 'A Prognostication of ye Westphalian Boore, named Michell Rochells, of the yeare. 1672' (pp. 262–4), 'A prophecy, or Merlins Riddle' (p. 456); 'A Prophecy pretended, to be made many yeares agone' (p. 540); 'Merlin reuiu'd' (p. 660), and the long Fifth-monarchist prophetic allegory, *The panther*, copied in April 1681 (pp. 689–95). My summary passes over a number of legal speeches, letters (real and bogus), administrative position papers, political pieces and facetiae of various kinds, but gives a fair sense both of the range of Haward's interests and the richness of the traditions of scribal publication on which he was able to draw from his rooms in Scotland Yard.

This very richness creates difficulties of interpretation of a kind which have already been raised with regard to Harington's *A supplie*. Granted that Haward shows a lively interest in contemporary poetry, has carefully preserved a number of important parliamentary records, was well supplied with political and legal separates, and was interested enough to copy a few documents of an antiquarian and geographical nature, one remains puzzled as to what his point of view was towards the texts he inscribed. It is

---

[83] A useful starting point would be Keith Thomas's chapter on 'Ancient prophecies', in *Religion and the decline of magic* (New York, 1971), pp. 389-432. During the Second World War, Goebbels encouraged the circulation of a doctored version of the prophecies of Nostradamus by what we would call scribal user publication, arguing that this would be more influential than an appearance in print.

likely enough that having become involved in a culture based on
barter, he found it prudent to take whatever it delivered to him,
but this would not require that material held as separates always
had to be copied into his private miscellany. If we could assume
that his interest was the undiscriminating one of the collector, and
that virtually any well-penned separate was grist to his mill, the
question would disappear but only to be replaced by that of what
point of view is *not* revealed by this remarkably catholic
assemblage of material. The interesting fact that he was consulted
on a matter of ducal nomenclature after the Revolution supports
the suspicion of Whiggish sympathies; but might indicate no more
than that he was an experienced survivor.[84] The temptation is to
assume either a Halifax-like cynicism towards all creeds and parties
combined with a fascination with the machinery by which they
operate, or a Harington-like ability to accommodate contradictory views of the same institution or individual.[85] Yet our most
important clue regarding Sir William is that he should have chosen
to preserve this topical, evanescent material with such devoted
care, providing an ark for much that would otherwise have been
lost. Here there is a striking similarity to Pepys in his capacity as a
collector of naval records and specimens of fine contemporary
handwriting. Relishing the written ephemera of the past, both
men could see a need to lay down new stores for the future.

The universities

> And yee who with more secrecie did write
> Lines which you thought too precious for the light,
> In reseru'd Manuscripts, for shame giue o're
> Your hard-strain'd numbers, and disperse no more
> Your heauy Rimes, which see[n]e by quicker Eie
> Would make one quite abiure all Poetrie,
> And studie *Stow* and *Hollinshed*, and make
> Tractates of Trauells, or an Almanake . . . [86]

---

[84] See his letter to Viscount Hatton of 23 Mar. 1689 written from Scotland Yard (BL
Add. MS 29563, ff. 453–4). The hand is that of the commonplace book.

[85] Collinson cites Harington's 'half-apology to the ghost of Bishop Aylmer, "whom in
mine own perticuler I loued very well, and yet . . . I shall shew perhaps no great signe of it" '
(*A supplie*, p. 46). Overall *A supplie* reveals an effortless accommodation of respect for the
episcopacy with a profound disrespect for many of its representatives.

[86] Davies of Hereford, *Works*, ii. 81.

217

These lines from Abraham Holland's *A continued inquisition against paper-persecutors* (1624/5) offer one unsurprising contemporary perception of scribally published verse—that it was a secret medium, and that it was crabbed and difficult in its style. While a fair range of such verse from the earlier years of the century might be held to fit this description, Holland's criticism would seem to be directed primarily at the Inns-of-Court and university wits who wrote in what we call the Metaphysical style, and, like their master Donne, actively preferred manuscript to print.

To find writing and reading of this nature pursued within these institutions is hardly surprising. They were for a start devoted to the training of readers, writers and speakers—the future clergy-men, lawyers and administrators. Beyond this they possessed a rich corporate culture, centred in the universities on the college and in the Inns of Court on the individual Inn. Much of the poetry there circulated in manuscript copies was innocent of Holland's charges, being light-hearted social verse, written for recitation on convivial occasions. (Swift in eighteenth-century Dublin belonged to a belated culture of this kind which had its origins in his student days at Trinity College.) Other pieces, especially the ubiquitous elegies and epitaphs, belong to the rites of passage of the institution and are the texts that testify most directly to its enduring ethos. These tend to marry a virtuosity in expression to thoroughly conventional subject matter. But the genuinely 'hard-strain'd' pieces reflect another aspect of university and Inns-of-Court verse, an insistent intellectuality, nourished by years of training in the arts of philosophical disputation and forensic argument. Much university verse was still written in Latin. Circulated as separates and carefully recorded in commonplace books, these texts represent an important but as yet little-studied creative initiative.[87]

Colleges and the Inns were also places where alliances between groups of the rising young could be formed which might persist through an entire lifetime or professional career. Indeed, many young men from aristocratic and gentry families attended for a year or two partly for that reason. On arrival, the novice student

---

[87] J. W. Binns's *Intellectual culture in Elizabethan and Jacobean England: the Latin writings of the age* (Leeds, 1990) presents an admirably thorough conspectus of the printed writings but gives only cursory attention to manuscript sources and hardly any to commonplace books and personal miscellanies.

would have been exposed to a series of partly authoritarian and partly peer-group pressures designed to instill a new sense of personal identity constructed round membership of both the immediate academic community (college or Inn) and the wider one (the university or profession). Yet, at a later stage it might well have become vital to resist these pressures by creating new communities within the community—a function in which writing and its controlled circulation might perform a central role. The membership of one such group is suggested by John Hoskins' 'Convivium philosophicum' in which the names of thirteen of the author's friends who attended a drinking party at the Mitre are given as Latin puns: Donne becomes 'Factus', Christopher Brooke 'Torrens' and Hugh Holland 'Hugo Inferior-Germanus'.[88] King at Oxford and Crashaw at Cambridge were each involved in active transcriptional cultures, while Oxford in the Laudian era also held the more convivial circle of Corbett and Strode. Later in the century Oxford gave birth to the 'invisible college' whose interest lay in experiments rather than epigrams, but which was equally the child of a process by which the larger institutions were continually giving birth to smaller more specialized ones involving the circulation of 'reserved' writings in manuscript. The reading of these texts could sometimes be a communal experience, as was often the case with printed texts. One widely attested practice was for members of a group to take turns in reading a text aloud with pauses for explication and discussion.

At this period, all areas of formal university scholarship—classical and scriptural languages, rhetoric, logic, theology, Aristotelian science, law, mathematics, medicine and music—were still reliant to a significant degree on the handwritten text transmitted from scholar to scholar and teacher to student. Rosemary O'Day cites several cases of tutors preparing manuscript materials for their students. In one instance from the first decade of the century we find Daniel Featley of Corpus Christi, Oxford worried that 'the many notes and directions' he had given his pupils might fall into the hands of other tutors whom he regarded as rivals.[89] Richard Holdsworth, fellow of Emmanuel, Cambridge, whose *Directions for a student in the universities* was

---

[88] Text in Aubrey, *Brief lives*, ii. 50–3.
[89] O'Day, *Education and society*, p. 116.

itself intended to be copied by his pupils, considered scribal textbooks to be more valuable than printed ones in the earlier stages of study. Of introductory works on logic he wrote:

This first Systeme may either be a printed one the shortest and exactest one that can be gott or else a written one of your Tutors own collecting: & for some reasons I should rather preferre the latter. First because those that are printed are most of them rather fitted to riper judgments, then for the capacitie & convenience of a young beginners containing many things either too difficult, or lesse necessary for such an one. An other reason is because it is found by experience, that a teacher is more carefull & earnest to inculcate his own notions thã an others, as best understanding why, & to what end every thing there is sayd & bec: there every thing fully agrees with his own judgment wch will scarce happen in an other's works. A third reason may be this, that a Scholar by writing it over shall have gott some knowledge of it, before his Tutor come to read, and explain it to him, w^{ch}: will make him understand it a great deale better, than if he had not looked over it at all.[90]

The user and entrepreneurial transmission of volumes of lecture summaries, already long established, was to prove one of the most enduring traditions of scribal publication, surviving in British and European universities until the late nineteenth century, and in the case of certain distinguished teachers (Saussure in linguistics; Wittgenstein in philosophy) even longer.[91] Outside curricular studies a shared interest in matters as varied as alchemy, astrology, heraldry, antiquarianism, topography, chronology, modern languages or the more arcane forms of hunting could easily lead to the exchange of epistles, separates or handwritten treatises. One strong incentive to devote time to the composition and reading of these pieces was that the two university cities were rather boring places. Another, more important one was that printed books were

[90] In Harris Francis Fletcher, *The intellectual development of John Milton* (Urbana, Ill., 1961), ii. 634.

[91] In 19th-cent. medical schools a lecturer might give the same lecture for an entire career, or even purchase those of his predecessor and deliver them. But what was actually spoken would not necessarily be the text as such (which students were assumed to have acquired by copying the notes of *their* predecessors) but a series of comments on and digressions around it, incorporating current clinical findings. One example of this is discussed in my *James Edward Neild: Victorian virtuoso* (Melbourne, 1989), p. 286. Among major scientific texts reconstructed with the aid of scribally published lecture notes was Joseph Black's *Lectures on the elements of chemistry*, 2 vols (Edinburgh, 1803).

not always easy to come by. Most instruction was still oral, and university and college libraries were open only to graduates. For the many students prevented by poverty from purchasing their own copies, standard texts could only be acquired through transcription.[92] John North, entering Jesus College, Cambridge, as a fellow-commoner in 1661, was 'early sensible of a great disadvantage to him in his studies by the not having a good library in his reach' and, like many others, ventured beyond his means in building his personal collection. Roger North deplored that 'the most pregnant lads, sons of ministers and others not able to buy for themselves, are lost for want of a little early access to books'.[93] When Henry Peacham counselled the newly-arrived student to seek out learned men 'whose conference and company may bee . . . a liuing and a mouing Library', it was in the understanding that he was unlikely to have access to real libraries.[94]

University reading of scribally published, as of print-published texts was ideally a serious and attentive pursuit. James Howell, writing in 1627 to a cousin at Oxford, is one of a number of writers who use the ancient metaphor of the digestion of food to describe the necessary stages of scholarly reading:

So in feeding your soul with Science, you must first assume and suck in the matter into your apprehension, then must the memory retain and keep it in, afterwards by disputation, discours, and meditation, it must be well concocted; then must it be agglutinated and converted to nutriment; All this may be reduc'd to these two heads, *tenere fideliter*, & *uti foeliciter*, which are two of the happiest properties in a student . . . [95]

The great emphasis laid on the strengthening of memory led to a pleasure in texts that exploited this capacity by being richly allusive and intricately structured. The study of classical rhetoric and

---

[92] Cf. O'Day, p. 124.

[93] *General preface and life*, pp. 105, 179. North's remark illustrates O'Day's point that universities were 'socially segregated communities' (p. 90). Up to half the students at some colleges at our period came from aristocratic or gentry families and had no intention of completing their degrees. The intending cleric who did actually complete his BA was usually from a 'plebeian' family.

[94] *The compleat gentleman* (London, 1622), p. 39. The few exceptions were fragile: one of Thomas Crosfield's first acts as librarian of the Queen's College was to ban scholars from the library on penalty of a shilling fine, and to purchase a new lock and keys (*Diary*, p. 46).

[95] James Howell, *Epistolae Ho-Elianae. Familiar letters domestic and forren* (London, 1655), ii. 206.

constant exposure to the sermons organized round the methodical 'division' of the text encouraged an acute sense of the relationship of part to whole within discourses of all kind. (Attendance at sermons, which was compulsory for undergraduates, might be followed by a demand to reconstitute their substance from memory.) Training in Aristotelian logic—the core subject of the seventeenth-century syllabus—made the ingenious manipulation of its procedures in Donne and the Metaphysicals a source of pleasure rather than difficulty. Since this was reading conducted within a community of readers that met corporately several times a day, it would both supply and receive matter from conversation; yet this conversation would itself be of a formal kind, often conducted in Latin, and influenced by the adversarial model of the formal disputation, which O'Day describes as 'the ordinary means of scholarly communication in the Elizabethan and Early Stuart period'. 'Students who intended to take the BA degree', she notes, 'could not evade this part of the course as they could the requirement to attend university lectures. Student notebooks are dominated by work for the disputations.'[96] Tim Yellowhammer in IV. i of Middleton's *A chaste maid in Cheapside* (1613) is ridiculed for disputing in Latin with his tutor, but is doing no more than would have been expected of him within the walls of his college. So disciplined a culture also lent itself to riotous festive inversion of revered methods, as in the speeches of the Oxford Terrae-filii, but even burlesque required its own kind of learned virtuosity.

The university reader was nearly always a writer, at least at the humble level of making notes of what was read or annotating the the margins of his text. '*The Study*', writes Comenius, 'is a place where *a Student*, a part from men, sitteth alone, addicted to his *Studies*, whilst he readeth *Books*, which being within his reach, he layeth open upon *a Desk* and picketh all the best things out of them into his own *Manual*, or marketh them in them with a dash, or *a little star*, in the *Margent*.'[97] The 'manual' was usually a common-place book in which material was entered under subject headings,

---

[96] p. 112.

[97] *Orbis sensualium pictus*, pp. 200–1: '*Muséum* est locus, ubi studiosus, secretus ab hominibus, solus sedet, *Studiis* deditus, dum lectitat *Libros*, quos penes se super *Pluteum* exponit, & ex illis in *Manuale* suum optima quaeque excerpit, aut in illis *Liturâ*, vel ad *marginem Asterico*, notat'. Cf. Holdsworth in Fletcher, ii. 638.

but John North 'noted as he went along, . . . not in the common way by commonplace, but every book severally, setting down whatever he found worthily to be observed in that book'.[98] Holdsworth was also sceptical about 'the toyle & the interuption it must needs creat to theyr studies, to rise evry foot to a great Folio book, & toss it and turn it for evry little passage y[t] is to be writt downe', preferring indexed 'bookes of Collections'.[99] The need to participate in the wider culture of writing within the university meant that texts were often assembled for their value as models. The don who might himself be called on to provide an elegy, an oration, a grace or a memorial inscription would be sure to have personal copies of work by admired practitioners. Writing of this kind was an advertisement for the wit of the donor community and the excellence of its Latinity, with rival authors competing in the display of their linguistic endowments.[100] In reading too, attention to style must sometimes have predominated over attention to matter, especially as fates and fortunes were not so intimately bound up as in the metropolis with the accurate prediction of future events.

Academic miscellanies, while invaluable, are unlikely to reveal the full range of what was read in scribal form because they do not generally include what we might think of as 'professional' texts as recorded in evanescent 'paper books' kept by students. But they do give us valuable insight into the shared culture that linked scholars of all ages and disciplines. The gift of a blank album to a student was a common practice: its pages would then be filled up with a greater or lesser degree of enthusiasm depending on the tastes of the recipient. Some from each generation of students would remain in the university to become fellows, sustaining the writing culture they had encountered in their student years and drawing contributions of texts from the wider world to which their contemporaries had dispersed. Advanced at last to church livings, they continued to serve as representatives of both formal and informal academic culture and as staging points for the transmission of manuscripts.

[98] North, *General preface and life*, p. 107.

[99] Fletcher, ii. 651. Earlier Holdsworth had given advice and models for note taking (pp. 635–6).

[100] For a socio-cultural analysis of this phenomenon, see Ong, *Fighting for life*. Holdsworth (p. 645) insists on the need to record 'quaint & handsome expressions' from

The most studied of university readers, Gabriel Harvey (1550–1630), is only vestigially of our period.[101] His vigorous faith in the political mission of humanist learning was one shared by the generation of his patrons Sidney and Leicester but, paradoxically, was not to survive the accession of the scholar-king James I, having already been called into question when Oxford's Henry Cuffe incited Essex to rebellion by the exposition of a passage from Lucan's *Pharsalia*. None the less, the practices noted by Lisa Jardine and Anthony Grafton in their study of Harvey's classical reading are worthy of note insofar as some will undoubtedly have been handed on to the academic generation of Donne and Marston.[102] For a start Harvey's readings are communal, both in the sense of often being conducted in the company of a patron or academic colleague, and in the wider sense of being offered to future readers through his copious marginalia. Secondly we should notice their synoptic nature: favourite texts were characteristically read in combination with a range of related texts, with many annotations specifically aimed at clarifying these connections. This latter aspect of Harvey's reading was encouraged by the culture of print with its capacity to provide the scholar with a wide range of learned writings and commentaries, but the resultant marginalia were a scribal phenomenon that might sometimes even be copied from volume to volume, though this is not known to have happened in his case. The next stage in the process was for the marginal commentary to be integrated into a scribally circulated abridgement, or a review essay of the kind represented by Filmer's *Quaestio quodlibetica*.[103]

The Inns of Court

The atmosphere of the Inns of Court, intermediate in position between the city and Westminster, was less solemn than that of the universities, especially since some students entered in order to gain experience of the metropolis rather than with any serious intention

Latin authors for use in the student's own writing and disputations.

[101] See *Gabriel Harvey's marginalia*, ed. G. C. Moore Smith (Stratford-upon-Avon, 1913) and Virginia F. Stern, *Gabriel Harvey. His life, marginalia and library* (Oxford, 1979).

[102] 'How Gabriel Harvey read his Livy', *P&P* 129 (Nov., 1990), 30–78.

[103] A commentary on Roger Fenton's *A treatise of usury*. For its circulation, see Laslett, 'Sir Robert Filmer', p. 528.

of preparing for a legal career.[104] But the fact that many students came from at least a year or two at the universities, and that the transition required an intitiation into a new institutional culture, meant that the forming of cliques and circles linked by the exchange of manuscripts was no less common. Moreover, these students were generally older now, and therefore closer to the choice to be made among the various careers offered by the great centre of patronage. If that choice was for the law, the Inn might remain their lifelong professional base, a matter that ensured that documents, as well as circulating among peer groups, also had a chance of surviving to new generations. The fact that the practice of the law was centred on the handwritten record, and that professional copyists existed to assist with the transcription of these records, was an encouragement to the scribal publication of non-legal texts. For those with an interest in literature (and it is remarkable how many poets and dramatists spent time at one of the Inns), the soliciting, exchanging or purchasing of separates of new poetry would be the counterpart of a student today becoming involved in the University literary magazine.

Reading in the Inns of Court would have been much more varied in its nature than University reading. Not only were the readers more mature and under laxer discipline, but they must have made a much sharper distinction between professional reading—the process of familiarizing themselves with a vast, imperfectly co-ordinated body of legal precedents—and reading for the purpose of intellectual development, self-cultivation or enjoyment. Reading of this first kind needed to be patient, industrious and, once again, responsive to the ways in which knowledge could be structured for memorization; however, it could also be more selective than, say, reading in science or theology. A very large part of the wording of legal documents has always been conventional and repetitive. Attention characteristically would be directed towards those relatively localized formulations within the conventionalized document that might provide the basis for a legal argument and could be filed for future use in the pages of a commonplace book. Roger North in the course of a

---

[104] For the Inns at this time, see W. R. Prest, *The Inns of Court under Elizabeth I and the early Stuarts 1590–1640* (London, 1972); David Lemmings, 'The student body of the Inns of Court under the later Stuarts', *BIHR* 58 (1985), 149–66; and O'Day, pp. 154–6.

valuable account of the reading habits of his brother, the future Lord Keeper, locates the skill of this activity in 'the judicious, but very contracted, Note of the Matter'. Francis North, like his other brother John, rejected the conventional method of ordering his materials under alphabetically arranged headings:

> It was his Lordship's constant Practice to commonplace as he read. He had no bad Memory, but was diffident, and would not trust it. He acquired a very small but legible Hand; for, where contracting is the main Business, it is not well to write, as the Fashion now is, uncial or semiuncial Letters, to look like Pigs Ribs. His writing in his Commonplaces was not by way of *Index*, but *Epitome*; because, as he used to say, the looking over the Commonplace Book on any Occasion, gave him a sort of Survey of what he had read about Matters not then inquisited, which refreshed them somewhat in his Memory: And that had not been obtained in a way of mere what and where, as the Style of most *Indexes* runs.[105]

Roger North regarded a commonplace book as 'of little Use to any but to him that made it. For the Law is inculcated by reading the long Arguments to be found in the Books, where Reasons are given *pro* and *con*, and not by any Extracts, however curiously made' (pp. 18–19) and thought that even such celebrated abridgements as Coke upon Littleton should not be put into the hands of students. Students predictably disagreed, sustaining a huge scribal circulation of abridgements and epitomes—many of the best-known text books of the century coming into print only after extensive copying, and often against their compilers' wishes. McKenzie observes: 'Of the hundreds of seventeenth-century editions of law books, many are wrongly attributed and only a few have reliable texts', the main reasons being 'the immense variety of manuscript sources, their wide textual divergence, and the reluctance of the best legal minds to accept that the law should be fixed in public print'.[106]

As was also the case at the universities, students were encouraged to 'digest' their reading through meditation, disputation (in the form of putting cases and mooting) and mutual discussion. Roger North, who held that 'Reading goes off with some Cloud, but Discourse makes all Notions limpid and just', thought that even

[105] *Life of Francis North*, pp. 6–17.
[106] 'Speech–manuscript–print', p. 98.

solitary speech could be of value 'for, in speaking, a Man is his own Auditor (if he had no others at Hand) to correct himself' (p. 16). His brother, being 'most sensible of the Benefit of Discourse' and having discovered that something well talked over never departed from his memory, made a point of making his day's reading the topic of 'his Night's Congress with his Friends, either at Commons or over a Chop' (p. 19). Francis North's regular programme was to spend the morning commonplacing from reports, and then at about noon to turn to 'institutionary' reading in general law books as well as 'some of the Antiquarian Books' which called for little note-taking. Besides these 'the Day afforded him Room for a little History, especially of *England*, modern Books, and Controversy in Print', though these 'Excursions into Humanity and Arts' were not to be regarded as 'suitable to the Genius of every young Student in the Law' (pp. 18–19). Similar programmes are recorded for Simonds D'Ewes and Edward Waterhouse.[107] Such disciplined study was important to the young student as there was no counterpart in the Inns to the tutorial system of the universities.

Despite Roger North's misgivings about his brother's 'Excursions', the study of the common law, for those who embraced it with enthusiasm, would almost invariably encourage an enlargement of interests in the area of English history and antiquities, matters that had little representation in the University curriculum. Working in a profession that made daily use of manuscripts led naturally to the study and transcription of manuscripts of the past, many of which were still of professional value. Simonds D'Ewes must have been among the most industrious of these reader/transcribers but should be seen as just one representative of a deeply historicist intellectual culture centred on the Inns. William Crashawe, the father of the poet, regarded them as 'the most comfortable and delightfull company for a scholler, that (out of the Universities) this kingdome yeelds'.[108] Legal training could also, especially when reinforcing university training in logic and theology, encourage the intense intellectuality that characterizes the work of such Inns-of-Court poets as Donne and Sir John Davies. The reading of such texts not only satisfied tastes formed

---

[107] O'Day, pp. 159–60.
[108] *Romish forgeries and falsifications* (London, 1606), P3ʳ; cited in R. M. Fisher, 'William Crashawe's library at the Temple 1605–1615', *Library*, 5:30 (1975), 117.

by earlier education, but was a mark of the mental qualities by which law students liked to see themselves as distinguished from their contemporaries at court, with whom they were in constant rivalry. (Following a playhouse scuffle in July 1673, it was noted that 'the Inns of Court men rayle horribly at the actions of the Court, and draw themselves into partyes to affront the courtiers anywhere'.[109])

None the less, it must be conceded that the intellectual seriousness of Inns-of-Court literary writing declined significantly in the later decades of the century. If a kind of poetry unique to the Inns still survived in the 1670s it was in the work of William Wycherley and Alexander Radcliffe. Wycherley's verse, though not published in print until the collections of 1704 and 1728, is clearly in many cases of much earlier date. Most of it professedly belongs to a genre of scribally published *vers de société* addressed to friends and acquaintances on the occasion of some event affecting them or some opinion they had uttered. The printed texts conceal the identities of most of these individuals; but poems addressed to Buckingham, Sedley, Etherege, Shadwell and Aphra Behn place themselves firmly within the Buckingham circle of the 1670s, and it is likely that much of the other verse also circulated there. For good reasons this verse remains little read even by those who admire Wycherley's plays. Its faults—merciless logic chopping and excessive length—are legal faults. Legal too is the insistently agonistic tone of the many poems which either contest an opinion delivered by another or defend one of the writer's against criticism. There is little of the ease, the realism or the brevity that characterizes the verse of his courtier friends, and when such qualities are encountered it may well be because they have been supplied by Pope who did a great deal of rewriting prior to eventual print publication.

Wycherley's contemporary, the Gray's Inn wit Alexander Radcliffe, also wrote initially for scribal circulation. The dedication to his printed collection, *The ramble: an anti-heroick poem* (London, 1682) refers to the prior circulation of some pieces 'in single Sheets',[110] and three pieces, 'The ramble', 'A call to the guard

---

[109] *Letters addressed . . . to Sir Joseph Williamson*, i. 87. Donne's fourth satire is an earlier testimony to this antagonism.

[110] p. (A3^{r-v}).

by a drum' and 'Upon a bowl of punch' are found in scribal miscellanies among work by court libertine poets. In this his verse reflects a situation in which the corporate intellectual life of the Inns had weakened under pressure from an evolving 'town' culture with its headquarters in the theatres, bookshops and coffee-houses of the Covent Garden area: two later Inns-of-Court writers, Southerne and Congreve, show virtually no impress from their legal training. As a token of this capitulation the Inns' elaborately theatrical Christmas rituals quietly fell into disuse to be replaced by mundane drinking and gambling. However, Rad-cliffe's 'Upon the Memory of Mr. John Sprat, late Steward of Grayes-Inn', a witty mock-epitaph, was clearly meant for readers within his Inn, and can not have made very much sense outside it.[111] Accompanying it at the end of his 1682 volume are a few other pieces of light comic verse written for legal, not courtly readers.

As a site of reading, then, the Inns changed considerably. In the early decades of the century they nourished a confident, highly intellectualized alternative to the literary culture of the court; but by the end of the century their only cultural distinctiveness was that directly imposed by the professional work of the law and a continuing concern with antiquarian research. At both periods scribal publication of new work was the norm, but by the latter the legal community had largely ceased to be a source of texts and styles and was content to become a transmitter. This process coincided with a decline in the social status of students entering the Inns which may in turn have brought a more narrow concentra-tion on preparation for a career in the law.[112]

CONCLUSION

The attempt to distinguish sites for reading and to identify styles of reading likely to have been carried out within those sites has several problematic aspects. One is its frankly *a priori* quality; another is the very obvious point that a single individual, like Calvino's hero, could easily move from one site to another, and presumably, as we

---

[111] Ibid. 126–7.
[112] The lowered status is documented in Lemmings, 'The student body'. He attributes to the increased inability of the home counties gentry to afford legal training for their sons.

do ourselves, from one style of reading to another. The prophecy of the Westphalian boor, which was transcribed by both Haward and John Watson, must have had one kind of significance read at court by the worldly Sir William and quite another read by Watson at his quiet vicarage in the country, but it is difficult to imagine what the difference would have been had the reader been a common acquaintance with access to both collections.

We are on safer ground when we direct our attention to the ways in which conditions imposed by the site would have determined the nature of the collections assembled within it and through this the possibilities of interpretation open to the reader of the individual item. Clearly a Pindaric ode on the bible means one thing read as part of a collection of godly verse and quite another wedged between two segments of 'Seigneur Dildoe': equally clearly it would not be within all communities of readers that such a juxtaposition would have been possible. Probably about two thirds of the contents of the Haward and Watson miscellanies exists in other manuscript sources—a few of them in thirty or more copies. Currently available bibliographical aids are too imperfect to permit more than a partial reconstruction of these connections, but it is likely that hundreds of other scribal collections, whether they were compiled by individuals or by professionals trying to anticipate the tides of fashion, share at least one item in common with them. Each of these collections can be read both centripetally as providing a unique context of interpretation for the individual item and centrifugally as a trace-bearing artefact of a site or community. To apply one set of results to the elucidation of the other would require great delicacy, since each would be derived from the same data, but need not be an impossible project so long as we were prepared to tread the circle warily. If we were also prepared to range comparatively over the widest practicable spread of collections, the prize to be won would be an understanding of reading as an activity that was always communal as well as individual, and through this a new way of understanding both individuals and communities of the Stuart century.

6

RESTORATION SCRIPTORIAL
SATIRE

PROBABLY the best documented tradition of scribal publication is
that of the 'state poems' and libertine verse circulated during the last
four decades of the century. With the work of David M. Vieth and
Keith Walker on the text and canon of Rochester, of W. J. Cameron
on an important scriptorium of the 1690s, and of the editors
(including Cameron) of the Yale *Poems on affairs of state* series having
already identified a large body of manuscript anthologies and
separates, Peter Beal's entries for Dorset, Etherege, Marvell and
Rochester in the *Index of English literary manuscripts* must have
brought us close to a complete knowledge of the surviving sources.[1]
Brice Harris's findings as the biographer and editor of Dorset, John
Harold Wilson's studies of the court satirists, and Paul Hammond's
detailed account of the 'Robinson' miscellany illustrate various
aspects of the cultures of authorship and production.[2] That an
important collection of this material is housed in the Beinecke
Library at Yale is due to the enthusiasm of a collector, the late James
M. Osborn, who was also an encourager of the *POAS* project. The
other major concentrations are at the British and Bodleian libraries
and the University of Nottingham library—the last of these the fruit
of a Duke of Portland's interest in the career of an ancestor.

[1] See Vieth, *Attribution*, and *Complete poems*, and Vieth and Bror Danielsson, eds, *The Gyldenstolpe manuscript miscellany of poems by John Wilmot, Earl of Rochester, and other Restoration authors* (Stockholm, 1967), *POAS (Yale)*, vols i–vii, and Cameron, 'Scriptorium'.
[2] Brice Harris, *Charles Sackville, sixth earl of Dorset, patron and poet of the Restoration* (Urbana, Ill., 1940) and *The poems of Charles Sackville*; John Harold Wilson, *The court wits of the Restoration* (Princeton, NJ, 1948) and *Court satires of the Restoration* (Columbus, Oh., 1976); Paul Hammond, 'The Robinson manuscript miscellany of Restoration verse in the Brotherton Collection Leeds', *Proceedings of the Leeds Philosophical and Literary Society*, Literary and historical section, 18/3 (1982), 277–324.

Part II

While a few more miscellanies will no doubt be discovered, it is unlikely that they will challenge the picture we already possess of this active and highly professionalized tradition. This makes the satire ideally suited to serve as a detailed case study of the practical workings of scribal publication. The term 'scriptorial satire' has been chosen because so many of the surviving examples were produced as part of scribal editions; however, the notion of the 'scriptorium' is once again used loosely. While some copying probably did take place in spaces organized for that purpose by scriveners or booksellers, much may equally well have been performed by scribes working on piecework in their own homes.

A marked feature of this material is its coherence as a canon of writing. The miscellanies in which it survives restrict themselves, for the most part, to three categories of material. The first of these is what has been referred to as the 'state poems' tradition—satires on politicians and politics. The second comprises satire directed at courtiers and court ladies, and the third erotic, sometimes pornographic, verse mostly written *by* courtiers—these last two categories comprising the 'court libertine' tradition. There are overlaps in subject matter between all three categories; and yet distinctions in tone and approach mean that there is rarely any real difficulty in distinguishing between a 'state' and a 'libertine' satire. The principal form encountered is the lampoon, a satirical attack on a group of victims, who are first addressed in general terms and then picked off one by one. This was in one sub-tradition a folk-form, deriving from much older models of improvised satirical balladry, and in another a pseudo-learned one, whose origin is to be found in Jacobean experiments at the naturalization of classical satire.[3]

Lampoons of the folk-derived class are stanzaic, usually written to a broadside ballad, country dance or playhouse tune. A Star

---

[3] For the folk aspects of the tradition, see in particular C. J. Sisson, *Lost plays of Shakespeare's age* (Cambridge, 1936), pp. 186–203. On p. 198 Sisson cites a Nottingham example of 1617 where the lampoon was sung to an accompaniment of candlesticks, tongs and basins, indicating its relationship to the 'rough music' of the skimmington. The Jacobean experiments of Hall, Marston and Donne are discussed in O. J. Campbell, *Comicall satyre and Shakespeare's 'Troilus and Cressida'* (San Marino, 1938); John Peter, *Complaint and satire in early English literature* (Oxford, 1956); Anthony Caputi, *John Marston, satirist* (Ithaca, NY, 1961); and Alvin Kernan, *The cankered muse: satire of the English renaissance* (New Haven, Conn., 1959).

Chamber bill of 1622 preserves a fragment of a 'naïve' lampoon directed at a Leicester couple Henry and Jane Skipwith:

John Pilkington did in the moneth of Aprill nowe last past most malitiously frame and contrive an vntrue scandelous and most infamous Libell in wrytinge agᵗ. Yoʳ said Subiecte and his said wife in theis words followinge (vizt) Henrie Skipwith his wife him Wippeth, because he Married a Twanger, Hee married her a riche Whoare, and hath made her full poore, and paies her olde debtes for anger.[4]

Pilkington sung the piece at various taverns and gatherings around Leicester. The rhythm is recognizable in literary examples such as this of 1667

> Good people, draw near
> If a ballad you'd hear,
>   It will teach you the new way of thriving.
> Ne'er trouble your heads
> With your books or your beads;
>   The world's ruled by cheating and swiving.[5]

or this of 1688

> The talk up and down
> In country and town
> Has been long of a parliament's sitting,
>   But we'll make it clear
>   Ne'er a month in the year
> Is proper for such a meeting.[6]

Only the last of these specifies its tune, 'Cold and raw, the north did blow', a version of a much earlier drinking song known as 'Stingo, or oil of barley'. Purcell's use of the piece as the ground bass of a movement in his 1692 birthday ode for Queen Mary has been

---

[4] PRO STAC8 261/25. For a similar sung text of 1632, see Gardiner, *Reports*, pp. 148–53.

[5] 'A ballad', Wilson, *Court satires*, p. 10.

[6] 'The statesman's almanac', *POAS (Yale)*, iv. 279. For the persistence of the form, compare the following stanza from a poem about the Collingwood Football Club, published in the Melbourne *Age*, 21 September 1990, p. 2:

> If the AFL's smart,
> They'll give the Magpies a start
> Each time that they enter the ring.
> It may create some gladness
> And help ease the sadness
> That comes with the wobbles of spring.

explained by her once having called for it in preference to his own songs; but its history as a lampoon melody suggests a more subversive explanation.[7]

Although it has not been customary for scholars to treat the stanzaic lampoon as a sung form, and the manuscript sources frequently neglect to identify the tune, musical performance will often give cogency to an otherwise nondescript text, besides solving problems of metre and accentuation. To hear Rochester's(?) 'Signior Dildo' sung to its original tune of 'Peggy's gone over sea with the soldier' locates it socially as an improvisatorial drinking song in a way that gives point to what on the page is a rather tedious repetition of a rudimentary joke.[8] One very common stanza form of three iambic tetrameter lines followed by a refrain usually implies a version of the melody known to us as 'Greensleeves'. A nine-line stanza in triple metre with lines five and six half the length of the others infallibly indicates 'Packington's pound'. These and other well-known ballad tunes could be heard daily in the streets and would be recognized by contemporary readers even when not specified in a title. The numerous lampoons using the 'litany' format may well have been chanted in a mock-ecclesiastical way with all present joining in the response (usually 'Libera nos domine').

The other lampoon mode is that which uses heroic couplets to suggest an alliance with the emerging tradition of classically derived satire. But the relationship is more one of show than of substance: if there is a classical influence at work it is the epigrams of Martial rather than the satires of Horace and Juvenal.[9] The usual pattern is for a perfunctory introduction to be followed by a series

---

[7] For the story see Claude M. Simpson's invaluable *The British broadside ballad and its music* (New Brunswick, NJ, 1966), p. 692.

[8] The tune is identified in Bodl. MS don. b 8, pp. 477–8, 480–2, the only text that survives from close to the time of composition. For the melody see Simpson, p. 572. Stanzaic lampoon tunes not found in Simpson should be sought in the six volumes of Thomas D'Urfey's *Songs compleat, pleasant and divertive* (London, 1719–20)—better known as *Pills to purge melancholy*—and *The complete country dance tunes from Playford's dancing master (1651–ca. 1728)*, ed. Jeremy Barlow (London, 1985). The attribution to Rochester does not seem to have been made until the 1690s.

[9] The influence is discussed in my 'Rochester and the traditions of satire' in my *Restoration literature: critical approaches* (London, 1972), pp. 145–75, drawing on Peter's discussion (*Complaint and satire*, pp. 155–6) of the influence of the classical epigram on the formal experiments of the Jacobean satirists.

of epigram-like attacks on a list of victims. The introduction often does little more than characterize the speaker of the satire as a plain-spoken enemy of cant, and sometimes even this can be dispensed with:

> This way of writing I observe by some
> Is introduced by an exordium,
> But I will leave to make all that ado,
> And in plain English tell you who fucks who.[10]

In other poems, particularly those using the 'ghost', 'dream', 'farewell' or 'advice' conventions, the exordium may be more sustained, but all comes in the end to the parade of personal attacks and it is rare to find a formal conclusion, a couplet or two normally sufficing to terminate the slaughter. Dorset's 'A faithful catalogue of our most eminent ninnies' (1688)—the longest and most vituperative essay in the genre—ends in mid-flight with a brusque 'Cetera desunt'. Alongside the two styles of lampoon, we encounter translations, songs (serious and 'mock'), a few true formal verse satires after classical and contemporary French models, and the occasional more serious political reflection, often using dialogue form. A few short prose satires also occur, usually employing the mock-auction-catalogue, mock-oration or mock-petition formula.

The victims of the satire are drawn from a world largely bounded by the court, the parliament, the Inns of Court, the theatres, and fashionable taverns and coffee houses. While scribally published satires were unquestionably read in the city there are not many cases of citizens being addressed as the primary audience. The writers adopt a tone of familiarity with the great and near-great which, while no doubt often bogus, has the appearance of allowing the reader vicarious entry to a select circle of all-knowing wits. The scribally published text had always attracted through its promise of revealing concealed knowledge, and when such knowledge was not actually available it would be manufactured. (No statement made in a lampoon should be accepted as a historical fact without supporting evidence.) Language is direct, colloquial, and frequently indecent. Names of writers appear more frequently

---

[10] 'Satire', Wilson, *Court satires*, p. 81.

than one would expect with such compromising works but must be regarded with the same scepticism as their substance. Most are probably speculative, and it is not exceptional for the same poem to appear in different sources attributed to two or three different authors. The editor of the 1704 edition of the second Duke of Buckingham's *Works* warns:

I might add, That several Copies of Verses in this Edition are now restored to their proper Authors, which were attributed before to Persons, to whom they [n]ever belong'd, the Transcribers of the last Age, as well as those of the former, either following common Report, which is often mistaken, or else setting any plausible Names before their Copies, (no matter with what justice this was done) provided it would but promote the value of their Manuscript.[11]

The practice is one that has already been noted in connection with early Stuart parliamentary separates: in this case the attempt to remedy it leads to several new errors. A sub-genre of lampoons satirizing lampooners is a useful source for names of minor poets active in the field, but should be used with caution in assigning authors to particular items.[12] More valuably for our present enquiry, authors of lampoons will frequently identify the scribal publisher who put the work into circulation—Robert Julian, Lenthal Warcup, John Somerton and Henry Heveningham being four so named.[13]

Satire of this kind had already been current during the reigns of James I and Charles I and the interregnum. It is to be regretted in this respect that Yale University Press have never thought to supplement their *Poems on affairs of state 1660–1714* with a preliminary series running from the accession of James I. The

---

[11] *Miscellaneous works, written by his grace George, late Duke of Buckingham*, 2nd edn (London, 1704), i. A4ʳ.

[12] Four examples conveniently available in Wilson, *Court satires* are 'The King, Duke and state' (pp. 92–6), 'Dear Julian, twice or thrice a year' (pp. 131–7), 'Mine and the poets' plague consume you all' (pp. 138–40) and 'Here take this, Warcup, spread this up and down' (pp. 159–65). To these should be added Buckingham's 'Thou common shore of this poetic town' (*POAS (Yale)*, i. 387–91), and 'On Monmouth, John Howe, and Lord Mulgrave' (*POAS (Yale)*, v. 4–6). Two lampooners, Roger Martin and John Howe, ingeniously work their names into the concluding couplet of poems (Wilson, pp. 119, 256).

[13] For Julian, Warcup and Somerton see below. Heveningham is the addressee of a prefatory letter to 'The divorce' (1691), quoted in *POAS (Yale)*, v. 534. For his literary career see W. J. Cameron, 'John Dryden and Henry Heveningham', *N&Q* 202 (June–Dec. 1957), 199–203.

events covered would have yielded nothing in interest, and, leaving Dryden and Marvell aside, the talents involved would, on the whole, have been mightier ones. The assassination of the first Duke of Buckingham in 1628 provoked a particularly rich harvest of oppositional verse, some of which occurs as linked groups in manuscript collections of that period.[14] After Milton's friend, Alexander Gill, had drawn attention to himself by claiming that 'if there were a hell and devil surely the Duke was there', a search was made of the 'chamber, study, and pockets' of his friend William Pickering, 'wherein they found divers libels and letters written by Alexander Gill and others, all of them touching on the late Duke of Buckingham'.[15] Bodleian MS Douce 357, acquired as a blank book by one 'A. P.' in 1642, is important for including political verse from both before and after the Restoration. The fifty-six items from the earlier period include linked groups of five poems on the death of Buckingham and nine on the execution of Strafford (including Cleveland's 'Here lies wise and valiant dust'). The 121 post-Restoration satires, written in a different hand, range in date of composition from the mid-1660s to the early 1690s, but are presented in no particular sequence. The collection appears to be unique among the larger anthologies in combining substantial bodies of verse from both the earlier and later seventeenth century.[16] It is possible that the later factors in lampoons no longer had access to the archives of their predecessors. The great fire of 1666, with the attendant destruction of the booksellers' stocks in the vaults under Saint Paul's, could well have been responsible for this. But it is also possible that the tradition of anti-court satire itself became dormant for some years, reviving only towards the end of

---

[14] Reprinted in *Poems and songs relating to George Villiers, Duke of Buckingham*, ed. F. W. Fairholt (London, 1850) and J. A. Taylor, 'Two unpublished poems on the Duke of Buckingham', *RES*, NS 40 (1989), 232–40. The second of the poems printed by Taylor, William Hemminge's 'Heere lyes thy vrne, O what A little blowe', passed as part of a linked group of three into the archive of the 'Cameron' scriptorium of the 1690s. See also V. L. and M. L. Pearl, 'Richard Corbett's "Against the opposing of the duke in parliament"', pp. 32–9.

[15] *CSP (Dom.) 1628–9*, pp. 338–9.

[16] The other examples known to me are the personal miscellanies, Society of Antiquaries MS 330, compiled by an unidentified Oxford don, BL Add. MS 18220, compiled by the Cambridge don and Sussex vicar, John Watson, and Yale MS Osborn b 52/1–2, compiled by John Pye. Such collections were written piecemeal over many years, whereas Douce 357 appears to have been produced in two or three concentrated acts of copying.

the decade. That tradition will now be considered under its main phases from its beginnings to the accession of Queen Anne in 1703.

'MARVELLIAN' SATIRE 1667–1678

Referring to the years immediately following the Restoration, George deF. Lord notes, not without reason, that 'except for one or two inferior squibs on the plight of the Cavaliers, who were bitter about the Restoration settlement . . . not a breath of criticism survives among all the commendatory verses on the royal family, on Lord Chancellor Hyde, or on Charles' reigning mistress, the Countess of Castlemaine'.[17] Even the savage anti-Dissenter measures of the early 1660s brought no evident reaction in the form of scribally circulated satire. The provocation that led to a revival of the earlier tradition was a printed poem, Waller's *Instructions to a painter*, which presented a flattering portrait of the behaviour of the Duke of York in the Battle of Lowestoft fought on 3 June 1665. This gave rise to a series of three further 'Advice to a painter' poems (1666–7), known as the second, third, and fourth Advices, which were followed by a 'Fifth advice', 'The last instructions to a painter' (both 1667) and 'Further advice to a painter' (1671).[18] Of these the 'Last instructions' (part of which is found in adapted form as 'The loyal Scot') is definitely by Marvell and one or more of the others could well be. A number of other satires of the late 1660s and early 1670s were also attributed to him, though often not until many years later. These are 'Clarendon's housewarming' (When Clarendon had discern'd beforehand'), 'The King's vows' ('When the plate was at pawn and the fob at low ebb'), 'A ballad called the Haymarket hectors' ('I sing a woeful ditty'), 'Upon His Majesty's being made free of the city' ('The Londoners gent'), 'On the statue erected by Sir Robert Viner' ('As cities that to the fierce conquerors yield') and 'The statue at Charing Cross' ('What can be the mystery why Charing Cross').[19]

---

[17] *POAS (Yale)*, i. 20.

[18] The genre continued to be a productive one until well into the nineteenth century. For its history see Mary Tom Osborne, *Advice-to-a-painter poems, 1633–1856* (Austin, 1949) and *POAS (Yale)*, passim.

[19] Annotated texts of these poems will be found in *POAS (Yale)*, i. 20–273 *passim*. The two extreme positions are those of Lord in *POAS (Yale)*, i, who attributes the second and third advices, 'Clarendon's housewarming', the 'Last instructions', 'Further advice to a painter', 'Upon Blood's attempt to steal the crown', 'Upon his Majesty being made free of

Although some of these poems were surreptitiously printed, their initial circulation was in manuscript. Together with such widely circulated satires as 'The downfall of the Chancellor' ('Pride, lust, ambition and the people's hate') and 'On the prorogation' ('Prorogu'd on prorogation—damn'd rogues and whores'), they constituted the core of a widely-read body of oppositional satire, which was soon consolidated into linked groups and sub-collections.

The early history of this 'Marvellian' tradition, can to some extent be reconstructed from its later copyings. Pepys is a witness to the role of user publication in this process. On 14 December 1666, he acquired a copy of what was evidently the 'Second advice', 'sealed up, from Sir H. Cholmly'. This suggests a folded separate rather than the surreptitiously printed broadside that was also in circulation. On 20 January 1667 John Brisbane, another naval official, showed him a copy of the 'Third advice', which he took home in order to copy it, 'having the former—being also mightily pleased with it'. On 1 July, while he was travelling from Rochester to London with John Creed, they 'fell to reading of the several *Advices to a Painter*, which made us good sport'—however, this may have been a printed collection.[20] The second, third and fourth advices are found together in a number of manuscripts in the company of other poems from the tradition. Several of these collections are of interest because the 'Marvellian' material occurs as an apparently self-contained unit within a larger structure. In Princeton MS Taylor 1 and its twin BL Harley 7315 (first compilation) it forms the opening items of a commercial anthology of state poems to 1680 whose other contents seem to have been drawn in no particular order from an assemblage of separates. (The satire immediately following, 'I sing the praise of a worthy wight', dates from the late 1670s.) In Harvard Eng. Misc. e 586, a private miscellany, the group is immediately followed by transcriptions from the 1680 Rochester *Poems on several occasions*

the city', 'On the statue erected by Sir Robert Viner' and 'The statue at Charing Cross' to Marvell, and that of Elizabeth Story Donno, in *Andrew Marvell, the complete poems* (Harmondsworth, 1972), who will allow him only 'The last instructions', with 'Blood and the crown' listed as of uncertain attribution. For discussion of the ascriptions see Donno, pp. 217–18 and Kelliher, *Andrew Marvell*, pp. 97–104.

[20] *Diary*, vii. 407; viii. 21, 313. See also *POAS (Yale)*, i, pp. xxxix–xli. Surreptitious printed editions, all dated 1667, survive of the second advice, the second and third advice

and those in turn by notes on legal cases. Harvard MS Eng. 624 and Society of Antiquaries MS 330 present alternative versions of an anti-Clarendon linked group, the first instance occurring at the beginning of a carelessly-written copy of an anthology compiled circa 1680 and the second in an anthology with both English and Latin sections commenced in 1671 by an Oxford don.

Bodleian MS Eng. poet. d 49 stands apart from the other sources in being a printed book, Marvell's posthumous *Miscellaneous poems* (London, 1681), with extensive manuscript additions. This volume has always been a problem to Marvell scholars since some of the additions are obviously derived from sources very close to Marvell (perhaps even his own copies), while others are satires that are not commonly accepted into the canon. The general assumption has been that they draw on Marvell's own archive of texts and that this included a mixture of his own and others' writing. It is also claimed that the hand of the additions is that of his nephew, William Popple. While there is nothing improbable about these claims, they fail to allow for the possibility that the volume was a publisher's made-up collection that may once have existed in more than one copy. An analogy might be drawn with an appendix of manuscript verse, discussed below, which was sold with some copies of the Rochester *Poems on several occasions* first published in the previous year.

What has been described so far has been an oppositional tradition; but as it evolved through the late 1670s it was increasingly a Whig, Exclusionist tradition. 'Loyal' satirists existed but it was not until the early years of the next decade that they commanded assured networks of entrepreneurial publication. The most telling testimony to the impact of the lampoonists was the attempt made in the new year of 1676 to close down the coffee houses. The author of 'The king, duke and state' (in yet another set of words to the ubiquitous 'stingo') was in no doubt that the lampooners were to blame for the banning.

> I must needs confesse,
> The King could doe no lesse,
>   To stop the mouth of Coffee poet,
> No great man or grave

together, and advices two to five with 'Clarendon's housewarming'. For these see *POAS (Yale)*, i. 447–8.

Could be dull fool or knave,
But straight all ye Citty must know it.[21]

The original proclamation of 29 December 1675 does not refer specifically to the availability of seditious manuscripts, merely objecting to 'the great resort of Idle and disaffected persons' including 'many Tradesmen and others' and that 'in such Houses, and by occasion of the meetings of such persons therein, divers False, Malitious and Scandalous Reports are devised and spread abroad, to the Defamation of His Majesties Government, and to the Disturbance of the Peace and Quiet of the Realm'.[22] But the coffee-house proclamation was followed on 7 January 1676 by another which indicates the government's real concern:

Whereas divers malicious and disaffected persons do daily devise and publish, as well by Writing, as Printing, sundry false, infamous, and scandalous Libells, endeavouring thereby, not only to traduce and reproach the Ecclesiastical and Temporal Government of this Kingdom, and the publick Ministers of the same, but also to stir up and dispose the minds of His Majesties Subjects to Sedition and Rebellion; For the discovery of such wicked Offenders, and to the intent that they may receive the severest Punishments which by the Laws of this Kingdom may be inflicted upon them, His Majesty (with the advice of His Privy Council) doth by this Royal Proclamation Publish and Declare, That if any person or persons shall discover and make known . . . the person or persons to whom any such Libell, at any time since the last Act of General Pardon, hath been, or shall hereafter be brought, and by him or them received, in order to Print or transcribe the same; Or the Place where such Libell shall be printing or transcribing, whereby the same shall happen to be seized; Or the person or persons by whom any such Libell at any time since the said Act hath been, or shall hereafter be printed or transcribed; Or shall discover and make known . . . any private Printing-Press . . . He or they making every such discovery, shall have and receive, as a reward from His Majesty, the sum of Twenty pounds.[23]

The proclamation has been carefully drafted to apply to both scribally published and print-published libels and to scriptoria as well as clandestine presses. If enforced with the firmness envisaged

---

[21] All Souls College, Oxford MS 116, ff. 44^r. There is a second text in Bodleian MS don. b 8, p. 556.

[22] *A proclamation for the suppression of coffee-houses* (London, 1675), p. 1.

[23] *A proclamation for the better discovery of seditious libellers* (London, 1676), p. 1.

by Roger L'Estrange in his 'Proposition concerning Libells' it might have done much to halt the flow of anti-court propaganda; but it is doubtful if this was regarded as practical, its true purpose being to create a means of controlling the coffee-houses short of actual suppression. On the day following the proclamation just quoted *An additional proclamation concerning coffee-houses* was issued which withdrew the earlier demand for abolition, replacing it with another by which each coffee-house proprietor was to take the oaths of allegiance and supremacy and enter into a recognizance of £500 to 'use his utmost endeavour to prevent and hinder all Scandalous Papers, Books or Libels concerning the Government, or the Publick Ministers thereof, from being brought into his House, or to be there read, Perus'd or Divulg'd'. From the outbreak of the Exclusion Bill crisis in 1678 parliament took care to remove what constraints remained on the free flow of both printed and scribal comment, refusing to renew the Licensing Act and encouraging the penny-post as an alternative method of conveying mail, and therefore libels, speedily and cheaply through the London area. By the early 1680s professionally written anthologies of oppositional satire, of the kind represented by BL Add. MS 34362, Harl. MS 7315[1] and Princeton MS Taylor 1, were already available.[24]

COURT LIBERTINE SATIRE OF THE 1670S

The restored court of 1660 was quick to claim its old responsibility for the patronage and supervision of literature. During the early years of Charles's reign, the elderly Duke of Newcastle reassumed the role of Maecenas he had held before the Civil War. Then, Jonson, D'Avenant and Shirley had come under his care. Under the new dispensation, an attempt to enlist Dryden came unstuck over the question of which of the two was to have the credit for *Sir Martin Mar-all*; but Shadwell was delighted to take up the vacancy, while Richard Flecknoe was a regular house guest with the Duke

---

[24] For the latter two see below. The first is a wide-ranging anthology of state verse compiled in 1682. The inscription on the title-page, 'Sam[ll] Danvers. 1664' seems to be a red herring: the most likely explanation is that the scribe was utilizing a blank book that had been so signed by Danvers.

and members of his very extended family.[25] Newcastle stood for an older concept of patronage but had not fallen too far behind in his tastes. In his championing of Ben Jonson against Shakespeare as the model of comic excellence and in his preference for an improvisatorial ideal of poetic wit, drawing its inspiration from courtly conversation, he was at one with the younger court poets of his time.[26] They in turn seem to have entertained an affectionate respect for both himself and his duchess.[27]

However, most of these younger writers preferred to attach themselves to a younger mentor in the person of George Villiers, second Duke of Buckingham (1628–87), whose wavering loyalties during the interregnum did not prevent him from wielding great influence at court, especially following the fall of Clarendon, which he helped engineer. The extraordinary excesses of Buckingham's private life, remembered through Dryden's portrait of him as 'Zimri' in *Absalom and Achitophel*, have blinded posterity to his very considerable political achievements.[28] A skilled intriguer, a malicious wit, and a man of real if erratic personal charm, he became the acknowledged leader of the group of court wits whose other prominent members were Rochester, Dorset, John, Lord Vaughan (later Earl of Carbery), Sir Charles Sedley, Etherege, Shadwell, Wycherley, Henry Savile and Fleetwood Sheppard. On 6 February 1668, Dorset, Sedley, Etherege and Buckingham sat together in the pit at the first performance of Etherege's *She would if she could*.[29] In 1670 Dorset and Sedley accompanied Buckingham, then at the height of his influence, on an embassy to Louis

[25] For these relationships, see my 'Shadwell, Flecknoe and the Duke of Newcastle' and 'Richard Flecknoe as author-publisher'.

[26] For Cavendish's life, see Geoffrey Trease, *Portrait of a cavalier: William Cavendish, first Duke of Newcastle* (London, 1979). His aesthetic ideals are explained by Douglas Grant in his introduction to *The phanseys of William Cavendish, Marquis of Newcastle* (London, 1956). The influence of the conversational ideal is discussed with reference to Restoration comedy in Robert Markley, *Two-edg'd weapons. Style and ideology in the comedies of Etherege, Wycherley, and Congreve* (Oxford, 1988).

[27] Evident in Etherege's 'To her Excellence the Marchioness of Newcastle after the reading of her incomparable poems', *The poems of Sir George Etherege*, ed. James Thorpe (Princeton, NJ, 1963), pp. 14–15.

[28] Buckingham's life is described in Hester Chapman's *Great Villiers* (London, 1949) and John Harold Wilson's *A rake and his times: George Villiers, second Duke of Buckingham* (New York, 1954). Of these Chapman gets closer to the man and Wilson is more reliable concerning the career.

[29] Pepys, *Diary*, ix. 54.

XIV. Sir Robert Howard should also be mentioned, for, although he and his brother Edward were butts of the wits' satire, he collaborated on *The country gentleman* with Buckingham and on a play about the Manchu conquest of China with Rochester, and was a political organizer for Buckingham in the House of Commons. Buckingham's witty client, Martin Clifford, and even wittier chaplain, Thomas Sprat (both coadjutors in *The rehearsal*), were also close to the circle, though never actual members.[30] Among the established living poets Waller and Butler had close links, while D'Avenant and Dryden were less respected, despite the latter's attempts to ingratiate himself. On Buckingham's departure from office in January 1674 most of the circle followed him into opposition.

But in the first decade following the Restoration, loyalty to the crown presented no problems. Dorset (then known as Lord Buckhurst) came to court aged seventeen in 1660 and began to establish himself as a writer from 1663 when he took part with a group that also included Waller and Sedley in a translation of Corneille's *La mort de Pompée* and engaged in a scribally circulated verse correspondence with Etherege.[31] Whereas the state lampoon took some years to regain its former vigour, the court lampoon was reportedly reinstated by early in the same year when an attempt by the Earl of Chesterfield to protect his wife from the attentions of the Duke of York by hurrying her off to the country set off an outburst of satirical balladry.[32] Anthony Hamilton remembered Dorset, Sedley, Etherege and Rochester as having been contributors, though the latter was actually still absent on the grand tour. Rochester arrived at court at Christmas 1664, immediately following his return from Europe. The period at

[30] Sprat's desertion to the Tories at the time of the Exclusion crisis must have severed his relationship with Buckingham, but letters discussed in Harris, *Charles Sackville*, pp. 137–40 show that after the Revolution he was quick to capitalize on an earlier friendship with Dorset. Clifford seems to have been the source of the greatly expanded version of Buckingham's 'commonplace book' preserved in Hertfordshire CRO MS D/EP F37.

[31] Harris, *Charles Sackville*, pp. 26–7 and 103–5. For the correspondence, see Dorset, *Poems*, ed. Harris, pp. 105–17 and Etherege, *Poems*, pp. 35-45.

[32] Anthony Hamilton, *Mémoires du chevalier de Gramont*, ed. Claire-Éliane Engel (Monaco, 1958), pp. 217–18. A surviving lampoon from 1663, 'Cary's face is not the best' (Wilson, *Court satires*, pp. 3–9), ignores the episode in presenting appraisals of the sexual potential of 18 leading women of the court, but shows all the features of the later misogynist lampoon.

which he began to establish himself as a writer is not clear. If the lyric 'This Bee alone of all his race', attributed to him in National Library of Ireland MS 2093, is authentic, it must have been written prior to the marriage of Lady Mary Stuart to Lord Richard Butler which had taken place by 16 March 1667; but otherwise, apart from three short pieces supposedly written as a schoolboy, no poem currently accepted into the Rochester canon can be confidently given a date earlier than 1670.[33] Testimony to his absorption into the Buckingham circle is given by the choice of Buckhurst (representing the king) and Sedley as godfathers at the christening of his son Charles on 2 January 1671 and the affectionate letter written by Buckhurst on that occasion.[34] The surviving letters from Buckingham himself to Rochester belong to 1676–7 but display an ease and informality that implies long friendship.

The earliest surviving group enterprise of the Buckingham circle was the series of mock-commendatory poems written in response to the publication during Easter term 1669 of Edward Howard's narrative poem, *The British princes*. The responses were probably assembled during the following summer by the time-honoured method of circulating the growing file from writer to writer.[35] It belongs to a tradition whose most notable prior landmarks were the printed collections inspired by *Coryate's crudities* in 1611 and Davenant's *Gondibert* in 1651, and the satires on Samuel Austin the younger collected in *Naps upon Parnassus* in 1658. In the fullest version, that of Bodleian MS Eng. poet. e 4, a private miscellany assembled by an Oxford man, the collection is as follows. Titles, first lines and ascriptions are all given as they appear in the original:

On M[r] Edward Howards New Utopia. ('Thou damn'd Antipodes to common Sense,') Charles L. Buckhurst [pp. 188–9]

[33] 'This bee alone' is addressed to Lady Mary under her maiden name. For the marriage, see Pepys, *Diary*, vi. 168n. The lines published under Rochester's name in *Britannia rediviva* (Oxford, 1660) and *Epicedia academiae Oxoniensis* (Oxford, 1660) were believed by Anthony à Wood to be the work of Robert Whitehall (*Athenae Oxonienses*, ed. Philip Bliss (London, 1813–20), iii. 1232).

[34] *Letters*, pp. 60–1.

[35] For the method, see Williams, 'Commendatory verses', pp. 8–9, and for the contributors A. J. Bull, 'Thomas Shadwell's satire on Edward Howard', *RES* 6 (1930), 312–15.

1 [*sic*]. To Mr Edward Howard on his British Princes. ('Come on, you Criticks, find one fault who dare;') Charles B. Buckhurst, now E. Dorsett [p. 190]

2. To the Honourable Ed. Howard Esq. upon his Incomparable, Incomprehensible Poem of the British Princes. ('Sir/ You have[36] oblig'd the British Nation more,') Edmund Waller [pp. 191–2]

3. On the British Princes. ('Your Book our old Knight Errants fame revives,') Th. Spratt [p. 192]

4. An Heroick Poem on the Names and Com[m]anders of England, Rome, and Gaul, or forty six Verses on forty six hundred. ('Our Bard most bravely draws up his Militia,') J. D. [pp. 193–4]

[Annotation to lines 5–6 of previous:] Two Verses left out in the Impression of the Poem. ('A Vest as wondrous Vortiger had on,') [p. 194]

[5.] On the British Princes ('With Envy (Criticks) you'l this Poem read,') Mart. Clifford [p. 194]

6. In Imitation of his most excellent Style ('Of all great Nature *fated* unto witt,') Tho. Shadwell [pp. 195–6]

7. On the same. ('Wonder not, Sir, that praises ne're yet due') L. Vaughan [p. 196]

8. On the British Princes ('As when a Bully draws his sword,') E[dmund] A[shton] [p. 197]

9. On these two Verses of Mr Howards. But Fame had sent forth all her nimble spies, / To blaze this Match, and lend to Fate some eyes. ('But wherefore all this pother about Fame') Buckingham [pp. 197–8]

On the humour in Mr Howards Play, where Mr Kinaston disputes his staying in, or going out of Town, as he is pulling on his Boots. In Imitation of the Earle of Orrerey. ('How hath my Passion made me Cupids scoff!') G. D Buckingham. [pp. 198–9]

This is actually a later recension of the series which has been augmented with poems by Dorset and Buckingham directed at Howard's play *The new Utopia*, published and, as far as is known, first performed in 1671. Buckingham's second contribution appears in variant form in III. ii of *The rehearsal*, written with the assistance of Sprat, Clifford and Butler and first performed in December 1671, and may even have been the germ of that work. The Howard linked-group adds the shadowy Edmund Ashton to our roll-call of the Buckingham circle, but omits Sedley, who could, however, well lurk behind the provocative initials 'J. D.'. (Dryden as Howard's brother-in-law would hardly have associ-

---

[36] Corrected in MS to 'Y'have'

ated himself with such a project.) Rochester is also missing, probably because of his absence in Paris during the spring and early summer of 1669. Despite the Howard satires having been circulated as a lengthy linked group, there is no evidence at this date of substantial anthologies of the verse of the circle being in circulation. It seems likely that for many years poems were transmitted only as separates and linked groups, and that only author and user publication were undertaken.

But Rochester, while continuing as late as 'An allusion to Horace' (1675–6) to argue the superiority of the intimate coterie audience, was finding a growing readership through user publication. In part this was purposive: poems written to wound enemies or to further his position at court would have failed in their aim if they had never spread beyond his own intimates.[37] He is known to have carried separates in his coat pockets and on one occasion late in 1673 or early in 1674 to have reached into the wrong pocket and handed the king a copy of 'I'th' isle of Great Britain', in which Charles was very roughly handled. In this case the desire to find a readership for his lampoons proved disastrous, but in others it was a necessary concomitant of writing. Two possible methods of spreading a lampoon are suggested in the anonymous 'Satyr unmuzzled' (1680) which speaks of 'lewd libels . . . / Which are i'th'streets by porters dropp'd and hurl'd; / Or else by Julian 'mongst the bullies spread—'.[38] It seems unlikely that handwritten lampoons would have been thrown around in the streets; and yet few compositions of this kind were ever printed.[39] Spreading amongst the bullies is well documented, and it is also known that poems were posted on doors and walls, inscribed as

[37] In his conversations with Burnet, he confirms that his lampoons were intended not merely to amuse his friends but to mortify his victims, something which could only happen if they were made generally available at Whitehall (*Some passages of the life and death of the Right Honourable John Earl of Rochester* (London, 1680), pp. 25–6).

[38] *POAS (Yale)*, ii. 209.

[39] However, H. J. Chaytor, *From script to print: an introduction to medieval vernacular literature* (Cambridge, 1945), p. 131 refers to 'dropping lampoons in public or private places, or fastening them up on walls' as common medieval practices. Proculus in Fletcher's *Valentinian*, IV. i. 84 produces a compromising letter which has been 'Scatterd belike i'th Court' (*Dramatic works*, iv. 338). Evelyn notes under 2 April 1668: 'Amongst other Libertine Libells, there was now printed & thrown about a bold Petition of the poore Whores, to the Lady *Castlemaine* &c:' (*Diary*, iii. 507). This was a printed version of a scribally published satire which continued to be widely copied independently of its printed transmission.

graffiti and strategically inveigled into the apartments of leading courtiers.[40] Once spoken of at Whitehall they would have been eagerly sought for private copying.

Moreover, by 1673 verse by Rochester was also circulating at those hotbeds of scribal publication, the Inns of Court. The young Theophilus, seventh Earl of Huntingdon, marooned at his family seat at Donnington Park, Leicestershire, was supplied with new lampoons by his town correspondent, Godfrey Thacker of Gray's Inn. By March of that year Thacker had already sent 'A ramble in St James's Park', 'Too long the wise commons' and an imperfectly memorized version of lines from 'I rise at eleven'. On 15 April Thacker wrote: 'I have been in quest of some more of my Ld Rochesters ingenuitie but cannot as yet accomplish my desires, but in the meanetime I present you with a coppy that is stolne from one to another a bout towne and fortunately this morning came to my hands'.[41] The poem enclosed ('Betwixt Father Patrick and's Highness of late') is probably not by Rochester, but the image of texts stealing 'from one to another' is a revealing one and suggests that other work beside that mentioned had already escaped into the wider possession of the town. A letter from Henry Ball to Sir Joseph Williamson of the same year is another piece of evidence for widening interest in the lampoons of the Buckingham circle:

But all men feare our officers of this army are not well pickt out, for the most of them debaucht profane persons and publique atheists which they say openly they learne of the Duke of Buckingham, one yesterday publickly in company I am told saying he believed neither Heaven nor Hell. These kinds of reports make the Town full of malicious libells. I am

---

[40] Examples given by the well-placed Sir William Haward and preserved in Bodl. MS don. b 8 are 'Haec Carmina in limine thalami Regis a quo, nescio, Nebulone, scripta reperiebantur' ('Bella fugis, Bellas sequeris, Belloque repugnas'), p. 183; 'Ouer the priuy Stayres att Whitehall found written wth a black-Lead-pen' ('Hobbs his Religion, Hyde his Moralls gaue'), p. 183; 'Written ouer Nell Gwins doore' ('These Lodgings are ready lett, & appoynted'), p. 212; the couplet, referred to in Ch. 5, which was found over the door of the king's bedchamber on 26 November 1675 ('In vaine for Ayde to yo^{ur}. old Freinds you call'), p. 539; 'The Inscription put ouer ye Gate att Marchant-Taylers Hall, when ye Duke dined there, die Martis. 21°. Octobr. 1679', p. 597; and two short poems fixed to the House of Commons door on 26 January and 15 April 1680 respectively, p. 644.

[41] Cited in Lucyle Hook, 'Something more about Rochester', *MLN* 75 (1960), 482. Lady Campden in 1682 was less fortunate. A letter of 20 April complains that new lampoons (not of course by Rochester) had appeared attacking the ladies but she was unable to get a copy of them (Wilson, *Court satires*, p. 81).

told of severall, and promised the copyes of some which I dare not venture by the Post.[42]

Ball's combination of horror at the libertinism of the circle with eagerness to obtain the manuscripts in which its blasphemies were expounded is a familiar one, albeit that, as an active scribal journalist and government spy, he was obliged to keep informed about such matters.

The transition from a limited to a more intense form of author and user publication and from that to entrepreneurial publication probably resulted from recourse to professional scribes to assist in the copying of lampoons for distribution at court. Rochester's household in 1675 apparently included at least one skilled scribe in the person of Thomas Alcock who later composed a narrative of an episode of 1675–6 in which Rochester set up as a mountebank under the name of Alexander Bendo.[43] But by this date Rochester may well have been in touch with the period's best-known scribal publisher, Robert Julian. Julian, a naval clerk, had previously been secretary to Admiral Sir Edward Spragge.[44] During engagements against the Dutch and the Algerines his place would have been by Spragge's side on the quarterdeck in order to take down messages (Nelson's secretary was killed at Trafalgar while performing this duty). Dorset and Rochester who, on different occasions, both served under Spragge's command, would have shared this perilous eminence and have had the responsibility of delivering some of the messages.[45] Following Spragge's death in action on 11 August

[42] *Letters addressed to Sir Joseph Williamson*, i. 67.

[43] Thomas Alcock and Rochester, *The famous pathologist or the noble mountebank*, ed. V. de Sola Pinto (Nottingham, 1961). Pinto asserts that the manuscript is in Alcock's own hand, which may well be the case, although the signatures reproduced on p. 9 can hardly be regarded as confirmation.

[44] For Julian see Brice Harris, 'Captain Robert Julian, secretary to the muses', *ELH* 10 (1943), 294–309; Mary Claire Randolph, ' "Mr Julian, secretary of the muses": Pasquil in London', *N&Q* 184 (Jan.–June 1943), 2–6; and Judith Slater, 'The early career of Captain Robert Julian, secretary to the muses', *N&Q* 211 (June–Dec. 1966), 260–2. The accounts indicate that he was fond of the bottle and heavily scarred. In 1685 he was described as 'an ancient man and almost blind' (*CTB*, viii, 1685–9, p. 231). A letter written by him in 1670 (PRO SP29/281A/226) asks for a message to be sent to his wife. Assuming a birth date *c*.1620–5, he may have been the Robert Julian who married Mary Blewitt at Saint Peter's upon Cornhill on 29 Apr. 1647 (*A register of all the christninges, burialles and weddinges within the parish of Saint Peeters upon Cornhill*, ed. G. W. G. Leveson Gower (London, 1877), p. 258).

[45] During the Four Days Battle of June 1666, Rochester carried a dispatch from Spragge under fire in a small boat. It was presumably written by Julian.

1673, Julian's post disappeared and he was imprisoned for debt. Among those to whom he applied for relief was Dorset, who is addressed in an undated letter as Earl of Middlesex, the title by which he was known between 4 April 1675 and 27 August 1677.[46] Julian speaks in this letter of having already received support from certain 'Persons of Honor', conceivably including Rochester, who is spoken of elsewhere as being linked with him in 'mutuall friendship'.[47] Another could well have been Pepys, to whom Julian had introduced himself in a finely penned letter of 30 June 1667 (see Plate 2) and who was a collector of the work of writing masters.[48] Dorset kept Julian's letter and seems subsequently to have been his principal patron. Certainly, by 1677 Julian was well recognized as a professional factor of lampoons, and Dorset's own poems were listed among his wares. A hypothesis which would account both for this and for the emergence of the poems of the court wits of the Buckingham circle into wider circulation during the mid-1670s is that he was initially employed by members of the group as a scribe in author publication, and moved by stages into the entrepreneurial publication first of separates and then of larger compilations.[49] The circle may also have helped supply the high-level protection that he must undoubtedly have possessed in order to continue as long as he did in his scandalous and highly illegal trade. For in the earlier years, at least, of his activities, Julian's primary affiliation was with the anti-Yorkist opposition.

Both the political and the literary ideals of the Buckingham circle are on display in Rochester's 'An allusion to Horace' written during the winter of 1675–6. The literary ideals (foreshadowed in Buckingham's own *The rehearsal*) include an emphasis on sense and plainness, hostility towards the heroic play and its chief proponent, Dryden, and an aristocratic belief in the supremacy of impromptu,

[46] Printed in Harris, *Charles Sackville*, pp. 178–9. The original was not able to be traced among the Sackville papers at the Kent CRO.

[47] 'Rochester's ghost addressing it self to the secretary of the muses' ('From the deep-vaulted Den of endless Night'), l. 9, *Poems on affairs of state, from the reign of K. James the first, to this present year 1703* (London, 1703), p. 128.

[48] PRO SP29/207/119, f. 181ʳ.

[49] Satirical accounts of Julian make frequent reference to his 'books' (for examples, see Harris 'Captain Robert Julian' and Randolph, 'Mr Julian'); however, no surviving anthology appears to contain his hand. Julian's script is represented in numerous documents of 1667–73 in the Public Record Office written as Spragge's secretary, some signed with his own name and some with Spragge's.

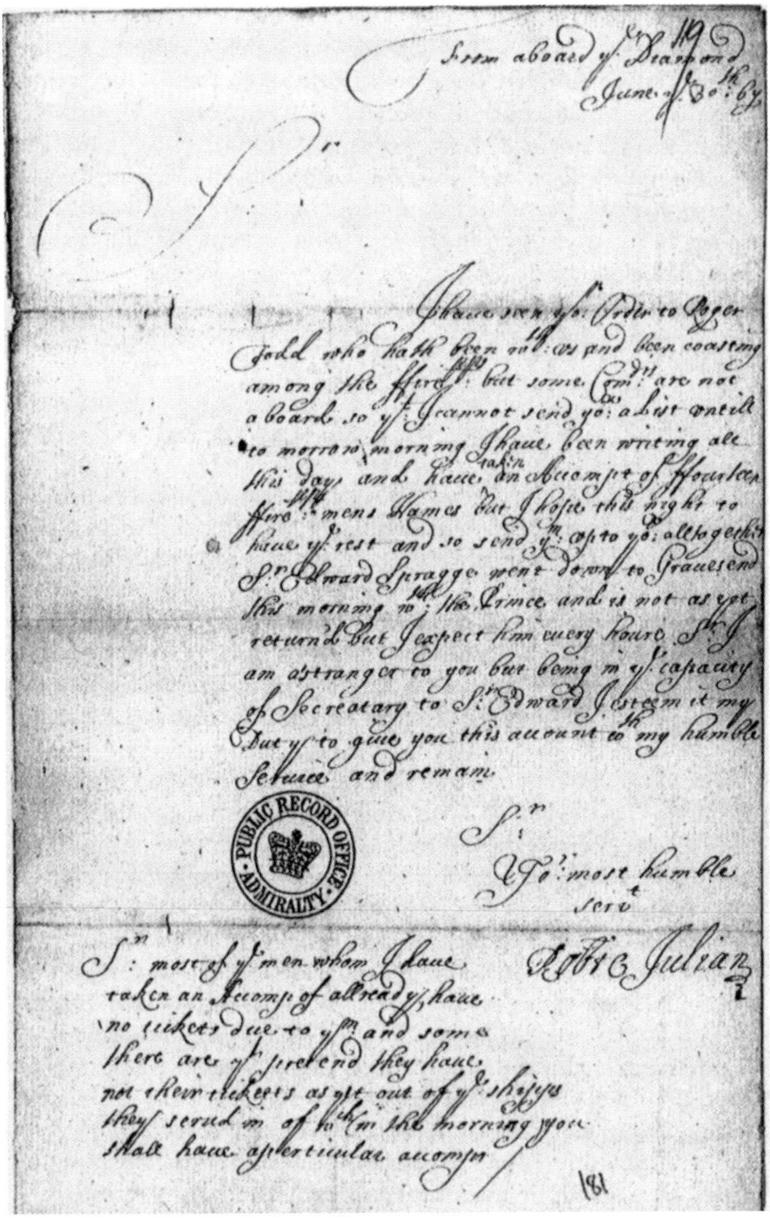

PLATE 2. Robert Julian to Samuel Pepys, 30 June 1667.

quasi-conversational wit over the laboured products of the professional pensmith. The circle shared Newcastle's preference for the Jonsonian style in comedy, and supported his protégé, Shadwell, who dedicated several times to its members. It also lent its assistance to Etherege and Wycherley, the two masters of the earlier phase of Restoration comedy of manners. The membership of the group as it stood in the mid-1670s is defined in the closing lines of the 'Allusion':

> I loath the Rabble, 'tis enough for me,
> If Sidley, Shadwell, Shepherd, Witcherley,
> Godolphin, Buttler, Buckhurst, Buckingham,
> And some few more, whom I omit to name
> Approve my Sense, I count their Censure Fame.[50]

The inclusion of the Tory, Godolphin, and the elderly Samuel Butler (if he is the individual intended) indicates that this is rather a list of Rochester's primary readership as an author-publisher than of the Buckingham faction per se; but otherwise the fit is exact. However, it still points to a political entity. While Wycherley and Etherege, for their own reasons, were to move into the Yorkist camp, Buckingham, Dorset, Sedley, Sheppard and Shadwell were all in separate ways to play a significant part in bringing about the great change of 1688, though Buckingham did not live to see it.

Buckingham had always been close to Marvell, his wife's former tutor, and, while a Francophile in his personal tastes, shared Shaftesbury's suspicion of the king's Catholic brother and heir, James Duke of York. By the crucial year of 1677 the position of Buckingham and his clients was one of Whig placemen in a Tory court, sceptical in religion but anti-Catholic in politics, French in culture but by now pro-Dutch in foreign policy, boon companions of the king yet resentful of the power of those unconstitutional ministers of state, his mistresses. They had been important to Charles as a counterpoise to the partisans of his brother, but by 1677 they were losing their usefulness through their association with Shaftesbury's anti-Yorkist extremism. Poetry, along with sceptical philosophy and practical debauchery, was the bonding agent of a group whose ultimate rationale was political—the

---

[50] Quoted in Walker's text (*Poems*, p. 102).

heterodox, Erastian wing of the Whig alliance. Rochester's cultivation during 1679–80 of the latitudinarian Protestant and Whig ideologue, Gilbert Burnet, is to be seen as a conscious political self-distancing from a Catholicizing court.

The concluding lines of the 'Allusion' suggest something of the closed, defensive position of the circle in the late 1670s within a court whose policies it was opposing in parliament and for whose leaders, if Rochester's letters are any guide, it had profound contempt. But the poem as a whole, although it argues for the priority of satire written for an intimate audience of cognoscenti, was also through the boldness of its cultural critique and its cultivation of a Horatian 'public' voice, addressing itself to an audience beyond these confines. One might even argue that it was presenting the values of frankness and clarity cultivated within the closed circle as the model for a critical public discourse that would address itself to matters of state as well as of taste. In this respect Rochester seems to accept even as he condemns the wider audience of opinion makers to which his work was now being brought by professional copyists.

ROBERT JULIAN AS SCRIBAL PUBLISHER

Whatever Julian's earlier relationship with his authors may have been, the close of the 1670s saw him well established as an entrepreneurial marketer of lampoons. Keeping no shop, his model for distribution was that adopted by other purveyors of luxury items of personal sale at the levees of the rich and powerful.[51] The increasing reliance of courtly authors on commercial factors of manuscripts inevitably brought its strains. In Julian's case it seems to have led to a temporary breakdown of trust over the scribe's mixing of work from the Buckingham circle with that of their Tory opponents.

Much of our knowledge of Julian comes from a considerable body of satires addressed to him by name.[52] Some of these also

---

[51] A practice well documented in Restoration comedy. Cf. Etherege, *The man of mode* (1676), I. i (oranges, shoes) and Vanbrugh, *The relapse* (1696), I. iii (clothes, shoes, stockings, wigs).

[52] Listed in Hugh Macdonald, *John Dryden, a bibliography of early editions and of Drydeniana* (Oxford, 1939), pp. 214–15. See also Harris, 'Captain Robert Julian' and Randolph, 'Mr Julian'.

claim to have been sent to him as a scribal publisher for circulation, as in the opening lines of the 'Letter to Julian' (1684):

> Dear Julian, twice or thrice a year
> I write to help thee in some gear;
> For thou by nonsense liv'st, not wit,
> As carps thrive best where cattle shit.[53]

The truth of such claims would be possible to accept if we could assume that he was reasonably thick-skinned and regarded the opportunity for advertisement as more important than the evidence the addresses provided of his involvement in an illegal trade. But there is one address that displays a vituperativeness towards Julian that makes it unlikely that he would have wished to publish it. This is 'A familiar epistle to Mr Julian secretary to the muses', apparently written before August 1677 (Dorset is still Middlesex) and attributable with reasonable certainty to Buckingham himself. Its opening lines will indicate the general tone of the piece, and also how active Julian had now become as a scribal publisher.

> Thou common shore of this poetic town,
> Where all our excrements of wit are thrown—
> For sonnet, satire, bawdry, blasphemy
> Are empti'd and disburden'd all on thee:
> The choleric wight, untrussing in a rage,
> Finds thee and leaves his load upon thy page—
> Thou Julian, O thou wise Vespasian, rather,
> Dost from this dung thy well-pick'd guineas gather.
> All mischief's thine; transcribing, thou dost stoop
> From lofty Middlesex to lowly Scroope.[54]

So far the references to Julian may be accepted as heavy-handed banter, but as the poem progresses it becomes clear that it is not only an address to Julian but an attack on him, and that his crime has been his association with the (then) Tory satirist, Sir Carr Scroope, who is the second target of the lampooner.

> This is the man ordain'd to do thee good,

---

[53] Wilson, *Court satires*, p. 131. Cf. also ll. 1–2 of 'A letter to Julian from Tunbridge' (ibid. 141): 'Dear friend, I fain would try once more / To help thee clear thy brandy score'.
[54] *POAS (Yale)*, i. 388–91, ll. 1–10.

The pelican to feed thee with his blood,
Thy wit, thy poet, nay thy friend! for he
Is fit to be a friend to none but thee. (ll. 87–90)

The rift between the Buckingham circle and Scroope had begun with an obscene parody by Rochester of Scoope's lyric, 'I cannot change as others do', and an attack on Rochester by Scroope in his widely copied 'In defence of satire' (1677). Rochester replied to this in 'On the supposed author of a late poem 'In defence of satire''; Scroope retorted in 'The author's reply' and Rochester delivered the *coup de grâce* in 'On poet Ninny'. The first three of these circulated as a linked group, but the fourth somehow became attached to another Rochester linked group directed at John Sheffield, Earl of Mulgrave.[55] More to the point is that Scroope was at least a temporary member of a rival group of Tory poets which had been formed in 1676 by Mulgrave, and which had Dryden as its principal professional luminary.[56]

The impetus to this new scribal community arose from the increasingly oppositional position of the Buckingham group and the consequent need to create a Yorkist centre of patronage. The formation of the group was made manifest in print by the publication of Lee's *The rival queens* in 1677 with a dedication to Mulgrave, a commendatory poem by Dryden and a prologue by Scroope, and confirmed by the 1680 *Ovid's epistles translated* whose contributors are a virtual roll-call of the Tory poets. In manuscript, the satirical scrapping with Scroope was paralleled in Rochester's poetical assaults on Mulgrave and Mulgrave's return of fire, with assistance from Dryden, in a long lampoon of 1679, 'An essay upon satire', whose targets are the wits of the Buckingham circle and their new political ally Halifax.[57] Dryden's attack on Shadwell in *Mac Flecknoe*, datable to mid-1676–77 though not appearing in

---

[55] For the poems and their sources, see *POAS (Yale)*, i. 364–75 and *Poems*, ed. Walker, pp. 109–10, 114–16 and notes. Aspects of the Rochester-Scroope imbroglio are discussed in Vieth, *Attribution*, pp. 137–63, 231–8 and 322–52.

[56] For the Mulgrave circle, see Vieth, *Attribution*, pp. 322–52 and *passim*. In March 1676 Scroope had still been close enough to the Buckingham circle to be entrusted with the prologue to Etherege's *The man of mode*. A snap at him in ll. 53–6 of Mulgrave and Dryden's 'An essay on satire' was probably prompted by his return to the Whig fold at the time of the Exclusion crisis. He is attacked as a Whig in 'A rambling satyr' ('Shall the world be thus abused and I sett still'), Lincolnshire Archives Office MS Anc 15/B/4, pp. 104–5.

[57] Text in *POAS (Yale)*, i. 396–413.

print until 1682 and surviving in sixteen manuscript copies independent of the printed text, represented a gauntlet thrown down by the leading professional of one faction to the leading professional of the other.[58] 'Advice to Apollo', for which a date late in 1677 would be plausible, praises Rochester and Dorset but is tart in its references to Scroope, Mulgrave and Dryden.[59] There is a tacit assumption in all these widely circulated poems that readers will be familiar with other writings allusively referred to and their putative authors, confirming that circulation had advanced beyond the simple passing of separates from friend to friend.

Julian's crime, and the cause of Buckingham's annoyance in his 'Epistle', was that he had begun to circulate work by both factions. Having been honoured with the opportunity to publish poems by Middlesex, he had intermingled them with the excremental outpourings of Scroope. Buckingham is thus justified in branding him as a 'poor apostate' (l. 20), though the allusion was a predictable one. We can also safely allow for a degree of aristocratic outrage that the choice sprouts of his own and his friends' wit had become objects of commerce: the poem takes care to indicate that it is Scroope's wares which are the proper ones for such a purpose. The caution seems to have been sufficient to put an end to Julian's truancy. A monologue put into his mouth in a satire of 1685, when the Tory ascendancy had removed his political protection, not only presents him as a Whig pensioner but contains a specific quotation of Buckingham's words of eight years earlier:

> Was't not hard measure, say, my Whiggish peers,
> Vending your nonsense to expose my ears?
> My pocket stuffed with scandal long has been
> The house of office to vend out your spleen,
> The common sink o'th' town, wherein you shit

---

[58] For the manuscripts see Beal, *IELM*, ii/1, 407–8. The sixteenth copy is in National Library of Ireland MS 2093, knowledge of which I owe to Dr Beal. Shadwell replied in the scribally published 'Upon a late fallen poet' ('A sad mischance I sing alas') and the printed *The medal of John Bayes* (London, 1682).

[59] Text in *POAS (Yale)*, i. 392–5. For a hypothesis regarding the origin of the poem, see Wilson, *Court wits*, p. 195. However, Wilson's belief that this was the group lampoon referred to in a letter of 1 Nov. 1677 from Henry Savile to Rochester is not reflected in any apparent stylistic feature. If permitted to guess at an author, I would suggest Sedley. A parting shot at Fleetwood Sheppard, a friend of both Buckingham and Dorset, indicates that none of these three was responsible.

To carry off your excrements of wit.
Such gallantry has not of late been shown;
To save your ears, poor Julian lost his own;
But if you ever catch me at that strain—
To vend your scurrilous scoundrel stuff again—
May infamy and scandal be my bane.[60]

Among the names of Julian's writers that follow are those of
Rochester's protégé, John Grubham Howe, at that time as
extreme a Whig as he was later to be a Tory, Etherege, and Julian's
'great Maecenas', Dorset, who is praised as having paid 'double
fees for what himself had writ'. The appearance in the list of the
most un-Whiggish Mulgrave and Dryden confirms that at the
period of their collaboration they had been numbered, albeit
briefly, among Julian's stable of authors.

A valuable picture of Julian in action is given in a rare Tory satire
of 1679–80, 'The visitt', here given complete from the apparently
unique source, Lincolnshire Archives Office MS Anc 15/B/4, with
the warning that the text shows signs of corruption:[61]

Pox on the Rhiming Fops that Plague the Town
with Libelling the Court and Rayling at the Gown
A man can make no visitt now but his Caresse
Is a Lewd Satyr shewn which Pray S^r. Guess
whose still [style?] it is: good Faith S^r. I dont care   5
For truly I read none that Treasons are
Then hee Replys Lord tis the wittyest thing
Tis smart on Nelly Portsmouth, and the King[62]
Just as he speakes comes Julian Passing by
His Pocketts stuft wth: scarrilous Poetry   10
my Freind Crys hee and adds to that a Bow
Thou slaue to th' muses, whats the newest now

---

[60] Wilson, *Court satires*, pp. 138–9. Julian is also included in the anti-Whig, 'A rambling satyr' (see n. 56).

[61] The manuscript, formerly in the possession of a John Brownloe, is a professionally prepared anthology of satires from the period 1679–82, possibly written as a series of separates rather than an integral volume. It is related textually to BL Harl. MS 6913 and Nottingham UL MS Pw V 38. The text is reproduced with the permission of the Trustees of the Grimsthorpe and Drummond Castle Trust.

[62] Satires that would qualify here are Rochester's 'When to the King I bid good Morrow', 1676 (*Poems*, ed. Walker, pp. 102–3) and Lacy's 'Preserved by wonder in the oak, O Charles', 1677 (*POAS (Yale)*, i. 425–8). It cannot be Mulgrave and Dryden's 'An essay upon satire' (ibid. 396–413) which is enquired for later in the poem.

S'Blood S^r. says he you're sicke oth old Disease
you want new Papers, dam mee where's my Fees
Of Guineys tost with Julian you're a Rogue   15
we'are straight Presented with whats new in vogue
There was obscene Rotchesters Cheife storys
of matrix Glances Dildo and Clittoris
With Dorsetts Tawdry Nonsense drest For sale
This motto on't Braue Buckhurst nere Faile   20
Gods Blood and wounds Crys Julian thats grown stale
I scarce can Put it off For nants and Ale
The next was smoothly writ by squinting Carr
Of Pembrooks drunken tricks, his Bull and Beare[63]
Behen was there with Bawdry in a vaile   25
But swearing Bloodily as in a Goale
Mulgraue appear'd with his base Borrowed witt
And Dryden at his heeles a owning it
There was Lewd Buckinghams slimb Poetry
But stufft so full of horrid Blasphemy
made Julian doubt there was no diety
Feirce Drydens satyr wee desir'd to veiw
For wee had heard he mourn'd in Black and Blew
Hee search'd for it but twas not to be Found
Twas Put ith Garett for a hundred Pound   35
The Taburn was the next resoult, where I
Quite weary of there Tipling company
went home a Cursing of this wretched age
That Couples each old Lady wth. her Page
And whores the Chastest virgin wth. her dog   40
And Calls the best of Kings a senceless Log[64]

The ambiguous use of 'he' in line 9 should not be allowed to
obscure the fact that it is Julian, not the friend, who is doing the
selling. The payment of guineas leads to his producing his wares

---

[63] Pembroke's menagerie is mentioned by Aubrey (*Brief lives*, ed. Andrew Clark
(Oxford, 1898), i. 317). Sir Carr Scroope appears to refer to Pembroke, but not his beasts, in
'In defense of satire', ll. 32–5, *POAS (Yale)*, i. 365 and n. 35.

[64] Citing an Aesopian allusion in a satire of 1680, 'The rabble' ('The rabble hates, the
gentry fear'), l. 17; text in *POAS (Yale)*, ii. 342–3, also found in the cited manuscript, p. 115,
with an attribution to Fleetwood Sheppard: 'England is Betwixt Thee and Yorke / The
Fabble of the Frogg / Hee is the feirce devouring storke / And thou the Lumpish Logg.' Cf.
also 'The history of insipids' (1674), ll. 163–8: 'Then farewell, sacred Majesty, / Let's pull all
brutish tyrants down! . . . / Mankind, like miserable frogs, / Is wretched, king'd by storks or
logs.' (*POAS (Yale)*, i. 251)

from his pockets. The writers mentioned were those popular at the close of the decade, all being represented in Yale MS Osborn b 105, the scribal sibling of the 1680 Rochester *Poems*. The poem must date from not long after the incident of 18 December 1679 when Dryden was attacked in Rose Alley, supposedly because of his share in 'An essay on satire'. The customers are keen to see a copy of the 'Essay' but learn that it has been suppressed by Julian in return for a bribe (and no doubt other kinds of pressure).

THE 1680 COMPILATIONS AND THEIR SCRIPTORIA

1680 sees the beginning of a new stage in the scribal publication of lampoons, characterized by the writing of substantial miscellanies. In part this simply indicates that a large enough body of poems was in circulation to permit the preparation of such collections, but it was also influenced by demand for work by Rochester in the year of his illness and death. The decision of parliament on 30 October to permit the printing of votes and transactions may also have contributed by closing down a busy area of scribal production.

Until this time the entrepreneurially published anthology of court-libertine (as of Marvellian) verse had been a rarity. Of surviving compilations only Harvard MS Eng. 636F, Princeton MS 14401 and BL MS Harl. 7312 appear to antedate 1680.[65] The raw materials for the new compilations were the separates and linked groups which had been circulated by Julian and whatever others had joined him in his trade. The work of these publishers seems always to have been uncoordinated, except insofar as they drew from time to time on each other's separates. It was also of brief duration with most ceasing to produce anthologies of court-libertine verse after the appearance of the printed Rochester *Poems on several occasions*, itself based on a scribally published anthology, late in 1680. There is no sense of the situation of the 1690s where a single agency was supplying most of the book-trade's requirement for scribally published satire. Since a number of these, admittedly scandalous, 1680 volumes survive with pages excised or poems and passages scribbled over, it is likely that the loss rate has been exceptionally high.

[65] MS Eng. 636F is considered below. Harl. 7312, an important source of libertine and pornographic verse, dates from 1678–9.

The fact that each anthologist was drawing on a restricted repertoire of separates and linked groups results in striking similarities in contents and sometimes order. The detailed collations presented in Keith Walker's edition of Rochester permit genealogical analysis of the textual interrelationships of several of the most widely copied poems. These have been supplemented, in my own case, by repetition and extension of some of Walker's collations, and selective collation of a number of other popular copied texts. The claim that any given pair of anthologies is the work of different compilers rather than representing varied selections from a body of separates held by a single scriptorium is based on this work, with a necessary acknowledgement of its incomplete character. A thorough investigation of these highly complex textual relationships would be a labour of many years. The archives so far identified and their surviving products are listed below.

(a) The 'Hansen' archive. The archive of this short-lived scriptorium was the source for at least four manuscripts, of which two survive, a third is known from a later scribal copy, and a fourth served as copy for the 1680 Rochester *Poems*.[66] Its most celebrated product is the important, though mutilated Rochester source, Yale MS Osborn b 105. The name 'Hansen' inscribed on its title page must surely refer to the diplomat, Friedrich Augustus Hansen, who visited England briefly in September 1680 in the entourage of Charles, the electoral prince Palatine.[67] It is a professional production which draws on excellent sources within the Buckingham circle and presents good texts and authoritative attributions. The collateral printed collection omits eleven poems which are present in the manuscript, of which four can be associated directly or by implication with the Mulgrave circle. These are Mulgrave's own 'Since now my Silvia, is as kind as faire', Dryden's *Mac Flecknoe*, and two vicious attacks on Buckingham, 'A new ballad to an old tune call'd Sage leafe' and the 'D: of B: letany'. The effect of these absences is to make the printed

---

[66] The relationship between the manuscript and the printed edition is exhaustively investigated in Vieth, *Attribution* pp. 56–100.

[67] For the evidence for this see Love, 'Scribal texts and literary communities: the Rochester circle and Osborn b. 105', *SB* 42 (1989), 232–3.

collection much more narrowly aligned with the Buckingham group, with its remaining adversarial poems (all by Scroope) embedded in linked groups where they are neutralized by answers. It is not at present clear whether this is the result of pruning— presumably by the print-publisher—or whether the manuscript copy for the printed text represented an earlier stage of the compilation which was subsequently augmented.[68] Whatever the case, that the collection was compiled in full awareness of the controversy is shown by the choice of Rochester's 'Epistolary essay' to Mulgrave as its opening item. The printed *Poems* has been stripped of attributions, presumably so as to suggest that its contents were entirely by Rochester.

The ready availability of this collection in its printed form led to some recopying of items into manuscript collections. However, the wider importance of Osborn b 105 for the history of scriptorial satire is that its writer was also concerned in the production of a companion volume of state poems which has survived in two copies. The first of these, Princeton MS Taylor 1, was written in the same hand as Osborn b 105 at almost exactly the same date and contains political satires from the Marvellian tradition, including four of the 'Advice to a painter poems', 'The downfall of the chancellor', 'Britannia and Raleigh' ('Ah! Raleigh, when thy breath thou didst resign'), 'The history of insipids' ('Chaste, pious, prudent Charles the Second') and 'A dialogue between the two horses' ('We read in profane and sacred records'). Only the two anti-Buckingham poems, 'The D: of B: letany' and 'A new ballad to an old tune call'd Sage leafe' are common to both collections. Another copy of the state-poems collection, lacking one item, is the first of two manuscript anthologies in the same hand bound as BL MS Harl. 7315, the second being a product of the later 'Cameron' scriptorium. The two 1680 compilations, the political and the libertine, define the scriptorial archive of a professional trader in manuscripts briefly active during that year but not apparently after it. They also make clear that, as with the 'Cameron' scriptorium, the publisher acknowledged a demand for

[68] There is a suggestion, explored in my 'Scribal texts', pp. 227–8, that any such compiler may have been associated with Gray's Inn. This is strengthened by Godfrey Thacker's activity there as a collector of Rochesterian verse.

two different kinds of product—witty, sexually explicit court satire and outspoken comment on the wider field of public events.

(b) The Gyldenstolpe archive. This has been named from an important anthology discovered by Bror Danielsson in the Riks-Bibliotheket, Stockholm (MS Vu. 69) and published in facsimile in 1967 by him and Vieth as *The Gyldenstolpe manuscript miscellany.* It belongs to a group of anthologies (not all of them textually related) which commence with Edmund Ashton's 'Gentle reproofs have long been tried in vain', apparently as an advertisement that the reproofs in what followed were going to be the reverse of gentle.[69] Its contents, predominantly from the court libertine tradition, contain a high degree of overlap with Osborn b 105, but, where the matter has been tested, there is no consistent textual affiliation. The collection must therefore be viewed as an independent garnering from the same corpus of material circulating as separates and linked groups. There is, however, an intermingling of recently written political satires, together with one or two earlier ones not usually associated with the Marvellian group. The *terminus ad quem* for compilation was set by Vieth as the 'late summer of 1680'.[70]

Here again we have a guide, though in this case not a complete one, to the scriptorial archive of a professional trader in manuscripts. A small collection of lampoons which was bound by Pepys with his copy of the 1680 *Poems* is revealed unmistakably by its variants to be drawn from the same archive.[71] Nottingham University Library MS Portland Pw V 32 is a very similar small collection from the same source, in this case explicitly titled *A supplement to some of my Lord Rochester's poems.* A third sub-collection, closely related in both order and contents to Pw V 32, provided the opening element of a later compilation, Princeton MS Taylor 3. It is likely that small collections of this kind were commissioned for sale with the printed 1680 collection. Nottingham University Library MS Portland Pw V 40 draws on

[69] Other anthologies having this as their first item are BL Add. MS 21094, BL Harl. MSS 6913 and 7312, Pepysian Library, Magdalene College Cambridge MS appendix to Rochester *Poems on several occasions* (1680), Nottingham UL MSS Pw V 32 and 38, and Princeton MS Taylor 3. The poem also appears in the Danchin manuscript (see below).

[70] *Gyldenstolpe miscellany*, p. xxiv.

[71] Richard Luckett, Pepysian Librarian, Magdalene College, has identified the handwriting as that of Pepys's secretary, Paul Lorrain.

another product of the scriptorium, intermingling poems from this source (identifiable by both stemmatological evidence and sequence) with others transcribed from the 'Pforzheimer' edition of the 1680 *Poems*—another case in which the work of the scriptorium is associated with the 1680 printed text.[72] Suggestive similarities in order plus a tendency to contiguity in stemmas also suggest a relationship with the Leeds 'Robinson' anthology; but in this case it is likely that the derivation was not direct but by the absorption of a sub-collection or a body of separates issued from the original 'Gyldenstolpe' scriptorium.

The scriptorium, then, was an apparently short-lived operation of 1680–1. There must be a high probability that it was run by a bookseller who also handled copies of the 1680 Rochester *Poems*.

(c) Harvard University Library MS Eng. 636F. This manuscript has been held in high regard by editors of Rochester and, after Osborn b 105, is the second most important contemporary source for his poems. It attracts through the elegant bravura of its hand, a pleasingly virtuosic exception to the blandness of much Restoration bookwork. Its contents, both Rochesterian and non-Rochesterian, overlap considerably with Osborn b 105, the poems not found in the Yale collection being mostly of a libertine or indecent nature. However, its texts are uneven in quality, despite the fact that it was compiled perhaps as early as December 1679. Once again we have an independent compilation from separates, linked groups and small sub-collections, which were already in general circulation. No further work deriving from this archive has so far been identified, though there is a tendency for it to group in collations with texts from the Edinburgh aggregation.

(d) The Danchin manuscript. This professionally written manuscript was acquired in Paris by Pierre Danchin and published by him in facsimile.[73] Although the excision of sexually objectionable material has left it seriously defective, it would seem to belong among the 1680 manuscripts. Its latest datable item is Scroope's

---

[72] This relationship was first pointed out by Vieth, *Gyldenstolpe manuscript*, p. xxvi.

[73] 'A late seventeenth-century miscellany—a facsimile edition of a manuscript collection of poems, largely by John Wilmot, Earl of Rochester', *Cahiers Élizabéthains*, no. 22 (Oct. 1982), 51–86.

'While *Phaon* to the flaming *Aetna* flies' in what appears to be a transcription from the Dryden–Tonson *Ovid's epistles, translated by several hands* (1680), which had been published by February 1680.[74]

(e) The Edinburgh aggregation. Edinburgh University Library MS D C 1 3, an oblong folio, is an unusual compilation which appears to record the contents of six separate smaller collections. They were copied throughout by the same scribe, who has given the texts a strong infusion of Scotticisms. Each sub-collection has its own title page and index, and the presence of a certain degree of overlap between the collections supports the premise that this was not simply a scribal convention to break up an otherwise unmanageable corpus of verse. Errors in pagination suggest that at least the first two collections were present in a consecutively written exemplar. With the exception of the sixth collection, which is solely composed of songs, the contents are a somewhat incoherent mixture of libertine verse, earlier state poems and current satire. Compilation would seem to have taken place late in 1683 though the bulk of the material dates from prior to 1680. The texts of the poems are, where tested, very poor: all the elements of the aggregation seem to stand at the end of a long succession of copyings. The manuscript appears to preserve the archive of an Edinburgh scriptorium, some of whose exemplars may well have come north with courtiers attending on York or Monmouth during their periods of residence in Scotland.

(f) The Dublin manuscript. A second regional compilation is represented by National Library of Ireland MS 2093, a professionally written pocket manuscript, principally of verse by Rochester, which is shown to be posthumous by the presence of Flatman's 'As on his deathbed gasping Strephon lay'. The collection draws partly on separates from the London scriptoria (its text of 'An epistolary essay' is from the same source as that of Harvard MS Eng. 636F) and partly on otherwise unrecorded material which appears to

---

[74] The volume is advertised in the *True domestic intelligence* for 10 Feb. 1680. The derivation is suggested by the sharing of an obvious error in the last line: 'But lett thy [for 'my'] Life here wth. thy Letter end'.

derive directly from the Rochester circle.[75] The most likely point of origin would be the vice-regal court at Dublin, a mimic Whitehall presided over by the elderly Duke of Ormond, one of whose daughters-in-law is the subject of a poem.

TOPICAL SATIRE OF THE 1680S

As mentioned earlier, the publication of the 1680 Rochester *Poems*, fairly late in that year, and its many surreptitious reprintings destroyed the market for collections solely or substantially devoted to court-libertine verse. From the following year court-libertine poems generally occur intermingled with political satires from the Marvellian and current traditions. An early example of these transitional volumes is Leeds University Library MS Brotherton 54, which was originally written by two scribes (later additions may be ignored for our present purposes).[76] The base collection (items 1–8 and 24–59) is an anthology of pre-1680 court-libertine verse with a strong contribution from Rochester; however, interpolated within this is a sub-collection of state satires of 1679–80 (items 9–23), all of this material being the work of hand A. The second collection, written by hand B, consists of state satires from 1683 to 1687 in rough chronological order, intermixed with some earlier libertine verse.

Alongside the collections which mixed current with retrospective lampoons, and which became increasingly prominent as the century progressed, other compilers concentrated on presenting volumes of material illustrating recent and current production, often with the items arranged chronologically. An example from the early 1680s (a boom period for lampoons[77]) is the pair BL MS Harley 6913 and Nottingham University Library Pw V 38, collections of topical satire from 1679–83, which, as Vieth was the first to point out, are substantially identical in contents and sequence. Both follow the example of the Gyldenstolpe manuscript by commencing with Ashton's 'Gentle reproofs have long

---

[75] In addition to three unique Rochester items listed by Beal, there is 'Chloe to Sabina', attributed to Mrs Jean Fox, whose title alludes to 'Artemisa to Chloe'.

[76] The manuscript is described and indexed in Hammond, 'Robinson miscellany'.

[77] Contemporary references to this are cited in *The prologues and epilogues of the Restoration 1660–1700*, ed. Pierre Danchin (Nancy, 1981–8), iii, pp. xviii–xix.

been tried in vain' but do not appear on present evidence to be textually dependent on the Gyldenstolpe archive. Lincolnshire Archives Office Anc. 15/B/4 shares a sequence of items with the pair. Another important source, National Library of Scotland Adv. MS 19.1.12, preserves three pre-existing compilations of which the first, covering 1680–84, survives independently as Nottingham University Library MS Portland Pw V 45. The second is a collection of state and libertine verse ranging from the late 1660s to 1680. At the end of this the scribe has copied the explicit of his exemplar, reading 'Exiatur. Fin de premier tome'.[78] The third collection opens in a new hand as a continuation of the second but then reverts to the first hand to become a continuation of the first. Within each section an attempt has been made to place the poems in chronological order, with dates given for most post-1677 items. Two further professionally written anthologies of topical satire are BL Add. MS 34362, containing satires from the late 1670s and early 1680s, and Yale MS Osborn b 113, a collection of the early 1680s with two token Rochester items from the earlier repertoire.

Although the publishers of these volumes have yet to be identified, the names of some individuals involved in the trade are known from a number of sources including the satires themselves. Robert Julian continued to market lampoons through the first half of the eighties. In the prologue to Ravenscroft's *The London cuckolds*, believed to have been first performed in October 1681, a lively picture is given of an outburst of lampoon writing:

> Now Fop may dine with Half-wit ev'ry noon,
> And reade his Satyr, or his worse Lampoon.
> *Julian*'s so furnished by these scribling Sparks
> That he pays off old Scores, and keeps two Clarks.[79]

And, indeed, it would seem from the evidence assembled by Harris and Randolph that his role at this period was more that of publisher than scribe. He waited personally on his upper-class clients both supplying newly copied lampoons, conveyed in his pockets, and collecting the contributions of authors for future copying. He would also deliver billets doux for a fee, wrote

[78] F. 109ᵣ. Ff. 109ᵛ–110ᵛ are blank, the text resuming on f. 111ᵣ.
[79] Danchin, *Prologues and epilogues*, iii. 329.

newsletters, and is reputed to have done some pimping on the side. An anecdote concerning Joe Haines indicates that he would pay, when necessary, for promising new copy.[80] In 1684 he finally succumbed to the law. On 31 May he was charged in the court of King's Bench and in November of that year fined and sentenced to the pillory 'for publishing several scandalous libells'.[81] He also suffered the humiliation of having one of his ears cropped. Unable to pay his fine, he remained in prison until the following June when an appeal for clemency to James II proved successful, no doubt because of his former sea service under James as Admiral. If he returned to his old trade, it was in an appropriately surreptitious fashion. The appearance of a burlesque epitaph in 1688 would suggest that this was the year of his death, were it not that Jack Howe's 'An epistle to Somerton', dated by Cameron 'possibly just before, but more probably just after the Revolution' speaks of him as alive and still working.[82]

Two other names also appear in verse addresses of the period, those of 'Captain' Warcup and John Somerton. Warcup is addressed in a lampoon of June 1686 couched in the form of advice about where writers of libels might be found.

> Here take this, Warcup, spread this up and down,
> Thou second scandal carrier of the Town;
> Thy trapstick legs and foolish, puny face
> Look as if nature meant thee for the place.
> In this vocation should grow greater far
> Than e'er should do by stratagems of war.[83]

Warcup has been convincingly identified by the editor of the satire, J. H. Wilson, as Captain Lenthal Warcup of the First Foot Guards, a son of the Whig justice, Edmund Warcup. Why an army officer would have traded in manuscripts is not clear—perhaps his role was rather that of a social circulator of lampoons—yet one

---

[80] In Tobyas Thomas, *The life of the late famous comedian, Jo Hayns* (London, 1701), pp. 45–6, Haines is said to have sold Julian a manuscript of 'On the three dukes killing the beadle' ('Near Holborne lies a park of great renown').

[81] Narcissus Luttrell, *A brief historical relation of state affairs* (Oxford, 1857), i. 319–20.

[82] 'Epitaph on the secretary of the muses' in *Poetical recreations . . . Part II* (London, 1688), p. 66 and several manuscript sources. A 'notched' scribe, suggestive of Julian, is referred to in the introductory epistle to 'The divorce' (1691), *POAS (Yale)*, v. 534. For 'An epistle to Somerton' see ibid., v. 535–6.

[83] Wilson, *Court satires*, p. 159.

large collection can be circumstantially linked with a regimental colleague of Warcup, Charles Robinson.[84]

Somerton is more mysterious. Howe's 'An epistle to Somerton' (1688–9) addresses him in terms that imply that he was a competitor of a still active Julian:

> Dear Somerton, once my beloved correspondent,
> Since scandal's so scarce, though the world is so fond on't
> That poor Brother Julian of pay does miscarry
> As well as the List, Civil, and Military,
> And the brains of our poets as empty are grown,
> As his Majesty's coffers, or (faith) as their own . . .[85]

The use of 'correspondent' suggests that Somerton may have moved into the lampoon field from being a newsletter writer—a logical enough progression. Our only other information comes from one of Tom Brown's *Letters from the dead to the living*, published in 1702, which is a reply from Will Pierre to the by then undoubtedly deceased Julian.[86] This tells us that 'since your death, and your Successor *Summerton*'s Madness, Lampoon has felt a very sensible decay'. An early hand has entered Somerton's name together with that of 'Bhen' on the title page of Bodleian MS Firth c 16, a substantial miscellany covering the years 1682–8. The title of the volume, *Astrea's booke for songs & satyr's*, confirms the connection with Aphra Behn, but leaves Somerton's role unclarified. The manuscript as originally copied contained 132 items. It is written in three main hands, two of them skilled book hands and the third a hurried and careless script, legible but revealing little concern with appearance. Mary Ann O'Donnell has identified the most frequent of the book hands as that of Aphra Behn, a discovery that greatly increases the interest of the volume but still leaves a mystery surrounding its function.[87] One explanation would be that it was the archive of the Somerton

---

[84] Leeds MS Brotherton Lt 54 contains two notes of direction to a Captain Robinson whose address is given as 'att Cpt Eloass [Elwes] near ye Watch house in Marlburrough street'. Assuming the reference was to a military and not a naval officer, Charles Robinson is the most likely candidate.

[85] *POAS (Yale)*, v. 535.

[86] (London, 1702), pp. 69–70.

[87] 'A verse miscellany of Aphra Behn: Bodleian Library MS Firth *c*. 16', *English manuscript studies* 2 (1990), 189–227.

(Behn?) scriptorium, similar to the great books of Starkey and Collins, with new items entered on acquisition by whichever scribe was available. What the book is not is a finished professional product intended for sale; but then neither is it a random, personal commonplace book: the concentration throughout is on topical, vendible lampoons.

As a coverage of satire to the eve of the Revolution, Firth c 16 can be grouped with Bodleian Douce 57 (second element) and Harvard Eng. 585 under the generic title of 'accession miscellanies'. By this is meant collections that present retrospective surveys of the satire of a particular reign or reigns on the occasion of the beginning of a new one. While the precise intentions of their compilers can only be guessed at, it is likely that the gathering of large numbers of potential customers in London for a coronation or first regnal parliament would create a demand for collections of this kind.

The wide readership achieved by scriptorial satire at this period is indicated by the casual way in which knowledge of particular scribally published pieces is assumed by writers for the theatre. An address to the 'Scribbling Beaus' in the epilogue to Aphra Behn's *The lucky chance* (1687) attempts a riposte to '*the late Satyr on Poetry*'—probably the 'Satyr on the poets' ('Wretch whosoe'er thou art that longst for praise') found in manuscripts of the Cameron scriptorium.[88] Southerne in the prologue *Sir Anthony Love* (1691) works a reference to a current lampoon into a lament for the absence of male theatregoers at the war in Ireland:

> *Some weak amends this thin Town might afford,*
> *If honest Gentlemen would keep their word.*
> *But your lewd* Tunbridge-Scandal *that was moving,*
> *Foretold how sad a Time wou'd come for Loving.*
> *Sad Time indeed when you begin to write:*
> *'Tis a shrewd sign of waning Appetite,*
> *When you forget your selves, to think of Wit.* [89]

Dryden's more general reproof in the prologue to *Amphitryon*

---

[88] Danchin, *Prologues and epilogues*, iv. 613. Danchin's candidates, two printed satires, were each several years out of date by this time. The context suggests strongly that lampoon-writers were intended.

[89] *The works of Thomas Southerne*, ed. Robert Jordan and Harold Love (Oxford, 1988), i. 172.

(1690) is linked by Richard Elias with the circulation of 'The female nine' ('What chance has brought thee into verse').[90] Lampoons of this kind, as well as proliferating in written form, were quickly appropriated by a culture of gossip shared between the male coffee house and the female tea table. News of the accusations made in a new lampoon would promote the desire to obtain a copy.

THE 1690S

Whereas the reign of James II had seen the satirists concentrating their venom on the court, the 1690s saw the recurrence of a healthy diversity of views, with Whigs and Tories, Williamites and Jacobites, belabouring each other in collections which display a surprising catholicity of viewpoints. The 'court Whig' tradition (so called to distinguish itself from its 'country' counterpart) was in many ways a derivative of the Buckingham circle in the 1670s. It is customary to think of the court of William and Mary as a rather dour place; but that was not the case as long as Purcell was in charge of its music, Kneller in charge of its art and Dorset in charge of its writers. Re-established at court in 1688 as Lord Chamberlain, a post he held until April 1697, and with the large revenues generated by that office at his service, Dorset moved into the last and most splendid decade of his career as a patron. With Fleetwood Sheppard as his *fidus Achates*, and Matthew Prior, Charles Montagu and George Stepney as protégés, he was once more at the centre of English literary culture, occupying a position not all that different from Newcastle's in the years following 1660, as an elder statesman of letters who was also a respected practitioner: moreover, he was younger than Newcastle had been, turning forty-five in the year of the Revolution. His circle included old Whig friends such as Shadwell, for whom he secured the laureateship stripped from Dryden, and Sedley who found a new lease of life as a translator and epigrammist; but he was also generous to former foes such as D'Urfey, a ready convert to the new order, and the unrepentant Jacobite, Dryden, whom Dorset personally recompensed for the loss of his official positions.

[90] *Works*, xv. 227; *POAS (Yale)*, v. 202–10.

The impact of the court group shows clearly in the miscellanies, especially those of the 'Cameron' scriptorium. Dorset remained one of the star authors, represented in the anthologies by the immense 'Faithful catalogue' of 1688 and a sprinkling of slighter satires and of the elegantly turned songs that were his forte.[91] However, although his influence was a strong one at the beginning of the decade, it was eventually to fade. In moving from opposition to become part of the establishment, the Dorset circle had offered itself as a target to both the Tories and those factions of his own party who were offended by Dorset's determination to extract every available guinea from his office. His master William III was also, on the whole, rather roughly handled, with the satirists routinely accusing him of a homosexual relationship with his favourite, Bentinck. Otherwise the satire of the decade reflects the vigour and many-sidedness of its politics. With a relatively small number of exceptions, of which the most notable is Yale MS Osborn b 111, a collection of 'Loyal poems' prepared for the exiled James II, the surviving miscellanies are unpartisan in their representation of competing points of view. Far from being factional collections they suggest a sophisticated interest in the political debate as debate, and in the artistry and malice of the satirist irrespective of the particular message. The satire in turn remains oppositional in a general tendency to denigrate those who currently hold power, but never seems able to speak with the authority of a movement which knows its time has come.

THE 'CAMERON' SCRIPTORIUM

The work of this scriptorium was first identified by W. J. Cameron while editing texts for volume 5 of the Yale *Poems on affairs of state* series, and was described by him in an important article of 1963 which has already been extensively cited.[92] Cameron's discussion of his material is extremely condensed, representing a preliminary report on a topic that would have justified a book-length study. While the essence of his method lay in the integration of textual, physical and historical data, his most telling evidence was derived

---

[91] For these, see Harris, *Charles Sackville*, and *Poems, passim*.
[92] Cameron, 'Scriptorium'; see also *POAS (Yale)*, v. 527–38.

from collations for the Yale edition, which the editorial policy of the series only permitted to be included in reduced form. Hopes that he might have returned to this material or given a fuller account of his evidence were dashed by his unexpected death in 1988.

In summarizing his findings I intend to begin where he did with an unusual manuscript in the Folger Library, MS M b 12, which is an aggregation of three originally separate manuscripts of state and libertine verse. The first two of these manuscripts were written by different scribes, with the third a joint effort in which the first-volume scribe was responsible for pp. 1–253 and the second-volume scribe for pp. 257–315. The care and similarity of the hands and the disciplined method of presenting the texts both suggest a conscious effort to achieve what Cameron calls 'an impersonal, professional norm' (p. 31). When the three manuscripts were originally written, there had been some overlap of contents between them, but, as part of the process of aggregation, the duplicated poems, along with some others, had been removed by a complicated mixture of excisions and pasteovers. Cameron had no trouble in demonstrating that the three sub-volumes represented the archive of a scribal publisher who offered his customers a choice of three different styles of miscellany, giving rise to what Cameron called the 'William' group, the 'Venus' group and the 'Restoration' group. Each of these groups is represented by a number of surviving manuscripts copied prior to the pruning of the archive and its incorporation into a single volume. These groups will be considered, as Cameron does, in the reverse order of their representation in the Folger manuscript, which will have the advantage of placing the most clearly defined group first and the most problematic last.

The 'William' group consists of satires of the reign of William and Mary and William alone and was continually updated during that reign. The earliest surviving member is Huntington MS Ellesmere 8770 whose title page reads: *A Collection of the best Poems, Lampoons, Songs & Satyrs from the Revolu[ti]on 1688. to 1692.* The other volumes known to Cameron were University of Nottingham Library MS Portland Pw V 47 (1695), Earl of Leicester's MS Holkham 686 (1695), BL Harl. MS 7315 (second element, 1701), Portland Pw V 48 (no date but also circa 1701),

University of Chicago MS PR1225f H5 c 7 (written after William's death in 1702), and Portland Pw V 44. The title page of the Folger sub-volume gives a date-range 1688–99 to which '1703/4' was later added, which the contents indicate was the date at which compilation ceased. Portland Pw V 44 is of the same period but Cameron was able to show that it derives from Folger as it was prior to its mutilation (or an immediate ancestor) and therefore preserves texts of the items excised during reconstruction. Detailed comparisons of watermarks made by Cameron provide strong evidence of origin within the scriptorium for all except the Chicago and Harleian manuscripts, which he classifies as extra-scriptorial copies ultimately derived from Pw V 48. Most of the manuscripts have the items in chronological order of years, with dates supplied when known, but this regularity sometimes breaks down towards the end of a manuscript.

The William group represents a continually evolving collection to which new items were regularly added and from which old ones were regularly discarded, a classic case of what I call a 'rolling archetype'. Beginning as an anthology of topical writing, it eventually turned into an 'accession' miscellany, recording the whole political history of William's reign and opening the way for a new topical compilation covering that of Anne—though it is not clear whether this was ever attempted. A manuscript unknown to Cameron was Leeds University Library Brotherton MS Lt q 38, which is a twin of BL Harl. 7315/2, though not in the same hand.

Cameron's second group, which is also represented second in the Folger manuscript, is a collection of chiefly libertine verse with a strong pornographic element. Its contents are signalled and its identity established by its opening item, the (otherwise innocuous) 'Venus her enquiry after Cupid'. Other manuscripts from this group, listed by Cameron, are Nottingham University Portland MS Pw V 42, Ohio State University MS Eng. 15, Princeton MS Taylor 2 and Bodleian MS Firth c 15. Cameron reports that there is much less variation in contents than in the case of the William group, but much variation in order within a broadly chronological arrangement. Portland Pw V 42 may well preserve the content of the Folger element as it was prior to mutilation. Watermark evidence confirms that all manuscripts originated within the scriptorium.

Part II

The third group is simultaneously the smallest, and the one that gave rise to the most substantial manuscripts. Called by Cameron the 'Restoration' group, it is an accession miscellany of libertine verse and state poems from the early 1670s to 1688, embracing much of the content of the 'Venus' group. The most imposing representatives of this group are Österreichische Nationalbibliothek MS 14090 and Victoria and Albert Museum MS Dyce 43, collections which in their original numbering contain 880 and 841 pages respectively. These are versions, in two different hands, of the same miscellany, except that the Vienna manuscript omits a few items found in the Dyce.[93] Selective collation shows that initially both scribes were working from a common exemplar; however, in at least some of the later texts Vienna is a descendent of Dyce. Vienna is also the less formally written, with such extensive use of contractions that it would have been difficult to make a completely accurate copy from it. The other representatives of the group, which are Folger MS M b 12 (first element) and Nottingham University Library Portland Pw V 43, represent selections from the earlier and the later part respectively of the huge primary compilation, the first ending with item 162 of the Dyce manuscript and the second beginning with item 164. (These are Cameron's numbers: mine would be 164 and 166; the corresponding numbers in the Vienna MS are 155 and 157.[94]) The contents of a lost manuscript are preserved in BL Harl. MS 6914, pp. 1–158, which is a copy made outside the scriptorium of fifty-seven poems from the Dyce/Vienna compilation.

In addition to the groups given, Cameron also identifies two other products of the scriptorium, a manuscript, Nottingham Pw V 46, and a printed book, *Poems on affairs of state: from Oliver Cromwell to this present time. Written by the greatest wits of the age . . .*

---

[93] Eighteen in Cameron's count and 22 in mine. (This discrepancy may arise from our differing definitions of an item.) The most likely reason for the omission is that the scribe of MS 14090, writing a larger hand than that of Dyce 43, was dropping material from time to time in order not extend what was already an enormous collection. (There is evidence in the index and the text itself (f. 40ᵛ) that some of the omitted material was available in his exemplar.) The Vienna scribe recognized and removed one appearance of a poem ('Satyr on the court ladies') that occurred twice in Dyce 43.

[94] See Rudolf Brotanek, 'Beschreibung der Handschrift 14090 (Suppl. 1776) der Nationalbibliothek in Wien', in *Festschrift der Nationalbibliothek in Wien. Herausgebeben zur Feir des 200jährigen Bestehens des Gebäudes* (Vienna, 1926), pp. 145–62.

Part III (London, 1698). The manuscript, compiled in 1695, is most closely related to the William group, but contains a preliminary selection of poems from previous reigns. A related manuscript which was unknown to Cameron was Bodleian MS Eng. poet. c 18, which differs only slightly in content and order from Pw V 46. A third manuscript linked with these is BL Add. MS 21094, a much larger anthology written in the reign of Queen Anne, and once owned by Fielding's uncle, the Earl of Denbigh. Items 82 to 162 of this are a selection, appearing in the same sequence, from the earlier compilation. Cameron classifies Add. MS 21094 as a 'copy of a scriptorium MS with additions' (*POAS (Yale)*, v. 542) and as descended from Portland Pw V 46 in respect of poems they have in common.[95] When the Nottingham and the Bodleian manuscripts were being written, two leaves were left blank at the same point in the sequence, presumably to permit the insertion of a text not currently available. In Eng. poet 18 (ff. 158^r–60^r) the first page of the first blank leaf was eventually filled in with a document dated 1718; in Pw V 46 (pp. 306–13), however, the gap was used, circa 1703, for a group of satires on the death of William III and the accession of Anne, four of which are present at the corresponding position in Add. MS 21094 (fols 129^r–30^v). The hands of Eng. poet. 18 and Pw V 46, while not the same, have enough detailed similarities to suggest that one was a conscious imitation of the other, which itself indicates a common origin.

The importance of the scriptorium manuscripts lies in the fact that their texts derive from a single archive of exemplars whose growth and decay can be mapped from the mutations of its products. The order of items is usually chronological with a high proportion dated by year of composition, though not always accurately. While there is a great deal of variation in order between anthologies, even sometimes when of similar date, most of this is within the limits of the year, suggesting that the publisher filed his material as far as possible in annual bundles. As these were untied to permit copying there would be inevitable changes of order, but as the separates would be returned after copying to the same bundle, the general shape of any later compilation would remain the same.

---

[95] Other poems are described as descending from a nonextant scriptorium collateral (*POAS (Yale)*, v. 554); see also 568, 585, 592–3, 595, 599.

The greater variability of the material in the Restoration group would be explained by the publisher being less certain of specific dates (certainly fewer appear attached to poems). The concern with dating also suggests something about the interests of readers. The scribally published state poem and court lampoon had come to comprise a kind of secret history of political events from the Restoration to the Revolution and beyond, which was in many ways more revealing than the conventional histories so far available. Huge compilations such as the Vienna and Dyce manuscripts were also a celebration of the scope and variety of the scribal medium which could still in the 1690s claim to have produced more satire of real distinction than had so far appeared in print. In each case the productions of the present gained in interest by being linked to those of the past, and, while topicality remained the *raison d'être* of the newly composed lampoon, the spirit of the large compilations is close to being an antiquarian one.

Before leaving the manuscripts it is necessary to mention one major anthology that Cameron certainly knew, but chose to exclude from his scriptorium—BL Harl. MS 7319. This has quite a high level of overlap in content with authentic scriptorium manuscripts and resembles them in its style of presentation; however, as far as I have tested the matter, I would agree that its texts do not derive from the scriptorium master copies. Two other questions I must defer are whether the scriptorium may also have published copies of single poems or small linked-groups of poems as separates, and scribal editions of prose texts. My expectation would be that it did both these things, but that, again, is a matter for further research.

THE SCRIPTORIUM AND THE BOOK TRADE

Having summarized and reviewed Cameron's findings, it is now necessary to consider whether the story of the scriptorium can be taken further than where he left it. Cameron's reconstruction of the work of his scriptorium rested on close physical examination of key manuscripts (including virtuoso analysis of watermarks), content and sequence analysis, and the meticulous collations prepared for his Yale *POAS* volume. Although none of this information (except that relating to watermarks) is reproduced in full in either of his two publications on the subject, he provides a magnificent platform for further study both of this and other scriptoria of the period. He also provides immaculate biographical and political annotations to the scriptorium texts included in his edition. What he does not do is to look at the work of his scriptorium within the larger context of scribal publication or writing for the scribal medium. Since the story is one that brings us close to the time when scribal publication ceased to be a major means of public communication, it will be useful to review his findings from this perspective.

The consolidation of the dispersed scriptorial activity of previous decades into the hands of a dominant well-organized agency poses an interesting parallel with tendencies in print publication which were seeing the emergence of large-volume specialist publishers such as Jacob Tonson and Thomas Parkhurst, along with the beginnings of wholesaling and the consolidation of much pamphlet publication into the hands of trade publishers such as Samuel Briscoe and John Morphew.[96] The period was also seeing a more co-operative attitude towards the marketing of copyrights and a tendency on the part of smaller booksellers to join together in congers to obtain a share in large-scale publication. Even as the regulatory power of the stationers' company declined, the trade was being restructured by a new body of co-operative relationships forged by the requirements of capitalist book production. Given this new context of mutuality, and the extent to which the scribal anthologies of the 1690s are dominated by the products of the Cameron scriptorium, it is tempting to hypothesize that the master of the scriptorium was not a furtive opportunist working on the fringe of the book trade, but a known specialist who could be approached by any bookseller who had received enquiries about such material. The distinguishing mark of such a businessman would not be his supervision of a writing room but his control of a body of exemplars and ability to obtain scribes willing to copy on a piecework basis.

This leaves us with the paradox that the master of our scriptorium may not in fact have had a scriptorium. That the archive was carefully preserved, regularly updated, and kept in

---

[96] Processes discussed in Feather, *A history of British publishing*, pp. 60–77.

good order is clear enough. The master had tidy habits and made sure he kept abreast of the market. The other thing he controlled was the paper used for copying. Cameron's 'Scriptorium' article gives us the results of very patient and detailed studies of watermarks, even going so far as to indicate when paper from the same pair of moulds is to be found in separate volumes. The judgement that a particular volume derived from the agency rather than being a secondary copy can be made with a high degree of certainty on the basis of this evidence.[97] But this does not mean that the master was the permanent employer of his scribes: simply that he found it wise to relieve them of an unnecessary overhead and ensure that a suitable grade of paper was used for these expensive products. In doing this he would again be following the practice of print publishers, who were expected to provide the printer with the paper required for a book.

The crucial question, then, becomes one of hands, and here the evidence falls well short of allowing us to posit a semi-permanent scriptorium with a stable staff. I note for a start that Cameron never himself claims that any two manuscripts from his list are written in the same hand. It is possible that he did not have the facilities for making proper comparisons, but if this was the case it would have been uncharacteristic of him not to tell us so, and I prefer to believe that this was a problem he had reserved for more mature consideration. Without having examined all the surviving scriptorium manuscripts, and being in no position to declare finally on this issue, I believe that a careful comparison would reveal at least fifteen distinct hands, and probably more. The only scribe whose work unmistakably recurs in more than two manuscripts is the one who wrote Portland Pw V 42, 43 and 44, which seem, in any case, to have been designed from the start as a group. Two scribes shared the work on the three Folger anthologies, and Bodleian Firth c 15 and Ohio State University MS Eng. 15 *may* have been written by a single hand, though, once again, the possibility cannot be ruled out that one versatile scribe was imitating the work of another.

Of course, judgements of this kind are often difficult to make.

[97] I take this opportunity to thank Dr Bryan Ward-Perkins of Trinity College, Oxford, and formerly librarian at Holkham Hall, for kindly listing the watermarks of Holkham 686 for me and assisting in the preparation of beta-radiograph prints.

Scribes of the period could frequently write a variety of hands quite distinct from each other; hands could vary greatly over time; institutionalized hands can be so conventional that the palaeographer may become hypersensitive to difference and blind to the weight of similarity; lastly, the surviving manuscripts may not be representative, in their variety of hands, of the total output—which is impossible in any case to quantify. But, on the evidence currently available, it seems unlikely that there was any permanent staff of scribes in the service of our scribal publisher. What seems more probable is that scribes were brought in on piecework rates whenever a new volume was bespoke, or that the work was contracted out to whichever scrivener, moonlighting scrivener's apprentice or newsletter scriptorium offered the lowest quotation.

CONCLUSION

What we have been following in this chapter is the origin and growth to maturity of one particular tradition of scribal publication. We have seen how the transmission of Restoration scriptorial satire began in the mid-1660s with the circulation of separates by author and user publication. From the mid-1670s we have evidence of professional involvement in the copying of court-libertine verse, and can assume the same with some confidence for the even more widely circulated state poems. 1679–80 sees the copying of the earliest surviving anthologies as enterprises of evanescent scriptoria with no apparent relationship to each other apart from that of drawing on a common stock of separates. From this period too the author-publisher yields place to the organized entrepreneur, selling directly to a clientele established through personal contact or to the customers of a particular bookseller but not, apparently, through the book trade to the public at large. The 1690s saw a decisive centralizing of activity into the hands of the Cameron scriptorium, a development that also suggests an integration of the production of manuscript books into the regular commerce of bookselling. With this the process is complete which has led us from the exchanging of single poems among friends to the writing of 800-hundred page anthologies by skilled professionals.

The development described in the publication of satirical verse is one which is paradigmatic for all scribal publication of topical texts. A tradition would evolve through a series of transitions of which the most important were the professionalization of writing and transmission, and the consolidation of scattered separates into substantial anthologies, which, by preserving many items which would otherwise have been lost, would widen the field of choice for subsequent compilers. The crucial factor in bringing about this latter transition was the growing mass of material available. If whole books of lampoons did not appear until the late 1670s it was largely because enough good satire was not yet in circulation to fill books. Once this was the case, the opportunity existed to present collections that were both current and retrospective, and which may well have been valued as chronological *aide-memoires* as well as for their polemics. The historical impulse was to prove a powerful incentive to purchase, as was the desire to present a whole tradition in its development. The same pattern will be found in other progressive compilations, such as collections of parliamentary reports and viol fantasias. Here we need to acknowledge the status of the scribally published text as a collectible alongside the better documented passions for coins, paintings, tulips and antiquarian manuscripts.

However, the professionalization of copying may well have been more advanced with regard to these highly saleable commodities than in the case of most other kinds of scribally circulated material. For this we can thank the aristocracy, who seem to have been the principal buyers of the large books. The humbler separate and newsletter drew their customers from the coffee houses and the unfailing hunger of country readers for fresh information from the town. In London itself the court lampoon had a place in the culture of gossip that ensured both that new compositions would be widely talked about and that women as well as men would be keen to secure copies. Once these avenues of transmission were in place, they could be manipulated in order to give special prominence to texts expounding a particular political position, Robert Julian's alliance with the 'Whiggish peers' being one example of this. A lampoon could be brought to attention by being displayed or discarded in places where it was likely to be read. Equally, one could be suppressed by the simple means of destroying copies or refusing access to exemplars.

The final stage in the life-cycle of the lampoon tradition was its transition to print. The work of the Cameron scriptorium, at the same time as it marks the culmination of a long tradition of scribal anthologies, also bears unmistakable signs of decadence. This is particularly evident in the 'Restoration' group whose two major representatives are monstrous in bulk and entirely retrospective— aged rakes grown fat and garrulous. Increasingly, the distinctive function of the scribally published lampoon—that of providing an arena of uninhibited critical expression within a culture premised on the strict control of public utterance—would join the other functions of script already appropriated by the press. A new generation of poets, by rejecting the outspokenness of lampoon for a manner based on irony and indirection, would show that a separate medium was no longer necessary for the performance of such a critique. Satire of the Popean kind could be publicly available through print while preserving a 'reserved' status by veiling its full import from those who had not acquired certain specialized reading skills. Meanwhile the lapse of time was making the older lampoon repertoire available to any bookseller bold enough to print it, in suitably censored versions, for the sake of its historical interest.

There is as yet no comprehensive study of the process by which this repertoire was progressively made available in printed form. A volume such as the 1680 Rochester *Poems on several occasions* is of little significance since it was simply a scribal miscellany in typographical dress. In the same way the various turn-of-the-century *Poems on affairs of state* volumes (one of which, as we saw, actually originated from the Cameron scriptorium) do little more than bring a mass of material together on an *omnium gatherum* principle. Greater interest attaches to Jacob Tonson's 1691 edition of Rochester in that its aim was to accommodate the writings of a scribal classic to an innovative print-publisher's conception of what constituted a vernacular literary 'works'—a field that Tonson was to make a specialism. In order to fulfil this aim, Rochester had to be reformulated ideologically as well as in terms of medium. To start with, *'every Block of Offence'* had to be removed, so that the volume might *'not unbecome the Cabinet of the Severest Matron'*.[98] And, while comparisons with Horace and Virgil

---

[98] *Poems, &c. on several occasions: with Valentinian, a tragedy. Written by the Right*

281

might seem far-fetched, a status that was both patriotic and elevated could be claimed through the prefacer's judgement that: '*Whatever Giant* Boileau *may be in his own Country, He seems little more than a Man of Straw with my Lord* Rochester' (p. A5').

Artistically the problem was how to confer an appearance of unity on the *œuvre* of an impenitently occasional writer—a solution being essayed through making him, in both his strengths and his weaknesses, an exemplary case of the aristocratic poet (as he was to remain). Whereas Horace had enjoyed the advantage of having his poetry '*over-look'd*' by 'Pollio, Mecænas, *and* Augustus, *the greatest Men, and the best Judges*', Rochester's high status left him with '*no Body of Quality or Severity so much above himself, to Challenge a Deference, or to Check the ordinary Licences of Youth, and impose on him the Obligation to copy over again, what on any Occasion had not been so exquisitely design'd*' (pp. A3ʳ⁻ᵛ). Yet there was a compensation for this special status in that '*No Imagination cou'd bound or prescribe whither his Flights would carry him*' (p. A6ʳ). Tonson also rearranged the poems into broad generic groupings of lyrics, satires, translations, and addresses (including the prologues and Bendo's bill), concluding with the tragedy *Valentinian*. This seems to reflect a conscious design to lead the reader progressively from the private and intimate to the most public of forms, the drama. There had also to be a renegotiation of class interests, for the readership of such editions was now a much broader one. Thus the Restoration court is roundly censured for its '*Ribaldry and Debauch*' (p. A3ᵛ).

Insofar as these print-engendered values could be imposed upon the Rochesterian corpus (or that part of it that was allowed to appear) this was done. And yet for some time Tonson's major outlet for the publication of new poetry was to remain the miscellany, in the series that began with Dryden's *Miscellany poems* of 1684 and concluded with the sixth volume of 1709. In this respect print publication had still to find its own organising principles to supplement the scribal anthologists' delight in mixture. The way in which these principles eventually evolved might be studied through patient comparison of the scribal

Honourable John late Earl of Rochester (London, 1691), 'The Preface to the Reader', p. A6ᵛ.

compilations detailed in Beal's volumes of the *Index of English literary manuscripts* with their printed counterparts; and by tracking both the manuscript and print appearances of satires recorded in David Foxon's *English verse 1701-1750: a catalogue of separately printed poems with notes on contemporary collected editions.*[99] But in the present study, it seemed more fruitful to look at the interactions of the two media in the work of a single writer, Jonathan Swift, who more than any other, was to recreate the political values of the scribally published text within the triumphant rival medium.

[99] 2 vols (Cambridge, 1975).

7

THE AMBIGUOUS TRIUMPH OF PRINT

THE city of Melbourne, where this book was written, is the home of a form of football played with four goalposts at each end of the field and eighteen players on each side. Although sometimes described as a cousin of Gaelic football it is in fact of at least as great antiquity, its origins having been scrutinized in this respect by a distinguished historian.[1] In the earlier years of the game the leading clubs had their grounds in working-class suburbs close to the city centre and drew their support from their own territories, matches at this stage having something of the quality of inter-tribal warfare. Like that of most team sports, the game's history has been one of continual subtle evolution within an overall dialogue between the framers of rules, whose intentions were sometimes conservative and sometimes reformist, and creative players and coaches, whose aim was to develop match-winning innovations, bending the rules when necessary. One important period of innovation occurred during the 1960s, a decade in which the teams' support base was transferred to a more dispersed constituency scattered through a vast exurbia.[2] Subject to new competitive pressures and an increased need to attract as a television spectacle, the game modified in the direction of greater player mobility, fewer interruptions to the movement of the ball, and enhanced physical skills, a process that still continues. Trevor

[1] Geoffrey Blainey, *A game of our own: the origins of Australian football* (Melbourne, 1990).
[2] This phase of the game's development, along with the attendant change from semi-professional to fully professional status, is the subject of David Williamson's drama, *The club* (Sydney, 1978). In performance the play has been adapted to other football codes, emphasizing that the predicament was a universal one.

Grant, in an article from which this section draws most of its material, has compared AFL football to 'a hyperactive child forever burrowing into unexplored territory' for whom 'the constant search for something new has rendered the past largely irrelevant'.[3]

Largely but not completely. While many of these changes, being a response to changing conditions, would have occurred anyway, there is a consensus that the essentials of the modern game were first formulated by a single, far-sighted coach, Len Smith (d. 1967), whose dicta are still treasured by present-day coaches. A friendly, civilized man in a brash profession, Smith did not himself win a premiership during his years as coach, but laid the tactical foundation for the later success of his own club Richmond and of Melbourne, the club coached by his brother Norman. Sporting coaches have always had a tendency to compile lists of 'do's' and 'dont's' for players and to keep written notes of their ideas about the game. In Len Smith's case the ideas were set down in eighty-eight pages of a black-covered exercise book.

From time to time other coaches were allowed to make transcriptions from this book. In 1965 Allan Jeans, then coach of St Kilda, went to see Smith for advice on how to prepare his team for an imminent grand final appearance. 'I remember hopping on the train', he told Grant, 'and going out to see Len at his place in Essendon. He welcomed me with open arms and brought out this old exercise book in which he had made all his coaching notes. I went through and jotted down everything he had written on confidence. I passed it on to the players and it formed the basis of the notes I used in the years to come.' Jeans's own notes, incorporating material from Smith's, were later deposited with the Victorian Coaches Association. Another coach, Colin Kinnear, went for advice some years after Len Smith's death to his brother Norm. Norm, he recalled, 'sat down with me for five hours and wrote out in longhand all those ideas from his brother's book', also adding some of his own. A third coach, John Northey, who had himself been coached by Len Smith, preserved notes received from him in a cardboard box. After a time Smith's text became a kind of cult object to be consulted for reasons other than immediate

[3] 'The father of modern football', *Sunday herald*, 22 Apr. 1990, p. 41.

practical advice: Kevin Sheedy described it as 'the sort of notes I look to when things aren't going right and I want to refresh my memory'. By 1990, according to Grant, a league coach who had not read some of the 'Smith manifesto' was a rarity. Smith's notebook may itself have incorporated material received from earlier coaches or during his own playing career. Certainly some of the principles quoted by Grant ('True friendship—one for all and all for one') have a time-honoured ring. But it is also clear that the game, at a period of transition but with a long history of orally transmitted football wisdom to draw on, was ready for the written *summa* that Smith provided. If he had not supplied it in so acceptable and forward-looking a form, some other coach would sooner or later have filled the vacuum.

What has just been described is a kind of scribal authorship and publication which should by now be perfectly familiar. Once the existence of Smith's manual came to be known, it was recognized as a means of winning games against coaches ignorant of its precepts. The ideal situation was one in which its reserved status was retained through certain coaches having access while others were denied it or given only partial access. For this reason it was deliberately withheld from the typewriter, the stencil duplicator and the photocopier. Personally generous, Smith was prepared to show it to enquirers of whom he approved but not, it would seem, until after he had retired from active coaching. His brother, to whom the book passed on Len's death, was also careful to restrict transmission. John Northey, although he was later to coach Norm's own club, Melbourne, could not be allowed to make his own transcription: instead Norm painstakingly copied out what he thought proper the younger man should receive. This was also a way of emphasizing Len Smith's status as a guru whose wisdom should not be undervalued through being acquired too lightly. Not all enquirers were interested in the entire document: Allan Jeans's special concern was material on building confidence. Ideas from the manual circulated back to players in a form analogous to seventeenth-century separates through coaches' notes and memoranda. Larger-scale copying seems generally to have been a form of re-creation as successive coaches incorporated their own insights into the received script and adjusted it to take account of new developments in the game. Fragmentary and interpolated

transmission led to a position where Smith could be invoked by
partisans of contradictory views—e.g. as favouring the 'flick pass',
later declared illegal by the rule-makers because it made the game
too fast-moving, and as deprecating handball as a poor alternative
to kicking. All of this can be parallelled in the scribal transmission
of earlier wisdom literatures, and must certainly have counterparts
in the histories of other modern team sports.

The example is given to show that even in an age when, with the
aid of the photocopier, the personal computer, and the modem,
reserved publication can be conducted quite effortlessly without
resort to the pen, transmission of texts through handwritten copies
still persists where there is a demand for its special capacity to
integrate privilege and presence. As late as the nineteenth century
the cultural role of scribal publication was still an important one.
During the lifetime of Gerard Manley Hopkins his writings were
distributed in a manner not essentially different from that
employed by Orinda in the seventeenth century, through separates
and small collections sent to a circle of readers, with only the
occasional appearance in print.[4] Even a text as important as
Wordsworth's *The prelude* could only be read by those to whom
the poet was prepared to give access to the manuscript. In our
terminology, recalling Donne's circulation of *Biathanatos*, it would
count as a case of author publication through one copy. The scribal
newsletter survived in the form of the handwritten ships'
newspapers produced on the lengthy intercontinental voyages of
this period: examples were also to be found in the trenches of the
first world war. Trevor Grant's article on Len Smith appeared in a
journal that was a successor to a handwritten newspaper circulated
on 1 January 1838 by John Pascoe Fawkner in Melbourne. The
political role of the scribally published text remained an important
one in Ireland until the present century, and continues to be
reasserted wherever the freedom to promulgate ideas through the
print and electronic media is denied. Samizdat publication in the
Soviet Union used the typewriter for Cyrillic texts but had no
alterative to the pen for those in Western languages.

The examples just given of late occurrences of scribal

---

[4] Since Hopkins also insisted that the true medium of his poetry was recitation, not silent
reading, he might well count as a case of what Ong calls the 'residual orality' of the
handwritten word.

publication could be enlarged very considerably; and yet it would be impossible to deny that in England, since 1800 at the very least, publication of this kind has been regarded as aberrant, or was the consequence of constraint rather than choice. In Hopkins's case, the choice of scribal publication was not his own, but forced on him by his religious superiors. Wordsworth, too, while reluctant to have *The prelude* printed while he was alive, fully intended to have it appear once he was dead. Handwritten newspapers, including Fawkner's, turned themselves into printed newspapers whenever it was possible to do so. This devaluation of the scribal medium can be detected as early as the reign of George I in the decline (though not total disappearance) of the entrepreneurially published newsletter and lampoon. The major writing of his reign was all circulated through the press, something that would not have held true for that of his predecessor, Anne, and certainly not for the reigns of Charles II and James II. What was kept in manuscript was increasingly what lacked the quality required for print publication. The taxing of newspapers from 1 August 1712 should have been of benefit to scribal publishers, and Defoe, in a passage quoted at the beginning of Chapter 1, foresaw it as likely to encourage a revival of 'Written Scandal' and an 'inconceivable Flood of written News-Letters'; but there is no evidence to date that this prediction was fulfilled.[5] More generally we can say that, while the institution survived the death of Anne, its centrality to the ideological debates of its society did not. It will be the task of this chapter to enquire why and how this happened.

'PRESENCE' AND 'AURA'

The most obvious reason is the rapid physical expansion of the printing trade during the early years of the eighteenth century and the accompanying diminution of the control governments were able or willing to exercise over it. The growth in the number of printers active, combined with the keenness of competition between them, led to an increase in surreptitious printing under fraudulent imprints, while the emergence of the trade publisher (usually a bookbinder or failed bookseller) permitted the real

[5] *A review*, viii. 708.

publishers of controversial works to hide their identities behind a third party.[6] Both of these developments encouraged the print publication of oppositional texts of a kind which would earlier have been circulated in manuscript. Inability to check the tide of pamphleteering led to competition for the services, or the silence, of the most able writers—those who could not be secured by money being courted, as in Swift's case, with flattery and the promise of preferment.[7] J. A. Downie's study of Harley's relationship with the press shows how an astute political manager could make use of this multiplicity of monitory voices for his own ends, influencing the conduct of his opponents' journals as well as those of his own party.[8] Harley's recognition of the need for political control of the press was no less keen than that of Clarendon or Danby; but he differed from them in appreciating that censorship and licensing were inefficient, self-defeating methods of achieving this.

Print and print culture were also extending their geographical spread. Terry Belanger has pointed out that by 1790 the aspiring author could send material to a local or a London newspaper or periodical, self-publish with a local or a London printer, or deal through a local or a London bookseller. In addition, the operations of the regional book-trade were supported throughout the kingdom by a vast mass of printing and publishing of a non-book kind. But prior to the expiry of the Licensing Act in 1695 the situation had been very different: even in London the newspapers were rudimentary, and magazines and journals rare, while outside London, with very few exceptions, they were simply absent.[9] That this was the case so long after the introduction of printing into

---

[6] For trade publishers, see Michael Treadwell, 'London trade publishers 1675–1750', *Library*, 6:4 (1982), 99–134. Where the trade publisher was a binder, he had a defence against prosecution in that, unlike the printer and the bookseller, he could not be assumed to have read the book that came out under his name (pp. 130–1).

[7] The subvention of writers by political factions is documented in Alexandre Beljame's *Le public et les hommes de lettres en Angleterre au dix-huitième siècle 1660–1744*, 2nd edn (Paris, 1897); English trans. by E. O. Lorimer as *Men of letters and the English public in the eighteenth century 1660–1744: Dryden, Addison, Pope* (London, 1948), pp. 212–22, 317–41. The practice declined sharply after Walpole's rise to power in 1721.

[8] *Robert Harley and the press. Propaganda and public opinion in the age of Swift and Defoe* (Cambridge, 1979).

[9] Terry Belanger, 'Publishers and writers in eighteenth-century England' in *Books and their readers in eighteenth-century England*, ed. Isabel Rivers (Leicester, 1982), p. 6.

England is a tribute to the efficiency of scribal methods of performing their functions; but it also points to the effects of repression and restricted literacy. Certainly after 1700 the domain of the pen contracts noticeably.

Citing Belanger's findings, Alvin Kernan, in an influential study of the social roles of the handwritten and the printed word in eighteenth-century England, goes on to consider the emergence of a 'print culture' based on 'print logic'.

> In this general transformation to a print culture, letters and the entire world of writing, which were directly and continuously involved with printing, underwent radical, even revolutionary, changes. To mention only some of the most familiar print-related changes in letters at this time, the novel became the major literary form, and prose challenged poetry as the most prestigious medium; the author's copyright was legalized and censorship was nearly abolished; enormous numbers of literary works, both new and old, were printed and made available to readers; large public and private libraries became common; criticism became a standard literary genre; patronage nearly disappeared as authors began to be able to live by selling their writing; literacy increased and a new public audience of readers appeared; literary histories were written for the first time. Changes of this magnitude were cumulatively as revolutionary in the world of letters as the events of 1688 and 1789, with which they were socially co-ordinate, were in the political world, and like the related political changes, the literary changes were not random but followed a particular logic.[10]

The 'print logic' which Kernan sees as powering these changes is that defined by McLuhan as 'the mechanical spirit of movable types in precise lines', whose effects may be further sublimed into abstraction, uniformity, repeatability, visuality and quantification.[11] In this Kernan's conclusions are close to those of Ong as outlined in Chapter four, though each has found his own way of accommodating the insights of McLuhan.

In another part of his study, Kernan distinguishes between the impact of manuscript and that of print by reference to Walter Benjamin's notion of 'aura'. Benjamin's argument defines aura as that quality possessed by a work of art while it remains unique in its

---

[10] *Printing technology*, p. 49. Kernan's concept of print-culture values is developed in Julie Stone Peters, *Congreve, the drama, and the printed word* (Stanford, Calif., 1990).

[11] Kernan, p. 50, citing McLuhan, *Gutenberg galaxy*, p. 244.

'Hier und Jetzt' but which is lost once it is multiplied through reproduction.[12] Benjamin's actual concern is with the relationship of theatre to film and painting to photography; but there is an obvious analogy with that between the manuscript exemplar for a printed book and the resultant edition. 'Aura' is also an outcome of the cult-status of the art-object, whether that status is conferred by magical or religious ritual or by its modern substitutes, the secular cult of beauty and the 'negative theology' of art for art's sake.[13] The transition from manuscript to the anonymous multiplicity of print deprives the book of its privileged uniqueness within a religiously valorized world, while simultaneously exposing it to the operation of the 'critical, judging spirit'.[14] The wider availability of books in the early decades of the eighteenth century led not only to an intensification of this spirit but a belief that anyone from the gentleman who writ with ease to the lowly Grub Street hack had the capacity to set up as an author.[15] To Kernan the problem of the eighteenth-century was to find a way of re-sacralizing printed texts, and 'rescuing them thereby from the imminent danger of being no more than ephemeral print commodities for sale in the marketplace' (p. 158).

Kernan's acceptance of 'aura' as that characteristic of the handwritten text which is lost by the transition to print is the main point of difference between him and Ong who allots that role to 'presence' in the sense established earlier. Both agree that *something* is lost and would relate it their own ways to the sacred, but these ways lead to quite different accounts of the change, one grounding it in loss of uniqueness and the other in greater remoteness from the human agents responsible for the creation of the text and document. From the point of view of a study of scribal publication, Kernan's view is less fruitful than Ong's. The notion of aura has little application to the most characteristic products of

[12] Walter Benjamin, *Das Kunstwerk im Zeitalter seiner technischen Reproduzierbarkeit* (Frankfurt, 1966), p. 12; English text as 'The work of art in the age of mechanical reproduction', in *Illuminations*, trans. Harry Zohn (London, 1973), pp. 219–53. Zohn's translation of the German phrase ('here and now') as 'presence' would have been confusing in the present context.
[13] *Illuminations*, p. 226.
[14] Kernan, pp. 152–4. See also McLuhan, pp. 69–71, drawing on Mercea Eliade's notion of 'desacralization'.
[15] Kernan, p. 155. Cf. *Illuminations*, pp. 232–4.

seventeenth-century scribal publication, the single or half-sheet separate and the private commonplace book. Even their enshrinement within rare-book libraries cannot disguise the functional, everyday quality of these documents. A few skilfully written miscellanies might enter a claim to aura on grounds of appearance, but it is one that, as Chapter 6 has shown, is usually undercut by their content. Dorset's lines from 'A faithful catalogue of our most eminent ninnies'

> Thy rammish, spendthrift buttock, 'tis well known,
> Her nauseous bait has made thee swallow down,
> Though mumbled and spit out by half the town.
> How well (my honest Lexington) she knows
> The many mansions in thy f—ing house;[16]

represent an extreme of desacralization in which the sacred (in this case the words of Christ in John 14:2) is subjected to obscene parody. (Dryden's parodies of Biblical language in the scribally published *Mac Flecknoe* are among many other examples which could be cited of the same tendency.) If volumes containing such passages were to be assimilated to a cultic conception of the inscribed word, it could only be by invoking a carnivalesque inversion of the sacred which acknowledged its privileged status even in the act of parody. By contrast, the notion of presence is one that has an immediate relevance to our physical experience of the manuscripts, at least in the non-philosophical sense that they retain much more intense traces of the human agents involved in their production and consumption than printed books. This is not said in order to deny validity to Kernan's argument, but simply to stress that it has less applicability to the matter in hand than Ong's.

A further difficulty is posed by Kernan's espousal of the idea that it was print and more specifically 'print logic' that was responsible for the emergence of a 'critical, judging spirit' in the writing of the early eighteenth century. Here the contention that such a spirit was dominant at this period is not in question—the careers of Swift, Addison and Pope would of themselves be enough to demonstrate it; but it is equally the case, and has been demonstrated many times in this book, that in a seventeenth-century context it was script and

---

[16] ll. 138–42, in *POAS (Yale)*, iv. 198. Harris, *Poems*, p. 141 incorrectly emends 'buttock' (= mistress) to 'buttocks'.

not print that was the critical, subversive medium. To some extent, as we saw in Chapter 5, this was the effect of state censorship. Attempts to use print in a critical role were ruthlessly suppressed whenever the authorities had the power to do so, and when they did not possess this power an oppositional print literature was quick to manifest itself. But the scribal medium must also be granted an inherent orientation towards a critical stance. The reserved nature of scribal publication and the fact that the initial readership of the scribally published text was usually a circle sympathetic to the author meant that opinions were uttered with a freedom and directness that would have been highly imprudent in print. It was also likely to be the case that the scribal community was a political community of an oppositional kind. The development of the lampoon as the most characteristic form of scribally published verse and the fact that a Suckling and a Rochester could devote their considerable talents to that genre is itself a strong objection to Kernan's model: we should also note the huge body of scribally published state poems, reaching back to the reign of James I, which collectively represent the most comprehensive and outspoken body of oppositional verse we possess from the Stuart century. If this tradition is to be reconciled with Kernan's reworking of Benjamin's insight it can only be in the form that a deprivation of aura experienced through print led to a critical reaction conveyed through script. As it stands, however, Kernan's model does not accommodate the historical phenomenon of scribal publication.

FROM LAMPOON TO SATIRE

What can be demonstrated, though, is a procedure by which as the vitality of scribal publication declined, a determined attempt was made to rescue forms of oppositional discourse which had been nourished within the scribal arena for use within the print medium. It will be maintained that the character of print culture was irreversibly changed as a result. The beginning of this process can be seen as early as Dryden's *Absalom and Achitophel* (1682), a print-published poem that draws boldly on the language and manner of the scribal lampoon. The opening lines, in their presentation of Charles II as an amoral libertine, strike a note which, while alien to print, was familiar from a long series of scribally published attacks:[17]

> In pious times, e'r Priest-craft did begin,
> Before *Polygamy* was made a sin;
> When man, on many, multiply'd his kind,
> E'r one to one was, cursedly, confind:
> When Nature prompted, and no law deny'd
> Promiscuous use of Concubine and Bride;
> Then, *Israel*'s Monarch, after Heaven's own heart,
> His vigorous warmth did, variously, impart
> To Wives and Slaves: And, wide as his Command,
> Scatter'd his Maker's Image through the Land. (ll. 1–10; *Works*, ii. 5)

The anti-clerical tone of these lines, their libertine critique of marriage, and their blasphemous inversion of Biblical language and values were features previously restricted to the scribal medium and must have had a considerable shock effect when first encountered in print.[18] The logic of lines 7–10 (recapitulated in 13–16), which, once applied to the year 1682, required Dryden's first readers to accept that the more Charles II committed adultery the more like God he became, represents a quite remarkable reversal of the teaching of the Church of England with regard to honourable marriage. The passage can certainly be read as ironic, but its irony is of a distinctly two-edged kind. In a printed text, some degree of irony would need to have been posited by a contemporary reader even to explain that it was being openly sold. Did not, after all, both civil and ecclesiastical courts exist to prosecute those responsible for the public utterance of blasphemies? But encountered in manuscript such lines would be accepted as a perfectly sincere statement of a familiar libertine critique of marriage as a human invention designed to privilege interest over nature. Where exactly then *did* Dryden stand in this puzzling mixture of discourses which were usually segregated off into separate media?

---

[17] A selection of these is given in Ch. 5, n. 81.

[18] The only exceptions to this would be surreptitious printed editions of scribal texts, such as the 1680 Rochester *Poems on several occasions*, and the speeches of theatrical villains, such as Don John in Shadwell's *The libertine*, in printed plays. While some mildly libertine philosophizing in plays (e.g. that of Phraartes in Crowne's *The destruction of Jerusalem*) is given to sympathetic characters, most was neutralized by either punishment or repentance.

Having seized our attention with his lampoon-style opening, Dryden swiftly withdraws into less disconcerting forms of discourse. Even when the lampoon manner is revived for the gallery of Charles's enemies in lines 543–681, print decorums are generally maintained. Still more reassuringly, by the end of his poem Dryden has become engaged in a full-scale exercise of resacralization—the presentation of the royal utterance in its by this time little-credited role as the metaphorical voice of God.[19] To return to the opening lines is to reveal that the poem is profoundly heteroglossial, exposing the reader to a variety of competing discourses and media (the vocal, the scribal and the typographical) with competing claims to authority. A discrepancy which has been noted by several commentators is that between the ironic use of 'godlike' in the reference to Queen Catherine as Michal

> *Michal*, of Royal blood, the Crown did wear,
> A Soyl ungratefull to the Tiller's care:
> Not so the rest; for several Mothers bore
> To Godlike *David*, several Sons before. (ll. 11–14; ii. 5–6)

and its 'serious' use in the concluding lines of the poem:

> Henceforth a Series of new time began,
> The mighty Years in long Procession ran:
> Once more the Godlike *David* was Restor'd,
> And willing Nations knew their Lawfull Lord. (ll. 1028–31; ii. 36)

The notion that these two usages need to be reconciled, or that one has to be valorized at the expense of the other, is a misconception: Dryden's poem is one whose unity lies in its acceptance of disunity, in its being a counterpoint of irreconcilable voices. This was in turn to be the condition of all writing in which what we would define, in Ong's or Kernan's sense, as script values were transferred into the medium of print, creating productions whose rationale was to question the certainties of print logic even as these were being invoked.

A critical perspective towards print was already established within the scribal medium through a fashion for texts parodying either the substance or the visual appearance of print forms. An early example is Francis Beaumont's 'Grammar lecture', a section

---

[19] Cf. Ch. 4, pp. 160–73.

by section send-up of William Lily's Latin grammar.[20] The Rochesterian *The destruction of Sodom* and *Actus primus, scaena prima* are burlesques not simply of conventional sexual mores and the conventions of the heroic play but also of the way these plays were set out on the page with their attendant title-pages, prologues and stage directions. The group of mock-commendatory verses circulated in 1669–71 on Edward Howard's *The British prince* and *The new Utopia* are an explicit example of scribally published burlesques directed at a printed text. Rochester's mock-songs and obscene lyrics mimic originals, both specific and generic, which formed the staple of the printed verse miscellany, while two of his satiric epistles appear to parody the Dryden-directed translation of *Ovid's epistles* (1680). The particular force of these parodies lies not simply in their somewhat mechanical reversals of received values but in their exposing the compromises and falsifications which had to be accepted by the print-publishing writer in order to take a stand in the public arena. From its shifting, indeterminate world, which is also, however, because it relies on penstrokes rather than machines for its perpetuation, a more human and in the Libertine sense 'natural' world, script mocks at the soulless fecundity of print. Dryden's scribally published *Mac Flecknoe* is in ways which have never fully been appreciated an anti-print poem, picturing a world choked up with the mighty yet evanescent products of the press:

> No *Persian* Carpets spread th' Imperial way,
> But scatter'd Limbs of mangled Poets lay:
> From dusty shops neglected Authors come,
> Martyrs of Pies, and Reliques of the Bum.
> Much *Heywood, Shirly, Ogleby* there lay,
> But loads of *Sh*— almost choakt the way.
> Bilk't *Stationers* for Yeomen stood prepar'd,
> And *H*— was Captain of the Guard. (ll. 98–105; ii. 56–7)

The press is a monster which once set in motion can never be halted—a perpetual action machine whose function, in a metaphor which was later to be adapted by Pope in *The dunciad*, is to convert mind into mountains of inky sheets. Being libertines in principle as well as in politics, the scribal poets of the Restoration

---

[20] Text in Mark Eccles, 'Francis Beaumont's *Grammmar lecture*', RES 16 (1940), 402–14.

were in no doubt that the print medium was their enemy; yet they must also have realized that it was ultimately unassailable through any medium but its own, and it was this project they handed on to their successors.

SWIFT, SCRIPT AND PRINT

The three eighteenth-century writers whose work reveals the sharpest sense of the relationship of the two media are Swift, Richardson and Sterne. It is interesting to note that both Swift and Sterne belonged to circles that engaged in some degree of scribal publication, Swift firstly as a Scriblerian and later as an exchanger of social verse with his friends Delany and Sheridan, and Sterne as a member of the Crazy Castle clique, presided over by John Hall Stevenson.[21] Richardson, paradoxically a printer by trade, was a compulsive letter-writer. Richardson's and Sterne's particular perception of the relationship emerges through an insistent foregrounding, within the fictional narrative, of the act of inscribing: their readers are rarely out of hearing of the scratching of a nib. In Sterne's case we should add his creation of a mode of storytelling which contradicts everything that has been proposed about print logic.

The case of Swift is especially pertinent in that his career spans the exact period in which the scribal medium ceased to be a central vehicle for ideological debate within the governing class and was reduced to a marginal function. What we see in the course of this career is a series of experiments by which the critical and parodic stance which had been perfected by writers for the medium is recreated within the culture of print. Born in 1667 he would undoubtedly have had some contact with the vigorous scribal culture of the closing decades of the century, though the links have yet to be explored in detail.[22] Certainly his own satirical verse is

[21] Apart from the handful of 'Jeux d'esprit of the Scriblerus club' (*The poems of Jonathan Swift*, ed. Harold Williams, 2nd edn (Oxford, 1958), pp. 184–8), the scribal phase of the circulation of Swift's Scriblerian writings is undocumented. For an interesting speculation that would assign elements of third voyage of *Gulliver's travels* to this period, see Christopher Worth, 'Swift's 'Flying Island': buttons and bomb-vessels', *RES* NS 42 (1991), 343–60. Manuscript circulation is recorded for several of the Irish pieces in the third volume of the *Poems*.

[22] It has not to my knowledge been suggested that his 'A pastoral dialogue' (*Poems*, 879–82) is a parody of Horace, *Carm.*, III. ix ('Donec gratus eram tibi'), but a connection

297

often very close to the manner of Rochester, Dorset and their
school. Poems such as 'The lady's dressing room', 'The problem'
and 'A beautiful young nymph going to bed' would have been
welcome additions to the archive of Robert Julian. They also have
an obvious parodic target in the idealizing love poems which were
the staple of the printed anthologies.

An equally important part of Swift's education was an initiation
into the duplicity of the print medium provided by his encounter
with John Dunton's Athenian Society. The Dunton episode shows
a surprisingly print-naïve young Swift falling into exactly the kind
of literary trap he was later to set himself with consummate skill.
Through a lively imagination, an incessantly active pen and a
masterly manipulation of the delusive authority of the typographic
page, Dunton had succeeded in conjuring into existence a largely
chimerical society of savants whose lucubrations, issued and
reissued in a variety of publications, so far prevailed upon Swift in
his isolation at Moor Park that he was moved to salute them with
an ode, his first published work, which was given pride of place in
The supplement to the fifth volume of the Athenian gazette on 1 April
1692. There is no trace of irony in this poem. Swift's tribute to
Dunton's semi-imaginary college (he did have his advisers but they
were scarcely the master-spirits pictured by Swift) appears to be a
perfectly sincere one. How soon after the publication of the ode
Swift was undeceived about the real nature of Dunton's operation
is not clear, but that the undeceiving was a bitter one is suggested
by the taunting reference in *A tale of a tub*, where Dunton is accused
of planning to publish 'a faithful and a painful Collection' of the
gallows speeches of criminals in twelve volumes in folio.[23] But
Dunton had at least taught Swift that, despite its prim visage and
air of impersonality, print could be made to lie and would be much
more effective in its lying than script or voice because in its
mechanical methodicalness and freedom from presence it seemed
to carry a guarantee of objectivity that was not available to its more
exposed and patently human rivals. Swift was himself in *Gulliver's
travels*, the *Modest proposal* and the Bickerstaffe papers (to look no

---

between the two poems would be more evident if we could introduce as an intermediary
term a cant version of Horace's ode ('Whilst thou hadst all my heart and I had thine'), widely
circulated in manuscript, in which the speakers are a Restoration rake and a prostitute.

[23] *Prose works of Jonathan Swift*, ed. Herbert Davis *et al.* (Oxford, 1939–68), i. 35.

further) to prove himself the most adroit of liars in print but always with the subsidiary aim of undermining the reaction by which readers unthinkingly attribute impersonality, authority and stability to the printed word. (We should take particular note here of his mastery of the parody title page.)

Swift's savaging of print genres and conventions may seem a strange attitude for an Anglican clergyman whose faith was anchored in the printed text of the Bible and the *Book of common prayer*. For reasons that will emerge, this was not as serious a problem as we might expect it would be; but it did complicate the profounder problem of how the democratically distributed sacred texts were to be protected from partial, sectarian interpretations. Here Swift's response was simply to deny that they should be interpreted at all. For a writer whose own works pose such stringent hermeneutic challenges he was surprisingly conservative in his overt attitude to the texts of others. His stylistic ideals, largely acquired from Sir William Temple, rest on admiration for a dignified plainness of expression, while his theological principles reflect an undeviating, churchmanly regard for the thirty-nine articles of the Churches of England and Ireland. Any Modern rash enough to cast doubt on either of those ideals was likely to be very vigorously handled. With regard to the Bible Swift exhibits a positively Brobdingnagian hostility to interpretation, branding it as impious, unorthodox and abhorrent to good sense 'to attempt explaining the Mysteries of the Christian Religion'.[24] Clive Probyn has pointed to the significance of his *Abstract of Mr C—ns's discourse of free-thinking* to an understanding of this attitude.[25] Anthony Collins's *A discourse of free-thinking, occasion'd by the rise and growth of a sect called free-thinkers*, published in 1713, had argued that Biblical meanings were incapable of final determination either at the philological/codicological level (due to uncertainties about the meanings of ancient words and the large number of variants among the source manuscripts) or at the interpretative where he denied the right of a self-perpetuating caste of hierophants to

---

[24] *Prose works*, ii. 77.

[25] "Haranguing upon texts': Swift and the idea of the book', in *Proceedings of the first Münster symposium on Jonathan Swift*, ed. Hermann J. Real and Heinz J. Vienken (München, 1986), pp. 187–97. See also his 'Swift and typographic man: foul papers, modern criticism, and Irish dissenters', in Peter Shakel ed., *Critical approaches to teaching Swift* (New York, 1991), pp. 1–17.

impose their reading on the world as the only valid one. In the light of this he argues for the liberty of individual readers to generate their own meanings in a way which, if not quite permitting the free play of meanings, was at least in accord with the principles of free trade.[26] To reduce Probyn's argument to its simplest terms, Collins's aim was to free the English Bible from an institutionalized and legally sanctioned form of closure imposed by the Anglican clergy and Swift's aim to reimpose closure both on the Bible and on Collins in a way that would protect the clerical hegemony over interpretation. This was not solely a matter of occupational self-interest on Swift's part: in his nostalgia for an originary signified, he seems genuinely to have regarded the urge to interpret what he saw as the plain and evident sense of the scriptures as a preliminary symptom of madness.

Division over such matters was not new even within the Church of England. The Bible, after having been both transmitted and interpreted by various communities of hierophants for 1500 years in the case of the New Testament and some centuries longer in the case of the Old, had unsettlingly been made available in the vernacular and distributed in enormous numbers by the printing press. Printing and, in England, the issue of an 'authorized' translation had brought a stability to the text to replace the disagreements over readings endemic to manuscript transmission, while also endowing it with a new kind of authority by virtue of Kernan's 'print logic'. After the Reformation, the Church of England, having rejected the Roman Catholic canons of Biblical interpretation resting ultimately on Papal authority, was in the awkward position of having to create a comparable consensus for its own, a task at which it was never particularly effective. (An acute analysis of its problems from a contemporary Catholic point of view will be found in the second part of Dryden's *The hind and the panther*.) Differences over the role of the bishops in controlling the interpretation of the text led first to the Puritan secession and then, following the Puritan victory in the Civil Wars, to the actual dismantling of the state church; however, the Puritan movement was itself already divided into a Presbyterian wing which favoured the supervision of interpretation by a national assembly and an

---

[26] *A discourse of free-thinking* (London, 1713), pp. 46–7 and *passim*.

Independent wing which defended the right of the individual congregation and individual believer to interpret the text as they were directed by inner conviction. 1660 and the years following saw the state church restored, interpretation once more under the supervision of the bishops, and a ruthless purge of all clergy who would not accept episcopal direction. But, since the motives behind this purge were as much political as theological, the dominant tone with regard to interpretation was increasingly set by the Church's rationalist, Latitudinarian party for whom knotty questions of faith were to be ignored as disruptive of social order or reduced to the lowest common denominator of reasonableness. In such a climate the way was open to assault from a more radical rationalism—a secular Independency judging by the light of sense rather than that of inspiration. It is to this movement that Collins belongs. Like earlier independents, in the expanded sense of those whose aim was to democratize interpretation, he set out to encourage a personal liberty of enquiry in all matters relating to the text. Swift's aim, on the other hand, was to deny Collins's pretence to authority (including the authority of print) while, at the same time, not yielding ground to those other arch-foes of mainstream Anglican divinity, the Papists and the Dissenters.

In performing this task, the last thing that Swift wished to do was to validate Collins's criticism by engaging him in his own rationalistic and historiographical kind of discourse. Others, including Swift's other foe, Richard Bentley, did do so and were able to identify flaws in Collins's scholarship and mastery of his sources, but were in this conceding his point that the authority of the Bible *could* be assailed on codicological, historical and philological grounds. One should add that Collins's emphasis on the transmissional instability of the Bible had been anticipated by the Catholic, Père Simon, whose *Histoire critique de la vieux testament*, translated into English in 1682, was praised by Dryden but deplored by Evelyn who rightly saw it as a serious threat to a faith premised on a belief in a stable, unvarying text preserved in the pristine purity of print.[27] Swift may also have anticipated difficulty in rebutting an attack on the rightness of a clerical

[27] Letter to Bishop Fell, 19 March 1682, *Diary and correspondence of John Evelyn Esq.*, F. R. S., ed. William Bray and H. B. Wheatley (London, 1906), iii. 410–13. Dryden's approval is signified in *Religio laici*, ll. 224–75.

monopoly of interpretation when he had himself argued in very similar terms to Collins in the history of Peter in *A tale of a tub*. The target therefore was not to be Collins's ideas but his claim to the authority of print logic—that is his claim to be speaking freely, rationally and objectively. To this end Swift, in an unashamed *tu quoque*, countered Collins's image of the clergy as self-interested manipulators of the sacred text with one of a burlesque Collins sputtering out his anti-clerical heterodoxies in a restructured version of his own phraseology through which, in Probyn's words, 'the formal dignity of the printed text' could be driven back into 'the disordered personality of an individual ego' (p. 190). The self-proclaimed man of reason is transformed, if not quite into an intellectual yahoo, at least into a recognizable variant of Swift's other satirical protagonists, the mad Modern author and the monomaniac projector.

Swift's strategy in this case is essentially one of transposing Collins from the medium of print into the medium of voice. Reordered and abstracted, his *Discourse* becomes a kind of monodrama—a performance text. Voice, because it is instinct with presence, permits discriminations to be made concerning sincerity and truthfulness that are not possible through print. To hear the voice of a printed text, whether that text was a discourse of freethinking or the Bible itself, was therefore essential to a proper appraisal of its moral tendency. It is likely that much 'silent' reading at this period was still strongly subvocal. Probyn suggests that Swift may himself have read in this way, citing *Thoughts on various subjects*: 'When I am reading a Book, whether wise or silly, it seemeth to me to be alive and talking to me.'[28] What was heard was not just the sound of the word but its wisdom or silliness.

Where the Bible was concerned we need to remember that most seventeenth-century readers had heard the principal passages read aloud many times in the course of divine service before they ever saw them on the page. Much Anglican theological literature, even if not in sermon form, must likewise have been reconstituted subaudially in the impersonal tones of the pulpit and lectern. Vocal

---

[28] Probyn, p. 190; *Prose works*, iv. 253. Cf. 'My Lady's lamentation and complaint against the Dean', ll. 155–6 which implies that Lady Acheson was also accustomed to read to herself aloud. This would be no more than a continuation of the medieval practice of vocal reading described in Chaytor, *From script to print*, pp. 5–21.

reading of this kind had internalized its own kind of institutional closure which protected the reader from the dangerous freedoms offered by the text that was merely scanned. The danger of Collins's text was that it came without a voice: few if any of its potential readers had ever been to a freethought sermon or had any clear idea what freethinking words should sound like. Collins and his kind used print as if it was somehow independent of voice, an assumption that must have been seriously disorienting to readers with Swift's kind of training in language. Freedom from voice implied a freedom from presence that helped activate the impersonality of print logic. Swift sets about the task of demolishing Collins by searching for the kind of voice that would have been audible if it were not hindered by the typographical filter from reaching the reader's ear, discovering that it was that of a prating buffoon. Probyn sums up the matter perfectly in describing the essential technique of Swift's satirical metafiction as being 'to expose those texts which seek to blur the reader's awareness of a medium, or narrative personality, or identifiable voice behind the authority of the printed word' (p. 90). The Bible was to be defended by essentially the same means, but with the aim of revealing an authoritative, originary voice rather than an unauthoritative and deferred one.

THE BIBLE AS MANUSCRIPT

But countering Collins in this way had not answered his central point that the Bible, despite having made the transition to the world of print logic, remains, when all is said, a printed manuscript and as such subject to all the indeterminacy of scribal transmission. This was an argument that Swift could hardly contest since it was, again, one he had used himself, most notably in *The battle of the books*. But there was no reason that he would have wanted to, since the *Battle* itself provided a sufficient answer to Collins.

Whatever Swift may have learned from the scriptorium poets about the unstable nature of scribal transmission will undoubtedly have been reinforced by the events that gave occasion for the *Battle*. As is well known, his patron, Sir William Temple, had announced (in print) his admiration for the *Epistles* of Phalaris as representing a noble simplicity characteristic of the earliest and most laudable period of Greek civilization. A Greek text of the work had been edited by Charles Boyle with the help of Atterbury and other Oxonians, only to be savaged by Cambridge's Richard Bentley on the grounds that the *Epistles* were not the work of a genuine 'ancient', but were a late-Greek forgery, an opinion which despite a spirited reply by the Oxford party has never since been doubted. The dispute raised the issue of the relative authority of print and script in an unusually acute way. The manuscripts of Phalaris were shown to be deceptive not only in the uncertainty of their readings but in their language, morality and ascription. The authority of Temple's printed essay had thus been subverted by the mendacity of its sources in much the same way as Collins was later to argue the Bible was vitiated by the ambiguities of the scribal medium. Bentley's superior acumen, on the other hand, was obviously a product of the print medium in that it rested on an understanding of the historical development of the Greek language which had been impossible to acquire before an immense corpus of ancient writings had become available in printed editions to the individual researcher.[29] Moreover, the press had not only provided the huge bodies of data that fuelled Bentley's phenomenal learning but had also fostered the spirit of enquiry which was so brilliantly exemplified in his critique. It was only to be expected that, as we will see in Chapter 8, Bentley scorned the evidence of manuscripts in favour of *ratio et res ipsa*.

In terms of the values that underlie the *Battle* things, as seen at first glance, are disastrously the wrong way round. Truth, identified by Swift with the ancients, with an unproblematic simplicity, with wax and honey which produce sweetness and light, comes to us tattered and torn while the arrogance of modern error, whose reality, according to the *Battle*, is the flybane and cobweb of speculation, comes clothed in the seamless garment of mechanically multiplied letterpress. Surely in a just world it would have been the thoughts of the ancients which would have enjoyed the authority and permanence of the printed page, while the egotistical whimsies of the magotty-headed moderns would have found their proper outlet in the labile, quizzical medium of script? In the case of the *Battle* and its companion tracts, Swift sets out to

---

[29] A point made by McLuhan, pp. 142–3.

reverse the cruel joke played by history, and by doing so to make a point about the nature of ancient truth and modern error which goes some way towards righting the reckoning in favour of the offended party.

Swift, as far as is known, never publicly conceded the duplicity of the chirographic medium in this instance, maintaining an unswerving allegiance to Temple's and Boyle's original judgements; but his method of assailing Bentley in the *Battle* shows that at a deeper level he had taken his lesson very much to heart. Whereas later with Collins the design would be to collapse the authority of print back into the vulnerability of voice, his technique with Bentley is to assert the proposition that *all* alphabetically reproduced texts are subject to the imperfections of manuscript. In the course of his career he was to devise several ways of doing this. In the *Battle*, the moderns (including the modern 'author' of *A tale of a tub* and editor of the *Battle*) have been for once consigned to their proper medium through Swift's insistence that his own printed text is only a transcript of a defaced and imperfect manuscript. His victims, Bentley, Wotton and their allies, become figures in a garbled, chirographically transmitted epic, their history degenerating, as the text proceeds, into a progressively more fragmentary state until in the end they are swallowed up in a *hiatus valde deflendus*. The ancients of the *Battle* are equally victims of the ravages of time and the lability of language in scribal transmission, but can be shown—now that the conditions of transmission are equalized—to be better equipped than the moderns to survive the rigours of transmission, because their ideas are simpler, stronger and less subject to manic elaboration (a line of defence also applied by Latitudinarian scholars to the imperfections of the Biblical text). Since the basic values of the ancients, like the fundamental values of Christianity, are so much more hiatus-proof than the complexities of the moderns, these very transmissional hazards may be seen as a test of truth—fatal to the speculative and intricate, which for Swift is also the false, if not the mad, but incapable of distorting the truths that emanate from an ancient or a divine simplicity. That where a modern was subjected to the rigours of chirographical transmission the result must be a very imperfect account of his thought is further demonstrated by the companion tracts, especially *A tale of a tub* and *The mechanical operation of the spirit.* A hiatus in *A tale of a tub* is supplied with the footnote: 'Here is another Defect in the Manuscript, but I think the Author did wisely, and that the Matter which thus strained his Faculties, was not worth a Solution; and it were well if all Metaphysical Cobweb Problems were no otherwise answered'.[30]

Chirography, then, can be used to explode the presumptions of print through the satirical device of a facsimile manuscript; but it can also serve as a kind of sieve which will not harm simple and clear conceptions but will do irreparable damage to over-complex ones. Finally, and crucially, it can remind us that the printed text only pretends to have entered an autonomous sphere of print logic, for there can be no printed text that can be anything more than a copy of the author's manuscript, and truth, if it resides anywhere, must do so in the original, not the copy. Moreover, in the course of print production the readings of the manuscript may suffer from a multitude of additional causes. At a vital moment of *The mechanical operation of the spirit* we encounter the 'editorial' rubric: '*Here the whole Scheme of spiritual Mechanism was deduced and explained, with an Appearance of great reading and observation; but it was thought neither safe nor Convenient to Print it*' (i. 181). Captain Gulliver's prefatory letter to his *Travels* reveals an even more deplorable situation. Cousin Sympson and his assistant, a young graduate, entrusted with preparing the text for print publication, had cut, interpolated, and so 'minced or changed' circumstances (xi. 5) that Gulliver hardly knew his own work:

I find likewise, that your Printer hath been so careless as to confound the Times, and mistake the Dates of my several Voyages and Returns; neither assigning the true Year, or the true Month, or Day of the Month: And I hear the original Manuscript is all destroyed, since the Publication of my Book. (xi. 7)

Additional errors include the consistent mis-spelling of 'Brob-dingrag' ('for so the Word should have been spelt, and not erroneously *Brobdingnag*') (xi. 8). Sympson, in his separate prefatory letter, impenitently insists that the book would have been twice as long if he had not removed large quantities of purely nautical information. The joke is not sustained beyond these missives, but the strategy is the same as in the cases just

[30] *Prose works,* i. 107.

considered—to remind us that a printed book is nothing more than a printed manuscript and may distort that manuscript just as radically as any chirographic transcription. Indeed, the greater amount of collaborative work involved in print publication means that a whole variety of parties—censors, capitalists, publishers, booksellers, compositors, pullers, beaters and binders—may all have an opportunity to influence the fidelity of what is transmitted. But fidelity to what?—in Swift's case it was fidelity to blatant lies which none the less took it upon themselves to assume the truth-conferring dress of typography.

Pertinently, Swift was to find that the printed text of his own *Travels* required manuscript emendation.[31] Equally pertinent is an episode which has also been studied by Probyn involving the first Dublin printing of the 'Verses on the death of Dr Swift'.[32] When these were printed, large white spaces were left in the notes, apparently signalling material that might get the printer into trouble, but also pointedly reminding the reader of the fact that the completion and truth of the text must reside in the manuscript original, not the printed edition. What is interesting is that, although many of these white spaces were filled in by hand in the surviving copies, the chirographical supplementations are never complete and never quite coincide. Whoever was responsible took care that the full version of the notes, preserved in Swift's manuscript, was never made available in any single copy of the edition, thereby ensuring that the derived status of the printed text could never be ignored.

CONCLUSION

The final point that needs to be emphasized is that Swift's two strategies for countering print logic, the reduction to voice and the reduction to script, are themselves dependent for their effect on being conducted through the medium of print. It is possible, as a thought exercise, to imagine the answer to Collins's discourse performed as a monodrama and the *Modest proposal* circulating as a scribal separate; but this would be to deprive them of something

[31] See David Woolley, 'Swift's copy of *Gulliver's travels*: the Armargh *Gulliver*, Hyde's edition, and Swift's earliest corrections' in *The art of Jonathan Swift*, ed. Clive Probyn (London, 1978), pp. 131–78.

[32] 'Swift's *Verses*', pp. 47–61.

which is an essential part of their power—a sense that dignity is being withdrawn not just from the victim but from the medium, or, if we like, that the power of the medium is being turned against itself. In their burlesques of a misused authority they are themselves the work of a great misuser, a hijacker of genres which in an ideal world would always be exercised with the seriousness and objectivity promised by print logic, but which have now become untrustworthy both at the level of the ostensible authors, the philosopher and the projector, and that of the unknown ventriloquist who pulls the strings and does the voices. Whoever this ventriloquist is, he can surely not be the disembodied spirit of print logic: indeed the whole basis of his art is that he sets out to deceive us from within a form of inscription that (falsely) promises truth.

The force of Swift's satire, then, can be seen to depend crucially on his involvement in the historical project of translating script values into the medium of print. The emergence of the ironic mode in satire was itself an effect of this transference. Prior to 1700 satirists had no particular need of irony for the simple reason that most of their work was directed toward the scribal medium, where views could be expressed without disguise. The decorum of the lampoon was one of outspokenness in all things, a fact that helps explain why so productive a genre produced so few lasting masterpieces. That, among the print-publishing satirists, John Oldham, Robert Gould, Richard Ames and Tom Brown should cultivate a similar bold directness is a token of their parallel involvement in scribal publication and a wish to appeal to patrons (principally Dorset) who were themselves scribally publishing satirists. Where irony makes an appearance in scriptorial satire it is usually in the form of heavy sarcasm. One satire of 1680 is actually headed 'An ironical satire', as if this was necessary to prevent its statements being taken seriously; but its 'irony', quickly discarded, amounts to no more than a bare mechanical, reversal of the writer's true opinion of Charles II:

> Not Rome in all her splendour could compare
> With those great blessings happy Britons share.
> Vainly they boast their kings of heav'nly race:
> A god incarnate England's throne does grace.
> Chaste in his pleasures, in devotion grave,

To his friends constant, to his foes he's brave;
His justice is through all the world admir'd,
His word held sacred, and his scepter fear'd.
No tumults do about his palace move,
Freed from rebellion by his people's love.[33]

This kind of thing is chainsaw-like in comparison with Pope's scalpel in *To Augustus*. Not to speak one's mind in a genre whose whole rationale was the speaking of minds about topics forbidden to the print medium was to invite total misunderstanding.

Print, even when used surreptitiously, encouraged greater subtlety in addressing readers, who in turn soon learned to read below and against the surface of the writing. Lois Potter's account of the reading habits of Cavaliers during the interregnum explores an earlier case in which readers were prepared to master strategies for placing a private, partial interpretation on outwardly innocuous public utterances.[34] But the decoding of Swiftian satire is of a different nature, resting on the recognition that an authorial persona valid in the print medium has been usurped by a malicious imposter who is consuming it, caterpillar-like, from within. Having communicated this primary awareness, each separate text then develops its own rules for decoding attitudes, which the reader has to be smart enough to discover. At a very simple level this procedure is made necessary by the fact that the satirist, having taken his stand in the forum, has to discover acceptably disguised ways of uttering the unacceptable truths he has come to deliver; but in Swift's case it is also the consequence of his desire to subvert the pretensions of print logic.

The important aspect of this subversion, as far as the present study is concerned, is that it was conducted in the name of another medium which had never claimed to be other than personal and partial in what it uttered. Writers such as Swift who had come to maturity in the age of the scribally published lampoon remained fifth-columnists for the medium of frankness long after they had abandoned it as a mode of addressing readers. By contrast, the irony of Pope, younger and less marked by scribal consciousness, is socially rather than inscriptionally based and reveals no discomfort

---

[33] *POAS (Yale)*, ii. 200.
[34] Potter, *Secret rites*, pp. 38–71 and *passim*.

about the print medium as such. It is also the case that Pope's irony is usually resolvable into a coherent authorial attitude whereas Swift's draws the reader towards deeper and deeper contradictions. Yet Pope was eventually to create the *Dunciad variorum* (the four-book version of the poem) which, through the medium of an elaborate burlesque of the typographical conventions of scholarly editions, was to deliver the most crushing of all attacks on the culture of print publishing as it existed in his time.[35] It is hard to see how the poem could have been written without some knowledge of the lampooners, even if it was only through the heavily censored anthologies in which their verse was eventually brought to the press. What Pope regained for satire in *The dunciad* was the sense of an inscriptional space in which attitudes could be expressed without reservation and disguise. In the previous century that space had existed within the scribal medium; by the mid-eighteenth century it had been re-established within the print medium, and perceptions of that medium definitively altered as a result. After the work of Swift and Pope, print could no longer pretend to be innocent.

The triumph of print, then, was an ambiguous one which, while it left 'print logic' intact, saw readers fully alerted to the fact that the printed word was always an irredeemably self-interested word, and instinct with disguise—as it remains.

[35] Cf. McLuhan, pp. 255–63.

PART III

EDITING SCRIBALLY
PUBLISHED TEXTS

8

EDITING SCRIBALLY
PUBLISHED TEXTS

THE manuscripts considered in this book offer a huge field for editorial work. We cannot go on for ever reading important writings either in early printed texts taken from randomly encountered manuscripts, or modern editions taken from such early printed texts. If we wish to know what Sir Robert Cotton was really arguing in *The danger in which this kingdom standeth and the remedy* we will need to edit the text from the fifty or more copies rather than supinely relying on Rushworth, *Cottoni posthuma* or the incredibly corrupt 1628 printings. The capacity of scribes to turn sense into nonsense should never be underestimated. The name of a man who called himself 'Wolseley' appears in the fourteen surviving scribal texts of Dorset's 'A faithful catalogue of our most eminent ninnies' as 'Wolesley', 'Woosely', 'Worsley', 'Woosly', 'Wosly', 'Oosly' and 'Oosy', with the best represented form being 'Oosly'.[1] What Rochester put into circulation as something like

> The great man's gratitude to his best friend,
> King's promises, whores' vows—towards thee they bend,
> Flow swiftly into thee and in thee ever end.

emerges at the end of one line of descent as

An earlier version of some of the material of this chapter appeared as 'The editing of Restoration scriptorial satire' in *Editing in Australia*, ed. Paul Eggert (Canberra, 1990), pp. 65–84.

[1] Sources in Beal, *IELM*, ii/1, pp. 357–8. Fiennes, *Journeys*, in referring to the place of that name (mod. Wolseley), employs the additional variants: 'Woolsely', 'Woolsley' and 'Woolsly'.

The Great Mans gratitude to his best Friend,
Court promises, *Whores* vows tow'rds thee, I bend,
Flow Swift, Fly into Thee, and severs in the End.[2]

Errors no less grave but simply less apparent lurk in many texts which have entered modern anthologies and collections of documents.

The scribes' difficulties arose from the average human brain's maladaptation to the task of exact copying.[3] In most historical situations, copying took place by transient memorization of a section of text either read or heard. The scribe would place a group of words in short-term memory, and the transcription would be made from the memorial record, not the original. Medieval evidence suggests that scribes would sometimes mumble the texts aloud to themselves as they often did in normal reading: in this case the intermediate record would be part aural, part visual and part muscular.[4] Touch-typing and the ability to write without taking one's eyes from the exemplar reduce copying from a three-stage to a two-stage process but disable the capacity to monitor what is being inscribed. While the record is held, it is subject to the process by which short-term memories are recorded for longer-term memorization as impressions or ideas—in effect a translation from the *parole* of speech to a highly generalized *langue* which is unavailable for conscious inspection. Thus, by the time the brain has to retrieve a word from late in the memorial group, that word may already have been processed, so that what is retrieved will be a reverbalization of the original concept. There will also be a tendency for the scribe's own verbal or syntactical preferences to override those of the author, even at the level of the initial perception and memorization. Added

---

[2] 'Upon nothing', ll. 49–51 in my own modern-spelling text and that of *Upon nothing. A poem* (London, 1679; A version), a pirated printing of a casually encountered manuscript. For the relationship of the two, see my *The text of Rochester's 'Upon nothing'*, Monash University Centre for Bibliographical and Textual Studies, Occasional papers, no. 1 (Melbourne, 1985).

[3] The standard guides to the psychology of copying are J. Stoll, 'Zur Psychologie der Schreibfehler', *Fortschritte der Psychologie* 2 (1913), 1–133, and Eugène Vinaver, 'Principles of textual emendation' in *Studies in French language and medieval literature presented to Professor Mildred K. Pope* (Manchester, 1939), pp. 351–69; repr. in *Medieval manuscripts and textual criticism*, ed. Christopher Kleinhenz (Chapel Hill, NC, 1976), pp. 139–66. See also Vinton A. Dearing, *Principles and practice of textual analysis* (Berkeley, Calif., and Los Angeles, 1974), pp. 25–58.

[4] See Chaytor, *From script to print*, pp. 13–21.

to this is the problem of relocating one's position in the exemplar (the source of eyeskips and repetitions of whole blocks of text) and mishaps in the largely autonomous functioning of the reflexes involved in the act of writing. The operation of all these systems will be further affected by the degree of care and responsibility the scribe brings to the task: the careless copyist may not even register the words of the exemplar correctly. Where copying is performed with complete accuracy, it will usually be because of rigorous systems of training which arise from a high cultural value placed on textual stability. The involvement of legal clerks in scribal publication would sometimes ensure this, but even they would often have had different standards for a separate and a writ. Scribes who realized that an error had been made would often delete it and continue with the correct text. Study of errors thus made and redeemed by a particular scribe will suggest what kinds of uncorrected errors may still lurk in the document.[5]

Apart from their involuntary lapses from accuracy, scribes would often have been active in adapting, repairing and revising texts. As we saw in Chapter 3, the document in chirographic transmission was open at every copying to purposive changes whose aim might be to refine or modernize expression, to remove perceived difficulties of meaning or to meet the expectations of new readers. Moral and political censorship was common, as was its opposite— the desire to make the text more shocking or more oppositional.[6] Many of these purposive changes are fascinating historical data in their own right, which is another reason why even workaday scribally published texts will often justify careful scholarly editing; but they greatly complicate the search for the authorial text. Variation, both involuntary and purposive, is particularly marked in texts whose scribal transmission was interrupted by episodes of oral transmission. The astonishing mutability of Rochester's 'I' th' isle of Great Britain' can only be explained on this assumption.[7]

The editor's first challenge is to locate the surviving copies—a

---

[5] For an example of this kind of analysis, see Peter Holloway, 'Scribal dittography: Daborne's *The poor man's comfort*', *Library*, 6:3 (1981), 233–9.

[6] Cameron (*POAS (Yale)*, v. 532) instances miscellanies of the 1690s whose compilers doctored texts 'in order to increase the force of Jacobite hatred of William and his new regime'.

[7] Walker notes (*Poems*, p. 185) that 'The texts are so divergent and corrupt I have not set out a table of variants, except in the case of the title'. Cf. Chaytor, pp. 125–9.

matter for which available bibliographical aids are still far from adequate. The indexes to the Historical Manuscripts Commission reports and the Calendars of State Papers are likely to be the starting point for most historical enquiries, with the *Index of English literary manuscripts* the source of first resort for literary scholars. *IELM* covers only a restricted canon of writers, but is of value for its brief descriptions of the sources in which their writings are contained. Used intelligently it will indicate which sources require to be searched for manuscripts of non-canonical writers. The work of earlier editors and scholars, bibliographies of special collections, union lists of manuscripts, the published catalogues of the major libraries and record offices, and whatever more specialized finding lists are relevant to the particular enquiry must be searched diligently. At the next stage, letters of enquiry need to be sent to all likely repositories. The value of these will depend on whether the library possesses a full author and title index to its corpus of texts held in manuscript: where it does not a personal visit may well be necessary to search all likely compilations. Scribal anthologies sometimes have contemporary tables of contents or even indexes, which can be obtained on microfilm. The value of these is limited by their endemic inaccuracy and the number of times texts appear with variant titles or ascriptions, but they at least give a sense of the scope and date range of a collection. Items in private hands, items in early printed collections, and items known only from appearances in auction catalogues all pose their own special challenges which will not always be solvable. It is always valuable to be able to tap the memories of experienced scholars and scholar-librarians in the field concerned: the world of manuscript studies is on the whole a friendly and co-operative one. The most serious problems likely to be encountered by the searcher are those posed by texts which are scattered through compilations of various kinds, since it is quite likely that they will also appear under unpredictable titles. It is also common for such texts to be misattributed or to appear without attribution. Here it is important that the editor's interest in a particular title is adequately advertised to other scholars.

Having assembled one's sources, to the very best of one's ability, there remains the crucial problem of choosing between the many ways by which a text might be presented to readers. Where there is only one source, facsimile is always to be preferred, with facing-page transcriptions when appropriate; but where there are several sources crucial questions of editorial choice arise. My aim in the present chapter is to address three topics which are at once the most challenging and the most contentious. The first is the value of genealogical reasoning to the editing of scribally transmitted texts in early modern English. There has been much negativism over this matter in recent decades, but it seems to me that the difficulties are not nearly so acute as is sometimes assumed. My second topic will be the special challenges posed to the constructor of transmissional histories by composite texts, such as miscellanies and anthologies. Finally it will be necessary to consider a range of problems attending the choice and treatment of the reading text. These topics will be raised at the appropriate points in a more general introduction to editorial procedure.

The work of editing begins with the collation of all manuscript and, when necessary, printed witnesses in order to prepare a list of variant readings, which must be both complete and totally accurate. A partial collation is useless for purposes of textual analysis and an inaccurate one a positive menace. It is the usual practice for editors to record only 'substantive' variants (those which actually affect meaning), ignoring spelling and punctuational differences as dependent on individual whim; but an exception can and should be made whenever an 'accidental' variant seems likely to have evidential value, as in variant spellings of an unusual proper name.[8] Study of the distribution of variant spellings of the same word over a group of texts can also be revealing. The master text for comparison is chosen purely for convenience and there is no reason for it to be the same as any eventual copy text, assuming that this method of editing is found appropriate.[9] In order that the dangers of comparing via a transient memorial image are avoided, a photocopy of the master text should be scrolled down the page bringing correspond-

---

[8] Cameron notes in *POAS (Yale)*, v. 529: 'When the texts in this volume were collated, all accidentals as well as substantive variants were recorded. Each text was established by applying Greg's principles, but before the text and its textual apparatus were modernized, the ranking of the textual witnesses according to their relative general authority was reviewed in the light of the evidence provided by the accidentals. Many modifications to the stemma were made clearer or more authoritative by the exercise.'

[9] Useful guidance on choice of base text and various practical aspects of collation will be found in John Whittaker, 'The practice of manuscript collation', *Text* 5 (New York, 1991), pp. 121–30.

ing verse lines or prose sentences into physical contiguity. The master is then moved laterally so that each individual pair of words can be sighted and compared as a single image. Collating from right to left will protect against the anticipation of known readings but inhibits the continuous reflection on matters of principle and detail which is the foundation of editorial wisdom.

Variations may be recorded in standard footnote form, in which the lemma is followed by a closing square bracket and the variants are separated by semi-colons

great] large *G*, *P2*; wide *Y9*

or in the more ample form invented by Greg:

10 thy pow'r *B2 uncorr.*, *B15 uncorr.*, *B22*, *BB*, *HE*, *I*, *LA*, *L31*, *W1* : the Nothing power *B4*, *C3*, *Y10* : thy Nothinge Pow'r *B15 corr.*, *L2*, *79A*, *79B* : thy mighty power *B7*, *B18*, *H7*, *H8*, *L11*, *L9*, *LO*, *W2*, *Y*, *YY*, *80*, *91* : at first thy power *E*, *G*, *P2*, *Y9* : att first thy Pow'rs *H6* : *om. W2*

In this case, where the best attested variant in the variation contains less than half the total number of sources, its members have to be specified in full; but, where it contains more than half the sources (which means that it has ceased to be of interest to the editor), it should be placed first in the record without its members:

5 When $\Sigma(-W2)$: by *B15*, *I*, *LA*, *79A*, *79B*

Here Σ indicates 'all sources not specified singly' and (-W2) instead of, say, '*om. W2*' that a source is not a witness for the passage that contains this reading (something that is not adequately signalled by many lists of variants). Greg's method, whether in the full or more condensed form, is to be preferred for the editor's own record, and 'footnote' format for the published collation. The well-equipped editor will have the variations entered on disk and a range of macros to shift entries from one format to another as required by the various stages of editing.[10]

---

[10] Computer packages also exist which assist with the collation of texts, recording of variants and the preparation of printer's copy. At the time of writing, Peter Shillingsburg's *CASE* programs, marketed by him through the English Department, Mississippi State University, and Peter Robinson's *Collate*, available from the Oxford University Computing Service, are the best-known and most versatile of these.

Sources are indicated by whatever sigla the editor regards as appropriate. In this case manuscripts are cited under a condensed library code and printed texts under the last two digits of the date of publication. Although more cumbrous, there is a lot to be said for the system by which manuscripts are cited under a truncated version of the call number, so that, for instance, Harvard MS Eng. 636F becomes *He36*. Sigla should remain constant throughout all the items of an edition so as not to impede the analysis of relationships between composite sources: the only exception to this would be when, as a temporary measure, an editor wants to approach a tradition without any influence from prior assumptions. In recording variants, there will often be a choice between using a whole phrase as the lemma, or breaking it down into a sequence of single-word variations. The second method is more exact in its indication of differences but may make it more difficult for the reader to grasp the gist of the matter. The longer example given above is a compromise: it does not have separate entries for the variants 'thy : the' or 'power : Pow'rs' but it does divide the 'nothing' and 'at first' variations between two separate entries. The assumption is that the reader can perform the requisite acts of integration or differentiation mentally; but this would not be true of a computer, and an editor who wishes to experiment with stemma-building software of the kind advocated by Vinton Dearing will need to specify variations with greater minuteness.[11] Since our first example is clearly an important variation one would expect to find a note explaining its significance.

After our list of variants between sources has been completed it is of the utmost importance that every reading on the list is rechecked for error against each one of the manuscripts. Once this is done, a few variants that occur in only one source may still have been overlooked but the chances will have been greatly reduced of any agreement *between* texts failing to be recorded. A list which has not been subjected to this test cannot be regarded as reliable. Since many published collations, whether for this or other reasons, are

---

[11] For Dearing's rules for defining variations see his *Principles and practice*, pp. 25–58. This book presents the result of long and deep reflection on editorial problems and has much to offer the reader who is prepared to grapple with its difficulties; but its larger theoretical claims are open to challenge. See also his 'Textual analysis: a kind of textual criticism', *Text* 2 (New York, 1985), pp. 13–23.

inaccurate or incomplete in their record of agreements (some grossly so), trial collations should be undertaken as a check on editors' work before it is made the basis of a textual argument.

GENEALOGICAL REASONING

A testimony to the low current status of the genealogical method is some words by Keith Walker from the introduction to his edition of Rochester:

The various versions of Rochester's texts . . . have been charted with increasing fullness and precision by Johannes Prinz, V. de Sola Pinto, James Thorpe, and David M. Vieth, but much is still to be investigated about their relation to each other. We do not even know the relations that Harvard MS Eng. 636F (which contains the texts of some twenty-seven of Rochester's poems), Nottingham MS Portland PwV 40, the recently available Leeds MS Brotherton Lt. 54, Victoria and Albert MS Dyce 43, and the Gyldenstolpe MS (merely to cite some of the largest of such collections) bear to each other. I hope that my tables of variants may stimulate enquiry upon these lines.[12]

The interesting point here is that Walker, although meticulous in his recording of variants between his many manuscript sources, did not himself regard the matter as worth pursuing. Rochester, as we saw in the previous chapter, was primarily a scribal-publishing poet. This would not trouble an editor if autographs of the poems had survived in any number, but this is not the case: shortly before his penitent death in 1680 he authorized the burning of his manuscripts, only a few stray leaves surviving.[13] The text of Rochester, then, like that of so many scribally publishing authors, has to be reconstructed from contemporary separates and manuscript miscellanies.

The collections that Walker mentions, along with Yale Osborn b. 105 and National Library of Ireland MS 2093, since they appear to have suffered least from corruption, are the ones on which—pending new information from Peter Beal—our texts of Rochester must chiefly depend. But they are very far from being the only manuscript sources. In an ideal world, where scribes always

---

[12] Walker, *Poems*, p. xvi.
[13] United in Nottingham UL, Portland MS Pw V 31, which is discussed in Vieth, *Attribution*, pp. 204–30.

introduced unique and irreversible alterations into the texts they copied, one could aspire to prepare a family tree (stemma) for each individual poem showing where each of its sources stood on lines of descent from their lost common ancestor. Armed with this information we might then look for evidence of wider relationships between the miscellanies, bearing in mind that these would be unlikely to be simple ones. But the world in which copies are made is not an ideal one in this respect: the scribe may not only fail to provide the kind of evidence that the method requires but make changes that lead the editor to wrong conclusions. One endemic problem is that of conflation (or contamination) which occurs when readings characteristic of one branch of a tradition are imported into a text descending in another branch. This may happen memorially as well as through the comparison of two written copies. In its simpler forms it is identifiable through a text wishing to appear at two (or three) different points in a stemma; however, when a tradition is largely or wholly composed of conflated texts, the whole rationale of the genealogical method is destroyed and the editor has to find other ways of divining the readings of the archetype.[14] Walker's reticence reflects a view widely held among Rochester scholars that no adequate methodology is available for dealing with these difficulties. Indeed, one might say both of his edition and that of David M. Vieth—the great reformer of the text and canon of Rochester—that they were prepared in an atmosphere of intense institutional suspicion of the genealogical method.

The origins of this suspicion are to be sought as early as the time of Karl Lachmann (1793–1851) who, in his capacity as an editor of Latin and Greek texts, is often credited with being the inventor of the method. Prior to his time editors of ancient texts had either placed their main reliance on a single favoured manuscript, or, in the tradition represented in England by Richard Bentley (1662–1742), had emended boldly on the basis of context and linguistic usage. If they explored the genetic relationships of

[14] The traditions of a number of Latin and Greek texts are radically conflated in this way. On the other hand, among 17th-cent. English texts circulated in manuscript, relatively uncontaminated traditions will often be found, with what conflation has taken place easy to diagnose. Genealogical analysis works best with new, rapidly expanding traditions and with those ancient traditions whose surviving copies derive from a single ancestor of the medieval or early Renaissance period.

manuscripts it was only to divide them loosely into 'families' defined by shared readings. The generation of Lachmann was the first to realize that under favourable circumstances the readings of the most recent common ancestor of a family of surviving texts could be restored through a systematic analysis of those of its descendants.[15] But Lachmann worked also on medieval German texts and was well aware that these were much less amenable to genealogical analysis than those of ancient authors. The reason arises from the circumstances of transcription. Classicists begin the work of analysis by deciding that certain readings are authentically ancient and others are scribal errors. They can do this because they are dealing with sources which were copied by scribes who were not speakers from birth of the tongues in which their texts were written, and whose alterations are therefore often easy to identify. Contemporary copyists of vernacular texts, on the other hand, can be assumed to have had just as good an understanding of the language as the author, which makes their interventions much harder to spot. They are also much more prone to alter the text in a purposive, creative way. The agreements in variation of vernacular texts, then, will often be too complex to permit the construction of clearly articulated trees ascending to an apex. On the other hand, such traditions are less likely to have been vitiated by conflation than texts which have been in scribal circulation for many centuries. Much of course depends on whether the surviving texts really descend from a single, finalized archetype, an assumption that is always risky to make in connection with a living vernacular tradition of author publication.

The greater lability of the vernacular text was one of the reasons which led first Joseph Bédier and later Eugène Vinaver to attack the very basis of the genealogical method as it had been applied to the editing of medieval French poetry. Bédier's initial misgiving, first stated in 1913 and developed in 1928, arose from the perceived reluctance of editors to include multi-branched junctions in their

---

[15] Traditional methods of textual criticism used by editors of Greek and Latin texts are described in Paul Maas, *Textual criticism*, trans. Barbara Flower (Oxford, 1958). For a fuller account of the history and varieties of the genealogical method, the reader is referred to G. Thomas Tanselle's magisterial 'Classical, biblical, and medieval textual criticism and modern editing', *SB* 36 (1983), 21–68. Michael Weitzman's 'The analysis of open traditions', *SB* 38 (1985), 82–120 searchingly surveys the major non-genealogical methods of textual analysis.

stemmas. Somehow when lines diverged (representing separate copyings from a single lost exemplar) it was nearly always into two rather than any larger number of branches.[16] Bédier accounted for this by editors wishing to enlarge their field of choice, rather than letting head-counting carry the day. But the more unsettling criticism, developed in his 1928 paper, was that in any situation where three manuscripts agreed in the patterns AB:C, AC:B and BC:A, four quite different stemmas could be offered to explain the phenomenon.[17] This reason for this had already been established by W. W. Greg in his analysis of 'the ambiguity of three texts'—a matter to be considered below.[18] Bédier's solution to the problem was that editors should eschew genealogical reasoning in favour of what is known as 'best manuscript' theory. Guided by this, they would simply reproduce the source that was judged to preserve the text in its most authentic form, emending its readings only when they were unmistakably in error.

Aussi la méthode d'édition la plus recommandable est-elle peut-être, en dernière analyse, celle que régit un esprit de défiance de soi, de prudence, d'extrême 'conservatisme', un énergique vouloir, porté jusqu'au parti pris, d'ouvrir aux scribes le plus large crédit et de ne toucher au texte d'un manuscrit que l'on imprime qu'en cas d'extrême et presque évidente nécessité: toutes les corrections conjecturales devraient être reléguées en quelque appendice.[19]

There remain many cases in which such conservatism is thoroughly justified.

Vinaver, in 1939, while accepting Bédier's critique of the genealogical method, recommended a more interventionist approach. Rather than relying on the readings of a single preferred text, the editor should use an understanding of the mechanics and psychology of copying to distinguish original readings from derived ones.[20] However, editors should still not aim at 'restoring

---

[16] Bédier's views are to be found in the introduction to his edition of the *Le lai de l'ombre par Jean Renart* (Paris, 1913) and his 'La tradition manuscrite du Lai de l'ombre, *Romania* 54 (1928), 161–96 and 321–56. Paul Maas, *Textual criticism*, pp. 47-8 questions the validity of Bédier's first criticism, but does not engage with his second.

[17] 'La tradition manuscrite', p. 338.

[18] W. W. Greg, *The calculus of variants. An essay on textual criticism* (Oxford, 1927), p. 21.

[19] 'La tradition manuscrite', p. 356.

[20] 'Principles of textual emendation', pp. 139–66.

the original work in every particular' but restrict themselves to 'lessening the damage done by the copyists'. In consequence Vinaver's attitude towards emendation was still relatively conservative: readings which were probably the result of scribal error were to be restored but 'improbable' readings which might or might not be those of the author were to be retained.[21]

A radical development of this view was adopted by George Kane and E. Talbot Donaldson for their editions of the A and B texts of *Piers plowman*, one of the most dazzling, but controversial, intellectual achievements of twentieth-century editing.[22] Their method involves the preparation of a conjectural text on the basis of one-by-one analyses of variations, and then accepting the existing text which most resembles this as their authority for spelling and minor grammatical variants. Variants are identified as original on the basis of an understanding of the psychology of copying and familiarity with the writer's *usus scribendi*. The result of this process, if it were wholly successful (which the editors do not pretend it could be), would be to reconstruct the author's own text of the work without any aid from genealogical controls: indeed, Kane and Donaldson argue, reversing the usual order of things, that a stemma can only be drawn *after* the work has been edited.[23] A claimed ability to distinguish Langland's own manner of writing from that of his scribes is the foundation of this approach. The high-risk status of such an assumption is acknowledged but the method is defended as the only one that makes the editing of this notoriously problematic text possible.[24] In the case of the A-text some groupings of texts are accepted as being genetic

[21] Ibid. 157–9. On this point, he takes issue with the still more interventionist Housman (pp. 158–9). The most influential study of the issue has been Greg's 'The rationale of copy-text', *SB* 3 (1950–1), 19–36 and in his *Collected papers*, ed. J. C. Maxwell (Oxford, 1966), pp. 374–91.

[22] *Piers plowman: the A version. Will's visions of Piers plowman and Do-well*, rev. repr. (London, 1988) and *Piers plowman: the B version. Will's visions of Piers plowman, Do-well, Do-better and Do-best* rev. repr. (London, 1988); originally pub. in 1960 and 1975 respectively.

[23] 'In this situation lodges the ultimate absurdity of recension as an editorial method: to employ it the editor must have a stemma; to draw the stemma he must first edit his text by other methods. If he has not done this efficiently his stemma will be inaccurate or obscure, and his results correspondingly deficient; if he has been a successful editor he does not need a stemma, or recension, for his editing' (*B-text*, pp. 17–18, n. 10). However, this only makes sense in terms of Kane and Donaldson's atomistic view of what constitutes 'successful' editing.

[24] *A-text*, pp. 54–64; *B-text*, pp. 130–1.

but are regarded as useless, because of convergent variation and other anomalies, for Lachmannian head-counting.[25] With the B-text, Kane and Donaldson insist that the incidence of genetically non-indicative variation is too great to permit anything more than a division of their eighteen sources into two families, one of which contains only two members.[26]

In its practical effects, this approach resembles that of the great but often mistaken Richard Bentley. Bentley maintained the view *'nobis et ratio et res ipsa centum codicibus potiores sunt'* ('meaning and content are more important to me than a hundred manuscripts'); a principle that he applied with great success to Greek texts, more controversially to Latin ones, and disastrously to Milton.[27] The difference between Bentley and the twentieth-century editors is the greater insight of the latter into the psychology of copying and the care with which the strengths and limitations of their method are explained to the reader. Their discussion is also valuable for its merciless demonstration that the Lachmannian method cannot be expected to work when applied to texts whose agreements lack the degree of genetic indicativeness necessary to support it. The weakness of their approach lies in its atomistic quality—decisions have to be made with regard to the individual reading without the editor possessing any theory of its relationship to other readings found in the same source. D. C. Greetham goes as far as to argue that the *Piers plowman* editions are not just prize examples of Bentleyism revived, but should be viewed as irrepressible outpourings of post-structuralist *jeu*, or, to put it less kindly, the eclectic method gone completely over the top.[28] In the end the only real recommendation for the Kane and Donaldson approach is the one they advance so passionately themselves: that dire straits call for desperate remedies.

---

[25] *A-text*, pp. 65–98.

[26] *B-text*, pp. 16–69.

[27] This maxim is quoted in Latin by Humphrey Palmer, *The logic of gospel criticism* (London, 1968), p. 61 and in English by R. F. Jones, *Lewis Theobald* (New York, 1919), p. 41, but in neither case with an indication of source. The sentiment, though not the precise wording, will be found in Q. *Horatius Flaccus ex recensione et cum notis atque emendationibus Richardi Bentleii* (Cambridge, 1711), p. c1[v]. For an account of Bentley's editorial method, see R. Gordon Moyles, 'Iconoclast and catalyst: Richard Bentley as editor of *Paradise lost*', in *Editing poetry from Spenser to Dryden*, ed. A. H. de Quehen (New York, 1981), pp. 77–98.

[28] Greetham, 'Textual and literary theory', pp. 11, 13–14, 23.

What makes this tradition pertinent to the present discussion is that the editing of Rochester—not quite so desperate a case—was conducted under these influences. Vieth, who published with Yale University Press, was advised early in his career by Donaldson, and took some years to struggle free from that influence.[29] He uses what is in effect the *Piers plowman* method of (1) creating a 'tentative text' by judging between variants on a one by one basis, and (2) accepting the existing text in closest sympathy with this as authority for indifferent readings. Genealogical reasoning was used during the first part of this process, but Vieth's general comments reveal the strong scepticism characteristic of the Yale school.[30] Walker, working at University College, London, under the long shadows of Kane and Vinaver, chose a form of 'best manuscript' theory closer to Bédier's ideal than Vinaver's in that it also involved fidelity to copy-text spelling and punctuation—Vieth's text being modernized. Walker, as well as being kind enough to reprint one of my own stemmas, sought advice during the preparation of his text from the distinguished textual theorist, Michael Weitzman, but emerged from this convinced that Weitzman's computer analyses of variation were merely confirming decisions he had already made on conjectural grounds. The editorial methods used in these two editions remain valid and workable models for editors of scribally published texts, and will continue to be used when circumstances are appropriate, but should not be regarded as the only ones available.

The scepticism towards the genealogical method which we see in Vieth's (1968) and Walker's (1984) editions of Rochester, but also much earlier in V. de Sola Pinto's (1953), was a pity for at least two reasons. The first is because one of the earliest things any Rochester scholar encounters is one of the great triumphs of

---

[29] An influence acknowledged by Professor Vieth in correspondence. Vieth's later 'Dryden's *Mac Flecknoe*: the case against editorial confusion', *Harvard Library bulletin*, 24 (1976), 204-44, shows how well he could employ genealogical reasoning when he set his mind to it.

[30] *Complete poems*, pp. xlvi–xlvii. They include the remark: 'Some aspects of textual criticism raise surprisingly philosophical questions, in this instance whether the universe (not to mention the human mind) is fundamentally rational' (p. xlvii). In the six-stage method of editing described on pp. xlix–li the earlier stages leading to the 'tentative text' are only of significance as a means of selecting the copy text, which is then awarded the authority of a 'best manuscript' whose readings are to be retained unless 'there is substantial reason to substitute a reading from other texts' (p. li).

genealogical reasoning in modern scholarship. I refer here to James Thorpe's demonstration of the genetic relationship of the editions of the 1680 Rochester *Poems on several occasions*.[31] Thorpe not only succeeded in establishing that what had once been regarded as a single edition was in fact no less than thirteen editions with near identical title pages; but successfully predicted that a mixed copy would be found combining sheets from the British Museum A and Sterling editions—which has since been done.[32] A further reason why this scepticism is to be regretted is that in 1963 W. J. Cameron, in an article already discussed at length, had presented a convincing account of how a sizeable group of manuscripts could plausibly be linked to a particular scriptorial archive.[33] Cameron provides a model of how the kind of enquiry Walker describes might be conducted using a combination of genealogical analysis, of which he is an enthusiastic advocate, with historical evidence, content analysis, bibliographical description and comparisons of watermarks.

Yet, despite these shining examples and the hardly less shining precedent of the Oxford English Texts editions of Donne (1952–78) and Suckling (1971), both of which laid strong reliance on the use of genealogical reasoning,[34] there was a widely-held assumption among editors of the 1950s, 1960s and 1970s that manuscript traditions of scribally published texts were too prone to non-genetic agreements and too sketchy and capricious in their documentation of the processes of change to be handled other than by free conjecture or some version of the 'best manuscript' approach. (More culpably some editors were still not prepared to edit from a manuscript at all, preferring the convenience of a

---

[31] *Rochester's Poems on several occasions*, ed. James Thorpe (Princeton, NJ, 1950), pp. xiii–xxii.

[32] See Nicholas Fisher and Ken Robinson, 'The postulated mixed "1680" edition of Rochester's poetry', *PBSA* 75 (1981), 313-15. There is rarely any difficulty in applying the genealogical method to printed sources.

[33] Cameron, 'Scriptorium', pp. 25-52.

[34] For the Donne editions, see Ch. 1, n. 5. *The works of Sir John Suckling* is in two volumes, *The non-dramatic works* edited by Thomas Clayton and *The plays* edited by L. A. Beaurline (Oxford, 1971). Beaurline's 'An editorial experiment: Suckling's *A sessions of the poets*', *SB* 16 (1963), 43-60 is one of very few studies available of the transmissional history of a representative scribally published text and the implications of this for editorial method. (J. B. Leishman's "You meaner beauties of the night': a study in transmission and transmogrification', *Library*, 4:26 (1945), 99-121 remains at the level of impressionism.)

printed copy text even when this was wholly unauthoritative.[35])
Editors of these persuasions did not try to apply genealogical
reasoning, and in doing so waived the possibility of developing
new methods specifically geared to the problems of traditions of
this kind and period. In the pre-Cameron volumes of the Yale
Poems on affairs of state series little effort is made to establish
transmissional histories, and what there is often leads to wrong
results. Collations of variants throughout the series are so
skeletonic that some editors do not even give a full record of the
emendations made to their copy texts. The editors of the 1628
Proceedings and debates, working from the same university, display
an even more marked disdain for the genealogy of sources,
announcing baldly that they have 'not tried to discover "families"
among the manuscripts'—'families' obviously being a dirty
word.[36] Here they are explicitly rejecting the precedent of
Notestein and Relf, who, while hampered by a primitive method,
had at least made a serious attempt to establish the main
distributional groupings of their sources.

There was also the problem in the 1960s and 1970s that editorial
theorists such as Vinton Dearing, Dom Froger and G. P. Zarri who
all accepted the validity of genealogical reasoning were also
intoxicated by the possibility that otherwise intractable volumes of
textual data might be analysed by computer.[37] This committed
them to a search for ways in which genealogies could be
constructed by purely quantitative means using very simple
algorithms. This was not a very plausible project at the time, and
has since come to appear even less so. Its effects can be followed in

---

[35] Examples are cited in Beaurline, 'An editorial experiment', p. 43.

[36] *CD 1628*, p. 7. They also reveal that one manuscript has been rejected from
consideration because it was a 'late copy' (p. 4) and another because of 'major defects' (p. 5);
however, neither factor in itself prohibits a source from being the sole bearer of an
archetypal reading.

[37] See Vinton A. Dearing, 'Computer aids to editing the text of Dryden' in *Art and error:
modern textual editing*, ed. Ronald Gottesman and Scott Bennett (Bloomington, Ill., 1970),
pp. 254–78; Dom. J. Froger, *La critique des textes et son automatisation* (Paris, 1968); and G. P.
Zarri, 'Algorithms, *stemmata codicum* and the theories of Dom. H. Quentin' in *The computer
and literary studies*, ed. A. J. Aitken, R. W. Bailey and N. Hamilton-Smith (Edinburgh,
1973), pp. 225–37. W. Ott, 'Computer application in textual criticism' in the Edinburgh
volume, pp. 199–23, is of greater value since it restricts the role of the computer to ordering
data for decision-making rather than actually making the decisions. Weitzman, 'The
analysis of open traditions', includes a critique of several of the methods proposed.

the writings of Vinton Dearing who devoted a very great amount of intellectual energy to discovering that gold could not, after all, be made out of sea water.[38]

The result of all this is that the theory of how the genealogical method is to be applied to scribally published texts is still pretty much where Greg left it in 1927. Greg's main innovation was his insistence that, before any decisions were made about the priority or posteriority of readings, the relationship of the sources should be expressed as a non-directional stemma, i.e. one that, excluding all assumptions about the direction of change, groups and filiates sources as a synchronic not a diachronic system. For Greg it is necessary that we determine the distributive relationships of texts before we attempt to show one as derived from the other. Of course, there will often be situations where directional judgements have to be made in order to resolve ambiguity or conflict in the evidence for distribution or where the relationship of the two kinds of judgement is a reciprocal rather than a linear one. But where evidence is plentiful and there is no serious problem with conflation, Greg's method of procedure is more satisfactory than the older alternatives.

Because of this many editors of medieval and Renaissance English texts with manuscript traditions still try to use *The calculus of variants* as a manual of editing. Unfortunately, this is something it was never meant to be. Greg does throw in some advice about the practical problems, but his aim in writing the book was a much more specialized one. What the *Calculus* is concerned with is the methods to be used in the formal analysis of variants within an ideal tradition in which all agreements are genetically significant—a tradition in which there is no irregular agreement and no conflation. His acknowledged intellectual influences were not editorial theorists but philosophers, particularly the team of Russell and Whitehead, though he also mentions Wittgenstein.[39] What we are given is a study in the logic of variant groupings, not

[38] See Tanselle, 'Classical, biblical, and medieval textual criticism', pp. 31–5 and Michael Weitzman's review of Dearing's *Principles and practice* in *Vetus testamentum* 27 (1977), 15–35. Dearing's reply to Weitzman, *VT* 29 (1979), 355–9, only partly deals with his criticisms. Dearing's method of eliminating conflict by breaking 'rings' at their weakest point leads not to a solution but to an endless deferral of the problems that the editor should be prepared either to resolve or to declare unresolvable.

[39] Greg, *Calculus*, pp. v–vi.

a manual of editorial practice. He does not deal systematically with how we are to determine the direction of change or with how genetically indicative variants are to be distinguished from those that are not. A further problem is that Greg's method is basically one of deductive investigation of the consequences which flow from a range of hypothetical stemmas. He is not a good guide to how one is to reason inductively from the evidence of real-life agreements (which can never be as clearcut as his examples), or how hypotheses derived from the textual evidence are to be tested against that same evidence, which is a crucial issue in editing of this kind.

Certainly the method described in the *Calculus* needs a great deal of development before it can help us with large, vernacular manuscript traditions. One crucial question is how we are to strike a balance between positive evidence and negative evidence. A very simple example is the process by which sources are classified as either terminal or intermediary. A terminal source is one that stands at the end of a line on the stemma, like the terminus of a railway line, while the intermediary is one of the stops or junctions along the line. (A textual railway line will often have a lot of little branch lines going for a stop or two.) The two are distinguished on the basis that a terminal source will possess unique variants which are not found in any other text, while an intermediary will possess no such variants. Now, while this is all perfectly logical, the two judgements are being made on the basis of two different, and incommensurate, criteria. Terminal status is determined by a presence and intermediary status by an absence. The positive argument is satisfied whenever evidence is to hand, irrespective of the length of the text, but the negative argument is much more cogent for a long text than for a short one. And, in any case, how is one to treat the manuscript that, as so often, shows two or three easily reversible unique variants—the one that could go either way? The problem here (as Bédier realized) is that when the two modes of argument come into collision it is usually the positive argument that wins. Yet any diagnosis of radial copying (where a number of manuscripts have been copied from a single exemplar) will inevitably rest on an argument from absences. These are real problems in the kind of traditions I am describing where there was probably a great deal of radial copying from scriptorial archetypes.

Under such circumstances one needs to give a special weight to negative evidence; but the problem is how this is to be done.

Here we encounter another cognitive problem not considered by Greg, which is the insufficiency of any linear model of textual reasoning. The issue is not simply that cases of irresolvable conflict over either distributive or directional evidence can only be dealt with by declaring certain agreements indicative and others non-indicative, but that the precise significance of some agreements must remain unclear until it is conferred by the stemma. (A simple example would be when what appeared initially to be a strong agreement has to be revalued in the light of fuller evidence that places the texts concerned at mutually remote arms.) In other words, decisions made at one stage of reasoning may have to be reviewed in the light of conclusions reached at a later stage which is itself dependent on those earlier decisions.[40] Until we have a sense of a possible structure, the data is only patterns without significance; and yet it is also the case that the structure is discovered through an analysis of that very same data. In this as in so many other aspects of historical scholarship it is difficult to escape from the hermeneutic circle. So while it is often possible to demonstrate a textual conclusion by means of linear argument, it is rarely that the conclusion has actually been arrived at in this way. Instead, 'hee that will

> Reach her, about must, and about must goe;
> And what th'hills suddennes resists, winne so . . .

RANKING OF VARIANTS

One mode of textual circumambulation is to divide the record of variation into two groups—a smaller one containing those classes of variation which one's experience of the particular tradition suggests can usually be relied on as genetically indicative, and a larger group of indifferent or trivial variations which are not, considered singly, an adequate basis for textual reasoning. The point here is that while members of this larger group are individually unable to provide a foundation for argument, they will still, collectively, tend to align themselves with the broad

---

[40] Vieth's Step 5 (*Complete poems*, p. li) is a rare acknowledgement of this.

genetic divisions of the tradition. So one can use the smaller group
to generate hypotheses (the more of them the better) that can then
be tested against the larger group. In cases where there is no smaller
group of putatively more reliable variations, or where the
agreements between those that there are radically contradict each
other, one has to work statistically from the whole body of
variants—a much more difficult matter.

The criteria that should govern the acceptance of some variants
as likely to be indicative and the rejection of others as less likely or
positively unlikely have been analysed by me with some care
elsewhere and will only be given here in outline.[41] The most prized
variant reading is that which is (1) likely to mark not only the
members of a particular 'family' within the overall tradition, but
all of the members of that family, and which (2) is not likely to
appear either spontaneously or through conflation in another
family. We may call the first of these criteria 'stability' and the
second 'unrepeatability'. The criterion of stability requires that the
reading should fit plausibly into its context. The persistence of a
glaring and obvious error (providing it is not of the kind to repeat
itself independently) is excellent evidence that the texts that
contain it stand in a close genetic relationship; but such a reading,
because of its vulnerability to correction, is unlikely to identify all
the texts of its group. The criterion of unrepeatability would give a
reduced value to variants produced by the commonly encountered
mechanisms of error—e.g. anticipation, perseveration, metathesis
and eyeskip—since there must always be a likelihood of the same
change being made by another scribe.[42] In many cases such changes
are context-promoted and will inevitably be repeated if copying
continues for long enough. Greg argues that 'the easier it is to
explain how an error arose, the less valid the assumption that it
only arose once'.[43]

The proneness of a reading to be transported to another family
by conflation must always be difficult to assess on probabilistic
grounds, but help may be had from the insight expressed by Greg

[41] 'The ranking of variants in the analysis of moderately contaminated manuscript
traditions', *SB* 37 (1984), 39–57. See also my 'The text of "Timon. A satyr"', *BSANZ
Bulletin* 6 (1982), 113–40, and *The text of Rochester's 'Upon nothing'*.
[42] These mechanisms are discussed in Stoll, 'Zur Psychologie der Schreibfehler'.
[43] *Calculus*, p. 20 n.

in the two forms: 'What usually happens is that collation and "correction" are confined to some of the more striking variants' and 'where conflation is suspected, the value of variants as an indication of ancestry is in inverse proportion to their intrinsic importance'.[44] Our ideal reading, then, should not be too obtrusive—with obtrusiveness a criterion that has to be derived afresh for each new work or tradition studied. In a religious text it might be the theologically charged word that required to be so defined whereas in verse the position of the word in the stanza might be significant. Where memorial contamination is suspected, the obtrusive word is simply the memorable word. A risk of conflation should also be assumed whenever the reading of the group of sources under consideration is notably superior to that of other groups—this assumption being necessary to allow for the case where a scribe, dissatisfied with an inferior reading, might come searching for a better alternative.[45] Our ideally indicative reading therefore would belong to a variation in which all the variants were plausible in their own way (as often happens as the result of authorial revision).

If some variants are to be preferred, others are firmly to be avoided. One should note, as stated earlier, that variations in spelling, since they depend so much on individual whim, are only of value in special instances. In practice the same volatility affects many kinds of variations which are formally classified as substantive. These include purely dialectical variations, many variations involving grammatical function words, most variations in which alterations to meaning are brought about by small changes to spelling or punctuation, and most variations in the wording of material ancillary to the text proper, such as titles, marginalia, author identifications or stage directions. To this we should add all variations involving words such as 'the', 'that', 'and', 'which' and 'when', which were frequently written in contracted form, and most variations between singular and plural forms,

---

[44] *Calculus*, p. 57. He continues: 'To the herd of dull commonplace readings we must look for the genetic source of the text, to the more interesting and striking for the source of the contamination. Nothing can be more misleading than to seek to "place" a manuscript on the evidence of a few "test" readings'.

[45] Maas (p. 8) notes the complementary principle that 'obvious corruptions, particularly *lacunae*, may easily be transmitted in the direct line but are hardly ever transferred by contamination'.

many of which appear to arise from the misreading of final 's' as a decorative flourish or of a decorative flourish as final 's'. The problem with such readings is that they are highly prone to reversal to the prior form (usually without any conscious awareness on the part of the scribes) and to spontaneous replication. Taken singly, variants of the kinds just described offer no basis at all for textual reasoning, though taken collectively, as has already been explained, they will show a general tendency to conform to the genetic distribution. Variations composed of synonyms or near-homonyms have some value but can still easily reverse more than once during a series of copyings, the vulnerability applying to both variants in the variation. In assessing the genetic indicativeness of variant groupings, it may be helpful to use an informal arithmetical scale with values assigned according to the criteria of stability, unrepeatability, obtrusiveness and relative plausibility.

CONSTRUCTING THE STEMMA

Our application of these principles begins with the investigation of distributional relationships expressed through a non-directional stemma. The variants are sorted out by hand or computer program into singletons, pairs, threes and so on, but with the full list always available for consultation, for the evidential value of an individual variant is always a function of its context in the work and the variation, and no two variants are exactly equivalent in this respect.[46] The editor must then classify each source as terminal, intermediary or ambiguous. A terminal text is defined, as we have seen, by the possession of unique readings and an intermediary by their absence. However, an easily reversible unique reading, or even a whole series of these, is not firm evidence of terminal status. Where this possibility cannot be excluded, one should withhold

---

[46] For pencil-and-paper analysis, this can be done by a simple computer program that rewrites the variations in the form 'list of sigla—line number—variant' and then resorts the list of sigla alphabetically, reverse alphabetically or from any given letter of the alphabet as required. If logical investigation of groups of sigla is undertaken by computer it should be solely with the aim of producing a range of hypothetical solutions to be tested against the actual readings. Before processing, each variant should be assigned an arithmetical estimate of indicativeness to be used in resolving conflict. The program should then produce a list of instances in which these estimates have been overridden.

judgement until more stable evidence is obtained. A helpful method is to grade variants for stability on a scale of 0, 1 and 2, with the 0 variant being that lacking real evidential value, and the 2 variant that least amenable to reversal. A 2-score variant would carry the evidential weight of a whole string of zeroes. The presence of copious evidence of terminal status in the earlier part of a text should not be made an excuse to suspend the testing of variants, in case the scribe may have switched to another exemplar.

The editor now turns to the variations which have been selected as most likely to be genetically indicative. Within these, some groupings of texts should immediately stand out as consistent and well attested. (Anomalous groupings among these texts, which can be assumed to be the result of non-genetic agreement, should be examined as evidence for the kinds of transmissional 'noise' likely to be encountered in the particular tradition.) Other groupings will be less certain, while at the lower extreme there will be agreements represented by only one or two trivial occurrences. A weakly attested pair may be non-evidential, or it may represent a true genetic link between two relatively invariant sources. Examination of other agreements involving each source should indicate which of these is the case. True genetic groups with a large number of members may never be attested by any single agreement, but always appear minus family members or in the company of interlopers. Irreconcilably conflicting groups will undoubtedly present themselves. Some conflicts will be the result of the same alteration being made independently or the spontaneous reversal of changes, but other cases will result from conflation, progressive copying, or successive copying from two exemplars. Conflation can usually be diagnosed when it has happened only once and sometimes if it has happened twice, but a source containing more than two levels of conflation is likely to remain inscrutable. It should not be included in the stemma but discussed separately. Note that a source which contains a large number of unique variants is also likely to enter into a large number of inconsistent agreements with other texts. This need not indicate conflation (which tends on the whole to reduce variation) but is simply what we would expect on a chance basis.

Beginning with the well-attested groups, we now construct our non-directional stemma. This relies primarily on the principle of intermediation, which holds that when three sources stand in the relationship A—B—C, they will generate the agreements AB and BC but not AC. Texts are arranged in order according to their membership of fields and sub-fields defined by the possession of common variant readings. The principle is the same as governs the use of Venn diagrams—which are another way of expressing the relationships concerned, as are the quasi-algebraic expressions used by Greg in *The calculus of variants*. It is often helpful to begin by placing texts along a linear 'spectrum' with vertical lines of division tagged with the indicative variants. One tries to begin with a well-attested and uncontradicted pair of texts which will be written as in Diagram 1. The existence of larger groups ABC and ABCD would permit us to extend the diagram to the form given in Diagram 2. In these diagrams it is assumed that all texts are terminal. If C, for instance, was an intermediary, it would be placed on the line instead of on a branch from it. The existence of additional groups DEF and EF would allow us to complete or stemma according to Diagram 3.

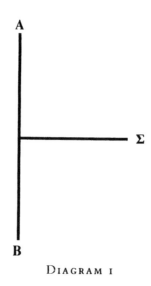

DIAGRAM 1

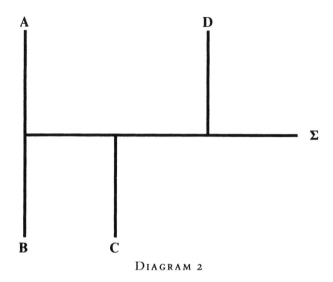

DIAGRAM 2

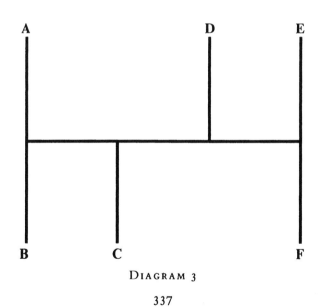

DIAGRAM 3

There is a certain fairy-tale quality about these examples, since in practice it may be hard to find pairs (let alone larger groups) that are both well-attested and uncontradicted. A little thought will show that the structure illustrated in Diagram 3 might well produce the pairs AC and BC as well as AB, and DE and DF as well as EF: all that would be required would be for the larger groups ABC and DEF to lose a member due to the mutation or reversal of a reading in one of the extreme pairs. In some instances, a large tradition will divide spectacularly at some key point into a series of consistent subfamilies characterized by a particular reading, greatly easing the work of the editor.[47] At other times we must work patiently from the smaller units up to the larger until we finally arrive at a testable hypothesis concerning the totality. Remember that at this stage relationships embody no assumptions about priority. The ancestor of the group could be at any point on the stemma or external to it.

To have a full appreciation of the significance of our diagram and how it is and is not to be used it will be necessary to give some consideration to what Greg called 'the ambiguity of three texts'. In its simplest form this is simply to say that the relationship of three terminal texts consistently agreeing AB:C, AC:B and BC:A may be any one of the four quite different directional stemmas shown in Diagram 4. This arises from the variety of points at which it is possible to insert the exclusive common ancestor of the pair. Inscribed on the non-directional stemma these are as indicated in Diagram 5.

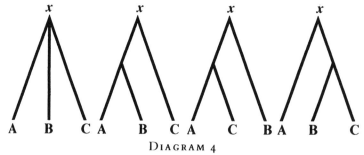

DIAGRAM 4

[47] In Rochester's 'Upon nothing' this occurs with the variant at line 10 quoted earlier in this chapter. The sources divide into four major groups arising from the loss of a word or words before 'power'. The variation does not indicate which, if any, of the variants is original. See my *The text of Rochester's 'Upon nothing'*, pp. 22–31.

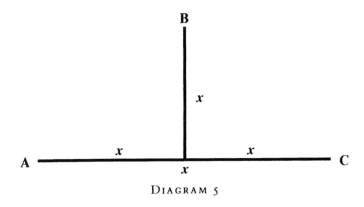

DIAGRAM 5

It will be seen that the term 'ambiguity of three texts' is inaccurate: the problem only arises when we try to insert the further text or texts that we require to supply the ancestor and any missing internal junctions or sub-ancestors. Greg realized, and Hruby has demonstrated more rigorously, that the presence of a larger number of texts in the non-directional stemma does not remove the problem, but simply alters its scale.[48] Thus, to borrow an example from Greg, a group of six terminal texts agreeing A:B:C:D:E:F (i.e. without any agreements in higher groups) permits one directional stemma in which all texts descend independently from the ancestor and a range of others which supply an intermediate common ancestor for all the sources except one.[49] Kane refers to the same problem when he warns against assigning a notional sub-ancestor to 'agreements in right readings, which are not evidence of descent from an exclusive common ancestor and would grievously mislead'.[50] In other words the relationship, ABCD:EF is equally satisfied by Diagram 6 and Diagram 7—to look no further. The moral of this is that all junctions entered on the non-directional stemma must be regarded as provisional, and that some may never be determined. What the stemma plots is intermediation, not filiation.

[48] Greg, *Calculus*, pp. 46–7; Antonín Hrubý, 'A quantitative solution of the ambiguity of three texts', *SB* 18 (1965), 147–82.

[49] *Calculus*, pp. 21–2.

[50] *A-text*, p. 63.

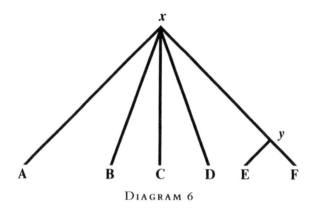

DIAGRAM 6

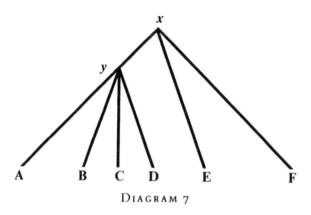

DIAGRAM 7

The next stage in stemma construction is the systematic examination of directional evidence in order to determine the position of the archetype and the nature of its relationship to the other surviving texts. As at the earlier stages we will almost certainly have to adjudicate cases of irresolvable conflict, and it is vital that our decisions in these instances and the considerations that led to our making them should be fully laid open to the reader. Reliable directional evidence is much less common than the school of Vinaver would have us believe.[51] For one thing, as has long been recognized, we have to be cautious about giving priority to a variant because it is 'better' than the alternative. Kane and Donaldson lay great stress on their ability to recognize Langland's *usus scribendi*; but this can never be more than an editorial construct from the fallible transcripts. In any case, the aim of recension is not to restore the author's lost autograph but simply the most recent common ancestor of the surviving copies—which may well itself have contained errors. Moreover, there is no reason why scribes should not be quite as good as editors in spotting a slip by one of their predecessors and either repairing it or replacing it with a plausible sophistication. Disappointingly, evidence often tends to diminish as we approach the position of the archetype. This is because a relatively good text gives the scribe a much better chance of producing an accurate copy than one riddled with oddities, errors and non-sequiturs, which will tend by their very nature to excite further alterations. The presence of conflation should have revealed itself at the stage of distributional analysis, but the matter of whether authorial revision has taken place is one that should be considered along with evidence of direction. We must also remain alert for evidence of progressive copying (discussed in Chapter 3) and mixed exemplars. Moreover, scriptorial exemplars could be altered between copyings—not an easy matter to diagnose but probably common enough. Some texts are found with readings from a second source entered marginally: subsequent copyists might well make their own selection of these. In others errors might be corrected between copyings, or attributions added or removed.

This will also be the point to review the evidence for the placing of intermediaries and the number of texts to be linked up to the various junctions within the stemma. Directional evidence will frequently permit resolution of these ambiguities.[52] However,

[51] A point searchingly considered in John M. Bowers, 'Hoccleve's two copies of *Lerne to dye*: implications for textual critics', *PBSA* 83 (1989), 437–72.

[52] Hrubý, 'A quantitative solution', offers an ingenious mathematical method to assist in the identification of intermediaries. This rests on the hypothesis that independent derivation (i.e. with no intervening sub-ancestor) will produce a different frequency · ·currence of the groupings ABC, AB:C, AC:B and BC:A than what he calls 'successive' derivation. ABC in this context represents the unaltered readings common to the three texts. The rates of occurrence of each of these groupings are expressed as decimals of the total number of

even when this evidence is clear and ample, there will sometimes be cases where the principle of intermediation permits texts to be isolated as a group but the evidence for branches within the group is irresolvably conflicting. Here the editor should simply box the texts on the stemma, sternly resisting any attempt to force the evidence of filiation within the box. Alternatively, the evidence could be presented in the form of an intermediation spectrum— still a useful tool—rather than a stemma of the Lachmannian type. Cases of less severe doubt should be footnoted so that readers are duly warned and can dissent as they see fit. Information about the historical circumstances of production is also of value in determining direction and derivation. Examples of this will be considered in the next section of this chapter.

Throughout our investigation, we will be looking for the directional stemma, or partial stemma, which yields the maximum plenitude of explanation, secured with the minimum need to declare agreements anomalous. If the truth of the matter fails to conform to this prescription it is unlikely that it will ever be known. The method of procedure will, as before, be one of reciprocal adjustments of models and data. Having established a hypothetical stemma or stemmas on the basis of the purportedly indicative subset, verification is sought by returning to the excluded variations and working through them one by one. If our hypothesis is correct, we will find that most of these conform to the predictions of the provisional stemma and that the remainder generally fail to do so as the result of some explicable scribal mechanism. Any completely anomalous variations should be checked at this point against the sources to make sure they have been correctly recorded: the discovery of an error that brings a reading into conformity with the stemma, while a sign of earlier carelessness, may none the less be reassuring to the editor. If this kind of fit is not encountered, the hypothesis should be regarded as

possible changes which is quantified as one. If the rate of ABC is given as f_1, that of AB:C as f_2, that of AC:B as f_3 and that of BC:A as f_4, the formula

$$\frac{f_1{}^2}{(f_1+f_4)\,(f_1+f_3)\,(f_1+f_2)}$$

should return a value of one in the case of independent variation and not one in the case of successive variation. However, it has never been shown how this might be applied in practice.

having failed and further possibilities be considered. When, as often happens, a choice between hypotheses rests on the interpretation given to two or three crucial variations, this should be explained to users of the edition in a way that makes it easy for them to review the editor's decision.

Our conclusions about these matters will always remain hypotheses even if they should be vastly more probable ones than any others we have been able to devise. Kane and Donaldson speak eloquently on this subject:

In any case our edition, as a hypothesis, continues subject to the classic test: whether it is the simplest that can be devised to account convincingly for the phenomena to which it applies. Like all hypotheses it is also essentially presumptive, that is subject to modification by the emergence of new data, or to replacement by a superior hypothesis.[53]

Having come so far, we will be as close to and as far from certainty as the facts of copying in the real world usually allow. It must be stressed that the theoretical aim of creating a full enough stemma to assist in the reconstruction of the readings of the archetype will by no means always be achievable. But this does not mean the exercise has not been worthwhile. To the extent that we are able to construct a convincing argument about the origin and growth of the tradition we will have gained a valuable aid to the other kinds of editorial decision making. We may also have acquired information that will cast light on other manuscripts and traditions.

THE TEXTUAL RELATIONSHIPS OF MISCELLANIES

Our discussion of the role of genealogical reasoning in the editing of scribally published texts has so far been concerned with single texts considered in isolation. But while these texts may well be encountered as separates, they will also as a rule be found as part of larger units. The simplest form of this is what W. J. Cameron called an 'aggregation', meaning a volume formed by binding together materials of diverse bibliographical origin.[54] Most surviving examples are the creations of later generations of

---

[53] *B-text*, p. 212.
[54] 'Scriptorium', pp. 27–9.

librarians, but collections will sometimes be found which were bound up in their own time, and there would have been many which were kept together by their original owners without actually being bound. For collections entered by their owners in a book reserved for that purpose, Beal's term 'personal miscellany' should be used rather than the traditional 'commonplace book', which should be reserved for actual collections of commonplaces in alphabetical order. 'Miscellany' is also to be used for all scribally published collections which would not more suitably be described as 'anthologies'. Little attention has so far been given to the significance of these larger units for the editor. Our starting point must be the realization that they possess a structure which is at once particulate, aggregative and, in many cases, evolving. Let me begin by explaining what I mean by these terms.

If one should wish to establish the textual relationship of two seventeenth-century manuscript miscellanies, whether of prose or verse, there would be no other way than by collating all the surviving copies of all their constituent items. This would yield a series of stemmas which might or might not be complete or, indeed, reliable, and which might or might not be consistent with each other. The chances are that they would not be complete, because there would probably be situations in which the available evidence would not support the procedural requirements of the method. But, assuming these stemmas were complete *and* reliable, they might still be inconsistent with each other. The reason, as we have seen, is that the compilers of these miscellanies, as well as acting as publishers for writers who brought them new material, were drawing on a body of separates already in circulation. Even when new pieces were sent to a scribal publisher by their authors, this would have nothing to do with their subsequent history, or with the condition or sequence in which they would be picked up by other scriptoria. So there is theoretically nothing to prevent each individual item from our pair of miscellanies having followed a different set of paths from agency to agency, or indeed for traditions of some complexity to have arisen within particular agencies through progressive copying. It is in this sense that the miscellanies are particulate.

But one would almost certainly find that a certain proportion of the contents of the miscellany had already been circulating as smaller sub-collections prior to their inclusion, that is as linked groups, sometimes consisting of several items on a particular topic, and sometimes of an item followed by others written in response to it.[55] It is in this sense that the miscellanies are aggregative. So as well as building stemmas for individual items, we would need to investigate the relationships of these linked groups. Moreover, when a number of versions of the same collection were the work of the same scribal agency, we would need to consider the overall collection as a transmissional unit. We are speaking, remember, of manuscript anthologies which are always one-off affairs. Of course they might be replicated in near-identical volumes with regard to their contents—though even here there will always be some alteration of readings—but it is much more common to find that collections issued by the same agency vary through items being added or removed. It is in this sense that they can be thought of as evolving. Because each manuscript is a separate production, the publisher can work in new material the moment it is acquired and discard the old the moment it grows out of date. There is also the opportunity to supply each customer with a product which is in some respects unique, or, less nobly, to force the purchase of material already possessed in order to secure the new and desired.

The moral of this is that, when dealing with the transmission of texts that were widely copied into composite sources, it can never be enough simply to analyse the transmissional history of the individual item. If that item has circulated as part of a linked group, then one must also study the history of that group through its growth and decay. If the miscellany exists in a series of evolving recensions one must also try to discover the sequence of those recensions. And then one has to see whether the three different histories agree or disagree. If they disagree one has to decide whether this is the result of a mistake in one's own analysis or whether the disagreement points to some undetected complication in the process of transmission. Not all these questions will be answerable.

To discuss these phenomena, we will need some terminology. The overall body of materials from which any particular volume is

---

[55] For linked groups of satires, see Vieth, *Attribution*, pp. 26–7, 76–80 and 322–52. The principle applies to all forms of scribally published composite texts.

compiled we have already called the *scriptorial archive*. Sometimes this archive would have been entered in a large book, as was done by Starkey and Collins and the creators of Folger MS M. b. 12. In this case there would have been a tendency for items to remain in the same order in any copy. But in other cases, as we saw in our discussion of the Cameron scriptorium, it is likely that the scriptorial archive existed in the form of separates—that is, of single leaves, half-sheets, folded sheets and small, stab-sewn booklets. In these cases, material removed from the archive might be lost permanently, and it would be a very easy matter for the order of items to become disturbed, either accidentally or by design. A scriptorial archive of this kind is in genealogical terms an archetype, but it is not a static archetype: I have called it a *rolling archetype*, and if it rolled long enough and vigorously enough it could even produce offspring that had no actual items in common.[56] The value of the terms scriptorial archive and rolling archetype is that they help us replace a very difficult question ('What is the transmissional history of this miscellany in respect both of its whole and its parts?') with a considerably simpler one ('Is there a known agency to which the production of this miscellany can be assigned?'). When the knowledge that given manuscript texts of a work derive from such an archive can be used in connection with the genealogical method, with each set of data serving as a control on the other, we can reason pretty conclusively.

The search for scriptorial archives and rolling archetypes makes use of many different kind of evidence. For a start there may be documentary information, of the kind considered in earlier chapters, about the publishers of texts. There also be bibliographical evidence concerning such matters as hands, layout styles, quiring and bindings. Watermarks and countermarks can offer evidence for common scriptorial origin. The composition dates of the items will also need to be considered: seeing the bulk of scribally circulated material is highly topical it is usually not hard to determine these. In addition much material in the sources is itself supplied with dates, which if they are not those of composition will

[56] The analogy would be with a bus or train which began its journey with one set of passengers and ended it with a completely different one, or with the turnover of staff within an organization.

at least be those of transcription or of the event that inspired the item. Most important of all, naturally, are the content of the collection and the order in which items appear, though it is necessary to realize that evidence of this kind is not always conclusive. Miscellanies will show strong similarities in content and also frequently order when they derive from the same scriptorial archive; but they will also show similarities whenever independent compilers of archives have been acquiring more or less the same items (including linked groups and formed sub-collections) over more or less the same period. Moreover, some compilers of retrospective miscellanies liked to impose a chronological arrangement on their material. In these cases order may not in itself offer a means of distinguishing the work of individual scriptoria. An obvious point is that collections formed in one scriptorium may become embedded, either in whole or in part, within a larger anthology produced by another scriptorium. Compilations of political and parliamentary material include many examples of this, as do the verse anthologies discussed in Chapter 6.

Otherwise, the challenge is to extend the methods of genealogical analysis from individual items and linked groups to embrace whole collections of items. Once again, we will try, by using the more reliable evidence, to generate hypothetical models and then test those models against the whole body of data. One strongly indicative pattern is when particular groups of sources maintain their integrity from stemma to stemma while appearing in constantly varying intermediary and terminal relationships with other identifiable groups. A fluidity of relationships *within* such a group may also be significant when it suggests the possibility of progressive copying. (When the fluidity arises from unexpected reversals of readings, these could well be due to a scriptorium scribe's memory of earlier copyings.) All this can yield no more than probabilities, but they can become powerful ones when we look at them, interactively, with other classes of evidence—the historical, the bibliographical and considerations of order and content. Once we are able to link miscellanies with particular scribal agencies, we possess a powerful tool for evaluating variants in items within those miscellanies in a way which will no longer be circular because it will now be conferred from a higher level of structural understanding. An example is the Rochesterian 'Signior Dildo', where problems of editorial judgement are vastly eased by the knowledge that all but three of the collections which contain the poem are derived directly or at second hand from the archive of the 'Cameron' scriptorium. Naturally, we should always be watchful for the possibility of a scriptorium's possessing two genetically unrelated copies of the same item.[57]

TEXT AND APPARATUS

The kind of edition that has been presented as an ideal in this chapter is one that represents the most probable hypothesis a present-day scholar is able to devise about what a seventeenth-century scribally-publishing author wrote. But the information necessary for a proper assessment of the edited text can only with some difficulty be displayed on the same page as that text. By the. use of diacritic signs of the kind invented by Hans Walter Gabler for his edition of Joyce's *Ulysses*, successive stages in the linear evolution of a work can be presented graphically—allowing the reader, in effect, to become the true editor of the text.[58] But the problem in our case is the very different one of recovering a lost text from the evidence of its descendants—something that is not merely a matter of the arrangement of states but rests on the construction and presentation of an argument. The challenge to the editor is to present that argument in such a way that the reader can appropriate it and if necessary revise it with the minimum of effort.

Such an aim requires that the data on which the argument rests—the list of variations—should not simply be presented but interpreted, whether it is by an introduction, physically separate explanatory notes, or notes and symbols embedded in the list itself. An uninterpreted list of variants is of very little value: only another editor is likely to be able to make much sense of it and even then it

---

[57] An example is the two highly variant texts of the Restoration 'Satyr on the court ladies' ('Curse on those critics ignorant and vain') in V&A MS Dyce 43, pp. 215–19 and 360–4, a product of the 'Cameron' scriptorium. Both are in the same hand. In the collateral manuscript, Österreichische Nationalbibliothek 14090, the first occurrence has been omitted.

[58] James Joyce, *Ulysses. A critical and synoptic edition*, ed. Hans Walter Gabler with Wolfhard Steppe and Claus Melchior (New York, 1984).

may take many hours of work before it can be put into usable form.[59] In practice, few editors do much to make their processes of reasoning intelligible. Many openly refuse accountability, presenting their text as the outcome of arcane processes of intellection which must always remain a mystery.[60] Such an approach is not only a manifestation of bad faith towards the reader, but leads to an unjustifiably final status being claimed for the resultant reading text. In fact the heart of the edition is not its text but the judgements that underlie the text. The edition that makes these judgements available for inspection will also acknowledge the necessarily provisional status of any reading text both with regard to the hypothetical nature of editorial decisions and the determining role of editorial policy. Here Kane and Donaldson provide a salutary model. As D. C. Greetham has pointed out 'the degree of license assumed by the editors requires that *all* of the evidence for reconstruction of the text be made available so that the editorial rationale can be continually tested against the documentary witnesses'.[61]

Having once accepted this primacy of the argument, the editor is rewarded with a considerable latitude in adapting the reading text to the requirements of its users. This can affect both substantive and incidental readings. Literary readers by and large are happy with the notion of the eclectic text constructed from a variety of witnesses; but there will always be strong resistance among historians towards this ideal since such a text has ceased to be what they would recognize as a document—i.e. something firmly assignable to a particular place and time.[62] In such cases it is

[59] The listing of variations in the form in which the lemma is the reading of the edited text is itself a source of confusion as it renders the variation less amenable to analysis. The form used by Greg for the demonstrations of *The calculus of variants* would be the ideal one with some typographical means used to single out the preferred variant.

[60] As in Vieth, *Complete poems*, p. xlvi: 'Although Rochester scholarship has shown encouraging progress in recent years, its level of accomplishment does not yet warrant incorporating into this edition a complete textual apparatus, including lists of all variants in the independently descended versions of each poem and a detailed account of the procedure, sometimes quite elaborate, by which these variants were used to establish text'.

[61] D. C. Greetham, 'Normalisation of accidentals in Middle English texts: the paradox of Thomas Hoccleve', *SB* 38 (1985), 123 n.

[62] This attitude is both defended and assailed in the papers presented in *Literary and historical editing*, ed. George L. Vogt and John Bush Jones (Lawrence, Kan., 1981). The wider ramifications of the debate are considered in Mary-Jo Kline, *A guide to documentary editing*

probably kindest to reserve speculation concerning the readings of the archetype for the report on transmissional history and provide a reading text which is a particular scribal version from as close as possible to the origin of the tradition, presented with only minimal intervention. But this will not be 'the text' so much as a means of interrogating the transmissional history, first of all for evidence as to the nature of the archetype, and secondly (and perhaps more importantly in a historical text) for the story of how the text has been conceived, promulgated, used, misused, understood, misunderstood, and revised to suit new circumstances. In other words, the critical old-spelling edition compiled (where practicable) on genealogical principles is not only a concatenation of hypotheses about what might once have been written but a record of the various forms in which the text was *read*—and rewritten—by its contemporaries.

As an example of the way in which records of variation illuminate the use of the text by its first readers, I would like to take two cases from poems by the sixth Earl of Dorset. A state poem of the Stuart century normally emerged from within a political clique which had highly privileged information about circumstances at court or in parliament, but whose aim was not to share this information so much as to use it as the basis of a sophisticated kind of disinformation which would influence the future course of events. From the point of view of the clique, the poem would soon be rendered obsolete by their acquiring hotter information and adopting new political strategies. But long before this happened, the satire would have moved out into circles which did not possess the privileged information of the writer and where readers would indulge in various kinds of creative *mis*reading in order to adjust the text to their own understanding of politics and desires to influence the future. They would do this by altering names, by filling in deliberate blanks with their own guesses, and, of course, by rewriting what seemed to them to be meaningless so that it made better sense—to themselves.

Dorset's 'Colon' is a satire on Charles II and his mistresses, written when the leading royal mistress, the Duchess of Ports-

(Baltimore, 1987), pp. 8–21 and G. Thomas Tanselle, 'Historicism and critical editing', *SB* 39 (1986), 1–46.

350

mouth, was under attack from parliament. The writer imagines that Portsmouth has resigned from her post, and that Charles is holding interviews to select her successor—the poem being a narrative of these interviews. At lines 56-9 we find the following passage:

> Next in stepp'd pretty Lady Grey,
> Offer'd her lord should nothing say
> 'Gainst the next treasurer's accus'd
> So her pretense were not refus'd:[63]

Elias Mengel in Volume two of the Yale *Poems on affairs of state* cites a variant reading for the third line ' 'Gainst next the treasurer's accus'd'.[64] He further suggests that if, as is quite likely, the poem was written between December 1678 and March 1679, the variant would allude very precisely to the plight of the then treasurer, the Earl of Danby, who had been saved from impeachment only by the proroguing of parliament on 30 December and was attacked at once by the new parliament which met on 6 March, dismissed from his post and on 16 April sent to the Tower. Mengel presents this simply as a piece of dating evidence, but the variation in the line can also be seen as marking a shift in the relationship between the text and the events it was both recording and trying to influence. We might refine this insight further by proposing that the change corresponds to a movement outwards of the satire from an internal court faction, to which Dorset belonged and for whom the poem was an attempt to influence internal court politics, to a wider public who would read it, in Whig terms, as an attack on the court as an institution. So the variant reflects both misunderstanding of the precise allusion intended by the writer, and a wresting of the poem by its new readers to an altered political function.

The second example is from Dorset's 'A faithful catalogue of our most eminent ninnies', dated 1686 and 1687 in some manuscripts but assigned by Brice Harris and Galbraith Crump to early in 1688.[65]

---

[63] *POAS (Yale)*, ii. 170–1.

[64] Ibid. 171.

[65] *Poems*, ed. Harris, p. 136; *POAS (Yale)*, iv. 190. Line 17 addresses Charles II (d. 1685) as if he was still living. The text given here is Crump's. Harris's contains several misprints as well as being marred by retention of inferior readings on a 'best manuscript' basis. His record of variants is much fuller than Crump's but still incomplete, as well as containing

> Proud Oxford justly thinks her Dutch-built shape
> A little too unwieldy for a rape;
> Yet, being conscious it will tumble down,
> At first assault surrenders up the town;
> But no kind conqueror has yet thought fit
> To make it his belov'd imperial seat;
> That batter'd fort, which they with ease deceive,
> Pillag'd and sack'd, to the next foe they leave;
> And haughty Di in just revenge will lig,
> Although she starve, with any senseless Whig . . . (ll. 368–77)

Early in the process of transmission, the fourth couplet of the passage was omitted and then added at the foot of the page with a mark to indicate its proper position. As a result of failure to observe the mark, the majority of the manuscripts have it in the wrong position, creating the following:

> But why to Ireland, Braithwait? Can the clime,
> Dost thou imagine, make an easy time?
> That batter'd fort, which they with ease deceive,
> Pillag'd and sack'd, to the next foe they leave.
> Ungratefully, indeed thou didst require
> The skillful goddess of the silent night
> By whose kind help thou wast so oft before
> Deliver'd safely on thy native shore. (ll. 394–9)

The error is obvious enough to modern readers with the full textual history of the poem available and should also have been obvious to a reader in 1688 since the errant couplet would have had no relationship to its context. But most of the surviving manuscripts are from anthologies written in the 1690s, and for their scribes the couplet would have seemed a perfectly apt, if somewhat oddly phrased, comment on the state of Ireland in the aftermath of William's invasion. In this case a sexual insult in a poem attacking members of the court of James II has been metamorphosed into a sneer at Anglo-Dutch conduct in Ireland.

Textual change of this kind has to be recorded because it is itself a part of the historical process. The Yale *Poems on affairs of state* series has good explanatory notes which illuminate many issues of

---

inaccuracies. Neither editor gives a proper record of the sidenotes which the manuscripts show were an integral part of the work.

this kind; but it is only in the Cameron and Ellis volumes that a real attempt is made to illustrate and explain transmissional histories. If a parallel series of the political poetry of the earlier part of the century should ever be attempted (now a major desideratum) it is to be hoped that the nexus between an understanding of textual genealogies and an understanding of how the text was used and understood by its early readers will be foregrounded for attention. The same should also apply to editions of historical documents. A precedent for this is the Notestein and Relf edition of the 1629 *Commons debates* which anticipates a number of techniques of present-day *textes génétiques*. In this, as in other respects, it is vital that the reader should not be confined to walking the decks of the edited text but should be given easy access to both the bridge and the engine room.

The secondary status of the reading text *vis-à-vis* the textual argument will also be reflected in the choices to be made concerning spelling and punctuation. It will be helpful in sorting out the issues if we return to the case of Rochester and the way in which the problem has been handled by his two most distinguished editors, Vieth and Walker. Vieth's edition of 1968 starts from the premise that what readers are primarily interested in is the personality of Rochester. The poems are grouped under sections headed Prentice Work, Early Maturity (1672–1673), Tragic Maturity (1674–1675), and Disillusionment and Death (1676–1680). The more substantial poems are introduced by headnotes relating them in a more particular way to the biography of the poet. For instance, at the beginning of 'Leave this gaudy gilded stage' Vieth has the note: 'It is tempting to imagine that this lyric, which survives in Rochester's own handwriting, was addressed to some actress who was his mistress, perhaps Elizabeth Barry'—which makes it rather difficult *not* to read the poem in a biographical way, or at least to test the offered proposition as one reads it.[66] An apparent inconsistency of the edition, in view of its strong assertion of the authorial rationale, is that it uses modern spelling and heavy, often actively interpretative, modern punctuation. Vieth's argument for modern spelling is that 'there is virtually no basis for an old-spelling text of Rochester's poems'—an

---

[66] *Collected poems*, p. 85.

argument which looks rather odd now that Walker has produced such a text.[67] But clearly what Vieth meant by an old-spelling edition was an edition that preserved the author's own accidentals, rather than simply accidentals from the historical period. This choice of modern spelling and punctuation is one of a number of features of Vieth's edition—the headnotes are another—that tend to submerge the personality of the author under that of the editor. In other words, it represents an arbitrary choice which is in conflict with the wider rationale of the edition. But my concern here is not to criticize that choice, but to use it to illustrate the kind of latitude which is validly available to the editor who acknowledges the secondary and provisional status of the reading text. Any disappointment felt with this edition will not be over its radical rehandling of incidentals but in its failure to provide its readers with a usable record of transmissional history.

Walker's edition of 1984, which deserves always to be remembered with gratitude as the first to present an *apparatus criticus*, was based on the alternative assumption, accepted much earlier by de Sola Pinto, that what is interesting about Rochester is his contribution to the development of the major genres of Augustan poetry. So in this case the text is arranged in sections headed Juvenilia, Love Poems, Translations, Prologues and Epilogues, Satires and Lampoons, Poems to Mulgrave and Scroope, and Epigrams, Impromptus, Jeux d'Esprit etc. Walker presents versions which are very faithful to their manuscript copy-texts, except when the accidentals of these would pose severe difficulties for a modern reader. This gives his edition a valuable sense of the flavour and variability imparted by scribal publication. Walker has also, very commendably in my view, included whole variant manuscript texts of a number of poems, and also poems by other writers which formed part of linked groups to which Rochester contributed, again emphasizing the conditions of the poems' first circulation as scriptorial satire. Yet here one is again conscious of a conflict of rationales. In de Sola Pinto's case the texts had been based on the edition of 1691, which was the form in which they were probably read by most later Augustan writers. This is clearly an advantage if one is looking at Rochester as a

[67] Ibid., p. xlv.

source of influences on the subsequent history of the genres he pioneered, and was one of a number of other policies which might legitimately have been chosen.

Both editors had their reasons for these choices which they would wish to defend. None the less, the choices actually made suggest the possibility of others which might have been considered. In Walker's case, a text presenting the accidentals of a series of 'best manuscripts' might well have ordered its contents not under genres but under the sources in which the poems made their first or most significant appearance. Vieth likewise might have reinforced the biographical thrust of his edition by using a synthetic spelling system based on Rochester's known preferences as revealed by the handful of verse holographs and, more revealingly, the manuscripts of the correspondence. As it happens, Rochester was remarkably consistent in both his spellings and his punctuation and such an approach would be perfectly feasible for a new edition. This could have been done either in a conservative way as in the Latham and Matthews *Pepys*, which uses spellings characteristic of the author when known but otherwise modern spelling, or more radically by employing the method accepted for the text of Hoccleve's *Regement of princes* in which probabilistic methods are used to replicate the author's use of variant spellings for the same word.[68] Such a choice would not be made on the assumption that one was actually restoring what the author originally wrote, but in the belief that, since some arbitrary system had to be used, it could more usefully be one the author approved of than modern spelling. Once again, these comments are not meant as criticisms of the choices actually made by Walker and Vieth, to both of whom future editors of Rochester will owe an immeasurable debt, but simply to illustrate the range of possibilities open to all editors of scribally published texts who set out to do more than reproduce a particular historical document.

Behind the freedom available in suiting or not suiting the accidentals to the wider aims of the edition lies Greg's liberating argument in 'The rationale of copy-text' that the authority for accidentals need not inhere in the same text as the authority for substantives.[69] His aim in proposing this was to ensure that the text

[68] *Diary*, i, p. cl; D. C. Greetham, 'Normalisation of accidentals', pp. 121–50.
[69] *SB* 3 (1950–1), 19–36. This modest paper has spawned a huge secondary literature, for

which best preserved the author's accidentals was available to be used as copy-text for the edition. In the cases just considered, and indeed most of the writings discussed in this book, there is no authorial text available in the first place, nor in many cases any text which is known to stand sufficiently close to the authorial fair copy as to preserve anything of its accidentals. Indeed, the authors of the majority of scribally published texts remain unknown or only to be guessed at. This makes the degree of options available unusually wide—even to the extent of abandoning any notion of copy-text in Greg's sense and supplying a conjecturally reconstructed text with editorial accidentals. One would not, of course, wish to see freedom degenerate into caprice. All things considered, it is preferable that the choice of a system of accidentals for the edition should grow from a sense of its function and purpose, and that this should also govern the ordering of items and the relationship established between the textual apparatus, the explanatory notes and the words on the page. But where there are good reasons for departing from this principle of consistency, they should be followed. What makes this freedom possible is a view of editing which sees its central and defining function not as the presentation of a text but the creation of an argument or a series of arguments embodied in a record of transmissional history. My own rider to this view is simply that the argument should be presented in a form which allows the reader to monitor and where necessary to revise its conclusions. A bare list of variants is of little use when the tradition is of any complexity. Editors must explain not only their general policy concerning the texts, but how and why they have chosen to resolve particular cases of conflict. This can best be done by direct annotation of the record of variation.

which see G. Thomas Tanselle, 'The editorial problem of final authorial intention', *SB* 29 (1976), 167–211.

BIBLIOGRAPHY OF MAJOR
REFERENCES

What are here listed are secondary, and a few primary, sources of major relevance to the topic, and those which are referred to by short title at scattered locations throughout the text. Other sources may be located through the index.

ASHBEE, ANDREW. 'A further look at some of the Le Strange manuscripts'. *Chelys* 5 (1973–4), 24–41.

AUBREY, JOHN. *'Brief lives', chiefly of contemporaries, set down by John Aubrey, between the years 1669 and 1696*, ed. Andrew Clark. 2 vols. Oxford, 1898.

BAUMAN, RICHARD. *Let your words be few: symbolism of speaking and silence among seventeenth-century Quakers.* Cambridge, 1983.

BEAL, PETER, comp. *Index of English literary manuscripts. Volume 1 1450–1625* and *Volume 2 1625–1700.* London, 1980– .

BEAUMONT, FRANCIS and JOHN FLETCHER. *Comedies and tragedies written by Francis Beaumont and John Fletcher gentlemen.* London, 1647.
—— *The dramatic works in the Beaumont and Fletcher canon,* gen. ed. Fredson Bowers. Cambridge, 1966– .

BÉDIER, JOSEPH. 'La tradition manuscrite du Lai de l'ombre'. *Romania* 54 (1928), 161–96 and 321–56.

BELANGER, TERRY. 'Publishers and writers in eighteenth-century England' in Isabel Rivers, ed., *Books and their readers in eighteenth-century England,* pp. 5–25. Leicester, 1982.

BELJAME, ALEXANDRE. *Men of letters and the English public in the eighteenth century.* London, 1948.

BENJAMIN, WALTER. *Illuminations,* introd. Hannah Arendt, trans. Harry Zohn. London, 1973.

BRAUNMULLER, A. R., ed. *A seventeenth-century letter-book.* Newark, Del., 1983.

BRETT, PHILIP. 'Edward Paston (1550–1630): a Norfolk gentleman and his musical collection'. *Transactions of the Cambridge Bibliographical Society* 4 (1964), 51–69.

CAMERON, W. J. 'A late seventeenth-century scriptorium'. *Renaissance and modern studies* 7 (1963), 25–52.

CHAYTOR, H. J. *From script to print: an introduction to medieval vernacular literature.* Cambridge, 1950.

COMENIUS, JOANNES AMOS. *Orbis sensualium pictus,* facsim. edn, introd. James Bowen. Sydney, 1967.

Commons debates for 1629, ed. Wallace Notestein and Frances Helen Relf. Minneapolis, 1921.

CORAL, LENORE F. 'Music in English auction sales, 1676–1750'. University of London Ph.D. thesis, 1974.

CRESSY, DAVID. *Literacy and the social order: reading and writing in Tudor and Stuart England.* Cambridge, 1980.

CROFT, P. J. *Autograph poetry in the English language.* 2 vols. London, 1973.

CROFT, PAULINE. 'Annual parliaments and the long parliament'. *Bulletin of the Institute of Historical Research* 59 (1986), 155–71.

CROSFIELD, THOMAS. *The diary of Thomas Crosfield,* ed. Frederick S. Boas. London, 1935.

CUST, RICHARD. 'News and politics in early seventeenth-century England'. *Past and present* 112 (Aug. 1986), 60–90.

CUST, RICHARD, and ANN HUGHES, eds. *Conflict in early Stuart England: studies in religion and politics 1603–1642* (London, 1989).

CUTHBERT, DENISE. 'A re-examination of Andrew Marvell'. Sydney University Ph.D. thesis, 1987.

DANCHIN, PIERRE, ed. *The prologues and epilogues of the Restoration 1660–1700.* 7 vols. Nancy, 1981–8.

DAVIES, JOHN, OF HEREFORD. *The complete works of John Davies of Hereford,* ed. Alexander B. Grosart. Edinburgh, 1878.

DAVIES, ROY. 'The creation of new knowledge by information retrieval and classification'. *Journal of documentation* 45 (1989), 273–301.

DAWSON, GILES E., and LAETITIA KENNEDY-SKIPTON. *Elizabethan handwriting 1500–1650.* London, 1966.

DEARING, VINTON A. *Principles and practice of textual analysis.* Berkeley, Calif., and Los Angeles, 1974.

DE BEAU CHESNE, JOHN, and JOHN BAILDON. *A booke containing divers sortes of hands.* London, 1602 (facsim. repr. Amsterdam, 1977).

DEFOE, DANIEL. *A review of the state of the British nation.* London, 1712 (facsim. ed. A. W. Secord, New York, 1938, book 21).

DERRIDA, JACQUES. *Of grammatology,* trans. G. C. Spivak. Baltimore, 1976.

D'EWES, SIR SIMONDS. *The autobiography and correspondence of Sir*

Simonds D'Ewes, Bart., during the reigns of James I and Charles I, ed. James Orchard Halliwell. London, 1845.

DODD, GORDON, comp. *Thematic index of music for viols*. First instalment (London, 1980), with further instalments 1982, 1984 and 1987.

DONNE, JOHN. *Letters to severall persons of honour*. London, 1651.

DORSET, CHARLES SACKVILLE, EARL OF. *The poems of Charles Sackville, sixth earl of Dorset*, ed. Brice Harris. New York, 1979.

DOUGLAS, DAVID. *English scholars 1660–1730*. 2nd rev. edn. London, 1951.

DOWNIE, J. A. *Robert Harley and the press. Propaganda and public opinion in the age of Swift and Defoe*. Cambridge, 1970.

DRAYTON, MICHAEL. *The works of Michael Drayton*, ed. J. William Hebel. 5 vols. Oxford, 1961.

DRYDEN, JOHN. *The works of John Dryden*, gen. eds. H. T. Swedenberg, jun., and Alan Roper. Los Angeles, 1956– .

DUGDALE, SIR WILLIAM. *The life, diary, and correspondence of Sir William Dugdale*, ed. William Hamper. London, 1827.

EVELYN, JOHN. *The diary of John Evelyn*, ed. E. S. de Beer. 6 vols. Oxford, 1955.

FEATHER, JOHN. *A history of British publishing*. London, 1988.

FIENNES, CELIA. *The journeys of Celia Fiennes*, ed. Christopher Morris. London, 1947.

FINLAY, MICHAEL. *Western writing implements in the age of the quill pen*. Wetheral, 1990.

FLETCHER, HARRIS FRANCIS. *The intellectual development of John Milton*. 2 vols. Urbana, Ill., 1961.

FRASER, PETER. *The intelligence of the secretaries of state and their monopoly of licensed news 1660–1688*. Cambridge, 1956.

FULLER, THOMAS. *Ephemeris parliamentaria*. London, 1654.

—— *The history of the worthies of England*. London, 1662.

GAIR, W. R. 'The politics of scholarship: a dramatic comment on the autocracy of Charles I' in David Galloway, ed., *The Elizabethan theatre III. Papers given at the third international conference on Elizabethan theatre held at the University of Waterloo, Ontario, in July 1970*, pp. 100–18. Waterloo, Ont., 1973.

GASKELL, PHILIP. *A new introduction to bibliography*, rev. impression. Oxford, 1974.

GOLDBERG, JONATHAN. *Writing matter: from the hands of the English Renaissance*. Stanford, Calif., 1990.

GREETHAM, D. C. 'Normalisation of accidentals in Middle English texts: the paradox of Thomas Hoccleve'. *SB* 38 (1984), 121–50.

GREETHAM, D. C. 'Textual and literary theory: redrawing the matrix'. *SB* 42 (1989), 1–24.

GREG, W. W. *The calculus of variants. An essay on textual criticism.* Oxford, 1927.

—— *A companion to Arber, being a calendar of documents in Edward Arber's 'Transcript of the registers of the Company of Stationers of London 1554–1640'.* Oxford, 1967.

—— 'The rationale of copy text'. *SB* 3 (1950-1), 19-36. Also in his *Collected papers*, ed. J. C. Maxwell, pp. 374–91. Oxford, 1966.

GUBAR, SUSAN. ' "The blank page" and the issues of female creativity' in Elizabeth Abel, ed., *Writing and sexual difference*, pp. 73–93. Brighton, 1982.

The Gyldenstolpe manuscript miscellany of poems by John Wilmot, Earl of Rochester, and other Restoration authors, ed. Bror Danielsson and David M. Vieth. Stockholm, 1967.

HABERMAS, JÜRGEN. *The structural transformation of the public sphere: an enquiry into a category of bourgeois society*, trans. Thomas Burger with the assistance of Frederick Lawrence. Cambridge, Mass., 1989.

HAMMOND, PAUL. 'The Robinson manuscript miscellany of Restoration verse in the Brotherton Collection, Leeds'. *Proceedings of the Leeds Philosophical and Literary Society, Literary and historical section*, 18/3 (1982), 277-324.

HARBAGE, ALFRED, rev. S. SCHOENBAUM and SYLVIA STOLER WAGENHEIM. *Annals of English drama 975–1700.* 3rd edn. London, 1989.

HARINGTON, SIR JOHN. *Nugae antiquae: being a miscellaneous collection of original papers.* 2 vols. London, 1769-75.

—— *A supplie or addicion to the catalogue of bishops, to the yeare 1608*, ed. R. H. Miller. Potomac, 1981.

HARRIS, BRICE. *Charles Sackville, sixth earl of Dorset, patron and poet of the Restoration.* Urbana, Ill., 1940.

—— 'Captain Robert Julian, secretary to the muses'. *ELH* 10 (1943), 294–309.

HEAL, SIR AMBROSE. *The English writing-masters and their copy-books 1570–1800: a biographical dictionary and a biography*, introd. Stanley Morison. London, 1931.

HEAWOOD, EDWARD A. 'Papers used in England after 1600. I. The seventeenth century to *c.* 1680'. *Library*, 4:11 (1930), 263–99.

HECTOR, L. C. *The handwriting of English documents.* 2nd edn. London, 1966.

HOBBS, MARY. 'An edition of the Stoughton manuscript (an early seventeenth-century poetry collection in private hands, connected with Henry King and Oxford) seen in relation to other contemporary poetry and song collections'. London University Ph.D. thesis, 1973.

HOBBS, MARY. 'Early seventeenth-century verse miscellanies and their value for textual editors'. *English manuscript studies 1100–1700* 1 (1989), 182–210.

HRUBÝ, ANTONÍN. 'A quantitative solution of the ambiguity of three texts'. *SB* 18 (1965), 147–82.

HUGHES, EDWARD. 'A Durham manuscript of the *Commons debates* of 1629'. *English historical review* 74 (1959), 672–9.

HYDE, HENRY, SECOND EARL OF CLARENDON. *The correspondence of Henry Hyde, Earl of Clarendon, and of his brother Laurence Hyde, Earl of Rochester*, ed. Samuel Weller Singer. 2 vols. London, 1828.

JENKINSON, SIR HILARY. *The later court hands in England from the fifteenth to the seventeenth century.* 2 vols. Cambridge, 1927.

JONSON, BEN. *Ben Jonson*, ed. C. H. Herford and Percy and Evelyn Simpson. 11 vols. Oxford, 1925–52.

JOWETT, JOHN. 'Jonson's authorization of type in *Sejanus* and other early quartos'. *SB* 44 (1991), 254–65.

KAY, DENNIS. 'Poems by Sir Walter Aston, and a date for the Donne/Goodyer verse epistle "alternis vicibus".' *RES* ns 37 (1986), 198–210.

KELLIHER, HILTON, comp. *Andrew Marvell, poet and politician 1621–78. An exhibition to commemorate the tercentenary of his death.* London, 1978.

KENYON, J. P. *Stuart England.* 2nd edn. Harmondsworth, 1985.

KERNAN, ALVIN. *Printing technology, letters and Samuel Johnson.* Princeton, NJ, 1987.

KINNAMON, NOEL. 'The Sidney psalms: the Penshurst and Tixall manuscripts'. *English manuscript studies 1100–1700* 2 (1990), 139–161.

KIRKMAN, FRANCIS. *The unlucky citizen: experimentally described in the various fortunes of an unlucky Londoner.* London, 1673.

LANGLAND, WILLIAM. *Piers plowman*, ed. George Kane and E. Talbot Donaldson. *The A version. Will's visions of Piers plowman and Do-well.* London, 1960 (rev. repr. 1988). *The B version. Will's visions of Piers plowman, Do-well, Do-better and Do-best.* London, 1975 (rev. repr. 1988).

LASLETT, PETER. 'The gentry of Kent in 1640'. *Cambridge historical journal* 9 (1947–9), 148–64.

—— 'Sir Robert Filmer: the man versus the Whig myth'. *William and Mary quarterly*, 3:5 (1948), 523–46.

—— *The world we have lost: further explored.* Cambridge, 1983.

LEMMINGS, DAVID. 'The student body of the Inns of Court under the later Stuarts'. *BIHR* 58 (1985), 149–66.

LE STRANGE, SIR NICHOLAS. *'Merry passages and jeasts': a manuscript jestbook of Sir Nicholas Le Strange (1603–1655)*, ed. H. F. Lippincott. Salzburg, 1974.

Letters addressed from London to Sir Joseph Williamson while plenipotentiary at the congress of Cologne in the years 1673 and 1674, ed. W. D. Christie. Camden Society publications, NS, 8–9. 2 vols. London, 1874.

LEVY, F. J. 'How information spread among the gentry, 1550–1640'. *Journal of British studies* 21 (1982), 11–34.

LILLYWHITE, BRYANT. *London coffee houses: a reference book of coffee houses of the seventeenth, eighteenth and nineteenth centuries*. London, 1963.

LOVE, HAROLD. *Restoration literature: critical approaches*. London, 1972.

—— 'Preacher and publisher: Oliver Heywood and Thomas Parkhurst'. *SB* 31 (1978), 227–35.

—— 'The text of "Timon. A satyr".' *BSANZ bulletin* 6 (1982), 113–40.

—— 'The ranking of variants in moderately contaminated manuscript traditions'. *SB* 37 (1984), 39–57.

—— 'Manuscript versus print in the transmission of English literature, 1600–1700'. *BSANZ bulletin* 9 (1985), 95–107.

—— 'Shadwell, Flecknoe and the Duke of Newcastle: an impetus for *Mac Flecknoe*'. *Papers on language and literature* 21 (1985), 19-27.

—— *The text of Rochester's 'Upon nothing'*. Monash University Centre for Bibliographical and Textual Studies. Occasional Papers, no. 1. Melbourne, 1985.

—— 'Scribal publication in seventeenth-century England'. *Transactions of the Cambridge Bibliographical Society* 9 (1987), 130–54.

—— 'Scribal texts and literary communities: the Rochester circle and Osborn b. 105'. *SB* 42 (1989), 219–235.

—— 'The editing of Restoration scriptorial satire', in Paul Eggert, ed. *Editing in Australia*, pp. 65–84. Canberra, 1990.

—— 'Richard Flecknoe as author-publisher'. *BSANZ bulletin* 14 (1990), 41–50.

LOVELACE, RICHARD. *The poems of Richard Lovelace*, ed. C. H. Wilkinson. Oxford, 1953.

LUTTRELL, NARCISSUS. *A brief historical relation*. 6 vols. Oxford, 1857.

MAAS, PAUL. *Textual criticism*, trans. Barbara Flower. Oxford, 1958.

MACCOLL, ALAN. 'The circulation of Donne's poems in manuscript', in A. J. Smith, ed., *John Donne: essays in celebration*, pp. 28–46. London, 1972.

MCKENZIE, D. F. *The Cambridge University Press 1696–1712: a bibliographical study*. 2 vols. Cambridge, 1966.

—— *Bibliography and the sociology of texts*. London, 1986.

McKenzie, D. F. 'Speech–manuscript–print', in Dave Oliphant and Robin Bradford, eds., *New directions in textual studies*, pp. 87–109. Austin, Tex., 1990.

McKenzie, D. F. and J. C. Ross, eds. *A ledger of Charles Ackers: printer of 'The London magazine'*. Oxford, 1968.

McLuhan, Marshall. *The Gutenberg galaxy: the making of typographic man*. Toronto, 1962.

Marotti, Arthur F. *John Donne, coterie poet*. Madison, Wis., 1986.

Marvell, Andrew. *The poems and letters of Andrew Marvell*, ed. H. M. Margoliouth, 3rd edn, rev. Pierre Legouis with the collaboration of E. E. Duncan-Jones. Oxford, 1971.

Maslen, K. I. D., and John Lancaster. *The Bowyer ledgers*. London, 1991.

Monson, Craig. *Voices and viols in England, 1600–1650. The sources and their music*. Ann Arbor, Mich., 1982.

Morison, Stanley. *Politics and script*, ed. Nicholas Barker. Oxford, 1972.

Morrill, J. S. 'William Davenport and the "silent majority" of early Stuart England'. *Journal of the Chester Archaeological Society* 18 (1975), 115–29.

Moxon, Joseph. *Mechanick exercises on the whole art of printing (1683–4)*, ed. Herbert Davis and Harry Carter. 2nd edn. London, 1962.

Muddiman, J. G. *The king's journalist 1659–1689: studies in the reign of Charles II*. London, 1923.

Nashe, Thomas. *The works of Thomas Nashe*, ed. R. B. McKerrow, rev. F. P. Wilson. 5 vols. Oxford, 1958.

Nicholl, Charles. *A cup of news: the life of Thomas Nashe*. London, 1984.

North, Roger. *The life of the right honourable Francis North, Baron of Guilford*. London, 1742.

—— *Roger North on music*, ed. John Wilson. London, 1959.

—— *General preface and life of Dr John North*, ed. Peter Millard. Toronto, 1984.

O'Day, Rosemary. *Education and society 1500–1800: the social foundations of education in early modern Britain*. London, 1982.

Ong, Walter J. *Fighting for life: contest, sexuality, and consciousness*. Ithaca, NY, 1981.

—— *Orality and literacy: the technologizing of the word*. London, 1982.

Patterson, Annabel. *Censorship and interpretation: the conditions of writing and reading in early modern England*. Madison, Wis., 1984.

Pearl, V. L. and M. L. 'Richard Corbett's "Against the opposing of the Duke in parliament, 1628" and the anonymous rejoinder, "An answer to the same, lyne for lyne": the earliest dated manuscript copies'. *RES* NS 42 (1991), 32–9.

PEBWORTH, TED-LARRY. 'John Donne, coterie poetry, and the text as performance'. *SEL* 29 (1989), 61-75.

PECK, LINDA LEVY. *Northampton: patronage and policy at the court of James I.* London, 1982.

PEMBROKE, MARY, COUNTESS OF. *The triumph of death and other unpublished and uncollected poems by Mary Sidney, Countess of Pembroke (1561–1621)*, ed. G. F. Waller. Salzburg, 1977.

PEPYS, SAMUEL. *The diary of Samuel Pepys*, ed. Robert Latham and William Matthews. 11 vols. London, 1970–83.

PETER, JOHN. *Complaint and satire in early English literature.* Oxford, 1956.

PETTI, ANTHONY G. *English literary hands from Chaucer to Dryden.* London, 1977.

PHILIPS, KATHERINE. *The collected works of Katherine Philips*, ed. Patrick Thomas. Stump Cross, 1990– .

PINTO, DAVID. 'The music of the Hattons'. *RMA Research chronicle* 23 (1990), 79–108.

PLANT, MARJORIE. *The English book trade. An economic history of the making and sale of books.* 2nd edn. London, 1965.

Poems on affairs of state. Augustan satirical verse, 1660–1714, gen. ed. George deF. Lord. 7 vols. New Haven, Conn., 1963–75.

POTTER, LOIS. *Secret rites and secret writings: royalist literature, 1641–1660.* Cambridge, 1989.

POWELL, WILLIAM S. *John Pory 1572–36. The life and letters of a man of many parts.* Chapel Hill, NC, 1977.

PRITCHARD, ALLAN. 'Marvell's "The garden": a Restoration poem?'. *SEL* 23 (1983), 371–88.

PROBYN, CLIVE. '"Haranguing upon texts": Swift and the idea of the book', in Hermann J. Real and Heinz J. Vienken, eds., *Proceedings of the first Münster symposium on Jonathan Swift*, pp. 187–97. München, 1985.

—— 'Swift's *Verses on the death of Dr Swift*: the notes'. *SB* 39 (1986), 47–61.

Proceedings of the short parliament of 1640, ed. Esther S. Cope in collaboration with Willson H. Coates. Camden Society, 4:19. London, 1977.

RANDALL, DALE B. J. *Gentle flame: the life and verse of Dudley, fourth Lord North (1602–1677).* Durham, NC, 1983.

RANDOLPH, MARY CLAIRE. '"Mr Julian, secretary of the muses": Pasquil in London'. *N&Q* 184 (Jan–June 1943), 2–6.

Bibliography

Reports of cases in the courts of Star Chamber and High Commission, ed. S. R. Gardiner. Camden Society, NS 39. London, 1886.

ROCHESTER, JOHN WILMOT, 2ND EARL OF. *The complete poems of John Wilmot, Earl of Rochester*, ed. David M. Vieth. New Haven, Conn., 1968.

—— *The letters of John Wilmot, Earl of Rochester*, ed. Jeremy Treglown. Oxford, 1980.

—— *The poems of John Wilmot, Earl of Rochester*, ed. Keith Walker. Oxford, 1984.

ROSTENBERG, LEONA. *English publishers in the graphic arts 1599–1700. A study of the printsellers and publishers of engravings, art and architectural manuals, maps and copy books.* New York, 1963.

SAUNDERS, J. W. 'The stigma of print: a note on the social bases of Tudor poetry'. *Essays in criticism* 1 (1951), 139–64.

SAVILE, GEORGE, MARQUESS OF HALIFAX. *The works of George Savile, Marquess of Halifax*, ed. Mark N. Brown. 2 vols. Oxford, 1989.

Scriveners' company common paper 1357–1628 with a continuation to 1678, ed. Francis W. Steer. London, 1968.

SHAKESPEARE, WILLIAM. *The complete works: original spelling edition*, ed. Stanley Wells and Gary Taylor. Oxford, 1986.

SHARPE, KEVIN. *Sir Robert Cotton 1586–1631: history and politics in early modern England.* Oxford, 1979.

SIMPSON, CLAUDE M. *The British broadside ballad and its music.* New Brunswick, NJ, 1966.

SNYDER, HENRY L. 'Newsletters in England, 1689–1715. With special reference to John Dyer—a byway in the history of England', in Donovan H. Bond and W. Reynolds McLeod, eds. *Newsletters and newspapers: eighteenth-century journalism.* Morgantown, 1977.

SOUTHERNE, THOMAS. *The works of Thomas Southerne*, ed. Robert Jordan and Harold Love. 2 vols. Oxford, 1988.

The spectator, ed. Donald F. Bond. 5 vols. Oxford, 1965.

STOLL, J. 'Zur Psychologie der Schreibfehler'. *Fortschritte der Psychologie* 2 (1913), 1–133.

STONE, LAWRENCE. *The crisis of the aristocracy 1558–1641.* Oxford, 1965.

STYLES, PHILIP. *Sir Simon Archer 1581–1662.* Oxford, 1946.

The first and second Dalhousie manuscripts: poems and prose by John Donne and others, a facsimile edition, ed. Ernest W. Sullivan II. 2 vols. Columbia, Mo., 1988.

SWANSON, DON. 'Undiscovered public knowledge'. *Library quarterly* 56 (1986), 103–118.

SWIFT, JONATHAN. *Prose works of Jonathan Swift*, ed. Herbert Davis et al. 14 vols. Oxford, 1939–68.

TANSELLE, THOMAS. 'Classical, biblical, and medieval textual criticism and modern editing'. *SB* 36 (1983), 21–68.

THOMPSON, ANN and JOHN. *Shakespeare: meaning and metaphor.* Brighton, 1987.

THOMPSON, ROBERT P. 'English music manuscripts and the fine paper trade, 1648–1688'. London University Ph.D. thesis, 1988.

TREADWELL, MICHAEL. 'London trade publishers 1675–1750'. *Library*, 6:4 (1982), pp. 99–134.

TURNBULL, G. H. *Hartlib, Dury and Comenius: gleanings from Hartlib's papers.* Liverpool, 1947.

VIETH, DAVID M. *Attribution in Restoration poetry: a study of Rochester's 'Poems' of 1680.* Yale studies in English, no. 153. New Haven, Conn., 1963.

—— 'Dryden's Mac Flecknoe: the case against editorial confusion'. *Harvard Library bulletin* 24 (1976), 204–44.

VINAVER, EUGÈNE. 'Principles of textual emendation', in *Studies in French language and medieval literature presented to Professor Mildred K. Pope*, pp. 351–69. Manchester, 1939; repr. in Christopher Kleinhenz, ed., *Medieval manuscripts and textual criticism*, pp. 139–66. Chapel Hill, NC, 1976.

WANLEY, HUMFREY. *The diary of Humfrey Wanley 1715–1726*, ed. C. E. Wright and Ruth C. Wright. 2 vols. London, 1966.

WATSON, ANDREW G. *The library of Sir Simonds D'Ewes.* London, 1966.

WEITZMAN, MICHAEL. 'The analysis of open traditions'. *SB* 38 (1985), 82–120.

WHALLEY, JOYCE IRENE. *The pen's excellencie: a pictorial history of Western calligraphy.* New York, 1980.

WILKINSON, D. R. M. *The comedy of habit.* Leiden, 1964.

WILLETTS, PAMELA. 'Sir Nicholas Le Strange and John Jenkins'. *Music and letters* 42 (1961), 30–43.

WILLIAMS, FRANKLIN B., jun. 'Commendatory verses: the rise of the art of puffing'. *SB* 19 (1966), 1–14.

WILLIAMS, WILLIAM P. 'The Castle Ashby manuscripts: a description of the volumes in Bishop Percy's list'. *Library*, 6:2 (1980), 391–412.

WILSON, JOHN HAROLD, ed. *The court wits of the Restoration.* Princeton, NJ, 1948.

—— *Court satires of the Restoration.* Columbus, Oh., 1976.

INDEX

Index

368

Index

Index

Index

Maitland, John, Duke of Lauderdale 215
Maitland, Richard, Earl of Lauderdale 53
Manwaring, Roger 14
Manifold, John 24
Manne, Thomas 52
Manuche, Cosmo 59
Markley, Robert 243
Marmion, Shackerley 85
Marotti, Arthur F. 5–6, 51, 62, 79, 181
Marriott, Richard 67
Marsh, Narcissus 25
Marston, John 181, 224, 232
Martin, Roger 236
Marvell, Andrew 4, 44, 50, 57, 62–3, 113, 116, 155, 174, 189, 231, 237, 238–240, 252
    Marvellian tradition in satire 213, 238–42, 259, 261, 262, 265
Mary II 182, 233–4, 270, 272
Maslen, Keith 90, 127
Massinger, Philip 51, 67
Matteis, Nicola 27, 64–65
Maule family 25
Meautys, Thomas 169
Mengel, Elias 351
Meres, Francis 68
Merro, John 25
Meyer, Ernst 24
Middleton, Thomas 66, 222
Miege, Guy 156–7
Milgate, Wesley 4
Millard, P. T. 28, 204
Miller, E. H. 67
Milton, John 48, 58, 187, 237, 325
Milward, Richard 49, 77
miscellanies 5–7, 16, 47, 52, 79, 189, 211–17, 231–83 passim, 296
    accession 269, 274
    textual relationships of 343–8
    see also rolling archetype; scriptoria
Monck, George, Duke of Albermarle 215
Monson, Craig 25, 180–1
Montagu, Charles, Earl of Halifax 270
Moore, John (scribe) 17
Moore, John, Bishop 78
Moore, Robert 113
Morison, Stanley 11, 109, 114
Morphew, John 277
Morrill, J. S. 180, 190–1, 202
Moseley, Humphrey 65, 67

Moxon, Joseph 90, 105, 113, 119, 127, 129
Moyles, R. Gordon 325
Muddiman, Henry 11, 12, 18, 126, 204
Mulgrave, Earl of, see Sheffield, John
Musgrove, S. 79
music, scribal publication of, see composers; lampoons, libels and satires; Oxford; viol consort music
music paper 105–7
Myriell, Thomas 25

Nalson, John 17
Nashe, Thomas 61, 72, 76–7, 79, 95
Neild, James Edward 220
Nelson, Horatio 249
Newdigate, Sir John 198
Newman, Thomas 72
newsletters 3, 9–22 passim, 49, 96, 123, 124–6, 129, 130–1, 190–1, 202, 204, 205, 206, 267–8, 279
    see also Chamberlain, John; Collins, Thomas; Dawks, Ichabod; Dyer, John; Hancock, Giles; Muddiman, Henry; Pory, John; Proby, Peter; Rossingham, Edward; Somerton, John; Urwin, Will; Williamson, Sir Joseph
Newton, Isaac 33
Nicholl, Charles 61, 72, 79
Norris, Christopher 143
North, Digby, Lord North 28
North, Dudley, Lord North 28, 41, 43
North, Francis, Baron Guilford 225–7
North, Sir Henry 28–9, 52, 179
North, John, Dr 111, 221, 223, 226
North, Roger 23–8, 33, 53, 63–4, 67, 75, 113, 184, 201, 203–4, 221, 225–7, 233, 264
North, Sara, Dame 28
Northey, John 285, 286
Nostradamus 216
Notestein, Wallace 10, 15–20, 135, 328, 353

Oates, Titus 171–3, 184
O'Day, Rosemary 93, 198, 219, 221, 222, 225, 227
O'Donnell, Mary Ann 268
Oldenburg, Henry 147, 182
Oldham, John 308

374

AU BORD DE LA RIVIÈRE

Michel David

AU BORD DE LA RIVIÈRE

TOME 3. XAVIER

Roman historique

Hurtubise

Catalogage avant publication de Bibliothèque et Archives nationales du Québec et Bibliothèque et Archives Canada

David, Michel, 1944-2010

Au bord de la rivière : roman historique

Édition originale : 2011-2012.

Sommaire : t. 1. Baptiste -- t. 2. Camille -- t. 3. Xavier -- t. 4. Constant.

ISBN 978-2-89723-387-7 (vol. 1)
ISBN 978-2-89723-388-4 (vol. 2)
ISBN 978-2-89723-389-1 (vol. 3)
ISBN 978-2-89723-390-7 (vol. 4)

I. David, Michel, 1944-2010. Baptiste. II. David, Michel, 1944-2010. Camille. III. David, Michel, 1944-2010. Xavier. IV. David, Michel, 1944-2010. Constant. V. Titre. VI. Titre : Baptiste. VII. Titre : Camille. VIII. Titre : Xavier. IX. Titre : Constant.

PS8557.A797A9 2014   C843'.6   C2013-942658-2
PS9557.A797A9 2014

Les Éditions Hurtubise bénéficient du soutien financier des institutions suivantes pour leurs activités d'édition :

- Conseil des Arts du Canada;
- Gouvernement du Canada par l'entremise du Fonds du livre du Canada (FLC);
- Société de développement des entreprises culturelles du Québec (SODEC);
- Gouvernement du Québec par l'entremise du programme de crédit d'impôt pour l'édition de livres.

Graphisme de la couverture : René St-Amand
Illustration de la couverture : Luc Normandin
Maquette intérieure et mise en pages : Andréa Joseph [pagexpress@videotron.ca]

Copyright © 2012, 2014 Éditions Hurtubise inc.

ISBN : 978-2-89723-389-1 (version imprimée)
ISBN : 978-2-89647-881-1 (version numérique PDF)
ISBN : 978-2-89647-882-8 (version numérique ePub)

Dépôt légal : 2e trimestre 2014
Bibliothèque et Archives nationales du Québec
Bibliothèque et Archives Canada

Diffusion-distribution au Canada :
Distribution HMH
1815, avenue De Lorimier
Montréal (Québec) H2K 3W6
www.distributionhmh.com

Diffusion-distribution en Europe :
Librairie du Québec/DNM
30, rue Gay-Lussac
75005 Paris FRANCE
www.librairieduquebec.fr

Imprimé au Canada
www.editionshurtubise.com

L'érable symbolise bien
La surnaturelle endurance
De cette âpre race de France
Qui pousse en plein sol canadien :
Robuste et féconde nourrice
Dont le flanc, tant de fois blessé,
Des rudes coups d'un fier passé
Porte l'illustre cicatrice.

Nérée Beauchemin
L'érable

Les principaux personnages

Anatole Blanchette: cultivateur et membre du conseil

Évariste Bourgeois: forgeron

Angèle Cloutier: veuve âgée d'une cinquantaine d'années, occupant le terrain voisin de la chapelle

Antonius Côté: cultivateur et membre du conseil

Télesphore et Alexandrine Dionne: propriétaires du magasin général et parents d'Angélique

Samuel Ellis: cultivateur âgé de 50 ans, époux de Bridget (également ménagère du curé) et président du conseil

Thomas Hyland: membre du conseil, tanneur, cultivateur et propriétaire de la scierie

Antonin Lemoyne: homme engagé de Xavier Beauchemin

Rang Saint-Paul

Hormidas Meilleur: facteur

Agénor Moreau: bedeau et père de Delphis

Eudore Valiquette: notaire nouvellement établi à Saint-Bernard-Abbé

Autres

Armand Beauchemin: cultivateur de Sainte-Monique, frère de Baptiste et époux d'Amanda

Mathilde Beauchemin: sœur de Baptiste, religieuse sous le nom de sœur Marie du Rosaire

Josaphat Désilets: curé de Saint-Bernard-Abbé

Amédée Durand: inspecteur scolaire

Sœur Émérentienne: sœur Grise, cousine de Laura Benoît

Anthime Lemire: organisateur conservateur dans le comté de Drummond-Arthabasca

Eugène Samson: docteur de Saint-Zéphirin

Chapitre 1

La dernière veillée

Le soleil se couchait derrière de lourds nuages plongeant progressivement les maisons du rang Saint-Jean dans l'ombre. Les eaux de la rivière Nicolet que longeait la petite route étroite et enneigée étaient figées dans un carcan de glace. De loin en loin, de la fumée s'élevait des cheminées des maisons, c'était le seul signe de vie en ce début de soirée hivernale.

Une *sleigh*, à peine éclairée par un fanal suspendu à l'avant, quitta la ferme de feu Baptiste Beauchemin. Le bruit des grelots de son attelage vint briser le silence pesant qui écrasait la campagne. Les derniers visiteurs se retiraient pour laisser à la famille du disparu le temps de se reposer un peu avant la longue soirée qui l'attendait.

— M'man veut pas venir manger, dit à voix basse Bernadette à sa sœur Camille qui était en train de vérifier si les deux pâtés à la viande qu'elle venait de sortir du four étaient suffisamment chauds.

La femme de Liam Connolly referma la porte du fourneau après y avoir remis les deux pâtés.

— Les tourtières sont pas encore prêtes, dit-elle à mi-voix. Va voir ce qu'Eugénie a à traîner en haut, je m'occupe de m'man. Dis-lui de descendre avec le petit. Le souper est presque prêt. De toute façon, les garçons sont à la veille de revenir des bâtiments.

La jeune institutrice de vingt ans monta à l'étage pour aller prévenir sa belle-sœur pendant que sa sœur s'approchait de la porte ouverte du salon.

La pièce n'était éclairée que par une lampe à huile et deux cierges à demi consumés, placés à la tête et au pied du cercueil posé sur des tréteaux. Baptiste Beauchemin y reposait depuis un peu plus de deux jours, en ce lendemain de Noël 1871. Avec sa disparition, Saint-Bernard-Abbé venait de perdre son premier habitant et celui à qui la mission devait son école et sa chapelle. Lourdement handicapé douze mois auparavant par ce que le docteur Samson avait appelé un «coup de sang», son départ n'en était pas moins inattendu pour les siens et son entourage.

Vêtue d'une robe noire, sa veuve était assise, seule, près de la dépouille de son mari, apparemment absente à tout ce qui l'entourait. La petite femme bien en chair aux traits tirés par la fatigue avait posé une main sur les mains jointes de son mari défunt.

— M'man, c'est le temps de venir manger, lui dit sa fille aînée en s'approchant d'elle.

— J'ai pas faim, fit Marie Beauchemin sans se donner la peine de tourner la tête vers elle.

La quinquagénaire «avait pris un coup de vieux», comme l'avait chuchoté sa bru à son mari, le matin même. Le départ de son compagnon de vie la laissait totalement désemparée. Les siens avaient du mal à reconnaître la maîtresse de maison aux idées très tranchées qui avait toujours dirigé sa maisonnée d'une main de fer.

— Écoutez, m'man, c'est pas en vous laissant mourir de faim que vous allez arranger quelque chose, reprit patiemment Camille. Vous avez rien mangé de la journée. Vous allez finir par tomber malade.

— Ça me dit rien de manger, répliqua sa mère dans un souffle.

— Il faut vous forcer, insista la jeune femme au visage rond dont les yeux bruns étaient largement cernés par la fatigue des derniers jours. Il y a encore toute la soirée et toute la nuit à veiller. Si vous mangez rien, vous allez vous évanouir. Soyez raisonnable, venez.

Marie Beauchemin finit par se lever et suivit sa fille aînée. Au moment où elles sortaient du salon, la porte de la cuisine d'été s'ouvrit sur Donat et Hubert de retour des bâtiments.

— On gèle tout rond dehors, déclara Donat en s'approchant du poêle. J'espère qu'on n'aura pas de neige demain, ajouta-t-il, apparemment inquiet.

— Il manquerait plus que ça, dit Bernadette.

— Je vous sers dans deux minutes, annonça Camille aux nouveaux arrivants.

— On va d'abord aller chercher une couple de brassées de bois dans la remise, dit Hubert. C'est pas le temps de laisser s'éteindre le poêle dans la cuisine d'été parce qu'on risque d'avoir encore pas mal de monde à soir.

Son frère l'accompagna dans la remise voisine et tous les deux revinrent les bras chargés de bûches qu'ils laissèrent tomber bruyamment dans chacun des coffres à bois placés près des poêles. Après s'être lavé les mains, les deux hommes prirent place à table. Leur mère s'était assise à l'extrémité habituellement occupée par leur père décédé. Durant la dernière année, elle avait dû s'installer là, près de son mari, pour le faire manger à chaque repas.

Bernadette descendit de l'étage des chambres, suivie de près par Eugénie portant Alexis dans ses bras.

— Elle était tellement fatiguée qu'elle s'était endormie avec le petit, expliqua Bernadette en s'approchant de Camille pour l'aider à servir le repas.

Camille lança un regard à la jeune femme au chignon noir qui venait d'installer son fils âgé d'un peu plus d'un an dans sa chaise haute dans l'intention de lui donner à manger. L'épouse de Donat arborait un visage fatigué que rien ne justifiait. Fidèle à son habitude d'en faire le moins possible, Eugénie s'était reposée sur ses belles-sœurs pour recevoir tous les gens venus offrir leurs condoléances. Elle avait trouvé le moyen de s'esquiver chaque fois qu'il avait fallu préparer et servir de la nourriture. Bref, elle avait su largement profiter du fait que sa belle-mère n'était pas en mesure de la houspiller pour disparaître très souvent dans sa chambre.

Marie récita le bénédicité, puis le souper se prit dans un silence que l'épuisement de tous, après deux nuits et trois jours de veille, expliquait aisément.

— Il y a personne avec votre père, dit soudain Marie au milieu du repas en esquissant le geste de se lever.

— Restez assise, m'man, intervint Donat. On va y aller dans cinq minutes. Il faut d'abord manger.

— Est-ce qu'on a tout ce qu'il faut pour la soirée? demanda Bernadette à sa sœur Camille.

— Avec le pain que j'ai fait à matin, on devrait être capables de se débrouiller. Emma est supposée apporter deux gâteaux. En plus, il nous reste encore des tartes.

Pendant cet échange, Hubert ne dit rien, se contentant de regarder sa mère qui avait peine à garder les yeux ouverts. Le jeune homme de vingt et un ans disait avoir quitté définitivement les frères de Saint-Joseph et n'était de retour à la maison paternelle que depuis quelques jours. Ce grand jeune homme bien découplé avait du mal à concevoir qu'il n'était revenu que pour assister au départ de son père.

— Bon, moi, je vais nettoyer un peu la cuisine d'été pendant que vous remettez de l'ordre ici dedans, déclara-t-il en se levant. Vous, m'man, vous devriez aller vous coucher une heure avant que le monde commence à arriver. Si vous faites pas ça, vous serez pas capable de veiller cette nuit.

Marie commença par refuser, mais devant l'insistance de ses enfants, elle finit par céder contre la promesse des siens de la réveiller dès que le premier visiteur se présenterait.

Elle disparut dans l'unique chambre du rez-de-chaussée, située au pied de l'escalier.

—Je pense que je vais faire la même chose, déclara Eugénie en essuyant le visage d'Alexis.

— Tu dois pas être si fatiguée que ça, intervint vivement sa belle-sœur Bernadette en lui tendant un linge. T'as fait un somme tout à l'heure. Donne-nous d'abord un coup de main à laver la vaisselle et à replacer la cuisine.

La jeune mère prit le linge à contrecœur et dut se mettre au travail. Pour sa part, son mari alla rejoindre son frère dans la cuisine d'été pour l'aider, laissant les femmes dans la cuisine d'hiver.

— Comment est-ce que les enfants se débrouillent sans toi ? demanda Bernadette à sa sœur aînée qui avait entrepris de laver la vaisselle.

— Ils risquent pas de mourir de faim, laissa tomber Camille. Ils ont du manger en masse et je peux compter sur Ann pour voir à ce que la maison soit pas trop à l'envers quand je vais revenir.

— Ça dérange pas trop Liam que tu restes à dormir ici dedans depuis la mort de p'pa ?

— Il comprend, se contenta de répondre Camille.

En fait, Liam Connolly comprenait surtout que Camille profitait de l'occasion pour l'éviter. Il n'acceptait pas du tout que la femme, qu'il avait épousée moins de deux mois auparavant, le repousse régulièrement quand il voulait l'obliger à accomplir son devoir conjugal. Il n'avait toujours pas compris en revanche qu'elle ne lui avait pas pardonné de l'avoir violée dès le premier soir de leur mariage. Si le veuf, père de quatre enfants, avait cherché une mère pour eux en l'épousant, il avait surtout désiré une femme capable de le satisfaire, ce qui était loin d'être le cas. Le manque d'enthousiasme évident de Camille pour tout ce qui touchait les relations physiques le frustrait au plus haut point.

L'après-midi même, il avait fait une courte apparition chez les Beauchemin avec les enfants. À la vue de ces derniers, Camille avait regretté d'avoir été obligée de gâcher involontairement le premier Noël qu'elle aurait dû passer avec eux. Elle les aimait comme s'ils étaient ses propres enfants.

La veille de Noël, quelques heures après le décès de Baptiste, Liam et ses enfants, en route pour la messe de minuit, s'étaient arrêtés quelques instants chez les Beauchemin pour offrir leurs condoléances aux membres de la famille. Liam, nouveau maître-chantre de la mission, ne pouvait rater cette cérémonie religieuse. Par ailleurs, les enfants avaient semblé bouleversés de constater à quel point cette mort faisait de la peine à leur mère adoptive. Rose et Ann, en particulier, s'étaient empressées de venir l'embrasser pour la consoler.

Le jour même, avant de retourner à la maison pour faire le train, Liam avait parlé à sa femme en aparté et lui avait pratiquement ordonné de venir coucher à la maison.

— Il y a pas de raison que tu couches ici quand ta maison est à une dizaine d'arpents, lui avait-il chuchoté, furieux.

— C'est la dernière nuit où je peux veiller mon père, s'était-elle bornée à dire, sans paraître impressionnée par sa colère. J'irai dormir chez nous après les funérailles, demain avant-midi.

— Et moi, là-dedans? avait-il fini par demander sèchement.

— Ben toi, t'attendras, avait-elle déclaré sur le même ton, révoltée par autant d'égoïsme.

Il l'avait quittée, incapable de dissimuler sa colère.

Camille revint à la réalité en entendant sa sœur lui parler.

— D'après toi, est-ce que Xavier a fait sa demande hier soir, comme il en avait l'intention? lui demanda Bernadette à voix basse.

— Ça me surprendrait pas mal. Il a passé la soirée avec nous autres, répondit Camille sur un ton neutre. Là, c'est vraiment pas le temps de parler de cette affaire-là. M'man en a déjà bien assez sur le dos sans ça.

Le mois précédent, le curé Désilets avait appris à Marie Beauchemin que son fils Xavier s'apprêtait à demander la main de Catherine Benoît, une fille-mère, objet de scandale dans Saint-Bernard-Abbé. Cette nouvelle avait donné lieu à une scène pénible entre la mère et le fils et ce dernier avait juré de ne plus remettre les pieds dans la maison de ses parents, tant et aussi longtemps que la jeune fille serait rejetée par les siens. Bien entendu, Xavier avait mis fin à sa bouderie la veille de Noël quand son beau-frère Rémi était venu lui apprendre la mort subite de son père. Depuis, il n'avait quitté la maison que pour aller soigner ses bêtes dans sa ferme du rang Sainte-Ursule, et aucun membre de la famille n'avait songé à l'interroger sur son intention de demander la main de sa jeune voisine.

Le bruit d'un attelage pénétrant dans la cour attira Bernadette à l'une des deux fenêtres de la cuisine d'hiver.

— Tiens, en parlant du loup, annonça-t-elle. V'là Xavier et Antonin qui arrivent.

Peu après, il y eut des bruits de pieds frappant la galerie pour faire tomber la neige des bottes, et la porte de la cuisine d'été s'ouvrit sur le jeune cultivateur et son homme engagé.

— Emma et Rémi s'en viennent, annonça Xavier en retirant son manteau et en le suspendant à un crochet derrière la porte. Ils sortaient de chez eux quand je suis passé devant leur maison.

— Avez-vous eu le temps de souper? demanda Camille aux nouveaux arrivants.

— Oui, on a mangé un reste de fricassée, lui répondit son frère.

Quelques instants plus tard, la porte s'ouvrit de nouveau pour livrer passage à Emma et à son mari.

— On a fait garder les deux petits par la femme de Tancrède Bélanger, déclara Rémi Lafond. Elle va s'en occuper jusqu'après le service, demain avant-midi.

— Il commence à neiger, dit Emma en secouant quelques flocons qui s'étaient déposés sur son manteau de drap gris. Où est m'man ?

— On l'a obligée à aller se reposer un peu, lui répondit Bernadette.

Tout le monde se regroupa dans la cuisine d'hiver. À la vue des six enfants de Baptiste et Marie Beauchemin, il était étonnant de constater qu'ils se ressemblaient par paire. Xavier et Hubert étaient grands, séduisants et plutôt costauds, le second avait étonnamment gagné en force depuis son retour à la ferme. Camille et Donat, les deux aînés, étaient plus trapus et dotés d'un visage rond assez agréable, comme l'était celui de leur père. Alors que Bernadette et Emma, la femme de Rémi Lafond, étaient deux jeunes femmes élancées aux traits particulièrement fins : l'une était brune alors que l'autre était la seule blonde de la famille.

— Est-ce qu'il y a quelque chose que je peux faire en attendant le monde ? demanda Emma, toujours aussi vaillante.

— Non, tout est prêt, l'informa Camille. Toi, tu ferais peut-être mieux de te ménager un peu dans ta situation.

La jeune femme blonde, même si elle était enceinte de son troisième enfant, était toujours la première au travail. Pendant que les quatre hommes allumaient leur pipe, les femmes se dirigèrent vers le salon et prirent place sur les chaises et les bancs disposés autour de la pièce.

~

Quand les premiers visiteurs apparurent peu après sept heures, Bernadette alla réveiller sa mère. Celle-ci n'avait retiré que ses souliers avant de s'enfouir sous les épaisses couvertures.

— M'man, le monde commence à arriver, lui chuchota-t-elle après avoir allumé la lampe de service sur la table de nuit. Vous levez-vous ?

Pendant un bref moment, Marie, les yeux ouverts, sembla perdue, se demandant où elle était exactement. Puis elle parut reprendre pied dans la réalité et elle s'empressa de s'activer. Du bout des doigts, elle vérifia l'état de son chignon poivre et sel et quitta sa chambre sur les talons de sa fille. Elle retrouva Angélina et Alcide Proulx dans le salon où Camille venait de les faire entrer en même temps que les voisins immédiats des Beauchemin, les Gariépy.

Quelques minutes plus tard, la porte s'ouvrit sur Armand Beauchemin et sa femme Amanda qui avaient été les premiers membres de la famille à se présenter à la maison la veille de Noël. Il était visible que le gros cultivateur de Sainte-Monique était passablement affecté par la perte de son frère cadet. Cependant, en cette dernière soirée de veillée au corps, sa femme et lui étaient accompagnés de deux sœurs Grises, sœur Marie du Rosaire et sœur Sainte-Anne. La première, une grande et grosse femme au geste impérieux et à la voix de stentor, était la sœur du disparu. Elle embrassa rapidement sa belle-sœur, ses neveux et ses nièces avant de s'emparer du meilleur siège du salon.

— Comment ça se fait que j'ai pas été avertie de la mort de ton père ? demanda-t-elle à Camille avec une voix remplie de reproches.

— Comment vouliez-vous qu'on vous prévienne, ma tante ? répondit l'aînée de la famille. Vous êtes à Sorel, c'est pas la porte à côté. J'ai pensé que mon oncle Armand irait vous chercher…

— Pantoute, ma petite fille. J'ai appris la nouvelle par hasard, déclara la religieuse assez fort pour être entendue par les autres membres de la famille regroupés dans le salon. J'avais prévu d'aller passer la semaine du jour de l'An chez ton oncle. Il m'a appris la mort de ton père quand je suis arrivée là avec ma compagne cet après-midi. Je te dis pas le choc que ça m'a fait. On a juste deux ans de différence…

— Il était bien malade, ma tante, dit Camille dans une vaine tentative pour endiguer le flot de paroles qui allait se déverser sur elle.

— Quand même! laissa sèchement tomber son interlocutrice.

Et la religieuse, une bavarde impénitente, se mit à raconter des souvenirs de jeunesse dans lesquels son frère défunt jouait un rôle.

— Vous m'excuserez, ma tante, je dois aller m'occuper du monde qui arrive, finit par lui dire Camille après quelques minutes d'écoute impatiente.

L'épouse de Liam Connolly attira sa sœur Emma à l'écart et lui demanda de se dévouer et de s'occuper un peu de leur tante de manière à ce qu'elle n'aille pas embêter leur mère avec son bavardage incessant.

Dans les minutes suivantes, la maison se remplit peu à peu de parents éloignés, de voisins et de connaissances venus offrir leurs condoléances à la famille en cette dernière veillée. Ce soir-là, Anselme Camirand et sa femme Françoise vinrent de Saint-Zéphirin en compagnie de leurs deux grands enfants. Les deux sœurs de Marie arrivèrent ensuite de Nicolet en même temps que les Boudreau et les Paquette.

Les syndics Samuel Ellis, Anatole Blanchette, Antonius Côté et Thomas Hyland se présentèrent aussi sur les lieux avec leur épouse, peu après Télesphore Dionne, le marchand général, accompagné de sa femme Alexandrine et de leur fille Angélique. Le facteur Hormidas Meilleur suivait la veuve Angèle Cloutier, et Liam Connolly pénétra dans la maison de ses beaux-parents au même moment que ces derniers.

En le voyant, Camille s'approcha de lui.

— Où sont les enfants? lui demanda-t-elle à voix basse.

— Je les ai laissés à la maison. Je me doutais qu'il y aurait ben du monde ici dedans à soir et ils auraient été une nuisance plus qu'autre chose. Ann s'en occupe.

Sur ces mots, il lui tourna le dos et se glissa tant bien que mal dans le salon pour saluer quelques parents de sa femme avant de retraiter dans la cuisine d'été où les hommes s'étaient déjà rassemblés.

Soudain, sœur Marie du Rosaire quitta sa chaise pour s'agenouiller au milieu du salon.

— On va dire un chapelet pour le salut de mon frère, déclara-t-elle sur un ton péremptoire ne donnant aucun choix aux personnes qui l'entouraient.

Elle attendit patiemment que les femmes s'agenouillent à côté d'elle. Les hommes présents dans la pièce se glissèrent dans la cuisine d'hiver et disparurent dans la cuisine d'été où Donat venait de sortir un cruchon de bagosse pour en servir aux visiteurs. Évidemment, Hormidas Meilleur fut le premier à demander une seconde rasade sous le prétexte qu'il devait combattre une bien vilaine grippe, ce qui fit sourire tous les gens de Saint-Bernard-Abbé qui connaissaient bien son goût pour l'alcool. En quelques minutes, un nuage de fumée se mit à flotter près du plafond, la plupart des invités ayant allumé leur pipe.

Hubert alla fermer la porte de communication pour que les conversations bruyantes de cette pièce ne troublent pas la prière récitée dans le salon et la cuisine d'hiver.

Xavier avait rejoint son oncle Armand et deux cousins Camirand avec qui il s'entretenait du prix offert par les compagnies forestières pour le bois qu'ils couperaient durant l'hiver. Un peu plus loin, Donat avait temporairement rangé le cruchon d'alcool et s'était joint à titre de plus jeune syndic de la mission aux autres membres du conseil.

— Demain matin, je vais venir à huit heures, lui déclara Anatole Blanchette, propriétaire du corbillard.

— Je vais venir avec lui pour visser le couvercle, intervint Thomas Hyland qui avait confectionné le cercueil en pin dans lequel reposait Baptiste Beauchemin.

— C'est ben correct, fit Donat. Le service est à neuf heures. Après ça, on va monter au cimetière de Sainte-Monique.

— Le curé Lanctôt était pas plus content qu'il faut qu'on vienne mettre p'pa dans le charnier de sa paroisse, intervint Xavier qui venait de s'approcher du groupe.

— Il a rien à dire, fit sèchement son frère aîné. Les Beauchemin ont un lot dans son cimetière. Il a pas le choix de le garder.

— Je pense que ce qu'il a moins aimé, c'est que je lui ai dit que p'pa serait pas enterré là, mais ici, dans notre nouveau cimetière, le printemps prochain.

— Il me semble qu'il devrait comprendre qu'on n'a pas encore trouvé le temps ni l'argent pour bâtir un charnier à Saint-Bernard, déclara Samuel Ellis. On est déjà endettés jusqu'au cou avec le jubé que monsieur le curé a voulu à tout prix faire construire cette année.

Les syndics présents hochèrent la tête. Le jubé imposé par le curé Désilets au début de l'automne allait peser lourd sur les finances de la mission. Comme le prêtre leur avait fait comprendre que sa construction était nécessaire pour que l'inspecteur délégué par monseigneur Laflèche fasse un rapport favorable à leur demande de devenir une paroisse, ils avaient accepté bien malgré eux cette lourde dépense. Cependant, ils avaient l'impression d'avoir été manipulés et cela les agaçait prodigieusement.

~

On frappa à la porte. Xavier quitta le groupe en faisant signe à son frère de ne pas bouger. Le jeune homme ne fut qu'à moitié surpris de découvrir sur le pas de la porte la famille Benoît au complet venue présenter ses respects aux Beauchemin. À Saint-Bernard-Abbé, comme dans toute la région, les inimitiés s'estompaient devant le deuil. À l'occasion de la mort de Léopold Benoît, un an et demi auparavant, pratiquement tous les habitants de la mission s'étaient déplacés pour venir prier au corps, même si la famille Benoît avait été mise à l'index à cause de la mauvaise réputation de Catherine.

Un bref silence accueillit l'entrée de Laura Benoît accompagnée de sa fille Catherine, de son fils Cyprien et de sa femme. Xavier leur souhaita la bienvenue, les remercia d'être venus et s'empressa de les débarrasser de leur manteau. Cyprien et Marie-Rose lui offrirent leurs condoléances du bout des lèvres. À les voir, il était évident qu'une antipathie naturelle les séparait. Le couple ne lui pardonnait pas d'être responsable du retour de Catherine à Saint-Bernard-Abbé. Si celle-ci n'avait pas été amoureuse de lui, elle serait demeurée à Montréal et les gens de la mission auraient fini par oublier qu'elle avait eu un enfant de leur homme engagé. De plus, Cyprien, un être fruste et rancunier, n'avait pas oublié que son jeune voisin l'avait sévèrement secoué l'année précédente et lui avait promis une raclée si jamais il le reprenait à lever la main sur sa sœur.

Les conversations un moment interrompues reprirent dès que Xavier eut entraîné les nouveaux arrivants dans la cuisine d'hiver. Celui-ci les précéda et leur ouvrit un chemin jusqu'au salon. Tous les quatre s'immobilisèrent un instant devant la dépouille de Baptiste Beauchemin pour une courte prière avant que le jeune homme les conduise jusqu'à sa mère, alors encadrée par Bernadette et Emma.

Marie ne sursauta même pas en les apercevant. Elle les remercia sans aucune chaleur d'être venus et échangea quelques mots avec eux. La veuve ne fit aucune allusion au fait que son fils cadet s'apprêtait à demander la main de Catherine. Xavier, les traits figés par la colère, se tenait sans rien dire près de la jeune fille, qui semblait profondément mal à l'aise. Dans cette pièce surpeuplée, au milieu du brouhaha des conversations échangées à mi-voix, il allait de soi que plusieurs surveillaient les Benoît du coin de l'œil.

L'arrivée du curé Désilets créa une heureuse diversion qui permit à Xavier de les entraîner un peu à l'écart.

Le prêtre âgé d'une quarantaine d'années compensait un front passablement dégarni par d'épais favoris poivre et sel. De taille moyenne, il avait de petits yeux noirs fureteurs dissimulés en partie par des lunettes à fine monture de métal.

Dès qu'il se présenta à l'entrée du salon, sœur Marie du Rosaire abandonna les dames avec qui elle s'entretenait depuis plusieurs minutes pour se porter à sa rencontre et se présenter.

— J'ignorais que monsieur Beauchemin avait une sœur chez les religieuses, dit le curé de Saint-Bernard-Abbé.

— Oui, monsieur le curé, et son garçon Hubert est chez les frères de Saint-Joseph, déclara fièrement Mathilde Beauchemin.

— Ah oui! fit Josaphat Désilets, surpris. Est-ce qu'il est ici?

— Hubert, viens donc ici une minute, fit la religieuse en faisant un signe de la main à son neveu qui s'apprêtait à aller rejoindre les hommes dans la pièce voisine.

— Oui, ma tante?

— Je viens de dire à monsieur le curé que t'étais chez les frères.

Hubert réalisa que sa tante ignorait qu'il avait quitté définitivement la communauté et il allait mettre les choses au point quand le prêtre l'apostropha avec autorité.

— Est-ce que je peux savoir, mon garçon, comment il se fait que tu portes pas ta soutane?

— Monsieur le curé, je dois vous…

— Est-ce que par hasard t'aurais honte de ton état de religieux?

— Non, monsieur le curé, j'ai pas ma soutane parce que je suis plus chez les frères, expliqua Hubert, un ton plus bas, bien conscient que plusieurs têtes s'étaient tournées vers eux pour savoir de quoi il s'agissait.

— Es-tu en train de me dire que ma paroisse a un défroqué? demanda Josaphat Désilets en montant le ton de sa voix.

— Pantoute, répondit sèchement Hubert à qui la moutarde commençait à monter au nez, j'ai jamais prononcé de vœux.

— Comment ça se fait que tu nous l'as pas dit? intervint sœur Marie du Rosaire, scandalisée.

— Parce que ça vous regarde pas, ma tante, répondit abruptement son neveu d'une voix cassante. Le seul que ça regarde, c'est moi, ajouta-t-il en visant clairement le prêtre qu'il dominait presque d'une tête.

Sur ces mots, le jeune homme fit demi-tour et se dirigea vers la cuisine d'été. Angélique Dionne, la fille unique du marchand général de Saint-Bernard-Abbé, l'intercepta avant qu'il passe dans la pièce voisine.

— T'as bien fait de les remettre à leur place, lui souffla la jeune fille à qui il n'avait parlé qu'en deux occasions depuis son retour à la ferme.

Angélique Dionne, sûre de son charme, lui proposa de s'asseoir quelques instants pour parler. Revenue chez ses parents depuis peu, après être demeurée plusieurs années auprès d'une vieille tante, la fille de Télesphore était dotée de magnifiques yeux bleus et d'une épaisse chevelure brune bouclée qui mettait en valeur ses traits fins. Dès qu'elle l'avait vue, quelques jours avant Noël, Bernadette Beauchemin avait tout de suite compris qu'elle se trouvait devant une concurrente au titre de plus belle fille de Saint-Bernard-Abbé.

Pour sa part, Hubert avait surtout fait la connaissance de la jeune fille lors d'une excursion en raquettes qui avait eu lieu la veille de Noël.

Le tête-à-tête entre les deux jeunes gens fut plutôt bref puisque sœur Marie du Rosaire venait de se charger de rassembler toutes les personnes installées dans les deux cuisines pour la récitation d'une prière que le curé Désilets s'apprêtait à prononcer. Les conversations se turent et tout le monde se mit à genoux pour se recueillir en pensant à Baptiste Beauchemin.

Un peu plus tard, Camille entraîna ses sœurs et sa belle-sœur Eugénie vers la cuisine d'hiver pour offrir de la nourriture aux visiteurs encore présents. Les femmes servirent non seulement les deux gâteaux d'Emma et les tartes cuisinées par Camille et Bernadette, mais aussi quelques mets apportés par des voisines charitables.

Vers dix heures et demie, après le départ du curé Désilets, les gens commencèrent à quitter les lieux en souhaitant bon courage aux parents du défunt. Constant Aubé, l'amoureux de Bernadette, partit l'un des derniers, au moment où il ne restait plus sur place que la parenté toute proche.

— Il vous reste pas mal de monde à coucher, dit-il à voix basse à la jeune institutrice. Si ça peut vous arranger, je peux toujours en héberger quelques-uns pour la nuit.

Bernadette s'empressa de transmettre son offre à ses oncles, tantes et cousins.

— Chez moi aussi, il y a de la place à coucher, s'empressa d'offrir Emma, qui demeurait au bout du rang.

Les gens sur place se consultèrent et déclinèrent ces offres. Ils avaient décidé de veiller le disparu durant la nuit. Ils allaient occuper les lits de la maison à tour de rôle, si besoin était.

Pour sa part, Liam Connolly attendit pour voir si son épouse avait changé d'idée et allait le suivre à la maison. Comme elle s'était mise à remettre la cuisine et le salon en ordre avec l'aide des autres femmes présentes, il endossa son manteau en cachant mal son mécontentement et rentra seul chez lui. Constant quitta la maison peu après en promettant à Bernadette d'être de retour très tôt le lendemain matin. Cette dernière le regarda par la fenêtre quitter la cour de la ferme en boitant, engoncé dans son épais manteau d'étoffe du pays.

D'un commun accord, on laissa s'éteindre le poêle de la cuisine d'été et on s'installa tant bien que mal dans le salon. Xavier sortit chercher du bois dans la remise pour alimenter le poêle et il s'attarda un long moment dans la cuisine. Camille s'en rendit compte et vint le retrouver.

Le jeune homme s'était versé une tasse de thé et était assis au bout de la table, solitaire, l'air si profondément malheureux que sa sœur se sentit obligée de venir le consoler.

— P'pa était bien malade depuis un an. C'est peut-être mieux qu'il soit parti comme ça, sans souffrir, lui dit-elle en s'assoyant près de lui.

— Je le sais ben, répliqua-t-il à voix basse. C'est pas ça, reprit son jeune frère en secouant la tête après un court silence. M'man lui a pas dit un mot. Rien. Elle a presque fait comme si elle avait pas été là.

— De qui est-ce que tu parles? lui demanda Camille, intriguée.

— De Catherine... Si elle pense que ça va m'empêcher de la marier, elle se trompe en blasphème, ajouta-t-il, l'air buté.

— Écoute, m'man est au bout du rouleau. Elle a presque pas dormi depuis trois jours. Donne-lui le temps de s'habituer à l'idée, reprit sa sœur d'une voix apaisante.

— Ça fait plus qu'un an que je la fréquente. Tu me feras pas croire qu'elle se doutait pas que je finirais par la demander en mariage, répliqua son frère.

— Tu la connais, elle est fière. C'est pas facile pour elle d'accepter dans la famille une fille comme ta Catherine. Le temps finira bien par arranger les choses.

Xavier se borna à secouer la tête et sa sœur le quitta pour retourner dans le salon où elle entreprit de convaincre sa mère d'aller dormir quelques heures.

— Allez vous coucher un peu, m'man. La nuit va être longue. J'irai vous réveiller tout à l'heure.

Marie finit par accepter d'aller s'étendre une heure ou deux. Après son départ, on résolut de se diviser en trois groupes, chacun assurant la veillée du corps durant trois heures.

— Moi, je veux pas rester debout en même temps que ma tante Mathilde, chuchota Bernadette à sa sœur aînée et à son frère Donat. J'ai pas envie de me faire étourdir pendant des heures en l'entendant me raconter sa vie.

— Dans ce cas-là, t'es mieux de monter te coucher tout de suite parce qu'elle vient de me dire qu'elle veut rester debout jusqu'à une heure du matin, lui conseilla son frère.

— Moi, je vais rester avec elle, sœur Sainte-Anne, mon oncle Armand et Emma, annonça Camille, malgré la fatigue.

Les gens venaient à peine de monter à l'étage pour se partager les lits disponibles que sœur Marie du Rosaire vint s'asseoir près de sa nièce.

— Je savais pas que ton frère Hubert était sorti de chez les frères, murmura-t-elle.

— ...

— Ça a dû faire tout un choc à ta mère, poursuivit la religieuse, non découragée par l'absence de réaction de son interlocutrice.

— Elle en a pas parlé, ma tante, se borna à dire Camille.

— Qu'est-ce que ton frère va faire?

— Il paraît qu'il va donner un coup de main à Donat. C'est pas l'ouvrage qui manque. Est-ce qu'on dit un chapelet, ma tante? demanda la jeune femme pour mettre un frein à la curiosité insatiable de la sœur Grise.

— C'est une bonne idée. On va prier pour ton père.

Un peu après une heure, Eugénie, Donat et d'autres parents vinrent prendre la relève. À voix basse, on décida de laisser dormir Marie encore quelques heures.

— Demandez à quelqu'un de venir me réveiller vers quatre heures, demanda Camille. À ce moment-là, je réveillerai m'man.

Elle retira discrètement ses souliers et entra dans la chambre de sa mère dont elle partageait le lit depuis la veille de Noël. Elle prit grand soin de ne faire aucun bruit et se glissa silencieusement sous les couvertures.

Les yeux ouverts dans le noir, elle songea d'abord à Liam dont la sécheresse de cœur ne cessait de la peiner. Lorsque Bernadette, en larmes, était venue la prévenir de la mort subite de leur père, son mari s'était contenté de dire :

— C'est aussi ben pour tout le monde. De toute façon, arrangé comme il l'était, il était plus utile à grand chose.

Durant les trois derniers jours, il n'avait fait que des visites sporadiques chez les Beauchemin, et jamais dans le but de lui apporter son soutien. Chaque fois, c'était pour l'inciter à revenir le plus tôt possible à la maison. Puis, sa pensée dériva vers Xavier et ses projets d'avenir avec Catherine. Bien sûr, le passé de la fille de Laura Benoît la choquait. Elle ne concevait pas qu'une jeune fille comme il faut ait manqué de principes au point d'être tombée enceinte sans être mariée. Cela allait trop à l'encontre de son éducation. Il n'existait pas de mots assez durs pour condamner un tel comportement... Par ailleurs, Xavier avait l'air de tellement l'aimer qu'il semblait prêt à surmonter tous les obstacles sur sa route pour la conduire au pied de l'autel. Il l'aimait sûrement plus que Liam ne l'aimait. Peut-être devrait-elle essayer de convaincre sa mère d'adoucir ses positions et de donner une chance au jeune couple...

Le sommeil l'emporta avant qu'elle prenne une décision.

Chapitre 2

Les funérailles

Camille se réveilla en sursaut en entendant des chuchotements de l'autre côté de la porte de la chambre à coucher. Elle se leva sans bruit et ouvrit la porte au moment où Bernadette s'apprêtait à frapper.

— Il est presque quatre heures, murmura la jeune fille. Je venais te réveiller. Est-ce que m'man dort encore?

— Je la réveille, se borna à lui répondre sa sœur en refermant la porte.

Camille alluma une lampe, ce qui eut pour effet de réveiller sa mère qui se fâcha un peu en apprenant l'heure.

— Mais vous m'avez laissée dormir presque toute la nuit, reprocha-t-elle à sa fille aînée.

— Il est même pas quatre heures, m'man, se défendit Camille. Vous aviez besoin de sommeil pour passer à travers ce qui vous attend.

Les deux femmes prirent quelques instants pour remettre un peu d'ordre dans leur tenue et dans leur coiffure avant de rejoindre ceux qui étaient descendus un peu après trois heures pour prendre la relève.

La porte de la cuisine d'été s'ouvrit soudainement sur Xavier, les épaules couvertes de neige.

— Bon, j'ai attelé. Je m'en retourne chez nous faire le train avec Antonin. Je vais revenir aussitôt que j'en aurai fini, annonça-t-il, ajoutant qu'il neigeait à plein ciel.

Un peu plus tard, Donat et Hubert quittèrent la maison à leur tour pour aller soigner les animaux pendant que les femmes qui ne dormaient pas venaient aider Camille et Bernadette à préparer le déjeuner. En quelques minutes, le poêle de la cuisine d'été fut rallumé. Quand tout fut prêt, on alla réveiller ceux qui se reposaient, et les gens, le visage chiffonné par une nuit trop brève, s'entassèrent autour des tables dans les deux cuisines. Tous levèrent la tête en entendant des bruits de bottes sur la galerie. La porte s'ouvrit sur Donat et Hubert, couverts de neige.

— Torrieu ! il est tombé au moins un pied de neige et ça a pas l'air de vouloir se calmer, déclara Donat en secouant sa casquette qu'il venait d'enlever. J'espère qu'on n'aura pas de misère à monter la côte du rang Sainte-Ursule.

— Au moins, il vente pas trop, ajouta Hubert en retirant son manteau.

Peu après, le bruit des grelots d'un attelage attira Bernadette à l'une des fenêtres. Elle vit son frère Xavier descendre de sa *sleigh*, déposer une épaisse couverture sur le dos de son cheval et se diriger vers la maison.

— De quoi a l'air le chemin ? se dépêcha de lui demander Donat.

— Ça peut encore aller, répondit celui dont la ferme était située à l'extrémité du rang Sainte-Ursule, juste après le long virage.

— Et la côte ? fit Hubert.

— Pour la descendre, il y a pas de problème, mais pour la monter tout à l'heure, ça va être une autre paire de manches.

À sept heures, bien avant le lever du soleil, tout le monde avait mangé et la vaisselle était lavée et rangée. Chacun s'empressa alors de faire sa toilette avant l'arrivée de Blanchette et de Hyland. Lorsque les gens étaient prêts, ils venaient se joindre à Marie déjà assise dans le salon près de la dépouille de son mari.

Comme prévu, dès huit heures, Anatole Blanchette vint immobiliser son grand traîneau devant la porte principale de la maison des Beauchemin. Le cocher avait pris la peine de doter la tête de son cheval d'un long plumet noir. Il se joignit à la famille en attendant Thomas Hyland. Celui-ci arriva quelques minutes plus tard en compagnie de son employé. Les deux hommes furent suivis par Liam Connolly et ses quatre enfants ainsi que par Constant Aubé et Rémi Lafond.

— Il faudrait penser à y aller si on veut arriver à temps à la chapelle, murmura Blanchette à Donat.

Ce dernier hocha la tête et s'approcha du cercueil dans lequel son père reposait.

— Faisons une dernière prière, se contenta-t-il de dire aux gens entassés dans la pièce.

Aussitôt, tous s'agenouillèrent et sœur Marie du Rosaire récita trois *Ave Maria*. Thomas Hyland et son employé s'avancèrent pour visser le couvercle de la bière. Camille et Bernadette s'empressèrent alors d'entraîner leur mère à l'extérieur de la pièce et toutes les autres personnes présentes les suivirent. Blanchette referma la porte du salon.

Quand Hyland sortit, tout le monde avait déjà endossé son manteau et chaussé ses bottes. On attendait patiemment dans les deux cuisines le signal du départ. Les trois fils de Baptiste Beauchemin et Rémi Lafond s'avancèrent pour soulever le cercueil. Emma leur ouvrit la porte de la façade et les quatre hommes allèrent déposer la dépouille sur le long traîneau-corbillard noir.

En quelques instants, la maison se vida et les gens s'entassèrent dans les *sleighs* et les traîneaux. Ann, l'aînée de Liam Connolly, fut la seule à demeurer sur place pour garder le petit Alexis. On avait retiré les couvertures déposées sur le dos des bêtes dont les naseaux fumaient. La neige tombait dru au point de cacher la rivière qui serpentait à une centaine de pieds à gauche de la route étroite.

Le convoi d'une dizaine de véhicules se mit lentement en marche derrière le corbillard. Il parcourut tout le rang Saint-Jean jusqu'au petit pont et s'engagea dans la côte abrupte du rang Sainte-Ursule. Les chevaux peinèrent et dérapèrent en quelques occasions avant de parvenir au sommet de la pente. La plupart des conducteurs durent descendre, la neige à mi-jambe, et s'emparer du mors de leur cheval pour inciter la bête à avancer. Quelques arpents plus loin, la chapelle, que le défunt était parvenu à faire ériger à force d'entêtement, se dressait fantomatique, comme reposant sur un épais linceul blanc.

La famille Beauchemin ne fut qu'à moitié étonnée de constater qu'un bon nombre de *sleighs* étaient déjà stationnées près du temple. Baptiste avait toujours été un homme fort apprécié pour son dévouement dans la petite communauté de Saint-Bernard-Abbé. Anatole Blanchette arrêta son long traîneau noir devant le parvis en bois que le vieil Agénor Moreau, le bedeau, venait tout juste de déneiger. Immédiatement, les quatre porteurs soulevèrent le cercueil et le transportèrent dans la chapelle où une quarantaine de personnes étaient déjà assises.

Samuel Ellis, le président du conseil des syndics, avait pensé à apporter les deux tréteaux qui avaient été utilisés lors du service funèbre du curé Ouellet au mois de juillet précédent. On déposa le cercueil sur les tréteaux devant la sainte table. La famille immédiate prit place dans les premiers bancs, face à l'autel. Camille laissa ses sœurs Bernadette et Emma s'asseoir de chaque côté de leur mère dans le premier banc. Elle s'agenouilla dans le second en compagnie de Liam et de ses trois enfants adoptifs. La petite Rose, sentant sa peine, se colla contre elle, ce qui contribua à la réconforter quelque peu.

Vêtu de ses ornements noirs, le curé Désilets traversa la nef, encadré par deux enfants de chœur, et entreprit de célébrer les funérailles du fondateur de Saint-Bernard-Abbé.

Lors de son bref sermon, le prêtre adressa des paroles de réconfort à la famille éprouvée et fit l'éloge du disparu. À la fin de la cérémonie, il endossa sa chape noire et accompagna la dépouille du défunt jusqu'à la porte de la chapelle. Sur son passage, les fidèles présents se levèrent en signe de respect.

La petite foule recueillie sur le parvis se dispersa rapidement. Les voisins et les connaissances venus assister à la cérémonie funèbre rentrèrent chez eux tandis qu'un petit convoi d'une demi-douzaine de *sleighs* et de berlots prenait la direction de Sainte-Monique, malgré la neige qui n'avait pas cessé de tomber.

Enfouis sous d'épaisses couvertures de fourrure, les gens tentaient de se protéger le mieux possible du froid, mais le mauvais état de la route rendait le déplacement lent et pénible.

Dès la seconde côte rencontrée par le cortège, le lourd corbillard de Blanchette s'immobilisa au milieu de la pente. Son cheval, pourtant un solide percheron, semblait incapable de la gravir. Aussitôt, tous les hommes du convoi se précipitèrent hors de leur véhicule pour prêter main-forte au cocher en difficulté.

— Mon Dieu! s'exclama Emma. Il manquerait plus qu'il arrive quelque chose à p'pa.

En fait, le corbillard s'était mis à reculer dangereusement et le cercueil en pin risquait de basculer hors du véhicule. Même s'ils étaient engoncés dans de lourds vêtements, les six hommes présents parvinrent à pousser le traîneau pendant qu'Anatole Blanchette tirait sa bête par le mors en l'injuriant abondamment. Quand le corbillard se retrouva sur le faîte, on poussa un soupir de soulagement et chacun regagna sa *sleigh* ou son berlot. Cependant, pour éviter un accident, on attendit que chaque véhicule ait escaladé la pente avant qu'un second se mette à monter.

On dut pousser le corbillard à deux autres reprises dans des côtes et le berlot d'Armand Beauchemin versa même dans un virage, au grand dam de son propriétaire qui ne put s'empêcher d'échapper un «Christ d'hiver!» retentissant en reprenant pied sur la route.

— Armand! Tu devrais avoir honte! se scandalisa sœur Marie du Rosaire qui l'avait entendu sacrer.

— Toi, achale-moi pas! répliqua son frère hors de lui, en secouant la neige qui le couvrait.

Quelques commentaires furent échangés entre les passagers des autres véhicules immobilisés derrière, attendant que le convoi reprenne la route.

— Ce serait pas arrivé si ma tante Mathilde et sœur Sainte-Anne avaient voyagé avec vous plutôt qu'avec Constant Aubé, dit Hubert, narquois, à son oncle après avoir aidé à remettre sur ses patins le lourd véhicule en bois.

— Pourquoi tu dis ça, mon garçon? demanda sœur Marie du Rosaire, qu'il n'avait pas vue s'approcher. Est-ce parce que je suis grosse? ajouta-t-elle, l'air mauvais.

— Pantoute, ma tante, se borna à répondre le jeune homme, tout de même satisfait de s'être un peu vengé de celle qui l'avait placé dans une situation gênante la veille lors de sa rencontre avec le curé Désilets.

Durant une bonne partie du trajet, Donat jura à mi-voix contre Anatole Blanchette dont le corbillard, en tête du convoi, ne cessait de s'embourber.

— Tu parles d'un sans-génie, répétait-il pour la troisième fois. Il me semble qu'il aurait dû penser à matin à atteler deux chevaux à son maudit corbillard. Il devait ben savoir que juste un suffirait pas à la besogne.

Finalement, tous les véhicules vinrent s'immobiliser à l'entrée du cimetière de Sainte-Monique un peu après midi.

— Qu'est-ce qu'on fait? demanda Xavier en descendant de sa *sleigh* pour rejoindre les autres hommes qui avaient mis pied à terre. Pour moi, monsieur le curé a pas fini de dîner.

— C'est vrai qu'on est en retard sans bon sens, fit remarquer sa mère qui avait pleuré tout au long du trajet.

— Je veux ben le croire, m'man, fit Donat, mais on est gelés ben dur et on n'est tout de même pas pour attendre que le curé Lanctôt ait fini de digérer pour venir s'occuper de p'pa.

— Qui va y aller? demanda Bernadette, qui grelottait depuis quelques minutes, même si son visage était en grande partie dissimulé derrière une épaisse écharpe de laine.

— On y va tous les trois, déclara Hubert en secouant la neige qui le couvrait.

Les trois fils de Baptiste Beauchemin montèrent l'escalier qui conduisait à la porte d'entrée de l'imposant presbytère. Donat sonna. La servante du curé Lanctôt, l'air toujours aussi revêche, vint leur ouvrir. En apercevant le corbillard stationné devant le presbytère, elle comprit immédiatement la raison de leur présence.

— Entrez, mais essayez de pas mettre de la neige partout sur mes planchers, leur dit-elle. Je vais prévenir monsieur le curé que vous êtes enfin arrivés. Il a pas fini de manger.

La dame se rendit au bout du couloir, entrouvrit une porte et dit quelques mots à voix basse. Il y eut un raclement de pattes de chaise sur le parquet en bois et un prêtre au ventre confortable, suivi par sa ménagère, vint vers les trois hommes demeurés près de la porte d'entrée.

— Je suppose que c'est pour Baptiste Beauchemin? leur demanda l'ecclésiastique.

— Oui, monsieur le curé, répondit Donat. On s'excuse pour le retard, mais avec la neige qui arrête pas de tomber, on a fait du mieux qu'on a pu.

— C'est correct, je vous attendais, dit le prêtre d'une voix étonnamment conciliante. Madame Lapierre, mettez le reste de mon dîner au réchaud. Je le mangerai en revenant, ajouta-t-il en se tournant vers sa servante et en tendant une main vers son épais manteau de chat sauvage suspendu à la patère près de la porte d'entrée.

Xavier aida le prêtre à endosser son manteau.

— C'est dommage, fit Louis-Georges Lanctôt, j'ai renvoyé mes deux enfants de chœur. Toi, dit-il en s'adressant à Hubert, tu vas aller chercher la croix, le bénitier et le goupillon qui ont été laissés dans la sacristie. Viens nous rejoindre au cimetière.

Hubert s'éclipsa pour aller chercher ce que le prêtre venait de lui demander pendant que ses deux frères accompagnaient le curé de Sainte-Monique à l'extérieur.

— Le bedeau avait pelleté un chemin jusqu'au charnier hier après-midi, déclara le prêtre en descendant l'escalier, mais j'ai bien peur qu'il soit disparu avec toute cette neige-là.

— C'est pas ben grave, monsieur le curé, répliqua Donat, on va se débrouiller.

En fait, le jeune homme avait du mal à reconnaître le prêtre irascible qui avait si souvent mis son père en colère. Durant les dernières années, les affrontements entre les deux hommes avaient été nombreux.

Jusqu'à l'automne précédent, Louis-Georges Lanctôt ne semblait pas prêt à pardonner à Baptiste Beauchemin de lui avoir fait perdre une cinquantaine de familles de sa paroisse en faisant signer une pétition pour la création de Saint-Bernard-Abbé. Inutile de préciser que les Beauchemin n'étaient guère en odeur de sainteté à Sainte-Monique depuis ce temps et le curé n'avait jamais raté une occasion de déblatérer contre eux. En cette froide matinée de décembre, tout laissait croire que la mort du cultivateur de Saint-Bernard-Abbé avait finalement eu raison de la rancune de l'ecclésiastique.

Dès l'apparition du prêtre, tous les gens du convoi se rassemblèrent près de lui.

— Ce sera pas long, dit le curé Lanctôt. L'un d'entre vous s'en vient avec la croix et le bénitier.

Hubert apparut peu après, portant les objets du culte demandés. Louis-Georges Lanctôt tendit la croix à Patrick, le fils de Liam Connolly âgé de onze ans, en lui disant de marcher lentement devant eux et il confia le bénitier et le goupillon à son frère cadet Duncan.

— On peut y aller, dit-il aux hommes prêts à soulever le cercueil. Vas-y, mon garçon, ordonna-t-il à Patrick en lui montrant le charnier au bout du cimetière.

Liam et Constant Aubé se joignirent aux trois frères Beauchemin et à leur beau-frère Rémi pour porter la bière devant le curé Lanctôt. Tout le monde avançait lentement, de la neige à mi-jambe.

— Ouvrez la porte. Il y a deux chevalets à l'intérieur, dit le prêtre à Armand Beauchemin.

Ce dernier sortit les deux trépieds et le cercueil fut posé dessus. Le curé fit signe aux gens de se rassembler autour de lui. Il aspergea la bière d'eau bénite et récita quelques prières avant de confier la dépouille de son ancien paroissien au charnier d'où elle ne serait retirée qu'au printemps suivant lorsque le sol serait dégelé.

Marie se serait effondrée si deux de ses fils ne l'avaient soutenue. Camille, stoïque, tapa doucement dans le dos de Bernadette qui ne pouvait s'arrêter de pleurer. Elle avait toujours été l'enfant préférée du disparu. La gorge étreinte par l'émotion, les autres membres de la famille regardèrent Constant Aubé, Liam Connolly et deux cousins soulever le cercueil pour le porter à l'intérieur du charnier. Quand ils sortirent de l'édicule, le bruit de la porte se refermant derrière eux eut quelque chose de définitif. Beaucoup de membres de la famille Beauchemin avaient l'impression qu'une partie importante de leur passé venait de disparaître avec l'homme qu'on avait déposé à l'intérieur.

Tous les gens présents quittèrent lentement les lieux. Parvenu à la sortie du cimetière, le curé Lanctôt eut quelques paroles d'encouragement pour la veuve et ses enfants avant d'attirer Donat à l'écart pour lui dire :

— Le printemps prochain, préviens-moi une semaine à l'avance quand t'auras l'intention de venir chercher ton père pour l'enterrer à Saint-Bernard.

— Oui, monsieur le curé. Et merci pour tout.

Le prêtre le salua de la tête et rentra dans son presbytère. Armand Beauchemin, dont la ferme était située à la sortie du village, invita tout le monde à venir se réchauffer à la maison avant de reprendre la route pour rentrer.

— Venez, notre homme engagé est supposé avoir chauffé la maison pendant qu'on était partis. On va ben trouver quelque chose à manger en cherchant un peu, insista-t-il, insensible au regard meurtrier que lui adressa sa femme de nature peu hospitalière.

Les gens étaient si frigorifiés après toutes ces heures passées sous la neige qu'ils s'empressèrent d'accepter l'invitation du gros homme.

— Seigneur, ma tante va bien en faire une maladie ! chuchota Bernadette à sa sœur Emma. Voir autant de monde débouler dans sa cuisine en même temps, elle va avoir une attaque.

— En tout cas, j'en connais un qui a pas fini d'en entendre parler, répliqua la femme de Rémi Lafond en songeant à son oncle Armand.

— Je pense que je vais rentrer, annonça Constant Aubé, gêné à l'idée d'aller s'imposer chez de parfaits inconnus.

— Fais pas le fou, lui ordonna Bernadette, t'es aussi gelé que tout le monde. En plus, c'est peut-être la seule chance de ta vie de voir de quoi a l'air le dedans de la maison de ma tante Amanda. Viens.

En montant dans la *sleigh* de Liam avec les trois enfants déjà enfouis sous la couverture de fourrure, Camille ne put s'empêcher de dire à son mari :

— J'espère juste que ma tante Mathilde s'est pas mis dans la tête de revenir s'installer quelques jours chez ma mère. Là, ce serait trop pour elle.

— C'est pas de nos affaires, laissa-t-il tomber, apparemment indifférent.

— Peut-être pas des tiennes, mais moi, ça me regarde, rétorqua-t-elle sèchement.

Il lui jeta un regard étonné, peu habitué à la voir se rebiffer aussi vite.

Les gens s'empressèrent d'envahir la maison ancestrale des Beauchemin, trop heureux de trouver enfin un peu de chaleur. Les manteaux furent empilés sur le lit de la chambre des maîtres.

Armand sortit un cruchon de bagosse pour réchauffer tout le monde pendant que les femmes offraient leur aide à la maîtresse de maison débordée par une telle affluence dans sa cuisine. De toute évidence, Amanda Beauchemin n'avait pas prévu recevoir beaucoup durant la période des fêtes puisqu'elle n'avait pratiquement rien cuisiné. Chez elle, les invités durent se contenter d'une soupe chaude et des restes d'un rôti de porc à qui ils eurent tôt fait de réserver un sort. Faute de mieux, on mangea beaucoup de pain trempé dans du sirop d'érable et on but de grandes tasses de thé noir pour faire descendre le tout.

Anatole Blanchette avait été le premier à s'éclipser après s'être restauré. Un peu plus tard, vers deux heures trente, Donat donna le signal du départ.

— Je pense que je vais aller passer quelques jours avec ta mère pour l'aider à remonter la pente, déclara sœur Marie du Rosaire à Camille, horrifiée par une telle éventualité.

— Ma pauvre ma tante, c'est dommage, ma mère vient justement d'accepter de venir passer la semaine chez nous pour se changer les idées, mentit Camille sans vergogne.

— Si c'est comme ça, je pense que je vais rester chez ton oncle Armand, fit la religieuse, dépitée.

Liam avait assisté à toute la scène sans rien dire. Dès que Mathilde Beauchemin se fut un peu éloignée, il ne put s'empêcher de lui demander :

— C'est pas vrai ! J'espère que t'as pas invité ta mère chez nous ?

— Inquiète-toi pas, répondit sa femme. Elle viendra pas te déranger. C'était juste pour que ma tante vienne pas l'encombrer.

Les gens quittèrent peu à peu la grande maison d'Armand Beauchemin après avoir remercié leurs hôtes. Marie endossa son manteau à son tour et s'approcha de sa fille Camille.

— Dis donc, toi, l'apostropha-t-elle à voix basse, la prochaine fois que tu conteras une menterie, avertis-moi.

— Pourquoi vous me dites ça, m'man ? s'étonna sa fille aînée.

— Ta tante Mathilde avait l'air bien déçue de pas pouvoir revenir rester à la maison une couple de jours.

— Je peux aller lui dire que vous avez changé d'idée et que vous aimez mieux rester chez vous pour la recevoir, si vous le voulez, plaisanta Camille.

— Laisse faire, je pense que t'as eu une bonne idée. Je suis pas pantoute d'humeur à l'endurer.

Eugénie et sa belle-mère montèrent avec Donat. Camille alla rejoindre Liam et les enfants, qui l'attendaient déjà dans la *sleigh*. Hubert aurait bien aimé faire le trajet avec Xavier à qui il n'avait guère eu l'occasion de parler depuis son retour à la maison, mais sa mère, malgré son chagrin, avait encore l'œil. Quand elle vit Bernadette s'apprêter à monter dans la *sleigh* de son amoureux, elle ordonna à son fils de monter avec eux.

— Une vraie tête folle ! ne put-elle s'empêcher de dire à Donat. Comme si ça se faisait de voyager toute seule avec un homme, sans chaperon.

Heureusement, la neige avait cessé de tomber durant le repas improvisé chez Armand Beauchemin et le retour s'annonçait tout de même un peu moins périlleux que l'aller.

— J'espère que Blanchette a pas eu de problème avec son traîneau sur le chemin, dit Donat à sa mère. Tout seul dans une côte, ça peut être compliqué s'il reste coincé.

— De toute manière, il est parti il y a juste une heure, lui fit remarquer sa femme. S'il est pris quelque part, on va le rencontrer et vous allez être capables de l'aider.

Toutefois, tout laissa croire que le lourd traîneau noir du cultivateur du rang Saint-Paul était parvenu à bon port parce qu'on ne le rencontra pas en cours de route.

Alors que Constant laissait Bernadette et son frère Hubert devant leur porte, il leur suggéra :

— Peut-être que ce serait une bonne idée de ranger au grenier le fauteuil roulant de votre père. Le voir continuellement dans la place va être pas mal difficile pour votre mère.

— T'as raison, l'approuva l'institutrice, on va s'en occuper en entrant.

— Si vous avez besoin de quelque chose, gênez-vous pas, leur offrit le meunier. Jusqu'à samedi, j'ai pas l'intention de bouger de la maison. J'ai des bottes à faire.

— Parles-tu des bottes neuves de la belle Angélique ? lui demanda Bernadette, toujours taraudée par la jalousie.

— Non, elle a eu ses bottes la veille de Noël. Elle tenait absolument à les étrenner à la messe de minuit, tint à lui préciser Constant.

Quelques minutes plus tard, Liam Connolly immobilisait sa *sleigh* devant la galerie des Beauchemin au moment où Constant rentrait chez lui. Il ne se donna pas la peine de descendre ; Camille alla rapidement chercher Ann et toute la famille rentra à la maison.

Ce soir-là, Marie Beauchemin sembla retrouver toute son énergie, malgré son épuisement. Elle houspilla sa bru et Bernadette pour que la literie de tous les lits soit changée avant même que le souper soit sur le feu.

— Voyons, m'man, il y a rien qui presse, se rebiffa Bernadette qui ressentait durement le manque de sommeil des derniers jours.

— Les hommes sont déjà aux bâtiments à soigner les animaux. Nous autres, on doit remettre la maison d'aplomb. Il est pas question qu'on couche dans des lits où tout un chacun est venu dormir depuis trois jours.

Déjà, Donat et Hubert s'étaient empressés de faire disparaître le fauteuil roulant ainsi que les deux tréteaux sur lesquels le cercueil de leur père avait été posé. Bernadette avait fait de même avec les restes des cierges.

Ce soir-là, le souper se prit en silence. Subitement, on réalisait que le père ne viendrait plus jamais occuper sa place habituelle au bout de la table et l'atmosphère en était appesantie.

Après le repas, les femmes remirent de l'ordre dans la maison pendant que Donat et Hubert se chargeaient du déneigement, ce qui les occupa une bonne partie de la veillée. À leur retour à la maison, ils étaient si fatigués qu'ils allèrent se coucher, même s'il était à peine neuf heures. Eugénie, Bernadette et sa mère décidèrent de les imiter.

Comme il en avait pris l'habitude depuis l'infarctus de son père, Donat remonta le mécanisme de l'horloge et déposa dans le poêle deux grosses bûches d'érable alors que son frère et sa sœur montaient l'escalier conduisant aux chambres. Eugénie les suivit de près après avoir recommandé à son mari de ne pas faire de bruit en venant la rejoindre pour ne pas réveiller Alexis.

Pour la première fois depuis la mort de Baptiste, Marie se retrouva seule dans son lit. Depuis la veille de Noël, Camille l'avait partagé avec elle. Elle souffla sa lampe après s'être étendue sur le côté gauche de la paillasse, comme si son mari était encore là, à sa place habituelle. Elle pleura durant de longues minutes, seule dans le noir, et le sommeil finit par l'emporter.

Dans la chambre bleue, au-dessus d'elle, Donat avait rejoint sa femme. Eugénie l'attendait, beaucoup moins fatiguée que lui. La petite femme au chignon noir s'était beaucoup ménagée durant les derniers jours, comme à son habitude. Dès qu'elle sentit son mari près d'elle, elle ne put s'empêcher de lui chuchoter :

— J'espère que ta mère va comprendre que la grande chambre du bas nous revient à cette heure. On est trois tassés sans bon sens ici dedans. Elle est toute seule dans la grande chambre.

— Tu vas au moins laisser la place du père se refroidir avant de l'achaler avec ça, j'espère ? dit Donat en se soulevant sur un coude.

— Bien oui.

— Dans ce cas-là, il y a rien qui presse. Là, j'en peux plus. Laisse-moi dormir tranquillement.

Deux fermes plus loin, Liam Connolly venait de terminer le déneigement de sa portion de la route et il rentra dans la maison après avoir dételé et soigné son cheval. Il avait espéré que sa femme l'ait attendu avant de se mettre au lit, mais il n'en était rien. Camille dormait déjà profondément depuis une heure quand il retira son manteau et ses bottes. La jeune femme avait dormi à peine trois heures par nuit les trois derniers jours et elle avait travaillé sans relâche pour nourrir tous les visiteurs.

Liam mit du bois dans le poêle avant de se diriger vers leur chambre à coucher. Il ne prit aucune précaution pour ne pas réveiller Camille. Il se déshabilla rapidement et se glissa sous les épaisses couvertures. Incapable de se retenir, il l'attira à lui avec une certaine brusquerie. Sa femme était si épuisée qu'elle ne se réveilla à moitié que lorsqu'il entreprit de lui faire l'amour avec sa brutalité habituelle. Elle ne réagit pas et attendit qu'il en ait fini avant de lui dire sur un ton lourd de reproches :

— T'aurais pas pu attendre que je sois moins fatiguée, non ?

— Je commence à te connaître, Camille Beauchemin, rétorqua-t-il en se tournant de l'autre côté, satisfait d'être parvenu à ses fins, tu te serais encore trouvé une défaite.

La jeune femme ne se donna pas la peine de répliquer. Elle se leva péniblement et sortit de la pièce pour aller faire un brin de toilette. Quand elle rentra dans la chambre, elle fut accueillie par les ronflements sonores de celui qu'elle avait épousé à peine deux mois auparavant.

Chapitre 3

La vie après Baptiste

Le lendemain, la vie reprit son cours tant bien que mal chez les Beauchemin. Donat et Hubert retournèrent bûcher dans le bois après le déjeuner alors que Marie tentait de surmonter son chagrin en reprenant le contrôle de ce qu'elle appelait « sa maisonnée ».

— À matin, il va falloir faire du pain. Il en reste presque plus dans la huche, dit-elle à Eugénie et Bernadette. Je vais m'en occuper. Toi, Bernadette, tu vas faire le lavage et étendre le linge dans la cuisine d'été. Pendant ce temps-là, Eugénie, tu vas t'occuper du ménage des chambres. Ça a pas d'allure, la maison est tout à l'envers.

— Mais, madame Beauchemin, c'est pas nécessaire de tout faire le même jour, fit sa bru d'une voix geignarde.

— Demain, on va faire le ménage en bas et il va falloir cuisiner pour le jour de l'An.

— Pourquoi, m'man? lui demanda Bernadette. Avez-vous l'intention d'inviter du monde?

— Non, on est en deuil. Mais on va tout de même recevoir Camille, Emma et Xavier avec Antonin. Le garde-manger est presque vide. Il va falloir se grouiller.

Cette dernière précision mit fin à toute contestation et les trois femmes se mirent au travail. Si Bernadette avait remarqué, la veille, à quel point sa mère avait vieilli depuis le départ de son père – des mèches blanches étaient apparues dans son chignon et sur ses tempes et de nouvelles rides sillonnaient son front –, cela n'avait en rien atténué son caractère déterminé de maîtresse de maison.

La jeune institutrice alla chercher les deux cuves et la planche à laver qu'elle posa sur un banc. Elle remplit les cuves d'eau chaude tirée du réservoir du poêle. Elle agita un peu de bleu à laver dans l'une des cuves avant de trier les vêtements sales de la famille et de se mettre à les frotter vigoureusement sur la planche après les avoir enduits de savon. Dès qu'un certain nombre de vêtements étaient lavés et rincés, elle quittait la cuisine d'hiver pour aller les étendre dans la cuisine d'été où des cordes avaient été préalablement tendues.

— Mets-toi une veste sur le dos quand tu vas de l'autre côté, lui ordonna sa mère quand elle la vit rentrer. On gèle dans la cuisine d'été, tu vas attraper ton coup de mort. Avec tout ce qui nous arrive, on n'a pas besoin de ça, ajouta-t-elle.

— Avez-vous déjà fini de préparer votre pâte à pain ? lui demanda la jeune fille.

— Oui, j'attends juste qu'elle lève. Là, je vais aller faire le ménage du salon avant de commencer à préparer le dîner.

— Je traînerai pas avec le lavage, lui promit sa fille.

— Parlant de traîner, reprit sa mère, où est passé le fauteuil de ton père ? Je l'ai pas vu nulle part.

— Hubert est allé le porter dans le grenier, m'man. C'est une idée de Constant. Il trouvait que ça vous ferait de la peine pour rien si vous deviez le voir tout le temps.

Marie ravala sa salive et ses yeux s'embuèrent. Elle finit tout de même par dire, la voix un peu changée :

— C'est une bonne idée, je trouve que ce garçon-là est pas mal délicat.

Bernadette hocha la tête. Sa mère avait raison. Constant boitait et n'était peut-être pas le plus beau, mais il était attentionné et jamais à court de ressources. De plus, il fallait reconnaître que le jeune meunier de Saint-Bernard-Abbé était un homme intéressant qui possédait plus d'une corde à son arc. Elle n'était pas encore certaine de l'aimer, mais elle n'acceptait pas qu'une autre fille cherche à l'attirer dans ses filets. En admettant cela, elle songeait surtout à la belle Angélique Dionne dont elle se méfiait particulièrement. La fille des propriétaires du magasin général lui semblait tourner un peu trop autour de son cavalier, et cela l'énervait au plus haut point. D'accord, Constant ne lui avait encore donné aucune raison précise d'être jalouse, mais elle l'était tout de même.

❦

Deux fermes plus loin, après le dîner, Liam Connolly avait exigé que ses deux fils le suivent dans la forêt au bout de sa terre pour l'aider à charger le bois débité durant les derniers jours. Camille, demeurée seule à la maison avec Ann et Rose, avait entrepris de regarnir le garde-manger mis à mal durant ses trois jours d'absence.

— On n'est tout de même pas pour se priver de manger durant les fêtes, dit-elle à ses deux filles adoptives en s'efforçant de mettre dans sa voix une joyeuse animation. Il nous reste quatre jours avant le jour de l'An, on a amplement le temps de faire à manger.

— P'pa trouve qu'on gaspille bien trop en manger, laissa tomber Ann.

— Et toi, qu'est-ce que t'en penses? lui demanda Camille en s'essuyant les mains sur son tablier.

— Je trouve qu'on mange bien, répondit l'adolescente sans la moindre hésitation.

— Moi aussi, ajouta la petite Rose du haut de ses six ans.

— C'était pas comme ça quand m'man vivait, poursuivit l'adolescente sur un ton attristé. Chaque fois qu'elle faisait une tarte ou un gâteau, p'pa s'enrageait après elle et la faisait pleurer.

— Ben, mes petites filles, c'est pas comme ça que ça va se passer avec moi, déclara Camille sur un ton décidé.

Si vous voulez dire comme moi, on n'en fera pas un drame et on va continuer comme avant. On ne se laissera pas mourir de faim pour faire plaisir à votre père.

Un éclat de rire des deux sœurs salua cette phrase de celle qu'elles considéraient comme leur confidente.

Depuis son mariage célébré à la fin du mois d'octobre précédent, la jeune femme avait découvert que son mari avait tendance à être brutal autant qu'avaricieux. Pendant un an, elle était venue aider Ann à cuisiner et jamais elle ne l'avait entendu se plaindre que cela lui coûtait trop cher. Soudain, voilà qu'il trouvait que les provisions disparaissaient trop rapidement. Durant un instant, elle se demanda comment sa défunte femme avait pu supporter un tel homme. En tout cas, il allait trouver à qui parler s'il entendait commencer à rationner les siens. Elle venait d'une famille où, sans être riche, on mangeait à sa faim tous les jours.

— Pour moi, sa Julia était une sainte femme, murmurat-elle dès qu'elle se retrouva seule dans la cuisine en train de placer ses boules de pâte à pain dans des moules avant de les déposer dans le fourneau.

Un bruit de grelots attira Rose à l'une des deux fenêtres de la cuisine.

— Il y a quelqu'un qui arrive, Camille, dit la gamine tout excitée.

— C'est un homme, précisa Ann, qui venait de rejoindre sa petite sœur à la fenêtre. Je le connais pas.

— Va lui ouvrir, lui dit Camille. Si c'est un *peddler*, dis-lui qu'on n'a besoin de rien.

L'homme frappa à la porte et l'adolescente alla lui répondre. On entendit des voix et la fille de Liam revint dans la cuisine, suivie par un petit homme engoncé dans un épais manteau de fourrure qui s'immobilisa sur le pas de la porte, la figure rougie par le froid et fendue d'un large sourire.

— Camille, il dit qu'il est l'oncle de p'pa, annonça Ann à la jeune femme.

— Bonjour, fit l'inconnu. Tu me connais pas, je suis Paddy Connolly, l'oncle de ton mari.

Stupéfaite, la jeune femme demeura un bref moment sans voix, hésitant sur le comportement à adopter. Puis elle s'avança rapidement vers le nouvel arrivant pour lui souhaiter la bienvenue et le prier d'enlever son manteau. L'homme s'exécuta volontiers et retira ses bottes. Ensuite, il empoigna son hôtesse par les deux épaules et l'embrassa sans façon sur les deux joues en manifestant une bonne humeur communicative.

— Venez vous réchauffer proche du poêle, l'invita Camille, tout de même un peu surprise par une telle familiarité de la part de quelqu'un qu'elle ne connaissait pas cinq minutes auparavant. Vous devez être gelé.

— C'est pas si pire, déclara l'oncle en prenant place dans l'une des deux chaises berçantes placées près du poêle.

Paddy Connolly était un petit homme âgé d'une cinquantaine d'années, bien en chair et doté d'un visage rubicond encadré par de larges favoris blancs. Il était vêtu d'une longue jaquette noire passée sur une veste de satin gris perle assez élégante. Une chaîne en or barrait son ventre confortable. Il avait des petits yeux gris et vifs dissimulés en partie sous d'épais sourcils. Il possédait surtout une voix de stentor et la timidité ne semblait pas faire partie de ses faiblesses.

— Voulez-vous boire une tasse de thé? lui offrit Camille, alors que Rose et Ann demeuraient à l'écart.

Elles regardaient avec curiosité cet étranger qui se disait l'oncle de leur père.

— Avec plaisir. Est-ce que ce sont les enfants de mon neveu? demanda Paddy Connolly en examinant les deux filles de Liam.

— Oui, Ann est l'aînée et Rose la cadette, répondit Camille. Il a aussi deux garçons, Duncan et Patrick, qui ont dix et onze ans.

— *God*, que le temps passe vite ! déplora le visiteur. La dernière fois que j'ai vu Liam, c'était à ses premières noces. J'aurais ben aimé venir à vos noces cet automne, mais j'ai pas pu.

— C'est pas grave, monsieur Connolly, fit la jeune femme. On fait pas toujours ce qu'on veut dans la vie.

— À qui le dis-tu, l'approuva-t-il.

Un long silence assez gênant s'installa dans la cuisine, comme si tout avait été dit entre ces inconnus. Finalement, l'épouse de Liam Connolly, mal à l'aise, demanda au visiteur :

— Êtes-vous l'un des deux oncles de Liam qui restent à Montréal ?

— En plein ça, mon frère Glen est mort à la fin de l'été passé, et il m'a fait promettre de venir voir Liam parce qu'il est le seul Connolly qui reste, à part moi, ben entendu.

— Vous êtes pas marié ?

— Non, j'ai toujours été vieux garçon, comme mon frère. Il faut croire qu'on n'avait pas le caractère qu'il faut pour qu'une femme nous endure, ajouta-t-il avec un gros rire communicatif.

— Et si je comprends bien, vous venez tenir votre promesse, reprit Camille. Ann, sers donc à ton grand-oncle une pointe de tarte aux raisins, dit-elle en se tournant vers l'adolescente qui écoutait sans rien dire depuis un bon moment.

Ann alla chercher une tarte dans le garde-manger, en découpa un morceau qu'elle déposa sur une assiette et l'apporta au visiteur qui ne se fit pas prier pour le manger.

— C'est toi qui fais aussi ben à manger ? demanda-t-il à Camille.

— Non, c'est Ann.

— *God*! Ça va faire ben vite une fille bonne à marier, dit Paddy avec un sourire.

Cette remarque fit rougir l'adolescente qui s'empressa d'aller ranger la tarte.

— Est-ce que vous restez toujours à Montréal? lui demanda Camille, curieuse.

— Certain.

— Travaillez-vous encore?

— Non, j'ai arrêté cet automne. J'avais plus le goût de continuer après la mort de mon frère. On était dans le commerce du fer depuis plus que trente ans, précisa-t-il. Il était temps que je vende ma *business* pour me reposer un peu. C'est ben beau faire de l'argent, mais il faut prendre le temps de vivre aussi.

— Vous avez bien raison, admit sa nièce par alliance du bout des lèvres.

— Ça fait que hier matin, en me levant, je me suis dit qu'il était temps que je vienne voir Liam, sa nouvelle femme et ses enfants. J'ai couché à Sorel et me v'là.

— Je suis certaine que ça va faire plaisir à votre neveu, mentit Camille, qui ne savait pas vraiment quel accueil son mari réserverait à ce vieil oncle qui ne s'était jamais soucié de son sort ni de celui de sa famille.

— Est-ce que tu penses que ce serait trop te demander que de coucher chez vous à soir? s'enquit l'oncle.

— C'est certain qu'on va vous garder à coucher, lui promit la maîtresse de maison, prise de court par la requête.

— Si c'est comme ça, je vais aller dételer.

— Il y a de la place dans l'écurie pour votre cheval.

Paddy Connolly se leva et endossa son manteau avant de sortir s'occuper de sa bête. Dès qu'il fut dehors, Camille envoya Ann changer la literie du lit de Rose.

— Tu vas coucher avec ta grande sœur, à soir, la prévint-elle. Tu vas prêter ton lit à l'oncle de ton père.

Quelques minutes plus tard, l'invité rentra dans la maison en portant une petite valise.

— Vous pouvez suivre Ann en haut, monsieur Connolly, lui annonça Camille. Ann vous a préparé une chambre. Installez-vous. Liam devrait pas tarder à rentrer avec les garçons.

À la fin de l'après-midi, Camille entendit Liam et ses fils pénétrer dans la cour de la ferme. Par la fenêtre, elle vit son mari immobiliser le traîneau surchargé de billes de bois devant la porte de la remise. Il entreprit ensuite de dételer son cheval pour l'entraîner vers l'écurie.

— Est-ce que tu veux que j'aille prévenir p'pa qu'on a de la visite ? lui demanda Ann.

— C'est pas nécessaire, fit Camille d'une voix neutre en adressant un sourire à Paddy Connolly qui était parvenu à amadouer Rose avec qui il parlait. Il va bien voir qu'il y a un cheval dans l'écurie.

De fait, quand Liam poussa la porte de la maison moins de cinq minutes plus tard, il s'enquit avec humeur :

— Veux-tu ben me dire à qui est le cheval qui est dans l'écurie ?

— À notre visite, se borna à répondre sa femme.

Liam s'arrêta sur le seuil et mit un bon moment avant de reconnaître son oncle qu'il n'avait pas vu depuis près de quinze ans.

— Calvas ! ça parle au diable ! Si c'est pas mon oncle Paddy.

— En chair et en os, mon garçon, déclara le petit homme en quittant sa chaise pour aller à la rencontre du maître de la maison.

— Savez-vous qu'un peu plus et je vous reconnaissais pas pantoute, ajouta Liam en s'avançant à son tour pour lui serrer la main.

— Viens pas me dire, toi, que j'ai vieilli à ce point-là, plaisanta le visiteur.

— Pantoute, mon oncle.

— Comme tu vois, j'étais pas à plaindre. Je me fais gâter par toutes les femmes de la maison depuis que je suis arrivé.

— Dis donc aux garçons d'entrer se réchauffer, suggéra Camille à son mari. T'as bien le temps de jaser un peu avec la visite avant d'aller faire ton train.

— Beau dommage! fit Liam avec une bonne humeur forcée en ouvrant la porte pour crier à Patrick et Duncan d'entrer.

Ses deux fils obéirent et il les présenta à son oncle avant d'accepter la tasse de thé que sa femme venait de lui verser.

Camille sentait qu'il y avait quelque chose de peu naturel dans l'enthousiasme manifesté par son mari. Ce dernier s'assit dans l'autre chaise berçante sans prendre la peine de retirer son manteau. Il prit des nouvelles de son oncle Glen. La nouvelle de sa mort récente sembla le peiner passablement, ce qui était plutôt étrange de la part d'un neveu à qui le disparu n'avait pas donné de nouvelles depuis une quinzaine d'années.

Profitant d'une courte pause dans les échanges entre l'oncle et le neveu, Camille annonça à son mari que son oncle avait accepté de coucher chez eux ce soir-là.

— Je vais même rester une couple de jours de plus pour fêter le jour de l'An avec vous autres si vous m'invitez, dit Paddy Connolly avec un sans-gêne renversant. C'est assez rare que je retrouve de la famille, je vais prendre le temps d'en profiter un peu.

— Bien sûr que vous êtes invité, monsieur Connolly, s'empressa de lui dire sa nièce par alliance.

— Tu vas me faire le plaisir d'abord d'arrêter de m'appeler monsieur Connolly. Appelle-moi mon oncle, lui ordonna-t-il, jovial, en se tournant vers elle.

— C'est correct, mon oncle.

Durant quelques minutes, l'invité monopolisa l'attention de tous les membres de la famille en racontant comment son frère et lui étaient devenus des membres plus que respectés de la communauté irlandaise de Montréal.

— Ton oncle et moi, on a brassé de ben grosses affaires. On s'est fait un nom en passant des gros contrats de fourniture avec les compagnies de chemins de fer, déclara le petit homme, sur un ton avantageux, les pouces passés dans les entournures de son gilet. À Montréal, tu peux demander à n'importe qui qui sont Paddy et Glen Connolly, on est connus comme Barabbas dans la Passion, ajouta-t-il, l'air suffisant.

— Mais pendant que vous êtes pas là, qui s'occupe de vos affaires, mon oncle? lui demanda un Liam nettement impressionné.

— Personne. Comme je venais de le dire à ta femme, après la mort de ton oncle Glen, j'avais plus le goût pantoute de continuer à faire des affaires. J'ai vendu ma *business*. J'ai tellement d'argent que je vivrai jamais assez vieux pour en dépenser même la moitié. Là, j'ai gardé juste cinq maisons et j'ai demandé à mon notaire de voir s'il pourrait pas les vendre un bon prix, prit-il soin d'ajouter.

— Qu'est-ce que vous faites à cette heure?

— Je me repose, affirma le petit homme, je profite des dernières années de ma vie.

— Vous faites bien, mon oncle, l'approuva Camille. Tout cet argent-là, vous l'emporterez pas dans votre tombe.

— C'est en plein ce que j'arrête pas de me dire, avoua Paddy Connolly en sortant de la poche de poitrine de sa jaquette un énorme cigare qu'il se mit en frais d'allumer.

Les enfants de Liam le regardèrent faire, les yeux ronds. Ils n'avaient jamais vu de cigare et son odeur prenante les surprit.

— Bon, c'est ben beau tout ça, mais il va falloir aller faire le train, déclara Liam en quittant sa chaise.

Ses deux fils l'imitèrent et endossèrent leur manteau.

Ce soir-là, Camille servit du pâté à la viande et des pommes de terre au souper. L'invité mangea avec appétit et la félicita pour son ketchup vert dont il avait versé un quart du pot dans son assiette pour accompagner le mets principal. Au dessert, il ne se fit pas prier pour accepter une deuxième pointe de tarte.

Durant toute la soirée, Paddy Connolly se raconta en long et en large et parla abondamment de la vie à Montréal et de tous les divertissements qu'une aussi grande ville pouvait offrir. Il décrivit les tramways qui sillonnaient maintenant quelques-unes des artères principales de la ville ainsi que le nouvel éclairage au gaz que les autorités venaient de faire installer. Il mentionna les élections municipales qui allaient avoir lieu au mois de février et parla aussi de monseigneur Bourget avec qui, s'il fallait le croire, il s'était entretenu à plusieurs reprises durant les dernières années.

À neuf heures, Camille annonça qu'on allait faire la prière pour permettre aux enfants d'aller au lit.

— On pourrait ben laisser faire pour à soir, intervint Liam, sous le charme de tout ce que racontait son oncle.

— Il y a pas de raison, répliqua-t-elle en s'agenouillant déjà.

Paddy l'approuva et tous durent imiter la maîtresse de maison. Après la prière, les enfants montèrent dans leur chambre et les adultes continuèrent à parler. Quand Liam mentionna la mort toute récente du père de Camille, l'invité offrit sans manifester trop de sympathie ses condoléances à son hôtesse. Peu après, le maître de la maison parla d'aller au lit. De toute évidence, il était fatigué par sa longue journée passée à bûcher.

— Je mangerais ben un petit quelque chose avant d'aller me coucher, déclara Paddy en affichant une mine gourmande.

— C'est pas trop dans nos habitudes de manger avant d'aller nous coucher, mon oncle, lui fit remarquer Camille, agacée par son sans-gêne. Si vous avez une petite faim, je peux toujours vous donner une tranche de pain avec de la graisse de rôti.

— Ça va faire l'affaire. Je me reprendrai demain matin au déjeuner.

L'oncle s'assit à table et attendit que Camille eût déposé sur la table une miche cuite le matin même et un bol de graisse de rôti. Pendant ce temps, Liam remonta le mécanisme de l'horloge et alluma une lampe de service avant de jeter deux rondins dans le poêle.

— Bon, nous autres on va aller se coucher, annonça-t-il à son oncle. Quand vous aurez fini de manger, vous aurez juste à prendre la lampe et à monter. Bonne nuit.

Le mari et la femme disparurent dans leur chambre à coucher, laissant seul leur invité attablé. Ils se déshabillèrent rapidement dans la pièce glaciale, pressés d'aller se réchauffer sous les couvertures.

— Sais-tu que je le trouve pas mal effronté, ton oncle, chuchota Camille, après avoir soufflé la lampe.

— Pourquoi tu dis ça ?

— Tu m'as dit que t'en as pas entendu parler depuis des années et v'là qu'il arrive et qu'il s'installe chez nous comme s'il était chez eux.

— C'est de la famille, murmura Liam.

— Je trouve ça drôle qu'il s'en rappelle seulement aujourd'hui… laissa-t-elle tomber. Il me semble qu'il aurait pu penser apporter un petit quelque chose aux enfants pour les fêtes ou encore un cadeau de noces, non ?

— Il y a pas pensé. À part ça, c'est pas important pantoute. Dis-toi que ce qui est important, c'est qu'il est pas mal riche et qu'on est sa seule famille, ajouta-t-il, laissant deviner ce à quoi il songeait.

— Je veux pas être regardante, dit sa femme, mais d'après moi il va rester riche longtemps s'il dépense pas plus que ça.

— S'il avait passé sa vie à dépenser à gauche et à droite, c'est sûr qu'il serait pauvre, assura Liam avec une certaine impatience. En plus, il y a rien qui dit qu'il nous donnera pas un gros montant au jour de l'An.

— En tout cas, je commence à comprendre pourquoi tu lui fais une si belle façon, dit-elle, sarcastique. Je suppose que t'espères hériter.

— C'est sûr, reconnut-il sans la moindre honte. C'est mon oncle et je suis le seul Connolly qui reste après lui. Ce serait normal que j'hérite.

— Moi, je me demande si c'est vrai tout ce qu'il nous a raconté à soir, conclut-elle en lui tournant le dos.

— Pourquoi ça le serait pas?

— A beau mentir qui vient de loin, comme le disait mon père, répliqua-t-elle. Tiens, pendant que j'y pense, viens pas te lamenter que les provisions baissent vite. Si tu veux savoir pourquoi, t'as juste à regarder manger ton oncle.

Liam Connolly ne jugea pas utile de répondre et se tourna sur le côté pour trouver une position plus confortable pour dormir.

❧

Deux jours plus tard, Xavier Beauchemin, assis à table, finissait de se raser avec soin devant un petit miroir. En ce dernier samedi de décembre, le jeune homme avait houspillé son employé pour faire le train dès quatre heures.

— Je vais veiller à soir et je veux souper de bonne heure, lui avait-il déclaré.

Antonin n'avait rien dit, mais il était heureux de voir que son patron et ami avait cessé de broyer du noir. Depuis le décès de son père la semaine précédente, Xavier parlait à peine et rien ne semblait l'intéresser. Il n'avait pas voulu retourner bûcher et il n'avait accepté de travailler à la finition des chambres de sa maison neuve que parce que l'adolescent s'en occupait quand ils n'allaient pas bûcher.

Après le souper, les deux hommes avaient lavé la vaisselle et préparé un rôti de porc dont Antonin devait surveiller la cuisson pendant que Xavier irait passer la soirée à la ferme voisine, chez Catherine Benoît.

Xavier disparut dans sa chambre quelques minutes et revint endimanché dans la cuisine pour se peigner.

— Sacrifice ! s'exclama l'adolescent en regardant son patron se pomponner. Est-ce qu'il y a quelque chose de spécial à soir ?

— C'est à soir que je fais ma grande demande, déclara Xavier Beauchemin en montrant une assurance qu'il était bien loin d'éprouver.

— Est-ce que ça veut dire que je suis à la veille de faire mon paquetage ? s'enquit Antonin, soudainement inquiet.

— Pantoute, répondit Xavier sans hésiter. Tu vas toujours avoir ta place ici dedans aussi longtemps que tu vas vouloir travailler avec moi.

Soulagé, l'orphelin le regarda endosser son épais manteau d'étoffe du pays et coiffer sa casquette.

— Souhaite-moi bonne chance, lui ordonna Xavier, la main sur la poignée de la porte.

— Je suis sûr qu'elle va dire oui, fit Antonin.

Dès qu'il se retrouva dehors à marcher en direction de la ferme des Benoît, le jeune homme perdit passablement de sa superbe. Il avait conscience de s'apprêter à faire une démarche qui allait être lourde de conséquences pour toute sa vie. Dans quelques minutes, il allait demander la main d'une fille qu'aucune maison honnête de Saint-Bernard-Abbé n'accepterait de recevoir. Pire, sa propre mère la rejetait et désapprouvait ses projets, comme son père l'aurait fait s'il avait été encore vivant. Pour le reste de sa famille, il était incapable de deviner la réaction de chacun quand on apprendrait qu'il épousait la honte de la paroisse.

— Je m'en sacre ! dit-il à haute voix en serrant les dents. C'est elle que je veux et je vais l'avoir. Ils la connaissent pas. Moi, je sais que c'est une bonne femme.

Il eut une pensée fugitive pour Cyprien Benoît et sa Marie-Rose. Tous les deux allaient certainement être heureux de voir partir Catherine. Ils ne pouvaient la souffrir et étaient intimement persuadés d'être boudés par le voisinage parce qu'ils l'abritaient.

— Eux autres, que le diable les charrie! fit-il en frappant à la porte de la maison grise de la ferme voisine, située à l'entrée de la longue courbe du rang Sainte-Ursule.

Catherine vint lui ouvrir et s'empressa de l'inviter à entrer. Comme chaque fois qu'il posait les pieds dans la maison des Benoît, il salua les personnes présentes dans la pièce. Seule Laura Benoît lui rendit son salut. Le fils et la bru de la veuve firent comme s'ils n'avaient rien entendu. Catherine s'empara d'une lampe et l'entraîna dans le salon dès qu'il eut retiré son manteau et ses bottes.

Ils prirent place tous les deux sur le vieux canapé rembourré de crin. Après avoir pris des nouvelles de la jeune fille, Xavier passa tout de suite au vif du sujet.

— Tu te rappelles qu'on avait convenu que je demanderais ta main à ta mère le soir de Noël.

Catherine hocha la tête.

— Je l'ai pas fait à cause de la mort de mon père. Si t'es toujours d'accord, je vais le faire à soir.

— Penses-tu que c'est convenable en plein deuil? s'inquiéta Catherine à voix basse.

— Pourquoi pas? répondit Xavier. On se mariera pas demain matin. Qu'est-ce que tu dirais si on annonçait à ta mère qu'on veut se marier le dernier samedi de juin?

— C'est correct, accepta-t-elle après une légère hésitation.

— Dans ce cas-là, demande à ta mère de venir dans le salon, dit-il en se levant.

La jeune fille quitta la pièce un court moment et revint en compagnie de sa mère. Debout au centre du salon, ne sachant trop quoi faire de ses mains et le visage un peu pâle, le fils de Baptiste Beauchemin attendit que Catherine vienne le rejoindre pour s'adresser à la veuve de Léopold Benoît:

— Madame Benoît, j'aimerais vous demander la main de votre fille. Ça fait plus qu'un an qu'on se fréquente et je pense qu'on se connaît ben.

— Je te la donne si Catherine est d'accord, dit Laura Benoît sans la moindre hésitation.

— Je lui ai dit oui, m'man, fit sa fille.

— Qu'est-ce que ta mère dit de ça ? s'enquit la maîtresse de maison.

— Je lui en ai pas encore parlé, avoua le jeune fermier, mais je vois pas pourquoi elle serait contre, mentit-il effrontément.

La veuve ne fut pas dupe de cette réponse, mais cette demande en mariage était si inespérée qu'elle n'osa pas insister.

— Quand avez-vous l'intention de vous marier ?

— J'en ai parlé avec votre fille tout à l'heure, répondit Xavier. Je pense que ce serait plus convenable d'attendre après la Saint-Jean à cause de la mort de mon père. En même temps, ça me permettrait de finir le dedans de ma maison.

— Et Catherine trouvera aussi le moyen d'ajouter quelques morceaux à son trousseau, poursuivit Laura. Cyprien ! Marie-Rose ! venez donc dans le salon une minute, héla Laura Benoît en faisant un pas vers la porte.

Son fils et sa bru apparurent à l'entrée du salon sans montrer le moindre empressement et en affichant leur visage fermé habituel.

— Xavier vient de me demander Catherine en mariage. J'ai accepté. Qu'est-ce que vous attendez pour les féliciter ?

Tous les deux ne purent que présenter des félicitations, mais ils le firent du bout des lèvres, même si ce mariage était leur vœu le plus cher.

À son retour à la maison en fin de soirée, Xavier exultait. Le temps des hésitations était terminé. Il avait franchi le pas. Plein d'optimisme, il se répétait qu'il avait près de six mois pour habituer les siens à l'idée qu'il allait épouser Catherine.

~

Le lendemain, avant-veille du jour de l'An, Camille réalisa en préparant les enfants pour la messe que la *sleigh* ne pourrait accommoder tout le monde plus l'oncle Paddy. Ce dernier allait devoir atteler, mais, comme l'invité n'avait pas l'air de vouloir bouger de la chaise berçante qu'il s'était appropriée depuis la veille, elle dut le lui rappeler.

— Mon oncle, il va falloir que vous alliez atteler parce qu'on n'a pas assez de place dans notre *sleigh*.

— Ton plus vieux pourrait peut-être le faire quand il aura fini d'aider son père à faire le train.

— Il aura pas grand temps. Il va falloir qu'il se change pour aller à la messe, lui fit remarquer Camille.

— Il aura juste à faire ça un peu plus vite, répliqua Paddy Connolly en allumant son premier cigare de la journée.

Camille ne dit rien, mais elle lui lança un regard sans aménité. Elle commençait à trouver que le célibataire montréalais manifestait un sans-gêne assez agaçant. Évidemment, Liam ne trouva rien à redire quand son oncle ordonna à Patrick d'aller atteler son cheval pendant qu'il continuait à se chauffer béatement près du poêle.

À leur arrivée à la chapelle, Liam exigea que Patrick aille se trouver une place au jubé pour permettre à son oncle de s'asseoir dans le banc loué par la famille. Lui-même devait monter au même endroit pour remplir son tout nouveau rôle de maître-chantre de la chorale paroissiale. Camille remarqua que, pour la première fois, son frère Xavier avait pris place aux côtés de Catherine Benoît dans le banc des Benoît. Elle en déduisit immédiatement qu'il avait demandé sa main et elle se demanda comment sa mère allait réagir en le voyant s'afficher ouvertement avec cette fille devant tout le monde. Heureusement, elle n'aperçut que Donat,

Eugénie et Bernadette dans le banc familial, signe que sa mère était demeurée à la maison pour prendre soin d'Alexis.

— Tant mieux, murmura-t-elle, elle l'apprendra bien assez vite.

— Qu'est-ce que tu dis? lui demanda Paddy en se tournant vers elle.

— Rien, mon oncle, je parlais à Rose, mentit-elle.

En ce dernier dimanche de l'année, le curé Désilets réservait une surprise à ses fidèles après son long sermon portant sur les occasions de pécher durant la période des fêtes. Il était revenu encore une fois sur les danses lascives et sur les malheurs engendrés par l'alcool. Il avait aussi lourdement insisté sur les responsabilités des parents de bien surveiller leurs enfants et de leur donner l'exemple de la vertu. À la stupéfaction des visiteurs étrangers, pas un seul homme n'avait osé sortir pour aller fumer durant le prône pour l'excellente raison que le bedeau et Anatole Blanchette, à la demande de leur curé, étaient postés près de la porte de la chapelle pour décourager tout contrevenant.

Au moment où les fidèles s'attendaient à voir leur curé retourner à l'autel pour poursuivre la célébration de la messe, le prêtre demeura sur place.

— Avant de poursuivre la sainte messe, déclara Josaphat Désilets, je dois vous lire une lettre pastorale de monseigneur notre évêque adressée spécifiquement aux fidèles de la mission Saint-Bernard-Abbé. Il m'est demandé expressément de vous la lire du haut de la chaire.

Les gens dans l'assistance se regardèrent, étonnés. Ils ne se rappelaient pas que cela se soit déjà produit par le passé. Pour leur part, Samuel Ellis et Thomas Hyland, l'air réjoui, tournèrent la tête vers Donat Beauchemin et murmurèrent en même temps: «Ça y est, monseigneur a accepté qu'on devienne une paroisse.» Le curé fit comme s'il ne remarquait pas l'agitation de la foule et entreprit la lecture de la lettre pastorale que monseigneur Laflèche lui avait fait parvenir quelques jours plus tôt.

Dans la missive, le prélat encourageait ses ouailles à faire montre de fermeté dans la foi et à résister à toutes les idées fausses véhiculées par ceux qui se disaient libéraux. Il les encourageait à obéir à leur prêtre et à suivre ses directives, ce qui était le meilleur moyen pour trouver le chemin du ciel.

> « *Chers enfants de Dieu de la mission de Saint-Bernard-Abbé, je profite de l'occasion pour vous rappeler qu'il est de votre responsabilité de loger convenablement votre pasteur et de lui assurer un minimum de confort.*
>
> *Enfin, je vous souhaite de la santé et le paradis à la fin de vos jours à l'aube de la nouvelle année.* »

— J'espère que tous ont compris le message de notre évêque, prit la peine de déclarer Josaphat Désilets avant de se signer et de retourner à l'autel.

À la fin de la messe, les gens se rassemblèrent sur le parvis malgré le froid intense pour commenter les dernières nouvelles. Pour leur part, les cinq syndics de la mission, entourés de quelques fermiers, n'avaient pas le cœur à rire.

— Torrieu! j'étais sûr que monsieur le curé allait nous annoncer que monseigneur faisait de Saint-Bernard-Abbé une paroisse comme les autres, s'exclama Antonius Côté, ouvertement dépité.

— Ben, c'était pas ça pantoute, laissa tomber Anatole Blanchette, l'air sombre.

— Moi, j'ai comme l'idée que notre curé a écrit à monseigneur qu'il gelait dans la sacristie et que c'était pas vivable, fit Donat Beauchemin après avoir allumé sa pipe. Ça peut pas être autre chose.

— Je dirais comme toi, le jeune, intervint Thomas Hyland. Du temps du curé Ouellet, on n'a jamais reçu une lettre comme ça.

— Mais pourquoi il s'est pas plaint à nous autres ? demanda Samuel Ellis, président des syndics.

— Entre nous, Sam, ça aurait changé quoi ? lui demanda Hyland sur un ton raisonnable. On le sait que la sacristie est trop grande pour être ben chauffée juste par le poêle, mais on peut pas faire plus.

— Le curé Ouellet a vécu là l'hiver passé et il en est pas mort, fit remarquer Blanchette.

— Bon, qu'est-ce qu'on fait ? demanda Côté.

— Moi, je serais d'avis de faire le mort, déclara Donat. Après tout, il nous en a pas parlé. On va attendre qu'il vienne se plaindre…

— C'est ça, approuva Ellis, et là, je lui dirai qu'on peut pas faire plus.

Camille s'approcha de son frère Donat et lui adressa un signe discret lui indiquant qu'elle voulait lui parler. Donat s'avança vers elle.

— Je suppose que t'as remarqué comme moi où Xavier était assis à matin ? lui demanda-t-elle.

— Oui, j'ai vu, répondit-il, l'air sombre.

— Qu'est-ce que tu dirais si on n'en parlait pas à m'man ? fit-elle. Il me semble qu'elle en a bien assez à endurer ces temps-ci.

— C'est correct, je vais avertir les autres.

Au même moment, elle vit Liam descendre les marches du parvis en compagnie de Céleste Comtois, l'accompagnatrice au clavecin de la chorale. Elle l'attendit et tous les deux allèrent rejoindre les enfants déjà réfugiés sous les épaisses couvertures en fourrure dans la *sleigh*. Au passage, ils virent Paddy Connolly en grande conversation avec Tancrède Bélanger, Évariste Bourgeois et Télesphore Dionne.

— Il y a pas à dire, dit-elle à son mari, ton oncle a pas pris trop de temps pour se faire connaître.

— C'est un homme habitué à brasser des grosses affaires et à parler au monde. Il y a pas grand-chose qui le gêne, affirma Liam, avec une certaine fierté.

Ce dimanche-là et le lendemain, veille du jour de l'An, Paddy Connolly ne rentra à la maison qu'à l'heure des repas. À voir sa trogne rouge, il était assez évident qu'il avait fait honneur à l'alcool que ses nouvelles connaissances lui avaient offert. À l'entendre, il y avait du monde bien intéressant qui se tenait au magasin général.

— Le magasin général est fermé le dimanche, mon oncle, lui fit remarquer Camille, étonnée.

— Pas pour tout le monde, ma petite fille, lui répondit le marchand de Montréal. Télesphore Dionne et sa femme ont l'air ben intéressés par tout ce qui se passe en ville.

— En tout cas, on peut pas dire que vous avez l'air de vous ennuyer de Montréal, dit-elle.

— Pantoute, je pense même que je commence à aimer mieux la campagne.

La jeune femme ne dit rien, mais elle se demanda si l'invité n'allait pas chercher à s'incruster un peu plus longtemps. Déjà chargée de quatre enfants et d'un mari peu facile à vivre, elle se voyait mal ajouter à sa tâche l'entretien de cet oncle plutôt effronté.

Chapitre 4

Ressentiments et rivalités

Bien peu de gens de la région songèrent à se plaindre du froid mordant qui régnait en ce 1er janvier 1872. Les années précédentes, tant de tempêtes de neige avaient empêché les réunions familiales du jour de l'An qu'il aurait été mal vu d'en vouloir au mercure ce jour-là.

Marie avait repris sa routine et avait été la première à se lever. Elle s'était réveillée peu après cinq heures et la pensée de son premier jour de l'An sans son mari la fit longuement pleurer, étendue dans son lit, dans le noir. Elle dut se secouer pour mettre fin à sa crise de larmes et se décider à poser les pieds sur le parquet glacial. Elle s'empressa ensuite de jeter un châle sur ses épaules et d'allumer la lampe avant de quitter sa chambre qui lui semblait si grande maintenant en l'absence de Baptiste.

Elle déposa la lampe sur la table de la cuisine et alla jeter deux rondins sur les tisons qui achevaient de se consumer dans le poêle. Comme elle ne se rappelait pas s'être levée après deux heures du matin, Donat avait dû descendre plus tard et mettre une bûche dans le poêle. Mais, malgré cela, la maison était glaciale.

En s'approchant de l'une des fenêtres, elle se rendit compte qu'elle était couverte d'une épaisse couche de givre. Elle y appliqua la paume de sa main afin de faire fondre celui-ci pour tenter de voir à l'extérieur. Tout était blanc et le fond de l'air semblait bien froid.

— Ces pauvres enfants, dit-elle à mi-voix en songeant aux siens, ils vont avoir un jour de l'An bien triste. L'année passée, on a chanté et on s'est raconté des histoires durant toute la soirée. Cette année, on pourra rien faire de tout ça.

Elle se retourna dans l'intention d'aller déposer la théière sur le poêle qui s'était mis à ronfler, puis elle réalisa qu'elle ne pourrait pas boire de thé si elle désirait aller communier. Elle eut la tentation de s'asseoir dans l'une des chaises berçantes en attendant que l'eau du réservoir soit assez chaude pour sa toilette, mais elle résista et décida de retourner dans sa chambre faire son lit et s'habiller.

Quand elle revint dans la cuisine, elle y trouva Donat et Hubert en train d'endosser leur manteau pour aller faire le train.

— C'est toi qui t'es levé pendant la nuit pour mettre du bois dans le poêle? demanda-t-elle à son fils aîné.

— Oui, il était en train de s'éteindre, répondit ce dernier. Je vous dis que c'est pas pratique pantoute de descendre chaque fois que le poêle a besoin de bois, sentit-il le besoin d'ajouter.

Marie saisit l'allusion et répliqua sèchement :

— T'es pas obligé de t'en occuper. L'hiver passé, je me suis levée durant tout l'hiver pour chauffer et j'en suis pas morte.

— Moi aussi, je peux le faire, offrit Hubert avant d'enfoncer une tuque sur sa tête.

Les deux jeunes hommes quittèrent la maison et leur mère prit un broc d'eau chaude dans le réservoir pour se laver.

— Ça, il y a de l'Eugénie en dessous de cette affaire-là, murmura-t-elle pour elle-même. La petite maudite veut avoir ma chambre depuis un bon bout de temps. Même du vivant de Baptiste, elle se gênait pas pour faire remarquer que leur chambre en haut était pas mal petite pour trois. Mais elle se trompe si elle pense l'avoir. C'est ma chambre et c'est ma terre. Il y a personne qui va m'obliger à les donner si je le veux pas.

Forte de cette décision, elle s'attaqua à son chignon qu'elle voulait impeccable. Quand Bernadette et sa belle-sœur descendirent à leur tour dans la cuisine, elles la trouvèrent en train de réciter son chapelet, habillée, coiffée, prête à partir pour la messe, même si cette dernière n'aurait lieu qu'une heure trente plus tard. En voyant arriver les deux jeunes femmes, elle remit son chapelet dans son étui et se leva.

— J'ai sorti un jambon tout à l'heure. On va le mettre au fourneau avant de partir pour la messe. Je pense qu'on devrait en avoir assez avec les tourtières pour tout le monde au souper.

— Je me demande bien pourquoi il faut que ce soit toujours nous autres qui recevions durant les fêtes, osa dire Eugénie en déposant son fils sur une couverture sur le parquet.

— Tout simplement parce qu'Emma est en famille et en arrache et parce que Camille a déjà les quatre enfants de Liam et son oncle sur le dos, répondit sèchement sa belle-mère en ne dissimulant pas son mécontentement. En plus, c'est normal que les enfants viennent chez leurs parents au jour de l'An, il me semble.

Remise à sa place, Eugénie n'osa rien dire.

— Et qu'est-ce qu'on va manger à midi? s'enquit Bernadette, désireuse de détourner la colère de sa mère.

— Il reste un peu de lard du souper d'hier. On va se contenter de ça avec de la galette de sarrasin. Eugénie, tu prépareras le mélange pendant qu'on va être à la messe, ordonna-t-elle à sa bru.

❧

Ce matin-là, Donat fit en sorte d'arriver à la chapelle du rang Sainte-Ursule une bonne trentaine de minutes avant le début de la grand-messe. Il avait été convenu avec les autres syndics de la mission qu'ils iraient présenter leurs vœux de bonne année au curé Désilets avant la célébration de la messe.

À son entrée dans le temple, il laissa sa mère, Hubert et Bernadette aller s'installer dans leur banc pour se joindre à Ellis, Hyland, Côté et Blanchette. Plusieurs bancs étaient déjà occupés par des fidèles et les membres de la chorale tenaient une courte répétition au jubé avant la célébration de la cérémonie religieuse. Les syndics allèrent frapper à la porte de la sacristie. Bridget Ellis vint leur ouvrir. L'épouse de Samuel, fidèle à son rôle de ménagère du curé, était là depuis près de deux heures à préparer les repas de la journée du prêtre.

Josaphat Désilets, déjà vêtu de son aube blanche, déposa son bréviaire sur une crédence et s'avança vers les visiteurs.

— On est venus vous souhaiter une bonne année, déclara Samuel Ellis en tendant la main au curé de Saint-Bernard-Abbé.

Le prêtre serra la main de chacun des administrateurs de la mission et formula des vœux de bonne santé et d'une nouvelle année remplie de bonheur. Il semblait d'excellente humeur.

— Allez-vous chez de la parenté aujourd'hui, monsieur le curé? lui demanda Antonius Côté.

— C'est possible que j'aille souper chez ma sœur, mais rien n'est décidé encore, dit le prêtre sans préciser où elle demeurait.

— Ça va vous permettre de vous réchauffer, ajouta malencontreusement Anatole Blanchette, s'attirant immédiatement des regards réprobateurs de ses compagnons.

— C'est certain, s'empressa d'approuver Josaphat Désilets. Comme vous pouvez le voir, c'est pas chaud ce matin dans la sacristie, même si j'ai chauffé toute la nuit.

— C'est tout de même pas pire que dans ben des maisons de la mission, voulut temporiser Samuel Ellis.

— Oui, c'est pire, déclara le curé en élevant légèrement la voix. Il y a des nuits où je suis obligé de dormir avec mon manteau sur le dos. Vous trouvez ça normal, vous autres ?

— Et c'est de ça que vous vous êtes plaint à monseigneur ? s'enquit Donat, uniquement pour s'assurer du fait.

— En plein ça… Et comme vous avez pu vous en rendre compte par sa lettre, il a pas l'air de trouver ça plus normal que moi.

— Bon, je pense qu'on va vous laisser finir de vous préparer pour la messe, dit Samuel Ellis en jetant un coup d'œil à l'horloge.

Les syndics prirent congé et rentrèrent dans la chapelle qui était maintenant presque entièrement occupée par les fidèles. En levant la tête vers le jubé, Donat aperçut ses beaux-frères Liam et Rémi debout près du clavecin avec les autres membres de la chorale.

— T'avais ben besoin de lui faire remarquer que c'était pas chaud dans la sacristie, reprocha Ellis à Blanchette.

— En tout cas, ça nous a au moins permis de savoir qu'il s'était ben lamenté d'avoir froid à monseigneur, intervint Donat avant de quitter les syndics pour aller rejoindre les siens.

À son entrée dans le banc, il se rendit compte immédiatement que quelque chose n'allait pas. Sa mère, le regard obstinément fixé vers l'avant et les traits figés, se tenait toute droite. Il saisit le signe discret de Bernadette.

— Qu'est-ce qui se passe encore ? demanda-t-il, excédé, à sa mère.

— Regarde en arrière et tu vas le savoir, fit-elle abruptement sans tourner la tête.

Donat regarda et ne vit rien de spécial.

— Je vois rien.

— Ton frère est là, dans le banc des Benoît, à côté de la Jézabel, expliqua-t-elle en ne faisant aucun effort pour cacher son mépris.

Donat se retourna à nouveau et remarqua cette fois-là que son frère était assis près de Catherine Benoît. Sans approuver la chose, il n'était pas prêt à en faire un drame.

Deux jours plus tôt, sur la recommandation de Camille, il avait prévenu les autres membres de la famille de ne pas mentionner ce fait à sa mère. Maintenant que celle-ci avait vu Xavier assis à côté de Catherine, elle était persuadée à son tour qu'il lui avait demandé sa main.

— Écoutez, m'man, reprit-il à voix basse sur un ton raisonnable. Vous êtes pas pour en faire une maladie. On dirait ben qu'il est décidé à la marier, même si vous êtes pas d'accord. Vous aurez beau mener le diable, je pense pas qu'il va changer d'idée. Il fait pas ça pour vous faire de la peine ni pour vous faire enrager.

— Il sait pas pantoute ce qui l'attend, le niaiseux, répliqua Marie, l'air mauvais.

— Il est pas fou pantoute, m'man. Il se rend compte qu'il y a personne à Saint-Bernard qui veut avoir affaire avec les Benoît. Mais comme vous pouvez le voir, ça a pas l'air de le déranger. Moi, je pense que si vous l'étrivez trop là-dessus, il va finir par ne plus venir nous voir. On est peut-être mieux de laisser faire le temps, vous pensez pas ?

L'entrée du célébrant dans le chœur dispensa Marie de répondre. Hubert avait tout entendu de l'échange entre son frère et sa mère et hocha la tête en signe d'approbation.

À ses côtés, Bernadette broyait du noir depuis quelques minutes, c'est-à-dire depuis qu'Angélique Dionne s'était arrêtée un court moment à leur banc pour chuchoter quelques mots à l'oreille de son frère Hubert. La fille cadette de Marie Beauchemin avait feint de ne pas la voir et, age-nouillée, avait fait comme si elle priait. Elle se rassit dès qu'Angélique eut regagné le banc occupé par ses parents.

— Qu'est-ce qu'elle te voulait ? avait-elle demandé à son frère.

— Elle m'a juste invité à une fête que son père organise cet après-midi. Il va y avoir de la danse.

— Dis-moi pas que t'es tombé dans l'œil de la belle Angélique ? avait-elle fait, moqueuse.

— Pantoute, s'était empressé de dire Hubert. Je pense qu'elle a invité tous les garçons de Saint-Bernard. Elle m'a dit qu'elle a invité Amable Fréchette et Constant Aubé. Elle a dû inviter aussi des filles.

Bernadette n'avait pu que noter que la fille de Télesphore Dionne ne l'avait pas invitée.

— Lui as-tu dit que t'étais en deuil ?

— Ben oui. Elle le savait que je refuserais, mais elle m'a invité par politesse.

— La maudite vache ! marmonna-t-elle en se levant pour accueillir le prêtre qui venait de s'arrêter au pied de l'autel, face au tabernacle.

Bernadette était persuadée que la belle Angélique n'avait nullement renoncé à séduire son cavalier, même si elle savait très bien que Constant Aubé la fréquentait depuis plusieurs mois. Elle ne cessa de retourner dans sa tête toutes sortes d'idées de vengeance.

— Si elle vient me souhaiter une bonne année à la fin de la messe, je lui arrache les yeux, se dit-elle, folle de rage.

À la fin de la messe, la plupart des fidèles firent fi du froid qui régnait à l'extérieur et prirent le temps de s'adresser de bons vœux à l'occasion de la nouvelle année. Pour sa part, Camille entraîna ses quatre enfants vers sa mère, sa sœur et ses frères pour qu'ils leur souhaitent une bonne année. Comme l'oncle Paddy l'avait suivie, elle ne put faire autrement que de leur présenter l'oncle de son mari. Ce dernier, toujours aussi à l'aise avec les gens, se montra si charmant que Marie l'invita à se joindre aux siens pour le souper qu'elle allait offrir. Rémi Lafond et Liam rejoignirent le petit groupe après avoir salué les autres membres de la chorale.

Marie fit un signe discret à sa fille aînée. Cette dernière comprit et s'éloigna de quelques pas pour lui parler.

— T'as remarqué Xavier ? se contenta-t-elle de lui demander.

— Oui.

— D'après toi, est-ce que ça veut dire qu'il l'a demandée en mariage ?

— C'est ce qu'il avait dit qu'il ferait, m'man, répondit sa fille aînée sur un ton raisonnable.

— Bondance de tête de cochon ! s'emporta-t-elle, les dents serrées. Combien de fois je…

— M'man, la coupa Camille, vous pensez pas qu'il est temps de vous faire à l'idée qu'il va la marier, que vous le vouliez ou pas ?

— …

— Nous autres, on s'est tous fait à l'idée, même si ça nous fait pas plaisir pantoute.

— Il est là-bas, avec les Benoît, reprit Marie, malheureuse. Dis à un de tes gars d'aller me le chercher.

— Vous allez pas lui faire une crise devant tout le monde, j'espère ? fit Camille, inquiète.

— Ben non, la rassura sa mère.

Camille héla Duncan et lui demanda d'aller prévenir Xavier que sa mère voulait lui parler. Le fils de Liam revint un moment plus tard en compagnie du jeune homme. Il était évident que Xavier craignait un esclandre devant les gens de Saint-Bernard-Abbé. A son arrivée, la conversation avait cessé dans le petit groupe de la famille Beauchemin et chacun épiait ce qui allait se produire entre la mère et le fils rebelle. Seul Paddy Connolly continuait à pérorer, inconscient du fait que son auditoire ne l'écoutait plus.

— Eh bien, mon garçon, est-ce que c'est rendu qu'il faut t'envoyer chercher pour que tu te décides à venir offrir tes vœux de bonne année à ta mère ? demanda Marie, agressive, à son fils.

— Pantoute, m'man, je vous avais pas oubliée. Je m'en venais. Je vous souhaite une bonne année, s'empressa-t-il d'ajouter en se penchant pour déposer deux baisers sonores sur les joues froides de sa mère.

— Moi aussi, mon garçon, je te souhaite une bonne santé, le paradis à la fin de tes jours… et un peu de jugeote avant qu'il soit trop tard.

— M'man, je…

— Pendant que j'y pense, le coupa-t-elle, tu viendras souper à la maison à soir avec toute la famille.

— Je sais pas si…

— T'emmèneras ta fiancée avec toi. Bon, là, je suis gelée d'un bord à l'autre. On se reverra cet après-midi, ajouta-t-elle précipitamment avant que son fils ne soit revenu de sa stupéfaction.

Là-dessus, la petite femme le planta là et fit signe à Donat qu'il était temps de rentrer. Ce dernier adressa un clin d'œil à Xavier avant d'aller chercher la *sleigh* stationnée au bout du terrain. Pendant ce temps, le jeune cultivateur du rang Sainte-Ursule, transporté de joie à l'idée que sa mère avait invité Catherine, embrassa ses sœurs et serra la main de Hubert et de ses deux beaux-frères en leur souhaitant une bonne année. Sa joie faisait plaisir à voir.

De retour à la maison, Bernadette se dépêcha d'apprendre la grande nouvelle à Eugénie, demeurée sur place pour prendre soin d'Alexis pendant que sa mère allait changer de robe.

— On chantera et on dansera peut-être pas à cause de notre deuil, déclara la jeune institutrice au retour de sa mère dans la cuisine, mais on va passer tout de même un bien beau jour de l'An.

Le fait que sa mère ait accepté de recevoir la fiancée de Xavier lui avait fait oublier sa rage contre Angélique Dionne.

De retour dans la cuisine, Marie se rendit compte de l'euphorie de sa fille cadette et en devina la raison.

— En vieillissant, ma fille, tu vas vite t'apercevoir qu'on est obligé bien souvent de piler sur son orgueil pour ses enfants.

— Je comprends, m'man.

— Ça me surprendrait que tu comprennes, reprit sèchement sa mère, les traits durcis. C'est pas de gaieté de cœur pantoute que je reçois Catherine Benoît chez nous. Ici dedans, c'est une maison honnête et une fille comme elle y a pas sa place. Je la reçois parce que ton insignifiant de frère s'est mis dans la tête de la marier. Tout ce qu'il me reste à faire, c'est de continuer à prier pour qu'il change d'idée avant que l'irréparable se fasse.

Là-dessus, la maîtresse de maison entreprit d'aider Eugénie à mettre le couvert. Quand elle passa dans la cuisine d'été pour aller y chercher quelque chose, Bernadette ne put s'empêcher de murmurer à sa belle-sœur :

— Je te dis qu'on va avoir un drôle de souper à soir si m'man fait cette tête-là.

⤙

Deux fermes plus loin, dans le rang Saint-Jean, Liam avait laissé sa femme et ses enfants près de la maison avant de poursuivre sa route jusqu'à l'écurie où son oncle l'avait devancé avec son attelage.

Camille s'empressa de jeter une bûche dans le poêle qui était en train de s'éteindre, après avoir enlevé son manteau et ses bottes. Elle était heureuse d'avoir aidé à rétablir les ponts entre son frère et sa mère et elle se promit de se montrer vigilante et de faire son possible pour éviter tout affrontement entre sa mère et Catherine lors du souper.

— Gardez vos beaux habits, dit-elle aux enfants qui s'apprêtaient déjà à monter à l'étage pour aller changer de vêtements. Vous vous changerez après avoir reçu la bénédiction de votre père.

— C'est quoi, ça ? demanda Patrick, intrigué.

— Comment ? Venez pas me dire que vous avez jamais demandé la bénédiction paternelle au jour de l'An ? fit leur mère adoptive, réellement stupéfaite.

— On n'a jamais fait ça, reconnut Ann.

— Bien, mais ça va changer à partir de cette année. Dans toutes les familles, les enfants demandent à leur père de les bénir au jour de l'An. Ici dedans, ça va être comme partout ailleurs.

— On sait pas comment faire ça, nous autres, intervint Duncan, en passant ses doigts dans sa tignasse rousse.

— T'as juste à te mettre à genoux devant ton père avec ton frère et tes sœurs. Ton père va être content de te bénir. Tu vas voir, ça va te porter chance durant toute l'année.

— Est-ce que ça veut dire qu'il nous donnera plus la volée ? demanda Patrick, intrigué.

— Seulement si vous le méritez, répondit Camille, le cœur serré à l'idée que les enfants voient leur père comme quelqu'un d'uniquement intéressé à les frapper.

— Qui va demander ça ? demanda Duncan.

— Normalement, c'est l'enfant le plus vieux.

— Ça me gêne de faire ça, reconnut Ann, apparemment mal à l'aise.

— Voyons, Ann, c'est à toi que ça revient de le faire. Ton père te mangera pas. Il va être content. Dis-toi que j'ai toujours fait ça chaque année chez nous parce que j'étais la plus vieille et j'en suis pas morte.

Ses traits s'assombrirent brusquement et ses yeux se remplirent de larmes à la pensée que c'était la première fois qu'elle ne recevrait pas la bénédiction paternelle.

— Là, vous allez rester tranquilles et me laisser dire deux mots à votre père quand il va rentrer, avant de lui demander sa bénédiction.

Lorsque Liam rentra en compagnie de son oncle, elle suivit son mari jusque dans la chambre à coucher dont elle referma la porte derrière eux.

— Les enfants t'attendent pour te demander ta bénédiction, lui dit-elle.

— C'est quoi cette niaiserie-là ? On n'a jamais fait ça dans ma famille.

— Dans la mienne, on l'a toujours fait. Ce serait normal que tu le fasses. C'est une façon pour tes enfants de te prouver qu'ils t'aiment et qu'ils te respectent.

— C'est pas nécessaire pantoute, se défendit-il, de toute évidence très embarrassé et aussi vaguement tenté.

— Je peux pas t'obliger à le faire si tu veux pas, finit par dire Camille.

— C'est correct, je vais les bénir, fit-il sur un ton agacé.

Il enleva son veston et ouvrit son collet de chemise avant de la suivre dans la cuisine où Paddy Connolly venait de s'asseoir sur l'une des chaises berçantes placées entre la fenêtre et le poêle. Camille fit un signe discret à Ann avant de se diriger vers le garde-manger d'où elle sortit un gâteau cuisiné la veille.

— P'pa, est-ce que vous voulez nous bénir ? demanda l'adolescente à son père d'une voix un peu tremblante.

— Certain, répondit-il, visiblement mal à l'aise en regardant ses quatre enfants s'agenouiller en demi-cercle devant lui.

L'oncle arrêta de se bercer et fixa la scène aussi intensément que Camille qui, les yeux humides, regardait ceux qu'elle considérait maintenant comme ses propres enfants. Liam murmura une courte prière et posa les mains sur la tête de chacun de ses quatre enfants agenouillés devant lui avant de se signer. Les enfants se signèrent à leur tour et se relevèrent.

Liam avait les yeux embués et, pour cacher son émotion, il s'empressa d'aller chercher le cruchon de bagosse.

— On a le temps de boire un petit remontant avant le dîner, déclara-t-il à son oncle. Après tout, on est au jour de l'An.

— Tu vois, mon garçon, c'est en voyant des affaires comme ça que je regrette parfois d'être resté vieux garçon, lui dit Paddy d'une voix changée.

Camille ordonna aux enfants d'aller changer de vêtements. Quand ils revinrent dans la cuisine, elle demanda à Ann et à Rose de finir de mettre la table pendant qu'elle s'éclipsait un court moment dans sa chambre à coucher. Elle revint avec différents petits paquets. Liam sursauta légèrement en la voyant les déposer sur un coin de la table.

— Qu'est-ce que c'est, toutes ces affaires-là? demanda-t-il, intrigué.

— T'oublies qu'on est au jour de l'An, lui fit remarquer sa femme avec bonne humeur. C'est la fête des enfants.

— Ben…

— Laisse faire, le coupa-t-elle. Approchez, ordonna-t-elle aux enfants, votre père et moi, on a des cadeaux pour vous autres.

Tous les quatre s'approchèrent, très excités. Elle tendit à chacun un paquet qui fut rapidement déballé.

— Hé! C'est un sucre d'orge! s'exclama Duncan, les yeux brillants de plaisir.

— Moi aussi, fit son frère.

Les deux filles de la maison avaient, elles aussi, reçu comme étrennes un gros sucre d'orge rouge. Les enfants, heureux, se mirent à comparer les animaux qu'ils représentaient. Puis ils remercièrent leurs parents avec effusion. Liam se borna à hocher la tête.

— Tant mieux s'ils font votre affaire, déclara Camille. À cette heure, vous allez les mettre de côté, c'est le temps de dîner.

Le repas se prit dans une joyeuse animation, pour le plus grand plaisir de Camille. L'oncle de son mari sembla faire un peu grise mine en constatant que la maîtresse de maison servait une simple fricassée, mais cette dernière ne se donna pas la peine de lui expliquer que, le soir même, il pourrait manger tant et plus chez sa mère.

Après le repas, Camille encouragea les enfants à aller se reposer une heure ou deux dans leur chambre pour pouvoir veiller plus tard. Ceux-ci furent précédés à l'étage par Paddy Connolly, grand amateur de sieste après le repas du midi.

Quand la cuisine fut correctement rangée, elle alla rejoindre son mari qui venait de se déchausser dans l'intention de s'offrir une sieste.

— Veux-tu ben me dire ce qui t'a pris de gaspiller de l'argent pour acheter des cochonneries aux enfants? demanda-t-il à sa femme en se laissant tomber sur le lit.

— C'est le jour de l'An, fit-elle. On donne des cadeaux aux enfants d'habitude.

— Voyons donc!

— Es-tu en train de me dire que t'as jamais donné d'étrennes à tes enfants ce jour-là?

— Avec quel argent tu penses que j'aurais pu faire ça? répliqua-t-il, vindicatif.

— Sais-tu qu'on peut pas dire que tu les gâtes trop, ces enfants-là! dit-elle sur un ton convaincu.

— Toi, où est-ce que t'as pris l'argent pour acheter ça? lui demanda-t-il, soupçonneux.

— Aie pas peur, c'est pas avec ton argent, répondit-elle sèchement. C'est avec de l'argent que je me suis fait l'hiver passé en cousant des courtepointes.

— Il aurait manqué juste ça, fit-il, l'air mauvais.

— C'est certain, rétorqua-t-elle, sarcastique. Toi, je suppose que si t'as des cennes, tu vas faire comme ton oncle et les garder pour toi.

— Pourquoi tu dis ça?

— Au cas où tu l'aurais pas remarqué, ton oncle a rien donné aux enfants. D'ailleurs, il a rien donné à personne.

— Il est pas obligé.

— Bien non, nous autres, on est obligés de l'héberger et de le nourrir pour rien, fit-elle d'une voix acide. Lui, il doit rien à personne.

— Bon, si t'as fini, j'aimerais ben que tu me laisses dormir un peu. Il y a déjà ben assez que je vais être obligé d'aller endurer ta famille toute la soirée.

— T'es pas obligé pantoute de venir. Si t'aimes mieux passer la soirée avec ton oncle, les pieds sur la bavette du poêle, t'es bien libre, rétorqua-t-elle en lui tournant le dos après s'être glissée sous les épaisses couvertures.

Durant de longues minutes, la jeune femme chercha vainement le sommeil. Cet après-midi du jour de l'An ne ressemblait en rien à ceux qu'elle avait connus dans le passé. Après deux mois de vie commune avec son mari, elle découvrait peu à peu ce à quoi allait ressembler sa vie près de lui.

— Comme des animaux, murmura-t-elle pour elle-même. Travailler, manger et dormir. C'est tout ce qu'il veut qu'on fasse. C'est bien de valeur, mais c'est pas comme ça que ça va se passer ici dedans.

Elle prit la ferme résolution de faire de sa nouvelle famille une vraie famille où on a du plaisir à vivre.

— S'il veut pas changer, il restera tout seul dans son coin, murmura-t-elle pour elle-même alors qu'elle entendait les premiers ronflements de son mari.

Quelques minutes plus tard, incapable de trouver le sommeil, elle finit par se relever et s'habiller. Avant de quitter la chambre à coucher, elle prit une épaisse paire de moufles qu'elle avait tricotées et elle les déposa près de la tête de son mari. C'était là le cadeau qu'elle lui avait préparé avec l'espoir qu'il aurait pensé à lui en offrir un. Pendant un instant, elle avait songé à ne pas le lui donner puisqu'il n'avait apparemment rien prévu pour elle. Puis elle avait réalisé que ce n'était pas ainsi qu'il commencerait à lui offrir quelque chose.

À son entrée dans la cuisine, elle entendit des rires en provenance des chambres à l'étage. De toute évidence, les enfants n'avaient pas du tout envie de dormir. Elle monta et les invita à venir jouer aux cartes avec elle.

À la fin de leur sieste, Liam et son oncle les trouvèrent tous les cinq en train de s'amuser. Déjà le soleil baissait à l'horizon.

— Si ça te fait rien, je vais prendre de l'avance avec les filles et on va s'en aller chez ma mère, annonça-t-elle à son mari. Je vais pouvoir donner un coup de main à préparer le souper. Tu viendras nous rejoindre avec les garçons quand le train sera fini.

— C'est correct. Et vous, mon oncle ? Est-ce que vous m'attendez ? demanda-t-il à Paddy.

— Je pense que je vais y aller avec ta femme, si ça te fait rien. Ça va me permettre de faire la connaissance de tout le monde, ajouta-t-il.

— Vous les avez pas mal tous rencontrés à matin après la messe, mon oncle, lui fit remarquer Camille, peu contente de voir venir le quinquagénaire aussi tôt chez sa mère.

❧

Cet après-midi-là, Xavier s'était dépêché d'aller passer quelques heures chez sa promise après avoir prévenu Antonin qu'il serait revenu vers trois heures et demie pour faire le train.

— Après ça, on va se changer et on va aller souper chez ma mère. Elle nous attend.

À son arrivée chez les Benoît, il était passé au salon en compagnie de Catherine à qui il avait appris l'invitation inattendue de sa mère. Immédiatement, le visage de la jeune femme blonde changea d'expression et prit un air préoccupé.

— Je sais pas si je devrais y aller, dit-elle à Xavier.

— Mais t'es invitée, insista-t-il.

— Oui, mais probablement juste parce que ta mère tient à ce que tu y ailles, répliqua-t-elle avec bon sens. Je voudrais pas être la cause d'une chicane en plein jour de l'An. Je te connais. Si ta mère ou quelqu'un de ta famille m'insulte ou me reçoit mal, t'es capable de t'enrager, et on sera pas plus avancés qu'avant.

— Ben non, tu sais ben que personne va faire ça, dit-il sur un ton peu convaincu.

Catherine le regarda longuement et, devant son air malheureux, finit par se résigner à affronter sa future belle-famille.

— C'est correct. Je vais y aller avec toi, mais je t'aurai prévenu. Je veux pas de chicanes avec personne à cause de moi.

— Crains pas, il arrivera rien.

— Bon, j'aimerais te demander quelque chose de difficile, moi aussi, fit-elle en baissant sensiblement la voix.

— Quoi ?

— Ma mère et moi, on aimerait bien que tu fasses la paix avec mon frère et sa femme.

— Mais je suis pas en chicane avec eux autres, protesta Xavier. Ils me boudent. Moi, la seule fois où j'ai parlé à ton frère, c'est quand il s'est mis à te bardasser. Tout ce que j'ai fait, c'est que je lui ai promis une volée s'il recommençait. Rien de plus. Quant à ta belle-sœur, j'ai rien contre elle, même si elle me fait un air de beu depuis que j'ai commencé à te fréquenter.

— Ça nous soulagerait pas mal, ma mère et moi, si vous vous entendiez.

— Ben…

— Je te demande pas de les aimer, reprit Catherine en posant une main sur son bras. J'aimerais juste que vous arrêtiez de vous regarder de travers chaque fois que vous vous rencontrez.

Xavier réfléchit un bon moment avant de se lever. Piler sur son orgueil n'était pas chose facile pour lui, mais il aimait tellement la jeune femme qu'il consentit finalement à faire ce qu'elle venait de lui demander.

Il quitta le salon et passa sans un mot devant Laura Benoît qui les chaperonnait, assise non loin de la porte de la pièce. Le fils de Baptiste Beauchemin s'approcha de la table près de laquelle était installé Cyprien Benoît. En le voyant arriver, ce dernier se leva brusquement, prêt à se défendre.

— J'ai oublié de te souhaiter une bonne année, lui dit Xavier en lui tendant la main.

Surpris, le jeune fermier mit quelques secondes à serrer la main tendue et à souhaiter, à son tour et sans grande chaleur, une bonne année à son futur beau-frère. Sur sa lancée, Xavier s'approcha de Marie-Rose, la femme de Cyprien, et lui offrit aussi ses vœux.

Après avoir fait ce geste, il alla rejoindre Catherine qui était demeurée dans l'embrasure de la porte du salon pour assister à la scène. Au passage, Laura Benoît adressa un sourire de reconnaissance à l'amoureux de sa fille.

❧

Camille et ses deux filles arrivèrent chez les Beauchemin en même temps que les Lafond. À sa grande surprise, l'épouse de Liam Connolly découvrit en pénétrant dans la maison qu'on avait décidé de chauffer la cuisine d'été.

— Seigneur! s'exclama-t-elle en retirant ses bottes, vous avez l'air d'attendre pas mal de monde, si je me trompe pas.

— Pas tant que ça, fit sa mère qu'elle venait d'embrasser. Mais j'ai pensé que ce serait pas une vilaine idée d'envoyer les hommes boucaner de l'autre côté quand ce sera rendu irrespirable dans la cuisine, expliqua-t-elle.

— Je suis arrivée plus de bonne heure avec mes deux filles pour donner un coup de main.

— C'est fin d'y avoir pensé, intervint Bernadette, mais tout est presque prêt. Hubert a même trouvé un moyen d'allonger la table pour qu'on puisse faire deux tablées dans la cuisine.

— Ça va faire moins de voyages qu'avec une autre table dans la cuisine d'été, fit Eugénie en train de disposer des marinades dans des bols.

— Bon, je pense qu'on est aussi ben de s'installer de l'autre côté, déclara Rémi, avec bonne humeur, s'adressant à l'oncle de son beau-frère. J'ai comme l'impression que les femmes tiennent pas trop à nous voir dans leurs jambes.

— S'il y a un bon petit boire de l'autre côté, je suis ben prêt à te suivre, répliqua Paddy avec son sans-gêne habituel.

— Inquiétez-vous pas pour ça, intervint Marie. Donat et Hubert sont à la veille de revenir du train. Ils l'ont fait plus de bonne heure que d'habitude. Donat va vous servir un peu de bagosse pour vous ouvrir l'appétit.

Rose entraîna Flore et Joseph, les deux enfants d'Emma, dans la cuisine d'été, à la suite des deux hommes, en leur promettant de jouer à l'école. La petite fille de six ans avait un an de plus que Flore et trois de plus que son jeune frère.

Quand la porte se fut refermée derrière eux, Camille s'empressa de demander à Emma comment elle allait. La troisième grossesse de la jeune femme blonde semblait être passablement plus difficile que les deux précédentes.

— Il me reste trois mois à faire, répondit Emma, les traits tirés. Je vais passer à travers, inquiète-toi pas.

— Et toi, Bernadette, as-tu passé la journée toute seule? lui demanda sa sœur aînée.

— Bien oui, comme une dinde, répondit l'institutrice, sans grand entrain.

— Prends pas cet air de martyre, l'enjoignit sa mère en tendant une miche de pain à Ann pour qu'elle aille la déposer sur la table. Si tu voulais que le petit Aubé vienne passer l'après-midi avec toi, t'avais juste à l'inviter hier soir quand il est venu veiller. Je t'avais dit qu'il pourrait rester à souper, si ça le tentait.

— Tu l'as pas invité ? s'étonna Eugénie.

— Non.

— Pourquoi ? s'enquit sa sœur aînée, intriguée.

— Il y avait une fête chez les Dionne cet après-midi et Angélique Dionne l'a invité. Ça fait que j'ai pas voulu qu'il se sente obligé de venir chez nous.

— T'es drôle, toi, ne put s'empêcher de lui dire Camille. C'est ton cavalier et t'es prête à laisser la fille de Télesphore Dionne te le voler.

— À la place de ce garçon-là, intervint sa mère, je me dirais que ma blonde tient pas trop à moi si elle fait ça.

— C'est pas ça, m'man, protesta Bernadette, mais…

Des bruits de bottes sur la galerie l'empêchèrent de compléter sa pensée. Elle fit trois pas vers la fenêtre pour tenter de voir qui venait d'arriver, comme si elle espérait, contre toute attente, que ce soit Constant.

— Ça peut pas être Xavier, laissa tomber Marie. On aurait entendu les grelots de son attelage.

D'ailleurs les voix de Donat et de Hubert confirmèrent ce qu'elle venait de dire. Peu après, ce dernier pénétra dans la cuisine pour y prendre des tasses dans lesquelles il allait servir de la bagosse.

— On n'est pas plus bêtes que les hommes, déclara soudainement Marie. Eugénie, sors donc le vin de cerise, on va en boire un peu.

Quelques minutes plus tard, Liam arriva en compagnie de ses deux fils. À peine venaient-ils tous les trois de retirer leur manteau que Xavier arriva avec Catherine et Antonin.

La jeune fille attendit que son compagnon ait jeté une épaisse couverture sur le dos de son cheval avant de se mettre en route vers la maison en sa compagnie et celle de l'adolescent.

— T'as pas à t'en faire, lui murmura Xavier. Tout va ben se passer, tu vas voir.

Les trois derniers invités poussèrent la porte de la cuisine d'été déjà passablement enfumée par Hubert, Paddy, Rémi et Donat.

— Blasphème! s'écria Xavier en guise de plaisanterie, il y a tellement de fumée ici dedans qu'on penserait qu'il y a le feu.

— Dis-toi que ça va être pire dans une couple de minutes parce que Antonin, Liam et toi vous fumez vous aussi, répliqua Donat en venant accueillir les nouveaux arrivés.

La porte séparant les deux cuisines s'ouvrit pour livrer passage à Marie. À la vue de sa future belle-mère, le visage de Catherine devint plus pâle et Xavier sentit la main de la jeune femme posée sur son bras trembler légèrement.

— Entrez, mettez vos manteaux sur le lit de ma chambre, leur ordonna-t-elle. Restez pas ici dedans à vous faire emboucaner. Et vous autres, les hommes, allez-y doucement avec la bagosse, prit-elle soin d'ajouter avant de faire signe à Catherine d'entrer dans la cuisine d'hiver.

— Bonsoir, madame Beauchemin, dit Catherine d'une toute petite voix, je vous souhaite une bonne année.

— Moi aussi, ma fille, dit Marie en lui plaquant un baiser sur une joue.

Mais les vœux de l'hôtesse étaient plutôt froids. Eugénie, Emma, Bernadette, Camille et Ann furent un peu plus chaleureuses dans leur accueil, autant envers Antonin, qu'elles n'avaient pas vu le matin même, qu'envers la fiancée de Xavier.

— Viens enlever ton manteau dans la chambre, proposa Camille à sa future belle-sœur.

Elle l'entraîna dans la chambre située au pied de l'escalier. Xavier les suivit. Catherine, consciente de la froideur de la mère de Xavier, retira son manteau. La jeune femme était mal à l'aise et se demandait comment elle allait pouvoir supporter cela durant toute la soirée. Camille se rendit compte de son malaise et lui souffla :

— Inquiète-toi pas trop, ça va passer. Ma mère est souvent comme ça avec le monde qu'elle connaît pas, mentit-elle.

Xavier lui adressa un sourire de reconnaissance avant d'entraîner Catherine dans la cuisine.

— Toi, tu vas pas traîner dans nos jambes pendant qu'on finit de préparer le souper, l'apostropha sa mère. Va donc rejoindre les hommes de l'autre côté et laisse-nous tranquilles un peu.

Xavier haussa les épaules et disparut dans la pièce voisine avec Antonin pendant que Bernadette entreprenait de mettre la table.

— Avez-vous un tablier pour moi, madame Beauchemin ? demanda Catherine en faisant un effort pour s'intégrer au groupe de femmes en train de préparer le repas.

— On devrait être capables de te trouver ça, répondit Marie. Bedette, il y en a un propre derrière la porte du garde-manger, ajouta-t-elle en se tournant vers sa fille cadette.

— On est six femmes ici dedans, déclara Emma. Jamais je croirai qu'on n'est pas capables de nourrir la bande de fainéants qui sont en train de jaser de l'autre côté.

L'éclat de rire général qui salua cette saillie eut le don de détendre un peu l'atmosphère empruntée qui s'était installée dans la cuisine.

Quand tout fut prêt, Marie décida qu'on devait faire manger les plus jeunes à une première tablée. Elle ouvrit la porte de la cuisine d'été pour déclarer aux enfants qui s'étaient réfugiés là :

— Les jeunes, on va vous servir à manger d'abord. Nous autres, les plus vieux, on se tassera à la deuxième tablée.

— Moi, ça me dérange pas pantoute de manger en premier, intervint Hubert en calculant qu'il y aurait beaucoup trop d'adultes au deuxième service.

— Je vais y aller avec lui, si ça vous arrange, madame Beauchemin, proposa Antonin.

— Vous êtes bien fins tous les deux, fit l'hôtesse. Consolez-vous en vous disant que vous allez manger la même chose que les autres. Il y a de la soupe aux légumes, des patates, du jambon et de la tourtière. Pour le dessert, vous verrez.

— C'est ben correct pour nous autres, affirma Hubert avec bonne humeur. En plus, on va surveiller ceux qui mangent mal et on va leur taper sur les doigts, ajouta-t-il en adressant un regard féroce aux enfants que cette mimique fit rire.

Bref, Hubert et Antonin prirent place à table en même temps que les sept enfants. Ils furent rapidement servis, surveillés de près par une Emma armée d'une grosse louche, l'air mauvais.

— Veux-tu bien me dire ce que t'as à rester plantée près de la table avec ta grosse cuillère? lui demanda sa mère.

— J'attends d'en entendre un seul critiquer ce qu'on vient de lui servir, il va en manger un bon coup.

Les enfants de Liam se figèrent pendant que la petite Flore se mettait à rire.

— M'man fait une farce, dit la petite fille de cinq ans, contente de la plaisanterie de celle qu'elle considérait maintenant comme sa mère.

— Enlève-toi de là, ordonna Marie à sa fille, et arrange-toi pas pour leur couper l'appétit.

Après le mets principal, les enfants eurent droit à un morceau de gâteau et à des beignets. Pendant qu'ils mangeaient leur dessert, Bernadette commença à laver la vaisselle et Catherine, sans dire un mot, s'empara d'un linge pour l'essuyer en compagnie de Camille. Il y avait beaucoup de bruit dans la cuisine et on parlait fort.

— Xavier t'a-t-il fiancée? murmura Camille à la fille de Laura Benoît.

— Non, pas encore, répondit la jeune fille sur le même ton.

— Il t'a demandée en mariage, non?

— Oui, samedi passé, mais je sais que ça fait pas l'affaire de tout le monde, ajouta Catherine d'une voix un peu tremblante.

— Laisse faire, fit Camille d'une voix apaisante. L'important, c'est que vous vous aimiez tous les deux. Le reste va s'arranger.

Catherine lui adressa un sourire de reconnaissance pour la remercier de son encouragement.

— Bon, les enfants, vous allez à côté pendant que nous autres on va manger, annonça Marie quand le dernier eut avalé son dessert. Ann, est-ce que tu peux t'occuper d'Alexis pendant qu'on mange?

— Oui, madame Beauchemin.

— Antonin et moi, on va rester ici dedans, proche du poêle, pour vérifier que vous mangez proprement, déclara Hubert à l'instant où les hommes venaient s'installer autour de la table à leur tour.

— Vous pouvez rester, mais vous nous emboucanez pas pendant qu'on mange, ordonna la maîtresse de maison.

— Tiens, toi, tu peux aussi bien nous surveiller en essuyant un peu de vaisselle, ajouta Bernadette en lui tendant un linge.

— C'est ça, et moi, je vais laver, dit Antonin, plein de bonne volonté. Ça va nous aider à digérer ce qu'on a mangé.

— J'aime pas ben ça, cette affaire-là, déclara Hubert. C'est donner un ben mauvais pli aux femmes que de commencer à faire leur ouvrage. Elles sont une demi-douzaine ici dedans…

— Si tu veux pas, t'es pas obligé, intervint sa mère au moment de remplir une assiette. C'est vrai que c'est pas un ouvrage d'homme. La même chose pour toi, Antonin.

— Mais vous pouvez faire un spécial au jour de l'An, les taquina Camille.

— C'est correct, on va le faire, consentit Hubert en faisant signe à l'adolescent de se mettre à laver la vaisselle empilée près de lui.

Camille, Emma, Eugénie et Marie eurent tôt fait de déposer une assiette bien garnie devant chacun des convives.

— Catherine, lâche ton linge à vaisselle et va t'asseoir à côté de Xavier, dit Marie à la jeune fille qui n'avait pas osé s'approcher. Tout le monde est servi, il est temps qu'on mange. Donat, dis le bénédicité avant que ça refroidisse, commanda-t-elle à son fils.

Le silence tomba sur la pièce et seule la voix de Donat se fit entendre. On se signa à la fin de la prière. Entassés sur le banc placé derrière la table, Catherine et Xavier étaient assis aux côtés d'Emma et de Rémi. En face d'eux mangeaient Liam, Camille et Paddy Connolly, alors qu'à une extrémité Bernadette et sa mère faisaient face à Donat et à Eugénie.

Si certains avaient craint que la présence de la fille de Laura Benoît ne jette un froid sur ce repas de fête, ils furent rassurés. Il y eut bien un moment de tristesse engendré par une remarque de l'hôtesse qui mentionna, la gorge apparemment nouée, l'absence de son mari pour la première fois à cette fête de famille, mais Paddy Connolly, avec sa verve habituelle, se chargea de dérider les convives entassés autour de lui. Pendant tout le repas, on n'entendit pratiquement que lui. Il raconta, entre autres, le grand incendie de Montréal en 1852 dans lequel avait brûlé la cathédrale Saint-Jacques, située au coin des rues Saint-Denis et Sainte-Catherine. Il parla longuement de la décision plutôt controversée de monseigneur Bourget de faire construire la nouvelle cathédrale dans l'ouest de la ville. Selon ses dires, le clergé montréalais n'était pas peu fier de clamer que le nouvel édifice allait ressembler à Saint-Pierre-de-Rome.

— Cette construction-là est supposée commencer dans deux ou trois ans, déclara l'oncle en adoptant un air avantageux.

— Comment vous êtes au courant de tout ça? lui demanda Rémi, impressionné autant par la faconde que par les grands airs du quinquagénaire rubicond.

— L'ingénieur est passé me voir pour savoir si je serais à même de fournir une partie du fer qui va entrer dans cette construction-là, laissa-t-il tomber.

Plusieurs convives, admiratifs, hochèrent la tête. Paddy Connolly en profita aussi pour parler de la grande patinoire ouverte sur le port de Montréal ainsi que des nouveaux tramways tirés par des chevaux, dont la ville venait de se doter. Son long monologue dériva ensuite sur les récentes exigences sanitaires des autorités municipales pour lutter contre les épidémies de variole qui frappaient trop souvent la population montréalaise.

Alors que l'oncle de Liam se taisait un court instant pour boire une gorgée de thé, Xavier se leva pour prendre la parole. Il était visiblement ému. Il tira une petite bourse en tissu de l'une des poches de son veston. Un lourd silence tomba immédiatement sur la pièce et Marie, les traits figés, fixa son fils, se doutant un peu de ce qui allait suivre à la vue de ce qu'il tenait à la main. Catherine, mal à l'aise d'être le point de mire de toute la tablée, baissait les yeux.

— J'ai attendu que toute la famille soit réunie pour vous annoncer que j'ai demandé la main de Catherine à sa mère, dit Xavier, la voix changée. Elle a accepté et nous avons décidé de nous marier au mois de juin, le dernier samedi.

Cette annonce ne suscita aucune réaction. Le jeune homme regarda les gens assis autour de la table les uns après les autres avant de poursuivre.

— À soir, j'en ai pas encore parlé à Catherine, mais ce sont nos fiançailles, ajouta-t-il sur un ton déterminé en obligeant la jeune femme à se lever à ses côtés.

Puis, sans plus attendre, il sortit une petite bague en or blanc de la bourse et la passa à l'annulaire de la main droite de sa promise, rougissante.

Il y eut un temps mort avant que Paddy, ignorant de tout ce qui entourait cette histoire, se mette à applaudir bruyamment, imité avec un temps de retard par tous les autres invités. Marie fut la dernière à s'exécuter.

On quitta bientôt la table et les hommes se réfugièrent dans la cuisine d'été pendant que les femmes rangeaient la pièce et lavaient la vaisselle. Catherine s'empressa de se rapprocher de Camille dont elle sentait intuitivement la sympathie. Pour sa part, Marie était allée chercher Alexis dans la cuisine d'été et avait annoncé qu'elle montait le préparer pour la nuit.

— Je le savais pas qu'il ferait ça, murmura Catherine à Camille.

— C'est pas important, lui dit sa future belle-sœur à voix basse. Inquiète-toi pas, il fallait que ce soit fait. Ma mère va finir par s'habituer à l'idée d'avoir une nouvelle bru, sentit-elle le besoin d'ajouter pour apaiser l'angoisse de la fiancée de son frère.

Quelques minutes plus tard, on frappa à la porte et Hubert alla ouvrir à Constant Aubé, le visage rougi par le froid.

— Dis-moi pas que t'es venu à pied, même s'il gèle à pierre fendre, dit-il au cavalier de sa sœur.

— C'est pas si pire. J'espère que j'arrive pas en plein milieu du repas, s'inquiéta le meunier en enlevant sa tuque et ses moufles.

— Inquiète-toi pas, on a fini de manger depuis un bon bout de temps. La vaisselle est même lavée, dit Bernadette qui venait d'apparaître dans le dos de son frère.

Hubert se retira pour aller rejoindre les hommes installés autour de la table de la cuisine d'été, les laissant seuls.

— Ça me surprend que tu sois venu me voir à soir, fit la jeune fille d'une voix acide pendant que son cavalier déboutonnait son manteau.

— Pourquoi tu me dis ça? s'étonna Constant à mi-voix.

— Je pensais jamais que tu lâcherais la fête chez les Dionne assez de bonne heure pour venir veiller.

— Mais je suis pas allé là, se défendit le jeune homme.

— T'es pas allé passer l'après-midi avec la belle Angélique? demanda Bernadette, incapable de dissimuler plus longtemps sa jalousie.

— Pantoute.

— Qu'est-ce que t'as fait d'abord toute la journée?

— Ben, je suis resté chez nous en attendant de venir te voir.

— Avoir su, je t'aurais invité à venir passer l'après-midi avec moi, regretta Bernadette, repentante. J'étais certaine que t'étais allé chez Dionne.

— Ben non, si je me fie à ce que j'ai entendu à matin, les Dionne avaient invité tellement de monde que la maison devait être pleine à craquer.

— T'aurais bien pu y aller, consentit à dire la jeune institutrice maintenant rassurée. Tu sais bien qu'ici on chantera pas et on dansera pas à cause de notre deuil.

— J'avais pas le temps, je devais finir tes étrennes, murmura Constant en lui tendant un paquet qu'il avait conservé sous l'un de ses bras.

— Qu'est-ce que c'est? demanda-t-elle, tout excitée en cherchant à s'emparer du colis.

— Si t'es assez fine pour m'inviter à enlever mon manteau, je vais te le donner, dit-il, taquin.

Elle prit son épais manteau d'étoffe du pays et, pendant qu'elle allait le déposer sur le lit de sa mère, Constant souhaita une bonne année aux hommes dans la pièce. À son retour dans la cuisine d'été, la jeune fille l'entraîna dans la pièce voisine. En rougissant un peu, il dut faire le tour de toutes les femmes présentes pour les embrasser sur une joue après leur avoir offert ses vœux. S'il fut étonné de voir Catherine Benoît, il le cacha bien.

— J'espère que vous avez pas l'intention de passer la soirée tout seuls dans le salon comme des coqs d'Inde ? plaisanta Emma.

— C'est Bernadette qui décide, déclara Constant avec un sourire.

— Laissez-lui le temps de me donner mes étrennes et on va venir s'amuser avec vous autres, fit Bernadette en prenant une lampe et en faisant signe à son amoureux de la suivre au salon.

— Ann, va surveiller ce qui va se passer là, ordonna Emma pour plaisanter.

— Toi, arrange-toi pas pour faire haïr ma fille, intervint Camille en riant. Bouge pas, Ann.

Dans le salon, Constant n'avait pas pris la peine de s'asseoir sur le canapé. Il s'était borné à tendre à Bernadette le paquet qu'il n'avait pas encore lâché.

— C'est pour aller avec les bottes de l'année passée, dit-il.

La jeune fille déchira l'emballage assez grossier et découvrit un magnifique manchon dont l'extérieur était fait du même cuir que ses bottes. Il était doublé d'une épaisse fourrure.

— Aïe, mais c'est bien beau ça ! s'exclama Bernadette, ravie.

— Je sais pas si c'est beau, mais ça devrait être pas mal chaud. Ah ! pendant que j'y pense, ajouta-t-il en sortant une lanière de cuir souple de la poche de son veston, je t'ai fait une courroie pour ton sac d'école. Comme ça, tu pourras le porter sur l'épaule et mettre tes deux mains dans ton manchon. Tu te gèleras plus les doigts.

Incapable de se retenir, Bernadette l'embrassa avec fougue pour le remercier. Le jeune meunier en resta pantelant.

— Ouf! une chance que ma mère m'a pas vue, s'empressa-t-elle de déclarer. Je te dis que je me ferais parler. Attends-moi une minute, j'ai quelque chose pour toi, dit-elle avant de sortir du salon.

Elle revint dans la pièce moins d'une minute plus tard, portant un paquet joliment emballé. Elle le lui tendit.

— C'est pour moi? demanda-t-il, étonné.

— Oui, tu peux l'ouvrir.

Constant trouva dans le paquet une tuque et une paire de chaussettes en laine grise qu'elle avait tricotées. Il la remercia, apparemment très ému qu'elle ait songé à lui donner quelque chose.

— C'est la première fois qu'une fille me fait un cadeau, murmura-t-il.

— Je l'espère bien… rétorqua-t-elle en prenant un air sévère. Comme ça, tu vas avoir chaud aux deux extrémités, ajouta-t-elle, mutine.

À leur sortie du salon, Bernadette ne put s'empêcher de montrer le cadeau qu'elle avait reçu de son amoureux. Chacune voulut essayer le manchon et s'extasia sur sa beauté et son confort.

— Il y en a qui sont chanceuses de se faire gâter comme ça, ne put s'empêcher de déclarer Camille.

Sa mère remarqua son dépit et sa peine et s'empressa de dire:

— Quand ça vient pas tout seul à son mari, il faut le dompter.

— C'est ce que j'ai fait, déclara Emma à voix basse. Il faut surtout pas l'habituer à tout recevoir sans jamais rien donner, précisa-t-elle.

Peu à peu, les hommes revinrent dans la cuisine d'hiver pour tenir compagnie aux femmes. On parla des jours de l'An passés et des mésaventures survenues à des membres de la famille durant l'année. Ensuite, on se mit à raconter des histoires en les enjolivant. Le meilleur dans ce domaine fut naturellement Paddy, peut-être parce qu'il s'agissait de récits que personne ne connaissait.

Au milieu de la soirée, l'hôtesse offrit du sucre à la crème et des fondants. Ensuite, Liam et son oncle se mirent à raconter des légendes où le diable jouait un grand rôle. Le premier conta *Le diable bâtisseur d'église* et Paddy enchaîna avec *Rose Latulippe*, ce qui impressionna beaucoup les enfants. Pour ne pas être en reste, Rémi les relança en contant *La chasse-galerie*. Les enfants écoutaient, tentant de combattre bravement leur peur. Quand l'horloge indiqua dix heures, Liam se leva.

— Bon, il est pas mal tard, déclara-t-il. Je pense qu'il est temps d'y aller.

— Et il y en a qui vont faire des cauchemars en dormant, poursuivit Camille en faisant allusion aux enfants.

Sans le vouloir, le couple avait donné le signal de la fin de la soirée. En quelques minutes, tous les invités se retrouvèrent avec leur manteau sur le dos, prêts à partir.

— Je peux ben aller vous conduire chez vous avant de rentrer à la maison, proposa Xavier à Camille et Liam.

— Ben non, refusa son beau-frère. On reste juste à quelques arpents. Ça va juste nous faire du bien de prendre l'air un peu avant d'aller nous coucher.

— C'est comme tu veux. Toi, Constant, veux-tu qu'on te laisse en passant ?

— C'est pas de refus, accepta le jeune meunier.

Au moment de partir, Catherine, comme les autres invités, remercia chaleureusement Marie de son invitation et de son bon repas.

— Si t'as aimé ça, t'as juste à revenir, dit l'hôtesse assez froidement.

Dès que le dernier invité eut quitté la maison, Hubert et Donat enlevèrent la rallonge temporaire de la table et se chargèrent de remplir le coffre de bûches pendant que

Bernadette, Eugénie et Marie remettaient un peu d'ordre dans la cuisine.

— Catherine avait l'air bien contente d'avoir été invitée, fit remarquer Bernadette sans s'adresser directement à sa mère.

— Tu sauras, ma fille, que je l'ai reçue pour que ton frère se sente pas rejeté par la famille en plein jour de l'An. Mais fais-toi pas d'idée, j'ai pas changé d'avis. Cette fille-là est pas pour lui.

— M'man ! je…

— Parle pas pour rien dire, lui ordonna sèchement sa mère. Il y a pas un garçon qui se respecte qui marierait une fille comme elle… Bon, je suis fatiguée. Vous direz votre prière tout seuls. Je vais me coucher.

Là-dessus, la maîtresse de maison disparut dans sa chambre, à la grande surprise de tous.

— Torrieu ! j'étais sûr que c'était fini cette histoire-là, s'exclama Donat à mi-voix.

— On dirait bien que c'est pas l'idée de ta mère, fit sa femme en allumant une lampe de service avant de monter à l'étage.

— Elle va ben finir par se calmer, intervint Hubert, optimiste.

Le retour à la maison chez les Connolly fut beaucoup moins agréable parce que le poêle avait eu le temps de s'éteindre quelques heures plus tôt. Comme la température était bien au-dessous du point de congélation en ce 1er janvier 1872, la maison était glaciale et humide.

— Vous gardez votre manteau sur votre dos et vous attendez que je vous dise de l'ôter, dit Camille aux enfants en s'empressant d'allumer le poêle.

— Moi, je boirais ben une bonne tasse de thé pour me réchauffer, dit Paddy Connolly en se laissant tomber dans l'une des deux chaises berçantes.

— Pour ça, mon oncle, vous allez devoir attendre que le poêle chauffe, lui dit-elle avec un rien d'impatience dans la voix.

— Les enfants ont de la misère à garder les yeux ouverts, dit Liam en apercevant Rose qui somnolait.

— Les enfants, vous pouvez aller vous coucher, mais restez habillés, dit Camille après une courte hésitation.

Ils ne se firent pas prier et montèrent se coucher, laissant les trois adultes près du poêle dans lequel les bûches enflammées s'étaient mises à crépiter.

— Ta famille, c'est du ben bon monde, dit Paddy à sa nièce par alliance.

— C'est vrai, reconnut Camille, et ils sont généreux. Ils sont toujours prêts à rendre service et à donner tout ce qu'ils ont.

— Ça empêche pas que ta mère a eu l'air d'avoir invité Catherine Benoît pas mal à reculons, laissa tomber Liam en allumant sa pipe.

— Peut-être, mais elle l'a fait quand même. En passant, as-tu vu le beau cadeau que Constant Aubé a fait à ma sœur ?

— Le manchon ?

— Oui.

— C'est facile pour lui, il travaille le cuir, dit son mari sur un ton désinvolte.

— Peut-être, mais c'est le geste qui est important, répliqua-t-elle. Il a du cœur, cet homme-là.

— Moi, je trouve ça niaiseux de passer son temps à se donner des cadeaux, laissa-t-il tomber.

Paddy hocha la tête comme s'il approuvait ce que son neveu venait de dire.

— Si c'est comme ça, je vais garder le foulard et les mitaines que je t'ai tricotés, riposta-t-elle abruptement. Quand t'auras changé d'idée sur les étrennes, je te les donnerai.

Surpris par cet éclat, Liam jeta un coup d'œil à son oncle qui ne broncha pas. Camille alluma une autre lampe.

— Je vous souhaite une bonne nuit. Je suis fatiguée, je m'en vais me coucher.

La jeune femme entra dans sa chambre et referma la porte derrière elle. Pendant un court moment, elle songea à se déshabiller pour passer son épaisse robe de nuit, mais elle y renonça tant il faisait froid dans la pièce.

Au moment où elle s'asseyait sur son lit pour enlever ses chaussures, elle aperçut quelque chose sur son oreiller. C'était un mouchoir et une feuille ornée de quatre belles roses dessinées de façon un peu malhabile sur laquelle on avait écrit : «Bonne année ! Nous t'aimons très fort». Elle était signée des quatre enfants.

Les larmes lui vinrent immédiatement aux yeux tant le geste la touchait. Elle se leva, prit la lampe et quitta la chambre.

— Où est-ce que tu vas ? lui demanda Liam.

— Voir si les enfants ont pas trop froid, se borna-t-elle à lui répondre.

Camille entra d'abord dans la chambre des filles. Rose dormait déjà, pelotonnée contre sa grande sœur. Elle remercia Ann et les embrassa toutes les deux après les avoir bordées. Elle passa ensuite dans chacune des chambres des garçons. Ils ne dormaient pas encore. Elle les remercia pour leur cadeau et les embrassa aussi avec reconnaissance avant de descendre au rez-de-chaussée. Ce simple geste de ses enfants adoptifs la consolait du peu d'égards de leur père à son endroit. Quand elle se mit au lit, elle sombra immédiatement dans un sommeil réparateur, malgré l'humidité et le froid qui régnaient dans la pièce.

Chapitre 5

La peur

Le lendemain matin, Paddy Connolly fut le dernier membre de la famille à se présenter dans la cuisine. Il s'approcha de l'une des fenêtres et devant l'épaisseur du givre qui couvrait la moitié de la vitre, il eut du mal à réprimer un frisson.

— Calvinus ! ça a pas l'air d'être ben chaud dehors, dit-il à Camille, occupée à préparer le gruau qu'elle allait servir au déjeuner.

— On gèle à matin, mon oncle. Je viens juste d'aller nourrir les cochons et les poules. Je vous dis que c'est pas le temps de traîner dehors.

— Liam a pas encore fini son train ?

— Il devrait achever. J'ai vu les garçons sortir de l'étable il y a deux minutes. Ils doivent être en train d'apporter du bois pour le poêle.

Peu après, la porte s'ouvrit sur Patrick et Duncan, les bras chargés de bûches qu'ils laissèrent tomber bruyamment dans le coffre à bois.

— Va me chercher de l'eau au puits avant de te déshabiller, demanda Camille à Patrick.

— Ann pourrait ben y aller, elle, se rebiffa-t-il.

— Ta sœur est en train de trancher le pain pour le déjeuner. Grouille avant que ton père rentre.

Le garçon de onze ans sortit avec un seau et revint en même temps que son père. Tout le monde passa à table et

Camille servit à chacun un bol de gruau chaud. À la fin du repas pris dans un silence presque complet, Liam déclara qu'il n'irait pas bûcher ce jour-là et qu'il nettoierait plutôt l'étable et l'écurie avec ses deux fils.

Camille ne fit aucun commentaire. Quand il avait mis les pieds dans la cuisine ce matin-là, elle s'était empressée de lui montrer le cadeau que lui avaient fait les enfants. Il n'avait rien dit, mais elle avait deviné à son air renfrogné qu'il n'appréciait pas de n'avoir rien reçu de leur part.

— Nous autres, on va remettre de l'ordre dans les chambres et faire le lavage, annonça Camille.

— En plein milieu de la semaine ? s'étonna son mari.

— Lundi, c'était la veille du jour de l'An. Je l'ai passée à cuisiner et à cuire le pain, lui rappela-t-elle.

— Et vous, mon oncle, qu'est-ce que vous allez faire ? demanda-t-il à Paddy qui venait d'allumer l'un de ses cigares malodorants.

— Je sais pas trop, répondit son oncle en hésitant.

— Avez-vous dans l'idée de partir cet avant-midi ou cet après-midi ? lui demanda plus directement Camille, qui commençait à en avoir assez de le servir depuis près d'une semaine sans jamais recevoir le moindre remerciement pour sa peine.

— À ce propos, je voulais te dire deux mots, mon neveu, dit Paddy Connolly en s'adressant exclusivement à Liam.

— Qu'est-ce qu'il y a, mon oncle ?

— Sais-tu, j'ai pensé à mon affaire, répondit le retraité. J'ai rien de pressant qui m'attend à Montréal. Qu'est-ce que tu dirais si j'hivernais avec vous autres ?

Camille sentit le sang se retirer de son visage. La dernière chose qu'elle souhaitait était bien d'avoir continuellement dans ses jupes cet homme qui allait traîner dans la maison du matin au soir. Elle sentit son mari hésiter et elle décida d'intervenir.

— Ce serait pas bien intéressant pour vous, mon oncle, déclara-t-elle. Liam passe d'habitude ses journées dans le bois et les enfants sont tous à l'école.

— C'est pas ben grave, répliqua Paddy avec un grand sourire. Quand je m'ennuierai, j'attellerai et j'irai passer une heure ou deux au magasin général.

— Je veux bien le croire, mais vos affaires ?

— Je te l'ai déjà dit, j'ai tout vendu. À mon âge, je pense avoir le droit de me reposer un peu.

— Mais il vous reste vos maisons à Montréal. Qui va s'en occuper ? demanda-t-elle, à court d'arguments.

— Inquiète-toi pas pour ça. J'ai un homme de confiance ben capable, répondit-il avant de se tourner vers Liam. Puis, mon neveu, qu'est-ce que tu penses de mon idée ?

— Ben…

— Tu peux être certain que tu y perdras rien, ajouta l'ex-homme d'affaires montréalais en affichant un air bon enfant.

— C'est correct, mon oncle. Ça va nous faire plaisir de vous garder, accepta finalement le maître de maison en évitant de croiser le regard furieux de sa femme.

— T'as juste à le dire si ça vous dérange, dit sans trop insister l'importun.

— Pantoute, mon oncle, vous êtes chez vous ici dedans.

Le sourire suffisant de l'homme ne fit qu'ajouter à la colère de Camille, qui entreprit de laver la vaisselle du déjeuner avec ses deux filles pendant que son nouveau pensionnaire décidait de monter à sa chambre pour y faire sa toilette.

Dès qu'elle entendit la porte de la chambre se refermer à l'étage, elle déposa l'assiette qu'elle s'apprêtait à laver.

— J'aimerais te dire deux mots dans notre chambre, dit-elle à mi-voix à son mari.

— Ben là, je m'en vais aux bâtiments, fit-il en s'approchant du crochet auquel était suspendu son manteau.

— Si ça te fait rien, ça va attendre un peu, répliqua-t-elle, les dents serrées, en se dirigeant vers leur chambre à coucher.

Liam laissa son manteau et la suivit. Il referma la porte derrière lui.

— Veux-tu bien me dire à quoi tu penses de garder ton oncle tout l'hiver ? lui demanda-t-elle, agressive. Il me semble que t'aurais pu me demander mon avis, non ?

— Il dérangera rien.

— Toi, il te dérangera pas parce que c'est pas toi qui vas l'avoir dans les jambes toute la sainte journée, riposta-t-elle, exaspérée.

— Tu commences à le connaître, il va toujours être à gauche et à droite.

— Oui, et il va rentrer pour chaque repas. Et moi, la folle, je vais être sa servante. Je vais le nourrir et le blanchir. As-tu pensé qu'il prend la chambre de Rose ?

— La petite peut ben coucher avec Ann cet hiver, elle en mourra pas.

— C'est bien beau tout ça, mais t'as même pas parlé du montant de sa pension.

— C'est de la famille, se justifia-t-il.

— Est-ce que ça veut dire qu'on va le garder ici dedans sans rien lui demander ? fit-elle stupéfaite. Si c'était un parent dans la misère, je comprendrais, mais il est riche, bien plus riche qu'on le sera jamais.

— Tu comprends rien, toi, dit-il en élevant la voix. Je te l'ai déjà dit. Je suis sa seule famille. Tout son argent va me revenir. À qui veux-tu qu'il le donne ? Ça fait que tu vas arrêter de faire ta tête de cochon et lui faire une belle façon. Arrange-toi pas pour qu'il nous déshérite, tu m'entends ?

Sur ces mots bien sentis, Liam quitta la chambre et alla endosser son manteau. Patrick et Duncan l'avaient précédé à l'extérieur. Folle de rage, Camille revint à l'évier poursuivre sa tâche. Elle avait la nette impression que Paddy Connolly les exploitait et cela la mettait dans tous ses états. Quand l'oncle de son mari annonça quelques minutes plus tard qu'il s'en allait au magasin général, elle ne dit pas un mot.

❧

Les jours suivants, un froid sibérien s'abattit sur la région, rendant tout travail à l'extérieur très pénible. Camille sentait que Patrick et Duncan avaient hâte de retourner à l'école pour échapper aux durs travaux que leur père exigeait d'eux chaque jour. Il était évident que les deux garçons redoutaient surtout les jours où ils devaient l'accompagner en forêt pour charger le traîneau avec le bois débité. Les longues heures d'exposition au froid semblaient les épuiser.

— Sois pas trop dur avec les garçons, finit-elle par dire à son mari après avoir remarqué leur fatigue au retour d'une longue journée de travail.

— C'est pas en les gardant sous tes jupes qu'ils vont apprendre ce que c'est que l'ouvrage, rétorqua-t-il avec humeur.

— Ils sont encore pas mal jeunes, lui fit-elle remarquer sur un ton maternel.

— Ils ont l'âge pour apprendre à gagner ce qu'ils mangent, laissa-t-il tomber sur un ton définitif.

À la fête des Rois, Camille se leva tôt pour préparer la galette dans laquelle elle dissimula un pois et une fève. Au retour de la messe dominicale, elle servit aux siens des pommes de terre et du rôti de bœuf. Quand arriva le moment du dessert, elle déposa devant chacun un morceau de galette après avoir expliqué que ceux qui allaient découvrir le pois et la fève dans leur galette seraient le roi et la reine du jour et pourraient se permettre de faire ce qu'ils désiraient le reste de la journée, dans les limites du raisonnable, bien entendu.

Liam poussa un soupir d'exaspération en adressant une grimace d'agacement à son oncle, qui n'avait rien dit.

Évidemment, la maîtresse de maison savait exactement qui allait hériter du pois et de la fève. Elle avait fait en sorte de servir les morceaux de galette les contenant à Rose et à Duncan.

— Faites bien attention de pas vous casser une dent sur le pois ou la fève en mangeant, prévint la cuisinière en reprenant sa place au bout de la table.

Tous les convives se mirent à manger leur dessert avec précaution. Camille appréciait à leur juste valeur les regards brillants de plaisir des quatre enfants assis à table.

— Moi, j'ai quelque chose, s'écria brusquement Duncan en retirant le pois de sa bouche.

— Bravo ! fit Camille.

— Moi aussi ! s'exclama la petite Rose, tout excitée.

— Parfait, on a une reine et un roi, dit leur mère adoptive en feignant de ne pas voir l'air dépité de Patrick et de sa sœur aînée.

— Est-ce que ça veut dire que je peux décider de rester dans la maison tout le reste de la journée ? demanda Duncan en tournant sa tête rousse vers son père.

Ce dernier allait refuser quand sa femme le prit de court et répondit à sa place qu'il était le roi pour la journée et qu'il avait le droit de ne rien faire, s'il le voulait. Liam sembla avoir du mal à ne pas la contredire.

— Et moi, déclara Rose, je pense que j'essuierai pas la vaisselle.

— T'as le droit, ma puce, fit Camille.

— Je vais faire comme mon oncle et passer ma journée à rien faire, affirma Duncan en se dirigeant vers l'une des chaises berçantes.

— Toi, mon petit désespoir, essayes-tu de me faire passer pour un sans-cœur ? demanda Paddy, finalement amusé par le jeu.

— Il y a pas à dire, t'as eu une autre bonne idée, dit Liam à sa femme.

Il quitta la table de fort mauvaise humeur.

— Tu sauras, Liam Connolly, que la galette des Rois, c'est une tradition, s'empressa-t-elle de répliquer. Je te gage qu'il y a pas deux maisons à Saint-Bernard où on la fait pas.

— Si ça avait été moi qui avais trouvé le pois, j'aurais fumé la pipe toute la journée, dit Patrick, envieux. Là, c'est pas ben juste, je vais être tout seul à travailler avec p'pa cet après-midi.

— Toi, arrête de dire n'importe quoi et avance, lui ordonna durement son père. On a assez perdu de temps avec ces niaiseries-là.

Camille adressa un clin d'œil de connivence à Ann avant de commencer à desservir la table. Quand Patrick eut suivi son père à l'extérieur et après que l'oncle fut monté faire sa sieste, Ann lui demanda à voix basse :

— Est-ce que c'était arrangé ?

— Pantoute, pourquoi tu me demandes ça ?

— Si c'est pas arrangé, comment ça se fait que c'est pas deux garçons ou deux filles qui trouvent le pois et la fève ? lui fit remarquer l'adolescente.

— Voyons, Ann ! Quand on fait la galette, on met le pois dans une moitié de la galette et la fève dans l'autre et on fait un tout petit signe sur la pâte pour reconnaître chaque partie. Quand on la sert, on s'organise pour servir une moitié aux filles et l'autre aux garçons.

En cette dernière journée des vacances scolaires, Camille occupa une bonne partie de son après-midi à vérifier l'état des vêtements qu'allaient porter les enfants le lendemain pour leur retour à l'école. Elle était heureuse qu'Ann ait accepté de retourner en classe après les fêtes.

Au début du mois de décembre, la mère de famille avait dû déployer des trésors de patience pour persuader son aînée d'aller s'asseoir sur les bancs de la classe de sa sœur Bernadette. L'adolescente de treize ans n'avait jamais fréquenté l'école. Elle était demeurée à la maison pour aider sa mère malade aussi longtemps qu'elle avait vécu, puis elle était restée avec sa grand-mère durant les deux années suivantes. Après le départ de celle-ci, Ann avait dû finalement se charger seule de la maisonnée malgré son jeune âge.

Quand Camille lui avait suggéré d'aller à l'école quelques semaines plus tôt, Ann avait craint de devenir la risée des enfants beaucoup plus jeunes qui fréquentaient l'école au bout du rang Saint-Jean. La jeune mère adoptive avait dû employer toutes sortes d'arguments autant pour convaincre l'adolescente de faire un essai que pour persuader son nouveau mari de la laisser y aller. Elle avait même avancé qu'ainsi Ann pourrait lui apprendre à lire et à écrire quand elle aurait fini ses devoirs et ses leçons à son retour à la maison.

Pour amener Liam à laisser sa fille fréquenter l'école, Camille avait plaidé qu'elle n'avait pas besoin d'elle à la maison toute la journée et que ce ne serait que justice qu'Ann jouisse des mêmes avantages que ses trois autres enfants. Il avait cédé de guerre lasse tout en déclarant qu'une fille n'avait pas besoin de savoir lire ni écrire pour tenir une maison.

Les jours suivants, Camille avait été heureuse d'apprendre par Bernadette que l'adolescente était très douée et qu'elle apprenait très rapidement. Mieux, l'institutrice l'utilisait déjà pour l'aider dans sa tâche, ce qui la valorisait encore plus. Bref, l'avant-veille de Noël, Ann avait déclaré à Camille qu'elle entendait retourner en classe après les fêtes, ce qui avait comblé de joie la jeune femme.

Ce soir-là, le roi et la reine virent leur règne singulièrement raccourci quand Camille annonça vers sept heures trente qu'il était temps de faire la prière et de monter se coucher.

— Est-ce que j'ai le droit de dire non ? demanda Rose.

— Non, la fête des Rois est finie. À cette heure, tu es redevenue ma petite Rose et tu obéis, répondit Camille en riant.

Le lendemain matin, il faisait encore plus froid que la veille quand les enfants s'habillèrent pour aller à l'école. Le soleil venait de se lever dans un ciel dépourvu de nuages et on entendait les têtes de clous éclater dans les murs. Avant le départ des enfants, Camille vérifia qu'ils avaient bien enfoncé leur tuque sur les oreilles et leur recommanda de se protéger le visage avec leur écharpe.

À leur départ, elle dut poser sa paume contre une vitre de la fenêtre pour faire fondre un peu le givre qui la couvrait presque entièrement afin de les voir partir. Elle les regarda s'engager sur la route avec un léger serrement au cœur.

— J'espère qu'ils gèleront pas trop, dit-elle à Liam et à son oncle en train de fumer près du poêle. Ça leur fait tout de même un peu plus qu'un mille à marcher.

— Ils en mourront pas, déclara Liam. Il faut qu'ils s'endurcissent.

— C'est sûr, la vie est pas facile pour personne, ajouta Paddy Connolly, croyant qu'il était autorisé à le faire.

— Vous, mon oncle, je suis pas certaine pantoute que vous en ayez arraché tant que ça durant votre vie, laissa-t-elle tomber, sceptique.

— Eh bien là! ma petite fille, si tu savais, répliqua-t-il en affichant un air très satisfait de lui.

❧

En ce début d'année, la routine reprit ses droits. Saint-Bernard-Abbé semblait figé dans une gangue de glace, et la fumée se dégageant des cheminées des maisons était le seul signe de vie. Durant les deux semaines suivantes, la température se maintint entre 20 et 25 degrés sous zéro, incitant souvent les bûcherons à ne travailler à l'extérieur qu'une demi-journée tant le froid était insupportable.

Chaque midi, quand Bridget Ellis revenait à la maison, elle disait à son mari que monsieur le curé se plaignait sans arrêt du froid qui régnait dans la sacristie.

— Il dit que ses pieds ont pas dégelé depuis trois jours, dit-elle au président des syndics.

— Voyons donc ! fit Samuel, qui avait bûché toute la matinée au bout de sa terre. C'est pas si froid que ça. T'as ben travaillé tout l'avant-midi dans la sacristie et t'es pas morte gelée.

— C'est vrai, reconnut-elle, mais c'était pas chaud.

— Dans ce cas-là, il a juste à se mettre les pieds sur la bavette du poêle, trancha son mari, mécontent d'entendre toujours les mêmes plaintes. Il a fait aussi froid l'hiver passé et j'ai jamais entendu le curé Ouellet se lamenter une seule fois. En plus, avant-hier, on a eu une réunion du conseil dans la sacristie, et on n'a pas eu froid pantoute, ajouta-t-il avec tout de même une certaine mauvaise foi.

Au bout du rang Sainte-Ursule, Xavier et son jeune employé auraient eu bien plus de raisons de se plaindre du froid. En effet, poussés par l'ambition de remplir le contrat qui les liait à la compagnie Price qui avait promis d'acheter la plus grande partie du bois abattu, ils travaillaient toute la journée à l'extérieur.

— Travailler, ça réchauffe, avait déclaré Xavier à Donat et à Hubert, rencontrés le dimanche précédent à la sortie de la chapelle.

— Le seul problème, c'est de garder la maison chaude, sacrifice ! était intervenu Antonin. La plupart du temps, le poêle a eu le temps de s'éteindre quand on revient dîner ou souper, et la maison est gelée ben dur.

— C'est sûr que c'est pas comme notre cabane de l'année passée, avait repris son jeune patron. C'est pas mal plus grand à réchauffer.

Pour sa part, Paddy Connolly avait trouvé un moyen de faire plaisir à son hôtesse à peu de frais. Parfois, il s'arrangeait pour aller passer une heure ou deux au magasin général de Télesphore Dionne et attendait la sortie des enfants de l'école, située en face, pour les ramener à la maison. C'était la seule utilité que Camille reconnaissait à son pensionnaire. Par ailleurs, l'épouse de Liam Connolly avait entrepris de «dompter le vieux garçon», comme elle disait, en cessant d'aller faire son lit chaque matin et de ramasser ses vêtements qui traînaient un peu partout dans sa chambre. L'oncle s'était fait sèchement rabrouer quand il avait osé s'en plaindre le premier jour où cela s'était produit.

— As-tu oublié de faire ma chambre, ma nièce? avait-il demandé en prenant place à table en même temps que Liam, ce midi-là.

— Non, mon oncle, avait-elle répondu, désinvolte.

— Ben, mon lit a pas été fait et mon linge a pas été ramassé, avait-il eu le culot de lui faire remarquer.

— Écoutez, mon oncle, avait-elle sèchement répliqué, les mains sur les hanches. C'est pas une auberge, ici dedans, et je pense pas que vous soyez infirme.

Les enfants l'avaient regardée, les yeux ronds d'étonnement.

— Ben non, avait marmonné le pensionnaire.

— Dans ce cas-là, moi, je suis pas votre servante. Si les enfants sont capables de faire leur lit et de ranger leur chambre le matin, je pense que vous en êtes capable, vous aussi.

— Et pour mon lavage? avait-il demandé à demi dompté.

— Quand vous aurez un morceau à faire laver, vous le descendrez le lundi matin et vous le laisserez sur la table dans la cuisine d'été. Je le laverai avec le reste du linge.

Paddy Connolly ne revint pas sur le sujet et mangea le contenu de son assiette. Durant l'échange, Liam avait semblé avoir du mal à se retenir d'intervenir, mais il s'était tu, se contentant d'adresser à sa femme un regard furieux.

Quand le couple se retrouva seul ce soir-là, Liam, mécontent, lui reprocha sa sortie.

— Tu donnes tout un exemple aux enfants en parlant comme ça à mon oncle, lui dit-il.

— Je me suis contentée de lui dire ce que j'avais sur le cœur, répliqua-t-elle en brossant ses cheveux avant de se mettre au lit. Il y a tout de même des limites à ambitionner sur le pain bénit.

— Faire sa chambre, c'est pas la fin du monde, osa-t-il dire.

— Ah bien là, j'aurai tout entendu! explosa-t-elle. Comme je l'ai dit à ton oncle, je suis pas une servante ici dedans. À part ça, c'est pas moi qui pense hériter. Si t'imagines qu'il va te laisser plus d'argent en faisant sa chambre, tu peux y aller, ça me dérange pas.

— T'as un vrai caractère de cochon! s'emporta-t-il. C'est pas surprenant que pas un gars a voulu te marier, à part moi.

— Si c'est juste ça que tu penses, t'aurais pu faire comme les autres et me laisser tranquille chez mon père. J'étais pas malheureuse pantoute et j'étais pas mal mieux traitée, rétorqua-t-elle sur le même ton.

Quand il voulut se faire pardonner à sa façon dès qu'elle eut éteint la lampe, elle ne montra aucun empressement à le satisfaire.

❧

À l'heure du souper le lendemain, toute la famille mangeait de bon appétit.

— Ça fait du bien d'avoir un peu de temps doux après avoir gelé aussi longtemps, fit Paddy en se servant une seconde portion de fèves au lard.

— C'est juste le redoux de la fin de janvier, mon oncle, lui fit remarquer son neveu. Ça va durer une journée ou deux et, après ça, le froid va revenir.

— À soir, on va en profiter. On va aller faire un tour chez ma mère, déclara Camille. C'est sa fête et j'ai préparé un gâteau pour elle.

— Dis-moi pas qu'à cette heure on est poignés pour nourrir la famille Beauchemin au complet, dit le maître de maison.

— J'espère que c'est une farce, répliqua sèchement Camille en le foudroyant du regard.

Son mari n'ajouta rien.

En ce 22 janvier, Marie Beauchemin célébrait son cinquante-deuxième anniversaire et Camille savait fort bien que ses frères et sœurs ne laisseraient pas passer l'occasion sans souligner l'événement.

— Moi, je bouge pas de la maison, affirma Liam sur un ton sans appel.

Camille refusa de commencer une scène à ce sujet et s'adressa plutôt aux enfants.

— Qui veut venir avec moi ? demanda-t-elle en se tournant vers eux.

Tous les quatre s'empressèrent d'accepter de l'accompagner.

— Je vais attendre que vous ayez fini vos devoirs et on va y aller tous ensemble, dit-elle.

Quand vint le moment de partir moins d'une heure plus tard, Camille eut la surprise de voir Paddy Connolly quitter sa chaise berçante en annonçant :

— Je vais y aller avec vous autres. Ta mère m'a ben reçu au jour de l'An. Elle mérite au moins que je lui souhaite une bonne fête.

Liam esquissa une grimace de contrariété et ne put qu'imiter son oncle.

Quelques minutes plus tard, toute la famille Connolly vint frapper à la porte de Marie Beauchemin et trouva sur place Rémi Lafond et les siens.

— Il manque juste Xavier pour que tout le monde soit là, dit Bernadette à sa sœur aînée en se chargeant des manteaux des enfants pour aller les déposer sur le lit de sa mère.

— Vous êtes bien fins de vous être dérangés pour venir me souhaiter bonne fête, déclara Marie, rayonnante.

— On pouvait pas laisser passer une occasion comme ça, madame Beauchemin, dit Rémi, et…

— Fais bien attention à ce que tu vas dire sur mon âge, toi, le mit en garde sa belle-mère, en riant. Je suis pas si vieille que ça.

— Mais j'ai rien dit, belle-mère, se défendit le mari d'Emma. Moi, je vous trouve encore ben jeune.

— Je te dis que t'as un beau licheux comme mari, plaisanta Camille en s'adressant à sa sœur Emma.

— Je le connais. Il sait de quel côté son pain est beurré, dit Emma en riant. En plus, il prie pour m'man chaque soir pour remercier le bon Dieu de lui avoir donné une si bonne femme.

— Il faudrait peut-être pas exagérer, fit Rémi, taquin.

— En tout cas, ça a tout l'air qu'on manquera pas de gâteau de fête à soir, intervint Bernadette en déposant sur la table un troisième gâteau. Eugénie et moi, on en a fait un avant le souper, Emma en a fait un et t'arrives avec un autre, dit-elle à Camille.

Le bruit de grelots d'un attelage entrant dans la cour incita Donat à soulever le rideau de cretonne qui masquait l'une des fenêtres.

— On dirait ben qu'on aura pas trop à s'en faire avec les gâteaux, v'là de l'aide pour les manger, dit-il. C'est Xavier et Antonin qui arrivent.

Le fils cadet pénétra dans la maison à la suite de son employé qui portait, lui aussi, un gâteau enveloppé dans une serviette.

— Ben, voyons donc! s'exclama Marie. Dis-moi pas que vous vous êtes donné le mal de me cuisiner un gâteau, vous autres aussi.

— Je vous dirais ben oui, m'man, mais ce serait une menterie, déclara Xavier en l'embrassant sur les deux joues après lui avoir souhaité un bon anniversaire. C'est Catherine qui vous envoie ça pour votre fête.

Les femmes présentes dans la pièce se jetèrent des regards avertis.

— T'aurais bien pu l'amener avec toi, dit Marie sans grand enthousiasme.

— J'y ai pas pensé, m'man, mentit son fils.

— En tout cas, on dirait ben que Rémi est pas tout seul à vouloir absolument faire plaisir à la belle-mère, déclara Liam.

— Je trouve ça normal d'être aimée par tous ceux à qui je donne mes enfants, affirma Marie à demi sérieuse. Ça prouve juste que j'ai pas affaire à des ingrats.

À cet instant, Camille ne put s'empêcher d'adresser un sourire narquois à son mari.

Ensuite, Marie s'occupa un peu des sept enfants regroupés autour d'elle, ne faisant apparemment aucune distinction entre Alexis, ceux d'Emma et ceux de Liam. Un peu plus tard, on servit un morceau de gâteau à chacun et la maîtresse de maison parla longuement de son enfance et de sa jeunesse.

Vers neuf heures trente, Camille donna le signal du départ en rappelant que les enfants devaient aller se coucher pour être frais et dispos le lendemain à l'école. Pendant que les invités s'habillaient, Marie eut un geste qui fit énormément plaisir à son fils cadet. Elle trancha un morceau de chacun des gâteaux, les déposa dans l'assiette qui avait contenu le dessert offert par Catherine et couvrit le tout avec un linge.

— Tiens, tu donneras ça à ta fiancée et tu la remercieras pour moi pour son gâteau. Dis-lui que tout le monde l'a bien aimé.

❧

Le surlendemain, comme l'avait prédit Liam, le redoux n'était plus qu'un souvenir. Après les abondantes chutes de neige la veille, le froid était revenu en force sur la région.

Vers trois heures, Camille entendit bouger au-dessus de sa tête, signe que l'oncle Paddy était en train de se lever après une longue sieste. Au moment où elle passait devant l'une des fenêtres de la cuisine, elle vit se déplacer une ombre à l'extérieur. Elle poursuivit pourtant son chemin vers la table avant de s'immobiliser, soudain alertée par le fait qu'elle n'avait pas entendu de bruit de pas sur la galerie.

— Veux-tu bien me dire ce qui vient de passer là ? se demanda-t-elle à haute voix avant de rebrousser chemin pour aller soulever le rideau.

Elle eut beau scruter la cour dans toutes les directions alors que le soleil commençait déjà à baisser, elle ne vit rien. Elle allait retourner à son repassage quand un hurlement tout proche la fit sursauter.

— Voyons donc ! s'exclama-t-elle en regardant plus attentivement.

Elle aperçut alors une sorte de gros chien un peu efflanqué qui venait de contourner le poulailler. Immédiatement, elle songea à Rose et à sa peur depuis qu'elle avait été mordue par un chien errant l'été précédent. Il ne fallait pas qu'elle aperçoive cette bête-là près de la maison.

— Lui, il va décamper et ça prendra pas goût de tinette, dit-elle, prête à s'habiller pour aller chasser l'animal.

Un autre hurlement à glacer le sang se fit à nouveau entendre et Camille aperçut alors quatre autres bêtes, identiques à la première, se diriger vers la maison.

— Seigneur, mais ce sont des loups ! s'écria-t-elle. D'où est-ce qu'ils sortent ?

Il arrivait, certains soirs d'hiver, d'entendre les hurlements des loups dans la région, mais ils semblaient toujours provenir des bois environnants et bien peu d'habitants en avaient vu ces dernières années. De temps à autre, l'hiver, des bûcherons trouvaient une carcasse de chevreuil à moitié dévorée par les loups, mais tout laissait croire qu'ils fuyaient l'homme.

— D'où ça vient, ce cri-là? demanda Paddy Connolly, qui se tenait au pied de l'escalier menant aux chambres à coucher.

Camille sursauta violemment, elle ne l'avait pas entendu descendre.

— Je pense qu'il y a des loups qui rôdent dans la cour, lui répondit-elle dans un souffle.

— C'est pas possible, dit-il en se penchant à la fenêtre à son tour. T'es sûre de ça, toi?

— C'est pas des chiens, en tout cas, répondit-elle en se dirigeant vers le crochet auquel était suspendu son manteau.

— Qu'est-ce que tu fais là? fit-il, étonné.

— Les enfants s'en reviennent bientôt de l'école, mon oncle. Je sais pas pantoute ce que ces bêtes-là vont faire quand elles vont les voir.

— Tu sais ben qu'elles vont prendre le bord.

— Non, mon oncle, je le sais pas. Il y a rien qui dit que les loups les attaqueront pas s'ils sont affamés, expliqua-t-elle en chaussant ses bottes.

Elle se dirigea vers le garde-manger au fond duquel Liam suspendait son fusil et elle prit une poignée de balles qu'elle enfouit dans l'une de ses poches.

— Qu'est-ce que t'as dans l'idée de faire? lui demanda Paddy.

— Je vais les faire partir et, après ça, je vais atteler pour aller chercher les enfants.

L'oncle sembla hésiter un court moment avant de se décider à dire:

— Attends une minute, je vais sortir avec toi. Laisse-moi le temps d'aller chercher ma grosse canne en haut. Je reviens tout de suite.

Moins de cinq minutes plus tard, Paddy et Camille ouvrirent la porte de la maison avec mille précautions, craignant qu'un ou des loups ne soient en embuscade sur la galerie. Il n'y avait aucune bête là, uniquement de nombreuses pistes qui prouvaient leur passage.

— Il faut que ces loups-là aient faim en jériboire pour s'approcher comme ça d'une maison habitée, dit Paddy dans un souffle en inspectant la cour devant lui, tous ses sens en alerte.

Camille, le fusil à la main, dut faire un effort extraordinaire pour quitter la galerie et s'avancer prudemment dans la cour d'où les loups avaient subitement disparu.

— Où est-ce qu'ils sont passés ? lui demanda l'oncle de son mari.

— Ils doivent pas être loin. Et Liam qui est dans le bois. J'espère qu'il lui est rien arrivé. Il est tout seul là-bas.

— À l'heure qu'il est, il doit être sur le chemin du retour, lui fit remarquer l'oncle de son mari. Pour moi, on est mieux de l'attendre avant de faire quelque chose.

— Non, mon oncle, on peut pas attendre, le contredit Camille. Il y a rien qui dit que ces bêtes-là sont pas tout près et qu'elles sauteront pas sur les enfants.

Un hurlement tout proche parut lui donner raison et les incita à presser le pas vers l'écurie où ils pénétrèrent en catastrophe. Les chevaux semblaient avoir senti la présence des prédateurs parce qu'ils étaient particulièrement nerveux.

— Tenez, mon oncle, prenez le fusil, lui ordonna Camille en lui tendant l'arme. Je vais atteler notre cheval.

La jeune femme parvint à calmer un peu la bête en lui parlant doucement, puis elle lui passa une bride et l'entraîna avec peine à l'extérieur. Elle eut beaucoup de mal à faire reculer le cheval entre les brancards de la *sleigh* abandonnée près de la porte pour l'atteler. Pendant ce temps, Paddy regardait nerveusement autour d'eux à la recherche du moindre signe de la présence des loups.

Au moment où ils montaient tous les deux dans le véhicule, ils en aperçurent un au coin de l'étable. Immédiatement, Camille tendit les guides à l'oncle de son mari et lui arracha le fusil des mains avant même qu'il songe à l'utiliser. Elle prit à peine le temps d'épauler et tira. Elle rata la cible, mais le loup décampa et disparut derrière le bâtiment.

— Envoyez, mon oncle ! Il faut aller chercher les enfants, ordonna-t-elle à Paddy que le coup de feu semblait avoir paralysé.

Il fouetta alors le cheval qui traversa rapidement la cour et tourna sur le rang Saint-Jean. Pendant que la *sleigh* avançait sur le chemin étroit balisé par des branches de sapinage, Camille ne lâchait pas son arme et regardait attentivement de chaque côté comme si des bêtes se préparaient à attaquer.

Un peu avant d'arriver au pont, elle aperçut une *sleigh* venant dans leur direction et elle reconnut Constant Aubé.

— Arrêtez, mon oncle. Il faut que je lui parle. C'est le cavalier de Bernadette.

Paddy immobilisa son véhicule. Constant fit de même et sursauta en apercevant l'arme sur les genoux de la passagère.

— Tabarnouche ! Qu'est-ce que tu fais avec un fusil ? lui demanda-t-il, stupéfait.

— Il y a une bande de loups qui rôde. On est venus chercher les enfants.

— Je viens de les voir en train de sortir de l'école, lui apprit-il. Je tourne dans la cour de Bélanger et je vous suis pour aller chercher Bernadette.

— C'est correct.

— En revenant, arrêtez juste une minute en passant devant chez nous. Je vais prendre mon fusil, moi aussi.

Constant Aubé fit demi-tour avec son attelage dans la cour de Tancrède Bélanger, voisin des Lafond, et il suivit de près la *sleigh* conduite par Paddy Connolly. Ce dernier arrêta son véhicule dès qu'il aperçut les quatre enfants de son neveu, une centaine de pieds après le pont.

— Montez, leur ordonna Camille.

— Pourquoi t'as le fusil de p'pa? lui demanda Duncan qui avait remarqué l'arme.

— Au cas où, se borna-t-elle à répondre.

Pendant ce temps, Constant avait dépassé leur *sleigh*, traversé le pont et immobilisé la sienne devant la petite école blanche située en face du magasin général. Il se précipita vers la porte. Celle-ci s'ouvrit avant même qu'il eût à frapper.

— Qu'est-ce qui se passe? lui demanda l'institutrice qui s'apprêtait à quitter sa classe pour rentrer chez elle.

— Je suis venu te chercher.

— T'es bien fin, Constant, mais tu sais bien que ma mère appréciera pas trop de me voir arriver toute seule dans une *sleigh* avec un garçon.

— Ben là, elle va l'endurer parce qu'il paraît qu'il y a des loups qui rôdent.

— Mon Dieu, les enfants! s'écria Bernadette, atterrée.

— Aie pas peur, j'en ai pas vu dans le rang en venant. Dépêche-toi, ta sœur Camille et l'oncle de son mari nous attendent de l'autre côté du pont. Ils ont fait monter les enfants. Je vais aller les aider à rentrer à la maison.

Bernadette ne se fit pas répéter l'invitation. Elle saisit son manchon, enfonça sa tuque et ferma la porte derrière elle après avoir saisi son sac. Elle monta dans la *sleigh* de son amoureux et se couvrit les jambes de l'épaisse couverture de fourrure pendant qu'il incitait son cheval à reprendre la route. Ils rejoignirent la *sleigh* de Camille à l'arrière de laquelle les quatre enfants s'étaient entassés. Les deux véhicules se remirent en route et s'arrêtèrent à l'entrée de la cour de chez Constant, située quelques arpents avant la ferme des Beauchemin, du côté de la rivière.

Constant confia les guides à Bernadette et disparut dans sa maison quelques instants, le temps de revenir armé d'un fusil qu'il déposa entre eux. Il laissa descendre Bernadette à la porte de la maison de sa mère et reprit la route derrière la *sleigh* conduite par Paddy.

Leur arrivée coïncida avec celle de Liam, de retour du bois. Il eut du mal à dissimuler sa surprise en apercevant Camille armée de son fusil en train de faire descendre les enfants.

— Calvaire! Veux-tu ben me dire ce qui se passe? demanda-t-il à sa femme en s'avançant vers les *sleighs*.

— Il y a une bande de loups qui est venue tourner autour de la maison et des bâtiments cet après-midi, lui dit-elle en lui tendant son fusil.

— Voyons donc! J'ai jamais vu ça, fit-il, incrédule.

— Demande à ton oncle, fit-elle.

— Il y en avait une demi-douzaine, répondit Paddy. C'est pour ça qu'il a fallu que ta femme tire une fois pour leur faire peur. On a attelé pour aller chercher les enfants. T'as juste à regarder, il y a des pistes partout autour de la maison et des bâtiments.

— Et moi, je suis venu au cas où ils auraient continué à rôder, poursuivit Constant. On sait jamais. Ces animaux-là, en bande et affamés, peuvent être dangereux.

— Ah ben, on aura tout vu! s'exclama Liam. Je passe mes journées dans le bois et j'en ai jamais vu un. Si c'est comme ça, il va falloir faire une battue pour s'en débarrasser avant qu'ils fassent des dégâts.

— Il faudrait peut-être pas trop tarder, fit remarquer Constant. Qu'est-ce que tu dirais si on s'en occupait demain matin?

— C'est correct, accepta Liam, au grand soulagement de sa femme. À soir, après le souper, je vais faire le tour du rang pour essayer de ramasser le plus de monde possible.

Un peu avant huit heures le lendemain, la cour de la ferme des Connolly fut prise d'assaut par une dizaine d'hommes armés chaussés de raquettes et engoncés dans d'épais manteaux.

Constant Aubé eut la délicatesse de rassurer Camille en offrant d'aller conduire les enfants à l'école. Évidemment, le jeune meunier s'arrêta au passage chez les Beauchemin pour faire monter Bernadette.

— On va être ben chaperonnés par les petits Connolly, prit-il soin de dire à Marie avant d'entraîner Bernadette vers la *sleigh* immobilisée devant la galerie.

— Ça, c'est toi qui le dis, se moqua la mère de famille en vérifiant tout de même par la fenêtre la présence des enfants dans le véhicule.

Constant Aubé revint chez les Connolly à temps pour participer au départ de la battue vers le boisé situé au bout de la terre de Liam.

À peu de chose près, les participants étaient les mêmes que ceux qui avaient pris part à la battue, l'année précédente, pour traquer l'incendiaire Ignace Houle. Toutefois, au lieu de constituer de petits groupes, les hommes se déployèrent sur une seule ligne dès l'orée de la forêt, à la recherche des pistes laissées par les loups.

Durant toute la matinée, ils s'enfoncèrent profondément dans le bois, ne relevant que quelques pistes de renards et de chevreuils. Il fallut attendre un peu avant onze heures pour que Joseph Gariépy et Conrad Boudreau, les voisins immédiats des Beauchemin, trouvent quelques empreintes ayant probablement été laissées par des loups. Finalement, harassés et passablement gelés, les hommes se consultèrent et décidèrent de mettre fin à la battue.

— Pour moi, ils ont dû traverser de l'autre côté de la rivière sur la glace, déclara Rémi Lafond. On les reverra plus dans le coin de sitôt.

— C'est ça, approuva John White. Si jamais on aperçoit des traces de loup sur nos terres, on fera une autre battue.

Les hommes revinrent lentement dans la cour de Liam Connolly. Dès leur arrivée, Camille s'empressa de les inviter à se réchauffer à l'intérieur où les attendaient du thé bouillant et des biscuits à la mélasse frais sortis du four.

Chapitre 6

Du nouveau

En ce début du mois de février 1872, Paddy Connolly pouvait se vanter d'avoir trouvé un moyen imparable de devenir le centre d'intérêt des quelques traîne-savates de Saint-Bernard-Abbé qui passaient une bonne partie de leurs journées assis près de la fournaise du magasin général de Télesphore Dionne. L'oncle de Liam s'était abonné au journal *La Minerve* le lendemain de la fête des Rois et le facteur, Hormidas Meilleur, le lui apportait chaque avant-midi, après en avoir pris livraison à la gare avec le reste du rare courrier à distribuer dans la mission.

À sa plus grande satisfaction, le Montréalais était devenu la principale source des informations circulant dans la paroisse, et il n'en était pas peu fier. Il monopolisait ainsi toute l'attention et il pouvait donner libre cours à son bagout en commentant abondamment chaque nouvelle, ce qui n'était pas peu dire.

Ainsi, le retraité prit rapidement l'habitude de guetter l'arrivée du facteur qu'il régalait d'un petit verre de bagosse de son neveu dès qu'il lui tendait son journal. Selon le petit homme au nez rubicond, Paddy Connolly était le seul abonné à un journal dans la région, ce qui en faisait un être à part qui méritait beaucoup de considération. Dès le départ du facteur, l'oncle s'installait dans sa chaise berçante et lisait attentivement les nouvelles qu'il jugeait importantes à transmettre. Habituellement, il avait terminé sa lecture à l'heure du dîner. Après sa sieste, il s'habillait avec soin et vérifiait qu'il avait bien en poche un ou deux cigares avant d'aller atteler sa *sleigh*.

Quand Camille le voyait partir, engoncé dans son épais manteau de chat sauvage, elle poussait un soupir de soulagement. C'était le seul moment de la journée où elle se retrouvait enfin seule dans sa maison.

Parvenu au magasin général, Paddy Connolly déposait une couverture sur le dos de sa bête et entrait, salué par les habitués de la place. Le nouvel arrivant prenait le temps de retirer son manteau et sa toque de fourrure avant de s'asseoir au bout de l'un des deux bancs qui flanquaient la grosse fournaise ventrue qui réchauffait les lieux. Habituellement, on lui laissait le temps d'allumer son cigare.

— Puis, qu'est-ce qu'il y a de nouveau dans le journal? lui demandait Télesphore.

C'était ainsi que les habitants de Saint-Bernard-Abbé avaient appris qu'une épidémie de petite vérole avait fait dix-huit morts à Valleyfield à la fin du mois précédent, que Charles-Louis Coursol venait d'être élu maire de Montréal et qu'on discutait sérieusement au gouvernement de ne plus permettre qu'un député ait un double mandat. Si on se fiait aux derniers articles parus dans le journal de Paddy, les politiciens allaient être obligés de choisir de représenter leurs électeurs à Québec ou à Ottawa, mais pas aux deux endroits en même temps.

Évidemment, la notoriété dont jouissait l'Irlandais faisait des envieux et certains ne se gênaient pas pour mettre en doute tout ce qu'il disait, particulièrement quand il se vantait de sa richesse. À dire vrai, Paddy Connolly jouait facilement au citadin qui connaissait tout au milieu de cultivateurs ignorants.

En fait, Hormidas Meilleur avait dû baisser pavillon depuis l'arrivée du nouveau venu. Il n'était plus l'unique source des informations circulant à Saint-Bernard-Abbé.

Bien sûr, il aurait pu montrer de la mauvaise volonté à livrer le journal ou même essayer de couper l'herbe sous le pied de l'abonné en révélant aux gens les nouvelles avant lui, mais cela aurait exigé des efforts qu'il n'était pas prêt à déployer. Secrètement mortifié de voir son rôle diminué, le facteur n'avait tout de même pas renoncé à rapporter tous les ragots circulant dans la mission, un domaine où Paddy ne pouvait le concurrencer.

Bref, au fil des jours et sans se consulter, les deux hommes firent en sorte d'occuper chacun un domaine bien particulier. Cependant, il était évident que le petit facteur au visage de gnome n'aurait jamais le panache de l'oncle de Liam Connolly.

Deux jours auparavant, le retraité avait donné un aperçu de son caractère quand Samuel Ellis et Thomas Hyland, présents au magasin lors de son passage, s'étaient mêlés d'interrompre l'un de ses longs commentaires.

— Vous, vous êtes un vrai Irlandais ! lui avait déclaré Samuel Ellis pour flatter celui qui commentait les dernières nouvelles à la poignée de clients rassemblés près de la fournaise.

— Pantoute, s'était contenté de rétorquer le retraité. Moi, je suis un Canadien. Mon père était Irlandais, mais moi, je suis venu au monde proche de Québec.

— Mais vous êtes l'oncle de Liam Connolly, lui avait fait remarquer Hyland, surpris par cette déclaration.

— Lui aussi est Canadien, pas Irlandais. La preuve, essayez de lui parler en anglais pour voir s'il va vous comprendre, avait répondu Paddy en riant.

Les deux hommes, un peu dépités, n'avaient pas insisté.

— *Goddam !* c'est une vraie honte d'entendre des affaires de même, avait dit Samuel au patron du moulin à bois quand ils s'étaient retrouvés seuls à l'extérieur. C'est la première fois que j'entends un Irlandais refuser de dire qu'il en est un.

Hyland s'était contenté de hausser les épaules.

Maintenant, presque tous les après-midi, Paddy Connolly s'arrangeait pour quitter son auditoire dès qu'il apercevait les premiers enfants qui sortaient de l'école située en face du magasin. Il faisait monter Bernadette et les enfants de Camille et les ramenait chez eux.

— C'est bien le seul temps où il sert à quelque chose, se répétait Camille en voyant descendre les enfants de la *sleigh*, devant la maison.

━━◆━━

Le mois de février suivait son cours et rien n'indiquait que le froid avait l'intention de relâcher son étreinte. De mémoire d'habitant de Saint-Bernard-Abbé, on n'avait pas connu un hiver aussi rigoureux depuis près de quinze ans. Fait étonnant, même s'il n'y avait eu aucune tempête importante durant le mois de janvier, les petites chutes régulières de neige faisaient en sorte que les piquets de clôture avaient disparu depuis longtemps sous l'épaisse couverture blanche.

Dans la maison des Beauchemin du rang Saint-Jean, la lueur d'une lampe à huile venait d'apparaître à l'une des fenêtres. Comme d'habitude, Marie Beauchemin était la première à s'être levée en ce mardi matin et elle était occupée à tisonner les braises qui restaient dans le poêle quand elle entendit la porte de la cuisine d'été s'ouvrir dans son dos. La veuve sursauta, se tourna tout d'une pièce et découvrit sa bru, les épaules couvertes d'un châle de laine, tenant une lampe à la main.

— Ma foi du bon Dieu, tu m'as fait peur ! s'exclama la veuve en jetant une bûche sur les tisons. Je t'ai pas entendue pantoute descendre.

— J'étais aux toilettes, se contenta d'expliquer Eugénie d'une voix si misérable qu'elle piqua la curiosité de sa belle-mère.

— Pourquoi tu t'es pas servie du pot de chambre? lui demanda-t-elle.

— J'étais malade et je voulais pas risquer de réveiller le petit.

— Tu digères pas?

— Ça fait trois matins que j'ai mal au cœur, avoua la femme de Donat en s'approchant du poêle pour se réchauffer un peu.

— Bon, dis-moi pas que t'attends du nouveau, déclara Marie en regardant la petite femme au chignon noir à demi défait.

— On le dirait bien, madame Beauchemin.

— C'est normal, conclut la veuve. T'es jeune et ta famille commence à peine. Ça, ça veut dire que cette année, la famille Beauchemin va augmenter de deux enfants, ajouta-t-elle, comme si elle se parlait à elle-même. Emma attend ça pour la fin de mars. Toi...

— Si je me trompe pas, ce serait pour l'automne prochain, compléta Eugénie. Bon, je pense que je vais remonter dormir un peu. Je me sens pas bien.

Sur ces mots, la jeune femme monta l'escalier et disparut dans sa chambre.

— On n'a pas fini d'en entendre parler, murmura Marie à mi-voix pour elle-même.

Elle se rappelait trop bien tous les embarras que sa bru avait faits quand elle était enceinte d'Alexis. À la voir, on aurait cru qu'elle était la première femme à attendre un enfant et, selon elle, Eugénie en avait largement profité pour cesser complètement de travailler à l'intérieur et autour de la maison. Tout avait alors été prétexte pour aller se reposer dans sa chambre. Il ne s'était guère passé de jour où la femme de Baptiste Beauchemin n'avait pas été obligée d'élever la voix pour inciter sa bru à faire sa part des travaux ménagers. L'indolence de la femme de son fils l'avait rendue folle et, plus d'une fois, Camille et Bernadette avaient dû intervenir pour l'empêcher de faire une crise. Elle avait eu beau répéter à la femme de son fils qu'attendre un petit était quelque chose de naturel et que cela ne faisait pas d'elle une infirme incapable de travailler, il n'y avait rien eu à faire. Elle jouait les martyres et disparaissait durant des heures dans sa chambre pour se reposer.

— Seigneur, on n'est pas sortis du bois ! s'exclama-t-elle. J'espère qu'elle va se montrer plus raisonnable que quand elle a attendu son premier.

Quand le thé fut chaud, elle s'en versa une tasse et le but à petites gorgées, toujours debout devant le poêle. Sa pensée dériva vers son aînée. Camille la préoccupait depuis quelque temps. Elle sentait que sa fille n'était pas très heureuse et s'en voulait de ne pas avoir tenté de l'empêcher d'épouser Liam Connolly. Bien sûr, la jeune femme de vingt-neuf ans ne se plaignait pas, mais elle avait la nette impression que ça n'allait pas très bien entre elle et son mari.

— Lui, il va falloir que je lui dise deux mots, murmura-t-elle. S'il est pas capable d'en prendre soin, il va avoir affaire à moi.

Des pas dans l'escalier la tirèrent de ses pensées. Donat, Bernadette et Hubert entrèrent dans la cuisine dans l'intention d'aller soigner les animaux.

— Eugénie descend pas ? demanda la maîtresse de maison à son fils.

— Elle se sent fatiguée, m'man. Je lui ai dit de dormir encore un peu.

— Le petit dort encore ? s'étonna-t-elle.

— Non, il est réveillé.

— Je suppose que s'il se met à brailler, sa mère va au moins se lever pour s'en occuper, fit-elle remarquer d'une voix acide.

— Ben oui, m'man, répondit Donat en finissant de chausser des bottes alors que son frère, son manteau sur le dos, venait d'allumer un fanal.

Hubert précéda son frère à l'extérieur et prit la direction de l'étable. Donat quitta à son tour la maison quelques instants plus tard.

— Est-ce qu'Eugénie est malade? demanda Bernadette, curieuse, à sa mère.

— Non.

— Pourquoi elle se lève pas d'abord pour aider?

— Il paraît qu'elle attend du nouveau, lui répondit sa mère.

— Dites-moi pas ça! s'exclama la jeune institutrice, excitée par la nouvelle.

— Il y a pas de quoi en faire toute une histoire, fit sèchement sa mère. Est-ce que t'as déjà oublié ce qui s'est passé quand elle attendait Alexis? Il y avait pas moyen de rien lui faire faire ici dedans.

— ...

— Là, ma fille, si t'as oublié, tu vas vite t'en rappeler parce que Camille est plus dans la maison pour faire sa part de besogne et que c'est toi et moi qui allons être obligées de faire son ouvrage.

— Il faudrait tout de même pas qu'elle exagère.

— Je vais y voir, promit sa mère.

Ce matin-là, au déjeuner, Eugénie annonça avec une fierté évidente qu'elle attendait un enfant.

— À cette heure que tu sais ce que c'est que d'avoir un petit, je suppose que ça va moins t'énerver, lui fit remarquer sa belle-mère.

— Ayez pas peur, madame Beauchemin, je me rappelle encore à quel point c'est épuisant de porter un enfant.

— Ce qui est important, c'est surtout de pas trop s'écouter, rétorqua la veuve de Baptiste Beauchemin. Toutes les femmes mariées connaissent ça et arrêtent pas pour autant de s'occuper de leur maisonnée.

Eugénie fit semblant de ne pas avoir entendu la remarque. Il y eut un court silence avant qu'elle ne déclare:

— Avec l'arrivée de cet enfant-là, on va avoir un sérieux problème de place en haut, dit-elle sans avoir l'air d'y toucher.

— Comment ça ? lui demanda sa belle-mère en feignant, à son tour, de ne pas saisir l'allusion.

— Ben, deux enfants avec nous autres dans la petite chambre verte…

— Voyons donc, Eugénie ! la réprimanda Marie. Tu sais bien que l'ancienne chambre de Camille est vide et que tu vas pouvoir mettre là le lit d'Alexis l'automne prochain, quand l'autre va arriver. Inquiète-toi donc pas pour rien.

La maîtresse de maison saisit le regard de dépit que la jeune femme adressa à son mari assis au bout de la table et elle s'en réjouit secrètement. De toute évidence, la femme de son fils avait cru pouvoir la chasser de sa grande chambre du rez-de-chaussée en prenant pour prétexte sa nouvelle grossesse.

❧

Ce soir-là, Donat fit sa toilette après le souper en enviant son frère Hubert de pouvoir se reposer en fumant sa pipe bien au chaud pendant qu'il allait devoir assister à une autre réunion du conseil à la sacristie.

— Après toute une journée dans le bois, je serais ben resté tranquille, à me chauffer proche du poêle, ne put-il s'empêcher de dire en endossant son manteau.

— Quand on court les honneurs, il faut en payer le prix, le taquina Bernadette, déjà installée à la table pour préparer ses classes du lendemain.

— En plus, on gèle ben dur dehors, ajouta son frère comme s'il n'avait pas entendu la remarque de la jeune fille.

— Tu salueras monsieur le curé pour nous autres, intervint sa mère qui venait de prendre place derrière son métier à tisser.

— Ça dépendra de son humeur, m'man, répliqua Donat en allumant le fanal qu'il allait suspendre à l'avant de la *sleigh*.

Il sortit de la maison et attela la Noire. L'attelage quitta la cour au bruit des grelots et emprunta le rang Saint-Jean. Au moment où il passait devant la maison de Constant Aubé, il aperçut trois raquetteurs se déplaçant lentement sur les eaux gelées de la rivière. Au bout du rang, il traversa le pont et fit escalader la pente abrupte du rang Sainte-Ursule à son cheval en déplorant de ne pas avoir songé à s'entendre avec Antonius Côté pour faire route ensemble.

Il s'arrêta dans la cour de la sacristie en même temps qu'Anatole Blanchette du rang Saint-Paul.

— On dirait ben que les autres sont déjà arrivés, lui fit remarquer le gros homme en jetant une couverture sur le dos de son cheval.

Deux *sleighs* étaient stationnées tout près de la sacristie pour mettre les chevaux à l'abri du vent qui soufflait. Il s'agissait sûrement des voitures de Côté et de Hyland.

Thomas Hyland vint leur ouvrir quand ils frappèrent à la porte. Samuel Ellis et Antonius Côté étaient debout près du poêle, aux côtés du curé Désilets. Les deux hommes s'empressèrent d'enlever leur manteau et de les rejoindre.

— Bon, le conseil est complet, déclara Josaphat Désilets. Je pense qu'on peut commencer la réunion. Il est déjà sept heures et quart.

Tous les hommes se dirigèrent vers la table placée près d'une fenêtre et attendirent que le prêtre récite la courte prière habituelle avant de se signer et de s'asseoir. Quelques minutes suffirent aux syndics pour regretter d'avoir enlevé leur manteau tant l'endroit était glacial. L'air froid de l'extérieur s'infiltrait dans la pièce et le poêle ne suffisait pas à réchauffer convenablement les lieux.

Samuel Ellis, président du conseil, donna la parole à Thomas Hyland, le seul syndic capable de lire et d'écrire.

Ce dernier lut un résumé de la dernière réunion et mentionna les sommes que les quêtes des quatre derniers dimanches avaient rapportées.

— Est-ce que vous avez des besoins particuliers, monsieur le curé? demanda Samuel Ellis.

— Il va falloir commander d'autres cierges pour l'autel, une douzaine de lampions et du vin de messe.

— Est-ce qu'on a assez d'argent en caisse pour payer ça? demanda le président à Hyland, devenu trésorier de la mission par la force des choses.

— Juste assez, se borna à répondre le propriétaire du moulin à bois.

— En passant, est-ce qu'on a enfin eu des nouvelles de monseigneur au sujet de notre demande de devenir une vraie paroisse? demanda le président au curé Désilets.

— Non, pas encore, répondit le pasteur en repoussant ses lunettes qui avaient glissé sur son nez. Pourtant, je suis certain que l'abbé Desmeules a remis son rapport.

— Je trouve que ça prend ben du temps, cette affaire-là, déclara Blanchette.

— L'abbé a dit que ça prendrait à peu près trois mois, ça fait pas encore tout à fait trois mois depuis qu'il a fait son enquête, lui fit remarquer Donat.

— Mais monseigneur nous a écrit, annonça Josaphat Désilets en tirant une feuille d'une enveloppe qu'il avait déposée ostensiblement devant lui dès le début de la réunion.

— Il nous a écrit? s'étonna Antonius Côté.

Le visage de Samuel s'était rembruni, comme s'il avait deviné le contenu de la missive.

— Je vais vous la lire avant de la lire en chaire dimanche prochain, comme l'exige monseigneur, déclara le curé de Saint-Bernard-Abbé en dépliant la feuille et en attirant vers lui la lampe à huile déposée au centre de la table.

« *Mes bien chers frères, mes bien chères sœurs de Saint-Bernard-Abbé,* commença à lire le prêtre.

Votre évêque n'ignore pas les difficultés auxquelles on doit faire face dans l'établissement d'une nouvelle mission. Il comprend tous les sacrifices que vous avez déjà consentis tant pour la construction d'une chapelle que pour l'entretien d'un prêtre. Toutefois, je manquerais à mon devoir en ne me préoccupant pas du bien-être de mes représentants.

Le mois dernier, j'ai demandé à votre pasteur de vous lire un court message dans lequel je vous faisais part de mon inquiétude face aux conditions de vie qui mettaient en danger la santé de votre curé. Il semble que mon appel n'ait pas été entendu. Par conséquent, je me vois obligé de vous faire savoir qu'il est hors de question que votre pasteur ou tout autre prêtre passe un autre hiver dans les conditions actuelles. Il faudra absolument voir à la construction d'un presbytère dans les prochains mois. Si rien ne change, je me verrai dans l'obligation de ne plus faire desservir votre mission.

Votre frère en Jésus-Christ,
Louis-François Richer Laflèche,
Évêque de Trois-Rivières »

Un long silence suivit cette lecture. Josaphat Désilets, le visage neutre, replia la feuille et la remit dans l'enveloppe d'où il l'avait tirée.

— Qu'est-ce que ça veut dire? demanda finalement Donat Beauchemin.

— Ça veut tout simplement dire que vous n'avez plus à vous préoccuper si monseigneur va accepter ou non que Saint-Bernard devienne une paroisse, laissa tomber froidement le prêtre. Il n'est même plus certain que ça reste une simple mission, si rien ne change, bien sûr.

—Je comprends pas pourquoi monseigneur nous envoie tout à coup cette lettre-là, intervint Antonius, stupéfait.

On fait pourtant de la bonne besogne. On a fait construire un jubé avant les fêtes et…

— Tu comprends rien à l'affaire, intervint Samuel Ellis, les dents serrées. Monsieur le curé s'est plaint à monseigneur avant les fêtes qu'il gelait dans la sacristie et que c'était pas vivable. Ça a tout l'air qu'il a écrit une nouvelle lettre à monseigneur pour lui faire savoir que rien avait changé et qu'il gelait toujours autant. Est-ce que je me trompe, monsieur le curé ?

— Non, c'est vrai, reconnut le prêtre sans fausse honte. Comme vous pouvez le constater vous-mêmes ce soir, on gèle dans la sacristie et ça fait deux jours que je sens même plus mes pieds tellement ils sont glacés. Il y a tout de même des limites.

— Mais on peut pas faire plus ! s'écria Anatole Blanchette.

— C'est ben ce que je pense, moi aussi, ajouta Côté.

— On est déjà endettés jusqu'au cou avec la chapelle et le jubé qu'on vient d'ajouter, fit le président du syndic.

— On a peut-être vu trop grand trop vite, avança Thomas Hyland sur un ton raisonnable.

— C'est ben ce que je suis en train de me dire, avoua Samuel avec un rien de rancune envers le prêtre qui lui faisait face.

Donat avait été le seul à ne rien dire et Antonius Côté avait remarqué le silence du plus jeune membre du conseil.

— Et toi, Donat, qu'est-ce que t'en penses ? lui demanda-t-il.

Le jeune homme prit quelques secondes avant de s'exprimer d'une voix hésitante.

— Moi, je me dis qu'on s'énerve peut-être trop vite pour rien. Il y a un moyen de se sortir de là sans perdre la mission.

— Je voudrais ben le connaître, ce moyen-là ! s'écria le président.

— Si j'ai ben entendu, monseigneur dit qu'il a ben compris toute la misère qu'on a à trouver l'argent pour payer la chapelle et l'entretien de monsieur le curé.

— Oui, puis après ? demanda Anatole.

— Il veut qu'on construise un presbytère et, je suppose, qu'on achète un terrain sur lequel on va le bâtir.

— C'est ce qui est écrit, reconnut Thomas Hyland, mais on n'a pas d'argent pour payer ça.

— Et c'est pas demain la veille qu'on va l'avoir, intervint sèchement Samuel Ellis en jetant un regard de réprobation au prêtre qui, les bras croisés, se contentait d'assister à la discussion.

— Monseigneur doit ben savoir que la mission est endettée, reprit Donat, comme s'il réfléchissait à haute voix. Je suppose qu'il est prêt à nous aider à trouver l'argent qu'il faut.

— Ça veut dire quoi, ce que tu nous dis là ? lui demanda Samuel, intrigué.

— Ça veut dire qu'il est peut-être prêt à garantir l'argent que Saint-Bernard-Abbé va être obligé d'emprunter pour construire un presbytère.

Cette déclaration fut suivie par un court silence que brisa Josaphat Désilets.

— Je trouve pas ça bête, cette idée, dit-il. Et le meilleur moyen de savoir si ça pourrait marcher, c'est d'envoyer le président du conseil à l'évêché pour voir si c'est possible.

— Whow ! monsieur le curé, fit Samuel en élevant légèrement la voix. Avant de faire ça, il va falloir réunir tous les cultivateurs de Saint-Bernard pour savoir s'ils acceptent qu'on s'endette encore plus pour garder la mission ouverte. Moi, j'ai dans l'idée qu'il y en a pas mal qui vont plutôt choisir de retourner dans la paroisse où ils étaient avant. Sainte-Monique et Saint-Zéphirin sont des vieilles paroisses où l'église est payée depuis ben longtemps. Si le monde veut pas embarquer, on n'aura pas le choix de fermer la chapelle et ce sera fini, ajouta le président du conseil, l'air sombre.

— Il faudrait peut-être voter au conseil pour savoir si on doit tenir une réunion là-dessus, suggéra Thomas Hyland.

Tous les membres du conseil hochèrent la tête en signe d'approbation. Le vote ne posa aucun problème. On décida de tenir une assemblée le dimanche suivant, à la chapelle, immédiatement après la grand-messe. Josaphat Désilets accepta d'annoncer la réunion à la fin des deux messes après avoir fait la lecture de la lettre pastorale de l'évêque du diocèse, comme il en avait reçu l'ordre de son supérieur.

La réunion du conseil prit fin un peu après huit heures trente et les cinq syndics quittèrent la sacristie après avoir souhaité assez froidement une bonne nuit à leur pasteur.

— Bout de cierge, on n'aurait aucun de ces troubles-là s'il avait pas passé son temps à se plaindre à monseigneur qu'il gelait dans la sacristie ! déclara Anatole Blanchette, de fort mauvaise humeur, dès que la porte de la sacristie se fut refermée derrière lui.

— Moi, j'en reviens pas, poursuivit Côté. Le curé Ouellet a passé l'hiver là, l'année passée, et pas une fois il s'est plaint et, pourtant, il a ben fait aussi froid que cet hiver.

— Qu'est-ce que tu veux qu'on y fasse, intervint Donat. On est tombés sur un curé feluette qui peut rien endurer.

— En attendant, on risque de se ramasser avec une chapelle qui servira plus à rien si le monde veut pas payer un presbytère, conclut Samuel, l'air inquiet.

— Avant de s'énerver, on va voir ce que les gens de Saint-Bernard vont décider dimanche prochain, fit Thomas d'une voix apaisante en montant dans sa *sleigh* où venait de prendre place son voisin, le président du conseil.

⌐

Cinq jours plus tard, Josaphat Désilets lut la lettre de monseigneur Laflèche avant d'insister lourdement sur l'importance de l'assemblée convoquée par les syndics immédiatement après la grand-messe.

— Vu l'urgence de la réunion, il n'y aura pas de salut au Saint-Sacrement après la grand-messe, prit-il soin de préciser.

L'objet de la réunion n'était plus un mystère pour personne depuis plusieurs jours puisque le contenu de la lettre de l'évêque avait été rapporté par les membres du conseil et amplement commenté durant toute la semaine. Chaque franc-tenancier était bien conscient des conséquences cruciales de la réunion et il n'était pas question de ne pas y participer, même si les leurs devaient les attendre à l'extérieur dans le froid glacial de ce dimanche matin de février. Les gens qui avaient assisté à la basse-messe quelques heures plus tôt attendirent la sortie d'une bonne partie des fidèles après la grand-messe pour se glisser de nouveau dans la chapelle.

— Maudit que j'ai faim! se plaignit le gros Tancrède Bélanger en prenant place dans un banc aux côtés de John White, son voisin du rang Saint-Jean.

— T'es pas tout seul, se contenta de lui dire l'Irlandais.

Comme la plupart des participants étaient à jeun depuis la veille pour pouvoir communier à la messe, la faim les tenaillait en cette fin d'avant-midi.

Les syndics, l'air important, circulaient dans la chapelle et s'adressaient à voix basse à certaines de leurs connaissances en attendant que le curé Désilets ait retiré ses habits sacerdotaux dans la sacristie. Quand ce dernier revint dans le chœur, vêtu de sa soutane noire sur laquelle il avait passé un surplis, les murmures se turent et les syndics vinrent le rejoindre à l'avant de la sainte table.

— Je vous ai lu, ce matin, la lettre que notre évêque m'a fait parvenir cette semaine, déclara le prêtre d'une voix forte. Quand j'en ai fait lecture au syndic de la mission lors de notre dernière rencontre, il a été décidé de réunir tous les cultivateurs de Saint-Bernard pour savoir ce qu'il convenait de faire. Je laisse le président du conseil vous expliquer ce qui se passe.

Sur ces mots, Josaphat Désilets céda la place à Samuel Ellis qui lissa nerveusement l'un de ses larges favoris roux avant de s'éclaircir la voix.

— Si vous avez ben écouté la lettre lue par monsieur le curé à matin, vous avez tous compris que monseigneur est décidé à fermer la mission si on construit pas un presbytère le printemps prochain.

— Il peut pas faire ça, le coupa Tancrède Bélanger. Il sait qu'on a fait construire une chapelle l'année passée.

— On a même ajouté un jubé, ajouta un nommé Comtois du rang Saint-Paul.

— Tout ça, c'est de l'argent en Jupiter ! s'exclama Angèle Cloutier.

— Où est-ce que monseigneur pense qu'on va le trouver, cet argent-là ? ajouta Rémi Lafond, le mari d'Emma.

— On est déjà endettés par-dessus la tête, intervint Cléomène Paquette.

— Ce qui est certain, c'est qu'on peut pas donner plus, fit Léon Allaire sur un ton définitif. Déjà, ça nous coûte le double de ce qu'on payait dans notre vieille paroisse. Il y a tout de même des limites.

— En plus, je fais remarquer à tout le monde qu'on m'a même pas encore remboursé la moitié de l'argent que le conseil me doit pour le lot où on a construit la chapelle et où se trouve le cimetière, reprit Angèle Cloutier, vindicative.

— Aie pas peur, Angèle, on n'est pas des voleurs, dit Antonius Côté d'une voix moqueuse. Tu vas être payée.

— Ben oui ! fit-elle, sarcastique. Dans la semaine des quatre jeudis, je suppose.

Le curé Désilets frappa du plat de la main sur la sainte table pour ramener l'ordre.

— Là, c'est pas le temps de se chicaner, reprit Samuel, l'air grave. On doit décider ce qu'on va faire...

— Le choix est pas ben compliqué, reprit avec autorité Donat Beauchemin, qui parlait pour la première fois depuis le début de la réunion. Ou on accepte de s'endetter encore plus en achetant un autre lot pour construire le presbytère que monseigneur veut absolument, ou Saint-Bernard disparaît et on retourne à nos deux vieilles paroisses... C'est clair, non ?

Les murmures reprirent de plus belle dans l'assistance et il en ressortait que les avis étaient partagés.

— Attendez ! ordonna le président du conseil en élevant la voix. Tout est peut-être pas si noir que ça. Je pourrais aller voir monseigneur à Trois-Rivières pour lui demander de garantir les emprunts de Saint-Bernard. Il me semble qu'il devrait comprendre qu'on commence et qu'on n'est pas ben riches.

— S'il dit non, qu'est-ce que tu vas faire ? lui demanda Angèle.

— On fera une autre réunion et ce sera à vous autres de décider ce qu'on va faire, déclara Samuel.

— En tout cas, ce serait ben dommage d'avoir gaspillé autant d'argent et de temps pour rien, conclut Hormidas Meilleur, assis dans le même banc que la veuve.

L'assistance l'approuva.

— Il vous faudrait quelqu'un habitué à brasser de grosses affaires pour aller discuter à l'évêché, intervint Paddy Connolly en se levant, l'air avantageux.

Apparemment, personne n'avait osé dire à l'oncle de Liam Connolly qu'il n'avait aucun droit de faire partie de l'assemblée puisqu'il n'était pas propriétaire à Saint-Bernard-Abbé.

— Qu'est-ce qui vous fait dire ça ? lui demanda Donat, tout de même étonné de le voir là.

— Voyons donc ! C'est clair qu'un homme d'affaires en imposerait ben plus qu'un simple cultivateur qui connaît pas grand-chose aux finances, rétorqua le retraité sur un ton un peu méprisant.

À voir les réactions, les gens dans l'assistance ne semblaient pas loin de partager son opinion. Thomas Hyland se pencha à l'oreille de Samuel Ellis pour lui murmurer quelques mots. Le président du conseil n'avait pas pardonné à l'homme d'avoir renié ses racines irlandaises et c'est sur un ton sans appel qu'il reprit la parole.

— Je suis pas sûr pantoute que vous ayez raison, monsieur Connolly. En plus, monseigneur trouverait pas mal drôle qu'on envoie un pur étranger qui est même pas un franc-tenancier de la mission quand il y a un conseil des syndics à Saint-Bernard. Si les gens sont d'accord pour demander à l'évêché de garantir nos emprunts, moi, le président du conseil, j'irai à Trois-Rivières.

Paddy, toujours debout, haussa les épaules et se rassit aux côtés de son neveu. Il paraissait tout de même un peu dépité qu'on ait refusé si cavalièrement son offre de service.

— Je pense qu'il est temps de passer au vote, reprit Samuel. Je vous rappelle que seuls les propriétaires ont le droit de voter, prit-il soin d'ajouter en jetant un regard mauvais en direction de Paddy Connolly.

Les gens votèrent à main levée. À la stupéfaction de certains membres du conseil, la grande majorité se déclara en faveur d'une démarche auprès de l'évêque. Cette décision prouvait bien que les gens tenaient à la survie de Saint-Bernard-Abbé.

Chapitre 7

Le notaire Valiquette

Dès le lundi matin, à la suggestion du curé Désilets, Thomas Hyland écrivit une lettre à l'évêché pour demander une audience à monseigneur Laflèche.

— Il aurait ben pu l'écrire lui-même, cette lettre-là, fit remarquer Samuel Ellis d'une voix acide quand le propriétaire du moulin à bois le mit au courant de son geste quelques jours plus tard.

— Monsieur le curé m'a dit que ça paraîtrait mieux que ce soit un membre du conseil qui écrive cette lettre-là plutôt que lui.

— En tout cas, j'espère que monseigneur se pressera pas trop pour répondre. Moi, j'ai du bois à bûcher et je peux pas passer mon temps à courir les chemins pour la mission.

Le président du conseil des syndics en avait gros sur le cœur depuis quelque temps. Ce poste qu'il avait tant envié à Baptiste Beauchemin lui pesait et il avait de plus en plus souvent envie d'y renoncer. Il avait cru naïvement qu'il lui conférerait un prestige enviable à Saint-Bernard-Abbé. Or, il lui avait principalement apporté des ennuis et des critiques, surtout depuis l'arrivée du curé Désilets, qui n'était jamais satisfait de rien. De plus, celui-ci ne faisait pas mystère qu'il continuait à chercher dans la mission une ménagère qui lui conviendrait mieux que sa femme. Il n'acceptait pas d'avoir une servante à mi-temps qui s'éclipsait chaque jour avant midi, après avoir préparé ses repas pour le reste de la journée.

— Il comprend pas que Bridget ne demande rien au conseil pour toute cette besogne-là, répétait-il aux syndics.

— Sauf ta dîme, lui faisait remarquer Anatole Blanchette.

— Ben oui, mais c'est tout de même pas mal moins que les gages qu'une ménagère va exiger, par exemple, rétorquait-il.

Ce jour-là, Samuel Ellis venait à peine de rentrer à la maison après avoir soigné ses bêtes qu'on vint frapper à sa porte.

— Veux-tu ben me dire qui vient nous déranger juste à l'heure du souper? demanda-t-il à Bridget en quittant la chaise berçante où il venait à peine de s'asseoir.

— Va ouvrir, c'est le meilleur moyen de le savoir, lui répondit sa femme, occupée aux derniers préparatifs du repas.

Samuel alla ouvrir et se retrouva nez à nez avec un parfait inconnu.

— Entrez, vous allez faire geler toute la maison, ordonna-t-il à l'homme en s'effaçant pour le laisser passer.

L'étranger pénétra dans la cuisine et enleva le casque à oreillettes qu'il portait.

— Bonsoir, est-ce que je suis chez monsieur Ellis?

— En plein ça, répondit l'Irlandais, intrigué.

— Je ne veux pas vous déranger longtemps, dit-il d'une voix grave et bien timbrée. Je m'arrête juste en passant. Je suis le notaire Eudore Valiquette et je viens de m'installer dans la maison d'un cousin germain de mon père, Euclyde Bérubé du rang Saint-Paul. Tout à l'heure, j'ai croisé monsieur le curé et il m'a dit que vous étiez le président des syndics et l'un des hommes les plus influents de Saint-Bernard-Abbé.

En entendant ces paroles, Samuel se rengorgea et Bridget s'empressa d'offrir au notaire de retirer son manteau et de s'approcher du poêle pour se réchauffer un peu. Le nouveau venu ne se fit pas prier et enleva sa pelisse de chat sauvage qu'il suspendit à l'un des crochets fixés au mur près de la porte d'entrée.

— Vous êtes bien aimable, madame, dit-il avec un sourire.

La bonhomie et la politesse de l'étranger sonnaient faux au point de susciter la méfiance du président du conseil.

Pendant qu'il retirait son manteau, Samuel examina le visiteur avec curiosité. L'homme était petit et paraissait très maigre, sanglé dans un strict costume noir. Durant un court moment, l'attention de l'hôte fut attirée davantage par la pomme d'Adam saillante de l'homme, qui montait et descendait au-dessus de son col dur, que par son étrange menton fuyant. En outre, l'homme de loi avait un visage étroit passablement ridé éclairé par de petits yeux bleus et encadré de longs favoris gris. Son crâne n'était couvert qu'en partie de quelques rares mèches de cheveux soigneusement étalés. Comme la plupart des personnes de petite taille, Eudore Valiquette se tenait très droit, soucieux de ne pas perdre un centimètre.

— J'espère que je ne vous dérange pas dans votre souper, s'excusa le visiteur.

— Il est pas encore prêt, mentit Bridget pour le mettre à l'aise.

— Mon cousin germain m'a parlé des problèmes du conseil avec monseigneur et je me suis dit que je pourrais peut-être vous être utile.

— Vous êtes ben bon de venir offrir votre aide, fit le président des syndics, mais vous savez, on a l'habitude de faire affaire avec le notaire Letendre de Sainte-Monique.

— Oui, je comprends, dit l'homme de loi en levant les mains en signe d'apaisement. Je ne viens pas essayer de voler la clientèle d'un confrère. En réalité, je ne pratique plus. Ma santé ne me le permet plus. Non, je me suis dit, après avoir écouté tout à l'heure ce que monsieur le curé me racontait, que je pourrais bien vous faire un prix spécial pour rédiger les actes de la mission. Comme vous n'avez pas l'air d'avoir de l'argent à jeter par les fenêtres, ce serait toujours ça de sauvé. Je vous ferais ça pour une partie du prix exigé par mon confrère, uniquement pour aider la mission et faire ma part, même si je suis encore un étranger.

— Ah ben, là! Ça, c'est une autre paire de manches, déclara Samuel, ravi. Si vous pouvez nous sauver de l'argent, le conseil refusera pas votre aide, c'est certain.

— Bon, c'est une affaire entendue.

— Est-ce que vous venez de la région? se hasarda à demander Bridget Ellis en tendant une tasse de thé au visiteur.

— Non, madame. J'ai vécu toute ma vie à Saint-Hyacinthe.

— Votre femme va trouver que c'est pas mal plus tranquille à Saint-Bernard.

— Je suis veuf depuis plus de dix ans et je n'ai pas d'enfant.

Pendant qu'il parlait, Samuel ne pouvait s'empêcher de fixer la pomme d'Adam du visiteur qui montait et descendait sans arrêt.

— En tout cas, monsieur le curé va être content d'avoir un autre bon paroissien, intervint la ménagère.

— Pas si bon que ça, rétorqua Eudore Valiquette avec un petit rire. Au risque de vous choquer, madame, je n'ai rien d'une grenouille de bénitier et je dois admettre que mon départ de Saint-Hyacinthe a dû faire pas mal plaisir à mon curé. J'ai bien peur qu'il ne m'ait jamais aimé bien gros.

— Vous exagérez certainement, protesta son hôtesse.

— Pas du tout, ma bonne dame. Je n'ai jamais beaucoup aimé les soutanes et ne m'en suis jamais caché. Je trouve que nos curés prennent trop de place dans nos villages et se mêlent de bien des affaires qui ne les regardent pas. Comme mon curé n'aimait pas se le faire dire, il m'en voulait. Pour être clair, mon offre de service s'adresse au syndic de la mission, pas à votre curé.

Samuel regarda sa femme, mais ne dit rien.

— Pendant que j'y pense, ajouta le visiteur. Si vous avez de l'argent à placer, je suis à votre disposition. Vous pourriez trouver ça pas mal plus pratique de venir me voir plutôt que d'aller courir à Sainte-Monique et, en plus, vous allez vite vous apercevoir que j'offre des intérêts pas mal intéressants.

— Vous venez pas de dire que vous pratiquiez plus? s'étonna Samuel.

— C'est vrai, affirma Eudore Valiquette, et j'ai pas l'intention de me faire une autre clientèle à Saint-Bernard. Non, à mon âge, j'ai décidé de me reposer un peu. Mais je vais continuer à prêter et à placer de l'argent pour les gens qui sont intéressés, juste pour me tenir un peu occupé.

Là-dessus, le petit homme se leva.

— Bon, je vous dérangerai pas plus longtemps, déclara-t-il avec un large sourire.

— Vous dérangez pas pantoute, lui dit Samuel par politesse en l'aidant à endosser son lourd manteau de fourrure.

Le notaire Valiquette quitta la maison du rang Sainte-Ursule après avoir salué les Ellis.

— Drôle de bonhomme! se borna à décréter le maître des lieux après avoir refermé la porte derrière lui. C'est à se demander pourquoi il est venu s'enterrer à Saint-Bernard s'il a toujours vécu en ville.

— En tout cas, j'ai pas aimé l'entendre parler contre les prêtres, décréta Bridget.

— Moi, ce que je comprends pas, c'est pourquoi il nous dit qu'il fait plus l'ouvrage de notaire quand il nous offre de faire des contrats et même de placer de l'argent, conclut son mari, un pli soucieux au front. Il a beau raconter que c'est pour se désennuyer, je trouve ça bizarre.

Le lendemain, à la fin de l'après-midi, le président du conseil esquissa une grimace en apercevant Paddy Connolly en train de commenter les dernières nouvelles au magasin général. Il salua de la tête Blanchette, Paquette, Bélanger et l'oncle de Liam avant de demander à Télesphore Dionne un gallon de mélasse. Il aurait bien consacré quelques minutes à discuter avec les hommes sur place si Paddy n'avait pas été là, mais il n'aimait vraiment pas le nouveau venu dans la paroisse.

Il allait prendre congé après avoir pris possession de son gallon de mélasse quand Hormidas Meilleur fit son entrée dans les lieux. Le visage rougi par le froid, le petit homme semblait de fort mauvaise humeur.

— Maudit Hérode! on gèle tout rond, jura-t-il en s'approchant de la grosse fournaise sans se soucier de couper la parole à celui qui commentait les nouvelles. À part ça, je dois être le seul facteur du comté à desservir du monde aussi gratteux! Pas un capable de m'offrir une goutte de bagosse depuis que j'ai commencé ma tournée!

— C'est sûr que c'est un manque de charité chrétienne, se moqua Télesphore Dionne en riant.

— Toi, tu peux ben rire, mon Hérode! s'emporta le facteur. Tu passes ta journée les fesses ben au chaud dans ton magasin.

— Attention à ce que vous dites, le père, le mit en garde le propriétaire. Il y a une créature ici dedans, précisa-t-il en lui indiquant sa fille Angélique en train de garnir une tablette avec de nouveaux produits.

— Mes excuses, mam'zelle, fit Hormidas, en décochant à la jeune fille un regard égrillard.

— Il y a pas d'offense, monsieur Meilleur.

— Bon, j'allais oublier de vous en apprendre une bonne, s'empressa d'ajouter Hormidas avant que Paddy reprenne la parole. Vous devinerez jamais qui vient de s'installer dans le rang Saint-Paul…

— Le notaire Eudore Valiquette, annonça Samuel, l'air sérieux.

— Comment ça se fait que tu sais ça, toi ? demanda le facteur, frustré d'être privé de son petit succès.

— Parce qu'il est venu me voir à la maison hier après-midi.

Tous se turent, curieux.

— En quel honneur ? osa demander Hormidas.

— Si on vous le demande, le père, vous direz que j'ai pas voulu vous le dire. C'est confidentiel.

— Je suppose que tu sais aussi qu'il a l'air en moyens, le notaire ? reprit le facteur, l'air narquois.

— Ça, je pourrais pas vous le dire, le père.

— Moi, je peux te le dire. Hé ! quand je l'ai croisé, il avait attelé en flèche deux chevaux à sa catherine… pas à une *sleigh* ou à un berlot comme tout le monde. Non, à une catherine. C'était de toute beauté à voir. En plus, moi, j'ai jamais vu deux beaux chevaux comme les siens. Des vrais chevaux pour la course avec des pattes fines…

— Une catherine ! intervint Cléomène Paquette. C'est pas pratique pour deux cennes, cette affaire-là. C'est trop haut sur patins et ça verse à rien. On m'en donnerait une et j'en voudrais pas, ajouta-t-il, l'air dédaigneux.

— Ben oui, Cléomène, fit Anatole, goguenard. Tout le monde de Saint-Bernard sait que t'aimes ben mieux ton vieux berlot à moitié rafistolé.

Le cultivateur pris à partie piqua un fard alors que les hommes présents ricanaient.

— En attendant, le ciel est en train de devenir ben noir et je serais pas surpris pantoute qu'on ait une bonne tempête la nuit prochaine, pronostiqua un Paddy Connolly désireux de reprendre le contrôle de son auditoire.

— Ça se peut qu'il tombe rien avant un bon bout de temps, le contredit le facteur, un rien agressif. La température a encore baissé.

— Vous saurez me le dire, s'entêta le retraité.

— Depuis quand le monde de la ville connaît quelque chose à la température ? se moqua Samuel, trop heureux de rabaisser ce faux Irlandais.

— Tu sauras… commença Paddy.

— Ah, j'y pense, l'interrompit Hormidas, j'ai une lettre pour toi, Samuel.

Sur ces mots, l'homme fouilla dans le vieux sac en cuir qu'il portait en bandoulière et il en tira une enveloppe qu'il lui tendit. Ellis la prit et la regarda un court moment, comme s'il était en mesure de déchiffrer ce qui était écrit dessus. Hormidas, toujours aussi curieux, attendit qu'il l'ouvre. Quand il se rendit compte que le président du conseil s'apprêtait à quitter les lieux, il lui proposa :

— Veux-tu que je te lise ce que ça dit ?

— Merci, père Meilleur, mais il y a rien qui presse, répondit Samuel qui venait d'apercevoir par la fenêtre du magasin Bernadette Beauchemin sur le point de verrouiller la porte de son école, en face.

Ellis salua les gens présents et sortit précipitamment du magasin général. Il héla la jeune institutrice alors qu'elle s'apprêtait à partir avec les quatre enfants de Liam Connolly qui l'attendaient au bord de la route. Au moment où il traversait le chemin, il se rendit compte que la porte du magasin venait de s'ouvrir dans son dos pour livrer passage à Paddy qui, comme il en avait pris l'habitude, avait l'intention de faire monter les enfants et leur institutrice dans sa *sleigh* pour les ramener à la maison.

— Est-ce que je peux te demander de me lire une lettre que je viens de recevoir ? demanda-t-il à la fille de Baptiste Beauchemin au moment où les grelots de l'attelage de Paddy se faisaient entendre dans son dos.

— Bien sûr, monsieur Ellis, répondit gentiment Bernadette. Les enfants, montez dans la *sleigh*, j'en ai pour une minute, ajouta-t-elle en tendant son manchon et son sac à Ann pour se libérer les mains.

La jeune fille décacheta la lettre et la lut à voix basse de manière à ce que le conducteur de la *sleigh*, qui venait de s'immobiliser quelques pieds plus loin, ne puisse pas l'entendre.

— Ça dit : «*Monsieur, monseigneur sera heureux de recevoir le ou les syndics de Saint-Bernard-Abbé jeudi, le 14 février prochain, à deux heures.*» Et c'est signé : *Eugène Dupras, secrétaire.*

— Merci, ma belle fille. Tu pourras raconter à ton frère ce que tu viens de me lire parce que ça regarde tout le conseil.

— J'aime autant pas, monsieur Ellis. Comme c'est votre lettre, je vais vous laisser lui raconter vous-même ce qui est écrit dedans. Je voudrais pas que mon frère me prenne pour un porte-panier, rétorqua l'institutrice avec un sourire avant de s'éloigner pour monter à bord de la *sleigh*.

❧

La tempête de neige annoncée par Paddy Connolly ne tomba finalement que vingt-quatre heures plus tard, comme si le ciel avait eu besoin de faire plus ample provision de neige avant d'ouvrir ses vannes sur la région. Un ciel couleur de plomb aux allures menaçantes empêcha certains hommes d'aller bûcher sur leur terre de crainte de devoir revenir précipitamment pour échapper à la tempête.

Ce répit inattendu permit aussi aux syndics de la mission de se réunir chez Samuel Ellis, hors de la présence du curé Désilets, ce qui était très inhabituel, pour ne pas dire désobligeant. Les cinq hommes se rassemblèrent donc après le souper. Samuel avait pris la peine d'avertir son épouse de ne pas répéter au curé un mot de ce qui se dirait ce soir-là dans sa cuisine.

Le président du conseil apprit aux quatre syndics qu'il avait reçu une réponse de l'évêché à la lettre envoyée par Thomas Hyland et que monseigneur les invitait à le rencontrer le 14 février, à l'évêché, à Trois-Rivières.

— Est-ce qu'on peut savoir pourquoi tu fais la réunion chez vous plutôt qu'à la sacristie, comme on fait d'habitude ? lui demanda Antonins Côté, apparemment intrigué.

— Parce que je voulais pas que monsieur le curé vienne mettre son grand nez dans l'affaire. Je suis à peu près certain qu'il voudrait venir avec nous autres et moi, je pense que c'est pas sa place, déclara tout net le président.

— Pourquoi pas ?

— Parce qu'il arrête pas de demander toutes sortes d'affaires et nous autres, on est poignés pour payer. S'il vient, comme je le connais, il va être le seul à parler, et nous autres, les niaiseux, on n'aura rien à dire. Moi, je me dis que comme c'est nous autres qui allons payer, c'est à nous autres de dire ce qu'on pense.

— Sans parler qu'il pourrait ben demander un gros presbytère et là, on serait pris pour le lui construire si monseigneur accepte, poursuivit Donat. Là, est-ce que ça veut dire que vous voulez pas qu'on dise un mot de la lettre à monsieur le curé et qu'on s'arrange entre nous autres pour aller à Trois-Rivières sans qu'il le sache ?

— Pourquoi pas ! fit Ellis.

— Moi, j'ai rien contre, même si je sais que ça fera pas plaisir à monsieur le curé quand il va le savoir, conclut Donat.

Le fils de Baptiste Beauchemin était le seul membre du conseil à vouvoyer Samuel Ellis parce qu'il avait l'âge d'être son fils. Mais il ne fallait pas se méprendre sur cette politesse toute de façade. À titre d'organisateur du parti conservateur dans la mission, le jeune homme de vingt-six ans n'éprouvait guère de sympathie – tout comme son père avant lui – pour l'Irlandais, organisateur libéral et adversaire politique.

Il n'avait pas oublié l'existence d'un sérieux contentieux entre eux depuis les dernières élections provinciales. Donat soupçonnait toujours le vieux roux d'une cinquantaine d'années d'avoir mis du séné dans la bagosse servie aux partisans conservateurs réunis à Sainte-Monique l'année précédente.

Les autres syndics se consultèrent du regard et acceptèrent la suggestion de Samuel à l'unanimité.

— Bon, c'est ben beau tout ça, mais qui va aller là-bas? demanda le président. Est-ce qu'on y va tous?

Un silence embarrassé suivit cette question.

— Je pensais qu'il avait été entendu que t'étais pour être tout seul à y aller, finit par répondre Blanchette.

Les autres membres approuvèrent en hochant la tête.

— Moi, aller là, tout seul...

— Est-ce que tu penses que tu vas être gêné devant monseigneur? osa lui demander Hyland, qui n'avait pas encore parlé.

— Pantoute, mentit l'Irlandais, mais j'aimerais ben qu'il y en ait au moins un parmi vous autres qui vienne avec moi au cas où j'oublierais quelque chose.

Chacun s'empressa de se trouver une excuse pour éviter ce déplacement difficile et onéreux, ce qui dépita passablement le président du conseil.

— À ben y penser, je pense que je vais y aller avec vous, monsieur Ellis, finit par dire Donat après un long moment de réflexion.

— Ah oui! fit Samuel, surpris.

— Ben oui, confirma Donat, ce serait pas normal que monseigneur parle à un libéral sans être surveillé de près par un bon conservateur.

— Aïe! le jeune, c'est pas de la politique qu'on va aller faire là-bas, se rebiffa le mari de Bridget Ellis.

— Je le sais, dit en souriant le jeune cultivateur, mais c'est au cas où monseigneur voudrait pas vous parler parce que vous êtes un Rouge.

— Ah ben, je voudrais ben voir ça! rétorqua Ellis, menaçant.

Le visage de Samuel se rembrunit tout de même à cette pensée. Il n'était pas sans savoir que le clergé voyait d'un très mauvais œil tous les libéraux, qu'il avait tendance à considérer comme des suppôts de Satan parce qu'ils prônaient divers moyens pour restreindre son rôle dans la société.

— Pendant que j'y pense, finit-il par dire aux quatre hommes assis autour de sa table de cuisine, le notaire Valiquette est passé me voir.

— Qui ça? demanda Antonius Côté.

— Le notaire Valiquette, répéta patiemment le président du conseil.

— D'où est-ce qu'il sort, ce notaire-là?

Samuel fut d'abord obligé d'expliquer à ceux qui ne le savaient pas déjà qu'Eudore Valiquette venait de s'installer dans la demeure de son cousin germain Euclyde Bérubé.

— C'est qu'on commence à être importants en bout de cierge! s'exclama Blanchette. On a un notaire à cette heure. Saint-Zéphirin en a même pas encore un.

— Fais pas le coq trop vite, Anatole, lui ordonna Samuel. Il m'a dit qu'il a pas l'intention de pratiquer et de voler la clientèle du notaire Letendre.

— C'est de valeur, il aurait pu être pas mal utile au monde de Saint-Bernard, regretta Donat à haute voix.

— Il va peut-être nous être ben utile, reprit le président. Il est venu me proposer de faire tous les contrats que le conseil pourrait passer en chargeant ben moins cher que le notaire Letendre. Qu'est-ce que vous dites de ça?

— Enfin une bonne nouvelle! déclara Antonius, la mine réjouie.

— Il va nous être utile tant que Saint-Bernard va continuer à exister, ajouta Donat Beauchemin, ce qui eut pour effet d'éteindre la flambée d'enthousiasme de ses confrères.

— En plus, il m'a dit qu'il était prêt à placer l'argent de ceux qui en auraient à placer, se sentit obligé d'ajouter Samuel.

— Ben, dans ce cas-là, je comprends pas pourquoi tu nous as dit qu'il voulait plus pratiquer, lui fit remarquer Anatole avec un certain bon sens. Si je me fie à ce que tu viens de dire, il est prêt à faire tout ce qu'un notaire fait d'habitude.

— C'est vrai, ça, fit Côté.

— Moi, je vous ai juste rapporté ce qu'il m'a dit, tint à préciser Samuel.

Avant de clore la réunion, il fut donc entendu que Samuel et Donat quitteraient Saint-Bernard-Abbé très tôt le matin de l'entrevue à moins qu'il n'y ait apparence d'importantes chutes de neige. Si c'était le cas, les deux hommes partiraient la veille et dormiraient dans une auberge de Trois-Rivières de manière à être sur place pour rencontrer le prélat à l'heure prévue.

On se sépara en jurant de garder le silence sur cette ambassade à laquelle Josaphat Désilets ne serait pas invité à se joindre.

À leur sortie de la maison du président du conseil, les hommes se rendirent compte qu'il faisait soudainement plus doux et que la neige s'était enfin mise à tomber doucement.

Chapitre 8

Une naissance

Le lendemain, la pire tempête de l'hiver 1872 ensevelit la région sous près de trois pieds de neige. Des vents violents soufflèrent durant vingt-quatre heures, paralysant toute activité humaine. Claquemurés dans leur maison, les habitants de Saint-Bernard-Abbé attendaient avec impatience que la neige cesse enfin de tomber.

Chez Xavier Beauchemin, la poudrerie avait fait en sorte que la neige recouvrait les fenêtres du rez-de-chaussée jusqu'aux deux tiers.

— Blasphème ! si ça arrête pas, il va falloir passer par les fenêtres du deuxième pour sortir de la maison, déclara le jeune homme à Antonin.

— Il y a pas de danger si on continue à pelleter le devant de la porte toutes les heures, répondit l'adolescent en rejoignant son jeune patron à l'étage où ils étaient occupés à terminer la construction des chambres.

— Regarde par la fenêtre, lui ordonna Xavier. Tout est blanc. On voit pas plus le chemin que la rivière. Je te dis que ça va prendre du temps pour nous désembourber de tout ça.

Antonin ne dit rien. Il devinait que malgré la tempête son patron n'aurait pas la moindre hésitation à chausser ses raquettes après le souper pour aller veiller chez sa fiancée.

La situation était identique chez Liam Connolly. Les hurlements du vent qui fouettait la neige contre les vitres donnaient l'impression qu'il essayait d'arracher la maison de son solage. Aller chercher de l'eau au puits ou des bûches dans la remise devenait une véritable expédition pour les garçons qui se plaignaient de ne voir qu'à quelques pouces devant eux. Par conséquent, inquiète, Camille ne quittait pas la fenêtre pour les surveiller quand ils devaient aller dehors. Pour y parvenir, elle devait s'étirer sur la pointe des pieds tant la neige couvrait une bonne partie des fenêtres de la cuisine.

Depuis son lever, la jeune femme était tiraillée par l'angoisse. Elle ne cessait de penser à sa sœur Emma dont l'heure de la délivrance approchait dangereusement. Elle n'osait pas en parler ouvertement devant les enfants, mais…

— Il faudrait pas que Rémi soit pris tout seul à ce moment-là, finit-elle par dire à son mari en train de se bercer près du poêle en compagnie de son oncle.

— De quoi tu parles ? lui demanda Liam.

— Je parle d'Emma.

— Arrête donc de t'en faire pour ça, lui ordonna-t-il, désinvolte. Tu sais ben que ta mère doit être là pour l'aider.

— Je suis pas sûre pantoute de ça. Elle rajeunit pas et c'est pas certain que Donat l'ait laissée prendre le chemin en pleine tempête.

— Elle reste plus près des Lafond que nous autres, lui fit remarquer Liam.

— Ça change rien.

Durant de longues minutes, Camille demeura debout devant la fenêtre, comme si sa présence allait inciter la tempête à se calmer. Soudain, elle se dirigea vers ses bottes placées sous les crochets auxquels étaient suspendus les manteaux et elle entreprit de les chausser.

— Qu'est-ce que tu fais là, ma nièce ? lui demanda Paddy en retirant son cigare de sa bouche.

— Je m'habille et je m'en vais chez ma sœur, lui répondit-elle sur un ton déterminé.

— Es-tu devenue folle ? s'insurgea son mari. On voit même pas l'étable au fond de la cour.

— J'y vais pareil. Je suis pas pour la laisser toute seule. Les derniers temps ont été difficiles pour elle et je suis certaine qu'il y a personne pour l'aider. S'il y a des complications et qu'elle perd son petit, je vais m'en vouloir jusqu'à la fin de mes jours.

— T'es complètement folle, laissa tomber Liam. En tout cas, il est pas question d'atteler pour aller te conduire là. Il y a pas une *sleigh* capable de passer sur le chemin avec toute la neige qui est tombée.

— Tu seras jamais capable de te rendre chez ta sœur, déclara Paddy d'une voix docte. On voit même pas à un pied en avant. Tu vas sortir du chemin sans t'en apercevoir et on va te retrouver morte gelée. Ta sœur sera pas plus avancée.

— Laissez faire, mon oncle. Les raquettes, c'est pas pour les chiens et je suis capable de faire attention.

— Veux-tu que j'y aille avec toi ? proposa Ann en s'avançant vers elle.

— T'es bien fine, mais j'aime mieux que tu restes ici dedans pour prendre soin de ta sœur et de tes frères et pour t'occuper des repas. Je sais pas quand je vais pouvoir revenir.

— Tu trouves ça normal, toi, de laisser ta famille se débrouiller toute seule pendant que tu t'en vas courir les chemins ? lui demanda son mari, exaspéré. J'ai ben envie de te défendre de sortir de la maison.

— Tu peux toujours le faire, répliqua-t-elle en endossant son manteau, mais il y a rien qui te dit que je t'obéirais.

Avant même que Liam ait trouvé une réplique cinglante, elle enfonça une tuque sur sa tête et sortit. Elle dut se battre contre le vent et la neige pour pouvoir refermer la porte derrière elle. Liam quitta sa chaise berçante et s'approcha de l'une des fenêtres de la cuisine assez rapidement pour la voir se frayer un chemin vers la remise voisine où étaient entreposées les raquettes. Peu après, il l'aperçut avançant lentement et péniblement, la tête penchée vers l'avant pour lutter contre le vent. Elle disparut très vite au milieu des tourbillons de neige et il ne put s'empêcher d'éprouver une certaine admiration pour celle qu'il avait épousée à la fin de l'automne.

— Maudite tête dure! se contenta-t-il de dire en regagnant sa chaise berçante.

Il feignit d'ignorer les regards réprobateurs que lui décochèrent ses enfants.

— Tu devrais te faire obéir pas mal mieux que ça par ta femme, fit Paddy. J'ai beau avoir jamais été marié, je sais ben qu'il doit y avoir juste un maître dans une maison pour que ça marche comme du monde… surtout quand ça se passe devant les enfants. Je pense que c'est pas un ben bon exemple à leur donner.

Liam ne dit rien, mais il se promit d'imposer plus sévèrement son autorité. Son oncle avait raison. Camille Beauchemin n'allait pas faire tout ce qu'elle voulait dans sa maison.

Pendant ce temps, la jeune femme marchait à l'aveuglette sur la route étroite du rang Saint-Jean. Même si on n'était qu'au début de l'après-midi, on aurait juré que le soir était déjà en train de tomber. La bouche couverte par une épaisse écharpe de laine, elle n'ouvrait les yeux qu'à demi pour se protéger des flocons que le vent poussait à l'horizontale, attentive avant tout à ne pas sortir du chemin. Le souffle coupé, elle s'efforçait de soulever ses raquettes qui s'enfonçaient profondément dans la neige.

Après ce qui lui sembla une éternité, elle crut apercevoir la maison de sa mère, étonnée de n'avoir pas parcouru plus de chemin depuis son départ. Le trajet de quelques arpents lui avait pris presque une demi-heure. Pendant un court moment, elle se demanda si elle allait s'arrêter à la maison paternelle ou si elle allait tenter de poursuivre jusque chez sa sœur, qui résidait presque à l'autre extrémité du rang.

Elle décida finalement qu'il était plus sage de faire un arrêt pour se réchauffer avant de continuer sa route.

À bout de souffle et à demi aveuglée, elle frappa à la porte. Donat vint lui ouvrir. Le jeune cultivateur ne cacha pas sa stupéfaction de la découvrir sur le pas de la porte en pleine tempête.

— Dis-moi pas qu'il est arrivé un malheur chez vous! s'exclama-t-il en s'effaçant pour la laisser entrer.

— Pantoute, le rassura Camille en tentant de reprendre son souffle tout en secouant la neige qui couvrait sa tuque et son manteau. Je voulais juste m'assurer qu'Emma était pas toute seule.

— Mais t'es complètement folle d'avoir pris le chemin dans une tempête pareille, intervint sa belle-sœur Eugénie en s'approchant d'elle. Des plans pour te perdre!

— Bien non, c'est pas si pire que ça, fit Camille pour la rassurer.

— En tout cas, pour Emma, crains rien, fit Hubert. Tu connais m'man. Quand le temps a commencé à se gâter hier matin, elle m'a obligé à atteler pour aller la conduire chez Rémi. Elle est là depuis hier soir. Quand Donat est rentré de sa réunion, elle était déjà partie.

— Ça me rassure pas mal, fit Camille en poussant un soupir de soulagement.

— Là, qu'est-ce que tu vas faire? s'enquit Donat. Tu t'en retournes chez vous?

— Non, je vais aller donner un coup de main à m'man. Je pense qu'on sera pas trop de deux pour aider Emma.

— Je vais y aller avec toi, annonça Bernadette avec détermination. T'es pas pour aller là toute seule.

— T'es bien fine, Bedette, mais c'est pas une place pour toi. Tu sais bien que m'man serait pas contente de te voir arriver pour aider Emma à accoucher. Elle a toujours eu pour son dire que c'était pas la place d'une femme pas mariée.

— Je pourrais toujours prendre soin de Flore et de Joseph, s'entêta l'institutrice.

— Il y a Rémi pour ça.

— Camille a raison, intervint Donat. Je pense que t'es mieux de rester ici dedans. Mais, toi, Camille, t'es pas pour aller là à pied, poursuivit-il. Tu te rendras jamais.

— Je pense être capable, s'entêta sa sœur aînée.

— Non, c'est trop risqué, déclara Hubert. Tu vas attendre un peu et je vais aller atteler le traîneau. La Noire devrait être capable de nous amener tous les deux jusqu'au bout du rang.

— Voyons donc! protesta faiblement Camille, reconnaissante. Penses-tu que la Noire va être capable de tirer le traîneau jusque chez Rémi dans une tempête où on voit ni ciel ni terre?

— Inquiète-toi pas, elle est vaillante. Je vais apporter des raquettes au cas où je serais obligé de l'aider à avancer, prit-il la précaution d'ajouter. Attends et réchauffe-toi un peu. Ce sera pas long.

— C'est ça, fit Bernadette d'une voix acide. M'man va être encore plus contente de te voir arriver là, toi, un homme.

— J'ai pas pantoute l'intention de rester là. Je vais aller mener Camille et je vais revenir, expliqua le jeune homme.

Il s'habilla rapidement et quitta la maison au moment où Eugénie tendait une tasse de thé bouillant à sa belle-sœur.

— Emma est bien chanceuse de pouvoir compter sur sa mère et sur toi, dit-elle à sa belle-sœur.

— T'as pas à t'en faire, répliqua Camille. On va faire la même chose pour toi quand ton heure sera venue.

Quelques minutes plus tard, la jeune femme entendit le bruit de grelots de l'attelage qui approchait de la maison. Elle boutonna rapidement son manteau, coiffa sa tuque et sortit après avoir souhaité le bonsoir aux trois adultes demeurés dans la pièce.

— Prends tes raquettes et monte, lui cria Hubert, debout en équilibre instable sur le gros traîneau en bois utilisé par les frères Beauchemin pour le transport du bois.

Camille obtempéra.

— Envoye ! Avance, ma Noire ! cria-t-il dans la tourmente pour inciter sa bête à se remettre en route.

La jument, les naseaux fumants et de la neige presque jusqu'au poitrail, se mit lentement en route en tirant difficilement sa charge. Debout devant la fenêtre obstruée en grande partie par la neige, Donat ne put s'empêcher de dire à Bernadette et à sa femme, qui s'apprêtait à aller mettre au lit le petit Alexis :

— Je sais pas trop quelle sorte d'homme est Liam Connolly, mais il m'a pas l'air de tellement tenir à Camille. Pour la laisser partir comme ça en pleine tempête, il faut être un maudit sans-cœur ! Il me semble qu'il aurait pu au moins essayer d'atteler pour aller la conduire chez Emma.

— Moi, j'en reviens pas, fit Bernadette.

— C'est vrai que c'est un drôle d'homme, reconnut Eugénie.

— En tout cas, il me semble que ma sœur mériterait d'être mieux traitée. Après tout, elle prend soin de ses enfants comme si c'étaient les siens, torrieu !

Au milieu des bourrasques de neige aveuglantes, le traîneau sortit de la cour de la ferme et tourna à droite. Hubert conduisait au jugé puisqu'il lui était impossible d'apercevoir les branches de sapinage qui balisaient la route étroite longeant la rivière. Sa bête peinait à tirer le traîneau sur lequel Camille avait beaucoup de mal à se tenir assise tant il risquait de verser lorsqu'il escaladait les congères. Hubert aperçut une lueur sur sa gauche et en déduisit que sa sœur et lui se trouvaient devant la maison de Constant Aubé, seule maison construite du côté gauche de la route dans le rang Saint-Jean. Il devina plus qu'il ne vit la maison de Conrad Boudreau quelques minutes plus tard, puis celle de son voisin, John White. Avant d'arriver face à la ferme de Gratien Ménard, le conducteur dut descendre du traîneau, chausser ses raquettes et aller saisir la Noire par le mors pour l'aider à sortir du banc de neige dans lequel elle venait de s'enliser. Camille quitta le véhicule à son tour pour l'alléger.

Plus loin, après avoir dépassé la ferme d'Ernest Gélinas, le voisin de Rémi Lafond, le traîneau versa. Par chance, Camille et son frère eurent le temps de sauter avant qu'il ne bascule, mais ils ne furent pas trop de deux pour le remettre à l'endroit.

— Coliboire de maudite misère noire! jura Hubert, aveuglé par la neige qui continuait à tomber. Est-ce qu'on va finir par arriver?

— Je pense qu'on y est presque, lui cria Camille pour l'encourager. Regarde, c'est chez Rémi.

De fait, il ne leur restait que quelques centaines de pieds à parcourir avant de pénétrer dans la cour de la ferme de leur beau-frère où Hubert prit la précaution d'immobiliser son attelage près de la remise, à l'abri du vent. Pendant que Camille se dirigeait vers la maison, son frère jeta une couverture sur le dos de la Noire avant de la suivre.

Rémi, stupéfait, vint leur ouvrir.

— Sacrifice! J'étais sûr que c'était le diable qui venait frapper à la porte par un temps pareil.

— Je suis certaine que t'es déçu, se moqua Camille en secouant la neige qui la couvrait de la tête aux pieds.

— Un peu, plaisanta son beau-frère. Ce qui m'a fait penser au diable, c'est la tête de Hubert.

— Toi, laisse-moi le temps de dégeler un peu avant de m'étriver, plaisanta le frère de sa femme.

— Dégreyez-vous et venez vous réchauffer, proposa le maître de maison. Mais qu'est-ce qui vous a fait sortir sur le chemin en pleine tempête?

— L'état de ta femme, se borna à répondre sa belle-sœur. Où sont passées m'man et Emma ? demanda-t-elle en ne les voyant pas dans la pièce où trônait un gros poêle à deux ponts.

— Emma est partie se reposer il y a une heure et ta mère est montée avec les enfants pour leur faire faire un somme. Elle devrait être à la veille de se lever. En attendant, je vais aller vous chercher quelque chose à boire qui va vous réchauffer, annonça-t-il en se dirigeant vers la porte du garde-manger.

Il sortit un cruchon de grès et entreprit de servir des petits verres de bagosse.

— Pas pour moi, si ça te fait rien, le prévint Camille, j'aimerais mieux une tasse de thé bien chaud.

— Sers-toi, lui proposa Rémi. La théière est sur le poêle. Toi, qu'est-ce que t'attends pour ôter ton manteau ? demanda-t-il à Hubert qui le dominait de plus d'une demi-tête.

— Je reste pas longtemps, répondit le jeune homme. Juste le temps de me réchauffer un peu et de laisser la Noire retrouver son souffle. L'heure du train approche et je vais retourner donner un coup de main à Donat. À part ça, cette maudite tempête-là va ben finir par arrêter un jour. À ce moment-là, je pense que l'ouvrage pour tout nettoyer manquera pas.

Rémi ne chercha pas à retenir son jeune beau-frère trop longtemps, sachant fort bien que le cheval devait souffrir du froid, même à l'abri de sa remise.

Quelques minutes plus tard, Hubert se leva et annonça son intention de retourner à la maison. Camille le remercia d'avoir eu le courage de venir la conduire chez Emma et lui conseilla la plus grande prudence pour le retour.

— Il commence déjà à faire noir, lui fit-elle remarquer alors qu'il enfonçait son casque sur sa tête.

— Ça fera pas une ben grosse différence, rétorqua le jeune homme. Il me semble qu'il a fait noir toute la journée. Bon, j'y vais, fit-il en ouvrant la porte pour sortir, à la revoyure !

Camille se posta devant la fenêtre et le vit passer peu après, debout sur le traîneau et invectivant sa bête pour l'inciter à avancer plus vite. Quand il eut disparu de sa vue, elle se retourna vers Rémi pour lui demander ce qui avait été prévu pour le souper.

— Je le sais pas trop, admit ce dernier.

— Bon, laisse faire, je vais bien trouver quelque chose, décida-t-elle. Tu peux aller faire ton train, je m'en occupe.

Le maître des lieux venait à peine de quitter la maison, un fanal à la main, pour se rendre à l'étable que Camille entendit des voix à l'étage. Peu après, elle vit la petite Flore descendre lentement l'escalier qui conduisait aux chambres, suivie de près par sa grand-mère qui portait le petit Joseph dans ses bras.

— Mais qu'est-ce que tu fais là, toi ? demanda abruptement Marie en apercevant sa fille aînée occupée à peler les pommes de terre, assise à la table de la cuisine. J'étais sûre que c'était Emma qui venait de se lever.

— Bien non, m'man, c'est juste moi. Comme vous pouvez le voir, je suis venue vous donner un coup de main.

— Où est Liam ?

— Il n'est pas là, se contenta de répondre Camille sur un ton neutre. Je suis allée chez vous à pied et c'est Hubert qui est venu me conduire en traîneau. Il vient juste de repartir.

— Bonne sainte Anne, si ça a du bon sens ! s'exclama Marie. Veux-tu bien me dire ce qui t'a pris de prendre le chemin par un temps pareil ?

— J'avais peur qu'Emma soit toute seule. J'étais trop inquiète. J'étais bien décidée à venir jusqu'ici pour lui donner un coup de main. Il me semble qu'elle en a pas mal arraché depuis une couple de mois.

— C'est ce que je pense aussi, admit sa mère, le front soudain barré par un pli soucieux. J'espère juste que tout va bien se passer quand son heure arrivera.

Les deux enfants vinrent s'asseoir à table, attendant la tartine de sucre du pays que leur grand-mère leur avait promise pour les inciter à faire une sieste. Tout en coupant deux épaisses tranches dans une miche de pain frais, Marie poursuivit à mi-voix pour ne pas réveiller Emma.

— Il aurait ben fallu que les enfants soient ailleurs, déclara-t-elle. C'est pas normal qu'ils soient ici dedans quand ça sera le moment.

— C'est certain. Pourquoi Hubert les a pas ramenés à Eugénie ou même chez nous quand il est venu vous conduire hier, avant la tempête ?

— C'est Emma qui a refusé. Elle a dit qu'elle voulait pas encombrer la famille avec ses enfants avant que le temps soit venu. D'après elle, il y a rien qui prouve que ça va arriver avant le commencement de la semaine prochaine… mais moi, j'en doute pas mal. En tout cas, si ça se produit après la tempête, Rémi aura juste à atteler pour aller les mener à la maison. Eugénie et Bernadette s'en occuperont.

La grand-mère tendit les tartines aux deux enfants en leur recommandant de ne pas faire de bruit pour ne pas réveiller leur mère.

— On va laisser Emma dormir pendant qu'on prépare le souper, suggéra Camille. J'ai vu qu'il y avait un reste de bœuf. On pourrait faire une fricassée.

— Parfait, accepta Marie. Je vais juste aller voir si Emma est correcte, ajouta-t-elle en se dirigeant vers la porte de la chambre des maîtres située au fond de la cuisine.

Elle entrouvrit doucement la porte et tendit l'oreille. La future mère avait l'air de dormir profondément.

— On la réveillera pour souper, annonça-t-elle à Camille en allant chercher un couteau pour l'aider à peler les pommes de terre.

Rémi revint à la maison près d'une heure plus tard après avoir soigné ses animaux. Il secoua la neige qui le couvrait et éteignit son fanal qu'il suspendit à un clou, près de la porte.

— On dirait que le vent commence à tomber, mais il neige toujours autant, annonça-t-il à sa belle-mère et à sa belle-sœur. Il y a de la neige jusqu'en haut de la porte de l'étable. J'ai jamais vu ça. Une chance que j'ai entré du bois en masse pour chauffer jusqu'à demain matin, conclut-il en retirant ses bottes.

— J'espère que Hubert a pas eu trop de misère à retourner à la maison, fit Camille en finissant de dresser le couvert.

La cuisine baignait dans une agréable odeur de nourriture en train de mijoter sur le poêle.

— Je pense qu'il est temps d'aller réveiller Emma, dit Marie en se dirigeant vers la chambre.

Elle resta absente deux ou trois minutes avant de revenir dans la pièce après avoir refermé la porte derrière elle.

— Est-ce qu'elle se lève ? lui demanda Camille.

— Elle dit qu'elle a pas faim et qu'elle aime mieux dormir encore un peu, lui répondit sa mère. Approchez, les enfants, venez souper, ajouta-t-elle. Toi aussi, Rémi.

Tous s'assirent autour de la table éclairée par une unique lampe à huile. À l'extérieur, les hurlements du vent avaient brusquement cessé, faisant place à un silence inquiétant.

— Je serais pas surprise pantoute que ce soit pour la nuit prochaine, avança Marie au moment où elle déposait un plat de fricassée au centre de la table.

— Qu'est-ce qu'on va faire des enfants ? s'inquiéta brusquement Rémi.

— On va faire ce qu'on va pouvoir, déclara Camille sur un ton ferme. Tu vas t'en occuper dans leur chambre en haut. On peut rien faire de mieux. T'es tout de même pas pour prendre la chance d'aller les conduire chez m'man ou chez nous.

Le repas se prit en silence et les deux femmes s'empressèrent de ranger la cuisine dès que Rémi et ses deux enfants eurent fini de manger. Quand Emma, les traits tirés et les yeux largement cernés, apparut dans la pièce un peu avant sept heures, elle s'étonna de trouver sa sœur aînée chez elle.

— Je suis venue voir si je pouvais être utile à quelque chose, expliqua l'épouse de Liam Connolly en taisant les difficultés qu'elle avait eues à se rendre chez sa sœur.

— Veux-tu manger quelque chose ? lui proposa sa mère.

— Non, m'man, j'ai pas faim. On dirait que le dîner passe mal.

— C'est correct. Je vais te servir une bonne tasse de thé et juste un ou deux biscuits à la mélasse. Ça va te faire du bien.

Camille regarda sa jeune sœur se déplacer lourdement, l'air pataud. Elle ne se rappelait pas l'avoir vue aussi mal en point lors de ses deux précédentes grossesses.

— Assois-toi proche du poêle et berce-toi, lui conseilla Camille. Non, mon cœur, maman peut pas te bercer, elle est fatiguée, prit-elle soin d'ajouter à l'intention du bambin de trois ans qui voulait prendre place sur les genoux de sa mère. Ma tante va te bercer, elle, ajouta-t-elle en prenant Joseph dans ses bras.

À huit heures, on décida de mettre au lit les deux enfants. Emma annonça son intention de retourner se coucher. Camille se chargea de préparer son neveu et sa nièce pour la nuit et revint dans la cuisine où il ne restait plus que sa mère et son beau-frère. Les trois adultes discutèrent durant un long moment à mi-voix avant de se retirer pour la nuit.

— Au moindre signe, viens m'avertir, ordonna Marie à son gendre avant de suivre Camille à l'étage. Les deux femmes se séparèrent sur le palier et allèrent se coucher.

La veuve de Baptiste Beauchemin avait l'impression de venir à peine de s'endormir quand elle entendit frapper doucement à la porte de sa chambre. Celle-ci s'ouvrit et Rémi apparut, une lampe à la main.

— Madame Beauchemin, je pense que le petit s'en vient, murmura-t-il sans oser entrer dans la pièce.

— Quoi? Qu'est-ce qu'il y a? demanda-t-elle, mal réveillée.

— Emma commence à avoir des douleurs.

— Quelle heure il est?

— Un peu plus que deux heures.

— Bon, je descends, lui dit-elle. Va t'occuper de bien chauffer la maison.

La porte se referma et elle alluma en tâtonnant la lampe déposée sur l'unique bureau de la pièce. Elle s'habilla rapidement, sortit de sa chambre et alla réveiller Camille, dans la chambre voisine.

— Camille, c'est commencé, se contenta-t-elle de dire à sa fille aînée en la secouant doucement par une épaule.

Un peu plus tard, les deux femmes entrèrent dans la chambre d'Emma, laissant dans la cuisine un Rémi nerveux à qui elles avaient confié le soin de s'occuper du poêle. Dehors, le vent était définitivement tombé et la neige avait cessé. En cette nuit glaciale du mois de février, le monde entier semblait enseveli sous une épaisse couche blanche surveillée par une lune qui venait enfin d'apparaître entre les nuages.

— Va chercher une autre lampe, ordonna Marie à Camille après avoir demandé à la future mère comment elle se sentait.

Emma lui apprit qu'elle avait ressenti les premières contractions quelques minutes plus tôt et qu'elle avait déjà perdu ses eaux. Au moment où Camille rentrait dans la pièce en tenant une autre lampe, de nouvelles contractions firent grimacer sa jeune sœur qui avait empoigné à pleines mains son ventre alourdi.

— Tu vas te lever une minute, dit Marie une fois passée la douloureuse crampe, on va changer ton drap.

On aida la jeune femme à s'asseoir sur le coffre placé au pied du lit et on s'empressa de changer le drap. Elle put regagner son lit à l'instant où une autre vague de contractions surgissait. Haletante, la sueur au front, Emma crispa les poings et émit une plainte étouffée pour ne pas réveiller les enfants qui dormaient à l'étage.

— Ça revient rapidement, déclara Marie. Prends courage, pour moi, ton petit va arriver vite.

— Si c'est comme ça, je vais aller préparer tout ce qu'il faut sur la table de cuisine, annonça Camille.

— J'ai tout mis dans l'armoire, lui apprit sa sœur.

Camille, les bras chargés d'un drap et de tout ce qui serait nécessaire pour laver et vêtir le nouveau-né, quitta la chambre. Elle trouva Rémi en train de faire les cent pas dans la cuisine. Sans rien dire, elle se dirigea vers le réservoir d'eau du poêle pour en vérifier le contenu.

— C'est dommage, le beau-frère, mais tu vas être obligé de t'habiller pour aller me chercher une chaudière d'eau au puits. On va avoir besoin de plus d'eau chaude que ça.

— J'y vais, fit Rémi, apparemment soulagé d'avoir quelque chose à faire.

L'épouse de Liam Connolly entreprit de placer sur la table de cuisine tout ce qu'elle avait rapporté de la chambre et, avant de revenir dans celle-ci, elle prit la précaution d'apporter un bol à main rempli d'eau tiède et une serviette. À son arrivée auprès de sa sœur, celle-ci sortait d'une série de contractions qui l'avaient laissée pantelante. Sans dire un mot, Camille trempa la serviette dans l'eau tiède et essuya le visage de sa sœur qui semblait au bord de l'épuisement. Pourtant, elle donnait l'impression d'attendre courageusement les prochaines douleurs qui ne manqueraient pas d'arriver.

— Restez pas debout à côté du lit, finit-elle par dire à sa mère et à sa sœur avec un pauvre sourire. Je me sens obligée d'accoucher tout de suite. Allez chercher les deux chaises dans le salon.

Marie hésita quelques instants avant d'obtempérer. Les douleurs étaient si rapprochées que la délivrance allait sûrement se produire dans les minutes suivantes. Finalement, quand elle se rendit compte que les contractions se faisaient soudainement attendre, elle décida de demander à Rémi de les apporter.

Et l'attente commença. Inexplicablement, le travail cessa. À tel point qu'Emma commença à somnoler puis s'endormit. Une heure passa sans que sa mère ni Camille n'osent quitter la chambre.

— J'aime pas ça pantoute, murmura Marie à sa fille aînée en regardant les traits tirés d'Emma. C'est pas normal, cette affaire-là.

Les deux femmes n'entendaient que le bruit du rond du poêle quand Rémi y jetait une bûche. Un peu avant trois heures trente, de vives contractions arrachèrent un cri à Emma brutalement tirée de son sommeil et le travail reprit. Puis les douleurs revinrent, plus rapprochées cette fois, au point que sa mère et sa sœur crurent que le moment de la délivrance approchait enfin.

Malheureusement, au bout d'une heure, tout s'arrêta encore une fois, laissant la future mère, trempée de sueur et au bord de l'épuisement total.

— Ça a pas d'allure, chuchota Camille. Elle passera jamais à travers si ça continue comme ça.

— On va prier, décida sa mère en tirant un chapelet de la poche de son tablier.

Les deux femmes se mirent à prier à voix basse pendant qu'Emma cherchait à récupérer suffisamment de forces pour enfin donner naissance à son enfant. Vers cinq heures trente, Camille sortit de la chambre alors que son beau-frère endossait son manteau et chaussait ses bottes.

— Je vais aller faire mon train, lui annonça-t-il en allumant un fanal. Là, je sers à rien et ça me rend fou.

— C'est ça, vas-y, l'encouragea Camille. Elle est en train de se reposer. Ça sera pas pour tout de suite.

— Mais veux-tu ben me dire ce qui se passe ? lui demanda-t-il. Pour les deux premiers, ça a jamais pris autant de temps.

— Je le sais pas, mais inquiète-toi pas, elle va finir par l'avoir, son petit.

Rémi enfonça sa tuque sur sa tête et quitta la maison. Quand Camille rentra dans la chambre, sa mère lui dit d'une voix basse chargée d'inquiétude :

— Je serais bien plus tranquille si le docteur Samson était ici dedans pour s'occuper de ta sœur.

— Là, m'man, on va bien être obligées de se débrouiller sans lui. Je serais surprise que les chemins soient ouverts avant la fin de la journée avec toute la neige qui est tombée. Je pense que...

La plainte sourde émise par Emma lui coupa la parole. Marie se leva et s'approcha de sa fille. Les contractions reprirent, mais cette fois-ci elles se firent de plus en plus violentes et rapprochées. La mère se mit à encourager la jeune femme en douleur à pousser de plus en plus fort pendant que Camille rafraîchissait le front de sa sœur avec un linge humide.

— Envoye, Emma, il s'en vient, lui ordonna Marie. T'en as plus pour longtemps. C'est presque fini.

Emma gémissait de plus en plus fort, en proie à ce qui semblait des douleurs insupportables.

— Continue, tu y es presque, fit sa mère quelques minutes plus tard alors que la tête du bébé venait enfin d'apparaître. Vas-y, je le vois.

Dans un effort suprême, la jeune mère expulsa enfin l'enfant qu'elle portait et perdit conscience, épuisée par les efforts qu'elle avait dû déployer pour donner naissance à son bébé.

— Occupe-toi de ta sœur, ordonna sèchement Marie à sa fille aînée qui fixait sans réaction le nouveau-né encore rattaché à sa mère. Éponge-lui le visage pendant que je coupe le cordon. Dépêche-toi !

— C'est un garçon ou une fille ?

— Une fille.

Sans plus s'occuper d'elle, la veuve de Baptiste Beauchemin coupa le cordon ombilical, saisit le bébé par les pieds et lui donna une tape sur le derrière pour le faire crier et ainsi dégager ses voies respiratoires. Une fois qu'il eut crié, elle s'empressa de l'envelopper dans un linge et le tendit à Camille au moment où Emma reprenait pied dans la réalité.

— À cette heure, va nettoyer le petit, commanda-t-elle à sa fille. Je vais finir de m'occuper de ta sœur.

Camille prit l'enfant tout rouge et quitta la chambre. La cuisine était suffisamment chaude pour ne pas mettre la santé du bébé en danger. Elle allait le déposer sur la table quand elle aperçut Flore, à demi réveillée, debout sur la première marche de l'escalier. Elle s'empressa de lui tourner le dos pour qu'elle ne voie pas ce qu'elle tenait dans ses bras.

— Qu'est-ce qu'il y a, ma tante ? demanda la petite fille de cinq ans.

— Rien, ma belle fille. Reste en haut et retourne te coucher. Il est trop de bonne heure pour que tu te lèves.

— J'ai entendu m'man crier.

— Ta maman a fait un cauchemar. Elle s'est rendormie. Fais la même chose qu'elle. Va te recoucher. Ma tante va aller te chercher tout à l'heure. Et fais attention de pas réveiller Joseph.

Camille attendit que sa nièce ait obéi avant de déposer le poupon sur la table. Elle s'empressa de préparer un bol d'eau tiède et se mit en frais de le laver et de l'emmailloter soigneusement. Le visage de l'enfant n'avait pas été trop marqué par sa naissance, mais sa largeur, ses yeux légèrement bridés ainsi que le petit bout de langue rose qui dépassait de ses lèvres avaient quelque chose de surprenant. Par ailleurs, sa tête lui semblait un peu plus grosse que la normale. Tout en préparant le nouveau-né avant d'aller le déposer dans les bras de la mère, la jeune femme ne cessait de se dire qu'il ne ressemblait en rien à sa sœur et à son frère qu'elle avait vus bébés.

La porte de la chambre s'ouvrit sur Marie portant des linges souillés ainsi que le placenta. Elle avait les traits tirés par la fatigue.

— Ta sœur est correcte, dit-elle à sa fille aînée en se débarrassant de son fardeau. Sa toilette est faite et je pense qu'elle a juste envie de dormir. J'ai soufflé une des deux lampes.

— Le bébé dort déjà, lui fit remarquer Camille en lui montrant l'enfant qu'elle tenait dans ses bras.

— Montre-moi donc ce bout de chou que je voie de quoi elle a l'air une fois bien propre, demanda Marie en retrouvant le sourire malgré sa fatigue.

Camille lui présenta l'enfant et guetta la réaction de sa mère. Celle-ci eut un léger sursaut à la vue du visage de sa petite-fille, ce qui ne l'empêcha pas de déposer un baiser sur le front du bébé.

— Vous trouvez pas qu'elle ressemble pas à Flore et à Joseph quand ils sont venus au monde? chuchota Camille.

— Ça veut rien dire, répondit sa mère d'une voix neutre. Un enfant, ça change vite. Déjà dans deux ou trois jours, on va avoir de la misère à le reconnaître.

Mais Camille ne se trompait pas. Elle était certaine que sa mère cherchait surtout à se rassurer.

— Bon, va le porter à Emma. Elle a hâte de voir sa fille, lui ordonna Marie. Rémi devrait être à la veille de rentrer, et lui aussi va être content de la voir.

— Pas juste lui, Flore est déjà réveillée et j'ai bien l'impression que Joseph va suivre.

Camille retrouva sa sœur souriante malgré son épuisement. Elle la félicita en déposant le bébé dans ses bras. La pièce était mal éclairée et tout de même assez fraîche parce qu'on avait tenu la porte fermée durant tout l'accouchement. Emma serra son enfant contre elle et l'embrassa, apparemment sans remarquer quoi que ce soit d'anormal. Elle allait demander si Rémi l'avait vue quand elle l'entendit entrer dans la maison. Marie l'invita à aller voir sa femme et sa fille, et Camille s'esquiva pour laisser le couple vivre ensemble ce moment privilégié.

Quelques instants plus tard, Flore apparut avec son petit frère sur la première marche de l'escalier.

— Vous pouvez descendre, leur permit leur grand-mère. Venez voir ce que les sauvages vous ont apporté pendant la nuit.

Les deux enfants descendirent l'escalier et Marie les fit entrer dans la chambre où ils retrouvèrent leur père, assis près de leur mère étendue. Il y eut des exclamations excitées. La grand-mère laissa passer quelques minutes avant de revenir dans la chambre.

— Bon, vous allez laisser votre mère dormir un peu, et moi je vais coucher votre petite sœur dans son berceau, annonça-t-elle sur un ton sans réplique. Vous autres, vous allez rejoindre votre tante Camille qui va vous aider à vous habiller avant de déjeuner.

Rémi Lafond comprit que le message s'adressait aussi à lui. Fatigué par sa nuit de veille, il sortit de la pièce derrière ses enfants. Pendant que Camille montait à l'étage avec Joseph et Flore, sa belle-mère lui dit :

— Il va falloir que tu trouves le moyen d'aller chercher le docteur Samson à Saint-Zéphirin.

— Est-ce que c'est pressant ? lui demanda son gendre, soudain inquiet. Il y a pas un chemin ouvert à matin.

— C'est sûr qu'à matin, tu pourras jamais te rendre, mais il faudrait que ce soit fait aujourd'hui, insista Marie. Il faut qu'il voie Emma et surtout la petite. L'accouchement a pas été facile pantoute et on sait jamais. On a fait notre possible, mais ce serait mieux si le docteur venait les voir, ajouta-t-elle, cherchant à faire taire l'inquiétude perceptible chez le mari d'Emma.

— C'est correct, madame Beauchemin. Je déjeune et, après ça, je déneige ma cour et mon bout de chemin. Après le dîner, je pense que les chemins devraient être pas mal ouverts. À ce moment-là, je vais y aller.

— Fais donc ça, mais garde-toi une heure ou deux pour dormir un peu, lui conseilla sa belle-mère. Si un de mes garçons vient aujourd'hui, je lui demanderai d'aller prévenir monsieur le curé pour qu'il vienne ondoyer la petite. Il faudrait pas prendre le risque que cette enfant-là aille dans les limbes s'il lui arrivait quelque chose.

— Vous m'inquiétez, madame Beauchemin, on dirait que vous avez peur que…

— Ben non, Rémi, c'est juste une précaution. C'est pas parce qu'on l'a pas fait pour Flore et Joseph qu'il faut pas le faire. À part ça, penses-tu que je vais finir par savoir un jour comment va s'appeler cette enfant-là ? ajouta-t-elle sur un ton léger qui sonnait un peu faux.

— On a pensé l'appeler Marthe.

— C'est un bien beau nom, fit Marie avec un sourire. C'est le nom de ma grand-mère Camirand.

Chapitre 9

L'épreuve

Après le déjeuner, Camille exigea que sa mère aille dormir quelques heures pendant qu'elle s'occuperait des deux enfants.

— Tu veux pas rentrer chez vous ? lui demanda Marie.

— Je pense que je vais être plus utile ici dedans qu'à la maison, lui répondit sa fille. Là-bas, ils sont pas en perdition, il y a Ann pour s'occuper de la maisonnée.

Fatiguée par sa nuit de veille, Marie ne se fit pas prier pour aller dormir et Rémi quitta la maison pour procéder au déneigement. Camille vit à ce que Flore et Joseph n'empêchent pas sa mère, Emma et le bébé de dormir.

Un peu après onze heures, Marie apparut dans la cuisine en déclarant qu'elle avait assez dormi et insista pour que sa fille aille se reposer à son tour. Cette dernière monta à l'étage et, sans se déshabiller, s'enfouit sous les épaisses couvertures encore chaudes qui couvraient le lit que sa mère venait de quitter. Elle mit quelques instants avant de trouver le sommeil, taraudée par ce à quoi elle avait assisté durant la nuit. Courageuse, elle était moins habitée par la crainte des souffrances de l'enfantement que par la terreur de donner naissance à un bébé… à un bébé différent des autres.

Camille fut tirée du sommeil sur le coup de trois heures par des voix masculines en provenance du rez-de-chaussée. Elle se leva rapidement, remit de l'ordre dans sa coiffure et ses vêtements et se dépêcha de descendre à la cuisine où elle trouva Rémi en train d'aider le curé Désilets à retirer son manteau.

— J'ai été chanceux, madame Beauchemin, dit le maître de la maison à Marie. Au moment où j'arrivais à la sacristie, j'ai rencontré Xavier qui s'en allait au magasin général. Le rang Sainte-Ursule est déjà ouvert sur toute sa longueur. Quand je lui ai dit qu'on venait d'avoir du nouveau et que je devais aller avertir le docteur Samson, il m'a dit qu'il s'en chargeait et de me contenter d'aller prévenir Antonin qu'il rentrerait pas avant le début de la soirée.

— Il est bien de service, se borna à dire Marie.

— Il va arrêter voir sa sœur et sa nièce en revenant, ajouta le jeune père.

— Bon, où sont la mère et l'enfant? demanda Josaphat Désilets, en manifestant une certaine impatience.

Le prêtre avait assisté à l'échange sans dire un mot.

— Je dois vous dire qu'il était pas nécessaire que je vienne ondoyer l'enfant, tint-il à préciser. N'importe qui dans la maison aurait pu le faire à ma place s'il jugeait la vie du bébé en danger ou si l'accouchement a été particulièrement difficile.

— Il a été difficile, monsieur le curé, répliqua la mère de l'accouchée, mais je savais pas quoi faire pour ondoyer la petite. J'ai pas voulu prendre de chance.

— C'est correct, laissa-t-il tomber sèchement.

Marie le précéda jusqu'à la chambre de sa fille pour lui ouvrir la porte et elle l'invita du geste à entrer en compagnie de Rémi. Elle referma la porte derrière eux.

— Seigneur qu'il est bête, ce prêtre-là! ne put s'empêcher de dire Camille.

— C'est un bon prêtre, ma fille. C'est ça qui est le plus important, la tança sa mère.

La cérémonie fut très brève et le curé de Saint-Bernard-Abbé revint dans la cuisine moins de dix minutes plus tard. Pendant qu'il endossait son manteau avec l'aide de Camille, il s'adressa à Rémi en train de s'habiller lui aussi.

— Est-ce que le docteur a vu cet enfant-là ?

— Pas encore, monsieur le curé, répondit le père.

— En tout cas, ce serait une bonne idée de venir le faire baptiser après-demain, dimanche après-midi.

— On va faire ça, monsieur le curé.

Après le départ du prêtre et de Rémi, Camille annonça à sa mère qu'elle allait rentrer chez elle avant que Liam perde patience. Elle la laissa à la préparation du souper pour aller dire quelques mots à sa sœur avant de partir.

Les traits un peu moins tirés, Emma avait la mine rayonnante de la nouvelle mère. Fait étonnant, elle ne semblait pas du tout inquiétée par le fait qu'on avait jugé bon d'ondoyer son bébé.

— Monsieur le curé est parti ? demanda-t-elle à sa sœur aînée.

— Il vient de partir avec Rémi. Il veut que le baptême se fasse dimanche.

— Mais il vient de baptiser la petite, protesta la mère.

— Il l'a ondoyée, pas baptisée, Emma, la corrigea Camille. C'est pas la même chose. Pour le baptême, il faut un parrain et une marraine.

Le visage d'Emma se rembrunit légèrement. Elle ne s'était pas inquiétée parce qu'elle avait confondu ondoiement et baptême.

— Qui avez-vous choisi comme parrain et marraine ? poursuivit Camille.

— Si ç'avait été un garçon, c'est le frère de Rémi qui aurait été dans les honneurs, mais là, c'est une fille. Les honneurs vont être dans ma famille. Est-ce que Liam et toi, vous voulez être le parrain et la marraine de Marthe ?

— Rien pourrait nous faire plus plaisir, accepta Camille avec un large sourire.

Il y eut un bref silence dans la chambre. Le bébé bougea dans son berceau et Camille vérifia s'il était bien couvert.

— Je viens de penser à quelque chose, murmura-t-elle à sa sœur. As-tu songé que tu pourrais demander à Xavier et à sa Catherine d'être dans les honneurs?

— T'es pas sérieuse? fit Emma, surprise par la suggestion de sa sœur aînée.

— Ça serait un bon moyen d'obliger m'man à accepter Catherine dans la famille.

— Je suis certaine qu'elle serait enragée bien noir, protesta sa jeune sœur.

— Peut-être sur le coup, mais après, elle aurait plus le choix. Moi, ce que je t'en dis... Va surtout pas croire que je veux pas être dans les honneurs... Je pensais seulement à la famille.

— Là, je le sais plus, admit Emma d'une voix hésitante. Normalement, ça devrait être toi la marraine, t'es la plus vieille de la famille. P'pa et m'man ont été dans les honneurs pour Flore.

— Écoute, parles-en à Rémi, lui conseilla sa sœur. Si vous acceptez, Liam et moi, on sera pas pantoute insultés. Ann pourrait même être la porteuse, si tu le veux. Tu nous feras savoir ce que vous aurez décidé. Bon, là, je rentre à la maison. M'man reste pour tes relevailles, mais si jamais t'as besoin de quelque chose, envoie-moi Rémi.

Celui-ci rentra à la maison au moment où sa belle-sœur s'apprêtait à partir. Il alla la conduire chez elle après avoir promis à sa belle-mère de s'arrêter en chemin pour annoncer à Bernadette, Donat et Eugénie la bonne nouvelle.

— Dis-leur tout de même d'attendre demain pour venir voir Emma et la petite, prit-elle soin de préciser. Explique-leur qu'on attend le docteur Samson et qu'Emma est encore pas mal faible.

Le soleil commençait à se coucher au-dessus des eaux gelées de la rivière quand la *sleigh* de Rémi Lafond quitta la ferme. Le chemin du rang Saint-Jean avait déjà été non seulement tapé par les rouleaux des cultivateurs, mais aussi soigneusement balisé avec des branches de sapinage. Il était stupéfiant de voir avec quelle rapidité les gens de l'endroit étaient parvenus à se sortir de l'énorme tempête qui avait laissé derrière elle près de trois pieds de neige. De loin en loin, seuls les toits des maisons semblaient émerger de toute cette neige.

À son arrivée à la maison, Camille trouva la table mise et le souper en train de cuire sur le poêle. L'oncle de Liam se berçait tranquillement près du poêle pendant qu'Ann était occupée à trancher du pain. Quand elle entra dans la maison, la petite Rose se précipita dans ses bras et le sourire de bienvenue de la petite fille réchauffa le cœur de sa mère adoptive.

— P'pa est à la veille de revenir du train, lui annonça Ann. Duncan et Patrick sont avec lui.

— C'est parfait.

— Est-ce que tout va ben ? finit par lui demander Paddy Connolly, sans manifester trop d'intérêt.

— Tout est rentré dans l'ordre, mon oncle, se borna-t-elle à dire. Ma sœur a eu une belle petite fille.

Ann et sa sœur furent tout excitées par la nouvelle. Quand Liam rentra quelques minutes plus tard, il arborait son visage fermé des mauvais jours. Il retira son manteau et ses bottes sans dire un mot alors que ses fils semblaient heureux de revoir Camille et ne le cachaient guère. Celle-ci remarqua que Duncan arborait une joue enflée et elle en déduisit qu'il avait été encore frappé par son père. Aidée par Ann, elle servit le repas puis mangea. Le silence régna autour de la table durant tout le souper. Comme son mari ne semblait pas désireux de savoir comment les choses s'étaient passées pour elle depuis la veille, Camille ne lui dit rien.

Après le repas, Ann et Rose l'aidèrent à laver la vaisselle et à ranger la cuisine pendant que les deux garçons remplissaient le coffre à bois avec des bûches qu'ils allaient chercher dans la remise voisine.

Un peu avant huit heures, Camille annonça aux enfants qu'ils allaient faire la prière parce qu'elle avait trop sommeil pour continuer à veiller.

— Tu peux aller te coucher tout de suite sans t'occuper de nous autres, lui proposa Patrick. Hier soir, Ann nous a fait faire notre prière. Elle peut faire la même chose à soir.

Camille eut un sourire d'appréciation à l'endroit de l'adolescente et la remercia d'y avoir pensé.

— J'ai pas dormi la nuit passée, expliqua-t-elle, davantage à l'intention des enfants qu'à celle de Liam et de son oncle. Si Ann veut bien vous faire réciter votre prière, je pense que je vais aller me coucher tout de suite.

Sur ces mots, elle embrassa chacun des enfants, alluma une lampe et disparut dans sa chambre.

❧

Après avoir déposé Camille chez elle et annoncé aux Beauchemin la naissance de son troisième enfant, Rémi Lafond revint à la maison. Il alla soigner ses animaux et il rentra chez lui quelques minutes avant que le repas soit prêt. Il retira son manteau et ses bottes avant d'aller jeter un coup d'œil dans la chambre pour s'assurer que sa femme avait tout ce dont elle avait besoin. Marie le regarda faire sans dire un mot, attendrie par l'attachement que son gendre manifestait à l'endroit de sa fille.

— Entre, chuchota Emma à son mari.

Rémi pénétra dans la pièce plongée dans l'obscurité et s'assit sur le bord du lit.

— Est-ce que t'es correcte ? lui demanda-t-il à voix basse.

— Oui, mais je veux te parler de quelque chose.

— De quoi ?

— Du parrain et de la marraine de la petite.

— Qu'est-ce qu'il y a ? Il avait pas été entendu que ce serait Liam et Camille si c'était une fille ?

— Oui, mais j'ai pensé à quelque chose. Qu'est-ce que tu dirais si on demandait à Xavier et Catherine d'être dans les honneurs ?

— T'es pas sérieuse ? fit son mari. Tu vas insulter Camille et Liam à mort si tu fais ça.

— Bien non, le contredit sa femme. C'est même Camille qui me l'a suggéré. Elle pense que ce serait une bonne façon de faire accepter Catherine Benoît dans la famille. En plus, je suis sûre que ça ferait bien plaisir à Xavier.

— Écoute, fit Rémi sur un ton qui se voulait raisonnable, j'aime ben ton frère, mais je voudrais pas mettre la chicane avec ta mère. Tu sais à quel point elle peut pas sentir la petite Benoît...

— Moi, je pense que m'man va peut-être ruer un peu dans les brancards en apprenant ça, puis après elle va s'habituer à l'idée. Qu'est-ce que t'en penses ?

— Fais ce que tu veux, finit-il par dire après une brève hésitation. Mais, à ta place, je lui en parlerais avant.

— Je vais même le faire tout de suite, dit Emma sur un ton résolu. Dis-lui que j'aimerais lui parler.

Rémi quitta la pièce et demanda à sa belle-mère d'aller voir sa fille. Marie s'empressa d'entrer dans la chambre, croyant que la nouvelle maman avait un besoin particulier à satisfaire.

— M'man, j'aimerais vous dire quelque chose, chuchota Emma en faisant signe à sa mère de s'asseoir sur le bord du lit.

— Qu'est-ce qu'il y a ?

— On avait décidé de demander à Camille et Liam d'être la marraine et le parrain du bébé si c'était une fille.

— C'est normal, c'est leur tour. Camille est la plus vieille de la famille.

— C'est vrai, mais Camille m'a donné une idée. Je viens d'en parler à Rémi, il est d'accord.

— Quelle idée ? demanda Marie, soudainement sur ses gardes.

— Qu'est-ce que vous diriez qu'on demande plutôt à Xavier et à Catherine ? fit Emma, s'attendant à ce que sa mère explose en entendant ses paroles.

Il y eut un long silence entre les deux femmes dans le noir.

— Vous êtes bien libres de faire ce que vous voulez, déclara sèchement la femme d'une cinquantaine d'années. Après tout, c'est votre enfant.

— C'est pas parce qu'on veut faire un passe-droit, m'man, se défendit la jeune femme. On essaye juste de faire comprendre à Xavier qu'il fait toujours partie de la famille, comme les autres, même s'il va marier une fille qu'on n'aime pas bien gros.

— Ouais, se borna à laisser tomber sa mère.

— Je sais que ça vous fait pas plaisir, mais…

— C'est correct, laisse faire, la coupa-t-elle. Je suppose qu'on va s'habituer à l'idée, et qu'à la longue il va bien falloir qu'on endure cette fille-là.

— Je savais que vous comprendriez, m'man.

— Bon, à cette heure, t'as assez jacassé. Dors un peu avant d'avoir à nourrir la petite. De toute façon, j'ai bien l'impression que le docteur est à la veille d'arriver, si Xavier a pu se rendre jusqu'à Saint-Zéphirin, comme de raison.

Marie sortit de la chambre. À vrai dire, la quinquagénaire était beaucoup plus préoccupée par la visite du médecin que par le fait qu'Emma ait décidé de demander à son plus jeune frère d'être le parrain de la petite.

⌐

Vers sept heures, un « Whow ! » sonore crié à l'extérieur attira Rémi à la fenêtre. Il faisait un magnifique clair de lune et il aperçut deux berlots qui venaient de s'immobiliser près de la galerie de sa maison.

— V'là Xavier et le docteur Samson, annonça-t-il à sa belle-mère qui venait d'aller coucher Flore et Joseph à l'étage.

— Ça, c'est une bonne nouvelle, fit la veuve de Baptiste Beauchemin en retirant son tablier.

Son gendre ouvrit la porte aux deux hommes avant même qu'ils aient eu à frapper et il les invita à entrer.

— Bonsoir, docteur, fit Marie en s'avançant pour le débarrasser de sa vieille trousse en cuir et ainsi lui permettre de retirer son épais manteau.

— Bonsoir, madame Beauchemin, fit l'homme au visage sévère en la reconnaissant.

— Maudit blasphème! jura le grand Xavier en secouant bruyamment ses pieds pour en faire tomber la neige, on gèle ben dur à soir.

— Pas tant de bruit, lui ordonna sa mère, tu vas réveiller la petite.

— Toutes mes excuses, j'y pensais pas, reprit-il un ton plus bas.

— C'est vrai qu'il fait pas mal plus froid que cet après-midi, reconnut Eugène Samson en tendant son manteau à Rémi, qui le suspendit derrière la porte. Mais au moins, ce froid-là a durci le chemin et le cheval a eu moins de misère à tirer le berlot.

— C'est presque pas humain de vous forcer à faire autant de chemin en plein hiver, s'excusa Rémi.

— Ça fait partie de la vie d'un docteur de campagne, répliqua le médecin sans sourire.

— Vous allez bien prendre quelque chose pour vous réchauffer un peu, proposa Marie.

— Peut-être après avoir vu la mère et l'enfant, fit Eugène Samson en mettant son lorgnon et en s'emparant de sa trousse.

— Je vous montre le chemin, dit Marie.

Alors que le médecin disparaissait dans la chambre, Marie revint dans la cuisine et sortit du réchaud une assiette de pommes de terre et de saucisses qu'elle déposa sur la table à l'intention de Xavier.

— Approche et viens manger, lui ordonna-t-elle.

— C'est pas de refus, accepta le jeune homme en s'attablant.

— En tout cas, je te remercie ben gros d'être allé chercher le docteur, fit Rémi, très reconnaissant, en déposant devant lui un demi-verre de bagosse. J'espère que t'en as pas trop arraché pour te rendre là-bas.

— Non, c'était pas si pire. Il y a juste dans le bas des côtes où la neige s'était pas mal ramassée, mais il y avait moyen de passer avec un berlot. Avec une *sleigh*, ça aurait été une autre paire de manches, par exemple.

Rémi et Marie le laissèrent manger en paix durant quelques minutes. À l'instant où le jeune homme finissait son repas, Eugène Samson sortit de la chambre à coucher en portant le bébé dans ses bras.

— Allez donc me chercher une couverture. Je vais examiner la petite ici dedans, déclara le praticien.

Marie s'empressa d'aller chercher une couverture qu'elle étala sur la table pendant que Rémi débarrassait celle-ci de la vaisselle sale.

— C'est correct. Vous pouvez me laisser faire, fit le médecin, incitant ainsi les trois adultes présents dans la pièce à se retirer à l'écart pour qu'il puisse examiner l'enfant.

Il déshabilla le bébé et l'ausculta longuement, apparemment hésitant à poser un diagnostic. Finalement, le front soucieux, il se tourna vers la grand-mère pour lui demander de rhabiller l'enfant et de le remettre dans son berceau.

— Venez dans la chambre avec moi, monsieur Lafond, commanda le docteur Samson en retirant son lorgnon. J'ai à vous parler, à vous et à votre femme.

Sans plus attendre, le médecin se dirigea vers la pièce voisine, suivi de Rémi. Il prit la précaution de refermer la porte de la chambre derrière le père dès que Marie eut quitté la pièce. Emma, adossée contre ses oreillers, regarda les deux hommes s'approcher d'elle sans rien dire.

— Votre femme va bien, déclara d'entrée de jeu le médecin de Saint-Zéphirin. Elle est faite forte. Dans trois ou quatre jours, elle va pouvoir reprendre sa besogne.

— C'est une bonne nouvelle, reconnut Rémi.

— Pour la petite, j'ai une moins bonne nouvelle, poursuivit Eugène Samson, le visage assombri.

— Qu'est-ce qu'elle a, ma petite ? demanda Emma, soudain alertée par le ton grave du praticien.

— Il va falloir que vous vous montriez courageux tous les deux, prit la précaution d'ajouter le médecin.

Angoissée, la jeune mère mit une main devant sa bouche, comme pour s'empêcher de crier.

— Écoutez, leur ordonna Samson, vous avez dû remarquer que votre petite fille était différente des autres enfants que vous avez eus.

Un coup d'œil vers la mère lui apprit qu'elle s'en était déjà rendu compte.

— La petite souffre de ce qu'on appelle en médecine le mongolisme.

— C'est quoi, ça ? demanda Rémi, dont le visage avait pâli.

— Ça veut dire qu'elle va rester toute sa vie une enfant attardée. Elle va apprendre à s'asseoir, à marcher et à parler bien plus lentement qu'un enfant normal. La science connaît pas grand-chose sur le mongolisme, mais ce qui est certain, c'est que votre fille va avoir besoin de vous durant toute sa vie qui va être beaucoup plus courte qu'une vie normale.

— Non ! s'écria Emma, horrifiée. Qu'est-ce que j'ai fait au bon Dieu pour mériter ça ? demanda-t-elle en se mettant à pleurer convulsivement.

Rémi demeura silencieux, comme tétanisé par la nouvelle qu'il venait d'apprendre.

— Qu'est-ce qu'on peut faire? finit-il par demander d'une voix éteinte au médecin.

— Rien, monsieur Lafond. Il y a rien à faire, sauf l'accepter. Votre femme et vous n'êtes pas à blâmer. Vous n'êtes pas responsables. C'est un accident de la nature. Votre fille n'est pas malade à proprement parler. Elle sera tout simplement pas comme les autres.

— J'ai mis au monde un monstre, hoqueta Emma.

— Non, madame, répliqua sèchement Eugène Samson. Vous avez donné naissance à un petit enfant différent des autres. Il va vous falloir du courage et l'accepter.

Le médecin laissa planer un long silence dans la chambre avant de reprendre la parole, un ton plus bas.

— Écoutez, dit-il aux parents. Si vous pensez pas être capables de supporter ce qui vous arrive, vous aurez toujours la possibilité d'aller porter votre fille à l'orphelinat de Sorel. Les sœurs refusent aucun enfant… Mais pensez-y bien avant de faire ce geste. Donnez-vous le temps de bien réfléchir. C'est tout ce que je peux vous dire.

Sur ces mots, il sortit de la chambre en compagnie de Rémi, conscient du drame que le couple vivait. Il fit signe à Marie de s'approcher de lui.

— Vous êtes la mère de madame Lafond? lui demanda-t-il.

— Oui, docteur.

Il lui annonça alors la terrible nouvelle qu'il venait d'apprendre à sa fille.

— Je m'en doutais, fit-elle.

— Ce serait une bonne idée que vous alliez lui parler, conclut-il.

Marie n'eut pas la moindre hésitation. Elle se dirigea vers la chambre alors que le médecin acceptait la tasse de thé que lui offrait Rémi. Son cœur se serra à la vue de sa fille en larmes et elle dut faire un effort énorme pour ne pas se mettre à pleurer à son tour. Elle tira un mouchoir de l'une des manches de sa robe et le tendit à Emma.

— Essuie-toi les yeux et écoute-moi, lui dit-elle avec une certaine brusquerie.

Emma obéit. Elle s'essuya les yeux et renifla bruyamment.

— Là, tu vas arrêter de te lamenter pour rien, ma fille.

— Mais, m'man…

— Le bon Dieu vous envoie une épreuve et t'as pas le choix de l'accepter. Cette enfant-là, même retardée, c'est ta fille et tu dois l'aimer comme tes autres enfants, même plus que tes autres enfants parce qu'elle a été moins chanceuse en venant au monde, tu m'entends?

— Oui.

— C'est ni de ta faute ni de la faute de Rémi si elle est comme ça… Et c'est encore moins de la sienne!

Emma sécha encore ses larmes.

— T'es sa mère, c'est ton devoir de la protéger. T'as pas le choix, tu dois remonter le moral de ton mari et voir à ce que Flore et Joseph aiment leur petite sœur.

— Qu'est-ce que les voisins vont dire quand ils vont s'en apercevoir? finit par dire Emma.

— Ça les regarde pas pantoute, déclara Marie sur un ton définitif. Ils diront ce qu'ils voudront, ça changera rien.

Marie continua à parler à sa fille durant quelques minutes et quand elle sortit de la chambre, elle découvrit que le docteur Samson était déjà parti.

— J'ai invité le docteur à venir coucher à la maison, dit Xavier, mais il tenait absolument à rentrer à Saint-Zéphirin. Il paraît qu'il y a un vieux qui est très malade au village.

— C'est presque pas humain de l'obliger à faire tout ce chemin-là à soir, dit-elle.

— Est-ce qu'Emma prend ça un peu mieux? demanda-t-il, apparemment inquiet pour sa sœur.

Marie comprit que Rémi lui avait tout raconté.

— Je pense que oui.

— Et toi, Rémi? demanda-t-elle, inquiète, à son gendre.

— C'est ma fille, et moi, je veux la garder, déclara-t-il, l'air résolu. Viens voir Emma, dit-il à son jeune beau-frère en se tournant vers lui.

— Je serais peut-être mieux d'attendre demain.

— Non, viens. Ça va lui changer les idées et je pense qu'elle a quelque chose à te demander, insista Rémi.

Les deux hommes pénétrèrent dans la chambre où ils trouvèrent Emma en train de s'essuyer les yeux, la tête tournée vers le berceau dans lequel dormait paisiblement son bébé.

— Je voulais juste savoir comment t'allais avant de partir, fit Xavier en s'approchant du lit. J'ai vu la petite tout à l'heure dans la cuisine, elle est loin d'être laide, ajouta-t-il assez maladroitement.

— T'es bien fin d'être allé chercher le docteur, fit Emma en faisant un effort pour sourire malgré sa tristesse.

— Rémi vient de me dire que tu voulais me demander quelque chose…

Il y eut un bref silence, le temps qu'elle se rende compte qu'elle devait lui parler du baptême à venir.

— Oui, on voulait te demander si t'accepterais d'être le parrain de la petite.

— Et qui serait la marraine? demanda son jeune frère, surpris.

— Ta fiancée.

— C'est sûr que j'accepte, dit-il, enthousiaste, mais est-ce que ça insultera pas personne? Là, tu me fais passer devant Camille et Donat qui sont plus vieux que moi.

— Ça a aucune importance. C'est vous deux qu'on veut comme parrain et marraine. Camille est déjà au courant et ça la dérange pas.

— Et m'man, elle? demanda-t-il, un ton plus bas.

— M'man a rien dit, mentit Emma.

— Comme ça, c'est correct, fit-il, rassuré. Quand est-ce que vous la faites baptiser ?

— Après-demain, au commencement de l'après-midi.

— Vous pouvez être certains qu'on va être là, affirma Xavier, incapable de cacher sa fierté.

Au moment où le jeune homme, de retour dans la cuisine, allait prendre congé pour rentrer chez lui, Marie prit sur elle de lui demander de passer à la maison.

— Arrête donc une minute pour dire à Donat, à Eugénie et à Bernadette que le docteur est passé et qu'Emma va bien.

— Dis-leur aussi pour la petite, poursuivit Rémi, un ton plus bas de manière à ce que sa femme ne l'entende pas. Je voudrais pas qu'ils aient l'air surpris quand ils vont venir la voir, précisa-t-il.

Xavier se contenta de hocher la tête avant de leur souhaiter une bonne nuit. Il sortit et, quelques minutes plus tard, alla frapper à la maison paternelle. Donat vint lui ouvrir.

— Torrieu ! Tu fais tes visites tard, mon frère, s'exclama-t-il.

— Je fais juste arrêter, déclara Xavier sans esquisser le geste d'enlever son manteau.

— Prends au moins le temps de te dégreyer, lui proposa son frère Hubert, assis au bout de la table en train de faire une réussite.

— J'ai pas le temps, fit le visiteur en restant planté près de la porte. Je voulais juste vous dire que je suis allé chercher le docteur Samson pour Emma. Il vient de partir.

— Puis ? demanda Bernadette en s'approchant.

— Emma est ben correcte.

— Tant mieux, fit Eugénie.

— On peut pas dire la même chose pour la petite, par exemple, poursuivit Xavier.

— Qu'est-ce qu'elle a ? lui demanda sa belle-sœur.

Xavier expliqua l'état du bébé qui venait de naître.

— Pauvre Emma! s'exclama Bernadette, émue par la mauvaise nouvelle.

— C'est toute une épreuve, dit Hubert en secouant la tête.

— Mon Dieu! fit Eugénie. S'il fallait que…

Donat comprit tout de suite que sa femme enceinte pensait que la même chose pourrait lui arriver.

— Commence pas à t'imaginer toutes sortes d'affaires! lui ordonna-t-il.

— Bon, je vous ai fait la commission que Rémi voulait que je vous fasse, déclara Xavier. Ah! En passant, Emma et Rémi m'ont demandé d'être le parrain de la petite. Le baptême est supposé être dimanche après-midi.

— Qui va être la marraine? demanda Bernadette, curieuse.

— Voyons, Bedette, Catherine, répondit son frère, comme si la chose allait de soi.

Sur ces mots, le jeune homme prit congé et partit.

— Je sais pas comment m'man a pris une affaire comme ça, fit Bernadette.

— Est-ce que tu parles de la petite ou d'avoir demandé à Xavier d'être parrain? lui demanda Hubert.

— Que Catherine Benoît devienne la marraine, expliqua l'institutrice en entreprenant de ranger ses effets scolaires éparpillés à un bout de la table.

— Je le sais pas, mais au fond, c'est pas de ses affaires, intervint Donat.

— En tout cas, je trouve ça pas mal drôle que ta sœur Emma et Rémi soient passés par-dessus Camille et nous autres pour demander à ton frère d'être parrain, fit Eugénie. On est tous plus vieux que lui.

— Ils devaient avoir leurs raisons pour faire ça, déclara Hubert en remettant les cartes à jouer dans leur boîte.

Deux jours plus tard, au retour de la grand-messe, Liam ne put s'empêcher de dire à sa femme d'une voix acide :

— Une chance que monsieur le curé a annoncé que ta sœur avait accouché, sinon je l'aurais jamais su.

— Tu me l'as pas demandé, répliqua-t-elle sur le même ton en retirant la grande épingle qui retenait son chapeau en place.

— Et pour le baptême, cet après-midi ? demanda-t-il sur un ton rogue.

— Naturellement, on va y aller. T'étais pas encore descendu du jubé quand ma mère nous a invités. Bedette est allée lui donner un coup de main pour préparer un peu à manger chez Rémi. En plus, Rémi a demandé tout à l'heure à Ann d'être la porteuse.

— Comment ça se fait que je suis toujours le dernier à connaître les nouvelles ? s'enquit-il sèchement.

— Là, c'était parce que t'étais encore avec la chorale.

— C'est pas ce que je veux dire. Si je me trompe pas, t'es la plus vieille chez vous et comme c'est une fille que ta sœur a eue, c'est nous autres qui allons être dans les honneurs. Rémi Lafond a chanté avec moi à matin et il m'a pas demandé si j'acceptais.

— Il te l'a pas demandé parce que c'est pas nous autres qui allons être parrain et marraine. Ils ont demandé à Xavier et à Catherine de l'être.

— Comment ça ? C'est insultant en maudit, une affaire comme ça ! s'emporta-t-il.

— Calme-toi donc un peu, lui conseilla sa femme, excédée. C'est moi qui l'ai suggéré à Emma. C'était pour faire plaisir à Xavier et aider à faire accepter Catherine dans la famille.

— Ça va se savoir dans Saint-Bernard et ça va faire jaser.

— Eh bien, ça jasera, fit-elle sur un ton définitif.

— En tout cas, je pense que j'irai pas à ce baptême-là.

— T'es bien libre de rester ici. J'irai toute seule avec les enfants, déclara-t-elle en faisant signe à Ann de commencer à dresser le couvert pour le dîner.

Pendant tout cet échange, Paddy Connolly ne dit pas un mot. Il s'était contenté d'allumer l'un de ses cigares malodorants et de s'asseoir dans l'une des chaises berçantes. Au moment de passer à table quelques minutes plus tard, l'oncle finit par demander à sa nièce par alliance :

— Moi, est-ce que je suis invité au baptême ?

— Je suppose que, comme n'importe qui, vous pouvez venir à la chapelle si ça vous tente, mon oncle, répondit Camille. Pour la petite fête après, là, je le sais pas.

En fait, Camille ne tenait pas du tout à voir l'oncle de son mari participer à la petite fête familiale. Il verrait le bébé et il colporterait probablement qu'il n'était pas normal. Elle s'estimait déjà chanceuse qu'il n'ait pas entendu Bernadette lui chuchoter après la messe ce que le docteur avait appris à Emma et à Rémi à propos de l'enfant.

Après le repas, la maîtresse de maison houspilla les enfants pour qu'ils l'aident à remettre de l'ordre dans la cuisine et aillent se préparer. Quand elle se rendit compte que son mari n'avait apparemment pas l'intention d'aller atteler la *sleigh*, elle décida de le faire elle-même avec l'aide de Patrick. Quand elle rentra dans la maison pour presser les enfants de monter dans le véhicule, Liam et son oncle s'étaient esquivés dans leur chambre pour leur sieste dominicale.

— Il va me payer ça, lui, murmura-t-elle, folle de rage.

Il faisait beau et froid. Un léger vent de l'ouest soulevait une petite neige folle. Patrick, Duncan et Rose s'entassèrent sur la banquette arrière et prirent soin de se couvrir jusqu'à la taille avec l'épaisse couverture de fourrure un peu mitée qui s'y trouvait. Ann monta aux côtés de la conductrice et celle-ci incita sa bête à avancer.

Alors qu'elle pénétrait dans la cour de la ferme de Rémi Lafond, Donat en sortait, transportant uniquement Eugénie et Hubert. Ils venaient de laisser le petit Alexis aux soins de Marie, chez Emma. Elle salua son frère et sa belle-sœur au passage et s'arrêta à son tour chez Rémi pour laisser descendre Ann, la porteuse du bébé.

— Tu diras à mon beau-frère qu'on vous attend à la chapelle, recommanda-t-elle à l'adolescente avant de reprendre la route.

À son arrivée à la chapelle, elle retrouva Catherine, Xavier et Antonin en compagnie de Donat, de Hubert et d'Eugénie sur le parvis.

— Où est passé ton mari? lui demanda son plus jeune frère, surpris de la voir arriver seule avec les trois enfants.

— Il doit couver quelque chose, mentit-elle. Il était pas dans son assiette en revenant de la messe. Je lui ai dit qu'on pouvait se passer de lui.

Xavier ne fit pas de commentaires, mais le coup d'œil qu'il échangea avec Hubert en disait long sur ce qu'il pensait de ce malaise.

— Où est Bedette? l'interrogea-t-elle à son tour.

— Elle s'en vient avec Constant Aubé. Pour éviter que Rémi soit obligé d'atteler, il a proposé de transporter Bedette, Rémi et la porteuse, expliqua Donat.

— Seigneur! voulez-vous bien me dire ce qu'on a à rester dehors à grelotter avec ce vent-là? fit Camille en réprimant difficilement un frisson. Pourquoi vous entrez pas?

— Parce que le père Moreau a pas encore débarré la porte, répondit Donat avec humeur.

— Tu parles d'un vieux sans-dessein, fit Hubert. Il sait pourtant ben qu'il y a un baptême à deux heures. Je vais aller le chercher.

Au moment où il descendait les quelques marches du parvis, prêt à traverser la route pour se rendre chez Delphis

Moreau, il aperçut le vieil homme venant tranquillement dans leur direction.

— Ça va être chaud encore pour la petite là-dedans, fit remarquer Xavier. Le poêle va être éteint.

— Les voilà, annonça Catherine en montrant la *sleigh* conduite par Constant Aubé qui venait d'apparaître au sommet de la côte du rang Sainte-Ursule.

— On va geler dans la chapelle, monsieur Moreau, dit Donat au vieux bedeau.

— C'est pas important, déclara le père de Delphis Moreau, monsieur le curé m'a dit qu'il baptiserait dans la sacristie. Là, je suis pas venu pour chauffer. Je veux juste balayer le jubé. Vous feriez mieux de vous en aller à la sacristie. Monsieur le curé doit vous attendre.

— Ah bon! fit Donat. Constant! continue jusqu'à la porte de la sacristie, cria-t-il au meunier alors qu'il arrêtait son attelage près de la chapelle. C'est là que ça va se faire. On vous rejoint tout de suite.

Constant Aubé fit un signe de la main pour indiquer qu'il avait entendu et il poursuivit son chemin jusqu'à la sacristie, une soixantaine de pieds plus loin. Ann, toute fière, descendit en serrant contre elle le bébé bien emmitouflé, aussitôt rejointe par Rémi, Bernadette et Constant. Rémi frappa à la porte de la sacristie que Josaphat Désilets s'empressa d'ouvrir pour les laisser entrer.

— Êtes-vous tout seuls? demanda-t-il.

— Non, monsieur le curé, lui répondit Rémi. Les autres s'en viennent. Ils attendaient à la porte de la chapelle.

Pendant que le reste de la famille pénétrait dans la pièce, le curé de Saint-Bernard-Abbé se rendit à l'armoire d'où il tira un surplis et une étole blanche qu'il passa. Il plaça ensuite au centre de la table un grand bol de pierre faisant office de fontaine baptismale pendant que les gens se débarrassaient de leur lourd manteau. Sans perdre un instant, Ann avait entrepris de dévêtir le bébé. Quand Bernadette et

Eugénie s'étaient avancées pour aider l'adolescente, Camille leur avait fait signe de la laisser faire.

— Est-ce que tout le monde est arrivé ? demanda Josaphat Désilets avec un rien d'impatience dans la voix.

— Oui, monsieur le curé, répondit Rémi.

— Qui sont les parrain et marraine ? Qu'ils s'avancent avec l'enfant.

Un peu intimidés, Catherine et Xavier s'approchèrent de la table en compagnie d'Ann portant le bébé. Le silence tomba sur la pièce et la cérémonie religieuse commença.

— Le parrain et la marraine répondront au nom de l'enfant qui va s'appeler…

— Marthe, monsieur le curé, répondit Catherine d'une voix claire.

Le prêtre prononça des exorcismes en latin dans le but de chasser le démon avant de tracer un petit signe de croix sur le front de l'enfant avec de l'huile sainte. Il enchaîna avec d'autres prières et mit quelques grains de sel dans la bouche de l'enfant avant de faire signe à la porteuse de confier le bébé au parrain et à la marraine. Il leur demanda de le tenir au-dessus de la fontaine baptismale pendant qu'il versait trois fois de l'eau sur la tête de l'enfant en disant : « *Ego te baptizo in nomine Patris, et Filii et Spiritus Sancti.* » Marthe, bien réveillée, la langue à demi sortie de sa petite bouche rose, ne pleura pas, ce qui fit sourire l'assistance. Un peu en retrait, Camille, les traits impénétrables, fixait l'enfant.

À la fin de la courte célébration liturgique, le curé rappela le rôle essentiel que le parrain et la marraine allaient être appelés à jouer auprès de l'enfant qui venait d'être baptisée. Pendant qu'il parlait, Ann avait repris Marthe et s'était empressée de la vêtir pour qu'elle ne prenne pas froid. La température régnant dans la sacristie était loin d'être confortable.

Rémi remercia le prêtre et lui glissa quelques sous dans la main en signe de reconnaissance avant de sortir, suivi par le reste de l'assistance. Donat s'apprêtait à quitter les lieux comme les autres quand Josaphat Désilets le retint en posant une main sur son bras.

— Dis-moi, mon garçon, si j'ai bien compris, cette enfant-là est ta nièce?

— En plein ça, monsieur le curé.

— Le docteur l'a vue?

— Mon beau-frère m'a dit qu'il était passé, oui, lui répondit Donat qui devinait où le prêtre voulait en venir.

— Je suppose qu'il a dû dire que cette enfant-là était pas normale?

— Oui, fit sèchement le jeune syndic en serrant les dents.

— Les parents ont dû commettre une faute bien grave pour mériter une pareille épreuve, ajouta le prêtre sur un ton pénétré.

— Ça, c'est vous qui le dites, monsieur le curé, fit Donat sur un ton rageur avant d'ouvrir la porte et de sortir dans le même élan sans prendre la peine de saluer le prêtre.

Il était si en colère contre Josaphat Désilets qu'il ne desserra les dents qu'à son arrivée chez son beau-frère.

— Veux-tu ben me dire ce que t'as à faire cette face-là? lui demanda Eugénie en descendant de la *sleigh*.

— Laisse faire, laissa-t-il tomber. C'est encore une niaiserie du curé Désilets qui m'a fait enrager.

Hubert, passager du véhicule, ne dit rien et les précéda dans la maison de sa sœur.

Si Marie remarqua l'absence de Liam Connolly à la petite fête qu'elle avait préparée avec l'aide de Bernadette, elle n'en fit pas mention. Dès leur arrivée, les gens furent invités à déposer leur manteau dans le salon avant d'aller voir la mère encore alitée.

Emma s'était soigneusement coiffée et sa mère avait fait en sorte que la chambre à coucher soit impeccable quand les invités vinrent la voir. On vanta Marthe qui n'avait pas pleuré durant son baptême et on félicita la mère pour sa bonne mine. Les hommes se retirèrent dans un coin de la cuisine pour boire un verre de bagosse et fumer leur pipe pendant que les femmes déposaient de la nourriture sur la table.

Emma remercia Catherine d'avoir accepté d'être la marraine de son bébé. La jeune fiancée tendit à la mère un petit mantelet en laine blanche à titre de cadeau pour Marthe. La fille de Marie Beauchemin comprit que ce vêtement avait probablement été destiné à son propre enfant…

— Inquiétez-vous pas, madame Lafond, on va toujours aimer Marthe et en prendre soin comme si c'était notre propre enfant, promit-elle à la mère.

Debout à ses côtés, Xavier se borna à hocher la tête en signe d'approbation.

— Tu vas commencer par m'appeler Emma et pas madame Lafond, dit la sœur de Xavier, émue. Quand tu m'appelles comme ça, j'ai l'impression d'être une vieille grand-mère.

De retour dans la cuisine avec les autres femmes quelques instants plus tard, Catherine ne put faire autrement que se rendre compte que Camille et Bernadette la traitaient comme un membre de la famille. Si leur mère montrait encore quelques signes de froideur, il y avait une nette amélioration dans son comportement à son égard.

À la fin de l'après-midi, les invités prirent congé des Lafond. Il était entendu que Marie allait demeurer chez sa fille au moins jusqu'au jeudi suivant pour lui offrir des relevailles décentes. Sur le chemin du retour à la maison, Camille ne put que convenir que sa sœur semblait apparemment avoir surmonté le choc. Elle n'avait décelé chez elle aucun signe de dépression. À son arrivée à la ferme, son mari était déjà en train de soigner les animaux, elle se chargea de dételer le cheval avec l'aide de Patrick.

Une heure plus tard, quand Liam rentra, il découvrit qu'il n'y avait que deux couverts sur la table.

— Les enfants mangent pas ? demanda-t-il alors que son oncle venait s'asseoir à table.

— Ils ont pas faim. Il y avait en masse à manger chez Rémi.

S'il avait imaginé qu'elle lui raconterait la cérémonie et la petite fête qui avait eu lieu durant l'après-midi, il dut déchanter. Elle ne lui raconta rien.

— Comment ça a été ? finit par demander Paddy Connolly, curieux.

— Bien, mon oncle, comme tous les baptêmes, fut le seul commentaire qu'il reçut de Camille qui, leur tournant le dos, avait entrepris de laver la vaisselle.

Chapitre 10

La surprise

Trois jours plus tard, au petit matin, Samuel Ellis vint immobiliser sa *sleigh* près de la maison des Beauchemin. Le soleil n'était pas encore levé et il faisait toujours aussi froid. L'homme descendit et jeta une couverture sur le dos de sa bête. Au moment où il allait frapper à la porte, celle-ci s'ouvrit et Donat, tout endimanché, invita le visiteur à entrer.

— Venez boire une tasse de thé pendant que je finis de me préparer, offrit Donat au président du conseil en s'effaçant pour le laisser entrer.

— C'est pas de refus, ça pince à matin, accepta l'Irlandais.

Ce dernier salua Bernadette et Eugénie qui finissaient de déjeuner. L'épouse de Donat se leva et lui versa une tasse de thé pendant que Donat disparaissait un bref instant dans sa chambre. Il revint, endossa son manteau et attacha son casque à oreillettes avant de signifier à son compagnon de voyage qu'il était prêt à partir.

— S'il fait beau, on devrait revenir au commencement de la soirée, dit-il à Eugénie en prenant avec précaution les deux briques qu'il avait mises au fourneau. S'il neige, on couchera en chemin.

Là-dessus, les deux hommes sortirent de la maison et montèrent dans la *sleigh* d'Ellis. Ils posèrent les pieds sur les briques chaudes avant de se couvrir les jambes avec une épaisse couverture de fourrure. Le cocher fouetta légèrement son cheval pour qu'il se mette en marche.

Durant de longues minutes, les deux hommes gardèrent le silence. Seul le crissement des patins de la *sleigh* sur la neige durcie troublait la paix de ce matin de février.

— J'espère que ça va ben se passer, finit par dire Donat.

— On va faire notre possible, rétorqua Samuel. On va présenter notre affaire à monseigneur de manière à ce qu'il nous donne un coup de main.

— C'est certain que ça va ben nous aider de pas avoir monsieur le curé dans les pattes, laissa tomber son jeune compagnon.

— *You bet!* confirma le président du conseil. Mais je me demande comment il va prendre ça quand il va apprendre qu'on est allés rencontrer monseigneur sans lui. Pour moi, il va faire une sainte crise.

— Ben, il la fera, déclara Donat d'une voix indifférente. Ça aura plus aucune importance, ce sera fait. C'est facile de demander toutes sortes d'affaires quand on n'a pas à se casser la tête pour savoir comment ça va être payé, ajouta-t-il.

— T'as raison là-dessus et on va faire comprendre à monseigneur que les gens de Saint-Bernard peuvent pas faire plus que ce qu'ils font déjà.

Lorsqu'ils entrèrent dans Sainte-Monique, Donat convainquit facilement Ellis de s'arrêter chez son oncle Armand pour se réchauffer et permettre au cheval de se reposer un peu. Le gros cultivateur fut heureux de recevoir des visiteurs, cela lui donnant l'occasion de souffler un peu. Il offrit une tournée de bagosse à son neveu et à Samuel Ellis avant de prendre des nouvelles de la famille qu'il n'avait pas vue depuis l'enterrement de son frère Baptiste. Donat lui apprit la naissance de l'enfant d'Emma en prenant bien garde de faire allusion à son anomalie.

Peu après, les deux syndics reprirent la route. Arrivés à Nicolet, ils apprirent que le pont de glace était passablement plus loin, à Bécancourt, où ils ne parvinrent qu'un peu après onze heures.

— On est aussi ben de traverser tout de suite avant de manger quelque chose, suggéra Samuel. On sait jamais, on peut être retardés et il est pas question d'arriver en retard.

Un passant indiqua à l'Irlandais où se trouvait le pont de glace qui franchissait le fleuve jusqu'à Trois-Rivières. En descendant sur la berge quelques minutes plus tard, les cultivateurs de Saint-Bernard-Abbé découvrirent un chemin assez large soigneusement balisé par des sapins se dirigeant en droite ligne vers la rive opposée. Le cours d'eau à cet endroit était si large que les deux voyageurs devinèrent plus qu'ils ne virent des habitations de l'autre côté.

— J'ai entendu dire par le père Meilleur qu'il y a ben une centaine d'hommes qui l'entretiennent ce chemin de glace là, dit Donat. Il paraît qu'ils mettent même des billots un peu partout pour qu'il soit plus solide.

— Moi, ce que raconte le père Meilleur, j'en prends et j'en laisse, se contenta de répondre le président du conseil, la tête rentrée dans les épaules pour mieux se protéger du vent.

Dès que la *sleigh* fut engagée sur le pont de glace, ses passagers durent subir les assauts d'un vent glacial auquel rien ne faisait obstacle. Durant le trajet, ils croisèrent trois traîneaux lourdement chargés et les conducteurs les saluèrent de la main au passage.

Parvenus enfin sur l'autre rive du fleuve, les deux hommes durent demander encore une fois leur chemin pour se rendre à la cathédrale. Ils auraient pu s'en abstenir tant l'imposant édifice inauguré à peine quatorze ans auparavant par le premier évêque du diocèse de Trois-Rivières, monseigneur Cooke, se voyait de loin. Lorsqu'ils furent enfin à proximité, rassurés, Samuel Ellis et Donat Beauchemin décidèrent d'aller manger dans une auberge voisine, dans la rue Royale. Cet arrêt leur permit de se restaurer et leur offrit surtout l'occasion de se réchauffer les mains et les pieds.

Après un repas frugal composé de fèves au lard et d'une tranche de jambon, Samuel consulta sa montre de gousset et découvrit qu'il était déjà un peu plus d'une heure.

— Il faut y aller, déclara-t-il à son jeune compagnon. J'aime mieux attendre un peu que risquer d'arriver en retard.

Donat quitta la table sans protester et paya son repas à la servante de l'auberge avant de suivre son aîné. Les deux hommes revinrent devant la cathédrale, donnèrent une ration d'avoine au cheval et le couvrirent d'une couverture. Avant de s'éloigner de la *sleigh*, Samuel prit un sac de toile sous la banquette avant.

— Je pense qu'on a ben le temps de jeter un coup d'œil dans la cathédrale, suggéra Samuel. On est encore pas mal en avance et c'est pas tous les jours qu'on peut voir ça.

Ils montèrent les marches conduisant au parvis de la cathédrale de l'Assomption et pénétrèrent dans le temple somptueusement éclairé par de magnifiques vitraux. Ils se rendirent à l'un des bénitiers placés à l'arrière pour y tremper le bout de leurs doigts et se signer.

— Une petite prière pour que monseigneur décide de nous aider sera pas de trop, déclara Donat en fixant le maître-autel à l'avant.

— T'as raison, se borna à dire son compagnon.

Ils restèrent pieusement silencieux durant quelques instants avant de se signer à nouveau et de sortir. Ils dirigèrent ensuite leurs pas vers ce qui ressemblait plus à un gros presbytère qu'à un palais épiscopal. Samuel sonna et une petite religieuse vint leur ouvrir.

— Bonjour, ma sœur, la salua l'Irlandais en retirant vivement sa tuque, on a rendez-vous avec monseigneur.

— Entrez, les invita la religieuse.

Les deux cultivateurs de Saint-Bernard-Abbé pénétrèrent dans l'entrée.

— Comment vous appelez-vous ? demanda-t-elle à Samuel.

Il se nomma.

— Je vais vérifier si monsieur l'abbé Dupras, le secrétaire de monseigneur, peut vous recevoir. En attendant, vous pouvez enlever vos bottes et suspendre votre manteaux à la patère, ajouta-t-elle aimablement en indiquant un porte-manteau près de la porte.

La religieuse parcourut une douzaine de pieds dans le couloir avant de frapper discrètement à une porte. Elle chuchota quelques paroles à une personne à l'intérieur de la pièce, referma la porte et revint vers les visiteurs.

— Monsieur l'abbé va vous recevoir. Suivez-moi, ordonna-t-elle aux deux hommes à l'allure empruntée dans leur costume noir, le cou un peu étranglé par leur col dur.

Donat et Samuel la suivirent jusqu'à la porte qu'elle leur ouvrit. Ils se retrouvèrent devant un jeune abbé aux traits ascétiques retranché derrière un bureau. L'ecclésiastique ne leva même pas les yeux à leur entrée dans la pièce. Il finit de rédiger ce qu'il avait entrepris d'écrire et déposa sa plume avant de s'intéresser aux deux visiteurs debout devant son bureau.

— Qu'est-ce que je peux faire pour vous ? demanda-t-il d'une voix haut perchée pendant que ses petits yeux gris les fixaient, à travers des lunettes à fine monture métallique.

— Nous sommes supposés rencontrer monseigneur à deux heures, monsieur l'abbé, répondit Samuel en tirant de son sac de toile la lettre d'invitation qu'il avait reçue.

L'abbé Dupras s'en empara et prit soin de la lire avant de la lui rendre.

— Bon, encore un visiteur de Saint-Bernard-Abbé pour monseigneur, laissa-t-il tomber de sa petite voix de fausset. Et vous, monsieur ? ajouta-t-il en s'adressant à Donat.

— Je suis avec lui, lui répondit le fils de Baptiste. Je suis un syndic de la mission.

— Très bien, vous pouvez aller vous asseoir dans la salle d'attente à côté, leur dit-il en désignant une porte ouvrant au fond de son bureau. Il est possible que vous ayez à attendre un peu parce que monseigneur a un peu de retard sur son horaire.

Tous les deux remercièrent le jeune prêtre, traversèrent son bureau et pénétrèrent dans une petite salle éclairée par deux hautes fenêtres et autour de laquelle une quinzaine de chaises étaient disposées. À leur entrée, Donat et Samuel sursautèrent violemment en découvrant Josaphat Désilets en train de lire tranquillement son bréviaire, près de l'une des fenêtres.

— Le monde est petit, hein! fit le curé de Saint-Bernard-Abbé en refermant son bréviaire avec un sourire acide.

— Monsieur le curé! Je m'attendais pas pantoute à vous voir ici! ne put s'empêcher de s'exclamer Samuel, le premier à retrouver son aplomb.

— Avoir su que vous aviez à faire à Trois-Rivières, on aurait pu faire le chemin tous les trois, finit par dire Donat d'une voix changée.

— Bien sûr, fit sèchement le prêtre. Mais pour ça, il aurait fallu que je sache que vous veniez à Trois-Rivières… et que vous m'invitiez à votre dernière réunion, pas vrai?

— Allez surtout pas croire que c'était par malveillance, monsieur le curé, reprit le président du conseil en prenant tout de même soin de s'asseoir assez loin de son curé.

— Je m'en suis douté, répliqua Josaphat Désilets, mi-figue, mi-raisin. J'ai supposé que c'était surtout pour pas me fatiguer. Une chance que le secrétaire de monseigneur m'a fait parvenir une lettre pour me faire savoir que monseigneur recevrait un syndic de la mission cet après-midi. Je pensais pas que vous seriez deux.

— Je suis juste venu pour lui tenir compagnie, se justifia Donat, sans se donner la peine d'essayer de se montrer agréable.

Il avait encore sur le cœur la remarque du curé au sujet de sa sœur Emma et de son beau-frère Rémi, le dimanche précédent, après le baptême.

— J'ai décidé, moi aussi, de venir rencontrer monseigneur. Je voudrais pas qu'il croie que je m'entends pas bien avec mon conseil, ajouta le curé sur un ton perfide.

Puis, il sembla tout à coup se désintéresser de ses deux paroissiens. Il rouvrit son bréviaire et se remit à le lire. Samuel jeta un regard d'intelligence à Donat qui se contenta de hausser les épaules en signe d'ignorance. Le silence retombé sur la salle d'attente fut brisé quelques minutes plus tard par l'arrivée de deux religieuses venues rencontrer, elles aussi, l'évêque de Trois-Rivières.

Un peu avant deux heures trente, l'abbé Dupras ouvrit la porte et invita les deux syndics et le curé Désilets à le suivre. Les trois hommes se levèrent et lui emboîtèrent le pas. Le secrétaire s'arrêta devant une porte, frappa et l'ouvrit :

— Monsieur le curé Désilets et deux syndics de Saint-Bernard-Abbé, monseigneur, annonça-t-il à l'occupant de la pièce.

Très intimidés, les trois hommes pénétrèrent dans le vaste bureau de l'évêque qui se leva pour les accueillir. Quand Josaphat Désilets s'avança pour embrasser la bague de son évêque, Donat et Samuel s'empressèrent de l'imiter.

Le prélat âgé d'une cinquantaine d'années était de taille moyenne et d'apparence robuste. Cet ancien missionnaire avait un visage glabre aux traits énergiques et des yeux bruns dissimulés en partie sous d'épais sourcils. Ses cheveux étaient blancs et courts.

— Assoyez-vous et voyons ce qu'on peut faire pour régler votre problème, déclara monseigneur Laflèche en leur indiquant les chaises placées devant son grand bureau en chêne. Si je me rappelle bien, monsieur Désilets, vous m'avez écrit à deux ou trois reprises depuis le début de l'hiver pour vous plaindre du froid de la sacristie où vous vivez. Est-ce exact?

— Oui, monseigneur, acquiesça le prêtre.

— J'ai envoyé moi-même une lettre à vos paroissiens pour les prévenir qu'il n'était pas question que vous passiez un autre hiver dans ces conditions et qu'il fallait, de toute urgence, qu'ils fassent bâtir un presbytère pour leur curé.

— C'est exact, monseigneur, fit Josaphat Désilets avec une humilité inhabituelle.

— Alors, je ne vois pas pourquoi le conseil de la mission a demandé à me rencontrer.

— Moi non plus, mentit le curé de Saint-Bernard-Abbé, l'air faux.

Comme Samuel Ellis semblait tétanisé depuis le début de la rencontre et serrait contre lui l'enveloppe de toile qu'il n'avait pas lâchée, Donat se décida à prendre la parole d'une voix d'abord hésitante qui se raffermit cependant peu à peu.

— Monseigneur, les syndics vous ont écrit parce qu'on a un gros problème sur les bras. On n'a pas d'argent pantoute pour faire construire. C'est aussi simple que ça. On voudrait bien, mais on peut pas.

— On a fait construire la chapelle l'année passée, monseigneur, intervint enfin le président du conseil. Il a fallu acheter un lot en plus.

— N'avez-vous pas reçu un don important pour la chapelle? demanda le prélat, prouvant ainsi qu'il était bien au fait de ce qui se passait dans son diocèse.

— C'est vrai, monseigneur, reconnut Donat, mais il a fallu faire construire en plus un jubé pas plus tard que l'automne passé parce que la chapelle était déjà pas assez grande pour le monde de Saint-Bernard. Ça a ajouté un gros montant à notre dette, conclut-il.

Josaphat Désilets allait prendre la parole quand Samuel Ellis le devança.

— J'ai apporté le registre de la mission où toutes les dépenses de Saint-Bernard sont notées depuis le commencement, monseigneur, dit-il en tirant de son sac de toile le grand cahier noir dans lequel Thomas Hyland notait tout depuis le début.

Il le tendit au prélat qui l'ouvrit et le consulta rapidement. Un pli soucieux apparut sur son front quand il lut la somme totale due par la mission.

— Bon, je vois, fit-il en se grattant le menton d'un air songeur.

— Si on est pris pour bâtir un presbytère, intervint Donat, il va falloir aussi acheter un autre lot.

— Je vois.

— Il va de soi, monseigneur, qu'il va me falloir aussi une écurie et une remise où entreposer les produits de la dîme et le bois de chauffage, crut bon de spécifier le curé Désilets.

Les deux syndics sursautèrent et se regardèrent, surpris. Leur étonnement n'échappa pas à l'évêque.

— Tout ça, ça va coûter cher sans bon sens, monseigneur, et Saint-Bernard n'aura jamais les moyens de payer autant, s'empressa de dire Donat.

— Il faut ce qu'il faut quand on veut devenir une paroisse, laissa tomber sèchement le curé Désilets, l'air désagréable.

— C'est vrai, fit l'évêque de Trois-Rivières. J'allais oublier que vous avez demandé l'automne dernier de devenir une paroisse.

— Oui, monseigneur, reconnut Samuel Ellis.

— L'abbé Desmeules ne m'a pas encore remis son rapport, mais quand je l'ai rencontré il y a quelques semaines, il m'a dit qu'il y avait un certain nombre de francs-tenanciers de la mission qui avaient demandé de retourner dans leur paroisse d'origine.

La nouvelle abasourdit aussi bien les deux syndics que le curé de la mission.

— J'espère que ça met pas notre demande en danger, monseigneur ? fit Josaphat Désilets.

— Il est encore trop tôt pour le dire, admit le prélat. Je n'ai pas encore le rapport de l'enquêteur.

— Est-ce que ça veut dire qu'on s'énerve pour rien avec l'histoire du presbytère ? demanda carrément Donat.

— Pourquoi me demandez-vous ça ? fit l'évêque, intrigué.

— Ben, si la mission doit perdre ben du monde, c'est certain qu'on va avoir encore moins les moyens de faire construire le presbytère. Et si on le fait pas, vous nous dites qu'on n'aura plus de prêtre l'hiver prochain.

Monseigneur Laflèche réprima un sourire avant de poursuivre.

— Écoutez, on ne mettra pas la charrue devant les bœufs. L'abbé Desmeules va me remettre sous peu son rapport et je serais étonné qu'il y ait assez de cultivateurs de Saint-Bernard-Abbé qui demandent de quitter la mission pour mettre sa survie en danger.

— Vous nous soulagez ben gros, monseigneur, admit Samuel.

— Attention ! Je n'ai pas dit que j'allais accepter de faire de la mission une paroisse, prit-il soin de préciser aux trois visiteurs assis devant lui.

— C'est certain, fit Donat.

— Qu'est-ce que vous voulez faire ? finit par demander le prélat en jetant un coup d'œil vers l'horloge installée dans un coin de son bureau. Voulez-vous renoncer à la mission ou bien essayer de trouver le moyen de construire le presbytère ?

— Je pense que tout le monde de Saint-Bernard est prêt à se serrer la ceinture pour construire ce qu'il faut, annonça le président du conseil. Le problème, c'est qu'on n'a plus une cenne et qu'on est tellement endettés qu'on trouvera jamais assez d'argent pour y arriver.

— C'est un gros problème, reconnut l'évêque.

— Le seul moyen de s'en sortir, monseigneur, ce serait que vous serviez de garantie à notre emprunt, suggéra Donat. Je suis sûr qu'on trouverait un prêteur de cette façon-là.

— J'avoue que vous tombez bien mal, dit le prélat, l'air soucieux. Le diocèse s'est tellement endetté qu'il n'a pas les moyens de loger convenablement son évêque dans un palais épiscopal. On remet sa construction d'année en année. On ne prévoit pas être capable de le bâtir avant sept ou huit ans.

L'évêque se leva et alla se planter devant l'une des fenêtres. Un silence pesant tomba sur la pièce. Après une ou deux minutes de réflexion, il finit par se tourner vers ses visiteurs comme s'il venait de prendre une décision.

— Bon, c'est entendu. Je vais vous faire confiance. Le diocèse va se porter garant de votre prochain emprunt. Le syndic recevra d'ici quelques jours une lettre de garantie et je demanderai qu'on y ajoute les noms de trois ou quatre institutions qui prêtent déjà au diocèse en pratiquant des taux d'intérêt très bas.

En entendant ces paroles, les visages du curé Désilets, de Samuel et de Donat s'illuminèrent. Tous les trois se levèrent pour remercier l'évêque, qui prit tout de même la précaution de les mettre en garde avant de leur donner congé.

— Je vous recommande toutefois la plus grande prudence, crut-il bon de spécifier. N'oubliez pas que l'argent est rare et ne faites pas de dépenses inconsidérées. Dites-vous que l'argent prêté, il faut finir par le remettre.

— Si c'est pas abuser de votre patience, monseigneur, intervint Josaphat Désilets au moment où son supérieur les reconduisait jusqu'à la porte de son bureau, j'aurais voulu vous parler de la cloche qu'il faudrait bien finir par acheter. Saint-Bernard a un clocher, mais pas de cloche et ça…

— Si ça vous fait rien, monsieur Désilets, votre cloche peut attendre. À ce que je viens de comprendre, Saint-

Bernard-Abbé s'apprête à faire des dépenses autrement plus onéreuses pour votre confort.

Les visiteurs saluèrent leur évêque et se dirigèrent en silence vers le porte-manteau. Ils s'habillèrent et sortirent à l'extérieur.

— Est-ce qu'on fait route ensemble, monsieur le curé ? proposa un Samuel Ellis, euphorique.

— Non, je couche à Trois-Rivières, répondit abruptement le prêtre.

— Dans ce cas-là, au revoir, monsieur le curé.

— C'est ça, au revoir, fit Josaphat Désilets en descendant les marches devant ses deux paroissiens.

Donat regarda autour et ne vit pas trace de la *sleigh* du curé de Saint-Bernard-Abbé. Ellis avait suivi son regard et s'apprêtait probablement à proposer au prêtre de le faire monter pour le laisser là où il comptait passer la nuit quand Donat lui fit signe de n'en rien faire.

Au pied de l'escalier, les deux syndics tournèrent le dos à l'ecclésiastique et se rendirent à leur *sleigh*. Après avoir enlevé la couverture qui protégeait le cheval, ils montèrent à bord et se mirent en route.

— Je comprends pas qu'il ait l'air aussi bête après ce que monseigneur vient de nous donner, fit Samuel, encore tout heureux d'avoir obtenu l'appui de l'évêque du diocèse.

— Comme vous avez pu l'entendre avant de partir, il voulait une cloche en plus. Torrieu ! Est-ce qu'il va comprendre un jour qu'il y a des limites à ce qu'on peut payer ?

— Ouais ! On dirait que monseigneur comprend plus vite que lui, rétorqua Ellis.

— En tout cas, on n'a pas fait le voyage pour rien et on revient pas les mains vides, déclara Donat en ne faisant aucun effort pour réprimer un sourire satisfait.

— Moi, j'ai ben hâte de voir la tête de Hyland, de Côté et de Blanchette quand on va leur apprendre la nouvelle.

— Moi aussi, reconnut le fils de Baptiste Beauchemin, mais je me demande encore qui a mis le curé au courant de notre petite réunion de la semaine passée.

À son retour à la maison, Donat Beauchemin retrouva sa mère en train de tisser à la lueur vacillante d'une lampe à huile. Bernadette tricotait, assise non loin de Hubert occupé à réparer un attelage, la pipe à la bouche.

— À ce que je vois, m'man, les relevailles d'Emma sont finies, dit-il en enlevant son manteau.

— En plein ça, mon garçon. Et je te dis qu'il était temps que je revienne ici dedans mettre de l'ordre. Une chatte y retrouverait plus ses petits.

Bernadette adressa à son frère un léger signe de tête et celui-ci comprit que le retour de sa mère après une semaine d'absence ne s'était pas fait dans l'harmonie. Elle avait dû faire sentir à Bernadette et surtout à Eugénie qu'elles avaient mal tenu la maison pendant qu'elle n'était pas là.

— Et toi, est-ce que ton voyage à Trois-Rivières s'est bien passé ? demanda-t-elle à son fils.

— Tout est arrangé, se contenta-t-il de dire.

— Veux-tu manger quelque chose ? proposa Bernadette, prête à abandonner son tricot pour le servir.

— Non, on a mangé en chemin. Où est passée Eugénie ?

— Elle vient de monter, lui répondit sa mère.

— Je pense que je vais faire la même chose, fit-il. Le voyage m'a éreinté.

Il souhaita une bonne nuit aux siens et monta à l'étage rejoindre sa femme. À sa grande surprise, il la trouva, assise sur leur lit, les épaules couvertes d'un épais lainage et un tricot à la main.

— Veux-tu ben me dire pourquoi tu tricotes en haut quand on gèle tout rond pendant que tu serais si ben en bas, proche du poêle ? lui demanda-t-il.

— Tout simplement parce que j'en pouvais plus d'endurer ta sainte mère, admit la petite femme au chignon noir d'une voix acide.

— Bon, qu'est-ce qui s'est encore passé? fit-il, excédé.

— Il s'est passé qu'elle a pas arrêté de critiquer tout ce que j'ai fait dans la maison depuis qu'elle a remis les pieds ici. À l'entendre, tout a été fait de travers et la maison est une vraie soue à cochons. Même Bernadette a fini par se fâcher.

— Tu la connais…

— Oui, je la connais, ta mère! Et je te dis qu'elle commence à me tomber sérieusement sur les nerfs, ajouta-t-elle, les larmes aux yeux. Mautadit! On dirait qu'elle comprend pas que je fais le mieux que je peux…

Donat s'assit sur le lit, prit sa femme par les épaules et la berça doucement pour la consoler.

— Là, c'est ton état qui te rend nerveuse sans bon sens. Ma mère est pas si pire. Puis, inquiète-toi pas, je vais lui parler demain matin.

Eugénie renifla et mit de côté son tricot. Son mari éteignit la lampe et entreprit de se déshabiller dans le noir.

Chapitre 11

Un concours

Les syndics de Saint-Bernard-Abbé purent constater que le curé Désilets avait la rancune tenace quand ils allèrent lui rendre visite à la sacristie le dimanche suivant pour lui demander s'il ne convenait pas d'annoncer aux fidèles les résultats de la rencontre avec monseigneur Laflèche.

— Tiens! Tout à coup, vous vous rendez compte que votre curé peut vous être utile, leur fit-il remarquer d'une voix coupante en mettant sa chasuble.

— C'est pas ça, monsieur le curé, dit le président du conseil, mais il me semble que le monde a le droit de savoir ce qui s'est passé.

— Il y a rien qui presse dans cette affaire-là, trancha le prêtre en posant sa barrette sur sa tête. S'il doit y avoir une construction, elle va se faire seulement au printemps, je suppose. On aura bien le temps d'en parler. En attendant, il me semble qu'il serait plus avisé d'aller demander à madame Cloutier combien elle voudrait pour le lot à côté de la chapelle.

En entendant le nom de la veuve d'Herménégilde Cloutier, Samuel Ellis ne put réprimer une grimace.

— Il y a rien qui oblige à acheter son lot, monsieur le curé, protesta Anatole Blanchette, guère plus enchanté qu'Ellis à la perspective d'aller discuter avec cette femme au caractère bouillant.

— Ah non! fit Josaphat Désilets, sarcastique. Je suppose que vous allez construire le presbytère à l'autre bout du village…

— On sait ben, intervint Antonius Côté, l'air songeur.

— Peut-être pourriez-vous en toucher un mot à la veuve, monsieur le curé? suggéra Thomas Hyland sur un ton raisonnable.

— Il en est pas question, trancha le prêtre. Vous avez vous-mêmes décidé que vous étiez capables de vous passer de moi pour aller rencontrer monseigneur. Bien, continuez et débrouillez-vous.

Sur ces mots, il fit signe à ses deux servants de messe qui s'étaient tenus à l'écart durant ce bref entretien et il se dirigea vers la porte qui communiquait avec le chœur.

— Il y a pas à dire, on a un curé qui est ben d'adon, laissa tomber Donat au moment où la porte se refermait derrière le prêtre.

— Qu'est-ce qu'on va faire? demanda Anatole Blanchette.

— On va faire ce qu'on a à faire, et pas plus tard que cet après-midi, déclara Ellis. Je vais aller voir Angèle Cloutier pour voir si elle est intéressée à vendre une couple d'arpents à la fabrique.

— Au fond, c'est peut-être mieux comme ça, reconnut son ami Hyland. J'ai comme l'impression qu'elle aime pas trop notre curé.

— Elle n'est pas la seule, se sentit obligé de compléter Donat.

— Qui va venir avec moi? demanda Samuel.

Les syndics se consultèrent rapidement du regard, mais aucun ne se proposa pour accompagner le président du conseil à la petite maison située au pied de la pente du rang Sainte-Ursule.

— Êtes-vous en train d'essayer de me faire croire que l'Angèle vous fait peur? demanda-t-il, sarcastique.

— Pantoute, déclara Anatole, mais j'ai pas le goût d'aller là.

— Moi, j'attends du monde cet après-midi, fit Hyland.

— Moi, je peux ben y aller avec vous, dit Donat, après une courte hésitation.

— Moi aussi, je vais y aller, décida Antonius Côté. Tu me prendras en passant, Donat.

— C'est parfait. On se retrouve là vers une heure et demie, dit Samuel, apparemment très soulagé de ne pas devoir affronter seul la veuve Cloutier.

La grand-messe dura deux bonnes heures, allongée assez considérablement par un sermon prononcé dans les deux langues, comme c'était maintenant coutume à Saint-Bernard. Les célébrations incontournables du Mardi gras deux jours plus tard inspirèrent de sévères mises en garde au pasteur qui se méfiait des débordements habituels, la veille du mercredi des Cendres.

— C'est bien long, se plaignit Bernadette à voix basse à l'oreille de son frère assis près d'elle.

— On lui a suggéré de faire son sermon une semaine en français et une semaine en anglais, il a pas voulu écouter, chuchota Donat.

— Il a tellement l'air d'avoir peur qu'on s'amuse un peu.

— Là, il fait juste sa besogne, lui fit remarquer son frère.

— Chut! fit leur mère en leur faisant les gros yeux.

Ce matin-là, Josaphat Désilets ne dit pas un mot de la rencontre qui avait eu lieu quelques jours auparavant à l'évêché. Par contre, il annonça qu'à compter du dimanche suivant, soit le 25 février, il célébrerait le salut au Saint-Sacrement immédiatement après la grand-messe.

— De cette manière, vous aurez plus à donner comme excuse que ça fait un trop long chemin à parcourir pour venir honorer Dieu puisque vous allez déjà être sur place, conclut-il d'une voix cinglante.

Après la messe, les gens assemblés sur le parvis de la chapelle discutèrent plus de cette décision de leur curé que du fait qu'on ne leur avait communiqué aucune nouvelle de la visite du syndic à monseigneur Laflèche. La raison en était probablement que les membres du conseil avaient largement diffusé la décision de l'évêque de garantir tout emprunt de la mission pour la construction d'un presbytère.

— Je trouve que monsieur le curé a eu une bien bonne idée, déclara Marie à Camille et à Alexandrine Dionne, arrêtée auprès d'elle pour prendre des nouvelles d'Emma et de son bébé.

— C'est vrai que c'est pas bête, reconnut la mère d'Angélique. Comme ça, le monde va se sentir obligé de rester. Ça va même être pas mal gênant de sortir de la chapelle.

— Après tout, ça va prendre juste un peu plus qu'une demi-heure, précisa la veuve de Baptiste Beauchemin.

— Avez-vous pensé, m'man, que bien des hommes seront jamais capables de se priver de fumer pendant trois heures ? Si je me trompe pas, on pourra pas sortir de là avant midi, midi et demi.

— Ils en mourront pas, fit la femme du propriétaire du magasin général. En plus, ça tombe bien. Dimanche prochain, ça va être juste trois jours avant le mercredi des Cendres. Nos hommes vont enfin commencer à se priver un peu.

Sur le chemin du retour, Liam ne cessa de pester contre cette nouvelle idée du curé de la mission.

— Calvaire ! jura-t-il. Est-ce qu'il s'imagine qu'on va passer notre journée du dimanche à genoux ?

— Fais attention à ce que tu dis devant les enfants, le mit en garde sa femme.

— En tout cas, s'il pense que je vais rester après la grand-messe, il se trompe, reprit-il sans tenir compte de ce qu'elle venait de dire.

— Je sais pas comment tu vas faire pour t'en aller sans te faire remarquer, fit Camille. La chorale va sûrement avoir à chanter pendant le salut au Saint-Sacrement.

Liam ne répliqua pas, mais il était de fort mauvaise humeur au moment de laisser les siens près de la maison avant d'aller dételer son cheval.

❧

Un peu avant une heure et demie, Donat Beauchemin alla chercher Antonius Côté, parcourut tout le rang Saint-Jean, traversa le petit pont et vint immobiliser sa *sleigh* à l'entrée de la cour de la ferme d'Angèle Cloutier, voisine de la forge. Au même moment, l'attelage de Samuel Ellis dévala la pente du rang Sainte-Ursule et les deux hommes décidèrent d'attendre le président du conseil avant de frapper à la porte de la veuve.

— On dirait qu'il y a personne, dit Antonius, surpris de ne pas apercevoir la maîtresse des lieux à l'une de ses fenêtres.

— Il y a certainement quelqu'un, le contredit Samuel en descendant de sa *sleigh*. J'ai vu un berlot attelé entre l'étable et la remise quand j'étais en haut de la côte.

— C'est drôle pareil, fit Donat en se mettant en marche vers la maison en compagnie des deux autres. Est-ce que ça veut dire qu'il y a quelqu'un qui veut pas que ça se sache qu'il est chez madame Cloutier?

— Dis-moi pas qu'elle reçoit un galant en cachette, plaisanta Antonius, sur un ton paillard. Si c'est ça, il doit avoir de la santé, le bonhomme, parce que l'Angèle, c'est tout un morceau.

— Hé! Fais pas de farce avec ça, lui ordonna Samuel. C'est pas le temps pantoute de chercher à l'étriver. On s'en vient lui demander de nous vendre un morceau de sa terre. Tu la connais. Si on la prend à rebrousse-poil, elle va nous jeter dehors avant même qu'on ait pu s'expliquer et après ça, ça va être la croix et la bannière pour la décider à nous reparler.

— C'est correct, j'ai compris, fit Côté en adressant un clin d'œil égrillard à Donat qui feignit de ne pas le remarquer.

Samuel frappa à la porte de la petite maison blanche et les trois hommes attendirent en tapant du pied sur la galerie pour faire tomber la neige qui couvrait leurs bottes. La porte s'ouvrit sur une Angèle Cloutier endimanchée qui ne sembla pas particulièrement heureuse de voir les visiteurs.

La veuve d'Herménégilde Cloutier n'avait jamais été une jolie femme. Son visage aux traits très accusés était paré depuis quelques années d'un soupçon de moustache, qui ne le rendait guère attirant. Toutefois, c'était une grande et forte femme à qui le dur travail de la terre n'avait jamais fait peur. Après le décès de son mari, cinq ans plus tôt, elle n'avait jamais songé à vendre son bien. Elle avait continué seule à cultiver courageusement sa terre.

— Dites-moi donc, c'est presque la moitié de Saint-Bernard qui vient me déranger en plein dimanche après-midi! s'exclama-t-elle, l'air un peu revêche.

— Ben, on a pensé que ça vous dérangerait moins dans votre ouvrage si on venait vous voir un dimanche après-midi, intervint poliment Donat.

— Qui est-ce qui est à la porte, ma douce? fit une voix d'homme au fond de la pièce voisine.

Quand Antonius Côté entendit cette voix, ses yeux s'arrondirent et il fallut un solide coup de coude de Donat pour l'empêcher de parler.

— De la visite, p'tit père, répondit la veuve d'une voix douce qu'aucun des visiteurs ne lui connaissait. Bon, ben, entrez puisque vous êtes là. Restez pas plantés là comme des piquets, finit-elle par dire, comme à contrecœur, en ouvrant plus grand la porte pour les laisser passer devant elle.

— Écoute, Angèle, on voudrait pas te déranger si t'as de la visite, fit Samuel Ellis.

— Vous dérangez pas pantoute. On jouait aux cartes. Ôtez votre manteau et passez dans la cuisine, à côté.

Ellis, Beauchemin et Côté obéirent et la suivirent dans la pièce voisine où ils découvrirent Hormidas Meilleur, assis à table, devant un paquet de cartes à jouer. L'air contrarié, le petit homme à la tête ronde se leva.

— On dirait ben que notre partie de cartes est sur le diable, dit-il à la maîtresse de maison.

— Tu peux rester si tu veux, p'tit père, minauda Angèle d'un air tout aussi contrarié.

— C'est pas ben grave, ma douce, on se reprendra une autre fois, dit le facteur célibataire en lui adressant un sourire enjôleur.

Angèle accompagna Hormidas jusqu'à la patère placée près de la porte et l'aida à endosser son manteau. Il y eut quelques chuchotements entre les deux dans l'entrée avant que le facteur ne quitte la maison après avoir salué, apparemment mal à l'aise, les trois visiteurs.

Dès que la porte se fut refermée, le visage d'Angèle se transforma du tout au tout. Toute trace de douceur et de féminité disparut comme par enchantement.

— Bon, assoyez-vous et dites-moi pourquoi vous êtes là, ordonna-t-elle aux trois syndics en prenant place au bout de la table.

— Angèle, t'as entendu comme nous autres ce que monseigneur racontait dans sa dernière lettre, dit Samuel Ellis. Il est pas question que notre curé passe un autre hiver dans la sacristie. Ça veut dire que si on lui construit pas un presbytère ce printemps, Saint-Bernard risque de disparaître parce qu'il y aura plus personne pour venir dire la messe dans notre chapelle.

— Ben oui, je sais tout ça, fit abruptement la veuve. Puis après?

— À ce moment-là, tu dois ben te douter pourquoi on est venus te voir, reprit Samuel.

— Tu veux encore un morceau de ma terre, c'est ça ?

— En plein ça. Mais on va te payer le prix que ça vaut, crains rien, voulut la rassurer le président du conseil.

— Et si je suis pas intéressée de vendre ?

— Ben, on n'aura pas le choix. Il y aura pas de presbytère. Tu connais monsieur le curé, il voudra jamais que son presbytère soit loin de la chapelle. Penses-y ! Si on n'arrive pas à s'entendre avec toi, on va être poignés pour acheter une couple d'arpents à Delphis, mais sa terre est ben trop loin pour que ce soit pratique pour notre curé.

— Ouais, fit Angèle, l'air songeur.

Il y eut un long silence dans la cuisine de la veuve. Donat et Antonius n'osaient pas intervenir. Ils préféraient laisser Samuel discuter avec Angèle. Ils avaient à peu de chose près le même âge et semblaient se comprendre.

— En admettant que j'accepte de te vendre. De combien d'arpents t'as besoin ?

— Pour moi, trois arpents de front feraient l'affaire, annonça le président du conseil.

— Trois arpents, mais sur toute la profondeur de ma terre, en haut de la côte, tint à préciser Angèle. Pourquoi autant ?

— Ben, monseigneur a eu l'air de nous dire qu'on ferait mieux de construire une remise et une écurie avec le presbytère, expliqua Samuel.

— Et qu'est-ce que t'as en tête exactement ?

— Je pensais que si tu vendais au syndic trois arpents à droite de la chapelle, ce serait parfait. On aurait là toute la place qu'il faut pour bâtir. Penses-y, tu cultives rien sur ce bout-là, lui fit-il remarquer.

— Ça, c'est pas de tes affaires, Samuel Ellis, fit-elle sèchement. Où est-ce que tu penses que je prends mon foin ?

— C'est correct, j'ai rien dit.

— Et si je décidais de vendre au conseil, combien tu serais prêt à me donner ?

— Soixante piastres.

— Soixante piastres! s'exclama-t-elle en adoptant un air horrifié.

— Oui, et dis-toi que tu serais payée en signant le contrat chez le notaire, à part ça, dit-il en prenant un air avantageux. Monseigneur a accepté de garantir tous les emprunts de Saint-Bernard.

— Ben, tes soixante piastres, tu peux les garder, Samuel Ellis! fit la veuve. T'auras jamais un bout de ma terre à ce prix-là. C'est rire du monde…

— Voyons, madame Cloutier, intervint Donat. Combien vous demandez pour les trois arpents qu'on veut?

— Au moins le double, mon garçon, déclara-t-elle sur un ton décidé.

— Vous savez, madame, que le conseil pourra jamais donner autant pour trois arpents, même si c'est de la ben bonne terre. Monseigneur comprendrait pas qu'on ait dépensé autant juste pour le terrain.

— Je donnerai jamais mon bien, répliqua-t-elle, catégorique.

— Je comprends, mais est-ce que vous pourriez pas faire un petit effort pour Saint-Bernard?

— Un petit effort jusqu'où? demanda-t-elle, l'air peu commode.

— Je sais pas, moi, madame, mais qu'est-ce que vous diriez si on coupait la poire en deux? Quatre-vingt-dix piastres. C'est ben de l'argent pour le conseil, mais on pourra jamais donner plus que ça, c'est certain.

Samuel secouait la tête en signe de dénégation, mais il se gardait bien de parler.

— Voulez-vous y penser, madame Cloutier? reprit Donat Beauchemin sur un ton raisonnable. On peut vous donner tout le temps qu'il faut pour vous faire une idée. De toute façon, on fera pas construire avant trois bons mois, pas vrai? demanda-t-il à ses deux confrères.

— Je vais y penser, consentit Angèle en se levant pour signifier que la réunion avait assez duré.

Les trois hommes la suivirent dans l'entrée, endossèrent leur manteau et chaussèrent leurs bottes, puis ils la saluèrent et sortirent.

— *Goddam!* Elle est complètement folle, la mère Cloutier! s'écria Samuel dès qu'il se fut suffisamment éloigné de la maison de cette dernière. Voyons donc! Il y a pas une maudite terre de Saint-Bernard qui vaut cent vingt piastres pour trois arpents! En plus, il y en a une partie qui va être perdue de l'autre côté du chemin parce que ça descend trop à pic vers la rivière pour servir à quelque chose. Si elle pense qu'on va se laisser voler tout rond, elle se trompe, moi, je vous le garantis.

— Mais si elle accepte de vendre pour quatre-vingt-dix piastres… commença Antonius.

— Ce serait encore trop cher pour ce que ça vaut, déclara le président du conseil avec mauvaise humeur.

Il n'avait pas approuvé la proposition de Donat, et là, il le lui faisait savoir.

— Peut-être pas si cher que ça, se défendit le fils de Baptiste Beauchemin. Oubliez pas, monsieur Ellis, que si on n'arrive pas à lui acheter les trois arpents qu'on veut, il y aura tout simplement pas de presbytère.

— C'est vrai, ce qu'il dit, approuva Antonius en montant dans la *sleigh* de son voisin.

— En tout cas, il y a rien de décidé. Elle va y penser, reprit Donat. On verra ben.

— On pourrait peut-être demander à monsieur le curé de lui parler, suggéra Antonius.

— T'es pas malade, toi! s'écria Samuel. Elle peut pas le sentir. Ce serait assez pour qu'elle dise carrément non.

Durant la semaine suivante, il y eut quelques chutes de neige sans conséquence et la plupart des hommes de Saint-Bernard-Abbé profitèrent de la légère hausse de la température pour bûcher plus longtemps chaque jour.

Le jeudi après-midi, un peu après quatre heures, plus d'une demi-douzaine d'hommes se retrouvèrent au magasin général de Télesphore Dionne pour une raison ou une autre. La rencontre était si animée que Paddy Connolly en oublia Bernadette et les enfants qui durent rentrer à pied à la maison.

Chacun comparait la quantité de bois abattu et scié depuis le début de l'hiver sur sa terre et on en vint à parler des hommes forts de la région.

— Moi, je me dis qu'on devrait organiser un beau jour un concours de tir au poignet, déclara le forgeron Évariste Bourgeois qui avait toujours été passablement fier de sa force physique.

Il faut reconnaître que l'homme était pratiquement aussi large que haut et qu'il possédait une musculature impressionnante.

— C'est la place qu'on n'a pas pour organiser ça, fit remarquer Athanase Auger, un solide gaillard lui aussi qui ne le cédait en rien à ses trois frères.

— Pourquoi vous feriez pas ça dans votre forge, monsieur Bourgeois? lui demanda Xavier Beauchemin. Il me semble qu'il y aurait là ben assez de place pour une trentaine d'hommes, si vous faites un peu de ménage, comme de raison.

— Tu peux être certain, mon jeune, que si on fait ça là, tous ceux qui vont vouloir entrer vont venir aider au ménage, prit soin de préciser l'homme à la figure rubiconde.

— Moi, je suis partant n'importe quand, affirma Amable Fréchette, l'ex-petit ami de Bernadette, l'air toujours aussi avantageux.

— Vous devriez faire ça dimanche après-midi, suggéra Paddy. Je me propose même comme juge.

— Comment ça! Vous voulez pas tirer au poignet! s'exclama Xavier pour se moquer de lui.

Le jeune homme n'était pas loin de partager l'antipathie que sa sœur Camille éprouvait à l'endroit du petit homme bedonnant qu'il jugeait un peu trop suffisant et effronté.

— Ce serait peut-être mieux d'avoir quelqu'un qui connaît ça, osa-t-il dire devant le groupe d'hommes rassemblés près de la fournaise de Télesphore Dionne.

— J'ai l'expérience de ce genre d'affaire-là, fit Paddy avec hauteur, peu habitué à se faire contester.

— Je sais pas trop si… reprit Xavier.

— Tu sauras, mon garçon, que dans la vie il y a des gens qui ont une tête et d'autres qui ont juste des bras, le coupa le retraité en le mettant au défi de le contredire.

— Et vous, je suppose, vous avez une tête, fit Xavier.

— En plein ça. Puis, qu'est-ce que vous pensez de mon idée de faire ça dimanche après-midi, monsieur Bourgeois? demanda l'oncle de Liam à Évariste en se tournant vers le forgeron.

— Ben…

— Envoyez donc, monsieur Bourgeois, le supplia Fréchette. Mercredi, ça va être le commencement du carême et c'est pas sûr pantoute que monsieur le curé va accepter qu'on fasse une affaire comme ça pendant le carême.

Le forgeron hésita encore un bref moment avant de dire, bourru:

— C'est correct, mais à la condition que j'aie du monde samedi après-midi pour nettoyer la forge.

— On va y être, promit Paddy.

La discussion venait à peine de prendre fin qu'Hormidas Meilleur pénétra dans le magasin général, suivi, un moment plus tard, par Antonius Côté. Lorsqu'il aperçut le facteur coiffé de son casque à oreillettes et portant en bandoulière son vieux sac de cuir avec lequel il distribuait quotidiennement le courrier, un air malicieux se peignit sur les traits du cultivateur. Il laissa le vieux célibataire se frotter longuement les mains au-dessus de la fournaise pour les réchauffer, mais il adressa quelques signes de connivence aux hommes présents qui se demandaient ce qu'il pouvait tramer.

— Hé, vous autres ! Avez-vous su que monsieur le curé va célébrer ce printemps les premières noces dans notre chapelle ? demanda Antonius à la cantonade.

— Qui se marie ? s'enquit Angélique Dionne, retranchée derrière son comptoir, comme d'habitude.

— Tu me feras pas croire, ma belle, que t'es pas au courant pantoute, feignit de s'étonner Antonius.

— Non.

— Ta voisine, la belle affaire, lui apprit le plaisantin sur un ton triomphant.

— La sœur de Xavier Beauchemin ? demanda Alexandrine Dionne, qui venait d'apparaître aux côtés de sa fille.

— Pas ma sœur, déclara tout net Xavier. En tout cas, moi, j'en ai pas entendu parler pantoute.

— Ben non, pas la petite maîtresse d'école, reprit Côté. Je vous ai dit votre voisine.

— Pas madame Cloutier quand même ! s'écria Angélique, prête à se mettre à rire.

— Ben oui, ma belle.

Les traits du visage d'Hormidas Meilleur s'étaient soudainement figés, mais il choisit de ne rien dire.

— Là, tu fais une farce, fit Télesphore en se mettant à rire.

— Pantoute, je suis sérieux comme un pape, protesta le cultivateur, la main sur le cœur.

Il y eut des murmures de stupéfaction parmi les clients présents.

— Qui est le brave ? demanda Amable Fréchette.

— Il est juste devant toi, le jeune, déclara Antonius en montrant le facteur.

— C'est pas vrai ! intervint Évariste Bourgeois, hilare. Moi, j'ai ben de la misère à croire ça.

— T'as raison, Évariste, déclara le petit homme en se tournant tout d'une pièce vers ceux qui ricanaient. Vous voyez ben que Côté rit de vous autres.

— Pourquoi il raconte une affaire comme ça, si c'est pas vrai, père Meilleur ? lui demanda Xavier.

— Parce que c'est une langue sale et parce qu'il aime raconter n'importe quelle niaiserie, fit le facteur en élevant la voix. Il m'a vu chez Angèle Cloutier dimanche après-midi. On jouait aux cartes quand il est arrivé avec Ellis et ton frère.

— C'est vrai, reconnut Antonius, sans se démonter. Et vous savez pas comment notre Angèle l'appelle ?

— Non, répondirent plusieurs.

— Elle l'appelle « p'tit père ». C'est pas beau, ça ?

Un éclat de rire général accueillit la révélation, ce qui fit violemment rougir le facteur.

— Tu joues aux cartes avec Angèle ? répéta le forgeron, le premier à retrouver son sérieux, en s'adressant à Hormidas.

— Ben oui, c'est pas un crime, bout de corde ! protesta le célibataire en retirant son casque à oreillettes pour passer ses doigts dans sa maigre chevelure poivre et sel.

— Et il l'appelle « ma douce », se moqua Antonius.

— Ayoye ! s'écria Fréchette. Pour moi, le père, vous buvez trop.

— Toi, mêle-toi de ce qui te regarde, le jeune, répliqua sèchement le facteur, exaspéré. Ça a même pas le nombril sec et ça se mêle des affaires des grands.

— Tu fais juste ça, hein ? Tu joues aux cartes avec elle ? intervint John White, qui n'avait pas dit un mot depuis le début de la discussion.

— Oui, monsieur ! proclama Hormidas. Madame Cloutier est une femme honnête.

— Et qui a tout ce qu'il faut pour se défendre, renchérit Évariste, goguenard.

— C'est sûr, confirma Hormidas qui ignora volontairement le sarcasme.

— Quand même, c'est pas ben correct que vous soyez tous les deux tout seuls, sans chaperon, affirma Antonius en feignant subitement d'être sérieux. Ça pourrait faire jaser si ça se savait.

— On dirait ben que là, ça se sait à cause de ta grande gueule, répliqua le facteur, de mauvaise humeur. En tout cas, partez pas de ragots. Je fréquente pas madame Cloutier et il y aura pas de mariage ce printemps, même si une commère de Saint-Bernard répand la rumeur.

Sur ces mots, le petit homme remit son casque sur sa tête, boutonna son manteau et quitta les lieux en claquant la porte derrière lui.

— Ah ben, petit Jésus! s'exclama Bourgeois. J'aurai tout entendu. Si c'est vrai que le père Meilleur va veiller avec ma voisine, il va falloir faire brûler un lampion pour lui, le pauvre homme. Il va passer par là avec elle. Avec les battoirs qu'elle a, il va avoir intérêt à marcher droit.

Un éclat de rire général salua la saillie. Chacun visualisait la différence importante de taille entre la veuve d'Herménégilde Cloutier et le petit facteur.

Quand Samuel Ellis apprit le lendemain avant-midi qu'Antonius Côté s'était moqué du facteur devant un groupe d'habitants de Saint-Bernard-Abbé, il piqua une belle colère.

— Le maudit sans-dessein! s'emporta-t-il devant sa femme. Ça, c'est peut-être le meilleur moyen pour pousser la Cloutier à refuser de nous vendre son lot. Trop bête pour fermer sa grande gueule quand il le faut.

Inutile de dire que lorsqu'il vit le syndic le dimanche matin, il l'attira à l'écart pour lui passer un savon.

— C'était pas ben méchant, se défendit Antonius, secoué par la colère du président du conseil.

— Peut-être, mais t'as pas pensé que si le bonhomme va raconter cette affaire-là à la Cloutier, elle va nous envoyer chez le diable, répliqua sèchement l'Irlandais, toujours aussi furieux.

— Tu sais ben qu'il lui dira rien.

— Je l'espère pour nous autres, rétorqua Samuel avant de lui tourner le dos pour regagner son banc dans la chapelle.

En ce dernier dimanche de février, Josaphat Désilets avait toutes les raisons du monde d'être dépité et mécontent. Tout d'abord, son idée de célébrer le salut au Saint-Sacrement immédiatement après la grand-messe ne connut pas le succès escompté. Il avait cru que l'ensemble des fidèles déjà sur place pour assister à la grand-messe n'oserait pas quitter les lieux à la fin de la célébration du saint sacrifice et demeurerait pour la cérémonie qui durerait, tout compte fait, moins d'une heure. Il s'était lourdement trompé. Dès qu'il eut prononcé l'*Ite missa est*, il vit des hommes se lever et se diriger vers la porte de la chapelle. Le mouvement d'abord hésitant prit peu à peu de l'ampleur. Plusieurs femmes suivies de leurs enfants leur emboîtèrent finalement le pas.

Quand le prêtre entreprit la célébration de la cérémonie, plus de la moitié des bancs avaient été désertés.

Il était encore furieux quand il prit place à table pour dîner dans sa sacristie, alors que son bedeau, Agénor Moreau, vint remplir de bûches le coffre placé près du poêle.

— Vous auriez bien pu attendre après le dîner, lui dit le curé de Saint-Bernard-Abbé en faisant un effort pour se montrer aimable envers le vieil homme.

— Je le sais, monsieur le curé, mais cet après-midi, j'ai l'intention d'aller voir le concours de tir au poignet chez Bourgeois.

— Quel concours ? demanda le prêtre, surpris.

— Les hommes de la paroisse ont décidé de faire un concours de tir au poignet. Il paraît qu'il va y avoir pas mal de monde, répondit le père de Delphis Moreau sans se rendre compte de la frustration de son curé.

Après le départ de l'homme, Josaphat Désilets remâcha longuement sa rancœur. Personne n'avait jugé bon de le prévenir de l'événement, comme si on souhaitait ne pas l'y voir. À ses yeux, c'était absolument inadmissible et cela représentait un manque de considération inexcusable envers leur pasteur. Puis il se demanda durant de longues minutes s'il n'allait pas se rendre quand même à la forge pour assister à la compétition, songeant que ce serait une agréable distraction à la veille du carême. Mais sa rancœur était telle qu'il choisit de bouder le concours tout en se promettant de parler du respect dû à son curé lors de son prochain sermon.

❧

Un peu après une heure, la cour commune entre la forge et le magasin général commença à être envahie de berlots et de *sleighs* occupés uniquement par des hommes. Peu à peu, la forge d'Évariste Bourgeois se remplit d'une foule bruyante d'hommes de tous âges.

La veille, une demi-douzaine de jeunes hommes de Saint-Bernard-Abbé s'étaient présentés sur les lieux pour aider le forgeron à ranger et à installer de longs bancs de fortune à l'aide de vieux madriers.

Chez les Beauchemin, Marie avait dû élever la voix pour empêcher Bernadette d'assister à la compétition.

— Voyons, m'man, avait-elle protesté. Il va y avoir là les plus beaux hommes de la paroisse. C'est pas un crime de vouloir aller voir comment ça va se passer.

— Bedette, je t'ai déjà dit hier que c'était pas la place d'une jeune fille.

— Je suis sûre que Constant va dire oui si je lui demande de m'emmener, plaida l'institutrice.

— Non, veux-tu faire rire de toi, Bedette Beauchemin? lui demanda sa mère, excédée. Il y aura pas une fille qui se respecte qui va mettre les pieds dans cette place-là cet après-midi. Voyons donc! Il va y avoir juste des hommes.

— Et tu vas avoir l'air d'une écornifleuse, intervint son frère Hubert.

— Toi, mêle-toi pas de ça. Ça te regarde pas, répliqua Bernadette, déçue. Les dimanches après-midi sont ennuyants à mourir, ajouta-t-elle dans une dernière tentative de persuader sa mère de la laisser y aller.

— Tu feras comme nous autres, tu tricoteras ou tu fileras. Tiens, tu pourras même commencer à assembler la courtepointe.

— De l'ouvrage, par exemple, ça, j'ai toujours le droit d'en faire, fit-elle d'une voix acide.

Bernadette aurait probablement été un peu consolée si elle avait su qu'Angélique Dionne avait rencontré la même résistance de la part de ses parents quand elle s'était approchée de la patère dans l'intention de mettre son manteau.

— Où est-ce que tu vas ? lui avait demandé Alexandrine, intriguée.

— Je vais juste jeter un coup d'œil à côté, m'man.

— Il en est pas question, déclara son père en train de chausser ses bottes. Tu restes ici dedans avec ta mère. Il y a pas de femme là-dedans.

— Mais, p'pa…

— T'as entendu ce que ton père vient de te dire. Tu vas pas aller faire rire de toi là-dedans.

Au moment où Télesphore Dionne quittait sa maison, une catherine attelée à un magnifique cheval vint s'immobiliser près de la galerie de son magasin. Le conducteur, un petit homme frêle, le salua avant d'entraver sa bête et il le suivit dans la forge déjà envahie par un épais nuage de fumée.

— Bonjour, notaire, salua Évariste en s'approchant d'Eudore Valiquette. Trouvez-vous une place. Ça commence dans une couple de minutes.

Il y avait déjà une quarantaine d'hommes sur place. Si plusieurs jeunes se défiaient ouvertement, quelques vieillards avaient entrepris de rappeler le souvenir d'hommes forts du passé et des tours de force qu'ils se plaisaient à réaliser.

— Monsieur Bourgeois, il me faudrait une chaise, demanda Paddy Connolly qui venait de retirer son épais manteau de chat sauvage.

— Quoi? Un bon banc en bois est trop dur pour des fesses de la ville? se moqua Rémi Lafond en adressant un clin d'œil à son beau-frère Donat.

— C'est pas ça, se défendit l'oncle de Liam, mais le juge doit être mieux installé que les spectateurs, et surtout, il doit être assis plus près.

— Il y a des quarts de clous en masse pour vous asseoir, intervint Cléomène Paquette.

— Non, il a raison, déclara le forgeron. Fréchette, va me chercher une chaise à la maison, demanda-t-il à Amable Fréchette, debout près de la porte.

— Moi, ça me dérangerait pas d'être juge quand vous serez fatigué, monsieur, se proposa Eudore Valiquette en s'approchant de Paddy.

Les deux hommes avaient la même taille et, à peu de chose près, le même âge. Cependant, le notaire était maigre alors que l'Irlandais était plutôt grassouillet.

— Qu'est-ce que le gagnant remporte? demanda Eudore Valiquette que la plupart des hommes présents ne connaissaient pas.

Les spectateurs se regardèrent, incapables de répondre à la question du nouveau venu.

— Ce serait normal qu'il y ait un prix, insista celui-ci.

Après un instant d'hésitation, le maître des lieux répondit:

— Je suis tellement sûr de gagner, que j'offre de ferrer gratis le cheval du gagnant.

— Tu t'organises pour que ça te coûte pas trop cher, mon Évariste, plaisanta Ellis.

— Je peux même te dire que ça me coûtera rien pantoute, plastronna le forgeron, parce qu'il y en a pas un qui va me battre.

Amable Fréchette revint avec une chaise qui fut placée près d'une table en bois. À chacune des extrémités de celle-ci, Évariste avait disposé un vieux quart de clous qui allait servir de siège aux concurrents.

— Comme c'est moi qui reçois, déclara Évariste Bourgeois en prenant place à un bout de la table, je vais être le premier à tirer au poignet. Qui veut venir m'essayer? demanda-t-il, sûr de sa force.

— Moi, déclara Cléomène Paquette en s'avançant pour prendre place en face de lui.

— T'es pas sérieux, Cléomène, s'écria Antonius Côté. Tu vas te faire manger tout rond. T'es pas de taille!

— Il va pas souffrir longtemps, dit Xavier Beauchemin en riant.

En fait, le cultivateur du rang Saint-Jean fut écrasé en quelques secondes et dut céder sa place à Delphis Moreau. Celui-ci offrit une meilleure opposition au forgeron, mais finit par déclarer forfait après quelques instants d'efforts.

— Un autre! cria Évariste après avoir récupéré durant quelques secondes.

Samuel Ellis vint s'asseoir devant lui. Les deux hommes plantèrent résolument un coude sur la table, présentant à leur adversaire une main que l'autre empoigna. Paddy posa une main sur les deux mains de manière à s'assurer qu'elles étaient bien à la verticale et il donna le signal de l'engagement. Durant un bon moment, l'Irlandais parvint à résister à la poussée du forgeron, puis, peu à peu, son bras se mit à pencher et sa main finit par venir claquer sèchement contre le bois de la table. Le président du conseil s'était défendu honorablement et obtint quelques applaudissements mérités.

— Thomas, ouvre une porte, bout de cierge! On est en train de mourir emboucanés, cria soudainement Anatole

Blanchette. C'est rendu qu'on voit même plus qui tire au poignet, exagéra-t-il.

Le maître des lieux vainquit trois autres adversaires sans trop de peine et il ne cachait pas son orgueil. C'était rendu au point où la compétition avait perdu passablement de son intérêt et plusieurs parlaient déjà de rentrer à la maison.

— Un autre brave? demanda Évariste en tournant sa grosse tête vers les spectateurs.

— Moi, je veux ben essayer, déclara Constant Aubé en s'avançant.

— Vas-y, Constant! Fais-le souffrir un peu! l'encouragea Rémi Lafond.

L'ami de cœur de Bernadette Beauchemin prit place sur le quart de clous libéré par le dernier vaincu, releva la manche droite de sa chemise, planta solidement son coude sur la table et tendit la main vers celle de son adversaire. La musculature du bras de Constant était surprenante pour un meunier, peut-être pas l'égale de la largeur du bras du forgeron, mais tout de même de quoi imposer le respect.

Dès le début de l'affrontement, les bras des deux hommes demeurèrent à la verticale durant un très long moment, chacun étant apparemment incapable de faire fléchir l'autre. Si le visage du meunier demeurait impénétrable alors que tous ses muscles étaient bandés, une grosse veine bleue finit par apparaître au front d'Évariste, signe qu'il déployait tous ses efforts pour vaincre son adversaire. Puis, les bras commencèrent à s'incliner lentement, très lentement. De toute évidence, le forgeron commençait à faiblir, même s'il parvint, à un certain moment, à redresser son bras. Mais cela ne dura guère. Peu à peu, son bras baissa, accompagné par les acclamations des spectateurs excités par le duel. Finalement, le bras d'Évariste entra en contact avec la table et son poignet claqua contre le meuble.

Essoufflés par tant d'effort, les deux adversaires demeurèrent un instant sans bouger. La surprise était si grande que, durant un court instant, la foule demeura sans réaction. Puis des cris d'excitation se firent entendre alors que le forgeron quittait lentement son siège.

— Là, je commençais à être un peu fatigué, déclara Évariste Bourgeois. Ça fait trois quarts d'heure que je tire au poignet. Lui était reposé.

— C'est certain, monsieur Bourgeois, reconnut Constant Aubé, de bonne grâce. Ça aurait été une autre paire de manches si vous aviez été reposé.

Cette déclaration de son adversaire mit un peu de baume sur l'orgueil écorché du forgeron qui dit aux hommes près de lui avec une admiration évidente :

— Ce petit calvaire-là, il est raide en pas pour rire.

Le meunier remporta trois victoires rapides avant d'affronter Amable Fréchette qui ne lui avait pas pardonné de l'avoir remplacé dans le salon des Beauchemin, aux côtés de la belle Bernadette. Par ailleurs, Constant n'avait pas oublié que l'autre avait délibérément cherché à le frapper avec son boghei alors qu'il transportait une boîte au magasin général.

C'est donc avec des yeux pleins de feu que les deux jeunes hommes s'empoignèrent, chacun bien décidé à terrasser l'autre pour lui prouver qu'il ne le craignait nullement. Amable résista près de cinq minutes avant de céder. Rouge autant à cause de l'effort fourni que de rage, il quitta immédiatement les lieux après sa défaite sous les quolibets de certains spectateurs. Il fut finalement remplacé par Hubert Beauchemin que Constant parvint tout de même à vaincre non sans difficulté.

— Ôte-toi, mon petit frère, je vais m'occuper de lui, moi, ordonna Xavier à son frère cadet. Il sera pas dit que ce maudit meunier-là va faire manger de l'avoine à tous les Beauchemin, ajouta-t-il pour plaisanter en donnant une bourrade à Constant qu'il aimait bien.

— C'est ça, viens faire le jars, répliqua Constant. Si tu me bats, je vais crier partout que c'est parce que j'étais fatigué.

— Tu vas pas te servir de l'excuse de notre forgeron. On la connaît celle-là.

Ce fut la rencontre la plus intéressante de l'après-midi parce que les adversaires étaient de force égale. Il fallut attendre de longues minutes avant que Constant Aubé ne cède la victoire à un Xavier Beauchemin qui n'en revenait pas de la force et de la résistance de celui qu'on avait si longtemps surnommé « la Bottine » dans le village.

— Blasphème ! Je sais pas ce que t'as mangé à midi, toi, s'écria-t-il après que Paddy l'eut déclaré grand vainqueur, mais on peut pas dire que t'es feluette.

Le sourire aux lèvres, l'ami de Bernadette lui serra la main et quitta le quart de clous sur lequel il était assis depuis de longues minutes.

— Il était temps que tu te lèves de là, plaisanta Anatole Blanchette. T'étais en train de prendre racine.

Après cette rencontre, Xavier n'eut à affronter que le fils aîné de Samuel Ellis avant d'être couronné champion de la compétition, faute de concurrents prêts à lui faire face.

— Ben là, je peux dire que c'est un bon après-midi, déclara le jeune homme. Je viens de gagner de faire ferrer mon cheval gratis.

— Je vais le ferrer gratis, mais tu vas payer les fers, répliqua Évariste.

— Il a jamais été question de faire payer les fers au gagnant, lui fit remarquer Dionne.

— C'est vrai, ça, intervint Hyland, qui avait été un spectateur très intéressé durant tout l'après-midi.

— Vous êtes sûrs de ça, vous deux ?

— C'est certain.

— Bon, ben, c'est correct, le jeune, je vais te donner aussi les fers neufs, calvaire !

En quelques minutes, la forge se vida de ses spectateurs qui partirent en commentant les affrontements qu'ils avaient le plus appréciés. Rémi Lafond et Donat s'approchèrent de Constant Aubé en compagnie de Hubert. Les deux premiers avaient perdu aux mains du forgeron.

— C'est ben de valeur que t'aies laissé gagner le grand fanal, déclara Rémi en désignant de l'index Xavier qui venait vers eux. Il me semble que ça lui aurait fait du bien une petite leçon d'humilité. Qu'est-ce que vous en pensez, vous autres ? demanda-t-il à ses deux beaux-frères.

— Là, t'as raison. On n'a pas fini d'en entendre parler, fit Donat.

— Et il va s'en vanter pendant des mois, ajouta Hubert, narquois.

— Vous pouvez ben parler, vous trois, intervint Xavier avec bonne humeur. Vous allez être les premiers dans Saint-Bernard à aller raconter ça partout.

— C'est dommage que Liam ait pas pu venir, fit remarquer Rémi.

— Il a aimé mieux passer l'après-midi avec sa femme, dit Paddy, au passage. Vous oubliez que c'est un nouveau marié. Il y a un paquet d'affaires qui l'intéressent plus que le tir au poignet.

Les hommes qui l'entendirent se mirent à rire. Déjà le soleil baissait à l'horizon et le vent venait de se lever.

Durant le souper ce soir-là, Paddy raconta en détail la compétition qui avait opposé les hommes forts de la mission. À l'entendre, il y avait joué un rôle de premier plan comme arbitre. Quand il mentionna que Xavier avait gagné le concours en battant de peine et de misère le meunier, Camille ne put s'empêcher de dire avec un sourire :

— On n'a pas fini d'en entendre parler.

— Pourquoi, p'pa, vous y êtes pas allé ? demanda Patrick à son père. C'est certain que vous auriez gagné.

— J'ai pas de temps à perdre avec ces niaiseries-là, laissa tomber Liam.

Ce soir-là, Constant eut à subir les moqueries de Hubert et de Donat lorsqu'il se présenta chez les Beauchemin pour veiller au salon avec Bernadette.

— Je sais pas si on doit laisser entrer un perdant ici dedans, déclara Donat en l'accueillant à la porte.

— Ben, je pense qu'il y en a déjà un dans la place, non? fit le meunier en désignant Hubert qu'il avait battu au tir au poignet.

— Aïe! Ça va faire, vous deux, intervint Bernadette en aidant le visiteur à se débarrasser de son manteau. Laissez-le donc tranquille. Vous avez dit qu'il avait battu monsieur Bourgeois et trois autres hommes avant de perdre.

— Whow, la petite sœur! Monte pas sur tes grands chevaux! fit Donat en riant. Nous autres, c'était juste pour l'étriver un peu.

— Moi, je trouve qu'elle le protège pas mal trop, son cavalier, fit Hubert, moqueur.

— C'est vrai, ça. Il me semble qu'il est capable de se défendre tout seul.

— Vous deux, ça va faire, fit Marie. Allez donc me remplir le coffre à bois qui est presque vide. Ça fera au moins quelque chose d'utile que vous aurez fait dans votre journée.

Bernadette en profita pour entraîner son amoureux à sa suite après avoir allumé une lampe qu'elle transporta au salon.

Chapitre 12

Le Mardi gras

Deux jours plus tard, tout travail sembla cesser à Saint-Bernard-Abbé pour qu'on puisse célébrer dignement le Mardi gras. Comme chaque année, la perspective de devoir se priver durant les quarante jours du carême incitait les gens à manger et à s'amuser tout leur soûl ce jour-là.

— T'aurais pu me permettre de dire aux petits de rester à la maison aujourd'hui, fit Bernadette, dépitée, alors qu'elle finissait son déjeuner.

— Il y a pas de raison de fermer l'école, déclara tout net son frère, président de la commission scolaire. T'es payée pour faire l'école, pas pour te reposer à la maison.

— Mais c'est Mardi gras, bonyenne! Les enfants vont avoir bien plus le goût de se déguiser pour passer d'une maison à l'autre que de travailler, plaida-t-elle.

— L'école doit rester ouverte, trancha Donat.

— Ton frère a raison, intervint Marie. En plus, tu sais très bien que monsieur le curé aurait été le premier à en parler à l'inspecteur si t'avais pas fait l'école aujourd'hui.

— Je te gagerais même qu'il va passer ce matin, plaisanta Hubert, juste pour voir si tu fais la classe.

— De toute façon, Bedette, les enfants s'amuseront à soir, comme nous autres, lui fit remarquer Eugénie en essuyant la bouche d'Alexis, assis sur ses genoux.

— Pendant que vous allez avoir de la visite et vous bourrer, moi, la folle, je vais avoir les enfants sur les bras.

— T'oublies qu'on est en deuil, fit sa mère, sévère.

La jeune institutrice quitta la maison pour l'école sans grand enthousiasme et la neige qui s'était mise à tomber doucement ce matin-là n'avait rien pour la réjouir, malgré l'atmosphère féérique qu'elle conférait au paysage. Cependant, la fille cadette des Beauchemin ne rata pratiquement rien parce que les célébrations ne débutèrent vraiment qu'avec le coucher du soleil. Joseph Gariépy fit la tournée des voisins du rang Saint-Jean au début de l'après-midi pour inviter tout le monde chez lui pour une soirée. À l'entendre, deux cousins de Saint-Zéphirin allaient venir jouer du violon et de l'accordéon pour faire danser tout le monde jusqu'aux petites heures du matin. Il recommanda aux hommes d'apporter de la bagosse parce qu'il n'était pas certain d'avoir une provision suffisante pour désaltérer tous ses invités. Un peu plus tard, on apprit que Delphis Moreau avait lancé une invitation identique à tous ceux qui voulaient célébrer le Mardi gras.

Marie Beauchemin avait remercié le jeune voisin pour son invitation et avait argué du deuil récent qui avait frappé la famille pour décliner.

— Si on fête pas, pourquoi on fait à manger depuis le matin ? demanda Eugénie à sa belle-mère.

— J'ai jamais dit qu'on fêterait pas, se défendit Marie. On peut pas danser et chanter à cause du deuil, mais il y a rien qui nous empêche de jouer aux cartes et de jaser jusqu'aux petites heures du matin, si ça nous tente.

En entendant cela, Hubert et Donat décidèrent d'un commun accord qu'ils ne travailleraient pas cet après-midi-là.

— Si c'est comme ça, on est aussi ben de commencer à fêter tout de suite, déclara l'aîné avec bonne humeur.

— Qu'est-ce que vous diriez si on invitait toute la famille chez nous, à soir ? leur demanda leur mère.

— Moi, j'ai rien contre, s'empressa de répondre Hubert.

— Là, on n'a pas arrêté de cuisiner depuis qu'on est levés à matin, on a de quoi nourrir une armée, intervint Eugénie.

— Ça fait que vous pourriez peut-être atteler et aller inviter Camille et Emma à venir souper avec nous autres. Après, on jouera aux cartes et on se racontera des histoires.

— C'est ben correct, accepta Hubert en quittant la chaise berçante sur laquelle il venait de s'asseoir. Qu'est-ce que je fais pour l'oncle de Liam? Lui, il va vouloir suivre, ça me surprendrait pas pantoute.

— Il y a pas moyen de faire autrement que de l'inviter avec les autres, consentit un peu à contrecœur la maîtresse de maison.

Depuis quelque temps, la veuve de Baptiste Beauchemin nourrissait de sérieuses réserves à l'endroit de l'oncle de son gendre. À la lumière de ce que lui racontait avec une certaine réticence son aînée, elle trouvait l'homme particulièrement effronté et sans cœur. Par ailleurs, elle avait de plus en plus de mal à cacher ses véritables sentiments à l'égard de celui qui avait épousé Camille. Si elle n'avait pas autant craint qu'il défende à sa femme la fréquentation de sa mère, elle lui aurait dit ses quatre vérités depuis longtemps. Toutefois, elle avait de plus en plus de mal à se retenir en sa présence.

«Il mériterait que je lui envoie un de mes garçons lui parler dans la face», se répétait-elle parfois.

— Arrête donc chez le petit Aubé en passant, recommanda-t-elle à Hubert. Dis-lui qu'on l'invite à souper, lui aussi. Il est tellement de service, ce garçon-là…

— Et ça vous ferait peut-être un bien bon gendre, pas vrai, madame Beauchemin? se crut autorisée à dire sa bru.

— Ça, c'est pas de mes affaires, fit Marie, cassante. Bedette choisira bien qui elle veut marier.

— Et pour Xavier, qu'est-ce qu'on fait? intervint Donat.

Marie garda le silence un bref moment avant de répondre.

— Tu peux aller inviter ton frère, mais insiste pas trop s'il a prévu d'aller fêter chez les Benoît.

— S'il y a rien chez les Benoît?

— Ben, tu lui diras qu'on l'attend pour souper avec Antonin.

— Et qu'est-ce que je fais pour Catherine?

— Tu lui diras de l'emmener, s'il y a pas moyen de faire autrement, conclut sa mère d'une voix lasse. Mais insiste pas, tu m'entends?

Donat jeta un coup d'œil vers sa femme. Il était évident que sa mère n'acceptait toujours pas sa future bru.

— Si c'est comme ça, finit-il par dire à son jeune frère, je vais atteler la Noire à la *sleigh* pour aller inviter Xavier. Je te laisse le Blond et le berlot.

Hubert commença sa tournée en s'arrêtant chez sa sœur Emma. Son mari et elle acceptèrent l'invitation sans se faire prier. Au retour, il alla chez le meunier qu'il trouva en train de réparer un attelage dans ce qui était appelé à devenir une cuisine d'été.

— Pour moi, t'es dans les petits papiers de ma mère pour qu'elle t'invite comme ça, lui fit remarquer un Hubert narquois.

— Pour te dire la vérité, j'aimerais mieux être dans les petits papiers de ta sœur, répliqua Constant avec un grand sourire.

— Es-tu en train de me dire que Bedette te maltraite? demanda le jeune homme.

— Pantoute, se défendit Constant, mais il y a des fois que je me demande si elle tient un peu à moi.

— Inquiète-toi pas pour ça, voulut-il le rassurer. Tant qu'elle accepte que t'ailles veiller avec elle au salon, il y a de l'espoir.

En sortant de chez Constant Aubé, Hubert se rendit compte que la petite neige folle qui tombait sur la région depuis le début de l'avant-midi n'avait pas cessé. Il passa devant la ferme paternelle et poursuivit son chemin jusque chez les Connolly. Quand il frappa à la porte, ce fut Camille qui vint lui ouvrir.

— Dis-moi pas que ton mari est parti bûcher ? fit-il en entrant dans la maison.

— Penses-tu ! répondit-elle avec le sourire. Il est comme tout le monde. Il fête, lui aussi. Il dort dans la chambre. Si tu veux lui parler, je peux bien aller le réveiller, proposa-t-elle.

— Non, c'est pas nécessaire. J'arrête juste pour t'inviter à souper à la maison. M'man et Eugénie ont cuisiné pas mal et on a dans l'idée de ramasser toute la famille à soir.

— Dis à m'man qu'on va y être dès que les enfants vont revenir de l'école.

— Attends-les pas. Avertis seulement l'oncle de Liam de les laisser à la maison en passant. Pendant que j'y pense, il est invité, lui aussi.

— Il est à la veille de finir son somme de l'après-midi, déclara la maîtresse des lieux. Je vais lui dire ça. Tu pourras dire à m'man que je vais arriver de bonne heure pour donner un coup de main à préparer le souper.

Quelques minutes après le départ de Hubert, Liam sortit de la chambre à coucher, ses bretelles battant sur ses cuisses et bâillant sans retenue.

— On est invités à souper chez ma mère à soir, lui apprit Camille.

— C'est correct, accepta-t-il sans manifester un grand enthousiasme.

— Quand il se lèvera, tu diras à ton oncle d'arrêter chez ma mère avec les enfants en revenant du magasin général.

— Une chance qu'il est là pour rendre service, lui fit remarquer Liam en se versant une tasse de thé bouillant après avoir passé ses bretelles.

— Je pense que c'est pas trop lui demander si on calcule qu'on le garde, lui et son cheval, sans jamais rien exiger, répliqua-t-elle d'une voix égale. En passant, moi, je commence à trouver ça pas mal gênant de me faire recevoir tout le temps par ma famille sans jamais la recevoir à manger.

— On n'est pas obligés d'y aller, laissa tomber son mari.

— Non, mais on n'arrête pas d'y aller quand même, lui fit-elle remarquer. C'est pas toujours aux mêmes de recevoir, tu sauras. On arrive six et même sept chaque fois. Là, je vais avertir tout le monde à soir que je vais les recevoir à souper à Pâques.

— T'es pas malade, toi ! s'exclama son mari. Combien ça va nous coûter, cette folie-là ?

— Pas plus cher que ce que ça leur coûte quand ils nous reçoivent, répliqua-t-elle sèchement. Puis, Seigneur, arrête d'être regardant comme ça ! Tu me fais honte.

Liam choisit de ne rien dire, mais à voir sa mine renfrognée, il était évident qu'il était loin d'être enchanté par la perspective de recevoir tous les Beauchemin.

— Là, je m'en vais chez ma mère aider à préparer le souper, déclara Camille à son mari en endossant son manteau. Oublie pas de dire à ton oncle de prendre les petits et de s'arrêter chez ma mère.

— Et s'il a pas le goût de souper chez ta mère ? demanda Liam, sans trop y croire.

— Là, ça me surprendrait bien gros, ne put s'empêcher de dire sa femme sur un ton sarcastique. Mais si jamais il dit qu'il a pas le goût, il aura juste à revenir se faire à souper lui-même ici dedans. Mais à ta place, je m'en ferais pas trop avec ça.

Un peu avant quatre heures, Paddy Connolly arrêta son attelage dans la cour de la ferme des Beauchemin pour laisser descendre Bernadette et les enfants. Pendant que le retraité s'occupait de sa bête, la jeune institutrice entra dans la maison en compagnie des enfants. Elle avait les traits légèrement tirés par la fatigue.

— Mautadit que les enfants étaient pas endurables aujourd'hui ! s'exclama-t-elle en enlevant son manteau. Je le savais qu'ils seraient pas tenables.

Camille adressa un regard de reproche aux quatre enfants en train de retirer, eux aussi, leur manteau.

— Pas nous autres, Camille, se défendit Patrick, en prenant la défense de ses deux sœurs et de son jeune frère.

— C'est vrai, reconnut Bernadette. Tes enfants ont été tranquilles, eux autres.

— En tout cas, t'en es tout de même pas morte, fit sa mère, occupée à touiller la soupe sur le poêle. Arrête de te lamenter pour rien.

— C'est correct, j'ai rien dit, reprit Bernadette en adressant un clin d'œil de connivence à ses quatre élèves qui la regardaient. Vous autres, les enfants, j'espère que vous trouvez que ça sent bon quand on entre ici.

L'institutrice obtint des « oui » enthousiastes qui firent sourire toutes les personnes présentes dans la cuisine.

— On a cuisiné toute la journée parce qu'on attend plein de monde pour souper, annonça Eugénie, occupée à dresser le couvert.

— Comment ça ? s'étonna Bernadette.

— On a invité toute la famille pour fêter un peu. On dansera pas, mais on s'ennuiera pas pour autant, lui expliqua sa mère. J'ai même invité Constant Aubé.

— Vous auriez pu m'en parler avant de faire ça, m'man, s'offusqua la jeune fille.

— Pourquoi ? Tu t'es chicanée avec lui ?

— Non, mais j'aurais aimé l'inviter moi-même, par exemple.

— T'auras pas à le faire, intervint Hubert, il m'a dit qu'il arriverait aussitôt après avoir soigné ses animaux.

— Je pense que nous autres aussi, on va aller faire notre train de bonne heure, déclara Donat en se levant.

Après le départ des deux hommes, Bernadette parla de ses élèves qui avaient l'intention de célébrer le Mardi gras en passant de porte en porte, déguisés, pour obtenir des friandises.

— Ça se fait aussi à Montréal, déclara Paddy en suspendant son manteau à un crochet près de la porte.

— Ça se fait à Montréal? répéta Eugénie, surprise.

— Il y a pas juste les enfants qui se déguisent à Mardi gras, poursuivit l'oncle de Liam. Il y a ben des adultes qui le font pour jouer des mauvais tours aux voisins et s'amuser.

— Nous autres, on n'a jamais fait ça, avoua Duncan en masquant mal ses regrets.

— C'est vrai, confirma son frère.

— Nous autres non plus, reconnut Bernadette, mais on aurait aimé ça.

— Ici, ça se faisait pas quand vous étiez jeunes, lui fit remarquer sa mère.

Camille était restée silencieuse durant cet échange entre ses enfants et sa sœur. Puis elle sembla prendre une décision.

— Au fond, m'man, il y a rien qui empêche les enfants de passer aujourd'hui. On pourrait prendre un peu de suie sur le poêle pour leur faire des moustaches et des barbes…

Marie tourna la tête vers les quatre jeunes dont les yeux s'étaient soudainement mis à briller et elle ne put résister à la tentation de leur faire plaisir.

— Pourquoi pas! Bedette, va me chercher la boîte de vieux linge dans l'armoire de la chambre jaune, en haut, et descends-la, commanda-t-elle à sa fille cadette. On va trouver quelque chose pour chacun.

— Moi, est-ce que je suis pas trop vieille pour faire ça? demanda Ann, mourant d'envie d'accompagner ses frères et sa jeune sœur.

— Pantoute, fit Camille en commençant à lui dessiner une magnifique moustache avec la suie recueillie sous le rond du poêle.

En moins de dix minutes, les quatre enfants, vêtus d'oripeaux et le visage grossièrement maquillé avec de la suie et un peu de poudre de riz, furent prêts à partir. Au moment de leur départ, Emma et sa famille entrèrent dans la maison en même temps que Constant Aubé, qui fit semblant d'avoir peur en voyant ceux que Marie appelait les «quêteux».

Immédiatement, la petite Flore voulut accompagner ses cousins.

— Tu vas y aller, toi aussi, lui promit Camille.

— Il commence à faire noir dehors, lui fit remarquer sa mère.

— Si ça peut vous rassurer, madame Beauchemin, je peux ben aller faire la tournée avec les enfants, proposa Constant.

— Tu serais pas mal fin de faire ça. Je serais moins inquiète. Je les trouve bien trop jeunes pour être sur le chemin à la noirceur.

— Le souper est prêt, m'man. Je peux y aller moi aussi, offrit Bernadette. On va faire juste une couple de voisins dans le rang avant de revenir.

Sa mère hésita un court moment avant d'accepter.

— Je vais aller vous rejoindre avec Flore dès qu'elle va être prête, promit Rémi.

Les enfants passèrent moins d'une heure à l'extérieur, mais ils s'amusèrent beaucoup des faux airs effrayés des gens qui leur ouvrirent leur porte. Quand ils revinrent à la maison, ils avaient fait ample provision de sucre à la crème, de bonbons aux patates et de fondants. Leur retour coïncida avec l'arrivée de Xavier et de Catherine Benoît.

— Ça aurait été ben plus utile qu'ils viennent me donner un coup de main à faire le train plutôt que de courir les chemins, fit Liam, mécontent, en voyant rentrer ses enfants, le visage maculé de suie.

— Ils vont passer leur vie à faire le train, le beau-frère, intervint Rémi. Mais ils vont être jeunes juste une fois.

Dès qu'elle eut retiré son manteau, Catherine s'approcha d'Emma en train de bercer la petite Marthe. Apparemment, elle ne semblait pas trop affectée par l'accueil assez peu chaleureux de la mère de son fiancé.

— Comment va ma filleule? demanda-t-elle à la mère.

— Une vraie soie, répondit Emma. Elle fait déjà ses nuits. On l'entend pas.

— Est-ce que je peux la bercer un peu?

— À ta guise, répondit Emma en quittant la chaise berçante qu'elle occupait.

Elle lui tendit l'enfant. Immédiatement, le visage de la fiancée de Xavier se transforma. Il exprimait un tel bonheur de serrer contre elle un enfant qu'il aurait fallu être aveugle pour ne pas le voir. Camille s'en rendit compte et fit signe à sa mère de regarder la scène. À son tour, son air s'adoucit lorsqu'elle vit la fille de Laura Benoît murmurer des mots tendres au bébé qu'elle berçait doucement.

— Elle va faire toute une mère, chuchota Emma à Eugénie et Camille qu'elle venait de rejoindre près des armoires.

Donat et Hubert furent les derniers à rentrer dans la maison et ils furent l'objet de quelques plaisanteries des invités déjà sur place.

— Sacrifice, les beaux-frères! s'exclama Rémi, avez-vous fait un somme dans la grange avant de rentrer. On vous attend depuis une éternité. Un peu plus, vous passiez sous la table.

— C'est le Blond qui nous a retardés, déclara Donat en cachant mal son inquiétude.

— Qu'est-ce qu'il a? intervint sa mère.

— Je le sais pas trop, il veut pas manger et il a pas l'air d'équerre pantoute.

— On lui a préparé un mélange de soufre et de mélasse pour le remettre d'aplomb, poursuivit Hubert. On verra ben comment il va demain matin.

Encore une fois, les hôtes durent faire deux tablées. Les femmes servirent d'abord les enfants qu'elles envoyèrent jouer ensuite dans la cuisine d'été après le repas. On avait allumé le poêle dans la pièce depuis le milieu de l'après-midi pour la rendre confortable.

Les cuisinières servirent aux invités une généreuse portion de bœuf et de pommes de terre après qu'ils eurent savouré un bol de soupe aux pois. Pour terminer, chacun eut droit à une grosse portion de gâteau.

Si le repas se prit dans un silence relatif, les langues se délièrent à la fin du dessert. Marie raconta aux siens une fête de Mardi gras organisée par ses beaux-parents la première année de son mariage. La veille, toute la parenté des environs était venue coucher dans la grande maison de Sainte-Monique et on avait commencé à manger et à boire dès le début de l'avant-midi. Après le souper, de nombreux voisins s'étaient joints à la fête et tout le monde avait dansé jusqu'aux petites heures du matin, pour le plus grand déplaisir du curé de l'époque.

— Si vous trouvez le curé Désilets sévère, vous autres, vous avez pas connu le curé Tremblay, affirma-t-elle aux gens réunis autour de la table. Vous auriez dû voir la crise qu'il a faite en chaire le lendemain quand on est allés recevoir les cendres. Il a obligé mon beau-père à se lever en pleine église pour le traiter de tous les noms et le menacer d'aller brûler en enfer pour avoir pas mis tout le monde dehors avant minuit. Pas nécessaire de vous dire que le père de mon mari était blanc comme un drap parce que tout le monde le regardait. Finalement, le curé Tremblay a obligé monsieur et madame Beauchemin à aller se confesser de ça.

— Blasphème ! il était pire que le curé Lanctôt, je crois ben, ne put s'empêcher de s'écrier Xavier. Moi, à leur place…

— T'aurais fait la même chose, mon garçon, le coupa sa mère. Dans ce temps-là, quand monsieur le curé parlait, t'avais intérêt à faire ce qu'il te disait.

— Moi, mon meilleur souvenir de Mardi gras, intervint Rémi Lafond en déposant sa tasse de thé vide, c'est quand mes deux frères ont pris un gros cruchon de bagosse de mon père et qu'on s'est retrouvés tous les trois dans la grange pour le vider.

— Puis? demanda Hubert, curieux.

— Ben, mon homme, on a été tellement malades, lui avoua son beau-frère, que mon père, pour nous punir, nous a laissés passer la nuit dans la grange. Mais on s'est ben amusés quand même.

À tour de rôle, chacun finit par raconter le Mardi gras dont il se souvenait avec le plus grand plaisir, même si toutes les femmes de la maison avaient entrepris de laver la vaisselle et de ranger la cuisine. Quand tout fut remis en ordre, Ann accepta de se charger d'amuser les plus jeunes. Les adultes, eux, constituèrent des équipes qui s'affrontèrent dans une partie de cartes endiablée. D'ailleurs, lors d'une main, Bernadette s'emporta contre Catherine, sa partenaire, qui venait de se faire ravir une levée sans réagir.

— Bondance, défends-toi! lui cria-t-elle, mécontente. Laisse-toi pas manger la laine sur le dos sous prétexte que c'est Xavier qui joue contre toi. Ce grand fanal-là est en train de nous battre.

— Laisse faire, j'ai une surprise pour lui, lui promit Catherine en cachant bien ses cartes.

En fait, fine joueuse, elle emporta la manche grâce aux deux atouts qui lui restaient.

Un peu avant onze heures, Camille déclara qu'il était temps de rentrer parce que les enfants devaient aller à l'école le lendemain matin et aussi parce que la maîtresse avait besoin de se reposer un peu si elle voulait avoir la patience de les endurer toute la journée.

— C'est vrai qu'il est pas mal tard, reconnut Xavier en levant les yeux vers l'horloge. La mère de Catherine va finir par penser que j'ai enlevé sa fille.

Tous les invités commencèrent à se lever. Pendant qu'Emma habillait chaudement son bébé, ses sœurs aidaient Joseph et Flore à s'emmitoufler.

— Je vous annonce tout de suite que je vais tous vous attendre pour le souper de Pâques, déclara Camille en endossant son manteau.

— Blasphème! tu fais tes invitations de bonne heure, ne put s'empêcher de dire Xavier. Le carême est même pas commencé.

— C'est pour être certaine que personne va accepter d'aller ailleurs que chez nous, à Pâques, précisa l'épouse de Liam.

Ce dernier se garda bien d'insister.

Ce soir-là, tout le monde se coucha très fatigué, mais satisfait de sa journée. Si Camille était heureuse d'avoir offert aux enfants de passer de porte en porte dans le rang, pour sa part, sa sœur Emma était contente d'avoir effectué sa première sortie depuis son accouchement.

Après le départ des invités, Donat s'habilla pour aller jeter un coup d'œil aux bâtiments et surtout pour vérifier l'état de son cheval. Il eut l'agréable surprise de constater que le Blond semblait beaucoup mieux et il rentra à la maison, rassuré.

Seule dans sa chambre, la veuve de Baptiste Beauchemin ne s'endormit pas avant d'avoir prié pour la petite Marthe. Son cœur de grand-mère avait souffert toute la soirée chaque fois qu'elle avait regardé la figure aux traits mongoloïdes du bébé. Elle aimait cette enfant autant que ses autres petits-enfants.

Chapitre 13

Le carême

Le lendemain, l'atmosphère avait changé du tout au tout dans la plupart des foyers de Saint-Bernard-Abbé. On était entré dans la longue période des sacrifices du carême.

Ce matin-là, Marie Beauchemin crut bon de rappeler aux siens de ne pas oublier de prendre une résolution qu'il leur faudrait tenir durant les quarante jours à venir.

— Ça, c'est le temps que j'haïs le plus dans l'année, fit Bernadette dans un souffle en tartinant sa rôtie avec de la confiture de fraises. Comme si l'hiver était pas déjà assez long…

— J'espère que votre promesse de carême va être assez difficile pour vous valoir des indulgences, poursuivit la mère en feignant de ne pas avoir entendu la remarque de sa fille cadette.

— Torrieu, m'man, je pense que si vous étiez un homme, vous feriez un ben bon curé! tenta de plaisanter Donat.

— Fais pas de farce avec ça, mon garçon. C'est le rôle d'une mère de voir à ce que tout un chacun dans sa maison soit un bon catholique. Moi, si vous voulez le savoir, j'ai promis de réciter à genoux mon chapelet tous les soirs pendant le carême.

— En plus de la prière? demanda Eugénie, surprise.

— Oui.

— Pauvre vous, vous allez bien avoir les genoux usés à l'os rendue à Pâques.

Cette remarque légère lui mérita un regard furieux de sa belle-mère.

— Et toi, Bedette, quelle résolution vas-tu prendre ? voulut savoir sa mère.

— J'y ai pas encore pensé, m'man, avoua l'institutrice en quittant la table pour se préparer à aller à l'école.

— Tu pourrais promettre de faire la vaisselle tous les soirs, lui suggéra Eugénie, avec un rien d'espoir dans la voix.

— Laisse faire, toi. Je suppose que pendant ce temps-là, t'aurais juste à te reposer.

Rabrouée, l'épouse de Donat se tut.

— Bon, m'man, je pense qu'on est tous assez vieux pour décider nous-mêmes de notre résolution de carême, vous pensez pas ? fit Hubert.

— Je veux bien te croire, mon garçon, mais en autant que vous en preniez une, laissa tomber sa mère, mécontente. Moi, j'avais espéré que ton frère et toi vous vous seriez privés de tabac durant le carême.

— Non, je promets pas ça ! ne put s'empêcher de dire Donat. L'année passée, c'était ma promesse et...

— T'as pas été endurable du carême, compléta Bernadette, sérieuse.

— En plein ça, reconnut son frère.

— En tout cas, comme chaque année, il va y avoir de la viande juste au souper, prévint Marie.

— Torrieu ! On va encore travailler le ventre vide toute la journée, déclara Donat.

— Il faut faire maigre, lui rappela sa mère. Déjà, on est chanceux de pouvoir manger de la viande un repas par jour parce que, normalement, ça devrait être maigre et jeûne jusqu'à Pâques.

— C'est drôle, mais j'ai l'impression qu'on va manger pas mal de binnes, dit Hubert sur un ton léger.

— Tu te trompes pas, mon frère, reconnut Donat. Mais oublie pas que m'man enlève le lard du chaudron avant de nous les servir.

—◆—

Chez les Connolly, plus loin dans le rang Saint-Jean, les résolutions de carême étaient aussi l'objet de la conversation autour de la table. Camille, en digne fille de sa mère, se préoccupait de ce que ses enfants adoptifs avaient décidé de promettre durant les prochains quarante jours.

— C'est quoi, cette affaire-là ? demanda Ann, qui n'avait apparemment jamais entendu parler de promesse de carême.

— Comment ! Votre père vous a jamais demandé de prendre une résolution au commencement du carême ? s'étonna Camille.

— Imagine-toi donc que j'avais ben d'autres choses à faire que ça, se défendit Liam, la mine renfrognée.

— J'en reviens pas, fit sa femme. Mais t'es un vrai petit païen !

Elle prit la peine d'expliquer aux quatre enfants assis autour de la table ce qu'était une résolution du carême ainsi que son but.

— Mais on est libres de promettre ce qu'on veut ? demanda Duncan, tout de même un peu inquiet d'avoir à s'imposer une obligation durant aussi longtemps que quarante jours.

— Oui, reconnut Camille, mais il faut pas que ce soit trop facile parce que tu vas perdre tout mérite. À cette heure, pensez à ce que vous allez promettre, ordonna-t-elle aux siens.

Durant quelques instants, le silence se fit autour de la table. Liam et son oncle ne disaient rien. Ils attendaient.

— Je promets de m'occuper de Rose tous les soirs pour l'aider à faire ses devoirs et ses leçons, déclara finalement Ann, sans la moindre hésitation.

— Moi, je vais faire mon lit tous les matins, affirma Duncan.

— Tu peux pas promettre ça, tu le fais déjà, comme tu fais ton ménage de chambre, lui rappela Camille. Qu'est-ce que tu dirais de remplir le coffre à bois tous les jours et sans chialer ?

— Ben, si je fais ça, il restera rien à faire à Patrick, plaida le garçon de dix ans.

— Inquiète-toi pas, ton frère va trouver quelque chose. Pas vrai, Patrick ?

— Je pourrais balayer la cuisine après le souper.

— C'est une bonne idée, approuva Camille. En plus, tu pourrais te charger d'aller chercher l'eau au puits.

— D'accord, fit-il, peu enthousiaste.

— Et toi, Rose ?

— Je voulais balayer, dit la petite fille de six ans.

— Ton frère le fait déjà, mais tu pourrais épousseter le salon, par exemple.

— C'est correct.

— Est-ce que je peux savoir maintenant ce que les hommes vont faire ? demanda Camille en se tournant vers son mari et son oncle. Moi, je mangerai pas de sucré durant tout le carême.

— Moi, à mon âge… commença Paddy en déposant sa tasse de thé sur la table.

— Justement, mon oncle, à votre âge, insista la maîtresse de maison sur un ton léger, il est important de vous préparer une belle place au ciel.

— Whow ! s'offusqua le petit homme bedonnant en devenant tout rouge. Es-tu en train de m'enterrer déjà ? J'ai pas pantoute l'intention de mourir demain matin.

— Je le sais, mon oncle, mais un petit sacrifice pendant le carême vous tuera pas.

— Je vais y penser, déclara le retraité sur un ton définitif.

— Et toi, Liam? demanda-t-elle à son mari qui venait d'allumer sa pipe après avoir essuyé un reste de sirop d'érable dans son assiette avec un morceau de pain.

— Moi, je travaille d'une étoile à l'autre, répondit sèchement son mari. J'ai pas de temps à perdre avec des promesses inutiles.

— C'est pas inutile, lui fit-elle remarquer, sévère. T'oublies que t'as à donner l'exemple à tes enfants.

— Calvaire! explosa-t-il. Est-ce que je pourrais au moins déjeuner tranquille le matin?

— Tiens! tu viens de la trouver ta résolution, répliqua-t-elle, peu impressionnée par sa saute d'humeur.

— Quoi?

— Pas sacrer devant les enfants durant tout le carême.

Liam prit le temps de jeter un regard à ses enfants qui le fixaient avant de dire :

— Je verrai ça.

~

Ce soir-là, un peu avant sept heures, la chapelle de Saint-Bernard-Abbé fut prise d'assaut par les fidèles impatients de recevoir les Cendres. Agénor Moreau avait allumé une demi-douzaine de lampes et les cierges de l'autel avant de s'occuper du poêle placé au fond du temple. Une heure auparavant, le vieil homme avait déneigé les marches du parvis. Depuis quelques minutes, les berlots et les *sleighs* ne cessaient d'arriver et les gens s'engouffraient à l'intérieur, heureux de trouver un peu de chaleur en cette avant-dernière soirée glaciale du mois de février.

Le curé Désilets, vêtu de ses habits sacerdotaux violets, apparut dans le chœur, encadré par deux servants de messe. La foule se leva et les murmures cessèrent. Avant de procéder à la bénédiction des Cendres, le prêtre expliqua qu'en recevant les Cendres chacun reconnaissait être un pécheur, et il rappela sur un ton apocalyptique que la mort pouvait survenir n'importe quand, comme un voleur. Il récita quelques prières, aspergea les Cendres en les bénissant puis commença l'imposition.

Les syndics virent à ce que les fidèles se placent en une seule file, sans bousculade, avant de venir s'agenouiller devant la sainte table où le prêtre déposait sur la tête de chacun une petite pincée de Cendres. Quand l'imposition eut pris fin, le célébrant retourna à l'autel et récita une dernière prière, non sans avoir insisté sur l'importance du jeûne comme moyen de purification durant le carême.

À la sortie de la chapelle, Angèle Cloutier se dirigea vers Samuel Ellis. Quand ce dernier vit la veuve approcher, il crut immédiatement qu'elle avait eu vent des plaisanteries d'Antonius Côté à son sujet et il se prépara à faire face à l'assaut.

— Si t'as le temps cette semaine, tu pourrais peut-être t'arrêter une minute à la maison, lui dit-elle, sans donner plus de précision.

— Si ça te dérange pas, je passerai demain après le souper, fit le président du conseil, soulagé de ne pas avoir à affronter la colère de la mégère.

Le lendemain soir, Samuel Ellis se prépara à aller chez la veuve, sitôt son souper terminé.

— Pour moi, elle veut discuter du prix du terrain que le conseil veut lui acheter, avait-il dit à sa femme avant de partir.

Dès son arrivée à la petite maison située au pied de la pente du rang Sainte-Ursule, Angèle le fit passer dans la cuisine où tout était soigneusement rangé.

— Ôte ton manteau et assois-toi, lui dit-elle en lui montrant l'un des deux grands bancs placés de chaque côté de la table.

Elle prit place en face de lui.

— J'ai bien réfléchi à ton offre, fit-elle. Je suis même allée en parler au notaire Letendre lundi après-midi.

Si elle s'était donné la peine d'aller à Sainte-Monique pour en parler au notaire, c'était un signe qu'elle était intéressée. Cette constatation réconforta l'Irlandais qui ne put empêcher un sourire d'illuminer sa figure. Angèle remarqua immédiatement sa réaction et se renfrogna un peu.

— C'est sûr que ton offre de soixante piastres pour trois arpents de bonne terre a bien fait rire le notaire, prit-elle soin de préciser.

— Bon, d'après lui, combien ça vaut? demanda le visiteur.

— Je le lui ai pas demandé, fit la veuve d'une voix tranchante. C'est pas lui qui vend, c'est moi.

— C'est correct, oublions les soixante piastres, consentit Samuel, apparemment plein de bonne volonté et prêt à négocier. Combien tu veux pour ton morceau de terre?

— Il me semble te l'avoir dit quand t'es venu avec le petit Beauchemin et Côté.

— Oui, t'as parlé de cent vingt piastres, mais tu sais ben qu'on n'a pas pantoute les moyens de te donner ça, laissa tomber le président du conseil.

— Tu l'as déjà dit.

— Fais-moi un prix plus raisonnable, Angèle, lui demanda-t-il sur un ton légèrement suppliant. Donne-nous une chance…

— Si je comprends bien, tu me demandes de faire un gros sacrifice, reprit la veuve.

— Ça nous aiderait ben gros. Tu le sais aussi ben que nous autres qu'on n'a pas d'argent et qu'on est endettés jusqu'au cou.

— Qu'est-ce que tu dirais si j'acceptais l'offre faite par le petit Beauchemin?

— Quelle offre? fit-il, feignant de ne pas s'en souvenir.

— Aïe, Samuel Ellis! fais-moi pas parler pour rien. Tu sais aussi bien que moi qu'il a parlé de quatre-vingt-dix piastres.

— C'est ben de l'argent, fit Samuel, l'air sombre.

— Je le sais que c'est ben de l'argent, reconnut-elle, mais c'est mon dernier prix. Déjà, je fais un gros sacrifice pour aider Saint-Bernard, m'en demande pas trop. Je te laisse jusqu'à vendredi de la semaine prochaine pour accepter. Si le contrat est pas signé vendredi, tu peux oublier ma terre. Je te vendrai rien. Est-ce que c'est clair ?

— C'est bien clair, accepta Ellis. Je vais réunir le conseil. Si tout le monde accepte, je vais revenir te voir avec le notaire pour signer le contrat.

— C'est correct comme ça, fit-elle en se levant pour lui signifier qu'elle n'avait plus rien à lui dire.

Samuel l'imita, mit son manteau et rentra chez lui.

🙣

Deux jours plus tard, le président des syndics convoqua une réunion extraordinaire du conseil après avoir mis le curé Désilets au courant de l'offre de la veuve Cloutier.

Quand les syndics apprirent qu'elle était prête à céder trois arpents de sa terre à droite de la chapelle pour la construction du presbytère et de certaines dépendances pour quatre-vingt-dix dollars, ils furent unanimes à s'en réjouir.

— Mais ça empêche pas que quatre-vingt-dix piastres pour trois arpents, c'est payer ce bout de terre là la peau et les os, ronchonna Anatole Blanchette.

— Elle en demandait cent vingt, lui fit remarquer Donat.

— Là, il est pas question d'essayer de la faire descendre plus bas, prit la peine de préciser le président. C'est son dernier prix et il faut que le contrat soit signé la semaine prochaine, sinon elle nous vendra rien pantoute.

— Il faut accepter, déclara Josaphat Désilets, qui n'avait rien dit depuis le début de la réunion. Le conseil peut emprunter ce montant-là sans problème puisqu'il a la garantie de monseigneur.

— C'est ben beau la garantie, monsieur le curé, mais il va falloir avoir les moyens de rembourser, par exemple, laissa tomber Côté, qui se méfiait de la propension du prêtre à endetter facilement la mission. Oubliez pas qu'on a encore et la chapelle et le jubé à payer à Bélisle. On n'a même pas encore payé le contrat du notaire Letendre pour le jubé, si je me trompe pas.

— Parlant de notaire, intervint le président, on va faire affaire avec le notaire Valiquette qui nous fera presque rien payer pour le contrat. Je vous l'ai dit qu'il est venu me voir pour me l'offrir.

Si Samuel continuait à éprouver de la méfiance envers le nouveau venu, son offre de rédiger les contrats à moitié prix lui semblait fort intéressante dans les circonstances.

— C'est ben beau d'avoir affaire à lui, mais qui est-ce qui va nous trouver l'argent? demanda Thomas Hyland. Si je me rappelle ben, tu m'as dit que Valiquette pratiquait plus. Je te rappelle que c'est Letendre qui nous a trouvé de l'argent pour financer la chapelle et le jubé.

— Je suppose que Valiquette est au courant et qu'il peut nous trouver l'argent qu'il faut, fit Samuel d'une voix pas trop assurée.

— Moi, en tout cas, j'ai pas trop confiance dans le bonhomme, déclara Donat. D'abord, on le connaît pas pantoute. Il vous a dit qu'il avait plus l'intention de s'occuper d'affaires et qu'il voulait se reposer… C'est drôle, mais j'ai entendu dire qu'il a commencé à offrir à du monde de Saint-Bernard de placer leur argent s'ils en avaient. Mon oncle Armand de Sainte-Monique a même appris qu'il était allé voir du monde de là-bas.

— C'est vrai ce qu'il dit, confirma Anatole Blanchette. Il est arrêté me voir samedi passé pour m'offrir de placer mon argent, si j'en avais.

— Je vois pas ce qu'il y a d'effrayant là-dedans, s'entêta Samuel Ellis. Il est notaire. Il y a rien qui l'empêche de faire ça. Au fond, on devrait être contents d'en avoir un à

Saint-Bernard. C'est pas mal plus pratique que d'avoir à courir à Sainte-Monique chaque fois qu'on en a besoin.

— En tout cas, mon père a toujours fait ses affaires avec le notaire Letendre et il a toujours été satisfait, déclara le jeune cultivateur du rang Saint-Jean. Moi, j'ai ben l'intention de continuer avec lui.

À la fin de la réunion, il fut entendu que le président du conseil allait rencontrer Eudore Valiquette et lui demander s'il pouvait trouver un prêteur et rédiger un contrat de vente pour la fin de la semaine suivante.

Quand les syndics croisèrent Ellis quelques jours plus tard, celui-ci leur apprit, la mine réjouie, que tout était réglé. Valiquette avait vite trouvé un créancier qui avait accepté de prêter à un intérêt de quatre pour cent et le contrat avait été rédigé et signé. Bref, la vente était conclue et il ne restait qu'à contacter l'architecte Bélisle de Saint-Zéphirin pour lui demander de tracer les plans d'un modeste presbytère, d'une remise et d'un petit bâtiment qui pourrait aussi bien servir d'étable que d'écurie.

— Je vais m'occuper de ça avant la fin du carême, promit le président du conseil. Là, j'ai demandé à Thomas d'écrire une lettre à monseigneur pour l'informer qu'on avait déjà acheté le terrain.

— Ce serait peut-être pas une mauvaise idée de savoir si Saint-Bernard va être une vraie paroisse avant de se lancer dans d'autres dépenses, lui fit remarquer Donat.

— Inquiète-toi pas. J'ai aussi demandé à Thomas de rappeler à monseigneur qu'on attendait toujours des nouvelles au sujet de notre demande de devenir une paroisse.

Chapitre 14

La chambre

Durant la plus grande partie du mois de mars, la vie à Saint-Bernard-Abbé sembla tomber dans une sorte de léthargie. On eut à subir deux tempêtes majeures qui laissèrent derrière elles près de deux pieds et demi de neige, et à aucun moment on n'eut l'impression de l'arrivée prochaine du printemps.

À la fin de la troisième semaine, Xavier Beauchemin et Antonin arrivèrent très tôt chez le meunier, devançant de quelques minutes Hubert, Donat et Rémi Lafond.

— Au moins, on n'aura pas à endurer du vent, déclara Donat en déposant sur son traîneau deux tarières et trois scies que son frère Xavier venait de lui tendre.

— C'est la première année où je coupe ma glace si tard, dit Donat, hors de propos. D'habitude, je fais toujours ça en février.

— Moi aussi, reconnut Xavier, mais cet hiver, on a eu tellement de mauvais temps...

— De toute façon, la glace est encore ben épaisse sur la rivière et il est pas trop tard, affirma Rémi. Et on est mieux de s'y mettre si on veut faire une bonne journée, ajouta-t-il.

— Pour moi, on va perdre ben du temps à pelleter la neige, déclara Antonin.

Le dimanche précédent, les frères Beauchemin et Rémi Lafond avaient convenu avec Constant de faire ensemble une corvée de coupe de glace sur la rivière.

— Et ce serait pas une mauvaise idée de faire ça proche de la roue de ton moulin de manière à ce que quand les glaces vont lâcher, elles l'arrachent pas, se crut obligé d'expliquer Xavier. C'est fort en maudit, les glaces. On se rappelle encore comment elles ont démoli le pont de Tancrède Bélanger il y a deux ans.

— C'est sûr que ça pourrait être ben utile de dégager la roue en coupant la glace autour, avait acquiescé le meunier. Si on fait ça, la semaine prochaine, je vais faire comme Hyland, en face, avec son moulin à bois. Il a toujours bâti une sorte de mur avec des billots en avant de sa roue pour faire dévier les glaces qui descendent le courant.

— Au fond, couper la glace proche de ta roue ou ailleurs, pour nous autres, c'est la même besogne, avait conclu Rémi avec bonne humeur. Pourvu qu'on se fasse notre provision de glace pour conserver notre viande, on demande pas plus.

— C'est dommage que Liam ait pas voulu venir, déplora Hubert.

— Il m'a dit qu'il aimait mieux finir de bûcher son bois avant de s'occuper de ça, dit Donat.

Ce matin-là, personne ne monta sur le traîneau tiré par le Blond. Les hommes, chaussés de raquettes, le firent descendre la pente douce qui conduisait à la rivière et ils l'entravèrent avant de s'emparer des pelles déposées sur le large traîneau en bois. Même s'il ne ventait pas, il faisait tout de même zéro.

— On a intérêt à se grouiller si on veut pas geler tout rond, déclara Rémi en enfonçant plus profondément sa tuque sur sa tête pour mieux couvrir ses oreilles.

— On est chanceux en blasphème ! s'exclama Xavier en constatant qu'il y avait moins d'un pied de neige qui couvrait la glace de la rivière près de la roue du moulin. Pour moi, le vent a soufflé fort depuis la dernière tempête pour qu'on n'ait pas plus à pelleter avant de rejoindre la glace.

En moins d'une demi-heure, les six hommes parvinrent à déneiger une importante portion de la rivière autour de l'énorme roue en bois du moulin. Constant Aubé s'empara de l'une des tarières et se mit en frais de percer la glace alors que Xavier faisait de même une vingtaine de pieds plus loin.

— Sacrifice! elle a au moins deux pieds d'épaisseur, déclara le meunier en retirant son outil qui venait d'atteindre l'eau sous la glace.

— C'est correct, fais un autre trou plus loin, suggéra Hubert en s'emparant de l'une des scies dont il glissa la lame dans le trou que Constant venait de forer.

En quelques minutes, les hommes constituèrent trois équipes de deux travailleurs qui scièrent en alternance. Dès que le premier bloc fut dégagé de la rivière, le travail devint beaucoup moins ardu. Tout en faisant bien attention de ne pas glisser dans l'eau glaciale, ils découpaient des blocs de deux à trois pieds de longueur qu'ils déposaient sur le traîneau en s'armant de pinces et de leviers.

Quand ils jugèrent que le traîneau était suffisamment chargé, Donat et Rémi décidèrent de faire escalader la faible pente de la rive au cheval pour transporter la première demi-douzaine de blocs.

— Comme on est chez vous, Constant, ces blocs-là sont pour toi, déclara Rémi. On va aller les porter dans un coin de ta grange. Tu t'organiseras toi-même pour les couvrir avec une bonne épaisseur de grain.

Le meunier fit signe qu'il avait compris et il poursuivit sa tâche avec les autres, demeurés sur place. Lorsque midi approcha, le second transport était prêt et destiné à Donat.

— Qu'est-ce que vous diriez de dîner avec moi? demanda Constant aux hommes avec qui il travaillait déjà depuis plusieurs heures.

— Les femmes doivent nous attendre, fit Rémi, indécis.

— J'ai fait chauffer un plein chaudron de binnes pendant toute la nuit, expliqua le meunier.

— C'est ce qu'on allait manger chez nous, intervint Hubert.

— Peut-être, répliqua Constant. Mais moi, je mets plein de jambon dans mes binnes. J'ai entendu dire par Bernadette que vous mangiez des binnes pas mal maigres par les temps qui courent, ajouta-t-il en riant.

— C'est pas vrai! s'exclama Rémi, la main sur le cœur. Ah ben là, t'as un client. Ma femme…

— Emma fait comme m'man, le coupa Donat. Elle a peur que tu manges de la viande le midi.

— En plein ça.

— Si ça te dérange pas, on va manger avec toi, déclara Hubert. Des bonnes binnes avec de la viande, c'est ce qu'il nous faut pour nous réchauffer le dedans.

— Nous autres, on pensait aller manger chez ma mère, dit Xavier en parlant de lui et de son jeune employé, mais je pense qu'on va plutôt aller goûter à tes binnes, nous aussi.

— En apportant la glace chez m'man, oublie pas de la prévenir qu'on reste à dîner chez Constant, recommanda Donat à Hubert qui avait décidé d'aller porter la glace dans leur grange en compagnie d'Antonin.

Les quatre hommes ne travaillèrent que quelques minutes après le départ du traîneau. D'un commun accord, ils décidèrent qu'ils avaient besoin de se réchauffer. Ils laissèrent leurs outils sur place, remirent leurs raquettes et traversèrent le champ jusqu'à la maison du meunier. Une odeur appétissante de fèves au lard flottait dans la cuisine.

Dès que ses invités eurent retiré leur manteau et leurs bottes, Constant leur servit un verre de bagosse.

— Ça, c'est pour vous réchauffer en attendant les deux autres.

On l'aida à dresser le couvert et Donat sortit chercher quelques brassées de bûches pour alimenter le poêle. Quand Hubert et Antonin arrivèrent, on passa à table. Après avoir déposé au centre de la table une grosse miche de pain, le maître de la maison servit une généreuse portion de fèves au lard à chacun en prenant soin de déposer dans chaque assiette un bon morceau de jambon.

— Mangez à votre faim, il en reste, les invita Constant.

— Calvinus! Veux-tu ben me dire qui t'a montré à cuisiner? demanda Rémi Lafond en se tapant sur la panse après avoir dévoré une seconde assiettée de fèves.

— Un peu tout le monde, répondit Constant. Ma mère est morte de bonne heure. Mon père, mes frères et, plus tard, mon grand-père m'ont montré à faire à manger. Il le fallait ben si on voulait pas mourir de faim.

— Joualvert, je trouve que t'as le tour en pas pour rire, fit Hubert.

— Parle pas trop vite, lui ordonna Constant en riant. J'ai juste un peu de crème et du sirop d'érable pour dessert.

— Ça va faire l'affaire, déclara Rémi. Chez nous, ma femme mange pas de sucré du carême et…

— Et naturellement, elle fait pas de dessert, le coupa Donat en riant. C'est la même chose chez nous.

Après une courte pause, les hommes reprirent leur travail sur la rivière et parvinrent, cet après-midi-là, à découper toute la glace dont ils auraient besoin pour conserver la viande quand la chaleur reviendrait. Rémi et Xavier rapportèrent chez eux une demi-douzaine de blocs, comme les autres.

Après leur départ, Constant prit la peine de planter des branches de sapinage autour du trou important fait sur la glace de la rivière pour éviter que quelqu'un ne tombe à l'eau en traversant. La probabilité d'un tel accident près de son moulin était plutôt faible, mais il ne voulait courir aucun risque.

Le lundi suivant, Marie finissait le lavage des vêtements quand elle aperçut sa bru pliée en deux, appuyée contre la table, le front couvert de sueur.

— Veux-tu bien me dire ce qui t'arrive encore ? lui demanda-t-elle en déposant son panier rempli de vêtements mouillés qu'elle s'apprêtait à aller étendre sur les cordes à linge tendues dans la cuisine d'été.

— Je le sais pas, madame Beauchemin, répondit la jeune femme sur un ton misérable.

Marie se méfiait. Elle connaissait assez bien la femme de Donat pour savoir qu'elle ne reculait habituellement devant rien pour pouvoir s'octroyer quelques heures de repos. Depuis le début de sa deuxième grossesse, il n'y avait guère eu de semaine sans qu'elle se soit plainte d'un malaise ou d'un autre.

— Bon, assois-toi un peu, ça va passer, lui ordonna-t-elle, un peu excédée.

Là-dessus, elle quitta la pièce et alla étendre le linge. Quand elle revint quelques minutes plus tard, Eugénie était assise dans une chaise berçante, le teint blafard et grimaçante.

— Je pense que j'ai des contractions, madame Beauchemin, haleta-t-elle.

— Ben voyons donc ! T'as juste trois mois de faits, protesta la veuve de Baptiste Beauchemin.

— Ça revient, se contenta de dire la jeune femme en se pliant en deux de douleur.

Soudain inquiète, Marie se décida à agir.

— Bouge pas de là, commanda-t-elle. Je vais aller avertir Donat. Il doit être en train de nettoyer l'étable.

Elle mit son manteau et sortit prévenir son fils. Ce dernier revint en courant à la maison.

— Arrête de bretter, fit sa mère, légèrement essoufflée, en entrant dans la maison derrière lui. Attelle et va chercher le docteur Samson. On sait jamais.

Son fils n'hésita pas un instant. Il sortit atteler la Noire à la *sleigh*, prévint Hubert et partit pour Saint-Zéphirin. Aussitôt après son départ, sa mère décida d'installer Eugénie dans son propre lit, dans sa chambre à coucher. Il n'était pas question de prendre le risque de faire monter la future maman à l'étage. Elle s'empressa de changer les draps et les taies d'oreiller avant d'aller chercher Eugénie pour l'aider à s'étendre.

— Reste tranquille, ça va finir par passer, conseilla-t-elle à la jeune femme avant de retourner dans la cuisine autant pour confectionner le dîner que pour surveiller le petit Alexis en train de s'amuser avec des blocs de bois.

Tout en préparant la soupe qu'elle avait l'intention de servir aux siens ce midi-là, elle songeait à sa bru étendue dans son lit.

— Je le savais donc qu'elle finirait par arriver à ses fins, la petite démone ! murmura-t-elle avec rage. Mais ça se passera pas comme ça ! Il y a personne qui va venir mener dans ma propre maison ! Il y a tout de même des limites.

Par ailleurs, en même temps que la maîtresse de maison se parlait, elle savait fort bien que son combat était perdu d'avance. Elle le savait depuis le jour où sa bru lui avait annoncé qu'elle attendait un deuxième enfant.

Jusque-là, elle avait farouchement résisté aux tentatives de Donat et de sa femme de s'approprier la chambre des maîtres située au rez-de-chaussée, au pied de l'escalier. C'était la plus grande chambre de la maison et elle lui revenait de droit. C'était là qu'elle avait mis au monde ses cinq enfants. Elle y dormait depuis plus de trente ans… Elle avait tellement de souvenirs rattachés à cette pièce qu'elle ne pouvait envisager le jour où elle en serait chassée.

Et pourtant, elle le savait, ce jour viendrait bientôt. Quand Eugénie aurait mis au monde son deuxième enfant, il allait être impossible, sinon inconvenant, que son fils, sa femme et les deux enfants s'entassent à l'étage, même avec la petite pièce libérée depuis le départ de Camille, alors qu'elle prendrait ses aises, seule, dans la plus grande chambre de la maison. Non ! Mais le fait de le savoir ne rendait pas le sacrifice moins pénible.

— La vie est donc mal faite ! dit-elle avec rage à mi-voix.

Elle se rendait compte tout à coup que son père avait probablement vécu la même chose après le décès de sa mère puisqu'il avait abandonné à son frère aîné et à sa femme la grande chambre du rez-de-chaussée de la vieille maison de Saint-Zéphirin.

— Pauvre p'pa ! Il a pas dû aimer ça plus que moi, murmura-t-elle en ayant une pensée attendrie pour le grand vieillard disparu plusieurs années auparavant.

Donat revint avec le docteur Samson un peu après l'heure du dîner. L'homme d'une quarantaine d'années, le visage rougi par le froid, retira son manteau et ses bottes après avoir salué Marie et Hubert qui s'étaient levés à son entrée.

— Il me semble que je viens souvent chez les Beauchemin depuis quelque temps, dit le praticien au visage glabre en s'emparant de sa trousse qu'il avait déposée à ses pieds.

— C'est pas pour le plaisir, docteur, lui fit remarquer Marie.

— Où est la malade ?

— Je l'ai installée dans ma chambre, expliqua la maîtresse de maison en lui indiquant la pièce voisine de la cuisine, dont la porte était ouverte.

— Bon, je vais aller l'examiner, déclara Eugène Samson en se dirigeant vers la chambre dont il referma la porte derrière lui.

Le médecin ne demeura que quelques minutes avec la patiente. Quand il sortit de la chambre de Marie, il retira son lorgnon et déposa sa trousse sur un banc. Donat, Hubert et leur mère attendaient avec une impatience mal déguisée son diagnostic.

— Énervez-vous pas, prit-il la précaution de dire, la petite dame est épuisée et elle a besoin de se reposer.

— Épuisée! s'étonna Marie. Pourtant, elle fait pas grand-chose dans la maison par les temps qui courent.

Eugénie avait dû parler au médecin des exigences de sa belle-mère parce que le praticien se fit beaucoup plus sévère quand il s'adressa à elle.

— Écoutez, madame Beauchemin, c'est pas toutes les femmes qui ont votre constitution. La femme de votre garçon est pas faite forte. Elle est capable de rendre son bébé à terme, mais en se ménageant.

— Si vous le dites, répliqua Marie, un peu sceptique.

— Là, je veux qu'elle reste au lit durant quinze jours.

— Deux semaines complètes? demanda Marie, interloquée.

— En plein ça, deux semaines. Et pour elle, il est pas question de jeûner ou de faire maigre, sauf le vendredi, bien sûr.

— J'ai porté cinq enfants, et ça m'a jamais empêchée de faire mon carême, protesta la maîtresse de maison.

— Vous, peut-être, mais votre bru est pas faite comme vous, madame Beauchemin. Je viens de vous le dire, riposta sèchement le médecin. À part ça, il vaudrait mieux qu'elle évite de monter et de descendre des escaliers. On sait jamais. S'il lui prenait un étourdissement et qu'elle perde l'équilibre…

— Seigneur! s'exclama Marie, qui n'en revenait pas.

— Inquiétez-vous pas, madame, tout va finir par se replacer si la jeune mère prend ces précautions-là et fait tout ce que je viens de vous dire, tint à préciser Eugène Samson en se méprenant sur le sens de l'exclamation de la quinquagénaire.

— On va y voir, docteur, promit Donat.

Après le départ du docteur, le jeune cultivateur prit la peine d'aller s'assurer que sa femme avait bien tout ce dont elle avait besoin, avant de retourner travailler avec son frère Hubert.

Le visage impassible, Marie alla retirer le linge sec étendu sur des cordes dans la cuisine d'été et entreprit de le plier. Ensuite, elle monta à l'étage autant pour laisser sur les lits de Bernadette et de Hubert leurs vêtements propres que pour changer les draps du lit de sa bru.

Quand Bernadette rentra à la fin de l'après-midi, cette dernière fut surprise de trouver sa mère seule dans la cuisine.

— Où est passée Eugénie ? demanda-t-elle.

— Dans ma chambre, se borna à lui répondre sa mère sans cesser de peler les pommes de terre qui allaient être servies au souper.

— Qu'est-ce qu'elle fait là ? s'étonna l'institutrice.

— Elle dort.

— Dans votre lit ? Ah ben, j'aurai tout vu, reprit la jeune fille, franchement stupéfaite.

— Elle est malade, poursuivit sa mère. Ton frère a dû aller chercher le docteur qui a décidé de la mettre au repos complet pour les deux prochaines semaines. Il a peur qu'elle perde son petit. Elle peut pas monter et descendre l'escalier.

— Pauvre vous ! la plaignit sincèrement Bernadette à mi-voix. Ça veut dire que vous allez être obligée de lui prêter votre chambre et…

— C'est ça, la coupa sa mère avec un rien d'agacement. Là, j'ai fini d'éplucher les patates. Tu vas venir m'aider à descendre le petit lit d'Alexis, et après ça on va monter mes affaires en haut et descendre les affaires de ta belle-sœur et de ton frère.

— Donat aurait pu s'en charger, quand même, protesta la jeune fille, fatiguée par sa journée d'enseignement.

— Il est aux bâtiments en train de soigner les animaux. Il a pas le temps de s'occuper de tout. Arrive qu'on en finisse, ajouta Marie sur un ton exaspéré.

Bernadette se rendit compte que ce n'était pas le temps de discuter avec sa mère. Elle la suivit à l'étage après avoir allumé une lampe parce que le soleil se couchait lentement. À leur entrée dans la chambre du rez-de-chaussée transportant avec quelque difficulté le petit lit d'Alexis, elles trouvèrent Eugénie confortablement adossée à deux oreillers en train d'amuser le garçon d'un an et demi.

— Vous êtes bien fines de descendre le lit du petit, fit la future maman.

— C'est normal qu'il dorme avec toi et Donat, répliqua Marie assez sèchement. S'il se réveille la nuit, vous pourrez vous en occuper.

— On est en train de vider vos tiroirs en haut. On va descendre toutes vos affaires, lui apprit Bernadette.

— Je vais t'apporter aussi tes oreillers parce que je veux reprendre les miens, poursuivit Marie. J'y suis habituée.

Quelques minutes suffirent pour descendre le contenu des quelques tiroirs et même échanger les couvertures.

— Il restera juste le gros coffre au pied de votre lit, en haut. Les hommes se chargeront de le descendre quand ils rentreront, déclara la maîtresse des lieux. Comme t'es là pour deux semaines, prit-elle soin d'ajouter, le visage fermé, c'est aussi bien que t'aies toutes tes affaires à portée de la main.

— Là, on a mis ça un peu n'importe comment dans les tiroirs, intervint Bernadette. Mais quand tu te sentiras mieux, tu pourras placer ça à ton goût.

— Merci, je suis mal à l'aise de vous donner autant de dérangements.

— C'est pas grave, dit sa jeune belle-sœur. Est-ce qu'on te laisse la porte de la chambre ouverte ? demanda-t-elle à l'alitée.

— Oui, ça va être plus chaud ici dedans.

De retour dans la cuisine, l'institutrice ne put s'empêcher de faire remarquer à sa mère :

— Je me demande bien comment elle et Donat vont faire avec un deuxième petit dans leur chambre en haut.

— Mêle-toi surtout pas de ça, la rembarra sa mère. Au lieu de te poser des questions inutiles, commence donc à mettre la table.

Au moment de se séparer pour la nuit, Marie ne manqua pas de rappeler à Donat que, puisqu'il dormait dans la grande chambre du rez-de-chaussée, il devrait se lever à deux ou trois reprises durant la nuit pour alimenter le poêle.

Cette nuit-là, elle se réveilla plusieurs fois, prête à aller jeter une bûche dans le poêle. Elle le faisait depuis si longtemps que c'était devenu un automatisme. Les oreilles aux aguets, elle guetta les bruits de la maison silencieuse jusqu'à ce qu'elle entende son fils aîné se lever pour accomplir le travail qu'elle avait fait durant les deux derniers hivers.

Dépaysée dans cette petite chambre, elle dormit mal, mettant son insomnie sur le compte d'une paillasse mal remplie. En fait, elle n'était pas habituée à ne pas voir son mobilier de chambre en chêne, cadeau de noces de ses parents. À son réveil, bien avant le lever du soleil, elle se pencha à la petite fenêtre pour découvrir qu'elle donnait sur les toits givrés de la ferme de Conrad Boudreau au loin.

Chapitre 15

De bonnes nouvelles

Au moment où on pensait ne jamais le voir arriver, le printemps fit une entrée timide dans la région à la fin du mois de mars. Quelques jours à peine après une grosse giboulée, la température s'adoucit sensiblement alors que la plupart des cultivateurs de la région travaillaient déjà à percer les érables pour planter des chalumeaux auxquels ils allaient suspendre des seaux destinés à recueillir l'eau d'érable. Il faisait encore froid la nuit, mais le soleil se mit à réchauffer suffisamment l'air durant la journée pour faire enfin couler les érables. Par ailleurs, on vit avec plaisir les piquets de clôture se dégager progressivement de leur gangue de neige.

— Pour moi, le beau temps est arrivé pour rester, déclara Xavier à sa fiancée ce samedi soir là. Le pied des arbres commence déjà à être cerné.

— Est-ce que tu vas faire du sirop? lui demanda Catherine en venant prendre place à ses côtés sur le canapé.

— Ben là, j'ai installé des chaudières, mais je suis pas sûr pantoute d'être capable d'en faire du bon, reconnut le jeune homme. Tu comprends, chez nous, c'est ma mère et Camille qui ont toujours fait bouillir. Nous autres, les hommes, on s'occupait du reste.

— Comment tu t'es débrouillé l'année passée?

— J'ai pas fait les sucres. Je suis allé donner un coup de main à Donat et il m'a donné une couple de gallons pour mes besoins.

— Mais cette année, il faudrait s'organiser autrement, lui fit-elle remarquer. Dans trois mois, on va être mariés et je vais avoir besoin de sirop pour cuisiner. Moi, j'irais bien faire bouillir, mais chez nous, ça a toujours été mon père et mon frère qui s'en sont toujours occupés.

— Ta mère ?

— Ma mère a jamais eu le don de faire du bon sirop, avoua Catherine. Elle se fiait à mon père.

— Écoute. Est-ce que tu pourrais pas demander à Cyprien de te montrer comment faire ? Après, tu pourrais venir faire bouillir dans notre cabane.

— Ce serait pas correct que je sois toute seule avec toi, lui dit-elle.

— Tu pourrais venir avec ta mère, si tu veux, si elle pense qu'Antonin fait pas un bon chaperon.

— Attends, je vais aller lui demander, fit-elle en se levant.

Catherine s'éclipsa un moment et revint quelques instants plus tard, la mine sombre.

— Il dit qu'il a pas de temps à perdre à me montrer ça, déclara-t-elle à voix basse.

— Toujours aussi de service, à ce que je vois, fit Xavier, sarcastique. Je vais me débrouiller autrement, ajouta-t-il sans trop savoir ce qu'il allait faire pour arriver à obtenir du bon sirop.

Ses relations avec son futur beau-frère et sa femme ne s'étaient vraiment pas améliorées, même s'il avait fait l'effort de leur tendre la main au jour de l'An. Ils étaient séparés par une antipathie naturelle que rien ne semblait en mesure de faire disparaître.

Le lendemain avant-midi, après la grand-messe, Xavier s'approcha des membres de sa famille en compagnie de sa fiancée pour les saluer, comme il le faisait pratiquement tous les dimanches. Laura Benoît avait signifié à son fils et à sa bru qu'ils pouvaient rentrer sans elle. Elle monterait dans le berlot de son futur gendre pour chaperonner le couple.

— Ça a tout l'air que cette année, on va avoir droit à une retraite, dit Marie après avoir salué Catherine et sa mère du bout des lèvres.

— Ça va nous rappeler des souvenirs de la vieille paroisse, poursuivit Camille.

— Pas tant que ça, la contredit sa sœur Emma. Au moins, à Sainte-Monique, on avait droit à un missionnaire qui venait prêcher. Cette année, c'est monsieur le curé qui va s'en occuper. Il va peut-être trouver ça dur de prêcher une retraite pour les femmes mariées, une pour les hommes, une pour les filles et une autre pour les gars de la paroisse.

— Je me demande pourquoi les deux premières vont durer trois soirs, tandis que celles pour les jeunes vont durer juste deux soirs, poursuivit Camille.

— Parce qu'on fait moins de péchés, cette affaire, plaisanta Hubert.

— En tout cas, moi, ce que je comprends pas, c'est pourquoi il fait pas comme le curé Ouellet, l'année passée, intervint Xavier. Lui, il nous avait dit qu'il y aurait pas de retraite à Saint-Bernard tant et aussi longtemps qu'on serait pas une paroisse.

— Il y avait aussi une autre bonne raison, ajouta Donat. On n'avait pas de place où faire coucher le prêtre qui serait venu prêcher.

— Moi, j'haïs ben ça d'avoir à m'habiller et à venir m'écraser sur un banc après une journée d'ouvrage, déclara Xavier.

— Voyons, Xavier, t'es plus un enfant, lui reprocha Catherine. Pâques s'en vient. C'est normal que tu te prépares à faire tes pâques. À part ça, ça dure juste trois soirs, du jeudi au samedi.

Cette remarque lui attira un signe d'approbation de sa future belle-mère.

— Ça fait rien, j'haïs ça quand même, riposta son fiancé.

— J'espère que tu feras un effet pour y aller, fit sa mère, sévère. Nous autres, les femmes, on ira.

Les femmes présentes l'approuvèrent bruyamment.

On se mit ensuite à parler de la saison des sucres puisque, la veille, on avait pu récolter la première eau de la saison.

— Ça coulait ben hier, dit Hubert. Chez vous ? demanda-t-il à son frère.

— Ça coulait aussi. Mais là, même si Antonin et moi, on s'est organisés pour faire bouillir dans notre ancienne cabane, sur le vieux poêle, j'ai un blasphème de problème.

— Lequel ?

— Je sais pas comment faire bouillir et Antonin est comme moi.

— J'irais bien t'aider, dit Bernadette, mais je fais l'école toute la journée.

— Catherine est ben prête à venir, mais il y a personne qui veut lui montrer comment on fait bouillir, reprit Xavier.

— J'aurais bien aimé être utile, fit Laura Benoît, mais c'est mon mari qui a toujours fait le sirop. J'ai pas la main.

Pendant un moment, les membres du petit groupe se turent, comme s'ils cherchaient une solution.

— Viens chez nous, finit par proposer Emma à Catherine. Moi, je suis prise à la maison avec la petite, mais Rémi est pas mal bon pour faire bouillir. Il va te montrer ça.

— Non, laisse faire, intervint Camille. Ce serait pas convenable. Viens donc passer la journée avec moi demain, tu vas voir que c'est pas compliqué pantoute. Après ça, tu vas être capable de faire du bon sirop. Oublie pas d'apporter tes raquettes.

— Si Xavier accepte de m'emmener chez vous demain et si tu penses que je te dérangerai pas, je vais y aller, c'est certain, accepta Catherine, reconnaissante.

Quand Camille apprit à Liam qu'elle avait proposé à Catherine de venir passer la journée avec elle le lendemain, ce dernier se renfrogna.

— J'aime pas trop l'idée qu'une fille comme ça vienne traîner chez nous, laissa-t-il tomber.

— Aïe, Liam Connolly ! s'emporta-t-elle. Catherine Benoît a pas la lèpre, que je sache.

— Ouais, mais calvaire on sait quelle sorte de fille c'est, par exemple ! dit-il en élevant la voix.

— Tu sacres encore en plein carême, lui fit-elle remarquer, sévère. Une chance qu'il y a une retraite qui s'en vient, ajouta-t-elle.

— Achale-moi pas avec ça et mêle-toi de tes maudites affaires, dit-il sèchement. En tout cas, arrange-toi pour que cette fille-là traîne pas plus longtemps que nécessaire à la maison, lui commanda-t-il.

Camille haussa les épaules. Depuis plus de deux semaines, son mari affichait une mauvaise humeur qui ne se démentait pas. Tout était sujet à ses critiques. La nourriture n'était pas assez chaude, les enfants perdaient leur temps à l'école, sa chemise du dimanche était mal repassée et, surtout, elle ne montrait pas assez d'empressement envers lui.

— Tu sauras qu'on n'attire pas les mouches avec du vinaigre, lui avait-elle dit la veille quand il s'était plaint de sa passivité au lit.

En fait, il n'y avait que son oncle qui échappait à ses critiques. Paddy Connolly était leur hôte depuis deux mois et demi. À aucun moment il n'avait offert un peu d'argent à titre de cadeau ou de pension. Il suivait la même routine chaque jour. En matinée, il lisait le journal. Après le dîner, il s'éclipsait durant deux bonnes heures pour sa sieste quotidienne avant d'aller pérorer au magasin général. Il rentrait à la maison à la fin de l'après-midi avec les enfants, soupait et allait se coucher tôt après avoir fumé l'un de ses cigares malodorants.

Camille avait supporté cet oncle par alliance durant tout l'hiver, mais elle cachait de moins en moins son impatience de le voir retourner chez lui à Montréal au début du printemps, comme il l'avait laissé entendre quand il s'était invité chez les Connolly en décembre.

— Le printemps est arrivé, bondance! avait-elle fait remarquer à son mari en se déshabillant ce soir-là avant de se mettre au lit. Est-ce que ton oncle est à la veille de partir?

— Il y a rien qui presse, avait laissé tomber Liam en se glissant sous les couvertures.

— On voit bien que c'est pas toi qui es obligé de le blanchir et de le nourrir. C'est moi qui l'ai dans les jambes du matin au soir. J'ai hâte aussi que les filles aient chacune leur chambre en haut. Ça fait des mois que ça dure, il y a tout de même des limites.

Tôt le lundi matin, Camille vit arriver son frère Xavier et Antonin en compagnie de Catherine. Les enfants venaient de partir pour l'école.

— T'es bien fine de me montrer à faire du sirop, déclara sa future belle-sœur.

— Tu vas voir, c'est pas sorcier pantoute, dit Camille en la faisant entrer dans la maison.

— À quelle heure est-ce que je dois revenir? demanda Xavier.

— Au milieu de l'après-midi, ça devrait faire l'affaire, répondit sa sœur.

Dès que son frère et son employé furent partis, Camille endossa son manteau. Normalement, elle aurait dû être en train de faire son lavage hebdomadaire, mais sa promesse d'aider Catherine l'avait obligée à bousculer son horaire.

— J'ai demandé à mon mari d'allumer le poêle dans la cabane avant d'aller chercher du bois. Il a ramassé pas mal d'eau à la fin de l'après-midi, hier. On va pouvoir faire bouillir. Mon oncle, votre dîner est dans le fourneau, dit-elle à Paddy en prenant un panier déposé sur la table. Essayez d'entretenir le poêle le temps qu'on va être parties.

— Inquiète-toi pas, se contenta de dire le petit homme en train de noter des choses dans un vieux cahier.

Les deux femmes sortirent et chaussèrent leurs raquettes. Même si on n'était qu'au début de l'avant-midi, l'air était étrangement doux et une petite brise de l'ouest charriait des effluves agréables. On n'en était pas encore au point de voir des îlots de terre noire dans les champs, mais si le temps doux se poursuivait, cela ne devrait pas trop tarder. De l'autre côté de la rivière, elles pouvaient voir la fumée sortant des cheminées.

Elles longèrent sans se presser les deux grands champs qui séparaient les bâtiments de la ferme du boisé au milieu duquel Liam avait construit une cabane rudimentaire en bois pourvue d'une unique petite fenêtre. À leur arrivée, les deux femmes retirèrent leurs raquettes qu'elles appuyèrent contre un mur.

Dès que Camille ouvrit la porte, elle fut accueillie par une agréable chaleur provenant du vieux poêle passablement rouillé installé contre l'un des murs. Elle déposa son panier sur une table bancale placée sous la fenêtre avant de déposer sur le poêle une énorme marmite. Avec l'aide de Catherine, elle remplit celle-ci avec l'eau d'érable recueillie la veille.

— On va attendre à cette heure que ça bouille et que ça réduise.

— Mon père disait toujours qu'il faut à peu près quarante gallons d'eau d'érable pour faire un gallon de bon sirop, dit Catherine.

— Pour moi, il était pas loin d'être dans le vrai. Viens dehors, on va aller voir s'il fait assez chaud pour que ça coule.

Elle entraîna la jeune femme à l'extérieur et elles firent une courte tournée des seaux pour voir si la sève coulait. C'était le cas. Elle coulait abondamment.

— D'ici midi, Liam va venir faire une tournée pour ramasser l'eau, annonça Camille quand elles rentrèrent dans la cabane pour jeter quelques bûches dans le poêle et vérifier le degré d'évaporation de l'eau en train de bouillir.

Avant l'heure du dîner, l'épouse de Liam Connolly avait eu le temps d'enseigner à la jeune fille tout ce qu'elle savait sur l'art de faire du bon sirop.

— On va même y goûter à midi, annonça-t-elle à la fiancée de son frère. J'ai apporté de la pâte à crêpe. On va manger ça avec notre sirop qu'on vient de faire.

Quand Liam rentra dans la cabane en portant une pleine barrique d'eau d'érable, Camille fit d'abord des crêpes avant de l'aider à remplir la marmite servant d'évaporateur. Elle dit ensuite à son invitée :

— À toi, à cette heure. Je te laisse faire.

Tous les trois mangèrent avec un bon appétit. Étrangement, Liam faisait une belle façon à sa future belle-sœur et il poussa même l'amabilité, ce midi-là, jusqu'à féliciter sa femme pour son sirop d'érable.

— C'est la première fois que je mange de ton sirop, lui dit-il. Il est meilleur que le mien.

Après le repas, il retourna à son travail en promettant de recueillir encore de l'eau d'érable avant d'aller soigner les animaux.

— Si la récolte vaut la peine, je vais rester le temps qu'il faudra pour faire bouillir, lui annonça sa femme. T'auras juste à prévenir Ann de faire le souper. Il y a du lard sur la table de la cuisine d'été.

Au milieu de l'après-midi, Camille et Catherine virent arriver Xavier et Antonin en raquettes.

— Liam nous a dit qu'on n'avait qu'à suivre vos pistes pour vous trouver, dit Xavier avec bonne humeur. Puis, comment ça s'est passé ? demanda-t-il à sa fiancée.

— Inquiète-toi pas pour elle, s'empressa de répondre Camille à la place de la jeune fille. Elle est capable de faire du bon sirop. Attends, je vais te faire goûter à celui qu'elle vient de faire.

Elle lui présenta un morceau de pain qu'il trempa dans une soucoupe où elle venait de verser une petite quantité de sirop blond. Xavier mangea la bouchée de pain en prenant l'air d'un connaisseur.

— Ouais, il est pas mal ! déclara-t-il, l'air pénétré.

— Espèce de grand fendant! feignit de s'emporter sa sœur. C'est tout juste capable de faire la différence entre de la mélasse et du sirop et ça vient prendre des grands airs.

L'éclat de rire d'Antonin fut communicatif.

— Il est ben bon, reconnut Xavier, redevenu sérieux. Je faisais ça juste pour t'étriver, dit-il à Catherine, heureuse. Demain, si t'es d'accord, tu pourras venir faire du sirop chez nous. Ta mère m'a dit qu'elle était pour venir avec toi. On n'aura pas besoin pantoute de ton frère, comme tu peux le voir.

Avant de partir, Catherine Benoît remercia chaleureusement Camille et lui promit une pinte de son premier sirop.

— J'espère qu'il sera pas trop mauvais, fit-elle avec un sourire.

— Je crains rien. Il va être bon, dit Camille pour la rassurer.

❧

Le surlendemain, le beau temps n'avait pas cessé et c'est sans grand enthousiasme que Donat entreprit de faire sa toilette le mercredi soir pour aller participer à la réunion statutaire du conseil des syndics à la sacristie.

— Torrieu! Il me semble qu'on pourrait ben laisser faire cette réunion-là quand il y a rien de spécial à discuter, maugréa-t-il en finissant de se raser devant le petit miroir de la cuisine. En plein temps des sucres! On pourrait faire bouillir une bonne partie de la soirée; mais non, on est pris pour aller au conseil.

— Si on avait encore en masse d'eau d'érable à faire bouillir, Hubert et moi, on serait capables de s'en occuper, lui fit remarquer sa mère. On n'aurait pas besoin de toi. Mais avec l'eau qui reste dans le baril, ça vaut pas la peine. On fera ça demain.

— Ça fait rien, poursuivit-il, de mauvaise humeur. Moi, quand j'ai rien de spécial, je fais pas de réunion pour rien pour la commission scolaire.

— Saint Donat, priez pour nous, se moqua Bernadette en train de préparer ses classes sur la table de la cuisine.

Le jeune cultivateur ne releva pas le sarcasme. Il se dirigea vers la chambre à coucher située au pied de l'escalier pour aller changer de vêtements. En quittant la pièce, il entraîna avec lui un Alexis récalcitrant.

— Je vous laisse le petit. Il empêche Eugénie de dormir.

— Ce serait peut-être mieux qu'elle se tienne réveillée une couple d'heures, fit sa mère, acide. Elle a dormi toute la journée. Pour moi, elle arrivera jamais à fermer l'œil la nuit prochaine.

— Viens voir ma tante Bedette, commanda l'institutrice au petit garçon en lui faisant signe de venir la rejoindre.

— Je serai pas parti longtemps, prévint Donat avant de sortir.

Quelques minutes plus tard, le fils de Baptiste Beauchemin retrouva les autres membres du conseil à la porte de la sacristie où Josaphat Désilets les fit entrer. Dès les premiers instants, Donat remarqua avec surprise l'air étrangement heureux de Samuel Ellis, de Thomas Hyland et même du curé de Saint-Bernard-Abbé.

— Qu'est-ce qui se passe ? chuchota-t-il à Anatole Blanchette et à Antonius Côté.

Ces derniers se contentèrent de hausser les épaules en signe d'ignorance. On s'assit autour de la grande table éclairée par une unique lampe et le prêtre récita la courte prière habituelle, face au crucifix suspendu au mur avant d'inviter les cinq hommes à s'asseoir. Thomas, Samuel et le curé Désilets affichaient un si large sourire que Donat demanda à haute voix si c'était indiscret de savoir ce qui les rendait de si bonne humeur.

— Une ben bonne nouvelle, déclara le président du conseil.

— C'est vrai, une ben bonne nouvelle, répéta Thomas Hyland, pourtant peu exubérant d'habitude.

— Bout de cierge! Est-ce qu'on va finir par savoir ce qui arrive? s'exclama Anatole Blanchette, réellement intrigué.

— On va laisser monsieur le curé l'annoncer, fit Samuel en invitant le prêtre à parler.

— On a reçu lundi une lettre de monseigneur, précisa Josaphat Désilets sur un ton théâtral. Le 15 mai prochain, Saint-Bernard va devenir officiellement une paroisse du diocèse. Il va venir lui-même procéder à l'érection canonique de Saint-Bernard-Abbé.

— C'est pas vrai! s'écria Antonius Côté, ravi.

— Il était temps, conclut Donat, aussi content que le prêtre et ses confrères. Enfin, on sait qu'on n'a pas fait bâtir cette chapelle-là pour rien, et surtout qu'on n'a pas acheté inutilement un autre terrain à madame Cloutier.

— Viens-tu de nous dire que tu connais la nouvelle depuis lundi et que t'as pas trouvé le moyen de nous avertir avant à soir? demanda un Anatole Blanchette furieux au président du conseil.

— Whow, Anatole! Je peux pas passer mon temps sur le chemin, se défendit Samuel. Oublie pas que moi aussi, je fais les sucres.

— Ça fait rien, t'aurais dû trouver le moyen de nous faire savoir ça, s'entêta le gros homme.

— La nouvelle est pas sortie du village, fit l'Irlandais, parce qu'on a pensé que c'était à monsieur le curé que revenait l'honneur de l'annoncer à tout le monde dimanche prochain, en chaire. Il paraît même qu'il doit le faire deux dimanches d'affilée, en anglais et en français.

— De quel village vous parlez? demanda Donat, l'air mauvais.

— On va pas recommencer, s'interposa Thomas qui se rappelait encore trop bien les prises de bec mémorables entre Baptiste Beauchemin et Samuel Ellis à ce propos. On est encore juste une mission. Quand on sera une vraie paroisse, il sera toujours temps de savoir où se trouve le village.

Samuel Ellis eut un petit sourire déplaisant qui fit serrer les poings à Donat.

— Il y avait pas juste une bonne nouvelle dans la lettre envoyée par monseigneur, rappela Thomas qui avait dû lire la missive à son voisin Ellis parce que ce dernier ne savait pas lire.

— C'est vrai, reconnut le président, l'air soudain assombri.

— Passe-moi la lettre, Samuel. Je vais finir de la lire aux autres.

— C'est inutile, intervint Josaphat Désilets en chaussant ses petites lunettes rondes et en tirant deux feuilles de papier d'une enveloppe déposée devant lui. Je vais le faire.

«*Selon le rapport remis par l'abbé Desmeules, quatorze francs-tenanciers de Saint-Bernard-Abbé ont demandé à retourner à leur paroisse d'origine. À leur avis, la distance pour se rendre à la chapelle de la mission est beaucoup plus longue que celle les séparant de leur église paroissiale. Par conséquent, les limites de la nouvelle paroisse ont été ramenées de manière à exclure ces familles.*»

— Sur la deuxième feuille, le nom des familles qui ont demandé à retourner à Sainte-Monique et à Saint-Zéphirin et les nouvelles bornes de Saint-Bernard-Abbé sont indiqués, ajouta Josaphat Désilets avant de replier la lettre.

— C'est fin en bout de cierge, cette affaire-là ! explosa Anatole. Quatorze familles de moins pour nous aider à payer les dettes qu'on s'est mises sur le dos !

— Et celles qu'on va ajouter ce printemps, poursuivit Côté, tout aussi secoué que son confrère.

— Faut se mettre à leur place, intervint Donat. Ces gens-là auraient été ben bêtes de rester avec nous autres si notre chapelle est plus loin que leur église. En plus, pourquoi venir s'endetter quand Sainte-Monique et Saint-Zéphirin sont des vieilles paroisses qui doivent probablement plus rien ?

— Ça fait rien, s'entêta Blanchette. Moi, je serais d'avis d'aller les voir pour essayer de les faire changer d'idée.

— Ce serait perdre son temps, laissa tomber le président. À cette heure qu'ils ont demandé officiellement à retourner dans leur paroisse, ils changeront pas d'idée pour nos beaux yeux.

— Il vaut mieux laisser faire, déclara le curé Désilets.

— Malgré tout ça, on a reçu la nouvelle qu'on attendait depuis des mois, reprit Samuel Ellis, et ça veut dire qu'il va falloir arrêter de bretter pour le presbytère. Là, avant tout, on va tous promettre de pas dire un mot de tout ça jusqu'à ce que monsieur le curé l'annonce, dimanche prochain.

Tous promirent et un sourire de contentement illumina le visage du prêtre, qui alluma sa pipe sans se presser.

— Avant la prochaine réunion, je vais essayer de trouver le temps d'aller voir Bélisle pour qu'il nous fasse les plans d'un presbytère, annonça Ellis.

— Et d'une bonne remise et d'un bâtiment qui pourra me servir d'étable et d'écurie, prit soin d'ajouter Josaphat Désilets.

— Calvince ! ça va nous coûter la peau des fesses, tout ça, ne put s'empêcher de s'exclamer Antonius Côté.

— Pas nécessairement, voulut le rassurer Thomas Hyland.

— J'ai une idée, intervint Donat. Est-ce qu'un presbytère de trente pieds par vingt-six pieds sur deux étages, avec une remise et une étable feraient pas l'affaire ?

— Voyons donc! protesta sèchement le curé de Saint-Bernard-Abbé, un presbytère comme ça serait bien trop petit.

— Comment ça, monsieur le curé? s'étonna le jeune homme.

— Tu oublies, mon jeune ami, qu'un presbytère, c'est pas seulement l'endroit où vit le curé de la paroisse. C'est aussi là où se font les réunions. Il y a des prêtres visiteurs. Un curé est même souvent obligé d'héberger des vicaires ou même des missionnaires venus prêcher une retraite. En plus, il a besoin d'un bureau pour recevoir les paroissiens qui veulent le rencontrer.

— Je comprends ben ça, monsieur le curé, mais un presbytère de cette grandeur-là devrait ben faire l'affaire. Après tout, normalement il y aura de la place pour quatre chambres en haut et, en bas, vous pourriez avoir une cuisine, un salon, un bureau et une petite salle de réunion.

— Je le penserais pas, fit sèchement Josaphat Désilets, mécontent.

— Vous connaissez tous la maison de Constant Aubé dans Saint-Jean? demanda Donat en s'adressant aux autres membres du conseil. Ben, si je me trompe pas, il me semble qu'il m'a dit que la maison que lui a construite Bélisle le printemps passé a ces dimensions-là. En plus, il lui a bâti une remise et un bâtiment qui lui sert aussi ben d'étable que d'écurie. Au fond, notre meunier a fait construire exactement ce qui nous conviendrait.

— Mais c'est tellement petit que c'est pas digne d'un presbytère, s'entêta le prêtre.

— Voyons, monsieur le curé, vous allez vivre tout seul là-dedans. Vous viendrez pas nous faire croire que c'est trop petit. Vous allez peut-être avoir la visite d'un ou deux prêtres de temps en temps, mais vous allez quand même avoir en masse de la place pour loger ce monde-là. Oubliez pas qu'il va falloir le chauffer, ce presbytère-là. Si on fait construire trop grand, vous allez geler l'hiver et vous serez pas plus avancé que vous l'êtes aujourd'hui. Ça va être comme ici, dans la sacristie.

— Je suppose, en plus, qu'il va être en brique et non en pierre? fit le curé en se gourmant.

— À mon avis, ni l'un ni l'autre, monsieur le curé, répondit Donat sans se donner la peine de consulter les autres membres du conseil. Il me semble qu'il devrait être en bois, comme la chapelle. Le monde de Saint-Bernard pourrait trouver drôle que notre curé reste dans une maison qui a l'air plus riche que la maison du bon Dieu.

Comme les hommes autour de la table paraissaient approuver ouvertement la proposition du cadet du conseil, Josaphat Désilets n'osa pas poursuivre. Il se borna à jeter un regard venimeux au fils de Baptiste Beauchemin.

— On pourrait même économiser un peu d'argent, continua Donat, rassuré de voir l'appui dont il bénéficiait et peu impressionné par l'air buté du prêtre assis au bout de la table.

— Comment ça? lui demanda le président du conseil.

— Ben, Bélisle aura pas à faire de plans parce qu'on va lui demander de nous construire la même chose qu'à Aubé.

— Il fréquente ta sœur, intervint Antonius. Est-ce que tu pourrais pas lui demander ce que ça lui a coûté?

— J'ai pas besoin de lui demander, je le sais déjà, affirma Donat. Bélisle lui a chargé sept cents piastres.

— Bout de cierge! s'écria Blanchette. C'est de l'argent en maudit.

— C'est vrai, mais il faut pas oublier que c'est pour trois bâtiments, lui fit remarquer Donat.

— C'est pas mal d'argent, dit Côté, l'air préoccupé.

— Quand monsieur Ellis va aller voir Bélisle, peut-être qu'il va accepter de nous charger un peu moins cher quand il va savoir que c'est pour la paroisse et qu'il a pas de plans à dessiner.

— As-tu noté les mesures, Thomas? demanda Samuel à Hyland. Je vais aller le voir aussitôt que je vais en avoir le temps.

— S'il pouvait construire pour un peu moins cher, on pourrait envisager de se payer une cloche et peut-être même un chemin de croix dans la chapelle, ajouta le curé de la paroisse avec un rien d'espoir dans la voix.

— Sacrifice, monsieur le curé, je pense ben que vous êtes plus dépensier que ma femme! plaisanta Antonius Côté.

— J'ai ben peur qu'avant que monseigneur accepte que la fabrique dépense pour commander une cloche ou un chemin de croix, mes poules vont avoir des dents, conclut Samuel. Oubliez pas, monsieur le curé, que Bélisle est un ben bon homme, mais on le paiera pas avec des prières. Après être allé le voir, il va falloir que j'aille rencontrer le notaire Valiquette pour savoir s'il peut nous trouver encore de l'argent pour payer tout ça. Il y a rien qui dit qu'il va y arriver.

Quand les membres du conseil se séparèrent ce soir-là dans le stationnement de la chapelle, ils étaient soulagés. Saint-Bernard-Abbé allait devenir une vraie paroisse et ils s'étaient entendus pour brider un peu la folie des grandeurs de leur pasteur. Il aurait son presbytère et ses deux autres bâtiments, mais ils allaient avoir des dimensions raisonnables.

— Moi, je serais ben curieux de savoir quelle résolution notre curé a prise pour le carême, fit Antonius Côté, hors de propos, avant de monter dans la *sleigh* de Donat.

— Je pense que t'es mieux de pas aller lui poser la question à soir, mon Antonius, lui répondit son voisin en mettant son cheval en marche. J'ai comme l'impression qu'il nous a pas pantoute en odeur de sainteté.

— Parle pour toi, rétorqua Côté en riant. Je suis sûr qu'il est pas prêt de te pardonner le petit presbytère qu'on va lui faire construire. Quand on est partis, il faisait une vraie face de carême.

— Ça tombe ben, on est en plein dedans, se borna à dire le conducteur de la *sleigh*.

~

Le lendemain, à la fin de l'après-midi, le vent changea de direction et se mit à souffler en provenance du nord, poussant devant lui de lourds nuages.

— On n'a pas trop à s'en faire pour la nuit prochaine, déclara Liam en pénétrant dans la maison après avoir soigné ses animaux. Ça va geler encore et demain, avec le soleil, les érables vont couler.

— Tant mieux, fit Camille en train de découper un rôti de bœuf pour le souper. On est déjà rendus à une douzaine de gallons de sirop.

Liam allait rejoindre son oncle assis près du poêle pour attendre le souper quand sa femme se tourna vers lui.

— Dis donc, j'ai pas vu de fumée sortir de la cheminée de la cabane à sucre des voisins. Ils font pas les sucres, eux autres?

— Éloi Provost? Ben oui, je l'ai encore aperçu aujourd'hui, répondit son mari en allumant sa pipe.

— Non, les Paquette.

— Cléomène Paquette? Ça me surprendrait pas. Il doit rester chez eux, ben au chaud, à s'inventer une raison pour pas les avoir faits. Je te gagerais qu'on va le voir arriver avant la fin de la semaine prochaine pour quêter un gallon de sirop en prenant un air miséreux. Il fait ça une année sur deux.

— C'est drôle, il est souvent venu quêter du tabac à mon père, mais jamais du sirop, répliqua-t-elle.

— Si ça vous intéresse, il a passé une partie de l'après-midi au magasin général, intervint Paddy en éteignant son mégot de cigare après avoir craché dans le crachoir placé à gauche de sa chaise berçante.

— En tout cas, cette année, mon oncle, je vais avoir une surprise pour lui. Je vais lui en donner un gallon.

Deux jours auparavant, Liam Connolly avait profité du fait que sa femme avait quitté la cabane à sucre un peu plus tôt que d'habitude pour prélever un gallon d'eau d'érable à demi réduit. De retour à la maison, il y avait ajouté deux grandes cuillérées de mélasse et un demi-verre d'eau dans lequel avait trempé un peu de son tabac à pipe. Le tout avait été brassé de manière à ce que le mélange un peu brunâtre ait la consistance du sirop.

— Tu vas lui donner un gallon complet de sirop? demanda Camille, surprise de le voir soudain aussi généreux.

— Beau dommage! dit-il, la mine réjouie.

La jeune femme aurait bien eu envie de lui dire que ce don ne ferait qu'encourager la paresse bien connue de leur voisin, mais elle s'en garda, ne voulant pas lui ôter le mérite d'un acte aussi charitable.

Ce soir-là, la plupart des femmes de Saint-Bernard-Abbé se présentèrent à la chapelle malgré le froid pour assister au début de la retraite que le curé Désilets allait prêcher. Entassées dans les premiers bancs de la chapelle, elles eurent droit à un véritable sermon d'une sévérité exemplaire.

Durant deux longues heures, leur pasteur les menaça des flammes de l'enfer si elles ne remplissaient pas convenablement leurs devoirs de mère chrétienne et d'épouse. Il insista lourdement sur l'acte de chair qui ne devait être fait qu'en vue de donner naissance et il les encouragea à sanctifier tout cela en y prenant le moins de plaisir possible. Puis il passa aux pensées impures et à leurs effets pernicieux pour la pureté de l'âme. Il termina en leur rappelant leur responsabilité du respect de la religion et de ses prêtres dans leurs foyers respectifs.

À leur sortie de la chapelle, certaines femmes ne purent s'empêcher de commenter à voix basse ce qu'elles venaient d'entendre.

— Sainte Vierge! s'exclama Angèle Cloutier en s'adressant à Alexandrine Dionne et à la femme de Tancrède

Bélanger, je pense que notre curé est encore plus sévère que le curé Lanctôt.

— Les plaisirs de la couchette! chuchota Maria Bélanger, mariée depuis près de quarante ans. Pauvre homme! S'il savait…

— Parlez-moi pas de ça, moi, je suis une veuve et je me souviens plus de rien, déclara Angèle en riant.

— En tout cas, j'ai l'impression que la retraite va être longue, intervint Alexandrine.

— T'es pas obligée d'y aller les trois soirs, lui fit remarquer sa voisine.

— Si je fais ça, Télesphore va en profiter pour se servir de ça comme excuse pour pas y aller.

Étrangement, Camille disait la même chose à sa mère alors qu'elle la ramenait chez elle.

— J'espère juste que la retraite qu'il a l'intention de faire pour les jeunes au commencement de la semaine sainte ressemblera pas à celle d'aujourd'hui, poursuivit-elle quand elle se rendit compte que sa mère ne se décidait pas à critiquer le curé Désilets. Si c'est du même genre que ce qu'on a entendu à soir, Bedette va ruer dans le bacul, c'est certain.

— Elle ruera, se contenta de lui dire sa mère. Ça va lui faire du bien de se faire brasser un peu. Je trouve qu'elle a la vie pas mal facile depuis un bout de temps.

— Monsieur le curé va sûrement parler aux jeunes de leurs fréquentations, ajouta Camille.

— Là aussi, ça lui fera pas de tort. Avec elle, il y a pas moyen de savoir si c'est sérieux ou pas avec le petit Aubé. Il y a des fois que je me demande s'il se découragera pas de venir veiller avec elle et s'il choisira pas une fille plus sage.

Cette semaine-là, il n'y eut guère de surprise. Le curé Désilets fut égal à lui-même et sa dernière prédication fut aussi sévère que la première. Cependant, le dimanche matin, la joie des habitants de Saint-Bernard-Abbé faisait plaisir à voir quand il leur annonça que le 15 mai suivant la mission allait devenir une véritable paroisse et que déjà les syndics planifiaient la construction du futur presbytère. Inutile de mentionner que les discussions étaient joyeuses à la fin du salut au Saint-Sacrement, à la sortie de la chapelle.

— On doit aller dire deux mots à monsieur le curé, annonça Donat à son frère, sa sœur et sa mère. Ça devrait pas être long.

— Fais ça vite, lui dit Bernadette. Il est déjà passé midi.

Dès que le célébrant se retrouva dans la sacristie, les membres du conseil vinrent le rejoindre, ce qui l'étonna passablement.

— Qu'est-ce qui se passe? demanda le curé en commençant à retirer ses vêtements sacerdotaux.

— C'est moi qui ai demandé aux autres de venir, monsieur le curé, répondit Samuel Ellis. Je voulais juste vous dire que je suis allé voir Bélisle, à Saint-Zéphirin, hier avant-midi.

— Puis? demanda Donat.

— Il a rien contre l'idée de bâtir un presbytère et des bâtiments comme ceux qu'il a construits chez Aubé.

— C'est parfait, déclara Blanchette.

— Il y a juste le prix qui accroche, poursuivit le président du conseil comme s'il ne l'avait pas entendu.

— Vous lui avez rappelé qu'il avait fait la besogne pour sept cents piastres pour le meunier? demanda Donat.

— Certain, mais il m'a répondu qu'il pouvait pas nous faire ça en bas de sept cent vingt piastres.

— Pourquoi? demanda le curé Désilets.

— Il paraît que Constant Aubé l'a payé comptant avant même de commencer les travaux et, en plus, Saint-Bernard lui doit déjà pas mal d'argent. Il dit qu'il peut vraiment pas faire mieux.

— Bon, qu'est-ce qu'on fait? dit Hyland.

— En revenant, je me suis arrêté chez le notaire Valiquette, dans Saint-Paul.

— Puis?

— Une bonne nouvelle. Le notaire peut emprunter pour nous autres non seulement les sept cents piastres, mais tout ce qu'on doit déjà à Bélisle de façon à ce que la paroisse ait une seule dette à la même place.

— Les intérêts? demanda Hyland.

— Cinq pour cent.

— Crédié! s'exclama Côté. C'est ben haut.

— Il m'a expliqué que c'est parce que le montant est gros, répondit Samuel. Il paraît que les risques sont plus importants, même si Saint-Bernard est une paroisse.

— Est-ce que vous pensez, monsieur le curé, que monseigneur va accepter une affaire comme ça? demanda Anatole Blanchette au prêtre. Après tout, c'est lui qui garantit.

— Je le sais pas, avoua Josaphat Désilets.

— D'après le notaire, le diocèse acceptera pas un prêt à cinq pour cent, poursuivit le président du conseil.

— Ben, à ce moment-là, pourquoi il le propose? demanda Côté, qui ne comprenait plus rien.

— Le notaire va emprunter un peu plus que ce qui est nécessaire et il va se servir de cet argent-là pour payer le un pour cent de plus que d'habitude. Officiellement, dans les papiers, ça va être quatre pour cent, mais en réalité, ça va être cinq pour cent.

— Moi, j'aime pas ben gros des affaires comme ça, laissa tomber Donat. C'est pas clair et ça a pas l'air trop honnête.

— Il y a rien de malhonnête dans ça, s'insurgea Ellis. C'est juste une façon de faire accepter notre emprunt par monseigneur.

Chacun sembla s'abîmer dans une profonde réflexion jusqu'à ce que le président du conseil reprenne la parole.

— Comme on est tous là et que ça servirait à rien de tourner autour du pot pendant des jours et des jours, je suggère qu'on vote là-dessus. Si on vote contre, je vois pas comment on peut faire construire un presbytère. Oubliez pas qu'on peut faire confiance au notaire Valiquette. Il nous a trouvé de l'argent pour le terrain et il nous a fait un contrat à la moitié du prix demandé par le notaire Legendre, d'habitude. Il dit qu'il va faire la même chose pour le contrat à passer avec Bélisle.

Le vote fut pris à main levée. Tous levèrent la main, sauf Donat qui ne parvenait pas à faire confiance à ce notaire. Le seul qui sembla hésiter fut le curé Désilets. Le prêtre, soucieux, mit quelques secondes avant de lever la main à son tour.

— Bon, Thomas, quand t'écriras le rapport de notre réunion dans le cahier, t'oublieras pas de mentionner que Donat Beauchemin a voté contre, tint à préciser Ellis à celui qui servait de secrétaire au conseil. Si le notaire parvient à nous avoir cet argent-là, ça veut dire que Bélisle aura pas le choix de baisser son prix parce qu'on va lui avoir remboursé tout ce que Saint-Bernard lui doit.

Chapitre 16

Un peu de sirop

La semaine suivante, plus d'une femme mariée de Saint-Bernard-Abbé dut harceler son mari pour qu'il assiste aux prédications du curé Désilets prévues pour les trois premiers soirs de la semaine.

— Ça va durer juste trois soirs, avait plaidé Camille auprès de Liam. C'est pas la fin du monde.

— J'ai pas le temps. On est en plein dans le temps des sucres, répliqua-t-il, agacé par son insistance.

— Je vais m'arranger pour faire bouillir avant le souper. Si tu y vas pas, tu peux être certain que monsieur le curé va s'apercevoir que t'es pas là et, tu le connais, tu vas en entendre parler longtemps.

— Calvaire! explosa son mari.

— T'as promis de pas sacrer, lui rappela Camille, sévère.

— Toi, lâche-moi et occupe-toi du souper, lui ordonna-t-il. Comme si le curé avait des conseils à donner aux hommes mariés, maudit cal…

— Liam! le prévint sa femme en lui montrant de la main ses enfants qui écoutaient. Moi, je peux te dire que tu pourrais peut-être faire ton profit de ce qu'il va dire.

— Ben sûr! Toi, t'es comme ta sainte mère, rétorqua-t-il, sarcastique. S'il y avait moyen, tu passerais ta vie à genoux à l'église…

— Et vous, mon oncle, j'espère que vous irez avec votre neveu, reprit Camille qui ne désarmait pas. Je pense que ça va vous faire du bien à vous aussi.

— J'haïrais pas ça, déclara Paddy à la plus grande surprise de sa nièce par alliance. Mais t'oublies, ma nièce, que je peux pas aller là. J'ai jamais été marié.

— Est-ce que ça veut dire que vous êtes prêt à aller à celles des gars à partir de jeudi?

— Là aussi, je peux pas y aller. Je suis ben trop vieux. Tout le monde va rire de moi.

— Si je comprends bien, vous allez vous sauver de la retraite, lui fit-elle remarquer d'une voix acide.

— Oui, mais si ça peut te consoler, j'ai ben l'intention de faire mes pâques.

— Ici ou en ville? s'empressa-t-elle de demander à son locataire encombrant pour savoir s'il entendait plier bagages incessamment.

— *Goddam!* À Saint-Bernard, répondit-il, comme si la réponse allait de soi.

Encore la veille, la fille de Marie Beauchemin avait mentionné à son mari qu'il n'y aurait probablement pas grand-chose à mettre sur la glace qu'il avait enfouie sous une bonne épaisseur de grain, dans la grange.

— On n'a pourtant pas mangé tant de viande que ça, cet hiver, lui avait-il fait remarquer, apparemment surpris.

— C'est vrai, avait-elle reconnu, mais t'oublies qu'on a nourri ton oncle tout l'hiver et qu'il a pas l'air d'être bien pressé de partir.

Liam n'avait rien dit, mais elle espérait qu'il se déciderait bientôt à mettre les choses au point avec son parent envahissant. Il ne le fit pas, mais le maître-chantre de Saint-Bernard-Abbé assista toutefois à contrecœur à la retraite des hommes, ce qui consola sa femme.

Quelques jours plus tard, le jeudi soir, c'était la deuxième et dernière soirée consacrée à la retraite des jeunes filles.

— Grouille-toi, Bedette. À force de te traîner les pieds, tu vas finir par arriver en retard, dit Marie à sa fille cadette. Hubert est allé atteler pour toi. Arrête de te regarder dans le miroir et vas-y.

— Mautadit! Comme si on avait bien besoin de ça, bougonna Bernadette Beauchemin, de mauvaise humeur. J'ai mes classes à préparer, moi. Avec ça, je vais être obligée de me coucher tard sans bon sens.

— Ça dure juste deux soirs, lui rappela sa mère. Arrête de te lamenter pour rien.

La jeune institutrice avait assisté à la première des deux soirées consacrées aux jeunes filles et n'était revenue à la maison que sur le coup de neuf heures.

— Puis? lui avait demandé sa mère en train de réparer une culotte d'Alexis.

— Bah! C'est la même chose qu'un sermon du dimanche, m'man, lui avait-elle répondu sans grand enthousiasme.

— Est-ce qu'il y avait bien des filles?

— Pas mal. J'ai vu Catherine Benoît et même Angélique Dionne. Je leur ai parlé en sortant de la chapelle.

— Est-ce que c'est Xavier qui conduisait la fille de Laura Benoît? s'enquit Marie Beauchemin.

— Non, elle conduisait elle-même sa *sleigh*.

— J'espère que le beau Xavier va suivre la retraite des garçons, la semaine prochaine, répliqua sa mère.

— D'après Catherine, c'est bien son intention. Dis donc, Hubert, ajouta-t-elle en se tournant vers son frère occupé à réparer une chaise dans un coin de la cuisine, on dirait bien que la belle Angélique te trouve pas mal à son goût.

— Pourquoi tu dis ça? lui demanda immédiatement sa mère.

— Aussitôt qu'elle m'a vue, elle s'est dépêchée de me demander de ses nouvelles et elle s'est même plaint qu'il venait pas assez souvent au magasin général.

Hubert ne broncha pas, mais il était évident qu'il se sentait flatté d'être l'objet de l'attention de l'une des plus belles filles de Saint-Bernard-Abbé.

— J'espère que tu gardes ta place quand tu vas là, laissa tomber sa mère, sévère.

— Voyons, m'man, vous savez bien que monsieur et madame Dionne sont toujours là, intervint Bernadette.

— Toi, occupe-toi de tes affaires, la rembarra Marie.

◆

La période des sucres prit fin de façon inattendue au début de la semaine sainte après trois jours de pluies incessantes. Brusquement, la température s'était adoucie au point qu'il ne gela plus la nuit, la sève monta et l'eau d'érable devint amère. Des îlots de terre noire apparurent çà et là dans les champs, alternant avec des mares impressionnantes d'eau de fonte. En même temps, les chemins de la région devinrent presque impraticables tant ils étaient ravinés et envahis par l'eau que les fossés ne parvenaient plus à absorber.

— Pour moi, demain ou après-demain, les glaces vont lâcher sur la rivière, prédit Hormidas Meilleur en pénétrant dans le magasin général où Paddy et quelques hommes discutaient paisiblement.

C'était un temps de l'année où on pouvait souffler un peu, dans la région. Soudain, il n'y avait plus aucun travail pressant : les sucres étaient finis et il fallait attendre quelques semaines avant de pouvoir travailler la terre.

— Dites donc, père Meilleur, l'apostropha Xavier, comment ça se fait qu'on vous a pas vu à la retraite des jeunes ?

— Parce que je suis pas jeune, laissa tomber le facteur en secouant sa casquette mouillée par la petite pluie fine qui tombait depuis le début de l'avant-midi.

— Je veux ben le croire, poursuivit le jeune homme, mais monsieur le curé nous a donné de ben bons conseils pour avoir des fréquentations pures… Il paraît que c'est ben important de pas toucher à la fille chez qui on va veiller.

— Veux-tu ben me dire pourquoi tu me dis toutes ces niaiseries-là, le jeune? demanda Hormidas, apparemment intrigué.

— Ben, je vous dis ça parce que le bruit court dans Saint-Bernard que vous fréquentez sérieusement madame Cloutier.

Il y eut des ricanements chez les hommes présents.

— C'est pas vrai, affirma le petit homme avec force en fixant le jeune homme d'un œil féroce.

— Dans ce cas-là, voulez-vous ben me dire comment ça se fait que j'arrête pas de voir votre berlot proche de la maison de la veuve? demanda Cléomène Paquette, hilare.

—J'arrête là comme j'arrête partout ailleurs, pour lui remettre son courrier.

— Baptême, le père, la veuve en reçoit en maudit des lettres, se moqua Évariste Bourgeois. Pour moi, ça cache quelque chose, cette affaire-là.

— Monsieur le curé devrait être mis au courant de tout ça, intervint le gros Tancrède Bélanger. Je trouve que des fréquentations sans chaperon, c'est pas un exemple à donner aux jeunes de la paroisse.

— Faites-moi pas étriver avec ça, vous autres! s'emporta Hormidas, à demi sérieux. Il manquerait plus que monsieur le curé…

Soudain, le facteur se tut, incitant la demi-douzaine d'hommes présents près du comptoir à tourner la tête vers la porte du magasin qui venait de s'ouvrir sur Josaphat Désilets.

— Bonjour, salua le prêtre en refermant derrière lui.

Les personnes présentes s'empressèrent de lui rendre son salut, mais la conversation ne reprit pas.

— Monsieur Dionne, mon bedeau m'a dit tout à l'heure qu'il vous arrivait d'avoir du sirop d'érable à vendre, fit le curé de Saint-Bernard-Abbé.

— Oui, monsieur le curé, répondit Télesphore, le crayon sur l'oreille et la taille ceinte de son éternel grand tablier blanc. Je m'arrange toujours pour en avoir un ou deux gallons. Aujourd'hui, j'en ai un gallon, si ça vous tente. Je le vends cinquante cennes.

— Je vais le prendre, dit le prêtre après une courte hésitation.

Le propriétaire du magasin se pencha derrière son comptoir pour en sortir une cruche. Il la déposa sur le comptoir pendant que Josaphat Désilets tirait d'une vieille bourse en cuir la somme demandée.

— Est-ce que c'est pour manger tout de suite ou juste après le carême, monsieur le curé? demanda impudemment Paddy Connolly.

— Si on vous le demande, vous répondrez que ça vous regarde pas, répondit sèchement le prêtre avant de prendre la cruche. Messieurs, je vous souhaite encore une fois le bonjour, ajouta-t-il à l'adresse des gens qui l'entouraient.

— *Shitt!* Il entend pas à rire pantoute, déclara Paddy, dépité.

— C'est ce qu'on appelle se faire remettre à sa place, ne put s'empêcher de dire Hormidas Meilleur, pas mécontent d'avoir vu cet étranger se faire rembarrer.

— Dis donc, Télesphore, c'est le gallon de sirop que tu m'as acheté hier que t'as vendu à monsieur le curé? demanda Cléomène Paquette.

— Oui.

— Sacrifice! Tu m'as donné trente-cinq cennes et tu le vends cinquante cennes.

— Aïe! Cléomène, c'est ça, le commerce. Il faut vendre un peu plus cher que ce qu'on a payé, se défendit le marchand général.

— Avoir su, j'aurais fait le tour de la paroisse pour le vendre moi-même, ce sirop-là, fit l'autre, ne faisant rien pour cacher son dépit.

— C'est sûr, fit le commerçant, agacé. Mais je te ferai remarquer que je t'ai pas cassé un bras pour prendre ton sirop. C'est toi qui as insisté pour que je te l'achète.

La figure de fouine de Cléomène Paquette se ferma et il haussa les épaules avant de se mettre à écouter distraitement Paddy Connolly qui s'était remis à commenter les dernières nouvelles du journal, activité qui avait été interrompue par l'arrivée du facteur.

Le cultivateur du rang Saint-Jean s'était bien gardé de mentionner à Télesphore Dionne que le sirop qu'il désirait lui vendre venait de lui être donné par Liam Connolly. Depuis une semaine, il avait entrepris la tournée de ses voisins immédiats et de vagues connaissances de Sainte-Monique pour les inciter à lui donner un peu de sirop en arguant qu'il n'avait pu « faire les sucres » cette année à cause de son cœur qui lui causait de bien grandes inquiétudes. Même si plusieurs des personnes sollicitées ne l'avaient guère cru, elles lui avaient tout de même fait don d'un peu de sirop en se disant le plus souvent qu'il s'agissait d'un acte de charité chrétienne.

— Après tout, c'est pas sa faute s'il est sans-dessein comme pas un, avait dit Camille, étonnée de voir son mari s'empresser d'aller chercher un gallon de sirop dans la cuisine d'été pour le remettre au voisin.

Liam n'avait rien dit, mais le petit sourire qu'il affichait aurait dû alerter sa femme.

En fait, ce midi-là, Cléomène avait dit à sa Germaine avec un petit air satisfait :

— D'après moi, on va avoir un peu trop de sirop pour nos besoins cette année. Je vais en vendre un gallon à Dionne. Il enlèvera ça sur l'argent qu'on lui doit.

Moins d'une heure après son arrêt au magasin général, Josaphat Désilets rentra dans sa sacristie après avoir laissé son cheval et sa *sleigh* chez les Moreau, comme d'habitude. S'il n'avait eu à aller que chez les Dionne, le prêtre ne se serait pas donné la peine de faire atteler, mais il avait dû visiter deux dames malades dans le rang Saint-Paul, et cc déplacement avait été long à cause de l'état du chemin. Les ornières remplies d'eau avaient rendu le trajet particulièrement pénible. C'était le premier printemps qu'il vivait à Saint-Bernard-Abbé et il apprenait à la dure à quel point ses nombreuses côtes rendaient la route presque impraticable quand l'eau de fonte se mettait à les descendre.

Dès qu'il eut retiré son manteau et ses bottes, Josaphat Désilets déposa le cruchon de sirop d'érable sur la table en se promettant d'en manger un peu avec un croûton de pain au souper. Toutefois, quelques minutes plus tard, poussé par la gourmandise, il alla chercher une soucoupe pour y faire couler un peu de sirop dans l'intention d'y goûter.

Dès qu'il eut retiré le bouchon de liège du cruchon, une étrange odeur lui monta au nez et il s'empressa de renifler avec circonspection le contenu du contenant en grès.

— Mais bonyenne! Qu'est-ce qui sent aussi mauvais que ça? ne put-il s'empêcher de s'exclamer en fronçant le nez de dégoût.

Il se décida à laisser couler un mince filet de sirop dans la soucoupe et il sursauta devant le liquide brunâtre et malodorant. Il s'empressa de reposer le bouchon sur le contenant en ne faisant rien pour réprimer une grimace.

— Qu'est-ce que c'est que cette cochonnerie-là? fit-il, en colère, en allant rincer dans le lavabo la soucoupe. Est-ce que Télesphore Dionne rit du monde? demanda-t-il à haute voix. Attends donc, toi!

Sans perdre un instant, le prêtre remit son manteau et ses bottes, empoigna le cruchon et quitta le presbytère, bien décidé à en avoir le cœur net.

— Il y a personne qui va venir me rire en pleine face comme ça! marmonna-t-il en prenant le direction de la côte au bas de laquelle était situé le magasin général.

Le curé de Saint-Bernard-Abbé, faisant fi de la route détrempée et en partie boueuse, parcourut les quelque cent cinquante pieds qui le séparaient de la fameuse côte du rang Sainte-Ursule et il entreprit de la descendre avec certaines précautions pour éviter de s'étaler en glissant sur une plaque de glace dissimulée sous la neige. Arrivé en bas, il longea la ferme d'Angèle Cloutier ainsi que la maison et la forge d'Évariste Bourgeois avant d'entrer dans la cour du magasin général au moment même où les premiers enfants quittaient l'école construite de l'autre côté de la route étroite.

À sa grande surprise, le curé Désilets retrouva le même groupe d'hommes qu'une heure auparavant. La réaction de ces derniers fut identique à celle qu'ils avaient eue lors de sa précédente entrée. On le salua et le silence tomba encore une fois dans la grande pièce encombrée de toutes sortes de produits. Cette fois-ci, ce fut Alexandrine qui s'avança vers lui pour le servir.

— Qu'est-ce que je peux faire pour vous, monsieur le curé? lui demanda-t-elle.

— J'aimerais bien dire deux mots à votre mari, répondit Josaphat Désilets, l'air peu commode, en déposant bruyamment son cruchon de sirop sur le comptoir devant lui.

— Je vais vous le chercher. Il vient de passer à côté, dit-elle, affable.

La femme fit quelques pas, ouvrit la porte de communication entre le magasin et sa maison et cria à son mari que monsieur le curé désirait lui parler. Moins d'une minute plus tard, Télesphore vint la rejoindre derrière le comptoir, affichant un sourire de circonstance.

— Vous voulez me dire quelque chose, monsieur le curé? demanda-t-il.

— Oui, j'aimerais que vous alliez vous chercher une cuillère pour goûter au sirop que vous m'avez vendu tout à l'heure.

— Je peux ben faire ça, monsieur le curé, accepta le commerçant, tout de même assez surpris par la requête.

Il disparut un court moment et revint en brandissant une cuillère. Le prêtre attendit qu'il la tende pour déboucher le cruchon et en faire tomber quelques gouttes dans l'ustensile.

— Goûtez à ça, ordonna-t-il à Télesphore qui avait pris une mine dégoûtée en sentant l'odeur qui se dégageait du produit.

— Attendez, monsieur le curé, fit-il en se tournant vers Cléomène Paquette, j'ai justement ici dedans celui qui l'a fait, ce sirop-là. Approche, Cléomène ! Viens goûter à ton sirop.

Les hommes sur place reculèrent légèrement pour laisser passer le cultivateur du rang Saint-Jean.

— Goûte à ton sirop, lui commanda le commerçant, monsieur le curé a pas l'air de le trouver pantoute à son goût.

Et sans lui laisser le temps de s'esquiver, Télesphore porta aux lèvres de l'homme la cuillère remplie du liquide brunâtre malodorant. L'interpellé ouvrit la bouche, goûta le liquide, eut un haut-le-cœur et cracha précipitamment ce qu'il avait en bouche.

— Ah ben, maudit bout de Christ ! jura-t-il. C'est quoi cette cochonnerie-là ?

— C'est le sirop que tu m'as vendu hier et que j'ai vendu à monsieur le curé tout à l'heure, désespoir ! répondit Télesphore, en colère. Comment tu fais ton sirop, toi ?

— Ben, j'en ai pas fait pantoute cette année, reconnut l'homme d'une quarantaine d'années au visage chafouin. J'avais pas le cœur assez solide pour faire une besogne aussi dure. Ce gallon-là, c'est Liam Connolly qui me l'a donné.

Il y eut des regards de connivence entre les hommes présents. Ils devinèrent que son voisin avait voulu donner une leçon à celui qu'ils appelaient entre eux « le quêteux ».

— S'il te l'a donné, comment ça se fait que t'es venu me le vendre? s'entêta Dionne, en faisant un effort méritoire pour ne pas rire de la mésaventure de son client le moins solvable.

— Le monde a été ben bon avec moi cette année, reconnut Cléomène. Ils m'ont donné trop de sirop. J'ai pensé qu'au lieu d'en perdre, j'étais aussi ben de t'en vendre un gallon ou deux.

— Sais-tu, je pense que tu vas laisser faire, déclara Télesphore en adoptant un air sévère. J'ai pas envie de perdre mes clients en leur vendant du sirop comme celui que tu m'as vendu. Là, je vais rajouter les trente-cinq cennes que j'avais enlevées à ton ardoise. Tu peux reprendre ton sirop.

Là-dessus, le marchand remboursa le curé Désilets qui n'avait pas ouvert la bouche durant tout l'échange.

— Monsieur le curé, je peux vous apporter un gallon de sirop demain matin, si le cœur vous en dit, proposa Xavier. Et je vous garantis que le mien sent pas ce que je viens de sentir.

— C'est correct, consentit le prêtre. Et vous, monsieur Paquette, oubliez pas de venir vous confesser pour avoir voulu rire de votre curé et pour avoir blasphémé le nom de Dieu. Vous devriez avoir honte, un homme de votre âge.

— Mais, monsieur le curé, j'ai…

— Laissez faire, lui jeta sèchement le prêtre.

Josaphat Désilets quitta le magasin après avoir adressé un sec signe de tête aux personnes présentes. Paddy le suivit de près, il venait d'apercevoir les enfants de son neveu entourant l'institutrice en train de verrouiller la porte de l'école.

— Lui, Liam Connolly, il l'emportera pas au paradis! s'exclama Cléomène, furieux. Il a voulu rire de moi et c'est à cause de lui que je me suis fait engueuler par monsieur le curé.

— Moi, je suis pas sûr de ça pantoute, intervint Xavier qui venait de voir entrer Samuel Ellis. Le mari de ma sœur est un Irlandais et ce monde-là aime peut-être le sirop qui a ce goût-là. On le sait pas.

— Ça se pourrait, fit Hormidas Meilleur, entrant dans le jeu du jeune homme. Ils sont ben surprenants, des fois.

— Qu'est-ce qu'ils ont, les Irlandais ? demanda Samuel en s'approchant du petit groupe.

— Ben, on se demandait s'ils aimaient pas un sirop d'érable un peu plus fort que le nôtre, répondit Xavier en faisant des efforts pour garder son sérieux. Monsieur Paquette a reçu un gallon de sirop en cadeau de mon beau-frère et il a pas l'air de trop l'aimer.

— Dis-moi pas, Cléomène, que t'es rendu difficile à cette heure ? fit Ellis en se tournant vers le petit homme.

— Pantoute, se défendit l'autre.

— Fais-lui goûter, lui commanda Hormidas Meilleur en faisant un clin d'œil à Télesphore. Il va te le dire si c'est comme ça que les Irlandais aiment leur sirop.

Sans attendre que Cléomène se décide à déboucher le cruchon, Xavier retira le bouchon du contenant, s'empressa de verser une pleine cuillérée de sirop et tendit l'ustensile à Samuel Ellis qui grimaça.

— Envoye, goûtes-y, Sam, l'invita Télesphore.

— *Shitt !* C'est quoi cette cochonnerie-là ? demanda le président des syndics en repoussant la cuillère malodorante.

— C'est le sirop de Connolly, répondit Paquette.

— Pour moi, t'es mieux de jeter ça au plus sacrant, lui conseilla Samuel. Il l'a manqué, c'est sûr. J'ai jamais senti un sirop qui sent aussi mauvais.

— Il paraît qu'il goûte la même chose qu'il sent, plaisanta Xavier.

Ce soir-là, au souper, Paddy attendit le dessert pour raconter la scène qui s'était déroulée au magasin général quelques heures plus tôt.

— C'est pas vrai! s'exclama Liam. Il a eu le front d'aller vendre mon sirop à Dionne. Tu parles d'un maudit effronté!

— Il a dit qu'on lui en avait donné trop, lui expliqua son oncle. Mais c'est effrayant comme ton sirop sent mauvais, ajouta le retraité en affichant une mine dégoûtée. Quand on l'a senti au magasin, c'était à lever le cœur.

Camille se leva précipitamment, alla chercher un cruchon de sirop dans le garde-manger et s'empressa de l'ouvrir pour en sentir le contenu.

— Mais mon sirop a l'air bon, dit-elle en en faisant couler une petite quantité dans son assiette.

Elle y trempa le bout d'un doigt et porta ce dernier à sa bouche.

— Il est bon, il y a rien à lui reprocher. Dis-moi pas que je vais être obligée d'aller ouvrir tous les cruchons pour vérifier s'il y a une cuvée que j'ai manquée.

— Ben non, calme-toi donc, lui commanda son mari. Le cruchon que j'ai donné à Paquette, c'était un mélange spécial pour lui.

— Comment ça? s'étonna-t-elle.

— Ben, je suis écœuré de le voir venir quêter ici à tout bout de champ. Ça fait que j'ai pris un peu de réduit et je l'ai mêlé à de la mélasse et à de l'eau où j'avais mis à tremper un peu de tabac. On dirait que ce sirop-là a pas été du goût de monsieur le curé, ajouta-t-il en se mettant à rire.

— J'espère que tu vas avoir encore le goût de rire quand il va te parler dimanche matin, lui annonça son oncle.

— Pourquoi il me parlerait?

— Tu penses tout de même pas que Cléomène Paquette s'est laissé manger la laine sur le dos quand monsieur le curé lui est tombé dessus. Il lui a dit que le sirop venait de toi. À mon avis, tu vas te faire parler.

— Ça m'inquiète pas pantoute, répliqua Liam. Il entend à rire.

— À ta place, je serais pas trop sûre de ça, intervint Camille sur un ton désapprobateur. Monsieur le curé a pas dû apprécier de retourner au magasin général pour se faire rembourser.

Ce soir-là, au moment de se mettre au lit, Camille se contenta de dire à son mari :

— Je suis pas fière pantoute de cette histoire-là.

— De quoi tu parles ? demanda-t-il en retirant son pantalon.

— Du sirop que t'as donné au voisin. C'est pas un exemple à donner aux enfants. Rire du monde, c'est pas charitable.

— Pour moi, t'étais faite pour être servante de curé ou bonne sœur comme ta tante Mathilde, toi, se contenta-t-il de lui dire en soufflant la lampe posée sur la table de chevet.

Chapitre 17

L'embâcle

Le mardi soir suivant, Hubert rentra trempé du second et dernier soir de la retraite consacrée aux jeunes gens non mariés.

— Salament! Ça a pas d'allure. Il mouille à boire debout! dit-il en suspendant son manteau trempé à l'un des crochets fixés derrière la porte après avoir éteint le fanal qu'il tenait. Pour moi, c'est fini pour la *sleigh* et le berlot cette année. Il y a presque plus de neige sur le chemin et la Noire en a arraché à me traîner. Le chemin est à moitié défoncé. Il va falloir sortir le boghei.

— As-tu jeté un coup d'œil aux bâtiments avant de rentrer? lui demanda sa mère.

— Oui, tout est correct.

— Si c'est comme ça, je monte me coucher, annonça-t-elle aux siens en se levant péniblement de sa chaise. Vous ferez votre prière sans moi.

Marie alluma l'une des lampes de service et monta lentement à l'étage, laissant derrière elle ses trois enfants et sa bru. Eugénie, qui avait quitté son lit une dizaine de jours plus tôt ses malaises ayant disparu, s'était attendue à ce que sa belle-mère lui signifie de regagner son ancienne chambre à l'étage, mais elle n'en avait rien fait, ce qui n'était pas sans l'intriguer. Bien sûr, elle aurait pu demander à la mère de Donat ses intentions, mais elle craignait trop que celle-ci exige de récupérer sa chambre dès maintenant, puisque ses deux semaines de repos étaient écoulées.

— Pour moi, ta mère est sur le point de nous dire de lui laisser sa chambre, avait-elle dit à Donat la veille avec une trace d'inquiétude dans la voix. Ce serait bien dommage parce que je trouve ça pas mal pratique de pas avoir à monter en haut cent fois par jour pour m'occuper du petit.

— C'est sa maison, et elle a encore le droit de choisir sa chambre, lui avait fait remarquer son mari.

— C'est sûr que tant qu'elle se sera pas donnée à nous autres...

— Commence pas avec cette affaire-là, lui avait-il ordonné en haussant la voix. Je t'ai déjà répété cent fois que c'était pas le temps de mettre ça sur le tapis.

Eugénie n'était pas revenue sur le sujet, mais il n'en restait pas moins que la possibilité que sa belle-mère exige d'un jour à l'autre de réintégrer son ancienne chambre l'obsédait.

La future mère avait bien tort de s'en faire. Marie avait fini par se faire une raison et avait définitivement renoncé à rentrer en possession de son ancienne chambre. En fait, elle aurait eu mauvaise conscience d'exiger que sa bru monte et descende constamment les escaliers durant les derniers mois de sa grossesse difficile. D'ailleurs, après la naissance du bébé, elle se serait sentie coupable de garder pour elle seule la plus grande chambre de la maison.

Au rez-de-chaussée, on attendit d'entendre la porte de la chambre se refermer avant de parler à mi-voix.

— Bonyenne, m'man vieillit ! murmura Bernadette. Elle a l'air fatiguée sans bon sens. Ça fait longtemps que je l'ai pas vue aller se coucher la première sans faire la prière.

— Il faut dire qu'elle fait de bien grosses journées d'ouvrage, lui rappela Eugénie. Dans mon état, je suis pas d'une grosse aide.

— C'est peut-être le changement de saison, suggéra Donat en se levant pour aller remonter le mécanisme de l'horloge murale.

— Parlant de saison, reprit son jeune frère, j'ai l'impression que les glaces sur la rivière tiendront pas indéfiniment avec le poids de l'eau qu'il y a dessus.

— C'est normal, il arrête pas de mouiller depuis quatre jours, intervint Bernadette. Vous devriez voir dans quel état les enfants arrivent à l'école. Ils ont les pieds tellement crottés que je suis obligée de les faire déchausser dans l'entrée, sinon ils mettent de la boue partout sur mon plancher.

Pour confirmer ce qui venait d'être dit dans la cuisine des Beauchemin, il y eut comme un bruit violent à l'extérieur qui fit sursauter tous les occupants de la maison. Cette détonation fut suivie par plusieurs autres, un peu moins fortes cependant. Donat alla précipitamment vers l'une des fenêtres de la cuisine dont il souleva le rideau pour chercher à voir à l'extérieur.

— On voit rien dehors, annonça-t-il aux autres, mais je suis certain que ce sont les glaces qui viennent de lâcher.

Une heure plus tard, la dernière lampe s'éteignit chez les Beauchemin après que Donat eut jeté deux bûches dans le poêle.

❦

Le lendemain matin, les premières lueurs de l'aube tirèrent Marie du sommeil. La pluie crépitait autant sur le toit que contre les vitres de la fenêtre. Fidèle à son habitude, elle ne traîna pas au lit. Elle repoussa ses couvertures, se leva et déposa un châle épais sur ses épaules avant de s'approcher de la fenêtre. Dans le petit matin blafard, elle crut d'abord avoir mal vu et elle se frotta énergiquement les yeux.

— Ben voyons donc! s'exclama-t-elle à mi-voix. C'est pas Dieu possible!

Elle avait devant elle un spectacle absolument incroyable. Des blocs de glace de presque deux pieds d'épaisseur enchevêtrés les uns sur les autres avaient été poussés par la rivière sur sa terre. Aussi loin que portait la vue, elle ne voyait que de l'eau grise. Il y avait sûrement un gros embâcle pour que les eaux soient sorties du lit de la rivière et aient envahi aussi bien les champs de l'autre côté de la route que la route elle-même.

Même en cherchant bien dans ses souvenirs, elle ne se rappelait pas avoir vu l'eau monter si haut et menacer ainsi sa maison pourtant située sur une légère hauteur à plus de quatre cents pieds de la rivière.

Sans perdre un instant, elle alla réveiller Bernadette et Hubert qui dormaient dans les chambres voisines. Ensuite, elle descendit rapidement au rez-de-chaussée et jeta une bûche sur les tisons du poêle.

— Donat, lève-toi, ordonna-t-elle à son fils après avoir entrouvert la porte de sa chambre. Dépêche-toi. L'eau monte.

En quelques minutes, tous les Beauchemin étaient réunis dans la cuisine. Penché à la fenêtre, Donat maugréait.

— Torrieu! On avait ben besoin de ça. C'est sûr qu'il y a au moins un embâcle sur la rivière. Ça peut être aussi ben aux petites chutes, un peu plus haut que chez Xavier, que proche du pont. Peut-être même aux deux places.

— Seigneur, mon école! s'exclama soudain Bernadette qui venait de réaliser que l'école de rang située au pied de la côte devait avoir été envahie par les eaux durant la nuit.

— Ton école, le magasin général, chez Bourgeois et chez la veuve Cloutier. Tout ça doit être dans l'eau, poursuivit Hubert.

— Reste à savoir si le pont a pas été emporté comme celui de Tancrède Bélanger il y a deux ans, fit remarquer Donat. Là, on n'a pas le choix. On va aller soigner les animaux, et après ça il va falloir se débrouiller pour sortir de la cour et aller voir les dégâts.

— Qu'est-ce qu'on va faire si l'eau continue à monter? demanda Marie, nettement dépassée par les événements.

— Il reste encore une bonne centaine de pieds avant qu'elle arrive à la maison, m'man, lui fit remarquer Bernadette. Si on voit qu'elle continue à monter, on ira essayer de sauver les légumes qui sont dans la cave. On n'aura pas le choix.

— J'espère que tout est correct chez Emma, fit sa mère, soudain inquiète pour sa fille qui demeurait au début du rang.

— On va aller voir après le déjeuner, lui promit Donat. Mais même si la maison de Rémi est un peu plus basse que la nôtre, ça me surprendrait pas mal que l'eau soit rendue là.

— Comment on va faire pour aller là? l'interrogea son frère.

— On va sortir la vieille chaloupe qui est au fond de la grange. Elle devrait flotter encore, même si ça fait des années qu'elle a pas servi.

Marie ne s'interrogea pas au sujet de Camille parce que les berges de la rivière étaient beaucoup plus hautes de l'autre côté de la route, en face de la maison de Liam Connolly.

Donat et Hubert allèrent soigner les animaux pendant que les femmes remettaient un peu d'ordre dans la maison et préparaient le déjeuner. Plantée devant l'une des fenêtres de la cuisine, Eugénie vit Donat conduire par la bride le Blond qui tirait derrière lui la vieille embarcation. Le cultivateur immobilisa sa bête quand la barque à fond plat ne fut plus qu'à quelques pieds de l'eau.

Lorsque les deux hommes rentrèrent, le jour était définitivement levé et l'eau miroitait à perte de vue sur la route et dans les champs en face de la maison. De l'autre côté de la rivière, les maisons du rang Sainte-Ursule bâties au sommet de la rive abrupte n'étaient en rien menacées par l'embâcle.

— Je vous dis que ceux qui se sont installés dans Sainte-Ursule ont eu le nez creux, déclara Donat, envieux, en rentrant. Eux autres, tout ce qu'ils risquent, c'est de perdre un peu de terrain si la berge est minée par les glaces.

— Toi, t'es chanceux que p'pa soit plus là pour t'entendre, dit Bernadette en déposant le beurre sur la table. T'aurais reçu une claque sur les oreilles s'il était encore ici. T'as oublié que pour lui, il y avait rien de plus beau que notre rang et qu'il fallait être malade pour aller s'installer en haut de la côte.

— Il a pourtant rien dit quand Xavier s'est installé là, répliqua son frère.

— Oui, mais parce qu'il y avait pas de terre à vendre dans Saint-Jean quand Xavier a voulu s'établir.

— Approchez, le déjeuner est prêt, annonça leur mère en déposant sur la table un plat contenant une grande omelette.

Donat et Hubert vinrent prendre place à table.

— Pour moi, Aubé a dû pâtir de ce coup d'eau là, dit Donat à son frère dès que le bénédicité eut été récité.

— Si l'eau est montée sur le chemin dans son coin, c'est sûr qu'il a été touché, déclara Hubert. C'est le seul du rang à avoir sa maison de ce côté-là du chemin.

Sans dire un mot, Bernadette monta précipitamment à l'étage et entra dans la chambre de sa mère pour regarder par la fenêtre. De là, elle pouvait apercevoir la maison de son cavalier et son moulin, plus loin, sur le bord de la rivière. Moins d'une minute plus tard, elle descendit.

— Je suis allée voir en haut. On dirait qu'il y a de l'eau tout autour de la maison de Constant, annonça-t-elle sans parvenir à dissimuler son inquiétude.

— Ça veut rien dire, fit Donat, il faut pas oublier qu'il a construit sur une butte. C'est ben possible que l'eau soit pas arrivée à entrer dans sa maison.

— Est-ce que je peux monter dans la chaloupe avec vous autres pour aller voir? demanda la jeune fille.

— Voyons donc, Bedette, c'est pas ta place pantoute, la réprimanda sa mère. À part ça, à quoi tu servirais si c'était le cas?

— Est-ce que je peux au moins aller voir les dégâts que l'eau a faits dans l'école? insista-t-elle.

— Ça te servirait à rien, décréta Donat en se versant une tasse de thé. Si l'eau est entrée dans la bâtisse, tu pourras rien faire.

— À la hauteur où est l'école, les murs ont ben pu être défoncés par les glaces, intervint Hubert, malicieux. Si ça se trouve, toutes les cochonneries qui étaient dans ta classe flottent dans le courant. Installe-toi devant une fenêtre, tu vas peut-être les voir passer.

— T'es pas drôle pantoute, Hubert Beauchemin, répliqua sa sœur avec humeur.

Évidemment, cela était impossible puisque l'école était située en aval, à l'autre bout du rang, à une centaine de pieds du pont.

— On va le savoir quand on sera allés voir, intervint Donat pour la rassurer.

— En tout cas, on dira ce qu'on voudra, mais quand il arrive une affaire comme ça, c'est Xavier qui est encore le plus chanceux, poursuivit Hubert. Là où il est, il risque rien. Je pourrais même gager que l'eau a à peine monté sur son terrain de l'autre côté du chemin. C'est pas comme nous autres. Avant que l'eau se soit retirée de notre champ, ça va prendre du temps.

Le reste du repas du matin se prit en silence. La pluie continuait à fouetter les vitres des fenêtres quand les deux frères endossèrent leurs manteaux pour aller voir ce qui se passait.

— Faites bien attention, vous deux, les mit en garde leur mère. Pas d'imprudence.

Ils la rassurèrent et sortirent. Ils traversèrent la cour en évitant les flaques d'eau et, arrivés à l'embarcation, ils la poussèrent jusqu'à ce qu'elle se mette à flotter. Alors, Hubert monta et s'empara des rames pendant que son frère prenait place à l'avant. Une petite pluie froide continuait à tomber.

— Cette maudite pluie-là va ben finir par arrêter un jour, dit Donat en remontant le col de son manteau.

À plus d'un endroit, la route étroite était occupée par des blocs de glace que le rameur devait contourner avec circonspection. Cependant, les frères Beauchemin finirent par arriver, quinze cents pieds plus loin, devant la maison de Constant Aubé, cernée de toutes parts par les glaces.

Le meunier devait guetter à l'une de ses fenêtres parce que, au moment où les deux jeunes hommes s'approchèrent, il sortit sur sa galerie.

— Tu parles d'une façon de se faire réveiller, leur cria-t-il alors qu'ils maintenaient difficilement la chaloupe à une vingtaine de pieds de la maison.

— As-tu des dégâts en dedans ? lui demanda Donat.

— Pantoute, répondit Constant. Bélisle a eu une sacrifice de bonne idée de me bâtir sur une butte comme ça. Par contre, comme vous pouvez le voir, je suis cerné par les glaces. Je pense que je risque rien tant que l'eau se remettra pas à monter. Si elle monte encore d'un pied, ça va être une autre paire de manches, par exemple.

— Et ton moulin ? lui demanda Hubert en regardant le moulin qui se dressait au loin, au bord de la rivière.

— Je peux pas dire. J'ai pas de chaloupe pour aller voir. De toute façon, ce serait peut-être pas mal dangereux de trop m'approcher.

— Je pense que t'as raison, l'approuva Donat.

— En tout cas, mon idée de protéger ma roue avec un muret de billes de bois, comme le fait toujours Hyland, a pas servi à grand-chose, poursuivit Constant. Les glaces l'ont écrasé comme rien. Regardez, le bois flotte partout dans le champ.

— Écoute, reprit Donat. Si tu peux rien faire, monte avec nous autres, on s'en va voir ce qui est arrivé au pont et à l'école. En revenant, si on peut, on essaiera d'aller voir de plus près si tout est correct au moulin.

— J'arrive, déclara Constant.

Il rentra chez lui un instant pour mettre un manteau et sortit en refermant la porte de la maison derrière lui. Donat et Hubert, un peu inquiets, le virent s'avancer en boitillant dangereusement sur les blocs de glace instables qui le séparaient de l'embarcation.

— Fais attention ! le mit en garde Hubert. Tu vas te casser la gueule.

Constant fit comme s'il ne l'avait pas entendu et finit par atteindre la chaloupe dans laquelle il se laissa glisser avec soulagement.

— Ce qui est certain, c'est qu'il sera pas tard ce printemps que je vais me greyer d'une chaloupe, moi aussi, affirma l'ami de cœur de Bernadette. J'ai pas aimé pantoute aller soigner mes animaux à matin avec de l'eau à mi-jambe.

Les trois hommes se relayèrent pour manier les rames. Tel qu'ils l'avaient envisagé, aucun des cultivateurs du rang n'avait eu sa maison ou ses bâtiments touchés par la soudaine montée de l'eau. Dans les pires cas, l'eau et les glaces avaient envahi la cour de la ferme, sans toutefois se rendre jusqu'à un édifice. Ils passèrent devant les fermes de Conrad Boudreau, de John White, de Gratien Ménard et d'Ernest Gélinas en suivant approximativement la route sauf quand un bloc de glace les obligeait à faire un détour.

— Pour moi, le niveau de l'eau est au moins cinq ou six pieds au-dessus de la normale, déclara Hubert en arrivant enfin devant la ferme de Rémi Lafond. On vient de passer au-dessus des piquets de la clôture de Rémi.

La chaloupe toucha terre une vingtaine de pieds avant le seuil de la maison. Ils descendirent tous les trois et ils allaient frapper à la porte de la petite maison en bardeaux quand Emma sortit, passablement agitée.

— Arrivez, vous trois, leur ordonna-t-elle. Restez pas dehors à la pluie. Il y a déjà bien assez de Rémi qui est parti tout à l'heure en canot vers le pont pour voir ce qui se passe. Ça m'énerve sans bon sens.

Les trois enfants d'Emma étaient près du poêle et la maîtresse de maison offrit une tasse de thé aux visiteurs avant de s'enquérir des dégâts causés dans le rang par cette inondation.

— Il faudrait pas que l'eau monte encore, finit-elle par dire. Là, il faudrait s'installer en haut et j'ose même pas penser aux dégâts que ça ferait en bas.

— Pour moi, t'as pas à t'en faire, dit Donat. L'eau a plus l'air de vouloir monter.

Les trois hommes ne demeurèrent que quelques minutes chez les Lafond avant de reprendre place dans leur chaloupe.

— Vous direz à m'man de pas s'en faire. Les enfants sont corrects.

— On va lui faire la commission, lui promit Hubert qui venait de s'emparer des rames. En plus, on va dire à ton Rémi que tu t'inquiètes pour lui.

— Je le connais, c'est pas ça qui va le faire revenir plus vite à la maison, rétorqua-t-elle avec un sourire.

La chaloupe passa devant la dernière ferme du rang, celle de Tancrède Bélanger, avant de bifurquer à gauche vers le pont.

— Salament! ne put s'empêcher de s'écrier Hubert. Avez-vous vu l'épaisseur de glace qu'il y a sur le pont? Les garde-fous ont été arrachés.

— C'est un miracle qu'il soit pas encore parti avec la glace, comme l'ancien pont, fit Donat, catastrophé. Approche, Hubert, commanda-t-il à son frère qui maniait les rames. Veux-tu ben me dire ce qui est poigné entre les deux plus gros blocs, à gauche?

Ces mots attirèrent l'attention de Constant Aubé qui chercha à mieux voir ce dont il s'agissait.

— Ah ben, taboire! s'exclama le meunier. Mais on dirait ben que c'est une partie de la grande roue de mon moulin.

— T'es pas sérieux? fit Donat en cherchant à reconnaître la grosse section en bois écrasée entre deux énormes blocs de glace.

— Je suis à peu près sûr, fit Constant, la mine sombre. Ça, ça veut dire que la grande roue va être à reconstruire et peut-être même le mur du moulin qui donne sur la rivière si la glace l'a défoncé. Maudite misère noire! ne put-il s'empêcher de s'écrier, à l'évidence découragé par la catastrophe qui venait de le frapper.

Au moment où ils atteignaient le pont, ils aperçurent Rémi Lafond, de l'autre côté de la rivière, qui se dirigeait vers le magasin général.

— Par où t'es passé pour arriver là? lui cria Donat.

— En avant de l'embâcle, à droite du pont. L'eau est libre. C'est pas dangereux pantoute.

Constant remplaça Hubert et se mit à ramer lentement pour contourner le pont et traverser la rivière à l'endroit où elle était le plus étroite et pratiquement dégagée de toute glace flottante.

— Vous avez vu l'école de Bernadette? demanda le rameur aux deux frères. Il y a de l'eau jusqu'à la moitié des fenêtres.

— Ça doit être beau à voir en dedans, se borna à dire Hubert.

L'attention des trois hommes fut soudainement attirée par les cris de Xavier qui venait d'immobiliser sa vieille voiture à foin aux deux tiers de la pente du rang Sainte-Ursule. Le jeune homme et Antonin avaient déposé sur le véhicule l'embarcation qu'ils utilisaient chaque automne pour la chasse aux canards et ils s'apprêtaient à la mettre à l'eau.

Les deux chaloupes et le canot se rejoignirent devant la maison d'Angèle Cloutier.

— Est-ce qu'il y a un autre embâcle proche de chez vous? demanda Donat à son frère.

— Non, s'il y en a un, il doit être pas mal plus haut sur la rivière parce que, devant chez nous, les glaces sont descendues et l'eau a presque pas monté.

— Si c'est comme ça, ce sera pas beau à voir quand ces glaces-là vont lâcher et venir s'empiler sur les glaces qui sont déjà devant le pont, intervint Hubert, l'air préoccupé. Pour moi, ce pont-là résistera pas.

— On verra ben, fit Constant.

— Blasphème! jura Xavier en montrant la maison de la veuve. Il y a de l'eau à la moitié de la porte. Il manquerait plus qu'on retrouve l'Angèle noyée dans son lit. Si l'eau a monté vite, ça se peut qu'elle ait pas pu ouvrir la porte pour sortir à temps.

Les trois embarcations se rapprochèrent de la maison et on les attacha à un poteau de la galerie. Les six hommes descendirent et avancèrent péniblement dans l'eau. Sans se donner la peine de frapper, ils unirent leurs efforts pour forcer la porte malgré la résistance de l'eau à l'intérieur.

Ils découvrirent, stupéfaits, la maîtresse de maison assise sur l'une des plus hautes marches de l'escalier conduisant à l'étage en compagnie de nul autre qu'Hormidas Meilleur. Tous les deux étaient en train de manger paisiblement des tartines, enfouis sous d'épaisses couvertures.

— Il était temps que quelqu'un se décide à venir nous aider à sortir d'ici, déclara la veuve sur un ton revêche. Un peu plus et on mourait noyés.

— On a ben cru notre dernière heure arrivée, ajouta le petit homme en quittant la marche sur laquelle il était assis.

Apparemment, l'homme n'était pas gêné d'être découvert en compagnie de la veuve si tôt le matin. Comme il n'y avait aucune embarcation près de la maison, les sauveteurs ne pouvaient que déduire qu'il était sur place bien avant l'inondation survenue la nuit précédente…

— Blasphème, père Meilleur ! C'est une drôle d'heure pour jouer aux cartes, ne put s'empêcher de dire Xavier en riant.

— Fais pas le comique, le jeune, lui ordonna sèchement le facteur. C'est pas le temps de rire pantoute.

— Bon, madame Cloutier, nos chaloupes sont dehors, sur le bord de votre galerie. Je vais vous porter jusque-là, proposa Hubert en s'avançant vers elle.

— C'est pas nécessaire pantoute, mon garçon. Je suis pas infirme. À cette heure que la porte est ouverte je suis encore capable de marcher sur mes deux jambes. Aide plutôt p'tit père.

Sur ces mots, elle descendit l'escalier et, malgré l'eau qui lui montait jusqu'à la taille, elle se dirigea vers la chaloupe dans laquelle elle monta sans aide. Hormidas Meilleur aurait eu de l'eau à mi-poitrine si Hubert et Xavier ne l'avaient pas soulevé pour l'aider à se rendre jusqu'à l'embarcation.

— Laisse la porte ouverte, commanda Angèle Cloutier à Constant Aubé. Cette maudite eau-là va bien finir par sortir un jour.

On ramena les deux sinistrés vers la côte du rang Sainte-Ursule en leur recommandant de chercher refuge pour se réchauffer chez les Moreau ou à la chapelle. Au moment où on les abandonnait sur la route boueuse, le curé Désilets descendait justement d'un pas précautionneux, apparemment peu désireux de couvrir de boue sa soutane.

— En passant, père Meilleur, chuchota Xavier au facteur avant de s'éloigner, ça serait peut-être pas une mauvaise idée de demander à monsieur le curé ce qu'il pense de vos parties de cartes la nuit avec la veuve…

L'homme lui décocha un regard meurtrier avant de suivre Angèle Cloutier qui avait entrepris d'escalader la côte.

— On va aller voir comment notre forgeron se tire d'affaire, déclara Donat.

Quelques minutes plus tard, ils aperçurent Évariste Bourgeois qui revenait de son étable, assis dans une vieille barque. À l'entendre, il n'y avait qu'à attendre que l'eau se retire. Sa femme était cantonnée à l'étage et lui s'apprêtait à aller prêter main-forte à Dionne dont le magasin était envahi par l'eau. Tous décidèrent alors de se rendre au magasin général pour aider.

À leur entrée dans le commerce, ils constatèrent qu'il y avait près d'un pied et demi d'eau à l'intérieur. Le propriétaire, sa femme et leur fille s'affairaient à mettre hors de portée de l'eau tous les produits qu'elle pouvait détériorer. L'arrivée soudaine des sept hommes leur fit le plus grand plaisir. Alexandrine demanda immédiatement de l'aide pour mettre quelques meubles à l'abri dans la maison attenante et Angélique s'empressa de choisir Hubert Beauchemin pour les accompagner de l'autre côté de la porte de communication.

En moins d'une heure, tout ce que Télesphore Dionne pouvait espérer sauver de l'inondation avait été rangé sur des tablettes que l'eau ne pouvait atteindre.

— J'aime autant pas penser à ce qui est dans la cave, dit le marchand en servant un verre de bagosse aux hommes qui lui étaient venus en aide.

— J'ai dans l'idée qu'il faudrait commencer à faire sauter l'embâcle, suggéra Constant. On peut pas attendre que la pluie fasse fondre la glace.

— C'est ben beau, ton idée, fit Rémi Lafond, mais comment tu veux faire ça ?

— Une année, il y en a eu un proche de chez mon grand-père. On a pris des pioches, des barres de fer et des pelles et on a dégagé un chenal. La glace a fini par partir. Aussitôt que ça s'est fait, l'eau a baissé.

Les hommes présents convinrent que c'était probablement l'unique moyen de sauver le pont et surtout d'éviter que l'eau fasse encore plus de dégâts. Avant de quitter le magasin, Donat demanda à Hubert s'il revenait avec lui. Son jeune frère lui répondit qu'il y avait encore pas mal à faire chez les Dionne et qu'il trouverait bien le moyen de revenir à la maison plus tard. Un coup d'œil vers Angélique apprit au fils aîné de Baptiste Beauchemin qu'il n'y avait pas que le travail qui retenait Hubert chez les Dionne.

À leur sortie du magasin général, les sauveteurs se rendirent compte qu'une quarantaine de cultivateurs s'étaient massés tant dans la côte du rang Sainte-Ursule qu'en face, près de la maison de Tancrède Bélanger.

Après une rapide consultation, il fut décidé qu'Évariste Bourgeois allait expliquer aux gens de Sainte-Ursule le travail à faire pour se débarrasser de l'embâcle et que Donat ferait la même chose avec ceux des rangs Saint-Jean et Saint-Paul prêts à venir aider.

Avant la fin de la matinée, presque tous étaient revenus sur les lieux de l'embâcle à bord d'embarcations diverses et armés de lourdes barres de fer, de pioches, de pelles et même de haches.

— On devrait commencer par dégager le pont avant qu'il s'écrase, déclara Évariste. Il y a au moins trois pieds de glace dessus.

Sans perdre un instant, les plus braves approchèrent leur embarcation du pont et les quittèrent pour monter sur la glace. Ils se mirent à frapper en cadence les énormes blocs qui, une fois morcelés, furent basculés dans le courant libre en aval. Moins d'une heure plus tard, la chaussée du pont était dégagée, mais toujours menacée par les glaces entassées contre ses piliers.

— Bout de cierge ! il fait chenu, ce pont-là, sans ses garde-fous, dit Anatole Blanchette en s'essuyant le front.

Maintenant, les hommes qui s'étaient éparpillés par petits groupes sur les glaces devant le pont ressemblaient à des fourmis. Ils frappaient à coups redoublés pour briser les plus gros blocs et quand ils y arrivaient, ils unissaient leurs efforts pour les repousser avec les barres de fer dans le courant qui contournait le pont.

— Une chance que l'eau fait son chemin partout, déclara le gros Tancrède Bélanger, confortablement installé dans sa chaloupe, à l'écart des travailleurs.

Ce disant, il montrait l'eau qui finissait par s'écouler à chacune des extrémités du petit pont qui enjambait la Nicolet.

— J'espère que vous vous fatiguez pas trop, monsieur Bélanger ? lui demanda Xavier, sarcastique, en soulevant sa casquette pour s'éponger le front.

— Moi, mon garçon, je suis pour la prudence, répliqua le cultivateur. Je suis là pour repêcher celui qui va tomber à l'eau.

— Ouais, intervint le forgeron, sceptique. Si t'es aussi vite pour ramer que tu l'es pour marcher, le pauvre gars va avoir le temps de boire une bonne tasse avant que tu le récupères.

Constant Aubé avait suivi Amable Fréchette et Rémi Lafond à l'un des postes les plus dangereux, entre les piliers du pont.

— Je vais prendre ta place, dit le boiteux au mari d'Emma.

— Pourquoi ça ? s'étonna ce dernier alors qu'il s'apprêtait à donner un grand coup de barre.

— T'es père de trois enfants. Il manquerait plus qu'il t'arrive quelque chose. Laisse-moi la place.

Rémi reconnut le bien-fondé des paroles de l'ami de Bernadette et ignora le regard méprisant que lui adressa Amable Fréchette quand il céda sa place au meunier.

— Ah ben, moi… commença l'autre.

— Toi, ferme ta gueule ou ben tu vas partir avec le prochain morceau de glace, lui ordonna sèchement Constant, qui détestait toujours autant le bellâtre.

Puis, sans plus se préoccuper de lui, il se mit à frapper à grands coups la glace devant lui.

En ce mercredi saint, il n'y eut pas de pause pour le repas du midi. Au milieu de l'après-midi, on vit enfin un coin de ciel bleu, signe que la pluie ne reprendrait pas ce jour-là. Les hommes travaillèrent sans relâche jusqu'au coucher du soleil. En unissant leurs efforts, ils étaient parvenus à creuser un étroit chenal entre les deux piliers principaux du pont et, jusqu'au moment d'abandonner leur travail, ils avaient œuvré à l'élargir avec succès.

Sur le chemin du retour, Donat put constater que l'eau avait commencé à se retirer de la route, mais elle couvrait toujours la plus grande partie des champs. La bonne nouvelle était qu'elle avait baissé suffisamment pour libérer les alentours de la maison de Constant Aubé, laissant derrière elle de gros blocs de glace grisâtre.

— Si le chenal bloque pas pendant la nuit, je vais revenir demain et on va pouvoir aller voir les dommages à ton moulin, annonça Donat au meunier, apparemment très soulagé de constater le retrait des eaux.

Donat n'entra pas dans la maison après être descendu de son embarcation de l'autre côté de la route, en face de la ferme paternelle. Il se dirigea immédiatement vers les bâtiments pour soigner ses animaux. À peine venait-il de commencer son travail qu'il vit arriver sa sœur Bernadette dans l'étable.

— Où est passé Hubert ? lui demanda-t-elle.

— Il est resté chez Dionne pour aider à sauver leurs affaires. Il va revenir tout à l'heure.

— Et mon école ?

— Il y a de l'eau jusqu'au milieu des fenêtres. Pour moi, tu vas avoir tout un ménage à faire là-dedans avant de pouvoir faire l'école là, lui annonça-t-il.

— Sainte bénite! s'exclama-t-elle, catastrophée.

— Il y a pire, reprit son frère. Il y a une grosse partie de la roue du moulin qui a été arrachée. Constant est pas mal découragé. Surtout qu'il peut même pas encore savoir s'il y a pas un mur complètement défoncé.

— Et là, qu'est-ce qu'on va faire?

— On a déjà fait ce qu'on a pu. On a creusé un chenal et comme t'as pu voir, l'eau a commencé à baisser. Il reste juste à prier, comme dirait m'man, pour que le chenal se bloque pas.

— Bon, je suis sortie pour te donner un coup de main. Tu dois être pas mal fatigué.

Donat ne se donna pas la peine de lui répondre, mais sa sœur vit qu'il était content de pouvoir profiter de son aide. Durant le repas du soir, le jeune père de famille dut raconter aux siens tout ce qui avait été fait pour juguler la montée des eaux durant la journée.

— Mais veux-tu ben me dire ce que Hubert a à bretter comme ça chez les Dionne? finit par demander Marie en terminant de laver la vaisselle du souper.

— J'ai dans l'idée que la belle Angélique commence à l'intéresser un peu, répondit Donat en allumant sa pipe après avoir pris son jeune fils sur ses genoux.

— Tiens! Tiens! laissa tomber Eugénie.

— Comme ça, elle va peut-être arrêter de faire de l'œil aux cavaliers des autres filles de la paroisse, fit remarquer Bernadette d'une voix acide.

— Et Liam, lui, qu'est-ce qu'il a dit de ce coup d'eau là? demanda Eugénie à son mari.

— Je le sais pas, on l'a pas vu pantoute de la journée, répondit Donat. On était plus qu'une quarantaine à travailler sur l'embâcle, mais lui, on l'a pas vu.

Ce matin-là, Liam Connolly avait bien vu que la rivière était sortie de son lit et il en avait tout de suite déduit la présence d'un embâcle important. Quand il quitta la maison avec ses deux fils, il se dirigea vers la route pour tenter de voir à quel endroit l'eau avait commencé à l'envahir. À première vue, c'était à mi-chemin entre la ferme de Gariépy et celle des Beauchemin. Devant chez lui, l'eau s'était arrêtée au milieu des champs, de l'autre côté de la route.

— Grouillez-vous! ordonna-t-il sèchement à Duncan et Patrick qui l'avaient suivi. Le train se fera pas tout seul.

Évidemment, Camille avait aperçu toute cette eau et s'était vivement inquiétée pour ses parents établis plus loin dans le rang Saint-Jean.

— Vas-tu aller voir si tout est correct chez ma mère et chez Emma? demanda-t-elle à son mari quand il s'assit à table en compagnie des enfants et de Paddy.

— Ça servirait à quoi? lui demanda-t-il.

— À me rassurer.

— Ben là, il va falloir que tu te fasses une raison, déclara-t-il tout net. J'ai pas l'intention pantoute de perdre ma journée à ramer. En plus, ça fait des années que je me suis pas servi du vieux canot au fond de la grange. Si ça se trouve, il est à moitié pourri.

Sa femme ne dit rien et prit place à l'autre bout de la table pour déjeuner.

— Aujourd'hui, j'ai une table à finir pour Aubé, ajouta son mari à titre d'excuse.

Depuis le début de l'hiver, Liam avait tenu parole. Il avait occupé toutes les journées où il n'avait pas pu aller bûcher à construire des meubles pour le meunier. Pour les premiers, ce dernier l'avait payé en attelages et en souliers, mais depuis la fin du mois de février il lui avait donné de l'argent pour chacun des meubles livrés.

Durant la matinée, Camille, aidée par ses deux filles, remit la maison en ordre et procéda au reprisage hebdomadaire. Après avoir mis le dîner sur le feu, elle s'habilla et se rendit dans la grange pour examiner le canot enfoui sous toutes sortes de matériaux. Il lui fallut plusieurs minutes pour le dégager. À première vue, il lui sembla en assez bon état pour flotter.

Elle rentra dans la maison et confia la garde de Rose à Paddy avant d'entraîner Ann à sa suite à l'extérieur.

— As-tu déjà ramé? demanda-t-elle à l'adolescente.

— Non.

— T'es chanceuse, lui dit-elle, tu vas commencer aujourd'hui. Viens avec moi. On va atteler la voiture à foin et on va mettre le canot dessus. D'après ton père, l'eau est montée sur la route en arrivant chez Gariépy. On va prendre le canot pour aller chez ma mère.

Quelques minutes plus tard, Liam sortit de la remise où il travaillait quand il entendit la voiture dans la cour.

— Veux-tu ben me dire où tu t'en vas avec ça? demanda-t-il à sa femme quand il aperçut l'embarcation.

— Voir si tout est correct chez ma mère.

— C'est fin, ton affaire, fit-il, sarcastique. Et tu vas faire quoi avec le cheval et la voiture?

— Patrick va venir nous conduire et il va les ramener.

Au lieu de se proposer pour aller voir chez les Beauchemin, il se borna à hausser les épaules et à rentrer dans son atelier improvisé. Un moment plus tard, Patrick sortit et monta dans la voiture.

— J'aimerais ça, moi, y aller avec vous autres, ne put-il s'empêcher de dire alors que la voiture quittait la cour de la ferme.

— T'as juste à venir, fit Camille.

— Je peux pas. P'pa m'a dit de revenir tout de suite après.

Camille et Ann n'eurent aucun mal à parcourir les quelques centaines de pieds qui les séparaient de la ferme des Beauchemin. Comme Donat était revenu chercher des outils pour travailler à l'embâcle quelques minutes avant l'arrivée des visiteuses, il avait pu rassurer sa mère sur le sort d'Emma et des enfants. Camille et sa fille étaient restées moins d'une heure et elles étaient rentrées sans problème. À aucun moment Marie n'avait demandé à sa fille où était Liam, persuadée qu'il travaillait avec les autres cultivateurs de la paroisse à démolir l'embâcle. Évidemment, peu fière du comportement de son mari, Camille s'était bien gardée de dire qu'il était à la maison. Cependant, avant de quitter sa mère, elle avait proposé d'aller aider Bernadette à nettoyer l'école le lendemain s'il faisait assez beau et si l'eau s'était retirée. Ainsi, elle compenserait la conduite égoïste de Liam.

❧

Dieu dut entendre les prières des habitants de Saint-Bernard-Abbé. Durant la soirée et la nuit, le chenal, loin de se refermer, s'ouvrit plus largement et permit aux glaces de suivre librement le courant et de descendre la rivière. Mieux, tout laissait croire que l'embâcle formé plus haut avait cédé sans faire de dégâts. À la plus grande satisfaction des riverains, le lendemain matin l'eau avait pratiquement regagné le lit de la rivière, laissant cependant d'importants blocs de glace dans les champs et sur la route, comme des îlots perdus dans une mer de boue.

— C'est un signe que le bon Dieu veut qu'on aille aux cérémonies à la chapelle à soir, déclara Marie. C'est jeudi saint. Pour moi, tout le monde va être là, ajouta-t-elle.

— Avant de pouvoir y aller, il va falloir atteler les chevaux et leur faire tirer les blocs de glace restés sur le chemin, lui fit remarquer Hubert. Si on fait pas ça, il y a pas un boghei qui va être capable de passer dans le rang Saint-Jean.

— C'est ce qu'on va faire cet avant-midi, annonça Donat. À part ça, il faut pas oublier que pour aller à la chapelle, il va falloir qu'on puisse grimper la côte, ajouta-t-il.

— Si le cheval peut pas, on la montera à pied, dit sa mère sur un ton sans appel. Après tout, ce sera pas la première fois qu'on arrivera tout crottés à la chapelle.

Pendant cet échange, Bernadette s'était approchée de l'une des fenêtres de la cuisine pour scruter le ciel où quelques nuages s'éloignaient.

— On dirait qu'il va faire beau, déclara-t-elle. Je m'en vais à l'école faire du ménage.

— Je vais t'emmener, lui proposa Donat. Hyland est supposé apporter du bois pour qu'on fasse de nouveaux garde-fous au pont à matin.

— Si c'est comme ça, je vais aller donner un coup de main à Bedette, déclara Marie.

— Mais m'man, vous avez déjà de la besogne par-dessus la tête ici dedans, lui fit remarquer l'institutrice. Je suis bien capable de me débrouiller.

— Laisse faire. Ça va être moins décourageant.

— Et toi, Hubert ? Qu'est-ce que tu vas faire ? lui demanda Donat.

— Moi, je vais partir en avant de vous autres avec le Blond. Je vais apporter des chaînes et je vais tirer une couple de blocs de glace en dehors du chemin parce qu'ils empêchent de passer. Si j'ai trop de misère, je t'attendrai.

— Après ça, j'espère que tu vas pas disparaître chez les Dionne ?

— Crains rien, dit son jeune frère, le visage mi-figue, mi-raisin.

— Mais t'es rentré bien tard hier soir, intervint Bernadette. On a cru que tu t'étais perdu en chemin, ajouta-t-elle, sarcastique.

— Monsieur et madame Dionne ont insisté pour que je soupe avec eux autres, se défendit Hubert en lui jetant un regard peu amène.

— Mais ils soupent ben tard, eux autres, dit Donat, moqueur.

— C'est pas ça, mais on a pas mal jasé à table.

— Est-ce qu'on peut te demander de quoi vous avez parlé ? lui demanda sa mère, curieuse.

— Ben, monsieur Dionne a ben des idées. Là, il m'a parlé d'un cousin qui a ouvert une fromagerie à Dunham. Il paraît que ça marche ben, cette affaire-là.

— Puis ? lui demanda son frère, intrigué.

— Il m'a dit que, s'il avait pas à s'occuper du magasin, il irait apprendre à faire du fromage chez son cousin et qu'après il ouvrirait une fromagerie à Saint-Bernard.

— T'es pas sérieux ? fit sa mère. Il me semble que ce serait une belle perte de temps. Toutes les femmes de la paroisse savent comment faire ça, du fromage.

— Peut-être, m'man, mais du bon fromage, il paraît que c'est autre chose, répliqua Hubert. D'après monsieur Dionne, tous les cultivateurs finissent par être pris avec des surplus de lait et ils seraient ben contents de le vendre à la fromagerie. En plus, selon lui, ben des femmes se donneraient plus la peine de faire leur fromage si elles étaient sûres d'en trouver du bon dans une fromagerie pas trop loin à un prix raisonnable.

— Ouais, c'est pas bête, reconnut Donat.

— Ça fait que j'ai proposé à monsieur Dionne d'aller à Dunham apprendre à faire du fromage si son cousin acceptait de me montrer comment faire, reprit Hubert avec fierté. Il est supposé lui écrire.

— C'est ben beau, ton affaire, intervint sa mère, mais une fois que tu vas savoir faire ça, qu'est-ce que tu vas faire ?

— Monsieur Dionne est intéressé à faire bâtir une petite fromagerie et je serais son fromager.

— Si je comprends ben, je pourrai pas compter sur toi pour travailler sur la terre ce printemps ? demanda Donat, passablement ennuyé par cette perspective.

— Ah ! Il y a encore rien de fait, le rassura son frère. Il va falloir d'abord que le cousin accepte de m'apprendre.

— Es-tu bien certain que les Dionne essayent pas surtout de caser leur Angélique ? lui demanda sa mère, l'air sévère.

— Puis après, madame Beauchemin ? rétorqua sa bru. Angélique Dionne est loin d'être laide et c'est surtout un bien beau parti.

— Un beau parti, c'est vite dit, répliqua sa belle-mère en lui décochant un regard venimeux.

— En tout cas, c'est une belle fille, dit Hubert.

— Tiens ! On dirait que l'ancien frère se déniaise, se moqua Bernadette.

— Toi, surveille ton langage, la mit en garde sa mère.

Quelques minutes plus tard, Eugénie chuchota à son mari :

— As-tu pensé que ce serait une bien bonne affaire que ton frère marie Angélique Dionne ?

— Pourquoi tu dis ça ?

— Comme ça, il s'incrusterait pas ici dedans et plus rien empêcherait ta mère de se donner à nous autres.

— Et Bernadette, elle ?

— Elle, elle m'inquiète pas trop, répliqua sa femme. Elle va bien finir par se décider avec son boiteux.

— Je trouve que tu vas vite en baptême, toi, lui reprocha-t-il. Hubert a même pas encore parlé d'aller veiller avec la fille de Télesphore Dionne et ma sœur, aux dernières nouvelles, a jamais parlé de fiançailles.

Chapitre 18

Les jours saints

Moins d'une heure plus tard, Eugénie se retrouva seule dans la maison. Donat était parti quelques minutes après son jeune frère. Il avait attelé le boghei pour la première fois de l'année et il y avait fait monter Bernadette et sa mère.

— J'espère juste que Hubert est arrivé à ôter la glace du chemin pour qu'on puisse passer, dit Donat en quittant la cour de la ferme avec son attelage.

— Tu vas bien le voir, fit Bernadette, assise sur la banquette arrière du véhicule. Si ça passe pas, je vais continuer à pied. Il faut absolument que j'aille voir les dégâts qu'il y a eu dans mon école.

En fait, la route, bien que très boueuse, était carrossable. Au passage, Bernadette poussa un cri quand elle vit les amoncellements de glace qui cernaient encore partiellement la maison de Constant Aubé.

— Il a été pas mal chanceux de pas avoir de dégâts dans sa maison neuve, fit-elle, aussi stupéfaite que sa mère devant le spectacle offert par tant de blocs de glace si près de la route.

Quand le boghei arriva au pont, Donat ne fut pas étonné de voir une demi-douzaine d'hommes déjà sur place, à l'entrée du pont, en train de décharger une voiture sur laquelle étaient empilés des madriers et des planches. Thomas Hyland, encore une fois, avait donné la preuve de son efficacité et de sa générosité.

Dès que Donat immobilisa son boghei, Hubert s'avança vers lui.

— Je sais pas si le moulin de Hyland a été magané par les glaces comme celui d'Aubé, dit-il. Après tout, ces deux moulins-là sont presque en face l'un de l'autre.

— En tout cas, comme tu peux voir, ça l'a pas empêché de nous donner pas mal de bois, répliqua Donat.

— Il en a pas parlé hier quand je l'ai vu, se contenta de dire son jeune frère. Il paraît que ce bois-là était dans sa remise.

— Laisse-nous descendre, ordonna Marie au conducteur. On va traverser le pont à pied. Moi, j'ai peur de passer là-dessus en voiture quand il y a pas de garde-fous.

Donat aida sa mère et sa sœur à descendre et les regarda traverser le pont à pied.

— Je vous dis que ça doit être beau à voir en dedans, dit Bernadette à sa mère en arrivant devant son école dont les murs extérieurs portaient les marques de larges traînées de boue. Regardez, m'man. Le perron a été à moitié arraché.

Les deux femmes se hissèrent difficilement sur le perron et l'institutrice, le cœur battant, déverrouilla la porte, en espérant, contre toute logique, que l'eau n'avait pas pénétré à l'intérieur de sa classe. Dès le premier coup d'œil, ses espoirs furent déçus. Le parquet disparaissait sous quelques pouces d'eau qui n'était pas parvenue à s'écouler à l'extérieur et, à voir les traces laissées sur les murs en planches bouvetées, elle était montée jusqu'à trois pieds au moins. Elle avait bousculé plusieurs pupitres et même déplacé la vieille fournaise installée au fond du local. De la suie s'était écoulée des tuyaux de la fournaise et tout était souillé par la boue.

— Seigneur, que c'est décourageant! s'écria Bernadette, les larmes aux yeux. On n'arrivera jamais à remettre tout ça d'aplomb pour mardi prochain.

— On a le temps, la contredit sèchement sa mère. T'as une couple de jours pour y arriver. Là, on se met à l'ouvrage.

— Il va falloir d'abord replacer la fournaise et installer les tuyaux si on veut faire chauffer de l'eau, dit Bernadette en rassemblant son courage. Là, je sais pas si je vais être capable de trouver du bois sec dans la remise pour allumer le poêle, par exemple.

— Si t'en trouves pas, tu demanderas à un de tes frères d'aller en chercher à la maison.

Pendant que Marie entreprenait de remettre sur pied les pupitres qui avaient été bousculés par l'eau, sa fille sortit de l'école. Elle l'entendit s'exclamer. Il y eut ensuite un bruit de pas sur le perron et la porte s'ouvrit sur un Constant Aubé de bonne humeur.

— M'man, ça a tout l'air qu'on n'aura pas à aller courir le bois. Constant y a pensé avant nous autres et il nous en apporte.

— T'es bien fin, mon garçon, dit Marie. Comme tu peux le voir, il y a tout un barda à faire ici dedans avant que ce soit convenable.

— C'est aussi pour ça que je suis venu, madame Beauchemin. Je suis venu vous donner un coup de main.

— Mais t'as pas la roue de ton moulin à réparer ? lui demanda Bernadette.

— C'est sûr, mais il y a rien qui presse. C'est pas demain la veille que je vais avoir à m'en servir. Ça peut attendre. Ensemble, on devrait être capables de tout remettre d'aplomb dans la journée.

— Que Dieu t'entende, conclut Marie.

Constant aida d'abord à éponger toute l'eau répandue sur le parquet. Il apporta ensuite plusieurs brassées de bois dans l'école, replaça les tuyaux et alluma la fournaise avant d'aller chercher de l'eau au puits situé derrière l'école. Quand il revint, il était accompagné de Camille et de ses quatre enfants.

— Je vous amène de l'aide ! annonça-t-il en faisant passer devant lui les nouveaux arrivants.

— Ben voyons donc! s'écria Bernadette en s'avançant pour accueillir sa sœur et ses enfants.

— On a pensé qu'on serait pas de trop pour tout remettre d'aplomb, déclara Camille. Les enfants aussi tenaient à faire leur part. Après tout, c'est leur école.

— Vous serez pas de trop, confirma Bernadette. Il y a de la besogne pour tout le monde.

— Comme sur le pont, à ce que j'ai pu voir, répliqua sa sœur en retirant son manteau. Ils sont au moins une douzaine à scier et à clouer. Pour moi, ça va être réparé aujourd'hui.

— On l'espère tous, intervint sa mère. Moi, ça me fait peur sans bon sens, un pont sans garde-fous. Il suffirait que le cheval bronche pour envoyer la voiture en bas du pont.

Bernadette et sa mère confièrent des tâches à chacun pendant que Constant allait emprunter quelques bouts de madrier aux hommes en train de construire les garde-fous du pont, dans l'intention de réparer le perron endommagé. À midi, Camille invita tous les travailleurs dans l'école à dîner. Elle demanda à Patrick et Duncan d'aller chercher le panier de provisions laissé dans la voiture. Assis sur les marches de l'escalier qui conduisait à l'appartement à l'étage, tous mangèrent de bon appétit des tartines et des cretons.

— On mange de la viande à midi, ça veut dire qu'il va falloir faire maigre à soir, fit remarquer Marie.

Après ce repas improvisé, on se remit au travail. On finit de laver les murs, les pupitres, les fenêtres et les ardoises et on nettoya à fond le parquet. À la fin de l'après-midi, l'école du rang avait retrouvé son apparence habituelle. Patrick et Duncan avaient même trouvé le temps de faire disparaître les traces de boue qui maculaient les murs extérieurs. Quand vint le moment de rentrer, Bernadette se confondit en remerciements, heureuse de voir son école aussi propre.

Quand ils passèrent sur le pont, ils se rendirent compte que les nouveaux garde-fous avaient été installés.

Toutefois, ce soir-là, comme prévu, il fut impossible aux habitants des rangs Saint-Jean et Saint-Paul d'escalader la pente abrupte du rang Sainte-Ursule avec leur attelage pour se rendre à la chapelle. Le chemin était trop boueux. Ils durent donc se résigner à laisser leur voiture en bas, chez Dionne et Bourgeois, et à monter la côte à pied tant bien que mal.

— Ça, c'est à mon goût! fit Bernadette en affichant un air dégoûté devant ses bottes maculées de boue jusqu'à mi-jambe. Je vais en avoir pour une heure à les nettoyer. Puis regardez le bas de ma robe!

— Veux-tu bien arrêter de te lamenter, lui ordonna sèchement sa mère, au moment où elles entraient dans la chapelle. On n'est pas pires que les autres.

Elles allèrent rejoindre Eugénie dans le banc familial. Ce soir-là, Hubert avait proposé de garder Alexis pour lui permettre d'assister à l'office des ténèbres.

Quelques minutes plus tôt, le curé de Saint-Bernard-Abbé avait envoyé le bedeau chercher les syndics qui aidaient les gens à trouver des places dans la chapelle prise d'assaut par les fidèles.

— Prenez chacun une chaise et assoyez-vous dans le chœur, leur ordonna-t-il.

— Pourquoi, monsieur le curé? osa lui demander Donat, surpris.

— On est jeudi saint. Vous allez personnifier les apôtres lors de la dernière Cène.

Hyland, Côté, Blanchette, Ellis et Donat Beauchemin s'exécutèrent sans trop comprendre ce que voulait dire le prêtre. Ils précédèrent celui-ci de peu dans le chœur pendant qu'il revêtait sa chasuble violette.

Alors commença la longue célébration. Il y eut de nombreuses lectures et des psaumes avant que le pasteur ne célèbre la messe. Un peu avant l'offertoire, il annonça aux gens réunis qu'il allait procéder au lavement des pieds des syndics de la mission pour rappeler le geste plein d'humilité posé par le Christ le soir de la dernière Cène. Sur ce, il se retourna et fit signe aux servants de messe de lui apporter un bol d'eau et une serviette, et il s'agenouilla devant Samuel Ellis pour lui laver les pieds.

— Enlève tes souliers, commanda-t-il à l'Irlandais qui n'avait pas encore bougé.

Dès que Samuel eut enlevé ses souliers, un fumet assez peu appétissant fit froncer le nez au célébrant qui remarqua que son président du conseil portait d'épaisses chaussettes trouées dont le dernier lavage datait quelque peu.

— Ôte tes bas aussi, batèche! lui ordonna tout bas Josaphat Désilets au bord de la nausée. Il me semble que t'aurais pu changer de bas, ajouta-t-il les dents serrées en lui lavant les pieds.

— …

— Rechausse-toi vite avant qu'on sente ça dans toute la chapelle, poursuivit le prêtre en passant à Donat.

Rouge de honte, Samuel Ellis s'empressa de remettre ses chaussettes et ses souliers, sous le regard goguenard des autres membres du conseil.

À la fin de la messe, les gens demeurèrent sur place pour assister au dépouillement solennel des autels. Avant de quitter le chœur, Josaphat Désilets prit soin de rappeler à ses ouailles l'obligation, sous peine de péché mortel, de se confesser afin de communier pour Pâques. Il annonça qu'il confesserait le lendemain et le surlendemain, tant l'après-midi que le soir.

Quand Samuel Ellis rejoignit sa femme à la fin de la cérémonie, Bridget s'empressa de lui demander ce que les autres syndics avaient à le regarder de travers durant le lavement des pieds.

— Monsieur le curé a pas aimé pantoute la senteur de mes pieds, se borna-t-il à dire, comme si la chose avait peu d'importance. En plus, il a trouvé que mes bas étaient pas mal sales.

— Bonyenne de sans-dessein! s'emporta-t-elle, rouge de colère. Là, c'est fin! Tu me fais passer pour une malpropre et tout ça, c'est ta faute. Je t'ai répété trois fois de changer de bas à matin quand tu t'es levé.

— C'est pas grave pantoute, laissa tomber Samuel. L'année prochaine, il aura juste à me sacrer patience quand il voudra laver les pieds du monde.

＞

Le lendemain matin, les habitants de Saint-Bernard-Abbé furent accueillis à leur réveil par un ciel gris et un petit vent frisquet de mauvais augure.

— Il peut ben mouiller tant que ça va pouvoir à cette heure que les glaces sont parties, dit Hubert en se préparant à sortir de la maison pour aller aider Donat à soigner les animaux.

— J'aimerais autant pas, rétorqua son frère en chaussant ses bottes. J'ai dans l'idée d'aller voir si Constant a besoin d'un coup de main. L'eau s'est retirée assez pour qu'on soit capables de se rendre jusqu'au moulin. Il serait peut-être temps de voir les dégâts que les glaces ont faits là.

— J'ai entendu Hyland hier matin dire que depuis chez eux, il y avait pas apparence d'y avoir d'autres dommages que la roue. De toute façon, je vais y aller avec toi.

— Vous avez raison d'y aller, les garçons, approuva leur mère. Il y a pas plus serviable que ce garçon-là. Qu'est-ce que tu fais là, Bedette? demanda-t-elle à sa fille cadette qui avait entrepris de mettre le couvert.

— Je mets la table.

— À quoi tu penses, ma fille? On est vendredi saint. C'est maigre et jeûne toute la journée.

— Salament! C'est pas vrai! s'exclama Hubert.

— Pour un ancien frère, je trouve que t'oublies pas mal vite, mon garçon, lui fit remarquer sa mère, sévère.

— J'ai pas oublié, m'man, mais je trouve que ça tombe mal quand on a de l'ouvrage dur à faire aujourd'hui.

— Tu travailleras pas bien longtemps, lui rappela sa mère. Oublie pas que monsieur le curé a bien dit qu'on devait arrêter toutes nos besognes au commencement de l'après-midi.

— En attendant, ça changera rien à nos plans, conclut Donat. Il faut aller donner un coup de main à Aubé.

En fait, les frères Beauchemin trouvèrent Constant Aubé déjà affairé dans son moulin ce matin-là. Le meunier était en train de nettoyer les dégâts causés par l'eau à l'intérieur.

— Puis, ta roue ? lui demanda Donat en entrant.

— Il y a une douzaine de pieds qui ont été arrachés, dit Constant, l'air sombre.

— On va t'aider à réparer ça, déclara Hubert, plein de bonne volonté.

— Je pense pas qu'on soit capables, lui apprit Constant. Le seul moyen d'y arriver, c'est de demander à Bélisle de revenir avec ses hommes. Eux autres ont les échafaudages et les treuils qu'il faut.

— Dans ce cas-là, on va te donner un coup de main à nettoyer ici dedans.

— Je peux ben le faire tout seul.

— Pantoute, t'es venu nous aider, c'est à notre tour.

En ce vendredi saint, tout travail cessa à l'heure du midi. Chez les Beauchemin, comme dans beaucoup de familles de la paroisse, on s'endimancha dès la fin du repas pour aller à la chapelle dans l'intention de se confesser avant la cérémonie célébrée traditionnellement à trois heures.

Comme prévu, un nombre impressionnant de fidèles faisait la queue patiemment, debout près du confessionnal dans lequel officiait Josaphat Désilets, vêtu de son surplis blanc et de son étole violette. À tour de rôle, chacun pénétrait dans la petite alcôve séparée du confesseur par un guichet et tenue à l'abri des regards des gens par un rideau.

— Il y a presque vingt-cinq personnes qui attendent, fit remarquer Eugénie à son mari. On en a au moins pour une heure à rester debout.

— On n'a pas le choix, on est rendus. Moi, j'ai pas le goût pantoute de revenir à soir.

Marie et Bernadette, résignées, avaient pris place derrière eux. L'institutrice avait même imité sa mère en sortant de sa bourse un chapelet et s'était mise à réciter.

— T'es rendue pieuse sans bon sens, lui chuchota sa belle-sœur, un peu moqueuse, en apercevant son chapelet.

— Ben non, je prends de l'avance sur la punition que monsieur le curé va me donner, lui expliqua Bernadette, sérieuse. En plus, ça fait passer le temps et…

— Quoi ? Qu'est-ce que vous venez de me dire là ? gronda la voix tonnante du confesseur qui fit sursauter les gens présents dans la chapelle.

Beaucoup de fidèles tournèrent la tête vers le confessionnal, cherchant à deviner à qui le prêtre s'adressait. Chacun ne pouvait voir que les pieds du pécheur dépassant sous le rideau qui masquait l'alcôve. On se regardait les uns les autres avec une certaine inquiétude, craignant soudainement que le confesseur ne fasse un éclat semblable quand son tour serait venu d'aller confesser ses péchés.

— J'ai jamais entendu une affaire comme ça ! Vous devriez avoir honte, vous m'entendez ! C'est du vice, ça ! poursuivit Josaphat Désilets, oubliant, à l'évidence, qu'on pouvait l'entendre. Si ça a de l'allure ! Un homme de votre âge !

Bernadette, curieuse, tendait le cou pour tenter de deviner qui était celui qui se faisait ainsi rabrouer. Elle n'eut pas à attendre très longtemps. Le rideau s'écarta finalement pour livrer passage à un Hormidas Meilleur au teint blafard qui alla s'agenouiller dans l'un des premiers bancs à l'avant de la chapelle, bien conscient que tous les regards le suivaient. Samuel Ellis vint prendre place dans la file et, au passage, il ne put s'empêcher de murmurer à Donat sur un ton moqueur :

— On dirait ben que le père Meilleur vient de se faire tirer les oreilles.

— Il paraît que ça arrive souvent aux hommes de plus de quarante ans, monsieur Ellis, répliqua le fils de Baptiste Beauchemin en prenant un air très sérieux.

— Petit baptême d'effronté ! jura l'Irlandais avant de poursuivre son chemin vers le bout de la file.

Quand les gens purent enfin quitter les lieux après la cérémonie religieuse, il était un peu plus de cinq heures.

— Maudit que c'est long la lecture de la Passion, se plaignit Bernadette. J'ai mal aux pieds.

— Arrête donc de te lamenter pour des niaiseries, la rabroua sa mère.

— Les vaches doivent ben se lamenter, elles aussi, fit remarquer Donat à son tour en s'emparant des guides après que tous les siens furent montés dans le boghei. L'heure du train est passée depuis un bon bout de temps.

— Qu'elles se lamentent, laissa tomber Marie. Le vendredi saint arrive juste une fois par année.

— En plus, m'man, on devrait pas leur donner à manger à soir, poursuivit Bernadette, sarcastique. Après tout, il y a pas de raison qu'on jeûne et qu'elles mangent.

— Et que t'es insignifiante, Bedette ! se contenta de dire sa mère.

— En tout cas, moi, j'ai bien hâte à Pâques, intervint Eugénie. Il est temps que le carême finisse. Je l'ai jamais trouvé aussi dur que cette année.

— Pourtant, à ma connaissance, tu t'es pas privée tant que ça, fit sa belle-mère d'une voix acide.

Le lendemain, la cuisine de Camille embaumait de toutes sortes de bonnes odeurs. Dans le four cuisait un gros jambon arrosé de sirop d'érable pendant que la cuisinière et Ann confectionnaient deux gâteaux après avoir préparé quatre tartes à la farlouche.

— Calvinus que ça sent bon! s'écria Paddy Connolly qui venait de descendre de sa chambre.

Il s'approcha des casseroles dans lesquelles mijotait un mélange qui lui mettait l'eau à la bouche.

— Enlevez votre grand nez de mes chaudrons, lui commanda Camille.

— On peut pas goûter? demanda le retraité avec un air gourmand. C'est un vrai sacrifice…

— Ça en fera au moins un que vous aurez fait pendant le carême, mon oncle, rétorqua la maîtresse de maison, le plus sérieusement du monde.

Celle-ci avait du mal à dissimuler son énervement. Depuis la veille, elle subissait la mauvaise humeur de son mari, fâché de constater qu'elle n'avait pas du tout renoncé à inviter toute sa famille à souper le jour de Pâques.

— Bondance, c'est pas une surprise! lui avait-elle dit deux jours plus tôt quand il s'était plaint de la dépense. Je te l'ai dit après les fêtes que c'était temps qu'on invite, nous autres aussi. On peut tout de même pas passer notre temps à se faire recevoir par tout un chacun sans jamais remettre rien. Oublie pas qu'on arrive six quand on va quelque part.

— Mais t'es pas obligée de vider le garde-manger, calvaire!

— Jure pas, tu viens d'aller te confesser, lui ordonna-t-elle, agacée. On n'est tout de même pas pour recevoir le monde en leur servant de la soupane.

Bref, Liam s'était enfermé dans un mutisme bouldeur et les enfants faisaient les frais de ses sautes d'humeur depuis deux jours. Camille avait les nerfs à fleur de peau et ne se sentait aucune envie de tolérer l'oncle de son mari tournant autour d'elle et d'Ann dans la cuisine.

Ce soir-là, tous les Connolly participèrent à la cérémonie de la lumière et Camille en profita pour renouveler son invitation à souper aux membres de sa famille.

— Je sais pas trop, fit Xavier, hésitant.

Il avait remarqué que son beau-frère battait plutôt froid à Catherine chaque fois qu'il la rencontrait.

— Toi, tu te cherches pas de défaite, le prévint-elle. Je t'avertis que si t'arrives à la maison sans ta fiancée, tu vas t'en retourner la chercher, le menaça Camille, sérieuse. Et toi, Bedette, tu dis à Constant Aubé de venir souper. Il est invité, lui aussi.

Sur le chemin du retour, Liam ne put s'empêcher de manifester sa mauvaise humeur.

— T'avais ben besoin d'inviter la Benoît, lui reprocha-t-il.

— Oui, j'avais besoin de le faire, répliqua-t-elle sèchement. Dans deux mois, elle va faire partie de la famille et c'est normal qu'elle soit là. C'est pas une si mauvaise fille que ça, ajouta-t-elle.

— Pas une mauvaise fille ! s'exclama-t-il. Qu'est-ce qu'il te faut ?

— Laisse faire !

— Et l'autre, la Bottine à Aubé ! Je suppose qu'il va faire partie de la famille, lui aussi.

— Tu devrais avoir honte, Liam Connolly. Constant a pas arrêté de nous rendre service depuis qu'il est revenu à Saint-Bernard. En plus, il t'achète tous les meubles que tu fais.

— Il me fait pas la charité.

— Je le sais, mais c'est un bon garçon et il est pas question de le laisser de côté, trancha-t-elle.

Le matin de Pâques, Camille n'eut pas à rappeler à son mari son devoir du dimanche pascal. Quand elle se réveilla, la place à côté d'elle dans le lit était vide. Elle se leva et trouva le poêle déjà allumé dans la cuisine et Liam en train d'endosser son manteau. La veille, avant de se coucher, la maîtresse de maison avait pris soin de déposer sur la table une cruche vide destinée à recueillir l'eau de Pâques.

Au moment où Liam allait sortir, Patrick descendit l'escalier et demanda à son père s'il pouvait l'accompagner. Apparemment de meilleure humeur que les deux jours précédents, ce dernier accepta et ils quittèrent tous les deux la maison. Le père tenait le fanal allumé et le fils s'était chargé de la cruche. Ils se dirigèrent vers la source d'eau vive qui passait au bout de la terre de Conrad Boudreau. Contrairement à l'année précédente, ils n'avaient pas besoin de raquettes. Par chance, le froid de la nuit avait durci la boue et ils purent rejoindre sans mal la dizaine d'hommes qui attendaient le lever du soleil avant de plonger leur contenant dans l'eau froide.

Ce matin-là, bien peu de gens de Saint-Bernard-Abbé se plaignirent de la température. Le ciel était dégagé et les fidèles purent faire monter la côte du rang Sainte-Ursule à leur attelage sans grande difficulté parce que le sol était maintenant durci. La semaine précédente, la plupart des femmes avaient sorti leurs vieux chapeaux et les avaient transformés en leur ajoutant un ruban neuf, une nouvelle voilette, des plumes ou même une petite cocarde. Même si les gens n'avaient pas encore mangé pour pouvoir aller communier et ainsi faire leurs pâques, ils arboraient un air réjoui en cette matinée d'avril ensoleillée. On avait enfin laissé derrière soi quarante jours de privations et on allait pouvoir fêter le jour de la résurrection du Seigneur et s'en mettre plein la panse après la messe.

Dans son sermon prononcé en anglais et en français, le curé Désilets eut des accents lyriques pour parler de la résurrection du Christ, ce qui ne l'empêcha pas de brandir les flammes de l'enfer pour ceux qui n'avaient pas encore fait leurs pâques. Avant de retourner à l'autel pour terminer la célébration de la messe, le pasteur de Saint-Bernard-Abbé rappela à ses ouailles qu'il ne restait plus que sept jours pour se préparer à recevoir dignement monseigneur l'évêque et qu'il comptait sur la bonne volonté de chacun pour faire de cette visite un événement digne de figurer dans les annales de la nouvelle paroisse.

— Rappelez-vous qu'il n'est pas donné à tout le monde d'assister dans sa vie à la naissance d'une paroisse, dit-il à l'assistance. Il faut que la chapelle soit décorée et que chacun se fasse un devoir de venir accueillir notre évêque.

À cet instant, alors que tout le monde s'attendait à voir le curé retourner enfin à l'autel, il fit une annonce qui surprit toute l'assistance.

— Première publication des bans, dit le prêtre en consultant une feuille. Il y a promesse de mariage entre Hormidas Meilleur de Saint-Bernard-Abbé, fils d'Athanase Meilleur et de Clémence Rompré de Saint-Zéphirin, et veuve Angèle Cloutier de cette paroisse, fille de Léon Parenteau et de Maria Jutras de Sainte-Monique.

Des murmures s'élevèrent dans la foule et plus d'un chercha le facteur et la veuve du regard. L'un et l'autre étaient invisibles. Ils semblaient avoir pris sagement la précaution d'aller à la basse-messe.

— Il est à mentionner que ce mariage sera le premier à être célébré dans notre nouvelle paroisse, prit la peine de préciser le célébrant avant de retourner à l'autel.

À la sortie de la chapelle, ce mariage entre la veuve et le petit facteur célibataire défraya la plupart des conversations et suscita bien des commentaires souvent accompagnés de remarques ironiques.

— Blasphème! j'aurais jamais cru que c'était aussi dangereux de jouer aux cartes avec une créature, déclara Xavier Beauchemin à ses beaux-frères.

— Moi, j'ai dans l'idée qu'il sera pas tard que p'tit père va se faire secouer le prunier par la veuve, dit en riant Rémi.

— Ça m'étonnerait pas qu'elle lui mette vite le holà quand il va rentrer la première fois avec un coup de trop dans le nez.

— Un autre qui savait pas à quel point il était ben vieux garçon, osa dire Liam Connolly, qui venait de se joindre au petit groupe d'hommes debout sur le parvis.

— Moi, j'aurais ben voulu savoir pourquoi monsieur le curé l'a traité de «vicieux» quand il est allé se confesser jeudi passé, chuchota Donat, l'œil égrillard.

— Ça, c'est pas de tes affaires, Donat Beauchemin, intervint sa sœur Emma qui s'était rapprochée du groupe pour signifier à son mari qu'il était temps de rentrer.

— Pour moi, t'as une idée pourquoi monsieur le curé a dit ça, se moqua Xavier.

— Grand niaiseux! le rabroua la femme de Rémi. Laissez-le donc tranquille, le pauvre homme. Il devait être assez mal à l'aise quand il est sorti du confessionnal.

— Ah ça, c'est vrai! reconnut Donat. On peut même dire qu'il rasait les murs et qu'il avait l'air de trouver la porte de la chapelle pas mal loin.

— D'après vous autres, qui va aller les chaperonner tous les deux? s'enquit Liam. Vous, belle-mère? demanda-t-il à Marie qui venait de s'approcher à son tour.

— Arrêtez donc de parler pour rien dire, fit la veuve de Baptiste Beauchemin sur un ton sévère. Angèle Cloutier est une femme respectable et je suis certaine qu'elle va s'organiser pour que ses fréquentations fassent pas scandale.

— Ben là, m'man, c'est mal parti en maudit, fit Donat. Ça fait deux fois qu'on les poigne tous les deux tout seuls.

— Fais bien attention aux calomnies, mon garçon, le mit en garde sa mère.

Le groupe se sépara et chacun rentra chez soi après avoir promis à Camille d'arriver tôt à son souper.

Ce soir-là, on parla beaucoup de la visite de monseigneur Laflèche prévue pour le dimanche suivant et surtout des travaux de la terre qui allaient reprendre incessamment. Déjà, les journées allongeaient et le soleil commençait à se faire plus chaud au milieu de la journée. Les nombreux jours de pluie des deux semaines précédentes avaient fait disparaître les dernières traces de neige. La taille des blocs de glace laissés dans les champs par l'embâcle avait sérieusement diminué.

Les invités réunis autour de la table des Connolly ne tarirent pas d'éloge sur la nourriture qui leur fut servie. Camille en profita pour qu'une bonne partie des compliments soit adressée à Ann qui avait largement participé à la confection du repas.

Par ailleurs, si Marie et Liam continuèrent à battre froid à Catherine Benoît, Camille et Emma firent en sorte que la fiancée de leur frère se sente à l'aise et acceptée par les autres membres de la famille. La jeune marraine s'occupa beaucoup de la petite Marthe et sembla charmer Duncan qui ne la quitta pas des yeux de la soirée.

— Fais attention à ta fiancée, recommanda Hubert à son frère Xavier, j'ai l'impression qu'il y a un gars dans la place qui a un œil dessus.

Xavier eut un sourire quand il remarqua les attentions que le garçon de dix ans de Liam accordait à sa future femme. À l'autre bout de la pièce, Camille surveillait son mari. Depuis l'arrivée des premiers invités, elle le voyait fixer des yeux ses enfants, comme s'il cherchait une raison pour les disputer. Il avait l'air contraint et souriait peu. Finalement, elle parvint à lui parler sans témoin quand ils allèrent tous les deux chercher des victuailles dans la cuisine d'été.

— Tu sais, t'es pas obligé d'avoir l'air bête parce qu'on reçoit, lui murmura-t-elle. Le monde mangera pas moins si tu fais une face de beu.

— J'ai pas l'air bête, se défendit-il, le visage fermé.

— En tout cas, c'est bien imité… insista-t-elle. Puis, essaye de pas chercher à faire payer les enfants parce que t'es de mauvaise humeur.

Liam haussa les épaules avant de la suivre dans la cuisine d'hiver où étaient rassemblés tous les invités. Cependant, la mise au point de Camille eut de l'effet, car il se contraignit à faire meilleure figure devant les invités.

— Est-ce qu'il y a quelque chose qui va pas avec ton mari? demanda Marie à sa fille quelques minutes plus tard. Tout à l'heure, il avait pas l'air dans son assiette.

— Un petit accrochage avec son oncle, mentit Camille, mais c'est arrangé.

Évidemment, Paddy fut celui qu'on entendit le plus durant toute la soirée. Aussitôt qu'on lui en donnait la chance, il se mettait à pérorer, les pouces passés dans les entournures de son gilet de satin noir. De toute évidence, les quatre mois passés chez son neveu n'avaient fait que lui confirmer sa supériorité de citadin et d'homme d'affaires averti sur ceux qu'il appelait sur un ton un peu méprisant «les pauvres habitants ignorants». Il était intimement persuadé de leur faire un grand honneur lorsqu'il leur expliquait les nouvelles.

Ainsi, il commenta abondamment la dernière nouvelle voulant que le ministre fédéral George-Étienne Cartier s'apprêtait à présenter aux Communes un projet de loi autorisant la construction d'un chemin de fer allant de l'Atlantique au Pacifique.

— Ça, ça va nous coûter cher! déclara l'homme d'affaires retraité, l'air convaincu.

— Cartier est un Bleu, ça a nécessairement du bon sens pour nous autres, les Canadiens français, avança Donat, se sentant obligé de défendre les conservateurs dont il avait été l'organisateur de campagne aux dernières élections.

— T'es ben jeune pour croire ça, rétorqua Paddy avec une certaine hauteur.

— On verra ben, s'entêta Donat.

— Les p'tits chars d'un bout à l'autre du pays, ça va surtout être bon pour les Anglais qui sont dans les affaires, le contredit Paddy. À part ça, Cartier doit penser qu'il y a une cenne à faire avec cette affaire-là pour ses amis Bleus.

— Faites attention à ce que vous dites, vous! le mit en garde Donat en élevant la voix.

— L'avenir nous le dira ben, intervint Rémi, soucieux d'éviter que la discussion tourne en affrontement. Mais parlant affaires, est-ce que je suis tout seul dans le rang à avoir reçu la visite du notaire Valiquette?

— Pour placer de l'argent? demanda Xavier.

— Oui.

— Je sais pas dans Saint-Jean, mais il a fait presque toutes les maisons dans Sainte-Ursule, affirma Xavier. Il est passé me voir la semaine dernière, la veille de l'embâcle. Il venait de chez les Benoît.

— Puis? lui demanda Donat.

— Moi, j'ai rien contre cet homme-là, répondit Xavier, mais j'ai fait affaire avec le notaire Letendre quand j'ai acheté ma terre et j'ai confiance en lui. C'est ce que je lui ai répondu.

— La même chose pour moi, fit Donat. Mais je sais qu'il y en a, comme Samuel Ellis, Tancrède Bélanger et Anatole Blanchette, qui lui ont donné leur argent pour qu'il le place pour eux. Il paraît qu'il leur a promis de bons intérêts.

— Moi, je me méfie d'Eudore Valiquette, reprit Rémi Lafond. On le connaît pas, ce notaire-là.

— Est-ce que ça veut dire que t'as pas voulu qu'il place ton argent? lui demanda sa belle-mère.

— Voyons, madame Beauchemin, un petit cultivateur comme moi a pas d'argent à placer.

— Si je me fie à ce qu'on raconte partout dans Saint-Bernard, Eudore Valiquette est arrivé à emprunter tout l'argent qu'il fallait pour bâtir le presbytère et payer la dette de la chapelle, intervint Paddy. Moi, je suis habitué aux affaires, affirma-t-il en se rengorgeant. Je peux vous dire que s'il a pu trouver autant d'argent, ça signifie qu'il a les reins solides et qu'on a confiance en lui en dehors de la paroisse.

— En tout cas, ça doit marcher son affaire, si je me fie à ce que j'ai entendu, dit Constant Aubé. Il y a au moins cinq cultivateurs de Saint-Paul et John White de notre rang qui ont fait affaire avec lui.

Durant la soirée, Camille et Ann servirent du sucre à la crème, des bonbons aux patates et des fondants. Maintenant, on pouvait se sucrer le bec sans avoir mauvaise conscience puisque le carême était officiellement terminé.

Un peu avant le départ des invités, Hubert apprit aux gens présents son intention d'aller faire un stage dans une fromagerie si Télesphore Dionne lui obtenait l'autorisation de son cousin. Il sut immédiatement que l'idée du père d'Angélique d'ouvrir une petite fromagerie à Saint-Bernard-Abbé aurait du succès en voyant la réaction enthousiaste des femmes présentes dans la pièce.

— Avoir toujours du bon fromage frais sans avoir à le faire, ça nous sauverait pas mal de temps, déclara Emma.

Après le départ du dernier invité, Liam alluma un fanal pour aller jeter un coup d'œil aux bâtiments pendant que ses fils allaient remplir le coffre à bois. Camille, aidée par ses deux filles, remit un peu d'ordre dans la maison. Quand les enfants eurent regagné leur chambre, à l'étage, la jeune femme alla se préparer pour la nuit et son mari vint la rejoindre peu après.

— Une chance que ça revient pas trop souvent, une affaire comme ça, dit-il après avoir retiré ses pantalons. Calvaire, on aurait dit que certains avaient pas mangé depuis un mois.

Camille ne se donna pas la peine de lui répondre. Épuisée par sa journée de travail, elle se tourna sur le côté et le sommeil l'emporta.

Chapitre 19

Tel père, telle fille

Le surlendemain, Marie Beauchemin venait à peine de commencer son repassage quand elle entendit une voiture entrer dans la cour de la ferme et s'arrêter près de la maison. Elle déposa son fer sur le poêle et s'approcha de la fenêtre pour identifier le visiteur. Elle eut alors la surprise de voir descendre de son boghei son beau-frère Armand, encore engoncé dans son épais manteau d'hiver même si la température avait commencé à s'adoucir sérieusement.

— Il y a quelqu'un qui arrive, madame Beauchemin, lui cria Eugénie en train de remettre de l'ordre dans sa chambre.

— Je le sais, c'est mon beau-frère Armand, rétorqua-t-elle.

Toujours penchée à la fenêtre, elle vit Donat sortir de l'étable et se diriger vers son oncle. Les deux hommes entrèrent dans la maison en même temps.

— P'tit Jésus! s'exclama-t-il après avoir salué sa belle-sœur et sa nièce par alliance, je vous dis que c'est pas encore ben chaud pour un mois d'avril.

— Approche-toi du poêle si t'es rendu frileux à ce point-là, l'invita Marie. Je vais te servir une bonne tasse de thé, ça va te réchauffer.

— Avec une goutte de bagosse, mon oncle, ça va être encore mieux, fit Donat en adressant à l'invité un clin d'œil de connivence.

Armand Beauchemin ne refusa pas.

— Un peu plus, je vous amenais Mathilde hier matin, annonça le gros homme en guettant du coin de l'œil la réaction des personnes présentes.

Le visage à la fois inquiet et mauvais de sa belle-sœur lui apprit que cette visite n'était pas tellement souhaitée. Dans la famille, on ne le disait pas ouvertement, mais les visites de la religieuse autoritaire et bavarde impénitente étaient considérées comme des épreuves qu'on trouvait toujours trop longues et surtout trop fréquentes.

— Elle aurait bien pu venir, dit Marie du bout des lèvres.

— Elle a dit qu'elle se reprendrait ce printemps, lui apprit le frère de Baptiste Beauchemin. Là, elle était attendue à l'orphelinat et il paraît que les sœurs peuvent pas se passer d'elle plus qu'une couple de jours.

— Est-ce qu'elle est restée longtemps chez vous ?

— Elle est arrivée jeudi passé.

— Pourquoi t'as pas amené Amanda avec toi ? lui demanda sa belle-sœur.

— Tu la connais, elle a pas de santé. Depuis la semaine passée, elle tire de la patte. Le voyage entre Sainte-Monique et Saint-Bernard aurait été trop dur pour elle.

Marie eut du mal à dissimuler un petit sourire. Elle connaissait suffisamment sa belle-sœur pour savoir que c'était une hypocondriaque souffrant de tous les maux, à l'entendre. De plus, l'arrivée de Mathilde n'avait pas dû arranger les choses. Il était bien connu dans la famille que la femme d'Armand n'était pas particulièrement hospitalière.

— Ma pauvre tante ! fit Eugénie sans grande conviction.

— Mais je suis pas seulement venu pour une visite de politesse, reprit le cultivateur de Sainte-Monique. Le curé Lanctôt m'a fait venir samedi passé pour me dire qu'on allait vider le charnier du cimetière cette semaine. Il y a eu des enterrements hier et ça me surprendrait pas qu'il reste pratiquement juste Baptiste. Ça fait qu'il faudrait que vous veniez le chercher sans trop perdre de temps. Il paraît que la terre est ben dégelée.

Marie regarda Donat qui prit la parole.

— S'il y a pas d'empêchement, mon oncle, on va aller chercher p'pa après-demain, le temps que je m'entende avec monsieur le curé pour acheter un lot dans le cimetière et avec Blanchette pour aller chercher le cercueil avec son corbillard.

— Ça a ben de l'allure, l'approuva son oncle. T'oublieras pas de me prévenir en passant quand vous arriverez à Sainte-Monique. Je vais vous attendre.

Armand Beauchemin resta à dîner chez sa belle-sœur et ne quitta les lieux qu'au début de l'après-midi. Après son départ, Donat se rendit au presbytère pour acheter un lot au cimetière paroissial, un lot situé près de la grande croix plantée l'automne précédent au centre de l'endroit. Baptiste Beauchemin serait le premier habitant de Saint-Bernard-Abbé à aller tenir compagnie au défunt curé Ouellet, enterré dans le cimetière paroissial.

Le curé Désilets fut d'accord pour officier une courte cérémonie de mise en terre et promit de voir à ce que la fosse soit creusée à temps.

Satisfait, le jeune cultivateur alla ensuite jusqu'à la ferme de son frère Xavier pour le prévenir avant de passer chez Blanchette pour s'assurer qu'il viendrait chercher la bière à Sainte-Monique. Après s'être arrêté chez ses sœurs Emma et Camille, il rentra à la maison.

À titre de président de la commission scolaire, il permit à Bernadette de donner congé à ses élèves le surlendemain pour qu'elle puisse assister à la cérémonie funèbre.

❦

Le jour venu, Ann accepta de se charger de la surveillance des enfants de la famille regroupés chez Emma. Xavier fut le dernier arrivé. À la surprise de tous, Catherine l'accompagnait. Marie lui battit froid en l'apercevant, mais ses enfants firent sentir à la jeune fille qu'ils appréciaient son geste. Ce matin-là, Marie Beauchemin sembla attacher plus d'importance à l'air renfrogné de son gendre Liam.

Un peu avant neuf heures, les adultes endimanchés prirent place dans les bogheis qui se dirigèrent vers Sainte-Monique. Le ciel gris et la petite pluie froide allaient bien avec la tristesse des participants au cortège funèbre qui suivait le corbillard noir d'Anatole Blanchette.

Il fallut presque une heure pour arriver au village. Sans descendre de voiture, on s'arrêta quelques instants devant la maison de l'oncle Armand, le temps de lui permettre de se joindre à la famille en compagnie de sa femme. Quelques minutes plus tard, les bogheis s'immobilisèrent en bordure du cimetière et Hubert alla prévenir le curé Lanctôt de l'arrivée de la famille Beauchemin.

Le pasteur de Sainte-Monique sortit du presbytère, suivi de près par Hubert et par son bedeau quelques instants après. L'homme d'Église salua les gens avant de les inviter à le suivre. Il semblait avoir oublié toute la rancune qu'il avait longtemps nourrie à l'encontre de Baptiste Beauchemin qu'il accusait, à juste titre, d'avoir travaillé à amputer sa belle paroisse d'une partie importante de ses fidèles en lançant la pétition qui avait conduit à la création de ce qui allait bientôt devenir la paroisse Saint-Bernard-Abbé.

Toutes les personnes présentes suivirent le prêtre dans les allées étroites du cimetière. L'homme s'arrêta non loin du charnier et fit signe aux hommes d'aller aider le bedeau déjà affairé à déverrouiller le petit édicule en pierre. Il sortit d'abord deux chevalets et Donat, Hubert, Xavier et Rémi portèrent le cercueil de Baptiste et le déposèrent dessus. Le prêtre s'avança alors et récita une courte prière avant de faire signe qu'on pouvait mettre la bière dans le corbillard qui attendait à l'entrée du cimetière. Les porteurs soulevèrent le cercueil et allèrent le placer dans la longue voiture noire d'Anatole Blanchette. Celui-ci s'empressa ensuite de le recouvrir d'une épaisse toile goudronnée.

La famille remercia le prêtre avant de remonter dans les voitures qui prirent la direction de Saint-Bernard-Abbé. La pluie avait cessé temporairement, mais le vent s'était levé. Le convoi funèbre arriva devant le cimetière de Saint-Bernard-Abbé un peu avant l'heure du dîner.

Cette fois-ci, ce fut Donat qui alla prévenir le curé de l'arrivée de la famille. Josaphat Désilets se dirigea vers une penderie pour y prendre la lourde chape noire qu'il déposa sur ses épaules.

— Avertis donc en passant Delphis Moreau et son père, ils sont dans la chapelle en train de laver le plancher, lui demanda le prêtre. Dis-leur de pas oublier les câbles.

Les deux hommes avaient creusé la fosse, la veille, et ils étaient chargés de jouer le rôle de fossoyeurs. Donat passa par la chapelle et prévint le père et le fils de l'arrivée du convoi. Les Moreau se ressemblaient étrangement, même si près de trente ans les séparaient. C'étaient deux petits hommes maigres à la figure chafouine tout en nerfs et en muscles.

— C'est correct, on y va, déclara Delphis, mais marche pas sur notre plancher frais lavé.

Au retour de Donat au cimetière, le cercueil dans lequel reposait son père depuis la fin du mois de décembre avait été transporté à moins de deux pieds de la fosse et la pluie s'était remise à tomber. À son grand étonnement, le fils aîné de Baptiste Beauchemin s'aperçut que Samuel Ellis, Thomas Hyland, Constant Aubé, la veuve Cloutier ainsi que quelques voisins du rang Saint-Jean s'étaient déplacés pour assister à la mise en terre.

Les Moreau prirent place à chacune des extrémités du trou d'environ six pieds de profondeur pendant que les autres personnes présentes se tenaient près du prêtre qui avait entrepris de réciter une dernière prière sur la tombe de son paroissien décédé. À la fin de l'oraison, Josaphat Désilets ferma son livre de prières et fit un léger signe de tête aux Moreau pour leur signifier qu'ils pouvaient glisser les câbles sous la bière pour la descendre au fond de la fosse.

Un instant plus tard, il se produisit un événement imprévu qui causa un véritable choc à l'assistance. Delphis Moreau prit un câble et voulut gagner du temps en se glissant entre la fosse béante et l'amoncellement de terre, le câble sur l'épaule. Mal lui en prit, l'un de ses pieds glissa sur l'herbe détrempée et le fossoyeur improvisé disparut dans le trou, accompagné par un « oh ! » de stupéfaction de l'assistance.

Il fallut quelques secondes aux gens présents pour réaliser ce qu'ils venaient de voir et se précipiter vers le bord de la fosse.

— Christ de Christ ! jura Delphis Moreau du fond du trou où il avait disparu.

L'homme, assis dans quelques pouces d'eau boueuse, paraissait passablement étourdi et jetait des regards furieux autour de lui, comme si la fosse était responsable de sa mésaventure.

— T'es-tu cassé quelque chose ? lui demanda son père.

— Je pense pas, répondit Delphis en se remettant debout tant bien que mal.

— On va te sortir de là, lui promit Ellis qui avait déjà saisi l'autre câble pour lui en tendre un bout, alors que l'assistance laissait paraître un léger sourire devant la situation, malgré le caractère triste du cérémonial.

Xavier et Hubert s'empressèrent d'aider Delphis Moreau à sortir de sa fâcheuse position. C'est un homme au visage et aux vêtements maculés de boue que les gens présents virent apparaître.

— Bonyeu ! Il me semble que t'es assez vieux pour faire attention où tu mets les pieds, lui reprocha son père à mi-voix.

Le cultivateur allait lui répondre quand Josaphat Désilets, la mine réprobatrice, s'approcha du rescapé pour lui suggérer de venir se confesser durant la semaine pour les sacres qu'il venait de proférer.

Les hommes présents décidèrent alors d'un commun accord de donner un coup de main aux deux fossoyeurs amateurs en les aidant à passer les deux câbles sous le cercueil qu'ils descendirent lentement au fond de la fosse. Dès qu'Agénor Moreau jeta la première pelletée de terre, Bernadette et Camille entraînèrent leur mère vers le boghei. Les trois femmes furent suivies par tous les autres participants à la courte cérémonie. Quand les voitures quittèrent les lieux, les Moreau se retrouvèrent seuls pour finir de combler la fosse.

Marie n'avait guère ouvert la bouche de la matinée, retrouvant intacte toute la douleur que le départ de son compagnon de toujours lui avait causée trois mois auparavant. Revoir son cercueil lui avait fait sentir encore l'énorme perte vécue la veille de Noël.

Ses enfants avaient compris à quel point cet avant-midi avait été difficile et ils préférèrent lui laisser un peu de temps pour se remettre. C'est pourquoi ils refusèrent tous de venir dîner à la maison. Camille et Liam s'arrêtèrent un bref moment chez Emma pour permettre à leurs enfants de monter dans leur boghei et ils rentrèrent chez eux. Personne n'osa revenir sur l'incident cocasse qui venait de se produire au cimetière.

De retour à la maison, on s'empressa d'aller changer de vêtements chez les Beauchemin. On improvisa un dîner rapidement avalé dans un silence presque complet. Toutefois, à la fin du repas, Marie ne put s'empêcher de faire remarquer :

— Il va bien falloir trouver un moyen d'installer une pierre tombale pour votre père.

— Ça traînera pas, il va y en avoir une, promit Donat, la mine sombre.

— Vous avez remarqué, m'man, que Catherine est venue avec Xavier. Je trouve que c'est pas mal fin de sa part, dit Bernadette.

— Ouais, fit sa mère sans esquisser le moindre sourire. Il en reste pas moins que ça se fait pas qu'une fille se promène sur les chemins avec un garçon sans chaperon.

— Voyons, madame Beauchemin, intervint Eugénie. On était tous là. Qu'est-ce que vous vouliez qu'il lui arrive ?

— On n'était pas toujours là, la contredit sa belle-mère. Elle a été toute seule avec Xavier entre la maison et l'église.

Bernadette regarda sa belle-sœur et lui fit un signe discret de ne pas insister.

— T'avais pas invité le petit Aubé à venir à Sainte-Monique avec nous autres ? demanda Marie en se tournant vers sa fille.

— Pourquoi j'aurais fait ça ? Il fait pas partie de la famille, à ce que je sache.

— Depuis le temps qu'il vient veiller ici dedans et avec tout ce qu'il a fait pour ton père, il aurait pu vouloir venir.

— Ça me tentait pas, laissa tomber l'institutrice. De toute façon, il était au cimetière.

— Qu'est-ce qui se passe encore ? lui demanda sa mère. T'es-tu encore chicanée avec lui ?

— Vous saurez, m'man, qu'on se chicane jamais. Constant est trop fin. Il fait toujours ce que je lui demande. Il est toujours prêt à me donner la lune.

— Ah bon !

— C'en est fatigant, avoua la jeune fille. J'ai envie de respirer un peu.

— Pauvre Bedette ! la plaignit sincèrement sa mère. Je me demande bien quel jour tu vas vieillir. Reprocher à son cavalier d'être trop fin… J'aurai vraiment tout entendu !

Le lendemain après-midi, Bernadette était en train de faire épeler quelques mots à ses élèves quand Patrick Connolly lui signala l'arrivée d'un visiteur. Sans cesser de faire travailler les élèves, l'institutrice s'approcha d'une fenêtre. Elle eut la surprise de reconnaître Amédée Durand, l'inspecteur scolaire qu'elle n'avait pas vu depuis le printemps précédent.

Pendant que le jeune homme à la moustache conquérante entravait sa bête et prenait possession de son porte-document, Bernadette ne pouvait s'empêcher de l'admirer. L'inspecteur avait fière allure dans son strict costume noir un peu lustré et coiffé de son chapeau melon de la même couleur. Elle sortit de sa courte rêverie au moment où il se dirigea vers l'école. Elle demanda aux enfants de se lever et de saluer poliment le visiteur tout en faisant signe à Patrick d'ouvrir la porte.

Amédée Durand, le visage éclairé par un large sourire, salua l'enseignante et les élèves avant de prendre place derrière le bureau de Bernadette. Il interrogea les enfants tant en arithmétique qu'en français. Il posa de nombreuses questions à Ann, l'élève la plus âgée de la classe, et sembla grandement satisfait des réponses obtenues.

— Je vais laisser à monsieur le curé le soin de vous interroger sur le catéchisme, conclut-il en notant certaines choses dans un dossier tiré de son porte-documents.

Avant qu'il n'annonce aux enfants qu'ils auraient droit à un congé le lendemain, Bernadette se pencha vers lui pour lui expliquer qu'ils avaient joui d'un congé involontaire la veille. Le jeune inspecteur qui avait eu l'occasion de rencontrer Baptiste Beauchemin l'année précédente lui présenta ses condoléances tardives et l'assura qu'il comprenait la situation. Il se borna à écourter la journée de travail des enfants en les renvoyant à la maison au milieu de l'après-midi.

Au moment où les enfants partaient, l'institutrice demanda à Ann de dire à son oncle de ne pas l'attendre.

L'inspecteur avait à lui parler. Elle rentra ensuite dans l'école pour aller rejoindre le visiteur.

Comme lors de ses visites précédentes, Amédée Durand vérifia les préparations de classe de l'enseignante ainsi que son cahier de présences.

— Tout est parfait, conclut-il en passant un doigt sur sa moustache gominée. Mais j'ai remarqué, mademoiselle Beauchemin, que vous avez cinq élèves qui ne parlent pas couramment français.

— C'est vrai, monsieur Durand, il y en a même six, reconnut-elle. Ce sont de petits Irlandais qui font ce qu'ils peuvent en classe et ils ne comprennent qu'à moitié ce que je dis.

— C'est vraiment pas idéal. Ça doit retarder les autres enfants, dit Amédée Durand, songeur.

— C'est certain que ça aide pas. Moi, je parle pas anglais. Je le comprends juste un peu.

— Il faudrait une autre école à Saint-Bernard avec une maîtresse capable de parler anglais. Je vais voir ce que le président de la commission scolaire peut faire.

— C'est mon frère Donat qui est président, monsieur l'inspecteur.

— Pensez-vous que je pourrais le voir aujourd'hui, mademoiselle ? lui demanda-t-il.

— Il devrait être à la maison. C'est presque l'heure du train.

— Dans ce cas-là, vous me permettrez de vous ramener chez vous, fit-il aimablement.

— Là, je sais pas trop, monsieur Durand, dit Bernadette, un peu confuse. Ma mère aime pas beaucoup voir sa fille toute seule dans une voiture avec un étranger.

— Je comprends ça, mademoiselle Beauchemin. C'est tout à son honneur. Mais je suis certain qu'elle ne trouvera rien à redire si vous êtes assise sur le siège arrière du boghei. Je ne serai que votre conducteur.

Quelques minutes plus tard, l'inspecteur engagea son attelage dans le rang Saint-Jean après avoir traversé le petit pont. Lorsque la voiture passa devant la maison de Constant Aubé, le hasard voulut que le meunier aperçoive son amie de cœur lancée dans une conversation animée avec Amédée Durand. Elle ne tourna même pas la tête vers lui. Il en éprouva un pincement de jalousie.

À leur arrivée à la ferme, Marie et Eugénie, occupées à l'entretien de leurs serres chaudes, reconnurent immédiatement le visiteur. La maîtresse de maison appela Hubert qui était en train de corder du bois dans la remise et l'envoya chercher son frère dans la grange. À la vue du jeune homme qui venait à peine de célébrer ses vingt-sept ans, Amédée Durand ne put s'empêcher de le féliciter d'avoir été élu président de la commission scolaire malgré son âge.

— Il est aussi marguillier, intervint Bernadette avec une certaine fierté.

— Seigneur ! Vous êtes un homme occupé alors ! s'exclama l'inspecteur.

— Pas tant que ça, se défendit Donat.

— Je pense que vous êtes aussi bien de vous installer dans le salon pour parler, déclara Marie. Nous autres, on va préparer le souper dans la cuisine.

Donat indiqua le salon d'un signe de la main au visiteur. Quand la maîtresse de maison se rendit compte que Bernadette s'apprêtait à leur emboîter le pas, elle la retint.

— Reste ici dedans, lui ordonna-t-elle sèchement. Ce qu'ils ont à dire te regarde pas.

— Mais, m'man, …

— Va te changer. On a besoin de toi pour préparer le souper.

Dans la pièce voisine, Amédée Durand ne perdit pas de temps pour expliquer au jeune président de la commission scolaire que le moment était peut-être venu de songer à doter Saint-Bernard-Abbé d'une école de rang qui accueillerait surtout les Irlandais unilingues.

— Il faut comprendre que ces enfants-là n'apprennent pas grand-chose avec une institutrice qui ne parle pas anglais et ils retardent les autres enfants.

— Je comprends ça, le rassura Donat, mais là, c'est une grosse question d'argent. Je suis pas sûr pantoute que les Irlandais de Saint-Bernard aient les moyens de faire construire une école et de payer une maîtresse.

— Il va falloir le leur demander, et le plus tôt serait le mieux, lui fit remarquer l'inspecteur. La situation ne peut pas durer.

— Il va falloir aussi que j'en parle aux deux autres commissaires.

— Évidemment. Écoutez, monsieur Beauchemin, j'aimerais bien que tout ça soit réglé cette semaine, ajouta Amédée Durand. Est-ce que vous ne pourriez pas organiser une réunion demain soir ? J'y assisterai pour expliquer les choses, si c'est nécessaire.

— Une réunion de toute la paroisse prend plus de temps que ça à organiser, laissa tomber Donat, un peu embêté d'être ainsi bousculé.

— Pourquoi de toute la paroisse ? lui demanda l'inspecteur. Vous êtes président de la commission scolaire. Vous avez été nommé avec les deux autres commissaires pour gérer la commission scolaire. Vous n'avez pas à retourner auprès des électeurs. Vous avez le pouvoir de décider. Si les gens ne sont pas contents, à la prochaine élection, ils éliront quelqu'un d'autre… Mais, entre vous et moi, une seule école de rang pour trois grands rangs, c'est nettement insuffisant et tout le monde est capable de s'en rendre compte.

— C'est correct, accepta finalement Donat. On va se réunir demain soir à l'école. Je vais juste demander à Samuel Ellis et à Thomas Hyland de venir. Ce sont les deux Irlandais les plus pesants de Saint-Bernard.

Sur ces mots, les deux hommes quittèrent le salon. Par politesse, Marie invita le visiteur à partager le repas de sa famille. Amédée Durand la remercia, mais il devait rentrer chez lui.

— Vous avez une femme et des enfants qui vous attendent, fit-elle, compréhensive.

— Non, madame, je suis un célibataire de trente ans qui n'a pas encore trouvé la femme qui lui convient, rétorqua en riant Amédée Durand. On ne peut pas dire que ce soit bien facile de trouver aujourd'hui une jeune fille sérieuse.

— Vous êtes peut-être trop difficile, intervint Bernadette avec un sourire aguichant.

Sa mère lui adressa un regard sévère dont elle ne tint aucun compte.

— C'est bien possible, admit le visiteur en s'emparant de son porte-documents laissé sur une chaise.

— Vous êtes certain de ne pas vouloir rester ? insista-t-elle. Ça nous aurait fait bien plaisir.

— Certain, l'assura Amédée Durand. Vous êtes bien aimable.

Donat le raccompagna à l'extérieur, mais quand il rentra, ce fut pour assister à la réprimande que sa mère adressait à sa fille cadette.

— Quand est-ce que tu vas apprendre à te tenir comme du monde, Bedette ? demanda Marie, mécontente.

— J'ai rien fait de mal, se défendit l'enseignante.

— T'as une façon de manquer de tenue devant les hommes qui me fait honte. T'avais pas à tant insister pour garder cet homme-là à manger. C'est un étranger que j'invitais par simple politesse. D'ailleurs, lui, il l'a compris. Arrête de te jeter à la tête du premier venu, bondance !

— Mais m'man, c'est un inspecteur, protesta la jeune fille. En plus, il est pas laid pantoute.

— Il est pas laid et toi, t'as pas de plomb dans la tête, conclut sa mère en lui tournant résolument le dos.

Le lendemain après-midi, Bernadette eut du mal à se concentrer sur son enseignement. Chaque fois qu'elle entendait une voiture passer devant l'école, elle tournait la tête vers l'une des fenêtres, espérant voir Amédée Durand arriver. Pourtant, elle se doutait bien que le séduisant inspecteur n'avait aucune raison de s'arrêter à l'école ce jour-là puisqu'il ne devait assister à la réunion des commissaires qu'en soirée.

— Il va peut-être décider de venir souper à la maison, murmura-t-elle à plusieurs reprises durant la journée. Après tout, m'man l'a invité hier.

À la fin de l'après-midi, déçue, elle permit à ses élèves de partir et rentra à la maison en compagnie des enfants de Camille. Toute à sa déception, elle ne parla pratiquement pas durant le repas, mais quand elle vit Donat se préparer pour aller à la réunion, elle lui proposa de l'accompagner.

— Pourquoi t'irais là ? intervint sa mère, sévère.

— Ben, pour voir ce qui va être décidé, m'man.

— T'as pas d'affaire là pantoute, trancha son frère en endossant son manteau. C'est une réunion des commissaires avec l'inspecteur et le monde est pas invité.

— Mais je suis la maîtresse d'école, plaida-t-elle sur un ton qui n'était pas sans rappeler celui que prenait régulièrement, les années passées, Baptiste Beauchemin pour s'affirmer.

— Puis après ? T'es juste engagée par la commission, pas plus.

— Bonyenne ! Je suis toujours poignée pour rester enfermée ici dedans, soir après soir, se plaignit-elle.

Dépitée, la jeune fille ne trouva rien à ajouter et saisit son sac d'école avec mauvaise humeur dans l'intention de travailler à la préparation de sa classe du lendemain.

Quand Donat Beauchemin arriva à l'école, il retrouva Évariste Bourgeois et Télesphore Dionne, debout sur le perron, en grande conversation avec l'inspecteur Durand. Le temps de descendre de voiture, le jeune président de la commission scolaire aperçut le boghei de Samuel Ellis en train de descendre la grande côte du rang Sainte-Ursule.

— J'espère que vous m'attendez pas depuis trop long-temps, s'excusa-t-il auprès des trois hommes en déver-rouillant la porte.

— On vient juste d'arriver, le rassura Télesphore en s'empressant d'allumer la lampe à huile parce que le soleil était en train de se coucher à l'horizon.

— Est-ce qu'on a besoin d'attiser le poêle ? demanda Évariste.

— Si on garde notre manteau sur le dos, on devrait avoir assez chaud, répondit Donat en consultant les autres du regard.

Thomas Hyland et Samuel Ellis firent alors leur entrée dans le petit bâtiment. Donat leur présenta l'inspecteur qu'ils ne connaissaient pas. Chacun s'installa comme il le pouvait et Donat laissa la parole à Amédée Durand qui expliqua le motif de la réunion.

— Le problème, c'est de savoir si les Irlandais de Saint-Bernard sont prêts à payer cette école-là et les gages d'une maîtresse d'école.

— *Goddam !* Il faut avoir du front tout le tour de la tête pour poser cette question-là, s'insurgea Samuel en passant une main dans sa tignasse rousse. On dirait que vous oubliez que nous autres, les Irlandais, on a payé pour l'école où on est et pour le salaire de la maîtresse.

— C'est vrai ce qu'il dit, approuva Thomas Hyland sur un ton raisonnable.

— Si c'est vrai, je vois pas pourquoi on serait tout seuls à payer l'autre école, reprit Samuel en haussant le ton.

— Parce qu'il y aurait juste des enfants qui parlent anglais qui iraient là, intervint Évariste.

— On a juste à dire que n'importe quel enfant pourrait y aller, corrigea sèchement Samuel. Je suis certain que ça dérangerait pas que des Canadiens français envoient leurs enfants là.

— Au fond, si je te comprends ben, tu penses que tout le monde devrait payer pour une autre école, dit Télesphore après avoir retiré sa pipe de sa bouche.

— En plein ça, confirma Samuel.

— C'est vrai qu'on n'est pas obligés de dire que c'est une école pour les Irlandais. L'important, c'est que la nouvelle maîtresse soit bilingue et capable de s'expliquer en anglais quand c'est nécessaire, ajouta le propriétaire du magasin général.

— Je trouve que la proposition de monsieur Dionne est pleine de bon sens, fit Amédée qui n'avait pas encore pris part à l'échange.

— Moi, j'ai rien contre l'idée, accepta Donat, mais où est-ce qu'on va trouver une maîtresse qui parle anglais?

— Il est vrai qu'une institutrice bilingue, ça ne court pas les chemins, reconnut l'inspecteur, l'air songeur.

— Moi, j'ai peut-être la solution, dit Télesphore. Ma fille est bilingue et elle est instruite. Je suis presque certain qu'elle accepterait de faire la classe si on le lui demandait.

Tous les hommes présents parurent soulagés. Angélique Dionne serait une candidate idéale.

— Bon, admettons que la fille de monsieur Dionne accepte d'enseigner, reprit Donat, ça règle pas le problème de la construction d'une autre école.

— C'est sûr que c'est important de trouver la bonne place où la bâtir dans Sainte-Ursule, dit Samuel, sans avoir l'air d'y toucher.

— Dans Sainte-Ursule ou dans Saint-Paul, prit soin d'ajouter Donat pour l'agacer. Il faut pas oublier qu'il y a autant, sinon plus, d'Irlandais dans Saint-Paul que dans Sainte-Ursule.

— Oui, mais proche de la chapelle… commença Ellis.

— Les terrains proches de la chapelle appartiennent à Angèle Cloutier et là, je suis pas certain pantoute qu'elle va accepter de nous en vendre encore un morceau pour l'école. Déjà que ça a tout pris pour qu'elle accepte de nous vendre le terrain du presbytère.

Un lourd silence tomba dans le local. Les hommes présents cherchaient une solution au problème.

— Mais j'y pense, fit Évariste Bourgeois. Pourquoi on ferait pas une offre à Hormidas Meilleur pour sa maison? Il se marie à la fin de la semaine. C'est certain qu'il va aller rester chez Angèle Cloutier. Sa maison est la troisième du rang Saint-Paul. Ça ferait pas trop loin à marcher autant pour les enfants de Sainte-Ursule que pour ceux de Saint-Paul. Qu'est-ce que vous en dites?

— Ça, ça voudrait dire que les enfants de Sainte-Ursule seraient encore poignés pour monter et descendre la côte deux fois par jour, beau temps mauvais temps, fit remarquer Samuel avec humeur.

— De toute façon, ils le font déjà en venant à l'école de la petite Beauchemin, lui rappela le forgeron.

— Reste à savoir si le père Meilleur veut vendre et à quel prix, intervint Donat.

— Il m'a dit qu'il demanderait pas cher s'il se décidait à vendre, dit Évariste. En tout cas, ça nous coûterait moins cher que de bâtir une école neuve. Je connais sa maison, elle est d'aplomb et il y aurait pas grand-chose à faire pour en faire une bonne école.

La réunion prit fin quelques minutes plus tard à la plus grande satisfaction de tous. On s'était entendu pour tenter d'acheter la maison d'Hormidas Meilleur et engager Angélique Dionne à titre d'enseignante. On confia à Donat la tâche de négocier l'achat de la maison.

À son retour à la ferme, le président de la commission scolaire apprit aux siens les décisions qui avaient été prises.

— Je sais pas si tu vas pouvoir acheter la maison de monsieur Meilleur, lui fit remarquer Bernadette, mais pour Angélique Dionne, je suis pas certaine pantoute qu'elle soit capable de faire l'école.

— Là, tu parles sans savoir, lui dit sa mère. La fille d'Alexandrine Dionne est instruite et je vois pas pourquoi elle serait pas capable d'enseigner aux enfants de la paroisse.

— En plus, elle parle anglais, elle, lui signala son frère.

— Ça, c'est ce que son père dit, fit la jeune fille, qui cachait mal sa jalousie.

⤝

Trois jours plus tard, Donat était parvenu à acheter la maison d'Hormidas Meilleur pour un prix fort raisonnable, à la plus grande satisfaction des deux autres commissaires. Les trois hommes convinrent d'attendre la fin du mois de juin pour équiper les lieux du matériel nécessaire. Le lendemain de l'achat, Télesphore fit signer à sa fille son premier contrat d'enseignante.

— Ça va être comme pour ta sœur, dit le marchand à Donat. Ma fille aura pas à rester dans l'école le soir et on sera pas obligés de meubler le haut ni de le chauffer.

Chapitre 20

L'orgueil de Liam

La dernière journée du congé pascal des enfants fut pluvieuse et plutôt froide pour la mi-avril. Camille profita toutefois de la présence d'Ann qui l'aida à laver les vêtements et à les étendre dans la cuisine d'été pendant que la petite Rose balayait tout le rez-de-chaussée de la maison. Aussitôt le repas du matin terminé, les garçons suivirent, bien à contrecœur, leur père aux bâtiments pour une corvée de nettoyage.

Au milieu de l'avant-midi, l'oncle Paddy quitta sa chambre au moment même où Hormidas Meilleur s'arrêtait dans la cour de la ferme.

— Bon, v'là mon journal qui arrive, dit le retraité en contournant le banc sur lequel était déposé le bac rempli d'eau savonneuse où trempaient des vêtements sales.

Il ouvrit la porte au petit homme au nez bourgeonnant qui portait, pour la première fois de la saison, son vieux chapeau melon verdâtre. Comme d'habitude, l'oncle lui offrit une bonne rasade de la bagosse de Liam avec son sans-gêne coutumier.

— À la santé des habitants de la maison ! dit le facteur avec une bonne humeur qui n'était probablement pas étrangère aux nombreuses consommations prises depuis le début de sa tournée.

— Félicitations pour votre mariage prochain, monsieur Meilleur, lui dit Camille en s'essuyant les mains sur son tablier.

— Merci, mais il faut ben faire une fin, comme on dit.

— Je vous pensais plus intelligent que ça, plaisanta Paddy. Vous étiez pas ben, libre comme l'air ?

— Voyons, mon oncle, le rabroua Camille. Monsieur Meilleur a peut-être pas la chance d'avoir un neveu pour l'héberger et prendre soin de lui.

— En plein ça, reconnut Hormidas avec bonne humeur. Bon, c'est pas tout, mais c'est pas en brettant que je vais finir ma *run*. Là, je vous laisse pas juste votre journal, j'ai aussi une lettre pour vous, ajouta-t-il, en tendant une enveloppe d'aspect officiel au retraité.

Paddy Connolly prit le journal et l'enveloppe et scruta cette dernière avant de raccompagner le facteur à la porte. Après le départ d'Hormidas Meilleur, le plus vieux des Connolly prit le temps de se verser une tasse de thé et de tartiner de beurre une épaisse tranche de pain. Ensuite, il alla s'asseoir confortablement près du poêle avant d'allumer un cigare. Camille et Ann s'étaient remises au lavage, mais il ne pouvait ignorer la curiosité qui semblait les dévorer. Après tout, ce n'était que la deuxième fois qu'il recevait du courrier à la maison depuis le début de l'hiver.

Il finit tout de même par ouvrir l'enveloppe d'où il tira une lettre qu'il lut après avoir déposé sur son nez ses vieilles lunettes à fine monture d'acier. Le sourire épanoui qui se répandit sur ses traits n'échappa pas à Camille qui l'épiait à la dérobée depuis de nombreuses minutes.

— Est-ce que ce sont des bonnes nouvelles, mon oncle ? lui demanda-t-elle.

— Pas mal bonnes… Ouais, pas mal bonnes, répéta-t-il sans chercher à dissimuler son contentement.

Camille ne tenta pas d'en savoir davantage, sachant fort bien que le bavard ne saurait se taire bien longtemps au sujet du contenu de la missive. En fait, elle n'eut à attendre que quelques minutes avant qu'il lui déclare sur un ton pompeux:

— Ma fille, mon homme d'affaires m'a écrit qu'il a un acheteur sérieux pour mes cinq maisons, à Montréal. Il paraît qu'il m'en offre un ben bon prix, à part ça.

— C'est toute une bonne nouvelle, ne put s'empêcher de dire Camille, heureuse pour lui.

— Ça fait que je vais être obligé de partir demain matin de bonne heure. Il faut que j'aille signer toutes sortes de papiers pour régler ça, ajouta l'Irlandais, tout fier.

— Est-ce qu'il va vous rester au moins une maison où habiter? lui demanda-t-elle, réalisant soudain ce que cela pouvait signifier.

— Inquiète-toi pas pour ça, s'empressa-t-il de répondre en se méprenant sur le sens de sa question. J'ai l'intention de vendre mes meubles avant de revenir rester ici avec vous autres.

Camille déglutit et sentit ses jambes se dérober sous elle. Tous ses espoirs d'être enfin débarrassée de cet hôte encombrant et sans gêne venaient de s'évanouir. Elle n'allait tout de même pas capituler sans se battre.

— Là-dessus, mon oncle, il va falloir se parler sérieusement, lui dit-elle d'une voix blanche.

— Comment ça? s'étonna l'effronté.

— Écoutez. Si vous vous rappelez bien, vous êtes arrivé avant Noël pour deux ou trois jours et ça nous a fait plaisir de vous recevoir. Après les fêtes, vous avez décidé de rester jusqu'à la fin de l'hiver, même si, comme vous avez pu le voir, on roule pas sur l'or et qu'on n'a pas grand place pour vous garder avec les quatre enfants.

— Mon neveu m'a rien dit là-dessus, prétendit le retraité en exhalant la fumée de son cigare sur un ton indifférent.

— Vous avez jamais pensé que c'était parce que Liam était trop gêné pour vous le dire, mon oncle?

— Ça me surprendrait, laissa-t-il tomber sèchement.

— En tout cas, moi, je vous le dis, s'entêta la maîtresse de maison en se campant devant lui. Je pense que j'ai le droit de dire ce que je pense dans ma propre maison. Après tout, c'est moi qui vous nourris et qui lave votre linge depuis presque cinq mois.

— Pourquoi tu me dis ça, là, aujourd'hui ? lui demanda Paddy en quittant brusquement sa chaise berçante pour se retrouver debout, en face d'elle.

— Parce que si vous avez l'intention de revenir rester chez nous, il va bien falloir parler de votre pension, mon oncle, lui déclara-t-elle, tout net. Je veux pas être regardante, mais une bouche de plus à nourrir, ça paraît.

— Je mange tout de même pas tant que ça, se défendit le petit homme bedonnant.

— Et là, je parle pas du surplus de besogne que je dois faire pour prendre soin de votre linge et de votre chambre.

— Bon, c'est correct. Je vais parler de tout ça avec Liam quand il rentrera. On verra ben ce qu'il dira. Après tout, je vais vous laisser tout l'argent que j'ai quand je vais lever les pattes.

— Bâti comme vous l'êtes, mon oncle, ça peut bien arriver dans vingt-cinq ou trente ans. Ça règle rien.

— Quand tu parles de pension, t'aimerais que je te donne quel montant ? finit-il par lui demander.

— Au moins deux piastres par semaine, affirma-t-elle sans la moindre hésitation.

— Deux piastres par semaine ! s'écria Paddy, l'air horrifié. Mais c'est presque le prix d'une chambre dans un hôtel de Montréal.

— Avec vos trois repas par jour et le lavage de votre linge ? s'enquit Camille, suspicieuse.

— Certain ! répondit-il avec force.

— Si c'est comme ça, à votre place, je choisirais l'hôtel, mon oncle, fit-elle, l'air moqueur. Comme ça, vous seriez pas enterré à la campagne.

— Il me semble qu'une piastre et quart par semaine, ce serait pas mal ben payé, suggéra le retraité, sans tenir le moindrement compte qu'il était hébergé gratuitement depuis près de cinq mois.

— Pour un homme qui se vante d'avoir pas mal d'argent, je trouve que vous vous débattez pas mal pour sauver une couple de cennes, ne put s'empêcher de lui faire remarquer la jeune femme, excédée.

— En tout cas, ça, c'est une affaire d'hommes. Je vais en parler à mon neveu et c'est lui, le maître de la maison, qui va décider, trancha-t-il.

— Faites donc ça, l'encouragea-t-elle, sur un ton qui cachait mal son sarcasme.

Moins de dix minutes plus tard, Camille vit l'oncle de son mari endosser son manteau et quitter la maison en direction des bâtiments. Elle était hors d'elle. De toute évidence, son pensionnaire avait décidé d'éclaircir la situation tout de suite avec Liam et hors de sa présence.

— Ça se passera pas comme ça ! dit-elle à haute voix, les dents serrées.

Elle se préparait déjà à avoir une conversation orageuse avec son mari quelques minutes plus tard. Elle finit son lavage et, avec l'aide de sa fille aînée, elle alla vider l'eau savonneuse dans l'auge des porcs, dans la porcherie.

Elle venait à peine de rentrer qu'elle aperçut Liam venant vers la maison à grandes enjambées.

— Montez donc en haut, les filles, dit-elle à Rose et à Ann. J'ai l'impression que votre père est pas de bonne humeur.

L'adolescente et la petite fille s'empressèrent de monter à l'étage. Leur père entra dans la maison en claquant violemment la porte derrière lui.

— C'est quoi cette histoire de vouloir obliger mon oncle à payer une pension ? lui demanda-t-il sur un ton rageur. Je pensais que c'était réglé une fois pour toutes, cette affaire-là.

— Pas quand j'apprends qu'il a l'intention de venir s'installer pour tout le temps chez nous, rétorqua-t-elle sur le même ton, bien décidée à ne pas céder d'un pouce. Il y a tout de même des limites à être effronté, bondance!

— C'est mon oncle!

— C'est peut-être ton oncle, mais t'as aussi quatre enfants et une femme. Je suis pas intéressée à devenir sa servante et à priver mes enfants pour permettre à quelqu'un qui a les moyens de vivre à nos crochets. Au cas où tu t'en serais pas aperçu, il mange, ton oncle!

— Calvaire, combien de fois il va falloir te répéter qu'il va me laisser tout ce qu'il a? dit-il en colère.

— Répète-le tant que tu veux, mais à se ménager comme il le fait depuis qu'il reste ici dedans, il va tous nous enterrer, répliqua-t-elle, sans céder d'un pouce. Je lui demande pas la fin du monde. Juste deux piastres par semaine.

— Il dit que c'est le même prix qu'on lui chargerait à l'hôtel.

— Si c'est comme ça, qu'il nous débarrasse et qu'il aille vivre à l'hôtel, rétorqua-t-elle sur un ton définitif. Toi, ton oncle te dérange pas. C'est moi qui suis poignée pour le nourrir et le blanchir. S'il paie pas de pension, j'arrête ça. Tu lui feras à manger.

— Maudite tête de cochon! s'écria Liam Connolly en levant la main comme pour la frapper.

S'il s'imaginait lui faire peur, il connaissait bien mal la fille aînée de Marie Beauchemin. Au lieu de reculer, elle fit un pas en avant, les yeux étincelants de fureur.

— Essaye donc de lever la main sur moi une seule fois pour voir, le provoqua-t-elle, les poings serrés, prête au combat. Je suis pas un de tes enfants et tu me fais pas peur pantoute, Liam Connolly.

Le cultivateur du rang Saint-Jean se rendit compte subitement que la femme qui lui faisait face n'était pas la faible Julia, sa première épouse. Camille Beauchemin avait pratiquement la même taille que lui et il vivait maintenant depuis assez longtemps avec elle pour connaître sa force physique.

Fou de rage, il tourna les talons et quitta la maison. Camille s'approcha de la fenêtre et regarda son mari s'entretenir avec son oncle à la porte de la grange où le retraité avait trouvé refuge. Elle n'entendit pas ce que les deux hommes se disaient, mais l'entretien dura quelques minutes. Peu après, Paddy rentra dans la maison et retira son manteau avant de reprendre sa place dans sa chaise berçante. Il déplia son journal, mais avant de se consacrer à sa lecture, il dit sèchement à sa nièce par alliance :

— Comme t'as l'air à ben gros y tenir, je me suis entendu avec Liam. Je vais vous donner une piastre et demie de pension chaque vendredi, même si je continue à croire que ça vaut pas ça.

— C'est correct, mon oncle, dit Camille qui avait entrepris d'éplucher les pommes de terre alors qu'Ann redescendait lui donner un coup de main. De toute façon, dites-vous que vous êtes pas obligé de rester avec nous autres. Vous serez toujours libre de partir quand vous voudrez.

Quand Liam rentra dans la maison pour dîner, il affichait un air mécontent qui ne le quitta pas de la journée. Camille feignit d'ignorer cette bouderie, trop contente d'être parvenue à ses fins. Avant de souffler la lampe, ce soir-là, elle prit tout de même la précaution de demander à son mari :

— Est-ce que c'est à toi ou à moi que ton oncle va payer sa pension ?

— Je lui ai pas dit, répondit-il sèchement.

— Si c'est comme ça, tu peux me laisser m'en occuper. Je pense qu'il va être plus gêné avec moi. De toute façon, je suppose que t'as dû t'arranger pour lui dire que c'était moi, la méchante, qui en voulait à son argent…

— En plein ça, se borna-t-il à dire.

— Ça me dérange pas pantoute, fit-elle, frondeuse. Comme ça, j'aurai moins l'impression qu'il rit de nous autres en pleine face.

— Là, tu vas l'avoir, ton argent, ça fait que je veux plus en entendre parler.

— J'espère que t'as tout de même remarqué qu'il s'est arrangé pour te faire baisser le prix de sa pension, ajouta-t-elle d'une voix acide.

— Calvaire, on n'est pas des quêteux! protesta-t-il en élevant la voix.

— C'est vrai, mais ça empêche pas qu'on a besoin de cet argent-là pour les enfants.

— Whow! J'ai mon mot à dire là-dedans.

— C'est ça, on en reparlera.

Dès que la lampe fut soufflée, Camille ne put s'empêcher de sourire dans le noir. Elle avait enfin obtenu ce qu'elle voulait, même si l'oncle avait coupé du quart la pension qu'elle exigeait. Si Paddy Connolly devenait trop malcommode ou trop exigeant sous le prétexte qu'il payait une pension hebdomadaire, elle allait faire en sorte de lui rendre la vie si difficile qu'il n'aurait pas d'autre choix que de partir. Mais en attendant, tout l'argent qu'elle allait lui arracher, son mari n'en verrait pas la couleur. Il allait servir à la réalisation d'un rêve qu'elle caressait pour Ann.

Devant les très bons résultats scolaires de l'adolescente, elle envisageait sérieusement de l'envoyer dans un pensionnat de Nicolet pour la préparer à devenir institutrice. Elle avait d'ailleurs commencé les travaux d'approche auprès de sa fille… Il ne resterait qu'à persuader Liam, ce qui n'allait pas être facile, mais elle en faisait son affaire.

❦

Le lendemain matin, le ciel était encore nuageux, mais la pluie avait cessé depuis quelques heures quand les enfants partirent pour l'école. Quelques minutes après leur départ,

Paddy Connolly descendit dans la cuisine en portant un maigre bagage qu'il déposa près de la porte. Depuis leur discussion de la veille, le quinquagénaire battait froid à son hôtesse et ne lui adressait la parole que lorsqu'il y était obligé.

— Il faut croire que c'est dans le caractère des Connolly, murmura Camille, nullement impressionnée par cette bouderie.

L'homme finit sa toilette devant le miroir suspendu près de l'armoire et se décida enfin à ouvrir la bouche.

— Est-ce que Patrick est déjà parti pour l'école? demanda-t-il à sa nièce par alliance occupée à ranger la cuisine.

— Il vient de partir avec les autres, mon oncle.

— Tornon! J'aurais ben voulu qu'il attelle ma voiture pendant que je déjeune.

— Là, j'ai bien peur que vous deviez vous débrouiller tout seul, laissa tomber Camille d'une voix neutre. Liam vient de partir pour le bois. Approchez, je vais vous préparer à déjeuner.

Paddy mangea seul, au bout de la table, et Camille entreprit son repassage sans se soucier davantage de lui. À la fin de son repas, il quitta les lieux après avoir dit qu'il ne savait pas exactement quand il reviendrait. La maîtresse de maison n'émit aucun commentaire. Elle le regarda se diriger vers l'écurie, sa petite valise à la main. Elle n'avait pas été sans remarquer que son pensionnaire n'avait pas daigné la saluer et la remercier pour tout ce qu'elle avait fait pour lui durant les mois précédents.

— Je crois bien qu'il me prend pour sa servante, murmura-t-elle, fâchée. Bon débarras! J'espère qu'il reviendra pas trop vite!

Peu après, elle entendit passer le boghei de l'oncle de son mari près de la maison. Elle ne se dérangea pas pour le voir partir.

— Lui, quand il va remettre les pieds ici dedans, on va mettre les choses au clair, dit-elle à haute voix. J'ai déjà assez d'avoir à endurer le neveu sans m'encombrer de l'oncle.

❧

Ce soir-là, les syndics de Saint-Bernard-Abbé se réunirent dans la sacristie pour mettre la dernière main aux préparatifs de la fête qui allait être donnée à l'occasion de la visite de monseigneur Laflèche prévue le dimanche suivant. Josaphat Désilets, l'air sombre, fit entrer les cinq hommes et les invita à prendre place autour de la grande table après avoir récité la courte prière habituelle.

— J'ai une mauvaise nouvelle à vous annoncer, déclara d'entrée de jeu le prêtre.

— Bon, qu'est-ce qui nous arrive encore? demanda Anatole Blanchette à mi-voix.

— Monseigneur pourra pas venir dimanche prochain, comme il était entendu. Son secrétaire m'a envoyé une lettre pour m'informer que monseigneur est tombé malade.

— Est-ce que ça veut dire qu'on va être obligés d'attendre encore durant des mois pour devenir une paroisse, monsieur le curé? lui demanda Donat.

— Non, si je me fie au document officiel que j'ai reçu hier, l'érection canonique de la paroisse est faite. J'ai aussi reçu un exemplaire de la gazette officielle de Québec qui prouve que l'érection civile de Saint-Bernard a été enregistrée la semaine passée. De ce côté-là, il y a plus de problème. Maintenant, les limites définitives de notre paroisse sont fixées et plus personne va pouvoir dire qu'il appartient pas à Saint-Bernard s'il est sur notre territoire.

Ce dernier commentaire du prêtre fit comprendre aux hommes réunis dans la pièce que Josaphat Désilets n'avait pas plus apprécié qu'eux que certains francs-tenanciers aient exigé de retourner dans leur paroisse d'origine en prétextant que la distance les séparant de la chapelle du rang Sainte-

Ursule était encore plus grande que celle qui les séparait de leur vieille église paroissiale.

— Si je comprends ben, monsieur le curé, c'est juste la petite fête qu'on prévoyait qui tombe à l'eau, intervint Antonius Côté, la mine réjouie. C'est pas ben grave, non ?

— On pourrait juste dire au monde que la fête est remise à quand monseigneur pourra venir nous voir, suggéra Samuel Ellis, le président du conseil, pas du tout catastrophé, lui non plus, par la nouvelle.

Comme tous semblaient approuver la suggestion, Josaphat Désilets se rangea à l'opinion générale et dut promettre de faire l'annonce le dimanche suivant.

— Avec un peu de chance, vous allez peut-être être capable de recevoir monseigneur dans votre nouveau presbytère, monsieur le curé, l'encouragea Thomas Hyland, toujours positif. Ce serait tout de même mieux que dans votre sacristie.

— Pour ça, vous avez raison, reconnut le prêtre, visiblement très déçu d'être privé d'une belle cérémonie.

Il y eut un court silence et Samuel allait donner le signal de la fin de la réunion quand le prêtre reprit la parole en affichant un petit air supérieur.

— Avant de se quitter, il faut parler du nouveau conseil de fabrique qui doit remplacer le conseil des syndics, dit-il.

— Où est la différence ? demanda Ellis, surpris.

— Voyons, monsieur Ellis. C'est évident, il me semble. La mission Saint-Bernard-Abbé existe plus et donc son conseil de syndics non plus. Il va falloir retourner devant les francs-tenanciers pour élire le nouveau conseil de fabrique.

Les cinq hommes réunis autour de la table se regardèrent, médusés, durant un bref moment. Si le curé Désilets avait cru inquiéter et déstabiliser les membres de son conseil en annonçant sa dissolution, il en fut pour ses frais.

— C'est un bout de cierge de bonne nouvelle, ça, déclara Anatole Blanchette, apparemment content d'apprendre cela. Moi, en tout cas, je suis prêt à laisser ma place n'importe quand si quelqu'un la veut.

— Moi aussi, s'empressa de dire Côté avec le même enthousiasme.

— C'est sûr que je me battrai pas, moi non plus, pour devenir marguillier, fit Donat à son tour.

— C'est vrai que c'est ben des responsabilités sur le dos, expliqua Samuel.

— Pour ça, il y a pas de doute, reconnut Thomas Hyland.

L'air affiché par les deux Irlandais apprit au curé que les membres de son conseil pensaient la même chose que les autres, ce qui l'inquiéta sérieusement.

— Attention, prit-il la peine de préciser sur un tout autre ton, j'ai pas dit que vous deviez quitter le conseil. Vous avez fait bien des choses pour la mission et je suis certain qu'en bons chrétiens, vous êtes prêts à continuer à vous sacrifier pour les habitants de Saint-Bernard. On va réunir les gens après la grand-messe, dimanche prochain, à la place du salut au Saint-Sacrement, pour faire l'élection. Personnellement, je vais recommander de tous vous nommer marguilliers de la nouvelle paroisse.

L'ecclésiastique ne vit aucun sourire de reconnaissance apparaître sur les visages qui l'entouraient. Apparemment, le titre ne suscitait guère d'enthousiasme chez les syndics en place.

❧

Le dimanche suivant, Donat laissa sa femme, Bernadette et Hubert devant le parvis de la chapelle avant d'aller stationner son boghei près des autres véhicules dans le stationnement. Le jeune cultivateur se porta à la hauteur d'Anatole Blanchette et d'Antonius Côté qui venaient d'arriver.

— On a quelque chose à te dire, fit Antonius en abordant son jeune voisin du rang Saint-Jean.

— Quoi, monsieur Côté ?

— Ben, tous les deux, on se présentera pas pour faire partie du nouveau conseil. Moi, monsieur le curé m'énerve trop.

— Et moi, je trouve qu'à mon âge je peux laisser ma place à un plus jeune, compléta Anatole.

— Mais si vous faites ça, vous allez laisser la place aux Irlandais, protesta Donat. Vous pouvez être certains que Hyland et Ellis, eux autres, lâcheront pas.

— C'est pas sûr pantoute, dit Antonius.

— Non, mais c'est un maudit risque, par exemple. Si les Irlandais sont en majorité au conseil de fabrique, les décisions vont toujours être en leur faveur. Ça me surprendrait même pas que monsieur le curé soit obligé de faire de plus en plus d'affaires en anglais, même les réunions…

Les deux hommes se regardèrent, puis haussèrent les épaules.

— Tu sais ben qu'il va y avoir des Canadiens français qui vont se présenter, avança Anatole Blanchette au moment où ils arrivaient à la porte de l'église. Là, moi, en tout cas, je vais avertir monsieur le curé.

— Attends-moi, reprit Antonius, j'y vais avec toi.

Donat, mécontent et inquiet, alla rejoindre les siens dans le banc loué par la famille Beauchemin.

Quelques minutes plus tard, Josaphat Désilets entra dans le chœur en compagnie de ses servants de messe. En conclusion de son prône, il annonça en anglais et en français dans un même souffle l'annulation de la visite de monseigneur Laflèche pour des raisons de santé et le remplacement du salut au Saint-Sacrement par la tenue de l'élection du premier conseil de fabrique de Saint-Bernard-Abbé, immédiatement après la célébration de la grand-messe. Par conséquent, il demandait aux francs-tenanciers de la paroisse de demeurer sur place après l'*Ite missa est*.

À la fin de la cérémonie, les femmes et les enfants quittèrent la chapelle, laissant derrière eux les propriétaires des fermes de Saint-Bernard-Abbé, ou leurs représentants, appelés à voter pour l'élection du nouveau conseil de fabrique. Angèle Cloutier était la seule femme à rester. Pendant que le prêtre allait retirer ses habits sacerdotaux dans la sacristie, les fermiers discutèrent à voix basse entre eux. Quand le curé de la paroisse revint dans le chœur, vêtu de sa soutane noire sur laquelle il avait passé un surplis, le silence tomba sur les lieux.

— Saint-Bernard-Abbé est maintenant une paroisse, déclara-t-il. Comme dans toutes les paroisses, il appartient à un conseil de fabrique de s'occuper de gérer les biens matériels de la paroisse. Depuis plus d'un an, vous aviez un conseil des syndics qui a bien et beaucoup travaillé. J'avais l'intention de vous demander de réélire en bloc tous les membres de ce conseil.

— Pourquoi pas ! intervint Télesphore Dionne assez fort pour être bien entendu par une bonne partie de l'assemblée.

La majorité des gens présents approuvèrent.

— On peut pas faire ça parce que deux syndics m'ont appris ce matin qu'ils tenaient pas à faire partie de la fabrique. Monsieur Antonius Côté et monsieur Anatole Blanchette se retirent et je les remercie pour tous les services qu'ils ont rendus à la mission.

Quelques maigres applaudissements suivirent ces remerciements. Hormidas Meilleur, assis près de sa fiancée, se leva soudain pour demander au prêtre :

— Monsieur le curé, est-ce qu'on pourrait pas élire marguilliers les trois syndics qui restent, s'ils le veulent ? Il me semble qu'ils connaissent ben les affaires de la paroisse et qu'on peut leur faire confiance.

Devant l'approbation générale de l'assemblée, le curé Désilets, habile, demanda que ceux qui s'opposaient à cette élection automatique des trois syndics lèvent la main. Aucune main ne se leva et Donat Beauchemin, Thomas Hyland et Samuel Ellis furent élus marguilliers sans opposition.

— Il faut maintenant voir au remplacement des deux démissionnaires, poursuivit Josaphat Désilets, satisfait de la tournure des événements. Quelqu'un a-t-il un nom à proposer? demanda-t-il en regardant la foule devant lui.

— Je propose Liam Connolly, dit Rémi Lafond.

Le mari de Camille sursauta en entendant son nom, mais il ne put cacher la fierté qui illumina son visage.

— Qui vote pour notre maître-chantre? demanda le prêtre.

À peine quatre ou cinq mains se levèrent pour appuyer sa candidature, ce qui mortifia passablement l'Irlandais.

— Moi, je propose monsieur Meilleur, dit Angèle Cloutier d'une voix forte.

Il y eut quelques ricanements et on se poussa du coude dans l'assistance.

— L'Angèle pousse son p'tit père en avant, on dirait, chuchota Xavier Beauchemin à son frère, assis près de lui.

— Mieux vaut lui qu'un autre Irlandais, chuchota Donat.

— Aurais-tu dit la même chose si Liam avait été élu? lui demanda son jeune frère.

— Non, lui, c'est pas un vrai Irlandais. Il parle même pas anglais.

Le curé de la paroisse fit voter les gens et, au grand étonnement de plusieurs, Hormidas Meilleur fut élu marguillier. À voir son visage, le petit facteur semblait le premier surpris. Il se leva et salua les gens avant de se rasseoir.

— Il nous manque encore un marguillier, déclara Josaphat Désilets.

— Je me propose, fit une voix forte en provenance de l'arrière de la chapelle.

Toutes les têtes se tournèrent pour découvrir le notaire Eudore Valiquette, debout très droit pour ne rien perdre de sa petite taille. Son visage mince au menton fuyant encadré par ses épais favoris gris arborait un sourire sympathique.

— Il faut être propriétaire d'une terre pour être marguillier, s'interposa Tancrède Bélanger, humilié de constater que personne ne songeait à lui.

— Mais je suis propriétaire de la moitié de la terre d'Euclyde Bérubé du rang Saint-Paul, affirma avec aplomb le notaire.

— Première nouvelle, laissa tomber Bélanger, le visage renfrogné.

Eudore Valiquette avait beau s'être installé à Saint-Bernard-Abbé moins de trois mois auparavant, le rôle qu'il avait joué dans l'emprunt pour le presbytère et le fait qu'il avait contacté presque tous les habitants de la paroisse pour leur offrir ses services l'avaient rendu assez populaire. Il fut élu à la majorité.

— On a évité le pire, murmura Donat à Xavier. Au moins, nous autres, les Canadiens, on reste majoritaires au conseil.

Un peu plus loin, Samuel Ellis était moins préoccupé par le fait que les Irlandais soient demeurés en minorité que par la nomination de Valiquette et l'importance qu'il allait probablement tenter de se donner au sein du conseil.

— Pour moi, il va chercher à être le président, dit-il à voix basse à Thomas Hyland alors que les gens sortaient de la chapelle après l'élection.

— Ben non, il vient juste d'arriver à Saint-Bernard, dit le propriétaire du moulin à bois pour le rassurer.

— Tu sauras me le dire, affirma le mari de Bridget Ellis, dont l'inquiétude était palpable.

— On va ben voir à la prochaine réunion, rétorqua Thomas d'une voix égale.

Ce jour-là, Liam Connolly rentra à la maison avec sa famille après la messe en affichant un air renfrogné de mauvais augure. Camille, assise près de lui sur le siège avant du boghei, ne disait pas un mot. Avant de monter dans la voiture, elle avait eu le temps d'apprendre que son mari n'avait obtenu que de très rares votes pour faire partie du conseil. Elle comprenait ce que cela pouvait avoir d'humiliant, surtout du fait de l'élection du notaire Valiquette qui n'était qu'un nouveau venu dans la paroisse.

Son mari ne desserra pas les dents jusqu'au moment où il rentra dans la maison après avoir dételé son cheval.

— Enrage-toi pas pour rien, lui conseilla-t-elle, compréhensive. Regarde Rémi. Personne a pensé à le proposer, lui, et pourtant, c'est un bon père de famille comme toi. En plus, il est même pas maître-chantre.

— Je le sais, sacrement! Mais rien empêche que c'est insultant, une affaire comme ça, jura-t-il en conservant son visage fermé.

~

À la fin de la semaine, Télesphore Dionne eut beaucoup de mal à empêcher quelques hommes de la paroisse de préparer un enterrement de vie de garçon mémorable à Hormidas Meilleur dont on devait célébrer le mariage le samedi suivant.

Xavier Beauchemin était le plus enthousiaste. Il avait suggéré d'enivrer le facteur avant de le rouler dans du fumier et de le couvrir de plumes. Avec quatre complices, il projetait de promener ensuite le futur marié dans une voiture dans tous les rangs de la paroisse.

— Tu peux pas faire une niaiserie comme ça, le réprimanda le propriétaire du magasin général. T'oublies que le père Meilleur a presque l'âge qu'avait ton père quand il a disparu. C'est pas un jeune. Il a droit à plus de respect et là, tout le monde va rire de lui.

— Mais il se marie, fit Xavier, rieur. Il faut fêter ça.

— Penses-tu que l'Angèle va vous pardonner cette folie-là si son futur lui arrive tout magané le matin des noces? Moi, à votre place, j'y penserais deux fois plutôt qu'une avant de faire ça.

— Ce sera pas si pire, insista Xavier qui sentait déjà fléchir la volonté de ses complices.

— Ce que monsieur Dionne dit est pas bête, intervint son frère Hubert, conscient qu'Angélique, debout derrière le comptoir, le couvait des yeux. Pense que tu te maries dans deux mois. Tu risques de te faire faire la même chose, et tu trouveras pas ça drôle pantoute.

Après une discussion de quelques minutes, il fut entendu que l'enterrement de vie de garçon du facteur se limiterait à l'encourager à boire autant de bagosse qu'il le désirerait la veille de son mariage. Le tout se passerait à la forge d'Évariste Bourgeois.

Le vendredi soir, plusieurs jeunes se présentèrent sur les lieux avec un cruchon de bagosse et Hormidas, tout heureux qu'on ait songé à lui organiser une petite fête, profita sans retenue des libations. En fait, il en profita si largement qu'il s'endormit au début de la nuit sur une pile de vieilles couvertures dans un coin de la forge, assommé par tout l'alcool ingurgité. D'un commun accord, les participants à la fête décidèrent de le laisser sur place cuver tout ce qu'il avait bu.

— À mon avis, il sera ja… jamais capable de se lever de… demain matin, déclara Amable Fréchette, la voix hésitante.

— Tant mieux pour lui, dit Tancrède Bélanger. Ça va lui éviter de faire une erreur demain.

La demi-douzaine de fêtards quitta la forge et Évariste laissa derrière lui le fiancé d'Angèle Cloutier ronflant comme un sonneur.

Quand le forgeron vint réveiller Hormidas, aux petites heures, le lendemain matin, le futur marié sembla d'abord passablement perdu et eut du mal à poser un pied devant l'autre.

— Grouillez-vous, père Meilleur, lui ordonna Évariste Bourgeois, goguenard. Vous devez rentrer chez vous vous laver et vous habiller pour vos noces. Là, vous sentez le putois et si vous vous présentez comme ça à l'église, votre promise va vous envoyer coucher dans la grange à soir, je vous en passe un papier. J'ai attelé votre boghei. Il est devant la porte.

Le petit homme retrouva son chapeau melon verdâtre qui avait roulé dans un coin, secoua ses vêtements, remercia son hôte et quitta les lieux. En ce dernier samedi d'avril, l'air était frais, mais il n'y avait pas un nuage.

Trois heures plus tard, Xavier et ses complices se réunirent sur le parvis de la chapelle, prêts à se moquer de l'air malade qu'allait sûrement afficher le futur marié après une telle soirée de beuverie.

— Avec tout ce qu'il a bu hier soir, il aurait presque pu prendre un bain dans la bagosse, déclara le fils de Marie Beauchemin.

— Pour moi, à matin, le bonhomme a pas été capable de se lever, ajouta le fils aîné de Samuel Ellis.

— Ce serait la moindre des choses, conclut Amable Fréchette. Il nous a coûté assez cher en bagosse, le « p'tit père ».

Pendant ce temps, Marie Beauchemin avait déposé un gâteau dans une boîte et l'avait transporté dans le boghei où l'attendait Donat avec impatience.

— Vous étiez pas obligée de venir au mariage, m'man, dit-il à sa mère. Moi et les autres marguilliers, on y va parce que le père Meilleur est au conseil.

— Madame Cloutier est une bonne femme et c'est normal qu'on lui apporte quelque chose pour ses noces. Tu vas voir, je suis certaine que les Bélanger, les Dionne et les Bourgeois vont être là et vont avoir fait la même chose.

En fait, à leur arrivée à la chapelle, la mère et le fils découvrirent qu'une vingtaine de personnes s'étaient déplacées pour assister à la célébration du mariage entre le facteur et la veuve. Quand Marie aperçut Xavier en train de discuter avec des amis, elle lui fit signe d'approcher.

— Je savais pas que t'avais l'intention de venir aux noces, lui dit-elle.

— Ben non, m'man. Je veux juste voir de quoi ont l'air les futurs mariés.

— Ah bon! Mais comme t'es déjà là, j'espère que tu vas entrer assister à la messe.

— Ben…

— Arrive, mon garçon. Prier te fera pas de mal.

Au même instant, Évariste Bourgeois immobilisa son attelage devant la chapelle pour en laisser descendre Hormidas Meilleur et Tancrède Bélanger, son témoin. Les jeunes présents découvrirent avec stupéfaction un futur marié souriant aux traits détendus et ne portant aucun stigmate visible de la cuite mémorable prise la veille.

— Le vieux blasphème, il a même pas l'air d'avoir mal à la tête! jura Xavier en cachant mal son admiration pour l'homme.

— C'est vrai qu'il a l'air frais comme une rose, ajouta Fréchette, dépité.

— Attendez que la mère Cloutier lui mette la main dessus, conclut Donat en riant. Il va frétiller pas mal moins, le bonhomme.

Hormidas, l'allure fringante, pénétra dans la chapelle avec son témoin.

Angèle Cloutier arriva dans la voiture de Télesphore Dionne en compagnie du propriétaire du magasin général et de sa femme quelques instants plus tard. La veuve portait un léger manteau de printemps sur une robe grise ornée d'un peu de dentelle. Elle sourit aux personnes rassemblées sur le parvis avant d'entrer dans la chapelle à son tour.

La cérémonie de mariage fut toute simple et dura moins d'une heure. À la sortie des nouveaux époux, on leur fit un petit cortège jusqu'au bas de la côte du rang Sainte-Ursule. Même si aucune fête n'avait été prévue, la mariée invita les gens à entrer chez elle.

Elle eut alors l'agréable surprise de constater que la plupart des femmes avaient songé à préparer des desserts. Tous les invités présents eurent donc droit à une pointe de tarte ou à un morceau de gâteau accompagné d'une tasse de thé.

Au milieu de l'après-midi, les gens commencèrent à quitter les lieux, heureux d'avoir improvisé une petite fête pour les nouveaux mariés.

Chapitre 21

Un printemps occupé

Le mois de mai commença par quelques journées de pluie, ce qui aida le curé de Saint-Bernard-Abbé à faire accepter que la récitation quotidienne du chapelet se fasse à l'abri de la chapelle plutôt qu'au pied de la croix de chemin du rang Saint-Jean, comme cela s'était toujours fait. Bien entendu, l'épouse de Tancrède Bélanger avait rechigné, mais le prêtre ne faisait que tenir la promesse faite à ses ouailles l'année précédente.

— Voulez-vous bien me dire à quoi ça sert que je fleurisse notre croix si plus personne vient prier là ? répétait-elle chaque fois qu'elle rencontrait des voisins.

Tout le monde savait bien que ce que la fermière regrettait avant tout, c'était son rôle d'hôtesse parce que la croix était sur la terre de son mari.

Évidemment, cette pluie retardait également le redressement des clôtures, premier travail de la saison avant d'envoyer les vaches à l'extérieur.

Le premier mercredi du mois, Camille se réveilla avec la nette impression que quelque chose n'allait pas. Son mari ronflait à ses côtés et le jour commençait à peine à se lever. La jeune femme se passa une main sur le front : celui-ci était couvert de sueur et une nausée subite la fit se précipiter hors de la chambre. Frissonnante, elle se couvrit les épaules de son vieux châle et sortit rapidement de la maison pour aller dans les toilettes sèches situées près de la remise. Là, pendant plusieurs minutes, elle fut secouée par de douloureux spasmes. L'estomac vide et un peu flageolante, elle revint à la maison en se demandant ce qu'elle n'avait pas digéré dans le repas pris la veille.

Elle alluma le poêle et mit la théière sur le feu avant de se laisser tomber dans sa chaise berçante, encore toute secouée par cette indigestion anormale. Elle ne réveilla les siens qu'après avoir bu une tasse de thé bouillant.

Les deux jours suivants, Camille fut victime des mêmes malaises matinaux. Ce qu'elle avait tant redouté semblait s'être produit. Tout laissait croire qu'elle était enceinte de son premier enfant, elle qui aurait trente ans dans deux mois.

— Mon Dieu! Un cinquième enfant dans la maison! Comment les enfants vont prendre ça? Et Liam?

Ce matin-là, la fille aînée de Marie Beauchemin attendit que les enfants soient partis à l'école pour apprendre la nouvelle à son mari qui, apparemment, ne s'était pas aperçu de ses malaises matinaux.

— Ah ben, calvaire! jura-t-il. Il manquait plus que ça! Pas un autre!

Les traits du visage de sa femme se durcirent en entendant l'accueil qu'il faisait à ce qu'elle considérait comme une bonne nouvelle.

— Ça a l'air de te faire plaisir sans bon sens, répliqua-t-elle sèchement.

— On en a déjà quatre, dit-il en guise d'explication.

— Je te ferai remarquer qu'on est mariés et que c'est normal qu'on ait des enfants, rétorqua-t-elle. Il paraît que le mariage, c'est fait pour ça.

— Laisse faire tes sermons de curé, la rabroua-t-il. Je connais la chanson. En attendant, nous v'là poignés avec un autre petit qui s'en vient.

— Il y a un bien bon moyen pour que ça arrive plus, persifla-t-elle. T'as juste à aller dormir dans une des chambres en haut.

Liam ne se donna pas la peine de lui répondre. Il sortit de la maison en claquant la porte et se dirigea vers les bâtiments. Après son départ, Camille alla s'enfermer dans sa chambre et se laissa tomber sur son lit. Elle sanglota durant de longues minutes, incapable de contrôler la peine qui la submergeait.

— J'aurais jamais dû le marier, murmura-t-elle. Il a pas de cœur, cet homme-là !

Mais la femme énergique qu'elle était reprit rapidement le dessus. Elle finit par sécher ses larmes et mit de l'ordre dans la pièce avant de regagner sa cuisine où elle entreprit de préparer le repas du midi. À la fin de la matinée, elle alla bêcher son jardin.

Un peu avant l'heure du repas, un bruit de voiture approchant sur la route la fit se redresser pour identifier le voyageur qui passait.

— Ah non ! Pas lui ! Ça, c'est le restant des écus ! dit-elle à haute voix en reconnaissant l'oncle de son mari qui venait de faire entrer son attelage dans la cour de la ferme.

Paddy Connolly ne pouvait revenir chez son neveu à un pire moment. L'homme poursuivit son chemin jusqu'à l'écurie, détela sa bête et la fit entrer dans l'enclos, avant de revenir à la maison en portant sa valise cartonnée. Camille se remit à sa tâche en attendant que son pensionnaire se décide à la saluer. Celui-ci fit comme s'il ne l'avait pas vue dans le jardin. Il déposa sa valise sur la galerie et entreprit de transporter trois boîtes remplies de ses affaires personnelles qu'il monta dans sa chambre. Camille continua sa besogne jusqu'à ce qu'elle voie son mari se diriger vers la maison pour dîner. Elle lui emboîta le pas sans se presser.

— Mon oncle est arrivé ? lui demanda-t-il.

— Je l'ai pas vu, mentit-elle sur un ton indifférent.

— Son boghei est proche de l'écurie, lui fit-il remarquer.

Tous les deux pénétrèrent dans la maison et trouvèrent le retraité bedonnant confortablement installé dans l'une des chaises berçantes, en train de fumer l'un de ses cigares malodorants.

— Tiens ! Vous êtes arrivé, mon oncle, dit-elle en feignant la surprise. Vous m'avez pas vue dans le jardin ?

— Ben non, répondit Paddy avec une évidente mauvaise foi.

— Pour moi, vous avez besoin de lunettes, répliqua-t-elle d'une voix acide. À force de lire vos journaux, votre vue baisse.

Puis, sans plus se préoccuper de l'oncle de son mari, elle s'occupa de son dîner. Elle sortit du fourneau les fèves au lard et dressa le couvert, en écoutant d'une oreille attentive ce que son pensionnaire racontait à son mari.

À l'entendre, Paddy Connolly avait liquidé tous ses avoirs. Il avait obtenu un bon prix autant pour ses maisons que pour ses meubles. Dorénavant, plus rien ne l'appellerait à retourner à Montréal. Il avait même sur lui une lettre de crédit représentant toutes ses économies qu'il se proposait d'aller porter chez le notaire Valiquette après le dîner. Après mûre réflexion, il avait décidé de confier tous ses avoirs au notaire pour qu'il les fasse fructifier.

— Ça, mon neveu, c'est ben de l'argent, prit-il soin de préciser en adoptant un air important. Je serais pas surpris pantoute qu'Eudore Valiquette en ait jamais vu autant dans sa vie.

Il était visible que Liam mourait d'envie de demander à son oncle quelle somme il entendait confier au notaire, mais il n'osa pas. Il se contenta de lui dire :

— Vous savez, mon oncle, Valiquette a été nommé marguillier de la nouvelle paroisse, comme le facteur.

— *Shitt !* Si j'avais pu revenir à temps, le monde de Saint-Bernard aurait pu me nommer marguillier, moi aussi.

— Je pense pas, mon oncle. Il faut posséder des biens dans la paroisse pour être marguillier, intervint Camille.

— Ouais! On sait ben. En passant, j'ai remarqué qu'on avait l'air à travailler pas mal au moulin du cavalier de ta sœur.

— Ce sont les hommes de Bélisle de Saint-Zéphirin qui sont en train de réparer la grande roue du moulin. Elle est partie avec les glaces, expliqua Liam.

À la fin du repas pris dans un silence presque complet, Paddy ne put s'empêcher d'apprendre à son neveu la nouvelle qui défrayait les manchettes à Montréal depuis quelques jours.

— Tu devineras jamais ce qui se passe, dit-il à Liam. Il y a des ouvriers de l'Ontario qui viennent de se mettre avec des gars de chez nous pour essayer d'obliger les *boss* à les faire travailler juste neuf heures par jour. As-tu déjà entendu une affaire écœurante comme ça, toi?

— Ça va faire des petites semaines d'ouvrage, ça, reconnut Liam, surpris.

— Des semaines de cinquante-quatre heures au lieu de soixante-douze heures, au même salaire, à part ça. Il y a pas un *boss* qui va accepter ça. Moi, mes hommes travaillaient douze heures par jour et j'en ai jamais entendu un se lamenter. Les jeunes d'aujourd'hui veulent plus rien faire. Tous des paresseux!

Liam se borna à approuver en hochant la tête.

Après un court repos, le maître des lieux décida de retourner au travail pendant que sa femme finissait de ranger la cuisine.

— Si tu pouvais venir me donner un coup de main à placer mes affaires dans ma chambre, ma nièce, ça ferait ben mon affaire, déclara le retraité.

— Voyons, mon oncle, vous avez pas tant d'affaires que ça à placer, répliqua Camille. Je vais vous laisser cette besogne-là. Moi, j'ai du fumier à transporter dans mon jardin et je suis pas pantoute en avance. Il faut que je me grouille si on veut avoir des légumes cet été.

Sur ce, elle le laissa seul dans la maison et sortit. La jeune femme ignora si son oncle par alliance rangea ses effets personnels ou s'il se laissa aller à une sieste réparatrice, mais elle le vit atteler son cheval un peu après trois heures et se diriger vers l'extrémité du rang.

Ce soir-là, malgré une journée de travail épuisante, Camille servit le souper tôt dans l'intention de participer à la récitation du chapelet à la chapelle. Dès que la vaisselle fut lavée, elle se mit à houspiller son monde pour ne pas arriver en retard.

— Moi, je vais pas là, déclara tout net son mari.

— Moi non plus, s'empressa d'annoncer Paddy.

Elle jeta un regard désapprobateur aux deux hommes, mais elle se contenta de demander à Liam :

— Dans ce cas-là, est-ce que c'est trop te demander d'aller m'atteler le boghei ?

— Patrick est capable de faire ça, répondit-il sèchement avant de sortir s'asseoir sur la galerie.

Le garçon qui allait célébrer ses douze ans quelques semaines plus tard comprit et il se dirigea vers l'enclos où les deux chevaux paissaient. Peu après, Camille et les quatre enfants s'entassèrent dans la voiture qui prit la direction du village.

Après le chapelet, la jeune femme retrouva sa mère, Bernadette, Donat, Hubert, Emma et Rémi à la sortie de la chapelle.

— Liam est pas avec toi ? lui demanda sa mère.

— Non, il était trop fatigué pour venir, répondit Camille, évasive.

— Viens donc jouer aux cartes avec nous autres, l'invita sa sœur Emma. Eugénie est chez nous. Elle garde Alexis et mes enfants.

— T'es bien fine, mais je pense que je vais rentrer. J'ai eu une grosse journée, refusa sa sœur aînée.

Marie comprit intuitivement qu'il se passait quelque chose, car elle annonça à ses enfants qu'elle préférait rentrer à la maison, elle aussi.

— Si tes enfants veulent se tasser un peu, je monterais bien avec toi, dit-elle à Camille sur un ton détaché.

— On peut ben aller vous reconduire à la maison, proposa Hubert.

— Ben non, c'est pas utile, intervint Camille, je vais ramener m'man à la maison. Vous autres, allez vous amuser et essayez de pas trop tricher, pour une fois.

— Ah ben! T'es pas gênée, la belle-sœur, fit semblant de s'offusquer Rémi Lafond. Tu sauras que moi, j'ai jamais triché aux cartes.

— Aïe, Rémi Lafond! T'oublies que j'ai déjà joué avec toi. Je sais ce que t'es capable de faire, déclara Camille en riant.

— Je pense qu'on a intérêt à le surveiller, lui, dit Donat en se mettant en marche vers son boghei.

Les trois voitures descendirent la côte du rang Sainte-Ursule l'une derrière l'autre. Celle de Camille était la dernière. Au passage, Camille et sa mère saluèrent Angèle Cloutier, debout sur sa galerie. Quand le boghei entra dans la cour de la ferme des Beauchemin, Marie dit à sa fille, comme si elle venait d'y penser:

— Pourquoi tu passerais pas un petit bout de veillée avec moi? Je suis toute seule et j'ai bien l'impression que je verrai pas revenir les autres avant au moins deux heures.

Camille n'hésita qu'un court moment avant de confier les rênes à Patrick.

— Va pas trop vite, recommanda-t-elle au garçon. Ann, tu diras à ton père que je vais revenir tout à l'heure, ajouta-t-elle à l'intention de l'adolescente.

Les deux femmes descendirent de voiture et elles attendirent de la voir disparaître dans un léger nuage de poussière avant de monter sur la galerie.

— Je pense qu'on est aussi bien de s'asseoir en dedans, déclara Marie. Le soleil se couche et il commence à faire frais.

Elles entrèrent et la maîtresse de maison s'empressa de jeter un rondin sur les tisons dans le poêle avant de déposer dessus la vieille théière un peu noircie.

— Il me semble que ça fait un bon bout de temps qu'on n'a pas pu se parler toutes les deux, dit Marie d'entrée de jeu. Il y a toujours Eugénie ou une de tes sœurs dans les parages chaque fois qu'on se voit.

— C'est vrai, reconnut sa fille aînée. Vous m'avez jamais dit comment vous trouvez ça d'avoir votre chambre en haut.

— C'est pas la fin du monde et j'en mourrai pas, déclara sa mère. Il y a du pour et du contre. En haut, c'est plus petit, mais je suis plus obligée de me lever la nuit pour entretenir le poêle. En plus, il fallait bien que ça arrive un jour avec Eugénie qui attend son deuxième. Ça aurait pas été normal que je prenne la plus grande chambre de la maison toute seule…

— Vous avez pas tort, m'man.

— Parlant de petit, fit Marie en la scrutant. T'as rien de nouveau à m'annoncer ?

— Pourquoi vous me demandez ça ? feignit de s'étonner sa fille.

— Voyons, Camille. T'es mariée depuis six mois…

— Si ça peut vous contenter, m'man, je suis en famille, déclara sa fille d'une voix éteinte. Je l'ai annoncé à matin à Liam.

— Il y a pas à dire, ça a l'air de te faire plaisir sans bon sens, fit sa mère, un peu surprise.

— Moi, je suis bien contente, mais…

— Mais ton mari l'est pas mal moins. C'est ça que tu veux dire ?

— Oui, il trouve qu'on en a déjà quatre et que c'est bien assez.

— Je veux bien le croire, mais quatre enfants, c'est pas une bien grosse famille. À part ça, ces enfants-là, même si tu les aimes bien gros, ce sont pas les tiens.

Camille se contenta de pousser un gros soupir et sa mère se rendit compte qu'elle se retenait pour ne pas pleurer devant elle.

— À quoi il s'attendait exactement, Liam Connolly, quand il t'a mariée ?

— Je le sais pas, reconnut Camille d'une toute petite voix. Il y a des fois que je pense qu'il cherchait surtout une servante.

— Ah ben là, j'espère que tu te laisseras pas faire, ma fille, s'emporta soudainement Marie. Il y a tout de même des limites à ambitionner sur le pain bénit. Cet enfant-là, tu l'as pas fait toute seule. Que ça fasse plaisir ou pas à ton mari, il va venir au monde.

— C'est ce que j'arrête pas de me dire, l'approuva Camille avec un pauvre sourire.

— Si c'est comme ça, secoue-toi et le laisse pas te manger la laine sur le dos. S'il le faut, je vais envoyer un de tes frères lui parler dans le visage, moi, à Liam Connolly.

— Faites pas ça, m'man, la pria sa fille. Je suis capable de me défendre toute seule.

— Je l'espère pour toi. En tout cas, je veux pas que tu me fasses de cachette. Si ton mari se conduit pas comme du monde, je veux que tu m'en parles. On va y mettre bon ordre. Il est pas dit qu'un maudit Irlandais va faire manger du foin à une Beauchemin.

Camille ne put s'empêcher d'éclater de rire, ce qui eut le don de détendre l'atmosphère. Ensuite, les deux femmes parlèrent du degré d'avancement de leur jardin et de ce qu'elles planteraient bientôt dans leurs plates-bandes.

— Est-ce que vous avez un peu d'aide pour faire tout ça ? finit par demander Camille.

— Bedette m'aide un peu quand elle revient de l'école, avoua sa mère. Pour Eugénie, tu la connais comme moi. Moins elle en fait, mieux elle est. À l'écouter, c'est la première femme au monde à attendre un petit. Une chance qu'elle a pas ta besogne à faire, elle en mourrait, ajouta-t-elle, sarcastique.

Une heure plus tard, Camille prit congé de sa mère. Cette conversation entre mère et fille lui avait fait un bien énorme et elle rentrait à la maison bien décidée à se faire respecter par son mari. Elle trouva celui-ci en train de se bercer seul dans la cuisine éclairée par la lampe déposée au centre de la table.

— Je commençais à me demander où t'étais passée, lui dit-il en guise de bienvenue.

— Ann t'a pas dit que j'étais arrêtée chez ma mère ?

— Oui, mais je pensais pas que tu passerais toute la soirée là.

— T'étais pas obligé de m'attendre, répliqua-t-elle sur le même ton. Je suis encore capable de trouver mon chemin, même quand il fait noir.

— Ouais, je vois ben ça. Mon oncle vient de monter et les enfants sont couchés, précisa-t-il.

— C'est correct. Moi aussi, je suis fatiguée. Je vais aller me coucher, lui dit-elle en se dirigeant vers leur chambre.

Quelques minutes plus tard, Liam Connolly put réaliser à quel point sa réaction à l'annonce d'une prochaine naissance avait blessé sa femme. Celle-ci repoussa sèchement ses avances en lui disant carrément :

— Je sais pas comment t'étais avec ta défunte, mais si t'étais avec elle comme t'es avec moi, elle a dû finir par t'haïr.

— Qu'est-ce qui te prend ? lui demanda-t-il, tout étonné.

— Il me prend que je m'aperçois que t'as pas de cœur, Liam Connolly, répondit-elle au bord des larmes. T'es bête comme tes pieds et tu penses juste à toi.

Sur ces mots, elle lui tourna le dos.

Si Camille s'imaginait que cette scène aiderait son mari à prendre conscience de son manque de délicatesse, elle se trompait. Elle s'en rendit compte le lendemain matin à sa façon sèche de donner des ordres aux siens, sans prendre la peine de la consulter.

— À partir d'aujourd'hui, tout le monde ici dedans va travailler à ramasser les pierres dans nos champs. Vous retournerez à l'école seulement quand je vous dirai que j'ai plus besoin de vous autres. Il est dit nulle part que je vais être le seul à m'éreinter du matin au soir.

— Même moi, p'pa ? demanda la petite Rose.

— Toi, tu peux y retourner. T'es encore trop petite pour servir à quelque chose.

Les trois autres enfants ne bronchèrent pas. Après le lavage de la vaisselle, Ann alla rejoindre ses deux jeunes frères dans le champ. Moins d'une heure plus tard, Camille se joignit à sa famille et, malgré son état, abattit sa large part de cette besogne éreintante. Quand son mari annonça qu'il était l'heure d'aller manger, elle rentra à la maison avec sa fille pour préparer le dîner.

❧

En ce samedi soir, la chapelle se remplit aux trois quarts pour la récitation du chapelet. Le curé Désilets avait tout lieu d'être fier de la ferveur de ses paroissiens depuis le début du mois de Marie. Comme il faisait beau, les gens n'étaient pas pressés de rentrer chez eux après la courte cérémonie et des groupes se formèrent autant sur le parvis que sur le bord de la route.

Constant Aubé s'empressa de venir à la rencontre de Bernadette qu'il n'avait pas vue de la semaine.

— C'est ben ennuyant le mois de mai parce que ça coupe de moitié notre samedi soir, dit-il à la jeune institutrice.

— Il y a pas moyen de faire autrement avec ma mère, répliqua Bernadette sans enthousiasme en guettant son frère Hubert qui se dirigeait vers les Dionne. À part ça, c'est pas une obligation de veiller ensemble tous les samedis soir, ajouta-t-elle sur un ton indifférent.

Cette remarque sembla blesser le jeune homme et il fit un effort louable pour orienter autrement la conversation.

— Au moins, la vie va enfin redevenir normale, ajouta le meunier. Les hommes de Bélisle ont fini les réparations au moulin juste avant le souper.

— Tant mieux, intervint Donat, debout dans son dos, on se demandait quand est-ce qu'il commencerait la construction du presbytère.

— Si je me fie à ce que ses hommes m'ont dit aujourd'hui, ils sont supposés commencer au début de la semaine prochaine.

— Ça, c'est une bonne nouvelle, déclara le jeune cultivateur avant de s'éloigner du couple.

— Penses-tu, Bedette, qu'on va avoir le temps de passer une heure ensemble à soir? demanda Constant à son amie de cœur.

— On pourrait peut-être laisser faire à soir, je me sens fatiguée, répondit Bernadette, comme si la chose l'intéressait peu. J'espère juste que ma mère en a pas pour trop longtemps à jaser avec Bridget Ellis et Angèle Cloutier. J'aimerais bien pas être obligée de l'attendre encore une heure avant de retourner à la maison.

Constant se dit que la jeune fille avait l'une de ses sautes d'humeur inexplicables et s'efforça tout de même de se montrer aimable.

— Si t'es si fatiguée que ça, tu pourrais peut-être demander à ton frère Hubert de nous chaperonner pendant que je te ramènerais chez vous.

— Il voudra pas. Mon frère va veiller chez la belle Angélique à soir, à condition que les Dionne arrêtent, eux autres aussi, de jacasser avec tout un chacun.

— Bon, si c'est comme ça, je pense que je vais rentrer, lui annonça le meunier en ne parvenant pas à dissimuler totalement sa déception.

Depuis plusieurs semaines, le jeune homme se rendait compte que Bernadette soufflait alternativement le chaud et le froid. Souvent, il avait l'impression de l'importuner en venant veiller au salon. Il ne savait plus trop où il en était avec elle. Il était toujours aussi follement amoureux d'elle, mais il aurait juré qu'elle s'éloignait de plus en plus de lui, comme si elle cherchait ailleurs. Il s'en voulait de ne pas avoir le courage de lui demander carrément si elle préférait qu'il cesse ses fréquentations. Il avait bien trop peur qu'elle réponde par l'affirmative.

Malheureux comme les pierres d'avoir été encore une fois rabroué, Constant Aubé monta dans son boghei et rentra chez lui.

Après le départ de son amoureux, Bernadette s'approcha de sa mère pour lui faire sentir qu'elle l'attendait pour rentrer. Tout en suivant distraitement la conversation qu'elle avait avec Bridget Ellis et Angèle Cloutier, elle observait Hubert du coin de l'œil.

En fait, il n'y avait qu'à regarder le visage de Hubert Beauchemin pour se rendre compte que le jeune homme était follement heureux. Angélique lui avait chuchoté que son père avait reçu la veille la réponse de son cousin Antoine Grondin, fromager à Dunham, et que ce dernier acceptait de le prendre comme apprenti.

Quand Télesphore s'était finalement approché du jeune homme pour lui apprendre la nouvelle, Hubert, diplomate, avait feint de ne rien savoir.

— Là, mon jeune, t'es chanceux, lui fit remarquer le propriétaire du magasin général. Tu vas apprendre un beau métier qui a ben de l'avenir. Quand tu vas revenir, on fera des projets sérieux ensemble.

Hubert, rouge d'émotion, remercia le marchand, persuadé que la belle Angélique pourrait facilement trouver sa place dans les projets qu'il commençait à caresser.

— Quand est-ce que je peux y aller, monsieur Dionne? demanda-t-il au marchand.

— Pour moi, le plus vite sera le mieux, répondit le père d'Angélique. À ta place, je bretterais pas trop. Si t'arrives vite, ça va prouver à mon cousin que t'es ben intéressé et ça va faire bonne impression.

Quand Hubert apprit la nouvelle aux siens à son retour à la maison à la fin de la soirée, Donat se réjouit beaucoup moins que sa femme.

— Ça tombe mal en torrieu, cette affaire-là, déclara-t-il à celle-ci en se déshabillant dans leur chambre du rez-de-chaussée. Juste au moment où on a le plus d'ouvrage sur les bras.

— T'engageras quelqu'un, ce sera pas la première fois, répliqua Eugénie. Avant, quand il était chez les frères, tu te débrouillais sans lui. Là, il part et j'ai bien l'impression qu'il travaillera plus sur une terre. Il va être fromager. Tu te rends compte qu'il reste plus que Bedette ici dedans. Une fois qu'elle va être casée, ta mère aura plus le choix de se donner à toi.

— Recommence pas avec cette histoire-là, la mit-il en garde avec humeur. Là, j'en ai pas mal sur le dos... à commencer par la réunion du conseil demain après-midi. C'est sûr qu'on va parler de la construction du presbytère.

➥

Le lendemain après-midi, les marguilliers de la nouvelle paroisse se réunirent dans la sacristie. Il faisait si doux en ce deuxième dimanche de mai que le curé Désilets avait ouvert les fenêtres de la grande pièce pour aérer. L'air charriait toutes sortes d'effluves et on entendait les croassements assourdissants des corneilles qui avaient fait leur apparition dans la région quelques jours auparavant.

— Avant de parler de la construction du presbytère qui doit commencer mardi prochain, s'empressa de dire Josaphat Désilets, il faut élire un président du conseil et un secrétaire.

Donat jeta un rapide coup d'œil à Samuel Ellis assis au bout de la table, comme il en avait l'habitude, ainsi qu'à Thomas Hyland, qui servait de secrétaire au conseil depuis la fondation de la mission. Hormidas Meilleur, assis près de lui, gardait un silence prudent.

— Est-ce que le vote se fait à main levée ou en secret? demanda Eudore Valiquette, sanglé dans son costume noir et son cou maigre étranglé par son col dur.

— D'habitude, on fait ça à main levée, s'empressa de répondre Samuel, sans consulter le curé.

— Je propose monsieur le notaire comme président, intervint le petit facteur. Si j'ai ben compris, c'est lui qui a trouvé l'argent pour la construction du presbytère. En plus, il est instruit.

Les traits du visage d'Ellis se figèrent, mais il ne dit rien.

— On va voter, annonça le pasteur de Saint-Bernard-Abbé. Qui vote pour monsieur Valiquette?

Hormidas Meilleur leva immédiatement la main, imité par Josaphat Désilets. Donat Beauchemin hésita un court moment avant de se décider à les imiter. Il était trop heureux de se venger de son adversaire politique qu'il soupçonnait encore d'être celui qui avait trafiqué sa bagosse l'année précédente lors de la campagne électorale. Après s'être consultés du regard, Hyland et Ellis finirent par lever la main à leur tour.

— Je propose monsieur Hyland comme secrétaire, intervint ensuite le curé Désilets. Il a une belle écriture.

Thomas fut reconduit au poste qu'il occupait au conseil des syndics. Durant plusieurs minutes, il fut question du presbytère, mais Samuel Ellis ne participa guère à la discussion générale. Il était évident qu'il était blessé dans sa fierté de ne pas avoir été réélu à la présidence et, en même temps, l'homme aux cheveux roux semblait préoccupé.

— J'ai bien hâte de voir arriver les ouvriers de Bélisle mardi matin, déclara le prêtre avec enthousiasme.

— Je vais être là souvent pour surveiller les travaux, annonça le petit notaire en se rengorgeant. Contrairement à vous, messieurs, j'ai pas une terre à travailler et j'ai tout mon temps pour y voir.

— Moi aussi, je vais venir voir de temps en temps, déclara Hormidas Meilleur. J'oublie pas que ça va être construit sur un lot de ma terre…

— Comment ça, de votre terre, père Meilleur ? lui demanda Donat, étonné.

— Voyons, mon jeune ! Tu devrais savoir qu'en mariant Angèle Cloutier, son bien est devenu mon bien. Et là, je vais voir à ce qu'on respecte les bornes.

Samuel Ellis se rappela soudain que le facteur avait vendu son lopin de terre et sa petite maison du rang Saint-Paul à la commission scolaire et qu'il avait emménagé chez sa femme le jour même de son mariage. On racontait même qu'il avait confié au notaire Valiquette l'argent de cette vente. Soudain, tout s'éclaira. Il venait de comprendre pourquoi Meilleur avait proposé que la présidence soit confiée au notaire. Ils s'étaient entendus avant la réunion.

— Le vieux verrat ! Il va me payer ça, chuchota-t-il à Thomas Hyland qui ne comprenait apparemment pas de quoi il parlait.

— Il faudrait tout de même pas s'organiser pour qu'il y ait des changements aux plans qui ont été faits, intervint Donat qui se rappelait trop bien les interventions du curé lors de la construction du jubé. On le sait, à cette heure, que chaque changement coûte de l'argent, et de l'argent, on n'en a pas.

— Si vous êtes d'accord, je vais parler à monsieur Bélisle dès mardi matin, fit Eudore Valiquette. Et je vais lui dire que les seuls changements qui seront faits seront ceux que le conseil aura acceptés.

Un air de profond mécontentement se peignit sur le visage du prêtre quand il se rendit compte que tous approuvaient la suggestion. S'il avait imaginé avoir les coudées plus franches avec le nouveau président du conseil, il devait convenir que les choses se présentaient assez mal.

Après la réunion, Samuel rentra chez lui et laissa éclater sa mauvaise humeur devant Bridget.

— *Goddam!* que le diable les emporte tous! explosa-t-il. Valiquette est pas dans la paroisse depuis trois mois que tout le monde est en adoration devant lui. Ils l'ont nommé président du conseil à ma place.

— Voyons donc! fit sa femme, incrédule.

— Je te le dis! Le père Meilleur l'a proposé et il avait l'air de s'être entendu avec lui avant la réunion. Le petit Beauchemin a voté pour parce que c'est un maudit Bleu... Le pire, c'est monsieur le curé. Il a tout de suite voté pour le notaire. Arrache-toi donc le cœur pour aider, c'est comme ça qu'on te remercie.

— Si c'est comme ça, j'arrête d'aller travailler à la sacristie. Monsieur le curé se trouvera une autre servante.

Il y eut un bref silence dans la cuisine de la maison du rang Sainte-Ursule avant que Samuel reprenne la parole.

— Non, fais pas ça. Ça aurait trop l'air de vouloir se venger. On va attendre que monsieur le curé s'installe dans son presbytère. À ce moment-là, tu pourras toujours dire que c'est trop grand à entretenir pour toi et que t'as plus le temps.

Évidemment, la nouvelle de la nomination d'Eudore Valiquette à la présidence de la fabrique fit le tour de la paroisse et ce dernier en acquit un prestige certain.

Deux jours plus tard, les ouvriers de l'architecte Bélisle profitèrent du beau temps pour entreprendre l'excavation de la cave du futur presbytère. Avec cette nouvelle construction, le rang Sainte-Ursule allait évidemment devenir le village de Saint-Bernard-Abbé, ce que Baptiste Beauchemin avait craint.

Ce jour-là, Télesphore Dionne quitta son magasin général en compagnie de Hubert dans l'intention de l'accompagner jusqu'à Dunham où il désirait présenter le jeune homme à son cousin, le fromager. Angélique fut la dernière à rentrer dans le magasin après le départ de son père et du fils de Marie Beauchemin. Il était maintenant certain qu'un lien était en train de se tisser entre les deux jeunes gens. La meilleure preuve en était que, depuis un mois, Hubert apprenait à écrire sous la surveillance de sa sœur Bernadette auprès de qui il s'assoyait chaque soir quand la cuisine était rangée.

Chapitre 22

Une lutte à prévoir

Au milieu de la semaine suivante, Donat revint de chez le forgeron en affichant un air satisfait inhabituel.

— T'as l'air du chat qui vient de croquer une souris, lui dit sa mère. Qu'est-ce qui se passe?

— Je viens de parler à Elzéar Gingras. À partir de demain matin, son Ernest va venir travailler chez nous. Il a six autres garçons, m'man. Il dit qu'il peut se passer de celui-là aussi longtemps que j'en aurai besoin.

— Mais l'Ernest, c'est pas celui qui a le visage plein de tics et qui arrête pas de grouiller? demanda Eugénie.

— Peut-être, mais d'après son père, c'est un bon travaillant qui a pas peur de l'ouvrage dur.

— C'est correct, accepta Marie, on va lui préparer une chambre en haut.

Le lendemain avant-midi, Marie étendit un vieux drap sur la galerie pour y égrener les épis de maïs tressés et suspendus dans la grange depuis l'été précédent.

— On n'est pas en avance pantoute, déclara-t-elle à sa bru qui se traînait les pieds, comme à son habitude. Les hommes vont avoir besoin des semences de blé d'Inde et nous autres, on n'a plus de blé d'Inde à lessiver. Si on veut manger de la soupe aux pois qui a du goût, on a intérêt à se grouiller.

— On n'est pas obligées de tout faire aujourd'hui, madame Beauchemin, se défendit Eugénie, sans entrain.

— Si, il le faut. Viens m'aider à rapporter les tresses. Si on perd pas de temps, on devrait avoir fini pour midi.

Les deux femmes s'installèrent au-dessus du drap pour frotter les épis les uns contre les autres afin d'en détacher les grains. Elles jetaient les « cotons » dans un seau dans l'intention d'aller le vider ensuite dans l'auge des porcs. Elles avaient accompli la moitié de leur tâche quand le jeune Ernest Gingras se présenta à la ferme, portant un petit baluchon.

— C'est toi, l'Ernest d'Elzéar Gingras ? lui demanda Marie.

— Oui, madame Beauchemin, répondit le jeune homme, un peu intimidé.

Eugénie s'arrêta de travailler pour regarder le nouvel employé de la maison. Le garçon âgé d'environ dix-huit ans avait l'air solide malgré une relative maigreur. Cependant, la femme de Donat remarqua davantage les clignements de ses yeux et ses froncements de nez incessants que ses larges mains et ses bras musclés.

— Bon, suis-moi, je vais te montrer ta chambre, lui ordonna Marie en se dirigeant vers la porte de la cuisine d'été.

Le jeune homme la suivit à l'intérieur. La maîtresse de maison lui montra sa chambre et le laissa seul. Moins de cinq minutes plus tard, le jeune homme vint la rejoindre sur la galerie.

— Tu vas trouver mon garçon dans le champ, en arrière de la grange, dit Marie à l'adolescent qui quitta les deux femmes sur un signe de tête.

— Mon Dieu, ça va prendre du temps avant de l'engraisser, celui-là ! s'exclama Eugénie dès que le nouvel homme engagé se fut suffisamment éloigné pour ne pas l'entendre.

— J'aime mieux un homme engagé maigre comme lui qu'un Gros-Gras malfaisant et paresseux comme l'était

Ignace Houle, laissa tomber sa belle-mère en reprenant sa besogne.

Dès le premier repas, les deux femmes furent à même de se rendre compte qu'Ernest Gingras avait un solide appétit. Toutefois, Donat s'empressa de dire à sa mère, en dehors de la présence de l'intéressé, qu'il abattait sa large part de travail et qu'il n'était pas besoin de lui pousser dans le dos pour le faire avancer.

— Seigneur! c'est de quelqu'un comme ça que je voudrais dans ma cuisine, ne put s'empêcher de déclarer Marie.

Donat comprit que sa mère faisait allusion à sa femme, mais il fit comme s'il ne l'avait pas entendue.

Au souper, Ernest Gingras sembla perdre tous ses moyens quand il aperçut Bernadette dans la cuisine. Assis à ses côtés, il mangea si peu qu'Eugénie se sentit obligée de lui demander:

— Qu'est-ce qui se passe? T'aimes pas ce qu'on t'a servi?

— Non, madame, tout est ben correct, s'empressa-t-il de lui répondre en rougissant. C'est juste que j'ai moins faim à soir.

Quand l'employé se retira dans sa chambre après le repas, Bernadette s'approcha de sa mère et de sa belle-sœur.

— J'espère qu'il a pas l'intention de me regarder tout le temps comme un veau qui vient de retrouver sa mère, fit-elle.

— Il est pas habitué aux filles, lui expliqua sa mère. Les Gingras ont juste six garçons.

— S'ils sont tous aussi laids et pleins de tics, ça doit être beau à voir, rétorqua-t-elle.

— Tête folle! fit sa mère. Les Gingras sont du bon monde. Pour les tics, Ernest est pas responsable. Toi, je veux que tu restes bien à ta place et va surtout pas essayer de le gêner ou de lui faire de la façon. C'est un homme engagé et ton frère en a besoin.

Tout avait été dit et la jeune institutrice prit bien soin de ne pas susciter de problèmes dans la maison en adoptant un comportement neutre à l'endroit du nouvel employé de sa mère.

～

Le jour suivant, Donat et Ernest étaient occupés à la réparation de la porte de la grange quand un boghei vint s'immobiliser tout près des deux hommes. Donat sursauta quand il reconnut Anthime Lemire descendant difficilement de sa voiture.

— Ah ben, ça parle au diable ! s'exclama-t-il en s'avançant vers le gros homme vêtu de noir. Avez-vous perdu votre chemin, monsieur Lemire ?

— Pantoute, mon jeune, c'est ben chez vous que je m'en venais à matin, répondit l'homme qui arborait toujours les mêmes épais favoris poivre et sel qui contrastaient avec ses grosses joues rouges rebondies. C'est à toi que j'ai affaire, ajouta-t-il en soulevant son chapeau melon pour essuyer son front où perlait de la sueur.

C'était une magnifique journée de la mi-mai. Il faisait beau et chaud et les arbres portaient déjà leur épaisse frondaison de la belle saison.

— Si c'est comme ça, venez vous rafraîchir à la maison, lui offrit Donat en tendant son marteau à son homme engagé.

L'organisateur du parti conservateur dans le comté salua Marie et Eugénie en train de travailler dans le jardin, la tête protégée par un large chapeau de paille, et suivit Donat. Dès l'entrée du visiteur dans la fraîche cuisine d'été, le jeune cultivateur lui servit un verre de bagosse et l'invita à prendre un siège.

— Venez pas me dire qu'il va y avoir encore des élections, dit-il, mi-sérieux, au visiteur.

— Inquiète-toi pas. Il y aura pas d'élection de sitôt, en tout cas pas au Québec, prit-il la précaution de préciser.

Les Bleus font une ben trop bonne *job* pour que le monde pense à les ôter de là. Le garçon de Chauveau a même été élu dans Rimouski il y a quinze jours.

— Ça empêche pas que nous autres, dans Drummond, on est poignés avec un Rouge.

— Ça durera pas éternellement. Laurier est une grande gueule, mais j'ai entendu dire qu'il veut se présenter au fédéral aux prochaines élections.

— Ce serait une bonne nouvelle, reconnut Donat qui avait fait campagne l'été précédent pour le candidat conservateur Hemming.

— Mais c'est pas pour ça que je suis passé te voir, poursuivit Anthime Lemire avec une certaine impatience. Cette semaine, il y a quelqu'un du gouvernement qui va passer voir votre curé pour lui demander d'afficher une annonce à la porte de votre chapelle.

— Quoi?

— Es-tu au courant que Saint-Bernard est devenu une paroisse civile et que ça a été écrit dans la gazette officielle de Québec?

— Oui, je sais ça.

— Est-ce que tu sais ce que ça veut dire?

— Ben…

— Ça veut dire que Saint-Bernard-Abbé est devenu un village comme les autres et que le gouvernement va vous obliger à élire un maire et deux échevins, si je me fie à ce qu'on m'a dit.

— J'avais pas pensé à ça pantoute, reconnut Donat. Mais j'espère que vous avez pas fait tout le chemin entre Victoriaville et Saint-Bernard juste pour me raconter ça, ajouta-t-il pour plaisanter.

— Oui et non, fit l'autre, soudain mystérieux, ce qui eut pour effet d'alerter Donat. As-tu pensé qu'un maire dans un comté, c'est pas mal pesant? lui demanda Lemire.

— Ça se peut.

— Un maire qui est reconnu pour voter du bon bord peut apporter pas mal plus au monde de son village qu'un autre.

— C'est normal.

— Bon, je pense que tu commences à comprendre. Les gros du parti m'ont demandé qui je voyais comme maire de Saint-Bernard et j'ai tout de suite pensé à toi.

— Mais…

— Non, laisse-moi finir, le coupa l'organisateur du parti conservateur. On est au pouvoir depuis longtemps et il paraît que le premier ministre Chauveau apprécie pas pantoute que ce soit un Rouge qui est député de Drummond-Arthabasca. Il a demandé aux têtes dirigeantes du parti de s'organiser de manière à avoir au moins des maires Bleus dans le comté, quand c'était possible. Dans Saint-Bernard, je vois pas qui pourrait être un meilleur maire que toi, conclut le visiteur, sur le ton de la flatterie.

— Je veux ben vous croire, monsieur Lemire, dit Donat, mais là, je pense que ce serait un peu trop. Je viens d'avoir vingt-sept ans et je suis déjà marguillier et président de la commission scolaire. Vous trouvez pas que ça fait beaucoup pour un jeune de la paroisse ?

— Pantoute ! fit Anthime Lemire sur un ton péremptoire. Si t'es déjà marguillier et président de la commission scolaire, c'est que les gens de Saint-Bernard ont confiance en toi et pensent que t'es capable de faire la besogne. Je vois pas pourquoi ils t'éliraient pas maire.

— Mais ça a pas d'allure, déclara un Donat tout de même un peu tenté.

— T'as la carrure de ton père, le flatta le visiteur. Je suis certain qu'il serait ben fier de toi s'il te voyait.

— Si j'acceptais d'être candidat, qu'est-ce que j'aurais à faire ? finit par demander le jeune homme après une courte hésitation.

— Monsieur le curé va annoncer les élections dimanche prochain, si je me fie à ce que le fonctionnaire du gouvernement m'a dit avant-hier. Après, il devrait afficher la feuille des mises en candidature à la porte de votre chapelle. Chaque candidat doit s'inscrire sur la feuille, appuyé par deux secondeurs. Comme dans toutes les élections, il doit être propriétaire dans la paroisse. Si je me trompe pas, chez vous, l'élection est prévue pour le 30 juin.

— Je veux ben vous croire, mais là, il y a un maudit problème. Je suis pas pantoute propriétaire, déclara Donat, un peu dépité.

— Inquiète-toi pas pour ça, j'y ai pensé, fit Lemire en tirant une feuille de la poche de poitrine de son veston.

— Fais un « x » en bas de cette feuille-là, ordonna-t-il au jeune homme avec un bon gros rire.

— C'est quoi, cette affaire-là? demanda le jeune cultivateur, soudain méfiant.

— Ça, mon jeune, c'est une petite bande de terrain que tu possèdes dans la paroisse.

— Moi?

— Ben oui.

— Elle est à moi? Je peux la cultiver? demanda Donat, tout réjoui de posséder enfin de la terre.

— Là, je pense pas que tu sois capable de la cultiver, dit en riant Anthime Lemire. Le terrain que t'as a juste deux pieds de large par un demi-arpent de profondeur. À dire vrai, t'as acheté un bout de fossé du chemin de la Price…

— Si je comprends ben, j'ai pas de terre.

— En plein ça, mais ça te donne le droit de te présenter. Si j'ai un conseil à te donner, organise-toi donc pour que les deux hommes qui vont t'appuyer soient tes candidats comme conseillers. C'est toujours plus facile de mener une paroisse quand les échevins sont de ton bord.

— Mais j'ai pas encore accepté, protesta Donat.

— Voyons donc! Tu me feras pas croire que t'es pas tenté, se moqua Anthime Lemire. En plus, t'es certainement capable de trouver deux bons hommes pour t'appuyer.

— C'est sûr, reconnut Donat.

— Dans ce cas-là, présente-toi. Je peux te garantir que le parti est prêt à te donner un coup de main si t'en as besoin. Quand tu vas être élu, tu vas t'apercevoir que c'est pas mal intéressant d'être du bon bord. Tu vas voir que les emprunts sont pas mal plus faciles à obtenir. Pour les routes et les ponts, je pense que j'ai pas de dessins à te faire. Tu comprends.

L'organisateur garda le silence durant un long moment pour permettre au jeune cultivateur de prendre sa décision. Finalement, Donat se leva et tendit la main à son visiteur.

— Ça marche, je vais me présenter, lui annonça-t-il.

— Je suis sûr que tu vas y arriver, affirma le gros homme en se dirigeant vers la porte. Un conseil, laisse pas les Rouges prendre les devants. Là, t'as quelques jours d'avance sur eux. Ils sont pas encore au courant. Profites-en pour commencer à t'organiser. Trouve tes deux hommes au plus coupant.

Donat promit de s'en occuper très vite et reconduisit Lemire à sa voiture.

Après le départ de l'organisateur, Donat s'empressa de retourner au travail avant que sa mère et sa femme viennent l'interroger sur les raisons de la visite d'Anthime Lemire. Les deux femmes durent ronger leur frein jusqu'à l'heure du repas du midi.

Quand Donat leur apprit avec un certain orgueil qu'on voulait qu'il soit candidat à la mairie de Saint-Bernard-Abbé, elles eurent des réactions bien différentes. Si Eugénie ne cacha pas sa fierté de voir son mari sollicité pour occuper un si haut poste, par contre, sa mère était loin d'être enchantée.

— On dirait que t'as déjà oublié que ce Lemire-là t'avait fait un paquet de belles promesses l'été passé pour que tu t'occupes de l'élection de Hemming et il en a pas tenu une seule, lui dit Marie. Le lendemain des élections, il t'a complètement oublié.

— Je veux ben le croire, m'man, mais on a perdu.

— T'as pas remarqué qu'on lui voit la face seulement quand il a besoin de toi ?

— C'est la politique, m'man, fit Donat, un peu excédé. Il est arrivé la même chose à p'pa.

— T'as peut-être raison, concéda Marie, mais t'as pas le même âge qu'avait ton père quand il a commencé. Moi, je te le dis, mon garçon, tout ça, c'est des affaires pour se faire critiquer par tout un chacun.

— C'est certain, m'man, que si je reste tout seul dans mon trou, personne va rien avoir à redire sur moi. Ça me tente quand même d'essayer, avoua-t-il.

— Essaye, mais viens pas te plaindre après si ça marche pas à ton goût, conclut sa mère.

Ce soir-là, Donat Beauchemin quitta la maison assez tôt après le souper sans préciser aux siens l'objet de sa sortie. Il avait passé une bonne partie de l'après-midi à réfléchir aux deux hommes qui seraient prêts à se présenter avec lui à l'élection. Il avait rejeté d'emblée Liam Connolly au caractère un peu trop imprévisible pour jeter son dévolu sur son beau-frère, Rémi Lafond. Ensuite, il s'était dit qu'un conseiller un peu plus âgé rassurerait peut-être les électeurs de Saint-Bernard-Abbé et il avait pensé à Télesphore Dionne... Mais le marchand accepterait-il d'être associé à un parti, au risque de s'aliéner une partie de sa clientèle ? Finalement, il avait opté pour Anatole Blanchette parce qu'il le connaissait bien et qu'il habitait le rang Saint-Paul où il aurait besoin de trouver des appuis.

Son flair ne l'avait pas trompé. Rémi Lafond accepta sans discuter de se présenter comme conseiller, plus par esprit de famille que par soif de pouvoir. Quand Donat lui mentionna son intention d'aller proposer l'autre poste à Anatole Blanchette, ce choix le surprit.

— T'as pas pensé demander à Liam s'il serait intéressé ? lui demanda le mari d'Emma. Un Irlandais aurait pu t'attirer pas mal de votes, ajouta-t-il avec un certain bon sens.

— Oui, j'y ai pensé, mais là, à nous trois, ça aurait eu l'air surtout d'une affaire de famille et je suis pas certain que le monde de Saint-Bernard aurait ben aimé ça, mentit Donat.

— T'as peut-être raison, concéda un Rémi peu convaincu.

Donat n'eut pas à déployer beaucoup d'efforts pour convaincre Anatole Blanchette. L'homme semblait déjà regretter d'avoir refusé le poste de marguillier.

À son retour à la maison, Donat était très satisfait de sa soirée. Il était fin prêt, persuadé d'avoir une bonne longueur d'avance sur son ou ses adversaires. En l'occurrence, c'était faire preuve d'une belle naïveté. Deux jours auparavant, Samuel Ellis avait reçu la visite de Carolus Champagne, un conseiller de Wilfrid Laurier, le député du comté. Champagne était venu lui apprendre la tenue imminente d'une élection municipale à Saint-Bernard-Abbé et lui avait demandé conseil, à titre d'organisateur des libéraux dans la région.

La réponse d'Ellis aurait sûrement surpris Donat Beauchemin s'il l'avait connue. Cependant, fait certain, le choix du candidat libéral à la mairie ainsi que celui de ses deux conseillers étaient déjà arrêtés avant même la visite d'Anthime Lemire chez les Beauchemin.

Contrairement à ce qu'on aurait pu croire, Samuel Ellis avait déclaré sans ambages à Carolus Champagne qu'il était bien prêt à aider un bon libéral à se faire élire à la mairie, mais que le poste ne l'intéressait pas du tout.

—J'ai déjà assez d'être marguillier, affirma-t-il sur un ton résolu.

En réalité, l'homme à la tête rousse et aux tempes argentées en avait assez. Il était encore amer du fait qu'on lui ait préféré le notaire Valiquette pour occuper la présidence du conseil de fabrique. Toutefois, le conseiller de Wilfrid Laurier sut se montrer assez convaincant pour au moins l'inciter à briguer un poste d'échevin. Samuel dut accompagner son visiteur chez Thomas Hyland pour l'aider à persuader ce dernier de se présenter à la mairie de Saint-Bernard-Abbé.

Le propriétaire du moulin à bois mit plusieurs minutes à se laisser convaincre.

— Il faut qu'un Irlandais libéral soit maire, Thomas, insista Samuel. Si tu te présentes pas, c'est un Canadien français qui va l'être et on n'aura jamais un mot à dire.

Le propriétaire du moulin finit par accepter de poser sa candidature un peu à contrecœur à la condition que Samuel se présente comme conseiller municipal, à ses côtés.

— Il reste à trouver l'autre conseiller, leur fit remarquer Carolus Champagne, en dissimulant mal son impatience après avoir consulté sa montre de gousset.

— Il nous faut un autre bon Irlandais, suggéra Samuel, tout fier d'avoir pu convaincre son voisin et ami de postuler la mairie de Saint-Bernard-Abbé.

— Je sais pas trop, dit Thomas, le monde aimera peut-être pas trop ça qu'il y ait juste des Irlandais.

— Moi, je pense la même chose que vous. Il vaudrait mieux un bon libéral canadien-français, intervint Champagne.

— C'est pas ce qui manque à Saint-Bernard, déclara Ellis en exagérant un peu.

— Oui, mais il faut qu'il ait du répondant et que le monde ait confiance en lui, fit l'envoyé du député.

— Qu'est-ce que tu dirais du notaire? proposa soudainement Hyland.

— Tu parles de Valiquette?

— Oui.

— Moi, j'aime autant te dire tout de suite que j'aime pas trop le bonhomme, poursuivit Ellis sur un ton déterminé.

— Écoute, Samuel, je te demande pas de l'aimer, poursuivit son ami. Reconnais que les gens de Saint-Bernard ont pas l'air de l'haïr depuis qu'il est arrivé et qu'il est toujours prêt à rendre service au monde.

— Fais ce que tu veux, concéda Ellis.

— Bon, je vais passer le voir à soir pour voir s'il est intéressé, mais le contraire me surprendrait pas mal, conclut Hyland.

Le soir même, le notaire, approché par le candidat à la mairie, ne se fit pas prier pour accepter d'apposer son nom sur la liste des mises en candidature qui allait être affichée quelques jours plus tard. Hyland se garda bien, néanmoins, de rapporter à Ellis que l'homme de loi avait même été surpris qu'on n'ait pas songé à lui pour occuper le poste de maire.

Chapitre 23

Des choix

Le vendredi suivant, Amédée Durand arrêta son boghei dans la cour du magasin général en face de la petite école blanche occupée par Bernadette et une douzaine d'élèves. Depuis près d'un mois, dix enfants ne se présentaient plus que très tôt le matin pour venir réciter leurs leçons et remettre leurs devoirs. Ils travaillaient maintenant à la ferme toute la journée, c'était le cas, entre autres, de Patrick et Duncan Connolly.

En cette fin du mois de mai, il régnait une première véritable chaleur estivale et l'institutrice enseignait depuis quelques jours dans une classe dont toutes les fenêtres étaient grandes ouvertes pour permettre à un peu d'air de pénétrer. Dès que le jeune inspecteur descendit de voiture, il entendit les enfants ânonner les réponses du catéchisme, ce qui le fit sourire. Durant un bref moment, il sembla hésiter entre pénétrer dans le magasin général ou traverser la route. Finalement, il se décida à traverser la petite route poussiéreuse pour aller frapper à la porte de l'école.

Une élève vint ouvrir et, à la vue de l'inspecteur, tous les enfants se levèrent d'un bloc. Il les salua avec un large sourire en faisant un signe discret à Bernadette qu'il désirait lui dire quelques mots. Le cœur de la jeune fille bondit dans sa poitrine. Elle le voyait pour la quatrième fois depuis le début du mois et, chaque fois, elle était victime du même émoi. Se pouvait-il qu'un homme si beau et si instruit soit tombé amoureux d'elle? À cette seule pensée, elle sentait ses jambes se dérober un peu sous elle.

La jeune femme, le visage rosi, demanda aux enfants de s'asseoir et fit signe à Ann, son élève la plus âgée, de prendre la relève pendant qu'elle sortait sur le perron de l'école en refermant à demi la porte derrière elle.

— Bonjour, mademoiselle Beauchemin, la salua Amédée Durand. Vous allez finir par croire que je passe mon temps à venir vous déranger pour des riens, lui dit-il en enlevant son chapeau.

— Pas du tout, monsieur l'inspecteur, dit-elle, tout émue.

— Vous êtes vraiment très gentille. Ne vous inquiétez pas, je ne viens pas encore interroger vos élèves. Je veux seulement vous remettre un document pour votre frère, ajouta-t-il en tirant une enveloppe de son porte-documents. Dites-lui que je passerai le reprendre chez vous la semaine prochaine.

— Je vais le faire avec plaisir, minauda-t-elle en prenant l'enveloppe.

— Cet après-midi, je viens m'assurer que la demoiselle Dionne dont votre frère m'a parlé est vraiment bilingue. Elle demeure bien en face, n'est-ce pas?

— Oui, monsieur Durand. C'est l'amie de cœur de mon frère Hubert, ajouta-t-elle, au cas où il se laisserait charmer par la fille de Télesphore Dionne.

— Bon, j'espère que c'est la dernière fois que je vous dérange.

— Vous me dérangez jamais, déclara-t-elle, aguichante.

Amédée Durand lui décocha un sourire enjôleur et la salua avant de remettre son chapeau sur sa tête. Il traversa la route. Plantée devant la fenêtre, l'institutrice le regarda se diriger vers le magasin général. À cet instant précis, elle aurait donné tout ce qu'elle avait pour être à la place d'Angélique Dionne qui allait sûrement le recevoir dans son salon.

— Apprenez les cinq autres réponses, commanda-t-elle aux enfants sans se retourner vers eux.

«Pas de saint danger qu'une affaire comme ça me serait arrivée!» se dit-elle, toujours debout devant la fenêtre. Puis, elle se mit à s'inquiéter. Qu'est-ce qu'Amédée allait penser de la belle Angélique?

— J'espère qu'il sera pas assez niaiseux pour se laisser prendre par ses grands airs, murmura-t-elle, ce qui fit relever la tête des élèves tout près d'elle.

Si elle s'était écoutée, elle aurait fait une prière pour que celle qu'elle considérait comme sa rivale rate son examen avec l'inspecteur. À son avis, il était impossible que la fille de Télesphore Dionne soit bilingue alors qu'elle-même ne l'était pas. Comment la Dionne aurait-elle pu apprendre à parler anglais? Elle était certaine qu'elle s'était vantée et qu'Amédée allait s'en rendre compte immédiatement, pour la plus grande honte de la menteuse. Tant pis pour elle.

Un observateur aurait vite conclu, à voir le comportement de la fille cadette de Marie Beauchemin, qu'elle était tombée amoureuse d'Amédée Durand qui, sans le savoir encore, était appelé à succomber à son charme irrésistible. Il ne pouvait en être autrement, elle en était certaine.

À quatre heures, l'inspecteur était toujours chez les Dionne et Bernadette en déduisit, avec une joie mauvaise, que l'entrevue devait se dérouler difficilement. Elle signifia alors à ses élèves qu'ils pouvaient partir. Même si rien ne l'empêchait de quitter elle-même son école surchauffée, elle prit la peine de sortir sur le perron pour dire à Paddy Connolly, qui venait de faire monter Ann et Rose dans sa voiture, de ne pas l'attendre, qu'elle avait du travail à terminer. Sa mère allait probablement s'inquiéter de son retard, mais elle trouverait bien quelque chose à lui raconter à son retour à la maison.

Dès qu'elle se retrouva seule dans sa classe, elle ne laissa qu'une fenêtre ouverte et s'assit près de celle-ci de manière à voir Amédée Durand quitter la maison des Dionne. Elle projetait de sortir de l'école au moment même où il monterait dans sa voiture afin qu'il se sente obligé de la raccompagner à la maison. Une fois là, elle avait imaginé l'inviter à souper. À aucun moment elle n'eut une pensée pour Constant Aubé, son amoureux qui la fréquentait depuis près d'un an.

La jeune femme attendit près de quarante-cinq minutes avant que l'inspecteur sorte de chez les Dionne. Il était accompagné par une Angélique toute souriante et son père. Elle aurait bien aimé entendre ce qu'ils se disaient, mais ils ne parlaient pas assez fort. L'inspecteur salua le père et la fille et se dirigea vers son boghei. Immédiatement, Bernadette, saisie d'une sorte de frénésie, se jeta sur son sac d'école et se précipita vers la porte de peur qu'Amédée ne quitte les lieux sans la voir. Un peu essoufflée, elle ferma la porte de l'école derrière elle et s'empressa de descendre du perron pour qu'il ne puisse pas la manquer. L'inspecteur fit faire demi-tour à son attelage et aperçut la jeune femme qui se dirigeait vers la route. Il souleva poliment son chapeau et prit la direction de la côte du rang Sainte-Ursule.

Dépitée au-delà de toute expression de voir son beau plan tomber à l'eau, la fille de Marie Beauchemin entreprit de parcourir à pied le mille qui la séparait de chez elle. Tout au long du trajet, elle ne cessa de rager contre sa malchance et elle rentra à la maison de fort mauvaise humeur en laissant claquer la porte derrière elle.

— Veux-tu bien me dire d'où tu sors à une heure pareille ? l'apostropha sa mère, occupée à faire cuire des crêpes.

— De l'école, m'man. D'où voulez-vous que je vienne ? répondit-elle sur un ton hargneux.

— Bon, qu'est-ce qui se passe encore ? s'informa Marie en se tournant carrément vers sa fille.

— Il y a que j'ai dû chercher comme une folle quelque chose que je trouvais pas et j'ai été obligée de marcher, même s'il fait chaud à mourir, mentit-elle avec aplomb.

— Ça t'apprendra à avoir de l'ordre, fit sa mère d'une voix tranchante. En attendant, va te changer et viens nous donner un coup de main à mettre la table. Les hommes sont à la veille de rentrer.

Ce soir-là, Bernadette, incapable de cacher son exaspération et son anxiété, choisit de se retirer dans sa chambre. Par chance, le mois de mai prenait fin le lendemain, ce qui signifiait qu'elle ne serait plus obligée d'aller à la récitation du chapelet à la chapelle.

~

Une heure plus tôt, Camille, occupée à désherber ses plates-bandes, vit arriver le boghei conduit par l'oncle de son mari. Celui-ci immobilisa son attelage près de la maison pour laisser descendre ses deux petites-nièces et poursuivit son chemin jusque devant l'écurie pour y dételer sa bête et la faire entrer dans l'enclos voisin.

Fourbue, la jeune femme se redressa et invita Ann et Rose à aller changer de robe avant de venir l'aider à préparer le souper. Quelques instants après être rentrée dans la cuisine d'été, elle entendit son pensionnaire s'installer dans l'une des chaises berçantes sur la galerie.

Le retraité était revenu depuis trois semaines et, chaque vendredi, elle avait dû livrer une vraie bataille pour obtenir qu'il lui remette le dollar et demi que représentait le coût de sa pension. Chaque fois, c'était la même histoire : ou il n'avait pas l'argent sur lui ou il lui manquait vingt-cinq ou cinquante cents pour compléter la somme due. Évidemment, son mari s'était bien gardé d'intervenir, lui laissant, encore une fois, le mauvais rôle.

— Il me semble que c'est pas bien compliqué, murmura-t-elle à Ann. Il sait qu'on est le vendredi. Pourquoi il laisse pas sa pension sur la table, sans qu'on ait à le supplier?

Le fait d'être encore une fois obligée de supplier son pensionnaire la mettait de mauvaise humeur. Elle décida de lui demander tout de suite, avant le souper, le montant de sa pension hebdomadaire. Elle s'approcha de la porte moustiquaire.

— Mon oncle, vous oubliez pas qu'on est vendredi, lui rappela-t-elle sans se donner la peine de sortir à l'extérieur.

— Il y a pas de danger que je l'oublie avec toi, répliqua Paddy, d'une voix où perçait l'agacement.

— Je serais pas obligée de vous le dire si vous preniez l'habitude de laisser votre pension sur la table le vendredi matin, après le déjeuner, lui fit-elle remarquer d'une voix acide.

Sans plus insister, elle retourna à son fourneau pour vérifier si les fèves au lard étaient assez cuites. Elle entendit alors la porte s'ouvrir et vit l'oncle de son mari s'approcher de la table, fouiller dans l'une des poches de son pantalon et en extraire avec difficulté un dollar tout froissé qu'il jeta, avec un geste de grand seigneur, sur le meuble. Camille ne dit rien et attendit que le quinquagénaire sorte les cinquante cents qui manquaient. Il n'en fit rien. Il tourna les talons et retourna s'asseoir sur la galerie.

La jeune femme prit le dollar et alla le ranger dans l'un des tiroirs de la commode dans sa chambre avant de se diriger d'un pas résolu vers le grand panier d'osier placé près de l'escalier, dans lequel les membres de la famille déposaient leurs vêtements sales. Elle en renversa le contenu sur le parquet. Elle choisit dans le tas cinq chemises blanches, deux paires de chaussettes, deux sous-vêtements et trois mouchoirs avant de remettre le reste des vêtements dans le panier.

Quand elle revint dans la cuisine d'été en portant ces vêtements sales, elle entendit son mari qui échangeait quelques mots avec son oncle avant d'aller soigner les animaux.

Elle choisit d'attendre que son mari soit parti à l'étable en compagnie de Patrick et Duncan pour reprendre le tas de vêtements extirpés du panier. Après leur départ, elle entrouvrit la porte moustiquaire et déposa sans un mot les vêtements près de la chaise berçante où se prélassait son oncle par alliance. Elle referma la porte.

Moins d'une minute plus tard, l'oncle de son mari entra dans la cuisine, l'air furibond.

— C'est quoi, cette affaire-là, ma nièce?

— Moi, je dirais que c'est votre linge sale, mon oncle, répondit-elle d'une voix neutre.

— Pourquoi tu viens me mettre ça proche de ma chaise?

— Parce que pour une piastre par semaine, je vous nourris, mais je vous blanchis pas.

— Comment ça? fit-il en adoptant un air stupéfait.

— Voulez-vous arrêter de me prendre pour une folle, mon oncle? lui demanda-t-elle en haussant le ton à son tour, les mains sur les hanches. Quand je vous ai demandé deux piastres par semaine pour votre pension, vous vous êtes dépêché de faire baisser le prix en allant pleurer dans le gilet de Liam. Lui, il a accepté une piastre et demie, si je me trompe pas... pas une piastre.

— Je le sais! s'emporta le petit homme bedonnant.

— Si vous le savez, voulez-vous bien me dire pourquoi je dois me battre avec vous chaque vendredi pour l'avoir, cette piastre et demie là? rétorqua Camille, à bout de patience. Là, j'aime autant vous le dire, mon oncle, vous avez fini de rire de moi. Votre pension, c'est une piastre et demie, pas une piastre...

— Toute cette histoire pour cinquante cennes, fit Paddy, dédaigneux, en prenant un air supérieur.

— Si ces cinquante cennes-là sont pas plus importants que ça pour vous, voulez-vous ben me dire pourquoi il faut vous les arracher avec une paire de pinces une semaine sur deux?

— Aie pas peur, tu vas les avoir, tes cinquante cennes! répliqua-t-il. Mais avant, laisse-moi te dire, ma fille, que t'as pas l'air de savoir ce que c'est la charité chrétienne, ajouta-t-il, pontifiant.

— Comme on dit, mon oncle, charité bien ordonnée commence par soi-même. En plus, faire la charité, ça veut pas dire se laisser manger la laine sur le dos.

Paddy Connolly ouvrit la bouche comme s'il allait répliquer, puis il sembla changer d'idée. Il se contenta de tourner les talons et de monter à sa chambre. Lorsqu'il en descendit quelques minutes plus tard, il laissa cinquante cents sur la table.

❧

Le lendemain, Marie Beauchemin se rendit compte que sa Bedette n'était pas dans son état normal et elle évita de la houspiller trop souvent.

— Je sais pas ce qu'elle a, elle, mais elle file un mauvais coton depuis une couple de jours, déclara-t-elle à sa bru en finissant de peler les carottes qui allaient être servies au souper.

Sur le coup de sept heures, Constant Aubé arriva à pied dans la cour de la ferme des Beauchemin. Bernadette, assise dans la balançoire installée près de la maison, avait regardé froidement son amoureux s'avancer vers elle en boitillant légèrement. Dans sa tête, elle le comparait à Amédée Durand et, à ses yeux, le meunier ne pouvait supporter la comparaison.

— Il est laid et il boite, murmura-t-elle pour elle-même, sans se donner la peine de se lever pour aller au-devant de son cavalier.

Constant prit le temps de saluer et de prendre des nouvelles des Beauchemin, assis à l'ombre sur la galerie, avant de se diriger vers la balançoire d'où Bernadette n'avait pas bougé. Le jeune homme remarqua aussitôt son air boudeur et chercha à en connaître la cause. Elle ne lui répondit que par monosyllabes.

Pendant de longues minutes, il fit seul les frais de la conversation. Le ciel s'était passablement assombri à la fin de l'après-midi et le tonnerre grondait de temps à autre au loin.

— Une bonne pluie va faire du bien, finit-il par dire, ne sachant plus quel sujet aborder. Pour moi, on va avoir un orage avant la fin de la veillée.

— Ça se peut, se borna-t-elle à dire.

— Bon, est-ce que je peux savoir ce qui va pas? demanda-t-il enfin, à court d'imagination pour la faire parler.

— Je suis fatiguée de tout, avoua-t-elle.

— C'est normal, t'as enseigné toute l'année. Mais décourage-toi pas, l'école achève et tu vas avoir tout l'été pour reprendre le dessus.

— Non, c'est pas juste ça, poursuivit-elle, comme si elle venait de prendre une décision. J'étouffe. J'ai besoin de réfléchir.

— Réfléchir à quoi? l'interrogea-t-il, la voix un peu changée, n'osant envisager ce qui venait.

— À nous deux. Tu viens veiller depuis plus qu'un an et...

— Et quoi?

— Ben, j'aimerais ça qu'on arrête de se voir un bout de temps. Juste pour me permettre de voir clair, tu comprends?

En entendant ces paroles, Constant sentit son visage pâlir, mais il ne chercha pas à faire changer d'avis la jeune fille. La veille, il avait complété le mobilier de sa maison et il avait eu l'intention d'inviter celle qu'il aimait et sa mère à venir admirer ce qu'était devenu l'intérieur de la maison qu'il avait fait bâtir le printemps précédent. Il ravala sa déception et sa peine pour dire dans un souffle :

— Je comprends ça, t'as ben le droit de prendre le temps de voir clair. Si ça te fait rien, je pense que je vais m'en retourner lentement chez nous avant que la pluie se mette à tomber. J'aurais l'air fin de rentrer chez nous mouillé comme une soupe.

Sur ces mots, Constant se leva et descendit de la balançoire.

— Si ta mère veut savoir pourquoi je suis parti si de bonne heure, t'as juste à lui dire que j'avais de la misère à digérer mon souper.

Bernadette se contenta de hocher la tête et l'accompagna cette fois jusqu'au bord de la route. Il la quitta sans se tourner une seule fois vers elle. Après l'avoir regardé aller durant quelques instants, elle revint lentement vers la balançoire.

— Torrieu ! Aubé a pas veillé tard à soir, lui fit remarquer Donat, assis sur la galerie.

— Il pense avoir une indigestion, se contenta-t-elle de dire avant de reprendre place dans la balançoire.

Ernest Gingras, assis à l'écart sur la galerie, avait cessé momentanément de sculpter un bout de bois pour écouter l'explication. Pour sa part, sans rien dire, Marie se dirigea vers sa fille et vint s'appuyer contre l'un des montants de la balançoire.

— Le petit Aubé a pas plus une indigestion que moi, déclara-t-elle sur un ton assuré. T'es-tu chicanée avec lui ?

— Non, m'man, je lui ai juste dit que j'étais fatiguée de le voir venir veiller toutes les semaines, que je voulais respirer un peu, avoua la jeune fille.

— Tu lui as pas dit ça comme ça, j'espère ?

— Comment vouliez-vous que je lui dise ça ?

— Bedette, il y a des fois que je me demande si t'as toute ta tête. T'as pas pensé à la peine que tu viens de faire à ce garçon-là ? Depuis que tu le connais, il a jamais arrêté de te gâter et de te donner tout ce que tu voulais…

— Je le sais bien, m'man, mais à la longue, il me tombe sur les nerfs.

— J'espère pour toi, ma petite fille, que tu regretteras pas un jour ce que tu viens de faire là.

La mère n'attendit pas la réponse de sa fille et regagna la galerie où elle reprit le tricot commencé l'avant-veille pour le premier enfant de Camille.

Quelques minutes plus tard, Bernadette se retira dans sa chambre. Malgré la chaleur accablante qui régnait dans la petite pièce, elle n'eut aucun mal à trouver le sommeil. Elle était convaincue d'avoir fait le bon choix. À son avis, il était impossible qu'Amédée Durand songe à la fréquenter s'il savait qu'un autre venait veiller avec elle. Ainsi, la situation était maintenant claire et il pourrait se déclarer. Il devait venir à la maison la semaine suivante et elle allait faire en sorte qu'il n'ait aucun doute sur son intérêt à son endroit.

Après le départ de sa jeune belle-sœur, Eugénie ne put s'empêcher de demander à sa belle-mère ce qui se passait avec Bernadette.

— Avec elle, c'est toujours la même affaire, déclara Marie, mécontente. Elle vient de dire au petit Aubé qu'elle voulait plus le voir, qu'elle avait besoin de respirer.

— Voyons donc, madame Beauchemin ! Elle lui a pas dit ça pour vrai ? fit la femme de Donat, incrédule.

— C'est ce qu'elle m'a raconté.

— J'en reviens pas, un si beau parti.

— Ça, ma fille, t'iras essayer de lui faire comprendre ça quand tu lui parleras, reprit Marie avec une nuance de découragement dans la voix.

Quand Donat et sa femme regagnèrent leur chambre une heure plus tard, Eugénie fut incapable de se contenir plus longtemps tant elle était mécontente de la décision de sa jeune belle-sœur.

— Si ça continue à ce train-là, finit-elle par dire à son mari qui venait de fermer la fenêtre à moitié parce que la pluie commençait à tomber, la Bedette se mariera jamais et on va l'avoir sur les bras encore pendant des années.

— Whow! ma sœur est pas encore une vieille fille, fit Donat en retirant ses chaussures. Elle a eu vingt et un ans au mois de mars. Elle a encore ben le temps de se trouver quelqu'un à son goût.

— Je veux ben te croire, mais en attendant, elle reste encore ici dedans et tant qu'elle va être avec nous autres, on pourra pas décider ta mère à se donner.

— Il y a pas à dire, rétorqua son mari en repoussant les couvertures parce qu'il faisait trop chaud, toi, quand t'as une idée dans la tête… Arrête donc de t'en faire avec ça. Ce qui doit arriver arrivera, et on pourra rien changer.

Sur ces mots, il l'embrassa sur une joue et lui tourna le dos, à la recherche d'une position confortable pour dormir malgré la chaleur. Dehors, un coup de tonnerre roula au loin. Des éclairs zébrèrent la nuit et la pluie se mit à marteler les vitres de la fenêtre.

❧

Le lendemain matin, le soleil se leva dans un ciel chargé de lourds nuages. Pas la moindre petite brise ne faisait frissonner les eaux grises de la rivière. Les fortes pluies de la nuit n'avaient cessé qu'aux petites heures du matin et avaient laissé de larges flaques sur la route devenue boueuse.

— Un autre dimanche où on va arriver toutes crottées à l'église, ronchonna Marie en montant dans la *sleigh* où l'attendaient Donat et Bernadette.

Normalement, l'institutrice aurait dû demeurer à la maison ce dimanche-là pour garder Alexis, mais sa belle-sœur s'était découvert une terrible migraine quelques minutes avant de partir pour la messe. Durant le court trajet conduisant au sommet de la côte du rang Sainte-Ursule,

Donat ne cessa de s'interroger sur la tournure que prendrait, ce matin-là, la mise en candidature qu'allait annoncer le curé Désilets. Peut-être serait-il l'unique candidat à la mairie... Puis, non, les Irlandais allaient sûrement présenter un candidat et celui-là ne pourrait être que Samuel Ellis. Si Ellis se présentait contre lui, il était presque certain de pouvoir le battre. La majorité des habitants de Saint-Bernard-Abbé étaient tout de même des Canadiens français et ils voteraient pour l'un des leurs plutôt que de soutenir un étranger.

Dès son arrivée, Donat laissa sa mère et sa sœur prendre les devants pour aller demander à Rémi, déjà au jubé en compagnie des autres membres de la chorale paroissiale, de venir le rejoindre sans tarder sur le parvis après la messe pour inscrire sa candidature. Il descendit ensuite pour s'arrêter près d'Anatole Blanchette installé dans son banc et lui faire le même message.

La chapelle était déjà aux trois quarts pleine et Agénor Moreau était occupé à ouvrir les fenêtres du temple pour tenter d'en chasser la chaleur humide qui l'avait envahie. Dès qu'il eut pris place dans son banc, Donat jeta un regard à la dérobée à son possible adversaire maintenant installé dans le banc voisin. L'Irlandais avait dû céder le premier banc face à l'autel à Eudore Valiquette, le nouveau président du conseil de fabrique, ce qui lui rappelait chaque dimanche l'affront que les membres du conseil lui avaient fait quelques semaines plus tôt.

Pour sa part, Bernadette chercha discrètement à apercevoir Constant Aubé, mais elle ne le vit pas. Elle en déduisit qu'il avait choisi d'aller à la basse-messe ce dimanche-là. Tant mieux, elle n'aurait pas à supporter son air de chien battu.

Après son sermon, le célébrant annonça que madame Angèle Meilleur avait accepté de dresser un reposoir devant sa maison pour la Fête-Dieu, qui aurait lieu trois semaines plus tard.

— Qui c'est, Angèle Meilleur? demanda Bernadette à sa mère.

— Angèle Cloutier, Bedette. Elle s'appelle Meilleur à cette heure.

Ensuite, le célébrant annonça qu'à la fin du mois, Saint-Bernard-Abbé aurait comme toutes les paroisses de la province, un maire et un conseil. Le bedeau allait afficher à la porte de la chapelle, dès la fin de la messe, une feuille sur laquelle les candidats pourraient inscrire leur nom. L'élection était prévue pour le jeudi 27 juin. Il conclut en disant espérer que tout se passerait dans l'ordre et la dignité.

Dès la fin de la messe, Donat rejoignit son beau-frère et Anatole Blanchette et tous les trois s'avancèrent vers la feuille qu'Agénor Moreau venait de fixer à la porte de la chapelle. Beaucoup de gens encombraient le parvis et ils eurent du mal à s'approcher.

— Comment on va faire pour écrire notre nom? demanda Rémi à mi-voix. Aucun de nous trois sait écrire.

— Attends, lui ordonna Donat en faisant quelques pas pour saisir Bernadette par un bras.

— Qu'est-ce qu'il y a? lui demanda celle-ci, légèrement agacée.

— Viens écrire nos noms sur la feuille, l'enjoignit son frère.

— Je sais même pas si j'ai un crayon, dit-elle en ouvrant son sac à main.

Par chance, elle en découvrit un au fond de son sac et elle écrivit les trois noms sur la feuille en spécifiant que son frère postulait le poste de maire. À peine venait-elle de ranger son crayon que Samuel Ellis s'approcha de l'endroit d'où venaient de s'écarter Donat et ses deux candidats. L'Irlandais était accompagné de Thomas Hyland et d'Eudore Valiquette. Le propriétaire du moulin à bois écrivit trois noms sur la feuille sous ceux de Donat Beauchemin, Rémi Lafond et Anatole Blanchette.

— Torrieu, c'est ben ce que je pensais ! chuchota Donat à ses deux complices. Ellis a décidé de se présenter contre moi.

— C'est pas monsieur Ellis qui se présente contre toi, c'est monsieur Hyland, lui apprit sa sœur qui venait de consulter la feuille.

— Arrête donc, toi ! s'exclama-t-il à mi-voix.

— C'est ça qui est écrit sur la feuille. Monsieur Ellis et le notaire veulent juste se faire élire conseillers.

Aux yeux de Donat, cette nouvelle n'avait absolument rien de rassurant. Thomas Hyland était, d'abord et avant tout, un homme très apprécié dans la communauté tant pour sa pondération que pour sa générosité. Contrairement à Samuel Ellis, on le considérait beaucoup moins comme un Irlandais que comme un commerçant serviable toujours prêt à se dévouer.

Par conséquent, le fils de Baptiste Beauchemin rentra à la maison passablement inquiet de la tournure qu'allait prendre la campagne électorale. Évidemment, il n'était pas question d'essayer de décrier Thomas Hyland, ce qu'il ne se serait guère privé de faire s'il s'était agi de Samuel Ellis.

Bref, le jeune cultivateur passa le dimanche après-midi à chercher une façon de se faire élire malgré un adversaire aussi respectable. Finalement, il choisit de lui laisser faire les premiers pas et d'attendre au moins une semaine avant d'entreprendre une tournée des maisons de Saint-Bernard-Abbé.

Si Donat avait pu voir la tête qu'arborait son beau-frère Liam en retournant à la maison ce dimanche midi là, il aurait compris avoir fait un impair important. Le mari de Camille se tut durant la plus grande partie du trajet. Finalement, incapable de contrôler son caractère bouillant, il éclata.

— Je te dis qu'il est fin en maudit, ton frère, dit-il à sa femme sur un ton mordant.

— Pourquoi tu dis ça ? s'étonna-t-elle.

— Ben, il va demander à un pur étranger comme Blanchette de se présenter comme conseiller. Il me semble qu'il aurait pu me l'offrir avant.

— Viens pas me dire que cette affaire-là t'intéresse ? fit-elle.

— Un fou ! Je suis aussi capable que n'importe qui, tu sauras, reprit-il, l'air mauvais.

— Si tu penses être aussi bon que n'importe qui, t'as juste à te présenter comme maire, rétorqua-t-elle. T'as pas besoin de mon frère pantoute.

— Ben oui, j'aurais l'air fin, tout seul.

— Je suis certaine que tu finirais par trouver deux hommes dans la paroisse intéressés à t'appuyer.

— Si c'était pas de la famille, je le ferais, déclara-t-il comme si c'était une menace.

— Gêne-toi pas pour moi, répliqua-t-elle, un rien sarcastique. À part ça, inquiète-toi pas pour Donat. Je le connais assez pour savoir que ça le fâcherait pas.

Liam n'ajouta pas un mot, mais il garda son humeur sombre toute la journée et il s'isola dans un mutisme boudeur.

Cet après-midi-là, Camille alla rendre visite à sa mère. Bernadette, assise seule dans la balançoire, regardait les eaux de la rivière comme si elle ne les voyait pas.

— Qu'est-ce qui se passe avec Bedette ? demanda-t-elle à voix basse à sa mère en la rejoignant sur la galerie où elle tricotait. Elle a l'air d'une âme en peine. Constant Aubé est pas là. Est-ce que ça veut dire qu'elle s'est chicanée avec lui ?

— Elle lui a dit hier soir qu'elle veut plus le voir, répondit Marie sur le même ton.

— Qu'est-ce qui lui a pris ?

— Il était trop fin avec elle, d'après elle.

— Seigneur ! Il y a pas de danger que ça me serait arrivé, ça ! s'exclama Camille.

Sa mère comprit, mais elle se garda bien d'entamer une discussion sur le comportement de Liam. Cependant, sa fille ne put s'empêcher de lui demander pourquoi Donat n'avait pas proposé à Liam d'être candidat avec lui.

— Est-ce que ton mari s'est plaint de ça? s'inquiéta Marie.

— Non, m'man, mentit sa fille aînée, c'est moi qui viens d'y penser.

— Donat y a pensé, mais il m'a dit que s'il était arrivé avec Rémi et Liam, ça aurait trop eu l'air d'une affaire de famille.

❧

Au bout du rang Saint-Jean, Emma et Rémi recevaient à souper Xavier et sa fiancée. La température était redevenue très humide et le ciel s'était encore chargé de nuages menaçants à la fin de ce dimanche après-midi. Quand Rémi se leva pour aller soigner ses animaux, Xavier le suivit pour l'aider.

— Ben non, protesta son beau-frère, t'es pas habillé pour venir faire le train.

— Laisse faire, plaisanta Xavier, il manquerait plus qu'un de nos échevins arrive épuisé à l'élection.

Catherine et Emma virent les deux hommes se diriger vers le champ pour rassembler les vaches.

— Franchement, t'étais pas obligée de nous inviter avec une chaleur pareille, dit Catherine à sa future belle-sœur.

— Il le fallait bien si je veux pouvoir me souvenir de quoi t'avais l'air avant de devenir la servante de mon frère. C'est dans trois semaines, votre mariage. Ça vient vite.

— T'as raison et tu devrais voir comment ma mère s'énerve avec ça. Il faut dire que la femme de mon frère l'aide pas trop, avoua-t-elle en baissant la voix malgré elle.

Les deux femmes s'occupèrent du souper dans la chaleur dégagée par le poêle à bois qu'il avait bien fallu allumer pour cuire le morceau de bœuf.

— C'est le dernier morceau qu'on avait sur la glace, reconnut la maîtresse de maison. Depuis hier, tout ce qui me reste de viande, je l'ai mis dans une chaudière dans le puits. La glace a déjà toute fondu.

— C'est la même chose chez nous, dit Catherine en commençant à dresser le couvert avec les assiettes de pierre que lui tendait la maîtresse de maison.

Après le souper, Emma décida de coucher ses trois enfants assez tôt. Flore et Joseph avaient été à la limite du supportable tout l'après-midi et Marthe n'avait pas cessé de rechigner après sa toilette du soir, ce qui était plutôt inhabituel.

— Il faut bien que ça arrive quand vous êtes là, fit remarquer la mère. Marthe, c'est un bon bébé qu'on n'entend jamais.

— Tout le portrait de sa marraine, plaisanta Xavier.

— Mais tu vas finir par m'entendre, dit en riant Catherine, surtout si tu cherches à m'étriver.

Après avoir couché les enfants, les adultes décidèrent d'aller prendre le frais sur la galerie malgré la nuée de maringouins que le temps humide avait fait apparaître.

À un moment donné, Emma rentra dans la maison pour s'assurer que les enfants ne chahutaient pas à l'étage et pour jeter un coup d'œil à son bébé. La porte de sa chambre au rez-de-chaussée avait été laissée ouverte pour faciliter la circulation de l'air et lui permettre d'entendre Marthe si elle pleurait. L'enfant semblait dormir, mais en s'approchant elle perçut une toux qui ressemblait à une sorte de jappement en provenance du berceau.

Soudain inquiète, la jeune mère avança la main pour toucher le front du bébé, il était bouillant de fièvre. L'enfant semblait avoir du mal à respirer et son nez coulait.

— Voyons donc! Elle allait bien il y a pas une heure, murmura-t-elle pour elle-même. Dis-moi pas qu'elle a attrapé le rhume en plein été.

Une autre quinte de toux sèche secoua l'enfant qui semblait éprouver beaucoup de difficulté à respirer. Au moment où elle allait revenir sur la galerie pour prévenir son mari et ses invités, elle trouva Catherine debout derrière elle.

— Je sais pas ce qu'elle a tout à coup. On dirait qu'elle a attrapé le rhume.

La fiancée de son frère, soucieuse, s'approcha à son tour du berceau et se pencha sur sa filleule, écoutant avec attention sa respiration haletante.

— Je veux pas t'énerver pour rien, chuchota-t-elle, mais je pense pas que ce soit juste un rhume.

— Comment tu saurais ça, toi? lui demanda Emma.

— J'ai travaillé un an à l'orphelinat à Montréal. Ça ressemble bien plus au croup qu'à un rhume. Écoute la petite, elle a de la misère à respirer.

— Mon Dieu! s'écria Emma, paniquée. Je demande tout de suite à Rémi d'atteler et d'aller chercher le docteur Samson.

La jeune mère sortit en catastrophe de la chambre et alla prévenir son mari. Rémi ne se donna même pas la peine de venir vérifier à l'intérieur. Il se précipita vers l'écurie en compagnie de Xavier pour atteler son boghei. Quand Emma rentra dans la maison, Catherine était en train de rallumer le poêle qu'on venait de laisser éteindre.

— Qu'est-ce que tu fais? lui demanda-t-elle.

— Il faut faire bouillir de l'eau et approcher la petite de la vapeur. C'est ce que les sœurs faisaient pour aider les enfants malades à respirer.

Emma s'empressa de remplir la grosse bouilloire avec de l'eau qu'elle déposa sur le poêle qui s'était remis à ronfler pendant que son invitée était allée chercher Marthe dans son berceau et s'était mise à la bercer doucement près du poêle.

— As-tu de l'alcool à friction?

— Oui.

— On va la frotter avec ça pour faire baisser sa fièvre. Ça devrait aider.

Le boghei passa près de la maison alors que les deux femmes finissaient de frotter le bébé qui geignait doucement.

— Xavier a décidé d'aller à Saint-Zéphirin avec Rémi, déclara Emma, tout énervée.

Catherine ne dit rien, trop occupée à maintenir le bébé assis bien droit sur ses genoux, à faible distance de la vapeur dégagée par l'eau qui bouillait.

— La petite commence à respirer un peu plus facilement, dit-elle à la mère pour la rassurer.

— Je vais prendre ta place. Tu dois crever de chaleur proche du poêle, fit Emma en s'avançant vers elle.

— Non, laisse-moi faire, répliqua la jeune fille. Après tout, c'est ma filleule.

Quand Rémi et Xavier rentrèrent, la soirée était passablement avancée et quelques gouttes de pluie s'étaient mises à tomber depuis quelques minutes.

— Le docteur était parti pour un accouchement, déclara Rémi. Sa femme m'a promis de nous l'envoyer aussitôt qu'il rentrerait. Et la petite, comment elle va? demanda-t-il en s'approchant du bébé secoué soudain par une quinte de toux sèche qui le fit pleurer.

— Elle a ben l'air d'avoir de la misère à respirer, fit remarquer Xavier, aussi inquiet que le père.

— Ça va mieux, déclara Catherine en lui adressant un regard de reproche.

— Bon, il va falloir qu'on rentre avant que l'orage nous tombe dessus pour de bon, reprit le fils de Marie Beauchemin.

— Tu vas rentrer tout seul, lui dit Catherine. En passant, dis à ma mère que tu vas venir me chercher demain avant-midi.

— Mais t'es pas pour passer la nuit debout, protesta Emma.

— La petite est ma filleule, répéta Catherine. Le moins que je puisse faire, c'est de m'en occuper avec toi quand elle est malade.

Voyant que rien ne ferait changer d'avis sa fiancée, Xavier salua son beau-frère, sa sœur et Catherine avant de quitter les lieux. Rémi le suivit pour aller chercher des bûches qu'il laissa tomber dans le coffre placé près du poêle pendant que sa femme remplissait encore une fois la bouilloire dont toute l'eau s'était évaporée.

Les deux femmes prirent tour à tour la petite malade dans leurs bras, cherchant à la soulager chaque fois qu'elle semblait avoir plus de peine à respirer. Un peu avant onze heures, Emma se rendit compte que son mari s'était endormi à la table, la tête appuyée sur les bras. Elle alla le secouer doucement et lui conseilla de s'étendre une heure ou deux en promettant de le réveiller dès l'arrivée du médecin.

Quelques minutes plus tard, la mère offrit à Catherine de la décharger de l'enfant qu'elle berçait depuis près d'une heure.

— Laisse faire, chuchota son invitée. C'est comme si je berçais ma fille.

— Quand tu vas en avoir une… commença Emma.

— J'en ai une, dit tout bas Catherine. Elle est à la crèche, à Montréal.

Emma ne dit rien. Elle connaissait trop bien la rumeur qui avait circulé l'année précédente dans Saint-Bernard-Abbé. Catherine venait de reconnaître qu'elle était une fille-mère qui avait donné naissance à une petite fille. Cela ne changeait rien au fait qu'elle demeurait un sujet de honte et de scandale. Toute famille respectable refuserait toujours qu'elle franchisse le seuil de sa maison. Bien sûr, les Lafond lui avaient ouvert leur porte, mais cela n'avait pas été de gaieté de cœur. Emma et son mari n'avaient accepté de lui demander d'être la marraine de Marthe que parce qu'ils ne voulaient pas que Xavier soit rejeté par la famille alors qu'il s'apprêtait à épouser cette fille perdue.

Un silence contraint tomba dans la cuisine à peine éclairée par la lampe déposée à l'autre bout de la pièce pour ne pas nuire au sommeil agité du bébé. Dehors, la pluie avait redoublé d'intensité, mais comme il n'y avait aucun vent, les fenêtres pouvaient demeurer ouvertes sans que l'eau pénètre à l'intérieur.

— Elle s'appelle Constance, ajouta doucement Catherine dans un souffle. Tu peux pas savoir à quel point je m'ennuie d'elle. J'y pense tous les jours. Il y a pas un soir où je m'endors sans avoir prié pour elle. Je prie pour qu'elle soit adoptée par du bon monde.

— Comment tu peux savoir qu'elle a pas encore été adoptée ? lui demanda Emma, sans manifester grand intérêt.

— Sœur Émérentienne, une cousine de ma mère, s'occupe de la crèche où est ma petite. Elle m'a promis qu'elle me l'écrirait quand elle serait adoptée.

La mère de Marthe se borna à hocher la tête, espérant que le sujet était clos. Après tout, il s'agissait de l'enfant du péché. Mais tout indiquait que la fiancée de son frère, mise en confiance par son silence, avait décidé de tout lui révéler. Sans entrer dans les détails, elle se mit à lui raconter comment l'homme engagé de son père, Magloire Delorme, avait sauté sur elle alors qu'elle se baignait dans la rivière. Elle décrivit la réaction violente de son père devant les signes de plus en plus évidents de sa grossesse. Elle narra l'intervention de sœur Émérentienne qui l'avait ramenée avec elle à Montréal, son séjour à Sainte-Pélagie qui accueillait les femmes dans sa situation ainsi que les mois passés à travailler à la crèche avant de pouvoir revenir à Saint-Bernard-Abbé.

— Ça aurait été moins pire si j'avais pas vu ma petite fille grandir pendant ces mois-là, avoua-t-elle. Mais je la voyais

452

tous les jours et ça m'a fendu le cœur de partir en la laissant à la crèche.

Emma était une mère et n'imaginait que trop bien ce que la jeune femme avait vécu.

— Quand je suis retournée travailler à Montréal, au refuge, l'été passé, j'ai revu souvent ma petite. Elle avait déjà quinze mois et elle était belle comme un cœur, ajouta-t-elle en essuyant discrètement une larme.

— Comment ça se fait qu'on l'a pas encore adoptée ? lui demanda Emma, curieuse.

— Je le sais pas, reconnut Catherine. Il y a tellement d'orphelins à la crèche…

Catherine allait poursuivre quand elle entendit une voiture entrer dans la cour des Lafond.

— Ça doit être le docteur, dit Emma en se levant pour aller réveiller Rémi qui dormait dans la pièce voisine.

Ce dernier ouvrit la porte au médecin dont les vêtements trempés faisaient peine à voir. Emma s'empressa d'offrir une serviette à Eugène Samson pour qu'il puisse s'essuyer le visage et les mains.

— Pauvre vous ! le plaignit-elle. C'est vraiment pas un temps à être sur le chemin.

Le docteur, bien connu pour son caractère tranchant, ne se donna pas la peine de lui répondre.

— Lequel de tes enfants est malade ? lui demanda-t-il après s'être débarrassé de son manteau.

— La petite dernière, docteur, répondit Emma en montrant l'enfant que Catherine n'avait pas cessé de bercer.

— Bon, étends quelque chose sur la table que je puisse l'examiner, ordonna-t-il à la mère en s'emparant de sa trousse et en la déposant sur un banc à côté de lui.

Emma étendit une couverture sur la table et Catherine y déposa l'enfant qui fut secouée par la toux en quittant les bras de sa marraine. Eugène Samson sortit son stéthoscope et écouta le sifflement que faisait l'air en sortant des poumons de l'enfant.

— Ta fille a le croup, déclara le praticien sans aucun ménagement. Elle a la gorge enflée. C'est pour ça qu'elle a de la misère à respirer. Par contre, elle a pas l'air à faire trop de fièvre. Qu'est-ce que t'as fait pour la soulager avant que j'arrive ?

Emma expliqua ce que Catherine et elle avaient fait et le médecin approuva.

— Il y a pas autre chose à faire, continuez. Quand l'enfant se réveillera, vous pourrez lui faire boire un peu d'eau. Demain, je passerai dans le courant de la journée pour voir si tout est correct. D'après moi, ça devrait se replacer dans une couple d'heures.

Le médecin refusa de boire quelque chose avant son départ et il quitta les lieux aussi rapidement qu'il était arrivé. Soulagés, les parents voulurent que leur invitée monte dormir dans l'une des chambres libres à l'étage. Catherine n'accepta qu'à la condition qu'on la réveille vers trois heures trente pour qu'elle prenne soin à son tour du bébé malade. Rémi prit sa fille et Emma accompagna Catherine à l'étage après avoir allumé une lampe. Il avait été entendu que le père allait s'occuper de sa fille durant les deux prochaines heures avant de céder sa place à sa femme.

Catherine Benoît se réveilla seule dans une chambre obscure et il lui fallut quelques instants avant de se rappeler où elle se trouvait. Alors qu'elle se demandait quelle heure il pouvait bien être, elle entendit les quatre coups sonnés par l'horloge installée au pied de l'escalier. Elle alluma la lampe laissée par Emma, remit rapidement de l'ordre dans sa tenue et descendit dans la cuisine où elle trouva la jeune mère de famille sommeillant dans la chaise berçante, Marthe sur ses genoux. La fiancée de Xavier lui enleva doucement l'enfant avant de la secouer.

— Va te coucher, c'est à mon tour, lui chuchota-t-elle. Ça fait presque une heure que t'aurais dû me réveiller, ajouta-t-elle avec une nuance de reproche.

Emma se leva, apparemment un peu courbaturée d'être demeurée assise si longtemps dans la chaise berçante. Avant de prendre la direction de sa chambre, elle jeta quelques rondins dans le poêle et s'assura que la bouilloire contenait suffisamment d'eau. Catherine posa une main sur le front de sa filleule. La fièvre semblait avoir disparu et elle respirait beaucoup plus librement.

Il lui fallut combattre le sommeil jusqu'à ce que l'aube fasse timidement son apparition. Elle vit par la fenêtre les ténèbres reculer lentement. Voyant que Marthe dormait d'un sommeil profond qu'aucune quinte de toux ne venait troubler, elle se décida à aller la déposer sur la couverture sur la table, le temps de se glisser dans la chambre de ses parents pour en rapporter le berceau qu'elle déposa près du poêle.

Au moment où elle installait l'enfant dans son lit, elle vit Rémi sortir de sa chambre à coucher, la tête hirsute.

— Est-ce que j'ai rêvé ou tu viens de sortir de ma chambre? lui demanda-t-il en passant ses bretelles.

— T'as pas rêvé, je viens d'aller chercher le berceau de la petite pour qu'elle puisse dormir. Ça a l'air d'être fini. Elle ne fait plus de fièvre et elle tousse plus.

— Là, tu me soulages, avoua-t-il. Quand je l'ai surveillée pendant la nuit, elle toussait encore pas mal.

— Moi, ça fait deux heures que je la berce et elle a pas toussé une fois. Elle dort comme un ange, ajouta-t-elle en se penchant, attendrie, sur le berceau.

Rémi annonça qu'il allait faire son train. Catherine ne dit rien, mais dès son départ vers les bâtiments, elle entreprit de préparer le déjeuner. Quand Flore et Joseph apparurent dans la cuisine, elle leur demanda de ne pas faire de bruit pour laisser dormir leur mère et elle leur servit une omelette baignant dans du sirop d'érable. Quelques minutes plus tard, Rémi eut droit au même menu.

Quand Emma se réveilla au milieu de l'avant-midi, sa future belle-sœur avait quitté sa maison depuis près d'une heure en compagnie de Xavier venu la chercher pour la ramener chez elle.

— Elle a été pas mal fine de faire tout ce qu'elle a fait, reconnut la femme de Rémi Lafond.

— En tout cas, elle a l'air d'aimer ben gros les enfants, dit son mari. On peut avoir ben des choses à redire sur ce qu'elle a fait, mais on peut pas lui ôter ce qu'elle a : elle a du cœur.

Le surlendemain, Marie accourut chez sa fille quand elle apprit que sa petite-fille avait failli être emportée par le croup.

— Est-ce que c'est vrai ce que Rémi a raconté à Camille ? C'est Catherine Benoît qui a veillé la petite avec toi toute la nuit pour en prendre soin.

— C'est en plein ça, m'man. Elle a jamais voulu repartir avec Xavier à la fin de la soirée quand elle s'est aperçue que la petite était malade. Une vraie marraine !

— On sait bien, admit sa mère comme à contrecœur. Même une fille comme elle peut avoir une qualité ou deux.

— Je pense même, m'man, qu'elle en a plus qu'une ou deux, ajouta Emma, plus pour faire rager sa mère que parce qu'elle le croyait vraiment.

— Commence pas ça, toi ! la mit en garde Marie Beauchemin. Il y a déjà bien assez que tu l'aies choisie comme marraine de la petite.

Chapitre 24

Une visiteuse encombrante

Il était écrit quelque part que le début du mois de juin ne se passerait pas sans qu'une épreuve ne vienne frapper la famille Beauchemin.

Depuis quelques jours, le sujet de conversation favori était le mauvais temps qui frappait maintenant la région depuis près d'une semaine. Les pluies se succédaient à un tel rythme qu'il était impossible de se rendre dans les champs pour y travailler et on déplorait que la récolte de fraises risque de pourrir sur place, faute de soleil.

Paddy Connolly avait repris sa place et son rôle au magasin général de Télesphore Dionne. Chaque jour, il s'installait sur la galerie en compagnie des traîne-savates de la paroisse pour commenter les dernières nouvelles, comme il l'avait fait durant les mois précédents en arborant toujours le même air supérieur. Ainsi, il avait longuement expliqué la nouvelle loi du gouvernement fédéral sur le chemin de fer du Pacifique adoptée le premier juin précédent, attachant beaucoup plus d'importance à cette nouvelle qu'à la construction d'un collège à Trois-Rivières et à l'inauguration d'une nouvelle église à Nicolet.

L'arrivée de Constant Aubé sembla distraire quelques instants son auditoire. Le jeune homme, le visage sombre, salua de la tête la demi-douzaine d'hommes rassemblés sur la galerie avant de pousser la porte du magasin général.

— Cybole! s'exclama Ludger Courtois du rang Saint-Paul, je sais pas ce qu'a notre meunier depuis un bout de temps, mais on dirait qu'il y a des affaires qui vont pas à son goût.

— Peut-être ses amours, suggéra Évariste Bourgeois.

L'oncle de Liam Connolly allait reprendre la parole quand une autre voiture détourna l'attention des hommes qui l'entouraient. Un vieil homme descendit de son boghei et tira deux valises de derrière la banquette arrière.

— Je vais pas plus loin, mes sœurs, déclara-t-il sur un ton sans appel aux deux religieuses qui n'avaient pas bougé de leur siège. Là, je rentre chez nous dans le rang Saint-Paul. Je suis sûr que vous allez trouver quelqu'un pour vous laisser chez les Beauchemin.

Une grosse et grande religieuse appartenant à la communauté des sœurs Grises se leva et descendit lourdement de voiture; sa compagne, une femme beaucoup plus chétive, l'imita.

— Je vous trouve bien malcommode, monsieur, déclara haut et fort Mathilde Beauchemin qui dominait le conducteur de près d'une demi-tête. Il reste juste un mille à faire. Ça vous aurait pas fait mourir de nous amener chez ma belle-sœur.

— Peut-être, mais mon cheval est ben fatigué, ma sœur, dit l'homme en remontant dans son boghei.

— Merci quand même, lui jeta sèchement la religieuse, apparemment très mécontente d'être laissée en cours de route.

Le bon Samaritain ne se donna pas la peine de lui répondre et fit faire demi-tour à son attelage pour rejoindre le rang Saint-Paul, laissant les deux sœurs Grises plantées dans la cour du magasin général. Mathilde Beauchemin n'esquissa pas un geste pour s'emparer de sa valise. Elle se contenta de tourner la tête vers la galerie où elle sembla découvrir pour la première fois les hommes qui y étaient assis.

Elle s'avança résolument vers eux.

— Est-ce qu'il y en a un qui a affaire dans le rang Saint-Jean? demanda-t-elle avec aplomb.

Hormidas Meilleur reconnut immédiatement les deux religieuses qu'il avait conduites au moins à deux reprises chez Baptiste Beauchemin et un frisson rétrospectif le prit. Il pensa immédiatement à Paddy Connolly.

— Monsieur Connolly reste dans ce rang-là, affirma le petit homme, l'air réjoui. Je suis sûr qu'il va être ben fier de vous accommoder, ajouta-t-il en désignant le retraité de la main.

— Comme ça, ça vous dérangerait pas trop de nous laisser chez les Beauchemin? demanda la grande et grosse religieuse à l'Irlandais, sans sourire.

Visiblement, il n'était guère enthousiaste à l'idée de transporter les deux voyageuses après avoir assisté à la scène qui venait de se dérouler devant lui dans la cour du magasin général.

— Ben, là, j'attends la petite maîtresse d'école et mes petites-nièces, prétexta le petit homme bedonnant pour échapper à la corvée. L'école est à la veille de fermer et je voudrais pas que ce monde-là marche dans la bouette.

— Vous pouvez aller reconduire les sœurs, monsieur Connolly, intervint Hormidas Meilleur, qui avait terminé sa tournée quelques minutes auparavant. Quand on va voir les enfants sortir, on va les avertir de vous attendre.

Paddy lui jeta un regard assassin, mais ne put que quitter sa place pour se diriger vers son boghei stationné au fond de la cour. À aucun moment il n'esquissa le geste de prendre les deux valises au passage pour les déposer dans sa voiture. Fidèle à elle-même, Mathilde Beauchemin, toujours aussi altière, fit signe à sa compagne de la suivre jusqu'à la voiture et de ne pas toucher aux bagages demeurés au centre de la cour. Paddy attendit avec impatience que les deux femmes aient pris place dans sa voiture avant de mettre son cheval en marche.

— Oubliez pas, mon brave, de prendre nos valises en passant, ordonna Mathilde Beauchemin au conducteur.

L'homme dut descendre de son boghei pour s'emparer des deux valises en cuir bouilli qu'il lança plus qu'il ne les posa dans sa voiture avant de remonter. Le conducteur ne put placer un mot – ce qui était pour le moins inhabituel – durant tout le trajet entre le magasin général et la maison de feu Baptiste Beauchemin. Ce fut avec un soulagement évident qu'il laissa les deux religieuses près de la galerie. Il tendit leurs valises aux deux visiteuses et s'empressa de reprendre la route avant que quelqu'un sorte de la maison.

Marie n'avait pas vu sa belle-sœur et sa compagne arriver. Elle était dans la tasserie en train de retirer d'une auge remplie d'eau les tresses de paille longues de plusieurs dizaines de pieds confectionnées l'automne précédent, quelques semaines avant le mariage de Camille.

Par contre, sa bru avait aperçu les deux religieuses et s'était retirée en hâte dans sa chambre à coucher en faisant signe au petit Alexis de la suivre.

— Il manquait plus qu'elle! s'exclama-t-elle en faisant référence à la sœur de Baptiste. Je voudrais bien savoir pourquoi elle nous tombe toujours sur le dos… Elle pourrait bien aller s'installer chez Emma ou chez Camille.

La jeune femme, enceinte de six mois, s'était réfugiée au fond de sa chambre avec son fils de un an et demi et elle prit bien soin de ne pas bouger, même quand elle entendit que les visiteuses sondaient la porte pour vérifier si le crochet était mis.

— On dirait qu'il y a personne, sœur Marie du Rosaire, dit la petite religieuse à sa compagne demeurée debout au pied des marches conduisant à la galerie.

— Il doit y avoir quelqu'un, déclara tout net Mathilde Beauchemin. Ils doivent être aux bâtiments. Attendez-moi ici, ma sœur. Je vais revenir.

Mathilde Beauchemin eut à peine le temps de franchir la moitié de la cour de la ferme qu'elle vit sa belle-sœur sortir de la tasserie.

— Es-tu toute seule? lui cria la religieuse en faisant sursauter violemment la maîtresse de maison.

— Seigneur que tu m'as fait peur! fit Marie en apercevant sœur Marie du Rosaire devant elle. Je t'ai pas entendue arriver.

Elle réprima difficilement une grimace et s'avança vers sa belle-sœur pour l'embrasser légèrement sur une joue.

— Je suis pas toute seule, dit-elle à la visiteuse. Je comprends pas qu'Eugénie t'ait pas ouvert la porte, Donat et notre homme engagé sont dans le champ en train de creuser un canal pour permettre à l'eau de s'écouler. Il arrête pas de mouiller.

La maîtresse de maison salua sœur Sainte-Anne en arrivant à la galerie et invita les deux femmes à entrer.

— Eugénie! Eugénie! cria-t-elle à travers la porte moustiquaire. Où est-ce que t'es passée encore?

La jeune femme apparut dans la cuisine en se frottant les yeux comme si elle venait de se lever.

— Pourquoi t'as mis le crochet sur la porte? lui demanda sa belle-mère avec humeur.

— Je l'ai fait sans m'en rendre compte, madame Beauchemin. Le petit rechignait et cherchait à sortir de la maison. Je viens juste d'aller le coucher dans mon lit. Sans le vouloir, je me suis endormie avec lui, mentit-elle.

Eugénie souhaita la bienvenue aux deux sœurs Grises après avoir poussé la porte pour les laisser entrer.

— Comment ça se fait que tu dors en plein jour comme ça? lui demanda sœur Marie du Rosaire sur un ton inquisiteur.

— Je suis en famille, ma tante, répondit Eugénie sur un ton geignard.

— S'il fallait que toutes les femmes qui attendent un petit passent leurs journées dans leur lit, ce serait beau à voir, rétorqua la religieuse en s'arrêtant au milieu de la cuisine d'été. Pour moi, tu t'écoutes trop, ma fille.

— Laisse faire, Mathilde, lui ordonna sèchement sa belle-sœur en venant au secours de sa bru. Là, c'est presque le temps de préparer le souper. Je vais vous montrer votre chambre avant d'éplucher les patates. Vous allez avoir le temps de vous installer.

Sans plus attendre, la maîtresse de maison se dirigea vers la porte ouvrant sur la cuisine d'hiver.

— Et nos valises? lui demanda sa belle-sœur sur un ton impérial.

— Quoi, vos valises?

— Qui va les monter en haut?

— Vous autres, sinon elles vont rester sur la galerie, déclara tout net son hôtesse. Ici dedans, il y a pas de servante.

Sur ce, sans plus se préoccuper de ce qui se passait derrière elle, Marie traversa vers ce qu'elle appelait le «haut côté». Les deux religieuses la rejoignirent un instant plus tard après être allées prendre leurs bagages demeurés à l'extérieur.

— Où est-ce qu'on va coucher? demanda Mathilde Beauchemin en arrivant à l'étage, légèrement essoufflée, suivie de près par la petite sœur Sainte-Anne.

— Dans la chambre bleue, au fond, à côté de ma chambre.

— Dis-moi pas qu'on va être obligées de dormir dans la même chambre? s'offusqua la visiteuse.

— Bien oui, Mathilde, répondit Marie en cachant mal son impatience. Les trois autres chambres sont prises par Bernadette, moi et Ernest, notre homme engagé.

— Tu pourrais pas coucher avec ta fille une couple de jours? eut le culot de demander sa belle-sœur. Moi, je suis pas habituée de coucher avec quelqu'un dans mon lit.

— Moi, c'est pareil, trancha Marie. Mais si vous êtes pas capables de coucher dans le même lit, il y en a une qui peut toujours aller coucher dans la grange, suggéra-t-elle d'une voix acide.

— On va s'arranger, madame Beauchemin, intervint sœur Sainte-Anne avec un petit sourire.

— Parfait. Bon, prenez tout le temps qu'il vous faut pour vous installer. Je descends m'occuper du souper.

Elle retrouva sa bru dans la cuisine en train de peler les pommes de terre.

— Bonyenne, on avait bien besoin de ça! dit-elle à mi-voix en prenant place en face d'elle pour l'aider dans sa tâche.

— Il nous reste juste à prier pour qu'elle reste pas trop longtemps, poursuivit Eugénie sur un ton pénétré. Je veux pas être méchante, madame Beauchemin, mais chaque fois, tante Mathilde m'étourdit à me rendre malade.

— Penses-tu que ça me fait plaisir de l'avoir encore une fois sur les bras? Il faut croire que le bon Dieu nous donne à tous une croix à porter. La sœur de mon mari est la mienne et…

Elle allait poursuivre quand la porte moustiquaire s'ouvrit pour livrer passage à Bernadette dont les traits étaient légèrement tirés par la fatigue.

— Dites-moi que c'est pas vrai, m'man, chuchota-t-elle en déposant son sac en cuir près de la porte.

— Quoi?

— C'est pas ma tante Mathilde qui est là?

— Bien oui, ma fille. Elle vient passer une couple de jours avec nous autres, pour nous faire plaisir, à part ça.

— C'est bien ce que j'ai pensé quand l'oncle de Liam m'a dit tout à l'heure qu'il avait laissé deux sœurs chez nous. Mautadit qu'on n'est pas chanceux! se plaignit-elle.

— Arrête de te lamenter, lui ordonna sa mère. Ta tante est tout de même pas une des sept plaies d'Égypte.

— Elle en est pas loin en tout cas.

— Va te changer. On a le souper à préparer et t'iras nourrir les poules et les cochons pendant que les hommes vont faire le train.

Bernadette monta à sa chambre en faisant le moins de bruit possible pour ne pas attirer l'attention de sa tante.

Au souper, personne n'eut à faire un effort pour entretenir la conversation autour de la table. Sœur Marie du Rosaire en fit tous les frais en racontant tous les petits faits survenus à l'orphelinat de Sorel où elle œuvrait. Elle parla tant qu'on se demandait comment elle faisait pour manger en même temps.

Au moment du dessert, elle décida d'interroger à fond Ernest Gingras sur sa famille et elle osa même lui dire :

— Tu serais un assez joli garçon si t'avais pas tant de tics dans le visage.

Cette remarque mesquine fit violemment rougir l'employé des Beauchemin et attira à son auteure des regards courroucés de ses hôtes. Ensuite, fidèle à son habitude, la grande et grosse religieuse tourna son attention vers sa jeune nièce.

— Puis, Bernadette, est-ce que monsieur le curé est finalement satisfait de ta manière de montrer le catéchisme aux enfants ?

Évidemment, elle n'avait pas oublié la vague allusion du curé Lanctôt, plus d'un an auparavant, sur sa façon d'enseigner le catéchisme.

— Notre curé et l'inspecteur sont tous deux bien contents de moi, ma tante, répondit l'institutrice sans sourire.

— Et tes amours vont bien ? poursuivit la religieuse, toujours aussi curieuse.

— De quelles amours vous parlez, ma tante ?

— Je parle de ton boiteux, ma fille, répondit Mathilde Beauchemin avec un rien d'impatience.

— Ça, ma tante, c'est fini déjà depuis un bon bout de temps.

— Tant mieux, ma fille. C'était visible comme le nez au milieu du visage que ce garçon-là était pas fait pour toi.

— Qu'est-ce qui te fait dire ça? intervint sèchement Marie en se tournant vers sa belle-sœur.

— Il était pas bien beau et il était pas instruit.

— Un homme a pas besoin d'être beau pour faire un bon mari, rétorqua la maîtresse de maison d'une voix coupante. Pour l'instruction, ce garçon-là sait lire et écrire, ce qui est pas mal plus que la plupart des jeunes hommes de la paroisse. En plus, il est bien élevé.

Cette réprimande eut le mérite de faire taire durant quelques instants la visiteuse, ce qui permit à sœur Sainte-Anne de parler avec bonté au petit Alexis, assis près d'elle.

Pendant ce temps, le visage boudeur, Bernadette mangea sans appétit son dessert. Elle était mécontente et énervée. Rien ne se déroulait comme elle l'avait imaginé.

La semaine précédente, elle avait attendu avec une impatience croissante la visite d'Amédée Durand qui avait promis de venir chercher le document qu'il lui avait laissé à l'intention de Donat. Chaque après-midi, elle s'était attendue à le voir arriver à l'école, mais il n'en fut rien. Deux jours auparavant, à son retour de sa journée de travail, elle avait appris de sa mère que l'inspecteur était passé à la maison à la fin de l'avant-midi pour parler à Donat et reprendre le document en question. Comme le mois de juin était déjà entamé, il y avait de fortes chances que l'homme ne revienne pas à Saint-Bernard-Abbé avant l'automne suivant à moins que… Mais si elle l'avait vraiment intéressé, il aurait fait en sorte de s'arrêter au moins quelques instants à l'école.

Pire encore, elle avait appris par Paddy Connolly que l'inspecteur s'était arrêté le jour même au magasin général et avait parlé durant quelques minutes avec Angélique Dionne. Il était donc en face de l'école et ne s'était même pas donné la peine de venir la saluer. Elle n'y comprenait plus rien. Ne l'intéressait-elle pas?

— Je te parle, Bedette, entendit-elle sa mère lui dire.

— Quoi? Qu'est-ce qu'il y a?

— Je viens de te demander comment allait la petite de ta sœur. T'as pas dit à matin que t'irais la voir à midi?

— Oui, j'y suis allée. Marthe a l'air correcte.

— Marthe, c'est la petite dernière d'Emma? demanda sœur Marie du Rosaire.

— Oui.

— Il faudrait bien que j'aille la voir, déclara la religieuse, comme si c'était une nécessité.

— Vous aurez pas à vous déranger, ma tante, s'empressa de préciser Bernadette, Emma est supposée venir faire un tour à soir avec les enfants.

Un pli soucieux apparut au front de Marie. Elle songea soudain à la réaction de sa belle-sœur quand elle s'apercevrait que l'enfant était différent. L'idée dut effleurer aussi sa fille et sa bru parce que toutes les deux se lancèrent des regards vaguement inquiets avant de se lever pour commencer à ranger la cuisine. Ernest Gingras s'empressa de les imiter et s'esquiva dans sa chambre, probablement peu désireux d'être à nouveau la cible de la tante de son patron.

— Tenez, ma tante, vous allez m'aider à laver la vaisselle, dit Bernadette en tendant un linge à la religieuse qui s'apprêtait à s'asseoir dans l'une des chaises berçantes installées sur la galerie.

— Tu peux m'en donner un aussi, intervint sœur Sainte-Anne, prête à aider.

— Il fait pas mal chaud en dedans, se plaignit Mathilde Beauchemin en essuyant la sueur qui perlait à son front.

— Plus on va faire vite, plus on va pouvoir sortir vite sur la galerie pour prendre l'air, déclara Marie en train de desservir la table.

— Ça va être moins pire dans une couple de minutes, prédit Eugénie, le poêle est en train de s'éteindre.

En ce début de soirée, l'humidité rendait le fond de l'air lourd. Encore une fois, le ciel charriait de gros nuages menaçants et un autre orage se préparait.

Quelques minutes plus tard, Rémi arriva à la ferme avec sa petite famille. Flore et Joseph devancèrent leurs parents et vinrent embrasser leur grand-mère, leur oncle et leurs tantes qui venaient de prendre place sur la galerie. Toutefois, les deux enfants se tinrent prudemment à distance des deux religieuses dont les costumes semblaient les impressionner.

— Viens nous montrer cette petite merveille-là, ordonna Mathilde Beauchemin à sa nièce au moment où elle posait le pied sur la première marche de l'escalier conduisant à la galerie.

Emma tendit l'enfant à sa tante qui se pencha pour mieux l'admirer. À la vue de la petite langue qui pointait entre les lèvres entrouvertes et des yeux étirés à la paupière tombante, les traits de la religieuse se figèrent durant un bref moment.

— C'est un beau bébé, se contenta-t-elle de dire en donnant l'enfant à sœur Sainte-Anne qui tendait déjà les bras pour le prendre.

Cette réaction pleine de retenue soulagea et étonna beaucoup les membres de la famille. Donat sortit d'autres chaises pour les visiteurs et, durant les minutes suivantes, on parla surtout des candidatures à la mairie et à l'échevinage de Donat et Rémi. Ensuite, Mathilde s'informa longuement de Hubert, de Xavier et de Camille qu'elle espérait pouvoir rencontrer avant le dimanche après-midi, moment qu'elle avait choisi pour rentrer à Sorel.

Ses hôtes se jetèrent un regard exprimant un certain soulagement. En fin de compte, ils n'auraient à la supporter que deux jours.

— Armand le sait pas encore, mais il va venir nous conduire à Sorel, déclara sœur Marie du Rosaire sur un ton définitif.

— Il va venir vous chercher à Saint-Bernard ? lui demanda Donat, étonné.

— Bien non, mon garçon. Toi, tu vas nous emmener chez ton oncle à Sainte-Monique, dimanche.

— Dimanche, s'il ne pleut pas, je risque d'être trop occupé, déclara son neveu sur un ton qui n'acceptait pas la contestation. Je vais aller vous conduire samedi, si ça vous fait rien, ma tante.

Mathilde n'osa pas contester, trop occupée soudain à tuer les maringouins et autres insectes piqueurs qui l'avaient prise comme cible depuis quelques instants.

— Bonté divine ! je veux bien croire que c'est humide, mais voulez-vous bien me dire ce que les bibittes ont à être après nous autres comme ça, à soir ? finit-elle par déclarer en écrasant énergiquement un maringouin qui venait de la piquer sur une joue. Elles arrêtent pas de me piquer.

— C'est vrai que c'est humide, reconnut Marie, assise près d'elle, mais je me fais pas piquer pantoute. Vous autres ? demanda-t-elle aux autres personnes présentes sur la galerie.

Le « non » unanime surprit un court moment la religieuse.

— Vous vous faites pas piquer, vous, ma sœur ? demanda-t-elle, stupéfaite, en s'adressant à sa compagne.

— Non, ça va.

— Voyons donc ! Pourquoi juste moi ?

— Vous avez peut-être quelque chose dans le sang qui les attire, suggéra Emma.

— Mais j'y pense, ma tante, il me semble avoir vu sur une tablette dans la remise un reste de l'onguent qu'on se mettait pour pas se faire piquer quand on était jeunes avant d'aller pêcher au bord de la rivière, intervint Bernadette.

— De quel onguent tu parles, Bedette? lui demanda sa mère.

— De l'onguent que p'pa faisait. Venez en dedans, ma tante, je vais aller vous le chercher et vous allez pouvoir vous en mettre. Si je me souviens bien, c'était pas mal bon, cet onguent-là.

La femme à la carrure imposante suivit sa nièce à l'intérieur. Bernadette la laissa un bref instant dans la cuisine d'été, le temps d'aller chercher un petit pot en grès bouché par du papier huilé dans la remise communicante. De retour dans la pièce, Bernadette tendit l'onguent à la religieuse et revint s'asseoir sur la galerie.

— J'espère que ça sent moins mauvais que dans le temps, dit Donat à sa sœur au moment où elle reprenait son siège.

— Je le sais pas, le pot est bouché, déclara hypocritement l'institutrice.

Les Beauchemin n'eurent pas à attendre bien longtemps pour le savoir. Dès que sœur Marie du Rosaire revint sur la galerie, une odeur pestilentielle arriva avec elle.

— Mais ça sent bien mauvais, cette affaire-là! se plaignit-elle. Je m'en suis mis seulement sur le visage et sur les mains et le cœur me lève.

— C'est probablement pour ça que c'est bon pour chasser les maringouins, ma tante, dit Rémi en riant. Avec cette senteur-là, il y en a pas un maudit qui va oser s'approcher de vous.

— Mais est-ce qu'il y a quelqu'un qui sait avec quoi cet onguent-là est fait? demanda sœur Sainte-Anne en fronçant le nez de dégoût.

— Mon Baptiste faisait ça avec des herbes et du purin de porc, je crois bien, expliqua Marie.

— Ouach! fit sa belle-sœur. Je commence à comprendre pourquoi ça sent aussi mauvais. Dire que je m'en suis mis sur le visage!

L'odeur dégagée par la religieuse était si prenante que, dans les minutes suivantes, chacun trouva un prétexte pour éloigner sa chaise de la sienne. Une heure plus tard, les Lafond annoncèrent leur intention de rentrer sans tarder à la maison, car le ciel devenait menaçant.

Après leur départ, Bernadette s'empressa de se retirer dans sa chambre malgré l'humidité étouffante. Elle préférait encore cela plutôt que de continuer à sentir le fumet dégagé par sa tante. Donat et Eugénie l'imitèrent. Dès qu'ils eurent disparu à l'intérieur de la maison, sœur Marie du Rosaire se tourna vers sa belle-sœur, sans tenir compte de la présence de sa compagne, assise un peu à l'écart.

— Dis donc, Marie, la petite de ta fille est pas normale? demanda-t-elle sans aucun ménagement.

— Emma a pris l'enfant que le bon Dieu lui a envoyé, Mathilde, répondit Marie d'une voix neutre.

— Je veux bien le croire, mais rien l'oblige à la garder, par exemple, répliqua la religieuse.

— C'est sa fille.

— Tu sais comment ça se passe, reprit Mathilde Beauchemin. Quand cette enfant-là va vieillir, il y aura pas moyen de la cacher bien longtemps. Tout le monde de Saint-Bernard va s'en apercevoir qu'elle est pas normale et on va la montrer du doigt.

— Je le sais, laissa tomber sa belle-sœur d'une voix blanche.

— Tu serais bien mieux de lui conseiller de la placer, insista la religieuse. Sa sœur et son frère vont s'apercevoir à la longue qu'elle est pas comme eux autres et ils vont rejeter la pauvre enfant.

— La placer où?

— La placer dans un orphelinat. On en a deux ou trois comme elle chez nous, à Sorel. À mon avis, cette enfant-là serait mieux dans une institution.

— Écoute, Mathilde, dit Marie d'une voix soudain raffermie, Rémi et Emma accepteront jamais que leur fille parte. Ils l'aiment autant, sinon plus que les deux autres. Mêle-toi surtout pas de ça et va pas leur faire de la peine. C'est déjà assez dur comme ça.

— Bon, je ne dirai rien, fit la religieuse en haussant les épaules.

— Bien, la journée a été longue, conclut Marie en se levant. Pour moi, t'es mieux de te frotter avec du savon du pays avant de monter te coucher, conseilla-t-elle à sa belle-sœur. J'ai l'impression que sœur Sainte-Anne va trouver que tu sens un peu fort.

La petite religieuse eut un petit rire et se leva à son tour, prête à aller se préparer pour la nuit.

Le lendemain matin, la maîtresse de maison eut la surprise de découvrir sœur Sainte-Anne assise sur la galerie, même si le soleil n'était pas encore levé. La pluie venait de cesser et un petit vent doux en provenance du sud rafraîchissait l'air.

— Voulez-vous bien me dire ce que vous faites dehors aussi de bonne heure, ma sœur ? lui demanda Marie, étonnée.

— Disons que l'onguent de sœur du Rosaire dégage une odeur un peu trop forte, répondit la religieuse avec sa retenue habituelle.

— Êtes-vous en train de me dire qu'elle sent encore cette cochonnerie-là ? s'étonna-t-elle.

— Même si elle est descendue deux ou trois fois se laver, on dirait qu'il y a rien pour faire partir la senteur. Vers quatre heures, j'en pouvais plus. Je suis sortie de la chambre et je suis venue respirer du bon air. J'espère que je vous ai pas réveillée.

— Pantoute, ma sœur, affirma-t-elle, un peu gênée.

Quand Bernadette descendit à la cuisine pour participer à la préparation du déjeuner, sa mère ne put s'empêcher de lui dire :

— Je te dis, toi, que t'as eu une riche idée de faire mettre cet onguent-là à ta tante. Ça sent partout en haut.

— Je le sais, m'man. Quand je me suis levée, ça m'a pris à la gorge. Je pensais que c'était une mouffette qui était morte proche de la maison. Mais, bonyenne, il me semble qu'elle aurait dû se douter que la senteur resterait quand elle en a mis. En tout cas, c'est la première fois que je regrette d'avoir une journée de congé le vendredi. Je pense que la journée serait moins fatigante à faire l'école, ajouta-t-elle en pensant à la présence de sa tante dans la maison.

Ce jour-là, il fut encore impossible d'aller travailler dans le jardin détrempé. Après quelques moments d'hésitation, Marie décida de consacrer la matinée à dégermer les dernières pommes de terre qui restaient dans le caveau, sous la maison, et l'après-midi à confectionner les chapeaux de paille qui finiraient bien par servir quand le soleil daignerait sortir de l'épaisse couverture nuageuse derrière laquelle il se blottissait depuis plusieurs jours.

— J'aime mieux être avec vous dans le caveau que de rester en haut avec ma tante, déclara Bernadette. Même si elle est en train de s'arracher la peau du visage et des mains à force de se laver pour ôter l'odeur. Cette senteur-là continue à me tomber sur le cœur.

Quelques minutes auparavant, les deux visiteuses s'étaient offertes à aider Eugénie à préparer le dîner pendant que la mère et la fille travailleraient dans le caveau.

Après le repas du midi, Marie demanda à Bernadette d'aller chercher le pressoir et les tresses de paille suspendues dans la tasserie et d'apporter le tout sur la galerie. La pluie s'était remise à tomber et la maîtresse de maison crut que la confection des chapeaux de paille occuperait de façon utile cet après-midi pluvieux. Sœur Marie du Rosaire annonça qu'elle avait besoin d'une sieste parce qu'elle avait mal dormi la nuit précédente, mais sa consœur préféra s'installer avec les femmes de la maison sur la galerie pour les aider.

— Chaque printemps, j'aidais ma mère à faire ça quand j'étais chez mes parents, déclara-t-elle, tout heureuse. Ça va me rappeler des souvenirs.

— On fait ça à cette époque-là, nous autres aussi, déclara la maîtresse de maison, mais cette année on a eu tellement de dérangements qu'on n'a pas trouvé le temps de le faire.

Marie introduisit le bout d'une première tresse dans le pressoir constitué de deux rouleaux de bois et tourna la manivelle pour bien l'aplatir pendant qu'Eugénie, Bernadette et sœur Sainte-Anne passaient du fil dans le chas de leur aiguille, prêtes à coudre les tresses pour en faire des chapeaux de paille pour chacun des habitants de la maison. Évidemment, on conserva les plus belles tresses pour la confection des chapeaux du dimanche qu'on ornerait plus tard d'un ruban et d'un autre colifichet.

❧

Deux jours plus tard, le dimanche matin, tous les Beauchemin n'aspiraient plus qu'au départ de Mathilde tant son bavardage continuel leur donnait le tournis.

— Si encore elle pouvait se fermer la trappe juste cinq minutes, se plaignit Bernadette, au bord de la crise de nerfs. Là, j'en peux plus de l'entendre me donner des conseils et se mêler de tout ce qui la regarde pas.

— Bedette ! dit sèchement sa mère, l'air sévère. Oublie pas que tu lui dois le respect. C'est ta tante, et une religieuse, à part ça.

— Ça lui donne tout de même pas le droit de mettre son grand nez dans nos affaires, m'man, protesta la jeune fille.

— Prends patience, elle s'en va après le dîner.

Comme il avait encore plu la veille, Donat, au plus grand mécontentement des femmes de la maison, avait renoncé à aller reconduire sa tante à Sainte-Monique.

— Le chemin est ben trop détrempé, argua-t-il au début de l'après-midi. Même si ça m'arrange pas pantoute, on va attendre demain, après le dîner, pour aller chez mon oncle Armand.

Pour sa part, ce matin-là, Marie se préparait en silence pour aller assister à la grand-messe. Elle n'en disait rien, mais elle craignait que sa belle-sœur ne lui annonce son intention de revenir pour le mariage de Xavier qu'on s'était pourtant bien gardé de mentionner durant sa visite.

Peu avant l'heure de la messe, Rémi et Emma eurent la bonne idée de venir offrir une place dans leur boghei à une Bernadette soulagée de ne pas avoir à supporter sa tante durant le trajet jusqu'à la chapelle.

— Le chemin est pas mal moins pire que je le pensais, dit le mari d'Emma à Donat qui venait de faire avancer sa voiture près de la galerie pour y laisser monter les deux religieuses et sa mère. Il a venté pas mal depuis hier soir et on dirait que ça a asséché un peu la route.

Malgré tout, les chevaux peinèrent passablement en escaladant la côte du rang Sainte-Ursule ravinée par les pluies, donnant une bonne idée à Donat de ce que serait le trajet jusqu'à Sainte-Monique l'après-midi même.

Ce dimanche-là, un bon nombre de paroissiens de Saint-Bernard-Abbé assistèrent à une scène pour le moins gênante qui eut lieu dans leur chapelle. Donat venait à peine de prendre place dans le banc auquel lui donnait droit son titre de marguillier qu'il remarqua avec un certain étonnement que Samuel Ellis et sa femme étaient confortablement installés dans le premier banc, face à l'autel, place réservée au président de la fabrique. Pendant un court moment, il se dit que l'ancien président du conseil avait dû se rendre compte que le notaire Valiquette avait assisté à la basse-messe et que, par conséquent, il pouvait occuper son ancien banc sans inconvénient pour personne.

Soudain, des murmures incitèrent le fils de Baptiste Beauchemin à tourner la tête. Il aperçut alors Eudore Valiquette, plein de dignité, qui s'avançait dans l'allée centrale en direction de son banc. Arrivé à l'avant de la chapelle, le petit homme sec s'arrêta devant son banc et attendit sans esquisser le moindre geste que les deux occupants lèvent la tête et l'aperçoivent, ce qui se produisit quelques secondes plus tard. Bridget donna un coup de coude discret à son mari assis près d'elle pour lui signaler la présence du président de la fabrique.

Pendant un court moment, l'Irlandais eut la tentation de feindre de ne pas avoir vu le notaire et de continuer à regarder l'autel devant lui. Mais comme l'autre n'avait pas l'air de vouloir renoncer à son privilège d'occuper le premier banc, Samuel, le visage rouge de honte, dut faire signe à sa femme de se lever et de sortir du banc avec lui.

L'homme de loi se borna à saluer sèchement de la tête son confrère marguillier avant de prendre place dans son banc. Sous le regard goguenard des gens présents, Bridget et Samuel s'empressèrent d'aller s'asseoir dans le quatrième banc.

Une heure plus tard, à la fin de son sermon, le curé Désilets rappela l'importance de la procession de la Fête-Dieu et mentionna, pour la deuxième fois, que le reposoir allait être chez madame Angèle Meilleur.

— C'est qui, Angèle Meilleur ? demanda une Bernadette distraite à sa mère.

— Voyons, Bedette ! Je te l'ai dit la semaine passée, monsieur le curé parle de madame Cloutier.

— Je m'habitue pas, murmura la jeune fille.

L'institutrice tourna légèrement la tête pour apercevoir celle qu'elle appelait encore madame Cloutier. Celle-ci se tenait droite, assise aux côtés d'Hormidas Meilleur qu'elle dominait largement par sa stature. Le petit homme n'avait jamais eu l'air aussi soigné que depuis son mariage.

Avant de regagner l'autel, le prêtre annonça :

— Il y a promesse de mariage entre Catherine Benoît, fille de feu Léopold Benoît et de Laura Lacroix, de cette paroisse, avec Xavier Beauchemin, fils de feu Baptiste Beauchemin et de Marie Camirand, également de cette paroisse. Si quelqu'un voit un obstacle à cette union, qu'il le dise ou qu'il se taise pour toujours.

— Quoi ? Ton garçon se marie ? demanda à voix basse sœur Marie du Rosaire stupéfaite à sa belle-sœur assise à ses côtés.

Celle-ci se contenta de hocher la tête avant de se lever comme tous les autres fidèles alors que le prêtre se rendait à l'autel pour poursuivre le saint sacrifice.

— Comment ça se fait que je l'ai pas su ? chuchota la religieuse.

— Parce que les Benoît vont faire des petites noces, laissa tomber Marie en lui faisant comprendre qu'elle voulait suivre la messe.

Le visage de la religieuse se renfrogna et elle reprit son missel. Cependant, à la fin de la messe, sœur Marie du Rosaire ne perdit pas une seconde.

— Qu'est-ce que tu veux dire par des « petites noces » ? insista-t-elle auprès de sa belle-sœur alors qu'elles se dirigeaient lentement vers la sortie.

— Les Benoît n'invitent que la parenté proche, répondit Marie, pour couper court.

— C'est qui cette Catherine Benoît ? s'enquit sa parente.

— Une fille de la paroisse, fit-elle, évasive. Les Benoît ont une terre à côté de celle de Xavier.

La veuve de Baptiste Beauchemin s'en voulait d'avoir oublié que la première publication des bans allait nécessairement se faire ce dimanche-là. Si elle s'en était souvenu, nul doute qu'elle aurait tout fait en son pouvoir pour que

Donat conduise les religieuses la veille chez Armand Beauchemin. Là, il était trop tard. Le mal était fait. Il ne lui restait plus qu'à entraîner le plus rapidement possible sa belle-sœur et sa compagne vers le boghei avant qu'elles puissent entendre des commentaires sur la future mariée, que certaines personnes de la paroisse allaient sûrement échanger entre elles après avoir entendu la publication des bans du mariage prochain de son fils. Elle était persuadée que les mauvaises langues n'allaient pas se priver de parler en mal de la fiancée de son fils.

— Je pense qu'on est aussi bien de pas traîner, dit-elle aux deux religieuses en les houspillant un peu. J'aimerais que vous ayez au moins le temps de dîner comme il faut avant de partir pour Sainte-Monique.

Parvenues au pied des marches, le hasard voulut que Mathilde Beauchemin aperçoive Xavier qui se dirigeait avec sa promise et Laura Benoît vers sa voiture.

— Xavier! le héla-t-elle en laissant sur place sœur Sainte-Anne, Marie et Bernadette pour s'approcher rapidement de son neveu.

Le jeune homme interpellé se tourna et aperçut sa tante sans manifester grand plaisir. Il eut le temps de murmurer quelques mots à Catherine et à Laura Benoît avant de faire quelques pas vers sa tante.

— Bonjour, ma tante, la salua-t-il.

— Eh bien, mon garçon, tu me fais des cachettes, à cette heure, lui dit-elle en s'approchant des deux femmes qui étaient demeurées sur place.

— Je savais pas que vous étiez à Saint-Bernard, ma tante, se défendit le grand jeune homme au sourire franc.

— Je suis chez ta mère depuis trois jours et t'as même pas trouvé le temps de venir lui rendre visite, lui reprocha la religieuse.

— Je suis pas toujours sur le chemin, ma tante, dit-il dans un éclat de rire. Comme vous venez de l'entendre, je me marie dans deux semaines et je manque pas d'ouvrage pour tout préparer.

— Qu'est-ce que t'attends pour me présenter ta promise ? demanda sœur Marie du Rosaire avec son aplomb habituel.

Marie et sœur Sainte-Anne avaient eu le temps de rejoindre Xavier au moment où celui-ci présentait sa fiancée et sa mère à sa tante. Catherine eut un sourire charmant à l'endroit de la sœur Grise et la salua ainsi que les autres personnes qui venaient d'arriver. Sœur Marie du Rosaire allait commencer à poser ses questions indiscrètes quand la nature décida de se porter au secours du jeune couple. La pluie se mit à tomber.

— Bon, on va sûrement se revoir, ma tante, déclara Xavier, mais là, on va y aller avant d'être mouillés.

Au même moment, Donat immobilisa son boghei près des deux religieuses et de sa mère qui n'eurent d'autre choix que de monter.

— C'est bien de valeur que j'aie pas eu le temps de parler un peu avec la future de ton garçon, Marie, se plaignit sa belle-sœur en prenant place dans la voiture. C'est un beau brin de fille qui a l'air d'avoir une belle façon.

— Une bien belle façon, laissa tomber Marie sans manifester beaucoup d'entrain.

Alors que Donat entreprenait de descendre la côte du rang Sainte-Ursule, son frère s'éloignait vers l'autre extrémité du rang, en direction de la ferme des Benoît et de la sienne.

— Toi, tu sais pas à quel danger tu viens d'échapper, plaisanta Xavier en s'adressant à Catherine, assise près de lui.

— Pourquoi tu dis ça ?

— Plus écornifleuse que ma tante Mathilde, ça se fait pas.

— C'est une sœur Grise comme ma cousine Émérentienne, fit remarquer Laura Benoît assise sur la banquette arrière.

— Oui, mais je vous garantis que ma tante a pas le même genre, madame Benoît.

Dans la maison du rang Saint-Jean, Marie profita de ce que les deux religieuses étaient montées préparer leurs bagages pour dire à mi-voix à sa bru et à ses enfants :

— On l'a échappé belle, à matin. S'il avait fallu qu'elle apprenne quel genre de fille Xavier va marier, on aurait entendu votre tante à n'en plus finir.

— Mais ça la regarde pas pantoute, m'man, protesta Bernadette. Xavier a bien le droit de marier qui il veut.

— Ouais, mais il y a tout de même pas de quoi s'en vanter, conclut sa mère en se dirigeant vers le garde-manger pour y prendre le beurre.

— Bedette, tu vas aller me chercher un peu de ouate, demanda soudain Donat à sa jeune sœur.

— Pourquoi t'as besoin de ça ?

— Parce que je pense avoir attrapé mal aux oreilles, déclara Donat. Grouille-toi avant qu'elles descendent toutes les deux.

— Mal aux oreilles ? fit sa mère en s'approchant.

— Ben non, m'man, dit-il un ton plus bas, je veux me mettre ça dans les oreilles pendant le voyage, sinon je tiendrai pas. Moi, je serai pas capable de me faire crier dans les oreilles pendant deux heures.

— C'est pas bien fin pour ta tante, lui fit remarquer Marie.

— C'est ça ou je vous la laisse toute la semaine, la menaça-t-il, plus ou moins sérieux.

Sa mère n'osa rien dire, mais quand Bernadette revint avec un peu de ouate prélevée dans la pharmacie, elle tendit la main pour s'en emparer en disant à sa fille :

— Donne-moi ça, je vais m'en occuper.

Le dîner se prit dans la bonne humeur. Les Beauchemin étaient heureux à la pensée d'être débarrassés dans quelques minutes de leurs encombrantes visiteuses. On servit du poulet dans une sauce blanche et un morceau de tarte à la mélasse comme dessert qu'on fit passer avec une tasse de thé.

— Bon, il va falloir y aller, déclara Donat en se levant, dès qu'il eut fini d'avaler sa dernière bouchée.

— Attends, mon garçon, lui ordonna Marie, il est pas question que tu prennes le chemin sans te mettre quelque chose dans les oreilles.

Ce disant, elle sortit la ouate de la poche de son tablier.

— Mets-toi ça dans les oreilles.

— Qu'est-ce qu'il a ? demanda sa belle-sœur, curieuse.

— Je pense qu'il a attrapé de la fraîche. Il a mal aux oreilles sans bon sens.

— Oui, mais arrangé comme ça, il entendra rien, s'inquiéta la religieuse.

— Il se fera une raison, conclut sa belle-sœur.

Pendant que Donat sortait pour s'occuper de son cheval, sœur Marie du Rosaire ne put s'empêcher de regretter de ne pas être allée rendre une petite visite à sa nièce Camille.

— Tu te reprendras une autre fois, dit la veuve de Baptiste Beauchemin pour la consoler. De toute façon, ces temps-ci, elle a tellement d'ouvrage qu'on la voit presque pas.

— Elle attend pas du nouveau ? demanda la curieuse. Elle est mariée depuis déjà un bon bout de temps.

— Pas aux dernières nouvelles, mentit sa belle-sœur.

Les deux religieuses remercièrent avec effusion leurs hôtes et montèrent dans le boghei. La pluie avait cessé durant le repas, à la plus grande satisfaction de Donat.

— Je vous remercie encore beaucoup, madame Beauchemin, dit sœur Sainte-Anne de sa petite voix douce. Je pense que moi aussi, je commence à avoir mal aux oreilles comme votre garçon, mais je vais offrir ça au bon Dieu, ajouta-t-elle avec un petit sourire narquois.

Chapitre 25

L'été se fait attendre

La troisième semaine de juin, le temps ne s'améliora guère, au plus grand dépit du curé Désilets qui rongeait son frein depuis les premiers jours du mois.

— Batèche de batèche, on dirait que le bon Dieu veut pas que j'aie mon presbytère cette année ! ne cessait-il de répéter chaque fois que la pluie obligeait les ouvriers d'Eugène Bélisle à repousser le travail.

Il fallait tout de même reconnaître que le prêtre avait des raisons d'être mécontent de la situation qui perdurait depuis quelques semaines parce que les travaux étaient tout simplement au point mort.

Le maître d'œuvre de Saint-Zéphirin n'avait pu tenir parole. Il n'avait envoyé une équipe d'ouvriers qu'à la mi-mai en arguant qu'il avait été retardé par l'exécution d'un autre contrat. Une demi-douzaine d'hommes sous la direction d'un nouveau contremaître, un certain Théophile Dussault, parvinrent à creuser la cave et à édifier le solage du futur presbytère de Saint-Bernard-Abbé en profitant des quelques journées de beau temps du début du mois. Malheureusement, depuis que les ouvriers avaient entrepris de monter la charpente, le temps n'avait cessé d'être pluvieux, ce qui avait considérablement retardé les travaux.

Dès le premier jour où les ouvriers avaient fait leur apparition sur le chantier, Josaphat Désilets s'était fait un devoir de passer le plus clair de ses journées à surveiller de si près les travaux qu'il en était venu à mettre à rude épreuve la patience déjà fort limitée du nouveau contremaître de Bélisle.

Contrairement à Beaupré, l'ancien contremaître, celui-ci ne parvint pas à cacher longtemps son irritation d'avoir continuellement le curé de la paroisse dans les jambes. À plus d'une occasion, il mit Josaphat Désilets en garde contre les dangers de se déplacer au milieu de ses hommes en train de travailler, sans obtenir grand résultat.

Bref, les jours passaient et la construction n'avançait guère. On était parvenu à monter le plus gros de la charpente et on s'apprêtait à couvrir le toit ce matin-là, quand le ciel ouvrit encore une fois ses vannes, obligeant Dussault, un homme au caractère irascible, à crier aux hommes qui venaient de monter sur le toit de descendre. De dépit, un ouvrier lança un bout de madrier du haut de la toiture et le morceau de bois tomba à quelques pouces du curé Désilets qui fit un saut de carpe pour éviter d'être frappé. Il s'était imprudemment avancé pour voir comment les hommes allaient s'y prendre pour poser la tôle sur le toit.

— Attention, maudit sans-dessein! hurla Dussault à son ouvrier. Regarde où tu lances tes affaires. Et vous, monsieur le curé, je vous ai dit cent fois que vous aviez rien à faire sur le chantier. Voulez-vous ben me sacrer votre camp de là! lui cria-t-il hors de lui.

Secoué par ce qui venait d'arriver, Josaphat Désilets demeura un court moment sans réaction sous l'algarade. Puis, rouge de colère, il s'avança vers le contremaître.

— Savez-vous à qui vous parlez? demanda-t-il, l'air mauvais, à Théophile Dussault.

— Oui, à quelqu'un qui comprend rien à ce qu'on lui dit, répondit l'autre sur le même ton, apparemment nullement impressionné par la soutane de son vis-à-vis. Je vous ai dit et répété que vous aviez rien à faire sur mon chantier, est-ce que c'est clair, ça?

— J'ai le droit de voir comment vous bâtissez mon presbytère.

— Non, monsieur le curé, ça vous regarde pas pantoute. Eugène Bélisle m'a dit que je devais avoir affaire qu'au notaire Valiquette, le président de votre fabrique. Et là, je vous avertis, à partir d'aujourd'hui, aussitôt que vous allez mettre le pied sur le chantier, je vais commander aux hommes d'arrêter de travailler. Comme ça, je serai sûr qu'il vous arrivera pas d'accident.

— On va bien voir qui va gagner dans cette affaire-là, dit le curé Désilets avec hauteur avant de tourner les talons pour aller se mettre à l'abri dans sa sacristie.

La menace du prêtre ne sembla pas intimider le moins du monde Théophile Dussault qui se dirigea pesamment vers ses hommes rassemblés un peu plus loin.

— Vous êtes aussi ben de retourner chez vous, leur dit-il. Je pense que c'est parti pour la journée, ajouta-t-il en faisant allusion à la pluie qui s'était mise à tomber encore plus fort.

Les jours suivants, le curé de Saint-Bernard-Abbé n'eut d'autre choix que de regarder de loin les travailleurs. Il prit alors l'habitude de lire son bréviaire en faisant les cent pas sur le parvis de la chapelle d'où il avait une vue dégagée sur le chantier. Chaque fois qu'il se produisait quelque chose à cet endroit, il s'arrêtait brusquement de marcher et levait la tête pour tenter de voir ce qui se passait. De toute évidence, le contremaître était parvenu à le dompter et il avait eu beau se plaindre à Eudore Valiquette, le petit homme de loi lui avait répété avec ménagement qu'il était le seul à posséder le mandat de traiter avec Dussault.

—

Pour sa part, Donat Beauchemin avait longuement réfléchi à son avenir en revenant de Sainte-Monique le dimanche après-midi et il regrettait amèrement d'avoir trop rapidement accepté la proposition de Lemire de se présenter à la mairie de Saint-Bernard-Abbé. Il ne se sentait pas prêt à assumer de telles responsabilités et, surtout, il commençait à réaliser qu'il avait bien peu de chances de l'emporter sur Thomas Hyland. À son arrivée à la maison, il était pratiquement décidé à retirer sa candidature.

— J'espère que mon oncle était content de voir arriver ma tante Mathilde? plaisanta Bernadette quand il rentra dans la maison.

— S'il était content, il l'a pas trop montré, répondit-il. Je pense qu'il avait pas le goût pantoute d'atteler pour aller reconduire les sœurs à Sorel, mais ma tante Amanda lui a pas laissé le choix.

Une heure plus tard, pendant qu'il soignait ses animaux, le jeune cultivateur se rendit compte qu'il ne pouvait laisser la voie libre aux Irlandais de la paroisse et il imagina une stratégie pour se tirer d'affaires.

— Pourquoi je pourrais pas faire comme Ellis? se demanda-t-il à mi-voix. Au lieu de se présenter lui-même, il a demandé à Hyland de le faire. Pourquoi je ferais pas ça avec Rémi, ou mieux, avec Blanchette? Blanchette a une cinquantaine d'années et le monde le respecte. À ben y penser, il a plus de chances que moi d'être élu.

Ce soir-là, dès la dernière bouchée du souper avalée, Donat attela son boghei et se rendit chez les Lafond pour discuter avec son beau-frère à qui il proposa d'abord de prendre sa place comme candidat à la mairie. Rémi s'empressa de refuser. Alors, son parent lui expliqua son idée de se faire remplacer par Anatole Blanchette.

— Ça va faire drôle en maudit que t'aies changé d'idée comme ça, en chemin, lui fit remarquer Rémi, plus ou moins d'accord avec son jeune beau-frère.

— Peut-être, mais on n'a pas encore commencé à aller voir le monde. Si Blanchette accepte, je vais me présenter comme conseiller, comme toi.

Rémi, toujours de bonne composition, accepta finalement de l'accompagner chez Anatole Blanchette, dans le rang Saint-Paul. Le gros homme écouta les explications de Donat sans dire un mot. Son sourire était le signe évident que le changement lui plaisait assez et il ne s'y opposa pas.

— Je pense qu'on a juste à changer ça sur la liste qui est sur la porte de l'église, conclut Donat.

— Non, il va falloir déranger monsieur le curé, le corrigea Anatole. Il l'a rentrée dans la sacristie à cause de la pluie qui arrête pas.

— On est aussi ben de se débarrasser de ça tout de suite, à soir, suggéra Rémi.

Le soir même, les trois hommes allèrent frapper à la porte de la sacristie pour demander au curé Désilets de procéder aux changements dans les mises en candidature.

— C'est plutôt inhabituel, ce que vous me demandez là, leur fit remarquer le prêtre d'une voix désagréable.

— C'est vrai, reconnut Donat, mais ma sœur a fait une erreur en écrivant les noms aux mauvaises places. Je pense que vous allez dire comme nous autres, monsieur le curé, c'est bien plus normal que monsieur Blanchette soit candidat comme maire que moi.

— Je me mêle pas de politique, laissa tomber le prêtre en procédant tout de même aux corrections demandées.

Les hommes le remercièrent et prirent congé. Avant de déposer Anatole Blanchette chez lui, il fut entendu qu'ils se déplaceraient tous les trois ensemble un soir sur deux, dès le lendemain soir, pour faire la tournée des foyers de Saint-Bernard-Abbé.

Ce soir-là, Donat se mit au lit fatigué, mais satisfait d'être parvenu à se tirer de ce qu'il en était arrivé à considérer comme un mauvais pas. Avant de s'endormir, il se promit d'être beaucoup plus prudent à l'avenir avant de s'engager.

Cette semaine-là, aucun habitant de la paroisse ne pouvait se vanter d'avoir vu Hormidas Meilleur traîner au magasin général. Après sa tournée de facteur, le petit homme au chapeau melon verdi par les intempéries disparaissait rapidement chez lui.

Ce vendredi après-midi-là, le ciel était uniformément gris et les champs gorgés d'eau étaient d'un vert soutenu. Quant au niveau de l'eau de la rivière qui coulait sous le pont, il était particulièrement élevé.

Au début de l'après-midi, les élèves de Bernadette avaient quitté l'école en criant leur joie d'être enfin en vacances pour la durée de l'été. En face, quelques clients désœuvrés de Télesphore Dionne qui s'étaient rassemblés sur la galerie du magasin général s'étonnaient de ne plus voir le facteur venir fumer une pipe avec eux.

— Dis-moi pas que le père Meilleur est encore en pleine lune de miel! s'exclama le gros Tancrède Bélanger avec un sourire égrillard. On le voit nulle part. Si l'Angèle le ménage pas plus que ça, le pauvre homme fera pas long feu, ajouta-t-il dans un éclat de rire.

— Riez pas, vous autres, intervint Évariste Bourgeois, en prenant un air sérieux. Moi, son voisin, je peux vous dire qu'il chôme pas.

— Ah! Ah! fit Paddy Connolly.

— Non, c'est pas ce que vous pensez. L'Angèle le fait travailler comme un fou sur le reposoir. Écoutez! Vous pouvez l'entendre clouer. Il est en train de faire un autel que lui et sa femme vont mettre sur leur galerie. Il m'a dit hier qu'il va y avoir des anges en carton et des draperies. Il paraît que ça va être de toute beauté, ce reposoir-là. Tout le temps qu'Angèle passe pas dans ses champs à cause de la pluie, elle l'occupe à préparer son reposoir.

— Et s'il mouille encore dimanche? demanda White.

— Elle va avoir fait tout ça pour rien, conclut Paddy sur un petit rire.

Personne ne sembla trouver la remarque amusante.

En face, dans l'école désertée par les enfants, Bernadette avait entrepris les derniers rangements avant de laver le plancher de la classe et de verrouiller l'école jusqu'au mois de septembre. La veille, elle avait signé son contrat pour l'année suivante. Lors de la signature, elle avait appris, sans grand plaisir, qu'Angélique Dionne avait finalement été engagée pour enseigner dans la nouvelle école.

— Est-ce que l'inspecteur est venu pour lui apprendre cette nouvelle-là ? avait-elle demandé à son frère en train de ranger le contrat.

— Non, ça le regarde pas pantoute. Par contre, la fille de Dionne a eu une idée qui est pas trop bête, avait-il ajouté en guettant sa réaction.

— Quelle idée ?

— Elle a proposé d'enseigner dans ton école. Comme ça, elle serait juste en face de chez eux et comme pas mal de ses élèves vont venir de Sainte-Ursule, ça leur ferait moins loin à marcher.

— Ah ben là ! Elle a tout un front de beu, elle ! s'était-elle emportée, rouge de colère. Et moi, dans tout ça ? Comme une belle dinde, j'aurais à marcher du rang Saint-Paul jusqu'à chez nous matin et soir ? Je t'avertis, Donat, si tu penses faire ça, je vais rester dans l'appartement en haut de l'école et la commission scolaire va être obligée de le meubler et de me chauffer tout l'hiver.

— Énerve-toi pas pour rien, l'avait rassurée son frère. Je lui ai dit que t'avais le premier choix parce que t'étais celle qui était la plus ancienne.

Bernadette avait éprouvé un véritable soulagement en apprenant la nouvelle, mais cela n'avait pas fait disparaître son principal sujet de préoccupation : Amédée Durand. Si l'inspecteur ne se présentait pas à l'école avant la fin de l'après-midi, il était certain qu'elle ne le reverrait plus avant le début de l'automne suivant. Et dire qu'elle ne savait même pas où il demeurait. Si elle l'avait su, elle n'aurait pas hésité à lui écrire pour l'inviter discrètement à l'accompagner au mariage de son frère qui allait avoir lieu dans huit jours.

Cet après-midi-là, quitte à susciter la colère de sa mère, elle ne se pressa nullement de quitter son école après avoir achevé son ménage. Il existait encore une maigre chance qu'Amédée Durand passe à l'école et elle ne voulait surtout pas courir le risque de le rater.

Quand Paddy Connolly s'arrêta pour lui offrir de la laisser chez elle en passant, comme il le faisait habituellement, elle le remercia et lui mentit en lui disant qu'elle avait encore beaucoup de choses à faire avant de pouvoir fermer définitivement l'école.

À cinq heures, la jeune institutrice, à bout de patience, décida soudain qu'elle avait suffisamment attendu son prince charmant. Elle sortit sur le perron de l'école et verrouilla la porte.

— Lui, il va me payer ça un jour, marmonna-t-elle en rangeant la clé dans son sac avant de se diriger vers la route et de traverser le pont.

Au moment où elle quittait le pont, la pluie se mit à tomber et elle eut beau presser le pas, elle dut s'arrêter chez sa sœur Emma, complètement trempée.

— Veux-tu bien me dire à quoi tu penses en prenant le chemin sans parapluie avec le mois de juin qu'on connaît cette année ? lui reprocha sa sœur en repoussant Flore qui cherchait à sortir de la maison. Entre, viens te sécher un peu.

— Je l'ai oublié en partant à matin, dit Bernadette.

— En tout cas, on peut pas dire que t'as l'air trop contente pour une fille qui travaillera pas pendant au moins deux mois, fit Emma sur un ton narquois.

— Aïe, Emma Beauchemin ! Essaye pas de me faire croire que t'as déjà oublié comment m'man est capable de nous occuper du matin au soir pendant l'été. Si c'est pas travailler, je me demande bien ce que c'est.

— Dans ce cas-là, marie-toi, lui conseilla sa sœur. C'est sûr que tu vas travailler autant, mais au moins, il y a personne qui va te donner des ordres du matin au soir… à moins que t'aies un mari aussi détestable que…

— Que qui ?

— Ben, que Liam Connolly, par exemple.

— Il est comme ça, lui ? demanda naïvement l'institutrice.

— Voyons, Bedette, ouvre les yeux. M'man pense comme moi. Il est pas plus fin qu'il faut avec notre sœur. Entre Liam et Camille, ça doit faire des flammèches.

— C'est vrai qu'il a pas l'air d'avoir bon caractère, le beau-frère.

— C'est certain qu'il a pas le caractère de Constant Aubé, lui fit remarquer Emma en riant.

Bernadette ne répliqua pas. Quelques minutes plus tard, elle laissa sa sœur aux préparatifs de son souper et décida de rentrer à la maison au moment où la pluie avait temporairement cessé. Lors de son passage devant la maison de son ex-amoureux, elle tourna ostensiblement la tête de l'autre côté pour bien lui montrer son indifférence s'il était embusqué derrière l'une de ses fenêtres.

Toutefois, une averse la rattrapa alors qu'elle n'était plus qu'à quelques centaines de pieds de la ferme familiale. À son entrée dans la maison, elle trouva sa mère sur son chemin.

— As-tu vu dans quel état tu es, Bedette Beauchemin ? l'apostropha Marie. Si ça a de l'allure !

— Je pouvais pas savoir qu'il était pour mouiller encore, se défendit Bernadette en s'emparant d'une serviette pour essuyer son visage.

— Les gens du rang vont te prendre pour une vraie folle d'être sur le chemin par un temps pareil, lui reprocha sa mère. Ma foi du bon Dieu, on dirait que t'as pas de tête, ma pauvre fille !

— Bon, là, je vais aller changer de robe, fit sèchement Bernadette, excédée. J'ai pas arrêté de travailler de la journée et je suis fatiguée.

— C'est ça, va te changer. Après, tu viendras nous aider à préparer le souper.

Ce soir-là, la jeune fille se réfugia tôt dans sa chambre, mécontente d'elle et des autres. Elle commençait à réaliser qu'elle s'était fait des idées sur le jeune inspecteur et, pour la première fois, elle se demanda si elle n'avait pas agi trop précipitamment avec Constant Aubé. Mais lui, il ne posait pas de problème. Elle n'aurait qu'à claquer des doigts pour qu'il lui revienne.

— En attendant, j'ai l'air fine, se plaignit-elle à mi-voix, je vais aller aux noces de Xavier sans cavalier.

❧

Le lendemain avant-midi, Xavier s'arrêta quelques minutes chez sa mère. Le jeune homme venait de rapporter un outil emprunté à Rémi Lafond et profitait de l'occasion pour prendre des nouvelles de la famille. Depuis le début du mois, on l'avait peu vu dans le rang Saint-Jean.

— Entre boire une tasse de thé et souffler un peu, lui offrit sa mère en l'apercevant à travers la porte moustiquaire. Donat s'en vient, il est juste allé voir si notre homme engagé avait fini de nettoyer l'étable.

Xavier entra, embrassa sa mère, Eugénie et Bernadette avant de s'asseoir dans l'une des chaises berçantes.

— J'espère que vous avez pas encore invité ma tante Mathilde pour passer une couple de jours chez vous ? fit-il en guise de plaisanterie.

— Fais pas de farce avec ça, toi, lui ordonna sa mère. Je veux bien gagner mon ciel, mais il faut quand même pas exagérer. Comment est le chemin ? lui demanda-t-elle.

— Il devrait faire l'affaire pour la procession demain s'il mouille pas encore aujourd'hui, répondit-il, sachant pertinemment que sa mère posait la question pour cette unique raison.

— Tant mieux, ce serait bien de valeur qu'Angèle ait autant travaillé à son reposoir pour rien.

— Quand même, m'man, j'ai ben l'impression que le monde va se plaindre d'avoir à descendre et à monter la grande côte pour ça.

— C'est l'idée de monsieur le curé. Il a sûrement ses raisons, affirma Marie, toujours prête à prendre la défense d'un prêtre.

— En tout cas, je suis certain qu'il y aura pas grand monde dans la paroisse qui va savoir avant le temps de quoi a l'air son reposoir. Le père Meilleur était en train de clouer une toile goudronnée devant sa galerie à matin, quand je suis passé.

— Pour moi, il fait ça parce qu'il a peur que la pluie vienne gâcher le reposoir, supposa Marie avec un certain bon sens.

— Je voulais vous dire que Catherine a écrit un petit mot à mon oncle Armand et à mon oncle Anselme pour les inviter aux noces la semaine prochaine. Ils ont répondu tous les deux qu'ils allaient venir.

— C'est fin de sa part.

— Là, toute la famille a été invitée et madame Benoît a déjà commencé à se préparer.

— Tu lui offriras mon aide, dit sa mère.

— Camille a déjà offert de venir lui donner un coup de main, mais elle a dit qu'elle et Catherine allaient être capables de se débrouiller. Après tout, on sera pas si nombreux que ça. Ils vont être seulement quatre du côté des Benoît et nous autres.

— Il y a pas juste Catherine qui peut l'aider, fit sa mère. Sa bru aussi doit donner un coup de main.

— Pas trop, m'man. Marie-Rose est pas de service pantoute.

— C'est vrai qu'elle a pas l'air plus aimable que son mari, reconnut Marie Beauchemin.

— C'est le moins qu'on puisse dire.

— Et toi, as-tu tout ce qu'il te faut? intervint Donat en entrant.

— Je pense que oui, répondit son frère. La maison va être ben propre et tout est en ordre. Antonin et moi, on a tout nettoyé, c'est tellement propre qu'on pourrait manger à terre. Après les noces, on va partir deux ou trois jours et mon homme engagé va s'occuper de mes animaux.

— Où est-ce que t'as l'intention d'aller? demanda Bernadette, curieuse.

— Ça, c'est un secret, répondit son frère en riant. Une sorte de petit voyage de noces.

— Je pensais bien que tu viendrais me voir pour faire arranger ton linge avant ton mariage, reprit sa mère en faisant les gros yeux à sa fille.

— C'est ce que je voulais faire aussi, mais Catherine a pas voulu que je vous encombre avec mes guenilles. Elle a réparé ce qui était réparable et elle m'a obligé à m'acheter un habit neuf pour les noces.

Marie Beauchemin eut besoin d'un court moment pour combattre une certaine jalousie.

— Tant mieux si elle a été capable de faire ça, approuva-t-elle du bout des lèvres. Pour l'habit, elle a bien fait. C'est une grosse dépense, mais c'est pas le temps de faire pitié le jour de son mariage.

❧

À leur réveil, le lendemain matin, les paroissiens découvrirent que le vent de la nuit était enfin parvenu à chasser les nuages. Finalement, ce dimanche promettait d'être une belle journée ensoleillée.

Debout sur le pas de la porte de la sacristie, le curé Désilets n'était pas le dernier à se réjouir du beau temps. Sa paroisse allait enfin connaître sa première procession de la Fête-Dieu. Celle-ci n'aurait peut-être pas tout le panache qu'on lui donnait dans les vieilles paroisses, mais elle aurait le mérite d'être fervente.

Après avoir jeté un coup d'œil désenchanté vers la structure de son futur presbytère dont la construction n'avait pratiquement pas progressé depuis la semaine précédente, il rentra dans la sacristie pour relire une dernière fois son sermon rédigé à moitié en anglais à moitié en français. La veille, le prêtre avait pris la précaution de faire venir Hyland et Blanchette à la sacristie pour leur demander de ne pas faire de rencontre politique sur le parvis de l'église avant ou après les cérémonies du lendemain. Ils avaient promis.

Maintenant, il n'y avait plus un habitant de Saint-Bernard-Abbé qui ignorait qu'Anatole Blanchette était l'adversaire de Thomas Hyland et que Donat Beauchemin et Rémi Lafond étaient ses deux candidats aux postes de conseillers, face à Samuel Ellis et à Eudore Valiquette.

Après avoir relu son sermon, le curé se mit à noter ses projets pour l'été. Évidemment, son emménagement dans son nouveau presbytère allait occuper beaucoup de son temps, mais cela ne devrait pas l'empêcher de mettre sur pied des mouvements paroissiaux aussi importants que celui des Enfants de Marie et des Dames de Sainte-Anne. Cette année, il s'était limité à la création d'une chorale, mais il fallait comprendre que Saint-Bernard-Abbé n'était une véritable paroisse que depuis deux mois et qu'il fallait du temps pour tout mettre en place.

— C'est dommage, laissa-t-il tomber à voix haute au moment où Bridget Ellis frappait à la porte.

Le prêtre la fit entrer et la laissa aux préparatifs du dîner et du souper pendant qu'il allait trouver refuge dans la chapelle.

— C'est dommage, répéta-t-il pour lui-même, en reprenant le monologue interrompu par l'arrivée de sa ménagère. Là, j'aurai même pas de dais pendant la procession et il y aura pas une seule bannière. Mais ça va changer de poil l'année prochaine...

Deux heures plus tard, Josaphat Désilets, vêtu de ses vêtements sacerdotaux blancs, célébra la messe. Plus d'un cultivateur pria alors pour que le beau temps perdure enfin. Après le long sermon du pasteur, les gens présents eurent droit à la deuxième publication des bans pour le mariage de Xavier Beauchemin et à quelques recommandations pour assurer la bonne marche de la procession qui allait avoir lieu dès la fin de la grand-messe. Avant la célébration, le curé avait envoyé le bedeau chercher Donat Beauchemin qu'il venait de voir arriver avec sa famille. Il avait demandé à ce dernier de prévenir son frère Xavier et sa fiancée qu'il désirait les rencontrer au début de l'après-midi, le jour même.

Après l'*Ite missa est*, la chapelle s'était rapidement vidée et les gens s'étaient rassemblés en petits groupes dans le stationnement et sur le bord de la route pour parler entre eux en attendant les directives des marguilliers. Il faisait beau et le temps était frais. Une température idéale pour participer à une procession.

Finalement, les marguilliers prirent place sur le parvis et Eudore Valiquette, à titre de président de la fabrique, expliqua comment le curé Désilets voulait que les choses se passent. Il allait sortir dans un instant de la chapelle en portant l'ostensoir, précédé par les servants de messe et lui-même, porteur de la croix. Les membres de la chorale paroissiale suivraient et entonneraient des chants. Il demanda aux gens de prendre place derrière eux en manifestant leur piété en priant et en chantant.

— Comme vous le savez tous, la procession va s'arrêter devant la maison de monsieur et madame Meilleur.

— De « p'tit père » et « ma douce », se moqua Xavier à mi-voix.

— Chut ! fit sa mère en lui adressant un regard sévère.

Catherine tapa légèrement sur le bras de son fiancé pour faire bonne mesure.

— Monsieur le curé va déposer l'ostensoir sur le reposoir, poursuivit le président, faire quelques prières et nous remonterons la côte dans le même ordre qu'on l'aura descendue.

Sur ces mots, le petit homme prit la croix que lui tendait Agénor Moreau, descendit du parvis et s'arrêta au bord de la route. Quelques instants plus tard, le prêtre, vêtu de sa chape dorée et précédé de quatre jeunes servants de messe, fit son apparition sur le parvis, en descendit les marches avec une lenteur étudiée et vint prendre place derrière le porte-croix qui se mit lentement en marche alors que la chorale paroissiale entonnait un premier hymne. La foule de fidèles suivit le mouvement en silence, couvrant toute la largeur de la route étroite. À la fin du premier chant, le prêtre commença la récitation d'une première dizaine de chapelet, imité immédiatement par les fidèles. Les voix pleines de ferveur de ses paroissiens s'entendaient de loin.

Lorsque la procession arriva en haut de la côte, Josaphat Désilets se rendit compte rapidement qu'il n'allait pas être facile de tenir l'ostensoir à bout de bras et de maintenir son équilibre sur une route profondément ravinée par les pluies incessantes des derniers jours. Toutefois, il entreprit la descente en ralentissant le pas, soucieux de la foule qui le suivait. S'il entendit des protestations murmurées dans son dos durant la pénible marche, il ne le montra pas, concentré à diriger les prières et les chants des fidèles.

Quand il parvint enfin à la petite maison blanche des Meilleur, au bas de la pente, il jeta un regard derrière lui pour constater qu'il restait la moitié de la côte à parcourir à un bon nombre de fidèles. Soulagé d'être enfin rendu au reposoir, le curé de Saint-Bernard-Abbé s'empressa de monter les deux marches conduisant à la galerie et déposa l'ostensoir sur l'autel improvisé.

Avant que tous les participants aient pris place devant la maison, face au reposoir, Josaphat Désilets eut tout le loisir de détailler celui-ci. À sa plus grande satisfaction, la nouvelle épouse d'Hormidas Meilleur était parvenue à fabriquer un reposoir magnifique avec des moyens très limités. La façade de la maison était décorée de bandes de jute blanchie. Angèle avait étalé sur l'autel improvisé sa plus belle nappe brodée sur laquelle elle avait déposé deux énormes bouquets de pivoines. De plus, pour ajouter un peu de couleur, le tout était orné de nombreux angelots découpés dans du carton peint en rose et en bleu.

Le prêtre prononça une courte homélie dans les deux langues quand il vit tous ses paroissiens rassemblés devant lui. Avant d'entreprendre le retour vers la chapelle, il n'oublia pas de féliciter Angèle et Hormidas Meilleur pour le magnifique reposoir qu'ils avaient confectionné. La plupart des gens applaudirent le couple en signe d'appréciation, ce qui eut le don de faire rougir de plaisir une Angèle qu'on ne soupçonnait pas si timide.

Puis Josaphat Désilets reprit l'ostensoir et la procession se reforma derrière lui pour la dernière étape, soit le retour à la chapelle. En fait, la montée de la côte abrupte se révéla beaucoup plus difficile, surtout pour les personnes âgées qui avaient le souffle coupé. Le célébrant le premier, tenu de porter l'ostensoir à bout de bras, n'en pouvait plus quand il parvint enfin au sommet de la pente. Il dut même s'arrêter un moment avant de poursuivre sa route pour permettre à son cœur de retrouver un rythme normal.

Enfin, le curé de Saint-Bernard-Abbé ne put dissimuler son soulagement quand il s'immobilisa sur le parvis de la chapelle pour attendre l'arrivée des fidèles qui finissaient de se regrouper devant lui. Il brandit alors une dernière fois l'ostensoir et s'engouffra dans le temple, sur les talons de ses servants de messe et du notaire Valiquette.

— C'est la première et la dernière fois qu'on fait la procession de la Fête-Dieu en bas de la côte, déclara le prêtre en retirant sa pesante chape dorée. Je pensais que j'arriverais jamais à la remonter.

— Moi aussi, je l'ai bien cru, monsieur le curé, affirma Eudore Valiquette en s'épongeant le front. Pour moi, on n'a pas fini d'entendre les plaintes des vieux de la paroisse à ce sujet-là.

— C'est bien possible.

À l'extérieur, la foule se dispersa rapidement. Avant de quitter les lieux, Donat prévint son jeune frère que le curé Désilets désirait le rencontrer avec Catherine l'après-midi même.

— J'espère qu'il va au moins nous laisser le temps de dîner, dit Xavier, agacé par cette convocation.

— Moi, je te fais juste la commission, se défendit Donat avant de faire avancer son boghei.

— Qu'est-ce que monsieur le curé peut bien leur vouloir ? demanda Bernadette, curieuse, à sa mère, assise près d'elle à l'arrière de la voiture.

— Ça te regarde pas, ma fille, la rabroua Marie.

— Qu'est-ce que monsieur le curé peut ben nous vouloir ? demanda Xavier à sa fiancée en mettant son attelage en route.

— C'est probablement pour le certificat de confession, intervint Laura Benoît assise derrière le couple.

— Blasphème ! je pensais plus pantoute à cette affaire-là, s'exclama le jeune homme.

— Comme tu peux le voir, monsieur le curé, lui, l'a pas oublié, dit en riant sa future belle-mère.

Cette possibilité sembla rassurer Xavier Beauchemin. Si ce n'était que ça, il n'y aurait pas de problème. Il n'était pourtant pas entièrement rassuré. À plusieurs reprises durant les deux dernières semaines, il avait été effleuré par l'idée que la publication des bans pouvait amener quelqu'un à rapporter au curé de la paroisse une bonne raison pour s'opposer à son mariage. À cette seule pensée, son cœur se serrait.

Il n'avait pas oublié l'accueil du prêtre lors de son passage à la sacristie, quelques semaines plus tôt, pour la publication des bans. Il avait eu droit à un véritable sermon du prêtre qui l'avait mis en garde contre un entêtement qui, selon lui, était souvent le propre des jeunes.

— As-tu bien réfléchi à ce que tu vas faire là ? lui avait demandé Josaphat Désilets, sévère.

— Oui, monsieur le curé.

— Tu sais qu'une bonne partie du monde de la paroisse va te tourner le dos parce que tu maries une fille qui a mis au monde un enfant du péché.

— Ça m'empêchera pas de vivre, avait déclaré sèchement le fils de Baptiste Beauchemin.

— Est-ce que tu te rends compte que même certains membres de ta famille accepteront pas ça ?

— Tant pis pour eux autres, s'était-il entêté. J'ai l'intention de marier quand même Catherine Benoît, que ça fasse leur affaire ou pas.

— Et t'as pas peur pour l'avenir en mariant une fille qui a pas été honnête ?

— Pantoute, monsieur le curé. Allez-vous nous marier ? avait-il fini par demander, blanc de colère, en se levant.

— J'aurai pas le choix, si personne m'apporte une bonne raison de pas le faire. C'est à ça que sert la publication des bans, mon garçon. Mais réfléchis quand même à tout ce que je viens de te dire, avait insisté le prêtre.

Un peu après deux heures, cet après-midi-là, Xavier s'arrêta chez les Benoît pour faire monter sa fiancée dans son boghei et ils parcoururent tout le rang Sainte-Ursule avant de s'arrêter près de la sacristie. Le prêtre les vit arriver et eut un rictus en s'apercevant qu'ils s'étaient déplacés sans chaperon. Il se leva et alla ouvrir la porte à ses visiteurs.

— Vous vouliez nous voir, monsieur le curé ? lui demanda Xavier, sur ses gardes et un peu remonté.

— Oui, entrez.

— Est-ce qu'il y a quelque chose qui va pas ? poursuivit le jeune homme.

— Non, tout est correct, le rassura le prêtre en repoussant ses lunettes sur son nez. Mais on a dû vous dire que, pour vous marier, vous avez besoin d'un certificat de confession émis par un prêtre dans les sept jours avant la cérémonie. Il fallait que je vous le rappelle.

Soulagé, Xavier se tourna un bref moment vers Catherine, comme pour quêter son approbation. Puis, sur un signe discret de celle-ci, il demanda au curé de Saint-Bernard-Abbé :

— Est-ce qu'on pourrait pas se confesser cet après-midi, pendant qu'on est ici, monsieur le curé ?

Josaphat Désilets n'hésita qu'un instant avant d'accepter.

— Vous pouvez aller vous préparer à la chapelle. Je vais aller vous rejoindre dans quelques minutes, leur offrit-il en leur ouvrant la porte de communication.

Quand le prêtre pénétra dans la chapelle un peu plus tard, après avoir passé un surplis et son étole, il découvrit les futurs époux, agenouillés dans des bancs différents, apparemment plongés dans leur examen de conscience. Il alla s'asseoir dans le confessionnal et attendit que l'un ou l'autre des fiancés vienne s'agenouiller dans l'isoloir.

Catherine fut la première à aller se confesser et elle céda sa place à Xavier quelques minutes plus tard. Peu après, tous les deux quittèrent la chapelle où ils ne remettraient les pieds que six jours plus tard pour se marier.

Josaphat Désilets les vit remonter en voiture en hochant la tête, persuadé que le jeune homme prenait un bien grand risque en épousant la fille de Laura Benoît.

Chapitre 26

Avant les noces

Le surlendemain, Xavier et Antonin se présentèrent chez les Benoît en début de soirée pour prendre livraison du coffre renfermant le trousseau de Catherine. Le fiancé eut alors la surprise de découvrir dans la cuisine de Laura Benoît sœur Émérentienne en train de broder un napperon.

Un peu intimidé par la vieille religieuse au visage tout ridé, le jeune homme la salua ainsi que les autres membres de la famille réunis dans la pièce. Comme à leur habitude, Cyprien et sa femme, Marie-Rose, répondirent à peine à son salut.

— Tu te souviens de sœur Émérentienne ? lui demanda sa future belle-mère. Elle est venue exprès de Montréal pour assister à vos noces.

— Vous êtes ben fine de vous être dérangée, fit Xavier.

— En plus, elle va nous donner un coup de main à cuisiner, ajouta la maîtresse de maison.

— Et ça va quand même être mangeable, crut bon de préciser la petite religieuse en riant de bon cœur.

— Je suis sûr que ça va être bon, dit Xavier. Bon, je suis venu chercher le coffre de Catherine, poursuivit-il.

— T'étais pas obligé de venir avec ton homme engagé, lui fit remarquer Laura. Cyprien aurait pu te donner un coup de main pour le transporter chez vous.

— Antonin est plus un ami de Xavier que son homme engagé, tint à faire remarquer Catherine, en adressant à l'adolescent un sourire chaleureux.

— C'est vrai ce que votre fille dit, madame Benoît. C'est presque un frère pour moi.

Le jeune homme de dix-sept ans se rengorgea.

— Et comme je suis presque un frère, il a aimé mieux me déranger que de déranger votre garçon, plaisanta l'adolescent.

— En tout cas, le coffre est encore en haut, dans la chambre de Catherine. Ce serait plus convenable qu'Antonin monte avec Cyprien pour le descendre, précisa Laura avec la nette approbation de sa cousine.

Son fils se leva apparemment à contrecœur et monta lourdement à l'étage, suivi de près par Antonin. Les deux hommes descendirent le coffre avec une certaine difficulté tant il semblait lourd.

— Il a bien l'air pesant, ce coffre-là, fit la religieuse.

— Pour moi, ma sœur, Catherine a mis des pierres au fond pour qu'on soit certains qu'il y a quelque chose dedans, dit Antonin à mi-voix à sœur Émérentienne.

— Toi, mon haïssable, j'ai dans l'idée qu'il va falloir que je te dompte, dit Catherine en riant.

Ce rire fit plaisir à Xavier qui se chargea de transporter le coffre avec son homme engagé après avoir souhaité une bonne soirée aux Benoît.

Tout en regagnant sa maison, le jeune homme réalisa à quel point sa fiancée était triste et tendue à l'approche de leur mariage. Elle ne riait plus et souriait de moins en moins. Le mois précédent, la couleur de sa robe de mariée l'avait longuement préoccupée. Elle était tellement tiraillée à ce sujet qu'elle avait fini par le consulter.

— Qu'est-ce que les gens vont dire si je me marie en blanc? lui avait-elle demandé, angoissée.

— En quoi ça les regarde? avait-il répliqué.

— Ils sont tous au courant de…

— Pantoute, avait-il tranché. Ils savent rien et, en plus, c'est pas de leurs affaires. C'est moi que tu maries et je veux que tu portes une robe blanche.

Cette décision avait semblé la rassurer durant quelques jours. Puis elle avait commencé à s'en faire avec la réaction de certains membres de sa famille lors des noces.

— Inquiète-toi pas pour ça, l'avait-il prévenue sèchement. Chez nous, ils savent se tenir. Tu sais déjà que tu peux compter sur Camille et Emma. Ma mère t'haït pas non plus, même si elle le montre pas encore. Pour les autres, j'en fais mon affaire.

Et voilà que l'arrivée de sœur Émérentienne semblait avoir tout remis en question. À son entrée dans la maison, il avait tout de suite remarqué l'humeur sombre de sa fiancée. Serait-ce que celle-ci lui aurait apporté de mauvaises nouvelles au sujet de la petite ? L'enfant avait-elle été adoptée ? Était-elle malade ?

Tout en déposant le coffre au pied de son lit, Xavier se promit de s'arrêter quelques minutes chez sa promise le lendemain soir pour s'informer de ce qui la tracassait.

❧

Chez les Beauchemin du rang Saint-Jean, les femmes s'étaient réunies ce soir-là pour discuter de la toilette à porter pour le mariage le samedi suivant. Camille était venue rejoindre sa mère, ses sœurs et sa belle-sœur en compagnie d'Ann qu'elle se plaisait à traiter de plus en plus en adulte depuis qu'elle avait eu ses quatorze ans, le 28 mars précédent. Pour une rare fois, Liam avait accepté de rendre visite à sa parenté.

— Il faut surtout pas oublier qu'on est en deuil, tint à préciser Marie.

— Je veux bien le croire, m'man, déclara sa fille aînée, mais on peut au moins rafraîchir nos chapeaux et ajouter quelque chose à nos robes noires.

— C'est vrai ce qu'elle dit, approuva Bernadette, sinon on va toutes avoir l'air d'une bande de corneilles à ce mariage-là.

— Rien nous empêche d'ajouter un petit collet de dentelle, par exemple, madame Beauchemin, suggéra Eugénie. Je pense pas que ce serait trahir notre deuil.

— À part ça, est-ce que quelqu'un sait de quelle couleur va être la robe de la mariée? chuchota Bernadette de manière à ne pas être entendue par Xavier en train de veiller avec Donat, Rémi et Liam sur la galerie.

— Je vois pas pourquoi tu poses cette question-là, Bedette, lui reprocha Emma sur le même ton. Catherine Benoît a bien le droit de choisir la couleur de robe qu'elle voudra. Elle, elle est pas en deuil. D'après moi, sa robe devrait être blanche.

Les femmes présentes dans la pièce se regardèrent. Il était évident que toutes pensaient à la même chose. Finalement, on s'entendit pour orner de nouveaux rubans de couleur le chapeau du dimanche et pour ajouter un peu de dentelle ou des colifichets à sa robe pour l'occasion.

Pendant ce temps, les discussions allaient bon train sur la galerie. Après avoir parlé du retour de Hubert qui était attendu de Dunham le lendemain, on discuta de la tournée des foyers de Saint-Bernard-Abbé que Rémi et Donat allaient terminer en compagnie d'Anatole Blanchette la veille du mariage.

— Il y a pas moyen de savoir ce que ça va donner, déclara le mari d'Emma. Blanchette est un bon diable, mais je trouve qu'il a pas ben le tour de parler au monde.

— On a tout de même l'avantage d'être passés les premiers dans la plupart des maisons, lui fit remarquer son jeune beau-frère. Là, il nous reste juste à aller voir une demi-douzaine d'habitants du rang Saint-Paul.

— Et on a pu voir notre nouveau marié, dit Rémi en riant.

— Quel nouveau marié ? demanda Liam en intervenant pour une rare fois dans la conversation.

— Pas moi, en tout cas, se défendit en riant Xavier, je le suis pas encore.

— T'es ben chanceux, laissa tomber son beau-frère.

Ce commentaire créa un certain froid et Rémi reprit la parole pour parler du couple formé par Angèle Cloutier et Hormidas Meilleur.

— Je voulais parler du père Meilleur, expliqua-t-il à Liam et Xavier. J'en reviens pas encore ! dit le mari d'Emma avec un petit rire. J'aurais jamais cru qu'il parviendrait à dompter la veuve. Elle doit peser au moins cinquante livres de plus que lui et elle est plus grande d'au moins six pouces.

— S'il lui en prenait l'envie, elle pourrait te l'aplatir comme une crêpe n'importe quand, intervint Xavier. On le sait tous qu'elle est solide comme un homme et qu'il y a pas grand-chose qui lui fait peur.

— C'est vrai ce que tu dis là, affirma Donat, mais depuis son mariage, elle est plus reconnaissable. Aussitôt que son « p'tit père » parle, elle devient douce comme un agneau du printemps.

— Blasphème ! Il va falloir que je lui demande des conseils avant samedi, plaisanta Xavier.

— Reste à savoir si ça va durer ben longtemps, cette affaire-là, dit Liam en se levant pour faire savoir à sa femme et à sa fille qu'il était temps de rentrer.

Rémi consulta alors sa montre de gousset et décida, lui aussi, que le moment était venu de se retirer. Après le départ des visiteurs, Donat alla faire la tournée des bâtiments. De retour à la maison quelques minutes plus tard, il éteignit son fanal. Les trois femmes de la maison l'attendaient pour la prière en commun.

— Je sais pas ce que Liam Connolly a de travers depuis une couple de semaines, dit-il à haute voix sans s'adresser à quelqu'un en particulier, mais on dirait qu'il est pas content pantoute d'être marié.

— Pourquoi tu dis ça ? lui demanda sa mère, l'air sévère.

— Je le sais pas. Juste sa façon de parler contre le mariage. Encore à soir, il a dit qu'il trouvait ben chanceux ceux qui l'étaient pas.

— Lui, s'il se replace pas bien vite, il va avoir affaire à moi, déclara la veuve sur un ton menaçant. Camille lui élève ses quatre enfants. Elle entretient la maison et leur linge. Elle cuisine et donne un coup de main sur la terre quand il en a besoin. Toute la famille a jamais eu l'air si propre ! En plus, il trouve le moyen de critiquer ! Là, ça va faire ! Si jamais je l'entends, il va le regretter.

Sur ces fortes paroles, Marie s'agenouilla, imitée par les siens. Elle récita la longue prière du soir habituelle.

❧

La veille du mariage, le ciel était nuageux, mais la température était plutôt douce. À son lever, Camille avait éprouvé les nausées matinales coutumières depuis le début de sa grossesse. À son retour dans la cuisine, la jeune femme s'était longuement regardée dans le petit miroir suspendu près de l'armoire. À son avis, rien ne paraissait encore de son état de future mère.

Elle prépara le déjeuner avec Ann pendant que les garçons se chargeaient de soigner les animaux avec leur père. Après le repas, elle laissa les soins du ménage du vendredi à Ann pour aller désherber son jardin et ses plates-bandes avec Rose. Au début de l'après-midi, elle examina attentivement les vêtements des siens pour s'assurer que chacun serait correctement habillé au mariage de son frère.

— Ça en fait tout un aria pour des noces, laissa tomber Liam, l'air mécontent, en l'apercevant en train d'examiner un pantalon.

Le cultivateur, occupé dans le poulailler, venait d'entrer dans la maison pour y boire un verre d'eau.

— J'ai pas envie que les enfants fassent rire d'eux autres, se borna à répliquer sa femme.

— En attendant, ce serait peut-être une bonne idée que tu lâches le linge pour t'occuper des fraises qui sont en train de pourrir dans le champ, ajouta-t-il sur un ton revêche.

— Je suis allée voir avant-hier, et elles étaient pas prêtes.

— Ben là, elles le sont.

— Les garçons pourraient peut-être…

— J'ai besoin d'eux autres. Ils viennent travailler avec moi pour m'aider à remplacer une partie du plancher du poulailler, affirma-t-il sèchement.

Il sortit sur ces mots en laissant claquer la porte moustiquaire derrière lui. Camille poussa un soupir d'exaspération et déposa quelques vêtements sur une chaise.

— Venez, les filles, on va aller ramasser des fraises, dit-elle à Ann et à Rose. Le repassage, on pourra toujours le faire après le souper.

— Qu'est-ce qu'on va faire pour le souper ? lui demanda Ann.

— On va manger de la galette de sarrasin. La pâte est déjà prête. On n'aura qu'à faire cuire les galettes en revenant.

Quelques minutes plus tard, Camille et ses filles, armées de petits seaux, pénétrèrent dans le carré de fraises aménagé derrière la grange. C'était une mauvaise année pour les fraises à cause de la pluie et du faible ensoleillement des dernières semaines. Avec plusieurs jours de retard, les petits fruits avaient fini par rougir, mais la récolte était loin des attentes.

— Elles ont pas grand goût, se plaignit Ann après avoir mangé une grosse fraise. Je trouve qu'elles goûtent l'eau.

— Il a trop mouillé, laissa tomber Camille, penchée au-dessus d'un plant.

Pendant deux bonnes heures, Camille et ses filles ramassèrent des fraises. À un certain moment, la mère adoptive se releva en se massant les reins pour déclarer :

— Là, on arrête. Ça sert à rien de continuer, ce qui reste est pas mûr.

Elles rentrèrent toutes les trois à la maison et se mirent à équeuter les fruits cueillis. Le poêle fut allumé en vue du souper et la maîtresse de maison en profita pour préparer ses premières confitures de la saison avec les fraises équeutées et lavées. Quand Liam rentra avec ses fils, il demanda à sa femme :

— As-tu vu mon oncle ? Son cheval est pas dans le clos.

— Il est allé chez le notaire Valiquette. Inquiète-toi pas, il va être là pour souper. Je me souviens pas l'avoir vu manquer un repas.

— C'est ben le moins, il paie pour ça, laissa-t-il tomber d'une voix désagréable.

Cette remarque ne fit que rappeler à Camille à quel point Paddy Connolly demeurait un pensionnaire plutôt récalcitrant à acquitter sa pension. Malgré la leçon qu'elle lui avait donnée deux semaines auparavant, elle était toujours obligée de lui rappeler à plusieurs reprises qu'on était le vendredi… Le retraité avait toujours une bonne raison pour remettre à plus tard le paiement. La semaine précédente, exaspérée, elle avait fini par dire à l'oncle de son mari :

— Savez-vous, mon oncle, que je pense pas que le propriétaire d'un hôtel vous courrait après comme je suis obligée de le faire chaque semaine ?

— Certain, avait affirmé avec morgue l'Irlandais, mais il faut dire que je suis pas à l'hôtel, mais chez mon neveu.

Si elle n'avait pas autant craint une violente réaction de son mari, elle aurait mis depuis longtemps toutes les affaires du retraité sur la galerie en le priant d'aller se faire héberger ailleurs.

— Ann, mets une assiettée de galettes dans le réchaud pour l'oncle de ton père, ordonna Camille. Il mangera quand il arrivera. Nous autres, on n'a pas le temps de l'attendre à soir. Il y a le repassage à faire et il faut que chacun prenne un bain.

— Ah non, Camille! s'écrièrent Duncan et Patrick à l'unisson.

— Oh oui! répliqua-t-elle sur le même ton. Vous commencez à sentir le putois et vous avez besoin de vous laver les cheveux. Avant de t'asseoir à table, Patrick, tu vas aller me chercher de l'eau au puits. On va la faire chauffer pendant le souper.

Paddy ne parut pas à la maison durant le repas du soir. Camille servit des fraises avec un peu de crème pour le dessert. Dès que tous furent rassasiés, Patrick fut envoyé se laver pendant qu'Ann et sa jeune sœur aidaient à ranger la cuisine.

— Arrange-toi pour pas mettre de l'eau partout sur le plancher, le prévint sa mère. Et lave-toi bien, partout. Duncan, tu iras te laver après lui, ordonna-t-elle. En attendant, tu peux aller nettoyer tes souliers pour demain.

— Camille, je vais commencer le repassage pendant que tu raccommodes la robe de Rose, proposa Ann dès que la dernière pièce de vaisselle eut été lavé.

Sans plus attendre, l'adolescente sortit le fer à repasser et le déposa sur le poêle pour le faire chauffer avant d'aller chercher la vieille planche à repasser qu'elle installa tout près.

Liam avait quitté la cuisine pour la galerie après le repas et il se berçait tranquillement en regardant les eaux de la rivière qui coulaient paresseusement, en face de chez lui, au bout du champ, de l'autre côté de la route.

— Ah non! s'écria soudainement Ann.

L'exclamation de l'adolescente fit sursauter sa mère adoptive qui venait de s'asseoir sur la galerie dans l'intention de recoudre l'ourlet de la robe que Rose devait porter le lendemain.

— Qu'est-ce qu'il y a? demanda-t-elle en se levant déjà pour s'approcher de la porte moustiquaire. T'es-tu brûlée sur le fer?

— Non, j'ai brûlé une chemise, avoua la jeune fille tout énervée.

Camille ouvrit la porte et ne l'entendit pas se refermer derrière elle pour la bonne raison que son mari la suivait de près.

— Quelle chemise? demanda Camille en s'approchant.

— Celle de p'pa, dit nerveusement Ann en lui montrant la trace roussie du fer sur une manche. J'ai pas fait exprès…

— Maudite sans-dessein! hurla son père en s'avançant, fou de rage et la main levée, prêt à frapper sa fille.

La jeune fille recula peureusement de quelques pas, heurtant de la hanche la chaise sur laquelle étaient déposés les vêtements à repasser. Elle se mit à pleurer, attendant les premiers coups. Duncan, debout à l'autre extrémité de la cuisine, avait nerveusement lâché ses souliers qu'il venait d'entreprendre de nettoyer.

— Whow, Liam Connolly! s'interposa Camille en se campant devant lui, les traits durcis par la fureur.

— Toi, tu t'enlèves de mon chemin ou c'est toi qui vas en recevoir une, la menaça-t-il.

— Ah ben, je voudrais bien voir ça! s'écria-t-elle, les dents serrées, en le repoussant du plat de la main. Essaye donc pour voir!

Ce disant, elle lui empoigna durement le bras levé et, sans effort apparent, l'obligea à le baisser. Pour la première fois, Liam Connolly sembla réaliser que sa femme était dotée d'une force peu commune, probablement héritée de son père, et qu'elle n'hésiterait pas à l'utiliser pour se défendre ou pour protéger l'un des enfants.

— Tu m'empêcheras pas de dompter mes enfants! cria-t-il.

— Je t'ai déjà répété souvent que des enfants sont pas des chiens qu'on traite à coups de pied et à coups de poing. Va donc t'asseoir sur la galerie pour retrouver tes sangs, lui conseilla-t-elle sèchement.

— Elle vient de gâcher ma chemise, plaida-t-il. Tu penses tout de même pas que je vais laisser les enfants gaspiller mes affaires!

— C'est un accident. Elle a pas fait exprès. Le mal est fait, on va réparer les dégâts. Calme-toi donc un peu.

Fou de rage, il tourna les talons et retourna s'asseoir sur la galerie en l'invectivant. Camille prit quelques secondes pour retrouver son calme. Ann et Duncan semblèrent la regarder avec de nouveaux yeux. Ils réalisaient soudain que leur mère adoptive n'avait rien de commun avec leur défunte mère qui ne s'était jamais opposée à leur père quand il les frappait. Ils venaient de constater, stupéfaits, que leur père ne parviendrait pas à faire peur ni à faire reculer leur amie quand il se laissait emporter par l'une de ses colères imprévisibles.

— Comment t'as fait ton compte? demanda Camille d'une voix calme à l'adolescente, qui retrouvait peu à peu ses couleurs.

— Je sais pas ce qui est arrivé, reconnut celle-ci. La moitié du fer était trop chaude et l'autre moitié était correcte.

— Ça peut arriver, la consola sa mère adoptive. Arrête de pleurer pour rien. Donne-moi la chemise, elle est brûlée juste en dessous de la manche. Je vais la réparer pendant que tu finis le repassage. Mais fais attention au fer.

La jeune mère choisit de ne pas retourner prendre place aux côtés de son mari à l'extérieur. Elle s'installa à la table pour réparer les dommages causés à la chemise de son mari.

Quelques minutes plus tard, Paddy Connolly entra dans la cour de la ferme et immobilisa son boghei devant la galerie un court moment, le temps de demander que l'un de ses petits-neveux vienne dételer sa bête. La maîtresse de maison devança son mari qui s'apprêtait à répondre à son oncle.

— Ils iraient bien, mon oncle, lui dit-elle à travers la porte moustiquaire, mais ils sont tous les deux en train de se laver.

— C'est que j'ai pas encore soupé, moi, et il est ben près de huit heures, plaida le petit homme bedonnant.

— C'est correct, mon oncle, allez manger, dit Liam sur un ton contrarié. Je vais m'occuper de votre cheval.

Paddy Connolly descendit de voiture, tendit les guides à son neveu et entra dans la cuisine d'été, son éternel journal roulé sous le bras.

— Qu'est-ce qu'il y a de bon à manger ? demanda-t-il, tout content de ne pas avoir à dételer sa bête.

— Je vais vous dire ça, mon oncle, en échange de votre pension de la semaine, répondit Camille en souriant.

— Dis-moi pas qu'on est encore vendredi ? demanda le pensionnaire avec une évidente mauvaise foi.

— Il paraît que ça revient tous les sept jours, mon oncle, lui fit remarquer avec humour sa nièce par alliance.

— Maudit que la vie coûte cher ! s'exclama Paddy en fouillant dans l'une de ses poches de pantalon pour en extraire difficilement un dollar et demi qu'il laissa tomber sur la table.

— À qui le dites-vous, mon oncle, fit Camille en prenant l'argent et en le déposant dans la poche de son tablier. Assoyez-vous, je vous sers tout de suite.

Elle prit l'assiette laissée sur la table et alla la remplir de galettes laissées au fourneau. À la vue du contenu de son assiette, l'oncle de Liam esquissa une grimace, mais n'osa rien dire. C'était le plat servi habituellement chez son neveu le vendredi soir. Par contre, les fraises trempant dans de la crème fraîche semblèrent lui plaire.

Au moment où il finissait son dessert, Paddy dit à la maîtresse de maison assise en face de lui, occupée à son travail de raccommodage :

— J'ai rencontré ton frère. C'est ça qui m'a retardé.

— Donat ?

— Non, l'autre, Hubert.

— Tiens ! Il est revenu de Dunham.

— Ben oui. J'étais au magasin général quand il s'est arrêté pour saluer les Dionne.

Camille entendit Liam rapprocher sa chaise berçante de la porte moustiquaire. Sans le faire voir, il voulait entendre ce que racontait son oncle.

— Je te dis qu'il a l'air d'aimer ce qu'il fait, celui-là. Si je me fie à ce qu'il a raconté à Télesphore Dionne, il paraît qu'il est presque prêt à faire du bon fromage. Selon lui, le cousin de Dionne lui aurait dit que dans un mois ou deux, il aurait fini son apprentissage.

— Je suis bien contente pour lui.

— Je me suis laissé dire que c'est un ancien frère ? demanda Paddy, curieux.

— Oui, mais il a jamais prononcé ses vœux. Là, il a décidé de rester avec nous autres, affirma Camille.

— Je commence à comprendre pourquoi la petite Dionne a l'air si intéressée par ton frère. Elle l'a pas lâché des yeux tout le temps qu'il a été au magasin. Il paraît même qu'il lui a demandé de l'accompagner aux noces de ton autre frère, demain.

— Puis ?

— Elle a dit oui tout de suite, mais j'ai eu l'impression que son père et sa mère avaient pas l'air trop contents qu'elle ait accepté son invitation. As-tu une idée pourquoi, toi ?

— Je le sais pas, mon oncle, mentit Camille.

Elle avait tout de suite deviné que Télesphore et Alexandrine Dionne ne tenaient pas beaucoup à voir leur

Angélique assister au mariage d'une fille perdue comme Catherine Benoît.

◆

En cette veille de son mariage, Laura Benoît et sœur Émérentienne cherchaient à calmer l'angoisse qui semblait avoir envahi Catherine.

— T'as pas à t'inquiéter, tout va être prêt à temps, lui dit la petite religieuse avec un sourire rassurant. Ton frère a fini d'installer la table et les bancs dehors et on va avoir bien assez de place pour asseoir tout le monde demain midi.

Depuis le début de la semaine, Laura Benoît n'avait pas cessé de pousser dans le dos son fils Cyprien et sa femme pour qu'ils participent activement aux préparatifs de la noce. Devant le manque de bonne volonté évident du couple, sœur Émérentienne avait même dû élever la voix et les traiter de « sans-cœurs » pour les inciter à faire leur part.

Maintenant, la maison reluisait de propreté et la nourriture était prête. Les femmes de la maison avaient fait cuire trois grosses poules qu'elles avaient l'intention de servir dans une sauce blanche et elles avaient cuisiné huit tartes aux raisins et à la mélasse, en plus d'une soupe aux pois très nourrissante. Sœur Émérentienne avait même trouvé le temps de cuisiner deux recettes de bonbons aux patates pour sucrer le bec des invités. Les cruchons de vin de cerise et de bagosse étaient déjà rangés sur l'armoire.

— Vous pouvez pas savoir comment j'ai hâte que tout ça soit passé, finit par déclarer la fiancée d'une voix éteinte en séchant sa longue chevelure blonde qu'elle venait de laver.

— Il faut pas que cette journée-là passe trop vite, fit sa mère, réprobatrice. C'est supposé être la plus belle journée de ta vie. Tu dois en profiter… À moins que tu penses pas aimer assez Xavier Beauchemin, suggéra-t-elle en fixant sa fille.

Marie-Rose, debout un peu à l'écart, attendait la réponse qu'allait donner sa belle-sœur.

— C'est pas ça, m'man. C'est le reste qui m'énerve. Le monde qui vont venir fouiner pour…

— Dis-toi qu'ils auront plus rien à dire une fois que tu seras passée devant monsieur le curé, ma fille, intervint sœur Émérentienne. Le passé, c'est le passé. Pense seulement à toutes les belles années qui t'attendent avec le garçon que t'as choisi.

— C'est vrai, ma sœur, reconnut la jeune fille en lui adressant un sourire timide.

— Maintenant, si tu veux bien, reprit sa mère, tu vas aller accrocher ton chapelet sur la corde à linge pour être certaine qu'il va faire beau demain et après, tu devrais aller te coucher, pour être belle demain matin.

Catherine ne discuta pas. La journée avait été longue et fatigante. Après avoir suspendu son chapelet à la corde à linge, elle alluma une lampe et alla se réfugier dans sa petite chambre, à l'étage. Le soleil était en train de se coucher en ce dernier vendredi de juin. Elle resta longtemps debout devant sa fenêtre à regarder le paysage qu'elle ne verrait probablement plus jamais sous cet angle. Puis elle se secoua et entreprit de passer sa robe de nuit tout en se disant que son départ allait alléger l'atmosphère de la maison et, malheureusement, laisser les coudées franches à son frère et à sa femme. Elle espérait que sa mère n'aurait pas trop à souffrir de se retrouver seule face à ce couple peu aimable.

Chapitre 27

Le mariage

L'un des vœux de Catherine fut au moins exaucé. Lorsque sœur Émérentienne vint la tirer du sommeil le lendemain matin, la jeune fille se réveilla dans une chambre inondée par un soleil éblouissant.

— Debout, la paresseuse ! lui ordonna la petite religieuse avec bonne humeur. Je t'ai monté de l'eau chaude. Fais ta toilette et dépêche-toi de descendre pour que ta mère ait le temps de te coiffer avant de mettre ta robe.

Catherine remercia la cousine de sa mère, s'étira un bref moment et se leva pour procéder à sa toilette. Avant de quitter sa chambre, elle prit le temps de faire son lit et d'étaler la toilette de jeune mariée qu'elle endosserait un peu plus tard. Elle regarda ensuite par la fenêtre en direction de la maison qui allait devenir la sienne dans quelques heures. S'il n'y avait pas eu encore ce mince rideau d'arbres qui séparait la terre de Xavier de celle de sa mère, elle aurait vu facilement son futur foyer.

À son entrée dans la cuisine, elle découvrit sa mère déjà prête et Marie-Rose en train d'essayer de fermer le col de la chemise de son mari.

— Tu m'étouffes, baptême, lui reprocha Cyprien avec sa mauvaise humeur habituelle.

— C'est pas de ma faute, t'as encore engraissé, rétorqua la petite femme.

La future mariée prit place sur un banc devant sa mère qui lui faisait signe de s'asseoir. Laura se mit à brosser les longs cheveux blonds bouclés de sa fille avant de les rassembler dans une toque retenue par un ruban blanc.

— Je trouve que c'est faire ben des embarras pour pas grand-chose, laissa tomber Cyprien que son col enfin fermé étouffait à moitié.

— C'est probablement ce que les parents de ta femme ont dû se dire le matin de vos noces, laissa tomber sœur Émérentienne.

— Il reste encore une bonne heure et demie avant de partir pour la chapelle, intervint Laura Benoît. T'as le temps d'aller voir si le boghei est bien propre et d'atteler pendant que ta sœur va finir de s'habiller. Nous autres, on va voir si tout est paré pour recevoir le monde après le mariage.

La veille, il avait été décidé que la religieuse allait demeurer à la maison pour surveiller la cuisson de la nourriture et procéder aux derniers préparatifs pendant la cérémonie. La mariée aurait préféré que sœur Émérentienne, à qui elle devait tant, assiste à son mariage, mais elle n'ignorait pas que sa mère ne pouvait faire appel à aucune voisine ou à une autre parente pour se charger de cette tâche.

Tout en endossant la petite robe blanche toute simple ornée d'une petite dentelle à l'encolure et aux poignets, la future madame Xavier Beauchemin redoutait plus que jamais de se faire insulter à son arrivée ou à sa sortie de l'église par une ou des commères qui ne lui reconnaîtraient pas le droit de se marier en blanc. Avant de descendre rejoindre sa famille qui attendait dans la cuisine, elle se maquilla légèrement avec de la poudre de riz devant le petit miroir fixé au mur au-dessus de l'unique bureau de la pièce. Le miroir lui renvoya l'image d'une mince jeune femme blonde qui avait eu vingt et un ans au mois de février précédent. Son visage aux hautes pommettes était éclairé par deux grands yeux noisette un peu assombris par l'inquiétude.

— Est-ce que j'ai raison de me marier ? se demanda-t-elle à mi-voix.

Cette question mettait moins en doute son amour pour Xavier que son propre droit au bonheur.

Il était maintenant trop tard pour reculer. Elle secoua doucement la tête et mit son missel et son chapelet dans sa bourse avant d'aller rejoindre les siens qui étaient prêts à partir.

Avant de quitter la maison, la jeune fille posa un geste inhabituel. La tradition voulait qu'une fille demande à son père de la bénir le matin de son mariage, au moment de quitter définitivement le toit familial. Or, Léopold Benoît était décédé. Toutefois, à la plus grande surprise de Laura, sa fille vint s'agenouiller devant elle pour lui demander sa bénédiction. Émue, sœur Émérentienne cessa son va-et-vient dans la pièce pour regarder la scène. Marie-Rose elle-même eut un hochement de la tête en signe d'approbation.

Après une courte hésitation, la mère bénit sa fille avant de l'embrasser sur les deux joues en lui murmurant qu'elle lui souhaitait beaucoup de bonheur.

Quand Cyprien prit la route, transportant sa mère, sa femme et sa sœur, Xavier et Donat, son témoin, l'avaient devancé depuis près de vingt minutes. Au début de la matinée, Antonin avait attelé le boghei de son patron et ami et avait pris la direction du rang Saint-Jean pour aider au transport des membres de la famille Beauchemin. Pour leur part, les Lafond avaient carrément refusé l'offre de Camille qui avait proposé qu'Ann aille garder les enfants durant la cérémonie.

— J'ai demandé à la petite voisine de venir et elle va garder aussi Alexis, expliqua Emma à sa sœur. Il y a pas de raison que ta fille manque le mariage.

Un peu avant neuf heures trente, il n'y avait que trois ou quatre bogheis stationnés près de la chapelle. En descendant de voiture, Xavier et Donat découvrirent Anselme Camirand et leur tante Françoise en grande conversation avec leur oncle Armand et sa femme au milieu d'une douzaine de curieux rassemblés au bas du parvis.

— Comment ça se fait que vous vous êtes pas arrêtés à la maison ? s'étonna Donat après avoir serré la main de ses deux oncles.

— Parce qu'on était un peu juste dans le temps, expliqua l'oncle Anselme, le visage tout à fait sérieux. Tu sauras, mon jeune, que quand t'es pris avec une vieille femme, t'es mieux de lui donner ben des heures pour qu'elle ait le temps de se rendre présentable, sinon t'es toujours en retard partout.

— Vieux haïssable ! se borna à laisser tomber sa femme.

— On se revoit tout à l'heure, déclara Xavier en faisant signe à son témoin qu'il était temps d'entrer dans la chapelle.

Xavier retira son chapeau melon noir et pénétra dans le temple où quelques personnes avaient déjà pris place. Suivi par Donat et affichant un aplomb qu'il était bien loin d'éprouver, il parcourut l'allée centrale. Après une courte hésitation, il s'assit sur l'une des deux chaises placées face à la sainte table.

À l'extérieur, les voitures se mirent à arriver. Antonin déposa Bernadette, sa mère et Eugénie devant le parvis alors que Rémi s'arrêtait un peu plus loin pour revenir à la chapelle en compagnie de sa femme et de Hubert, tout fier de s'exhiber avec Angélique Dionne à son bras. Paddy Connolly les suivit de près avec ses petits-neveux, Liam et Camille ayant insisté pour que leurs deux filles soient assises dans leur voiture.

Camille se serait bien passée de la présence de l'oncle de son mari aux noces de son frère, mais Catherine avait tenu à lui faire plaisir ainsi qu'à Liam en l'invitant.

Quand Cyprien Benoît vint immobiliser sa voiture au pied des marches du parvis pour permettre aux deux femmes qu'il transportait de descendre, il y eut des murmures dans la petite foule rassemblée à la porte de la chapelle. Catherine eut un sourire un peu craintif et regarda à peine les quelques étrangers qui se tenaient à l'écart des membres de la famille Beauchemin qui avaient attendu son arrivée. Agénor Moreau, serviable, proposa au conducteur de lui laisser les guides et d'accompagner immédiatement sa sœur à l'intérieur.

Le jeune cultivateur, mal à l'aise dans ses vêtements du dimanche trop étroits, donna le bras à sa sœur et tous les deux pénétrèrent dans la chapelle, suivis de Marie-Rose et Laura Benoît. Les gens encore à l'extérieur s'empressèrent alors d'entrer et de prendre place dans les bancs.

Catherine vint s'asseoir à la gauche de Xavier devant la sainte table. Le regard admiratif de son fiancé la rassura quelque peu et la fit sourire. Derrière les deux futurs mariés, il y avait une nette disproportion entre les deux familles.

La famille Benoît n'occupait que deux bancs. Seuls l'oncle Ulric et sa femme se tenaient derrière Laura, son fils et sa bru. Cela contrastait étrangement avec les nombreux Beauchemin massés du côté droit de la chapelle.

Peu après, le curé Désilets fit son entrée dans le chœur pour célébrer le mariage du jeune couple. Une fois son calice déposé sur l'autel, le célébrant s'avança vers les futurs mariés et fit signe à leurs témoins de s'approcher. Il interrogea d'abord brièvement les futurs mariés, non sans leur avoir rappelé le caractère sacré du mariage. Il les bénit ainsi que les anneaux avant de les déclarer officiellement unis par les liens du mariage. Finalement, il retourna à l'autel pour la célébration de la messe.

Lors de son bref sermon, le prêtre tint à souligner les devoirs que les époux avaient l'un envers l'autre et le caractère indissoluble du mariage.

— Aux yeux de Dieu, vous ne faites plus qu'un, conclut-il avec une certaine grandiloquence. Vous avez le devoir d'aimer l'autre plus que vous-même et, surtout, d'élever vos enfants dans la foi chrétienne, ajouta-t-il.

Sur ces mots. il retourna à l'autel pour poursuivre la célébration du saint sacrifice.

Céleste Comtois, installée au clavecin dans le jubé, joua quelques morceaux durant la cérémonie. Quand le curé Désilets bénit l'assistance à la fin de la messe, les nouveaux époux empruntèrent l'allée centrale pour quitter la chapelle, suivis par leurs invités apparemment d'excellente humeur. Tous ces gens semblaient soudainement pressés de s'amuser et de se restaurer.

Antonin s'était empressé d'avancer le boghei pour le stationner devant le parvis et permettre aux jeunes mariés d'y prendre place dès leur sortie de la chapelle. L'ami de Xavier attendit que tout le monde ait eu le temps de monter à bord de sa voiture pour se mettre lentement en route vers la ferme de Laura Benoît, dans le rang Sainte-Ursule. Le convoi formé de près d'une dizaine de voitures soulevait un petit nuage de poussière sur la route.

Assise aux côtés de son nouveau mari sur la banquette arrière du boghei, Catherine était rayonnante de fierté. Tout s'était bien déroulé. Personne de la paroisse n'avait osé venir les chahuter ou la montrer du doigt à son entrée ou à sa sortie de la chapelle, ce dont elle avait tellement eu peur. Elle se lova dans les bras de Xavier, profitant au maximum de ce moment de pur bonheur.

À l'arrivée des invités chez les Benoît, la cour de la ferme fut vite encombrée par toutes ces voitures et Cyprien eut fort à faire pour que les cochers les stationnent loin des deux grandes tables installées sous les arbres, près de la maison. Rémi fut le seul à ne pas dételer sa bête. Après avoir laissé descendre de voiture Angélique Dionne et Hubert, il fit demi-tour en compagnie de sa femme pour aller chercher les enfants parce que Catherine avait beaucoup insisté pour qu'ils participent à la fête.

Laura Benoît avait déjà pris place sur la galerie aux côtés des nouveaux mariés pour remercier chacun des invités d'être venu aux noces. Chaque couple avait apporté un cadeau qui était déposé sur une table improvisée sur la galerie. Xavier et Catherine reçurent surtout des pièces tissées : des draps, des nappes, des linges à vaisselle, des taies d'oreiller et des serviettes. Armand et Amanda Beauchemin, pour leur part, s'étaient distingués en offrant un ensemble de vaisselle en pierre et Anselme Benoît et sa femme avaient eu la bonne idée et les moyens financiers de donner quatre belles marmites et une poêle.

À la demande de sœur Émérentienne, Marie-Rose se mit à offrir du vin de cerise aux femmes pendant que son mari distribuait sans entrain de la bagosse aux hommes rassemblés près des voitures.

— Bondance que ce couple-là a l'air bête, ne put s'empêcher de murmurer Camille à sa mère, debout près d'elle.

— Elle, je sais pas si elle a de la misère à digérer quelque chose, fit Marie à voix basse, mais on dirait que le Cyprien vient de se faire arracher une dent. Je te dis que ton frère vient d'entrer dans une drôle de famille, ma fille.

— En tout cas, m'man, je trouve que la mère de Catherine fait pitié, reprit la jeune femme. Elle a l'air à plus savoir où donner de la tête. Je vais aller lui donner un coup de main en dedans. Je viens de la voir entrer dans la maison.

— J'y vais avec toi, décida Marie.

Un peu en retrait, Bernadette s'ennuyait ferme. Elle n'avait personne à qui parler. Hubert et Angélique se tenaient à l'écart et semblaient échanger des secrets. Un peu plus loin, la tante Amanda avait entrepris de raconter ses récentes maladies à Catherine et à sœur Émérentienne. Au retour d'Emma, elle ne trouva rien de mieux à faire que d'aller aider Ann à s'occuper des enfants.

Paddy Connolly était parvenu à monopoliser l'attention d'un bon nombre d'hommes en leur apprenant que, d'après le journal, Macdonald avait annoncé des élections générales du 20 juillet au 12 octobre et que George-Étienne Cartier, un homme que tous admiraient, allait probablement se présenter dans un quartier de Montréal. Comme tous les hommes présents étaient d'allégeance conservatrice, il n'y eut pas de dispute. On s'interrogea seulement sur le nombre de députés que le premier ministre allait parvenir à faire élire.

— À la campagne, je pense pas qu'il va y avoir de problème, déclara Anselme Benoît, en parlant assez fort pour couvrir la voix de Paddy. Mais en ville, je suis pas si sûr que les Bleus vont se faire élire facilement.

— En tout cas, ce serait pas juste, dit Paddy avec une certaine hauteur. Le gouvernement a fait passer une loi qui rend légales toutes les unions. Si les ouvriers votent pas pour Macdonald après ça, je me demande ce qu'il va falloir faire pour les contenter. Moi, j'ai eu des employés toute ma vie, ajouta-t-il en prenant un air important. Je suis pas pour cette loi pantoute. Avec cette affaire-là, un *boss* est même plus maître. Ses employés ont le droit de se mettre en grève pour un oui ou pour un non et il est obligé de discuter avec eux autres. *Shit!* Il me semble que c'était pas nécessaire, cette loi-là. Si quelqu'un est pas content de son salaire, il a juste à aller voir ailleurs.

Comme ses auditeurs étaient tous des cultivateurs qui se sentaient peu concernés par le problème, on préféra parler de l'effet des dernières pluies abondantes sur les prochaines récoltes.

Laura Benoît mit fin aux discussions en invitant les gens à passer à table. La mère de la mariée aurait aimé compter le curé de la paroisse parmi ses convives, comme cela se faisait habituellement, mais Josaphat Désilets avait prétexté la nécessité de terminer la préparation de son sermon du lendemain pour refuser son invitation.

Camille et Emma exigèrent que leur mère et celle de Catherine aillent s'asseoir aux côtés des nouveaux mariés pendant qu'elles aidaient sœur Émérentienne et Marie-Rose à servir le repas. Au même moment, Angélique vint rejoindre Hubert après avoir aidé Ann et Bernadette à servir le repas aux enfants installés dans la cuisine, à l'intérieur.

Le repas ne donna pas lieu aux blagues à double sens habituelles. On tapa sur les tables pour demander aux nouveaux mariés de s'embrasser, ce qu'ils firent avec plaisir, mais ce furent bien les seules manifestations qui vinrent troubler les conversations qui allaient bon train.

C'était une magnifique journée de juin et une petite brise agréable rafraîchissait l'air et incitait à la bonne humeur. Après avoir fait aussi bonne chère, on déboutonna les cols de chemise et on recula les ceintures de quelques crans. Les hôtes furent félicités avec enthousiasme pour un si bon repas.

Quand on se mit à desservir les tables, les hommes s'éloignèrent pour fumer à leur aise et poursuivre les discussions entreprises à table. À un certain moment, Catherine se pencha pour dire quelque chose à l'oreille de son mari et se leva pour aider à desservir.

Xavier, désœuvré, se retrouva soudain en compagnie de ses beaux-frères Rémi et Liam et de Paddy Connolly. Ce dernier, plus par méchanceté que par besoin de se faire valoir, dit au nouveau marié :

— Je trouve que t'es pas mal courageux, mon jeune.

— Pourquoi vous me dites ça ? lui demanda Xavier, intrigué.

— De marier une fille avec la réputation qu'elle a à Saint-Bernard, eut le mauvais goût de poursuivre le petit homme bedonnant.

Immédiatement, les traits du visage de Xavier se figèrent. Il dominait les trois hommes de plusieurs pouces et sa musculature puissante mettait à dure épreuve les coutures de son costume neuf. Il se pencha lentement vers le retraité en arborant un air si menaçant que les trois hommes firent un pas en arrière.

— Écoutez-moi ben, monsieur Connolly, lui ordonna-t-il, les dents serrées, le premier enfant de chienne qui va dire un mot contre ma femme, il va avoir affaire à moi, même s'il a des cheveux blancs, vous m'entendez?

Paddy, secoué, se borna à hocher la tête.

— Là, vous allez m'excuser, il faut que j'aille voir où se cache ma femme, ajouta Xavier en tournant les talons, non sans avoir lancé au préalable un regard de défi au vieux Connolly.

☛

Xavier allait s'éloigner quand une voiture entra dans la cour. En même temps que Donat, il reconnut le gros Anthime Lemire qui descendit avec difficulté de son boghei sous le regard inquisiteur de la plupart des hommes présents dans la cour de la ferme. Donat et Xavier s'approchèrent en même temps du visiteur.

— Je sais que je tombe mal, dit l'organisateur conservateur. Je suis passé à Saint-Bernard pour voir Donat et le voisin m'a appris que je le trouverais ici. Je voudrais pas être effronté et venir déranger la noce, ajouta-t-il en guise d'excuse.

— Il y a pas de mal, fit Xavier.

— Je t'offre mes meilleurs vœux de bonheur, déclara Lemire en lui tendant la main. Inquiète-toi pas, j'ai pas pantoute l'intention de m'inviter à tes noces. Je veux juste dire deux mots à ton frère, si ça te dérange pas trop, tint-il à préciser en se tournant vers celui-ci.

— Je vous laisse parler de politique, dit Xavier en s'éloignant déjà. Je vais aller m'occuper de ma femme.

Liam Connolly dit quelques mots à l'oreille de son oncle qui ne quittait pas des yeux le nouvel arrivant. Quand il apprit qu'il s'agissait de l'un des organisateurs du parti conservateur du comté, le retraité fit quelques pas en direction de Donat et du gros homme. Donat l'aperçut et entraîna Anthime Lemire vers la route pour savoir ce qu'il lui voulait.

— J'ai appris que t'as changé d'idée et que tu te présentais plus comme maire, lui dit l'organisateur avec une note de reproche dans la voix.

— Je l'aurais fait si Ellis s'était présenté, lui expliqua le jeune cultivateur. Mais quand je me suis rendu compte que c'était un bon homme comme Hyland, j'ai décidé un bon Bleu comme Anatole Blanchette de se présenter et moi, j'ai choisi d'être conseiller, avec mon beau-frère. Hyland est ben aimé dans la paroisse, comme Blanchette.

— T'as ben fait, l'approuva Lemire en lui tapant sur l'épaule.

— Là, la campagne est presque finie. L'élection a lieu lundi. On va ben voir ce qui va arriver. Mais on a fait le tour des maisons et on a fait tout ce qu'on a pu pour se faire élire.

— C'est correct… Bon, tu devines un peu pourquoi je suis venu te voir ?

— Pourquoi ?

— On va avoir besoin de toi, on a des élections qui s'en viennent.

— Pas encore ! s'exclama Donat, peu enthousiaste.

— Ben oui et on a confiance en toi, à part ça. T'as ben travaillé aux provinciales la dernière fois. Je suis sûr que t'es capable de faire encore mieux.

— En plein été ! Moi, j'ai de l'ouvrage à faire sur ma terre.

— Inquiète-toi pas pour ça, voulut le rassurer le gros homme avec un bon rire. On est tous comme toi. Mais dis-toi que Macdonald sera pas un ingrat et qu'il oubliera pas ceux qui auront fait jeter dehors Sénécal. Ça fait cinq ans que ce Rouge-là nous fatigue. Il est temps qu'il aille se faire voir ailleurs.

— Qui est-ce que vous présentez contre lui ? demanda Donat, curieux.

— C'est pas un as de pique, mon garçon. C'est Pierre-Nérée Dorion, un arpenteur-géomètre ben connu qui parle ben et qui a de l'expérience. Tu vas voir, lui, il va entrer dans Drummond-Arthabasca comme dans du beurre.

— Ouais.

— Embarques-tu avec nous autres comme la dernière fois? Oublie pas que t'es en train de te faire tout un nom dans le parti. Ce serait de valeur que tu lâches déjà.

Donat réfléchit quelques instants avant d'accepter de se charger de Saint-Bernard-Abbé et de Sainte-Monique. Satisfait d'avoir bien rempli sa mission de recrutement, Anthime Lemire lui serra la main en lui promettant de lui donner des nouvelles quelques jours plus tard.

— Et bonne chance pour les élections à Saint-Bernard, lui souhaita-t-il au moment de remonter dans son boghei.

Paddy Connolly s'approcha dans l'intention évidente de s'entretenir avec Lemire, mais ce dernier l'ignora totalement et fit faire demi-tour à son attelage avant de reprendre la route.

❧

Xavier allait se diriger vers sa femme quand il se retrouva face à face avec sa sœur Camille.

— J'aimerais te dire deux mots, dit-elle à voix basse à son jeune frère en l'attirant à l'écart.

— Qu'est-ce qu'il y a? lui demanda-t-il, intrigué par son air sérieux.

— Je voudrais te parler de Catherine.

— De Catherine, qu'est-ce qu'elle a? s'étonna-t-il.

— Écoute-moi, lui ordonna-t-elle, c'est important, ce que je vais te dire là.

— Je t'écoute.

— À soir, sois pas brusque avec elle, sois pas trop pressé. Donne-lui le temps de s'habituer à toi. Vous avez toute la vie devant vous autres.

— C'est certain, reconnut-il, gêné par une telle conversation.

— Dis-toi que si tu sais la ménager, elle va juste t'aimer plus. C'est tout ce que je voulais te dire.

Xavier comprit soudain à quel point cette entrevue avait dû coûter à sa sœur plutôt prude et il lui en fut reconnaissant. Il se contenta de l'embrasser rapidement sur une joue pour la remercier avant d'aller retrouver sa femme.

Moins d'une heure plus tard, Antonin s'esquiva quelques minutes avant de revenir en conduisant par la bride le cheval de Xavier attelé à sa voiture. L'adolescent immobilisa l'attelage près de la maison au moment où Laura Benoît annonçait à ses invités que les nouveaux mariés s'apprêtaient à partir en compagnie de sœur Émérentienne parce qu'ils avaient un train à prendre pour Montréal.

— Montréal! s'exclama Bernadette. Mais ils sont donc chanceux d'aller là en voyage de noces, dit-elle, tout excitée, à sa sœur Emma debout près d'elle.

— Chaperonnés par une sœur, j'ai dans l'idée que ça va faire un voyage de noces où il se passera pas grand-chose, déclara d'une voix un peu avinée Armand Beauchemin.

— Armand, tiens-toi comme du monde! lui ordonna sa femme, mécontente. C'est pas des farces à faire.

Hubert abandonna un instant Angélique Dionne pour aller se charger de la valise que tenait Cyprien Benoît, debout derrière sa mère. Le jeune homme alla la déposer à l'arrière de la voiture. Après avoir quitté ses invités le temps d'enlever sa robe blanche, Catherine apparut vêtue de sa robe du dimanche et vint rejoindre un Xavier éclatant de fierté.

Le jeune couple prit la peine de faire une rapide tournée des convives pour les remercier d'avoir assisté à leur mariage. Marie embrassa sa nouvelle bru et recommanda la prudence à son fils quand le couple s'arrêta devant elle. Catherine et Xavier se retrouvèrent finalement devant Laura Benoît, les yeux gonflés de larmes. La jeune femme embrassa sa mère et la remercia avant de monter dans la voiture aux côtés de son mari. Antonin aida ensuite sœur Émérentienne à prendre place sur la banquette avant, près de lui, avant de reprendre les guides et de diriger l'attelage vers la route.

Le départ des jeunes mariés donna le signal de la fin de la fête. D'ailleurs, les enfants étaient de plus en plus agités et couraient partout. Les hommes se dirigèrent sans se presser vers le clos où paissaient tranquillement leurs chevaux et ils les attelèrent à leur voiture. On remercia les hôtes et on quitta les lieux.

— Au fond, il manquait juste ma tante Mathilde, déclara Eugénie, assise près de son mari, sur la banquette avant de la voiture conduite par Donat. C'est un peu dommage qu'elle ait pas été invitée.

— Torrieu, exagère pas! s'écria son mari avec un petit rire. T'aurais été la première à te plaindre si elle était venue. En plus, elle serait arrivée avec une autre sœur. Déjà avec la cousine de madame Benoît...

— On était très bien comme on était, se contenta de répondre sa mère, le visage sombre.

Marie Beauchemin avait subitement réalisé au départ des nouveaux époux que son fils avait uni pour de bon sa destinée à celle de Catherine Benoît, et elle était loin d'être rassurée sur l'avenir du couple. Qui sait quelle sorte d'épouse et de mère une fille comme ça allait faire. Si son mari avait encore été vivant, il n'aurait jamais accepté une telle union, elle en était persuadée. En participant à ce mariage, elle avait un peu l'impression de l'avoir trahi.

Pour sa part, Bernadette broyait du noir parce qu'elle n'avait nullement apprécié les noces de son frère.

— Qu'est-ce que t'as, toi, à faire la baboune? lui demanda soudain sa mère en sortant de ses réflexions moroses.

— Je suis jamais allée à des noces aussi plates, laissa tomber la jeune fille sur un ton désabusé.

— Pourquoi ? Parce que t'as pas pu danser ? intervint Eugénie, assise près de son mari.

— Pantoute, mais passer des noces à s'occuper des enfants, c'est pas ce que j'appelle un mariage amusant, moi.

— Personne te forçait à le faire, lui fit remarquer sa mère.

— J'avais pas autre chose à faire.

— T'avais juste à demander de te faire accompagner par Constant Aubé, fit sèchement Marie. Il aurait peut-être pas demandé mieux.

— Ça m'aurait surpris, dit Donat en tournant la tête vers sa mère. Rémi m'a dit qu'il est parti la semaine passée pour Québec.

— Qui s'occupe de ses animaux ? lui demanda Marie.

— Son homme engagé.

Bernadette aurait bien aimé savoir pour combien de temps son ex-amoureux devait s'absenter, mais elle eut peur qu'on devine son regret.

— C'est drôle pareil qu'il parte comme ça au commencement de l'été, fit remarquer Marie Beauchemin. Je me demande s'il aurait pas l'intention de retourner s'installer avec ses frères, ajouta-t-elle en jetant un regard en biais vers sa fille cadette.

— Il fera jamais ça, ne put s'empêcher de déclarer Bernadette avec une assurance qu'elle était loin d'éprouver. Il vient de se faire bâtir un moulin et une maison dans notre rang, m'man.

— Tout ça, ça se vend, dit sa mère.

— À moins qu'il soit allé se chercher une femme dans le coin où il a été élevé, poursuivit Eugénie. Il doit être connu là-bas pour avoir du bien et il y a bien des filles qui cherchent juste à s'établir. Moi, ça me surprendrait pas de le voir revenir, mais pas tout seul.

— C'est possible après tout, ajouta Marie. C'est un homme qui a une tête sur les épaules et je vois pas pourquoi il se trouverait pas facilement une femme, ici ou ailleurs.

À la vue de l'air de doute qui se peignit sur le visage de sa fille, la mère crut bon de préciser :

— Ça apprendra à certaines à se montrer capricieuses comme des enfants gâtées. Un homme, ça a aussi sa fierté et, à force de se faire rejeter, il finit par aller voir ailleurs.

➤

Les voitures de Liam et de son oncle arrivèrent l'une derrière l'autre dans la cour de la ferme du rang Saint-Jean. Dès leur entrée dans la maison, Camille s'empressa de demander aux enfants d'aller changer de vêtements. Avec l'aide d'Ann et de Rose, elle entreprit de préparer le souper pendant que les garçons allaient faire le train avec leur père. Pour sa part, Paddy s'était laissé tomber dans la chaise berçante placée près de l'une des fenêtres ouvertes de la cuisine et avait allumé un mégot de cigare qu'il venait de tirer de l'une de ses poches.

La maîtresse de maison venait à peine de s'installer à la table pour peler les pommes de terre et les carottes qui allaient être servies au souper que l'oncle de son mari lui dit :

— Sais-tu, ma nièce, que ton frère a pas l'air d'avoir trop bon caractère.

— Duquel de mes trois frères vous parlez ?

— De ton frère Xavier.

— Pourquoi vous dites ça ? s'étonna Camille en cessant momentanément de peler une pomme de terre.

— Ben, un peu plus, il me frappait quand je lui ai dit que je le trouvais pas mal brave de marier une fille comme Catherine.

— Vous êtes pas allé lui dire une affaire pareille ! s'exclama la jeune femme.

— Ben, il y avait rien de mal dans ce que je lui ai dit, protesta le retraité. C'est pas ma faute si sa femme a la réputation d'être une fille de rien.

— Faites bien attention à ce que vous dites, dit rageusement Camille. Là, vous faites juste rapporter des ragots. Si jamais ça vient aux oreilles de mon frère, vous allez passer un mauvais quart d'heure, ça, je peux vous le jurer.

Ce soir-là, elle profita de ce que Paddy Connolly s'était retiré assez tôt pour raconter à Liam ce que son oncle lui avait dit.

— Je le sais, j'étais là, lui apprit son mari sans s'émouvoir.

— Tu l'as laissé insulter mon frère sans rien dire ? s'étonna sa femme.

— Qu'est-ce que tu voulais que je fasse ? Après tout, c'était vrai, ce que disait mon oncle.

— Peut-être, reconnut Camille, mais ça le regarde pas pantoute et c'était surtout pas le temps de sortir ça en pleines noces.

— Ça change rien, s'entêta Liam après avoir allumé sa pipe. Le monde de Saint-Bernard va toujours se rappeler quelle sorte de fille était Catherine Benoît.

— C'est bien dommage, laissa tomber sa femme. Catherine a du cœur et je suis certaine qu'elle va faire une bien bonne femme à mon frère.

— J'espère que ce sera pas juste une bonne femme dans la cuisine, fit Liam, amer.

Camille comprit à quoi son mari faisait allusion et elle garda le silence un bon moment avant de dire :

— Elle pourra certainement être une bonne femme à Xavier ailleurs aussi, s'il sait s'y prendre, lui.

Le rictus qui apparut sur la figure de son mari lui apprit qu'elle avait fait mouche.

Chapitre 28

Le voyage de noces

Antonin avait laissé le jeune couple et sœur Émérentienne à la gare une trentaine de minutes avant l'arrivée du train et était reparti seul pour s'occuper de la ferme de son patron. À leur entrée dans la petite gare, ils trouvèrent une demi-douzaine de voyageurs attendant impatiemment le train.

Xavier jeta un coup d'œil agacé vers la religieuse qui venait de s'asseoir aux côtés de Catherine. Il aurait bien aimé trouver un moyen d'effectuer le voyage sans la présence encombrante de sœur Émérentienne, mais il n'y avait rien eu à faire. La religieuse devait rentrer à Montréal le jour même et comme il n'y avait qu'un train ce jour-là, il devait faire contre mauvaise fortune bon cœur.

Le jeune homme sursauta en entendant le train approcher de la gare. Immédiatement, les voyageurs se levèrent et sortirent sur le quai alors que l'énorme locomotive tirant cinq wagons s'arrêtait dans un nuage de vapeur. Xavier était mal à l'aise. Il n'avait jamais pris le train. Il dut suivre les deux femmes qui avaient l'habitude de prendre ce moyen de transport. Il se hissa dans un wagon derrière elles. Avant même de le réaliser, il se retrouva assis aux côtés de sa femme sur une banquette de bois, dans le sens contraire de la marche. En face, sœur Émérentienne avait pris place près d'un homme d'une cinquantaine d'années aux larges favoris poivre et sel. Après le «*All aboard!*» hurlé par un employé, le train se remit lentement en marche dans un bruit assourdissant.

Toutes les banquettes du wagon semblaient occupées par des voyageurs et un nuage de fumée de tabac stagnait près du plafond.

— On devrait ouvrir la fenêtre, suggéra Xavier, à demi levé, prêt à passer aux actes.

— Je pense que t'es mieux de pas faire ça, mon garçon, l'avisa le voyageur assis près de sœur Émérentienne. Quand on fait ça, on reçoit souvent de la suie ou des morceaux de charbon.

— C'est vrai, confirma la religieuse. C'est pour ça que la plupart préfèrent endurer la chaleur.

Xavier se rassit.

Le train ne se déplaçait pas très rapidement et le jeune cultivateur de Saint-Bernard-Abbé ne cessait de regarder le paysage qui défilait devant lui en ce début de soirée du mois de juin. Déjà, le soleil commençait à décliner quand le train passa lentement sur le pont traversant la rivière Richelieu. Beaucoup de voyageurs avaient commencé à manger les provisions qu'ils avaient apportées et rangées le plus souvent dans le compartiment au-dessus de leur tête.

Sœur Émérentienne ouvrit son grand cabas pour en extraire un paquet enveloppé dans un linge blanc. Il s'agissait d'épaisses tranches de pain qu'elle avait pris soin de beurrer. Elle en offrit aux jeunes gens et à l'étranger qui partageait son siège.

— Vous savez que c'est ici, en 46, qu'a eu lieu un des plus gros accidents de train au pays, dit l'homme après avoir avalé une grosse bouchée de pain.

— Quel accident? lui demanda Xavier, curieux.

— Ben, le train était rendu au milieu du pont quand on a commencé à le lever pour laisser passer un bateau. Le train a plongé dans la rivière. Il y a eu quatre-vingt-dix-neuf morts, si j'ai bonne mémoire.

— Mon Dieu ! s'exclama Catherine.

— Oui, madame, ça a été toute une histoire.

L'obscurité venait tout juste de tomber quand le train pénétra dans la gare Bonaventure de Montréal. Un peu étourdi par la foule de voyageurs qui venait d'envahir les quais, le fils de Baptiste Beauchemin agrippa sa valise et celle de la religieuse avant de suivre Catherine et sœur Émérentienne vers la sortie.

— On va prendre un tramway jusqu'à la crèche et je vais vous montrer une pension où vous allez pouvoir avoir une chambre pas trop chère, annonça la petite religieuse en prenant place dans une file constituée de trois ou quatre voyageurs.

— Émilia Boisvert reste juste dans la rue à côté, dit Catherine à son mari.

— Qui ?

— Tu sais, la fille avec qui j'ai travaillé au refuge l'été passé. Je t'en ai parlé souvent. On s'entendait bien. Elle s'est loué un appartement sur cette rue-là, proche de la gare. À cette heure, elle travaille plus au refuge. Elle est couturière, elle travaille chez eux. Elle m'écrit presque tous les mois. C'est dommage qu'il soit si tard, j'aurais aimé aller la saluer, ajouta-t-elle avec une note de regret dans la voix.

— Tu vas peut-être avoir la chance de la voir avant qu'on reparte, dit Xavier, sérieusement distrait par toute l'animation autour de lui.

Le jeune homme n'avait pas assez de ses deux yeux pour regarder tout ce qui l'entourait. Il ne remarqua pas le petit sourire entendu que les deux femmes échangèrent devant sa stupéfaction. Il n'avait jamais quitté la campagne. Pour la première fois de sa vie, Xavier prenait conscience d'un monde qu'il ne soupçonnait même pas. Il voyait autour de lui des immeubles de quatre ou cinq étages et une rue éclairée par des becs de gaz et pourvue de trottoirs en bois. Même à cette heure relativement tardive, il ne cessait de passer toutes sortes de voitures tirées par un, deux et même quatre chevaux.

Il ne put s'empêcher de sursauter violemment quand un tramway tiré par quatre chevaux s'immobilisa soudain devant lui. Catherine lui dit que cela coûtait un cent pour y prendre place. Il tendit l'argent au cocher et alla s'asseoir près de sa femme. Durant le trajet, la religieuse montra avec fierté les nouveaux magasins que les sœurs Grises venaient de faire construire dans les rues De la Commune et Saint-Pierre.

Quelques minutes plus tard, elle fit signe aux tourtereaux qu'ils étaient arrivés. Ils descendirent tous les trois devant la crèche d'Youville. Sœur Émérentienne fit quelques pas en compagnie des jeunes mariés pour leur montrer une maison à deux étages rue Saint-Amable, non loin.

— Vous devriez être capables de vous trouver une chambre là, dit-elle. Mais avant ça, vous allez entrer avec moi à la crèche et on va se trouver à manger. La cuisinière est une vieille amie.

Un peu intimidés, tous les deux pénétrèrent à sa suite dans l'institution et longèrent les longs couloirs. De loin en loin, ils entendaient les pleurs d'un enfant, ce qui avait pour effet de crisper Catherine qui jetait des regards nerveux autour d'elle.

Sœur Émérentienne les fit entrer dans le réfectoire réservé aux religieuses et s'esquiva quelques minutes pour aller parler à la cuisinière. Moins d'une demi-heure plus tard, celle-ci leur servit avec bonne humeur des pommes de terre rissolées et des saucisses. Ils la remercièrent et mangèrent ce repas avec un bel appétit. Au moment de se séparer, sœur Émérentienne fit promettre à Xavier et Catherine de venir la saluer avant de rentrer à Saint-Bernard-Abbé.

Lorsqu'ils se retrouvèrent enfin seuls, debout sur le trottoir, les deux jeunes gens hésitèrent un peu avant de se diriger vers la maison où il était possible de louer une chambre pour la nuit. Xavier se secoua, s'empara de leur valise et prit la direction de la maison en pierre. Il sentait Catherine nerveuse à ses côtés. Il sonna à la porte et une dame entre deux âges vint leur ouvrir.

— Est-ce qu'on peut vous louer une chambre pour une journée ou deux? lui demanda Xavier.

— C'est quarante cennes par jour, se borna à dire la logeuse, sans sourire, en leur faisant signe d'entrer.

— C'est correct, accepta-t-il en tirant la somme demandée de l'une de ses poches et en la lui tendant.

La femme prit l'argent et les invita à la suivre. Elle monta au second étage par un escalier vermoulu dont le centre des marches était pourvu d'un vieux tapis élimé. Arrivée à l'étage, le souffle un peu court, elle s'arrêta devant une porte qu'elle déverrouilla et ouvrit. Elle pénétra dans une petite pièce où presque tout l'espace était occupé par un grand lit. La logeuse se dirigea vers l'unique fenêtre pour l'ouvrir et aérer un peu les lieux qui sentaient le renfermé. Le mobilier de la chambre était aussi constitué de deux chaises et d'une commode sur laquelle trônaient un grand bol à main bleu et une cruche.

— Je vous donne la chambre 8, dit-elle à ses jeunes clients. Vous allez être bien tranquilles, il n'y a qu'un autre client à votre étage. Mais à l'étage en dessous, toutes les chambres sont occupées. Ça fait que si vous avez à sortir ou à rentrer tard, faites pas de bruit pour pas déranger les autres. Les toilettes sont au bout du couloir, prit-elle soin d'ajouter.

Sur ces mots, elle tendit la clé à Xavier et sortit après leur avoir souhaité une bonne nuit.

Une fois la porte refermée derrière la dame, Xavier et Catherine étaient seuls dans une pièce pour la première fois depuis qu'ils se connaissaient. Intimidés tous les deux, ils ne savaient pas trop comment se comporter.

— Ben, je pense qu'il est quasiment l'heure de se coucher, finit par dire Xavier d'une voix changée. Qu'est-ce que t'en dis ?

— C'est vrai qu'il est pas mal tard, reconnut Catherine qui s'était approchée de la fenêtre pour regarder à l'extérieur.

— Aimerais-tu que j'aille fumer dehors pendant que tu te prépares ? finit par lui offrir son jeune mari.

— Tu serais bien fin, répondit sa femme en lui adressant un sourire de reconnaissance.

— Bon, j'y vais, fit-il, mais si tu vois que je suis pas revenu demain matin, c'est que je me serai perdu en chemin.

— Éloigne-toi tout de même pas trop, lui conseilla-t-elle en riant un peu nerveusement. Montréal, c'est pas Saint-Bernard. C'est pas toujours du bon monde qui traîne tard dans les rues.

Xavier quitta la chambre et n'y revint que trois quarts d'heure plus tard. Il était tendu et vaguement inquiet. Il n'avait qu'une vague idée des gestes à poser pour faire de Catherine sa femme. Parvenu sur le palier, il prit une grande inspiration et se rappela les paroles de sa sœur aînée.

Il ouvrit sans bruit la porte de la chambre et découvrit que sa femme s'était endormie à la lueur de la lampe en l'attendant. Il trouva qu'elle avait l'air d'un ange avec ses cheveux blonds étalés sur l'oreiller. Il enleva ses souliers sans faire de bruit, alla souffler la lampe et se déshabilla dans le noir. Il fit tant bien que mal une toilette rapide, écarta l'unique couverture et se glissa doucement dans le lit.

Étendu près d'elle, il entendait sa respiration régulière et en fut tout ému. Même s'il mourait d'envie d'explorer son corps, il parvint à se contenir, se contentant de l'embrasser doucement sur une joue et d'écouter son souffle régulier jusqu'à ce que le sommeil finisse par l'emporter.

Au matin, comme il n'avait pas songé à tirer les rideaux, un rayon de soleil vint frapper l'une de ses paupières et le força à ouvrir les yeux. Il découvrit alors la tête de Catherine lovée sur son épaule. La jeune femme avait une pose abandonnée qui l'attendrit. Un vague sourire courait sur ses lèvres.

— Est-ce qu'on peut savoir à quoi tu rêves, la marmotte? lui chuchota-t-il.

Elle ouvrit les yeux et sembla soudain s'apercevoir que le jour était levé.

— Mon Dieu! Est-ce que je me suis endormie? demanda-t-elle, rouge de confusion.

— On le dirait ben, fit son mari avec bonne humeur. Il faut croire que t'as pensé que j'étais pas assez intéressant pour m'attendre, hier soir.

— J'en reviens pas! s'exclama-t-elle. Tu dois bien m'en vouloir, non?

— Ben non. J'ai ben aimé te regarder dormir, ajouta-t-il en l'embrassant sur le bout du nez. Là, par exemple, il va falloir se lever si on veut aller à la messe. Je vais essayer de trouver un peu d'eau chaude pour me raser et je vais aller m'habiller dans les toilettes au bout du couloir.

Sur ces mots, il mit son pantalon, prit ses effets personnels et quitta la chambre. Quand il revint, Catherine avait eu le temps de s'habiller, de se coiffer et de remettre de l'ordre dans la chambre.

— Je suis allé voir madame Legault, la propriétaire, dit-il à sa femme. Il y a une messe dans dix minutes à l'église au coin de la rue. On va pouvoir déjeuner en revenant. Elle sert des repas pour pas trop cher, ajouta-t-il.

Tous les deux assistèrent à la messe et revinrent lentement à la pension. Après un copieux déjeuner, Xavier accepta de se laisser piloter par sa femme dans un quartier de Montréal qu'elle semblait assez bien connaître. Pendant près de quatre heures, ils arpentèrent les rues environnantes afin d'admirer les vitrines des magasins qui ouvraient sur les rues Notre-Dame et de la Commune ainsi que les nouveaux grands immeubles en construction. Pour profiter du soleil, ils s'arrêtèrent quelques minutes place Jacques-Cartier pour y regarder les badauds se promener.

Un peu après trois heures, le couple, fatigué de toute cette agitation urbaine à laquelle il n'était pas habitué, décida de rentrer. Dès qu'ils se retrouvèrent dans leur petite chambre, Catherine tira les rideaux, enleva ses souliers et proposa à son mari de faire une sieste avant le souper. Elle replia soigneusement le couvre-lit et s'étendit.

Il vint la rejoindre. Quand il fut près d'elle, elle n'hésita pas une seconde à déposer sa tête sur son épaule et à lui tendre ses lèvres. Xavier comprit alors que le moment tant attendu était venu. Il déploya d'immenses efforts pour réfréner son envie et il se mit à la caresser doucement, attendant qu'elle guide ses mains pour aller plus loin. Après de longues minutes de préliminaires, Catherine exigea dans un souffle qu'il fasse d'elle sa femme. Même là, il sut se montrer délicat et procéder doucement, sans aucune violence, ce que sembla beaucoup apprécier celle qui partageait dorénavant sa vie. Tous les deux finirent par s'endormir dans les bras l'un de l'autre et se réveillèrent en sursaut un peu après six heures.

— On va passer en dessous de la table si on se grouille pas, dit Xavier avec entrain en se levant.

— Deux minutes et je suis prête, fit Catherine en l'imitant.

Toute espèce de gêne semblait maintenant disparue entre les nouveaux époux. Ils descendirent souper et allèrent ensuite faire une longue promenade avant de revenir s'enfermer dans leur petit nid d'amour.

❧

Le lundi matin, Xavier découvrit une Catherine à l'air inquiet et malheureux à leur réveil. Intrigué, il lui demanda ce qui n'allait pas. Elle refusa d'abord de le dire, mais devant son insistance, elle finit par lui avouer qu'elle ne cessait de penser à sa petite Constance et que le plus beau cadeau qu'il pourrait lui faire avant de rentrer à Saint-Bernard-Abbé serait de lui permettre de la revoir une dernière fois avant qu'elle soit adoptée.

Xavier, un peu mal à l'aise devant la situation, ne dit rien et la laissa finir sa toilette pendant qu'il fumait la pipe, sa première de la journée, debout devant la fenêtre ouverte. Peu après, ils descendirent déjeuner même si l'appétit n'était pas au rendez-vous. À la sortie de la petite salle à manger de madame Legault, le jeune homme, incapable de supporter plus longtemps de voir sa femme si malheureuse, consentit finalement à l'accompagner à la crèche d'Youville. Tout heureuse, elle lui sauta au cou pour le remercier.

Un peu après neuf heures, tous les deux se présentèrent à la crèche et demandèrent à parler à sœur Émérentienne. La sœur tourière les fit entrer dans un parloir qui sentait l'encaustique et les pria d'attendre.

— Vous êtes pas déjà sur votre départ? s'étonna la petite religieuse à la figure ridée quand elle vint les rejoindre, toute souriante.

— Non, ma sœur, la rassura Xavier. Ma femme aurait juste aimé voir Constance, si c'est possible.

Aussitôt le sourire s'effaça sur le visage de la sœur Grise.

— Es-tu bien certaine que c'est une bonne idée? demanda-t-elle à la jeune femme nerveuse qui se tenait debout devant elle.

— Je m'en ennuie trop, ma sœur.

— Oui, mais tu te fais du mal pour rien. Tu te souviens de ce que je t'ai dit chez vous la semaine passée. C'est cette semaine qu'un couple est supposé venir la voir. Il paraît que le mari et la femme sont même revenus la semaine passée et qu'ils sont bien intéressés, selon sœur Saint-Jérôme, expliqua-t-elle.

Catherine tourna un regard malheureux vers son mari.

— Vous êtes aussi ben de lui laisser voir la petite, si c'est ce qu'elle veut, dit-il à sœur Émérentienne.

— Bon, je vais aller la chercher, mais vous la gardez pas plus qu'un quart d'heure, ajouta-t-elle, intraitable.

Ils durent attendre une dizaine de minutes avant de voir la religieuse entrer dans le parloir en tenant par la main une petite fille qui faisait apparemment ses premiers pas. En la voyant, Catherine se mit à genoux et lui tendit les bras, mais la fillette blonde, intimidée, s'accrocha à la robe de la religieuse en refusant de faire un pas de plus.

— Viens-tu me voir? lui demanda sa mère d'une voix étranglée par l'émotion en lui tendant toujours les bras.

L'enfant sembla hésiter encore un court moment avant de se décider à s'avancer vers celle qui, les yeux pleins de larmes, voulait la prendre dans ses bras.

Ému, Xavier se tenait à l'écart et se taisait. Sœur Émérentienne se retira, pour les laisser tous les deux seuls avec l'enfant. Catherine prit sa fille dans ses bras et la serra contre elle en l'embrassant.

— Serre-la pas trop, lui conseilla Xavier, tu vas finir par l'étouffer, cette enfant-là.

Catherine finit par remettre par terre sa fille qui se dirigea vers Xavier en lui tendant les bras. Ce dernier ne put faire autrement que de la prendre et de l'asseoir sur ses genoux.

— Je te ferai remarquer que j'attire pas mal les blondes, plaisanta-t-il pour faire sourire sa femme. En tout cas, il y a personne qui peut dire qu'elle te ressemble pas, ajouta-t-il. Elle est belle comme un cœur.

Après quelques instants, Constance choisit de s'asseoir sur sa mère en jargonnant des mots incompréhensibles. Quand sœur Émérentienne réapparut dans le parloir, elle eut du mal à séparer la mère de l'enfant.

— Je te l'avais bien dit que c'était te faire du mal pour rien, dit la religieuse à la fille de sa cousine. Bon, embrasse-la et dis-toi qu'elle va être bien traitée chez les gens qui vont l'adopter.

En larmes, Catherine embrassa une dernière fois sa fille. Au moment où sœur Émérentienne quittait la pièce avec l'enfant, Xavier crut bon de préciser qu'ils rentreraient le lendemain à Saint-Bernard-Abbé. La religieuse leur souhaita un bon voyage de retour et disparut derrière la porte. Le jeune mari dut attendre quelques minutes pour permettre à sa femme de se remettre de ses émotions. Quand ils quittèrent la crèche, la porte de l'institution se referma derrière eux avec un bruit définitif.

Cette visite gâcha la dernière journée de leur voyage de noces. Rien de ce que put faire Xavier ne parvint à tirer Catherine de la tristesse dans laquelle elle s'était elle-même plongée. Ils firent une longue balade en tramway qui les conduisit jusqu'au pied du mont Royal et ils marchèrent longtemps sur les quais du port qui n'avaient jamais connu une activité aussi fébrile, mais au coucher du soleil Catherine proposa de se coucher tôt en prétextant la fatigue d'une longue journée.

Ils firent l'amour encore une fois et Catherine s'endormit dans ses bras. Incapable de trouver le sommeil, Xavier demeura éveillé durant de longues heures, à l'affût des bruits en provenance de l'extérieur.

❧

Étrangement, ce premier lundi de juillet ne semblait pas avoir éveillé beaucoup de passion dans la population de Saint-Bernard-Abbé, même si on allait élire le premier conseil de l'histoire de la paroisse.

D'un commun accord, on avait accepté que la surveillance du scrutin soit confiée à Hormidas Meilleur et qu'il se tienne dans l'école de rang, face au magasin général.

— Pas de saint danger qu'ils aient fait ça dans l'autre école, ronchonna Bernadette. Là, je suppose que c'est encore moi, la folle, qui vais être obligée d'aller remettre de l'ordre dans la classe et de laver le plancher que j'ai lavé il y a pas deux semaines.

— On pouvait pas faire ça ailleurs, affirma Donat. L'autre école est pas encore prête, ajouta-t-il en parlant de la maison d'Hormidas Meilleur que la commission scolaire avait achetée au printemps pour en faire la seconde école de rang de la paroisse.

Ce matin-là, dès neuf heures, le facteur, l'air important, avait pris place derrière le bureau de l'enseignante après avoir ouvert toutes grandes les fenêtres pour aérer. Il s'était levé un peu avant cinq heures pour aller chercher le courrier à la gare, mais il ne le distribuerait que le lendemain. Il avait aujourd'hui une tâche beaucoup plus importante à remplir.

Il faisait beau et chaud et toute la campagne était paisible. Un peu plus tard, avant d'aller récolter les dernières fraises, sa femme traversa la route et vint voir comment il se tirait d'affaire.

— Calvinus ! il est encore venu personne, se plaignit-il en passant une main sur son front où perlait un peu de sueur.

— Pauvre p'tit père ! le plaignit sa femme, pourquoi tu restes enfermé comme ça ? Ça fera pas venir le monde plus vite. À ta place, je sortirais une chaise sur le perron. Tu pourrais au moins prendre l'air.

Hormidas l'approuva et transporta sa chaise sur l'étroit perron de l'école pour s'y installer confortablement pendant que sa femme, chapeau de paille sur la tête, retournait au travail.

Le facteur finit par comprendre qu'il ne verrait probablement des électeurs qu'à l'heure du dîner et même, davantage, après le souper. Par une si belle journée, les cultivateurs de Saint-Bernard-Abbé allaient tous travailler dans leurs champs. Par conséquent, il finit par verrouiller la porte de l'école et traverser la route pour aller s'asseoir aux côtés de Télesphore Dionne sur la large galerie du magasin général.

— Je vois pas pourquoi je niaiserais tout seul dans l'école quand je peux aussi ben voir le monde arriver de chez vous, dit-il au propriétaire du magasin général qui s'étonnait de sa présence sur sa galerie. Quand quelqu'un viendra, je traverserai.

Cette journée s'écoula très lentement et le scrutateur volontaire ne vit arriver les premiers électeurs qu'à la toute fin de l'après-midi. Comme on ne lui avait pas prescrit d'heure de fermeture, il décida de prolonger les heures de scrutin jusqu'à neuf heures et ainsi de donner une chance aux retardataires d'exercer leur droit de vote.

Vers huit heures, on vit le curé Désilets descendre lentement la pente du rang Sainte-Ursule. Les deux candidats à la mairie lui avaient demandé, la veille, de superviser le comptage des votes. Le prêtre, d'abord un peu réticent à se mêler de politique, avait finalement accepté pour rendre service.

Le soleil était sur le point de se coucher quand les habitants de Saint-Bernard-Abbé commencèrent à se rassembler autour de l'école et dans la cour commune entre le magasin général et la forge d'Évariste Bourgeois. Thomas Hyland, Ellis, le notaire Valiquette et un fort groupe de partisans avaient pris place devant le magasin général. Un peu plus loin, Anatole Blanchette, Donat et son beau-frère Rémi échangeaient avec des cultivateurs du rang Saint-Jean sur leurs chances d'être élus.

Une quarantaine de minutes furent nécessaires à Hormidas Meilleur et au curé Désilets pour faire le décompte des votes. Quand les deux hommes parurent sur le perron de l'école, les gens se rapprochèrent immédiatement pour mieux entendre les résultats de l'élection.

L'air important et le chapeau melon incliné vers l'arrière, Hormidas Meilleur leva une main pour demander le silence.

— On a fini de compter. Je laisse monsieur le curé vous annoncer les résultats, ajouta-t-il en faisant signe au prêtre de parler.

— Pour le poste de maire de Saint-Bernard, monsieur Thomas Hyland est élu avec trente-deux votes de plus que monsieur Blanchette.

L'élection de l'Irlandais fut saluée par des applaudissements et des cris de victoire. Josaphat Désilets leva une main à son tour pour rétablir le silence.

— Il y avait quatre candidats pour les deux postes de conseillers. Celui qui a obtenu le plus de votes est monsieur Eudore Valiquette.

Autres applaudissements, tout de même un peu moins fournis que les précédents.

— Monsieur Rémi Lafond est le deuxième, conclut le curé.

— Est-ce qu'on peut demander à notre nouveau maire et à ses conseillers de venir nous rejoindre sur le perron ? demanda Hormidas, jouant au maître de cérémonie.

Thomas Hyland se dirigea lentement vers le scrutateur et attendit d'être rejoint par ses deux conseillers pour monter sur le perron. On applaudit les trois hommes et on réclama un discours du nouveau maire. Le propriétaire du moulin à bois avait toujours été un homme de peu de mots et, dans les circonstances, son comportement ne changea pas.

— J'ai jamais été maire, se borna-t-il à dire à ses électeurs attentifs. Tout ce que je peux vous promettre, c'est que je vais faire de mon mieux.

Le curé Désilets choisit de se retirer discrètement au moment où certains exhibaient des cruchons de bagosse qu'ils avaient dissimulés dans leur voiture pour célébrer l'événement.

Anatole et Donat se consultèrent à voix basse avant de s'avancer vers les élus pour les féliciter. L'un et l'autre ne manifestèrent aucune amertume devant leur défaite. En fait, ils n'avaient jamais cru être en mesure de battre Hyland. Donat était même presque soulagé d'avoir perdu. Ses responsabilités de marguillier et de président de la commission scolaire prenaient déjà beaucoup de son temps. De plus, il y avait les élections fédérales…

Le plus surpris parmi les élus était peut-être Rémi.

— Je comprends pas pourquoi j'ai été élu plutôt que toi, dit-il à voix basse à son beau-frère Donat.

— C'est parce qu'ils ont confiance en toi. Moi, je suis sûr que tu vas faire un bon conseiller.

— As-tu vu la tête d'Ellis?

— Ouais, on dirait ben qu'il est pas content pantoute, lui fit remarquer le fils de Baptiste Beauchemin. C'est à peine s'il a pris le temps de serrer la main de Hyland et du notaire avant de partir. Remarque que c'est pas mal insultant pareil d'être battu par Eudore Valiquette. Après tout, ça fait même pas six mois que le notaire reste à Saint-Bernard.

Ce soir-là, Liam Connolly rentra à la maison après avoir assisté au dévoilement des résultats de l'élection en compagnie de son oncle.

— Ton frère s'est fait battre, annonça-t-il sans faire aucun effort pour dissimuler une certaine jubilation.

— On dirait que ça te fait plaisir, fit Camille.

— Non, mais ça va lui faire du bien de s'être fait rabattre le caquet.

— J'espère que tu dis pas ça parce que t'es jaloux de lui, rétorqua-t-elle d'une voix acide.

Chapitre 29

Le cadeau

Lorsque Xavier rouvrit les yeux le lendemain matin, ce fut pour découvrir sa femme, déjà habillée, assise au bord du lit, les yeux rougis comme si elle avait pleuré.

— Qu'est-ce que t'as ? lui demanda-t-il en prenant appui sur un coude.

— C'est pas grave, répondit-elle en s'efforçant de sourire, juste un mauvais rêve.

Il feignit de la croire, se leva et alla faire sa toilette au bout du couloir pendant qu'elle déposait leurs affaires dans leur valise. Ils descendirent ensemble à la salle à manger pour prendre un dernier repas à la pension de madame Legault. Pendant le déjeuner, Catherine s'efforça de mettre une joyeuse animation dans sa voix, mais ses efforts ne trompèrent pas Xavier qui finit par lui dire :

— Écoute, il est neuf heures et le train part seulement à deux heures. Je pense que tu vas avoir tout le temps que tu veux pour aller voir ton amie Émilia.

— Tu viens avec moi.

— Ben non. Qu'est-ce que tu veux que je fasse là ? Vous allez être ben mieux si je suis pas dans vos jambes.

— Voyons, Xavier, on est en voyage de noces. Je peux pas te laisser comme ça, protesta-t-elle mollement, même si elle était visiblement attirée par la proposition.

— J'en mourrai pas. Moi, je vais me promener autour pour voir tout ce qu'il y a à regarder. J'ai dans l'idée que c'est pas demain la veille que je vais pouvoir revenir à Montréal. Aussi ben en profiter.

— T'es certain que ça te fait rien? lui demanda-t-elle, hésitante.

— Pantoute, vas-y. On va se rejoindre à la gare pour prendre le train. Inquiète-toi pas, je me perdrai pas.

Catherine l'embrassa sur une joue et quitta la salle à manger. Xavier attendit quelques instants avant d'acquitter la facture de leur repas. Il monta ensuite à leur chambre pour y prendre leur petite valise. Avant de partir, il salua la logeuse et quitta définitivement la petite pension de famille de la rue Saint-Amable.

Pendant plusieurs minutes, le jeune homme déambula dans le quartier sans jamais s'éloigner de la crèche d'Youville. Il était déchiré par des sentiments contradictoires qui le tourmentaient depuis la veille.

— Maudit blasphème! jura-t-il à haute voix. Ça va faire! Il n'y a qu'une chose à faire.

Sur ces mots, il se mit résolument en marche vers l'institution et s'arrêta devant la porte. Après une dernière hésitation, il sonna et demanda à la sœur tourière s'il pouvait parler à sœur Émérentienne. La religieuse sembla se souvenir de lui et ne fit aucune difficulté pour le conduire au parloir où elle le pria d'attendre.

Xavier se retrouva dans la grande pièce où il était venu le jour précédent en compagnie de sa femme. Il resta debout devant une haute fenêtre pour regarder les enfants qui s'amusaient dans la cour sous la surveillance de quelques religieuses. Le bruit d'une porte qui s'ouvrait dans son dos le fit se retourner.

— T'es tout seul? lui demanda la petite sœur Émérentienne, apparemment étonnée. Où est Catherine?

— Elle est partie voir son amie Émilia, ma sœur.

— Et toi, t'es venu me dire bonjour avant que vous repartiez pour Saint-Bernard, poursuivit-elle avec un sourire, c'est très gentil de ta part.

— Pas seulement ça, ma sœur, lui dit le jeune homme. J'aurais quelque chose à vous demander.

— Quoi ? fit la religieuse, intriguée.

— Pensez-vous que je pourrais adopter la fille de Catherine ?

— Es-tu sérieux, Xavier ?

— Oui, ma sœur. Catherine est malheureuse comme les pierres depuis qu'elle sait que sa fille sera loin d'elle. Moi, je veux que ma femme soit heureuse.

— Mais c'est pas ton enfant, lui rappela la sœur Grise.

— Elle va le devenir, si je l'adopte. Je ferai jamais la différence entre elle et les enfants que nous aurons ensemble. Elle va être traitée comme les autres.

— Je trouve que t'as bien bon cœur, mon garçon, ne put s'empêcher de dire sœur Émérentienne. Mais es-tu bien sûr que c'est ce que tu veux ?

— Oui, ma sœur, répondit Xavier sur un ton ferme qui cachait bien toute l'inquiétude qu'un tel geste spontané impliquait.

— N'as-tu pas peur de la réaction du monde de Saint-Bernard quand ils vont te voir revenir de Montréal avec une enfant ?

— Ça me dérange pas, s'entêta le fils de Baptiste Beauchemin. Mes affaires regardent pas personne.

— Bon, je sais pas si la directrice va accepter, mais je vais aller lui parler tout de suite. Attends-moi, je ne serai pas longue.

La petite religieuse quitta le parloir pour n'y revenir qu'un quart d'heure plus tard.

— Puis ? demanda Xavier, inquiet et impatient.

— Viens avec moi, la directrice t'attend, se contenta de répondre la cousine de Laura Benoît.

Ils longèrent un long couloir sombre avant de s'arrêter devant une porte à la vitre dépolie. Sœur Émérentienne frappa et une voix la pria d'entrer. Xavier se retrouva devant une religieuse de taille moyenne dont le visage rayonnait de bonté.

— Comme ça, c'est le jeune monsieur qui veut adopter notre Constance ? dit-elle d'entrée de jeu en priant ses visiteurs de s'asseoir sur les chaises disposées devant son bureau.

— Oui, ma sœur, répondit Xavier, impressionné.

— Sœur Émérentienne m'a expliqué que vous venez d'épouser la mère de Constance et que vous aimeriez avoir l'enfant.

— Oui, ma sœur.

— Un couple doit venir demain pour adopter l'enfant. Je suppose que vous êtes au courant.

— Oui, ma sœur, mais c'est la fille de Catherine.

— C'est certain que Constance serait mieux avec sa vraie mère... pourvu que vous, vous acceptiez bien l'enfant.

— Je promets de la traiter comme ma propre fille.

— Si c'est comme ça, vous pouvez l'adopter, déclara la religieuse avec un large sourire. J'ai déjà préparé les documents. Savez-vous lire et écrire ?

— Non, ma sœur.

— Voulez-vous que je vous lise ce qui est écrit ?

— C'est pas nécessaire. Je vous fais confiance.

— Dans ce cas-là, vous n'avez qu'à signer au bas de chacune des deux feuilles, précisa la directrice en lui tendant une plume.

Xavier traça un «x» au bas de chacune des feuilles. La religieuse plia l'un des documents et le glissa dans une enveloppe avant de le lui tendre et de se lever pour signifier que l'entrevue était terminée.

— Je suppose que vous aimeriez emmener l'enfant avec vous dès aujourd'hui ? demanda-t-elle.

— Oui, ma sœur. On doit prendre le train à deux heures pour retourner chez nous.

— Bon, sœur Émérentienne va voir à ce qu'on prépare les affaires de votre fille, monsieur Beauchemin. On va aussi la faire manger avant de partir. Si vous voulez l'attendre, vous pouvez aller vous asseoir au parloir. On va vous l'amener quand elle sera prête.

— Merci, ma sœur.

En regagnant le parloir, Xavier se sentait libéré. Il était persuadé maintenant d'avoir pris la meilleure décision pour le bonheur de Catherine... et le sien. Sœur Émérentienne le laissa pour s'assurer que Constance allait être prête à le suivre dans quelques minutes. Le nouveau père de famille dut tout de même attendre près d'une heure avant de voir la religieuse revenir dans la pièce en tenant par la main la petite Constance qui sembla le reconnaître dès qu'elle l'aperçut.

Quand il lui tendit les bras, l'enfant n'eut pas la moindre hésitation pour se rapprocher de lui. Il la souleva et l'embrassa sur le bout du nez avant de l'asseoir sur une chaise pour prendre le léger bagage que lui remettait sœur Émérentienne.

— Il y a pas grand-chose là-dedans, lui dit-elle. Deux robes et quelques couches. Je suis sûre que Catherine va vite arranger ça.

Xavier ouvrit sa valise et y glissa les maigres possessions de Constance avant de la refermer.

— Merci pour tout, ma sœur, fit Xavier reconnaissant.

— Avant que tu partes, mon garçon, je dois te dire que j'aurais jamais cru que Catherine soit tombée sur un homme avec un aussi grand cœur. Le bon Dieu va te récompenser pour le geste que tu poses aujourd'hui.

Xavier la remercia encore, prit sa fille dans ses bras et empoigna sa valise avant de se mettre en marche vers la sortie. Lorsqu'il se retrouva sur le trottoir au milieu de la cohue, il prit conscience qu'il était maintenant responsable d'une autre vie. La matinée tirait déjà à sa fin et il décida de prendre le tramway pour retourner à la gare Bonaventure.

À son arrivée à la gare, il confia sa valise à la consigne et, avec Constance dans les bras qui ne semblait pas avoir les yeux assez grands pour tout voir, il se mit en quête d'un endroit où se restaurer. Il trouva dans un petit marché voisin un étal où on vendait des tranches de pain tartinées de cretons. Il en mangea et en fit manger à la petite qui sembla apprécier cette nourriture.

Un peu avant une heure, le nouveau papa se rendit compte que sa fille s'endormait. Il décida de retourner s'asseoir à la gare avec l'enfant. De nombreux bancs étaient libres. Il en choisit un à l'écart après être allé récupérer sa valise et avoir acheté deux billets. Après s'être assis, il étendit Constance sur le banc, la tête sur l'une de ses cuisses. La fillette s'endormit en quelques instants.

Quelques minutes plus tard, il aperçut Catherine qui entrait dans la gare. La jeune femme s'était immobilisée près de la porte qu'elle venait de franchir, cherchant à le repérer des yeux. Xavier leva une main pour lui signaler sa présence. En l'apercevant, elle sembla soulagée et se mit en marche dans sa direction. Il ne se leva pas pour ne pas réveiller Constance.

— J'avais peur de pas pouvoir te… commença-t-elle à dire quand son mari, un doigt sur les lèvres, lui fit signe de se taire.

Stupéfaite, la jeune femme ne comprit pas tout d'abord pourquoi il avait un si étrange comportement. Puis, soudain, elle réalisa qu'un enfant était étendu sur le banc sur lequel il était assis. À la vue de la petite fille, le cœur de Catherine eut un raté et son visage s'illumina subitement.

— Mais c'est… c'est Constance ! parvint-elle à dire en se penchant vers sa fille, les yeux émerveillés par la surprise.

— En plein ça, reconnut son mari.

— Qu'est-ce qu'elle fait là? demanda-t-elle d'une voix rauque en tendant la main vers l'enfant, comme si elle voulait s'assurer qu'elle ne rêvait pas.

— Elle est à sa place, déclara Xavier. Elle est avec sa mère et son père.

— Comment ça? fit sa femme, incapable de demeurer plus longtemps debout tant ses jambes flageolaient.

— Je l'ai adoptée ce matin. C'est notre fille maintenant.

Constance choisit ce moment pour ouvrir les yeux. Catherine, émue au plus haut point, la prit dans ses bras et la serra convulsivement contre elle. Des larmes de joie jaillirent tout à coup de ses yeux et elle posa sa tête contre l'épaule de son mari.

— J'oublierai jamais ce que tu viens de faire, lui promit-elle à voix basse.

Au même moment, on annonça l'entrée en gare du train qu'ils attendaient. Xavier empoigna la valise et laissa sa femme porter leur fille.

— À cette heure, il est temps qu'on rentre chez nous, déclara-t-il, soulagé.

À suivre
Sainte-Brigitte-des-Saults
décembre 2009

Table des matières

Suivez-nous

Achevé d'imprimer en juin 2014
sur les presses de Marquis-Gagné
Louiseville, Québec